T0223371

Lecture Notes in Artificial Intelligence   10021

Subseries of Lecture Notes in Computer Science

More information about this series at http://www.springer.com/series/1244

Loizos Michael · Antonis Kakas (Eds.)

Logics in Artificial Intelligence

15th European Conference, JELIA 2016
Larnaca, Cyprus, November 9–11, 2016
Proceedings

 Springer

Editors
Loizos Michael
Open University of Cyprus
Nicosia
Cyprus

Antonis Kakas
University of Cyprus
Nicosia
Cyprus

ISSN 0302-9743   ISSN 1611-3349 (electronic)
Lecture Notes in Artificial Intelligence
ISBN 978-3-319-48757-1   ISBN 978-3-319-48758-8 (eBook)
DOI 10.1007/978-3-319-48758-8

Library of Congress Control Number: 2016955503

LNCS Sublibrary: SL7 – Artificial Intelligence

Printed on acid-free paper

This Springer imprint is published by Springer Nature
The registered company is Springer International Publishing AG
The registered company address is: Gewerbestrasse 11, 6330 Cham, Switzerland

Preface

These are the proceedings of the 15th European Conference on Logics in Artificial Intelligence (JELIA 2016), held during November 9–11, 2016, in Larnaca, Cyprus, and organized by the University of Cyprus and the Open University of Cyprus.

The European Conference on Logics in Artificial Intelligence (or Journées Européennes sur la Logique en Intelligence Artificielle — JELIA) began back in 1988, as a workshop, in response to the need for a European forum for the discussion of emerging work in this field. Since then, JELIA has been organised biennially, with proceedings published in the Springer series *Lecture Notes in Artificial Intelligence*. Previous meetings took place in Roscoff, France (1988), Amsterdam, The Netherlands (1990), Berlin, Germany (1992), York, UK (1994), Évora, Portugal (1996), Dagstuhl, Germany (1998), Málaga, Spain (2000), Cosenza, Italy (2002), Lisbon, Portugal (2004), Liverpool, UK (2006), Dresden, Germany (2008), Helsinki, Finland (2010), Toulouse, France (2012), and Madeira, Portugal (2014).

The aim of JELIA is to bring together active researchers interested in all aspects concerning the use of logics in artificial intelligence (AI) to discuss current research, results, problems, and applications of both theoretical and practical nature. JELIA strives to foster links and facilitate cross-fertilization of ideas among researchers from various disciplines, among researchers from academia and industry, and between theoreticians and practitioners.

The increasing interest in this forum, its international level with growing participation of researchers from outside Europe, and the overall technical quality have turned JELIA into a major biennial forum for the discussion of logic-based approaches to AI.

For the 2016 edition of JELIA, authors were invited to submit papers presenting original and unpublished research in all areas related to the use of logics in AI. To encourage a discussion of the links and synergies between AI and cognitive psychology, this year's edition of JELIA encouraged submissions on logics in AI and cognition, and included invited talks related to this topic.

There were 88 submissions, each reviewed by three Program Committee members. The committee decided to accept 32 full papers for regular presentations or system demonstrations, and ten short papers for spotlight/poster presentations. The accepted papers span a number of areas within logics in AI, including: belief revision, answer set programming, argumentation, probabilistic reasoning, handling inconsistencies, temporal logics and planning, description logics, and decidability and complexity results. The program also included five invited talks by Costas Bekas, Tarek R. Besold, Marc Denecker, Torsten Schaub, and Keith Stenning.

We would like to thank the authors of all the submitted papers and the members of the Program Committee and the additional experts who helped during the reviewing process, for contributing and ensuring the high scientific quality of JELIA 2016.

We would also like to acknowledge the support of the University of Cyprus, the Open University of Cyprus, the Cyprus Tourism Organisation, Austrian Airlines, IBM, Springer, and EasyChair.

September 2016   Loizos Michael
                                                           Antonis Kakas

Organization

Conference Chair

Antonis Kakas   University of Cyprus, Cyprus

Program Chair

Loizos Michael   Open University of Cyprus, Cyprus

Program Committee

Natasha Alechina	University of Nottingham, UK
Jose Julio Alferes	CENTRIA, New University of Lisbon, Portugal
Leila Amgoud	IRIT-CNRS, University of Toulouse, France
Carlos Areces	National University of Córdoba, Argentina
Franz Baader	Technical University of Dresden, Germany
Peter Baumgartner	NICTA, Australia
Salem Benferhat	CRIL-CNRS, University of Artois, France
Philippe Besnard	IRIT-CNRS, University of Toulouse, France
Alexander Bochman	Holon Institute of Technology, Israel
Gerhard Brewka	University of Leipzig, Germany
Jan Broersen	Utrecht University, The Netherlands
Nils Bulling	Delft University of Technology, The Netherlands
Pedro Cabalar	University of Coruna, Spain
Walter Carnielli	State University of Campinas, Brazil
Giovanni Casini	University of Luxembourg, Luxembourg
Mehdi Dastani	Utrecht University, The Netherlands
James Delgrande	Simon Fraser University, Canada
Marc Denecker	Katholieke Universiteit Leuven, Belgium
Didier Dubois	IRIT-CNRS, University of Toulouse, France
Barbara Dunin-Keplicz	Warsaw University and Polish Academy of Sciences, Poland
Paul Dunne	University of Liverpool, UK
Wolfgang Faber	University of Huddersfield, UK
Luis Farinas del Cerro	IRIT-CNRS, University of Toulouse, France
Eduardo Fermé	University of Madeira, Portugal
Raul Fervari	Universidad Nacional de Córdoba, Argentina
Michael Fisher	University of Liverpool, UK
Nina Gierasimczuk	University of Amsterdam, The Netherlands
Laura Giordano	University of Eastern Piemonte, Italy
Valentina Gliozzi	University of Turin, Italy

Lluis Godo	Artificial Intelligence Research Institute, CSIC, Spain
Valentin Goranko	Stockholm University, Sweden
Andreas Herzig	IRIT-CNRS, University of Toulouse, France
Tomi Janhunen	Aalto University, Finland
Tommi Junttila	Aalto University, Finland
Gabriele Kern-Isberner	Technical University of Dortmund, Germany
Sébastien Konieczny	CRIL-CNRS, University of Artois, France
Roman Kontchakov	Birkbeck, University of London, UK
Jérôme Lang	LAMSADE-CNRS, University of Paris-Dauphine, France
Joohyung Lee	Arizona State University, USA
Joao Leite	CENTRIA, New University of Lisbon, Portugal
Maurizio Lenzerini	University of Rome La Sapienza, Italy
Nicola Leone	University of Calabria, Italy
Vladimir Lifschitz	University of Texas, USA
Emiliano Lorini	IRIT-CNRS, University of Toulouse, France
Pierre Marquis	CRIL-CNRS, University of Artois, France
Jérôme Mengin	IRIT-CNRS, University of Toulouse, France
George Metcalfe	University of Bern, Switzerland
Thomas Meyer	University of Cape Town and CAIR, South Africa
Luís Moniz Pereira	CENTRIA, New University of Lisbon, Portugal
Angelo Montanari	University of Udine, Italy
Manuel Ojeda-Aciego	University of Malaga, Spain
Magdalena Ortiz	Vienna University of Technology, Austria
Jeff Z. Pan	University of Aberdeen, UK
David Pearce	Technical University of Madrid, Spain
Henri Prade	IRIT-CNRS, University of Toulouse, France
Maurício Reis	University of Madeira, Portugal
Christian Retoré	LIRMM-CNRS, University of Montpellier, France
Jussi Rintanen	Aalto University, Finland
Sebastian Rudolph	Technical University of Dresden, Germany
Vladislav Ryzhikov	Free University of Bozen-Bolzano, Italy
Torsten Schaub	University of Potsdam, Germany
Steven Schockaert	Cardiff University, UK
Theresa Swift	NOVALINKS, New University of Lisbon, Portugal
Jakub Szymanik	University of Amsterdam, The Netherlands
Paolo Torroni	University of Bologna, Italy
Mirek Truszczynski	University of Kentucky, USA
Leon van der Torre	University of Luxembourg, Luxembourg
Ivan Varzinczak	CRIL-CNRS, University of Artois, France
Joost Vennekens	Catholic University of Leuven, Belgium
Rineke Verbrugge	University of Groningen, The Netherlands
Carlos Viegas Damásio	CENTRIA, New University of Lisbon, Portugal
Toby Walsh	NICTA and UNSW, Australia
Mary-Anne Williams	University of Technology Sydney, Australia
Frank Wolter	University of Liverpool, UK
Stefan Woltran	Vienna University of Technology, Austria

Additional Reviewers

Alviano, Mario
Antoniou, Grigoris
Bogaerts, Bart
Cuteri, Bernardo
Dennis, Louise
Diller, Martin
Diéguez, Martín
Dvořák, Wolfgang
Fandinno, Jorge
Fernandez Gil, Oliver
Gonçalves, Ricardo
Hoffmann, Guillaume
Jansen, Joachim
Janssens, Laurent
Lagniez, Jean Marie
Lapauw, Ruben
Linsbichler, Thomas
Madrid, Nicolas
Manna, Marco
Maubert, Bastien

Mora Bonilla, Angel
Motik, Boris
Obermeier, Philipp
Ostrowski, Max
Peppas, Pavlos
Peñaloza, Rafael
Pieris, Andreas
Ricca, Francesco
Schellhorn, Sebastian
Schwind, Nicolas
Szalas, Andrzej
Tabatabaei, Masoud
Thiele, Sven
Valverde, Agustin
van der Hallen, Matthias
Velázquez-Quesada, Fernando R.
Vitacolonna, Nicola
Wheeler, Gregory
Zhuang, Zhiqiang

Abstracts of Invited Talks

Frontiers of Cognitive Computing

Costas Bekas

IBM Research - Zurich, Zurich, Switzerland
bek@zurich.ibm.com

Cognitive Computing is the new frontier of the information age. Computers have evolved into indispensable tools of our modern societies, having modernized numerous aspects of our everyday lives. Computers have facilitated the acquisition, storage and access of huge amounts of data since the very first electronic general purpose machines of the 1940s. Since then, we learned how to program computers in order to allow uses that even the wildest imagination of computer pioneers of the 50s and 60s did not capture, such as the internet, social networks and simulations of nature of incredible fidelity. Cognitive computing turns our trusted programmable machines, into cognitive companions. The systems are not programmed to simply achieve a task, but rather they are developed to reason with us in ways that are natural for us. They can debate with us, test our ideas, as these are expressed in natural language, against incredible volumes of data and give us insights that ultimately free us and let us focus on and use our deepest of human capabilities: intuition and intelligence. Cognitive systems mimic the way we humans reason, allowing us to express in unstructured ways, such as speech and vision in order to achieve in a small fraction of the previously required time feats such as pharmaceuticals and materials discovery, attacking cancer, understand complex natural ecosystems as well as man-made ecosystems such as the economy and technology. We will discuss the remarkable progress of cognitive computing and give a glimpse of what the future may look like.

To the Extent that You Are Like a Grape: Symbolic Models of Analogy and Concept Blending in Cognitive AI

Tarek R. Besold

University of Bremen, Bremen, Germany
tbesold@uni-bremen.de

Analogy is one of the most studied representatives of a family of non-classical forms of reasoning working across different domains, usually taken to play a crucial role in creative thought and problem-solving. In the first part of the talk, I will shortly introduce general principles of computational analogy models (relying on a generalisation-based approach to analogy-making). We will then have a closer look at Heuristic-Driven Theory Projection (HDTP) as an example for a theoretical framework and implemented system: HDTP computes analogical relations and inferences for domains which are represented using many-sorted first-order logic languages, applying a restricted form of higher-order anti-unification for finding shared structural elements common to both domains. The presentation of the framework will be followed by a few reflections on the "cognitive plausibility" of the approach motivated by theoretical complexity and tractability considerations.

In the second part of the talk I will discuss an application of HDTP to modeling essential parts of concept blending processes as current "hot topic" in Cognitive Science. Here, I will sketch an analogy-inspired formal account of concept blending — developed in the European FP7-funded Concept Invention Theory (COINVENT) project— which, among others, combines HDTP with mechanisms from Case-Based Reasoning.

The FO(.) Knowledge Base System Project

Marc Denecker

Katholieke Universiteit Leuven, Leuven, Belgium
Marc.Denecker@cs.kuleuven.be

The goal of this project is to build a Knowledge Base System for an expressive knowledge representation language. Such systems allow to separate declarative knowledge from the problems that arise in the application domain, allowing to reuse the knowledge base to solve different computational tasks by applying different forms of inference. On the logical level, we start from classical first order logic (FO) (the notation FO(.) is used here as a generic term to denote extensions of classical first order logic FO). In this logic, we integrate various language constructs from different computational logic paradigms: types, inductive definitions, aggregates, (bounded) arithmetic, ... The goal is to achieve an expressive, cleanly integrated knowledge representation language with possible world semantics and a well-understood informal semantics of mathematical precision. On the computational level, the project aims to integrate and extend technologies developed in various computational logic fields to build a Knowledge Base System that supports various forms of inference.

Motivations, principles and research questions raised by such a project will be discussed. I will give an overview and demonstration of the current IDP system and some applications. An application for interactive configuration will serve to highlight a principle that distinguishes declarative modelling from programming: the separation of knowledge from problems and the possibility to apply multiple forms of inference on the knowledge base to solve different computational tasks. We discuss how even interactive systems can be described and "run" within FO(.).

Hybrid Reasoning with Answer Set Programming

Torsten Schaub

University of Potsdam, Potsdam, Germany
Inria Rennes, Rennes, France
torsten@cs.uni-potsdam.de

Answer Set Programming (ASP) provides an approach to declarative problem solving that combines a rich yet simple modeling language with effective Boolean constraint solving capacities. This makes ASP a model, ground, and solve paradigm, in which a problem is expressed as a set of first-order rules, which are subsequently turned into a propositional format by systematically replacing all variables, before finally the models of the resulting propositional rules are computed. ASP is particularly suited for modeling problems in the area of Knowledge Representation and Reasoning involving incomplete, inconsistent, and changing information due to its non-monotonic semantic foundations. From a formal perspective, ASP allows for solving all search problems in NP (and NP^{NP}) in a uniform way. Hence, more generally, ASP is well-suited for solving hard combinatorial search (and optimization) problems. Interesting applications of ASP include decision support systems for NASA shuttle controllers, industrial team-building, music composition, natural language processing, package configuration, phylogenetics, robotics, systems biology, timetabling, and many more.

However, despite its growing popularity, ASP is not a silver bullet. For instance, it became clear early on that ASP fails to handle large numeric domains. This was addressed by Gelfond et al. in 2005 by proposing an integration of ASP and Constraint Processing (CP). This influential work has given rise to the subarea of Constraint ASP (CASP). Although this is an exemplar of hybridizing ASP, the need for integrating special-purpose reasoning is omnipresent when it comes to attacking real-world applications. This includes the integration of ASP with linear programming in bio-informatics, with geometrical reasoning in robotics, simulation in hardware design, and many more. This reveals the need for a principled way of integrating ASP with dedicated reasoning formalisms, both at the semantic and implementation level. Although this development has already been anticipated in the area of Satisfiability Testing (SAT), leading to the subfield of SAT Modulo Theories (SMT), it only serves as a limited blueprint for ASP. This is because (i) it only deals with solving and ignores modeling and grounding and (ii) it is monotonic and thus follows different semantic principles.

The talk will start with an introduction to CASP and sketch important aspects and insights gained in the development of the CASP solver *clingcon*. Building on this, we will describe the general framework for integrating theory reasoning into ASP offered by the fifth generation of the ASP system *clingo*. And finally we sketch a novel semantic approach to integrating ASP and CP, called the logic of *Here-and-There with constraints*.

We Reason in Uncertainty, But of What Kinds?

Keith Stenning

The University of Edinburgh, Scotland, UK
k.stenning@ed.ac.uk

If logic is to be helpful in analysing human reasoning, we first need to acknowledge the heterogeneity of the kinds of reasoning that people do. There has been a strong shift in the study of human reasoning away from classical logic toward probability theory as the formal framework, and for many researchers probability is all that is needed to analyse any human reasoning. Reasoning in this respect is held to be homogeneous. We have argued elsewhere that this move is from the frying pan into the fire, not because probability (or classical logic) cannot be useful, but because homogeneity is empirically and formally disastrous (Stenning et al. (submitted); Stenning and van Lambalgen (2008); Besold et al. (submitted)). We take it that in AI, this is all commonplace. But some of the insights arising in cognition may be of interest to AI researchers. Engaging with logical multiplicity focusses attention on qualitatively different kinds of uncertainty, and how to characterise them. This talk will present some current thinking on that question. The idea is to use logics to individuate kinds of uncertainty. In particular we contrast Logic Programming (LP) as a nonmonotonic logic, here specialised for analysing human discourse processing, and with some track record in modelling discourse semantics, with, on the one hand classical logic, and on the other probability. When examined close up, it is emerges just how what different kinds of things the uncertainties of these three system are.

References

Besold, T.R., Garcez, A., Stenning, K., Torre, L.V.D.: Reasoning in Non-probabilistic Uncertainty: Logic Programming and Neural- Symbolic Computing as Examples. Minds and Machines (submitted)

Stenning, K., Martignon, L., Varga, A.: Adaptive Reasoning: Integrating Fast and Frugal Heuristics with a Logic of Interpretation. Decision (submitted)

Stenning, K., van Lambalgen, M.: Human Reasoning and Cognitive Science. MIT Press, Cambridge (2008)

Over, D.E.: New paradigm psychology of reasoning. Think. Reason. 15(4), 431–438 (2009)

Contents

Short Papers

Full Papers

Metabolic Pathways as Temporal Logic Programs

Jean-Marc Alliot[1], Martín Diéguez[2(⊠)], and Luis Fariñas del Cerro[3]

[1] IRIT - Toulouse University, Toulouse, France
jean-marc.alliot@irit.fr
[2] IRIT - CIMI - Toulouse University, Toulouse, France
martin.dieguez@irit.fr
[3] IRIT - CNRS - Toulouse University, Toulouse, France
farinas@irit.fr

Abstract. Metabolic Networks, formed by series of metabolic pathways, are made of intracellular and extracellular reactions that determine the biochemical properties of a cell and by a set of interactions that guide and regulate the activity of these reactions. Cancers, for example, can sometimes appear in a cell as a result of some pathology in a metabolic pathway. Most of these pathways are formed by an intricate and complex network of chain reactions, and they can be represented in a human readable form using graphs which describe the cell signaling pathways.

In this paper we present a logic, called Molecular Equilibrium Logic, a nonmonotonic logic which allows representing metabolic pathways. We also show how this logic can be presented in terms of a syntactical subset of Temporal Equilibrium Logic, the temporal extension of Equilibrium Logic, called Splittable Temporal Logic Programs.

1 Introduction

Molecular Interaction Maps [20], formed by a series of metabolic pathways, are made of intracellular and extracellular reactions that determine the biochemical properties of a cell by consuming and producing proteins, and by a set of interactions that guide and regulate the activity of these reactions. These reactions are at the center of a cell's existence, and are regulated by other proteins, which can either activate these reactions or inhibit them. These pathways form an intricate and complex network of chain reactions, and can be represented using graphs. *Molecular Interaction Maps* (MIM's) [1] are such a representation, and it is possible to write these graphs using editors such as Pathvisio [17] (which outputs its own XML representation) or System Biology Markup Language (SBML) [2] editors.

This research was partially supported by the French Spanish Laboratory for Advanced Studies in Information, Representation and Processing (LEA-IREP). Martín Diéguez was supported by the Centre international de mathématiques et d'informatique (contract ANR-11-LABX-0040-CIMI).

L. Michael and A. Kakas (Eds.): JELIA 2016, LNAI 10021, pp. 3–17, 2016.
DOI: 10.1007/978-3-319-48758-8_1

These graphs can become extremely large, and although essential for knowledge capitalization and formalization, they are difficult to use because: (1) Reading is complex due to the very large number of elements, and reasoning is even more difficult; (2) Using a graph to communicate goals is only partially suitable because the representation formalism requires expertise; (3) Graphs often contain implicit knowledge, that is taken for granted by one expert, but is missed by another one.

Our aim consists in providing a logical framework that helps users to detect possible inconsistencies as well as reasoning on such kind of maps. We have chosen to use Pathvisio and its XML representation as our editor/representation of choice for representing these graphs, but this work could be extended to SBML and SBML editors. In [11], we modelled a restricted subclass of MIM's in terms of first-order logic with equality. This work was simplified into propositional logic in [6], which enabled to use all propositional calculus tools such as solving abductive queries on MIM's. Unfortunately that representation was unable to express the temporal properties of MIM, which are implicit in the formalisations. So we extended our work with temporal logic in [5]. This representation was enhanced with a naive approach to abductive temporal reasoning by assuming bounded time and the so-called *closed world assumption* [27], a concept tightly connected with Logic Programming and Non-Monotonic reasoning[1]. The use of non-monotonicity allows us to use defaults and inertia rules to express things like "a protein remains in the environment if it is not used in one reaction", which greatly enhances our temporal descriptions.

In order to incorporate such kind of defaults and to justify the use of the closed world assumption in [5], we present in this paper Molecular Equilibrium Logic (MEL), a reformulation of the temporal version of Molecular Interaction Logic [5] in terms of Equilibrium Logic [25], a well-known logical characterisation of *Stable Models* [15] and *Answer Sets* [9]. Moreover we show the existence of a connection between MEL and Temporal Equilibrium Logic (TEL) [3], the temporal extension of the Equilibrium Logic. By going one step further, we show that MEL can be encoded in a syntactic subclass of TEL called splittable temporal logic programs (STLP's) [4], which allows us to capture the set of Molecular Equilibrium Models (explained in Sect. 4) in terms of a Linear Time Temporal Logic (LTL) formula [22] (see Sect. 7).

The rest of this paper is organized as follows: Sect. 2 presents several biological concepts used along this paper as well as describes the problems to solve in layman's words and with a simple example. Section 3 describes the concepts of production and regulation which are the basic operations present in a MIM. Sections 4 and 5 respectively describe two different semantics based on equilibrium logic: Molecular Equilibrium Logic and Temporal Equilibrium Logic. The former is capable of describing general pathways while the latter is the best-known temporal

---

[1] Regarding non-monotonic approaches to model biological systems, there are several contributions in the area of *Answer Set Programming* [9,28], *action languages* [29] or *Inductive Logic Programming* [12]. In these contributions the temporal behaviour is considered in [29] but both representation and query languages are different.

extension of Equilibrium Logic. In Sect. 6 we establish the relation between the two aforementioned formalisms, which is studied in detail in Sect. 7 where we prove that the Equilibrium Models of our temporal theories can be expressed in Linear Time Temporal Logic [22] via Temporal Completion [4,10].

2   A Simple Classical Example

In this section we introduce the example of the regulation of the *lac* operon [19][2,3], which will be used and developed in the rest of this paper. The lac operon (lactose operon) is an operon required for the transport and metabolism of lactose in many bacteria. Although glucose is the preferred carbon source for most bacteria, the lac operon allows for the effective digestion of lactose when glucose is not available. The lac operon is a sequence of three genes (lacZ, lacY and lacA) which encode 3 enzymes. Then, these enzymes carry the transformation of lactose into glucose. We will concentrate here on lacZ. LacZ encodes the β-galactosidase which cleaves lactose into glucose and galactose. The lac operon uses a two-part control mechanism to ensure that the cell expends energy producing the enzymes encoded by the lac operon only when necessary. First, in the absence of lactose, the lac repressor halts production of the enzymes encoded by the lac operon. Second, in the presence of glucose, the catabolite activator protein (CAP), required for production of the enzymes, remains inactive.

Figure 1(a) describes this regulatory mechanism. The expression of lacZ gene is only possible when RNA polymerase (pink) can bind to a promotor site

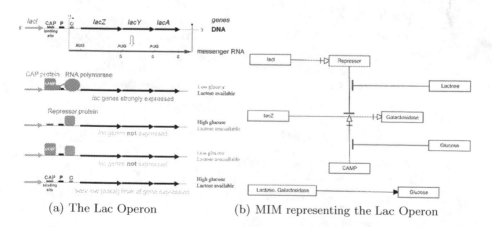

(a) The Lac Operon   (b) MIM representing the Lac Operon

Fig. 1. Graphical and MIM representation of the Lac Operon. (Color figure online)

---

[2] The Nobel prize was awarded to Monod, Jacob and Lwoff in 1965 partly for the discovery of the lac operon by Monod and Jacob [18], which was the first genetic regulatory mechanism to be understood clearly, and is now a "standard" introductory example in molecular biology classes.

[3] A less formal explanation can be found in https://en.wikipedia.org/wiki/Lac_operon.

(marked P, black) upstream the gene. This binding is aided by the cyclic adeno-
sine monophosphate (cAMP in blue) which binds before the promotor on the
CAP site (dark blue). The lacl gene (yellow) encodes the repressor protein Lacl
(yellow) which binds to the promotor site of the RNA polymerase when lactose
is not available, preventing the RNA polymerase to bind to the promoter and
thus blocking the expression of the following genes (lacZ, lacY and lacA): this is
a *negative regulation*, or *inhibition*, as it blocks the production of the proteins.
When lactose is present, the repressor protein Lacl binds with lactose and is
converted to allolactose, which is not able to bind to the promotor site, thus
enabling RNA polymerase to bind to the promotor site and to start expressing
the lacZ gene if cAMP is bound to CAP. cAMP is on the opposite a *positive
regulation*, or an *activation*, as its presence is necessary to express the lacZ gene.
However, cAMP is itself regulated negatively by glucose: when glucose is present,
the concentration of cAMP becomes low, and thus cAMP does not bind to the
CAP site, blocking the expression of lacZ. In this figure, we have three kinds of
entities which have different initial settings and temporal dynamics:

- lacl, lacZ and cAMP are initial external conditions of the model and they do
  not evolve in time.
- galactosidase and the repressor protein can only be produced inside the graph,
  and are always absent at the start (time 0) of the modeling. Their value will
  then evolve in time according to the processes described by the graph.
- glucose and lactose also evolve in time (like galactosidase and the repressor
  protein) according to the processes described by the graph, but they are also
  initial conditions of the system, and can either be present or absent at time
  0, like lacl, lacZ and cAMP.

So, an entity must be classified according to two main characteristics: **C1:**
It can evolve in time according to the cell reactions (appear and disappear), or
it can be fixed, such as a condition which is independent of the cell reactions
(temperature, protein always provided in large quantities by the external environment, etc. . .). **C2:** It can be an initial condition of the cell model (present *or*
absent at the beginning of the modeling), or can *only* be produced by the cell.
There are thus three kinds of entities, which have three kind of behaviour:

Exogenous entities: an *exogenous* entity satisfies $C1$ and $\neg C2$; their status
  never change through time: they are set once and for all by the environment
  or by the experimenter at the start of the simulation; the graph never modifies
  their value, and if they are used in a reaction, the environment will always
  provide "enough" of them.
Pure endogenous entities: on the opposite, a *pure endogenous* entity satisfies
  $\neg C1$ and $C2$; their status evolves in time and is set *only* by the dynamic of
  the graph. They are absent at the beginning of the reaction, and can only
  appear if they are produced inside the graph.
Weak endogenous entities: *weak endogenous* entities satisfy $C2$ and $C1$; they
  can be present or absent at the beginning of the process (they are initial
  conditions of the model), however their value after the start of the process is

entirely set by the dynamic of the graph. So they roughly behave like *pure endogenous* entities, but the initial condition can be set by the experimenter.

The status of a protein/condition is something which is set by the biologist, regarding his professional understanding of the biological process described by the graph[4]. However a rule of thumb is that exogenous entities are almost never produced inside the graph (they never appear at the right side of a production arrow), while endogenous entities always appear on the right side of a production arrow (but they can also appear on the left side of a production rule, especially weak endogenous entities). These distinctions are fundamental, because the dynamics of these entities are different and they will have to be formalized differently.

3   Fundamental Operations

The mechanism described in the previous section is summarized in the simplified graph in Fig. 1(b). This example contains all the relationship operators that will be used in the rest of this document. In order to make their presentation clearer, we will distinguish between productions and regulations:

Productions can take two different forms, depending on whether the reactants are consumed by the reactions or not: In Fig. 1(b), lactose and galactosidase produce glucose, and are consumed while doing so, which is thus noted ($galactosidase, lactose \rightarrow glucose$). On the opposite, the expression of the lacZ gene to produce galactosidase (or of the lacI gene to produce the LacI repressor protein) does not consume the gene, and we have thus ($lacZ \dashrightarrow galactosidase$). Generally speaking, If the reaction consumes completely the reactant(s) we write: $a_1, a_2, \cdots, a_n \rightarrow b$ while if the reactants are not consumed by the reaction, we write $a_1, a_2, ...a_n \dashrightarrow b$. In the former representation the production of b completely consumes $a_1, a_2...a_n$ whereas in the latter $a_1, a_2...a_n$ are not consumed when b is produced.

Regulations can also take two forms: every reaction can be either *inhibited* or *activated* by other proteins or conditions. In the Diagram of Fig. 1(b), the production of galactosidase from the expression of the lacZ gene is activated by cAMP (we use $cAMP \dashrightarrow$ to express activation). At the same time the same production of galactosidase is blocked (or inhibited) by the LacI repressor protein (noted $Repressor \dashv$).

Generally speaking, we write $a_1, a_2, ...a_n \dashrightarrow$ if the simultaneous presence of $a_1, a_2, ...a_n$ activates a production or another regulation. Similarly we write

---

[4] It is important here to notice that lactose can be either considered as a weak endogenous variable, or as an exogenous variable if we consider that the environment is always providing "enough" lactose. It is a simple example which shows that variables in a graph can be interpreted differently according to what is going to be observed.

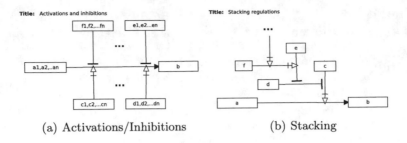

(a) Activations/Inhibitions   (b) Stacking

Fig. 2. Examples of activations and inhibitions and stacking contexts.

$a_1, a_2, ... a_n \dashv$ if the simultaneous presence of $a_1, a_2, ... a_n$ inhibits a production or another regulation. On Fig. 2(a), we have a summary of basic inhibitions/activations on a reaction: the production of b from $a_1, \cdots, a_n$ is activated by the simultaneous presence of $c_1, \cdots, c_n$ **or** by the simultaneous presence of $d_1, \cdots, d_n$, and inhibited by the simultaneous presence of $e_1, \cdots, e_n$ **or** by the simultaneous presence of $f_1, \cdots, f_n$. These regulations are often "stacked", on many levels (see Fig. 2(b)). For example in Fig. 1(b), the inhibition by the LacI repressor protein of the production of galactosidase can itself be inhibited by the presence of lactose, while the activation of the same production by cAMP is inhibited by the presence of glucose.

A final word of warning is necessary. Graphs pragmatically describe sequences of operations that biologists find important. They are only a model of some of the biological, molecular and chemical reactions that take place inside the cell; they can also be written in many different ways, depending on the functional block or operations that biologists want to describe, and some relationships are sometimes simply left out because they are considered not important for the function which is described in a particular graph.

4   Molecular Equilibrium Logic

In this section we introduce *Molecular Equilibrium Logic*. The syntax of this logic consists of two elementary building blocks: *pathway context* and *pathway formula*. The former corresponds to the representation of the activation and inhibition conditions while the latter allows representing the production of new substances (see Sect. 3). A *pathway context* is formed by expressions defined by the following grammar:

$$\alpha ::= \langle \{\alpha_1, \cdots, \alpha_n\} P \twoheadrightarrow, \{\alpha_{n+1}, \cdots, \alpha_{n+m}\} Q \dashv \rangle,$$

where P and Q are sets (finite and possibly empty) of propositional variables representing the conditions of activation ($\twoheadrightarrow$) and inhibition ($\dashv$) of the reaction. Every context can be associated with a (possibly empty) set of activation (α_i, with $1 \leq i \leq n$) and inhibition (α_j, with $1 \leq j \leq m$) contexts. One or both sets can be empty. Broadly speaking, the context associated with a pathway formula represents the set of substances that must be present or absent in order to make the reaction possible. As an example of context, let us consider the example of the Lac Operon, whose graph is displayed in Fig. 1(b). The context associated with the production rule $lacZ \rightarrow Galactosidase$ corresponds to the following expression:

$$\gamma = \langle \{ \langle \varnothing \rightarrow, \{Glucose\} \rightarrow \rangle \} \{CAMP\} \rightarrow, \{ \langle \varnothing \rightarrow, \{Lactose\} \rightarrow \rangle \} \{Repressor\} \rightarrow \rangle. \tag{1}$$

A *Pathway formula* is a rule built from the grammar $F ::= [\alpha] (P^\wedge \multimap q) \mid F \wedge F$, where α represents a context, $\multimap \in \{ \rightarrow, \rightarrow \}$, $P^\wedge$ stands for a conjunction of all atoms in the finite set P and q corresponds to a propositional variable. Regarding our running example, which is shown in Fig. 1(b), consists of three different pathways, each of them corresponds to one of the following pathway formulas:[5]

$$[\langle \varnothing \varnothing \rightarrow, \varnothing \varnothing \rightarrow \rangle] (Lactose, Galactosidase \rightarrow Glucose) \tag{2}$$

$$[\langle \varnothing \varnothing \rightarrow, \varnothing \varnothing \rightarrow \rangle] (lacl \rightarrow Repressor) \tag{3}$$

$$[\gamma] (lacZ \rightarrow Galactosidase). \tag{4}$$

From a biological point of view, substances can be created or destroyed by reactions that might take place in parallel. Therefore, we must take into account situations where a protein is produced and consumed at the same time or where a protein remains present because it was not involved in a reaction which would have consumed it. We model this aspect by extending the set of propositional variables Σ to the set $\widehat{\Sigma} = \Sigma \cup \{ \mathbf{Pr}(p_1), \cdots, \mathbf{Pr}(p_n) \} \cup \{ \mathbf{Cn}(p_1), \cdots, \mathbf{Cn}(p_n) \}$, where $p_1, \cdots, p_n$ are either a weak or pure endogenous variables. Informally speaking, every atom of the form $\mathbf{Pr}(p)$ means that p is produced as a result of a chemical reaction while $\mathbf{Cn}(p)$ means that the reactive p is consumed in a reaction. Regarding our running example, we notice that the production of $Glucose$ implies that $Galactosidase$ is consumed. However, $Lactose$, as an exogenous variable is never consumed. From now on, we will use the symbols Σ and $\widehat{\Sigma}$ referring to, respectively, the signature (set of entities occurring in a MIM) and its corresponding extension.

The semantics of MEL is based on the monotonic logic of Molecular Here and There (MHT) plus a minimisation criterion among the Here and There models. Given a set of propositional variables Σ we define a *Molecular Here and There*[6] *interpretation* $\mathbf{M}$ as an infinite sequence of pairs $m_i = \langle H_i, T_i \rangle$ with $i = 0, 1, 2, \ldots$ where $H_i \subseteq T_i \subseteq \widehat{\Sigma}$ satisfying the following properties: for all endogenous variable $p \in \Sigma$ and for all exogenous variable $q \in \Sigma$ and for all $i \geq 0$,

---

[5] Notice that only the pathway formula associated with the production of $Galactosidase$ has an associated context, defined in (1), while the rest of pathway formulas have an empty context.

[6] Here and There [16] is an intermediate logic which severs as a monotonic basis for the Equilibrium Models [25], a logical characterisation of the Stable Model semantics [15].

(A) if $\mathbf{Pr}\,(p) \in H_i$ then $p \in H_{i+1}$;

(B) if $p \in H_i$ and $\mathbf{Cn}\,(p) \notin T_i$ then $p \in H_{i+1}$;

(C) if $\mathbf{Pr}\,(p) \in T_i$ then $p \in T_{i+1}$;

(D) if $p \in T_i$ and $\mathbf{Cn}\,(p) \notin T_i$ then $p \in T_{i+1}$;

(E) if $q \in H_i$ then $q \in H_{i+1}$;

(F) if $q \in T_i$ then $q \in T_{i+1}$.

For simplicity, given a MHT interpretation, we write $\mathbf{H}$ (resp. $\mathbf{T}$) to represent the sequence of pair components $H_0, H_1, \ldots$ (resp. $T_0, T_1, \ldots$). Using this notation, we will sometimes abbreviate the interpretation as $\mathbf{M} = \langle \mathbf{H}, \mathbf{T} \rangle$. If $\mathbf{H} = \mathbf{T}$, we will call $\mathbf{M}$ *total* model.

Before presenting the satisfaction relation we introduce the *activation* ($\mathcal{A}(\alpha)$) and *inhibition* ($\mathcal{I}(\alpha)$) expressions associated with a pathway context $\alpha = \langle \{\alpha_1, \cdots, \alpha_n\} P \twoheadrightarrow , \{\beta_{n+1}, \cdots, \beta_{n+m}\} Q \dashrightarrow \rangle$. Informally speaking, $\mathcal{A}(\alpha)$ characterizes when the context α is active while $\mathcal{I}(\alpha)$ describes when it is inhibited. These expressions, which will be used in the definition of the satisfaction relation, are defined as follows:

$$\mathcal{A}(\alpha) = \bigwedge_{p \in P} p \wedge \bigwedge_{i=1}^{n} \mathcal{A}(\alpha_i) \wedge (\bigvee_{q \in Q} \neg q \vee \bigwedge_{j=n+1}^{m} \mathcal{I}(\beta_j))$$

$$\mathcal{I}(\alpha) = \bigvee_{p \in P} \neg p \vee \bigvee_{i=1}^{n} \mathcal{I}(\alpha_i) \vee (\bigwedge_{q \in Q} q \wedge \bigwedge_{j=n+1}^{m} \mathcal{A}(\beta_j)).$$

If one part of the context α is empty, then the corresponding part is of course absent in $\mathcal{A}(\alpha)$ and $\mathcal{I}(\alpha)$. For instance, the activation and inhibition expressions of the context γ described in (1) correspond to the Boolean expressions: $\mathcal{A}(\gamma) = CAMP \wedge \neg Glucose \wedge (\neg Repressor \vee Lactose)$ and $\mathcal{I}(\gamma) = \neg CAMP \vee Glucose \vee (Repressor \wedge \neg Lactose)$.

Given a MHT interpretation $\mathbf{M}$, $i \geq 0$ and a pathway formula F on Σ, we define the satisfaction relation ($\mathbf{M}, i \models F$) as follows:

- $\mathbf{M}, i \models p$ iff $p \in H_i$, for any variable $p \in \Sigma$;
- $\mathbf{M}, i \models \neg p$ iff $p \notin T_i$, with $p \in \Sigma$;
- disjunction and conjunction are satisfied in usual way;
- $\mathbf{M}, i \models [\alpha](P^\wedge \twoheadrightarrow q)$ iff for all $\mathbf{H}' \in \{\mathbf{H}, \mathbf{T}\}$ and $j \geq i$, if $\langle \mathbf{H}', \mathbf{T}' \rangle, j \models \mathcal{A}(\alpha)$ and $P \subseteq H'_j$, then $\{\mathbf{Pr}\,(q), \mathbf{Cn}\,(p) \mid p \in P$ an endogenous variable$\} \subseteq H'_j$;
- $\mathbf{M}, i \models [\alpha](P^\wedge \dashrightarrow q)$ iff for all $\mathbf{H}' \in \{\mathbf{H}, \mathbf{T}\}$ and $j \geq i$, if $\langle \mathbf{H}', \mathbf{T}' \rangle, j \models \mathcal{A}(\alpha)$ and $P \subseteq H'_j$, then $\mathbf{Pr}\,(q) \in H'_j$;

As in other equilibrium logic extensions, we relate two MHT models $\mathbf{M} = \langle \mathbf{H}, \mathbf{T} \rangle$ and $\mathbf{M}' = \langle \mathbf{H}', \mathbf{T}' \rangle$ as follows: $\mathbf{M}' \leq \mathbf{M}$ iff $\mathbf{T} = \mathbf{T}'$ and for all $i \geq 0$ $H'_i \subseteq H_i$. $\mathbf{M}' < \mathbf{M}$ if $\mathbf{M}' \leq \mathbf{M}$ and $\mathbf{M}' \neq \mathbf{M}$. We say that a MHT interpretation $\mathbf{M}$ is a *Molecular Equilibrium Model* of a set of pathway formulas Γ iff $\mathbf{M}$ is total, $\mathbf{M}, 0 \models \Gamma$ an there is no $\mathbf{M}'$ such that $\mathbf{M}' < \mathbf{M}$ such that $\mathbf{M}', 0 \models \Gamma$.

5 Temporal Equilibrium Logic

Temporal Equilibrium Logic (TEL) [3] extends Equilibrium Logic [25][7] with temporal operators from Linear Time Temporal Logic [22]. TEL can also be seen as a temporal extension of the stable models semantics [15] for logic programming. This formalism is very suitable for representing the temporal behaviour of biological systems, since the use of the laws of inertia allows us to avoid the specification of the large number of frame axioms [24] that should be considered in the representation. The TEL formulas we will consider along this paper are built from the following grammar:

$$\varphi ::= \bot \mid p \mid \varphi_1 \wedge \varphi_2 \mid \varphi_1 \vee \varphi_2 \mid \varphi_1 \rightarrow \varphi_2 \mid \bigcirc\varphi_1 \mid \Box\varphi_1 \mid \Diamond\varphi_2,$$

where φ_1 and φ_2 are also temporal formulas. Regarding the modal operators, $\bigcirc$ is read "next", $\Box$ is read "forever" and $\Diamond$ stands for "eventually" or "at some future point".

The semantics of TEL is defined, in the same spirit as in Equilibrium Logic, in terms of a temporal extension of the logic of Here and There [16], called Temporal Here and There (THT), plus a minimisation criterion among the THT models. We define a *Temporal Here and There interpretation* $\mathbf{M}$ as an infinite sequence of pairs $m_i = \langle H_i, T_i \rangle$ with $i = 0, 1, 2, \ldots$ where $H_i \subseteq T_i \subseteq \widehat{\Sigma}$. For simplicity, given a temporal interpretation, we write $\mathbf{H}$ (resp. $\mathbf{T}$) to represent the sequence of pair components $H_0, H_1, \ldots$ (resp. $T_0, T_1, \ldots$). Using this notation, we will sometimes abbreviate the interpretation as $\mathbf{M} = \langle \mathbf{H}, \mathbf{T} \rangle$. An interpretation $\mathbf{M} = \langle \mathbf{H}, \mathbf{T} \rangle$ is said to be *total* when $\mathbf{H} = \mathbf{T}$. The satisfaction relation $\models$ is interpreted as follows on THT models ($\mathbf{M}$ is a THT model and $k \in \mathbb{N}$):

1. $\mathbf{M}, k \models p$ iff $p \in H_k$, for any $p \in \widehat{\Sigma}$.
2. $\mathbf{M}, k \models \varphi \wedge \psi$ iff $\mathbf{M}, k \models \varphi$ and $\mathbf{M}, k \models \psi$.
3. $\mathbf{M}, k \models \varphi \vee \psi$ iff $\mathbf{M}, k \models \varphi$ or $\mathbf{M}, k \models \psi$.
4. $\mathbf{M}, k \models \varphi \rightarrow \psi$ iff for all $\mathbf{H}' \in \{\mathbf{H}, \mathbf{T}\}$, $\langle \mathbf{H}', \mathbf{T} \rangle, k \not\models \varphi$ or $\langle \mathbf{H}', \mathbf{T} \rangle, k \models \psi$.
5. $\mathbf{M}, k \models \bigcirc\varphi$ iff $\mathbf{M}, k+1 \models \varphi$.
6. $\mathbf{M}, k \models \Box\varphi$ iff for all $j \geq k$, $\mathbf{M}, j \models \varphi$.
7. $\mathbf{M}, k \models \Diamond\varphi$ iff there is $j \geq k$ such that $\mathbf{M}, j \models \varphi$.
8. never $\mathbf{M}, k \models \bot$.

Note that, as happens in Equilibrium logic, $\neg\varphi \stackrel{\text{def}}{=} \varphi \rightarrow \bot$.

Proposition 1. *Let* $\mathbf{M}$ *be a model. For all pathway context* α *and for all* $i \in \mathbb{N}$, *(a)* $\mathbf{M}, i \models_{MHT} \mathcal{A}(\alpha)$ *iff* $\mathbf{M}, i \models_{THT} \mathcal{A}(\alpha)$; *(b)* $\mathbf{M}, i \models_{MHT} \mathcal{I}(\alpha)$ *iff* $\mathbf{M}, i \models_{THT} \mathcal{I}(\alpha)$;

Proof. First note that $\mathcal{A}(\alpha)$ and $\mathcal{I}(\alpha)$ are build on the language p, $\neg p$ (with $p \in \Sigma$), $\wedge$ and $\vee$. Second, remark that, regarding the aforementioned language, MHT and THT have the same satisfaction relation (note that when negation only affects to atoms of Σ, $\mathbf{M}, i \models_{THT} \neg p$ iff $p \notin T_i$ iff $\mathbf{M}, i \models_{MHT} \neg p$). From all those facts it is easy to prove, by induction, (a) and (b). ∎

---

[7] Modal extensions of Equilibrium Logic and the logic of Here and There can be considered as promising lines of research which lead to several remarkable results, among others, [7,13].

A formula φ is THT-*valid* if $\mathbf{M}, 0 \models \varphi$ for any $\mathbf{M}$. An interpretation $\mathbf{M}$ is a THT-*model* of a theory Γ, written $\mathbf{M} \models \Gamma$, if $\mathbf{M}, 0 \models \varphi$, for all formula $\varphi \in \Gamma$. Notice that when we disregard temporal operators, we obtain the logic of HT. On the other hand, if we restrict the semantics to total interpretations, $\langle \mathbf{T}, \mathbf{T} \rangle \models \varphi$ corresponds to satisfaction of formulas $\mathbf{T} \models \varphi$ in LTL. Given two interpretations $\mathbf{M} = \langle \mathbf{H}, \mathbf{T} \rangle$ and $\mathbf{M}' = \langle \mathbf{H}', \mathbf{T}' \rangle$ we say that $\mathbf{M}'$ is *lower or equal than* $\mathbf{M}$, written $\mathbf{M}' \leq \mathbf{M}$, when $\mathbf{T}' = \mathbf{T}$ and for all $i \geq 0$, $H_i' \subseteq H_i$. As usual, $\mathbf{M}' < \mathbf{M}$ stands for $\mathbf{M}' \leq \mathbf{M}$ and $\mathbf{M}' \neq \mathbf{M}$. Finally, an interpretation $\mathbf{M}$ is said to be a *temporal equilibrium model* of a theory Γ if $\mathbf{M}$ is a total model of Γ and there is no other $\mathbf{M}' < \mathbf{M}$, such that $\mathbf{M}' \models \Gamma$.

6   From Molecular Equilibrium Logic to Temporal Equilibrium Logic

In this section we first show how MEL can be embedded in TEL by providing a translation between their monotonic basis, MHT and THT. The reader might have noticed that the only differences between MHT and THT interpretations are the constraints (A)-(F), which are imposed on the MHT. Those restrictions can be captured in THT by adding the following rule of *inertia*, for any variable $p \in \Sigma$ as follows:

$$inertia(p) \overset{\text{def}}{=} \begin{cases} \Box \left((\mathbf{Pr}\,(p) \vee (p \wedge \neg \mathbf{Cn}\,(p))) \to \bigcirc p \right) \text{ if } p \text{ is an endogenous variable} \\ \Box\,(p \to \bigcirc p) \qquad\qquad\qquad\qquad\quad \text{ if } p \text{ is an exogenous variable.} \end{cases}$$

Informally speaking, endogenous variables are true in the next state if they are produced or if they are present and not consumed. On the other hand, exogenous variables are automatically passed to the next state since they are never produced or consumed. They are just present in the environment.

Proposition 2. *Given a signature Σ, let $\mathbf{M}$ be a THT interpretation on $\widehat{\Sigma}$. $\mathbf{M}$ is a MHT model (that is, $\mathbf{M}$ satisfies conditions (A)–(F)) iff $\mathbf{M}, 0 \models_{THT} inertia(p)$, for all variable $p \in \Sigma$.*

Proof. From right to left, let us assume that $\mathbf{M}, 0 \models_{THT} inertia(p)$. It follows for all $i \geq 0$ $\mathbf{M}, i \models_{THT} \mathbf{Pr}\,(p) \vee (p \wedge \neg \mathbf{Cn}\,(p)) \to \bigcirc p$, if p is an endogenous variable or $\mathbf{M}, i \models_{THT} (p \to \bigcirc p)$ if p is exogenous. Using the THT satisfaction relation, it can be easily seen that satisfying both implications implies to meet conditions (A)–(F). Therefore $\mathbf{M}$ is a MHT model.

Conversely, if $\mathbf{M}$ is an MHT model, $\mathbf{M}$ satisfies conditions (A)–(F). It is easy to prove, by using the satisfiability of THT, that conditions (A)–(D) imply that $\mathbf{M}, 0 \models_{THT} inertia(p)$ for endogenous variables while conditions (E)–(F) imply that $\mathbf{M}, 0 \models_{THT} inertia(p)$ for exogenous. ∎

Given a pathway formula F, we define the THT formula $tr\,(F)$ (on $\widehat{\Sigma}$) as:

$$tr\,([\alpha]\,(P^{\wedge} \twoheadrightarrow q)) = \Box \left(\mathcal{A}(\alpha) \wedge P^{\wedge} \to \left(\mathbf{Pr}\,(q) \wedge \bigwedge_{p \in P} \mathbf{Cn}\,(p) \right) \right);$$

$$tr\,([\alpha]\,(P^{\wedge} \dashrightarrow q)) = \Box\,(\mathcal{A}(\alpha) \wedge P^{\wedge} \to \mathbf{Pr}\,(q));$$

$$tr\,(F_1 \wedge F_2) = tr\,(F_1) \wedge tr\,(F_1),$$

where F_1 and F_2 are arbitrary pathway formulas and both p and q are endogenous variables. Going back to our running example, the temporal theory associated with (2)–(4) would correspond to the following THT formula:

$$\Box\,(Lactose \wedge Galactosidase \rightarrow (\mathbf{Pr}\,(Glucose) \wedge \mathbf{Cn}\,(Galactosidase)))\,(2)$$
$$\wedge \Box\,(lacI \rightarrow \mathbf{Pr}\,(Repressor))\,(3)$$
$$\wedge \Box\,(\mathcal{A}(\gamma) \wedge lacZ \rightarrow \mathbf{Pr}\,(Galactosidase))\,(4)$$

Theorem 1 (Correspondence). *Let F be a pathway formula built on Σ and $\mathbf{M}$ be a THT interpretation on $\widehat{\Sigma}$. It holds that:*

(a) $\mathbf{M}, 0 \models_{MHT} F$ *iff* $\mathbf{M}, 0 \models_{THT} tr\,(F) \wedge \bigwedge\limits_{p \in \Sigma} inertia(p)$;

(b) $\mathbf{M}, 0 \models_{MEL} F$ *iff* $\mathbf{M}, 0 \models_{TEL} tr\,(F) \wedge \bigwedge\limits_{p \in \Sigma} inertia(p)$.

Proof. We first consider Case (a). Thanks to Proposition 2, we can reduce the whole proof to the claim: $\mathbf{M}, 0 \models_{MHT} F$ iff $\mathbf{M}, 0 \models_{THT} tr\,(F)$. It is easily to check that this claim for elements of Σ as well as conjuntion and disjunction of elements of Σ (see Proposition 1). For the case of pathway formulas we proceed by induction on the form of the pathway formulas: base cases, $[\alpha]\,(P^\wedge \rightarrow q)$ and $[\alpha]\,(P^\wedge \dashrightarrow q)$, are proved by means of the satisfaction relation of THT and MHT, Condition (A)-(F) and Proposition 1. The conjunction of pathway formulas follows directly from the induction hypothesis. Finally, Case (b) follows from (a) since the minimisation used for computing the equilibrium models is the same in both formalisms. ∎

7 MIM's as Splittable Temporal Logic Programs

In this section we show how $tr\,(F)$ can be turned into an *splittable temporal logic program* (STLP), a syntactical subset of TEL which has been studied in detail in [4]. A *Temporal Logic Program Π on $\widehat{\Sigma}$* is said to be *splittable* if Π consists of rules of any of the forms:

(1) $B \wedge N \rightarrow H$;

(2) $B \wedge \circ B' \wedge N \wedge \circ N' \rightarrow \circ H'$;

(3) $\Box(B \wedge N \rightarrow H)$;

(4) $\Box(B \wedge \circ B' \wedge N \wedge \circ N' \rightarrow \circ H')$,

where B and B' are conjunctions of atoms, N and N' are conjunctions of negative literals like $\neg p$ with $p \in \widehat{\Sigma}$, and H and H' are disjunctions of atoms. The *(positive) dependency graph*, of an STLP Π, noted $G(\Pi)$, is a graph whose nodes are the atoms of Π and the edges are defined by the expression below:

$$E = \{(p, p) \mid p \in E\} \cup \{(p, q) \mid \exists B \rightarrow H \in \Pi \text{ s.t. } p \in H \text{ and } q \in B\}.$$

A set of atoms L is called a *loop* of a logic program Π iff the subgraph of $G(\Pi)$ induced by L is strongly connected. Notice that reflexivity of $G(\Pi)$ implies that for any atom p, the singleton $\{p\}$ is also a loop. Every loop of $G(\Pi)$

generates an implication which is called *loop formula* [4,14,21][8]. By $LF(\Pi)$ we refer to the conjunction of all loop formulas of Π.

Theorem 2 (from [4]). *Let Π be an STLP and* **T** *an LTL model of Π. Then* $\langle \mathbf{T}, \mathbf{T} \rangle \models_{TEL} \Pi$ *iff* **T** $\models_{LTL} \Pi \wedge LF(\Pi)$. ∎

$tr(\Gamma) \wedge \bigwedge_{p \in \Sigma} inertia(p)$ can be expressed as a STLP, thanks to the following THT equivalences:

(1) $\Box(((\varphi_1 \vee \varphi_2) \wedge \psi) \leftrightarrow ((\varphi_1 \wedge \psi) \vee (\varphi_2 \wedge \psi)))$;
(2) $\Box(((\varphi_1 \wedge \varphi_2) \vee \psi) \leftrightarrow ((\varphi_1 \vee \psi) \wedge (\varphi_2 \vee \psi)))$;
(3) $\Box((\psi \rightarrow (\varphi_1 \wedge \varphi_2)) \leftrightarrow ((\psi \rightarrow \varphi_1) \wedge (\psi \rightarrow \varphi_2)))$;
(4) $\Box(((\varphi_1 \vee \varphi_2) \rightarrow \psi) \leftrightarrow ((\varphi_1 \rightarrow \psi) \wedge (\varphi_2 \rightarrow \psi)))$;
(5) $\Box(\varphi_1 \wedge \varphi_2) \leftrightarrow (\Box\varphi_1 \wedge \Box\varphi_2)$.

For example, the following STLP corresponds to rules (2)–(4) plus the rules of inertia for the atoms *Glucose, Repressor, Lac, LacZ, Galactosidase, Lactose* and $CAMP$:

$\Box(Lactose \wedge Galactosidase \rightarrow \mathbf{Pr}(Glucose))$
$\Box(Lactose \wedge Galactosidase \rightarrow \mathbf{Cn}(Galactosidase))$ $\Big\}$ (2)

$\Box(lacl \rightarrow \mathbf{Pr}(Repressor))$ $\}$ (3)

$\Box(CAMP \wedge \neg Glucose \wedge \neg Repressor \wedge lacZ \rightarrow \mathbf{Pr}(Galactosidase))$
$\Box(CAMP \wedge \neg Glucose \wedge Lactose \wedge lacZ \rightarrow \mathbf{Pr}(Galactosidase))$ $\Big\}$ (4)

$\Box(\mathbf{Pr}(Glucose) \rightarrow \bigcirc Glucose)$
$\Box(Glucose \wedge \neg \mathbf{Cn}(Glucose) \rightarrow \bigcirc Glucose)$ $\Big\}$ *inertia(Glucose)*

$\Box(\mathbf{Pr}(Repressor) \rightarrow \bigcirc Repressor)$
$\Box(Repressor \wedge \neg \mathbf{Cn}(Repressor) \rightarrow \bigcirc Repressor)$ $\Big\}$ *inertia(Repressor)*

$\Box(\mathbf{Pr}(Galactosidase) \rightarrow \bigcirc Galactosidase)$
$\Box(Galactosidase \wedge \neg \mathbf{Cn}(Galactosidase) \rightarrow$
$\bigcirc Galactosidase)$ $\Big\}$ *inertia(Galactosidase)*

$\Box(Lactose \rightarrow \bigcirc Lactose)$ $\}$ *inertia(Lactose)*
$\Box(CAMP \rightarrow \bigcirc CAMP)$ $\}$ *inertia(CAMP)*
$\Box(Lacl \rightarrow \bigcirc Lacl)$ $\}$ *inertia(Lacl)*
$\Box(LacZ \rightarrow \bigcirc LacZ)$ $\}$ *inertia(LacZ)*

Observation 1. *Let Γ be a set of pathway formulas and $\Pi = tr(\Gamma) \wedge \bigwedge_{p \in \Sigma} inertia(p)$, expressed as an STLP. Then*

---

[8] We refer the reader to [4] for details about the computation of such loop formulas.

(a) $G(\Pi)$ has only unitary loops;

(b) Since $G(\Pi)$ has only unitary loops, Temporal Equilibrium Models of Π coincide with the LTL models of the temporal extension of Clark's completion [4,10], denoted by $COMP(\Pi)$ [4]. ∎

Temporal Completion consists in specifying, along time, that the truth value of an atom $p \in \widehat{\Sigma}$ must be logically equivalent to the disjunction of all its possible causes (see [4] for details). More precisely, $COMP(\Pi)$ corresponds, in our case, to the following expression:[9]

$$COMP(\Pi) = \Box(\bigcirc p \leftrightarrow (\mathbf{Pr}\,(p) \vee (p \wedge \neg\mathbf{Cn}\,(p)))) \wedge \Box\left(\mathbf{Pr}\,(p) \leftrightarrow \bigvee_{[\alpha](P^\wedge \multimap p)\in F} P^\wedge \wedge \mathcal{A}(\alpha)\right)$$

$$\wedge\, \Box\left(\mathbf{Cn}\,(p) \leftrightarrow \bigvee_{[\alpha](P^\wedge \twoheadrightarrow p)\in F} P^\wedge \wedge \mathcal{A}(\alpha)\right).$$

Theorem 3 (Main result). *Let Γ be a set of pathway formulas, $\Pi = tr\,(\Gamma) \wedge \bigwedge_{p\in\Sigma} inertia(p)$ and $\mathbf{T}$ be an LTL model of Π.*

$$\langle \mathbf{T}, \mathbf{T}\rangle \models_{MEL} \Gamma \ \text{iff} \ \mathbf{T} \models_{LTL} COMP(\Pi).$$

Proof. From Theorem 1 we get that $\langle \mathbf{T}, \mathbf{T}\rangle \models_{MEL} \Gamma$ iff $\langle \mathbf{T}, \mathbf{T}\rangle \models_{TEL} \Pi$. From Theorem 2 it follows that $\langle \mathbf{T}, \mathbf{T}\rangle \models_{TEL} \Pi$ iff $\mathbf{T} \models_{LTL} \Pi \wedge LF(\Pi)$. Finally, regarding Observation 1 we can reduce $\Pi \wedge LF(\Pi)$ to $COMP(\Pi)$ so, therefore $\mathbf{T} \models_{LTL} COMP(\Pi)$. ∎

8   Conclusion and Future Work

In this paper we gave a formal representation of MIM's in terms of Temporal Equilibrium Logic. To do so, we first defined Molecular Equilibrium Logic, a nonmonotonic logic for dealing with general pathways. Then we showed that this logic can be captured by an LTL formula via a translation into Splittable Temporal Logic Programs under TEL semantics.

As a follow up, we are looking for a way to solve abductive temporal queries on MIM's. Abductive query express important properties; for example the abductive solution to $\Diamond\Box \bigwedge_{p\in\Sigma} (p \leftrightarrow \bigcirc p)$ is the set of all possible conditions that make the cell reach a stable state. An idea to undertake this problem is to combine the works on abduction in Equilibrium Logic [26] and in modal logic [23] in order to define a procedure for abduction in Temporal Equilibrium Logic. Furthermore, finding the complexity of our fragment of temporal equilibrium logic is an open problem. Although in the general case it is known to be EXPSPACE [8], this bound might be lower in our case as the problem is restricted to STLP's with only unitary loops.

---

[9] We omitted the completion at time step 0 since the formula at the initial state depends on the extensional database, which is not considered here.

References

1. Molecular interaction maps site. http://discover.nci.nih.gov/mim/. Accessed 6 Sept 2016
2. The systems biology markup language site. http://sbml.org/Documents. Accessed 6 Sept 2016
3. Aguado, F., Cabalar, P., Diéguez, M., Pérez, G., Vidal, C.: Temporal equilibrium logic: a survey. J. Appl. Non-Classical Logics **23**(1–2), 2–24 (2013)
4. Aguado, F., Cabalar, P., Pérez, G., Vidal, C.: Loop formulas for splitable temporal logic programs. In: Delgrande, J.P., Faber, W. (eds.) LPNMR 2011. LNCS (LNAI), vol. 6645, pp. 80–92. Springer, Heidelberg (2011). doi:10.1007/978-3-642-20895-9_9
5. Alliot, J.M., Demolombe, R., Diéguez, M., Fariñas del Cerro, L., Favre, G., Faye, J.C., Obeid, N., Sordet, O.: Temporal modeling of biological systems. In: Akama, S. (ed.) Towards Paraconsistent Engineering: From Pure Logic to Applied Logic. Springer (2016, to appear)
6. Alliot, J.M., Demolombe, R., Fariñas del Cerro, L., Diéguez, M., Obeid, N.: Abductive reasoning on molecular interaction maps. In: 7th European Symposium on Computational Intelligence and Mathematics. Springer, Cádiz, Spain (2015)
7. Balbiani, P., Diéguez, M.: Temporal here and there (2016, unpublished)
8. Bozzelli, L., Pearce, D.: On the complexity of temporal equilibrium logic. In: LICS 2015, pp. 645–656. IEEE, Kyoto, Japan (2015)
9. Brewka, G., Eiter, T., Truszczyński, M.: Answer set programming at a glance. Commun. ACM **54**(12), 92–103 (2011)
10. Clark, K.L.: Negation as failure. In: Logic and Databases, pp. 293–322. Plenum Press (1978)
11. Demolombe, R., Fariñas del Cerro, L., Obeid, N.: A logical model for molecular interactions maps. In: Fariñas del Cerro, L., Inoue, K. (eds.) Logical Modeling of Biological Systems, pp. 93–123. Wiley, New York (2014)
12. Doncescu, A., Yamamoto, Y., Inoue, K.: Biological systems analysis using inductive logic programming. In: AINA 2007, pp. 690–695, Niagara Falls, Canada (2007)
13. Fariñas del Cerro, L., Herzig, A., Su, E.I.: Epistemic equilibrium logic. In: IJCAI 2015, pp. 2964–2970. AAAI Press, Buenos Aires, Argentina (2015)
14. Ferraris, P., Lee, J., Lifschitz, V.: A generalization of the Lin-Zhao theorem. Ann. Math. Artif. Intell. **47**(1–2), 79–101 (2006)
15. Gelfond, M., Lifschitz, V.: The stable model semantics for logic programming. In: ICLP 1988, pp. 1070–1080. MIT Press, Cambridge (1988)
16. Heyting, A.: Die formalen Regeln der intuitionistischen Logik. In: Sitzungsberichte der Preussischen Akademie der Wissenschaften, Physikalisch-mathematische Klasse, pp. 42–56 (1930)
17. Iersel, M.V., Kelder, T., Pico, A., Hanspers, K., Coort, S., Conklin, B., Evelo, C.: Presenting and exploring biological pathways with PathVisio. BMC Bioinform. (2008). doi:10.1186/1471-2105-9-399
18. Jacob, F., Monod, J.: Genetic regulatory mechanisms in the synthesis of proteins. J. Mol. Biol. **3**, 318–356 (1961)
19. Kennell, D., Riezman, H.: Transcription and translation initiation frequencies of the Escherichia Coli lac operon. J. Mol. Biol. **114**(1), 1–21 (1977)
20. Kohn, K.W., Pommier, Y.: Molecular interaction map of the p53 and Mdm2 logic elements, which control the off-on swith of p53 response to DNA damage. Biochem. Biophys. Res. Commun. **331**(3), 816–827 (2005)

21. Lin, F., Zhao, Y.: ASSAT: computing answer sets of a logic program by SAT solvers. Artif. Intell. **157**(1–2), 112–117 (2002)
22. Manna, Z., Pnueli, A.: The Temporal Logic of Reactive and Concurrent Systems: Specification. Springer, New York (1991)
23. Mayer, M.C., Pirri, F.: Propositional abduction in modal logic. Logic J. IGPL **3**(6), 907–919 (1995)
24. McCarthy, J., Hayes, P.: Some philosophical problems from the standpoint of artificial intelligence. Mach. Intell. J. **4**, 463–512 (1969)
25. Pearce, D.: A new logical characterisation of stable models and answer sets. In: Dix, J., Pereira, L.M., Przymusinski, T.C. (eds.) NMELP 1996. LNCS, vol. 1216, pp. 57–70. Springer, Heidelberg (1997). doi:10.1007/BFb0023801
26. Pearce, D., Valverde, A.: Abduction in equilibrium logic. In: ASP 2001 Workshop, Stanford, USA (2001)
27. Reiter, R.: On closed world data bases. In: Logic and Data Bases, pp. 55–76 (1977)
28. Schaub, T., Thiele, S.: Metabolic network expansion with answer set programming. In: Hill, P.M., Warren, D.S. (eds.) ICLP 2009. LNCS, vol. 5649, pp. 312–326. Springer, Heidelberg (2009). doi:10.1007/978-3-642-02846-5_27
29. Tran, N., Baral, C.: Reasoning about non-immediate triggers in biological networks. Ann. Math. Artif. Intell. **51**(2–4), 267–293 (2007)

On Decidability of a Logic of Gossips

Krzysztof R. Apt[1] and Dominik Wojtczak[2(✉)]

[1] CWI, Amsterdam, The Netherlands
[2] University of Liverpool, Liverpool, UK
d.wojtczak@liverpool.ac.uk

Abstract. Gossip protocols aim at arriving, by means of point-to-point or group communications, at a situation in which all the agents know each other secrets, see, e.g., [11]. In [1], building upon [3], we studied distributed epistemic gossip protocols, which are examples of *knowledge based programs* introduced in [6]. These protocols use as guards formulas from a simple epistemic logic. We show here that these protocols are implementable by proving that it is decidable to determine whether a formula with no nested modalities is true after a sequence of calls. Building upon this result we further show that the problems of partial correctness and of termination of such protocols are decidable, as well.

1 Introduction

1.1 Background and Motivation

Knowledge-based programs were introduced in [6]—these are programs that use tests for knowledge. Examples are protocols for the sequence transmission problem, such as the alternating bit protocol, studied in [7]. A more recent example are the distributed epistemic gossip protocols introduced in [3] and further studied in a slightly different setting in [1].

In *gossip protocols* each agent holds a secret initially known only to him. The secrets spread by means of communications. During them, e.g., point-to-point or group communications, the participating agents exchange all secrets they know. The aim of the gossip protocols is to arrive at a situation in which all the agents know each other secrets, see, e.g., the early survey [8], the book coverage [10] or a more recent paper [11].

As shown in [1], the formulation of distributed gossip protocols as knowledge-based programs considerably simplifies the task of their verification. The reason is that these protocols are strikingly simple in their syntax based on epistemic logic (though not semantics)—they are just parallel compositions of loops in which the agents repeatedly perform a call assuming the corresponding epistemic guard evaluates to true. One issue ignored in [1] was the natural question: are these gossip protocols implementable?

In this paper we provide a positive answer to this question. More precisely, we show that it is decidable to determine whether a formula with no nested modalities is true after a sequence of calls. All gossip protocols studied in [3] use only such formulas as guards.

© Springer International Publishing AG 2016
L. Michael and A. Kakas (Eds.): JELIA 2016, LNAI 10021, pp. 18–33, 2016.
DOI: 10.1007/978-3-319-48758-8_2

We also study correctness and termination of these protocols. Building upon the just mentioned result we show that it is decidable to determine whether a given distributed epistemic gossip protocol is correct. Namely, the formula that expresses its correctness is with no nested modalities and we show that for such formulas truth is decidable. The final result allows us to solve the halting problem for these protocols. This shows that the distributed epistemic gossip protocols are very specific programs that in particular do not have the full power of the Turing machines.

The obtained results, while sufficient for a study of the considered protocols, do not address more general questions concerning both the logic itself and the protocols, which remain open and to which we return in the conclusions.

Finally, let us mention here some recent works on gossip protocols. In [2] a tool is presented that given a high level description of an epistemic protocol in the setting of [3] generates the characteristics of the protocol. The calls considered there differ from ours, so this approach is not applicable to our setting. Further, [13] presents a study of dynamic distributed gossip protocols in which the calls allow the agents not only to share the secrets but also to transmit the links. The purpose of the paper is to characterize such protocols in terms of the class of graphs for which they terminate. Such protocols then differ from the ones here considered, which are static. Next, in [9] gossip protocols are studied that aim at achieving higher-order shared knowledge. Finally, in [4] gossip protocols are studied as an instance of multi-agent epistemic planning that is subsequently translated into the classical planning language PDDL.

1.2 Plan

The paper is organized as follows. In the next two sections we recall the syntax and semantics introduced in [1]. Then, in Sect. 4 we introduce an alternative, equivalent, semantics, which helps us to prove the desired decidability results. In Sect. 5 we prove the decidability of checking whether a formula with no nested modalities is true after a given sequence of calls, and in Sect. 6 we show how to extend this result to checking whether such a formula is true (so true after any sequence of calls). In turn, in Sect. 7 we show that it is also decidable to determine whether a given gossip protocol terminates. Then, in the final section, we list some related open problems and clarify the difference between the type of calls studied in [1,3].

2 Syntax

Throughout the paper we assume a fixed finite set A of at least three *agents*. We assume that each agent holds exactly one *secret* and that there exists a bijection between the set of agents and the set of secrets. We denote by P the set of all secrets. Our aim is to analyze what the agents know after a sequence of calls took place. So first we introduce the calls and then consider an epistemic language allowing us to refer to agents' knowledge.

Assume a fixed ordering on the agents. Each **call** concerns two different agents, say a and b, and is written as ab, where agent a precedes agent b in the assumed ordering.

Calls are denoted by c, d. Abusing notation we write $a \in$ c to denote that agent a is one of the two agents involved in the call c (e.g., for c $:= ab$ we have $a \in$ c and $b \in$ c).

We consider formulas in a simple epistemic language defined by the following grammar:

$$\phi ::= F_a p \mid \neg \phi \mid \phi \wedge \phi \mid K_a \phi,$$

where $p \in$ P and $a \in$ A. Each secret is viewed a distinct constant. We denote the secret of agent a by A, the secret of agent b by B and so on. We denote the set of so defined formulas by $\mathcal{L}$ and we refer to its members as epistemic formulas.

We read $F_a p$ as 'agent a is familiar with the secret p' and $K_a \phi$ as 'agent a knows that formula ϕ is true'. So $F_a p$ is an atomic formula, while $K_a \phi$ is a compound formula. In fact, all atomic formulas of $\mathcal{L}$ are of the form $F_a p$.

In [1], as a follow up on [3], we also introduced distributed epistemic gossip protocols. We do not discuss them here and only mention that formulas of $\mathcal{L}$ are used in them as guards. All guards used in [1] are built from the formulas $F_a B$ and $K_a F_b C$, where a and b are different agents, by means of the Boolean connectives. Thus no nested modalities are used in the guards.

3   Semantics

We now recall from [1] semantics of the epistemic formulas. To this end we recall first the concept of a gossip situation.

3.1   Gossip Situations and Their Modifications

A **gossip situation** (in short a **situation**) is a sequence $s = (Q_a)_{a \in A}$, where $Q_a \subseteq P$ for each agent a. Intuitively, Q_a is the set of secrets a is familiar with in situation s. The **initial gossip situation** is the one in which each Q_a equals $\{A\}$ and is denoted by root. We say that an agent a is an **expert** in a situation s if he is familiar in s with all the secrets, i.e., if $Q_a =$ P. The initial gossip situation reflects the fact that initially each agent is familiar only with his own secret.

In this paper we do not study particular gossip protocols. We mention only that their goal is to reach a gossip situation in which each agent is an expert.

We will use the following concise notation for gossip situations. Sets of secrets will be written down as lists. e.g., the set $\{A, B, C\}$ will be written as ABC. Gossip situations will be written down as lists of lists of secrets separated by dots. E.g., if there are three agents, then root $= A.B.C$ and the gossip situation $(\{A, B\}, \{A, B\}, \{C\})$ will be written as $AB.AB.C$.

Each call transforms the current gossip situation by modifying the set of secrets the agents involved in the call are familiar with. Consider a gossip situation s $:= (Q_d)_{d \in A}$. Then $ab(s) := (Q'_d)_{d \in A}$, where $Q'_a = Q'_b = Q_a \cup Q_b$, $Q'_c = Q_c$, for $c \neq a, b$. This simply says that the only effect of a call is that the secrets are shared between the two agents involved in it.

3.2   Call Sequences

In [1] computations of the gossip protocols were studied, so both finite and infinite call sequences were used. Here we limit ourselves to the finite call sequences as we are only interested in the semantics of epistemic formulas.

So in this paper, in contrast to [1], a **call sequence** is a *finite* sequence of calls. The empty sequence is denoted by ϵ. We use **c** to denote a call sequence and **C** to denote the set of all call sequences. Given call sequences **c** and **d** and a call c we denote by **c.c** the outcome of adding c at the end of the sequence **c** and by **c.d** the outcome of appending the sequences **c** and **d**. We write $\mathbf{c} \preceq \mathbf{d}$ to denote the fact that **d** extends **c**, i.e., that for some **c'** we have $\mathbf{c.c'} = \mathbf{d}$.

The result of applying a call sequence to a situation s is defined inductively as follows:

[Base] $\epsilon(\mathsf{s}) := \mathsf{s}$,
[Step] $(\mathbf{c.c})(\mathsf{s}) := \mathbf{c}(c(\mathsf{s}))$.

Example 1. Let $\mathsf{A} = \{a, b, c\}$. Consider the call sequence (ac, bc, ac). It generates the following successive gossip situations starting from root:

$$A.B.C \xrightarrow{ac} AC.B.AC \xrightarrow{bc} AC.ABC.ABC \xrightarrow{ac} ABC.ABC.ABC.$$

Hence $(ac, bc, ac)(\mathsf{root}) = (ABC.ABC.ABC)$.   □

3.3   Gossip Models and Truth

A gossip situation is a set of possible combinations of secret distributions among the agents. As calls progress in sequence from the initial situation, agents may be uncertain about which one of such secrets distributions is the actual one. This uncertainty is captured by appropriate equivalence relations on the call sequences.

Definition 1. *A* **gossip model** *is a tuple* $\mathcal{M} := (\mathbf{C}, \{\sim_a\}_{a \in \mathsf{A}})$, *where each* $\sim_a \subseteq \mathbf{C} \times \mathbf{C}$ *is defined inductively as follows.*

[Base] $\epsilon \sim_a \epsilon$;
[Step] *Suppose* $\mathbf{c} \sim_a \mathbf{d}$.
  (i) If $a \notin \mathsf{c}$, *then* $\mathbf{c.c} \sim_a \mathbf{d}$ *and* $\mathbf{c} \sim_a \mathbf{d.c}$.
  (ii) If $a \in \mathsf{c}$ *and* $\mathbf{c}.c(\mathsf{root})_a = \mathbf{d}.c(\mathsf{root})_a$, *then* $\mathbf{c.c} \sim_a \mathbf{d.c}$.

A gossip model with a designated call sequence is called a **pointed gossip model**.

For instance, by *(i)* we have $ab, bc \sim_a ab, bd$. But we do not have $bc, ab \sim_a bd, ab$ since $(bc, ab)(\mathsf{root})_a = ABC \neq ABD = (bd, ab)(\mathsf{root})_a$.

We recall now from [1] the following two properties of $\sim_a$.

Fact 1

(i) Each $\sim_a$ is an equivalence relation;
(ii) For all $\mathbf{c}, \mathbf{d} \in \mathbf{C}$ if $\mathbf{c} \sim_a \mathbf{d}$, then $\mathbf{c}(\mathsf{root})_a = \mathbf{d}(\mathsf{root})_a$.

Finally, we recall the definition of truth.

Definition 2. *Let $(\mathcal{M}, \mathbf{c})$ be a pointed gossip model with $\mathcal{M} := (\mathbf{C}, (\sim_a)_{a \in \mathsf{A}})$ and $\mathbf{c} \in \mathbf{C}$. We define the satisfaction relation $\models$ inductively as follows (clauses for Boolean connectives are as usual and omitted):*

$$(\mathcal{M}, \mathbf{c}) \models F_a p \text{ iff } p \in \mathbf{c}(\mathsf{root})_a,$$
$$(\mathcal{M}, \mathbf{c}) \models K_a \phi \text{ iff } \forall \mathbf{d} \text{ s.t. } \mathbf{c} \sim_a \mathbf{d}, \ (\mathcal{M}, \mathbf{d}) \models \phi.$$

Further

$$\mathcal{M} \models \phi \text{ iff } \forall \mathbf{c} \ (\mathcal{M}, \mathbf{c}) \models \phi.$$

*When $\mathcal{M} \models \phi$ we say that ϕ is **true**.*   □

So formula $F_a p$ is true whenever secret p belongs to the set of secrets agent a is familiar with in the situation generated by the designated call sequence $\mathbf{c}$ applied to the initial situation root. The knowledge operator is interpreted as customary in epistemic logic using the equivalence relations $\sim_a$.

4   An Alternative Equivalence Relation

In this section we provide an alternative equivalence relation between the call sequences that is easier to work with. To this end we introduce a **view** of agent a of a call sequence $\mathbf{c}$, written as $\mathbf{c}_a$, and defined by induction as follows.
[Base]

$$\epsilon_a := \mathsf{root},$$

[Step]

$$(\mathbf{c}.\mathbf{c})_a := \begin{cases} \mathbf{c}_a \xrightarrow{\mathbf{c}} \mathsf{s} & \text{if } a \in \mathbf{c} \\ \mathbf{c}_a & \text{otherwise} \end{cases}$$

where for $d \in \mathsf{A}$

$$\mathsf{s}_d := \begin{cases} \mathbf{c}.\mathbf{c}(\mathsf{root})_d & \text{if } d \in \mathbf{c} \\ \mathsf{s}'_d & \text{otherwise} \end{cases}$$

where s' is the last gossip situation in $\mathbf{c}_a$.

Intuitively, a view of agent a of a call sequence $\mathbf{c}$ is the information he acquires by means of the calls in $\mathbf{c}$ he is involved in. It consists of a sequence of gossip situations connected by the calls in which a is involved in. After each such call, say ab, agent a updates the set of gossips he and b are currently familiar with.

Example 2. Let us return to Example 1. So $\mathsf{A} = \{a, b, c\}$ and we consider the call sequence (ac, bc, ac). We noticed there that it generates the following successive gossip situations starting from root:

$$A.B.C \xrightarrow{ac} AC.B.AC \xrightarrow{bc} AC.ABC.ABC \xrightarrow{ac} ABC.ABC.ABC.$$

We now compare it with the view of agent a of the sequence (ac, bc, ac), which is

$$A.B.C \xrightarrow{ac} AC.B.AC \xrightarrow{ac} ABC.B.ABC.$$

Thus, in the final gossip situation of this view, agent b is familiar with neither the secret A nor C. However, the final gossip situation of a view does not reflect agents' knowledge. In fact, as we shall see, according to the semantics, after the above sequence of calls, agent a knows that agent b is familiar both with A and C. □

We now introduce for each agent a an equivalence relation $\equiv_a$ between the call sequences, defined as follows:

$$\mathsf{c} \equiv_a \mathsf{d} \text{ iff } \mathsf{c}_a = \mathsf{d}_a.$$

So according to this definition two call sequences are equivalent for agent a if his views of them are the same. The following result shows that the equivalence relations $\sim_a$ and $\equiv_a$ coincide.

Theorem 2 (Equivalence). *For each agent a the relations $\sim_a$ and $\equiv_a$ coincide.*

Proof. Omitted. □

So two call sequences are $\sim_a$ equivalent iff their views by agent a coincide. This alternative definition of the equivalence relation between the call sequences makes it simpler to determine various properties of our semantics.

Below, given a call c, we denote by c^* a sequence consisting of zero or more calls c and by c^+ a sequence consisting of one or more calls c.

Example 3. Note that we have $(\mathcal{M}, (ac, bc, ac)) \models K_a F_b A$. To see this recall from Example 2 that the view of agent a of the sequence (ac, bc, ac) is

$$A.B.C \xrightarrow{ac} AC.B.AC \xrightarrow{ac} ABC.B.ABC.$$

So if $(ac, bc, ac) \equiv_a \mathsf{d}$, then d is of the form $ac, (bc)^+, ac, (bc)^*$, which implies that $(\mathcal{M}, \mathsf{d}) \models F_b A$.

We conclude that it is possible that an agent, here a, knows that another agent, here b, is familiar with his (so a's) secret even though no communication took place between them. The same argument shows that $(\mathcal{M}, (ac, bc, ac)) \models K_a F_b C$, as claimed in Example 2. □

In the examples and proofs below we use the $\equiv_a$ relation instead of $\sim_a$ and repeatedly appeal to the Equivalence Theorem 2. First we show that an immediate repetition of a call has no effect on the truth of the formulas. More precisely, the following holds.

Theorem 3 (Stuttering). *Suppose that* $\mathbf{c} := \mathbf{c}_1, \mathsf{c}, \mathbf{c}_2$ *and* $\mathbf{d} := \mathbf{c}_1, \mathsf{c}, \mathsf{c}, \mathbf{c}_2$. *Then for all formulas* ϕ, $(\mathcal{M}, \mathbf{c}) \models \phi$ *iff* $(\mathcal{M}, \mathbf{d}) \models \phi$.

Proof. We proceed by induction of the structure of ϕ. For the formulas of the form $F_a p$ it suffices to note that $\mathbf{c}(\text{root}) = \mathbf{d}(\text{root})$. The only induction step of interest is for the formulas of the form $K_a \phi$. Suppose first that $a \notin \mathsf{c}$. Then $\mathbf{c} \equiv_a \mathbf{d}$, so $(\mathcal{M}, \mathbf{c}) \models K_a \phi$ iff $(\mathcal{M}, \mathbf{d}) \models K_a \phi$.

Assume now that $a \in \mathsf{c}$. Suppose that $(\mathcal{M}, \mathbf{c}) \models K_a \phi$. Take $\mathbf{d}'$ such that $\mathbf{d} \equiv_a \mathbf{d}'$. Then $\mathbf{d}'$ is of the form $\mathbf{d}'_1, \mathsf{c}, \mathsf{c}, \mathbf{d}'_2$. Let $\mathbf{c}' := \mathbf{d}'_1, \mathsf{c}, \mathbf{d}'_2$. By the induction hypothesis $(\mathcal{M}, \mathbf{d}') \models \phi$ iff $(\mathcal{M}, \mathbf{c}') \models \phi$. Further, $\mathbf{d} \equiv_a \mathbf{d}'$ implies that $\mathbf{c} \equiv_a \mathbf{c}'$. So $(\mathcal{M}, \mathbf{c}') \models \phi$. Hence $(\mathcal{M}, \mathbf{d}') \models \phi$ and consequently $(\mathcal{M}, \mathbf{d}) \models K_a \phi$.

The proof in the other direction is analogous. $\square$

The above result cannot be extended to a repetition of the call sequences. Indeed, we have $(\mathcal{M}, (ab, bc)) \models \neg F_a C$, and $(\mathcal{M}, (ab, bc, ab, bc)) \models F_a C$. On the other hand a monotonicity result holds for positive formulas.

Theorem 4 (Monotonicity). *Suppose that* ϕ *is a formula that does not contain the* $\neg$ *symbol. Then*

$$\mathbf{c} \preceq \mathbf{d} \ and \ (\mathcal{M}, \mathbf{c}) \models \phi \ implies \ (\mathcal{M}, \mathbf{d}) \models \phi.$$

Proof. We proceed by induction on the structure of ϕ. The only case of interest is when ϕ is of the form $K_a \psi$. Suppose that $\mathbf{c} \preceq \mathbf{d}$ and $(\mathcal{M}, \mathbf{c}) \models \phi$. Take some call sequence $\mathbf{d}'$ such that $\mathbf{d} \equiv_a \mathbf{d}'$. Then for some call sequences $\mathbf{d}_1$ and $\mathbf{d}'_1$ such that $\mathbf{d}_1, \mathbf{d}'_1 = \mathbf{d}'$ we have $\mathbf{c} \equiv_a \mathbf{d}_1$.

We have by the assumption $(\mathcal{M}, \mathbf{d}_1) \models \psi$, so by the induction hypothesis $(\mathcal{M}, \mathbf{d}') \models \psi$. As $\mathbf{d}'$ was arbitrarily chosen we conclude that $(\mathcal{M}, \mathbf{d}) \models \phi$. $\square$

Here and below we say that a call is a b-*call* if agent b is involved in it. Before we deal with the decidability matters consider the formula $K_a F_b C$ for pairwise different agents a, b, c. The following example reveals that it can be true in some subtle ways.

Example 4

(i) First, note that a can learn (that is, know) that agent b is familiar with the secret C through a direct communication with b.

Indeed, we have $(\mathcal{M}, (bc, ab)) \models K_a F_b C$. Namely the view of agent a of the sequence (bc, ab) is

$$A.B.C \xrightarrow{ab} ABC.ABC.C.$$

So if $(bc, ab) \equiv_a \mathbf{d}$, then $\mathbf{d}$ is of the form $(bc)^+, ab, (bc)^*$, which implies that $(\mathcal{M}, \mathbf{d}) \models F_b C$.

(ii) Further, it is also possible that a learns that b is familiar with the secret C through a direct communication with c.

Indeed, we have $(\mathcal{M}, (bc, ac)) \models K_a F_b C$. To see this note that the view of agent a of the sequence (bc, ac) is

$$A.B.C \xrightarrow{ac} ABC.B.ABC.$$

So if $(bc, ac) \equiv_a \mathbf{d}$, then $\mathbf{d}$ is of the form $(bc)^+, ac, (bc)^*$, which implies that $(\mathcal{M}, \mathbf{d}) \models F_b C$.

(iii) Also, it is possible that a learns that b is familiar with the secret C without ever communicating with b or c.

Namely, we have $(\mathcal{M}, (cd, ad, bd, ad)) \models K_a F_b C$. Indeed, the view of agent a of the sequence (cd, ad, bd, ad) is

$$A.B.C.D \xrightarrow{ad} ACD.B.C.ACD \xrightarrow{ad} ABCD.B.C.ABCD.$$

So if $(cd, ad, bd, ad) \equiv_a \mathbf{d}$, then $\mathbf{d}$ is of the form $(cd)^+, (bc)^*, ad, \mathbf{d}', ad, \mathbf{d}''$, where in $\mathbf{d}'$ a call bd took place or a call bc followed by a call cd took place, and in $\mathbf{d}'$ and $\mathbf{d}''$ no a-call took place. This implies that $(\mathcal{M}, \mathbf{d}) \models F_b C$.

(iv) In *(iii)* agent a learned that b is familiar with c by communicating with agent d twice. But it is also possible that a learns that b is familiar with the secret C without communicating with any agent twice.

To see this note that $(\mathcal{M}, (cd, ad, bc, ac)) \models K_a F_b C$. Indeed, the view of agent a of the sequence (cd, ad, bc, ac) is

$$A.B.C.D \xrightarrow{ad} ACD.B.C.ACD \xrightarrow{ac} ABCD.B.ABCD.ACD.$$

So if $(cd, ad, bc, ac) \equiv_a \mathbf{d}$, then $\mathbf{d}$ is of the form $(cd)^+, ad, \mathbf{d}', ac, \mathbf{d}''$, where in $\mathbf{d}'$ a call bc took place or a call bd followed by a call cd took place, and in $\mathbf{d}'$ and $\mathbf{d}''$ no a-call took place. This implies that $(\mathcal{M}, \mathbf{d}) \models F_b C$.   □

We conclude by noting that the Monotonicity Theorem 4 does not hold when we extend the call sequences to the left. Indeed, as observed in Example 4 *(ii)*, $(\mathcal{M}, (bc, ac)) \models K_a F_b C$. However, $(\mathcal{M}, (cd, bc, ac)) \models \neg K_a F_b C$, since $(cd, bc, ac) \equiv_a (bd, cd, ac)$ and $(\mathcal{M}, (bd, cd, ac)) \models \neg F_b C$.

5   Decidability of Semantics

In this section we show that the definition of semantics given in Definition 2 is decidable for formulas that do not use nested modalities.

Consider a call sequence $\mathbf{c}$. If for some prefix $\mathbf{c}_1.\mathbf{c}$ of $\mathbf{c}$, $\mathbf{c}_1(\text{root}) = \mathbf{c}_1.\mathbf{c}(\text{root})$, then we say that $\mathbf{c}$ is **redundant** in $\mathbf{c}$. First note the following observation.

Lemma 1 (Semantic Stuttering). *Suppose that* $\mathbf{c} := \mathbf{c}_1, \mathbf{c}, \mathbf{c}_2$ *and* $\mathbf{d} := \mathbf{c}_1, \mathbf{c}_2$, *where* $\mathbf{c}$ *is redundant in* $\mathbf{c}$. *Then for all propositional formulas* ϕ, $(\mathcal{M}, \mathbf{c}) \models \phi$ *iff* $(\mathcal{M}, \mathbf{d}) \models \phi$.

Proof. We proceed by induction on the structure of ϕ. The only case of interest is when ϕ is of the form $F_a p$. The redundancy of $\mathbf{c}$ implies that $\mathbf{c}(\text{root}) = \mathbf{d}(\text{root})$. Hence $(\mathcal{M}, \mathbf{c}) \models F_a p$ iff $p \in \mathbf{c}(\text{root})_a$ iff $p \in \mathbf{d}(\text{root})_a$ iff $(\mathcal{M}, \mathbf{d}) \models F_a p$.   □

The following example shows that Lemma 1 does not extend to arbitrary formulas of $\mathcal{L}$.

Example 5. In the call sequence ab, ac, bc, ab the second call ab is redundant since $(ab, ac, bc, ab)(\text{root}) = (ab, ac, bc)(\text{root}) = ABC.ABC.ABC$.

However, $(\mathcal{M}, (ab, ac, bc, ab)) \models K_a F_b C$, because if $\mathbf{d} \equiv_a (ab, ac, bc, ab)$ then $\mathbf{d}$ is of the form (ab, ac, bc^+, ab, bc^*). At the same time, $(\mathcal{M}, (ab, ac, bc)) \models \neg K_a F_b C$ since $(ab, ac, bc) \equiv_a (ab, ac)$.   □

Now, consider an agent a and a call sequence $\mathbf{c}$. Starting from $\mathbf{c}$ we repeatedly remove from the current call sequence a redundant call that does not involve agent a. We call each outcome of such an iteration an *a-reduction* of $\mathbf{c}$.

Corollary 1. *Let $\mathbf{d}$ be an a-reduction of $\mathbf{c}$. Then*

(i) $\mathbf{c} \equiv_a \mathbf{d}$,
(ii) for all propositional formulas ϕ, $(\mathcal{M}, \mathbf{c}) \models \phi$ iff $(\mathcal{M}, \mathbf{d}) \models \phi$.

Proof

(i) It suffices to note that a removal of a redundant call that does not involve agent a does not affect his view of the call sequence.
(ii) By the repeated use of the Semantic Stuttering Lemma 1.   □

Given an agent a we now say that a call sequence $\mathbf{c}$ is *a-***redundant free** if no call c from $\mathbf{c}$ such that $a \notin c$ is redundant in it. Clearly each a-reduction is a-redundant free.

We now prove the following crucial lemma.

Lemma 2. *For each agent a and a call sequence $\mathbf{c}$ the set of a-redundant free call sequences $\mathbf{d}$ such that $\mathbf{c} \equiv_a \mathbf{d}$ is finite.*

Proof. Consider an a-redundant free call sequence $\mathbf{d}$ such that $\mathbf{c} \equiv_a \mathbf{d}$. Then $\mathbf{d}$ has the same number, say k, of a-calls as $\mathbf{c}$.

Associate with $\mathbf{d}$ the sequence of gossip situations $\mathbf{d}^0(\text{root}), \mathbf{d}^1(\text{root}), \ldots,$ $\mathbf{d}^m(\text{root})$, where m is the length of $\mathbf{d}$, $\mathbf{d}^0 = \epsilon$, and $\mathbf{d}^k = d_1, d_2, \ldots, d_k$ for $k = 1, \ldots, m$. This sequence monotonically grows, where we interpret the inclusion relation component wise. Moreover, for all calls d_i such that $a \notin d_i$ the corresponding inclusion is strict. Consequently, m, the length of $\mathbf{d}$, is bounded by $k + |A|^2$, the sum of the number of a-calls in $\mathbf{c}$ and of the total number of secrets in the gossip situation in which each agent is an expert.

But for each m there are only finitely many call sequences of length at most m. This concludes the proof.   □

We can now state and prove the desired result.

Theorem 5 (Decidability of Semantics). *For each call sequence* **c** *it is decidable whether for a formula* ϕ *with no nested modalities* $(\mathcal{M}, \mathbf{c}) \models \phi$ *holds.*

Proof. We use the definition of semantics as the algorithm. We only need to show that the case of the formulas of the form $K_a\phi$, where ϕ is a propositional formula, can be rewritten by referring to a finite set of call sequences **d** that can be explicitly constructed. Thanks to the Equivalence Theorem 2 and Corollary 1 we can rewrite the clause for $K_a\phi$ as:

$$(\mathcal{M}, \mathbf{c}) \models K_a\phi \text{ iff } \forall \mathbf{d} \text{ s.t. } \mathbf{c} \sim_a \mathbf{d} \text{ and } \mathbf{d} \text{ is } a\text{-redundant free, } (\mathcal{M}, \mathbf{d}) \models \phi,$$

and according to Lemma 2 this definition indeed refers to an explicitly constructed finite set of call sequences **d**. □

6 Decidability of Truth

Next, we show that truth for formulas that do not use nested modalities is decidable. This implies that the verification problem of gossip protocols, i.e., the problem of determining whether upon protocol's termination every agent is an expert, is decidable for protocols that do not use nested modalities. These include all protocols discussed in [1].

The key notion in our approach is that of an ***epistemic view***. It is a function of a call sequence **c**, denoted by $EV(\mathbf{c})$, defined by

– putting for each agent $a \in A$, $EV(\mathbf{c})(a) = \{\mathbf{d}(\text{root}) \mid \mathbf{c} \sim_a \mathbf{d}\}$, and setting
– $EV(\mathbf{c})(*) = \mathbf{c}(\text{root})$.

So $EV(\mathbf{c})(a)$ is the set of all gossip situations consistent with agent a's observations made throughout **c** and $EV(\mathbf{c})(*)$ is the actual gossip situation after **c** takes place. Note that if $\mathbf{c} \sim_a \mathbf{d}$ then $EV(\mathbf{c})(a) = EV(\mathbf{d})(a)$.

Lemma 3. *For each call sequence* **c** *and agent* a *the set* $EV(\mathbf{c})(a)$ *is finite and can be effectively constructed.*

Proof. Fix an agent a. By Corollary 1, Equivalence Theorem 2, and Fact 1(ii) to construct the set $EV(\mathbf{c})(a)$ it suffices to consider a-redundant free call sequences **d** and by Lemma 2 there are only finitely many such call sequences **d** for which $\mathbf{d} \sim_a \mathbf{c}$. □

Our interest in epistemic views stems from the following result.

Lemma 4. *Suppose that* $EV(\mathbf{c}) = EV(\mathbf{d})$. *Then for all epistemic formulas with no nested modalities* ϕ, $(\mathcal{M}, \mathbf{c}) \models \phi$ *iff* $(\mathcal{M}, \mathbf{d}) \models \phi$.

Proof. A simple proof by induction shows that for a propositional formula ψ and arbitrary call sequences $\mathbf{c}'$ and $\mathbf{d}'$, $\mathbf{c}'(\text{root}) = \mathbf{d}'(\text{root})$ implies that $(\mathcal{M}, \mathbf{c}') \models \psi$ iff $(\mathcal{M}, \mathbf{d}') \models \psi$. Since $EV(\mathbf{c})(*) = \mathbf{c}(\text{root})$ and $EV(\mathbf{d})(*) = \mathbf{d}(\text{root})$, this settles the case for $\phi = F_a p$.

The above observation also implies that for a propositional formula ψ and an agent a,

$$(\mathcal{M}, \mathbf{c}) \models K_a \psi \text{ iff } \forall \mathbf{c}' \text{ s.t. } \mathbf{c}'(\text{root}) \in EV(\mathbf{c})(a), (\mathcal{M}, \mathbf{c}') \models \psi.$$

Since $EV(\mathbf{c})(a) = EV(\mathbf{d})(a)$, this settles the case for $\phi = K_a \psi$.

The remaining cases of negation and conjunction follow directly by the induction. □

The above lemma is useful because the set of epistemic views is finite, in contrast to the set of call sequences. Next, we provide an inductive definition of $EV(\mathbf{c}.\mathsf{c})(a)$ the importance of which will become clear in a moment.

Lemma 5. *For any call sequence $\mathbf{c}$, call c, and agent a such that $a \in \mathsf{c}$*

$$EV(\mathbf{c}.\mathsf{c})(a) = \{\mathsf{c}(\mathsf{s}) \mid \mathsf{s} \in EV(\mathbf{c})(a) \text{ and } \mathsf{c}(\mathsf{s})_a = \mathsf{c}(\mathbf{c}(\text{root}))_a\}.$$

Proof. Intuitively the condition $\mathsf{c}(\mathsf{s})_a = \mathsf{c}(\mathbf{c}(\text{root}))_a$ states that s is consistent with the observation agent a gets after call c is made in the gossip situation $\mathbf{c}(\text{root})$.

($\subseteq$) Take $\mathsf{s}' \in EV(\mathbf{c}.\mathsf{c})(a)$. By the definition of $EV(\mathbf{c}.\mathsf{c})(a)$ there exists a call sequence $\mathbf{d}.\mathsf{c}$ such that $\mathbf{d}.\mathsf{c} \sim_a \mathbf{c}.\mathsf{c}$ and $\mathsf{s}' = \mathbf{d}.\mathsf{c}(\text{root})$. So $\mathsf{s}' = \mathsf{c}(\mathsf{s})$, where $\mathsf{s} = \mathbf{d}(\text{root})$. We also have $\mathbf{d} \sim_a \mathbf{c}$, so $\mathbf{d}(\text{root}) \in EV(\mathbf{c})(a)$. Moreover, $\mathsf{c}(\mathbf{d}(\text{root}))_a = \mathsf{c}(\mathbf{c}(\text{root}))_a$, because $\mathbf{d}.\mathsf{c} \sim_a \mathbf{c}.\mathsf{c}$.

($\supseteq$) Take $\mathsf{s}' \in \{\mathsf{c}(\mathsf{s}) \mid \mathsf{s} \in EV(\mathbf{c})(a) \text{ and } \mathsf{c}(\mathsf{s})_a = \mathsf{c}(\mathbf{c}(\text{root}))_a\}$. So for some gossip situation s we have $\mathsf{s}' = \mathsf{c}(\mathsf{s})$, $\mathsf{s} \in EV(\mathbf{c})(a)$ and $\mathsf{c}(\mathsf{s})_a = \mathsf{c}(\mathbf{c}(\text{root}))_a$. The second fact implies that there exists a call sequence $\mathbf{d}$ such that $\mathbf{d} \sim_a \mathbf{c}$ and $\mathsf{s} = \mathbf{d}(\text{root})$. Now, this and the third fact imply that $\mathbf{d}.\mathsf{c} \sim_a \mathbf{c}.\mathsf{c}$. So $\mathbf{d}.\mathsf{c}(\text{root}) \in EV(\mathbf{c}.\mathsf{c})(a)$. Consequently also $\mathsf{s}' \in EV(\mathbf{c}.\mathsf{c})(a)$, since $\mathsf{s}' = \mathsf{c}(\mathsf{s}) = \mathbf{d}.\mathsf{c}(\text{root})$. □

This brings us to the following important conclusion stating that $EV(\mathbf{c}.\mathsf{c})$ can be computed using $EV(\mathbf{c})$ and c only, i.e., without referring to $\mathbf{c}$. Denote the set of epistemic views by $\widetilde{EV}$ and recall that C denotes the set of calls.

Corollary 2. *There exists a function $f : \widetilde{EV} \times C \to \widetilde{EV}$ such that for any call sequence $\mathbf{c}$ and call c*

$$EV(\mathbf{c}.\mathsf{c})(a) = f(EV(\mathbf{c}), \mathsf{c}).$$

Proof. By the definition of $\sim_a$ we have $EV(\mathbf{c}.\mathsf{c})(a) = EV(\mathbf{c})(a)$ if $a \notin \mathsf{c}$, $EV(\mathbf{c}.\mathsf{c})(*) = \mathsf{c}(EV(\mathbf{c})(*))$. This in conjunction with the above lemma implies the claim. □

Consider a call sequence $\mathbf{c}$. If for some prefix $\mathbf{c}_1.\mathbf{c}_2$ of $\mathbf{c}$, we have $EV(\mathbf{c}_1) = EV(\mathbf{c}_1.\mathbf{c}_2)$, then we say that the call subsequence $\mathbf{c}_2$ is *epistemically redundant* in $\mathbf{c}$ and that $\mathbf{c}$ is *epistemically redundant*.

We say that c is ***epistemically non-redundant*** if it is not epistemically redundant. Equivalently, a call sequence $c_1.c_2.\ldots.c_k$ is epistemically non-redundant if the set

$$\{EV(c_1.c_2.\ldots.c_i) \mid i \in \{1,\ldots,k\}\}$$

has k elements.

We now show a counterpart of the Semantic Stuttering Lemma 1 for epistemic views.

Lemma 6 (Epistemic Stuttering). *Suppose that* $c := c_1.c_2.c_3$ *and* $d := c_1.$ c_3, *where* c_2 *is epistemically redundant in* c. *Then* $EV(c) = EV(d)$.

Proof. Let $c_3 = c_1.c_2.\ldots.c_k$. First note that thanks to Corollary 2 we have $EV(c_1.c_2.c_1) = EV(c_1.c_1)$, since $EV(c_1.c_2.c_1) = f(EV(c_1.c_2),c_1) = f(EV(c_1),c_1) = EV(c_1.c_1)$ due to the epistemic redundancy of c_2 in c. Repeating this argument for all $i \in \{1,\ldots,k\}$ we get that $EV(c_1.c_2.c_1.c_2.\ldots.c_i) = EV(c_1.c_1.c_2.\ldots.c_i)$.

In particular $EV(c) = EV(d)$.   □

Corollary 3. *For every call sequence* c *there exists an epistemically non-redundant call sequence* d *such that for all epistemic formulas with no nested modalities* ϕ, $(\mathcal{M},c) \models \phi$ *iff* $(\mathcal{M},d) \models \phi$.

Proof. By the repeated use of the Epistemic Stuttering Lemmas 4 and 6.   □

Next, we prove the following crucial lemma.

Lemma 7. *For any given model* $\mathcal{M}$, *there are only finitely many epistemically non-redundant call sequences.*

Proof. Note that each epistemic view is a function from $A \cup \{*\}$ to the set of functions from A to $2^{|P|}$ (this is an overestimation because for $*$ this set has only one element). There are $k = 2^{(|A|+1)\cdot 2^{|A|\cdot|P|}}$ such functions, so any call sequence longer than k has an epistemically redundant call subsequence. But there are only finitely many call sequences of length at most k. This concludes the proof.   □

Finally, we can establish the announced result.

Theorem 6 (Decidability of Truth). *For any formula* ϕ *with no nested modalities, it is decidable whether* $\mathcal{M} \models \phi$ *holds.*

Proof. Recall that $\mathcal{M} \models \phi$ iff $\forall c\ (\mathcal{M},c) \models \phi$. Thanks to Corollary 3 we can rewrite the latter as

$$\forall c \text{ s.t. } c \text{ is epistemically non-redundant, } (\mathcal{M},c) \models \phi.$$

But according to Lemma 7 there are only finitely many epistemically non-redundant call sequences and by Lemma 3 their set can be explicitly constructed.   □

As an easy consequence we obtain the following.

Corollary 4. *It is decidable to determine whether a given gossip situation can be an outcome of a call sequence.*

Proof. Each gossip situation $s = (Q_d)_{d \in A}$ can be encoded as a conjunction

$$\phi(s) = \bigwedge_{a \in A} \Big(\bigwedge_{B \in Q_a} F_a B \wedge \bigwedge_{B \notin Q_a} \neg F_a B \Big).$$

Then $\exists c(c(\text{root}) = s)$ iff $\exists c((\mathcal{M}, c) \models \phi(s))$ iff $\neg(\mathcal{M} \models \neg\phi(s))$. □

7 Decidability of Termination

Finally, we show that it is decidable to determine whether a gossip protocol terminates. First, we establish monotonicity of gossip situations and epistemic views with respect to call sequence extensions. Intuitively, we claim that as the call sequence gets longer each agent acquires more information. This can be seen as a counterpart of the Monotonicity Theorem 4. First we need to define suitable partial orderings $\leq_s$ and $\leq_{ev}$ over gossip situations and epistemic views, respectively.

Definition 3. *For any two gossip situations s, s' we write $s \leq_s s'$ if for all $a \in A$ we have $s_a \subseteq s'_a$.*

Note 1. For all call sequences c and d such that $c \preceq d$ we have $c(\text{root}) \leq_s d(\text{root})$.

Proof. For any gossip situation s and call c we have by definition $s \leq_s c(s)$. By induction this implies that for any call sequence c' we have $s \leq_s c'(s)$. Now $c \preceq d$ implies that $d = c.c'$ for some c'. Therefore, $c(\text{root}) \leq_s c'(c(\text{root})) = d(\text{root})$. □

Definition 4. *For any two epistemic views $V, V' \in \widetilde{EV}$ we write $V \leq_{ev} V'$ if for all $a \in A$ there exists $X \subseteq V(a)$ and an surjective (onto) function $g : X \to V'(a)$ such that for all $s \in X$ we have $s \leq_s g(s)$.*

Lemma 8. $\leq_{ev}$ *is a partial order.*

Proof. Omitted. □

The next lemma formalizes the intuition that epistemic information grows along a call sequence.

Lemma 9. *For all two call sequences such that $c \preceq d$ we have $EV(c) \leq_{ev} EV(d)$.*

Proof. Let $d = c.c'$. Take $a \in A$. Note that by a repeated application of Lemma 5 we can show that $EV(c.c')(a) = \{c'(s) \mid s \in EV(c)(a)$ and $\forall_{c'' \preceq c'} c''(s)_a = c''(c(\text{root}))_a\}$. It suffices then to pick $X = \{s \in EV(c)(a) \mid \forall_{c'' \preceq c'} c''(s)_a = c''(c(\text{root}))_a\}$, and set $g(s) = c'(s)$ for all $s \in X$. It is easy to check that such $g : X \to EV(d)$ is surjective, so $EV(c) \leq_{ev} EV(d)$. □

We can now draw the following useful conclusion.

Lemma 10. *Suppose that* $\mathbf{c}$ *is epistemically redundant. Then a prefix* $\mathbf{c_1}.\mathbf{c}$ *of it exists such that* $\mathbf{c_1}$ *is epistemically non-redundant and* $EV(\mathbf{c_1}.\mathbf{c}) = EV(\mathbf{c_1})$.

Proof. Let $\mathbf{c_1}.\mathbf{c_2}$ be the shortest prefix of $\mathbf{c}$ such that $EV(\mathbf{c_1}) = EV(\mathbf{c_1}.\mathbf{c_2})$. Then $\mathbf{c_1}$ is epistemically non-redundant. Let $\mathbf{c_2} = c_1.\ldots.c_l$. By Lemma 9 we have $EV(\mathbf{c_1}) \leq_s EV(\mathbf{c_1}.c_1) \leq_s EV(\mathbf{c_1}.c_1.c_2) \leq_s \ldots \leq_s EV(\mathbf{c_1}.c_1.c_2.\ldots.c_l) = EV(\mathbf{c_1}.\mathbf{c_2}) = EV(\mathbf{c_1})$. Since $\leq_s$ is a partial order, $EV(\mathbf{c_1}.c_1) = EV(\mathbf{c_1})$ holds. $\square$

Finally we can establish the desired result.

Theorem 7 (Decidability of Termination). *Given a gossip protocol it is decidable to determine whether it always terminates.*

Proof. We first prove that a gossip protocol may fail to terminate iff it can generate a call sequence $\mathbf{c}.c$ such that $\mathbf{c}$ is epistemically non-redundant and $EV(\mathbf{c}.c) = EV(\mathbf{c})$.

($\Rightarrow$) Let $\bar{\mathbf{c}}$ be an infinite sequence of calls generated by the protocol. There are only finitely many epistemic views, so some prefix $\mathbf{c}$ of $\bar{\mathbf{c}}$ is epistemically redundant. The claim now follows by Lemma 10.
($\Leftarrow$) Suppose that the protocol generates a sequence of calls $\mathbf{c}.c$ such that $\mathbf{c}$ is epistemically non-redundant and $EV(\mathbf{c}.c) = EV(\mathbf{c})$.

Let ϕ be the guard associated with the call c. By assumption $(\mathcal{M}, \mathbf{c}) \models \phi$. By the assumption about the gossip protocols the formula ϕ is without nested modalities, so by Lemma 4 $(\mathcal{M}, \mathbf{c}.c) \models \phi$. Hence by the repeated use of the Stuttering Theorem 3, for all $i \geq 1$, $(\mathcal{M}, \mathbf{c}.c^i) \models \phi$. Consequently, $\mathbf{c}.c^\omega$ is an infinite sequence of calls that can be generated by the protocol.

The above equivalence shows that determining whether the protocol always terminates is equivalent to checking that it cannot generate a call sequence $\mathbf{c}.c$ such that $\mathbf{c}$ is epistemically non-redundant and $EV(\mathbf{c}.c) = EV(\mathbf{c})$.

But given a call sequence, by the Decidability of Semantics Theorem 5, it is decidable to determine whether it can be generated by the protocol and by Lemma 3 it is decidable to determine whether a call sequence is epistemically non-redundant. Further, by Lemma 7 there are only finitely many epistemically non-redundant call sequences, so the claim follows. $\square$

8 Conclusions

In this paper we studied decidability questions concerning a natural epistemic logic appropriate for expressing gossip protocols. One of our aims was to show that the gossip protocols considered in [1] are executable. A self-contained summary is that the semantics of the introduced epistemic language $\mathcal{L}$ is decidable for formulas with no nested modalities. Another aim was to prove that partial correctness of the gossip protocols studied in [1] is decidable. To this end we showed that truth of formulas of $\mathcal{L}$ with no nested modalities is decidable. This implies the former since partial correctness of such a gossip protocol means that a specific epistemic formula, namely the conjunction of the negation of all guards implies that each agent is an expert, is true and such a formula has no nested modalities. Finally, we showed the problem of determining termination of a gossip protocol is decidable. An interesting open question is whether all of these results can be extended to arbitrary formulas of the language $\mathcal{L}$. The main stumbling block in generalizing our proofs is that, as Example 5 shows, the crucial Semantic Stuttering Lemma 1 cannot be extended to arbitrary formulas of $\mathcal{L}$.

These considerations lead to another interesting open problem. Gossip protocols studied in [1] are parametric in the sense that they are formulated in such a way that they do not depend on the underlying graph (for instance a ring). The results we proved allow us only to consider each specific gossip protocol (for example for a ring formed by 5 agents) separately. What is needed is a decision procedure that would allow us to consider all instances of a protocol (for example for all rings) simultaneously. We conjecture that this decision problem is undecidable both for partial correctness and for termination.

The semantics we introduced in Sect. 3 stipulates through the definition of $c(s)$ that a call ab is not noted by any agent $c \neq a, b$. In [3] different type of calls were studied, namely

- ab^-, which stipulates that every agent $c \neq a, b$ noted that a called b,
- ab^0, which stipulates that every agent $c \neq a, b$ noted that some call took place, though not between whom,
- ab^+ which stipulates that every agent $c \neq a, b$ noted that possibly some call took place, though not between whom.

It would be interesting to check whether our results hold for these types of calls, as well.

Another issue interesting to study is the synthesis of a distributed epistemic gossip protocol from epistemic specifications. For a related work on a synthesis of a knowledge-based programs see, e.g. [12]. Finally, it would be interesting to study the decidability of the problems considered here for a variant of our logic in which the only modal operator is the common knowledge operator $C_G\phi$. This operator states that the formula ϕ is commonly known among the group of agents G. The standard semantics of this operator is given in [5].

Acknowledgments. We thank the reviewers for helpful comments. First author is also a Visiting Professor at the University of Warsaw. He was partially supported by the NCN grant nr 2014/13/B/ST6/01807. The second author was partially supported by EPSRC grant EP/M027287/1.

References

1. Apt, K.R., Grossi, D., Van der Hoek, W.: Epistemic protocols for distributed gossiping. In: Proceedings of the 15th Conference on Theoretical Aspects of Rationality and Knowledge (TARK 2015). EPTCS, vol. 215, pp. 51–66 (2016)
2. Attamah, M., Ditmarsch, H., Grossi, D., Hoek, W.: A framework for epistemic gossip protocols. In: Bulling, N. (ed.) EUMAS 2014. LNCS (LNAI), vol. 8953, pp. 193–209. Springer, Heidelberg (2015). doi:10.1007/978-3-319-17130-2_13
3. Attamah, M., van Ditmarsch, H., Grossi, D., Van der Hoek, W.: Knowledge and gossip. In Proceedings of ECAI 2014. IOS Press (2014)
4. Cooper, M.C., Herzig, A., Maffre, F., Maris, F., Régnier, P.: A simple account of multiagent epistemic planning. In: Proceedings of ECAI 2016, pp. 193–201. IOS Press (2016)
5. Fagin, R., Halpern, J., Vardi, M., Moses, Y.: Reasoning About Knowledge. MIT Press, Cambridge (1995)
6. Fagin, R., Halpern, J.Y., Moses, Y., Vardi, M.Y.: Knowledge-based programs. Distrib. Comput. 10(4), 199–225 (1997)
7. Halpern, J.Y., Zuck, L.D.: A little knowledge goes a long way: knowledge-based derivations and correctness proofs for a family of protocols. J. ACM 39(3), 449–478 (1992)
8. Hedetniemi, S.M., Hedetniemi, S.T., Liestman, A.L.: A survey of gossiping and broadcasting in communication networks. Networks 18(4), 319–349 (1988)
9. Herzig, A., Maffre, F.: How to share knowledge by gossiping. In: Rovatsos, M., Vouros, G., Julian, V. (eds.) EUMAS/AT -2015. LNCS (LNAI), vol. 9571, pp. 249–263. Springer, Heidelberg (2016). doi:10.1007/978-3-319-33509-4_20
10. Hromkovic, J., Klasing, R., Pelc, A., Ruzicka, P., Unger, W.: Dissemination of Information in Communication Networks - Broadcasting, Gossiping, Leader Election, and Fault-Tolerance. Texts in Theoretical Computer Science. An EATCS Series. Springer, New York (2005)
11. Kermarrec, A., van Steen, M.: Gossiping in distributed systems. Oper. Syst. Rev. 41(5), 2–7 (2007)
12. Meyden, R., Wilke, T.: Synthesis of distributed systems from knowledge-based specifications. In: Abadi, M., Alfaro, L. (eds.) CONCUR 2005. LNCS, vol. 3653, pp. 562–576. Springer, Heidelberg (2005). doi:10.1007/11539452_42
13. van Ditmarsch, H., van Eijck, J., Pardo, P., Ramezanian, R., Schwarzentruber, F.: Dynamic gossip (2015). CoRR, abs/1511.00867

Hilbert-Style Axiomatization for Hybrid XPath with Data

Carlos Areces[(✉)] and Raul Fervari

FaMAF, Universidad Nacional de Córdoba, Argentina CONICET,
Córdoba, Argentina
{areces,fervari}@famaf.unc.edu.ar

Abstract. In this paper we introduce a sound and complete axiomatization for XPath with data constraints extended with hybrid operators. First, we define HXPath$_=$($\uparrow\downarrow$), an extension of vertical XPath with nominals and the hybrid operator @. Then, we introduce an axiomatic system for HXPath$_=$($\uparrow\downarrow$), and we prove it is complete with respect to the class of abstract data trees, i.e., data trees in which data values are abstracted as equivalence relations. As a corollary, we also obtain completeness with respect to the class of concrete data trees.

Keywords: XPath · Modal logic · Hybrid logic · Data tree · Axiomatization

1 XPath as a Modal Logic with Data Tests

XPath is arguably the most widely used XML query language. Indeed, XPath is implemented in XSLT and XQuery and it is used in many specification and update languages. XPath is, fundamentally, a general purpose language for addressing, searching, and matching pieces of an XML document. It is an open standard and constitutes a World Wide Web Consortium (W3C) Recommendation [14]. [21] adapts the definition of XPath to be used as a powerful query language over knowledge bases. Core-XPath [20] is the fragment of XPath 1.0 containing the navigational behavior of XPath. It can express properties of the underlying tree structure of the XML document, such as the label (tag name) of a node, but it cannot express conditions on the actual data contained in the attributes. In other words, it is essentially a *classical modal logic* [8,10]. Core-XPath has been well studied from a modal point of view. For instance, its satisfiability problem is known to be decidable even in the presence of DTDs [6,22]. Moreover, it is known that it is equivalent to FO2 (first-order logic with two variables over an appropriate signature on trees) in terms of expressive power [23], and that it is strictly less expressive than PDL with converse over trees [7]. Sound and complete axiomatizations for Core-XPath have been introduced in [12,13].

However, from a database perspective, Core-XPath is not expressive enough to define the most important construct in a query language: the *join*. Without the ability to relate nodes based on the actual data values of the attributes,

© Springer International Publishing AG 2016
L. Michael and A. Kakas (Eds.): JELIA 2016, LNAI 10021, pp. 34–48, 2016.
DOI: 10.1007/978-3-319-48758-8_3

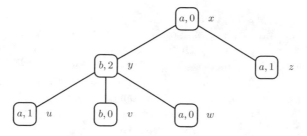

Fig. 1. An example of a data tree.

the logic's expressive power is inappropriate for many applications. The extension of Core-XPath with (in)equality tests between attributes of elements in an XML document is named Core-Data-XPath in [11]. Here, we will call this logic XPath$_=$. Models of XPath$_=$ are data trees which can be seen as XML documents. A data tree is a tree whose nodes contain a label from a finite alphabet and a data value from an infinite domain (see Fig. 1 for an example). We will relax the condition on finiteness and consider also infinite data trees, although all our results hold also on finite structures. The main characteristic of XPath$_=$ is to allow formulas of the form $\langle \alpha = \beta \rangle$ and $\langle \alpha \neq \beta \rangle$, where α, β are path expressions that navigate the tree using axes: descendant, child, ancestor, next-sibling, etc. and can make tests in intermediate nodes. The formula $\langle \alpha = \beta \rangle$ (respectively $\langle \alpha \neq \beta \rangle$) is true at a node x of a data tree if there are nodes y, z that can be reached by paths denoted by α, β respectively, and such that the data value of y is equal (respectively different) to the data value of z. For instance, in Fig. 1 the expression *"there is a one-step descendant and a two-steps descendant sharing the same data value"* is satisfied at x, given the presence of u and z. The expression *"there are two children with distinct data value"* is also true at x, because y and z have different data.

Notice that XPath$_=$ allows to compare data values at the end of a path, by equality or inequality. However, it does not allow the access to the concrete data value of nodes (in the example, 0, 1 or 2). Hence, it is possible to work with an abstraction of data trees: instead of having concrete data values in each node, we have an equivalence relation between nodes. In the data tree from Fig. 1, the relation consists of three equivalence classes: $\{x, v, w\}$, $\{u, z\}$ and $\{y\}$.

Recent articles investigate XPath$_=$ from a modal perspective. For example, satisfiability and evaluation are discussed in [15,16,19], while model theory and expressivity are studied in [2,3,17,18]. We will focus in the proof theory of XPath$_=$ extended with hybrid operators. In [5], a Gentzen-style sequent calculus is given for a very restricted fragment of XPath$_=$, named DataGL. In DataGL, data comparisons are allowed only between the evaluation point and its successors. An extension of the equational axiomatic system from [12] is introduced in [1], allowing downward navigation and equality/inequality tests.

In this article we will continue the investigation of axiomatic systems for XPath$_=$. In particular, we will introduce a Hilbert-style axiomatization for the logic with downward and upward navigation, where node expressions are extended with nominals (special labels that are valid in only one node), and path expressions are extended with the hybrid operator @ (allowing the navigation to some particular named node). We call this logic *Hybrid Vertical XPath* (denoted HXPath$_=$($\uparrow\downarrow$)). We will take advantage of hybrid operators to prove completeness using a Henkin-style model construction (see [8] for details).

The article is organized as follows. In Sect. 2 we introduce the syntax and semantics of HXPath$_=$($\uparrow\downarrow$). Then we define the axiomatic system HXP in Sect. 3 and we prove its completeness in Sect. 4. In Sect. 5 we extend HXP to prove completeness with respect to the class of data trees. To conclude, in Sect. 6 we introduce some remarks and future lines of research.

2   Preliminaries

In this section we introduce the syntax and semantics for the logic we call Hybrid Vertical XPath (HXPath$_=$($\uparrow\downarrow$) for short). We assume basic knowledge of classical modal logic (see [8] for further details).

We start by defining the structures that will be used to evaluate formulas in the language.

Definition 1 (Hybrid Data Models). *Let* LAB *(the set of labels) and* NOM *(the set of nominals) be two infinite countable sets. An* abstract hybrid data model *is a tuple* $\mathcal{M} = \langle M, \sim, \rightarrow, label, nom \rangle$, *where M is a non-empty set of elements, $\sim \subseteq M \times M$ is an equivalence relation between elements of M, $\rightarrow \subseteq M \times M$ is the accessibility relation, $label : M \rightarrow 2^{\mathsf{LAB}}$ is a labeling function and $nom :$ NOM $\rightarrow M$ is a function that assigns nominals to certain elements.*

A concrete hybrid data model *is a tuple* $\mathcal{M} = \langle M, D, \rightarrow, label, nom, data \rangle$, *where M is a non-empty set of elements, D is a non-empty set of data, $\rightarrow \subseteq M \times M$ is the accessibility relation, $label : M \rightarrow 2^{\mathsf{LAB}}$ is the labeling function, $nom :$ NOM $\rightarrow M$ is a function which names the nodes and $data : M \rightarrow D$ is the function which assigns a data value to each node of the model.*

We often write $w{\downarrow}v$ and $v{\uparrow}w$ when $w \rightarrow v$.

Concrete data models are most commonly used in application, where we encounter data from an infinite alphabet (e.g., alphabetic strings) associated to the nodes in a semi-structured database. It is easy to see that each concrete data model has an associated, equivalent abstract data model where data is replaced by an equivalence relation that links all nodes with the same data. Vice-versa, each abstract data model can be "concretized" by assigning to each node its equivalence data class as data. We will prove sound and completeness over the class of abstract data models and, as a corollary, obtain completeness over concrete data models.

We are now ready to introduce the syntax and semantics of HXPath$_=$($\uparrow\downarrow$).

Definition 2 (Syntax). *The set of path expressions (which we will note as α, β, γ, ...) and node expressions (which we will note as φ, ψ, θ, ...) of $HXPath_=(\uparrow\downarrow)$ are defined by mutual recursion as follows:*

$$\alpha, \beta ::= \ \downarrow \ | \ \uparrow \ | \ @_i \ | \ [\varphi] \ | \ \alpha\beta$$

$$\varphi, \psi ::= a \ | \ i \ | \ \neg\varphi \ | \ \varphi \wedge \psi \ | \ \langle \alpha = \beta \rangle \ | \ \langle \alpha \neq \beta \rangle, \qquad a \in \mathsf{LAB}, i \in \mathsf{NOM}.$$

Notice that path expressions occur in node expressions in *data comparison formulas* of the form $\langle \alpha = \beta \rangle$ and $\langle \alpha \neq \beta \rangle$, while node expressions occur in path expressions in *test formulas* of the form $[\varphi]$.

In what follows we will always use δ to represent the $\downarrow$ and $\uparrow$ operators and $*$ for $=$ and $\neq$. Other Boolean operators are defined as usual. We define the following operators as abbreviations.

Definition 3 (Abbreviations). *Let α, β be path expressions, γ_1, γ_2 path expressions or the empty string, φ a node expression, i a nominal, and p an arbitrary symbol in* LAB:

Node Expressions	Path Expressions
$\top \equiv p \vee \neg p$	$\epsilon \equiv [\top]$
$\bot \equiv \neg\top$	$\langle \gamma_1(\alpha \cup \beta)\gamma_2 * \gamma_3 \rangle \equiv \langle \gamma_1\alpha\gamma_2 * \gamma_3 \rangle \vee \langle \gamma_1\beta\gamma_2 * \gamma_3 \rangle$
$\langle \alpha \rangle \varphi \equiv \langle \alpha[\varphi] = \alpha[\varphi] \rangle$	$\langle \gamma_1 * \gamma_2(\alpha \cup \beta)\gamma_3 \rangle \equiv \langle \gamma_1 * \gamma_2\alpha\gamma_3 \rangle \vee \langle \gamma_1 * \gamma_2\beta\gamma_3 \rangle$
$[\alpha]\varphi \equiv \neg\langle \alpha \rangle\neg\varphi$	
$@_i\varphi \equiv \langle @_i \rangle\varphi$	

As a corollary of the definition below, the diamond and box expressions $\langle \alpha \rangle \varphi$ and $[\alpha]\varphi$ will have their classical meaning, and the same will be true for hybrid "at" formulas of the form $@_i\varphi$. Notice that we use $@_i$ both as a path expression and as a modality; the intended meaning will always be clear by context. Notice also that, following the standard notation in XPath logics and in modal logics, the $[\ ]$ operation is overloaded: for φ a node expression and α a path expression, both $[\alpha]\varphi$ and $[\varphi]\alpha$ are well-formed expressions; the former is a node expression where $[\alpha]$ is a box modality, the later is a path expression where $[\varphi]$ is a test.

Definition 4 (Semantics). *Let $\mathcal{M} = \langle M, \sim, \rightarrow, label, nom \rangle$ be an abstract data model, and $x, y \in M$. We define the semantics of $HXPath_=(\uparrow\downarrow)$ as follows:*

$$
\begin{aligned}
\mathcal{M}, x, y &\models \downarrow &&\text{iff} && x \rightarrow y \\
\mathcal{M}, x, y &\models \uparrow &&\text{iff} && y \rightarrow x \\
\mathcal{M}, x, y &\models @_i &&\text{iff} && nom(i) = y \\
\mathcal{M}, x, y &\models [\varphi] &&\text{iff} && x = y \text{ and } \mathcal{M}, x \models \varphi \\
\mathcal{M}, x, y &\models \alpha\beta &&\text{iff} && \text{there is some } z \in M \text{ s.t. } \mathcal{M}, x, z \models \alpha \text{ and } \mathcal{M}, z, y \models \beta \\
\mathcal{M}, x &\models a &&\text{iff} && a \in label(x) \\
\mathcal{M}, x &\models i &&\text{iff} && nom(i) = x \\
\mathcal{M}, x &\models \neg\varphi &&\text{iff} && \mathcal{M}, x \not\models \varphi \\
\mathcal{M}, x &\models \varphi \wedge \psi &&\text{iff} && \mathcal{M}, x \models \varphi \text{ and } \mathcal{M}, x \models \psi \\
\mathcal{M}, x &\models \langle \alpha = \beta \rangle &&\text{iff} && \text{there are } y, z \in M \text{ s.t. } \mathcal{M}, x, y \models \alpha, \ \mathcal{M}, x, z \models \beta \text{ and } y \sim z \\
\mathcal{M}, x &\models \langle \alpha \neq \beta \rangle &&\text{iff} && \text{there are } y, z \in M \text{ s.t. } \mathcal{M}, x, y \models \alpha, \ \mathcal{M}, x, z \models \beta \text{ and } y \not\sim z.
\end{aligned}
$$

Corollary 1

$$\mathcal{M}, x \models @_i\varphi \quad \text{iff} \quad \mathcal{M}, nom(i) \models \varphi$$
$$\mathcal{M}, x \models \langle\delta\rangle\varphi \quad \text{iff} \quad \text{there is some } y \in M \text{ s.t. } x\delta y \text{ and } \mathcal{M}, y \models \varphi$$
$$\mathcal{M}, x \models [\delta]\varphi \quad \text{iff} \quad \text{for all } y \in M, \ x\delta y \text{ then } \mathcal{M}, y \models \varphi.$$

The addition of the hybrid operators to XPath increases its expressive power. The following examples should serve as illustration.

Example 1. We list below some $\text{HXPath}_=(\uparrow\downarrow)$ expressions together with their intuitive meaning:

$\alpha[i]$	There exists an α path between the current point of evaluation and the node named i
$@_i\alpha$	There exists an α path between the node named i and some other node
$\langle @_i = @_j \rangle$	The node named i has the same data than the node named j
$\langle \alpha = @_i\beta \rangle$	There exists a node accessible from the current point of evaluation by an α path that has the same data than a node accessible from the point named i by a β path

3   Axiomatic System

In this section we introduce the axiomatic system HXP for $\text{HXPath}_=(\uparrow\downarrow)$. It is an extension of an axiomatic system for the hybrid logic HL(@) which adds nominals and the @ operator to the basic modal language (see [8]). In particular, we include axioms to handle data equality and inequality.

We present axioms and rules step by step, providing brief comments to help the reader understand their role. In all cases, we provide *axiom and rule schemes*, i.e., they can be instantiated with arbitrary path and node expressions (but always respecting types). In all axioms and rules φ, ψ and θ are node expressions, α, β and γ are path expressions, i, j and k are nominals. We use $\vdash \varphi$ to indicate that φ is a theorem of HXP.

In addition to an arbitrary set of axiom and rule schemes for propositional logic, we include generalizations of the K axiom and the *Necessitation* rule for the basic modal logic to handle modalities with arbitrary path expressions.

Axiom and rule for classical modal logic
$\mathsf{K} \ [\alpha](\varphi \to \psi) \to ([\alpha]\varphi \to [\alpha]\psi)$ $\qquad\qquad \dfrac{\vdash \varphi}{\vdash [\alpha]\varphi} \ Nec$

Then we introduce generalizations of the rules for the hybrid logic HL(@).

Hybrid rules
$\dfrac{\vdash j \to \varphi}{\vdash \varphi} \ name \qquad\qquad \dfrac{\vdash @_i\langle\gamma\rangle j \wedge \langle @_j\alpha * \beta\rangle \to \theta}{\vdash \langle @_i\gamma\alpha * \beta\rangle \to \theta} \ paste$
j is a nominal different from i that does not occur in $\varphi, \theta, \alpha, \beta, \gamma.$

Now we introduce axioms that handle @. Notice that $@_i$ is a path expression of $HXPath_=(\uparrow\downarrow)$ and as a result, some of the standard hybrid axioms for @ have been generalized. In particular, the K axiom and *Nec* rule above also apply to $@_i$. In addition, we provide axioms to ensure that the relation induced by @ is a congruence.

Axioms for @	Congruence for @	
	@-refl.	$@_i i$
	@-sym.	$@_i j \rightarrow @_j i$
@-self-dual $\neg @_i \varphi \leftrightarrow @_i \neg\varphi$	nom	$@_i j \wedge \langle @_i \alpha * \beta \rangle \rightarrow \langle @_j \alpha * \beta \rangle$
@-intro $i \wedge \varphi \rightarrow @_i \varphi$	agree	$\langle @_j @_i \alpha * \beta \rangle \leftrightarrow \langle @_i \alpha * \beta \rangle$
	back	$\langle \gamma @_i \alpha * \beta \rangle \rightarrow \langle @_i \alpha * \beta \rangle$

Axioms involving the classical XPath operators can be found below. We organize them in three groups. First, we have axioms for the interaction between $\downarrow$ and $\uparrow$. These axioms are the classical ones characterizing "future" and "past" modalities (see [8]). Then, we introduce axioms to handle complex path expressions in data comparisons. Finally, we introduce axioms to handle data tests.

Axioms for $\downarrow, \uparrow$-interaction	
down-up	$\varphi \rightarrow [\downarrow]\langle\uparrow\rangle\varphi$
up-down	$\varphi \rightarrow [\uparrow]\langle\downarrow\rangle\varphi$
Axioms for paths	
comp-assoc	$\langle(\alpha\beta)\gamma * \eta\rangle \leftrightarrow \langle\alpha(\beta\gamma) * \eta\rangle$
comp-neutral	$\langle\alpha\beta * \gamma\rangle \leftrightarrow \langle\alpha\epsilon\beta * \gamma\rangle$ (α or β can be empty)
comp-dist	$\langle\alpha\beta\rangle\varphi \leftrightarrow \langle\alpha\rangle\langle\beta\rangle\varphi$
Axioms for data	
equal	$\langle\epsilon = \epsilon\rangle$
distinct	$\neg\langle\epsilon \neq \epsilon\rangle$
@-data	$\neg\langle @_i = @_j\rangle \leftrightarrow \langle @_i \neq @_j\rangle$
ϵ-trans	$\langle\epsilon = \alpha\rangle \wedge \langle\epsilon = \beta\rangle \rightarrow \langle\alpha = \beta\rangle$
*-comm	$\langle\alpha * \beta\rangle \leftrightarrow \langle\beta * \alpha\rangle$
*-test	$\langle[\varphi]\alpha * \beta\rangle \leftrightarrow \varphi \wedge \langle\alpha * \beta\rangle$
@*-dist	$\langle @_i\alpha * @_i\beta\rangle \leftrightarrow @_i\langle\alpha * \beta\rangle$
comp*-dist	$\langle\alpha\rangle\langle\beta * \gamma\rangle \rightarrow \langle\alpha\beta * \alpha\gamma\rangle$

Proposition 1. *The following formulas are theorems in* HXP.

1. *test-dist* $\vdash \langle[\varphi] = [\psi]\rangle \leftrightarrow \varphi \wedge \psi$
2. *test-$\perp$* $\vdash \langle[\varphi] \neq [\psi]\rangle \leftrightarrow \langle\epsilon \neq \epsilon\rangle$
3. *@-swap* $\vdash @_i\langle\alpha * @_j\beta\rangle \leftrightarrow @_j\langle\beta * @_i\alpha\rangle$
4. *bridge* $\vdash \langle\alpha\rangle i \wedge @_i\varphi \rightarrow \langle\alpha\rangle\varphi$

Proof (test-dist and test-$\perp$). Let $*$ be $=$ or $\neq$. Then:

$$\vdash \langle[\varphi] * [\psi]\rangle \leftrightarrow \langle[\varphi]\epsilon * [\psi]\rangle \text{ by } comp\text{-}neutral.$$

$\vdash \langle [\varphi] \epsilon * [\psi] \rangle \leftrightarrow \varphi \wedge \langle \epsilon * [\psi] \rangle$ by *-test.
$\vdash \varphi \wedge \langle \epsilon * [\psi] \rangle \leftrightarrow \varphi \wedge \langle [\psi] * \epsilon \rangle$ by *-comm.
$\vdash \varphi \wedge \langle [\psi] * \epsilon \rangle \leftrightarrow \varphi \wedge \langle [\psi] \epsilon * \epsilon \rangle$ by comp-neutral.
$\vdash \varphi \wedge \langle [\psi] \epsilon * \epsilon \rangle \leftrightarrow \varphi \wedge \psi \wedge \langle \epsilon * \epsilon \rangle$ by *-test.

Replacing $*$ by $=$ we get $\varphi \wedge \psi$ by equal. Replacing it by $\neq$ we get $\langle \epsilon \neq \epsilon \rangle$. (@-swap).

$\vdash @_i \langle \alpha = @_j \beta \rangle \leftrightarrow \langle @_i \alpha = @_i @_j \beta \rangle$ by @ =-dist.
$\vdash \langle @_i \alpha = @_i @_j \beta \rangle \leftrightarrow \langle @_i @_j \beta = @_i \alpha \rangle$ by =-comm.
$\vdash \langle @_i @_j \beta = @_i \alpha \rangle \leftrightarrow \langle @_j \beta = @_i \alpha \rangle$ by agree.
$\vdash \langle @_j \beta = @_i \alpha \rangle \leftrightarrow \langle @_i \alpha = @_j \beta \rangle$ by =-comm.
$\vdash \langle @_i \alpha = @_j \beta \rangle \leftrightarrow \langle @_j @_i \alpha = @_j \beta \rangle$ by agree.
$\vdash \langle @_j @_i \alpha = @_j \beta \rangle \leftrightarrow @_j \langle @_i \alpha = \beta \rangle$ by agree.
$\vdash @_j \langle @_i \alpha = \beta \rangle \leftrightarrow @_j \langle \beta = @_i \alpha \rangle$ by =-comm.

(bridge). Using contrapositive, bridge is equivalent to $\langle \alpha \rangle i \wedge [\alpha] \varphi \rightarrow @_i \varphi$. Using the modal theorem $\vdash \langle \alpha \rangle \varphi \wedge [\alpha] \psi \rightarrow \langle \alpha \rangle (\varphi \wedge \psi)$, we reason:

$\vdash \langle \alpha \rangle i \wedge [\alpha] \varphi \rightarrow \langle \alpha \rangle (i \wedge \varphi)$.
$\vdash \langle \alpha \rangle (i \wedge \varphi) \rightarrow \langle \alpha \rangle (@_i \varphi)$ by @-intro.
$\vdash \langle \alpha \rangle (@_i \varphi) \rightarrow @_i \varphi$ by back.

4   Completeness

It is a fairly straightforward exercise to prove that the axioms and rules of HXP are sound for the intended semantics. We will now show that the axiomatic system is also complete. The completeness argument follows the lines of the completeness proof for HL(@) (see [8]), which is a Henkin-style proof with nominals playing the role of first-order constants.

In what follows, we will write $\Gamma \vdash \varphi$ if and only if φ can be obtained from a set of formulas Γ by applying the inference rules of HXP.

Definition 5. *Let Γ be a set of formulas, we say that Γ is an* HXP *maximal consistent set (*HXP-*MCS, or MCS for short) if and only if $\Gamma \nvdash \bot$ and for all $\varphi \notin \Gamma$ we have $\Gamma \cup \{\varphi\} \vdash \bot$.*

Proposition 2. *Let Γ be an* HXP-*MCS. Then, the following facts hold:*

1. *$\{i, \varphi\} \subseteq \Gamma$ then $@_i \varphi \in \Gamma$,*
2. *$@_i \langle \alpha = \beta \rangle \in \Gamma$ then $\langle @_i \alpha = @_i \beta \rangle \in \Gamma$, and*
3. *$\langle \alpha = @_i \beta \rangle \in \Gamma$ then $\langle \alpha = @_j @_i \beta \rangle \in \Gamma$.*

Proof. Item 1 is a consequence of @-*intro*, 2 follows from @=-*dist* and 3 can be proved using *agree* and =-*comm*.   □

The next corollary follows from the definition of MCS, as expected:

Corollary 2. *Let Γ be a MCS. Then for all φ, either $\varphi \in \Gamma$ or $\varphi \notin \Gamma$.*

In the same way as for hybrid logic, inside every MCS there are a collection of MCSs with some desirable properties:

Lemma 1. *Let Γ be an* HXP-*MCS. For any nominal $i \in \Gamma$, let us define $\Delta_i = \{\varphi \mid @_i\varphi \in \Gamma\}$. Then*

1. *Δ_i is an* HXP-*MCS.*
2. *For all nominals i, j, if $i \in \Delta_j$ then $\Delta_i = \Delta_j$.*
3. *For all nominals i, j, we have $@_i\varphi \in \Delta_j$ iff $@_i\varphi \in \Gamma$.*
4. *If $k \in \Gamma$ then $\Gamma = \Delta_k$.*

Proof. See [8, Lemma 7.24] for details.

Definition 6 (Named and Pasted MCS). *Let Γ be an* HXP-*MCS. We say that Γ is* named *if for some nominal i we have that $i \in \Gamma$ (and we will say that Γ is named by i). We say that Γ is* pasted *if the following holds:*

1. *$\langle @_i\delta\alpha = \beta\rangle \in \Gamma$ implies that for some nominal j, $@_i\langle\delta\rangle j \wedge \langle @_j\alpha = \beta\rangle \in \Gamma$*
2. *$\langle @_i\delta\alpha \neq \beta\rangle \in \Gamma$ implies that for some nominal j, $@_i\langle\delta\rangle j \wedge \langle @_j\alpha \neq \beta\rangle \in \Gamma$.*

Now we are going to prove a crucial property in our completeness proof: the *Extended Lindenbaum Lemma*. Intuitively, it says that the rules of HXP allow us to extend MCSs to *named and pasted* MCSs, provided we enrich the language with new nominals. This lemma will be useful to obtain the models we need from an MCS.

Lemma 2 (Extended Lindenbaum Lemma). *Let* NOM$'$ *be a (countably) infinite set of nominals disjoint from* NOM*, and let* HXPath$_=(\uparrow\downarrow)'$ *be the language obtained by adding these new nominals to* HXPath$_=(\uparrow\downarrow)$*. Then, every* HXP-*consistent set of formulas in* HXPath$_=(\uparrow\downarrow)$ *can be extended to a named and pasted* HXP-*MCS in* HXPath$_=(\uparrow\downarrow)'$*.*

Proof. Enumerate NOM$'$. Given Σ a consistent set in HXPath$_=(\uparrow\downarrow)$, define Σ_k to be $\Sigma \cup \{k\}$, where k is the first nominal in our enumeration. Σ_k is consistent, otherwise for some conjunction θ from Σ, $\vdash k \to \neg\theta$. By the *name* rule, $\vdash \neg\theta$, contradicting the consistency of Σ.

Now enumerate all formulas in HXPath$_=(\uparrow\downarrow)'$. Define Σ^0 to be Σ_k and suppose we have defined Σ^m, for $m \geq 0$. Let φ_{m+1} be the $m + 1$th formula in our enumeration of HXPath$_=(\uparrow\downarrow)'$. Define Σ_{m+1} as follows. If $\Sigma^{m+1} \cup \{\varphi_{m+1}\}$ is inconsistent, then $\Sigma^{m+1} = \Sigma^m$. Otherwise:

1. $\Sigma^{m+1} = \Sigma^m \cup \{\varphi_{m+1}\}$ if φ_{m+1} is not of the form $\langle @_i\delta\alpha * \beta\rangle$.
2. $\Sigma^{m+1} = \Sigma^m \cup \{\varphi_{m+1}\} \cup \{@_i\langle\delta\rangle j \wedge \langle @_j\alpha * \beta\rangle\}$, if φ_{m+1} is of the form $\langle @_i\delta\alpha * \beta\rangle$. Here j is the first nominal in the enumeration that does not occur in Σ^m or $\langle @_i\delta\alpha * \beta\rangle$.

Let $\Sigma^+ = \bigcup_{n \geq 0} \Sigma^n$. This set is named (by k), maximal and pasted. Furthermore, it is consistent as a direct consequence of the *paste* rule. $\square$

From a named and pasted HXP-MCS we can extract a model:

Definition 7 (Extracted Model). *Let Γ be a named and pasted HXP-MCS, then we define the* extracted model *from Γ, $\mathcal{M}_\Gamma = \langle M, \sim, \rightarrow, label, nom \rangle$ as:*

- $M = \{\Delta_i \mid \Delta_i\, was\ obtained\ from\, \Gamma\}$
- $\Delta_i \rightarrow \Delta_j$ *iff* $\langle\downarrow\rangle j \in \Delta_i$
- $a \in label(\Delta_i)$ *iff* $a \in \Delta_i$
- $nom(i) = \Delta_i$
- $\Delta_i \sim \Delta_j$ *iff* $\langle \epsilon = @_j \rangle \in \Delta_i$.

Proposition 3. *Let $\mathcal{M}_\Gamma = \langle M, \sim, \rightarrow, label, nom \rangle$ be the extracted model, for some Γ. Then,*

1. $\Delta_i \rightarrow \Delta_j$ *if and only if* $\langle\uparrow\rangle i \in \Delta_j$, *and*
2. $\Delta_i \not\sim \Delta_j$ *if and only if* $\langle \epsilon \neq @_j \rangle \in \Delta_i$.

Proof. Item 1 uses the same argument as for HL(@) in addition to the axioms for $\uparrow$; item 2 follows from @-*data*.

We need to prove that, in fact, $\mathcal{M}_\Gamma$ is an abstract hybrid data model.

Proposition 4. $\mathcal{M}_\Gamma$ *is well defined, i.e., the following properties hold:*

1. $nom(i) = \Delta_1$ *and* $nom(i) = \Delta_2$ *then* $\Delta_1 = \Delta_2$, *and*
2. $\sim$ *is an equivalence relation.*

Proof. Item 1 follows from the axioms for the hybrid operators in a standard way. Let us prove that $\sim$ is an equivalence relation.

- *Reflexivity:* $\Delta_i \sim \Delta_i$ iff $\langle \epsilon = @_i \rangle \in \Delta_i$ iff $@_i \langle \epsilon = \epsilon \rangle \in \Delta_i$, which is true because $\langle \epsilon = \epsilon \rangle$ is a theorem.
- *Symmetry:* $\Delta_i \sim \Delta_j$ iff $\langle \epsilon = @_j \rangle \in \Delta_i$. By definition of Δ_i, we have $@_i \langle \epsilon = @_j \rangle \in \Gamma$, and by *neutral* and =-*comm* we get $@_i \langle \epsilon = @_j \epsilon \rangle \in \Gamma$. Then, by @-*swap* $@_j \langle \epsilon = @_i \epsilon \rangle$. Therefore $\langle \epsilon = @_i \rangle \in \Delta_j$ (by neutral), iff $\Delta_j \sim \Delta_i$.
- *Transitivity:* Suppose $\Delta_i \sim \Delta_j$ and $\Delta_j \sim \Delta_k$, iff $\langle \epsilon = @_j \rangle \in \Delta_i$ and $\langle \epsilon = @_k \rangle \in \Delta_j$. This means that we have $@_i \langle \epsilon = @_j \rangle \in \Gamma$ iff (by @-swap) $@_j \langle \epsilon = @_i \rangle \in \Gamma$, and $@_j \langle \epsilon = @_k \rangle \in \Gamma$. Then $\langle \epsilon = @_i \rangle \wedge \langle \epsilon = @_k \rangle \in \Delta_j$, and by ϵ-*trans* we have $\langle @_i = @_k \rangle \in \Delta_j$. By *agree* and @=-*dist* we get $@_i \langle \epsilon = @_k \rangle \in \Delta_j$, iff by definition of Δ_j, $@_j @_i \langle \epsilon = @_k \rangle \in \Gamma$. By *agree* we obtain $@_i \langle \epsilon = @_k \rangle \in \Gamma$, then $\langle \epsilon = @_k \rangle \in \Delta_i$. Hence, we have $\Delta_i \sim \Delta_k$. □

Now, given a named and pasted MCS Γ we can prove the following Existence Lemma:

Lemma 3 (Existence Lemma). *Let Γ be an HXP-MCS and let $\mathcal{M}_\Gamma = \langle M, \sim, \rightarrow, label, nom \rangle$ be the extracted model from Γ. Suppose $\Delta \in M$ and $i \in \Delta$. Then*

1. $\langle \delta\alpha = \beta \rangle \in \Delta$ *implies there exists* $\Sigma \in M$ *s.t.* $\Delta\delta\Sigma$ *and* $\langle \alpha = @_i\beta \rangle \in \Sigma$,
2. $\langle \delta\alpha \neq \beta \rangle \in \Delta$ *implies there exists* $\Sigma \in M$ *s.t.* $\Delta\delta\Sigma$ *and* $\langle \alpha \neq @_i\beta \rangle \in \Sigma$.

Proof. We discuss the case for $=$ (the case for $\neq$ is similar). Because $\Delta \in M$, for some nominal i we have $\Delta = \Delta_i$. As $\langle \delta\alpha = \beta \rangle \in \Delta$, $@_i\langle \delta\alpha = \beta \rangle \in \Gamma$. Then, by Axiom @=-*dist*, $\langle @_i\delta\alpha = @_i\beta \rangle \in \Gamma$. Because Γ is pasted $@_i\langle\delta\rangle j \wedge \langle @_j\alpha = @_i\beta \rangle \in \Gamma$. As Γ is MCS, $@_i\langle\delta\rangle j \in \Gamma$ and $\langle @_j\alpha = @_i\beta \rangle \in \Gamma$. By Axiom *agree*, we have $\langle @_j\alpha = @_j@_i\beta \rangle \in \Gamma$. Then, $@_j\langle\alpha = @_i\beta\rangle \in \Gamma$ by @=-*dist*. By definition, $\langle\delta\rangle j \in \Delta_i$ and $\langle\alpha = @_i\beta\rangle \in \Delta_j$. Taking Σ as Δ_j, we complete the proof. □

Now we are ready to prove the Truth Lemma that states that membership in an MCS of the extracted model is equivalent to being true in that MCS.

Lemma 4 (Truth Lemma). *Let* $\mathcal{M}_\Gamma = \langle M, \sim, \rightarrow, label, nom \rangle$ *be the extracted model from a MCS* Γ, *and let* $\Delta_i \in M$. *Then, for any formula* φ,

$$\mathcal{M}_\Gamma, \Delta_i \models \varphi \quad iff \quad \varphi \in \Delta_i.$$

Proof. In fact we will prove a stronger result. Let $\Delta_i, \Delta_j \in M$, φ be a node expression and α be a path expression.

(IH1): $\mathcal{M}_\Gamma, \Delta_i \models \varphi$ iff $\varphi \in \Delta_i$.
(IH2): $\mathcal{M}_\Gamma, \Delta_i, \Delta_j \models \alpha$ iff $\langle\alpha\rangle j \in \Delta_i$.

The proof proceeds by induction in the complexity of φ and α. First, we prove the base cases:

- $\alpha = \downarrow$: Suppose $\mathcal{M}_\Gamma, \Delta_i, \Delta_j \models \downarrow$ iff $\Delta_i \rightarrow \Delta_j$ (by $\models$), iff $\langle\downarrow\rangle j \in \Delta_i$ (by definition of extracted model).
- $\alpha = \uparrow$: Suppose $\mathcal{M}_\Gamma, \Delta_i, \Delta_j \models \uparrow$ iff $\Delta_j \rightarrow \Delta_i$ (by $\models$), iff $\langle\uparrow\rangle j \in \Delta_i$ (by 1 of Proposition 3).
- $\alpha = @_k$: Suppose $\mathcal{M}_\Gamma, \Delta_i, \Delta_j \models @_k$ iff $nom(k) = \Delta_j$. But by definition of nom, $\Delta_j = \Delta_k$, and because we know $j \in \Delta_j$ we have $j \in \Delta_k$. Then, we have $@_k j \in \Gamma$, and by Axiom *agree*, $@_i@_k j \in \Gamma$. Therefore, $@_k j \in \Delta_i$.
- $\varphi = a$: $\mathcal{M}_\Gamma, \Delta_i \models a$ iff $a \in label(\Delta_i)$, iff $a \in \Delta_i$.
- $\varphi = j$: $\mathcal{M}_\Gamma, \Delta_i \models j$ iff $nom(j) = \Delta_i$, iff $\Delta_i = \Delta_j$ iff $j \in \Delta_i$.

Now we prove the inductive cases:

- $\varphi = \psi \wedge \rho$ and $\varphi = \neg\psi$: are direct from (IH1).
- $\alpha = [\psi]$: $\mathcal{M}_\Gamma, \Delta_i, \Delta_j \models [\psi]$ iff $\Delta_i = \Delta_j$ and $\mathcal{M}_\Gamma, \Delta_i \models \psi$. By (IH1), we have $\psi \in \Delta_i$ and $j \in \Delta_i$. By Δ_i MCS, we have $\psi \wedge j \in \Delta_i$, and by idempotence of the conjunction we have $\psi \wedge \psi \wedge j \in \Delta_i$. Also, we have $\langle \epsilon = \epsilon \rangle \in \Delta_i$, then we can use Axioms =-*test* and =-*comm* to obtain $\langle [\psi][j] = [\psi][j] \rangle \in \Delta_i$ (which is the same as $\langle [\psi]\rangle j$) as we wanted.
- $\alpha = \beta\gamma$: $\mathcal{M}_\Gamma, \Delta_i, \Delta_j \models \beta\gamma$ iff there is some Δ_k such that $\mathcal{M}_\Gamma, \Delta_i, \Delta_k \models \beta$ and $\mathcal{M}_\Gamma, \Delta_k, \Delta_j, \models \gamma$. By (IH2), we have $\langle\beta\rangle k \in \Delta_i$ and $\langle\gamma\rangle j \in \Delta_k$. We can conclude $@_i\langle\beta\rangle k \in \Gamma$ and $@_k\langle\gamma\rangle j \in \Gamma$, then $@_i\langle\beta\rangle k \wedge @_k\langle\gamma\rangle j \in \Gamma$. By *agree*, we have $@_i\langle\beta\rangle k \wedge @_i@_k\langle\gamma\rangle j \in \Gamma$, and with a very simple hybrid argument we get $@_i(\langle\beta\rangle k \wedge @_k\langle\gamma\rangle j) \in \Gamma$. By *bridge*, we have $@_i(\langle\beta\rangle\langle\gamma\rangle j) \in \Gamma$, and by Axiom *comp-dist* $@_i(\langle\beta\gamma\rangle j) \in \Gamma$. Hence, $\langle\beta\gamma\rangle j \in \Delta_i$.

For node expressions of the form $\langle \alpha * \beta \rangle$ we need to do induction on the length of α and β (defined in the obvious way).

First notice that by *-*comm*, $\langle \alpha * \beta \rangle \in \Delta_i$ iff $\langle \beta * \alpha \rangle \in \Delta_i$. And by the semantic definition, $\mathcal{M}_\Gamma, \Delta_i \models \langle \alpha * \beta \rangle$ iff $\mathcal{M}_\Gamma, \Delta_i \models \langle \beta * \alpha \rangle$. So we need only discuss the case for α. Moreover, by *comp-neutral*, $\vdash \langle \alpha * \beta \rangle \leftrightarrow \langle \alpha \epsilon * \beta \rangle$ which is also a validity. So we can assume that every path ends in a test. The base case then is when $|\alpha| + |\beta| = 2$, and both α and β are tests.

- $\varphi = \langle [\psi] = [\rho] \rangle$: direct from *test-dist*.
- $\varphi = \langle [\psi] \neq [\rho] \rangle$: it is a contradiction from *test-$\perp$*, then this case has not to be considered.

Now, let us consider $|\alpha| + |\beta| \geq 3$:

- $\varphi = \langle \downarrow\beta = \gamma \rangle$: $\mathcal{M}_\Gamma, \Delta_i \models \langle \downarrow\beta = \gamma \rangle$ iff there are Δ_j, Δ_k such that $\mathcal{M}_\Gamma, \Delta_i, \Delta_j \models \downarrow\beta$, $\mathcal{M}_\Gamma, \Delta_i, \Delta_k \models \gamma$ and $\Delta_j \sim \Delta_k$. Then, by (IH2) and definition of $\mathcal{M}_\Gamma$ we have:
  1. $\langle \downarrow\beta \rangle j \in \Delta_i$,
  2. $\langle \gamma \rangle k \in \Delta_i$, and
  3. $\langle \epsilon = @_k \rangle \in \Delta_j$.
     By 1 and the Existence Lemma, there is Δ_l such that both $\Delta_i \to \Delta_j$ and $\mathcal{M}_\Gamma, \Delta_l, \Delta_j \models \beta$ hold. Then by (IH2) we have
  4. $\langle \beta \rangle j \in \Delta_l$.

  ($\otimes$) From 2 we have $\langle \gamma \rangle k \in \Delta_i$ and from 3 we can obtain $\langle \epsilon = @_j \rangle \in \Delta_k$ then we have $\langle @_i \gamma \rangle k \wedge @_k \langle \epsilon = @_j \rangle \in \Gamma$, by definition and Axiom *comp-dist*. By *bridge*, $\langle @_i \gamma \rangle \langle \epsilon = @_j \rangle \in \Gamma$, then by *comp=-dist* and *back*, we get $\langle @_i \gamma = @_j \rangle \in \Gamma$. Applying =*-comm*, *comp-neutral*, *agree* and @*-dist*, $@_i \langle \epsilon = @_i \gamma \rangle \in \Gamma$.
  Also, from 4 we have $@_l \langle \beta \rangle j \in \Gamma$, then $@_j \langle \epsilon = @_i \gamma \rangle \wedge \langle @_l \beta \rangle j \in \Gamma$ (by MCS and *comp-dist*), and by *bridge* we get $\langle @_l \beta \rangle \langle \epsilon = @_i \gamma \rangle \in \Gamma$. By *comp=-dist* and *comp-neutral*, $\langle @_l \beta = @_l \beta @_i \gamma \rangle \in \Gamma$, then by *back* and @=*-dist* we have $@_l \langle \beta = @_i \gamma \rangle \in \Gamma$. Therefore, we have $\langle \beta = @_i \gamma \rangle \in \Delta_l$.
  Then, because $\Delta_i \to \Delta_l$ and the previous paragraph, we can use the Existence Lemma to obtain $\langle \downarrow\beta = @_i \gamma \rangle \in \Delta_i$, if and only if $\langle \downarrow\beta = \gamma \rangle \in \Delta_i$ (by @=-dist), hence $\langle \downarrow\beta = \gamma \rangle \in \Delta_i$, as we wanted.

- $\varphi = \langle \uparrow\beta = \gamma \rangle$ and $\varphi = \langle \delta\beta * \gamma \rangle$ are similar to the previous one but using also Proposition 3.
- $\varphi = \langle @_j \beta = \gamma \rangle$: $\mathcal{M}_\Gamma, \Delta_i \models \langle @_j \beta = \gamma \rangle$ iff there are Δ_k, Δ_l such that $\mathcal{M}_\Gamma, \Delta_i, \Delta_k \models @_j \beta$, $\mathcal{M}_\Gamma, \Delta_i, \Delta_l \models \gamma$ and $\Delta_k \sim \Delta_l$. Then, by (IH2) and definition of $\mathcal{M}_\Gamma$ we have:
  1. $\langle @_j \beta \rangle k \in \Delta_i$, iff $@_i \langle @_j \beta \rangle k \in \Gamma$ iff $@_j \langle \beta \rangle k \in \Gamma$,
  2. $\langle \gamma \rangle l \in \Delta_i$, iff $@_i \langle \beta \rangle l \in \Gamma$, and
  3. $\langle \epsilon = @_k \rangle \in \Delta_j$, iff $@_k \langle \epsilon = @_l \rangle \in \Gamma$.

By 1 and 2 we have $@_j\langle\beta\rangle\langle\epsilon = @_l\rangle \in \Gamma$, iff (by *comp=-dist*) $@_j\langle\beta = \beta@_l\rangle \in \Gamma$. By *back*, we get $@_j\langle\beta = @_l\rangle \in \Gamma$, which is equivalent to $@_l\langle\epsilon = @_j\beta\rangle \in \Gamma$ (by *agree* and =-*dist*). Together with 2 and *bridge* we get $@_i\langle\gamma\rangle\langle\epsilon = @_j\beta\rangle \in \Gamma$, hence $@_i\langle\gamma = \gamma@_j\beta\rangle \in \Gamma$ iff (by *back* and =-comm) $@_i\langle@_j\beta = \gamma\rangle \in \Gamma$. Using definition of Δ_i, we finally get $\langle@_j\beta = \gamma\rangle \in \Delta_i$.

- $\varphi = \langle[\psi]\beta = \gamma\rangle$: $\mathcal{M}_\Gamma, \Delta_i \models \langle[\psi]\beta = \gamma\rangle$ iff there are Δ_j, Δ_k such that $\mathcal{M}_\Gamma, \Delta_i, \Delta_j \models [\psi]\beta$, $\mathcal{M}_\Gamma, \Delta_i, \Delta_k \models \gamma$ and $\Delta_j \sim \Delta_k$. Then, by (IH2) and definition of $\mathcal{M}_\Gamma$ we have:
  1. $\langle\beta\rangle j \in \Delta_i$,
  2. $\langle\gamma\rangle k \in \Delta_i$,
  3. $\langle\epsilon = @_k\rangle \in \Delta_j$, and
  4. $\psi \in \Delta_i$.

Using the same argument as in ($\otimes$) the proof that $\langle[\psi]\beta = \gamma\rangle \in \Delta_i$ is straight-forward.

- Cases involving $\neq$ are analogous, using Proposition 3 to obtain $\langle\epsilon = @_k\rangle \notin \Delta_j$ in item 3 above. □

As a result we obtain the completeness result.

Theorem 1. *The axiomatic system* HXP *is complete for abstract hybrid data models.*

Proof. We need to prove that every HXP-consistent set of HXPath$_=$($\uparrow\downarrow$)-formulas Σ it satisfiable in a countable hybrid model. For any Σ, we can use the Extended Lindenbaum Lemma to obtain Σ^+ which is named and pasted in HXPath$_=$($\uparrow\downarrow$)′. Let $\mathcal{M} = \langle M, \sim, \rightarrow, label, nom\rangle$ be the extracted model from Σ^+. As Σ^+ is named, then $\Sigma^+ \in M$. Then by Truth Lemma, for all $\varphi \in \Sigma$ we have $\mathcal{M}, \Sigma^+ \models \varphi$. Because each state is named by some nominal from a countable set NOM′, the model is countable.

Because the class of abstract data models is a conservative abstraction of concrete data models, we can conclude:

Corollary 3. *The axiomatic system* HXP *is complete for concrete hybrid data models.*

5 Completeness for Tree Models

As we mentioned in the introductory section, XPath$_=$ is a query language for XML documents, and that it is possible to work with some abstractions called *data trees*. So far, we introduced an axiomatic system which is sound and complete with respect to a more general class of structures, which are the hybrid data models from Definition 1. We will show that it is possible to extend the axiomatic system HXP to handle data trees, the most interesting structures for HXPath$_=$($\uparrow\downarrow$) applications.

The table below introduces two groups of axioms. Those in the first column guarantee that the evaluation model is a tree. In the second column, we have two axioms which impose a standard property required in abstractions of XML documents: the set of labels LAB is assumed to be finite and each node is labeled exactly by one tag name.

Axioms for trees		Axioms for labels	
no-circle	$i \to \neg \langle \downarrow \rangle^n i, n \geq 1$	lab-some	$\bigvee_{a \in \mathsf{LAB}} a$
no join	$\langle \uparrow \rangle i \wedge \langle \uparrow \rangle j \to @_i j$	lab-uniq	$\neg(a \wedge b)$ (for $a \neq b$)

We need to consider a point-generated sub-model of $\mathcal{M}_\Gamma$ to ensure that the resulting model is a tree.

Definition 8 (Generated Sub-model). *Let Γ be a named and pasted MCS using the axiomatic system HXP extended with the axioms for trees and labels, and $\mathcal{M}_\Gamma = \langle M, \sim, \to, \text{label}, \text{nom} \rangle$ the extracted model from Γ. We define $\mathcal{T}_\Gamma$ as the point-generated sub-model of $\mathcal{M}_\Gamma$ obtained from Γ, i.e., $\mathcal{T}_\Gamma$ is the smallest sub-model of $\mathcal{M}_\Gamma$ that includes Γ in its domain, and such that for all points w, the following closure condition holds:*

$$\text{If } w \in \mathcal{T}_\Gamma \text{ and } w \to v, \text{ then } v \in \mathcal{T}_\Gamma.$$

Proposition 5. *$\mathcal{T}_\Gamma$ is a tree.*

Proof. By construction Γ is the root of $\mathcal{T}_\Gamma$. We have to prove that the accessibility relation is (*a*) irreflexive, (*b*) asymmetric and (*c*) that every node except the root has exactly one immediate predecessor. The proof is standard using axioms for $\downarrow, \uparrow$ interaction and the axioms for trees.   □

It should be obvious that the axioms for labels ensure that exactly one label holds in a node. Using $\mathcal{T}_\Gamma$ in the Truth Lemma gives the desired result.

Theorem 2. *The axiomatic system HXP extended with the axioms for trees and labels is complete for abstract named data trees (and consequently, for concrete named data trees).*

6   Final Remarks

We introduced a sound and complete axiomatization for HXPath$_=(\uparrow\downarrow)$, i.e., the language XPath with upward and downward navigation and data comparisons, extended with nominals and the hybrid operator @. The *hybridization* of XPath allowed us to replicate the completeness argument for the hybrid logic HL(@) shown, e.g., in [8].

As future work we would like to take advantage of the hybridization of XPath$_=$ to obtain general axiomatizations as in [4,9]. The idea is to define minimal proof systems that are not only complete for the class of all models, but which can also be extended with additional axioms that are *pure* in some sense, ensuring completeness with respect to the corresponding class of models. Our goal is to explore this general framework and obtain complete axiomatic systems for some natural extensions of $HXPath_=(\uparrow\downarrow)$:

- $HXPath_=(\uparrow\downarrow)$ with reflexive-transitive closure for downward/upward navigation (i.e., allowing $\downarrow^*$ and $\uparrow^*$), and sibling navigation.
- Exploring new kind of data comparisons, for instance, including the relation $<$ in addition to $=$ and $\neq$.

Another aspect we would like to explore is *decidability* and *complexity*. A filtration argument (see [8]) can be applied to prove that $HXPath_=(\uparrow\downarrow)$ is decidable over the class of all models, obtaining a NEXPTIME upper bound for the satisfiability problem. We conjecture that the satisfiability problem is also decidable over the class of finite data trees, and that this result can be proved adapting the automata proof given in [15], with the method used to account for hybrid operators presented in [24].

Acknowledgments. This work was partially supported by grant ANPCyT-PICT-2013-2011, STIC-AmSud "Foundations of Graph Structured Data (FoG)" and the Laboratoire International Associé "INFINIS."

References

1. Abriola, S., Descotte, M., Fervari, R., Figueira, S.: Axiomatizations for downward XPath on data trees. CoRR, abs/1605.04271 (2016)
2. Abriola, S., Descotte, M., Figueira, S.: Model theory of XPath on data trees. Part II: Binary bisimulation and definability. Information and Computation (to appear). http://www.glyc.dc.uba.ar/santiago/papers/xpath-part2.pdf
3. Abriola, S., Descotte, M.E., Figueira, S.: Definability for downward and vertical XPath on data trees. In: Kohlenbach, U., Barceló, P., Queiroz, R. (eds.) WoLLIC 2014. LNCS, vol. 8652, pp. 20–35. Springer, Heidelberg (2014). doi:10.1007/978-3-662-44145-9_2
4. Areces, C., ten Cate, B.: Hybrid logics. In: Blackburn, P., Wolter, F., van Benthem, J. (eds.) Handbook of Modal Logics, pp. 821–868. Elsevier, Amsterdam (2006)
5. Baelde, D., Lunel, S., Schmitz, S.: A sequent calculus for a modal logic on finite data trees. In: 25th EACSL Annual Conference on Computer Science Logic, CSL 2016, pp. 32:1–32:16 (2016)
6. Benedikt, M., Fan, W., Geerts, F.: XPath satisfiability in the presence of DTDs. J. ACM **55**(2), 1–79 (2008)
7. Benedikt, M., Koch, C.: XPath leashed. ACM Comput. Surv. **41**(1), 1–54 (2008)
8. Blackburn, P., de Rijke, M., Venema, Y.: Modal Logic. Cambridge Tracts in Theoretical Computer Science, vol. 53. Cambridge University Press, Cambridge (2001)
9. Blackburn, P., ten Cate, B.: Pure extensions, proof rules, and hybrid axiomatics. Studia Logica **84**(2), 277–322 (2006)
10. Blackburn, P., van Benthem, J.: Modal logic: a semantic perspective. In: van Benthem, J., Blackburn, P., Wolter, F. (eds.) Handbook of Modal Logic, pp. 1–84. Elsevier, Amsterdam (2006)

11. Bojańczyk, M., Muscholl, A., Schwentick, T., Segoufin, L.: Two-variable logic on data trees and XML reasoning. J. ACM **56**(3), 1–48 (2009)
12. ten Cate, B., Litak, T., Marx, M.: Complete axiomatizations for XPath fragments. J. Appl. Logic **8**(2), 153–172 (2010)
13. ten Cate, B., Marx, M.: Axiomatizing the logical core of XPath 2.0. Theory Comput. Syst. **44**(4), 561–589 (2009)
14. Clark, J., DeRose, S.: XML path language (XPath). Website. W3C Recommendation (1999). http://www.w3.org/TR/xpath
15. Figueira, D.: Reasoning on words and trees with data. Ph.D. thesis, Laboratoire Spécification et Vérification, ENS Cachan, France (2010)
16. Figueira, D.: Decidability of downward XPath. ACM Trans. Comput. Logic **13**(4), 34 (2012)
17. Figueira, D., Figueira, S., Areces, C.: Basic model theory of XPath on data trees. In: International Conference on Database Theory, pp. 50–60 (2014)
18. Figueira, D., Figueira, S., Areces, C.: Model theory of XPath on data trees. Part I: Bisimulation and characterization. J. Artif. Intell. Res. **53**, 271–314 (2015)
19. Figueira, D., Segoufin, L.: Bottom-up automata on data trees and vertical XPath. In: 28th International Symposium on Theoretical Aspects of Computer Science (STACS 2011), pp. 93–104 (2011)
20. Gottlob, G., Koch, C., Pichler, R.: Efficient algorithms for processing XPath queries. ACM Trans. Database Syst. **30**(2), 444–491 (2005)
21. Kostylev, E., Reutter, J., Vrgoč, D.: Xpath for DL ontologies. In: Proceedings of the Twenty-Ninth AAAI Conference on Artificial Intelligence, AAAI 2015, pp. 1525–1531. AAAI Press (2015)
22. Marx, M.: XPath with conditional axis relations. In: Bertino, E., Christodoulakis, S., Plexousakis, D., Christophides, V., Koubarakis, M., Böhm, K., Ferrari, E. (eds.) EDBT 2004. LNCS, vol. 2992, pp. 477–494. Springer, Heidelberg (2004). doi:10. 1007/978-3-540-24741-8_28
23. Marx, M., de Rijke, M.: Semantic characterizations of navigational XPath. ACM SIGMOD Rec. **34**(2), 41–46 (2005)
24. Sattler, U., Vardi, M.Y.: The hybrid μ-calculus. In: Goré, R., Leitsch, A., Nipkow, T. (eds.) IJCAR 2001. LNCS, vol. 2083, pp. 76–91. Springer, Heidelberg (2001). doi:10.1007/3-540-45744-5_7

Approximate Unification in the Description Logic $\mathcal{FL}_0$

Franz Baader[1(✉)], Pavlos Marantidis[1], and Alexander Okhotin[2]

[1] Theoretical Computer Science, TU Dresden, Dresden, Germany
{franz.baader,pavlos.marantidis}@tu-dresden.de
[2] Chebyshev Laboratory, St. Petersburg State University, Saint Petersburg, Russia
alexander.okhotin@utu.fi

Abstract. Unification in description logics (DLs) has been introduced as a novel inference service that can be used to detect redundancies in ontologies, by finding different concepts that may potentially stand for the same intuitive notion. It was first investigated in detail for the DL $\mathcal{FL}_0$, where unification can be reduced to solving certain language equations. In order to increase the recall of this method for finding redundancies, we introduce and investigate the notion of approximate unification, which basically finds pairs of concepts that "almost" unify. The meaning of "almost" is formalized using distance measures between concepts. We show that approximate unification in $\mathcal{FL}_0$ can be reduced to approximately solving language equations, and devise algorithms for solving the latter problem for two particular distance measures.

1 Introduction

Description logics [1] are a well-investigated family of logic-based knowledge representation formalisms. They can be used to represent the relevant concepts of an application domain using concept descriptions, which are built from concept names and role names using certain concept constructors. In this paper, we concentrate on the DL $\mathcal{FL}_0$, which offers the constructors conjunction ($\sqcap$), value restriction ($\forall r.C$), and the top concept ($\top$).

Unification in DLs has been introduced as a novel inference service that can be used to detect redundancies in ontologies, and was first investigated in detail for $\mathcal{FL}_0$ [5]. For example, assume that one developer of a medical ontology defines the concept of a *patient with severe head injury* as

$$\text{Patient} \sqcap \forall\text{finding.}(\text{Head\_injury} \sqcap \forall\text{severity.Severe}), \tag{1}$$

whereas another one represents it as

$$\text{Patient} \sqcap \forall\text{finding.}(\text{Severe\_finding} \sqcap \text{Injury} \sqcap \forall\text{finding\_site.Head}). \tag{2}$$

F. Baader—Supported by the Cluster of Excellence 'Center for Advancing Electronics Dresden'.
P. Marantidis—Supported by DFG Graduiertenkolleg 1763 (QuantLA).

© Springer International Publishing AG 2016
L. Michael and A. Kakas (Eds.): JELIA 2016, LNAI 10021, pp. 49–63, 2016.
DOI: 10.1007/978-3-319-48758-8_4

Formally, these two concept descriptions are not equivalent, but they are nevertheless meant to represent the same concept. They can obviously be made equivalent by treating the concept names Head_injury and Severe_finding as variables, and substituting the first one by Injury ⊓ ∀finding_site.Head and the second one by ∀severity.Severe. In this case, we say that the descriptions are unifiable, and call the substitution that makes them equivalent a *unifier*. Intuitively, such a unifier proposes definitions for the concept names that are used as variables: in our example, we know that, if we define Head_injury as Injury ⊓ ∀finding_site.Head and Severe_finding as ∀severity.Severe, then the two concept descriptions (1) and (2) are equivalent w.r.t. these definitions.

Of course, this example was constructed such that a unifier providing sensible definitions for the concept names used as variables actually exists. It is based on the assumption that both knowledge engineers had the same definition of the concept *patient with severe head injury* in mind, but have modeled certain subconcepts on different levels of granularity. Whereas the first knowledge engineer used Head_injury as a primitive (i.e., not further defined) concept, the other one provided a more detailed definition for *head injury*; and the other way round for *severe finding*. But what if there are more differences between the two concepts, maybe due to small modeling errors? For example, assume that a third knowledge engineer has left out the concept name Severe_finding from (2), based on the assumption that all injuries with finding site head are severe:

$$\text{Patient} \sqcap \forall\text{finding.}(\text{Injury} \sqcap \forall\text{finding\_site.Head}). \tag{3}$$

The concept descriptions (1) and (3) cannot be unified if only Head_injury is used as a variable. Nevertheless, the substitution that replaces Head_injury by Injury ⊓ ∀finding_site.Head makes these two descriptions quite similar, though not equivalent. We call such a substitution an *approximate unifier*.

The purpose of this paper is to introduce and investigate the notion of approximate unification for the DL $\mathcal{FL}_0$. Basically, to formalize approximate unification, we first need to fix the notion of a distance between $\mathcal{FL}_0$ concept descriptions. An approximate unifier is then supposed to make this distance as small as possible. Of course, there are different ways of defining the distance between concept descriptions, which then also lead to different instances of approximate unification. In this paper, we consider two such distance functions, which are based on the idea that differences at larger role depth (i.e., further down in the nesting of value restrictions) are less important than ones at smaller role depth. The first distance considers only the smallest role depth ℓ where the difference occurs (and then uses $2^{-\ell}$ as distance), whereas the second one "counts" all differences, but the ones at larger role depth with a smaller weight. This idea is in line with work on nonstandard inferences in DLs that approximate least common subsumers and most specific concepts by fixing a bound on the role depth [9].

Exact unification in $\mathcal{FL}_0$ was reduced in [5] to solving certain language equations, which in turn was reduced to testing certain tree automata for emptiness. We show that this approach can be extended to approximate unification. In fact, by linking distance functions on concept descriptions with distance functions on languages, we can reduce approximate unification in $\mathcal{FL}_0$ to approximately solving language equations. In order to reduce this problem to a problem for tree automata, we do not employ the original construction of [5], but the more sophisticated one of [6]. Using this approach, both the decision variant (is there a substitution that makes the distance smaller than a threshold) and the computation variant (compute the infimum of the achievable distances) of approximate unification can be solved in exponential time, and are thus of the same complexity as exact unification in $\mathcal{FL}_0$.

Due to space constraints, we cannot give detailed proofs of all our results. They can be found in the accompanying technical report [2].

2 Unification in $\mathcal{FL}_0$

We will first recall syntax and semantics of $\mathcal{FL}_0$ and describe the normal form of $\mathcal{FL}_0$ concept descriptions that is based on representing value restrictions as finite languages over the alphabet of role names. Then, we introduce unification in $\mathcal{FL}_0$ and recall how it can be reduced to solving language equations.

Syntax and Semantics. The *concept descriptions* C of the DL $\mathcal{FL}_0$ are built recursively over a finite set of concept names N_c and a finite set of role names N_r using the following syntax rules:

$$C ::= \top \mid A \mid C \sqcap C \mid \forall r.C, \tag{4}$$

where $A \in N_c$ and $r \in N_r$. In the following, we assume that $N_c = \{A_1, \ldots, A_k\}$ and $N_r = \{r_1, \ldots, r_n\}$.

The semantics of $\mathcal{FL}_0$ is defined in the usual way, using the notion of an *interpretation* $\mathcal{I} = (\Delta^{\mathcal{I}}, \cdot^{\mathcal{I}})$, which consists of a nonempty domain $\Delta^{\mathcal{I}}$ and an interpretation function $\cdot^{\mathcal{I}}$ that assigns binary relations on $\Delta^{\mathcal{I}}$ to role names and subsets of $\Delta^{\mathcal{I}}$ to concept names. The interpretation function $\cdot^{\mathcal{I}}$ is extended to $\mathcal{FL}_0$ concept descriptions as follows: $\top^{\mathcal{I}} := \Delta^{\mathcal{I}}$, $(C \sqcap D)^{\mathcal{I}} := C^{\mathcal{I}} \cap D^{\mathcal{I}}$, and $(\forall r.C)^{\mathcal{I}} := \{d \in \Delta^{\mathcal{I}} \mid \text{ for all } e \in \Delta^{\mathcal{I}} : \text{ if } (d, e) \in r^{\mathcal{I}}, \text{ then } e \in C^{\mathcal{I}}\}$.

Equivalence and Normal Form. Two $\mathcal{FL}_0$ concept descriptions C, D are *equivalent* (written $C \equiv D$) if $C^{\mathcal{I}} = D^{\mathcal{I}}$ holds for all interpretations $\mathcal{I}$.

As an easy consequence of the semantics of $\mathcal{FL}_0$, we obtain that value restrictions ($\forall s.\cdot$) distribute over conjunction ($\sqcap$), i.e., $\forall s.(C \sqcap D) \equiv \forall s.C \sqcap \forall s.D$ holds for all $\mathcal{FL}_0$ concept descriptions C, D. Using this equivalence from left to right, we can rewrite every $\mathcal{FL}_0$ concept description into a finite conjunction of descriptions $\forall s_1. \cdots \forall s_m.A$, where $m \geq 0, s_1, \ldots, s_m \in N_r$, and $A \in N_c$. We further abbreviate $\forall s_1. \cdots \forall s_m.A$ as $\forall(s_1 \ldots s_m).A$, where $s_1 \ldots s_m$ is viewed to be a word over the alphabet of all role names N_r, i.e., an element of N_r^*. For $m = 0$, this is the empty word ε. Finally, grouping together value restrictions that end with the same concept name, we abbreviate conjunctions $\forall w_1.A \sqcap \ldots \sqcap \forall w_\ell.A$

as $\forall\{w_1, \ldots, w_\ell\}.A$, where $\{w_1, \ldots, w_\ell\} \subseteq N_r^*$ is viewed to be a (finite) language over N_r. Additionally we use the convention that $\forall\emptyset.A$ is equivalent to $\top$. Then, any $\mathcal{FL}_0$ concept description C (over $N_c = \{A_1, \ldots, A_k\}$ and $N_r = \{r_1, \ldots, r_n\}$) can be rewritten into the *normal form* $\forall L_1.A_1 \sqcap \ldots \sqcap \forall L_k.A_k$, where $L_1, \ldots L_k$ are finite languages over the alphabet N_r. For example, if $k = 3$, then the concept description $A_1 \sqcap \forall r_1.(A_1 \sqcap \forall r_1.A_2 \sqcap \forall r_2.A_1)$ has the normal form $\forall\{\varepsilon, r_1, r_1 r_2\}.A_1 \sqcap \forall\{r_1 r_1\}.A_2 \sqcap \forall\emptyset.A_3$. Using this normal form, equivalence of $\mathcal{FL}_0$ concept descriptions can be characterized as follows (see [5] for a proof).

Lemma 1. *Let* $C = \forall L_1.A_1 \sqcap \ldots \sqcap \forall L_k.A_k$ *and* $D = \forall M_1.A_1 \sqcap \ldots \sqcap \forall M_k.A_k$ *be* $\mathcal{FL}_0$ *concept descriptions in normal form. Then*

$$C \equiv D \ iff \ L_1 = M_1, \ldots, L_k = M_k.$$

Consider the head injury example from the introduction, where for brevity we replace the concept and role names by single letters: (1) thus becomes $A \sqcap \forall r.(X \sqcap \forall s.B)$ and (2) becomes $A \sqcap \forall r.(Y \sqcap D \sqcap \forall t.E)$. The normal forms of these two concept descriptions are

$$
\begin{aligned}
\forall\{\varepsilon\}.A \sqcap \forall\{rs\}.B \sqcap \forall\emptyset.D \sqcap \forall\emptyset.E \sqcap \forall\{r\}.X \sqcap \forall\emptyset.Y, \\
\forall\{\varepsilon\}.A \sqcap \forall\emptyset.B \sqcap \forall\{r\}.D \sqcap \forall\{rt\}.E \sqcap \forall\emptyset.X \sqcap \forall\{r\}.Y.
\end{aligned}
\tag{5}
$$

Unification. In order to define unification in $\mathcal{FL}_0$, we need to introduce an additional set of concept names N_v, whose elements we call *concept variables*. Intuitively, N_v contains the concept names that have possibly been given another name or been specified in more detail in another concept description describing the same notion. From a syntactic point of view, concept variables are treated like concept names when building concepts. We call expressions built using the syntax rules (4), but with $A \in N_c \cup N_v$, *concept patterns*, to distinguish them from concept descriptions, where only $A \in N_c$ is allowed. The difference between elements of N_c and N_v is that concept variables can be replaced by substitutions.

A *substitution* σ is a function that maps every variable $X \in N_v$ to a concept description $\sigma(X)$. This function can be extended to concept patterns, by setting $\sigma(A) := A$ for $A \in N_c \cup \{\top\}$, $\sigma(C \sqcap D) := \sigma(C) \sqcap \sigma(D)$, and $\sigma(\forall r.C) := \forall r.\sigma(C)$. We denote the set of all substitutions as Sub.

Definition 1 (Unification). *The substitution* σ *is a* unifier *of the two* $\mathcal{FL}_0$ *concept patterns* C, D *if* $\sigma(C) \equiv \sigma(D)$. *If* C, D *have a unifier, then we call them* unifiable. *The* $\mathcal{FL}_0$ unification problem *asks whether two given* $\mathcal{FL}_0$ *concept patterns are unifiable or not.*

In [5] it is shown that the $\mathcal{FL}_0$ unification problem is ExpTime-complete. The ExpTime upper bound is proved by a reduction to language equations, which in turn are solved using tree automata. Here we sketch the reduction to language equations. The reduction to tree automata will be explained in Sect. 4. Without loss of generality, we can assume that the input patterns are in normal form (where variables are treated like concept names), i.e.,

$$
\begin{aligned}
C = \forall S_{0,1}.A_1 \sqcap \ldots \sqcap \forall S_{0,k}.A_k \sqcap \forall S_1.X_1 \sqcap \ldots \sqcap \forall S_m.X_m, \\
D = \forall T_{0,1}.A_1 \sqcap \ldots \sqcap \forall T_{0,k}.A_k \sqcap \forall T_1.X_1 \sqcap \ldots \sqcap \forall T_m.X_m,
\end{aligned}
\tag{6}
$$

where $S_{0,i}, T_{0,i}, S_j, T_j$ are finite languages over N_r. The unification problem for C, D can be reduced to (independently) solving the language equations

$$S_{0,i} \cup S_1 \cdot X_{1,i} \cup \ldots \cup S_m \cdot X_{m,i} = T_{0,i} \cup T_1 \cdot X_{1,i} \cup \ldots \cup T_m \cdot X_{m,i} \qquad (7)$$

for $i = 1, \ldots, k$, where "$\cdot$" stands for concatenation of languages. A *solution* σ_i of such an equation is an *assignment* of languages (over N_r) to the variables $X_{j,i}$ such that $S_{0,i} \cup S_1 \cdot \sigma_i(X_{1,i}) \cup \ldots \cup S_m \cdot \sigma_i(X_{m,i}) = T_{0,i} \cup T_1 \cdot \sigma_i(X_{1,i}) \cup \ldots \cup T_m \cdot \sigma_i(X_{m,i})$. This assignment is called *finite* if all the languages $\sigma_i(X_{j,i})$ are finite. We denote the set of all assignments as Ass and the set of all finite assignments as $finAss$.

As shown in [5], C, D are unifiable iff the language equations of the form (7) have finite solutions for all $i = 1, \ldots, k$. In fact, given finite solutions $\sigma_1, \ldots, \sigma_k$ of these equations, a unifier of C, D can be obtained by setting

$$\sigma(X_i) := \forall \sigma_i(X_{i,1}).A_1 \sqcap \ldots \sqcap \forall \sigma_i(X_{i,k}).A_k, \qquad (8)$$

and every unifier of C, D can be obtained in this way. Of course, this construction of a substitution from a k-tuple of finite assignments can be applied to arbitrary finite assignments (and not just to finite solutions of the Eq. (7)), and it yields a bijection ρ between k-tuples of finite assignments and substitutions.

Coming back to our example (5), where we now view X, Y as variables, the language equations for the concept names A and B are

$$\{\varepsilon\} \cup \{r\} \cdot X_A \cup \emptyset \cdot Y_A = \{\varepsilon\} \cup \emptyset \cdot X_A \cup \{r\} \cdot Y_A,$$
$$\{rs\} \cup \{r\} \cdot X_B \cup \emptyset \cdot Y_B = \emptyset \cup \emptyset \cdot X_B \cup \{r\} \cdot Y_B.$$

Among others, the first equation has $X_A = Y_A = \emptyset$ as a solution, and the second $X_B = \emptyset$ and $Y_B = \{s\}$. The equations for D, E are built in a similar way, and $X_D = \{\varepsilon\}, Y_D = \emptyset$ and $X_E = \{t\}, Y_E = \emptyset$ are solutions of these equations. Using (8), but leaving out the value restrictions for $\emptyset$, these solutions yield the unifier σ with $\sigma(X) = \forall\{\varepsilon\}.D \sqcap \forall\{t\}.E \equiv D \sqcap \forall t.E$ and $\sigma(Y) = \forall\{s\}.B \equiv \forall s.B$.

3 Approximate Unifiers and Solutions

As motivated in the introduction, it makes sense to look for substitutions σ that are actually not unifiers, but come close to being unifiers, in the sense that the distance between $\sigma(C)$ and $\sigma(D)$ is small. We call such substitutions *approximate unifiers*. In the following, we will first recall some definitions regarding distances from metric topology [15]. Subsequently, we will first introduce approximate unification based on distances between concept descriptions, and then approximately solving language equations based on distances between languages. Next, we will show how distances between languages can be used to define distances between concept descriptions, and that approximate unification for distances obtained this way can be reduced to approximately solving language equations.

Metric Topology. Given a set X, a *metric* (or *distance*) on X is a mapping $d\colon X \times X \to [0, \infty)$ that satisfies the properties:

$(M1)$ $d(a, b) = 0 \iff a = b$
$(M2)$ $d(a, b) = d(b, a)$
$(M3)$ $d(a, c) \leqslant d(a, b) + d(b, c)$

In this case, (X, d) is called a *metric space*. Given a metric space (X, d), a sequence (a_n) of elements of X is said to *converge* to $a \in X$ (written $a_n \xrightarrow{d} a$) if for every $\epsilon > 0$ there is an $n_0 \in \mathbb{N}$ s.t. $d(a_n, a) < \epsilon$ for every $n \geqslant n_0$.

Approximate Unification. In order to define how close $\sigma(C)$ and $\sigma(D)$ are, we need to use a function that measures the distance between these two concept descriptions. We say that a function that takes as input a pair of $\mathcal{FL}_0$ concept descriptions and yields as output an element of $[0, \infty)$ is a *concept distance* for $\mathcal{FL}_0$ if it satisfies the following three properties:

- equivalence closedness: $m(C, D) = 0 \iff C \equiv D$,
- symmetry: $m(C, D) = m(D, C)$,
- equivalence invariance: $C \equiv D \implies m(C, E) = m(D, E)$.

Note that equivalence closedness corresponds to $(M1)$ and symmetry to $(M2)$ in the definition of a metric. Equivalence invariance ensures that m can be viewed as operating on equivalence classes of concept descriptions.

Definition 2 (Approximate Unification). *Given a concept distance m, $\mathcal{FL}_0$ concept patterns C, D, and a substitution σ, the degree of violation of σ is defined as $v_m(\sigma, C, D) := m(\sigma(C), \sigma(D))$. For $p \in \mathbb{Q}$, we say that σ is a p-approximate unifier of C, D if $2^{-p} > v_m(\sigma, C, D)$.*

Equivalence closedness of m yields that $v_m(\sigma, C, D) = 0$ iff σ is a unifier of C, D.

The *decision problem* for approximate unification asks, for a given threshold $p \in \mathbb{Q}$, whether C, D have a p-approximate unifier or not. In addition, we consider the following *computation problem*: compute $\inf_{\sigma \in Sub} v_m(\sigma, C, D)$.

The following lemma, which is immediate from the definitions, shows that a solution of the computation problem also yields a solution of the decision problem.

Lemma 2. *Let m be a concept distance and C, D $\mathcal{FL}_0$ concept patterns. Then C, D have a p-approximate unifier iff $2^{-p} > \inf_{\sigma \in Sub} v_m(\sigma, C, D)$.*

The reduction of the decision problem to the computation problem obtained from this lemma is actually polynomial. In fact, though the size of a representation of the number 2^{-p} may be exponential in the size of a representation of p, the number 2^{-p} need not be computed. Instead, we can compare p with $\log_2 \inf_{\sigma \in Sub} v_m(\sigma, C, D)$, where for the comparison we only need to compute as many digits of the logarithm as p has.

Approximately Solving Language Equations. Following [6], we consider a more general form of language equations than the one given in (7). Here, all Boolean operators (and not just union) are available. *Language expressions* are built recursively over a finite alphabet Σ using union, intersection, complement, and concatenation of regular languages from the left, as formalized by the following syntax rules:

$$\phi ::= L \mid X \mid \phi \cup \phi \mid \phi \cap \phi \mid \sim\phi \mid L \cdot \phi, \tag{9}$$

where L can be instantiated with any regular language over Σ and X with any variable. We assume that all the regular languages occurring in an expression are given by finite automata. Obviously, the left- and the right-hand sides of (7) are such language expressions. As before, an *assignment* $\sigma \in Ass$ maps variables to languages over Σ. It is extended to expressions in the obvious way (where $\sim$ is interpreted as set complement). The assignment σ *solves* the *language equation* $\phi = \psi$ if $\sigma(\phi) = \sigma(\psi)$. For *finite solvability* we require the languages $\sigma(X)$ to be finite, i.e., σ should be an element of *finAss*.

In order to define approximate solutions, we need the notion of distances between languages. A function $d : 2^{\Sigma^*} \times 2^{\Sigma^*} \to [0, \infty)$ satisfying (M1), (M2), and (M3) is called a *language distance*.

Definition 3 (Approximate Solutions). *Given a language distance d, language expressions ϕ, ψ, and an assignment σ, the* degree of violation *of σ is defined as $v_d(\sigma, \phi, \psi) := d(\sigma(\phi), \sigma(\psi))$. For $p \in \mathbb{Q}$, we say that σ is a p-approximate solution of $\phi \approx \psi$ if $2^{-p} > v_d(\sigma, \phi, \psi)$.*

The *decision* and the *computation problem* for approximately solving language equations are defined analogously to the case of unification. In addition, the analog of Lemma 2 also holds in this case, and thus the decision problem can be reduced to the computation problem.

Recall that unification in $\mathcal{FL}_0$ is reduced to *finite* solvability of language equations. The above definition of approximate solutions and of the decision and the computation problem can also be restricted to finite assignments, in which case we talk about *finite approximate solvability*. However, we will show that finite approximate solvability can actually be reduced to approximate solvability. For this to be the case, we need the language distance to satisfy an additional property (M4). Given a natural number ℓ, we call two languages $K, L \subseteq \Sigma^*$ *equal up to length ℓ* (and write $K \equiv_\ell L$) if K and L coincide on all words of length at most ℓ.

(*M4*) Let L be a language and (L_n) a sequence of languages over Σ. Then, $L_n \equiv_n L$ for all $n \geq 0$ implies $L_n \xrightarrow{d} L$.

If (*M4*) is satisfied for d, then the computation problem for finite assignments has the same solution as for arbitrary assignments.

Lemma 3. *Let d be a language distance satisfying (M4) and ϕ, ψ language expressions. Then,*

$$\inf_{\sigma \in finAss} v_d(\sigma, \phi, \psi) = \inf_{\sigma \in Ass} v_d(\sigma, \phi, \psi).$$

Before showing that language distances can be used to construct concept distances, we give two concrete examples of language distances satisfying $(M4)$.

Two Language Distances Satisfying $(M4)$. The following two mappings from $2^{\Sigma^*} \times 2^{\Sigma^*}$ to $[0, \infty)$ are defined by looking at the words in the symmetric difference $K \triangle L := (K \setminus L) \cup (L \setminus K)$ of the languages K and L[1]:

$$d_1(K, L) := 2^{-\ell} \qquad \text{where} \quad \ell = \min \{|w| \mid w \in K \triangle L\},$$
$$d_2(K, L) := \mu(K \triangle L) \quad \text{where} \quad \mu(M) = \tfrac{1}{2} \sum_{w \in M} (2|\Sigma|)^{-|w|}.$$

The intuition underlying both functions is that differences between the two languages are less important if they occur for longer words. The first function considers only the length ℓ of the shortest word for which such a difference occurs and yields $2^{-\ell}$ as distance, which becomes smaller if ℓ gets larger. The second function also takes into account how many such differences there are, but differences for longer words count less than differences for shorter ones. More precisely, a difference for the word u counts as much as the sum of all differences for words uv properly extending u. The following lemma is easy to show (see [2] for details).

Lemma 4. *The functions d_1, d_2 are language distances satisfying $(M4)$.*

From Language Distances to Concept Distances. Based on the normal form of $\mathcal{FL}_0$ concept descriptions introduced in Sect. 3, we can use a language distance d to define a concept distance. Basically, given $\mathcal{FL}_0$ concept descriptions $C = \forall L_1.A_1 \sqcap \ldots \sqcap \forall L_k.A_k$ and $D = \forall M_1.A_1 \sqcap \ldots \sqcap \forall M_k.A_k$ in normal form, we can use the distances $e_i = d(L_i, M_i)$ to define a distance between C and D. For this, we need an appropriate function that combines the k values $e_1, \ldots, e_k$ into a single value. We say that the function $f : [0, \infty)^k \to [0, \infty)$ is a *combining function* if it is

- commutative: $f(a_1, \ldots, a_k) = f(a_{\pi(1)}, \ldots, a_{\pi(k)})$ for all permutations π of the indices $1, \ldots, k$,
- monotone: $a_1 \leqslant b_1, \ldots, a_k \leqslant b_k \implies f(a_1, \ldots, a_k) \leqslant f(b_1, \ldots, b_k)$,
- zero closed: $f(a_1, \ldots, a_k) = 0 \iff a_1 = \cdots = a_k = 0$,
- and continuous.

The following are simple examples of combining functions:

- $\max(a_1, \ldots, a_k)$,
- $\operatorname{sum}(a_1, \ldots, a_k) = a_1 + \cdots + a_k$,
- $\operatorname{avg}(a_1, \ldots, a_k) = \sum_{i=1}^{k} a_i / k$.

Given a language distance d and a combining function f, the *concept distance* $m_{d,f}$ induced by d, f is defined as follows. If C, D are $\mathcal{FL}_0$ concept descriptions with normal forms $C \equiv \forall L_1.A_1 \sqcap \ldots \sqcap \forall L_k.A_k$ and $D \equiv \forall M_1.A_1 \sqcap \ldots \sqcap \forall M_k.A_k$, then we set

$$m_{d,f}(C, D) := f\big(d(L_1, M_1), \ldots, d(L_k, M_k)\big).$$

---

[1] In the first line below we assume, as usual, that $\min \emptyset = \infty$ and $2^{-\infty} = 0$.

Using one of the language distances d_1, d_2 introduced above in this setting means that differences between the concepts C, D at larger role depth count less than differences at smaller role depth.

Lemma 5. *Let d be a language distance and f be a combining function. Then the concept distance induced by f, d is indeed a concept distance, i.e., it is equivalence closed, symmetric, and equivalence invariant.*

Reducing Approximate Unification to Approximately Solving Language Equations. In the following, we assume that d is a language distance, f a combining function, and $m_{d,f}$ the concept distance induced by f, d. Let C, D be $\mathcal{FL}_0$ concept patterns in normal form, as shown in (6), and (7) the corresponding language equations, for $i = 1, \ldots, k$. We denote the left- and right-hand sides of the equations (7) with ϕ_i and ψ_i, respectively. The following lemma shows that the degree of violation transfers from finite assignments $\sigma_1, \ldots, \sigma_k$ to the induced substitution $\rho(\sigma_1, \ldots, \sigma_k)$ as defined in (8).

Lemma 6. *Let $\sigma_1, \ldots, \sigma_k \in finAss$. Then $f(v_d(\sigma_1, \phi_1, \psi_1), \ldots, v_d(\sigma_k, \phi_k, \psi_k)) = v_{m_{d,f}}(\rho(\sigma_1, \ldots, \sigma_k), C, D)$.*

Since the combining function is continuous, the equality stated in this lemma is preserved under building the infimum. In addition, Lemma 3 shows that the restriction to finite assignments can be dispensed with if d satisfies $(M4)$.

Lemma 7. *Assume that d satisfies $(M4)$. Then,*

$$\inf_{\sigma \in Sub} v_{m_{d,f}}(\sigma, C, D) =$$

$$= f(\inf_{\sigma_1 \in finAss} v_d(\sigma_1, \phi_1, \psi_1), \ldots, \inf_{\sigma_k \in finAss} v_d(\sigma_k, \phi_k, \psi_k))$$

$$= f(\inf_{\sigma_1 \in Ass} v_d(\sigma_1, \phi_1, \psi_1), \ldots, \inf_{\sigma_k \in Ass} v_d(\sigma_k, \phi_k, \psi_k)).$$

In case f is computable (in polynomial time), this lemma yields a (polynomial time) reduction of the computation problem for approximate $\mathcal{FL}_0$ unification to the computation problem for approximately solving language equations. In addition, we know that the decision problem can be reduced to the computation problem. Thus, it is sufficient to devise a procedure for the computation problem for approximately solving language equations.

In our example, the normal forms of the abbreviated concept descriptions (1) and (3) are

$$\forall\{\varepsilon\}.A \sqcap \forall\{rs\}.B \sqcap \forall\emptyset.D \sqcap \forall\emptyset.E \sqcap \forall\{r\}.X,$$
$$\forall\{\varepsilon\}.A \sqcap \forall\emptyset.B \sqcap \forall\{r\}.D \sqcap \forall\{rt\}.E \sqcap \forall\emptyset.X.$$

It is easy to see that the language equations for the concept names A, D, E are solvable, and thus these solutions contribute distance 0 to the overall concept distance. The language equation for the concept name B is $\{rs\} \cup \{r\} \cdot X_B = \emptyset \cup \emptyset \cdot X_B$, and the assignment $X_B = \emptyset$ leads to the smallest possible symmetric difference $\{rs\}$, which w.r.t. d_1 yields the value $2^{-2} = 1/4$. It is easy to see that this is actually the infimum for this equation. If we use the combining function avg, then this gives us the infimum $1/16$ for our approximate unification problem.

4   Approximately Solving Language Equations

In the following, we show how to solve the computation problem for the language distances d_1 and d_2 introduced above. Our solution uses the automata-based approach for solving language equations introduced in [6].

The first step in this approach is to transform the given system of language equations into a single equation of the form $\phi = \emptyset$ such that the language expression ϕ is *normalized* in the sense that all constant languages L occurring in ϕ are singleton languages $\{a\}$ for $a \in \Sigma \cup \{\varepsilon\}$. This normalization step can easily be adapted to approximate equations, but in addition to a normalized approximate equation $\phi_a \approx \emptyset$ it also generates a normalized strict equation $\phi_s = \emptyset$.

Lemma 8. *Let ϕ, ψ be language expressions. Then we can compute in polynomial time normalized language expressions ϕ_a and ϕ_s such that the following holds for $d \in \{d_1, d_2\}$:*

$$\{v_d(\sigma, \phi, \psi) \mid \sigma \in Ass\} = \{v_d(\sigma, \phi_a, \emptyset) \mid \sigma \in Ass \wedge \sigma(\phi_s) = \emptyset\}.$$

This lemma shows that, to solve the computation problem for $\phi \approx \psi$, we must solve the computation problem for $\phi_a \approx \emptyset$, but restrict the infimum to assignments that solve the strict equation $\phi_s = \emptyset$.

In a second step, [6] shows how a normalized language equation can be translated into a tree automaton working on the infinite, unlabeled n-ary tree (where $n = |\Sigma|$). The nodes of this tree can obviously be identified with Σ^*. The automata considered in [6] are such that the state in each successor of a node is determined independently of the choice of the states in its siblings. These automata are called *looping tree automata with independent transitions (ILTA)*.

Definition 4. *An ILTA is of the form $A = (\Sigma, Q, Q_0, \delta)$, where Σ is a finite alphabet, Q is a finite set of states, with initial states $Q_0 \subseteq Q$, and $\delta \colon Q \times \Sigma \to 2^Q$ is a transition function that defines possible successors of a state for each $a \in \Sigma$. A run of this ILTA is any function $r \colon \Sigma^* \to Q$ with $r(\varepsilon) \in Q_0$ and $r(wa) \in \delta(r(w), a)$ for all $w \in \Sigma^*$ and $a \in \Sigma$.*

According to this definition, ILTAs do not have a fixed set of final states. However, by choosing any set of states $F \subseteq Q$, we can use runs r of A to define languages over Σ as follows: $L_r(A, F) := \{w \in \Sigma^* \mid r(w) \in F\}$.

Given a normalized language equation $\phi = \emptyset$ with variables $\{X_1, \ldots, X_m\}$, it is shown in [6] how to construct an ILTA $A^\phi = (\Sigma, Q^\phi, Q_0^\phi, \delta^\phi)$ and subsets $F, F_1, \ldots, F_m \subseteq Q^\phi$ such that the following holds:

Proposition 1. *If r is a run of A^ϕ, then the induced assignment σ_r with $\sigma_r(X_i) := L_r(A^\phi, F_i)$, for $i = 1, \ldots, m$, satisfies $\sigma_r(\phi) = L_r(A^\phi, F)$. In addition, every assignment is induced by some run of A_ϕ.*

The size of this ILTA is exponential in the size of ϕ. In order to decide whether the language equation $\phi = \emptyset$ has a solution, one thus needs to decide whether

A^ϕ has a run in which no state of F occurs. This can easily be done by removing all states of F from A^ϕ, and then checking the resulting automaton A^ϕ_{-F} for emptiness. In fact, as an easy consequence of the above proposition we obtain that there is a 1–1-correspondence between the runs of A^ϕ_{-F} and the solutions of $\phi = \emptyset$ (Proposition 2 in [6]).

This approach can easily be adapted to the situation where we have an approximate equation $\phi_a \approx \emptyset$ and a strict equation $\phi_s = \emptyset$. Basically, we apply the construction of [6] to $\phi_a \cup \phi_s$, but instead of one set of states F we construct two sets F_a and F_s such that $\sigma_r(\phi_a) = L_r(A^{\phi_a \cup \phi_s}, F_a)$ and $\sigma_r(\phi_s) = L_r(A^{\phi_a \cup \phi_s}, F_s)$ holds for all runs r of $A^{\phi_a \cup \phi_s}$. By removing all states of F_s from $A^{\phi_a \cup \phi_s}$, we obtain an automaton whose runs are in 1–1-correspondence with the assignments that solve $\phi_s = \emptyset$. In addition, we can make this automaton $trim^2$ using the polytime construction in the proof of Lemma 2 in [6].

Theorem 1. *Given an approximate equation $\phi_a \approx \emptyset$ and a strict equation $\phi_s = \emptyset$, we can construct in exponential time a trim ILTA $A = (\Sigma, Q, Q_0, \delta)$ and sets of states $F_a, F_1, \ldots, F_m \subseteq Q$ such that every run r of A satisfies $\sigma_r(\phi_a) = L_r(A, F_a)$ and $\sigma_r(\phi_s) = \emptyset$. In addition, every assignment σ with $\sigma(\phi_s) = \emptyset$ is induced by some run of A.*

The Measure d_1

Using Lemma 8, Theorem 1, and the definition of d_1, it is easy to see that the computation problem for an approximate language equation $\phi \approx \psi$ can be reduced to solving the following problem for the trim ILTA $A = (\Sigma, Q, Q_0, \delta)$ of Theorem 1: compute $\sup_{r \, run \, of \, A} \min\{|w| \mid r(w) \in F_a\}$.

In order to compute this supremum, it is sufficient to compute, for every state $q \in Q$, the *length $lpr(q)$ of the longest partial run of A starting with q that does not have states of F_a at non-leaf nodes*. More formally, we define:

Definition 5. *Let $\Sigma^{\leqslant \ell}$ denote the set of all words over Σ of length at most ℓ. Given a trim ILTA $A = (\Sigma, Q, Q_0, \delta)$, a partial run of A of length ℓ from a state $q \in Q$ is a mapping $p : \Sigma^{\leqslant \ell} \to Q$ such that $p(\varepsilon) = q$ and $p(wa) \in \delta(p(w), a)$ for all $w \in \Sigma^{\leqslant \ell-1}$ and $a \in \Sigma$. The leaves of p are the words of length ℓ.*

Lemma 9. *The function $lpr : Q \to \mathbb{N} \cup \{\infty\}$ can be computed in time polynomial in the size of A.*

Proof. In order to compute lpr, we use an iteration similar to the emptiness test for looping tree automata [7].

If $q \in F_a$, then clearly $lpr(q) = 0$ and otherwise q has an appropriate partial run of length > 0 (recall that A is trim). For this reason, we start the iteration with

$$Q^{(0)} := F_a.$$

---

^{2} An ILTA (Σ, Q, Q_0, δ) is *trim* if every state is reachable from an initial state and $\delta(q, a) \neq \emptyset$ for all $q \in Q, a \in \Sigma$.

Next, for $i \geq 0$, we define

$$Q^{(i+1)} := Q^{(i)} \cup \{q \in Q \mid \exists a \in \Sigma : \delta(q, a) \subseteq Q^{(i)}\}.$$

We have $Q^{(0)} \subseteq Q^{(1)} \subseteq Q^{(2)} \subseteq \ldots \subseteq Q$. Since Q is finite, there is an index $j \leq |Q|$ such that $Q^{(j)} = Q^{(j+1)}$, and thus the iteration becomes stable.

It is easy to show that

$$lpr(q) = \begin{cases} \min\{i \mid q \in Q^{(i)}\} & \text{if } q \in Q^{(j)} \\ \infty & \text{if } q \notin Q^{(j)} \end{cases}$$

Since the number of iterations is linear in $|Q|$ and every iteration step can obviously be performed in polynomial time, this completes the proof. □

The function lpr can now be used to solve the computation problem as follows:

$$\sup_{r \text{ run of } A} \min\{|w| \mid r(w) \in F_a\} = \max\{lpr(q) \mid q \in Q_0\}.$$

If this maximum is ∞, then the measure d_1 yields value 0 and the approximate equation was actually solvable as a strict one.

Theorem 2. *For the distance d_1 and a polytime computable combining function, the computation problem (for approximate $\mathcal{FL}_0$ unification and for approximately solving language equations) can be solved in exponential time, and the decision problem is ExpTime-complete.*

Proof. The ExpTime-upper bounds follow from our reductions and the fact that the automaton A can be computed in exponential time and is thus of at most exponential size. Hardness can be shown by a reduction of the strict problems, which are known to be ExpTime-complete [5,6]. In fact, the proof of Lemma 9 shows that d_1 either yields the value $0 = 2^{-\infty}$ (in which case the strict equation is solvable) or a value larger than $2^{-(|Q|+1)}$ (in which case the strict equation is not solvable). □

The Measure d_2

Recall that the value of d_2 is obtained by applying the function μ to the symmetric difference of the input languages. In case one of the two languages is empty, its value is thus obtained by applying μ to the other language. It is easy to show that $\mu(L)$ for $L \subseteq \Sigma^*$ satisfies the following recursive equation:

$$\mu(L) = \frac{1}{2}\chi_L(\varepsilon) + \frac{1}{2|\Sigma|} \sum_{a \in \Sigma} \mu(a^{-1}L), \qquad (10)$$

where $a^{-1}L := \{w \in \Sigma^* \mid aw \in L\}$ and χ_L is the characteristic function of the language L.

Using Lemma 8, Theorem 1, and the definition of d_2, it is easy to see that the computation problem for an approximate language equation $\phi \approx \psi$ w.r.t. d_2 can be reduced to solving the following problem for the trim ILTA $A = (\Sigma, Q, Q_0, \delta)$ of Theorem 1: compute $\inf_{r \, run \, of \, A} \mu(L_r(A, F_a))$.

Using (10), we now show that this infimum can be computed by solving a system of recursive equations that is induced by the transitions of A. Given an arbitrary (not necessarily initial) state $q \in Q$, we say that $r \colon \Sigma^* \to Q$ is a q-run of A if $r(\varepsilon) = q$ and $r(wa) \in \delta(r(w), a)$ for all $w \in \Sigma^*$ and $a \in \Sigma$. We denote the set of all q-runs of A with $R_A(q)$. Since each run of A is a q_0-run for some $q_0 \in Q_0$, we have

$$\inf_{r \, run \, of \, A} \mu(L_r(A, F_a)) = \min_{q_0 \in Q_0} \inf_{r \in R_A(q_0)} \mu(L_r(A, F_a)).$$

For all $q \in Q$, we define $\mu(q) := \inf_{r \in R_A(q)} \mu(L_r(A, F_a))$. The identity above shows that we can solve the computation problem for approximate language equations w.r.t. d_2 if we can devise a procedure for computing the values $\mu(q) \in \mathbb{R}$ for all $q \in Q$. The identity (10) can now be used to show the following lemma.

Lemma 10. *For all states $q \in Q$ we have*

$$\mu(q) = \frac{1}{2}\chi_{F_a}(q) + \frac{1}{2|\Sigma|} \sum_{a \in \Sigma} \min_{p \in \delta(q,a)} \mu(p),$$

where χ_{F_a} denotes the characteristic function of the set F_a.

By introducing variables x_q (for $q \in Q$) that range over $\mathbb{R}$, we can rephrase this lemma by saying that the values $\mu(q)$ yield a solution to the system of equations

$$x_q = \frac{1}{2}\chi_{F_a}(q) + \frac{1}{2|\Sigma|} \sum_{a \in \Sigma} \min_{p \in \delta(q,a)} x_p \quad (q \in Q). \tag{11}$$

Using Banach's fixed point theorem [8,12], one can show that the system (11) has a *unique* solution in $\mathbb{R}$. Thus, to compute the values $\mu(q)$ for $q \in Q$ it is sufficient to compute a solution of (11). This can be realized using Linear Programming [16]. The only non-trivial step in the translation of (11) into an LP problem is to express the minimum operator. For this, we introduce additional variables $y_{q,a}$, which intuitively stand for $\min_{p \in \delta(q,a)} x_p$. Then (11) is transformed into

$$x_q = \frac{1}{2}\chi_{F_a}(q) + \frac{1}{2|\Sigma|} \sum_{a \in \Sigma} y_{q,a} \quad (q \in Q). \tag{12}$$

To express the intuitive meaning of the variables $y_{q,a}$, we add the inequalities

$$y_{q,a} \leq x_p \quad \text{for all} \quad q \in Q \quad \text{and} \quad p \in \delta(q,a) \tag{13}$$

as well as the objective to maximize the values of these variables:

$$z = \max \sum_{q \in Q} \sum_{a \in \Sigma} y_{q,a}. \tag{14}$$

Lemma 11. *The LP problem consisting of the Eq. (12), the inequations (13), and the objective (14) has the unique solution*

$$\{x_q \mapsto \mu(q) \mid q \in Q\} \cup \{y_{q,a} \mapsto \min_{p \in \delta(q,a)} \mu(p) \mid p \in Q, a \in \Sigma\}.$$

Since LP problems can be solved in polynomial time and the size of the LP problem in the above lemma is polynomial in the size of A, we obtain an ExpTime-upper bound for the computation problem and the decision problem. ExpTime-hardness can again be shown by a reduction of the strict problem (see [2]).

Theorem 3. *For the distance d_2 and a polytime computable combining function, the computation problem (for approximate $\mathcal{FL}_0$ unification and for approximately solving language equations) can be solved in exponential time, and the decision problem is ExpTime-complete.*

For this theorem to hold, the exact definition of the distance d_2 is actually not important. Our approach works as long as the distance induces a system of equations similar to (11) such that Banach's fixed point theorem ensures the existence of a unique solution, which can be found using linear programming (see [2] for an example).

5   Conclusion

We have extended unification in DLs to approximate unification in order to enhance the recall of this method of finding redundancies in DL-based ontologies. For the DL $\mathcal{FL}_0$, unification can be reduced to solving certain language equations [5]. We have shown that, w.r.t. two particular distance measures, this reduction can be extended to the approximate case. Interesting topics for future research are considering approximate unification for other DLs such as $\mathcal{EL}$ [4]; different distance measures for $\mathcal{FL}_0$ and other DLs, possibly based on similarity measures between concepts [14,17]; and approximately solving other kinds of language equations [13]. Approximate unification has been considered in the context of similarity-based Logic Programming [10], based on a formal definition of proximity between terms. The definition of proximity used in [10] is quite different from our distances, but the major difference to our work is that [10] extends syntactic unification to the approximate case, whereas unification in $\mathcal{FL}_0$ corresponds to unification w.r.t. the equational theory $ACUIh$ (see [5]). Another topic for future research is to consider unification w.r.t. other equational theories. First, rather simple, results for the theory $ACUI$, which extend the results for strict $ACUI$-unification [11], can be found in [3].

References

1. Baader, F., Calvanese, D., McGuinness, D., Nardi, D., Patel-Schneider, P.F. (eds.): The Description Logic Handbook: Theory, Implementation, and Applications. Cambridge University Press (2003)
2. Baader, F., Marantidis, P., Okhotin, A.: Approximate unification in the description logic $\mathcal{FL}_0$. LTCS-Report 16-04, Chair for Automata Theory, Institute for Theoretical Computer Science, Technische Universität Dresden, Dresden (2016). http://lat.inf.tu-dresden.de/research/reports.html
3. Baader, F., Marantidis, P., Okhotin, A.: Approximately solving set equations. In: Ghilardi, S., Schmidt-Schauß, M. (eds.) Proceedings of the 30th International Workshop on Unification (UNIF 2016), Porto (2016)
4. Baader, F., Morawska, B.: Unification in the description logic $\mathcal{EL}$. Log. Methods Comput. Sci. **6**(3), 350–364 (2010)
5. Baader, F., Narendran, P.: Unification of concept terms in description logics. J. Symb. Comput. **31**(3), 277–305 (2001)
6. Baader, F., Okhotin, A.: On language equations with one-sided concatenation. Fundamenta Informaticae **126**(1), 1–35 (2013)
7. Baader, F., Tobies, S.: The inverse method implements the automata approach for modal satisfiability. In: Goré, R., Leitsch, A., Nipkow, T. (eds.) IJCAR 2001. LNCS, vol. 2083, pp. 92–106. Springer, Heidelberg (2001). doi:10.1007/3-540-45744-5_8
8. Banach, S.: Sur les opérations dans les ensembles abstraits et leur application aux équations intégrales. Fundamenta Mathematicae **3**(1), 133–181 (1922)
9. Ecke, A., Peñaloza, R., Turhan, A.-Y.: Computing role-depth bounded generalizations in the description logic $\mathcal{ELOR}$. In: Timm, I.J., Thimm, M. (eds.) KI 2013. LNCS (LNAI), vol. 8077, pp. 49–60. Springer, Heidelberg (2013). doi:10.1007/978-3-642-40942-4_5
10. Iranzo, P.J., Rubio-Manzano, C.: Proximity-based unification theory. Fuzzy Sets Syst. **262**, 21–43 (2015)
11. Kapur, D., Narendran, P.: Complexity of unification problems with associative-commutative operators. J. Autom. Reason. **9**, 261–288 (1992)
12. Kreyszig, E.: Introductory Functional Analysis With Applications. Wiley, New York (1978). Wiley Classics Library
13. Kunc, M.: What do we know about language equations? In: Harju, T., Karhumäki, J., Lepistö, A. (eds.) DLT 2007. LNCS, vol. 4588, pp. 23–27. Springer, Heidelberg (2007). doi:10.1007/978-3-540-73208-2_3
14. Lehmann, K., Turhan, A.-Y.: A framework for semantic-based similarity measures for $\mathcal{ELH}$-concepts. In: Cerro, L.F., Herzig, A., Mengin, J. (eds.) JELIA 2012. LNCS (LNAI), vol. 7519, pp. 307–319. Springer, Heidelberg (2012). doi:10.1007/978-3-642-33353-8_24
15. Munkres, J.: Topology. Featured Titles for Topology Series. Prentice Hall, Upper Saddle River (2000)
16. Schrijver, A.: Theory of Linear and Integer Programming. Wiley-Interscience Series in Discrete Mathematics and Optimization. Wiley, New York (1999)
17. Tongphu, S., Suntisrivaraporn, B.: On desirable properties of the structural subsumption-based similarity measure. In: Supnithi, T., Yamaguchi, T., Pan, J.Z., Wuwongse, V., Buranarach, M. (eds.) JIST 2014. LNCS, vol. 8943, pp. 19–32. Springer, Heidelberg (2015). doi:10.1007/978-3-319-15615-6_2

Inconsistency-Tolerant Query Answering: Rationality Properties and Computational Complexity Analysis

Jean François Baget[1], Salem Benferhat[2], Zied Bouraoui[3(✉)],
Madalina Croitoru[4], Marie-Laure Mugnier[4], Odile Papini[5], Swan Rocher[4],
and Karim Tabia[2]

[1] Inria, Paris, France
`baget@lirmm.fr`
[2] Artois University, Arras, France
`{benferhat,tabia}@cril.fr`
[3] Cardiff University, Cardiff, UK
`BouraouiZ@cardiff.ac.uk`
[4] Montpellier University, Montpellier, France
`{croitoru,mugnier,rocher}@lirmm.fr`
[5] Aix-Marseille University, Marseille, France
`odile.papini@lsis.org`

Abstract. Generalising the state of the art, an inconsistency-tolerant semantics can be seen as a couple composed of a modifier operator and an inference strategy. In this paper we deepen the analysis of such general setting and focus on two aspects. First, we investigate the rationality properties of such semantics for existential rule knowledge bases. Second, we unfold the broad landscape of complexity results of inconsistency-tolerant semantics under a specific (yet expressive) subclass of existential rules.

1 Introduction

Within the Ontology-Based Data Access [17,18] setting, this paper addresses the problem of query answering when the assertional base (which stores data) is inconsistent with the ontology (which represents generic knowledge about a domain). Recently, a general framework for inconsistency-tolerant semantics was proposed in [2]. This framework considers two key notions: modifiers and inference strategies. Inconsistency-tolerant query answering is seen as made out of a *modifier*, which transforms the original ABox into a so-called MBox, which is a set of consistent ABoxes (w.r.t. the TBox), and an *inference strategy*, which evaluates queries against this MBox knowledge base. Interestingly enough, such setting unifies main existing work and captures various semantics in the literature (see e.g., [1,6,16]). The obtained semantics were compared with respect to the productivity of their inference.

© Springer International Publishing AG 2016
L. Michael and A. Kakas (Eds.): JELIA 2016, LNAI 10021, pp. 64–80, 2016.
DOI: 10.1007/978-3-319-48758-8_5

This paper goes one step further in the characterization of these inconsistency-tolerant semantics by carrying out an analysis in terms of rationality properties and data complexity. The rationality properties are considered for existential rule knowledge bases [3,9] (a prominent ontology language that generalizes lightweight description logics). On the one hand we study basic properties of semantics such as their behaviour with respect to the conjunction and consistency of inferred conclusions. On the other hand, starting from the obvious observation that inconsistency-tolerant semantics are inherently nonmonotonic, we investigate their behaviour with respect to properties introduced for non-monotonic inference [14] that we rephrase in our framework. Entailment with general existential rules being undecidable, complexity is studied for a specific (yet expressive) subclass of existential rules known as *Finite Unification Sets* (FUS) [3], which in particular generalizes the description logic DL-Lite$_\mathcal{R}$ dedicated to query answering [10] (see also the *OWL2-QL* profile).

Before presenting our contributions, we provide some preliminaries on the logical setting and briefly recall the unified framework for inconsistency-tolerant semantics.

2   Preliminaries

We consider first-order logical languages without function symbols, hence a *term* is a variable or a constant. An *atom* is of the form $p(t_1, \ldots, t_k)$ where p is a predicate name of arity k, and the t_i are terms. A (factual) *assertion* is an atom without variables (also named a *ground* atom). A *Boolean conjunctive query*[1] (and simply *query* in the following) is an existentially closed conjunction of atoms, that we will consider as a set of atoms, leaving quantifiers implicit. Given a set of assertions $\mathcal{A}$ and a query q, the answer to q over $\mathcal{A}$ is yes iff $\mathcal{A} \models q$, where $\models$ denotes the standard logical consequence. Given two sets of atoms S_1 and S_2 (with disjoint sets of variables), a *homomorphism* h from S_1 to S_2 is a substitution of the variables in S_1 by the terms in S_2 such that $h(S_1) \subseteq S_2$ (where $h(S_1)$ is obtained from S_1 by substituting each variable according to h). It is well-known that, given two existentially closed conjunctions of atoms f_1 and f_2 (for instance queries and conjunctions of factual assertions), $f_1 \models f_2$ iff there is a homomorphism from the set of atoms in f_2 to the set of atoms in f_1.

A knowledge base can be seen as a database enhanced with an ontological component. Since inconsistency-tolerant query answering has been mostly studied in the context of description logics (DLs), and especially DL-Lite, we will use some DL vocabulary, like ABox for the data and TBox for the ontology. However, our framework is not restricted to DLs, hence we define TBoxes and ABoxes in terms of first-order logic (and more precisely in the existential rule framework). We assume the reader familiar with the basics of DLs and their logical translation.

---

[1] For readability, we restrict our focus to *Boolean* conjunctive queries, however the framework and the obtained results can be directly extended to general conjunctive queries.

An *ABox* is a set of factual assertions. As a special case we have DL assertions restricted to unary and binary predicates. A *positive axiom* is of the form $\forall \mathbf{x} \forall \mathbf{y}(B[\mathbf{x}, \mathbf{y}] \rightarrow \exists \mathbf{z}\, H[\mathbf{y}, \mathbf{z}])$ where B and H are conjunctions of atoms; in other words, it is a *positive existential rule*. As a special case, we have for instance concept and role inclusions in DL-Lite$_\mathcal{R}$, which are respectively of the form $B_1 \sqsubseteq B_2$ and $S_1 \sqsubseteq S_2$, where $B_i := A \mid \exists S$ and $S_i := P \mid P^-$ (with A an atomic concept, P an atomic role and P^- the inverse of an atomic role). A *negative axiom* is of the form $\forall \mathbf{x}(B[\mathbf{x}] \rightarrow \bot)$ where B is a conjunction of atoms; in other words, it is a *negative constraint*. As a special case, we have for instance disjointness axioms in DL-Lite$_\mathcal{R}$, which are inclusions of the form $B_1 \sqsubseteq \neg B_2$ and $S_1 \sqsubseteq \neg S_2$, or equivalently $B_1 \sqcap B_2 \sqsubseteq \bot$ and $S_1 \sqcap S_2 \sqsubseteq \bot$.

A *TBox* $\mathcal{T} = \mathcal{T}_p \cup \mathcal{T}_n$ is partitioned into a set $\mathcal{T}_p$ of positive axioms and a set $\mathcal{T}_n$ of negative axioms. Finally, a *knowledge base* (KB) is of the form $\mathcal{K} = \langle \mathcal{T}, \mathcal{A} \rangle$ where $\mathcal{A}$ is an ABox and $\mathcal{T}$ is a TBox. Such a KB is logically interpreted as the conjunction of its elements. $\mathcal{K}$ is said to be *consistent* if $\mathcal{T} \cup \mathcal{A}$ is satisfiable, otherwise it is said to be *inconsistent*. We also say that $\mathcal{A}$ is consistent (or inconsistent) with $\mathcal{T}$, which reflects the assumption that the TBox is reliable while the ABox may not. The answer to a query q over a consistent KB $\mathcal{K}$ is yes iff $\langle \mathcal{T}, \mathcal{A} \rangle \models q$. When $\mathcal{K}$ is inconsistent, standard consequence is not appropriate since all queries would be positively answered.

The notion of a (virtual) repair is a key notion in inconsistency-tolerant query answering. A repair is a subset of the ABox consistent with the TBox and inclusion-maximal for this property: $\mathcal{R} \subseteq \mathcal{A}$ is a *repair* of $\mathcal{A}$ w.r.t. $\mathcal{T}$ if (i) $\langle \mathcal{T}, \mathcal{R} \rangle$ is consistent, and (ii) $\forall \mathcal{R}' \subseteq \mathcal{A}$, if $\mathcal{R} \subsetneq \mathcal{R}'$ ($\mathcal{R}$ is strictly included in $\mathcal{R}'$) then $\langle \mathcal{T}, \mathcal{R}' \rangle$ is inconsistent. We denote by $\mathcal{R}(\mathcal{A})$ the set of $\mathcal{A}$'s repairs (for easier reading, we often leave $\mathcal{T}$ implicit in our notations). Note that $\mathcal{R}(\mathcal{A}) = \{\mathcal{A}\}$ iff $\mathcal{A}$ is consistent. The most commonly considered semantics for inconsistency-tolerant query answering, inspired from previous works in databases, is the following: q is said to be a *consistent consequence* of $\mathcal{K}$ if it is a standard consequence of each repair of $\mathcal{A}$ [1]. Several variants of this semantics have been proposed, which differ in their behaviour (cautiousness w.r.t. inconsistencies) and their computational complexity, see in particular [1,6,16].

3   A Unified Framework for Inconsistency-Tolerant Query Answering

In this section we recall the framework introduced in [2] for the study of inconsistency-tolerant query answering semantics. In this framework, semantics are defined by two components: a modifier and an inference strategy, applied on MBox knowledge bases. An *MBox KB* is simply a KB with multiple ABoxes of the form $\mathcal{K}_\mathcal{M} = \langle \mathcal{T}, \mathcal{M} \rangle$ where $\mathcal{T} = \mathcal{T}_p \cup \mathcal{T}_n$ is a TBox and $\mathcal{M} = \{\mathcal{A}_1, \ldots, \mathcal{A}_m\}$ is a set of ABoxes, called an MBox. A standard KB will be seen as an MBox with $m = 1$. An MBox KB $\mathcal{K}_\mathcal{M}$ is said to be *consistent*, or $\mathcal{M}$ is said to be consistent (with $\mathcal{T}$), if each $\mathcal{A}_i$ in $\mathcal{M}$ is consistent (with $\mathcal{T}$). A modifier transforms a possibly inconsistent MBox KB into an MBox KB such that, when the latter is consistent, it can be provided as input to the inference strategy that determines if the query is entailed.

A *(composite) modifier* is a finite combination of elementary modifiers. In [2] the three following kinds of elementary modifiers are introduced:

- **Expansion** modifiers, which expand an MBox by explicitly adding some inferred assertions to its ABoxes. A natural expansion modifier is the *ground positive closure* of an MBox, which computes the closure of each ABox with respect to the positive axioms of the TBox, keeping only ground atoms:

$$\circ_{cl}(\mathcal{M}) = \{Cl(\mathcal{A}_i)|\mathcal{A}_i \in \mathcal{M}\}, \text{ where } Cl(\mathcal{A}_i) = \{\text{ground atom } a \,|\langle \mathcal{T}_p, \mathcal{A}_i \rangle \models a\}.$$

- **Splitting** modifiers, which replace each $\mathcal{A}_i$ of an MBox by one or several of its maximally consistent subsets (hence, they always produce consistent MBoxes). A natural splitting modifier splits each ABox into the set of its *repairs*:

$$\circ_{rep}(\mathcal{M}) = \bigcup_{\mathcal{A}_i \in \mathcal{M}} \{\mathcal{R}(\mathcal{A}_i)\}.$$

- **Selection** modifiers, which select some elements of an MBox. A natural selection modifier is the *cardinality-based selection* modifier, which selects the largest ABoxes of an MBox:

$$\circ_{card}(\mathcal{M}) = \{\mathcal{A}_i \in \mathcal{M}|\forall \mathcal{A}_j \in \mathcal{M}, |\mathcal{A}_j| \leq |\mathcal{A}_i|\}.$$

Note that the cardinality-based selection function fully makes sense when inconsistency is due to the presence of multiple sources. Other selection functions, such as the ones based on rational closure or System Z [11] may be used, especially when inconsistency reflects the presence of exceptions in axioms of the TBox.

Many composite modifiers can be potentially defined using the three above "natural" modifiers, however this number is considerably reduced if we focus on non-equivalent modifiers: indeed, any composite modifier that produces a consistent MBox from a standard ABox, and obtained by combining the elementary modifiers $\circ_{rep}$, $\circ_{card}$ and $\circ_{cl}$, is equivalent to one of the eight modifiers listed in Table 1. To ease reading, these modifiers are also denoted by abbreviations reflecting the order in which the elementary modifiers are applied, and using the following letters: R for $\circ_{rep}$, C for $\circ_{cl}$ and M for $\circ_{card}$. Different kinds of inclusion relations hold between modifiers (see [2] for details).

Example 1. Let $\mathcal{K}_{\mathcal{M}} = \langle \mathcal{T}, \mathcal{M} \rangle$ be an MBox KB where $\mathcal{T}=\{A(x) \land B(x) \rightarrow \bot,$ $A(x) \land C(x) \rightarrow \bot,$ $B(x) \land C(x) \rightarrow \bot,$ $A(x) \rightarrow D(x),$ $B(x) \rightarrow D(x),$ $C(x) \rightarrow D(x),$ $B(x) \rightarrow E(x),$ $C(x) \rightarrow E(x)\}$ and $\mathcal{M}=\{\{A(a), B(a), C(a), A(b)\}\}$. With R, we get $\circ_1(\mathcal{M})=\{\{A(a), A(b)\},\{B(a), A(b)\},\{C(a), A(b)\}\}$. With CR: $\circ_5(\mathcal{M})=\{\{A(a),$ $D(a), A(b), D(b)\},$ $\{B(a), D(a), E(a),$ $A(b),D(b)\},$ $\{C(a), D(a), E(a), A(b),$ $D(b)\}\}$. With MCR: $\circ_6(\mathcal{M}) = \{\{B(a), D(a), E(a), A(b), D(b)\}, \{C(a), D(a),$ $E(a), A(b), D(b)\}\}$.

An inference strategy takes as input a consistent MBox KB $\mathcal{K}_{\mathcal{M}}=\langle \mathcal{T}, \mathcal{M} \rangle$ and a query q and determines if q is entailed from $\mathcal{K}_{\mathcal{M}}$. Four main inference strategies

Table 1. The eight composite modifiers for an MBox $\mathcal{K}_{\mathcal{M}}=\langle \mathcal{T}, \mathcal{M} = \{\mathcal{A}\}\rangle$

Modifier	Combination	MBox
R	$\circ_1 = \circ_{rep}(.)$	$\mathcal{M}_1 = \circ_1(\mathcal{M})$
MR	$\circ_2 = \circ_{card}(\circ_{rep}(.))$	$\mathcal{M}_2 = \circ_2(\mathcal{M})$
CMR	$\circ_3 = \circ_{cl}(\circ_{card}(\circ_{rep}(.)))$	$\mathcal{M}_3 = \circ_3(\mathcal{M})$
MCMR	$\circ_4 = \circ_{card}(\circ_{cl}(\circ_{card}(\circ_{rep}(.))))$	$\mathcal{M}_4 = \circ_4(\mathcal{M})$
CR	$\circ_5 = \circ_{cl}(\circ_{rep}(.))$	$\mathcal{M}_5 = \circ_5(\mathcal{M})$
MCR	$\circ_6 = \circ_{card}(\circ_{cl}(\circ_{rep}(.)))$	$\mathcal{M}_6 = \circ_6(\mathcal{M})$
RC	$\circ_7 = \circ_{rep}(\circ_{cl}(.))$	$\mathcal{M}_7 = \circ_7(\mathcal{M})$
MRC	$\circ_8 = \circ_{card}(\circ_{rep}(\circ_{cl}(.)))$	$\mathcal{M}_8 = \circ_8(\mathcal{M})$

are considered, namely universal (also known as skeptical), safe, majority-based and existential (also called brave). They are formally defined as follows:

- *universal* consequence: $\mathcal{K}_{\mathcal{M}} \models_\forall q$ if $\forall \mathcal{A}_i \in \mathcal{M}, \langle \mathcal{T}, \mathcal{A}_i \rangle \models q$.
- *safe* consequence: $\mathcal{K}_{\mathcal{M}} \models_\cap q$ if $\langle \mathcal{T}, \bigcap_{\mathcal{A}_i \in \mathcal{M}} \mathcal{A}_i \rangle \models q$.
- *majority-based* consequence: $\mathcal{K}_{\mathcal{M}} \models_{maj} q$ if $\frac{|\mathcal{A}_i : \mathcal{A}_i \in \mathcal{M}, \langle \mathcal{T}, \mathcal{A}_i \rangle \models q|}{|\mathcal{M}|} > 1/2$.
- *existential* consequence: $\mathcal{K}_{\mathcal{M}} \models_\exists q$ if $\exists \mathcal{A}_i \in \mathcal{M}, \langle \mathcal{T}, \mathcal{A}_i \rangle \models q$.

Given two inference strategies s_i and s_j, s_i is said to be *more cautious* than s_j, denoted $s_i \leq s_j$, if for any consistent MBox $\mathcal{K}_{\mathcal{M}}$ and any query q, if $\mathcal{K}_{\mathcal{M}} \models_{s_i} q$ then $\mathcal{K}_{\mathcal{M}} \models_{s_j} q$. The considered inference strategies are totally ordered by $\leq$ as follows: $\cap \leq \forall \leq maj \leq \exists$.

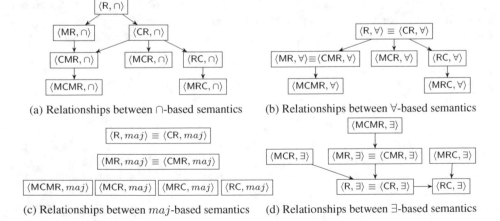

(a) Relationships between $\cap$-based semantics   (b) Relationships between $\forall$-based semantics

(c) Relationships between maj-based semantics   (d) Relationships between $\exists$-based semantics

Fig. 1. Productivity of inconsistency-tolerant semantics where $X \longrightarrow Y$ means that Y is strictly more productive than X.

An inconsistency-tolerant query answering semantics is then defined by a composite modifier and an inference strategy.

Definition 1. *Let* $\mathcal{K}=\langle\mathcal{T},\mathcal{A}\rangle$ *be a standard KB,* $\circ_i$ *be a composite modifier and* s_j *be an inference strategy. A query* q *is said to be an* $\langle\circ_i,s_j\rangle$-*consequence of* $\mathcal{K}$, *denoted by* $\mathcal{K}\models_{\langle\circ_i,s_j\rangle} q$, *if it is entailed from the MBox KB* $\langle\mathcal{T},\circ_i(\{\mathcal{A}\})\rangle$ *by the strategy* s_j.

Note that the main semantics from the literature [1,6,16] are covered by this definition: AR, IAR and ICR semantics respectively correspond to $\langle\mathsf{R},\forall\rangle$, $\langle\mathsf{R},\cap\rangle$, and $\langle\mathsf{CR},\cap\rangle$.[2]

Example 2. Consider the input KB $\mathcal{K}_{\mathcal{M}}=\langle\mathcal{T},\mathcal{M}\rangle$ from Example 1. $\circ_1(\mathcal{M}) = \mathcal{M}_1 = \{\{A(a),A(b)\},\{B(a),A(b)\},\{C(a),A(b)\}\}$. Since $A(b) \in \bigcap_{\mathcal{A}_i\in\mathcal{M}_1}$ and $A(x){\rightarrow}D(x)$, $\mathcal{K}\models_{\langle\circ_1,\cap\rangle} D(b)$ holds. Hence, we also have $\mathcal{K}\models_{\langle\circ_1,\forall\rangle} D(b)$. Furthermore $\mathcal{K}\models_{\langle\circ_1,\forall\rangle} D(a)$. By $\langle\circ_1,maj\rangle$, $E(a)$ is furthermore entailed. Indeed, $\langle\mathcal{T},\{B(a),A(b)\}\rangle \models E(a)$ and $\langle\mathcal{T},\{C(a),A(b)\}\rangle \models E(a)$ and $|\mathcal{M}_1|{=}3$. By $\langle\circ_1,\exists\rangle$, $A(a)$ is also entailed. Let $q = \exists xD(x){\wedge}E(x)$. Then q is a consequence of $\langle\circ_1,maj\rangle$ and $\langle\circ_1,\exists\rangle$.

The obtained semantics have been compared from a productivity point of view. Formally, a semantics $\langle\circ_i,s_k\rangle$ is *less productive* than a semantics $\langle\circ_j,s_l\rangle$ if, for any KB $\mathcal{K}=\langle\mathcal{T},\mathcal{A}\rangle$ and any query q, if $\mathcal{K}\models_{\langle\circ_i,s_k\rangle} q$ then $\mathcal{K}\models_{\langle\circ_j,s_l\rangle} q$. This productivity relation is a preorder, which can be established by considering on the one hand the inclusion relations between composite modifiers and on the other hand the cautiousness total order on inference, as detailed below. Figure 1 depicts the results about semantics defined with the same inference strategy (note that transitivity edges are not drawn and no other edges hold). Then Theorem 1 extends these results to semantics possibly based on different inference strategies. In particular, if $s_k < s_l$ then, for all modifiers $\circ_i$ and $\circ_j$, $\langle\circ_i,s_k\rangle$ is strictly less productive than $\langle\circ_i,s_l\rangle$, and $\langle\circ_j,s_l\rangle$ is at least as productive as $\langle\circ_i,s_k\rangle$.

Theorem 1 (Productivity of semantics [2]). *The inclusion relation* $\sqsubseteq$ *is the smallest relation that contains the inclusions* $\langle\circ_i,s_k\rangle \sqsubseteq \langle\circ_j,s_k\rangle$ *defined by the inclusions in Fig. 1a to d and satisfying the two following conditions: (1) for all* s_j, s_p *and* $\circ_i$, *if* $s_j \leq s_p$ *then* $\langle\circ_i,s_j\rangle \sqsubseteq \langle\circ_i,s_p\rangle$; *(2) it is transitive.*

It follows from Theorem 1 that 26 different semantics are obtained (out of the possible 32 inference relations used in Fig. 1). We point out that this result holds even when KBs are restricted to DL-Lite$_\mathcal{R}$ TBoxes. Finally, note that when the initial KB is consistent, all semantics correspond to standard entailment, i.e., given a consistent standard KB $\mathcal{K}$ and a query q, $\mathcal{K}\models_{\langle\circ_i,s\rangle} q$ iff $\mathcal{K}\models q$, for all $1 \leq i \leq 8$ and $s \in \{\cap,\forall,\exists,maj\}$.

---

[2] Note however that CAR and ICAR [16] are close to $\langle\mathsf{RC},\forall\rangle$ and $\langle\mathsf{RC},\cap\rangle$ resp., but not equivalent. They could be covered by considering other elementary modifiers.

4   Rationality Properties of Inconsistency-Tolerant Semantics

This section is dedicated to the logical properties of inconsistency-tolerant semantics. We first analyze the behaviour of these semantics w.r.t the conjunction (or set union) and the consistency of inferred conclusions for a fixed KB. We then turn our attention to the fact that these semantics are inherently non-monotonic. Indeed, if some query q is entailed from a KB using a semantics $\langle \circ_i, s_j \rangle$, then q may be questionable in the light of new factual assertions. We will assume that these new factual assertions are sure (and will speak of conditional inference, opposed to unconditional inference when the KB is fixed). Hence, we also analyze inconsistency-tolerant semantics w.r.t rationality properties introduced for nonmonotonic inference that we recast in our framework.

4.1   Properties of Unconditional Inference

Let $\mathcal{K}_{\mathcal{M}} = \langle \mathcal{T}, \{\mathcal{A}\} \rangle$ be a possibly inconsistent KB and $\langle o_i, s \rangle$ denote any semantics with $\circ_i \in \{$R, MR, CMR, MCMR, CR, MCR, RC, MRC$\}$ and $s \in \{\forall, \cap, \exists, maj\}$. We define the following desirable properties:

QCE (Query Conjunction Elimination) For any KB $\mathcal{K}_{\mathcal{M}}$ and any queries q_1 and q_2, if $\mathcal{K}_{\mathcal{M}} \models_{\langle \circ_i, s \rangle} q_1 \wedge q_2$ then $\mathcal{K}_{\mathcal{M}} \models_{\langle \circ_i, s \rangle} q_1$ and $\mathcal{K}_{\mathcal{M}} \models_{\langle \circ_i, s \rangle} q_2$.

QCI (Query Conjunction Introduction) For any KB $\mathcal{K}_{\mathcal{M}}$ and any queries q_1 and q_2, if $\mathcal{K}_{\mathcal{M}} \models_{\langle \circ_i, s \rangle} q_1$ and $\mathcal{K}_{\mathcal{M}} \models_{\langle \circ_i, s \rangle} q_2$ then $\mathcal{K}_{\mathcal{M}} \models_{\langle \circ_i, s \rangle} q_1 \wedge q_2$.

Cons (Consistency) For any set of assertions $\mathcal{A}'$, if $\mathcal{K}_{\mathcal{M}} \models_{\langle \circ_i, s \rangle} \mathcal{A}'$ then $\langle \mathcal{T}, \mathcal{A}' \rangle$ is consistent.

ConsC (Consistency of Conjunction) For any set of assertions $\mathcal{A}$, if for all $f \in \mathcal{A}$, $\mathcal{K}_{\mathcal{M}} \models_{\langle \circ_i, s \rangle} f$ then $\langle \mathcal{T}, \mathcal{A} \rangle$ is consistent.

ConsS (Consistency of Support) For any set of assertions $\mathcal{A}'$, if $\mathcal{K}_{\mathcal{M}} \models_{\langle \circ_i, s \rangle} \mathcal{A}'$ then there is $R \in \mathcal{R}(\mathcal{A})$, such that $\langle \mathcal{T}, R \rangle \models \mathcal{A}'$.

Note that in the three last properties, the sets of assertions could be extended to queries with a more complex formulation. We first remind that, when $\mathcal{K}_{\mathcal{M}}$ is consistent, all semantics correspond to standard entailment, hence $\mathcal{K}_{\mathcal{M}} \models_{\langle \circ_i, s \rangle} q_1 \wedge q_2$ iff $\mathcal{K}_{\mathcal{M}} \models_{\langle \circ_i, s \rangle} q_1$ and $\mathcal{K}_{\mathcal{M}} \models_{\langle \circ_i, s \rangle} q_2$. When $\mathcal{K}_{\mathcal{M}}$ is inconsistent, one direction is still true for all semantics, namely Property **QCE**, which relies on the consistency of a repair. The converse direction, namely Property **QCI**, is obviously satisfied by universal and safe semantics but not by brave and majority-based semantics, even when q_1 and q_2 are ground atoms and the TBox contains only disjointness inclusions as shown by the next examples.

*Example 3 (Majority-based semantics does not satisfy **QCI**).*[3] Let $\mathcal{T} = \{B \sqcap C \sqsubseteq \bot, A \sqcap D \sqsubseteq \bot, C \sqcap D \sqsubseteq \bot\}$ and $\mathcal{A} = \{A(a), B(a), C(a), D(a)\}$. The repairs are $\{A(a), B(a)\}$, $\{A(a), C(a)\}$ and $\{B(a), D(a)\}$. All modifiers give the same MBox since $\mathcal{T}_p = \emptyset$ and the repairs have the same size. $A(a)$ and $B(a)$ are each entailed by a majority of repairs but their conjunction is not.

---

[3] Most examples in this section are provided in DL-Lite$_{\mathcal{R}}$ in order to show that some rationality properties do not hold even in this simple fragment of existential rules.

Example 4 (Brave semantics does not satisfy properties **QCI** *and* **ConsC**). Let $\mathcal{T}=\{A\sqcap B\sqsubseteq\bot\}$ and $\mathcal{A}=\{A(a),B(a)\}$. The repairs are $\{A(a)\}$ and $\{B(a)\}$. All modifiers lead to the same MBox since $\mathcal{T}_p=\emptyset$ and the repairs have the same size. $A(a)$ and $B(a)$ are both brave consequences but their conjunction is not. Besides **ConsC** is not satisfied since $\langle\mathcal{T},\{A(a),B(a)\}\rangle$ is inconsistent.

Property **Cons** is true for any semantics (again by the consistency of a repair). Property **ConsC** holds for universal and safe semantics, and is false for any brave semantics, even for $|A_j|=|A_k|=1$ and DL-Lite TBoxes restricted to disjointness inclusions (see Example 3). Majority-based semantics are an interesting case, since the expressivity of the ontological language plays a role: Property **ConsC** is satisfied by all majority-based semantics when the language is restricted to DL-Lite$_\mathcal{R}$ and not satisfied as soon as we allow concept inclusions of the form $A\sqcap B\sqsubseteq C$ or ternary disjointness axioms of the form $A\sqcap B\sqcap C\sqsubseteq\bot$, even with ground queries (see Example 6). The fundamental reason why majority-based semantics satisfy Property **ConsC** over DL-Lite$_\mathcal{R}$ KBs is that, in these KBs, conflicts (i.e., minimal inconsistent subsets of the ABox) are necessarily of size two. When two ground atoms a_1 and a_2 are inferred with a majority-based strategy, at least one of element of the considered (consistent) MBox classically entails both a_1 and a_2, hence $a_1\wedge a_2$ is consistent; when conflicts are of size two, pairwise consistency entails global consistency. Note that this property still holds if we extend DL-Lite$_\mathcal{R}$ to n-ary predicates.

Example 5 (Majority-based semantics does not satisfy Property **ConsC** *for slight generalizations of DL-Lite$_\mathcal{R}$).* Let $\mathcal{T}=\{A\sqcap B\sqcap C\sqsubseteq\bot\}$ and $\mathcal{A}=\{A(a),B(a),C(a)\}$. The repairs are $\{A(a),B(a)\}$, $\{A(a),C(a)\}$ and $\{B(a),C(a)\}$. All modifiers give the same MBox since $\mathcal{T}_p=\emptyset$ and all the repairs have the same size. Each atom from $\mathcal{A}$ is entailed (by 2/3 repairs), however $\mathcal{A}$ itself is not.

Finally, Property **ConsS**, which expresses that every conclusion has a consistent support in the ABox, is satisfied by all semantics except those involving modifiers RC and MRC (as illustrated by the next example).

Example 6 ((M)RC-based semantics do not satisfy Property **ConsS**).[4] Let $\mathcal{T}=\{A\sqcap B\sqsubseteq\bot, A\sqsubseteq C_1, B\sqsubseteq C_2\}$ and $\mathcal{A}=\{A(a),B(a)\}$. The (maximal) repairs of the ABox' closure are $\{A(a),C_1(a),C_2(a)\}$ and $\{B(a),C_1(a),C_2(a)\}$. The set of atoms $A_j=\{C_1(a),C_2(a)\}$ is entailed by all semantics based on RC and MRC, however no consistent subset of $\mathcal{A}$ allows to entail A_j using $\mathcal{T}$.

Proposition 1 (Properties of unconditional inference). *The behaviour of semantics* $\langle\circ_i,s\rangle$, *with* $\circ_i\in\{$R, MR,CMR,MCMR, CR, MCR, RC, MRC$\}$ *and* $s\in\{\sqcap,\forall,maj,\exists\}$, *with respect to Properties* **QCE**, **QCI**, **Cons**, **ConsC** *and* **ConsS**, *is stated in Table 2.*

---

[4] This example also shows that CAR and ICAR [16] do not satisfy **ConsS** (although they do when the conclusion is a single atom).

Table 2. Properties of unconditional inferences.

Properties	$\langle \circ_i, \cap \rangle$	$\langle \circ_i, \forall \rangle$	$\langle \circ_i, Maj \rangle$	$\langle \circ_i, \exists \rangle$
QCE	√	√	√	√
QCI	√	√	×	×
Cons	√	√	√	√
ConsC	√	√	× [*]	×
ConsS $\circ_i \in \{\mathsf{RC}, \mathsf{MRC}\}$	×	×	×	×
otherwise	√	√	√	√

[*]: Except for languages where conflict sets involve at most two elements, like DL-Lite$_R$.

4.2   Properties of Conditional Inferences

We now analyze more finely the inconsistency-tolerant semantics by considering their properties in terms of nonmonotonic inference. Within propositional logic setting, several approaches have been proposed for nonmonotonic inference (e.g. [5,12,14]). In such approaches nonmonotonicity is essentially caused by the fact that initial knowledge used for inference process is incomplete, and thus, later information may come to enrich them, which generally leads to revise some of the a priori considered hypotheses.

Let $\mathcal{K_M} = \langle \mathcal{T}, \{\mathcal{A}\} \rangle$ be a possibly inconsistent KB and $\mathcal{A}_\alpha$, $\mathcal{A}_\beta$ be two sets of assertions such that $\langle \mathcal{T}, \mathcal{A}_\alpha \rangle$ and $\langle \mathcal{T}, \mathcal{A}_\beta \rangle$ are consistent. Assume that $\mathcal{A}_\alpha$ is the newly added knowledge. Since $\mathcal{A}_\alpha$ is considered as more reliable than the assertions in the KB, we have to keep $\mathcal{A}_\alpha$ in every selected repair of the KB. For the sake of simplicity, we define the notion of the set of repairs of $\mathcal{K_M}$ in presence of a new consistent set of assertions $\mathcal{A}_\alpha$ with respect to a modifier $\circ_i$: $\mathcal{M}_i^\alpha = \{R : R \in \circ_i(\{\mathcal{A} \cup \mathcal{A}_\alpha\}) \text{ and } \mathcal{A}_\alpha \subseteq R\}$. Now, we say that $\mathcal{A}_\beta$ is a *nonmonotonic consequence* of $\mathcal{A}_\alpha$ w.r.t. $\mathcal{K_M}$, denoted by $\mathcal{A}_\alpha \mid\!\sim_{\circ_i, s} \mathcal{A}_\beta$, if $\langle \mathcal{T}, \mathcal{M}_i^\alpha \rangle \models_s \mathcal{A}_\beta$.

In this study, we focus on the situation where the considered conclusions are sets of assertions, which can also be seen as conjunctions of ground queries. We first rephrase within our framework some KLM rationality properties [14]. Let $\mathcal{A}_\alpha$, $\mathcal{A}_\beta$ and $\mathcal{A}_\gamma$ be consistent sets of assertions w.r.t $\mathcal{T}$ and $\mid\!\sim$ be an inference relation, the *KLM* logical properties that we consider are the following[5].

R (Reflexivity) $\mathcal{A}_\alpha \mid\!\sim \mathcal{A}_\alpha$.
LLE (Left Logical Equivalence) If $\langle \mathcal{T}, \mathcal{A}_\alpha \rangle \equiv \langle \mathcal{T}, \mathcal{A}_\beta \rangle$ and $\mathcal{A}_\alpha \mid\!\sim \mathcal{A}_\gamma$ then $\mathcal{A}_\beta \mid\!\sim \mathcal{A}_\gamma$.
RW (Right Weakening)   If $\langle \mathcal{T}, \mathcal{A}_\alpha \rangle \models \langle \mathcal{T}, \mathcal{A}_\beta \rangle$ and $\mathcal{A}_\gamma \mid\!\sim \mathcal{A}_\alpha$ then $\mathcal{A}_\gamma \mid\!\sim \mathcal{A}_\beta$.
Cut   If $\mathcal{A}_\alpha \mid\!\sim \mathcal{A}_\beta$ and $\mathcal{A}_\alpha \cup \mathcal{A}_\beta \mid\!\sim \mathcal{A}_\gamma$ then $\mathcal{A}_\alpha \mid\!\sim \mathcal{A}_\gamma$.

---

[5] We have adopted here a formulation close to the one of *KLM* logical properties, even at the cost of simplicity. For instance $\langle \mathcal{T}, \mathcal{A}_\alpha \rangle \models \langle \mathcal{T}, \mathcal{A}_\beta \rangle$ could have been simplified in $\langle \mathcal{T}, \mathcal{A}_\alpha \rangle \models \mathcal{A}_\beta$. We remind that $\models$ and $\equiv$ denote standard logical entailment and equivalence.

CM (Cautious Monotony) If $\mathcal{A}_\alpha\!\mid\!\sim\!\mathcal{A}_\beta$ and $\mathcal{A}_\alpha\!\mid\!\sim\!\mathcal{A}_\gamma$ then $\mathcal{A}_\alpha \cup \mathcal{A}_\beta\!\mid\!\sim\!\mathcal{A}_\gamma$.
And If $\mathcal{A}_\alpha\!\mid\!\sim\!\mathcal{A}_\beta$ and $\mathcal{A}_\alpha\!\mid\!\sim\!\mathcal{A}_\gamma$ then $\mathcal{A}_\alpha\!\mid\!\sim\!\mathcal{A}_\beta \cup \mathcal{A}_\gamma$.

R means that the additional assertions have to be a consequence of the inference relation. **LLE** expresses the fact that two equivalent sets of assertions have the same consequences. **RW** says that consequences of the plausible assertions are plausible assertions too. **Cut** expresses the fact that if a plausible consequence is as secure as the assumptions it is based on, then it may be added into the assumptions. **CM** expresses that learning new assertions that could be plausibly inferred should not invalidate previous consequences. **And** expresses that the conjunction of two plausible consequences is a plausible consequence. The first five properties correspond to the system C [14] while the **And** property is derived from the previous ones. Clearly the **And** property is closely related to the **QCI** property given in Sect. 4.2. Indeed when $\mathcal{A}_\alpha = \emptyset$ (empty set, no additional information) and if q_1 and q_2 used in **CQI** are sets of assertions then **And** is equivalent to **CQI**. We now give the properties of the inference relations.

Proposition 2 (Properties of conditional inference). *The behaviour of inference relations* $\mid\!\sim_{o_i,s}$, *with* $o_i \in \{$R, MR,CMR,MCMR, CR, MCR, RC, MRC$\}$ *and* $s \in \{\cap, \forall, maj, \exists\}$, *with respect to Properties* **R**, **LLE**, **RW**, **Cut**, **CM**, **And**, *is given in Table 3.*

Proof: [Sketch of proof]. Properties **R**, **LLE** and **RW** follow from the definition of $\mathcal{M}_i^\alpha$. For $s \in \{\forall, \cap, \exists\}$ and for $o_i \in \{$R, MR$\}$ the satisfaction of Properties **Cut** and **CM** stems from the fact that $\forall R' \in \mathcal{M}_i^{\alpha\cup\beta}$ we have $R' = R \cup \mathcal{A}_\beta$ with $R \in \mathcal{M}_i^\alpha$. Moreover, for $o_i \in \{$CMR, CR, RC, MRC$\}$ the satisfaction of Properties **Cut** and **CM** holds due the fact that $\forall R' \in \mathcal{M}_i^{\alpha\cup\beta}$ we have $R' = R \cup Cl(\mathcal{A}_\beta)$ with $R \in \mathcal{M}_i^\alpha$. The following counter-examples show the non-satisfaction cases. □

Example 7 $(\mid\!\sim_{o_i,s}$ *with* $o_i \in \{$MCMR, MCR$\}$ *and* $s \in \{\forall, \exists, \cap\}$ *does not satisfy* **Cut**). For MCMR: Let $\mathcal{T} = \{A \sqsubseteq \neg B,\ A \sqsubseteq \neg G,\ F \sqsubseteq \neg B,\ B \sqsubseteq C,\ C \sqsubseteq D,\ A \sqsubseteq E\}$, and $\mathcal{A} = \{A(a), B(a),\ F(a),\ G(a)\}$, $\mathcal{A}_\alpha = \emptyset$,

Table 3. Properties of conditional inferences.

Properties	$\mid\!\sim_{o_i,\forall}$	$\mid\!\sim_{o_i,\cap}$	$\mid\!\sim_{o_i,\exists}$	$\mid\!\sim_{o_i,maj}$
R	✓	✓	✓	✓
LLE	✓	✓	✓	✓
RW	✓	✓	✓	✓
Cut $o_i \in \{$MCMR, MCR$\}$	×	×	×	×
otherwise	✓	✓	✓	×
CM $o_i \in \{$MCMR, MCR$\}$	×	×	×	×
otherwise	✓	✓	×	×
And	✓	✓	×	×

$\mathcal{A}_\beta=\{C(a),D(a)\}$, $\mathcal{A}_\gamma=\{A(a)\}$. We have $\mathcal{M}_4^\alpha=\{\{B(a),G(a),\ C(a),D(a)\}\}$ and $\mathcal{M}_4^{\alpha\cup\beta}=\{\{A(a),F(a),C(a),D(a),E(a)\}\}$. Thus $\langle\mathcal{T},\mathcal{M}_4^\alpha\rangle \models_\forall \mathcal{A}_\beta$ and $\langle\mathcal{T},\mathcal{M}_4^{\alpha\cup\beta}\rangle \models_\forall \mathcal{A}_\gamma$ but $\langle\mathcal{T},\mathcal{M}_4^\alpha\rangle \not\models_\forall \mathcal{A}_\gamma$. **Cut** is not satisfied even for $s \in \{\exists,\cap\}$. MCR: Let $\mathcal{T}=\{A \sqsubseteq \neg B,\ F \sqsubseteq \neg B,\ B \sqsubseteq C,\ C \sqsubseteq D\}$, $\mathcal{A} = \{A(a),B(a),F(a)\}$, $\mathcal{A}_\alpha=\emptyset$, $\mathcal{A}_\beta=\{C(a),D(a)\}$, $\mathcal{A}_\gamma = \{A(a)\}$. We have $\mathcal{M}_6^\alpha=\{\{B(a),C(a),D(a)\}\}$, $\mathcal{M}_6^{\alpha\cup\beta}=\{\{\ A(a),F(a),C(a),D(a)\}\}$. Thus $\langle\mathcal{T},\mathcal{M}_6^\alpha\rangle \models_\forall \mathcal{A}_\beta$ and $\langle\mathcal{T},\mathcal{M}_6^{\alpha\cup\beta}\rangle \models_\forall \mathcal{A}_\gamma$ but $\langle\mathcal{T},\mathcal{M}_6^\alpha\rangle \not\models_\forall \mathcal{A}_\gamma$. **Cut** is not satisfied either for $s \in \{\exists,\cap\}$.

Example 8 $(\mid\sim_{o_i,s}$ *with* $o_i \in \{\mathsf{MCMR},\mathsf{MCR}\}$ *and* $s \in \{\forall,\cap\}$ *does not satisfy* **CM**$)$.   Let $\mathcal{T}=\{A \sqsubseteq \neg B,\ B \sqsubseteq C\}$, and $\mathcal{A}=\{A(a),B(a)\}$, $\mathcal{A}_\alpha=\emptyset$, $\mathcal{A}_\beta=\{C(a)\}$, $\mathcal{A}_\gamma=\{B(a)\}$. We have $\mathcal{M}_4^\alpha=\mathcal{M}_6^\alpha=\{\{B(a),C(a)\}\}$, $\mathcal{M}_4^{\alpha\cup\beta}=\mathcal{M}_6^{\alpha\cup\beta}=\{\{A(a),C(a)\},\{B(a),C(a)\}\}$. Thus $\langle\mathcal{T},\mathcal{M}_4^\alpha\rangle \models_\forall \mathcal{A}_\beta$ and $\langle\mathcal{T},\mathcal{M}_4^\alpha\rangle \models_\forall \mathcal{A}_\gamma$ but $\langle\mathcal{T},\mathcal{M}_4^{\alpha\cup\beta}\rangle \not\models_\forall \mathcal{A}_\gamma$. Moreover, $\langle\mathcal{T},\mathcal{M}_6^\alpha\rangle \models_\forall \mathcal{A}_\beta$ and $\langle\mathcal{T},\mathcal{M}_6^\alpha\rangle \models_\forall \mathcal{A}_\gamma$ but $\langle\mathcal{T},\mathcal{M}_6^{\alpha\cup\beta}\rangle \not\models_\forall \mathcal{A}_\gamma$. **CM** is not satisfied even for $s=\cap$.

Example 9 $(\mid\sim_{o_i,maj}$ *with any* o_i *does not satisfy* **Cut**$)$.   For $i = 1$ (R), let $\mathcal{T}=\{A \sqsubseteq \neg B,\ A \sqsubseteq \neg C,\ A \sqsubseteq \neg D,\ B \sqsubseteq \neg D,\ C \sqsubseteq \neg D,\ A \sqsubseteq E,\ B \sqsubseteq E,\ C \sqsubseteq E,\ D \sqsubseteq \neg E,\ A \sqsubseteq G,\ B \sqsubseteq G\}$, and $\mathcal{A}=\{A(a),B(a),C(a),D(a)\}$, $\mathcal{A}_\alpha=\{F(a)\}$, $\mathcal{A}_\beta=\{E(a)\}$, $\mathcal{A}_\gamma=\{G(a)\}$. We have $\mathcal{M}_1^\alpha = \{\{A(a),F(a)\},\{B(a),F(a)\},\{C(a),F(a)\},\{D(a),F(a)\}\}$, thus $\langle\mathcal{T},\mathcal{M}_1^\alpha\rangle \models_{maj} \mathcal{A}_\beta$. Moreover, $\mathcal{M}_1^{\alpha\cup\beta}=\{\{A(a),F(a),E(a)\},\{B(a),F(a),E(a)\},\{C(a),F(a),E(a)\}\}$ and $\langle\mathcal{T},\mathcal{M}_1^{\alpha\cup\beta}\rangle \models_{maj} \mathcal{A}_\gamma$, however $\langle\mathcal{T},\mathcal{M}_1^\alpha\rangle \not\models_{maj} \mathcal{A}_\gamma$. **Cut** is not satisfied for any other o_i.

Example 10 $(\mid\sim_{o_i,\exists}$ *with any* o_i *does not satisfy* **CM**$)$.   For $i=1$ (R): Let $\mathcal{T} = \{A \sqsubseteq \neg C, A \sqsubseteq B, C \sqsubseteq B, A \sqsubseteq D, C \sqsubseteq E, D \sqsubseteq \neg C, E \sqsubseteq \neg A\}$, and $\mathcal{A} = \{A(a),C(a)\}$, $\mathcal{A}_\alpha = \{B(a)\}$, $\mathcal{A}_\beta = \{D(a)\}$, $\mathcal{A}_\gamma = \{E(a)\}$. We have $\mathcal{M}_1^\alpha = \{\{A(a),B(a)\},\{C(a),B(a)\}\}$, thus $\langle\mathcal{T},\mathcal{M}_1^\alpha\rangle \models_\exists \mathcal{A}_\beta$ and $\langle\mathcal{T},\mathcal{M}_1^\alpha\rangle \models_\exists \mathcal{A}_\gamma$. Moreover $\mathcal{M}_i^{\alpha\cup\beta}=\{\{A(a),B(a),D(a)\}\}$ and $\langle\mathcal{T},\mathcal{M}_1^{\alpha\cup\beta}\rangle \not\models_\exists \mathcal{A}_\gamma$. **CM** is not satisfied for any other o_i.

Example 11 $(\mid\sim_{o_i,maj}$ *with any* o_i *does not satisfy* **CM**$)$.   For $i=1$ (R): Let $\mathcal{T}=\{A \sqsubseteq \neg B,\ A \sqsubseteq \neg C,\ B \sqsubseteq \neg C,\ A \sqsubseteq D,\ B \sqsubseteq D, C \sqsubseteq D, A \sqsubseteq E, B \sqsubseteq E, C \sqsubseteq F, B \sqsubseteq F, A \sqsubseteq \neg F\}$, and $\mathcal{A} = \{A(a),B(a),C(a)\}$, $\mathcal{A}_\alpha = \{D(a)\}$, $\mathcal{A}_\beta = \{E(a)\}$, $\mathcal{A}_\gamma = \{F(a)\}$. We have $\mathcal{M}_1^\alpha = \{\{A(a),D(a)\},\{B(a),D(a)\},R_3 = \{C(a),D(a)\}\}$, thus $\langle\mathcal{T},\mathcal{M}_1^\alpha\rangle \models_{maj} \mathcal{A}_\beta$. Moreover $\langle\mathcal{T},\mathcal{M}_1^\alpha\rangle \models_{maj} \mathcal{A}_\gamma$. We have $\mathcal{M}_1^{\alpha\cup\beta}=\{\{A(a),D(a),E(a)\},\{B(a),D(a),E(a)\}\}$, thus $\langle\mathcal{T},\mathcal{M}_1^{\alpha\cup\beta}\rangle \not\models_{maj} \mathcal{A}_\gamma$. **CM** is not satisfied for any other o_i.

Example 12 $(\mid\sim_{o_i,s}$ *with any* o_i *and* $s \in \{\exists,maj\}$ *does not satisfy* **And**$)$.   For $i = 1$ and $s = \exists$ (R): Let $\mathcal{T}$ and $\mathcal{A}$ from Example 10. $\langle\mathcal{T},\mathcal{M}_1^\alpha\rangle \models_\exists \mathcal{A}_\beta$ and $\langle\mathcal{T},\mathcal{M}_1^\alpha\rangle \models_\exists \mathcal{A}_\gamma$ but $\langle\mathcal{T},\mathcal{M}_1^\alpha\rangle \not\models_\exists \mathcal{A}_\beta \cup \mathcal{A}_\gamma$. **And** is not satisfied for any other o_i. For $i = 1$ and $s = maj$ (R): Let $\mathcal{T}$ and $\mathcal{A}$ from Example 11. $\langle\mathcal{T},\mathcal{M}_i^\alpha\rangle \models_{maj} \mathcal{A}_\beta$ and $\langle\mathcal{T},\mathcal{M}_i^\alpha\rangle \models_{maj} \mathcal{A}_\gamma$. but $\langle\mathcal{T},\mathcal{M}_i^\alpha\rangle \not\models_{maj} \mathcal{A}_\beta \cup \mathcal{A}_\gamma$. **And** is not satisfied for any other o_i.

From Table 3, one can see that, for the composite modifiers $\circ_i \in$ {R,MR,CMR,CR,RC, MRC}, the semantics based on universal and safe consequence satisfy all the properties of the system C. In **LLE** $\mathcal{A}_\gamma$ can be replaced by a Conjunctive Query (CQ), in **RW** $\mathcal{A}_\alpha$ (resp. $\mathcal{A}_\beta$) can be replaced by CQ and **And** $\mathcal{A}_\gamma$ (resp. $\mathcal{A}_\beta$) can be replaced by a CQ.

5   Complexity of Inconsistency-Tolerant Query Answering

In this section we study the data complexity[6] of CQ entailment under the various semantics for classes of TBoxes $\mathcal{T} = \mathcal{T}_p \cup \mathcal{T}_n$ that fulfill the following property: $\mathcal{T}_p$ is a *Finite Unification Set* (FUS) of existential rules [3], while $\mathcal{T}_n$ remains any set of negative constraints. A set of rules $\mathcal{T}_p$ fulfills the *FUS* property when, for any CQ q, there exists a *finite* set of CQs $\mathcal{Q}$ (called the set of *rewritings* of q) such that for any ABox $\mathcal{A}$, $\langle \mathcal{T}_p, \mathcal{A} \rangle \models q$ iff $\exists q_i \in \mathcal{Q}$ such that $\mathcal{A} \models q_i$; in other words, q can be rewritten into a union of CQs $\mathcal{Q}$, which allows to forget the rules. Since query rewriting does not depend on any ABox, CQ entailment has the same data complexity as the classical database problem, which is in the low complexity class AC_0. Note also that when $\mathcal{T}_p$ satisfies the *FUS* property, the consistency of a standard KB can be checked by rewriting the query $\bot$ with $\mathcal{T}$ (or equivalently, rewriting each body of a negative constraint with $\mathcal{T}_p$) and checking if one of the obtained rewritings is entailed by $\mathcal{A}$. Such TBoxes encompass DL-Lite$_\mathcal{R}$ TBoxes as well as more expressive classes of existential rules, e.g., linear and sticky [8,9]. All the following membership results apply to *FUS* rules, while all hardness results hold as soon as DL-Lite$_\mathcal{R}$ TBoxes are considered.

We first briefly recall the definition of the complexity classes that we use. The class $\Delta_2^P = P^{NP}$ refers to problems solvable in polynomial time by a deterministic Turing Machine provided with an NP oracle, and its subclass $\Theta_2^P = \Delta_2^P[O(\log n)]$ is allowed to make only logarithmically many calls to an NP oracle. A Probabilistic Turing Machine (PTM) is a non-deterministic TM allowed to "toss coins" to make decisions: we will use the Probabilistic Polynomial-time (PP) class that contains the problems solvable in polynomial time with probability strictly greater than $\frac{1}{2}$ by a PTM [13].[7] We also recall that Δ_2^P, Θ_2^P and PP are all closed under complement. CQ entailment with DL-Lite$_\mathcal{R}$ TBoxes is *coNP-complete* under $\langle R, \forall \rangle$ and $\langle RC, \forall \rangle$ semantics, and in AC_0 under $\langle R, \cap \rangle$ and $\langle RC, \cap \rangle$ semantics (semantics respectively known as *AR*, *CAR*, *IAR* and *ICAR* [16]). It is *coNP-complete* under $\langle CR, \cap \rangle$ semantics (known as *ICR* [6]), and Θ_2^P-*complete* under $\langle MR, \forall \rangle$ and $\langle MR, \cap \rangle$ semantics [7]. We first show that these complexity results also hold for FUS existential rules.

Proposition 3. *If CQ-entailment under* $\langle R/RC/MR, \forall \rangle$ *and* $\langle R/RC/CR, \cap \rangle$ *belongs to some complexity class* $\mathcal{C}$ *for DL-Lite$_\mathcal{R}$ TBoxes, then CQ-entailment remains in the same complexity class* $\mathcal{C}$ *for the more general FUS existential rules.*

---

[6] This complexity measure is usually considered for query answering problems. Only the data (here the ABox) are considered in the problem input.

[7] PP includes NP, co-NP and Θ_2^P.

Table 4. Complexity: tight complexity results are in black font (completely new results marked by a star, the other being generalizations of known results to *FUS*). Membership results are in gray font.

Modifier	$\cap$	$\forall$	Maj	$\exists$
R	AC_0	$coNP$-c	PP-c *	AC_0 *
MR	Θ_2^P-c	Θ_2^P-c	$PP^{NP[O(log\ n)]}$	Θ_2^P
CMR	Θ_2^P	Θ_2^P-c *	$PP^{NP[O(log\ n)]}$	Θ_2^P
MCMR	Θ_2^P	Θ_2^P-c *	$PP^{NP[O(log\ n)]}$	Θ_2^P
CR	$coNP$-c	$coNP$-c	PP-c *	AC_0 *
MCR	Θ_2^P	Θ_2^P-c *	$PP^{NP[O(log\ n)]}$	Θ_2^P
RC	AC_0	$coNP$-c	PP	P
MRC	Θ_2^P	Θ_2^P-c *	$PP^{NP[O(log\ n)]}$	Θ_2^P

Proof: [Sketch] Let us first consider $\langle R/RC, \forall \rangle$. One can obviously guess a repair $\mathcal{R}$ and check in polynomial time (actually in AC_0) if $\langle \mathcal{T}, \mathcal{R} \rangle \models \bot$ (by rewriting all negative constraints and looking for a homomorphism from one of those rewritings into $\mathcal{R}$), and if $\langle \mathcal{T}, \mathcal{R} \rangle \not\models q$ via rewriting methods as well. Concerning $\langle MR, \forall \rangle$, the membership holds for any FUS rules for similar reasons, and by observing that one can compute the maximum size of a repair through logarithmically many calls to an NP oracle. For $\langle R/MRC, \cap \rangle$ the technique from [16] still holds; whereas for $\langle CR, \cap \rangle$, we guess a set of repairs $\mathcal{R} = \{\mathcal{R}_1, ..., \mathcal{R}_k\}$, with k polynomially bounded by the number of homomorphisms from rewritings of the query q to $Cl(\mathcal{A})$, such that: for any homomorphism h from a rewriting q' of q to $Cl(\mathcal{A})$ there is $\mathcal{R}_i \in \mathcal{R}$ with $h(q') \not\subseteq \mathcal{R}_i$. There is a polynomial number of rewritings (for data complexity), hence a polynomial number of homomorphisms from these rewritings to the $Cl(\mathcal{A})$. $\square$

The previous observations explain the complexity results written in black font without star in Table 4. We now provide some new complexity results for other universal-based and existential-based semantics.

Proposition 4. *CQ entailment under $\langle R, \exists \rangle$ (hence $\langle CR, \exists \rangle$) is in AC_0.*

Proof: [Sketch] We first compute a set $\mathcal{Q}$ that contains all the rewritings of q with the rules from $\mathcal{T}_p$, as well as all their specialisations according to all possible partitions on terms. We also rewrite $\bot$ (i.e., all negative constraints) into the set $\mathcal{N}$. We remove from $\mathcal{Q}$ all rewritings q' such that an element of $\mathcal{N}$ maps to q' by homomorphism. Finally, we add to each remaining rewriting $q'' \in \mathcal{Q}$ all inequalities between its terms, which yields $\mathcal{Q}'$. $\mathcal{Q}'$ can be seen as a union of CQs with inequality predicates, hence a first-order query. We have that $\mathcal{K} \models_{\langle R, \exists \rangle} q$ iff $\mathcal{A} \models \mathcal{Q}'$. Therefore q is first-order rewritable w.r.t. $\mathcal{T}$, under $\langle R, \exists \rangle$ semantics. $\square$

Proposition 5. *For $\circ_i \in \{CMR, MCMR, MCR, MRC\}$, CQ entailment under $\langle \circ_i, \forall \rangle$ and $\langle \circ_i, \exists \rangle$ semantics is in Θ_2^P.*

Proof: [Sketch] Notice that we can compute the maximum size of a repair and the maximum size of the ground positive closure of a maximum-sized repair through logarithmically many calls to an NP oracle. Then with one more call to this oracle, we can check whether there is a repair $\mathcal{R}$ that satisfies the cardinality constraints and such that $\langle \mathcal{T}, \mathcal{R} \rangle \not\models q$ (resp. $\langle \mathcal{T}, \mathcal{R} \rangle \models q$). Therefore, $\langle \circ_i, \forall \rangle$ (resp. $\langle \circ_i, \exists \rangle$) is in Θ_2^P. □

Proposition 6. *For* $\circ_i \in \{$CMR, MCMR, MCR, MRC$\}$, *CQ entailment under* $\langle \circ_i, \forall \rangle$ *semantics is* Θ_2^P-*hard.*

Proof: We adapt the reduction from the problem ParitySAT built in [7] (which is a reduction to $\langle$MR, $\forall\rangle$ with an instance query). We "tweak" the query and the $TBox$ so that the positive part of the $TBox$ is empty; this ensures that $(\circ_i, \forall) = (\circ_j, \forall)$ for any $\circ_i, \circ_j \in \{$MR, CMR, MCMR, MCR, MRC$\}$. □

For majority-based semantics, we rely on probabilistic algorithms and provide two completeness results, as stated by the next proposition.

Proposition 7. *Conjunctive Query entailment under* $\langle$R, $Maj\rangle$ *and* $\langle$CR, $Maj\rangle$ *semantics is* PP-*complete.*

Proof: [Sketch] Membership: We use the following algorithm: first choose a subset S of atoms from $\mathcal{A}$ randomly, then if S is not a repair of $\mathcal{K}$, output NO with probability $\frac{1}{2}$. Otherwise (S is a repair), if $(\mathcal{T}, S) \models q$, output NO with probability $\frac{1}{2^{n+1}}$; else $((\mathcal{T}, S) \not\models q)$, output NO with probability 1. This procedure obviously runs in polynomial time and the idea is that each repair has the same probability of being selected in the first step $(\frac{1}{2^n})$, and by answering NO a few times when $(\mathcal{T}, S) \models q$ we ensure that the algorithm will give the right answer with probability strictly greater than $\frac{1}{2}$.

Hardness: We consider the following problem coMajSAT: given a Boolean SAT formula, is the number of unsatisfying affectations strictly greater than half of all possible affectations? We recall that PP is closed under complement. We notice that the reduction from SAT to $\langle S, \forall \rangle$ built in [15], ensures that each repair corresponds exactly to an affectation of the SAT formula, and the obtained query q is evaluated to true iff there is at least one invalid affectation. Hence, the majority of affectations are invalid iff q is entailed by the majority of the repairs. Hence, this transformation yields a reduction from coMajSAT to $\langle$R, $Maj\rangle$. Since $\langle$R, $Maj\rangle = \langle$CR, $Maj\rangle$, the result also holds for $\langle$CR, $Maj\rangle$. □

To further clarify the complexity picture, we give some complexity class membership results for the remaining semantics (Table 4, in gray font). CQ entailment under $\langle$RC, $\exists\rangle$ semantics is clearly in P since we can first compute the ground positive closure of the ABox in polynomial time and $\langle$R, $\exists\rangle$ is in AC_0. For $\langle$MRC, $Maj\rangle$ semantics, the membership proof from Proposition 7 holds as soon as we have observed that we could first compute the ground positive closure of the ABox. For the remaining majority-based semantics, we use an argument similar to the one in Proposition 5 to show membership to $PP^{NP[O(log\ n)]}$: we only need logarithmically many calls to an NP oracle to get the maximum cardinality of a repair. Concerning the remaining intersection-based semantics $\langle\circ_i, \cap\rangle$, we observe that by calling independently the corresponding universal problem $(\circ_i, \forall)$ on each atom from the ABox, we can build the intersection of all repairs, hence the Θ_2^P membership. Finally, an interesting question is to what extent pre-processing the data, independently from any query, can reduce the complexity of query entailment. It seems reasonable to require that the result of this pre-processing step takes space at most linear in the size of the data. For instance, let us consider $\langle\mathsf{MR}, \forall\rangle$: if we precompute the maximum cardinality of a repair (stored in $log_2(|\mathcal{A}|)$ space), the complexity of CQ entailment drops from Θ_2^P-c to $coNP$-c, i.e., the complexity of $\langle\mathsf{R}, \forall\rangle$.

6   Concluding Remarks

The framework for inconsistency-tolerant query answering recently proposed in [2] covers some well-known semantics and introduces new ones. These semantics were compared with respect to productivity. We broaden the analysis by considering two other points of view. First, we initiate a study of rationality properties of inconsistency-tolerant semantics. Second, we complement known complexity results, on the one hand by extending them to the more general case of FUS existential rules, and on the other hand by providing tight complexity results on some newly considered semantics (computation of repairs or closed repairs with majority-based or brave inference, as well several cardinality-based modifiers with universal inference).

The most efficiently computable semantics are $\langle\mathsf{R}, \cap\rangle$ and $\langle\mathsf{R}, \exists\rangle$ (equal to $\langle\mathsf{CR}, \exists\rangle$). The $\langle\mathsf{R}, \cap\rangle$ semantics is the least productive semantics in the framework. However, if one considers the closure of the repairs to increase the productivity of $\langle\mathsf{R}, \cap\rangle$, i.e., $\langle\mathsf{CR}, \cap\rangle$, one obtains a semantics that computationally costs as the "natural" semantics $\langle\mathsf{R}, \forall\rangle$. At the opposite, $\langle\mathsf{R}, \exists\rangle$ may be considered as too adventurous and does not behave well from a rationality point of view since it produces conclusions that may be inconsistent with the ontology. More generally, universal and safe semantics satisfy the rationality properties for most modifiers, which is not the case of majority-based and existential semantics. In addition, for all semantics, RC and MRC, which compute the closure of an inconsistent ABox, may lead to consider as plausible a conclusion with a contestable support, and since they do not seem to bring any advantage compared to other semantics, they should be discarded. Despite majority-based semantics do not fulfil some desirable logical properties, they remain interesting for several reasons: they are only slightly more complex to compute than universal semantics (w.r.t. the same modifier) while being more productive, without being as adventurous as existential semantics. Hence, they may be considered as a good tradeoff between both semantics when the universal semantics appear to be insufficiently productive. We also recall that majority-based semantics behave better from a logical viewpoint when they are restricted to DL-Lite$_\mathcal{R}$ (and more generally, when the ontological language ensures that the size of the conflicts is at most two). Regarding the use of cardinality, cardinality-based modifiers can be used to counteract troublesome assertions that conflict with many others, however they behave strangely when the cardinality criterion is applied to closed repairs.

In summary, no semantics appears to outperform all the others in all of the considered criteria. Selecting a semantics means selecting a suitable trade-off between productivity (or, inversely, cautiousness), satisfaction of rationality properties and computational complexity. We believe that this choice depends on the applicative context.

In a future work, new semantics could be considered within the unified framework, like *no-objection* semantics [4]. Besides, the study of rationality properties could be extended to other properties, and the exact complexity of several semantics remains an open issue.

Acknowledgments. This work was supported by the projects ASPIQ (ANR-12-BS02-0003), PAGOGA (ANR-12-JS02-007-01) and the ERC Starting Grant 637277.

References

1. Arenas, M., Bertossi, L.E., Chomicki, J.: Consistent query answers in inconsistent databases. In: Proceedings of the Eighteenth ACM SIGACT-SIGMOD-SIGART Symposium on Principles of Database Systems, pp. 68–79 (1999)
2. Baget, J.-F., Benferhat, S., Bouraoui, Z., Croitoru, M., Mugnier, M.-L., Papini, O., Rocher, S., Tabia, K.: A general modifier-based framework for inconsistency-tolerant query answering. In: Proceedings of the Fifteenth International Conference on Principles of Knowledge Representation and Reasoning, KR (2016)
3. Baget, J.-F., Leclère, M., Mugnier, M.-L., Salvat, E.: On rules with existential variables: Walking the decidability line. Artif. Intell. **175**(9–10), 1620–1654 (2011)
4. Benferhat, S., Bouraoui, Z., Croitoru, M., Papini, O., Tabia, K.: Non-objection inference for inconsistency-tolerant query answering. In: Proceedings of the Twenty-Fifth International Joint Conference on Artificial Intelligence (2016)
5. Benferhat, S., Cayrol, C., Dubois, D., Lang, J., Prade, H.: Inconsistency management and prioritized syntax-based entailment. In: Proceedings of the 13th International Joint Conference on Artificial Intelligence, pp. 640–647 (1993)
6. Bienvenu, M.: On the complexity of consistent query answering in the presence of simple ontologies. In: Proceedings of the Twenty-Sixth Conference on Artificial Intelligence (2012)
7. Bienvenu, M., Bourgaux, C., Goasdoué, F.: Querying inconsistent description logic knowledge bases under preferred repair semantics. In: Proceedings of the Twenty-Eighth AAAI Conference on Artificial Intelligence, pp. 996–1002 (2014)
8. Calì, A., Gottlob, G., Pieris, A.: Towards more expressive ontology languages: the query answering problem. Artif. Intell. **193**, 87–128 (2012)
9. Calì, A., Gottlob, G., Lukasiewicz, T.: A general datalog-based framework for tractable query answering over ontologies. J. Web Sem. **14**, 57–83 (2012)
10. Calvanese, D., De Giacomo, G., Lembo, D., Lenzerini, M., Rosati, R.: Tractable reasoning and efficient query answering in description logics: the DL-Lite family. J. Autom. Reason. **39**(3), 385–429 (2007)
11. Casini, G., Straccia, U.: Rational closure for defeasible description logics. In: Janhunen, T., Niemelä, I. (eds.) JELIA 2010. LNCS (LNAI), vol. 6341, pp. 77–90. Springer, Heidelberg (2010). doi:10.1007/978-3-642-15675-5_9
12. Gärdenfors, P., Makinson, D.: Nonmonotonic inference based on expectations. Artif. Intell. **65**(2), 197–245 (1994)

13. Gill, J.: Computational complexity of probabilistic turing machines. SIAM J. Comput. **6**(4), 675–695 (1977)
14. Kraus, S., Lehmann, D.J., Magidor, M.: Nonmonotonic reasoning, preferential models and cumulative logics. Artif. Intell. **44**(1–2), 167–207 (1990)
15. Lembo, D., Lenzerini, M., Rosati, R., Ruzzi, M., Savo, D.F.: Inconsistency-tolerant semantics for description logics. In: Hitzler, P., Lukasiewicz, T. (eds.) RR 2010. LNCS, vol. 6333, pp. 103–117. Springer, Heidelberg (2010). doi:10.1007/978-3-642-15918-3_9
16. Lembo, D., Lenzerini, M., Rosati, R., Ruzzi, M., Savo, D.F.: Inconsistency-tolerant query answering in ontology-based data access. J. Web Sem. **33**, 3–29 (2015)
17. Lenzerini, M.: Ontology-based data management. In: Proceedings of the 6th Alberto Mendelzon International Workshop on Foundations of Data Management 2012, pp. 12–15 (2012)
18. Poggi, A., Lembo, D., Calvanese, D., De Giacomo, G., Lenzerini, M., Rosati, R.: Linking data to ontologies. J. Data Semant. **10**, 133–173 (2008)

Temporal Here and There

Philippe Balbiani[1(✉)] and Martín Diéguez[2(✉)]

[1] Institut de recherche en informatique de Toulouse, Toulouse University,
118 route de Narbonne, 31062 Toulouse Cedex 9, France
philippe.balbiani@irit.fr
[2] Centre International de Mathématiques et d'Informatique, IRIT,
Toulouse University, 118 route de Narbonne, 31062 Toulouse Cedex 9, France
martin.dieguez@irit.fr

Abstract. Temporal Here and There (THT) constitutes the logical foundations of Temporal Equilibrium Logic. Nevertheless, it has never been studied in detail since results about axiomatisation and interdefinability of modal operators remained unknown. In this paper we provide a sound and complete axiomatic system for THT together with several results on interdefinability of modal operators.

1 Introduction

In [10], Michael Gelfond and Vladimir Lifschitz introduced the so-called θ semantics that subsumed many of the existing Logic Programming alternatives but without the syntactic restrictions made by previous approaches. The model-based orientation of this semantics led to a paradigm suitable for constraint-satisfaction problems that is known nowadays as *Answer Set Programming* (ASP) [17,18] and that became one of the most prominent and successful approaches for Knowledge Representation. During the evolution of ASP, many hints have pointed out its relevance inside the theoretical foundations of Non-Monotonic Reasoning. One result had a particular success in the study of foundations of ASP: *Equilibrium Logic* (EQL). Introduced by David Pearce [19], this characterisation has shown interesting features such as the theorem of *Strong equivalence* [15] as well as extensions to first-order and modal logics [4,8,20] without imposing any syntactic restriction on the formulas.

Among this modal extensions, we remark Temporal Equilibrium Logic (TEL) [4], which extends the language of EQL with temporal operators from Linear Time Temporal Logic (LTL) [21]. Following the same spirit as EQL, TEL strongly relies on Logic of Temporal Here and There (THT), an extension of the logic of Here and There (HT) [12]. However, contrary to HT, THT has not been studied in detail. Only its role in the theorem of *Temporal Strong Equivalence* [2]

Special acknowledgement is heartly granted to Pedro Cabalar and Luis Fariñas del Cerro for their feedback on a preliminary version of our paper. Martín Diéguez was supported by the Centre international de mathématiques et d'informatique (contract ANR-11-LABX-0040-CIMI).

© Springer International Publishing AG 2016
L. Michael and A. Kakas (Eds.): JELIA 2016, LNAI 10021, pp. 81–96, 2016.
DOI: 10.1007/978-3-319-48758-8_6

and a pair of connections with other logics based on HT [5] are known. In this paper we deal with two problems that remained open in THT. The first problem consists in determining whether modal operators are interdefinable or not while the second problem corresponds to the definition of a sound an complete axiomatic system for THT.

The temporal constructs of THT will be $\square$, $\Diamond$, $\boxed{\star}$ and $\text{\textasteriskcentered}$, the constructs $\square$ and $\Diamond$ being interpreted by the successor relation between integers whereas the constructs $\boxed{\star}$ and $\text{\textasteriskcentered}$ being interpreted by the precedence relation between integers. As usual when one has to axiomatise modal logics where some modal constructs are interpreted by the reflexive transitive closure of the accessibility relation used to interpret other modal constructs, our axiomatisation will use inference rules for induction. In this setting, traditional proofs of completeness (see [11, Chap. 9]) are based on canonical model and filtration. In our HT setting, however, the usual filtration method does not allow to transform, as it is the case in ordinary temporal logic, the canonical model into a model where $\boxed{\star}$ and $\text{\textasteriskcentered}$ are interpreted by the precedence relation between integers. For this reason, we had to redefine the filtration method in an appropriate way (see Sect. 6 for details). Moreover, the determinisation of the filtrated model requires, in the case of ordinary temporal logic, the use of a characteristic formula that cannot be expressed in our language. As a result, we had to redefined the determinisation of the filtrated model.

This paper is organised as follows: in Sect. 2 we introduce syntax and two equivalent semantics for THT. In Sect. 3 we go through the problem of interdefinability by defining the notion of bisimulation in the HT setting. The proof of completeness of the axiomatic system described in Sect. 4 is described along Sects. 5–7 and we finish the paper with conclusions and future work.

2   Syntax and Semantics

Let At be a finite or countable set of atomic formulas (with typical members denoted by p, q, etc.). We inductively define the set of all formulas (with typical members denoted by ϕ, ψ, etc.) as follows:

$$\phi ::= p \mid \bot \mid (\phi \vee \psi) \mid (\phi \wedge \psi) \mid (\phi \rightarrow \psi) \mid \square\phi \mid \Diamond\phi \mid \boxed{\star}\phi \mid \text{\textasteriskcentered}\phi.$$

Note that, following the tradition in Intuitionistic Modal Logic, we have added the new temporal constructs $\square$, $\Diamond$, $\boxed{\star}$ and $\text{\textasteriskcentered}$ to the ordinary language of IPL. As it will soon become clear, the constructs $\square$ and $\Diamond$ are equivalent in THT while $\boxed{\star}$ and $\text{\textasteriskcentered}$ are independent. We define $\neg\phi$ as the abbreviation $\neg\phi ::= \phi \rightarrow \bot$. For all sets of formulas x, let $\square x = \{\varphi \mid \square\varphi \in x\}$ and $\Diamond x = \{\Diamond\varphi \mid \varphi \in x\}$. The sets $\boxed{\star}x$ and $\text{\textasteriskcentered}x$ are similarly defined. We shall say that a set Σ of formulas is closed if (1) Σ is closed under subformulas; (2) if $\boxed{\star}\varphi \in \Sigma$ then $\square\boxed{\star}\varphi \in \Sigma$; (3) if $\text{\textasteriskcentered}\varphi \in \Sigma$ then $\Diamond\text{\textasteriskcentered}\varphi \in \Sigma$; (4) if $\varphi \in \Sigma$ then $\neg\varphi \in \Sigma$. Remark that the least closed set of formulas containing a given formula is infinite. Nevertheless, its quotient by the relation of logical equivalence will be finite in the context of THT. We define the *degree* of a formula ϕ (in symbols $deg(\phi)$) by induction as follows: (i) $deg(p) =$

$deg(\bot) = 0$; (ii) $deg(\phi \vee \psi) = deg(\phi \wedge \psi) = deg(\phi \rightarrow \psi) = max\{deg(\phi), deg(\psi)\}$; (iii) $deg(\Box\phi) = deg(\Diamond\phi) = 1 + deg(\phi)$; (iv) $deg(\boxtimes\phi) = deg(\text{⟐}\phi) = deg(\phi)$. We define a temporal model as a structure $\mathcal{M} = \langle H, T \rangle$ where $H : \mathbb{N} \rightarrow 2^{At}$ and $T : \mathbb{N} \rightarrow 2^{At}$ are such that $H(i) \geqslant T(i)$ for all $i \geqslant 0$. If an atomic formula belongs to $H(i)$, $i \in \mathbb{N}$, then it means that p holds here in $\mathcal{M}$ at time i whereas if p belongs to $T(i)$ then it means that p holds there at time i. The satisfaction relation in a temporal model $\mathcal{M} = \langle H, T \rangle$ of a formula φ at the pair $(i, \alpha) \in \mathbb{N} \times \{h, t\}$, denoted by $\mathcal{M}, (i, \alpha) \models \varphi$, is inductively defined as follows:

- $\mathcal{M}, (i, h) \models p$ iff $p \in H(i)$;
- $\mathcal{M}, (i, t) \models p$ iff $p \in T(i)$;
- $\mathcal{M}, (i, \alpha) \models \varphi \wedge \psi$ iff $\mathcal{M}, (i, \alpha) \models \varphi$ and $\mathcal{M}, (i, \alpha) \models \psi$;
- $\mathcal{M}, (i, \alpha) \models \varphi \vee \psi$ iff $\mathcal{M}, (i, \alpha) \models \varphi$ or $\mathcal{M}, (i, \alpha) \models \psi$;
- $\mathcal{M}, (i, \alpha) \models \varphi \rightarrow \psi$ iff for all $\beta \in \{\alpha, t\}$ $\mathcal{M}, (i, \beta) \not\models \varphi$ or $\mathcal{M}, (i, \beta) \models \psi$;
- $\mathcal{M}, (i, \alpha) \models \Box\varphi$ iff $\mathcal{M}, (i+1, \alpha) \models \varphi$;
- $\mathcal{M}, (i, \alpha) \models \Diamond\varphi$ iff $\mathcal{M}, (i+1, \alpha) \models \varphi$;
- $\mathcal{M}, (i, \alpha) \models \boxtimes\varphi$ iff for all $j \geqslant i$, $\mathcal{M}, (j, \alpha) \models \varphi$;
- $\mathcal{M}, (i, \alpha) \models \text{⟐}\varphi$ iff there exists $j \geqslant i$ s.t. $\mathcal{M}, (j, \alpha) \models \varphi$;

We will say that a formula φ is THT-valid (denoted by $THT \models \varphi$) iff $\mathcal{M}, (0, h) \models \varphi$ for all THT models $\mathcal{M}$.

Proposition 1 (Persistence). *For all formulas φ, for all THT models $\mathcal{M}$ and for all $i \in \mathbb{N}$, if $\mathcal{M}, (i, h) \models \varphi$ then $\mathcal{M}, (i, t) \models \varphi$.*

Our aim, in this paper, is to completely axiomatise the set of all THT-valid formulas. This will be done from Sect. 4 on. In the meantime we study an alternative semantics for THT formulas that will be used in the proof of completeness of our axiomatisation. A *birelational model* is a structure of the form $\mathcal{M} = \langle W, \leqslant, R^{\Box}, R^{\boxtimes}, V \rangle$ such that:

- W is a non-empty set of worlds;
- $\leqslant$ is a partial order on W;
- $R^{\Box}$ and $R^{\boxtimes}$ are binary relations on W;
- $V : W \rightarrow 2^{At}$ is such that for all x, $y \in W$, if $x \leqslant y$ then $V(x) \subseteq V(y)$.

Given a birelational model $\mathcal{M} = \langle W, \leqslant, R^{\Box}, R^{\boxtimes}, V \rangle$, a world $x \in W$ and a formula φ, the satisfaction relation is defined as follows:

- $\mathcal{M}, x \models p$ iff $p \in V(x)$;
- $\mathcal{M}, x \models (\varphi \wedge \psi)$ iff $\mathcal{M}, x \models \varphi$ and $\mathcal{M}, x \models \psi$;
- $\mathcal{M}, x \models (\varphi \vee \psi)$ iff $\mathcal{M}, x \models \varphi$ or $\mathcal{M}, x \models \psi$;
- $\mathcal{M}, x \models \varphi \rightarrow \psi$ iff for all $x' \in W$, if $x \leqslant x'$ then $\mathcal{M}, x' \not\models \varphi$ or $\mathcal{M}, x' \models \psi$;
- $\mathcal{M}, x \models \Box\varphi$ iff for all $x', y \in W$, if $x \leqslant x' R^{\Box} y$ then $\mathcal{M}, y \models \varphi$;
- $\mathcal{M}, x \models \Diamond\varphi$ iff there exists $y \in W$ s. t. $x R^{\Box} y$ and $\mathcal{M}, y \models \varphi$;
- $\mathcal{M}, x \models \boxtimes\varphi$ iff for all $x', y \in W$, if $x \leqslant x' R^{\boxtimes} y$ then $\mathcal{M}, y \models \varphi$;
- $\mathcal{M}, x \models \text{⟐}\varphi$ iff there exists $y \in W$ s. t. $x R^{\boxtimes} y$ and $\mathcal{M}, y \models \varphi$.

Notice that the clauses concerning the temporal constructs $\square$ and $\boxed{\star}$ imitate the clause for the quantifier $\forall$ in first-order intuitionistic logic whereas the clauses concerning $\Diamond$ and $\hat{\Diamond}$ imitate the clause for $\exists$. See [7, Lemma 5.3.2] for details. We shall say that $\mathcal{M}$ is *normal* if (1) for all x, y, $z \in W$, if $x \leqslant y$ and $x \leqslant z$ then either $x = y$ or $x = z$ or $y = z$; (2) for all x, y, $z \in W$, if $x \leqslant y$ and $xR^{\square}z$ (respectively $xR^{\boxed{\star}}z$) then $yR^{\square}t$ (respectively $yR^{\boxed{\star}}t$) and $z \leqslant t$ for some $t \in W$; (3) for all x, y, $z \in W$, if $xR^{\square}y$ (respectively $xR^{\boxed{\star}}y$) and $y \leqslant z$ then $x \leqslant t$ and $tR^{\square}z$ (respectively $tR^{\boxed{\star}}z$) for some $t \in W$. If $\mathcal{M}$ is normal then for all $x \in W$, either x is a maximal element with respect to $\leqslant$, or there exists $y \in W$ such that $x \leqslant y$ and $x \neq y$. In the former case let $\widehat{x}$ be x. In the latter case, there exists exactly one $y \in W$ such that $x \leqslant y$ and $x \neq y$; let $\widehat{x}$ be this y. A normal model $\mathcal{M} = \langle W, \leqslant, R^{\square}, R^{\boxed{\star}}, V \rangle$ is said to be *standard* if $R^{\square}$ is serial, $R^{\square}$ is deterministic and $R^{\boxed{\star}}$ is equal to the reflexive transitive closure of $R^{\square}$. We say that a formula φ is *standard-valid* iff for all standard birelational models $\mathcal{M} = \langle W, \leqslant, R^{\square}, R^{\boxed{\star}}, V \rangle$ and for all $x_0 \in W$, $\mathcal{M}, x_0 \models \varphi$. We now relate this alternative semantics to the THT semantics. Let $\mathcal{M} = \langle H, T \rangle$ be a THT model. We define the birelational model $\mathcal{M}' = \langle W, \leqslant, R^{\square}, R^{\boxed{\star}}, V \rangle$ as follows:

- $W = \mathbb{N} \times \{h, t\}$;
- $(i_1, \alpha_1) \leqslant (i_2, \alpha_2)$ iff $i_1 = i_2$ and either $\alpha_1 = h$ or $\alpha_2 = t$;
- $(i_1, \alpha_1)R^{\square}(i_2, \alpha_2)$ iff $i_1 + 1 = i_2$ and $\alpha_1 = \alpha_2$;
- $(i_1, \alpha_1)R^{\boxed{\star}}(i_2, \alpha_2)$ iff $i_1 \leqslant i_2$ and $\alpha_1 = \alpha_2$;
- $V((i, \alpha)) = H(i)$ if $\alpha = h$ else $T(i)$.

Obviously, $\mathcal{M}'$ is a standard birelational model. Moreover, as the reader can show by structural induction, for all formulas φ, for all $i \in \mathbb{N}$ and for all $\alpha \in \{h, t\}$, $\mathcal{M}, (i, \alpha) \models \varphi$ iff $\mathcal{M}', (i, \alpha) \models \varphi$. Reciprocally, let $\mathcal{M}' = \langle W, \leqslant, R^{\square}, R^{\boxed{\star}}, V \rangle$ be a standard birelational model. Hence, $R^{\square}$ is serial, deterministic and for all $x \in W$ and for all $i \in \mathbb{N}$, there exists exactly one $y \in W$ such that $x \left(R^{\square}\right)^{i} y$; let $\left(R^{\square}\right)^{i}(x_0)$ be this y. Let $x_0 \in W$. We define the functions $H, T : \mathbb{N} \to 2^{At}$ as $H(i) = V(\left(R^{\square}\right)^{i}(x_0))$ and $T(i) = V(\widehat{\left(R^{\square}\right)^{i}}(x_0))$. Remark that for all $i \in \mathbb{N}$, $H(i) \subseteq T(i)$. Let $\mathcal{M} = \langle H, T \rangle$. Thus, $\mathcal{M}$ is a THT model. As the reader can show by structural induction, for all formulas φ and for all $i \in \mathbb{N}$, $\mathcal{M}', \left(R^{\square}\right)^{i}(x_0) \models \varphi$ iff $\mathcal{M}, (i, h) \models \varphi$ and $\mathcal{M}', \widehat{\left(R^{\square}\right)^{i}}(x_0) \models \varphi$ iff $\mathcal{M}, (i, t) \models \varphi$. As a result, THT semantics and the alternative semantics are equivalent.

3   Interdefinability

As it is well-known, disjunction is definable in terms of conjunction and implication within the context of HT [16].

Lemma 1. *For all formulas ϕ, ψ, $THT \models \phi \vee \psi \leftrightarrow ((\phi \to \psi) \to \psi) \wedge ((\psi \to \phi) \to \phi)$.*

Below, we show the non-interdefinability of conjunction in THT.

Lemma 2. *Let $\mathcal{M}_1 = \langle H_1, T_1 \rangle$, $\mathcal{M}_2 = \langle H_2, T_2 \rangle$ and $\mathcal{M}_3 = \langle H_3, T_3 \rangle$ be the THT models such that for all $i \in \mathbb{N}$, $H_1(i) = \{p, q\}$, $T_i(i) = \{p, q\}$, $H_2(i) = \{p\}$, $T_2(i) = \{p, q\}$, $H_3(i) = \{q\}$ and $T_3(i) = \{p, q\}$. For all $\wedge$-free formulas φ and for all $i \in \mathbb{N}$, $\mathcal{M}_1, (i, h) \models \varphi$ iff $\mathcal{M}_2, (i, h) \models \varphi$ or $\mathcal{M}_3, (i, h) \models \varphi$.*

Proof. By structural induction on φ.

Lemma 3. *Let $p, q \in At$. There is no $\wedge$-free formula ψ such that $THT \models p \wedge q \leftrightarrow \psi$.*

Proof. Remark that $\mathcal{M}_1, (0, h) \models p \wedge q$, $\mathcal{M}_2, (0, h) \not\models p \wedge q$ and $\mathcal{M}_3, (0, h) \not\models p \wedge q$. Hence, by Lemma 2, $p \wedge q$ is THT-equivalent to no $\wedge$-free formula.

In the HT setting, the non-interdefinability of $\wedge$ has also been proved by Aguado et al. [1] by means of a denotational semantics based on sets of models. Our proof is simpler, seeing that it does not require the use of sets of models. Before considering the interdefinability of the modal operators in THT, we must remark that the following equivalences are THT-valid:

- $\square\bot \leftrightarrow \bot$;
- $\square(\varphi \vee \psi) \leftrightarrow \square\varphi \vee \square\psi$;
- $\square(\varphi \wedge \psi) \leftrightarrow \square\varphi \wedge \square\psi$;
- $\square(\varphi \to \psi) \leftrightarrow (\square\varphi \to \square\psi)$;
- $\square\boxed{\star}\varphi \leftrightarrow \boxed{\star}\square\varphi$;
- $\square\boxed{\diamond}\varphi \leftrightarrow \boxed{\diamond}\square\varphi$;

- $\lozenge\bot \leftrightarrow \bot$;
- $\lozenge(\varphi \vee \psi) \leftrightarrow \lozenge\varphi \vee \lozenge\psi$;
- $\lozenge(\varphi \wedge \psi) \leftrightarrow \lozenge\varphi \wedge \lozenge\psi$;
- $\lozenge(\varphi \to \psi) \leftrightarrow (\lozenge\varphi \to \lozenge\psi)$;
- $\lozenge\boxed{\star}\varphi \leftrightarrow \boxed{\star}\lozenge\varphi$;
- $\lozenge\boxed{\diamond}\varphi \leftrightarrow \boxed{\diamond}\lozenge\varphi$.

As a result, every formula is equivalent to a formula in which $\bot$, $\vee$, $\wedge$, $\to$, $\boxed{\star}$ and $\boxed{\diamond}$ do not appear within the scope of $\square$ or $\lozenge$. In order to prove the non-interdefinability of $\boxed{\star}$ and $\boxed{\diamond}$, we introduce the notions of $\boxed{\star}$-bisimulation and $\boxed{\diamond}$-bisimulation between THT models. Let $\mathcal{D} = \{(i, \alpha) \mid i \in \mathbb{N} \text{ and } \alpha \in \{h, t\}\}$ and let $k \in \mathbb{N}$. A binary relation $\mathcal{Z}$ on $\mathcal{D}$ is said to be a k-$\boxed{\star}$-*bisimulation* between the THT models $\mathcal{M}_1$ and $\mathcal{M}_2$ if the following conditions are satisfied:

1. if $(i_1, \alpha_1) \mathcal{Z} (i_2, \alpha_2)$ then for all j, $0 \leqslant j \leqslant k$, and for all propositional variables p, $\mathcal{M}_1 (i_1 + j, \alpha_1) \models p$ iff $\mathcal{M}_2, (i_2 + j, \alpha_2) \models p$;
2. if $(i_1, \alpha_1) \mathcal{Z} (i_2, \alpha_2)$ then $(i_1, t) \mathcal{Z} (i_2, t)$ or both $(i_1, \alpha_1) \mathcal{Z} (i_2, t)$ and $(i_1, t) \mathcal{Z} (i_2, \alpha_2)$;
3. if $(i_1, \alpha_1) \mathcal{Z} (i_2, \alpha_2)$ and $i_1 \leqslant j_1$ then there exists $j_2 \in \mathbb{N}$ s.t. $i_2 \leqslant j_2$ and either $(j_1, \alpha_1)\mathcal{Z} (j_2, \alpha_2)$ or $(j_1, \alpha_1) \mathcal{Z} (j_2, t)$;
4. if $(i_1, \alpha_1) \mathcal{Z} (i_2, \alpha_2)$ and $i_2 \leqslant j_2$ then there exists $j_1 \in \mathbb{N}$ s.t. $i_1 \leqslant j_1$ and $(j_1, \alpha_1) \mathcal{Z} (j_2, \alpha_2)$ or $(j_1, t) \mathcal{Z} (j_2, \alpha_2)$.

A binary relation $\mathcal{Z}$ on $\mathcal{D}$ is said to be a k-$\boxed{\diamond}$-*bisimulation* between the THT models $\mathcal{M}_1$ and $\mathcal{M}_2$ if the following conditions are satisfied:

1. if $(i_1, \alpha_1) \mathcal{Z} (i_2, \alpha_2)$ then for all j, $0 \leqslant j \leqslant k$, and for all propositional variable p, $\mathcal{M}_1, (i_1 + j, \alpha_1) \models p$ iff $\mathcal{M}_2, (i_2 + j, \alpha_2) \models p$;

2. if $(i_1, \alpha_1)\ \mathcal{Z}\ (i_2, \alpha_2)$ then $(i_1, t)\ \mathcal{Z}\ (i_2, t)$ or both $(i_1, \alpha_1)\ \mathcal{Z}\ (i_2, t)$ and (i_1, t) $\mathcal{Z}\ (i_2, \alpha_2)$;

3. if $(i_1, \alpha_1)\ \mathcal{Z}\ (i_2, \alpha_2)$ and $i_1 \leqslant j_1$ then there exists $j_2 \in \mathbb{N}$ s.t. $i_2 \leqslant j_2$ and either $(j_1, \alpha_1)\ \mathcal{Z}\ (j_2, \alpha_2)$ or $(j_1, t)\ \mathcal{Z}\ (j_2, \alpha_2)$;

4. if $(i_1, \alpha_1)\ \mathcal{Z}\ (i_2, \alpha_2)$ and $i_2 \leqslant j_2$ then there exists $j_1 \in \mathbb{N}$ s.t. $i_1 \leqslant j_1$ and $(j_1, \alpha_1)\ \mathcal{Z}\ (j_2, \alpha_2)$ or $(j_1, \alpha_1)\ \mathcal{Z}\ (j_2, t)$;

The proof of the following lemmas can be done by induction on ϕ.

Lemma 4 (Bisimulation Lemma 1). *Given THT models $\mathcal{M}_1$ and $\mathcal{M}_2$ and a k-⊠-bisimulation $\mathcal{Z}$ between them, for all ⬦-free formulas ϕ, $deg(\phi) \leqslant k$, and for all (i_1, α_1) and $(i_2, \alpha_2) \in \mathcal{D}$, if $(i_1, \alpha_1)\ \mathcal{Z}\ (i_2, \alpha_2)$ then $\mathcal{M}_1, (i_1, \alpha_1) \models \phi$ iff $\mathcal{M}_2, (i_2, \alpha_2) \models \phi$.*

Lemma 5 (Bisimulation Lemma 2). *Given THT models $\mathcal{M}_1$ and $\mathcal{M}_2$ and a k-⬦-bisimulation $\mathcal{Z}$ between them, for all ⊠-free formulas ϕ, $deg(\phi) \leqslant k$, and for all (i_1, α_1) and $(i_2, \alpha_2) \in \mathcal{D}$. if $(i_1, \alpha_1)\ \mathcal{Z}\ (i_2, \alpha_2)$ then $\mathcal{M}_1, (i_1, \alpha_1) \models \phi$ iff $\mathcal{M}_2, (i_2, \alpha_2) \models \phi$.*

Proposition 2. *Let $p \in At$. There is no ⬦-free formula ψ such that $THT \models$ ⬦$p \leftrightarrow \psi$.*

Proof. Suppose that ψ is a ⬦-free formula such that $THT \models$ ⬦$p \leftrightarrow \psi$. Let $k \geqslant 0$ be the degree of ψ. Without loss of generality we can assume that $\bot$, $\vee$, $\wedge$, $\rightarrow$ and ⊠ do not appear in ψ within the scope of the connectives $\square$ and $\Diamond$. Let $\mathcal{M}_1 = \langle H_1, T_1 \rangle$ and $\mathcal{M}_2 = \langle H_2, T_2 \rangle$ be the THT models such that for all $i \in \mathbb{N}$, $H_1(i) = \varnothing$, $T_1(i) = \{p\}$ if $i \bmod k + 2 = k + 1$ and $\varnothing$ otherwise, $H_2(i) = \{p\}$ if $i = k + 1$ and $\varnothing$ otherwise, $T_2(i) = \{p\}$ if $i \bmod k + 2 = k + 1$ and $\varnothing$ otherwise. Let $\mathcal{Z}$ be the binary relation on $\mathcal{D}$ such that $(i_1, \alpha_1)\ \mathcal{Z}\ (i_2, \alpha_2)$ iff one of the following condition holds: (1) either $\alpha_1 = \alpha_2 = h$ and $i_1 = i_2 = 0$, or $\alpha_1 = \alpha_2 = t$ and $i_1 = i_2$; (2) $\alpha_1 = \alpha_2 = h$ and $i_2 = i_1 + k + 2$; (3) $\alpha_1 = \alpha_2 = t$ and $i_2 = i_1 + k + 2$; (4) $\alpha_1 = t$, $\alpha_2 = h$ and $i_1 = i_2 < k + 2$. The reader may easily verify that $\mathcal{Z}$ is a k-⊠-bisimulation between $\mathcal{M}_1$ and $\mathcal{M}_2$. Since $\mathcal{M}_1, (0, h) \models$ ⬦p, therefore $\mathcal{M}_1, (0, h) \models \psi$. Hence, by Lemma 4, $\mathcal{M}_2, (0, h) \models \psi$. Thus $\mathcal{M}_2, (0, h) \models$ ⬦p: a contradiction.

Proposition 3. *Let $p \in At$. There is no ⊠-free formulas ψ such that $THT \models$ ⊠$p \leftrightarrow \psi$.*

Proof. Similarly to the proof of Proposition 2, by using the THT models $\mathcal{M}_1 = \langle H_1, T_1 \rangle$ and $\mathcal{M}_2 = \langle H_2, T_2 \rangle$ such that for all $i \in \mathbb{N}$, $H_1(i) = \{p\}$, $T_1(i) = \{p\}$, $H_2(i) = \varnothing$ if $i = k + 1$ and $\{p\}$ otherwise, $T_2(i) = \{p\}$ and the binary relation $\mathcal{Z}$ on $\mathcal{D}$ such that $(i_1, \alpha_1)\ \mathcal{Z}\ (i_2, \alpha_2)$ iff one of the following condition holds: (1) either $\alpha_1 = \alpha_2 = h$ and $i_1 = i_2 = 0$; (2) $\alpha_1 = \alpha_2 = t$ and $i_1 = i_2$; (3) $\alpha_1 = \alpha_2 = h$ and $i_2 = i_1 + k + 2$; (4) $\alpha_1 = \alpha_1 = h$ and $i_1 = i_2 > k + 1$; (5) $\alpha_1 = h$, $\alpha_2 = t$ and $i_1 = i_2$.

4 Axiomatisation

The axiomatic system of THT consists of the axioms of Intuitionistic Propositional Logic [6, Chap. 5] plus the following axioms and inference rules:

Hosoi axiom: (1) $p \vee (p \rightarrow q) \vee \neg q$;

Axioms for $\square$ and $\Diamond$:

(2) $\square p \leftrightarrow \Diamond p$;

(3) $\square(p \rightarrow q) \leftrightarrow (\square p \rightarrow \square q)$;

(4) $\square(p \vee q) \leftrightarrow \square p \vee \square q$;

(5) $\square(p \wedge q) \leftrightarrow \square p \wedge \square q$;

(6) $\square \bot \leftrightarrow \bot$

Fisher Servi axioms for $\boxed{\ast}$ and $\Diamond\!\!\!\!\ast$:

(7) $\boxed{\ast}\bot \leftrightarrow \bot$

(8) $\boxed{\ast}(p \rightarrow q) \rightarrow (\boxed{\ast}p \rightarrow \boxed{\ast}q)$;

(9) $\boxed{\ast}(p \rightarrow q) \rightarrow (\Diamond\!\!\!\!\ast p \rightarrow \Diamond\!\!\!\!\ast q)$;

(10) $\Diamond\!\!\!\!\ast(p \vee q) \rightarrow \Diamond\!\!\!\!\ast p \vee \Diamond\!\!\!\!\ast q$;

(11) $(\Diamond\!\!\!\!\ast p \rightarrow \boxed{\ast}q) \rightarrow \boxed{\ast}(p \rightarrow q)$;

Axioms combining $\square$, $\Diamond$, $\boxed{\ast}$ and $\Diamond\!\!\!\!\ast$: (12) $\boxed{\ast}p \rightarrow p \wedge \square\boxed{\ast}p$; (13) $p \vee \Diamond\Diamond\!\!\!\!\ast p \rightarrow \Diamond\!\!\!\!\ast p$;

Induction: (14) $\dfrac{p \rightarrow \square p}{p \rightarrow \boxed{\ast}p}$; (15) $\dfrac{\Diamond p \rightarrow p}{\Diamond\!\!\!\!\ast p \rightarrow p}$;

Modus ponens: (16) $\dfrac{p \rightarrow q,\ p}{q}$. **Necessitation:** (17) $\dfrac{p}{\boxed{\ast}p}$; (18) $\dfrac{p}{\square p}$.

Proposition 4 (Soundness). *The axiomatic system presented in this section is sound.*

Proof. Left to the reader. It is sufficient to check that all axioms are valid and the inference rules preserve validity.

The Hosoi axiom corresponds to the fact that, in a normal model, $\mathcal{M} = \langle W, \leqslant, R^{\square}, R^{\boxed{\ast}}, V \rangle$, if $x \leqslant y$ and $x \leqslant z$ then either $x = y$ or $x = z$ or $y = z$. Axioms (2)–(4) correspond to the fact that in a standard model $\mathcal{M} = \langle W, \leqslant, R^{\square}, R^{\boxed{\ast}}, V \rangle$, $R^{\square}$ is serial and deterministic. The Fisher Servi axioms for $\boxed{\ast}$ and $\Diamond\!\!\!\!\ast$ are similar to the axioms considered in [9,22]. Remark that the corresponding Fisher Servi axioms for $R^{\square}$ are easily derivable. Axioms combining $\square$, $\Diamond$, $\boxed{\ast}$ and $\Diamond\!\!\!\!\ast$ correspond to the fact that, in a standard model $\mathcal{M} = \langle W, \leqslant, R^{\square}, R^{\boxed{\ast}}, V \rangle$, $R^{\boxed{\ast}}$ is reflexive and $R^{\square} \circ R^{\boxed{\ast}} \subseteq R^{\boxed{\ast}}$. As for the rules of inference (14) and (15), they will be used in the proof of Lemma 15, where the canonical model $\mathcal{M}_c = \langle W_c, \leqslant_c, R^{\square}_c, R^{\boxed{\ast}}_c, V_c \rangle$ of THT is filtrated into a model $\mathcal{M}_{\Sigma} = \langle W_{\Sigma}, \leqslant_{\Sigma}, R^{\square}_{\Sigma}, R^{\boxed{\ast}}_{\Sigma}, V_{\Sigma} \rangle$ such that $R^{\boxed{\ast}}_{\Sigma}$ is the reflexive transitive closure of $R^{\square}_{\Sigma}$.

Lemma 6. *For all $m, n \in \mathbb{N}$, the following rules are derivable:*

1. $\dfrac{\psi_1 \wedge \ldots \wedge \psi_m \rightarrow \phi \vee \chi_1 \vee \ldots \vee \chi_n}{\boxed{\ast}\psi_1 \wedge \ldots \wedge \boxed{\ast}\psi_m \rightarrow \boxed{\ast}\phi \vee \Diamond\!\!\!\!\ast\chi_1 \vee \ldots \vee \Diamond\!\!\!\!\ast\chi_n}$;

2. $$\frac{\phi \wedge \psi_1 \wedge \ldots \wedge \psi_m \to \chi_1 \vee \ldots \vee \chi_n}{\diamondsuit\!\!\!\!\!/\,\phi \wedge \boxed{\star}\psi_1 \wedge \ldots \wedge \boxed{\star}\psi_m \to \diamondsuit\!\!\!\!\!/\,\chi_1 \vee \ldots \vee \diamondsuit\!\!\!\!\!/\,\chi_n} \ .$$

Proof. These rules are derivable by means of Fisher Servi axioms. See [9,22].

Lemma 7. *The following formulas are derivable:* $\varphi \wedge \square\boxed{\star}\varphi \to \boxed{\star}\varphi \ \diamondsuit\!\!\!\!\!/\,\varphi \to \varphi \vee \Diamond\diamondsuit\!\!\!\!\!/\,\varphi$

5   Canonical Model Construction

As usual, we will base our proof of completeness on the canonical model construction.

5.1   Prime Sets

Given two sets of formulas x and y, we say that y is a consequence of x (denoted by $x \vdash y$) iff there exists $\phi_1, \ldots, \phi_m \in x$ and $\psi_1, \ldots, \psi_n \in y$ such that $\phi_1 \wedge \ldots \wedge \phi_m \to \psi_1 \vee \ldots \vee \psi_n \in THT$. We shall say that a set x of formulas is *prime* if it satisfies the following conditions: (1) $\bot \notin x$; (2) for all formulas ϕ, ψ, if $\phi \vee \psi \in x$ then either $\phi \in x$, or $\psi \in x$; (3) for all formulas ϕ, if $x \vdash \phi$ then $\phi \in x$.

Lemma 8 (Lindenbaum Lemma). *Let x and y be sets of formulas. If $x \nvdash y$ then there exists a prime set z of formulas such that $x \subseteq z$ and $z \nvdash y$.*

The next Lemma shows the connection between Hosoi axiom and the relation of inclusion between prime sets of formulas.

Lemma 9. *Let x, y, z be prime sets of formulas. If $x \subseteq y$ and $x \subseteq z$ then either $x = y$, or $x = z$, or $y = z$.*

Proof. By Hosoi axiom.

Proposition 5. *Let x be a prime set of formulas. There exists at most one prime set of formulas strictly containing x.*

Hence, for all prime sets x, either x is maximal, for inclusion, among all prime sets, or there exists a prime set y such that $x \subseteq y$ and $x \neq y$. In the former case, let $\widehat{x} = x$. In the latter case, there exists exactly one prime set y such that $x \subseteq y$ and $x \neq y$; let $\widehat{x}$ be this y. In our HT setting, one can easily show that for all formulas φ, $\varphi \in \widehat{x}$ iff $\neg\neg\varphi \in x$.

5.2   Canonical Model

The canonical model $\mathcal{M}_c$ is defined as the structure $\mathcal{M}_c = \langle W_c, \leqslant_c, R_c^{\square}, R_c^{\boxed{\star}}, V_c \rangle$ where:

- W_c is the set of all prime sets;
- $\leqslant_c$ is the partial order on W_c defined by: $x \leqslant_c y$ iff $x \subseteq y$;
- $R_c^{\square}$ is the binary relation on W_c defined by: $xR_c^{\square}y$ iff $\square x \subseteq y$ and $\Diamond y \subseteq x$;

– $R_c^{\boxed{\star}}$ is the binary relation on W_c defined by: $xR_c^{\boxed{\star}}y$ iff $\boxed{\star}x \subseteq y$ and $\textcircled{\star}y \subseteq x$;
– $V_c : W_c \to 2^{At}$ is the valuation function defined by: $p \in V_c(x)$ iff $p \in x$;

Proposition 6. $\mathcal{M}_c$ *is normal.*

Proof. The condition (1) of normality follows from Lemma 9. In order to prove the conditions (2) and (3) it suffices to prove that for all $x, y \in W_c$, if $xR_c^{\square}y$ then $\widehat{x}R_c^{\square}\widehat{y}$. Firstly remark that $\neg\neg\square p \to \square\neg\neg p$ and $\Diamond\neg\neg p \to \neg\neg\Diamond p$ are in THT seeing that these formulas are derivable in the axiom systems considered in [9,22]. Secondly, let x and y be prime sets such that $xR_c^{\square}y$ and suppose that $\widehat{x}R_c^{\square}\widehat{y}$. Hence, either $\square\widehat{x} \not\subseteq \widehat{y}$ or $\Diamond\widehat{y} \not\subseteq \widehat{x}$. Let φ be a formula such that either $\square\varphi \in \widehat{x}$ but $\varphi \notin \widehat{y}$ or $\varphi \in \widehat{y}$ but $\Diamond\varphi \notin \widehat{x}$. In the former case, $\neg\neg\square\varphi \in x$, $\square\neg\neg\varphi \in x$, $\neg\neg\varphi \in y$ and $\varphi \in \widehat{y}$: a contradiction. In the latter case, $\neg\neg\varphi \in y$, $\Diamond\neg\neg\varphi \in x$, $\neg\neg\Diamond\varphi \in x$ and $\Diamond\varphi \in \widehat{x}$: a contradiction.

Proposition 7. $R_c^{\square}$ *is serial and deterministic.*

Proof. **Seriality:** Let $x \in W_c$. We define $y = \square x$. By means of Axiom (2) the reader can easily show that y is a prime set such that $\square x \subseteq y$ and $\Diamond y \subseteq x$, thus $xR_c^{\square}y$. **Determinism:** Suppose that there exists $x, y, z \in W_c$ such that $xR_c^{\square}y$ and $xR_c^{\square}z$ but $y \neq z$. Without loss of generality, let $\varphi \in y$ be such that $\varphi \notin z$. As a consequence $\Diamond\varphi \in x$ but $\square\varphi \notin x$, which contradicts Axiom (2).

Proposition 8. $R_c^{\boxed{\star}}$ *is reflexive and transitive.*

Proof. **Reflexivity:** Use the first parts of Axioms (12) and (13). **Transitivity:** Use the second parts of Axioms (12) and (13) together with the induction rules.

Remark also that Axioms (12) and (13) guarantee that $\left(R_c^{\square}\right)^{\star} \subseteq R_c^{\boxed{\star}}$. Nevertheless, as it is usually the case when one axiomatises a modal logic in which one connective is interpreted by the reflexive transitive closure of the relation interpreting another connective, it might be the case that $\left(R_c^{\square}\right)^{\star} \neq R_c^{\boxed{\star}}$.

Lemma 10 (Truth Lemma). *For all formulas φ and for all $x \in W_c$, (1) If $\varphi \in x$ then $\mathcal{M}_c, x \models \varphi$; (2) if $\varphi \notin x$ then $\mathcal{M}_c, x \not\models \varphi$.*

Proof. By induction on φ. We only present the proof for the case of $\boxed{\star}$. Assume that $\boxed{\star}\psi \in x$ but $\mathcal{M}_c, x \not\models \boxed{\star}\psi$. From the latter assumption it follows that there exists $x', y \in W_c$ such that $x \leqslant_c x'$, $x'R_c^{\boxed{\star}}y$ and $\mathcal{M}_c, y \not\models \psi$. Since $x \leqslant_c x'$ then $\boxed{\star}\psi \in x'$. On the other hand, from $x'R_c^{\boxed{\star}}y$, $\mathcal{M}_c, y \not\models \psi$ and the induction hypothesis we conclude that $\boxed{\star}\psi \notin x'$, which is a contradiction.

Reciprocally, assume that $\mathcal{M}_c, x \models \boxed{\star}\psi$ but $\boxed{\star}\psi \notin x$. Let $u = \boxed{\star}x$. Remark that $u \not\vdash \{\psi\} \cup \{\chi \mid \textcircled{\star}\chi \notin x\}$. By Lindenbaum Lemma, let $y \in W_c$ be such that $u \subseteq y$ and $y \not\vdash \{\psi\} \cup \{\chi \mid \textcircled{\star}\chi \notin x\}$. Note that $\boxed{\star}x \subseteq y$ and $\textcircled{\star}y \subseteq x$. Hence, $xR_c^{\boxed{\star}}y$. Since $y \not\vdash \psi$, therefore $\psi \notin y$ and, by induction hypothesis, $\mathcal{M}_c, y \not\models \psi$, which contradicts $\mathcal{M}_c, x \models \boxed{\star}\psi$ and $xR_c^{\boxed{\star}}y$.

6   Filtration

In order to repair the main defect of $\mathcal{M}_c$, namely $\left(R_c^{\square}\right)^* \neq R_c^{\boxast}$, the traditional tool, filtration, consists in identifying prime sets in W_c that contain the same formulas from the least closed set of formulas containing a given formula. We had to change the definition of filtration, seeing that, within the context of THT, the ordinary definition of filtration as the one presented in [11, Chap. 9] is not appropriate. Given a normal THT model $\mathcal{M} = \langle W, \leqslant, R^{\square}, R^{\boxast}, V \rangle$ and a closed set Σ of formulas, we define the equivalence relation $\equiv_\Sigma$ on W as: $x \equiv_\Sigma y$ iff for all $\varphi \in \Sigma$, $\mathcal{M}, x \models \varphi$ iff $\mathcal{M}, y \models \varphi$.

Lemma 11. *For all $x, y \in W_c$, if $x \equiv_\Sigma y$ then $\widehat{x} \equiv_\Sigma \widehat{y}$.*

The equivalence class of $x \in W$ with respect to $\equiv_\Sigma$ is denoted by $[x]$. We say that a THT model $\mathcal{M}_\Sigma = \langle W_\Sigma, \leqslant_\Sigma, R_\Sigma^{\square}, R_\Sigma^{\boxast}, V_\Sigma \rangle$ is a filtration of $\mathcal{M}$, with respect to Σ, iff $W_\Sigma = W_{|\equiv_\Sigma}$ and for all $x, y \in W$:

1. if $x \leqslant y$ then $[x] \leqslant_\Sigma [y]$;
2. for all $\varphi \to \psi \in \Sigma$, if $[x] \leqslant_\Sigma [y]$, $\mathcal{M}, x \models \varphi \to \psi$ and $\mathcal{M}, y \models \varphi$ then $\mathcal{M}, y \models \psi$;
3. if $xR^{\square}y$ then there exists $z \in W$ s. t. $[x]R_\Sigma^{\square}[z]$ and $[y] \leqslant_\Sigma [z]$;
4. if $xR^{\square}y$ then there exists $t \in W$ s. t. $[t]R_\Sigma^{\square}[y]$ and $[x] \leqslant_\Sigma [t]$;
5. for all $\square\varphi \in \Sigma$, if $[x]R_\Sigma^{\square}[y]$ and $\mathcal{M}, x \models \square\varphi$ then $\mathcal{M}, y \models \varphi$;
6. for all $\lozenge\varphi \in \Sigma$, if $[x]R_\Sigma^{\square}[y]$ and $\mathcal{M}, y \models \varphi$ then $\mathcal{M}, x \models \lozenge\varphi$;
7. if $xR^{\boxast}y$ then there exists $z \in W$ s. t. $[x]R_\Sigma^{\boxast}[z]$ and $[y] \leqslant_\Sigma [z]$;
8. if $xR^{\boxast}y$ then there exists $t \in W$ s. t. $[t]R_\Sigma^{\boxast}[y]$ and $[x] \leqslant_\Sigma [t]$;
9. for all $\boxast\varphi \in \Sigma$, if $[x]R_\Sigma^{\boxast}[y]$ and $\mathcal{M}, x \models \boxast\varphi$ then $\mathcal{M}, y \models \varphi$;
10. for all $\varobslash\varphi \in \Sigma$, if $[x]R_\Sigma^{\boxast}[y]$ and $\mathcal{M}, y \models \varphi$ then $\mathcal{M}, x \models \varobslash\varphi$;
11. for all $p \in At \cap \Sigma$, $p \in V_\Sigma([x])$ iff $p \in V(x)$.

Lemma 12 (Filtration Lemma). *Let $\mathcal{M} = \langle W, \leqslant, R^{\square}, R^{\boxast}, V \rangle$ be a normal THT model, Σ be a closed set of formulas and $\mathcal{M}_\Sigma = \langle W_\Sigma, \leqslant_\Sigma, R_\Sigma^{\square}, R_\Sigma^{\boxast}, V_\Sigma \rangle$ be a filtration of $\mathcal{M}$ with respect to Σ. For all $\varphi \in \Sigma$ and for all $x \in W$, $\mathcal{M}, x \models \varphi$ iff $\mathcal{M}_\Sigma, [x] \models \varphi$.*

Proof. By induction on φ.

We will be interested in the filtration $\mathcal{M}_\Sigma$ of $\mathcal{M}_c$ with respect to the least closed set Σ containing a given formula φ_0. Remind that the quotient of W_c by $\equiv_\Sigma$ is finite. The relational structure $\mathcal{M}_\Sigma = \langle W_\Sigma, \leqslant_\Sigma, R_\Sigma^{\square}, R_\Sigma^{\boxast}, V_\Sigma \rangle$ is defined as follows:

1. $W_\Sigma = W_{c|\equiv_\Sigma}$;
2. $[x] \leqslant_\Sigma [y]$ iff $x \equiv_\Sigma \circ \leqslant_c \circ \equiv_\Sigma y$;
3. $[x]R_\Sigma^{\square}[y]$ iff $x \equiv_\Sigma \circ R_c^{\square} \circ \equiv_\Sigma y$;

4. $[x]R_\Sigma^{\boxast}[y]$ iff $[x]\left(R_\Sigma^{\square}\right)^*[y]$;

5. $V_\Sigma([x]) = V_c(x) \cap \Sigma$.

Lemma 13. *For all $x, y \in W_c$, $[x] \leqslant_\Sigma [y]$ iff $x \equiv_\Sigma y$ or $\widehat{x} \equiv_\Sigma y$.*

In the sequel, φ and ψ will be Σ-formulas. For each $t \in W_c$, let

$$\Phi_t = \bigwedge_{\varphi \in t} \varphi \wedge \bigwedge_{\varphi \notin t} \neg\varphi \wedge \bigwedge_{\varphi \in\, t \,\setminus\, t} \neg\neg\varphi \wedge \bigwedge_{\varphi,\, \psi \in\, t \,\setminus\, t} (\varphi \to \psi).$$

By using the results proved in [3] we can deduce that for all $s \in W_c$, $\mathcal{M}_c, s \models \Phi_t$ iff $[s] = [t]$ or $[s] = [\widehat{t}]$. Now W_Σ is finite, as Σ is, so for all $D \subseteq W_\Sigma$ let
$\Psi_D = \bigvee\limits_{[t] \in D} \Phi_t$.

Lemma 14. *For any set $D \subseteq W_\Sigma$ and for all $x \in W_c$, $\mathcal{M}_c, x \models \Psi_D$ iff $\exists [z] \in D$ s. t. $[x] = [z]$ or $[x] = [\widehat{z}]$.*

Lemma 15 (Filtrated Model). *The aforementioned filtrated model, $\mathcal{M}_\Sigma$, is a filtration of the canonical model $\mathcal{M}_c$.*

Proof. We only study the Conditions 7 and 9.

- **Condition 7**: Suppose $xR_c^{\boxtimes}y$ and let $D = \{[z] \in W_\Sigma \mid$ there exists $t \in W_c$ s.t. $[x]R_\Sigma^{\boxtimes}[t]$ and $[z] \leqslant_\Sigma [t]\}$. Let us prove that $[y] \in D$. Remark that for all $[z] \in W_\Sigma$, if $[\widehat{z}] \in D$ then $[z] \in D$. Suppose by contradiction that $[y] \in (W_\Sigma \backslash D)$. Remark that $[x] \in D$. Let $\Psi_{W_\Sigma \backslash D}$ be the characteristic formula of $W_\Sigma \backslash D$. Since $[y] \in (W_\Sigma \backslash D)$ then, by Lemma 14, $\mathcal{M}_c, y \models \Psi_{W_\Sigma \backslash D}$. Since $xR_c^{\boxtimes}y$, it holds that $\mathcal{M}_c, x \models \lozengedot \Psi_{W_\Sigma \backslash D}$. Since $[x] \in D$, then $\mathcal{M}_c, x \not\models \Psi_{W_\Sigma \backslash D}$ and, therefore, $\mathcal{M}_c, x \not\models \lozengedot \Psi_{W_\Sigma \backslash D} \to \Psi_{W_\Sigma \backslash D}$. Consequently $\lozengedot \Psi_{W_\Sigma \backslash D} \to \Psi_{W_\Sigma \backslash D} \notin THT$. From the Induction rule (15) we conclude that $\lozenge\Psi_{W_\Sigma \backslash D} \to \Psi_{W_\Sigma \backslash D} \notin THT$. This means that there exists $u \in W_c$ such that $\mathcal{M}_c, u \models \lozenge\Psi_{W_\Sigma \backslash D}$ and $\mathcal{M}_c, u \not\models \Psi_{W_\Sigma \backslash D}$ (therefore $[u] \in D$). From the latter it follows that there exists $t \in W_c$ s.t. $[x]R_\Sigma^{\boxtimes}[t]$ and $[u] \leqslant [t]$, while from the former we get that there exists $v \in W_c$ such that $uR_c^{\square}v$ and $\mathcal{M}_c, v \models \Psi_{W_\Sigma \backslash D}$ (thus $[v] \notin D$). Since $[u] \leqslant_\Sigma [t]$, therefore by Lemma 13 either $u \equiv_\Sigma t$ or $\widehat{u} \equiv_\Sigma t$. In the former case $[u] = [t]$ and we have: $[u]R_\Sigma^{\square}[v]$, $[t]R_\Sigma^{\square}[v]$ and $[x]R_\Sigma^{\boxtimes}[v]$. Thus $[v] \in D$ and $\mathcal{M}_c, v \not\models \Psi_{W_\Sigma \backslash D}$: a contradiction. In the latter case, $[t] = [\widehat{u}]$ and we have: $[\widehat{u}]R_\Sigma^{\square}[\widehat{v}]$, $[t]R_\Sigma^{\square}[\widehat{v}]$ and $[x]R_\Sigma^{\boxtimes}[\widehat{v}]$. Hence, $[v] \in D$ and $\mathcal{M}_c, v \not\models \Psi_{W_\Sigma \backslash D}$: a contradiction.

- **Condition 9**: Suppose $[x]R_\Sigma^{\boxtimes}[y]$ and let $\boxtimes\varphi \in \Sigma$. Suppose $\mathcal{M}_c, x \models \boxtimes\varphi$ and let $k \in \mathbb{N}$ be such that $[x]\left(R_\Sigma^{\square}\right)^k [y]$. Such k exists by definition of $R_\Sigma^{\boxtimes}$. By induction on k, we demonstrate $\mathcal{M}_c, y \models \varphi$. Firstly, assume $k = 0$, therefore $[x] = [y]$, which means that $x \equiv_\Sigma y$. From $\mathcal{M}_c, x \models \boxtimes\varphi$ and Axiom (12) we conclude that $\mathcal{M}_c, y \models \varphi$. For the inductive step, assume $k \geqslant 1$ and let $[z]$ be such that $[x]R_\Sigma^{\square}[z]$ and $[z]\left(R_\Sigma^{\square}\right)^{k-1} [y]$. From $\mathcal{M}_c, x \models \boxtimes\varphi$ and Axiom (12) we conclude that $\mathcal{M}_c, x \models \square\boxtimes\varphi$. Since Σ is closed and $\boxtimes\varphi \in \Sigma$, therefore $\square\boxtimes\varphi \in \Sigma$. From $[x]R_\Sigma^{\square}[z]$ and Condition 5 of Filtration we conclude that $\mathcal{M}_c, z \models \boxtimes\varphi$. Finally from $[z]\left(R_\Sigma^{\square}\right)^{k-1} [y]$ and the induction hypothesis it follows that $\mathcal{M}_c, y \models \varphi$.

Lemma 16. *For all* $[x], [y], [z] \in W_\Sigma$, *if* $[x] \leqslant_\Sigma [y]$ *and* $[x] \leqslant_\Sigma [z]$ *then* $[x] = [y]$ *or* $[x] = [z]$ *or* $[y] = [z]$.

Proof. Suppose that $[x] \leqslant_\Sigma [y]$ and $[x] \leqslant_\Sigma [z]$. Let x', x'', y' and z'' in W_c be such that $x \equiv_\Sigma x' \leqslant_c y' \equiv_\Sigma y$ and $x \equiv_\Sigma x'' \leqslant_c z'' \equiv_\Sigma z$. Moreover, suppose that $[x][y]$, $[x] \neq [z]$ and $[y] \neq [z]$. Without loss of generality, let ϕ, ψ and χ in Σ be such that $(\mathcal{M}_c, x \not\models \phi$ and $\mathcal{M}_c, y \models \phi)$, $(\mathcal{M}_c, x \not\models \chi$ and $\mathcal{M}_c, z \models \chi)$ and $(\mathcal{M}_c, y \models \psi$ and $\mathcal{M}_c, z \not\models \psi)$. Since $\mathcal{M}_c, y \models \psi$ then $\mathcal{M}_c, y \not\models \neg\psi$ and, together with the definition of $[x] \leqslant_\Sigma [y]$, $\mathcal{M}_c, x \not\models \neg\psi$. Moreover, from $x \equiv_\Sigma x''$ and $\mathcal{M}_c, x \not\models \phi$ we conclude that $\mathcal{M}_c, x'' \not\models \phi \vee \neg\psi$ and, by means of Hosoi axiom, it follows that $\mathcal{M}_c, x'' \models \phi \to \psi$. Since $x'' \leqslant_c z''$ then $\mathcal{M}_c, z'' \models \phi \to \psi$. Apart from this, since $z'' \equiv_\Sigma z$, $\mathcal{M}_c, z \models \phi$ and $\mathcal{M}_c, z \not\models \psi$ then $\mathcal{M}_c, z'' \not\models \psi$ and $\mathcal{M}_c, z'' \models \phi$. Finally, from $\mathcal{M}_c, z'' \models \phi \to \psi$ we reach a contradiction.

Proposition 9. $\mathcal{M}_\Sigma$ *is normal.*

Proof. Condition (1) of normality follows from Lemma 16. To prove Conditions (2) and (3) it is sufficient to prove that if $[x]R_\Sigma^\square[y]$ (respectively $[x]R_\Sigma^\square[y]$) then $[\widehat{x}]R_\Sigma^\square[\widehat{y}]$ (respectively $[\widehat{x}]R_\Sigma^{\boxed{\star}}[\widehat{y}]$). The proof for $R_\Sigma^\square$ follows from Lemma 11 and Proposition 6 while the proof for $R_\Sigma^{\boxed{\star}}$ follows a similar argument.

Lemma 17. *For any formula* φ *and* $x \in W_c$.

(1) *If* $\boxed{\star}\varphi \in \Sigma$ *and* $\boxed{\star}\varphi \notin x$ *then there exists* $y \in W_c$ *such that* $[x]R_\Sigma^{\boxed{\star}}[y]$ *and* $\varphi \notin y$;

(2) *If* $\Diamond\!\!\!\star\,\varphi \in \Sigma$ *and* $\Diamond\!\!\!\star\,\varphi \in x$ *then there exists* $y \in W_c$ *such that* $[x]R_\Sigma^{\boxed{\star}}[y]$ *and* $\varphi \in y$;

Proof. (1) From $\boxed{\star}\varphi \notin x$ and Lemma 10 we conclude that $\mathcal{M}_c, x \not\models \boxed{\star}\varphi$, so there exists $z \in W_c$ such that $xR_c^{\boxed{\star}}z$ and $\mathcal{M}_c, z \not\models \varphi$. From Condition 8 of filtration we conclude either $[x]R_\Sigma^{\boxed{\star}}[z]$ or $[\widehat{x}]R_\Sigma^{\boxed{\star}}[z]$. In the first case, take $y = z$. In the second case, we follow the argument as follows: from $\mathcal{M}_c, z \not\models \varphi$ and Condition 9 of filtration we conclude that $\mathcal{M}_c, \widehat{x} \not\models \boxed{\star}\varphi$. By following an argument as in Proposition 6 $\mathcal{M}_c, x \not\models \boxed{\star}\neg\neg\varphi$, thus there exists $t \in W_c$ such that $xR_c^{\boxed{\star}}t$ and $\mathcal{M}_c, t \not\models \neg\neg\varphi$ (as a consequence, $\mathcal{M}_c, t \not\models \varphi$ and $\mathcal{M}_c, \widehat{t} \not\models \varphi$). Finally by applying the Condition 7 of filtration, we conclude that $[x]R_\Sigma^{\boxed{\star}}[t]$ or $[x]R_\Sigma^{\boxed{\star}}[\widehat{t}]$. In the first case take $y = t$ while, in the second one take $y = \widehat{t}$. (2) From $\Diamond\!\!\!\star\,\varphi \in \Sigma$, $\Diamond\!\!\!\star\,\varphi \in x$ and Lemma 10 we conclude that $\mathcal{M}_c, x \models \Diamond\!\!\!\star\,\varphi$ and, therefore, there exists $y \in W_c$ such that $xR_c^{\boxed{\star}}y$ and $\mathcal{M}_c, y \models \varphi$ (and $\mathcal{M}_c, \widehat{y} \models \varphi$). Then, due to Condition 7 of filtration it follows that either $[x]R_\Sigma^{\boxed{\star}}[y]$ or $[x]R_\Sigma^{\boxed{\star}}[\widehat{y}]$. We conclude the proof by saying that it is sufficient to take y in the first case and $\widehat{y}$ in the second one to reach the condition.

Lemma 18. *Let* $\square\varphi \in \Sigma$ *be a temporal formula and* $x \in W_c$. *The following conditions are equivalent: (1)* $\mathcal{M}_c, x \models \square\varphi$. *(2)* $\forall y \in W_c$, *if* $([x]R_\Sigma^\square[y]$ *then* $\mathcal{M}_c, y \models \varphi)$ *(3)* $\exists y \in W_c ([x]R_\Sigma^\square[y]$ *and* $\mathcal{M}_c, y \models \varphi)$.

Proof. **(1)**⇒ **(2)**: Assume there exists $y \in W_c$ such that $[x]R_{\Sigma}^{\square}[y]$ and $\mathcal{M}_c, y \not\models \varphi$. Thanks to the Condition 5 of filtration we get $\mathcal{M}_c, y \models \varphi$: a contradiction. **(2)**⇒ **(3)**: Take $[x] \in W_c$. Since $R_{\Sigma}^{\square}$ is serial, there exists $[y] \in W_{\Sigma}$ such that $[x]R_{\Sigma}^{\square}[y]$. From 18 and $[x]R_{\Sigma}^{\square}[y]$ we obtain (3). **(3)** ⇒ **(1)**: By definition of $[x]R_{\Sigma}^{\square}[y]$, there exist $x', y' \in W_c$ such that $x \equiv_{\Sigma} x' R_c^{\square} y' \equiv_{\Sigma} y$. From $\mathcal{M}_c, y \models \varphi$ and Axiom (2) it follows that $\mathcal{M}_c, x \models \square\varphi$.

Lemma 19. *Let $\lozenge\varphi \in \Sigma$ be a temporal formula and $x \in W_c$. The following conditions are equivalent: (1) $\mathcal{M}_c, x \not\models \lozenge\varphi$. (2) $\exists y \in W_c \left([x]R_{\Sigma}^{\square}[y] \text{ and } \mathcal{M}_c, y \not\models \varphi\right)$ (3) $\forall y \in W_c$, if $\left([x]R_{\Sigma}^{\square}[y] \text{ then } \mathcal{M}_c, y \not\models \varphi\right)$.*

Proof. Similar to the proof of Lemma 18.

7   Determinisation

The filtrated model defined in Sect. 6 possesses the normality conditions (1) and (2). Since $R_{\Sigma}^{\square}$ is serial and $R_{\Sigma}^{\boxed{\star}}$ is equal to the reflexive transitive closure of the $R_{\Sigma}^{\square}$, $\mathcal{M}_{\Sigma}$ would be standard if $R_{\Sigma}^{\square}$ were deterministic. The property of determinism is not preserved by filtration. In this section we show how to extract a deterministic model from $\mathcal{M}_{\Sigma}$. Before that, we must introduce the concepts of chain and defect. Let $S = \mathbb{N} \times \{\boxed{\star}, \blacklozenge\} \times \Sigma$. Remark that S is countable. Let $(k_0, \sigma_0, \psi_0), (k_1, \sigma_1, \psi_1), \cdots$ be an enumeration on S where each triple is repeated infinitely many times. A *chain* consists of a finite sequence $([x_0], \cdots, [x_n])$ of elements of W_{Σ} such that for all $i < n$, $[x_i]R_{\Sigma}^{\square}[x_{i+1}]$. A triple $(k, \boxed{\star}, \psi) \in S$ is a *defect* of the chain $([x_0], \cdots [x_n])$ if (1) $k \leqslant n$; (2) $\boxed{\star}\psi \notin x_k$; (3) for all i, $k \leqslant i \leqslant n, \psi \in x_i$. Similarly, a triple $(k, \blacklozenge, \psi) \in S$ is a defect of the sequence $([x_0], \cdots [x_n])$ if (1) $k \leqslant n$; (2) $\blacklozenge\psi \in x_k$; (3) for all i, $k \leqslant i \leqslant n, \psi \notin x_i$. Let φ_0 be a formula such that $\varphi_0 \notin \text{THT}$. Let $x_0 \in W_c$ be such that $\varphi_0 \notin x_0$. We define an infinite sequence $([x_0], [x_1], \cdots)$ of elements of W_{Σ} such that $[x_0]R_{\Sigma}^{\square}[x_1]R_{\Sigma}^{\square}[x_3] \cdots$ as follows: let $S_0 = ([x_0])$. Let $a \geqslant 0$ and $S_a = ([x_0], \cdots, [x_m])$ be a sequence of elements of W_{Σ} such that $[x_0]R_{\Sigma}^{\square} \cdots R_{\Sigma}^{\square}[x_m]$. We consider the following cases:

- Case "(k_a, σ_a, ψ_a) is not a defect of S_a": In this case let $[y] \in W_{\Sigma}$ be such that $[x_m]R_{\Sigma}^{\square}[y]$ and define $S_{a+1} = ([x_0], \cdots, [x_m], [y])$.
- Case "(k_a, σ_a, ψ_a) is a defect of S_a and $\sigma_a = \boxed{\star}$": Hence, $k_a \leqslant x_m$, $\boxed{\star}\psi_a \notin x_m$ and for all i, $k_a \leqslant i \leqslant m$, $\psi_a \in x_i$. By Lemma 7, $\boxed{\star}\psi_a \notin x_m$. By Lemma 17, let $[y] \in W_{\Sigma}$ be such that $[x_m]R_{\Sigma}^{\boxed{\star}}[y]$ and $\psi_a \notin y$. Let $[y_0], \cdots, [y_n] \in W_{\Sigma}$ be such that $[y_0] = [x_m]$, $[y_n] = [y]$ and $[y_0]R_{\Sigma}^{\square}[y_1] \cdots R_{\Sigma}^{\square}[y_n]$. We define $S_{a+1} = ([x_0], \cdots, [x_m], [y_1], \cdots, [y_n])$.
- Case "(k_a, σ_k, ψ_k) is a defect of S_a and $\sigma_a = \blacklozenge$": This case is similar to the previous one.

Now, let $\mathcal{M}_d = \langle W_d, \leqslant_d, R_d^{\square}, R_d^{\boxed{\star}}, V_d \rangle$ be the model defined as follows:

- $W_d = \mathbb{N} \times \{h, t\}$;

- $(i_1, \alpha_1) \leqslant_d (i_2, \alpha_2)$ iff $i_1 = i_2$ and either $\alpha_1 = h$ or $\alpha_2 = t$;
- $(i_1, \alpha_1) R_d^{\square} (i_2, \alpha_2)$ iff $i_1 + 1 = i_2$ and $\alpha_1 = \alpha_2$;
- $(i_1, \alpha_1) R_d^{\boxed{\star}} (i_2, \alpha_2)$ iff $i_1 \leqslant i_2$ and $\alpha_1 = \alpha_2$;
- $V_d((i, \alpha)) = \{p \in At \mid p \in x_i \cap \Sigma\}$ if $\alpha = h$ and $\{p \in At \mid p \in \widehat{x_i} \cap \Sigma\}$ otherwise.

Lemma 20 (Truth Lemma). *Let $\varphi \in \Sigma$. For all $i \in \mathbb{N}$ and for all $\alpha \in \{h, t\}$, the following conditions are equivalent: (1) $\mathcal{M}_d, (i, \alpha) \models \varphi$; (2) $\mathcal{M}_\Sigma, [x_i] \models \varphi$.*

Proof. By induction on φ. The case for atomic formulas follows from the definition of V_d. The cases for $\bot$, $\wedge$, $\vee$ and $\rightarrow$ are left to the reader. The cases for $\square$ and $\lozenge$ follow from Lemmas 18 and 19. The cases for $\boxed{\star}$ and $\diamondsuit$ follow from the definition of $\mathcal{M}_d$.

And now, the grand finale:

Proposition 10. *Let φ be a formula. The following conditions are equivalent: (1) $\varphi \in THT$; (2) $THT \models \varphi$.*

Proof. (1) $\Rightarrow$ (2): By proposition 4. (2) $\Rightarrow$ (1): Suppose $\varphi \notin THT$. Let $x_0 \in W_c$ be such that $\varphi \notin x_0$. By Lemma 10, $\mathcal{M}_c, x_0 \not\models \varphi$. Let Σ be the least closed set of formulas containing φ. By Lemmas 12 and 15, $\mathcal{M}_\Sigma, [x_0] \not\models \varphi$. By Lemma 20, $\mathcal{M}_d, (0, \alpha) \not\models \varphi$. Since $\mathcal{M}_d$ is standard, therefore $THT \not\models \varphi$.

8   Conclusion

Much remains to be done. For example, suppose the language is extended by the temporal constructs $\mathcal{U}$ (until) and $\mathcal{R}$ (release). In that case, within the context of THT-models, can we demonstrate that these temporal constructs are not interdefinable? And how to axiomatise the set of all THT-valid formulas? One may also consider, for this extended language, a van Benthem characterization theorem. Its proof will probably necessitates the definition of an appropriate notion of bisimulation similar to the one considered by de Rijke and Kurtonina [14]. Now, what do these problems become when the language, restricted to the temporal constructs $\mathcal{U}$ and $\mathcal{R}$, is interpreted over the nonnegative rationals or the nonnegative reals? In that case, THT-models will be of the form $\mathcal{M} = \langle H, T \rangle$ where $H : \mathbb{Q}^+$ (or $\mathbb{R}^+) \rightarrow 2^{At}$ and $T : \mathbb{Q}^+$ (or $\mathbb{R}^+) \rightarrow 2^{At}$ are such that $H(i) \subseteq T(i)$ for each $i \geqslant 0$. In other respect, for the language extended by the temporal constructs $\mathcal{U}$ (until), $\mathcal{R}$ (release), $\mathcal{S}$ (since) and $\mathcal{T}$ (trigger), when interpreted over the set of all integers, can we demonstrate that these temporal constructs are not interdefinable? When interpreted over Dedekind-complete linear orders, can one obtain for this language a THT version of Kamp's Theorem [13]? Finally, if one prefers partial orders to linear orders then one may want to axiomatise the HT version of branching time logics like CTL.

References

1. Aguado, F., Cabalar, P., Pearce, D., Pérez, G., Vidal, C.: A denotational semantics for equilibrium logic. TPLP **15**(4–5), 620–634 (2015)
2. Cabalar, P., Diéguez, M.: Strong equivalence of non-monotonic temporal theories. In: Proceedings of the 14th International Conference on Principles of Knowledge Representation and Reasoning (KR 2014), Vienna (2014)
3. Cabalar, P., Ferraris, P.: Propositional theories are strongly equivalent to logic programs. Theory Pract. Log. Program. **7**(6), 745–759 (2007)
4. Cabalar, P., Pérez Vega, G.: Temporal equilibrium logic: a first approach. In: Moreno Díaz, R., Pichler, F., Quesada Arencibia, A. (eds.) EUROCAST 2007. LNCS, vol. 4739, pp. 241–248. Springer, Heidelberg (2007). doi:10.1007/978-3-540-75867-9_31
5. Cabalar, P., Diéguez, M., Vidal, C.: An infinitary encoding of temporal equilibrium logic. TPLP **15**(4–5), 666–680 (2015)
6. Dalen, D.V.: Intuitionistic logic. In: Gabbay, D., Guenthner, F. (eds.) Handbook of Philosophical Logic, vol. 166, pp. 225–339. Springer, Netherlands (1986)
7. van Dalen, D.: Logic and Structure. Universitext. Springer, Heidelberg (1989)
8. Fariñas del Cerro, L., Herzig, A., Su, E.I.: Epistemic equilibrium logic. In: Proceedings of the Twenty-Fourth International Joint Conference on Artificial Intelligence, IJCAI 2015, Buenos Aires, 25–31 July 2015, pp. 2964–2970 (2015)
9. Servi, G.F.: Axiomatisations for some intuitionistic modal logics. Rend. Sem. Mat. Univers. Polit. Torino. **42**, 179–194 (1984). Torino, Italy
10. Gelfond, M., Lifschitz, V.: The stable model semantics for logic programming. In: Proceedings of the 5th International Conference on Logic Programming (ICLP 1988), Seattle, pp. 1070–1080 (1988)
11. Goldblatt, R.: Logics of time and computation. No. 7 in CSLI Lecture Notes, Center for the Study of Language and Information, Stanford, 2 edn. (1992)
12. Heyting, A.: Die formalen Regeln der intuitionistischen Logik. Sitzungsberichte der Preussischen Akademie der Wissenschaften. Physikalisch-mathematische Klasse, Deütsche Akademie der Wissenschaften zu Berlin, Mathematisch-Naturwissenschaftliche Klasse (1930)
13. Kamp, H.: Tense logic and the theory of linear order. Ph.D. thesis, University of California, Los Angeles (1968)
14. Kurtonina, N., de Rijke, M.: Bisimulations for temporal logic. J. Log. Lang. Inf. **6**(4), 403–425 (1997)
15. Lifschitz, V., Pearce, D., Valverde, A.: A characterization of strong equivalence for logic programs with variables. In: Baral, C., Brewka, G., Schlipf, J. (eds.) LPNMR 2007. LNCS (LNAI), vol. 4483, pp. 188–200. Springer, Heidelberg (2007). doi:10.1007/978-3-540-72200-7_17
16. Lukasiewicz, J.: Die logik und das grundlagenproblem. Les Entreties de Zürich sur les Fondaments et la Méthode des Sciences Mathématiques **12**(6–9), 82–100 (1938)
17. Marek, V., Truszczyński, M.: Stable Models and an Alternative Logic Programming Paradigm, pp. 169–181. Springer, Heidelberg (1999)
18. Niemelä, I.: Logic programs with stable model semantics as a constraint programming paradigm. Ann. Math. Artif. Intell. **25**(3–4), 241–273 (1999)
19. Pearce, D.: Equilibrium logic. Ann. Math. Artif. Intell. **47**(1–2), 3–41 (2006)
20. Pearce, D., Valverde, A.: Quantified equilibrium logic and foundations for answer set programs. In: Garcia de la Banda, M., Pontelli, E. (eds.) ICLP 2008. LNCS, vol. 5366, pp. 546–560. Springer, Heidelberg (2008). doi:10.1007/978-3-540-89982-2_46

21. Pnueli, A.: The temporal logic of programs. In: Proceedings of the 18th Annual Symposium on Foundations of Computer Science, Providence, pp. 46–57 (1977)
22. Simpson, A.K.: The proof theory and semantics of intuitionistic modal logic. Ph.D. thesis, University of Edinburgh (1994). http://homepages.inf.ed.ac.uk/als/Research/thesis.ps.gz

On Logics of Group Belief
in Structured Coalitions

Philippe Balbiani[1], David Pearce[2], and Levan Uridia[3]([⊠])

[1] Université de Toulouse, Toulouse, France
Philippe.Balbiani@irit.fr
[2] Universidad Politécnica de Madrid, Madrid, Spain
david.pearce@upm.es
[3] Razmadze Institute of Mathematics, Tbilisi, Georgia
l.uridia@freeuni.edu.ge

Abstract. In the study of group belief formation, groups of agents are often assumed to possess a topological structure. Here we investigate some ways in which this topological structure may provide the semantical basis for logics of group belief. We impose a partial order on a set of agents first to be able to express preferences of agents by their doxastic abilities, secondly to express the idea of a coalition (well formed group) and thirdly to give a natural semantics for the group belief operator. We define the group belief of a set of agents in two different ways and study their corresponding logics. We also study a logic where doxastic preference is expressed by a binary operator. We prove completeness and discuss correspondences between the logics.

1 Introduction

An important concept in the study of collective intentionality as well as group reasoning is that of *group belief*. The nature of group belief has been analysed by a number of scholars and is of interest in areas such as philosophy, psychology, logic, social sciences and computer science. Quinton [9] for example discussed the *summative* view whereby a group G has a group belief in a proposition p if most of the members of G believe that p; here 'most' can refer to a simple numerical majority or perhaps to a majority of members of a certain kind. More recent work in the field of social ontology has taken a non-summative view according to which individual beliefs do not play such an important role in forming the group belief [6,10]. To have a group belief that p, in this kind of a non-summative, agreement-based sense, it is neither sufficient nor even necessary that the group members individually believe p. Instead, it is required that they together agree that as a group they believe that p. Different versions of the summative and non-summative views have recently been analysed by Gaudou *et al.* [5] who develop in detail a modal logic of group belief and compare their formal system to different philosophical accounts of the group belief concept.

In the discussion of group belief an important feature is that a group should be a constituted collective. In the approach of [5] the nature of the constituted

© Springer International Publishing AG 2016
L. Michael and A. Kakas (Eds.): JELIA 2016, LNAI 10021, pp. 97–111, 2016.
DOI: 10.1007/978-3-319-48758-8_7

group is given by the logic. More precisely, the logic is equipped with a possible worlds semantics whose accessibility relation determines the nature of the group. This idea seems to work well if one assumes that each group is constituted by a unique set of agents A, but it may be problematic if a given set of individuals constitutes two or more different groups. Suppose for example that the university darts team happens to be co-extensive with the graduate admissions committee. Their group beliefs will no doubt be different in the two contexts in which they act. For instance the judgement that Phil Taylor is the greatest ever darts player might be a belief of the darts team but not of the admission committee. This difference in group beliefs will not be manifest in approaches like that of [5]. The authors are aware of this limitation. In another paper devoted to the logic of group *acceptance* [8] they have introduced the idea of an *institutional context* that enters into the semantics of group attitudes. This is a formal device that allows one to distinguish the set of agents from the group or team situation in which they are acting. It supplies an additional parameter of evaluation but doesn't impose any structure on the groups themselves.

A different kind of approach has been explored in work on judgement aggregation. For example, List and Pettit [7] discuss group agency and group beliefs by assuming that some organizational structure is associated with the groups. This structure can be understood in at least two apparently different senses. In one sense it refers to mechanisms such as voting rights and procedures that may be in place in order for group judgements to be obtained by some rational process from the beliefs and preferences of individual group members. Such mechanisms may be thought of as external to the agents themselves, since they reflect group features that may persist even if the set of agents that constitutes the group changes over time. However, [7] also discusses ways in which a group may be structured in a more internal sense. An example is when large judgmental tasks are decomposed into several smaller tasks and the corresponding group judgements for these tasks are allocated to suitable subgroups. As List and Pettit observe [7] (pp. 94–97), not all group members may have the same level of expertise, so it may be rationally justified (at least in theory) to assign judgement subtasks to say expert subgroups and then use a further aggregation mechanism to form a final collective judgement for the whole group. In such cases the chosen decomposition may reflect properties of individual members (e.g. their expertise) and hence need not persist when members leave and enter the group. Nevertheless it seems clear that such structures are group-specific in kind, since if two different groups are composed of the same set of members, the associated group structures will carve up that set in different ways.

In this paper we also study the idea of groups having a structure, but using a different approach from that of [7]. We explore the effects of imposing a topological structure directly on the set of agents and without assuming that judgmental tasks are split into subtasks for resolution by a subgroup. One effect of our approach is that even if say the university darts team and the humanities graduate committee are composed of the same individuals, their constitution *qua* groups (hence their collective beliefs) may be different. Another effect is that the topological structure may reflect a natural ordering among agents, such as their level of knowledge of a certain domain, their abilities, their degree of commitment to a certain cause, or some other relevant criterion. We will deal with finite sets of agents and therefore the topological structure will amount to a partial ordering.[1] In real life situations one observes that arbitrary subsets of agents do not form a coalition. Usually coalitions are closed under some specific properties. Having structured groups makes it possible to formalise different versions of group belief and also explore the connections and differences between different approaches. In this paper we attempt to model both ideas simultaneously by considering partial orders on the sets of agents. It is known that such orders naturally model many existing real life social commitments.[2] Moreover with partial orders we may understand coalitions as those sets of agents which have certain properties according to the given order. In particular that they are downsets.

The paper is organised as follows. In Sect. 3 we define a logic $\mathcal{GB}1$ of group belief where group belief is defined in terms of shared belief. The group belief defined in this way inherits some properties of group belief discussed in [5] although it lacks the important property that group belief p implies that it is common belief that p is a group belief. To remedy this in Sect. 4 we define a logic $\mathcal{GB}2$ where group belief is defined in terms of common belief. This logic gains the property that was missing for the logic $\mathcal{GB}1$ but it loses another property satisfied by $\mathcal{GB}1$, in particular: that group belief does not imply the common belief of group members. In both Sects. 3 and 4 we extend the logics with a modal dependency axiom which links the partial order of agents to their belief sets. In both extended logics group belief collapses to the shared belief of group members. In Sect. 5 we consider pure multi-modal logic with an additional operator $a \preceq b$ to take control over the structure of agents. We prove several completeness results. Completeness for the logics $\mathcal{GB}1$ and $\mathcal{GB}2$ is relatively simple and closely based on already existing results, while completeness for the logic $\mathcal{GB}$ from Sect. 5 is nonstandard and uses a selection method.

2   Preliminaries

We recall some basic definitions and notions which will be used throughout the paper.

Definition 1. *A partial order on a set A is a relation $\leq \subseteq A \times A$ which is reflexive $\forall a \in A)(a \leq a)$ and transitive $(\forall a, b, c \in A)(a \leq b \wedge b \leq c \rightarrow a \leq c)$.*

Every partial order has a distinguished class of subsets called *downsets*

---

[1] Topological structures in groups are also used to formalise group attitudes in Dunin-Keplicz and Verbrugge [3]. As they emphasise, this structure may be based on power or dependency relations that reflect different social commitments. [3] considers different group topologies but the approach is somewhat different from ours. The topologies are mainly used to model different forms of communication between agents in a group. A related, formal account of group beliefs is studied in [2] using a concept of (group) epistemic profile to model doxastic reasoning. However epistemic profiles are an additional feature, not derived from the group topological structure.

[2] See e.g. [3] and further references given there.

Definition 2. *A subset D of a partial order $(A, \leq)$ is a downset if for every $d \in D$ and every $a \in A$ if $a \leq d$ then $a \in D$. The minimal downset containing the set $J \subseteq A$ will be denoted by $\overline{J}$. In other words $\overline{J} = \{a \in A \mid \exists b \in J \text{ s.t. } a \leq b\}$.*

Throughout the paper we will be working in a standard multimodal language enriched with different operators for common belief, shared belief group belief, etc. The language $\mathcal{L}$ is defined with an infinite set of propositional letters $p, q, r..$ and connectives $\vee, \wedge, \neg, \square_a$, for each $a \in A$, where A is a finite, partially ordered set $(A, \leq)$ of agents. Observe that the ordering of a set of agents A is common for both the syntax and semantics. Formulas are constructed in a standard way from the following recursive definition:

$$\phi := \mid p \mid \phi \vee \phi \mid \phi \wedge \phi \mid \neg \phi \mid \square_a \phi$$

for every $a \in A$ and $G \subseteq A$. For extensions of $\mathcal{L}$ with additional operators we will use the abbreviation $\mathcal{L}(\{O_i \mid 1 \leq i \leq n\})$ where each O_i is a new operator and the set of formulas is extended in an appropriate way i.e. in the construction of formulas we will have additional clauses

$$\phi := \mid p \mid \phi \vee \phi \mid \phi \wedge \phi \mid \neg \phi \mid \square_a \phi \mid O_i \phi$$

for every $a \in A$ and $i \in \{1, .., n\}$. For example $\mathcal{L}(\{E_J \mid J \subseteq A\}$ denotes the language $\mathcal{L}$ extended with operators E_J for each $J \subseteq A$. Throughout the paper the operators E_J, C_J and GB_J will stand for the *shared belief, common belief* and *group belief* operators respectively.

Shared belief is defined as the conjunction of beliefs of individual members of the group. i.e. a proposition p is a shared belief of the group J (abbreviated as $E_J p$) if every member of the group believes that p which means $\bigwedge_{i \in J} \square_i p$. The shared belief operator is definable in the basic language and hence the languages $\mathcal{L}$ and $\mathcal{L}(\{E_J \mid J \subseteq A\})$ have the same expressive power. This is not the case for common belief. Common belief is defined as the infinite iteration of individual beliefs of group members. Formally $C_J p$ iff $\bigwedge_{n \in \omega} E_J^n p$ which is an infinite conjunction and therefore is not a formula of the language $\mathcal{L}(\{E_J \mid J \subseteq A\}$. In general it is known that $\mathcal{L}(\{C_J \mid J \subseteq A\}$ is strictly more expressive then $\mathcal{L}$.

3   Logics of Group Belief

We define a modal logic of group belief in a structured set $(A, \leq)$ of agents, where the structure $\leq \subseteq A \times A$ is a partial order. Coalitions are formed by downsets. Therefore the structure of coalitions of agents will depend on the relation $\leq$ in question.

3.1   Syntax of $\mathcal{GB}1$

The language has two operators: for shared belief and for group belief. Shared belief (analogous to shared knowledge) has been considered and studied intensively, see for example [4]. We enrich the logic with a group belief operator where group belief is defined as the shared belief of the coalition to which the group belongs. Hence the two groups J and J' of agents have the same group belief if they both belong to the same coalition.

Definition 3. *The normal modal logic $\mathcal{GB}1$ is defined in a modal language $\mathcal{L}(\{E_J, GB_J \mid J \subseteq A\})$. Operators E_J and GB_J, stand for shared belief and group belief respectively.*

The axioms of $\mathcal{GB}1$ are all classical tautologies. Each box satisfies the K4 axioms for every $a \in A$, and in addition we have one axiom scheme for shared belief and one axiom scheme for the group belief,

$$\Box_a(p \to q) \to (\Box_a p \to \Box_a q) \tag{1}$$

$$\Box_a p \to \Box_a \Box_a p \tag{2}$$

$$E_J p \leftrightarrow \bigwedge_{a \in J} \Box_a p \tag{3}$$

$$GB_J p \leftrightarrow E_{\overline{J}} p \tag{4}$$

for every $J \subseteq A$. The rules of inference are: modus ponens, substitution and necessitation for each box modality.

Observe that the axiom of group belief operator uses symbol $\overline{J}$ from Definition 2, hence implicitly refers to the partial order on the set of agents A. As it was mentioned in the introduction the order on agents is needed to form coalitions and coalitions are exactly downsets according to the order on agents. In these terms the group belief axiom from Definition 3 says that p is a group belief of the a group of agents J if p is a shared belief of the minimal coalition $\overline{J}$ to which the group J belongs.

Example 4 *Every group forms a coalition. Assume that $\leq$ is an empty relation. In this case the downset $\overline{J} = J$. Hence every subset of agents forms a coalition and hence group belief coincides with shared belief. $GB_J p \leftrightarrow E_{\overline{J}} p \leftrightarrow E_J p$.*

Example 5 *The only coalition. Assume that $\leq = A \times A$. In this case we have only one coalition as far as $\overline{J} = A$ for every $J \subseteq A$. Hence something is a group belief only if it is a shared belief of all agents.*

Example 6. *Let $A = \{w, u, v\}$ and $\leq = \{(w, w), (u, u), (v, v), (w, u), (w, v)\}$. In this case we have 4 different coalitions $\{w, u\}$, $\{w, v\}$, $\{w, u, v\}$ and $\{w\}$. Group belief for this case depends on the group. If $J = \{u, w\}$, $J = \{v, w\}$ or $J = \{w\}$, group belief coincides with shared belief $GB_J p \leftrightarrow E_J p$, while when $J = \{u, v\}$ we have $GB_J p \leftrightarrow E_A p$ and in cases when $J = \{u\}$ or $J = \{v\}$ group belief is a shared belief of a corresponding coalition $GB_J p \leftrightarrow E_{\{u,w\}} p$ and $GB_J p \leftrightarrow E_{\{v,w\}} p$ respectively.*

3.2   Semantics

Semantics for the modal logics $\mathcal{GB}1$ is provided by OUR-models.

Definition 7. *An OUR-structure for a partially ordered set of agents $(A, \leq)$ is a tuple $(W, \{R_a | a \in A\})$ where W is a set of worlds, R_a for each $a \in A$ is a transitive relation on W. An OUR-model is an OUR-structure together with a valuation function $V : Prop \times W \to 2$.*

Notice that the structure on a set of agent as well as the set of agents itself is common both to the syntax and semantics. It is true that the syntax does not contain any symbol for the relation $\leq$ but it interacts with this relation by the group belief axiom. The semantics, as is clear from the next definition, has a more straightforward interaction with the structure on the set of agents.

Definition 8. *For a given OUR-model $M = (W, \{R_a | a \in A\}, V)$, the satisfaction of a formula at a point $w \in W$ is defined inductively as follows:*
$w \models p$ iff $w \in V(p)$;
the boolean cases are standard;
$w \models \Box_a \phi$ iff $(\forall v)(w R_a v \Rightarrow v \models \phi)$;
$w \models E_J \phi$ iff $(\forall v)(w R v \Rightarrow v \models \phi)$ where $R = \bigcup_{a \in J} R_a$;
$w \models GB_J \phi$ iff $(\forall v)(w R' v \Rightarrow v \models \phi)$ where $R' = \bigcup_{a \in \bar{J}} R_a$;
    A formula is valid in an OUR-structure if it is satisfiable at every point $w \in W$ under every valuation V. A formula is valid in a class $\mathfrak{C}$ of OUR-structures if it is valid in every OUR-structure $\mathfrak{F} \in \mathfrak{C}$.

What does the last definition imply in different examples? The idea is to think of coalitions as downsets. In such a setting each member of a group J may believe the sentence p but the coalition $\bar{J}$ may have additional members who do not share this belief and hence the group J as part of the coalition does not have p as a group belief of a coalition. In other words *only those sentences are believed by the group which are shared beliefs of the coalition to which the group belongs.* We might call this kind of belief "coalition dependent".

The group belief operator defined in this sense has the following properties discussed in [5]:

Proposition 9

1. *No combination of individual beliefs implies group belief;*
2. *Not all sets of agents form coalitions;*
3. *Group belief does not imply the common belief of the group;*

Proof. 2 follows by the definition of coalition. 3 is an easy application of the definitions of common belief and shared belief. See Sect. 2. For 1 let us consider a partial order $(\{a, b, c\}, \leq)$ of agents where $a \leq b \leq c$. Let $J = \{b, c\}$. As for the set of possible worlds and relations, let us take $W = \{w, u, v\}$, $R_a = \{(w, u), (w, v), (u, v)\}$ and $R_b = R_c = \{(v, u), (v, w), (u, w)\}$ let $w \models p$ and $v \not\models q$. See Fig. 1.

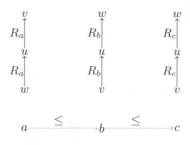

Fig. 1. .

In this case $u \models \Box_b p \wedge \Box_c p$ since the only successor of u both by R_b and R_c is w which on its own models p. This means that all members of the group J believe in p but still p is not a group belief of the group. This is because the coalition $\overline{J}$ containing the group also contains agent a. $u \not\models \Box_a p$ as there is an R_a successor v of u which does not model p. So $u \not\models E_{\overline{J}} p$.

Note that $\Box_b p \wedge \Box_c p$ is just one particular combination of individual beliefs and hence it is not enough to claim that no combination of individual beliefs implies group belief. But an easy argument shows that indeed no formula written in a restricted language which only contains $\Box_b$ and $\Box_c$ can imply group belief. The full proof of this claim needs additional definitions and properties and is given in the appendix.

The other two important properties from [5] "Goup belief does not imply individual beliefs of the group members" and "Group belief does not imply subgroup belief" are not satisfied. This is because the group is always contained in the coalition and as well every subgroup is contained in a coalition formed by a bigger group. Now what happens if we add the belief dependency axiom? Does it effect the structure. The answer is yes. The belief dependency axiom sets some constraints on the structure of frames.

3.3 Completeness

One way to prove completeness is via a standard canonical model construction. Here we use a different method and prove completeness by applying results from [11]. First we show that the axiom for the group belief modality is a relational modal definition. Secondly we will use the result that modal logic with the shared belief modality is complete, and lastly we will apply the result that extensions of complete logics with relational modal definitions yield complete logics.

Definition 10. *A modal definition* $\boxplus p \leftrightarrow \phi(p, p_1, \dots, p_n)$ *is called a* relational modal definition *if there exists a first-order formula* $\Psi_+(x, y)$ *with two free* *variables using only symbols that occur in* $ST_x[\phi(p, p_1, \ldots, p_n)]$ *such that for every formula* ψ *in the language without* ⊞ *it holds that*

$$(\forall y)(\Psi_+(x, y) \Rightarrow ST_y[\psi]) \text{ is logically equivalent to } ST_x[\phi(\psi, p_1, \ldots, p_n)].$$

Let $\Psi_+(x, y)$ be the first-order formula corresponding to a relational modal definition. Given a model $\mathfrak{M} = (\mathfrak{F}, V)$, we uniquely construct the model $\mathfrak{M}_+ = (\mathfrak{F}_+, V)$, where the underlying frame $\mathfrak{F}_+$ is obtained from $\mathfrak{F}$ by adding the binary relation $R_+ \subseteq W^2$ defined as:

$$(x, y) \in R_+ \text{ if, and only if, } \mathfrak{M} \models \Psi_+(x, y).$$

For a class $\mathcal{C}$ of models, we denote by $\mathcal{C}_+$ the class consisting of the models $\mathfrak{M}_+$, where $\mathfrak{M}$ ranges over the models in $\mathcal{C}$.

Fact 11. *Let* $\mathcal{L}$ *be the modal language for a signature* $\langle \Pi, M \rangle$, *and let* $\mathcal{L}_+$ *be the modal language for* $\langle \Pi, M \cup \{+\} \rangle$ *for some fresh symbol '+'. Let* $L \subseteq \mathcal{L}$ *be a modal logic that is complete w.r.t. a class* $\mathcal{C}$ *of models. Let* $L_+ \subseteq \mathcal{L}_+$ *be the modal logic obtained by extending* L *with the relational modal definition* ⊞$p \leftrightarrow \alpha(p, p_1, \ldots, p_n)$. *Then* L_+ *is complete w.r.t.* $\mathcal{C}_+$.

Another result which we are going to use is completeness of the modal logic obtained by eliminating the group belief operator from logic $\mathcal{GB}1$. The result as stated does not appear anywhere but an exact analog of the result is known for the shared knowledge operator, see [4]. And the distinction between the two is insignificant for these results.

Proposition 12. *The modal logic of shared belief (The logic obtained by eliminating operator* GB_J *together with the group belief axiom from* $\mathcal{GB}1$) *is sound and complete w.r.t. possible world structures (Kripke structures), where each relation is transitive.*

Lastly, to obtain the completeness for the logic $\mathcal{GB}1$ it remains to show that the group belief axiom is a relational modal definition and describe the class of frames it specifies.

Proposition 13. *The axiom* $GB_G\phi \leftrightarrow E_{\overline{G}}\phi$ *is a relational modal definition.*

Proof. Immediate if we take $\Psi_+(x, y)$ in Definition 10 to be xRy where $R = \bigcup_{a \in \overline{G}} R_a$. □

Corollary 14. *The modal logic* $\mathcal{GB}1$ *is sound and complete w.r.t. OUR-structures.*

3.4   Fibered Structures

By ordering the set of agents we want to reflect the intuition that not all agents have the same belief sets. Moreover it is natural to think that the structure of agents is connected with the structure of their belief sets. Which is not the case in OUR-frames from previous section. For instance if $a \leq b$, then belief set of a is smaller then belief set of b. At this point we don't have such a requirement. One could obtain this property by adding the law $a \leq b \Rightarrow \vdash \Box_b p \rightarrow \Box_a p$, which we encode by the following axiom:

- *Belief dependency axiom*

$$\Box_a p \rightarrow GB_{\{a\}} p$$

Now the meta-rule $a \leq b \Rightarrow \vdash \Box_b p \rightarrow \Box_a p$ becomes satisfied. For, assume $a \leq b$, by the belief dependency axiom we have $\Box_a p \rightarrow GB_{\{a\}} p$, and by the axiom for the group belief operator we get $\Box_b p \rightarrow E_{\overline{\{b\}}} p$ and, as $a \leq b$, we know that $a \in \overline{\{b\}}$. By the axiom for shared belief we obtain $E_{\overline{\{b\}}} p \rightarrow \bigwedge_{i \in \overline{\{b\}}} \Box_i p$ which on its own implies $\Box_a p$. Hence we get $\Box_b p \rightarrow \Box_a p$. Thus, despite the fact that our language does not contain the symbol $\leq$, it is strong enough to express the property of belief dependency. By $\mathcal{GB}1^{\leq}$ we denote the extension of $\mathcal{GB}1$ by the belief dependency axiom.

Definition 15. *Let us call an OUR-structure $(W, \{R_a | a \in A\})$ a fibered frame iff $a \leq b$ implies $R_a \subseteq R_b$.*

Proposition 16. *The belief dependency axiom is valid in an OUR-frame $\mathfrak{F} = (W, \{R_a | a \in A\})$ iff $\mathfrak{F}$ is a fibered frame.*

Proof. Assume for the contradiction that an OUR-structure $\mathfrak{F}$ is not fibered. By definition this means that there exists a and b in the set of agent A such that $a \leq b$ while $R_a \not\subseteq R_b$, i.e. there are points $w, u \in W$ such that $wR_a u$ while not $wR_b u$. Take a valuation such that p is true everywhere in a frame except at u, then it is clear that $w \models \Box_b p$ while $w \not\models \Box_a p$ sincet $wR_a u$ and $u \not\models p$. Hence $w \not\models GB_{\{b\}} p$ which falsifies the axiom.

Now assume that $\mathfrak{F}$ is a fibered OUR-structure. Let V be an arbitrary valuation on $\mathfrak{F}$. Let us take an arbitrary point $w \in W$ and show that $w \models \Box_b p \rightarrow GB_{\{b\}} p$ for an arbitrary $b \in A$. Assume that $w \models \Box_b p$. Hence for every R_b successor v of w it holds that $v \models p$. Let us show that $w \models E_{\overline{\{b\}}} p$. By the axiom of shared belief $E_{\overline{b}} p \leftrightarrow \bigwedge_{a \in \overline{b}} \Box_a p$, it suffices to show that $w \models \Box_a p$ for every $a \leq b$. Now since $\mathfrak{F}$ is fibered, $a \leq b$ implies that $R_a \subseteq R_b$. Hence every R_a successor u of w is also an R_b successor and we already know that every such u satisfies p.

The following proposition shows that fibered frames do not preserve the property of group belief from Proposition 9. Proof of the following proposition can be found in Appendix.

Proposition 17. *In every fibered OUR-structure, the group belief of a set of agents is implied by the conjunction of the individual beliefs of those agents that have maximal belief sets from the group.*

Corollary 18. *In every fibered OUR-structure, the group belief of a set of agents is equivalent to the shared belief of the same set of agents.*

This shows that the notion of group belief as defined above does not make much sense in the class of fibered frames and the language collapses to a simple modal language with many modalities. In Sect. 5 we will consider the logic of a pure modal language of ordered agents with an additional operator reflecting the order of agents and derive the completeness of the logic w.r.t. the class of fibered structures.

4   Syntax of $\mathcal{GB}2$

An important property of group belief discussed in [5], which our definition of group belief lacks, is the following: 'If p is a group belief of a group G, then it is a common belief that p is a group belief of the group'. As we saw from the example this property is not satisfied for $\mathcal{GB}1$. In this section is modify the logic $\mathcal{GB}1$ so that the desirable properties of $\mathcal{GB}1$ are preserved but additionally group belief satisfies the above condition. We consider a modal logic $\mathcal{GB}2$ in which shared belief is replaced by common belief.

4.1   Syntax

Definition 19. *The language of the normal modal logic $\mathcal{GB}2$ is $\mathcal{L}(\{C_J, GB_J \mid J \subseteq A\})$ where the operators C_J stand for common belief. The axioms are all classical tautologies, each box satisfies $K4$ axioms $\Box_a(p \to q) \to (\Box_a p \to \Box_a q)$ and $\Box_a p \to \Box_a \Box_a p$ for every $a \in A$. In addition we have an equilibrium axiom for common belief:*

$$(equi) : C_J p \leftrightarrow \bigwedge_{a \in J} \Box_a p \wedge \bigwedge_{a \in J} \Box_a C_J p$$

And a new axiom for the group belief operator

$$GB_J p \leftrightarrow C_{\overline{J}} p$$

for every $J \subseteq A$. The rules of inference are: modus ponens, substitution and necessitation for each box modality and additionally an induction rule for the common believe operator:

$$(ind) : \frac{\vdash p \to \bigwedge_{a \in J} \Box_a(p \wedge q)}{\vdash p \to C_J q}$$

4.2   Semantics

A semantics for $\mathcal{GB}2$ is provided by OUR-models. Let us first recall the definition of the transitive closure of a binary relation.

Definition 20. *The transitive closure R^+ of the relation R is defined in the following way: $xR^+y \Leftrightarrow (\exists x_1, \exists x_2, ..., \exists x_n)(x = x_1 \wedge x_1 R x_2 \wedge x_2 R x_3 \wedge ... \wedge x_n Ry)$ for some $n \in \omega$.*

Now we are ready to define the satisfaction of modal formulas on OUR-models.

Definition 21. *For a given OUR-model $M = (W, \{R_a | a \in A, V\})$, the satisfaction of a formula at a point $w \in W$ is defined inductively as follows:*

$w \models p$ *iff* $w \in V(p)$;

the boolean cases are standard;

$w \models \Box_a \phi$ *iff* $(\forall v)(w R_a v \Rightarrow v \models \phi)$;

$w \models C_J \phi$ *iff* $(\forall v)(w R v \Rightarrow v \models \phi)$ *where* $R = (\bigcup_{a \in J} R_a)^+$;

$w \models GB_J \phi$ *iff* $(\forall v)(w \overline{R} v \Rightarrow v \models \phi)$ *where* $\overline{R} = (\bigcup_{a \in \overline{J}} R_a)^+$;

    A formula is valid in an OUR-structure if it is satisfiable at every point $w \in W$ under every valuation V. A formula is valid in a class $\mathfrak{C}$ of OUR-structures if it is valid in every OUR-structure $\mathfrak{F} \in \mathfrak{C}$.

The following result for $\mathcal{GB}2$ shows that some of the good properties of group belief defined the previous section are preserved for the group belief operator of $\mathcal{GB}2$ and additionally the latter has the property that 'If p is a group belief of a group J then it is a common belief that p is a group belief of the group.' Proof is given in Appendix.

Proposition 22

1. *No combination of individual beliefs imply group belief;*
2. *Not all sets of agents form coalitions;*
3. *If a sentence p is a group belief of a set of agents J then is is common belief (of the set of agents J) that p is a group belief of the set of agents J;*

4.3 Completeness

The main result for this section is that the logic $\mathcal{GB}2$ is the logic of all OUR-structures with the given semantics. Observe that completeness for this case can not be obtained by the technique of Sect. 3.3 since the axiom $GB_J p \leftrightarrow C_{\overline{J}} p$ is not a relational modal definition. The reason is that the transitive closure used for defining the semantics of the common belief operator is not first order definable. Nevertheless we are able to prove the completeness of the logic $\mathcal{GB}2$ by a slight modification of the completeness proof for the logic of common belief [4]. A proof sketch can be found in Appendix.

Theorem 23. *The logic $\mathcal{GB}2$ is sound and complete w.r.t. the class of all OUR-structures.*

5 The Logic of Fibered Structures

In this section we introduce the logic of fibered structures in a simpler language which does not contain a group belief operator. Instead we have an operator $\preceq$ which captures the partial order of agents. An analogous approach with geometric interpretations of the operator $\preceq$ has been introduced in [1]. The set FOR of all formulas (with typical members denoted ϕ, ψ, etc.) is now inductively defined as follows:

– $\phi, \psi ::= p \mid \bot \mid \neg \phi \mid (\phi \vee \psi) \mid \Box_a \phi \mid a \preceq b.$

We define the other Boolean constructs as usual. The formula $a \npreceq b$ is an abbreviation for: $\neg a \preceq b$. We omit parentheses if this does not lead to any ambiguity. The notion of a subformula is standard. For all sets x of formulas, let $\Box_a x = \{\phi : \Box_a \phi \in x\}$.

5.1   Semantics

For a given OUR-model $M = (W, \{R_a \mid a \in A\}, V)$, the satisfaction relation is defined as follows for formulas of the form $a \preceq b$:

- $w \models a \preceq b$ iff $(\forall v)(w R_a v \Rightarrow w R_b v)$.

Therefore, in our setting, "$a \preceq b$" means that a believes everything that b believes.

We remark that

Lemma 24. *The following formulas are satisfied in any world of any model:*

- $\Box_a \phi \rightarrow \Box_a \Box_a \phi$,
- $a \preceq a$,
- $a \preceq b \wedge b \preceq c \rightarrow a \preceq c$,
- $a \preceq b \rightarrow (\Box_b \phi \rightarrow \Box_a \phi)$,
- $\Box_a \bot \rightarrow a \preceq b$.

Proof. Since OUR-models are based on transitive relations, formulas of the form $\Box_a \phi \rightarrow \Box_a \Box_a \phi$ are valid. The validity of formulas of the form $a \preceq a$ and $a \preceq b \wedge b \preceq c \rightarrow a \preceq c$ comes from the fact that the relation of inclusion between sets is reflexive and transitive. For formulas of the form $a \preceq b \rightarrow (\Box_b \phi \rightarrow \Box_a \phi)$, they are valid because in an OUR-model $M = (W, \{R_a \mid a \in A\}, V)$, if $w \models a \preceq b$ then $R_a(w) \subseteq R_b(w)$ where $R(w)$ denotes the set of all accessible porints from w. Concerning formulas of the form $\Box_a \bot \rightarrow a \preceq b$, they are valid because in an OUR-model $M = (W, \{R_a \mid a \in A\}, V)$, if $R_a(w) = \emptyset$ then $w \models a \preceq b$.

5.2   Axiomatization/Completeness

Let L be the least normal modal logic in our language containing the formulas of Lemma 24. We want to show that L provides a sound and complete axiomatization of the set of all valid formulas. By Lemma 24, L is sound. To prove completeness, we must show that every valid formula is in L. It suffices to prove that every consistent formula is satisfiable. To reach this goal, we use a step-by-step method. We define a subordination model to be a structure $S = (W, \{R_a \mid a \in A\}, \sigma)$ where W is a nonempty subset of $\mathbb{N}$, R_a is an irreflexive transitive relation on W and σ is a function assigning to each $x \in W$ a maximal L-consistent set $\sigma(x)$ of formulas such that

- if $\Box_a \phi \in \sigma(x)$ then for all $y \in W$, if $x R_a y$ then $\phi \in \sigma(y)$,
- if $a \preceq b \in \sigma(x)$ then $R_a(x) \subseteq R_b(x)$.

For all maximal L-consistent sets Γ of formulas, let $S^\Gamma = (W^\Gamma, \{R_a^\Gamma \mid a \in A\}, \sigma^\Gamma)$ be the structure where $W^\Gamma = \{0\}$, $R_a^\Gamma = \emptyset$, $\sigma^\Gamma(0) = \Gamma$. The reader may easily verify that

Lemma 25. S^Γ is a finite subordination model.

Consider a finite subordination model $S' = (W', \{R_a' \mid a \in A\}, \sigma')$. We define a $\Box$-imperfection in S' to be a triple of the form (x, a, ϕ) where $x \in W'$, a is an agent and ϕ is a formula such that $\Box_a \phi \notin \sigma'(x)$ and for all $y \in W$, if $xR_a' y$ then $\phi \in \sigma'(y)$.

Lemma 26. Let (x, a, ϕ) be a $\Box$-imperfection in S'. Let Γ be a maximal L-consistent set of formulas such that $\Box_a \sigma'(x) \subseteq \Gamma$ and $\phi \notin \Gamma$. Let y be a new nonnegative integer. Let $S = (W, \{R_a \mid a \in A\}, \sigma)$ be the structure where

- $W = W' \cup \{y\}$,
- $zR_b t$ iff one of the following conditions holds:
  - $z \in W'$, $t \in W'$ and $zR_b' t$,
  - $z \in W' \setminus \{x\}$, $t = y$, $zR_b' x$ and $a \preceq b \in \sigma'(x)$,
  - $z = x$, $t = y$ and $a \preceq b \in \sigma'(x)$,
- $\sigma(z) = $ if $z = y$ then Γ else $\sigma'(z)$.

Then, S is a finite subordination model. We shall say that S is the local completion of S' with respect to the $\Box$-imperfection (x, a, ϕ).

We define a $\preceq$-imperfection in S' to be a triple of the form (x, a, b) where $x \in W'$ and a, b are agents such that $a \preceq b \notin \sigma'(x)$ and $R_a'(x) \subseteq R_b'(x)$.

Lemma 27. Let (x, a, b) be a $\preceq$-imperfection in S'. Let Γ be a maximal L-consistent set of formulas such that $\Box_a \sigma'(x) \subseteq \Gamma$. Let y be a new nonnegative integer. Let $S = (W, \{R_a \mid a \in A\}, \sigma)$ be the structure where

- $W = W' \cup \{y\}$,
- $zR_c t$ iff one of the following conditions holds:
  - $z \in W'$, $t \in W'$ and $zR_c' t$,
  - $z \in W' \setminus \{x\}$, $t = y$, $zR_c' x$ and $a \preceq c \in \sigma'(x)$,
  - $z = x$, $t = y$ and $a \preceq c \in \sigma'(x)$,
- $\sigma(z) = $ if $z = y$ then Γ else $\sigma'(z)$.

Then, S is a finite subordination model. We shall say that S is the local completion of S' with respect to the $\preceq$-imperfection (x, a, b).

Let $(x_0, a_0, \phi_0), (x_1, a_1, b_1), (x_2, a_2, \phi_2), (x_3, a_3, b_3), \ldots$ be an enumeration of $(\mathbb{N} \times A \times FOR) \cup (\mathbb{N} \times A \times A)$ in which each item appears infinitely many times. For all maximal L-consistent sets Γ of formulas, let $T^0 = (W^0, \{R_a^0 \mid a \in A\}, \sigma^0)$, $T^1 = (W^1, \{R_a^1 \mid a \in A\}, \sigma^1)$, etc., be the infinite sequence of subordination models defined as follows. Let $T^0 = S^\Gamma$. Let n be a nonnegative integer. Given $T^{2 \times n}$, let $T^{2 \times n + 1}$ be the local completion of $T^{2 \times n}$ with respect to the $\Box$-imperfection $(x_{2 \times n}, a_{2 \times n}, \phi_{2 \times n})$ when $(x_{2 \times n}, a_{2 \times n}, \phi_{2 \times n})$ is a $\Box$-imperfection of $T^{2 \times n}$. Otherwise, let $T^{2 \times n + 1}$ be $T^{2 \times n}$. Now, let $T^{2 \times n + 2}$ be the local completion of $T^{2 \times n+1}$ with respect to the $\preceq$-imperfection $(x_{2 \times n+1}, a_{2 \times n+1}, b_{2 \times n+1})$ when $(x_{2 \times n+1}, a_{2 \times n+1}, b_{2 \times n+1})$ is a $\preceq$-imperfection of $T^{2 \times n+1}$. Otherwise, let $T^{2 \times n+2}$ be $T^{2 \times n+1}$. Now, we put $T^\omega = (W^\omega, \{R_a^\omega \mid a \in A\}, \sigma^\omega)$ to be the subordination model defined as follows:

- $W^\omega = \bigcup \{W^n \colon n \text{ is a nonnegative integer}\}$,
- if $x \in W^m$ for some nonnegative integer m and $y \in W^n$ for some nonnegative integer n then $xR_a^\omega y$ iff $xR_a^{m+n}y$,
- if $x \in W^n$ for some nonnegative integer n then $\sigma^\omega(x) = \sigma^n(x)$.

The reader may easily verify that T^ω has no imperfection. The result that emerges from the discussion above is:

Proposition 28. *The following conditions are equivalent for every formula ϕ:*

1. *ϕ is in L.*
2. *ϕ is valid.*

Proof. 1. $\Rightarrow$ 2.: By Lemma 24.
2. $\Rightarrow$ 1.: Suppose $\phi \notin L$. Let Γ be a maximal L-consistent set of formulas such that $\phi \notin \Gamma$. Let $T^\omega = (W^\omega, \{R_a^\omega \mid a \in A\}, \sigma^\omega)$ be the subordination model associated to Γ as above. Let $M = (W, \{R_a \mid a \in A\}, V)$ be the model defined as follows:

$$W = W^\omega, \quad xR_a y \text{ iff } xR_a^\omega y, \quad V(p) = \{x \mid p \in \sigma^\omega(x)\}.$$

By induction on ψ, the reader may easily verify that for all $x \in W$, $x \Vdash \psi$ iff $\psi \in \sigma^\omega(x)$. Since $\phi \notin \Gamma$, therefore $0 \nVdash \phi$. Consequently, ϕ is not valid.

6   Summary and Future Work

In this preliminary study we have explored different ways in which group belief might be modeled when a certain structure is imposed on the set of agent. Group belief in the resulting logics displays different properties, suggesting that the logics may have different types of application - a topic for further study in the future.

As we have seen both logics, $\mathcal{GB}1$ and $\mathcal{GB}2$, collapse to standard multi-modal languages when a belief dependency axiom is added. This shows that on a semantical level there is natural correspondence between the $\mathcal{GB}1^\leq$ and $\mathcal{GB}2^\leq$ and the logic of all fibered structures from Sect. 5. This suggests the possibility of syntactic connections between the three logics which we aim to explore in future work.

References

1. Balbiani, P., Gasquet, O., Schwarzentruber, F.: Agents that look at one another. Logic J. IGPL **21**(3), 438–467 (2013)
2. Dunin-Kęplicz, B., Szałas, A.: Epistemic profiles and belief structures. In: Jezic, G., Kusek, M., Nguyen, N.-T., Howlett, R.J., Jain, L.C. (eds.) KES-AMSTA 2012. LNCS (LNAI), vol. 7327, pp. 360–369. Springer, Heidelberg (2012). doi:10.1007/978-3-642-30947-2_40
3. Dunin-Kęplicz, B., Verbrugge, R.: Teamwork in Multi-Agent Systems: A Formal Approach, 1st edn. Wiley, New York (2010)
4. Fagin, R., Halpern, J., Moses, Y., Vardi, M.: Reasoning About Knowledge. MIT Press, Cambridge (1995)
5. Gaudou, B., Herzig, A., Longin, D., Lorini, E.: On modal logics of group belief. In: Herzig, A., Lorini, E. (eds.) The Cognitive Foundations of Group Attitudes and Social Interaction. SPS, vol. 5, pp. 75–106. Springer, Heidelberg (2015). doi:10.1007/978-3-319-21732-1_4
6. Gilbert, M.: Modelling collective belief. Synthese **73**(1), 185–204 (1987)
7. List, C., Pettit, P.: Group Agency: The Possibility, Design and Status of Corporate Agents. OUP, Cambridge (2011)
8. Lorini, E., Longin, D., Gaudou, B., Herzig, A.: The logic of acceptance: grounding institutions on agents' attitudes. J. Logic Comput. **19**(6), 901–940 (2009)
9. Quinton, A.: Social objects. In: Proceedings of the Aristotelian Society, pp. 1–27 (1976)
10. Tuomela, R.: Group beliefs. Synthese **91**(3), 285–318 (1992)
11. Uridia, L., Walther, D.: Completeness via modal definitions. In: Proceedings of TBILLS16. (submitted to)

A Three-Value Abstraction Technique for the Verification of Epistemic Properties in Multi-agent Systems

Francesco Belardinelli$^{(\boxtimes)}$ and Alessio Lomuscio$^{(\boxtimes)}$

Department of Computing, Imperial College London, London, UK
belardinelli@ibisc.fr, a.lomuscio@imperial.ac.uk

Abstract. We put forward an abstraction technique, based on a three-value semantics, for the verification of epistemic properties of agents participating in a multi-agent system. First we introduce a three-value interpretation of epistemic logic, based on a notion of order defined on the information content of the local states of each agent. Then, we use the three-value semantics to introduce an abstraction technique to verify epistemic properties of agents in infinite-state multi-agent systems.

Keywords: Logics in multi-agent systems · Epistemic logic · Formal verification by model checking

1 Introduction

Modal logics for knowledge representation and reasoning, including epistemic logics, have been proved to be a valuable formal tool for the modelling and analysis of multi-agent systems [15,21,29]. These logical languages typically include an operator K_i to represent the knowledge of an agent i, as well as possibly modalities for collective, common and distributed, knowledge. In combination with techniques for automated verification by model checking, epistemic logics have been used to model and verify complex multi-agents scenarios [26], among which communication and security protocols [6], auction-based mechanisms [5], business process workflows [4,20].

The application of methods from knowledge representation and reasoning to the verification of multi-agent systems (MAS) depends crucially on the development of efficient model checking methodologies and algorithms. In particular, abstraction techniques are key to tackle the state-space explosion problem [9,23]. Moreover, whenever agents manipulate infinite data types (e.g., natural numbers, integers, reals, lists, arrays, etc.), finite abstractions are often the only chance to obtain a decidable model checking problem [1,4,13].

Inspired by the considerations above, in this paper we put forward an abstraction technique, based on a three-value semantics, for the verification of epistemic properties of agents participating in a MAS. Specifically, the contribution of the paper is twofold. Firstly, we introduce a three-value interpretation of epistemic

© Springer International Publishing AG 2016
L. Michael and A. Kakas (Eds.): JELIA 2016, LNAI 10021, pp. 112–126, 2016.
DOI: 10.1007/978-3-319-48758-8_8

logic, which is based on a partial order $\leq$ defined on the information content of the local states of each agent. According to this intuition, agent i considers epistemically possible not just states that are indistinguishable to her, i.e., in which i's local state is identical, but also states comparable by order $\leq$. We illustrate the formal machinery with examples from agent-based systems, particularly infinite-state systems that are not directly amenable to standard model checking techniques. Secondly, we use the three-value semantics to introduce an abstraction technique to model check epistemic properties of agents in infinite-state MAS. As a result, our contribution is meant to advance the state-of-the-art both in the theory of epistemic logic and the verification of MAS.

Related works. The area of epistemic logics has reached such a level of maturity nowadays that it is extremely difficult to provide an exhaustive account. Here we only mention the contributions most closely related to the verification of multi-agent systems by abstraction. Techniques to model check epistemic properties of agents in MAS have witnessed a growing interest in recent years, with a number of tools made publicly available [18,22,27]. This work pursues the same research direction, but we target explicitly infinite-state MAS, for which the verification task is considerably more complex. Abstraction techniques for epistemic properties of MAS have appeared in [10,11], but the underlying logic is two-valued, and therefore only its "universal" fragment is preserved by the abstraction procedure. Instead, here we adopt the abstraction method via under- and over-approximations, which has been applied mainly to the verification of simple transitions systems against temporal properties [2,7,19,28]. Previous contributions on three-value abstractions for epistemic logics have appeared in [14,20,24,25]. However, the settings and the three-value semantics are different w.r.t. the account here put forward. Specifically, in [14] there is no notion of under- and over-approximation, as the three-value semantics follows [16,17]. This implies that only (universal and existential) fragments of the original language are preserved. Hence, the class of verifiable specifications is somewhat limited, while here we are able to verify the full language in principle. Further, in [24,25] the proposed three-value semantics is not a conservative extension of the standard two-value semantics for epistemic logic, in particular no analogue to Proposition 1 below can be proved. As a consequence, verification results available for the three-value semantics do not immediately transfer to the two-value semantics. Finally, differently from [20], we ground under- and over-approximations on a relation $\leq$ of order between local states, which provides guidance as to the definition of the abstract system, while making the abstraction process more transparent in our opinion.

Scheme of the paper. In Sect. 2 we introduce the multi-agent epistemic logic **K** that includes operators for distributed and common knowledge, and we provide **K** with a three-value semantics based on an order $\leq$ on the local states of each agent. We illustrate the formal machinery with examples of (infinite-state) multi-agent systems. In Sect. 3 we develop an agent-based abstraction technique that we prove to preserve the three-value interpretation of formulas in **K**. We conclude by discussing applications of these results to the verification of epistemic properties of infinite-state MAS.

2   Preliminaries

In this section we introduce the formalism of three-value epistemic logic. First, we present the language of multi-agent epistemic logic, including modalities for collective knowledge. Then, we provide this logic with a Kripke-style semantics, which allows to compare the local information possessed by agents, thus inducing a natural three-value semantics suitable for abstractions.

In the following $Ag = \{1, \ldots, m\}$ is a set of indexes for agents and AP is a set of atomic propositions. Also, we denote the $i + 1$-th element of a tuple v as v_i.

The Language. To reason about multi-agent systems and to describe properties pertaining to the agents' knowledge, we make use of the multi-modal epistemic logic **K** defined by the following BNF:

$$\varphi ::= q \mid \neg\varphi \mid \varphi \rightarrow \varphi \mid C_\Gamma\varphi \mid D_\Gamma\varphi$$

where $q \in AP$ and $\Gamma \subseteq Ag$.

The informal meaning of formulas $C_\Gamma\varphi$ is that "φ is *common* knowledge in group Γ"; while $D_\Gamma\varphi$ is read as "φ is *distributed* knowledge in group Γ". As customary, we can introduce individual knowledge formulas $K_i\varphi$ as shorthands for either $C_{\{i\}}\varphi$ or $D_{\{i\}}\varphi$. Also, we omit group Γ whenever $\Gamma = Ag$. Notice that **K** is not to be confused with the homonymous normal modal logic.

The Models. To provide a formal interpretation to the epistemic formulas in **K**, we introduce a notion of agent and interpreted systems.

Definition 1 (Agent). *Given a set Ag of agent indexes, an* agent *is a tuple $i = \langle L, Act, Pr, \tau \rangle$ such that*

- *L is the (possibly infinite) set of* local states *with a partial order $\leq$ on L;*
- *Act is the set of* actions;
- *$Pr : L \rightarrow (2^{Act} \setminus \{\emptyset\})$ is the* protocol function;
- *$\tau : L \times ACT \rightarrow 2^L$ is the* local transition function, *where $ACT = Act_1 \times \cdots \times Act_{|Ag|}$ is the set of* joint actions, *such that $\tau(l, a)$ is defined iff $a_i \in Pr(l)$.*

The notion of agent in Definition 1 is typical of the literature on interpreted systems [15,27]: each agent is assumed to be situated in some local state, and to perform the actions in Act according to protocol Pr. The evolution of her local state is determined by the transition function τ. Differently from the state-of-the-art, we also consider a partial order $\leq$ on local states, i.e., a reflexive, antisymmetric, and transitive relation on L. Intuitively, $l \leq l'$ means that in local state l' agent i has at least as much information as in l. The partial order $\leq$ is key to approximate the knowledge of agent i, whenever computing the exact information of i is too costly computationally, not dissimilarly to the use of over- and under-approximations in system verification [2,28]. Further, the standard notion of agent appearing in the literature can be seen as a particular case of Definition 1, in which the partial order $\leq$ is the identity. If this is the case, we say that the agent is *standard*.

Given a set Ag of agents, a *global state* is a tuple $s = \langle l_1, \ldots, l_{|Ag|} \rangle$ of local states, one for each agent in the system. We denote the set $L_1 \times \ldots \times L_{|Ag|}$ of all global states as $\mathcal{G}$. We now introduce interpreted systems to describe formally the interactions of agents in a multi-agent environment.

Definition 2 (IS). *An* interpreted system *is a tuple* $M = \langle Ag, I, \tau, \Pi \rangle$ *where*

- *every $i \in Ag$ is an agent;*
- *$I \subseteq \mathcal{G}$ is the set of* (global) initial states;
- *$\tau : \mathcal{G} \times ACT \to 2^{\mathcal{G}}$ is the* global transition function *such that* $\tau(s, a) = \tau_1(s_1, a) \times \ldots \times \tau_{|Ag|}(s_{|Ag|}, a)$;
- *$\Pi : \mathcal{G} \times AP \to \{tt, ff, uu\}$ is the* labelling function.

According to Definition 2, an interpreted system describes the evolution of a group Ag of agents from any initial state in I, according to the global transition function τ. By the constraint on each τ_i, $\tau(s, a)$ is defined iff $a_i \in Pr(s_i)$ for every $i \in Ag$. In the following we also make use of the local transition relation $\to$ such that $l \to l'$ iff $l' \in \tau(l, a)$ for some $a \in ACT$, as well as its reflexive and transitive closure $\to^*$. A global transition relation $\to$ and its reflexive and transitive closure $\to^*$ are defined similarly on global states in $\mathcal{G}$. Then, the set $\mathcal{S}$ of *reachable states* is introduced as the closure of I under $\to^*$, that is, $s \in \mathcal{S}$ iff $s_0 \to^* s$ for some initial $s_0 \in I$. Hereafter we assume that only reachable states count as epistemic alternatives for the agents in the interpreted system. That is, states that are not reachable in the system are not considered epistemically possible by the agents. This is in line with current accounts of IS [15,27].

Atomic propositions in AP can be assigned value true (tt), false (ff), or undefined (uu). This last value can be used to describe situations in which the truth of an atom is not set, or it is unknown, or underspecified. We will see examples of these instances at the end of the section. We say that the truth value t is *defined* whenever $t \in \{tt, ff\}$. If all agents in Ag are standard and the truth value of all atoms is defined, then we say that the IS is *standard* as well.

In the two-value semantics for epistemic logic the interpretation of knowledge formulas is normally given by means of an individual indistinguishability relation $\sim_i$ on global states, which is defined by the identity of local states, that is, $s \sim_i s'$ iff $s_i = s_i'$ [15]. Here we define over-approximation R_i^{may} and under-approximation R_i^{must} of relation $\sim_i$ by leveraging on the fact that we consider the partial order $\leq$ on local states, rather than simply their identity. Specifically, for each agent $i \in Ag$, we define relation R_i^{may} on global states such that $R_i^{may}(s, s')$ iff for some reachable $s'' \in \mathcal{S}$, $s_i'' \geq s_i$ and $s_i'' \geq s_i'$. Further, $R_i^{must}(s, s')$ iff $s_i' \leq s_i$. Notice that in particular $R_i^{must}(s, s')$ implies $R_i^{may}(s, s')$. Intuitively, R_i^{may} can be thought of as over-approximating the knowledge of agent i. Indeed, states s and s' are related by R_i^{may} if the information of agent i in s and s' can be consistently combined in some reachable state s_i'' (which is indeed an over-approximation of both s_i and s_i'); while $R_i^{must}(s, s')$ holds iff s_i' under-approximates the information contained in s_i. We remark that the use of over- and under-approximations R_i^{may} and R_i^{must} is customary in multi-valued logics and abstraction for transition systems [2,28]. Here we apply approximations to epistemic logic by grounding them on an order defined on information states.

To interpret common and distributed knowledge, for $x \in \{may, must\}$, we consider the intersection $R_\Gamma^{Dx} = \bigcap_{i \in \Gamma} R_i^x$ and the transitive closure $R_\Gamma^{Cx} = (\bigcup_{i \in \Gamma} R_i^x)^+$ of the union of accessibility relations. Then, $R_\Gamma^{Dx}(s, s')$ holds iff $R_i^x(s, s')$ holds for all $i \in \Gamma$; while $R_\Gamma^{Cx}(s, s')$ is the case iff for some sequence $s_0, \ldots, s_n$ of states, (i) $s_0 = s$ and $s_n = s'$; and (ii) for every $k < n$, $R_i^x(s_k, s_{k+1})$ for some $i \in \Gamma$. Finally, notice that R_i^{may} and R_i^{must} are both reflexive and R_i^{may} is also symmetric. However, they are not transitive in general, and therefore they are not equivalence relations. As a result, relations R_i^{may} and R_i^{must} do not define an S5-modality. This is to be expected and not really an issue in the present context, as we are interested in truth of formulas in a model as opposed to validity in a class of models. In particular, if the interpreted system is standard, then $R_i^{may} = R_i^{must}$ is an equivalence relation and we are back to the standard indistinguishability relation $\sim_i$ of the two-value semantics for epistemic logic.

Finally, we introduce a three-value interpretation of epistemic formulas in the logic **K**.

Definition 3 (Satisfaction). *The three-value satisfaction relation $\models^3$ for an IS M, state $s \in \mathcal{S}$, and formula ϕ is inductively defined as follows:*

$$
\begin{array}{ll}
((M, s) \models^3 q) = t & \text{iff } \Pi(s, q) = t, \text{ for } t \in \{tt, ff\} \\
((M, s) \models^3 \neg\phi) = tt & \text{iff } ((M, s) \models^3 \phi) = ff \\
((M, s) \models^3 \neg\phi) = ff & \text{iff } ((M, s) \models^3 \phi) = tt \\
((M, s) \models^3 \phi \to \phi') = tt & \text{iff } ((M, s) \models^3 \phi) = ff \text{ or } ((M, s) \models^3 \phi') = tt \\
((M, s) \models^3 \phi \to \phi') = ff & \text{iff } ((M, s) \models^3 \phi) = tt \text{ and } ((M, s) \models^3 \phi') = ff \\
((M, s) \models^3 C_\Gamma\varphi) = tt & \text{iff } \text{for all } s' \in \mathcal{S}, R_\Gamma^{Cmay}(s, s') \text{ implies } ((M, s') \models^3 \varphi) = tt \\
((M, s) \models^3 C_\Gamma\varphi) = ff & \text{iff } \text{for some } s' \in \mathcal{S}, R_\Gamma^{Cmust}(s, s') \text{ and } ((M, s') \models^3 \varphi) = ff \\
((M, s) \models^3 D_\Gamma\varphi) = tt & \text{iff } \text{for all } s' \in \mathcal{S}, R_\Gamma^{Dmay}(s, s') \text{ implies } ((M, s') \models^3 \varphi) = tt \\
((M, s) \models^3 D_\Gamma\varphi) = ff & \text{iff } \text{for some } s' \in \mathcal{S}, R_\Gamma^{Dmust}(s, s') \text{ and } ((M, s') \models^3 \varphi) = ff
\end{array}
$$

In all other cases, the value of ϕ is undefined (uu).

By Definition 3 we can derive the satisfaction clauses for individual knowledge formulas as follows:

$$
\begin{array}{l}
((M, s) \models^3 K_i\varphi) = tt \text{ iff for all } s' \in \mathcal{S}, R_i^{may}(s, s') \text{ implies } ((M, s') \models^3 \varphi) = tt \\
((M, s) \models^3 K_i\varphi) = ff \text{ iff for some } s' \in \mathcal{S}, R_i^{must}(s, s') \text{ and } ((M, s') \models^3 \varphi) = ff
\end{array}
$$

Intuitively, agent i knows ϕ at state s iff in all states s' that are epistemically compatible with s (in the sense that the information of s and s' can be consistently combined in a third reachable state s''), ϕ holds at s'. This can be seen as a conservative notion of knowledge, as ϕ has to be true in all such states s', in which i might have strictly more information than in s. Symmetrically, for $K_i\phi$ to be false at s, ϕ has to be false in some state s' in which i has at most as much information as in s.

We remark that the logic **K** does not contain temporal operators, and therefore in **K** we cannot describe notions pertaining to the evolution of knowledge, nor the knowledge of temporal facts. Nonetheless, we provided a dynamic account of agents and interpreted systems, which is apparent in Definition 3 as the interpretation of epistemic formulas is restricted to the set $\mathcal{S}$ of reachable states. Indeed, in line with the standard semantics of interpreted systems [15, 27], we assume that agents consider epistemically possible only the reachable states in $\mathcal{S}$, and therefore the dynamics of IS is accounted for also in the semantics of static epistemic properties. In Sect. 3 we will see that this has a major impact on the definition of abstractions.

The two-value satisfaction relation $\models^2$ for standard IS can be derived from $\models^3$ by considering clauses for tt only, as well as identity of local states and classic negation (clauses for propositional connectives are immediate and thus omitted):

$$(M,s) \models^2 q \qquad \text{iff} \quad \Pi(s,q) = \text{tt}$$
$$(M,s) \models^2 C_\Gamma\varphi \quad \text{iff} \quad \text{for all } s' \in \mathcal{S}, \; s \sim_\Gamma^C s' \text{ implies } (M,s') \models^2 \varphi$$
$$(M,s) \models^2 D_\Gamma\varphi \quad \text{iff} \quad \text{for all } s' \in \mathcal{S}, \; s \sim_\Gamma^D s' \text{ implies } (M,s') \models^2 \varphi$$

An IS M satisfies a formula φ, or $M \models^2 \varphi$, iff for all states $s \in \mathcal{S}$, $(M,s) \models^2 \varphi$. Similarly, $(M \models^3 \varphi) = \text{tt}$ (resp. ff) iff for all (resp. some) $s \in \mathcal{S}$, $((M,s) \models^3 \varphi) = \text{tt}$ (resp. ff). In all other cases, $(M \models^3 \varphi) = \text{uu}$.

We now state the model checking problem for this setting.

Definition 4 (Model Checking Problem). *Given an IS M and a formula ϕ in **K**, determine whether $M \models \phi$.*

Since we defined agents on possibly infinite sets of local states, interpreted systems are really infinite-state systems and the model checking problem is undecidable in general. In Sect. 3 we develop abstraction techniques to tackle the model checking problem. For the time being, we prove the following auxiliary result, which shows that for standard IS the two-value and three-value semantics for **K** coincide.

Proposition 1. *In every standard IS M, for every state s and formula ϕ in **K**,*

$$((M,s) \models^3 \phi) = \text{tt} \;\; iff \;\; (M,s) \models^2 \phi$$
$$((M,s) \models^3 \phi) = \text{ff} \;\; iff \;\; (M,s) \not\models^2 \phi$$

Proof. The proof is by induction on ϕ, the interesting cases concern the knowledge formulas. We prove the case for $\phi = K_i\varphi$. We remarked above that in standard IS the distinction between over- and under-approximations collapse, and $R_i^{may} = R_i^{must} = \sim_i$. Hence, $((M,s) \models^3 \phi) = \text{tt}$ iff for all $s' \in \mathcal{S}$, $R_i^{may}(s,s')$ implies $((M,s') \models^3 \varphi) = \text{tt}$. Since $R_i^{may}(s,s')$ iff $s \sim_i s'$ and by induction hypothesis, the above is equivalent to $s \sim_i s'$ implies $(M,s') \models^2 \varphi$, for all $s' \in \mathcal{S}$, that is, $(M,s) \models^2 \phi$. The case for $((M,s) \models^3 K_i\varphi) = \text{ff}$ is symmetric; while the inductive cases for $\phi = C_\Gamma\varphi$ and $\phi = D_\Gamma\varphi$ are proved similarly.

By Proposition 1 on standard IS the three-value semantics for **K** is a conservative extension of the typical two-value semantics. This result has a major impact on the abstraction procedure put forward in Sect. 3.

We conclude this section with two examples of interpreted systems. In particular, we consider two types of systems: (i) systems with a natural partial order defined on the local states of agents, and (ii) infinite-state IS for which we will define finite, three-value abstractions in Sect. 3.

Example 1. We first consider an example of an interpreted system with a partial order defined on each agent's local states. We introduce a variant of the muddy children puzzle [15], in which each child sees some of the other children, but she might not see all of them, and she does not know how many children are exactly taking part in the puzzle. Hence, we assume that the local state of child i is a tuple $\langle s_1, \ldots, s_{i-1}, s_{i+1}, \ldots, s_{|Agl|} \rangle$ that registers whether any other child $j \neq i$ is either clean (0), muddy (1), or unknown ($-$). We define an order $\leq$ on local states such that $l \leq l'$ iff $l'_j = l_j$ for every child $j \neq i$ with $l_j \neq -$.

Now consider a global state $s = (0, 1, -)$, in which child 1 sees that child 2 is muddy, while she has no information on 3. In particular, child 1 knows that, provided that child 2 is actually active in the puzzle (i.e., 2's local state is different from $-$), then she is not muddy, but 1 does not know this about child 3. Formally, we can check that $(s \models K_1(active_2 \rightarrow m_2)) = $ tt as for all states s', $R_1^{may}(s, s')$ implies that $s'_2 \in \{1, -\}$, and therefore 2 is muddy whenever she is active. On the other hand, we have that $(s \models K_1(active_3 \rightarrow m_3)) \neq $ tt, as for state $s'' = (0, 1, 0)$, $R_1^{may}(s, s'')$ holds, that is, child 3 is active but clean. Also, $(s \models K_1(active_3 \rightarrow m_3)) \neq $ ff, as for every s', $R_1^{must}(s, s')$ implies $s'_3 = -$, i.e., $active_3 \rightarrow m_3$ is vacuously true. As a result, $(s \models K_1(active_3 \rightarrow m_3)) = $ uu. By reasoning similarly, we can check that $(s \models D(active_2 \rightarrow m_2)) = $ tt, while $(s \models C(active_3 \rightarrow m_3)) = $ uu.

Furthermore, we consider the impact of the system's evolution on the epistemic properties of agents. In the classic muddy children puzzle, the father announces that at least one child is muddy. As a consequence, no child considers state $(0, 0, 0)$ epistemically possible any longer. In particular, after the father's announcement, at state $v = (1, 0, 0)$ child 1 knows that she is muddy, as for all reachable states v', $R_1^{may}(v, v')$ implies $v_1 = 1$. Hence, it is the case that $(v \models K_1 m_1) = $ tt. On the other hand, for state $u = (1, 0, -)$, we have that $(u \models K_1 m_1) \neq $ tt, as $R_1^{may}(u, (0, 0, 1))$ and $((0, 0, 1) \models m_1) = $ ff. Further, $(u \models K_1 m_1) \neq $ ff as, if $R_1^{must}(u, u')$, then $u'_1 = 1$ because at least one child has to be muddy, and therefore $(u' \models m_1) \neq $ ff. As a result, $(u \models K_1 m_1) = $ uu, that is, child 1 is not able to see any other muddy child, but she cannot infer that she is muddy, as she is unsure about 3. Most importantly, the epistemic properties of agents depends essentially on the states reachable in the system's execution.

Example 2. The second example we analyse hinges on a standard IS, but with an infinite number of states. In Sect. 3 we will show how a finite, three-value abstraction can be defined on such infinite-state IS, in order to make the model checking problem decidable.

In this scenario we consider agents 1 and 2, whose local states are represented by integer variables x and y respectively, taking values in $\mathbb{Z}$, together with the environment e. Agents 1 and 2 can increase or decrease the value of their integers at any time, but in selected cases the joint action takes effect only if they increase or decrease their values simultaneously. Formally, we define agents 1 and 2 so that (i) $L_1 = L_2 = \mathbb{Z}$; (ii) $Act_1 = Act_2 = \{inc, dec\}$; and (iii) $Pr_1(z) = Pr_2(z) = Act_1$ for all $z \in \mathbb{Z}$. Moreover, as regards the environment e, we have $L_e = \{(x, y) \mid x, y \in \mathbb{Z}\}$; and $Act_e = \{ok, no\}$ with $Pr_e((x, y)) = \{ok\}$ iff $x = -4 \Leftrightarrow y = -2$ or $x = 5 \Leftrightarrow y = 3$; $Pr_e((x, y)) = \{no\}$, otherwise. Then, the transition function τ_1 is given as follows. If $x \neq -4$, $x \neq 5$, and $a = (a_1, a_2, ok)$, then the updated value x' is obtained by applying the increase or decrease action a_1. Further, if $x = -4$ or $x = 5$, and $a_1 \neq a_2$ or $a_3 = no$, then the updated value x' is equal to x; else, if $a = (a_1, a_2, ok)$ for $a_1 = a_2$, then the updated value x' is obtained by applying the corresponding action a_1. The definition of τ_2 is symmetric for $y = -2$ and $y = 3$, and it is given as follows:

$$\tau_2(y, (a_1, a_2, ok)) = a_2(y) \qquad \text{for } y \neq -2 \text{ and } y \neq 3;$$
$$\tau_2(y, (a_1, a_2, a_3)) = y \qquad \text{for } y = -2 \text{ or } y = 3, \text{ and } a_3 = no \text{ or } a_1 \neq a_2;$$
$$\tau_2(y, (a_1, a_2, ok)) = a_2(y) \qquad \text{for } y = -2 \text{ or } y = 3, \text{ and } a_1 = a_2.$$

Intuitively, agents 1 and 2 freely increment and decrement their local variable, but synchronise in states $(-4, -2)$ and $(5, 3)$ to either increment or decrement simultaneously. Since each agent can only view her local variable, the environment e acts as to guarantee their synchronisation. In particular, the environment's transition function τ_e is given as follows:

$$\tau_e((x, y), (a_1, a_2, ok)) = (a_1(x), a_2(y)) \quad \text{for } (x, y) \neq (-4, -2) \text{ and } (x, y) \neq (5, 3);$$
$$\tau_e((x, y), (a_1, a_2, a_3)) = (x, y) \qquad \text{for } (x, y) = (-4, -2) \text{ or } (x, y) = (5, 3),$$
$$\text{and } a_3 = no \text{ or } a_1 \neq a_2;$$
$$\tau_e((x, y), (a_1, a_2, ok)) = (a_1(x), a_2(y)) \quad \text{for } (x, y) = (-4, -2) \text{ or } (x, y) = (5, 3),$$
$$\text{and } a_1 = a_2.$$

Finally, we introduce the interpreted system M on the set $Ag = \{1, 2, e\}$ of agents, starting from initial state $(0, 0)$.

By the definition of M, we can check informally that if $x \leq 3$, then agent 1 knows that $y \leq 3$, that is, the specification $(x \leq 3) \to K_1(y \leq 3)$ is true in M. Moreover, specification $(x \leq 3) \to D_{\{1,2\}}(y \leq 3)$ holds as well. However, to verify such formulas at some state $s = (x, y)$ such that $s \models x \leq 3$ we have in principle to check that $y \leq 3$ on an infinite number of states $s' = (x, y')$, for $y' \in \mathbb{Z}$, which are indistinguishable for agent 1. As a consequence, model checking epistemic specification on infinite-state IS is undecidable in principle. In the case in hand we can reason about the particular protocol and specification considered, and reach a conclusive answer. However, our aim is to develop an abstraction-based general-purpose verification procedure that does not rely on system-specific features and can be applied as generally as possible.

3   Abstraction

In this section we introduce an abstraction-based technique for the verification of epistemic properties on standard, possibly infinite interpreted systems. Specifically, for every agent $i \in Ag$ in a standard IS M, we define an abstract agent i^A and the corresponding abstract IS M^A. Then, we prove that any formula ϕ in $\mathbf{K}$ is preserved by the abstraction, that is, if ϕ receives a defined truth value in M^A, then this value is preserved in M. As a result, given an infinite-state standard IS M, we can define a verification procedure by model checking a suitable finite-state abstraction M^A. However, the abstraction M^A of a standard IS M is not necessarily standard, and some specification ϕ can receive an undefined truth value in M^A. Therefore, the outlined procedure defines a partial verification technique, which is to be expected given that model checking infinite-state systems is undecidable in the most general instance.

To define abstraction M^A we introduce some preliminary notions. Given a standard agent $i \in Ag$, we say that a set $\mathcal{U} = \{U_1, \ldots, U_k\} \subseteq 2^L \setminus \{\emptyset\}$ of non-empty subsets $U \subseteq L$ of local states is a *cover* of L iff for every $l \in L$, $l \in U$ for some $U \in \mathcal{U}$. Then, we define a partial order $\leq$ on sets U, U' in the cover $\mathcal{U}$ so that $U \leq U'$ iff $U' \subseteq U$. Intuitively, a set U' of local states contains more information than U iff U' is a subset of U. This is in line with the informal meaning of local states as epistemic alternatives: if agent i considers possible less epistemic alternatives, then she has more information about what the current state actually looks like. In the limit case, for U a singleton, i knows exactly the current state.

Given a cover $\mathcal{U}$ for a standard agent $i \in Ag$, we define the abstraction i^A.

Definition 5 (Abstract Agent). *Given a standard agent $i = \langle L, Act, Pr, \tau \rangle$ and a cover $\mathcal{U}$, we introduce the abstraction $i^A = \langle L^A, Act^A, Pr^A, \tau^A \rangle$ such that*

- *$L^A = \mathcal{U}$ with partial order $\leq$ such that $U \leq U'$ iff $U' \subseteq U$;*
- *$Act = Act^A$;*
- *for every $U \in L^A$, $Pr^A(U) = \bigcup_{l \in U} Pr(l)$;*
- *$U' \in \tau^A(U, a)$ iff for some $l \in U$, $l' \in U'$, we have $l' \in \tau(l, a)$.*

Notice that the size of an abstract agent i^A, given as the cardinality $|L^A|$ of the set L^A of her abstract local states, is finite although the set L of concrete local states might be infinite. Indeed, while in such a case cover L^A must contain at least one subset $U \subseteq L$ with infinitely many local states, the size $|L^A|$ of L^A given as its cardinality is finite. Further, an action a is enabled in abstract state U iff it is enabled in some local state in U; while a transition $U \to U'$ holds iff $l \to l'$ for some local states $l \in U$ and $l' \in U'$. Observe that the definition of the abstract transition function τ^A is in line with similar notions for the abstraction of simple transition systems [8]. As a consequence, it is also prone to some of the related issues. In particular, the abstract transition might generate reachable states for which there is no corresponding concrete transition and reachable states, that is, the abstract transition might be spurious. Hereafter, we impose constraints on our abstract agents and interpreted systems to avoid spurious transitions.

Next we define a kind of simulation relation between the global states built on the concrete and abstract agents respectively, and say that $s' \in \mathcal{G}^A$ *simulates* $s \in \mathcal{G}$, or $s \preceq s'$, iff for every $i \in Ag$, $s_i \in s'_i$. Notice that, since each $\mathcal{U}_i$ is a cover, for every $s \in \mathcal{G}$, $s \preceq s'$ for some $s' \in \mathcal{G}^A$.

We now introduce the abstraction M^A of a standard IS M, defined on abstract agents $i^A \in Ag^A$, as follows.

Definition 6 (Abstract IS). *Given a standard IS $M = \langle Ag, I, \tau, \Pi \rangle$, the abstract IS $M^A = \langle Ag^A, I^A, \tau^A, \Pi^A \rangle$ is such that*

- Ag^A *is the set of abstract agents i^A, for each agent $i \in Ag$;*
- $I^A = \{ s' \in \mathcal{G}^A \mid s \preceq s' \text{ for some } s \in I \}$;
- τ^A *is defined as in Definition 2;*
- *for every $s' \in \mathcal{G}^A$, for $t \in \{\text{tt}, \text{ff}\}$, $\Pi^A(s', p) = t$ iff for all $s \in \mathcal{G}$, $s \preceq s'$ implies $\Pi(s, p) = t$; otherwise, $\Pi^A(s', p) = \text{uu}$.*

Since each $\mathcal{U}_i$ is a cover, the set I^A of abstract initial states is non-empty whenever I is. Further, the global abstract transition function τ^A is indeed the composition of the various local τ^A_i, as per Definition 2; while an atom is either true or false at abstract state s' iff it is such in all concrete states simulated by s', otherwise it is undefined.

Above we mentioned that the abstract transition function can introduce reachable states in the abstract IS M^A, for which there is no corresponding concrete state reachable in M. In particular, in M^A an agent might consider reachable epistemic alternatives, that are not really such in M. This remark motivates the introduction of the following notion.

Definition 7 (Admissibility). *A set Ag^A of abstract agents is* admissible *iff for every $s' \in \mathcal{G}^A$ and $s, t \in \mathcal{G}$, if $s \preceq s'$ and $t \preceq s'$ then $s \rightarrow^+ t$.*

Intuitively, this condition on IS says that any state simulated by $s' \in \mathcal{G}^A$ is eventually reachable from any other state simulated by s'. Then, an abstraction M^A of an IS is *admissible* iff all its abstract agents in Ag^A are.

By this notion of admissibility we are able to prove the following key result, which intuitively states that the epistemic relations in IS M and abstraction M^A commute with the simulation relation $\preceq$.

Lemma 1. *Let M be a standard IS with admissible abstraction M^A. If $s \preceq s'$ and $R_i^{Amust}(s', t')$, then $s \sim_i t$ for some $t \in \mathcal{S}$ such that $t \preceq t'$. Moreover, if $s \preceq s'$ and $s \sim_i t$, then $R_i^{Amay}(s', t')$ for some t' such that $t \preceq t'$.*

Proof. Suppose that $s \preceq s'$. Then, $R_i^{Amust}(s', t')$ iff $t'_i \leq s'_i$, iff $s'_i \subseteq t'_i$. In particular, for $l = s_i$, $s \preceq s'$ and $s'_i \subseteq t'_i$ imply $l \in t'_i$. Further, if $t' \in I^A$ is initial, then either $t \preceq t'$ for some initial $t \in I$ such that $t_i = l$, and therefore $s \sim_i t$ for $t \in \mathcal{S}$; or for some $t^0 \in I$, $t^0 \preceq t'$, but $t_i^0 \neq l$. However, we assumed that M^A is admissible, that is, $t \preceq t'$ is reachable from $t^0 \preceq t'$. Hence, we obtain a reachable state $t \in \mathcal{S}^A$ such that $t \preceq t'$ and $t_i = l = s_i$, i.e., $s \sim_i t$.

On the other hand, suppose that t' is reachable in M^A via execution $t'^0 \to \ldots \to t'^k$ such that $t'^0 \in I^A$ and $t'^k = t'$. By induction on k, we can prove that there exists an execution $t^0, \ldots, t^{k'}$ in M, for $k' \geq k$, and integers $j' \leq k'$ such that $t^j \preceq t^{j'}$ and $t_i^{k'} = l$. The case for $k = 0$, that is, $t' \in I^A$, goes as above. Hence suppose that the induction hypothesis holds for $k - 1$. Further, we have $t'^{k-1} \to t'^k$. In particular, $v \to v'$ for some $v \preceq t'^{k-1}$ and $v' \preceq t'^k$. Since M^A is admissible, v is reachable from $t^{k'-1}$ and $t^{k'}$ is reachable from v'. Hence, by reasoning similarly to the case for $k = 0$, we obtain an execution $t^0 \to \ldots \to t^{k'}$ in M such that $t^k \preceq t^{k'}$ and $t_i^{k'} = l$. In particular, for $t = t^{k'} \in \mathcal{S}$, we have $s \sim_i t$ and $t \preceq t'$.

Finally, suppose that $s \sim_i t$, that is, $s_i = t_i$. Hence, for $t_i' = s_i'$ we have $t_i' \subseteq t_i'$ and $t_i' \subseteq s_i'$. Moreover, for every $j \neq i$, there exists U_j such that $t_j \in U_j$. Define $t' = \langle U_0, \ldots, U_{i-1}, t_i, U_{i+1}, \ldots, U_{|Ag|} \rangle$. By Definition 6 abstract state t' is reachable in M^A by the same sequence of joint actions as t in M. Hence, $t' \in \mathcal{S}^A$ and $R_i^{Amay}(s', t')$ holds.

Notice that the need for admissibility stems from the presence of spurious executions in the abstract system. Various methodologies have been put forward for refining abstractions w.r.t. spurious behaviours [8]. Here we remark that our notion of admissibility is only meant to preserve reachability, and in general it is not sufficient to preserve more elaborate temporal properties. Nonetheless, it is enough to preserve epistemic properties, as shown by the next result.

Theorem 1. *Let M be a standard IS with admissible abstraction M^A, $s \preceq s'$, and $t \in \{\text{tt}, \text{ff}\}$. Then for every formula ϕ in $\mathbf{K}$,*

$$((M^A, s') \models^3 \phi) = t \quad implies \quad ((M, s) \models^3 \phi) = t$$

Proof. The proof is by induction on the structure of ϕ. We only consider the cases for knowledge formulas, with $\phi = K_i \varphi$. If $((M, s) \models^3 \phi) \neq \text{tt}$ then for some $t \in S$, $s \sim_i t$ and $((M, t) \models^3 \varphi) \neq \text{tt}$. If $s \preceq s'$ and $s \sim_i t$, then by Lemma 1, for some $t' \in \mathcal{S}^A$, $R_i^{Amay}(s', t')$ and $t \preceq t'$. In particular, $((M, t) \models^3 \varphi) \neq \text{tt}$ implies $((M^A, t') \models^3 \varphi) \neq \text{tt}$ by induction hypothesis, that is, $((M^A, s') \models^3 \phi) \neq \text{tt}$. As regards the case for $\phi = K_i \varphi$ being false. If $((M^A, s') \models^3 \phi) = \text{ff}$ then for some $t' \in \mathcal{S}^A$, $R_i^{Amust}(s', t')$ and $((M^A, t') \models^3 \varphi) = \text{ff}$. If $s \preceq s'$ and $R_i^{Amust}(s', t')$, then again by Lemma 1, for some $t \in \mathcal{S}$, $s \sim_i t$ and $t \preceq t'$. In particular, by induction hypothesis we obtain $((M, t) \models^3 \varphi) = \text{ff}$, and therefore $((M, s) \models^3 \phi) = \text{ff}$. The cases for the distributed and common knowledge formulas are proved similarly.

By Proposition 1 and Theorem 1 the next result follows immediately.

Corollary 1. *Let M be a standard IS with admissible abstraction M^A, and $s \preceq s'$. Then for every formula ϕ in $\mathbf{K}$,*

$$((M^A, s') \models^3 \phi) = \text{tt} \quad implies \quad (M, s) \models^2 \phi$$
$$((M^A, s') \models^3 \phi) = \text{ff} \quad implies \quad (M, s) \not\models^2 \phi$$

By Theorem 1 and Corollary 1 we obtain the following (partial) decision procedure to verify a multi-agent epistemic specification ϕ against infinite-state IS. Given a standard IS M we build an admissible abstraction M^A and then model check ϕ against M^A. If the outcome is either true tt or false ff, then by Corollary 1 we obtain that ϕ is true (resp. false) in M as well. In case that ϕ is undefined in M^A, then no conclusive answer can be drawn. As we mentioned, this limitation is to be expected, since the state-space of M is infinite, and the model checking problem for infinite-state systems is undecidable in general. Nonetheless, we may think of refinement procedures on the abstraction M^A, in order to obtain a refined abstraction M'^A that is able to decide ϕ. We leave abstraction refinement for future work, while here we observe that the abstract IS M^A depends crucially on the cover $\mathcal{U}_i$ chosen for each agent $i \in Ag$. Here we did not provide details as to how such covers can be effectively found. In most cases of interest covers can be obtained by an analysis of the protocol and transition function of each agents, as well as the specification at hand. We consider an instance of such cases in the following example.

Example 3. We reconsider Example 2. By an analysis of the protocols and transition functions of agents 1 and 2, we identify predicates $p_1 := (x < -4)$, $p_2 := (x = -4)$, $p_3 := (-4 < x < 5)$, $p_4 := (x = 5)$, and $p_5 := (x > 5)$ regarding agent 1, as well as predicates $q_1 := (y < -2)$, $q_2 := (y = -2)$, $q_3 := (-2 < y < 3)$, $q_4 := (y = 3)$, and $q_5 := (y > 3)$ for agent 2. With an abuse of notation, we identify a predicate p with the set of local states satisfying p, as it is customary, for instance, in predicate abstraction [12].

Consider again specification $(x \leq 3) \rightarrow K_1(y \leq 3)$, and a new predicate $p_6 := (-4 < x \leq 3)$. Then, condition $x \leq 3$ can be rewritten as $p_1 \vee p_2 \vee p_6$, and $y \leq 3$ is tantamount to $q_1 \vee q_2 \vee q_3 \vee q_4$. Further, observe that $\mathcal{U}_1 = \{p_1, \ldots, p_6\}$ is a cover of L_1, and $\mathcal{U}_2 = \{q_1, \ldots, q_5\}$ is a cover of L_2 (actually a partition). Then, we define abstract agents 1^A and 2^A such that

- $L_1^A = \mathcal{U}_1 = \{p_1, \ldots, p_6\}$ with order $p_3 \leq p_6$, and $L_2^A = \mathcal{U}_2 = \{q_1, \ldots, q_5\}$;
- $Act_1^A = Act_2^A = Act_1 = Act_2$;
- $Pr_1^A(p) = Act_1$, for all $p \in L_1^A$; and $Pr_2^A(q) = Act_1$, for all $q \in L_2^A$;
- the abstract transition function τ_1^A is such that, for $1 \leq j \leq 5$, $j \neq 3$,

$$\tau_1^A(p_j, (dec, a_2, ok)) = \{p_j, p_{j-1}\} \qquad \tau_1^A(p_j, (inc, a_2, ok)) = \{p_j, p_{j+1}\}$$

with the proviso that $p_{j-1} = p_j$ for $j = 1$, and $p_{j+1} = p_j$ for $j = 5$. Moreover,

$$\tau_1^A(p_3, (dec, a_2, ok)) = \{p_2, p_3, p_6\} \qquad \tau_1^A(p_3, (inc, a_2, ok)) = \{p_3, p_4, p_6\}$$
$$\tau_1^A(p_6, (dec, a_2, ok)) = \{p_6, p_2, p_3\} \qquad \tau_1^A(p_6, (inc, a_2, ok)) = \{p_6, p_3\}$$

and for all $p \in L_1^A$, $\tau_1^A(p, (a_1, a_2, no)) = p$.
- the abstract transition function τ_2^A is defined similarly to τ_1^A.

Observe that the definitions of the abstract agents 1^A and 2^A are in accordance with Definition 5. Also, the abstract environment e^A is given as follows:

- $L_3^A = \{(p, q) \mid p \in L_1^A, q \in L_2^A\}$;
- $Act_e^A = Act_e$;
- $Pr_e^A((p_i, q_j)) = \{ok\}$ iff $i = 2 \Leftrightarrow j = 2$ or $i = 4 \Leftrightarrow j = 4$; otherwise, $Pr_e^A((p_i, q_j)) = \{no\}$
- we omit the detailed presentation of τ_e^A for reasons of space, but this can be obtained immediately by Definition 5.

Moreover, all agents 1^A, 2^A, and e^A are admissible, as in the concrete IS M, every state is reachable from any other state by an appropriate sequence of actions. The abstract IS M^A is defined on the set $Ag^A = \{1^A, 2^A, e^A\}$ of abstract agents as above, while the set I^A of abstract initial states contains pairs (p_3, q_3) and (p_6, q_3) only. The abstract global transition function τ^A is defined as in Definition 6, and the labelling of abstract states is immediate. In particular, M^A is a finite-state system.

Now, we check specification $(x \leq 3) \rightarrow K_1(y \leq 3)$ on abstraction M^A. Specifically, if $((M^A, s) \models x \leq 3) = \text{tt}$ then $s_1 = p_1$, $s_1 = p_2$, or $s_1 = p_6$. In the first case, $R_1^{Amay}(s, s')$ implies $s_1' = p_1$ and $s_2' = q_1$ or $s_2' = q_2$. In both cases $((M^A, s') \models y \leq 3) = \text{tt}$. Further, $s_1 = p_2$ and $R_1^{Amay}(s, s')$ imply $s_1' = p_2$ and $s_2' = q_2$, and again $((M^A, s') \models y \leq 3) = \text{tt}$. Finally, $s_1 = p_6$ and $R_1^{Amay}(s, s')$ imply $s_1' = p_6$ or $s_1' = p_3$. In the former case we have that $s_2' = q_2$ or $s_2' = q_3$, and therefore $((M^A, s') \models y \leq 3) = \text{tt}$. In the latter, $s_2' = q_2$, $s_2' = q_3$, or $s_2' = q_4$. In all these cases we obtain $((M^A, s') \models y \leq 3) = \text{tt}$. As a result, if $((M^A, s) \models x \leq 3) = \text{tt}$, then for all $s' \in \mathcal{S}^A$, $R_1^{Amay}(s, s')$ implies $((M^A, s') \models y \leq 3) = \text{tt}$, that is, $((M^A, s) \models K_1(y \leq 3)) = \text{tt}$. Hence, the specification is true in the abstract model, and by the transfer result Theorem 1 we obtain that it holds in the concrete IS M as well.

4   Conclusions

In this paper we introduced a three-value semantics for the multi-agent epistemic logic **K**, based on a notion of order defined on the local states of each agent. Intuitively, in the standard, two-value interpretation of epistemic logic, a notion of i-indistinguishability is defined on global states by the identity of the local states for agent i. Here we generalised this idea by considering a partial order $\leq$ on local state, instead of the identity $=$. This semantic choice allows us to define an abstraction technique, in which local states are bundled together in sets that are then compared according to set-theoretic inclusion. Most importantly, we are able to model check an epistemic specification ϕ on a concrete, infinite-state IS M, by verifying the same formula on some suitable abstraction M^A, and then transfer the result to M by means of Theorem 1. We observe that the abstraction technique developed in Sect. 3 has a key advantage over similar contributions in [3,25]. In fact, in [3,25] abstract states are defined as satisfiable cubes of predicates, which are generated by means of an SMT solver with considerable computational cost. Nothing similar is needed in the present context, where predicates, seen as sets of states, can be arbitrary as long as they satisfy the admissibility condition.

Admittedly, powerful as it is, the proposed methodology has a number of limitations. We provided an heuristic for building the abstraction M^A, by using the predicates mentioned in the system description as well as the specification at hand, but did not provide any algorithmic procedure to build a suitable, finite M^A, nor any correctness proof of such a procedure. Further, we require our predicates, agents, and interpreted system to be admissible, that is, being closed under reachability. While we conjecture that in most cases of interest, this property hold, further investigations are needed on this point. These are all directions we aim to explore in future work, in order to develop a fully automated verification methodology for epistemic properties of infinite-state multi-agent systems. Finally, we plan to implement this verification procedure as an extension of the MCMAS model checker [27].

References

1. Bagheri, B., Calvanese, D., Montali, M., Giacomo, G., Deutsch, A.: Verification of relational data-centric dynamic systems with external services. In: Proceedings of the 32nd Symposium on Principles of Database Systems (PODS13), pp. 163–174. ACM (2013)
2. Ball, T., Kupferman, O.: An abstraction-refinement framework for multi-agent systems. In: Proceedings of the 21st Annual IEEE Symposium on Logic in Computer Science (LICS06), pp. 379–388. IEEE (2006)
3. Belardinelli, F., Lomuscio, A., Michaliszyn, J.: Agent-based refinement for predicate abstraction of multi-agent systems. In: Proceedings of the 22nd European Conference on Artificial Intelligence (ECAI16), pp. 286–294. IOS Press (2016)
4. Belardinelli, F., Lomuscio, A., Patrizi, F.: Verification of agent-based artifact systems. J. Artif. Intell. Res. **51**, 333–376 (2014)
5. Belardinelli, F.: Model checking auctions as artifact systems: decidability via finite abstraction. In: Proceedings of the 21st European Conference on Artificial Intelligence (ECAI14), pp. 81–86 (2014)
6. Boureanu, I., Kouvaros, P., Lomuscio, A.: Verifying security properties in unbounded multi-agent systems. In: Proceedings of the 15th International Conference on Autonomous Agents and Multi-Agent Systems (AAMAS16), pp. 1209–1218. IFAAMAS (2016)
7. Bruns, G., Godefroid, P.: Model checking with multi-valued logics. Technical report ITD-03-44535H, Bell Labs (2003)
8. Clarke, E., Grumberg, O., Jha, S., Lu, Y., Veith, H.: Counterexample-guided abstraction refinement. In: Emerson, E.A., Sistla, A.P. (eds.) CAV 2000. LNCS, vol. 1855, pp. 154–169. Springer, Heidelberg (2000). doi:10.1007/10722167_15
9. Clarke, E.M., Grumberg, O., Peled, D.A.: Model Checking. MIT Press, Cambridge (1999)
10. Cohen, M., Dam, M., Lomuscio, A., Qu, H.: A data symmetry reduction technique for temporal-epistemic logic. In: Liu, Z., Ravn, A.P. (eds.) ATVA 2009. LNCS, vol. 5799, pp. 69–83. Springer, Heidelberg (2009). doi:10.1007/978-3-642-04761-9_6
11. Cohen, M., Dam, M., Lomuscio, A., Russo, F.: Abstraction in model checking multi-agent systems. In: Proceedings of the 8th International Conference on Autonomous Agents and Multiagent Systems (AAMAS09), pp. 945–952. IFAAMAS Press (2009)

12. Das, S., Dill, D.L., Park, S.: Experience with predicate abstraction. In: Halbwachs, N., Peled, D. (eds.) CAV 1999. LNCS, vol. 1633, pp. 160–171. Springer, Heidelberg (1999). doi:10.1007/3-540-48683-6_16

13. De Giacomo, G., Lespérance, Y., Patrizi, F.: Bounded situation calculus action theories and decidable verification. In: Proceedings of the 13th International Conference on Principles of Knowledge Representation and Reasoning (KR 2012), pp. 467–477 (2012)

14. Enea, C., Dima, C.: Abstractions of multi-agent systems. In: Burkhard, H.-D., Lindemann, G., Verbrugge, R., Varga, L.Z. (eds.) CEEMAS 2007. LNCS (LNAI), vol. 4696, pp. 11–21. Springer, Heidelberg (2007). doi:10.1007/978-3-540-75254-7_2

15. Fagin, R., Halpern, J.Y., Moses, Y., Vardi, M.Y.: Reasoning about Knowledge. MIT Press, Cambridge (1995)

16. Fitting, M.: Many-valued modal logics. Fundam. Inform. **15**(3–4), 335–350 (1991)

17. Fitting, M.: Many-valued modal logics II. Fundam. Inform. **17**, 55–73 (1992)

18. Gammie, P., Meyden, R.: MCK: model checking the logic of knowledge. In: Alur, R., Peled, D.A. (eds.) CAV 2004. LNCS, vol. 3114, pp. 479–483. Springer, Heidelberg (2004). doi:10.1007/978-3-540-27813-9_41

19. Godefroid, P., Jagadeesan, R.: On the expressiveness of 3-valued models. In: Zuck, L.D., Attie, P.C., Cortesi, A., Mukhopadhyay, S. (eds.) VMCAI 2003. LNCS, vol. 2575, pp. 206–222. Springer, Heidelberg (2003). doi:10.1007/3-540-36384-X_18

20. Gonzalez, P., Griesmayer, A., Lomuscio, A.: Verification of GSM-based artifact-centric systems by predicate abstraction. In: Barros, A., Grigori, D., Narendra, N.C., Dam, H.K. (eds.) ICSOC 2015. LNCS, vol. 9435, pp. 253–268. Springer, Heidelberg (2015). doi:10.1007/978-3-662-48616-0_16

21. van der Hoek, W., Meyer, J.J.C.: Possible logics for belief. Logique et Analyse **127–128**, 177–194 (1989)

22. Kacprzak, M., Nabialek, W., Niewiadomski, A., Penczek, W., Pólrola, A., Szreter, M., Woźna, B., Zbrzezny, A.: Verics 2007 - a model checker for knowledge and real-time. Fundam. Inform. **85**(1), 313–328 (2008)

23. Katoen, C.: Principles of Model Checking (Representation and Mind Series). MIT Press, Cambridge (2008)

24. Lomuscio, A., Michaliszyn, J.: Verifying multi-agent systems by model checking three-valued abstractions. In: Proceedings of the 14th International Conference on Autonomous Agents and Multiagent Systems (AAMAS15), pp. 189–198 (2015)

25. Lomuscio, A., Michaliszyn, J.: Verification of multi-agent systems via predicate abstraction against ATLK specifications. In: Proceedings of the 15th International Conference on Autonomous Agents and Multiagent Systems (AAMAS16), pp. 662–670 (2016)

26. Lomuscio, A., Penczek, W.: Model checking temporal epistemic Logic. In: van Ditmarsch, H., Halpern, J.Y., van der Hoek, W., Kooi, B. (eds.) Handbook of Epistemic Logic. College Publications, London (2015)

27. Lomuscio, A., Qu, H., Raimondi, F.: MCMAS: A model checker for the verification of multi-agent systems. Software Tools for Technology Transfer (2015). http://dx.doi.org/10.1007/s10009-015-0378-x

28. Shoham, S., Grumberg, O.: Monotonic abstraction-refinement for CTL. In: Jensen, K., Podelski, A. (eds.) TACAS 2004. LNCS, vol. 2988, pp. 546–560. Springer, Heidelberg (2004). doi:10.1007/978-3-540-24730-2_40

29. Wooldridge, M.: An Introduction to MultiAgent Systems, 2nd edn. Wiley, Chichester (2009)

A Relaxation of Internal Conflict and Defence in Weighted Argumentation Frameworks

Stefano Bistarelli, Fabio Rossi, and Francesco Santini[✉]

Dipartimento di Informatica e Matematica, Università di Perugia, Perugia, Italy
{bista,rossi,francesco.santini}@dmi.unipg.it

Abstract. In Weighted Abstract Argumentation Frameworks (WAAFs), weights on attacks bring more information. An advantage is the possibility to define a different notion of defence, which also checks if the weight associated with defence is compared with the weight of attacks. We study and merge together two different relaxations of classically crisp-concepts in WAAFs: one is related to a new notion of weighted defence (defence can be stronger or weaker at will), while the second one is related to how much inconsistency one is willing to tolerate inside an extension (which can be not totally conflict-free now). These two relaxations are strictly related and influence each other: allowing a small conflict may lead to have more arguments in an extension, and consequently result in a stronger or weaker defence. We model weights with a semiring structure, which can be instantiated to different metrics used in the literature (*e.g.*, fuzzy WAAFs).

1 Introduction

The aim of this work is to relax classically exact and sharp concepts in *Weighted Abstract Argumentation Frameworks* (*WAAFs*, see works in Sect. 6). This is accomplished *(i)* by allowing an internal conflict *inside* the extensions satisfying a given semantics (*e.g.*, admissible), and *(ii)* by relaxing the defence of arguments w.r.t. (the weight of) the attacks coming from *outside* an extension. Such two issues mutually influence each other, hence they need to be studied together: allowing a small conflict may lead to have one more argument inside an extension, which consequently may be more strongly defended by exploiting the attacks of this additional argument, or more weakly, in case such additional taken-argument receives attacks from external ones.

A flexible computational framework should consider *i* and *ii*, in order to let an agent cope with both such two factors simultaneously. In this way, an autonomous reasoning-agent has more instruments to understand, for instance, whether tolerating a small conflict among its arguments considerably changes its point of view: as a possible scenario, a debate can be permeated by arguments advanced by *trolls* [18], which can accordingly generate noise in an abstract framework. Internal inconsistency arises in many areas of AI and computing:

Research supported by: "VisColla" funded by Fondazione Cassa di Risparmio di Perugia, and "BitCoins" funded by Banca d'Italia and Cassa di Risparmio di Perugia.

L. Michael and A. Kakas (Eds.): JELIA 2016, LNAI 10021, pp. 127–143, 2016.
DOI: 10.1007/978-3-319-48758-8_9

merging information from heterogeneous sources, negotiation in multi-agent systems, or understanding natural language dialogues [4].

On the other hand, an agent could be interested in defending its arguments with a higher or lower level of strength. Even this choice impacts on the final outcome: by requiring a weaker defence one finds more extensions with the same given semantics. The strictest (not relaxed) level of defence corresponds to w-defence [7]. Differently from [14], where the aggregation of all the attack weights from a set of arguments $\mathscr{B}$ to an attacker a needs to be only stronger than the attack from a to b, in w-defence we aggregate all the attack weights from a to $\mathscr{B}$: attacks are collectively considered.

With such aims in mind, we design α^γ-semantics, where α is the amount of internal conflict tolerated inside an extension, and γ is the weight-difference between a "full" defence (we newly define and call it w-defence) and the "weaker" defence it holds instead. By progressively relaxing defence (i.e., increasing γ) we show that we reconnect to related definitions in the literature, as [14] and Dung's seminal work [15]. Hence, we define α^γ-conflict-free, α^γ-admissible, α^γ-complete, α^γ-preferred, and α^γ-stable. These new semantics nevertheless inherit some original properties [15], as their implications (e.g., α^γ-stable $\Rightarrow \alpha^\gamma$-preferred), or the fact that $\top^\perp$-semantics are equivalent to their correspondent in [15], and $\top^\top$-semantics are equivalent to [7].

To represent weights and operations (e.g., their aggregation), we adopt a parametric algebraic framework based on c-semirings [6]. Hence, it is possible to consider different metrics within the same computational framework (e.g., fuzzy or probabilistic).

The paper is structured as follows: in Sect. 2.1 we introduce c-semirings [6] (the general structure we adopt to represent weights) and we summarise the basic definitions of AAF given in [15]. Section 3 presents WAAFs and w-defence. Section 3.1 relaxes w-defence by proposing γ-defence, where γ is the amount by which defence is weakened. In Sect. 4 we propose α^γ-semantics (e.g., α^γ-admissible), which extend classical ones by considering an internal amount of conflict α, and γ at the same time. In Sect. 5 we describe an implementation of the proposed framework, and we show the tests obtained on a set of 100 random WAAFs; we also present an application scenario and contextualise the motivations behind the work. In Sect. 6 we describe related work, and, finally, Sect. 7 wraps up the paper by drawing final conclusions and suggesting future work.

2   Background

We first introduce c-semirings (Sect. 2.1), and then (Sect. 2.2) we recollect the main definitions behind AAFs [15]. C-semirings here represent a parametric framework where to evaluate and compose attack-weights. By changing the underlying c-semiring instantiation, it is possible to capture different metrics with the purpose to model e.g., fuzzy or probabilistic WAAFs (see Sect. 6).

2.1 Semirings

In practice, c-semirings [6] are *commutative* ($\otimes$ is commutative) and *idempotent* semirings (i.e., $\oplus$ is idempotent), where $\oplus$ defines a complete lattice: every subset of elements have a *least upper bound*, or *lub*, and a *greatest lower bound*, or *glb*. In fact, c-semirings are semirings where $\oplus$ is used as a preference operator, while $\otimes$ is used to compose preference-values together.

Definition 1 (C-semirings [6]). *A commutative semiring is a tuple* $\mathbb{S} = \langle S, \oplus, \otimes, \bot, \top \rangle$ *such that S is a set, $\top, \bot \in S$, and $\oplus, \otimes : S \times S \to S$ are binary operators making the triples $\langle S, \oplus, \bot \rangle$ and $\langle S, \otimes, \top \rangle$ commutative monoids (semigroups with identity), satisfying (i) $\forall s, t, u \in S.s \otimes (t + u) = (s \otimes t) + (s \otimes u)$ (distributivity), and (ii) $\forall s \in S.s \otimes \bot = \bot$ (annihilator). If $\forall s, t \in S.s \oplus (s \otimes t) = s$, the semiring is said to be absorptive. In short, c-semirings are defined as commutative and absorptive semirings.*

The idempotency of $\oplus$ leads to the definition of a partial ordering $\leq_{\mathbb{S}}$ over the set S (S is a poset). Such partial order is defined as $s \leq_{\mathbb{S}} t$ if and only if $s \oplus t = t$, and $\oplus$ returns the *lub* of s and t (defined also as $\sqcup$, while the *glb* is defined by $\sqcap$). This intuitively means that t is "better" than s. Some more properties can be derived on c-semirings [6]: *(i)* both $\oplus$ and $\otimes$ are monotone over $\leq_{\mathbb{S}}$, *(ii)* $\otimes$ is intensive (i.e., $s \otimes t \leq_{\mathbb{S}} s$), and *(iii)* $\langle S, \leq_{\mathbb{S}} \rangle$ is a complete lattice. $\bot$ and $\top$ are respectively the bottom and top elements of such lattice. When also $\otimes$ is idempotent, *(i)* $\oplus$ distributes over $\otimes$, *(ii)* $\otimes$ returns the *glb* of two values in S, and *(iii)* $\langle S, \leq_{\mathbb{S}} \rangle$ is a distributive lattice.

Well-known c-semiring instances are: $\mathbb{S}_{boolean} = \langle \{false, true\}, \vee, \wedge, false, true \rangle$[1], $\mathbb{S}_{fuzzy} = \langle [0, 1], \max, \min, 0, 1 \rangle$, $\mathbb{S}_{bottleneck} = \langle \mathbb{R}^+ \cup \{+\infty\}, \max, \min, 0, \infty \rangle$, $\mathbb{S}_{probabilistic} = \langle [0, 1], \max, \times, 0, 1 \rangle$ (or *Viterbi* semiring), $\mathbb{S}_{weighted} = \langle \mathbb{R}^+ \cup \{+\infty\}, min, +, +\infty, 0 \rangle$.

Although c-semirings have been historically used as monotonic structures where to aggregate costs (and find best solutions), the need of removing values has raised in local consistency algorithms and non-monotonic algebras using constraints (e.g., [5]). A solution comes from *residuation theory* [11], a standard tool on tropical arithmetics that allows for obtaining a division operator that represents a "weak" inverse of $\otimes$.

Definition 2 (Division [5]). *Let $\mathbb{S}$ be a tropical semiring. $\mathbb{S}$ is residuated if the set $\{x \in S \mid t \otimes x \leq s\}$ admits a maximum for all elements $s, t \in S$, denoted $s \oslash t$.*

Since a complete[2] tropical-semiring is also residuated, we have that all the classical instances of c-semiring presented above are residuated, i.e., each element in S admits an "inverse", which can be also unique:

---

[1] Boolean c-semirings can be used to model crisp problems and classical Argumentation [15].

[2] $\mathbb{S}$ is complete if it is closed with respect to infinite sums, and the distributivity law holds also for an infinite number of summands [5].

Definition 3 (Unique invertibility [5]**).** *If* $\mathbb{S}$ *is absorptive and invertible, then it is uniquely invertible iff it is cancellative, i.e.,* $\forall s, t, u \in S.(s \otimes u = t \otimes u) \wedge (u \neq 0) \Rightarrow s = t.$

Since all the previously listed instances of c-semirings are cancellative, they are uniquely invertible as well. For instance, the unique "inverse" $s \oslash t$ in the weighted c-semiring is $\top = 0$ if $t \geq s$ (e.g., $s = 7, t = 8$) and $s - t$ if $s > t$ (e.g., $8 - 7 = 1$), while in the fuzzy c-semiring it is $\top = 1$ if $t \leq s$ (e.g., $s = 0.8, t = 0.7$) and s if $s < t$ (e.g., $s = 0.7, t = 0.8$); this is also known as Gödel implication. In the following of the paper we will use "semiring" as a synonym of "c-semiring".

2.2   Argument Systems

In his pioneering work [15], Dung proposes *Abstract Argumentation Frameworks*:

Definition 4. *An Abstract Argumentation Framework (AAF) is a pair* $\langle \mathscr{A}_{rgs}, R \rangle$ *of a set* $\mathscr{A}_{rgs}$ *of arguments and a binary relation* R *on* $\mathscr{A}_{rgs}$ *called the attack relation.* $\forall a_i, a_j \in \mathscr{A}_{rgs}$, $a_i R a_j$ *(or* $R(a_i, a_j)$*) means that* a_i *attacks* a_j.

An *argumentation semantics* is the formal definition of a method (either declarative or procedural) ruling the argument evaluation process. In the *extension*-based approach, a semantics definition specifies how to derive from an AAF a set of extensions, where an extension $\mathscr{B}$ of an AAF $\langle \mathscr{A}_{rgs}, R \rangle$ is simply a subset of $\mathscr{A}_{rgs}$. In Definition 5 we define the first semantics, which is at the basis of all the others:

Definition 5 (Conflict-free). *A set* $\mathscr{B} \subseteq \mathscr{A}_{rgs}$ *is conflict-free iff no two arguments* a *and* b *in* $\mathscr{B}$ *exist such that* a *attacks* b.

All the other semantics presented in this section rely (explicitly or implicitly) upon the concept of defence:

Definition 6 (Defence $\mathbb{D}_0$**).** *An argument* b *is defended by a set* $\mathscr{B} \subseteq \mathscr{A}_{rgs}$ *(or* $\mathscr{B}$ *defends* b*) iff for any argument* $a \in \mathscr{A}_{rgs}$, *if* $R(a, b)$ *then* $\exists c \in \mathscr{B}$ *s.t.,* $R(c, a)$.

An admissible set of arguments is a conflict-free set that defends all its elements. Formally:

Definition 7 (Admissible). *A conflict-free set* $\mathscr{B} \subseteq \mathscr{A}_{rgs}$ *is admissible iff each argument in* $\mathscr{B}$ *is defended by* $\mathscr{B}$ *(from the arguments in* $\mathscr{A}_{rgs} \backslash \mathscr{B}$*).*

Three classical semantics [15] refining admissibility are defined in the following definitions:

Definition 8 (Complete). *An admissible extension* $\mathscr{B} \subseteq \mathscr{A}_{rgs}$ *is a complete extension iff each argument which is defended by* $\mathscr{B}$ *is in* $\mathscr{B}$.

Definition 9 (Preferred). *A preferred extension is a maximal (w.r.t. set inclusion) admissible subset of $\mathscr{A}_{rgs}$.*

Definition 10 (Stable). *A conflict-free set $\mathscr{B} \subseteq \mathscr{A}_{rgs}$ is a stable extension iff for each argument which is not in $\mathscr{B}$, there exists an argument in $\mathscr{B}$ that attacks it.*

If $\sigma = \{cf, adm, com, stb, prf\}$ respectively stand for conflict-free, admissible, complete, stable, and preferred semantics, we recall that given any framework F, $stb(F) \subseteq prf(F) \subseteq com(F) \subseteq adm(F)$ always holds. Moreover, for each σ except stb we have $\sigma(F) \neq \emptyset$ holds.

3   Weighted Abstract AFs

In the following of this section we rephrase some of the classical definitions given in [15], with the purpose to parametrise them with the notion of weighted attack and c-semiring. The following definition presents *semiring-based WAAF* [8]:

Definition 11 (Semiring-based WAAF [8]). *A semiring-based Weighted AAF (WAAF$_{\mathbb{S}}$) is a quadruple $\langle \mathscr{A}_{rgs}, R, W, \mathbb{S} \rangle$, where $\mathbb{S}$ is a c-semiring $\langle S, \oplus, \otimes, \bot, \top \rangle$, $\mathscr{A}_{rgs}$ is a set of arguments, R the attack binary-relation on $\mathscr{A}_{rgs}$, and $W : \mathscr{A}_{rgs} \times \mathscr{A}_{rgs} \longrightarrow S$ is a binary function. Given $a, b \in \mathscr{A}_{rgs}$, $\forall (a, b) \in R$, $W(a, b) = s$ means that a attacks b with a weight $s \in S$. Moreover, we require that $R(a, b)$ iff $W(a, b) <_{\mathbb{S}} \top$.*

In Fig. 1 we provide an example of a weighted interaction graph describing the $WAAF_{\mathbb{S}}$ defined by $\mathscr{A}_{rgs} = \{a, b, c, d, e\}$, $R = \{(a, b), (c, b), (c, d), (d, c), (d, e), (e, e)\}$, with $W(a, b) = 7, W(c, b) = 8, W(c, d) = 9, W(d, c) = 8, W(d, e) = 5, W(e, e) = 6$, and $\mathbb{S} = \langle \mathbb{R}^+ \cup \{\infty\}, \min, +, \infty, 0 \rangle$ (i.e., the weighted semiring).

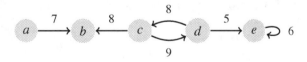

Fig. 1. An example of WAAF.

Hence, each attack is associated with a semiring value that represents the "strength" of an attack between two arguments. We can consider the weights in Fig. 1 as supports to the associated attack, as similarly suggested in [16,17]. A semiring value equal to the top element of the c-semiring $\top$ (e.g., 0 for the weighted semiring) represents a no-attack relation between two arguments. On the other side, the bottom element, i.e., $\bot$ (e.g., ∞ for the weighted semiring), represents the strongest attack possible.

In Definition 12 we define the attack strength for a set of arguments that attacks an argument, a different set of arguments, or an argument that attacks a set of arguments; the former and the latter are what we need to define w-defence. In the following, we will use $\bigotimes$ to indicate the $\otimes$ operator of the c-semiring $\mathbb{S}$ on a set of values:

Definition 12 (Attacks to/from sets of arguments). *Given a WAAF$_\mathbb{S}$, $\langle \mathscr{A}_{rgs}, R, W, \mathbb{S} \rangle$,*

- *a set of arguments $\mathscr{B}$ attacks an argument a with a weight of $k \in S$ if*
$$W(\mathscr{B}, a) = \bigotimes_{b \in \mathscr{B}} W(b, a) = k;$$
- *an argument a attacks a set of arguments $\mathscr{B}$ with a weight of $k \in S$ if*
$$W(a, \mathscr{B}) = \bigotimes_{b \in \mathscr{B}} W(a, b) = k;$$
- *a set of arguments $\mathscr{B}$ attacks a set of arguments $\mathscr{D}$ with a weight of $k \in S$ if*
$$W(\mathscr{B}, \mathscr{D}) = \bigotimes_{b \in \mathscr{B}, d \in \mathscr{D}} W(b, d) = k.$$

For example, looking at Fig. 1 we have that $W(\{a, c\}, b) = 15$, $W(c, \{b, d\}) = 17$, and $W(\{a, c\}, \{b, d\}) = 24$. We are now ready to introduce our version of weighted defence, i.e., w-defence:

Definition 13 (w-defence ($\mathbb{D}_w$)). *Given a WAAF$_\mathbb{S}$, $WF = \langle \mathscr{A}_{rgs}, R, W, \mathbb{S} \rangle$, $\mathscr{B} \subseteq \mathscr{A}_{rgs}$ w-defends $b \in \mathscr{A}_{rgs}$ from a iff, given $a \in \mathscr{A}_{rgs}$ s.t. $R(a, b)$, then $W(a, \mathscr{B} \cup \{b\}) \geq_\mathbb{S} W(\mathscr{B}, a)$; $\mathscr{B}$ w-defends b iff it defends b from any a s.t. $R(a, b)$.*

As previously advanced, a set $\mathscr{B} \subseteq \mathscr{A}_{rgs}$ defends an argument b, if the $\otimes$ of all the attack weights from $\mathscr{B}$ to a (for any a s.t. $R(a, b)$) is worse-equal (w.r.t. $\leq_\mathbb{S}$) than the $\otimes$ of the attacks from a to $\mathscr{B} \cup \{b\}$. For example, the set $\{c\}$ in Fig. 1 defends c from d because $W(d, \{c\}) \geq_\mathbb{S} W(\{c\}, d)$, i.e., $(8 \leq 9)$. On the other hand, $\{d\}$ in Fig. 1 does not defend d (i.e., itself) from c because $W(c, \{d\}) \ngeq_\mathbb{S} W(\{d\}, c)$.

Definition 13 can be seen as an extension of the defence in [14]: both proposals implement a collective defence from $\mathscr{B}$ to a (composing the weights of the counter-attacks together), but while in [14] the weight of the defence is compared against each single attack from a, in Definition 13 we consider the group of attacks from a to $\mathscr{B}$ as a single entity, i.e., with a single global weight; thus, the comparison is only against such a weight, leading to a more balanced approach between attack and defence. In Definition 14 we represent the defence in [14] in the same semiring-based framework.

Definition 14 ($\mathbb{D}_1$). *Given $WF = \langle \mathscr{A}_{rgs}, R, W, \mathbb{S} \rangle$, an argument b is defended by a subset of arguments $\mathscr{B}$ if $\forall a \in \mathscr{A}_{rgs}$ s.t. $R(a, b)$, we have that $W(a, b) \geq_\mathbb{S} W(\mathscr{B}, a)$.*

In Fig. 2 we show an example of the difference between $\mathbb{D}_w$ and $\mathbb{D}_1$. What we obtain is something stricter than both [14, 15]:

Proposition 1 (Defence implications [7]). $\mathbb{D}_w \Rightarrow \mathbb{D}_0$ *and* $\mathbb{D}_w \Rightarrow \mathbb{D}_1$.

A more detailed comparison of w-defence and the notions of defence in [14, 15, 24] can be found in [7]. For instance, we prove that, when using the Boolean semiring, w-defence and [14,15,24] are equivalent.

3.1   Relaxing w-Defence

Even if stricter than $\mathbb{D}_0$ [15] and $\mathbb{D}_1$ [14], w-defence can be relaxed in order to meet $\mathbb{D}_1$ and, ultimately, since $\mathbb{D}_1 \Rightarrow \mathbb{D}_0$ [7], the classical defence given by Dung, i.e., $\mathbb{D}_0$. This relaxation, called γ-defence, is parametrised on a threshold-value γ, which quantifies how much defence is relaxed: if γ grows then the relaxation is greater. γ-defence is used to reach and defend arguments that are not "fully" w-defended according to Definition 13, i.e., for which $W(a, \mathscr{B} \cup \{b\}) \not\geq_{\mathbb{S}} W(\mathscr{B}, a)$:

Definition 15 (γ-defence ($\mathbb{D}_\gamma$)). *Given* $\langle \mathscr{A}_{rgs}, R, W, \mathbb{S} = \langle S, \oplus, \otimes, \bot, \top \rangle \rangle$ *and* $\gamma \in S$, $\mathscr{B} \subseteq \mathscr{A}_{rgs}$ γ-*defends* $b \in \mathscr{A}_{rgs}$ *iff* $\forall a \in \mathscr{A}_{rgs}$ *such that* $R(a, b)$ *we have that* $W(\mathscr{B}, a) \neq \top$ *and* $(W(a, \mathscr{B} \cup \{b\}) \oslash W(\mathscr{B}, a)) \geq_{\mathbb{S}} \gamma$.

Considering the example in Fig. 1 ($\mathbb{S}_{weighted}$), for instance $\{d\}$ 1-defends d from c (i.e., $\gamma = 1$): $(W(c, \{d\}) - W(\{d\}, c)) \leq 1$, since $9 - 8 = 1$ and $1 \leq 1$. Next proposition shows how it is possible to reconnect γ-defence to w-defence (see Definition 13):

Proposition 2. $\top$-*defence* ($\gamma = \top$) *is equivalent to w-defence (Definition 13), i.e.* $\mathbb{D}_\top \Leftrightarrow \mathbb{D}_w$.

Next proposition shows how it is possible to reconnect γ-defence to Dung's original definition of defence.

Proposition 3. $\bot$-*defence* ($\gamma = \bot$) *is equivalent to the original definition of defence given by Dung [15], i.e.,* $\mathbb{D}_\bot \Leftrightarrow \mathbb{D}_0$.

In the following two propositions we relate $\mathbb{D}_\gamma$ and $\mathbb{D}_1$ when all the arguments attack at most one other argument (Proposition 4), and when there are more attacks (Proposition 5).

Proposition 4. *Given* $a \in \mathscr{A}_{rgs}$, *we define* T_a *as* $\bigcup_{b \in \mathscr{A}_{rgs}} R(a, b)$. *If* $\forall T_a$ *the cardinality is* $|T_a| \leq 1$, *then* $\mathbb{D}_1 \Leftrightarrow \mathbb{D}_\top$ *(by Proposition 2, also* $\mathbb{D}_1 \Leftrightarrow \mathbb{D}_w$ *holds).*

Proposition 5 ($\mathbb{D}_1 \Rightarrow \mathbb{D}_{\bar{\gamma}}$). *With* T_a *defined as in Proposition 4, if* $\exists T_a. |T_a| \geq 2$, *we find the* n *subsets* T_a^i *of* T_a *with cardinality* $|T_a| - 1$. *Then we define* $\gamma_a = \prod_{i=1..n} (\prod_{R(a,b) \in T^i} W(a, b))$, *and* $\bar{\gamma} = \prod \gamma_a$ *($\sqcap$ is the* glb *of* $\mathbb{S}$*). Finally, we obtain that* $\mathbb{D}_1 \Rightarrow \mathbb{D}_{\bar{\gamma}}$ *always holds.*

Finally, we can define an implication relation with respect to different γ:

Proposition 6. *If* $\mathscr{B}$ γ_1-*defends* b *and* $\gamma_1 \geq_{\mathbb{S}} \gamma_2$, *then* $\mathscr{B}$ γ_2-*defends* b, *i.e.,* $\mathbb{D}_{\gamma_1} \Rightarrow \mathbb{D}_{\gamma_2}$.

4 α^γ-Semantics

In this section we redefine all the classical semantics [15] by exploiting both the notion of *(i)* an inconsistency amount α inside an extension (to be tolerated), and *(ii)* the concept of γ-defence. In Definition 16 we redefine the notion of conflict-free semantics: conflicts can be now part of the solution up to a cost-threshold α.

Definition 16 (α-conflict-free semantics). *Given a* $WAAF_{\mathbb{S}}$, $WF = \langle \mathscr{A}_{rgs}, R, W, \mathbb{S} \rangle$, *a subset of arguments* $\mathscr{B} \subseteq \mathscr{A}_{rgs}$ *is* α-conflict-free *iff* $W(\mathscr{B}, \mathscr{B}) \geq_{\mathbb{S}} \alpha$.

With respect to the $WAAF_{\mathbb{S}}$ in Fig. 1, while the set $\{a, b, c\}$ is not conflict-free in the crisp version of the problem (since it includes the attacks between a and b, and between c and b), $\{a, b, c\}$ is instead 15-conflict-free because $W(a, b) + W(c, b) = 15$ (as a reminder, we are using $\mathbb{S}_{weighted}$ for such examples).

Hence, by raising α we further relax the requirements behind conflict-freeness. No constraint is given on the amount of conflict internal to an extension, thus all arguments can coexist together.

Proposition 7. *Given any* $\langle \mathscr{A}_{rgs}, R, W, \mathbb{S} \rangle$, *the set of* $\bot$-conflict free extensions *correspond to the power-set of* $\mathscr{A}_{rgs}$.

We now define two propositions that derive from Definition 16 and from the semiring properties explained in Sect. 2.1.

Proposition 8. *If an extension is* α_1-conflict-free *and* $\alpha_1 \geq_{\mathbb{S}} \alpha_2$, *then the same extension is also* α_2-conflict-free.

For instance, $\{a, b, c\}$ is 16-conflict-free because it is a 15-conflict-free ($15 \geq_{\mathbb{S}_{weighted}} 16$). Therefore, this states than in α-conflict-free extensions we tolerate an internal inconsistency-amount better than α.

The notion of γ-defence (see Definition 15) brings to the definition of the first semantics taking advantage of the notion of defence, that is the α^γ-admissible semantics:

Definition 17 (α^γ-admissible semantics). *Given* $WF = \langle \mathscr{A}_{rgs}, R, W, \mathbb{S} \rangle$, *an* α-conflict-free set $\mathscr{B} \subseteq \mathscr{A}_{rgs}$ *is* α^γ-admissible *iff the arguments in* $\mathscr{B}$ *are* γ-defended by $\mathscr{B}$ *from the arguments in* $\mathscr{A}_{rgs} \setminus \mathscr{B}$.

Considering the framework in Fig. 1 as unweighted, Dung's admissible sets are: $\emptyset, \{a\}, \{c\}, \{d\}, \{a, c\}, \{a, d\}$. $\top^\top$-admissible extensions (i.e., 0^0-extensions in $\mathbb{S}_{weighted}$) are $\{a\}$, $\{c\}$, and $\{a, c\}$ instead: $\{a\}$ because is not attacked by any other argument, $\{c\}$ and $\{a, c\}$ because they both w-defends c from the attack performed by d, i.e., $W(d, c) \geq_{\mathbb{S}_{weighted}} W(c, d)$ (i.e., $8 \leq 9$). For instance $\{d\}$ is not 0^0-admissible because it is not able to 0-defend (or to w-defend, see Proposition 2) itself from the attack of c. For the same reason, $\{a, d\}$ is not 0^0-admissible.

Considering an example with an internal inconsistency $\alpha \neq \top$, the extension $\{a, b, c\}$ is 15^0-admissible: it is 15-conflict-free, and $\{a, b, c\}$ 0-defends its arguments, i.e., c from d. All the 15^0-admissible extensions are $\emptyset$, $\{c\}$, $\{c, e\}$, $\{a\}$, $\{a, c\}$, $\{a, c, e\}$, and $\{a, b, c\}$. In order to provide an example with both $\alpha \neq \top$ and $\gamma \neq \top$ (still considering Fig. 1), the set $\{d, e\}$ is 11^1-admissible, since it is 11-conflict-free, and d defends itself (and the whole $\{d, e\}$) from c by paying a penalty of $9 - 8 \leq 1$.

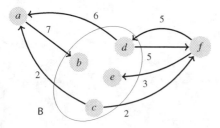 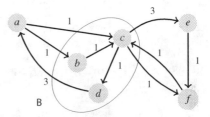

Fig. 2. A WAAF where $\mathscr{B} = \{b, c, d, e\}$ defends its arguments from f according to $\mathbb{D}_1$, but not according to $\mathbb{D}_w$ (using $\mathbb{S}_{weighted}$). The attack from a is defended according to both $\mathbb{D}_1$ and $\mathbb{D}_w$.

Fig. 3. An example of 2^0-complete extension, $\mathscr{B} = \{b, c, d\}$; $\mathscr{B} \cup \{f\}$ is 4^0-complete, while $\mathscr{B} \cup \{f\}$ and $\mathscr{B} \cup \{e\}$ are two 5^0-complete extensions (using $\mathbb{S}_{weighted}$).

Four further semantics, which refine α^γ-admissibility, are introduced from Definitions 18 to 20:

Definition 18 (α^γ-complete). *Given $\langle \mathscr{A}_{rgs}, R, W, \mathbb{S} \rangle$, an α^γ-admissible $\mathscr{B} \subseteq \mathscr{A}_{rgs}$ is α^γ-complete iff each argument $b \in \mathscr{A}_{rgs}$ that is γ-defended by $\mathscr{B}$ and s.t. $W(\mathscr{B} \cup \{b\}, \mathscr{B} \cup \{b\}) \geq_\mathbb{S} \alpha$ is in $\mathscr{B}$ (i.e., $b \in \mathscr{B}$).*

Therefore, in the α^γ-complete semantics we need to bring in all the γ-defended arguments while respecting the α-threshold at the same time. An example is given in Fig. 3 (we still suppose to adopt $\mathbb{S}_{weighted}$), where $\mathscr{B} = \{b, c, d\}$ is the only 2^0-complete extension: even if $\mathscr{B}$ 0-defends f from e, it is not possible to bring f in $\mathscr{B}$ because we can tolerate only 2 as internal conflict (already $W(b, c) + W(c, d) = 2$). However, by relaxing the problem to find 4^0-complete extensions, $\{b, c, d, e\}$ is sole solution, while both $\{b, c, d, e\}$ and $\{b, c, d, f\}$ are two 5^0-complete extensions.

Definition 19 (α^γ-preferred). *An α^γ-preferred extension is a maximal (with respect to set inclusion) α^γ-admissible subset of $\mathscr{A}_{rgs}$.*

Still considering Fig. 1, $\{a, c\}$ and $\{a, d\}$ are the two preferred extensions according to [15] (i.e., not considering weights). However, $\{a, c\}$ is the only 0^0-preferred extension, while $\{\{a, c\}, \{a, d\}\}$ is the set of 0^1-preferred extensions.

Definition 20 proposes Dung's stable semantics revisited in a *WAAF*$_\mathbb{S}$.

Definition 20 (α^γ-stable). *Given* $\langle \mathscr{A}_{rgs}, R, W, \mathbb{S} \rangle$, *an* α^γ-*admissible set* $\mathscr{B}$ *is also an* α^γ-*stable extension iff* $\forall a \notin \mathscr{B}, \exists b \in \mathscr{B}. W(b, a) \neq \top$, *and* $\mathscr{B} \cup \{a\}$ *is not* α^γ-*admissible.*

For example, the set $\{a, d\}$ is not 0^0-stable, because $W(c, d) \not\geq_{\mathbb{S}_{weighted}}$ $W(\{a, d\}, c)$, i.e., $9 \not\leq 8$. However, it is 0^1-stable, since $W(c, d) \oslash W(\{a, d\}, c) = 9 - 8 \leq 1$ satisfies $\gamma = 1$. Thus, in such example there is no 0^0-stable extension.

4.1 Properties of α^γ-Semantics

In the following we provide general considerations on α-semantics: for example, classical inclusion-relations [15] among the α-semantics are still valid:

Theorem 1 (α^γ-semantics inclusions). *Given any* $\langle \mathscr{A}_{rgs}, R, W, \mathbb{S} \rangle$, *with* $\mathbb{S} = \langle S, \oplus, \otimes, \perp, \top \rangle$, *and* $\alpha, \gamma \in S$,

1. *each* α^γ-*admissible extension is also* α-*conflict-free.*
2. *each* α^γ-*complete extension is also* α^γ-*admissible.*
3. *each* α^γ-*preferred extension is also* α^γ-*complete.*
4. *each* α^γ-*stable extension is also* α^γ-*preferred.*

Theorem 1 leads to Corollary 1, which states that the classical implication chain between semantics [15] also holds for α^γ-semantics.

Corollary 1. *By setting* $\alpha, \gamma \in S$, *the following implications hold between* α^γ-*semantics:* α^γ-*stable* $\Rightarrow$ α^γ-*preferred* $\Rightarrow$ α^γ-*complete* $\Rightarrow$ α^γ-*admissible* $\Rightarrow$ α-*conflict-free.*

Theorem 2 shows when α^γ-semantics can be used to exactly obtain the classical semantics [15].

Theorem 2. *Given* $F = \langle \mathscr{A}_{rgs}, R \rangle$, *and* $WF = \langle \mathscr{A}_{rgs}, R, W, \mathbb{S} \rangle$, *with* $\mathbb{S}$ *as desired, then*

1. *the set of* $\top$-*conflict-free extensions in* WF *is equal to the set of conflict-free extensions in* F.
2. *the set of* $\top^\perp$-*admissible extensions in* WF *is a equal of the set of admissible extensions in* F.
3. *the set of* $\top^\perp$-*complete extensions in* WF *is equal to the set of complete extensions in* F.
4. *the set of* $\top^\perp$-*preferred extensions is equal to the set of preferred extensions in* F.
5. *the set of* $\top^\perp$-*stable extensions in* WF *is equal to the set of stable extensions in* F.

Theorem 3 relates α^γ-semantics using $\top$-defence) and no internal conflict (i.e., $\alpha = \top$), to their counterpart in the classical ones [15].[3]

---

[3] Theorem 3 refines the results in [7].

Theorem 3. *Given $F = \langle \mathscr{A}_{rgs}, R \rangle$, and $WF = \langle \mathscr{A}_{rgs}, R, W, \mathbb{S} \rangle$, with $\mathbb{S}$ as desired, then*

1. *the set of $\top$-conflict-free extensions in WF is equal to the set of conflict-free extensions in F.*
2. *the set of $\top^\top$-admissible extensions in WF is a subset of the set of admissible extensions in F.*
3. *for each $\top^\top$-complete extension $\mathscr{B}_{WF}$ in WF, there exists a complete extension $\mathscr{B}_F$ in F, s.t., $\mathscr{B}_{WF} \subseteq \mathscr{B}_F$.*
4. *for each $\top^\top$-preferred extension $\mathscr{B}_{WF}$ in WF, there exists a preferred extension $\mathscr{B}_F$ in F, s.t. $\mathscr{B}_{WF} \subseteq \mathscr{B}_F$.*
5. *for each $\top^\top$-stable extension $\mathscr{B}_{WF}$ in WF, there exists a stable extension $\mathscr{B}_F$ in F, s.t. $\mathscr{B}_{WF} \subseteq \mathscr{B}_F$.*

Theorem 4 shows what happens to α^γ-semantics when α and γ change.

Theorem 4. *Given $\langle \mathscr{A}_{rgs}, R, W, \mathbb{S} = \langle S, \oplus, \otimes, \bot, \top \rangle \rangle$, and $\alpha_1, \alpha_2, \gamma_1, \gamma_2 \in A$ s.t. $\alpha_1 \geq_{\mathbb{S}} \alpha_2$ and $\gamma_1 \geq_{\mathbb{S}} \gamma_2$, then*

1. *the set of α_1-conflict-free extensions is a subset of the set of α_2-conflict-free extensions.*
2. *the set of $\alpha_1^{\gamma_1}$-admissible extensions is a subset of the set of $\alpha_2^{\gamma_2}$-admissible extensions.*
3. *for each $\alpha_1^{\gamma_1}$-complete extension $\mathscr{B}_1$, there exists an $\alpha_2^{\gamma_2}$-complete extension $\mathscr{B}_2$, such that $\mathscr{B}_1 \subseteq \mathscr{B}_2$.*
4. *for each $\alpha_1^{\gamma_1}$-preferred extension $\mathscr{B}_1$, there exists an $\alpha_2^{\gamma_2}$-preferred extension $\mathscr{B}_2$, such that $\mathscr{B}_1 \subseteq \mathscr{B}_2$.*
5. *for each $\alpha_1^{\gamma_1}$-stable extension $\mathscr{B}_1$, there exists an $\alpha_2^{\gamma_2}$-stable extension $\mathscr{B}_2$, such that $\mathscr{B}_1 \subseteq \mathscr{B}_2$.*

5   Implementation, Tests, and Applications

We have implemented α^γ-semantics in *ConArg*[4] [9,10], which is a tool that exploits *Gecode*[5] (a constraint-programming library) to solve several problems related to Argumentation. All the following tests have been collected on a benchmark of 100 graphs (25 arguments each) generated according to the Erdős-Rényi random model [19]: a generator in the *NetworkX* library[6] has been used. Each directed edge is added to a graph with an independent probability p. To each edge we associate a random natural number in the interval [1..10] (in order to test $\mathbb{S}_{weighted}$), and [1..10]/10 (to test $\mathbb{S}_{fuzzy}$).

Figures 4 and 5 respectively show the average number (on 100 graphs) of α^γ-admissible and α^γ-stable extensions (other semantics are omitted for the sake of space) for all the 78 combinations of $\alpha = \{0, 1, 2, 4, 6, 8, 9, \ 10, 11, 12\}$

---

[4] http://www.dmi.unipg.it/conarg/.
[5] http://www.gecode.org.
[6] https://networkx.github.io.

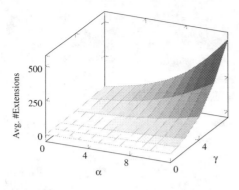

Fig. 4. Avg. number of α^γ-admissible ext. (changing α and γ); with $\mathbb{S}_{weighted}$.

Fig. 5. Avg. number of α^γ-stable ext. (changing α and γ); with $\mathbb{S}_{weighted}$.

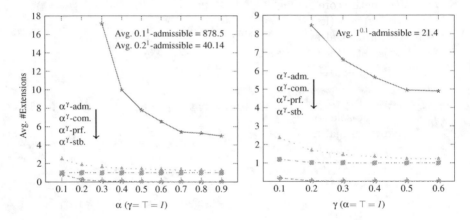

Fig. 6. α^γ-admissible (———), -complete ($\cdots\triangle\cdots$), -preferred ($-\blacksquare-$), and -stable ($-\diamond-$) number of average extensions (on 100 graphs), using the Fuzzy semiring.

and $\gamma = \{0, 1, 2, 4, 6, 8\}$ (using $\mathbb{S}_{weighted}$): hence we can appreciate what happens when both α and γ change. The two sets of extensions grow in the same way, even if they reach a cardinality of 525 and 21. Figure 6 reports instead the average number of α^γ-admissible, α^γ-complete, α^γ-preferred, and α^γ-stable extensions using $\mathbb{S}_{fuzzy}$. In the two plots we change only α (resp. γ) while we keep $\gamma = \top$ (resp. $\alpha = \top$). From these figures see that the number of extensions remains quite stable (except for the α^γ-admissible).

5.1 An Application Scenario

Relaxing a framework allows us to mitigate the disturbing effect of poorly specified or unsound attacks (*e.g.*, from *trolls*) [18]. In Fig. 7 we show the same framework (with the same weights) reported in [18], where several participants argue about the role of the government in what banning smoking is concerned

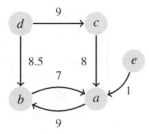

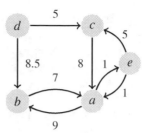

Fig. 7. The *troll* framework example in [18], using $\mathbb{S}_{weighted}$.

Fig. 8. $\{a, d\}$ is $\top^3$-admissible, $\{a, d, e\}$ is $2^\top$-admissible.

(please refer to [18] for a description of what arguments really stand for). Weights represent a strength score for each attack. The attack from e to a is meant to represent a troll attack (its strength is very low, i.e., 1). In [18] the authors show how their computational framework is able to mitigate the disturbing effect of such attack: e is not attacked, thus, with the classical semantics [15], it is capable of always ruling a out (its impact is strong).

However, we can mitigate it also by using our framework: if we compute the $\top^\perp$-stable extensions (by using $\gamma = \perp$ we consider classical defence [15]) we obtain $\{d, e\}$ as the sole solution: in [18] these are the same two most preferred arguments before mitigating the troll attack. If we instead relax the problem by computing the $1^\perp$-stable semantics, the solution becomes $\{a, d, e\}$. This extension contains the same three most preferred arguments in [18] (i.e., a, d, and e) after mitigating the troll attack: thus, we remove the effect of e on a in the framework. Note that e is a "good" argument in [18], thus it is not surprising it can be part of a "good" extension. It is the attack from e to a to be fake: the aim is to remove the effect of the attack from e, not e itself.

Figure 8 is instead presented to show how internal and defence relaxations are strictly linked together: the set $\{a, d\}$ is $\top^3$-admissible, since a is attacked by c with weight of 8, but only a counter-attack with weight 5 is present from d to c (hence, in the weighted semiring, the difference to be tolerated is $8 - 5 = 3$). However, if an internal inconsistency of 2 can be tolerated, the set $\{a, d, e\}$ is $2^\top$-admissible: by allowing a small internal conflict, the defence against b and c becomes stronger (no relaxation is needed to defend them). Therefore, we provide a means to an agent to decide between $\{a, d\}$ or $\{a, d, e\}$, satisfying either the first or the second semantics.[7]

6   Related Work

We begin by showing that a parametric structure to represent weights is useful, since other approaches in the literature are specialised on a single metric only.

---

[7] Defining a (multi-criteria) ranking is outside the scope of this work: see future work in Sect. 7.

For instance, an argument can be seen as a chain of possible events that makes a hypothesis true [23]. The credibility of a hypothesis can then be measured by the total probability that it is supported by arguments; to solve this problem we can use the probabilistic semiring. The *Fuzzy Argumentation* approach presented in [25] enriches the expressive power of the classical argumentation model by allowing to represent the relative strength of the attack relations between arguments, as well as the degree to which they are accepted. In this case, the fuzzy semiring can model such scenario.

We took inspiration from [16,17] for allowing internal inconsistency: the authors define the notion of inconsistency budget for the first time, even if with the purpose to compute more (than one [15]) grounded extensions (see Sect. 7 for an hint on this issue).

A recent quantitative study is proposed in [22], where the authors define *Social Abstract Argumentation Frameworks*, which basically associate positive and negative votes to each argument. Afterwards, it is defined how to aggregate these votes together, and how to associate it with an unique social model. This framework has been extended in [18] by considering weights on attacks as well.

In [24] attacks are relatively ordered by their force, i.e., $R(a,b) \gg R(b,a)$ means that the former attack is stronger than the latter. This is accordingly reflected by the defence definition, where considering $R(a,b)$ and $R(c,a)$ we can have that c is a *strong* or *weak* defender of b. Therefore, an argument b is defended by $\mathscr{B}$ if, and only if, for any argument a such that $R(a,b)$, there is an argument $c \in \mathscr{B}$ such that $R(c,a)$, and according to the desired defence strength, $R(c,a) \gg R(a,b)$ or $R(c,a) \ll R(a,b)$.

In [13] the authors review the works in [1,12,16,21], focusing on how to relate preference-values and weights, on either arguments or attacks. In [8], if $R(a,b)$ and $R(b,c)$, a defends c if $W(a,b)$ is worse than $W(b,c)$ (as in [21]), thus the defence is not collective as instead in [14] and this paper, and the attack is not collective as in this work. In [21] the difference between the weight associated with a is related to both the weights of b and c, with the purpose to check how much a defends b (thus obtaining *"varied-strength defeat relations"*).

In [2] the authors investigate the case where several weak attacks may compensate one strong attack. Then they propose new semantics that originate from this idea, i.e., α-BBS, which satisfy compensation at different degrees. The new semantics assign to every argument a score which represents how heavily the argument is attacked; a score increases when the number and/or the quality of the attackers increase.

The two principles in [20] are, *(i)* having fewer attackers is better than having more, and *(ii)* having more defenders is better than having fewer. The result is the definition of a graded defence $d_{m,n}(\mathscr{E})$, which defines different levels of defence-strength: if $d_{m,n}(\mathscr{E})$ holds, $\mathscr{E}$ is a set of arguments for which each $a \in \mathscr{E}$ does not have at least m attackers that are not counter-attacked by at least n arguments in $\mathscr{E}$.

Finally, it is worth to mention two well-known works that deal with values or preferences [1,3]. In [3], AAFs have been extended to *Value Based* AAFs (*VAFs*).

A VAF is a five-tuple $\langle \mathscr{A}_{rgs}, R, V, val, P \rangle$, where $\mathscr{A}_{rgs}$ is a finite set of arguments, R is an irreflexive binary relation on A (i.e. $\langle \mathscr{A}_{rgs}, R \rangle$ is a standard AAF), V is a non-empty set of values, val is a function which maps from elements of A to elements of V, and P is the set of possible audiences (i.e. total orders on V). We say that an argument a relates to value v if accepting A promotes or defends v: the value in question is given by $val(a)$. For every $a \in \mathscr{A}_{rgs}$, $val(a) \in V$. A *Preference Based* argumentation AAF [1] is a triplet $\langle \mathscr{A}_{rgs}, R, Pref \rangle$ where *Pref* is a partial pre-ordering (reflexive and transitive binary relation) on $\mathscr{A}_{rgs} \times \mathscr{A}_{rgs}$. The notion of defence changes accordingly: let a and b be two arguments, b attacks a iff $R(b, a)$ and not $a > b$.

7 Conclusion and Future Work

We have shown two different kinds of relaxations of classically crisp concepts in Abstract Argumentation. Firstly, arguments inside an extension can attack each other, and, secondly, a new notion of weighted defence (i.e., w-defence [7]) can be relaxed to γ-defence, with the purpose to be less restrictive. Classical implications between semantics [15] still hold also in this framework, which can be adopted to directly represent [15] and other works in the literature. Tests show that for small α or γ the average number of extensions slowly increases, thus permitting to catch few very "close" solutions characterised by a low amount of inconsistency (see Sect. 5). Relaxing internal conflict or defence (which are linked together, as exemplified in Sect. 5.1), or both at the same time, provides an agent with a much finer-grained level of analysis than it is typically possible, since inconsistency is ubiquitous in every-day life [4,17].

In the future we will investigate the α^γ-grounded semantics, which deserves separate considerations: a straightforward definition, along the line presented in Sect. 4, would lead to more than one grounded extension (as in [17]). To have a single extension requires a definition alternative to the minimal set-inclusion of α^γ-complete extensions; e.g., we can consider the set of all sceptically accepted arguments (in the α^γ-complete semantics). In the presented framework it is possible to define a single grounded extension that coincides with the intersection of all the α^γ-complete extensions (and with the union of all sceptically-accepted arguments). We will also study two-criteria (α and γ) decision-making procedures to help an agent choose between internal or defence relaxations (as for Fig. 8), as introduced at the end of Sect. 5.1.

References

1. Amgoud, L., Cayrol, C.: On the acceptability of arguments in preference-based argumentation. In: UAI 1998: Proceedings of the Fourteenth Conference on Uncertainty in Artificial Intelligence, pp. 1–7. Morgan Kaufmann (1998)
2. Amgoud, L., Ben-Naim, J., Doder, D., Vesic, S.: Ranking arguments with compensation-based semantics. In: Principles of Knowledge Representation and Reasoning: Proceedings of the Fifteenth International Conference, KR, pp. 12–21. AAAI Press (2016)

3. Bench-Capon, T.J.M.: Persuasion in practical argument using value-based argumentation frameworks. J. Log. Comput. **13**(3), 429–448 (2003)
4. Bertossi, L., Hunter, A., Schaub, T. (eds.): Inconsistency Tolerance. LNCS, vol. 3300. Springer, Heidelberg (2005)
5. Bistarelli, S., Gadducci, F.: Enhancing constraints manipulation in semiring-based formalisms. In: ECAI, Frontiers in Artificial Intelligence and Applications, vol. 141, pp. 63–67. IOS Press (2006)
6. Bistarelli, S., Montanari, U., Rossi, F.: Semiring-based constraint satisfaction and optimization. J. ACM **44**(2), 201–236 (1997)
7. Bistarelli, S., Rossi, F., Santini, F.: A collective defence against grouped attacks for weighted abstract argumentation frameworks. In: Proceedings of the Twenty-Ninth International Florida Artificial Intelligence Research Society Conference, FLAIRS 2016, pp. 638–643. AAAI Press (2016)
8. Bistarelli, S., Santini, F.: A common computational framework forsemiring-based argumentation systems. In: Coelho, H., Studer, R., Wooldridge, M. (eds.) ECAI, Frontiers in Artificial Intelligence and Applications, vol. 215, pp. 131–136. IOS Press (2010)
9. Bistarelli, S., Santini, F.: Conarg: a constraint-based computational framework for argumentation systems. In: IEEE 23rd International Conference on Tools with Artificial Intelligence, ICTAI 2011, pp. 605–612. IEEE (2011)
10. Bistarelli, S., Santini, F.: Modeling and solving AFs with a constraint-based tool: ConArg. In: Modgil, S., Oren, N., Toni, F. (eds.) TAFA 2011. LNCS (LNAI), vol. 7132, pp. 99–116. Springer, Heidelberg (2012). doi:10.1007/978-3-642-29184-5_7
11. Blyth, T.S., Janowitz, M.F.: Residuation Theory, vol. 102. Pergamon Press, Oxford (1972)
12. Cayrol, C., Devred, C., Lagasquie-Schiex, M.C.: Acceptability semantics accounting for strength of attacks in argumentation. In: ECAI 2010 - 19th European Conference on Artificial Intelligence, vol. 215, pp. 995–996. IOS Press (2010)
13. Cayrol, C., Lagasquie-Schiex, M.C.: From preferences over arguments to preferences over attacks in abstract argumentation: a comparative study. In: 2013 IEEE 25th International Conference on Tools with Artificial Intelligence, pp. 588–595. IEEE Computer Society (2013)
14. Coste-Marquis, S., Konieczny, S., Marquis, P., Ouali, M.A.: Weighted attacks in argumentation frameworks. In: Principles of Knowledge Representation and Reasoning: Proceedings of the Thirteenth International Conference, KR 2012, Rome, Italy, June 10–14, 2012. AAAI Press (2012)
15. Dung, P.M.: On the acceptability of arguments and its fundamental role in nonmonotonic reasoning, logic programming and n-person games. Artif. Intell. **77**(2), 321–357 (1995)
16. Dunne, P.E., Hunter, A., McBurney, P., Parsons, S., Wooldridge, M.: Inconsistency tolerance in weighted argument systems. In: Conference on Autonomous Agents and Multiagent Systems, pp. 851–858. IFAAMS (2009)
17. Dunne, P.E., Hunter, A., McBurney, P., Parsons, S., Wooldridge, M.: Weighted argument systems: basic definitions, algorithms, and complexity results. Artif. Intell. **175**(2), 457–486 (2011)
18. Eğilmez, S., Martins, J., Leite, J.: Extending Social abstract argumentation with votes on attacks. In: Black, E., Modgil, S., Oren, N. (eds.) TAFA 2013. LNCS (LNAI), vol. 8306, pp. 16–31. Springer, Heidelberg (2014). doi:10.1007/978-3-642-54373-9_2
19. Erdős, P., Rényi, A.: On the evolution of random graphs. Bull. Inst. Internat. Statist **38**(4), 343–347 (1961)

20. Grossi, D., Modgil, S.: On the graded acceptability of arguments. In: Proceedings of the Twenty-Fourth International Joint Conference on Artificial Intelligence, IJCAI, pp. 868–874. AAAI Press (2015)
21. Kaci, S., Labreuche, C.: Arguing with valued preference relations. In: Liu, W. (ed.) ECSQARU 2011. LNCS (LNAI), vol. 6717, pp. 62–73. Springer, Heidelberg (2011). doi:10.1007/978-3-642-22152-1_6
22. Leite, J., Martins, J.: Social abstract argumentation. In: IJCAI, Proceedings of the 22nd International Joint Conference on Artificial Intelligence, pp. 2287–2292. IJCAI/AAAI (2011)
23. Li, H., Oren, N., Norman, T.J.: Probabilistic argumentation frameworks. In: Modgil, S., Oren, N., Toni, F. (eds.) TAFA 2011. LNCS (LNAI), vol. 7132, pp. 1–16. Springer, Heidelberg (2012). doi:10.1007/978-3-642-29184-5_1
24. Martínez, D.C., García, A.J., Simari, G.R.: Anabstract argumentation framework with varied-strength attacks. In: Principles of Knowledge Representation and Reasoning: Proceedings of the Eleventh International Conference, pp. 135–144. AAAI Press (2008)
25. Schroeder, M., Schweimeier, R.: Fuzzy argumentation for negotiating agents. In: AAMAS, pp. 942–943. ACM (2002)

Decidability and Expressivity
of Ockhamist Propositional Dynamic Logics

Joseph Boudou[✉] and Emiliano Lorini

IRIT-CNRS, Toulouse University, Toulouse, France
{joseph.boudou,lorini}@irit.fr

Abstract. Ockhamist Propositional Dynamic Logic (OPDL) is a logic unifying the family of dynamic logics and the family of branching-time temporal logics, two families of logic widely used in AI to model reactive systems and multi-agent systems (MAS). In this paper, we present two variants of this logic. These two logics share the same language and differ only in one semantic condition. The first logic embeds Bundled CTL* while the second embeds CTL*. We provide a 2EXPTIME decision procedure for the satisfiability problem of each variant. The decision procedure for the first variant of OPDL is based on the elimination of Hintikka sets while the decision procedure for the second variant relies on automata.

1 Introduction

In [2] a new logic, called Ockhamist Propositional Dynamic Logic (OPDL) has been introduced. This logic connects the family of dynamic logics with the family of branching-time temporal logics, two families of logic that are traditionally used in artificial intelligence for the verification of programs and for modelling autonomous agents and multi-agent systems (MAS). On the one hand, dynamic logics have been used to model actions of agents and their consequences as well as deontic notions such as obligation and permission. On the other hand, branching-time temporal logics have been used to model the evolution of the agents' attitudes and dispositions including beliefs, preferences and intentions as well as to specify communication protocols and to model dynamics of commitments in a multi-agent setting.

As shown in [2], OPDL offers the right "bridge" between these two families of logics, as it embeds in a *natural* and *polynomial* way both Propositional Dynamic Logic (PDL) [10] and Full Computation Tree Logic (CTL*) [14]. Existing embeddings of both PDL and CTL* are rather complicated and unnatural. For example, it is well-known that PDL and CTL* can be embedded in modal μ-calculus. However, although the embedding of PDL into modal μ-calculus is simple and direct, the embedding of CTL* into modal μ-calculus is rather complicated and doubly exponential in the length of the input formula [5]. Another logic that links PDL with CTL* is the extension of PDL with a repetition construct (PDL-Δ) by [16]. But again, the embedding of CTL* into PDL-Δ is rather complicated and doubly exponential in the length of the input formula [19].

L. Michael and A. Kakas (Eds.): JELIA 2016, LNAI 10021, pp. 144–158, 2016.
DOI: 10.1007/978-3-319-48758-8_10

OPDL can be conceived as the logic in the dynamic logic family based on the Ockhamist view of time. Ockhamist semantics for temporal logic have been widely studied [4,17,20]. The logic of agency STIT (the logic of "seeing to it that") by Belnap *et al.* [3] is based on such semantics. According to the Ockhamist conception of time (also called *indeterminist actualist*, see [20]) the truth of statements is evaluated with respect to a moment and to a particular *actual* linear history passing through that moment.[1]

The original semantics for OPDL given by [2] is based on the concept of OPDL Ockhamist model, which can be seen as an extension with a program component of Zanardo's Ockhamist model for branching-time temporal logics [20]. Specifically, in an OPDL Ockhamist model, temporal transitions between states are labelled with sets of atomic programs. A second variant of OPDL is studied by [2], called OPDL^{lts}. Like PDL, OPDL^{lts} is interpreted in labelled transition systems (LTS). However, while in PDL the truth of a formula is evaluated with respect to a state, in OPDL^{lts} it is evaluated with respect to a path.

The present paper furthers the study of OPDL by providing complexity results of the satisfiability problems of its different variants. Specifically, we introduce a new path semantics for OPDL, which allows for finer analyses of its different variants. The OPDL Ockhamist semantics is proved to correspond to the fusion closure condition in the path semantics. Observing that OPDL^{lts} studied by [2] lacks the conservative property, a new variant of OPDL, called OPDL^{lc}, is devised by adding the limit closure property to the path semantics, thereby imitating the difference between the semantics for Bundled CTL* (BCTL*) and the semantics for CTL*. We show that the satisfiability problems of OPDL and OPDL^{lts} are both 2EXPTIME-complete, the same complexity as for CTL*.

The rest of the paper is organized as follows. In the next section, the OPDL language and the Ockhamist semantics for OPDL are recalled from [2]. The path semantics framework is also introduced. Then, optimal decision procedures for the satisfiability of OPDL and OPDL^{lc} are presented in Sects. 3 and 4, respectively. We conclude in Sect. 5.[2]

2   Ockhamist Propositional Dynamic Logics

OPDL and OPDL^{lc} share the same language which is the language of PDL where one special atomic program $\equiv$ called the branching program is distinguished. Formally, assume a countable set $Prop = \{p, q, \ldots\}$ of atomic propositions and a countable set $Atm = \{a, b, \ldots\}$ of atomic programs (or actions). The language $\mathcal{L}_{\mathsf{OPDL}}(Prop, Atm)$ of OPDL consists of a set Prg of programs and a set Fml of formulas, defined as follows:

$$Prg : \alpha ::= a \mid \equiv \mid (\alpha_1; \alpha_2) \mid (\alpha_1 \cup \alpha_2) \mid \alpha^* \mid \varphi?$$
$$Fml : \varphi ::= p \mid \neg\varphi \mid (\varphi_1 \wedge \varphi_2) \mid [\alpha]\varphi$$

---

[1] The Ockhamist view of branching time is traditionally opposed to the Peircean view [13,17]. According to the Peircean view, the truth of a temporal formula should be evaluated with respect either to some history or all histories starting in a given state.

[2] Due to space restriction, this version of the paper contains only sketches of proofs of some theorems.

where $\equiv$ is a syntactic symbol distinct from atomic programs. We adopt the standard definitions for the remaining Boolean operations. Implicit elimination of double negations is assumed: $\neg\neg\varphi$ is identified with φ. The dual $\langle\langle\alpha\rangle\rangle$ of the modality $[\![\alpha]\!]$ is defined by $\langle\langle\alpha\rangle\rangle\varphi \overset{def}{=} \neg[\![\alpha]\!]\neg\varphi$. We write $|\alpha|$ and $|\varphi|$ to denote the numbers of occurrences of symbols in the program α and the formula φ. Like for PDL, the formula $[\![\alpha]\!]\varphi$ has to be read as "φ holds after all possible executions of α".

2.1   Ockhamist Semantics

OPDL models are structures with two dimensions: a vertical dimension corresponding to the concept of history, a horizontal dimension corresponding to the concept of moment.

Definition 1. *An OPDL model is a tuple $M = (W, \mathcal{Q}, \mathcal{L}, \mathcal{R}_\equiv, \mathcal{V})$ where:*

- *W is a nonempty set of states (or worlds),*
- *$\mathcal{Q}$ is a partial function $\mathcal{Q} : W \longrightarrow W$ assigning a successor to states,*
- *$\mathcal{L}$ is a mapping $\mathcal{L} : W \times W \longrightarrow 2^{Atm}$ from pairs of states to sets of atomic programs such that $\mathcal{L}(w, v) \neq \emptyset$ iff v is the successor of w, i.e., $v = \mathcal{Q}(w)$,*
- *$\mathcal{R}_\equiv \subseteq W \times W$ is an equivalence relation between states in W,*
- *$\mathcal{V} : W \longrightarrow 2^{Prop}$ is a valuation function for atomic propositions,*

and such that for all $w, v, u \in W$:

(C1) *if $\mathcal{Q}(w) = v$ and $(v, u) \in \mathcal{R}_\equiv$ then there is $z \in W$ such that $(w, z) \in \mathcal{R}_\equiv$, $\mathcal{Q}(z) = u$ and $\mathcal{L}(z, u) = \mathcal{L}(w, v)$.*
(C2) *if $(w, v) \in \mathcal{R}_\equiv$ then $\mathcal{V}(w) = \mathcal{V}(v)$.*

$\mathcal{R}_\equiv$-equivalence classes are called *moments*. A *history* starting in w_1 is a maximal sequence $\sigma = w_1, w_2, \ldots$ of states such that $w_{k+1} = \mathcal{Q}(w_k)$ for all positive k less than the length of σ.

Constraint C1 corresponds to what in Ockhamist semantics is called property of *weak diagram completion*. This means that if two worlds v and u are in the same moment and world w is a predecessor of v then, there exists a world z such that (i) w and z are in the same moment, (ii) u is the successor of z, (iii) the transition from w to v and the transition from z to u are labeled with the same set of action names. Constraint C2 just means that two worlds belonging to the same moment agree on the truth values of the atoms.

The truth of an OPDL formula is evaluated with respect to a world w in an OPDL model M.

Definition 2. *Let $M = (W, \mathcal{Q}, \mathcal{L}, \mathcal{R}_\equiv, \mathcal{V})$ be an OPDL model. Given a program α, we define a binary relation $\mathcal{R}_\alpha$ on W with $(w, v) \in \mathcal{R}_\alpha$ (or $w \, \mathcal{R}_\alpha \, v$) meaning that v is accessible from w by performing α. We also define a binary relation $\models$*

*between worlds in M and formulas with $M, w \models \varphi$ meaning that formula φ is
true at w in M. The rules inductively defining $\mathcal{R}_\alpha$ and $\models$ are:*

$$\mathcal{R}_a = \{(w, v) \mid \mathcal{Q}(w) = v \text{ and } a \in \mathcal{L}(w, v)\}$$
$$\mathcal{R}_{\alpha_1;\alpha_2} = \mathcal{R}_{\alpha_1} \circ \mathcal{R}_{\alpha_2}$$
$$\mathcal{R}_{\alpha_1 \cup \alpha_2} = \mathcal{R}_{\alpha_1} \cup \mathcal{R}_{\alpha_2}$$
$$\mathcal{R}_{\alpha^*} = (\mathcal{R}_\alpha)^*$$
$$\mathcal{R}_{\varphi?} = \{(w, w) \mid M, w \models \varphi\}$$

and
$$M, w \models p \Longleftrightarrow p \in \mathcal{V}(w);$$
$$M, w \models \neg\varphi \Longleftrightarrow M, w \not\models \varphi;$$
$$M, w \models \varphi \wedge \psi \Longleftrightarrow M, w \models \varphi \text{ and } M, w \models \psi;$$
$$M, w \models [\alpha]\varphi \Longleftrightarrow \forall v \in W, \text{ if } w \, \mathcal{R}_\alpha \, v \text{ then } M, v \models \varphi.$$

An OPDL formula φ is OPDL valid, denoted by $\models_{\mathsf{OPDL}} \varphi$, iff for every OPDL
model M and for every world w in M, we have $M, w \models \varphi$. An OPDL formula φ
is OPDL satisfiable iff $\neg\varphi$ is not OPDL valid.

2.2 Path Semantics

In this section we describe the path semantics for $\mathcal{L}_{\mathsf{OPDL}}(Prop, Atm)$, inspired
by the path semantics for branching time temporal logics [14]. In this semantics,
the set of all histories is explicit in the model and formulas are interpreted
over histories. We show that one variant of this semantics is equivalent to the
Ockhamist semantics of the previous section, while another variant defines the
OPDL^{lc} logic.

Notation. Given an alphabet Σ, Σ^* denotes the set of finite words over Σ, Σ^ω
the set of infinite words and Σ^∞ the union of Σ^* and Σ^ω. Let $\sigma = w_1 w_2 \ldots$
be a finite or infinite word. The length of σ is denoted by $|\sigma|$. If σ is infinite
then $|\sigma| = \omega$. For any $i \in 1..|\sigma|$, we use σ^i, $\sigma^{\leq i}$ and $\sigma^{\geq i}$ to denote respectively
the ith element w_i in σ, the prefix $w_1 \ldots w_i$ of σ up to its ith element and the
suffix $w_i w_{i+1} \ldots$ of σ from its ith element. The notations $\sigma^{<i}$, $\sigma^{>i}$ and $\sigma^{i..j}$ are
shorthands for $\sigma^{\leq i-1}$, $\sigma^{\geq i+1}$ and $(\sigma^{\leq j})^{\geq i}$, respectively.

Definition 3. *A path model is a tuple $M = (W, \mathcal{L}, B, \mathcal{V})$ where W is non-
empty set of states, $\mathcal{L} : W \times W \longrightarrow 2^{Atm}$ is a function assigning a set of atomic
programs to each pair of states, the bundle $B \subseteq W^\infty$ is a non-empty set of
sequences of states (histories) such that for each sequence $\sigma = w_1, w_2, \ldots \in B$
and all $k \geq 1$ less than the length of σ, $\mathcal{L}(w_k, w_{k+1}) \neq \emptyset$ and $\mathcal{V} : W \longrightarrow 2^{Prop}$
is a valuation for the propositional variables. The binary relations $\mathcal{R}_\alpha$ over B*

for all programs α and the forcing relation $\models$ between M, sequences in B and formulas are defined by simultaneous induction such that:

$$\mathcal{R}_a = \{(\sigma_1, \sigma_2) \mid \sigma_2 = \sigma_1^{\geq 2} \text{ and } a \in \mathcal{L}(\sigma_1^1, \sigma_2^1)\}$$
$$\mathcal{R}_\equiv = \{(\sigma_1, \sigma_2) \mid \sigma_1^1 = \sigma_2^1\}$$

and
$$M, \sigma \models p \Longleftrightarrow p \in \mathcal{V}(\sigma^1)$$
$$M, \sigma \models \neg\varphi \Longleftrightarrow M, \sigma \nvDash \varphi;$$
$$M, \sigma \models \varphi \wedge \psi \Longleftrightarrow M, \sigma \models \varphi \text{ and } M, \sigma \models \psi;$$
$$M, \sigma \models [\alpha]\varphi \Longleftrightarrow \forall \sigma' \in B, \text{ if } \sigma \, \mathcal{R}_\alpha \, \sigma' \text{ then } M, \sigma' \models \varphi.$$

the missing cases being identical as to Definition 2.

The main interest in the path semantics is that, by adding additional conditions restricting the possible bundles, it gives a convenient framework to analyse and distinguish different logics based on the same language. We list some such conditions and discuss their impact on logics. We abusively write that a model has one of these conditions whenever its bundle has it.

Suffix closure. B is suffix closed iff for any sequence $\sigma \in B$ and any $k \in 1..|\sigma|$, $\sigma^{\geq k} \in B$. In contrast with CTL*, as long as seriality is not imposed, this condition does not change the logic. But since this condition makes the definition of $\mathcal{R}_a$ more natural, we will assume path models have it.

Fusion closure. B is fusion closed iff for any two sequences $\sigma_1, \sigma_2 \in B$, if $\sigma_1^k = \sigma_2^{k'}$ for some k and k' then the sequence $\sigma_1^{<k}\sigma_2^{\geq k'}$ is in B. This condition corresponds to condition (C1). Indeed, we have the following theorem.

Theorem 1. *OPDL is the logic obtained by interpreting $\mathcal{L}_{\text{OPDL}}(Prop, Atm)$ in the class of all suffix and fusion closed path models.*

Limit closure. B is limit closed iff whenever an infinite sequence $\sigma \in W^\omega$ is such that for all $k \geq 1$, there is a sequence $\sigma_k \in B$ such that $\sigma_k^{\leq k} = \sigma^{\leq k}$ then $\sigma \in B$. A similar condition makes the difference between BCTL* and CTL* [14]. The logic obtained by interpreting $\mathcal{L}_{\text{OPDL}}(Prop, Atm)$ in the class of suffix, fusion and limit closed models is called OPDL^{lc}.

Seriality. B is serial iff all paths in B are infinite ($B \subseteq W^\omega$). Combining this condition with the suffix closure corresponds, in the Ockhamist semantics, to enforcing $\mathcal{Q}$ to be a total function. If Atm is infinite, then any path model satisfying a formula φ_0 can be turned into a serial path model satisfying φ_0 by choosing an atomic program e not occurring in φ_0 and by adding for each finite sequence $\sigma \in B$ a state w_σ such that w_σ is a successor by $\{e\}$ of itself and of the last state in σ. This transformation preserves satisfiability and the suffix closed, fusion closed and limit closed conditions. Therefore, since OPDL and OPDL^{lc} are conservative, we can assume that these logics are interpreted in serial path models.

Total seriality. B is totally serial iff B is the set of all infinite paths. By the constructions used in the proofs of Corollary 1 or Theorem 4, we can prove as a corollary of any of these theorems that the logic obtained by interpreting $\mathcal{L}_{\text{OPDL}}(Prop, Atm)$ in the class of all suffix closed, fusion closed and totally serial models is OPDL^{lc}.

Total maximality. B is totally maximal iff B is the set of all maximal paths. In [2], the logic obtained by interpreting $\mathcal{L}_{\text{OPDL}}(Prop, Atm)$ in the class of totally maximal models, called $\text{OPDL}^{lts}(Prop, Atm)$, have been considered. But, in contrast with OPDL and OPDL^{lc}, $\text{OPDL}^{lts}(Prop, Atm)$ is not conservative. We define a logic $L1$ in the language $\mathcal{L}(Prop, Atm)$ as being *conservative* iff every extensions $L2$ of $L1$ to the language $\mathcal{L}(Prop', Atm')$ where $Prop \subseteq Prop'$ and $Atm \subseteq Atm'$, is a conservative extension, i.e., the set of validities of $L2$ in the language $\mathcal{L}(Prop, Atm)$ is exactly the set of validities of $L1$. Intuitively, a logic is conservative if the validity of any formula is independent of the propositional variables and atomic program which does *not* occur in the formula. To prove that $\text{OPDL}^{lts}(Prop, \{a\})$ is not conservative, consider the formula $[\![a]\!]\bot \wedge \langle\!\langle\equiv;a\rangle\!\rangle\top$. This formula is not $\text{OPDL}^{lts}(Prop, \{a\})$ satisfiable but is $\text{OPDL}^{lts}(Prop, \{a,b\})$ satisfiable. In the present work, we will study OPDL^{lc} (which is conservative) instead of $\text{OPDL}^{lts}(Prop, Atm)$. It can easily be proved that if Atm is infinite then OPDL^{lc} and $\text{OPDL}^{lts}(Prop, Atm)$ are the same logic. Moreover, the proof from [2] that CTL^* can be embedded into OPDL^{lts} can easily be adapted to prove that CTL^* can be embedded into OPDL^{lc}.

3   Optimal Decision Procedure for OPDL

We describe a decision procedure for the satisfiability problem of OPDL, based on the *elimination of Hintikka sets* procedure devised for PDL by Pratt [12] and adapted to BCTL^* by Reynolds [15]. The general idea is to construct a syntactic structure which contains all the possible states then to eliminate the states preventing the structure to be a model. For PDL the possible states are Hintikka sets (*hues* in [15]). For BCTL^*, states are sets of Hintikka sets, called *clusters* in this paper (*colors* in [15]). For OPDL, states must be clusters too, but because of formulas like $\langle\!\langle a\rangle\!\rangle p \wedge [\![b]\!]\neg p \wedge \langle\!\langle\equiv\rangle\!\rangle \langle\!\langle b\rangle\!\rangle p$, the atomic programs labeling edges have to be considered. Hence the syntactic structures are more involved than for PDL or BCTL^*. We study these syntactic structures before introducing the decision procedure for OPDL. Properties of syntactic structures are used for the automata-based procedure of Sect. 4 too.

3.1   Syntactic Structures

Given a formula φ_0, the Fischer-Ladner closure $FL(\varphi_0)$ of φ_0 is defined as for PDL (see [9] for details) except that we enforce $FL(\varphi_0)$ to be closed under negation: $\psi \in FL(\varphi_0)$ iff $\neg\psi \in FL(\varphi_0)$. Since implicit elimination of double negation is assumed, the well-known result that the cardinal of $FL(\varphi_0)$ is linear in $|\varphi_0|$ remains. We write $SP(\varphi_0)$ to denote the set $\{\alpha \mid \exists\varphi, \langle\!\langle\alpha\rangle\!\rangle\varphi \in FL(\varphi_0)\}$.

Definition 4. *A set* $\mathcal{H} \subset FL\,(\varphi_0)$ *is a* Hintikka set *for* φ_0 *iff all the following conditions are satisfied:*

- *for any* $\neg\varphi \in FL\,(\varphi_0)$, $\varphi \in \mathcal{H}$ *iff* $\neg\varphi \notin \mathcal{H}$
- *for any* $\varphi \wedge \psi \in FL\,(\varphi_0)$, $\varphi \wedge \psi \in \mathcal{H}$ *iff* $\varphi \in \mathcal{H}$ *and* $\psi \in \mathcal{H}$
- *for any* $[\alpha; \beta]\varphi \in FL\,(\varphi_0)$, $[\alpha; \beta]\varphi \in \mathcal{H}$ *iff* $[\alpha][\beta]\varphi \in \mathcal{H}$
- *for any* $[\alpha \cup \beta]\varphi \in FL\,(\varphi_0)$, $[\alpha \cup \beta]\varphi \in \mathcal{H}$ *iff* $[\alpha]\varphi \in \mathcal{H}$ *and* $[\beta]\varphi \in \mathcal{H}$
- *for any* $[\alpha^*]\varphi \in FL\,(\varphi_0)$, $[\alpha^*]\varphi \in \mathcal{H}$ *iff* $\varphi \in \mathcal{H}$ *and* $[\alpha][\alpha^*]\varphi \in \mathcal{H}$
- *for any* $[\varphi?]\psi \in FL\,(\varphi_0)$, $[\varphi?]\psi \in \mathcal{H}$ *iff* $\neg\varphi \in \mathcal{H}$ *or* $\psi \in \mathcal{H}$
- *if* $[\equiv]\varphi \in \mathcal{H}$ *then* $\varphi \in \mathcal{H}$

Definition 5. *A set* $\mathcal{C}$ *of Hintikka sets for* φ_0 *is a* cluster *for* φ_0 *iff* $\mathcal{C} \neq \emptyset$ *and for any* $\mathcal{H}_1, \mathcal{H}_2 \in \mathcal{C}$ *the following conditions are satisfied:*

- *for any propositional variable* $p \in FL\,(\varphi_0)$, $p \in \mathcal{H}_1$ *iff* $p \in \mathcal{H}_2$
- *for any formula* $[\equiv]\varphi \in FL\,(\varphi_0)$, $[\equiv]\varphi \in \mathcal{H}_1$ *iff* $[\equiv]\varphi \in \mathcal{H}_2$

Given a set $P \subseteq Atm$ of atomic programs, the successor relation S_P over Hintikka sets is defined such that $\mathcal{H}_1 \, S_P \, \mathcal{H}_2$ iff (i) for any formula $\langle\!\langle a \rangle\!\rangle\varphi \in \mathcal{H}_1$, $a \in P$ and (ii) for any formula $\langle\!\langle a \rangle\!\rangle\varphi \in FL\,(\varphi_0)$ such that $a \in P$, $\langle\!\langle a \rangle\!\rangle\varphi \in \mathcal{H}_1$ iff $\varphi \in \mathcal{H}_2$. This relation is extended to clusters: $\mathcal{C}_1 \, S_P \, \mathcal{C}_2$ iff for all $\mathcal{H}_2 \in \mathcal{C}_2$ there exists $\mathcal{H}_1 \in \mathcal{C}_1$ such that $\mathcal{H}_1 \, S_P \, \mathcal{H}_2$.

A syntactic structure is a pseudo-model where the valuation has been replaced with a function assigning clusters and where the bundle is implicit. Intuitively, each Hintikka set in the cluster associated to a state w corresponds to the set of formulas satisfied by a history starting at w.

Definition 6. *A syntactic structure for a formula* φ_0 *is a tuple* $\mathcal{S} = (W, \mathcal{L}, \mathfrak{C})$ *where* W *is a non-empty set of states,* $\mathcal{L}$ *assigns a set of atomic programs to each pair of states,* $\mathfrak{C}$ *assigns a cluster for* φ_0 *to each state such that for all* $w, x \in W$, *if* $\mathcal{L}(w, x) \neq \emptyset$ *then* $\mathfrak{C}(w) \, S_{\mathcal{L}(w,x)} \, \mathfrak{C}(x)$. *A syntactic structure is* standard *iff* (i) $\varphi_0 \in \mathcal{H}$ *for some* $\mathcal{H} \in \mathfrak{C}(w)$ *and some* $w \in W$ *and* (ii) *for all* $w \in W$, *there exists* $x \in W$ *such that* $\mathcal{L}(w, x) \neq \emptyset$.

A *path* in a syntactic structure $\mathcal{S}$ is a (possibly infinite) non-empty sequence π over the alphabet composed by the special *branching* symbol $\bullet$ and all the couples $(\mathcal{H}, w)$ where $w \in W$ and $\mathcal{H} \in \mathfrak{C}(w)$. Any path π must satisfy all the following conditions, for all $k \in 1.. \, |\pi|$:

- $\pi^1 \neq \bullet$ and if $|\pi| < \omega$, $\pi^{|\pi|} \neq \bullet$;
- if $\pi^k = \bullet$ then $\pi^{k-1} = (\mathcal{H}, w)$ and $\pi^{k+1}(\mathcal{H}', w)$ for some $w \in W$ and some $\mathcal{H}, \mathcal{H}' \in \mathfrak{C}(w)$;
- if $\pi^k = (\mathcal{H}_k, w_k)$ and $\pi^{k+1} = (\mathcal{H}_{k+1}, w_{k+1})$ then $\mathcal{L}(w_k, w_{k+1}) \neq \emptyset$ and $\mathcal{H}_k \, S_{\mathcal{L}(w_k, w_{k+1})} \, \mathcal{H}_{k+1}$.

Intuitively, a finite path π corresponds to a possible execution of some programs (different programs may have some common possible executions). When this is the case, we say that the path *carries* the program. This relation between a finite path and a program is defined formally as the least relation satisfying the following conditions:

- $(\mathcal{H}_1, w_1)(\mathcal{H}_2, w_2)$ carries a iff $a \in \mathcal{L}(w_1, w_2)$.
- $(\mathcal{H}_1, w) \bullet (\mathcal{H}_2, w)$ carries $\equiv$.
- $(\mathcal{H}_1, w_1)$ carries $\varphi?$ iff $\varphi \in \mathcal{H}_1$.
- π carries $(\alpha \cup \beta)$ iff π carries α or β.
- π carries $(\alpha; \beta)$ iff for some $m \in 1..|\pi|$, $\pi^{\leq m}$ carries α and $\pi^{\geq m}$ carries β.
- π carries α^* iff there is a non-empty list $k_0, \ldots, k_m$ such that $k_0 = 1$, $k_m = |\pi|$ and for all $i < m$, $k_i < k_{i+1}$ and $\pi^{k_i \cdots k_{i+1}}$ carries α.

An *unbranching path* is a path which contains no occurrences of the branching symbol $\bullet$. The *trunk* of a path is its longest unbranching prefix. The *support* of an unbranching path $(\mathcal{H}_1, w_1)(\mathcal{H}_2, w_2) \ldots$ is the sequence $w_1 w_2 \ldots$.

An *eventuality chain* is a non-empty sequence $\eta = \alpha_1 \ldots \alpha_n \varphi$ where the last element is a formula and the other elements are programs. To an eventuality chain $\eta = \alpha_1 \ldots \alpha_n \varphi$ corresponds the formula form $(\eta) = \langle\!\langle \alpha_1 \rangle\!\rangle \ldots \langle\!\langle \alpha_n \rangle\!\rangle \varphi$. This correspondence is not injective, for instance the eventuality chains aap, $a\langle\!\langle a \rangle\!\rangle p$ and $\langle\!\langle a \rangle\!\rangle \langle\!\langle a \rangle\!\rangle p$ all correspond to the same formula $\langle\!\langle a \rangle\!\rangle \langle\!\langle a \rangle\!\rangle p$. The *maximal eventuality chain* for a formula φ is the longest eventuality chain η such that form $(\eta) = \varphi$. *Fulfillment* of an eventuality chain η by a path π is defined inductively as follows:

- The path π fulfills a one-element eventuality chain $\eta = \varphi$ iff $\pi = (\mathcal{H}_1, w_1)$ and $\varphi \in \mathcal{H}_1$ for some state w_1 and some Hintikka set $\mathcal{H}_1 \in \mathfrak{C}(w_1)$;
- The path π fulfills an eventuality chain $\eta = \alpha\eta'$ iff there is $k \in 1..|\pi|$ such that $\pi^{\leq k}$ carries α and $\pi^{\geq k}$ fulfills η'.

For any eventuality chain $\eta = \alpha\varphi$ of length two, the corresponding formula $\langle\!\langle \alpha \rangle\!\rangle \varphi$ is called an *eventuality* and any path fulfilling η is said to *fulfill the eventuality* $\langle\!\langle \alpha \rangle\!\rangle \varphi$. A state $w \in W$ is fulfilling if for any Hintikka set $\mathcal{H} \in \mathfrak{C}(w)$ and any eventuality $\langle\!\langle \alpha \rangle\!\rangle \varphi \in \mathcal{H}$, there is a path π from $(\mathcal{H}, w)$ fulfilling $\langle\!\langle \alpha \rangle\!\rangle \varphi$. A syntactic structure $\mathcal{S}$ *fulfills all eventualities* iff all its states are fulfilling. A *justifying path* is an infinite unbranching path π such that for all k, if $\pi_k = (\mathcal{H}_k, w_k)$ for some $\mathcal{H}_k$ and w_k then for any eventuality $\langle\!\langle \alpha \rangle\!\rangle \varphi \in \mathcal{H}_k$, there is a fulfilling path π' for $\langle\!\langle \alpha \rangle\!\rangle \varphi$ starting at $(\mathcal{H}_k, w_k)$ such that the trunk of π' is a prefix of $\pi^{\geq k}$.

We can now state the main result of this section.

Theorem 2. *A formula φ_0 is OPDL satisfiable if and only if there is a standard syntactic structure for φ_0 fulfilling all eventualities.*

Proof (Proof sketch). We only detail the right-to-left direction. Given a standard syntactic structure $\mathcal{S} = (W, \mathcal{L}, \mathfrak{C})$ for φ_0 fulfilling all eventualities, we define the path model $M = (W, \mathcal{L}, B, \mathcal{V})$ such that B is the set of supports of the justifying paths in $\mathcal{S}$ and $\mathcal{V}(w) = \mathcal{H} \cap Prop$ for any $\mathcal{H} \in \mathfrak{C}(w)$. Two steps are difficult in proving that M is an OPDL path model satisfying φ_0: the proof that B is fusion-closed and the proof of the following Existence Lemma.

Lemma 1 (Existence Lemma). *For any finite unbranching path π in a standard syntactic structure $\mathcal{S}$ fulfilling all eventualities, there is a justifying path π' in $\mathcal{S}$ such that π is a prefix of π'.*

For BCTL*, these two points are resolved by the fact that any eventuality $\varphi \mathcal{U} \psi$ is either resolved at the current state or still satisfied in the successor state. For OPDL, we need the Witness Lemma below. To state this lemma, we inductively define the function next from eventuality chains to sets of pairs composed of a set of formulas (the guard) and an eventuality chain:

$$\text{next}(\varphi) = \{(\emptyset, \varphi)\} \qquad \text{next}(\psi?\eta) = \{(G \cup \{\psi\}, \eta') \mid (G, \eta') \in \text{next}(\eta)\}$$
$$\text{next}(a\eta) = \{(\emptyset, a\eta)\} \quad \text{next}((\beta_1 \cup \beta_2)\eta) = \text{next}(\beta_1\eta) \cup \text{next}(\beta_2\eta)$$
$$\text{next}(\equiv\eta) = \{(\emptyset, \equiv\eta)\} \quad \text{next}((\beta_1;\beta_2)\eta) = \text{next}(\beta_1\beta_2\eta)$$
$$\text{next}(\alpha^*\eta) = \text{next}(\eta) \cup \{(G, \beta_1 \ldots \beta_{n'-1}\alpha^*\eta) \mid n' > 1 \text{ and}$$
$$(G, \beta_1 \ldots \beta_{n'-1}\text{form}\,(\alpha^*\eta)) \in \text{next}(\alpha\text{form}\,(\alpha^*\eta))\}$$

Lemma 2 (Witness Lemma). *For any syntactic structure $\mathcal{S} = (W, \mathcal{L}, \mathfrak{C})$, any state $w \in W$, any Hintikka set $\mathcal{H} \in \mathfrak{C}(w)$, any eventuality chain η_1 such that $\text{form}\,(\eta_1) \in \mathcal{H}$ and any path π in $\mathcal{S}$ from $(\mathcal{H}, w)$, π fulfills η_1 if and only if there is $(G, \eta_2) \in \text{next}(\eta_1)$ such that $G \cup \{\text{form}\,(\eta_2)\} \subseteq \mathcal{H}$ and π fulfills η_2.*

The proof of the Witness Lemma is by induction on the sum $\sum_{k=1}^{|\eta_1|-1} \left|\eta_1^k\right|$ of the length of the programs in η.   □

In the proof of Theorem 2, we construct from a standard syntactic structure $\mathcal{S} = (W, \mathcal{L}, \mathfrak{C})$ for φ_0 the path model $M = (W, \mathcal{L}, B, \mathcal{V})$ in which B is the set of supports of the justifying paths in $\mathcal{S}$. Therefore if the set of the supports of the justifying paths in $\mathcal{S}$ is limit closed then B is limit closed too. Hence the following corollary can be deduced from Theorem 2.

Corollary 1. *A formula φ_0 is $OPDL^{lc}$ satisfiable if and only if there is a standard syntactic structure $\mathcal{S}$ for φ_0 which fulfills all eventualities and such that the set of the supports of the justifying paths in $\mathcal{S}$ is limit closed.*

3.2   The Optimal Decision Procedure

We describe a procedure which, given a formula φ_0, either fails or exhibits a standard syntactic structure for φ_0 fulfilling all eventualities. The procedure inductively constructs a finite sequence $\mathcal{S}_0, \ldots, \mathcal{S}_n$ of syntactic structures for φ_0. The initial syntactic structure $\mathcal{S}_0 = (W_0, \mathcal{L}_0, \mathfrak{C}_0)$ is defined such that:

- W_0 is the set of all pairs $(P, \mathcal{C})$ where P is a non-empty subset of $SP(\varphi_0) \cup \{e\}$ for some fixed $e \notin SP(\varphi_0)$ and $\mathcal{C}$ is a cluster for φ_0,
- $\mathcal{L}((P_1, \mathcal{C}_1), (P_2, \mathcal{C}_2)) = P_2$ if $\mathcal{C}_1 \, S_{P_2} \, \mathcal{C}_2$ and is empty otherwise,
- $\mathfrak{C}(P, \mathcal{C}) = \mathcal{C}$.

Then for all k, the syntactic structure $\mathcal{S}_{k+1}$ is constructed from $\mathcal{S}_k = (W_k, \mathcal{L}_k, \mathfrak{C}_k)$ by removing from W_k the states $(P, \mathcal{C})$ which are not fulfilling or such that for some $\mathcal{H} \in \mathcal{C}$, there is no $(P', \mathcal{C}') \in W_k$ and $\mathcal{H}' \in \mathcal{C}'$ such that $\mathcal{C} \; S_{P'} \; \mathcal{C}'$ and $\mathcal{H} \; S_{P'} \; \mathcal{H}'$.

There exists a constant C such that the number of states in W_0 for any φ_0 is bounded by $2^{2^{C \cdot \ell}}$ where $\ell = |\varphi_0|$. Therefore, for some $n \leq 2^{2^{C \cdot \ell}}$ no state can be eliminated from $\mathcal{S}_n$. The procedure terminates successfully iff there is a state $(P, \mathcal{C}) \in W_n$ and a Hintikka set $\mathcal{H} \in \mathcal{C}$ such that $\varphi_0 \in \mathcal{H}$. By Theorem 2, the decision procedure is sound and complete. Since the satisfiability problem of OPDL is 2EXPTIME-hard [2], we have the following theorem.

Theorem 3. *The satisfiability problem of OPDL is 2EXPTIME-complete.*

4 Optimal Decision Procedure for OPDL^{lc}

The procedure of the Sect. 3 is difficult to adapt to OPDL^{lc} because no simple condition can be checked during the construction of the syntactic structure to guarantee that the set of the supports of all justifying paths is limit closed. Therefore, we first prove that OPDL^{lc} has a particular tree model property. Then we use this property to reduce the satisfiability problem of OPDL^{lc} to the (dual of) the emptiness problem of an automaton on infinite trees. Because syntactic structures are more convenient than models for decision procedures, we prove a *tree syntactic structure property*, from which the usual tree model property can be deduced using the construction of Sect. 3.1.

4.1 Tree Model Property of OPDL^{lc}

An N-ary ω-tree over an alphabet Σ is a function $T : [1..N]^* \longrightarrow \Sigma$. In such a tree, nodes are labeled with elements of Σ. A *branch* in T is an infinite sequence $\sigma_1 = \lambda_1 \lambda_2 \ldots$ for which there exists $\sigma_2 \in [1..N]^\omega$ and $i \in \mathbb{N}$ such that for all $k > 0$, $\lambda_k = \sigma_2^{\leq i+k}$. Like in the previous section, we need nodes to be labeled with pairs $(P, \mathcal{C})$ where P is the set of atomic programs labeling the incoming edge and $\mathcal{C}$ is a cluster. To simulate incomplete trees, we allow P to be empty, in which case the branch is said to be pruned.

Definition 7. *An N-ary syntactic tree for a formula φ_0 is an N-ary ω-tree T over $\Sigma = 2^{Atm} \times Clusters(\varphi_0)$ where $Clusters(\varphi_0)$ is the set of clusters on φ_0 and such that:*

1. $T_P(\epsilon) = \emptyset$ and there is $\sigma \in [1..N]^\omega$ such that for all $i > 0$, $T_P(\sigma^{\leq i}) \neq \emptyset$;
2. for all $\lambda \in [1..N]^*$ and $k \in 1..N$, $T_P(\lambda k) = \emptyset$ or $T_C(\lambda) \; S_{T_P(\lambda k)} \; T_C(\lambda k)$.

where T_P and T_C are the projections of T on 2^{Atm} and $Clusters(\varphi_0)$, respectively. A branch σ in T is valid if for all $k > 1$, $T_P(\sigma^k) \neq \emptyset$ and pruned otherwise.

To any N-ary syntactic tree $T = (T_P, T_C)$ naturally corresponds the syntactic structure $\mathcal{S}(T) = ([1..N]^*, \mathcal{L}, T_C)$ where $\mathcal{L}(\lambda_1, \lambda_2) = T_P(\lambda_2)$ if $\lambda_2 = \lambda_1 k$ for some $k \in 1..N$ and is the empty set otherwise. Therefore, an N-ary syntactic tree can be seen as a tree syntactic structure. Indeed, we will abusively write about paths in syntactic trees. For the following definition of a good syntactic tree, since we do not assume that the corresponding syntactic structure fulfills all eventualities, we adapt the definition of a justifying path. A *pseudo-justifying path* is an infinite unbranching path π such that for all $k > 0$, if $\pi^k = (\mathcal{H}_k, w_k)$ then for any eventuality $\langle\!\langle \alpha \rangle\!\rangle \varphi \in \mathcal{H}_k$ there is $\ell \geq k$ such that $\pi^\ell = (\mathcal{H}_\ell, w_\ell)$ and either $\pi^{k..\ell}$ fulfills $\langle\!\langle \alpha \rangle\!\rangle \varphi$ or there is an eventuality chain η such that $\eta^1 = \equiv$, $\mathrm{form}(\eta) \in \mathcal{H}_\ell$ and for any path π_2 from π^ℓ fulfilling η, $\pi^{k..(\ell-1)}\pi_2$ fulfills $\langle\!\langle \alpha \rangle\!\rangle \varphi$. By the Witness Lemma, any justifying path is a pseudo-justifying path.

Definition 8. *An N-ary syntactic tree $T = (T_P, T_C)$ for a formula φ_0 is good iff all the following conditions hold:*

1. *any valid branch σ is the support of a pseudo-justifying path;*
2. *for any node λ in T, if $T_P(\lambda) \neq \emptyset$ and there is $\mathcal{H} \in T_C(\lambda)$ such that $\langle\!\langle \equiv \rangle\!\rangle \psi \in \mathcal{H}$ for some formula ψ, then there is a finite path π in T from $(\mathcal{H}', \lambda)$ fulfilling the maximal eventuality chain for ψ;*
3. *there is a pseudo-justifying path in T from $(\mathcal{H}, \epsilon)$ such that $\varphi_0 \in \mathcal{H}$.*

Let $N^{\equiv}_{\varphi_0}$ be the number of eventualities of the form $\langle\!\langle \equiv \rangle\!\rangle \psi$ in $FL(\varphi_0)$ plus one. The tree property of OPDL^{lc} is stated as follows.

Theorem 4. *A formula φ_0 is OPDL^{lc} satisfiable iff there is a good $N^{\equiv}_{\varphi_0}$-ary syntactic tree for φ_0.*

Proof (Proof sketch). We only detail the construction for the left-to-right direction, which is inspired by a similar construction for CTL^* [7]. Suppose φ_0 is satisfiable. By Corollary 1, there is a standard syntactic structure $\mathcal{S} = (W, \mathcal{L}, \mathfrak{C})$ for φ_0 which fulfills all eventualities and such that the set of the supports of the justifying paths in $\mathcal{S}$ is limit closed. Let $\langle\!\langle \equiv \rangle\!\rangle \psi_2, \ldots, \langle\!\langle \equiv \rangle\!\rangle \psi_{N^{\equiv}_{\varphi_0}}$ be an ordering of the eventualities of the form $\langle\!\langle \equiv \rangle\!\rangle \psi$ in $FL(\varphi_0)$. We first define the $N^{\equiv}_{\varphi_0}$-ary ω-tree T_{path} over the alphabet of all the paths in $\mathcal{S}$ plus the empty word ϵ. By Lemma 1, there is a justifying path π_0 from $(\mathcal{H}_0, w_0)$. We label the root of T_{path} with this path: $T_{\mathrm{path}}(\epsilon) = \pi_0$. For each node $\lambda \in [1..N^{\equiv}_{\varphi_0}]^*$, if $T_{\mathrm{path}}(\lambda) \neq \epsilon$, the labeling path continues with the first successor: $T_{\mathrm{path}}(\lambda 1) = T_{\mathrm{path}}(\lambda)^{\geq 2}$. For the other successors $k \in 2..N^{\equiv}_{\varphi_0}$ of λ, let $(\mathcal{H}_\lambda, w_\lambda) = T_{\mathrm{path}}(\lambda)^1$. If $\langle\!\langle \equiv \rangle\!\rangle \psi_k \in \mathcal{H}_\lambda$ then let π_1 be the shortest path fulfilling the maximal eventuality chain for ψ_k and such that $\pi_1^1 = (\mathcal{H}', w_\lambda)$ for some $\mathcal{H}'$. By Lemma 1, there is a justifying path $\pi_{\lambda k}$ whose prefix is the trunk of π_1. We label the kth successor of λ with it: $T_{\mathrm{path}}(\lambda k) = \pi_{\lambda k}^{\geq 2}$. Otherwise, if $\langle\!\langle \equiv \rangle\!\rangle \psi_{k-1} \notin \mathcal{H}_\lambda$ then $T_{\mathrm{path}}(\lambda k) = \epsilon$. All successors of a node labeled with ϵ are labeled with ϵ. Finally, the good $N^{\equiv}_{\varphi_0}$-ary syntactic tree T for φ_0 is constructed from T_{path} as follows. For the root node, $T(\epsilon) = (\emptyset, \mathfrak{C}(w_0))$. For $\lambda \in [1..N^{\equiv}_{\varphi_0}]^*$ and $k \in 1..N^{\equiv}_{\varphi_0}$, if $T_{\mathrm{path}}(\lambda)^1 = (\mathcal{H}_\lambda, w_\lambda)$ and $T_{\mathrm{path}}(\lambda k)^1 = (\mathcal{H}_{\lambda k}, w_{\lambda k})$ then $T(\lambda k) = (\mathcal{L}(w_\lambda, w_{\lambda k}), \mathfrak{C}(w_{\lambda k}))$. Otherwise, $T(\lambda k) = (\emptyset, \mathcal{C})$ for some arbitrary cluster $\mathcal{C}$. □

4.2   Automata-based Decision Procedure for OPDL^{lc}

By Theorem 4, whenever a formula φ_0 is satisfiable, there is a good $N_{\varphi_0}^{\equiv}$-ary syntactic tree for φ_0. Therefore, we construct an automaton which recognizes exactly the good $N_{\varphi_0}^{\equiv}$-ary syntactic trees for φ_0. We first recall the definitions of the automata used in the procedure before describing the construction of our automaton.

A Büchi word automaton is a tuple $\mathcal{A} = (\Sigma, S, \rho, S_0, F)$ where Σ is the input alphabet, S is the set of states of the automaton, $\rho : S \times \Sigma \longrightarrow 2^S$ is a non-deterministic transition function, $S_0 \subseteq S$ is the set of initial states and $F \subseteq S$ is the termination condition. Given an infinite word μ over Σ, a *run* of $\mathcal{A}$ on μ is a word r over S such that $r^1 \in S_0$ and for all $k \geq 1$, $r^{k+1} \in \rho(r^k, \mu^k)$. The set of states occurring infinitely often in a run r is denoted by $\inf(r)$. A word μ is accepted by $\mathcal{A}$ iff there is a run r of $\mathcal{A}$ on μ such that $\inf(r) \cap F \neq \emptyset$. By extension, a Büchi word automaton accepts a tree iff it accepts all its branches seen as words over the labels of the trees's nodes.

A Street tree automaton is a tuple $\mathcal{A} = (\Sigma, S, \rho, S_0, F)$ similar to a Büchi word automaton except that $\rho : S \times \Sigma \longrightarrow 2^{S^N}$ assigns a set of N-ary tuples of states and $F \subseteq 2^S \times 2^S$ is a set of pairs of set of states. Given an N-ary ω-tree T over Σ, a run of $\mathcal{A}$ on T is a tree T_r over S such that $T_r(\epsilon) \in S_0$ and for all $\lambda \in [1..N]^*$, $(T_r(\lambda 1), \ldots, T_r(\lambda N)) \in \rho(T_r(\lambda), T(\lambda))$. For all branch σ in T_r, the set of states occurring infinitely often in σ is denoted by $\inf(\sigma)$. A tree T is accepted by $\mathcal{A}$ iff there is a run T_r of $\mathcal{A}$ on T such that for any branch σ in T_r and any pair $(A, B) \in F$, if $\inf(\sigma) \cap A \neq \emptyset$ then $\inf(\sigma) \cap B \neq \emptyset$.

Given a formula φ_0 we devise a Streett tree automaton $\mathcal{A}$ which recognizes exactly the good $N_{\varphi_0}^{\equiv}$-ary syntactic trees for φ_0. We first describe three automata, each checking conditions from Definitions 7 and 8. Let $\Sigma = 2^{Atm} \times \text{Clusters}(\varphi_0)$.

Condition (2) of Definition 7 is checked by the "successor" Büchi word automaton $\mathcal{A}_S = (\Sigma, S_S, \rho_S, S_{S,0}, F)$ where S_S is the set of clusters on φ_0 plus the special state I, $S_{S,0} = \{I\}$, $F_S = S_S$ and $s_1 \in \rho_S(s_0, (P, \mathcal{C}))$ iff (i) $s_1 = \mathcal{C}$ and (ii) $P = \emptyset$ or $s_0\ S_P\ s_1$.

Condition (1) of Definition 8 is checked by the "justifying" Büchi word automaton $\mathcal{A}_J = (\Sigma, S_J, \rho_J, S_{J,0}, F_J)$ where

- S_J is the set of pairs $(\mathcal{H}, E)$ where E is a set of eventuality chains to be fulfilled and $\mathcal{H}$ is either a Hintikka set of the parent cluster or the empty set if the current node is the root or $FL(\varphi_0)$ if the current branch is pruned;
- $S_{J,0} = \{(\emptyset, \emptyset)\}$ and $F_J = \{(\mathcal{H}, E) \in S_J \mid \mathcal{H} \neq \emptyset \text{ and } E = \emptyset\}$;
- $(\mathcal{H}_1, E_1) \in \rho_J((\mathcal{H}_0, E_0), (P, \mathcal{C}))$ if one of the following condition holds:
  - $\mathcal{H}_0$ is a Hintikka set, $E_0 \neq \emptyset$, $\mathcal{H}_1 \in \mathcal{C}$, $P \neq \emptyset$, $\mathcal{H}_0\ S_P\ \mathcal{H}_1$ and for all $\eta_0 \in E_0$, $\text{form}(\eta_0) \in \mathcal{H}_1$ and there is $(G_1, \eta_1) \in \text{next}(\eta_0)$ such that $G_1 \cup \{\text{form}(\eta_1)\} \subseteq \mathcal{H}_1$ and if $\eta_1^1 \in Atm$ then $\eta_1^{\geq 2} \in E_1$.
  - $\mathcal{H}_0 \neq FL(\varphi_0)$, $E_0 = \emptyset$, $\mathcal{H}_1 \in \mathcal{C}$, if $\mathcal{H}_0 \neq \emptyset$ then $P \neq \emptyset$ and $\mathcal{H}_0\ S_P\ \mathcal{H}_1$ and for any eventuality $\langle\!\langle \alpha \rangle\!\rangle \varphi \in \mathcal{H}_1$, there is $(G_1, \eta_1) \in \text{next}(\alpha\varphi)$ such that $G_1 \cup \{\text{form}(\eta_1)\} \subseteq \mathcal{H}_1$ and if $\eta_1^1 \in Atm$ then $\eta_1^{\geq 2} \in E_1$.
  - $\mathcal{H}_1 = FL(\varphi_0)$ and $E_1 \neq \emptyset$.
  - $\mathcal{H}_1 = FL(\varphi_0)$, $E_1 = \emptyset$ and either $E_0 = \emptyset$ or $\mathcal{H}_0 \neq \emptyset$ and $P = \emptyset$.

Finally, the "existential" Büchi tree automaton $\mathcal{A}_E = (\Sigma, S_E, \rho_E, S_{E,0}, F_E)$ ensures that there is a pseudo-justifying path π from $(\mathcal{H}_1, \epsilon)$ where $\varphi_0 \in \mathcal{H}_1$ and such that the support of π is the branch obtained by always choosing the first successor (conditions (1) of Definition 7 and (3) of Definition 8). Moreover, $\mathcal{A}_E$ checks conditions (2) of Definition 8. It is defined such that:

- S_E is the set of triples $(\mathcal{H}, E, t)$ where $\mathcal{H}$ and E play the same role as in $\mathcal{A}_J$ and t is a Boolean value ($\top$ or $\bot$) indicating whether the state is final;
- $S_{E,0} = \{(\emptyset, \emptyset, \bot)\}$ and $F_E = \{(S_E, F)\}$ where $F = \{(\mathcal{H}, E, t) \in S_E \mid t = \top\}$.

The transition function ρ_E is defined such that if

$$((\mathcal{H}_1, E_1, t_1), \ldots, (\mathcal{H}_{N_{\varphi_0}^{\equiv}}, E_{N_{\varphi_0}^{\equiv}}, t_{N_{\varphi_0}^{\equiv}})) \in \rho_E((\mathcal{H}_0, E_0, t_0), (P, \mathcal{C}))$$

then all the following conditions hold:

- for all $k \in 1..N_{\varphi_0}^{\equiv}$, either $\mathcal{H}_k \in \mathcal{C}$ or $\mathcal{H}_k = FL(\varphi_0)$;
- if $\mathcal{H}_0 = \emptyset$ then $\mathcal{H}_1$ is a Hintikka set, $\varphi_0 \in \mathcal{H}_1$ and $P = \emptyset$;
- if $\mathcal{H}_0$ is a Hintikka set then $P \neq \emptyset$, $\mathcal{H}_1$ is a Hintikka set and $\mathcal{H}_0 \, S_P \, \mathcal{H}_1$;
- if $\mathcal{H}_1$ is a Hintikka set and $E_0 = \emptyset$ then for all eventuality $\langle\!\langle \alpha \rangle\!\rangle \varphi \in \mathcal{H}_1$ there is $(G_2, \eta_2) \in \text{next}(\alpha\varphi)$ such that $G_2 \cup \{\text{form}(\eta_2)\} \subseteq \mathcal{H}_1$, if $\eta_2^1 \in Atm$ then $\eta_2^{\geq 2} \in E_1$ and if $\eta_2^1 = \equiv$ and $E_k \neq \emptyset$ for k such that $\text{form}(\eta_2) = \langle\!\langle \equiv \rangle\!\rangle \psi_{k-1}$ then $t_k = \bot$;
- if $\mathcal{H}_1$ is a Hintikka set then for all $\eta_1 \in E_0$, $\text{form}(\eta_1) \in \mathcal{H}_1$ and there is $(G_2, \eta_2) \in \text{next}(\eta_1)$ such that $G_2 \cup \{\text{form}(\eta_2)\} \subseteq \mathcal{H}_1$, if $\eta_2^1 \in Atm$ then $\eta_2^{\geq 2} \in E_1$ and if $\eta_2^1 = \equiv$ and $E_k \neq \emptyset$ for k such that $\text{form}(\eta_2) = \langle\!\langle \equiv \rangle\!\rangle \psi_{k-1}$ then $t_k = \bot$;
- for all $k \in 2..N_{\varphi_0}^{\equiv}$, if $\mathcal{H}_1$ is a Hintikka set and $\langle\!\langle \equiv \rangle\!\rangle \psi_{k-1} \in \mathcal{H}_1$ then $\mathcal{H}_k$ is a Hintikka set, $\psi_{k-1} \in \mathcal{H}_k$ and there is $(G_2, \eta_2) \in \text{next}(\eta_1)$ where η_1 is the maximal eventuality chain for ψ_{k-1} such that $G_2 \cup \{\text{form}(\eta_2)\} \subseteq \mathcal{H}_k$ and if $\eta_2^1 \in Atm$ then $\eta_2^{\geq 2} \in E_k$;
- if $E_1 \neq \emptyset$ then $t_1 = \bot$.

$\mathcal{A}_S$ is deterministic and the number of its states is double exponential in $|\varphi_0|$. It can be directly translated into a Streett tree automaton with no termination pair. $\mathcal{A}_J$ has an exponential number of states but it must be determinized before being transformed into a tree automaton, because the choice of the Hintikka sets depends on the successor of the node. By the construction of Piterman [11], any nondeterministic Büchi word automaton with s states can be transformed into an equivalent deterministic Streett word automaton with s^{2s+2} states and s pairs. Hence, the resulting Streett tree automaton corresponding to $\mathcal{A}_J$ has a double exponential number of states and an exponential number of termination pairs. $\mathcal{A}_E$ has an exponential number of states and a single termination pair. The product of these three tree automata gives a Streett tree automaton $\mathcal{A}$ with a double exponential number of states and an exponential number of pairs. Emerson and Jutla [8] proved that the emptiness of a Streett tree automaton with s states and p termination pairs can be decided in deterministic time $(s \cdot p)^{\mathcal{O}(p)}$.

Since $\mathcal{A}$ recognizes exactly the good syntactic trees for φ_0, by Theorem 4, the satisfiability problem of OPDL^{lc} is in 2EXPTIME. Moreover, the proof from [2] that OPDL^{lts} is 2EXPTIME-hard can easily be adapted to OPDL^{lc}. Hence we have the following result.

Theorem 5. *The satisfiability problem of $OPDL^{lc}$ is 2EXPTIME-complete.*

5 Conclusion

In this work, we have first shown that the logic OPDL^{lts} proposed by [2] does not have the good property of being conservative. Using the more convenient path semantics framework, the semantics of this logic has been slightly modified to obtain the new logic OPDL^{lc} which is conservative and in which PDL and CTL^* can still be embedded. Then, we have answered the question, left open in [2], of the complexity of the satisfiability problems of OPDL and OPDL^{lc}. We have proved that both problems are 2EXPTIME-complete. However, the methods used to prove these results are quite different. Whereas for OPDL a finite model with bounded size is constructed, for OPDL^{lc} infinite branches must be considered using automata on infinite trees. This highlights the difference between OPDL and OPDL^{lc} as a consequence of the limit closure property of the path semantics.

Some questions about OPDL and OPDL^{lc} have been left open for future research. For instance, there is still no axiomatization for OPDL and OPDL^{lc}. Furthermore, it would be interesting to study the relative expressive power of these logics and other logics embedding both PDL and CTL^* like the automata-based logic YAPL [18] or the extension $\mathsf{PDL}{-}\Delta$ of PDL with repetition [16].

Another issue of future research is the relation between OPDL, OPDL^{lc} and ATL^*, the full version of Alternating-time Temporal Logic (ATL) introduced in [1]. There have recently been interesting results by [6], providing a tableau-based decision procedure for ATL^*, which has been proved to be in 2EXPTIME as well, and to also work for CTL^*. The procedure has been implemented. Future research will be devoted to verify whether a similar solution can be found for OPDL and OPDL^{lc} in order to have an implemented procedure for checking satisfiability in these logics.

References

1. Alur, R., Henzinger, T., Kupferman, O.: Alternating-time temporal logic. J. ACM **49**(5), 672–713 (2002)
2. Balbiani, P., Lorini, E.: Ockhamist propositional dynamic logic: a natural link between PDL and CTL*. In: Libkin, L., Kohlenbach, U., Queiroz, R. (eds.) WoLLIC 2013. LNCS, vol. 8071, pp. 251–265. Springer, Heidelberg (2013). doi:10.1007/978-3-642-39992-3_22
3. Belnap, N., Perloff, M., Xu, M.: Facing the Future: Agents and Choices in Our Indeterminist World. Oxford University Press, New York (2001)

4. Brown, M., Goranko, V.: An extended branching-time Ockhamist temporal logic. J. Logic Lang. Inform. **8**(2), 143–166 (1999)
5. Dam, M.: CTL* and ECTL* as fragments of the modal mu-calculus. Theoret. Comput. Sci. **126**(1), 77–96 (1994)
6. David, A., Schewe, S.: Deciding ATL* satisfiability by tableaux. Technical report, Laboratoire IBISC - Université d'Evry Val-d'Essonne (2016)
7. Emerson, E., Sistla, A.: Deciding full branching time logic. Inf. Control **61**, 175–201 (1984)
8. Emerson, E.A., Jutla, C.S.: The complexity of tree automata and logics of programs. SIAM J. Comput. **29**(1), 132–158 (1999)
9. Fischer, M.J., Ladner, R.E.: Propositional dynamic logic of regular programs. J. Comput. Syst. Sci. **18**(2), 194–211 (1979)
10. Harel, D., Kozen, D., Tiuryn, J.: Dynamic Logic. MIT Press, Cambridge (2000)
11. Piterman, N.: From nondeterministic Büchi and Streett automata to deterministic parity automata. In: Logic in Computer Science (LICS), pp. 255–264. IEEE Computer Society (2006)
12. Pratt, V.R.: Models of program logics. In: 20th Annual Symposium on Foundations of Computer Science, pp. 115–122. IEEE Computer Society (1979)
13. Prior, A.: Past, Present, and Future. Clarendon Press, Oxford (1967)
14. Reynolds, M.: An axiomatization of full computation tree logic. J. Symbol. Logic **66**(3), 1011–1057 (2001)
15. Reynolds, M.: A tableau for bundled CTL*. J. Logic Comput. **17**(1), 117–132 (2007)
16. Streett, R.S.: Propositional dynamic logic of looping and converse is elementarily decidable. Inf. Control **54**(1–2), 121–141 (1982)
17. Thomason, R.: Combinations of tense and modality. In: Gabbay, D., Guenthner, F. (eds.) Handbook of Philosophical Logic, vol. 2, 2nd edn, pp. 135–165. Reidel, Dordrecht (1984)
18. Vardi, M.Y., Wolper, P.: Yet another process logic (preliminary version). In: Clarke, E., Kozen, D. (eds.) Logic of Programs 1983. LNCS, vol. 164, pp. 501–512. Springer, Heidelberg (1984). doi:10.1007/3-540-12896-4_383
19. Wolper, P.: A translation from full branching time temporal logic to one letter propositional dynamic logic with looping (unpublished manuscript)
20. Zanardo, A.: Branching-time logic with quantification over branches: the point of view of modal logic. J. Symbol. Logic **61**(1), 143–166 (1996)

On the Expressiveness
of Temporal Equilibrium Logic

Laura Bozzelli[⊠] and David Pearce

Technical University of Madrid (UPM), Madrid, Spain
laura.bozzelli@fi.upm.es

Abstract. We investigate expressiveness issues of Temporal Equilibrium Logic (TEL), a promising nonmonotonic logical framework for temporal reasoning. TEL shares the syntax of standard linear temporal logic LTL, but its semantics is an orthogonal combination of the LTL semantics with the nonmonotonic semantics of Equilibrium Logic. We establish that TEL is more expressive than LTL, and captures a strict subclass of ω-regular languages. We illustrate the expressive power of TEL by showing that LTL-conformant planning, which is not expressible in LTL, can be instead expressed in TEL. Additionally, we provide a systematic study of the expressiveness comparison between the LTL semantics and the TEL semantics for various natural syntactical fragments.

1 Introduction

Answer Set Programming (ASP) is now well established as a successful paradigm for declarative programming, with its roots in the fields of knowledge representation (KR), logic programming, and nonmonotonic reasoning (NMR) [3]. An adequate and well-known logical foundation for ASP is provided by *Equilibrium Logic* [19,20], a nonmonotonic extension of the superintuitionistic logic of *here-and-there* (HT) [17]. This provides useful logical tools for the metatheory of ASP and a framework for defining extensions of the basic ASP language, for example to arbitrary propositional and first-order theories, to languages with intensional functions, and to hybrid theories that combine classical and rule-based reasoning [7,10,14,21].

ASP has been applied to a wide range of temporal reasoning problems, including prediction, planning, diagnosis and verification. However, since it is not an intrinsically temporal formalism, it suffers some important limitations. Most ASP solvers deal with finite domains, which hampers the solution of temporal reasoning problems dealing with unbounded time, like proving the non-existence of a plan. Temporal scenarios dealing with unbounded time are typically best suited for modal temporal logics, a fundamental framework for the specification

---

An authors' online version of this paper is available at https://www.dropbox.com/s/x0fnjzhjwira780/TEL%20Expression.pdf?dl=0. Its appendix includes proofs that are omitted here for lack of space.

L. Michael and A. Kakas (Eds.): JELIA 2016, LNAI 10021, pp. 159–173, 2016.
DOI: 10.1007/978-3-319-48758-8_11

of the dynamic behavior of reactive systems. However, standard modal temporal logics, such as propositional linear-time temporal logic LTL [22], are not designed to deal with many issues in KR. These logics (like classical logics) have a monotonic consequence relation, meaning that adding a formula to a theory never produces a reduction of its set of consequences. A monotonic logic cannot handle various commonsense reasoning tasks such as reasoning by default.

Temporal Equilibrium Logic (TEL). TEL was proposed by Cabalar and Vega [8] as a nonmonotonic temporal logic, able to capture temporal reasoning problems not representable in ASP. It is apparently the only nonmonotonic extension of a standard modal temporal logic (viz. LTL) that does not use additional operators or constructions.

TEL shares the syntax of standard LTL, but its semantics is an orthogonal combination of the LTL semantics with the nonmonotonic semantics of Equilibrium Logic. As for Equilibrium Logic, the non-monotonic semantics of TEL is based on a selection criterion (a kind of minimization) among the models of the intermediate monotonic temporal logic of Here-and-There (THT), a combination of LTL and the propositional superintuitionistic logic of Here-and-There (HT).

Many works have been dedicated to the theoretical study of TEL, and some tools have been developed for computing models of temporal programs under TEL semantics (see e.g. [5]). Theoretical key results include the use of TEL to translate action languages [8], an automata-theoretic approach for checking the existence of TEL models [4], a decidable criterion for proving strong equivalence of two TEL theories [6], and a systematic study of the computational cost of TEL satisfiability [2] (a problem which is in general EXPSPACE-complete).

Our Contribution. We investigate expressiveness issues for the TEL framework. It is known [4] that like LTL, TEL allows to specify only ω-regular temporal properties. As a first contribution, we show that TEL is in general more expressive than LTL. In particular, the class of TEL-definable languages strictly includes the class of LTL-definable languages and is strictly included in the class of ω-regular languages. We also illustrate the expressive power of TEL by considering the problem of finding conformant plans for temporal goals in dynamic systems in the presence of incomplete information[1] when the goal and the system behavior are specified in LTL [9]. We show that this problem, which is not expressible in LTL [9], can be instead expressed in TEL.

As an additional non-trivial theoretical contribution, we provide a systematic study of the expressiveness comparison between the LTL semantics and the TEL semantics for various natural syntactical fragments. The considered fragments are obtained by restricting the set of allowed temporal modalities and/or by imposing a bound on the nesting depth of temporal modalities. The expressive power of LTL semantics for these fragments has been made relatively clear by numerous researchers. Thus, since for some of these fragments, TEL satisfiability is known to be relatively tractable [2], the aim is also to understand what kind of temporal reasoning problems can be captured by these fragments under the TEL

---

[1] On both the initial situation and on the full effects of actions.

semantics. Furthermore, we consider the class of splittable temporal programs [5], a TEL fragment which is known to be LTL-expressible and for which a solver has been implemented [5]. We show that a slight syntactical generalization of this fragment, obtained by relaxing a constraint on the use of temporal literals in the dynamic rules (intuitively ensuring that "the past does not depend on the future"), already leads to a fragment more expressive than LTL.

Some of the expressiveness results obtained also point to a peculiar difference between LTL and TEL: due to the interpretation of the implication connective, in TEL, a temporal modality cannot be expressed in terms of its 'dual' modality. Thus, in TEL, dual temporal modalities, such as F ('eventually') and G ('always'), need to be considered independently from one another. This is illustrated by one of our results: while for the syntactical fragment whose allowed temporal modalities are F and X ('next'), the TEL semantics is less expressive than the LTL semantics, for the dual fragment, the TEL semantics already allows one to express non-LTL-definable requirements.

Related Work. Several research areas of AI have combined modal temporal logics with formalisms from knowledge representation for reasoning about actions and planning (see e.g. [12]). Combinations of NMR with modal logics designed for temporal reasoning are much more infrequent in the literature. The few exceptions are typically modal action languages with a nonmonotonic semantics defined under some syntactical restrictions. Recently, an alternative to TEL has been introduced, namely, Temporal Answer Sets (TAS), which relies on dynamic linear-time temporal logic [16], a modal approach more expressive than LTL. However, while the non-monotonic semantics of TEL covers any arbitrary theory in the syntax of LTL, TAS uses a syntactic transformation that is only defined for theories with a rather restricted syntax. A framework unifying TEL and TAS has been proposed in [1].

2   Preliminaries

Let $\mathbb{N}$ be the set of natural numbers and for all $i, j \in \mathbb{N}$, let $[i, j] := \{h \in \mathbb{N} \mid i \leq h \leq j\}$. For an infinite word w over some alphabet and for all $i \geq 0$, $w(i)$ is the ith symbol of w. Let P and P' be two disjoint finite sets of atomic propositions. Given an infinite word w over 2^P and an infinite word w' over $2^{P'}$, $w \oplus w'$ denotes the infinite word over $2^{P \cup P'}$ given by $w(0) \cup w'(0), w(1) \cup w'(1), \ldots$, and $w \oplus P'$ denotes the infinite word over $2^{P \cup P'}$ given by $w(0) \cup P', w(1) \cup P', \ldots$. A proposition p is *flat in* w if $p \in w(i)$ for all $i \geq 0$. Note that each proposition $p' \in P'$ is flat in $w \oplus P'$. We extend the operator $\oplus$ to ω-languages $\mathcal{L}$ over 2^P in the obvious way: $\mathcal{L} \oplus P'$ denotes the ω-language over $2^{P \cup P'}$ consisting of the infinite words of the form $w \oplus P'$ where $w \in \mathcal{L}$.

2.1   Temporal Equilibrium Logic

We recall the framework of Temporal Equilibrium Logic (TEL) [8]. TEL is defined by first introducing a monotonic and intermediate version of standard linear temporal logic LTL [22], the so-called logic of *Temporal Here-and-There* (THT) [8].

The nonmonotonic semantics of TEL is then defined by introducing a criterion for selecting models of THT.

Syntax and Semantics of THT. While the syntax of THT coincides with that of LTL, the semantics of THT is instead an orthogonal combination of the superintuitionistic propositional logic of Here-and-There (HT) [17] and LTL. Fix a finite set P of atomic propositions. The set of THT formulas φ over P is defined by the following abstract syntax.

$$\varphi := p \mid \bot \mid \varphi \vee \varphi \mid \varphi \wedge \varphi \mid \varphi \rightarrow \varphi \mid \mathsf{X}\varphi \mid \varphi\mathsf{U}\varphi \mid \varphi\mathsf{R}\varphi$$

where $p \in P$ and X, U, and R, are the standard 'next', 'until', and 'release' temporal modalities. Negation is defined as $\neg\varphi \stackrel{\text{def}}{=} \varphi \rightarrow \bot$ while $\top \stackrel{\text{def}}{=} \neg\bot$. The classical temporal operators G ('always') and F ('eventually') can be defined in terms of U and R as follows: $\mathsf{F}\varphi \stackrel{\text{def}}{=} \top\mathsf{U}\varphi$ and $\mathsf{G}\varphi \stackrel{\text{def}}{=} \bot\mathsf{R}\varphi$. The size $|\varphi|$ of a formula φ is the number of distinct subformulas of φ. The *temporal depth* of φ is the maximum number of nested temporal modalities in φ.

Recall that LTL over P is interpreted on infinite words over 2^P, called in the following *LTL interpretations*. By contrast, the semantics of THT is defined in terms of infinite words over $2^P \times 2^P$, which can also be viewed as pairs of LTL-interpretations. Formally, a *THT interpretation* is a pair $\mathsf{M} = (\mathsf{H}, \mathsf{T})$ consisting of two LTL interpretations: H (the 'here' interpretation) and T (the 'there' interpretation) such that

$$\text{for all } i \geq 0, \ \mathsf{H}(i) \subseteq \mathsf{T}(i)$$

Intuitively, $\mathsf{H}(i)$ represents the set of propositions which are true at position i, while $\mathsf{T}(i)\backslash\mathsf{H}(i)$ is the set of propositions which *may* be true (i.e. which are not falsified in an intuitionistic sense). A THT interpretation $\mathsf{M} = (\mathsf{H}, \mathsf{T})$ is said to be *total* whenever $\mathsf{H} = \mathsf{T}$. In the following, for *interpretation*, we mean a THT interpretation. Given an interpretation $\mathsf{M} = (\mathsf{H}, \mathsf{T})$, a position $i \geq 0$, and a THT formula φ, the satisfaction relation $\mathsf{M}, i \models \varphi$ is inductively defined as follows:

$\mathsf{M}, i \nvDash \bot$
$\mathsf{M}, i \models p \qquad \Leftrightarrow p \in \mathsf{H}(i)$
$\mathsf{M}, i \models \varphi \vee \psi \Leftrightarrow$ either $\mathsf{M}, i \models \varphi$ or $\mathsf{M}, i \models \psi$
$\mathsf{M}, i \models \varphi \wedge \psi \Leftrightarrow \mathsf{M}, i \models \varphi$ and $\mathsf{M}, i \models \psi$
$\mathsf{M}, i \models \varphi \rightarrow \psi \Leftrightarrow$ for all $\mathsf{H}' \in \{\mathsf{H}, \mathsf{T}\}$, either $(\mathsf{H}', \mathsf{T}), i \nvDash \varphi$ or $(\mathsf{H}', \mathsf{T}), i \models \psi$
$\mathsf{M}, i \models \mathsf{X}\varphi \qquad \Leftrightarrow \mathsf{M}, i+1 \models \varphi$
$\mathsf{M}, i \models \varphi\mathsf{U}\psi \ \Leftrightarrow$ there is $j \geq i$ so that $\mathsf{M}, j \models \psi$ and for all $k \in [i, j-1]$, $\mathsf{M}, k \models \varphi$
$\mathsf{M}, i \models \varphi\mathsf{R}\psi \ \Leftrightarrow$ for all $j \geq i$, either $\mathsf{M}, j \models \psi$ or $\mathsf{M}, k \models \varphi$ for some $k \in [i, j-1]$

We say that M is a (THT) model of φ, written $\mathsf{M} \models \varphi$, whenever $\mathsf{M}, 0 \models \varphi$. A THT formula φ is THT *satisfiable* if it admits a THT model. A formula φ is THT *valid* if every interpretation M is a THT model of φ. Note that the semantics of THT is defined similarly to that of LTL except for the clause for the implication connective $\rightarrow$ which must be checked in both the components H and T of M. As a consequence $\mathsf{M}, i \nvDash \varphi$ does not correspond to $\mathsf{M}, i \models \neg\varphi$ (i.e., $\mathsf{M}, i \models \neg\varphi$ implies that $M, i \not\models \varphi$, but the converse direction does not hold in general). However, if we restrict the semantics to total interpretations, $(T, T) \models \varphi$ corresponds to the satisfaction relation $T \models \varphi$ in LTL. More precisely, the LTL models T of φ correspond to the total interpretations (T, T) which are THT models of φ. With regard to THT validity, a THT valid formula is also an LTL valid formula, but the converse in general does not hold. For example, the *excluded middle* axiom $\varphi \vee \neg\varphi$ is not a valid THT formula since, as highlighted above, for an interpretation $M = (H, T)$, $M \not\models \varphi$ does not imply that $M \models \neg\varphi$. Similarly, the temporal formulas $F\varphi \leftrightarrow \neg G\neg\varphi$ and $\varphi_1 U\varphi_2 \leftrightarrow \neg\varphi_1 R\neg\varphi_2$, which are well-known valid LTL formulas (and allow to express, in LTL, a temporal modality in terms of its dual modality), are not THT valid formulas. Thus, in THT, dual temporal modalities, like F and G, or U and R, need to be considered independently from one another. The following proposition summarizes some observations made above, where we use $\models_{LTL}$ to denote the satisfaction relation in LTL.

Proposition 1. *Let* (H, T) *be an interpretation and* φ *be a THT formula.*

1. *If* $(H, T), i \models \varphi$, *then* $(T, T), i \models \varphi$ *(for all* $i \geq 0$*)*.
2. $(H, T), i \models \neg\varphi$ *iff* $(T, T), i \models \neg\varphi$ *(for all* $i \geq 0$*)*.
3. $(T, T) \models \varphi$ *iff* $T \models_{LTL} \varphi$.

***The non-monotonic logic* TEL.** This logic is obtained from THT by restricting the semantics to a subclass of models of the given formula, called *temporal equilibrium models*. For LTL interpretations H and T, $H \sqsubseteq T$ means that $H(i) \subseteq T(i)$ for all $i \geq 0$, and $H \sqsubset T$ means that $H \sqsubseteq T$ and $H \neq T$.

Definition 1 (Temporal Equilibrium Model). *Given a THT formula* φ, *a* (temporal) equilibrium model *of* φ *is a total model* (T, T) *of* φ *satisfying the following minimality requirement: whenever* $H \sqsubset T$, *then* $(H, T) \not\models \varphi$.

If we restrict the syntax to HT formulas (i.e., THT formulas where no temporal modality is allowed) and the semantics to HT interpretations $(H(0), T(0))$, then (non-temporal) equilibrium models coincide with stable models of answer set programs in their most general form [13]. In particular, the interpretation of negation is that of default negation in logic programming: formula $\neg\varphi$ holds (φ is false by default) if there is no evidence regarding φ, i.e., φ cannot be derived by the rules of the logic program. As a first example, let us consider the THT formula φ given by $\varphi = G(\neg p \rightarrow Xp)$. Its intuitive meaning corresponds to the first-order logic program consisting of rules of the form $p(s(X)) \leftarrow not\, p(X)$, where time has been reified as an extra parameter $X = 0, s(0), s(s(0)), \ldots$. Thus, at any time instant, if there is no evidence regarding p, then p will become true at the next instant. Initially, we have no evidence regarding p, so this will imply Xp. To derive XXp, the only possibility would be the rule $\neg Xp \rightarrow XXp$, an instance of φ. As the body of this rule is false, XXp becomes false by default, and so on. It is easy to see that the unique equilibrium model of φ is $((\emptyset\{p\})^\omega, (\emptyset\{p\})^\omega)$.

Note that an LTL satisfiable formula may have no temporal stable model. As an example, consider the formula φ given by $\varphi = G(\neg Xp \rightarrow p) \wedge G(Xp \rightarrow p)$. The unique LTL model is $T = \{p\}^\omega$. However, (T, T) is not an equilibrium model of φ, since the interpretation (H, T), where $H = (\emptyset)^\omega$ is a THT model of φ.

For a THT formula φ, we denote by $\mathcal{L}_{TEL}(\varphi)$ (resp., $\mathcal{L}_{LTL}(\varphi)$) the ω-language over 2^P consisting of the LTL interpretations T such that (T, T) is an equilibrium model of φ (resp., T is an LTL model of φ). Note that by Proposition 1, $\mathcal{L}_{TEL}(\varphi) \subseteq \mathcal{L}_{LTL}(\varphi)$. A TEL language (resp., LTL language) is an ω-language of the form $\mathcal{L}_{TEL}(\varphi)$ (resp., $\mathcal{L}_{LTL}(\varphi)$) for some THT formula φ. We now observe the following.

Remark 1. LTL-definable languages are TEL-definable.

Indeed, by Proposition 1, the set of LTL models of a THT formula φ over P corresponds to the set of TEL models of $\varphi \wedge \psi_{Tot}(P)$, where formula $\psi_{Tot}(P)$ (we exploit this formula in many parts of the paper) captures, under the THT semantics, the total interpretations over P.

$$\psi_{Tot}(P) := \bigwedge_{p \in P} G(p \vee \neg p)$$

Next, we observe that like LTL, the class of languages definable by TEL is strictly included in the class of ω-regular languages. Indeed, by [4], every TEL language is effectively ω-regular. Moreover, let us consider the ω-regular language $\mathcal{L}_{even}$ consisting of the LTL interpretations T over $P = \{a\}$ of the form $\emptyset^{2n} \cdot \{a\} \cdot \emptyset^\omega$ for some $n \geq 0$ (where the maximal prefix preceding the unique a-position has even length). One can trivially check that $\mathcal{L}_{even}$ is not TEL definable. Hence:

Proposition 2. *The class of TEL languages is strictly included in the class of ω-regular languages.*

2.2   Problems Investigated and Summary of the Main Results

In this paper, we compare the expressive power of the LTL semantics and the TEL semantics for full THT and various syntactical THT fragments.

In particular, we consider the syntactical fragments of THT obtained by restricting the set of allowed temporal modalities and/or by bounding the temporal depth. Formally, given $O_1, O_2, \ldots \in \{X, F, G, U, R\}$, we denote by $THT(O_1, O_2, \ldots)$ the fragment of THT for which only the temporal modalities $O_1, O_2, \ldots$ are allowed. For $k \geq 0$, $THT_k(O_1, O_2, \ldots)$ denotes the fragment of $THT(O_1, O_2, \ldots)$ where the temporal depth is at most k. We write nothing for k when no bound is imposed. For instance, $THT_2(G)$ denotes the fragment where the unique allowed temporal modality is G and the temporal depth is at most 2. We also consider a syntactical fragment of THT, we call *splittable* THT, corresponding to a generalization of splittable temporal programs introduced in [5]. A *temporal literal* is either an ordinary literal or a literal preceded by the next operator X. A splittable THT formula is a conjunction of formulas of the following types:

- *Initial rules:* a formula of the form $B \to H$, where B is a conjunction of temporal literals and H is a disjunction of temporal literals.
- *Dynamic rules:* formulas of the form $G\, r$, where r is an initial rule.
- *Constraints:* formulas of the form $\neg\varphi$ for arbitrary THT formulas φ (such formulas impose constraints only on the 'there' part of an interpretation).

THT fragments under TEL semantics	LTL	
THT, THT(X, R), splittable THT	$>$	Theorem 6
THT(X, U), THT$_{k+1}(X, U)$ $(k \geq 1)$	$\bot$	Theorem 6
THT(U), THT$_{k+2}(U)$ $(k \geq 1)$	$\bot$	Theorem 6
THT$_{k+1}(X, R)$, THT(R), THT$_{k+2}(R)$ $(k \geq 1)$	$\bot$	Theorem 6
THT(X, G), THT$_{k+1}(X, G)$ $(k \geq 1)$	$\not\leq$	Proposition 4
THT(X, F)	$<$	Theorem 3
THT(F, G)	$<$	Theorem 2
THT$_1$	$<$	Theorem 5

Fig. 1. Expressive comparison between TEL fragments and full LTL

For two THT fragments $\mathcal{F}$ and $\mathcal{F}'$ and $\mathcal{S}, \mathcal{S}' \in \{\text{LTL}, \text{TEL}\}$, we say that $\mathcal{F}$ under the $\mathcal{S}$-semantics is subsumed by $\mathcal{F}'$ under the $\mathcal{S}'$-semantics, written $(\mathcal{F})_{\mathcal{S}} \leq (\mathcal{F}')_{\mathcal{S}'}$, if for each $\mathcal{F}$-formula φ, there is a $\mathcal{F}'$-formula φ' s.t. $\mathcal{L}_{\mathcal{S}'}(\varphi') = \mathcal{L}_{\mathcal{S}}(\varphi)$. Moreover, $\mathcal{F}'$ under the $\mathcal{S}'$-semantics is more expressive than $\mathcal{F}$ under the $\mathcal{S}$-semantics, denoted by $(\mathcal{F})_{\mathcal{S}} < (\mathcal{F}')_{\mathcal{S}'}$, if $(\mathcal{F})_{\mathcal{S}} \leq (\mathcal{F}')_{\mathcal{S}'}$ but not $(\mathcal{F}')_{\mathcal{S}'} \leq (\mathcal{F})_{\mathcal{S}}$. Additionally, we say that $\mathcal{F}$ under the $\mathcal{S}$-semantics is expressively incomparable with $\mathcal{F}'$ under the $\mathcal{S}'$-semantics, written $(\mathcal{F}')'_{\mathcal{S}} \perp (\mathcal{F})_{\mathcal{S}}$, if neither $(\mathcal{F})_{\mathcal{S}} \leq (\mathcal{F}')_{\mathcal{S}'}$ nor $(\mathcal{F}')'_{\mathcal{S}} \leq (\mathcal{F})_{\mathcal{S}}$. Sometime, we simply write LTL to mean $(\text{THT})_{\text{LTL}}$.

Figure 1 summarises some of the obtained results concerning the expressiveness comparison between the considered THT fragments under the TEL semantics and full THT under the LTL semantics.

3   Expressing LTL-conformant Planning in TEL

In this section, we illustrate the expressive power of TEL by showing that the LTL-conformant planning problem considered in [9], which is not expressible in LTL [9], can be instead expressed in TEL. Some other approaches in ASP for the formalization of conformant planning can be reformulated in the LTL-conformant planning framework such as the one based on Gelfond's action language [15].

In the context of reasoning about actions and planning, we consider a setting where we have incomplete information on the dynamic system and the knowledge about the system is represented in LTL. In particular, the system is described by introducing a set of atomic facts, called fluents, whose truth value changes as the system evolves, and by specifying through LTL the effects of actions on such a set of facts. Thus, we consider two disjoint finite sets of atomic propositions: F – the set of fluents – and A – the set of actions. The behavior of the given system is specified by an LTL formula φ_s over $A \cup F$ which describes the set of possible evolutions of the system, each of which is represented as an infinite sequence of situations, where transitions from one situation to the next are caused by actions. Note that with this formalization, we may have incomplete information both on the initial situation and on the actual effects of actions so that, given a sequence of actions, we will have multiple possible evolutions, one of which is the actual one. The LTL-conformant planning problem consists in constructing a plan, i.e. a sequence of actions that guarantees the satisfaction of a temporal goal expressed in LTL whenever the conditions specified by φ_s are satisfied.

Formally, the LTL-conformant planning problem is the problem of finding, given two LTL formulas φ_s and φ_g over $A \cup F$ (representing the system specification and the temporal goal, respectively), an infinite sequence $\mathsf{T}_A = \{a_0\}, \{a_1\}, \ldots$ of actions such that for all LTL interpretations T_F over F (i.e. for all the possible infinite sequences of truth assignments to fluents), it holds that

$$\mathsf{T}_A \oplus \mathsf{T}_F \models \varphi_s \to \varphi_g$$

Let $Con(\varphi_s, \varphi_g)$ be the set of such conformant plans T_A. Such a set cannot be in general expressed in LTL [9]. Here, we show that, unless an additional set of flat propositions, $Con(\varphi_s, \varphi_g)$ can be instead expressed in TEL. We construct in *linear-time* a THT formula φ_{con} whose set of equilibrium models corresponds to $Con(\varphi_s, \varphi_g) \oplus F'$, where $F' = F \cup \{u\}$, and u is a fresh (dummy) proposition non in $A \cup F$.

Before defining φ_{con}, we need additional definitions. A THT formula is in negation normal form (NNF) if the implication connective occurs only as negation and, additionally, negation is applied only to atomic propositions. By using De Morgan's laws, the duality between U and R, and the fact that in LTL, $\xi_1 \to \xi_2$ can be rewritten as $\neg \xi_1 \vee \xi_2$, we can convert the THT formula $\neg(\varphi_s \to \varphi_g)$ into a THT formula $\overline{\psi}_{sg}$ in NNF having the same set of LTL models.

Let $K_u(\overline{\psi}_{sg})$ be the THT formula obtained from the NNF formula $\overline{\psi}_{gs}$ by replacing each occurrence of a negative literal $\neg p$ with $p \to u$. Intuitively, $p \to u$ is used to express negation on the 'here' part H of an interpretation (H, T) such that u is flat in T and $u \notin \mathsf{H}(i)$ for all $i \geq 0$. Formally, one can easily show by structural induction that for such an interpretation, $(\mathsf{H}, \mathsf{T}) \models K_u(\overline{\psi}_{gs})$ iff $\mathsf{H} \models_{\mathsf{LTL}} \overline{\psi}_{gs}$. Hence, $(\mathsf{H}, \mathsf{T}) \models K_u(\overline{\psi}_{gs})$ iff $\mathsf{H} \not\models_{\mathsf{LTL}} \varphi_s \to \varphi_g$.

The THT formula φ_{con} over $A \cup F'$ is then defined as follows:

$$\varphi_{con} := \mathsf{G}(\bigvee_{a \in A} (a \wedge \bigwedge_{a' \in A \setminus \{a\}} \neg a)) \wedge (\psi_{Tot}(A \cup F')) \to \bigwedge_{p \in F'} \mathsf{G}p) \wedge$$
$$(\mathsf{F}u \to \psi_{Tot}(A \cup F')) \wedge (u \vee K_u(\overline{\psi}_{gs}))$$

The first conjunct captures the THT interpretations (H, T) such that H and T agree over the set A of actions, and exactly one action occurs at any timestamp. The second and third conjuncts ensure that every proposition in $F' = F \cup \{u\}$ is flat in T and whenever $H \neq T$, $u \notin H(i)$ for every $i \geq 0$. Finally, the last conjunct is fulfilled iff whenever $H \neq T$, $H \models_{LTL} K_u(\overline{\psi}_{gs})$. Formally, the following holds, which proves the result (for details see the online version of this paper at https://www.dropbox.com/s/x0fnjzhjwira780/TEL%20Expression.pdf?dl=0).

Claim. $\mathcal{L}_{TEL}(\varphi_{con}) = Con(\varphi_s, \varphi_g) \oplus F'$.

4   Maximal Fragments Expressible in **LTL**

In this section, we individuate maximal THT fragments which under the TEL semantics are subsumed by full LTL.

The fragment **THT(F,G).** We show that full THT under the LTL semantics is more expressive than the fragment THT(F, G) under the TEL semantics. On the other hand, we additionally establish that for the considered fragment, the TEL semantics is more expressive than the LTL semantics. For the first result, we exploit a well-known characterization of the ω-regular languages which are LTL-expressible [18,24]. In the following, we also consider *finite* (THT) interpretations which are non-empty prefixes of (THT) interpretations.

Definition 2 (*N-stutter Closure* [18,24]). *For $N \geq 1$, an ω-language $\mathcal{L}$ over an alphabet Σ is N-stutter closed if for all finite words x, y, u, w and infinite words v over Σ,*

$$u \cdot w^N \cdot v \in \mathcal{L} \text{ iff } u \cdot w^{N+1} \cdot v \in \mathcal{L}$$

$$x \cdot (u \cdot w^N \cdot y)^\omega \in \mathcal{L} \text{ iff } x \cdot (u \cdot w^{N+1} \cdot y)^\omega \in \mathcal{L}$$

Proposition 3 ([18,24]). *If $\mathcal{L}$ is an ω-regular language over 2^P which is N-stutter closed for some $N \geq 1$, then $\mathcal{L}$ is LTL-expressible.*

For $\varphi \in$ THT(F, G), let $N_\varphi := n^2(h+1)^{2^n}$, where $n = 2^{2|P|}$ and h is the temporal depth of φ. We demonstrate that the language $\mathcal{L}_{TEL}(\varphi)$ is N_φ-stutter closed. For this, we use an additional notion, we call *h-bisimilarity*.

Definition 3 (*h-bisimilarity*). *Let w and w' be two finite words over an alphabet Σ and i and i' be two positions of w and w', respectively. Given $h \geq 0$, (w, i) and (w', i') are h-bisimilar if $w(i) = w'(i')$ and whenever $h > 0$, then:*

– for all $i \leq j < |w|$ (resp., $i' \leq j' < |w'|$), there exists $i' \leq j' < |w'|$ (resp., $i \leq j < |w|$) such that (w, j) and (w', j') are $(h-1)$-bisimilar.

We say that w and w' are h-bisimilar if $(w, 0)$ and $(w', 0)$ are h-bisimilar.

For each $h \geq 0$, a formula in THT$_h(F, G)$ cannot distinguish under the THT semantics two interpretations where one is obtained from the other one by replacing finite segments with h-bisimilar ones. Formally, we establish the following result.

Lemma 1. *Let $h \geq 0$, $\varphi \in THT_h(F, G)$, and N and N' be two finite h-bisimilar interpretations. For all finite interpretations M_1, M_2, M_3 and infinite interpretations M_4,*

$$M_1 N M_4 \models \varphi \text{ iff } M_1 N' M_4 \models \varphi$$
$$M_1(M_2 N M_3)^\omega \models \varphi \text{ iff } M_1(M_2 N' M_3)^\omega \models \varphi$$

The following lemma is based on a counting argument, asserts that for all $h \geq 1$ and finite interpretations consisting of concatenations of N segments, where $N \geq n^2(h+1)^{2^n}$ and $n = 2^{2|P|}$, there always exists a segment whose removal or pumping preserves h-bisimilarity.

Lemma 2. *Let $h \geq 1$ and M be a finite interpretation of the form $M = M_1 \ldots M_N$ such that $N \geq n^2(h+1)^{2^n}$, where $n = 2^{2|P|}$. Then,*

– *for some $j \in [1, N]$, M and $M' = M_1 \ldots M_{j-1} \cdot M_{j+1} \ldots M_N$ are h-bisimilar. Moreover, M' is non-total if M is non-total.*
– *for some $j \in [1, N]$, M and $M_1 \ldots M_j \cdot M_j \cdot M_{j+1} \ldots M_N$ are h-bisimilar.*

By Lemmas 1 and 2, we deduce the desired result.

Theorem 1. *For each $\varphi \in THT(F, G)$, $\mathcal{L}_{TEL}(\varphi)$ is N_φ-stutter closed.*

Proof. Let $\varphi \in THT(F, G)$ and h be the temporal height of φ. We assume that $h > 0$ (otherwise, the result is obvious). Recall that $N_\varphi = n^2(h+1)^{2^n}$, where $n = 2^{2|P|}$. Let T and T' be two LTL interpretations such that

$$T = u \cdot w^N \cdot v \text{ and } T' = u \cdot w^{N+1} \cdot v$$
$$(\text{resp., } T = x \cdot (u \cdot w^N \cdot y)^\omega \text{ and } T' = x \cdot (u \cdot w^{N+1} \cdot y)^\omega)$$

for some finite words x, u, y, w and infinite words v, where $N \geq N_\varphi$ and $n = 2^{2|P|}$. We show that $T \in \mathcal{L}_{TEL}(\varphi)$ iff $T' \in \mathcal{L}_{TEL}(\varphi)$. By Lemma 2, w^N and w^{N+1} are h-bisimilar. Thus, by Lemma 1, (T, T) is a THT model of φ iff (T', T') is a THT model of φ. We prove the following, hence, the result follows:

1. for all $H \sqsubset T$, there is $H' \sqsubset T'$ such that $(H, T) \models \varphi$ iff $(H', T') \models \varphi$.
2. for all $H' \sqsubset T'$, there is $H \sqsubset T$ such that $(H, T) \models \varphi$ iff $(H', T') \models \varphi$.

We focus on Condition 1 (the proof of Condition 2 being similar). Let $H \sqsubset T$ and $M = (H, T)$. Assume that $T = u \cdot w^N \cdot v$ (the other case, where $T = x \cdot (u \cdot w^N \cdot y)^\omega$, being similar). Then, M can be written in the form $M = M_1 N_1 \ldots N_N M_2$ such that $|M_1| = |u|$ and $|N_i| = |w|$ for all $i \in [1, N]$. By Lemma 2, there exists $j \in [1, N]$ such that $N_1 \ldots N_N$ is h-bisimilar to $N_1 \ldots N_j \cdot N_j N_{j+1} \ldots N_N$. Let $M' = M_1 N_1 \ldots N_j N_j N_{j+1} \ldots N_N M_2$. Since M is non-total, M' is non-total too, and by Lemma 1, $M \models \varphi$ iff $M' \models \varphi'$. Moreover, since $T' = u \cdot w^{N+1} \cdot v$, the non-total interpretation M' is of the form (H', T'), and we are done.   □

We now establish the main result for the fragment $THT(F, G)$.

Theorem 2. $(THT(F, G))_{TEL} < LTL$ and $(THT(F, G))_{TEL} > (THT(F, G))_{LTL}$.

Proof. One can easily show that the LTL-expressible ω-language consisting of the LTL interpretation $\emptyset \cdot \{a\} \cdot \emptyset^{\omega}$ cannot be expressed by any THT(F, G) formula under the TEL semantics. Thus, since TEL languages are ω-regular, by Proposition 3 and Theorem 1, we obtain that $(\mathsf{THT}(F, G))_{\mathsf{TEL}} < \mathsf{LTL}$. For the second part of the theorem, first, we observe that for a THT(F, G) formula φ, the set of LTL models of φ corresponds to the set of TEL models of the THT(F, G) formula $\varphi \wedge \psi_{Tot}(P)$. Hence, $(\mathsf{THT}(F, G))_{\mathsf{TEL}} \geq (\mathsf{THT}(F, G))_{\mathsf{LTL}}$. It remains to show that $(\mathsf{THT}(F, G))_{\mathsf{TEL}} \not\leq (\mathsf{THT}(F, G))_{\mathsf{LTL}}$. For this, let $P = \{b, u\}$ and (T_1, T_1) and (T_2, T_2) be two total interpretations defined as follows: $T_1 = \{u\}\{b, u\}^2\{u\}^{\omega}$ and $T_2 = \{u\}\{b, u\}\{u\}^{\omega}$. No THT$(F, G)$ formula can distinguish T_1 and T_2 under the LTL semantics. On the other hand, we show that there exists a THT$_1(F, G)$ formula φ such that (T_2, T_2) is a TEL model of φ, and (T_1, T_1) is not.

$$\text{Let } \varphi := G(\neg\neg u) \wedge Fb \wedge (Fu \rightarrow \psi_{Tot}(P)) \wedge F((b \rightarrow u) \wedge \neg\neg b)$$

Under the THT semantics, the first three conjuncts capture the interpretations (H, T) such that (i) for all $i \geq 0$, $u \in T(i)$, (ii) if $H \neq T$, then for all $i \geq 0$, $u \notin H(i)$, and (iii) there is $h \geq 0$ such that $b \in H(h)$. Additionally, the fourth conjunct is fulfilled whenever either $T = H$, or there is $k \geq 0$ such that $b \notin H(k)$ and $b \in T(k)$. It easily follows that the set of TEL models of φ is $\{u\}^* \cdot \{b, u\} \cdot \{u\}^{\omega}$, where there is exactly one occurrence of $\{b, u\}$, and the result follows. $\square$

The fragment THT(X,F). For the fragment THT(X, F), we crucially use the following known result [2], where for a total interpretation (T, T), a position $i \geq 0$ is *non-empty* in (T, T) if $T(i) \neq \emptyset$.

Lemma 3 ([2]). *Let φ be a THT(X, F) formula. Then, every equilibrium model of φ has at most $|\varphi|^2$ non-empty positions.*

Since there are THT(X, F) formulas whose LTL models contain infinite occurrences of non-empty positions (for example, the formula $\neg F \neg p$), by Lemma 3 we easily deduce the following result.

Theorem 3. *Given a THT(X, F) formula φ, one can build a THT(X, F) formula ψ such that $\mathcal{L}_{LTL}(\psi) = \mathcal{L}_{TEL}(\varphi)$. Moreover, $(THT(X, F))_{TEL} < (THT(X, F))_{LTL}$.*

The fragment THT$_1$. For the fragment THT$_1$, where there is no nesting of temporal modalities, we first establish the following result.

Theorem 4. *Given a THT$_1$ formula φ, one can construct a THT formula whose LTL models correspond to the TEL models of φ.*

Sketched Proof. For the fixed finite set P of atomic propositions, it is possible to define an equivalence relation of *finite* index on total interpretations such that the following holds: (1) each equivalence class C is finitely representable and no THT$_1$ formula over P can distinguish elements of C under the TEL semantics, (2) given an equivalence class C and a THT$_1$ formula φ over P, one can effectively check whether C is associated with TEL models of φ, and (3) each equivalence class C is effectively LTL-characterizable.   □

The construction in Theorem 4 cannot be done remaining in THT_1. Indeed, the following holds.

Theorem 5. $(THT_1)_{TEL} < LTL$ *and* $(THT_1)_{TEL} > (THT_1)_{LTL}$.

Proof. Let us consider the LTL-expressible ω-language consisting of the LTL interpretation $\emptyset^3 \cdot \{a\} \cdot \emptyset^\omega$. One can easily show that such a language cannot be expressed by any THT_1 formula under the TEL semantics. Thus, by Theorem 4, we obtain that $(\mathsf{THT}_1)_{\mathsf{TEL}} < \mathsf{LTL}$. For the second part of the theorem, first, we observe that for a THT_1 formula φ, the set of LTL models of φ corresponds to the set of TEL models of the THT_1 formula $\varphi \wedge \psi_{Tot}(P)$. Hence, $(\mathsf{THT}_1)_{\mathsf{TEL}} \geq (\mathsf{THT}_1)_{\mathsf{LTL}}$. It remains to show that there exists a THT_1 formula whose set of TEL models cannot be captured by any THT_1 formula under the LTL semantics. For this, let $P = \{b, u\}$, $\mathsf{T}_1 = \{u\}\{b, u\}^2\{u\}^\omega$, and $\mathsf{T}_2 = \{u\}\{b, u\}\{u\}^\omega$. Evidently, no THT_1 formula can distinguish T_1 and T_2 under the LTL semantics. On the other hand, by the proof of Theorem 2, there exists a $\mathsf{THT}_1(\mathsf{F}, \mathsf{G})$ formula φ such that $(\mathsf{T}_2, \mathsf{T}_2)$ is a TEL model of φ, and $(\mathsf{T}_1, \mathsf{T}_1)$ is not. Hence, the result follows.   □

5   TEL Fragments Non-subsumed by LTL

In this section, we derive an almost complete picture of the TEL fragments (w.r.t. the considered THT syntactical hierarchy) which are expressively incomparable with LTL. We also show that under the TEL semantics, the fragment $\mathsf{THT}(\mathsf{X}, \mathsf{R})$ and splittable THT are more expressive than LTL. We conclude the section by providing a characterization of ω-regular languages in terms of TEL languages.

We first individuate minimal THT fragments which under the TEL semantics are not subsumed by LTL.

Proposition 4. *Let $\mathcal{F}$ denote any of the following THT fragments: $THT_2(X, U)$, $THT_3(U)$, $THT_3(R)$, and splittable $THT_2(X, G)$. Then $(\mathcal{F})_{TEL} \not\leq LTL$.*

Proof. Here, we focus on splittable $\mathsf{THT}_2(\mathsf{X}, \mathsf{G})$ (for the other fragments, see the authors' full paper online). Let $\mathcal{L}_{odd}$ be the ω-regular language given by

$$\mathcal{L}_{odd} := \{\mathsf{T} \mid \mathsf{T} = \{a, b, u\}^{2n+1} \emptyset^\omega \text{ for some } n > 0\}$$

where a, b, and u are distinct atomic propositions. One can easily show that $\mathcal{L}_{odd}$ is not LTL expressible (see e.g. [11]). We exhibit a splittable $\mathsf{THT}_2(\mathsf{X}, \mathsf{G})$ formula φ_{odd} over $P = \{a, b, u\}$ whose set of TEL models corresponds to $\mathcal{L}_{odd}$.

Formula φ_{odd} is the conjunction of the following three splittable $\mathsf{THT}_2(\mathsf{X}, \mathsf{G})$ formulas, where $\psi_\emptyset := \neg a \wedge \neg b \wedge \neg u$ characterizes the empty positions of the "there" interpretation.

$$\neg\neg u \;\wedge\; \neg\neg\mathsf{G}(\psi_\emptyset \vee (a \wedge b \wedge u)) \;\wedge\; \neg\neg\mathsf{G}(\psi_\emptyset \to \mathsf{X}\psi_\emptyset) \tag{1}$$

$$\mathsf{G}(u \to a \wedge b) \ \wedge \ \mathsf{G}(\mathsf{X}u \to u) \ \wedge \ \mathsf{G}(u \to \mathsf{X}u \vee \mathsf{X}\neg u) \tag{2}$$

$$a \ \wedge \ \mathsf{G}(a \wedge b \to u) \ \wedge \ \mathsf{G}(a \to \mathsf{X}b) \ \wedge \ \mathsf{G}(b \to \mathsf{X}a \vee \mathsf{X}\neg u) \tag{3}$$

Formula (1), which is a conjunction of constraints in a splittable THT formula, captures the interpretations (H, T) such that $\mathsf{T} \in \{a, b, u\}^+ \emptyset^\omega$. Formula (2) additionally ensures that whenever $\mathsf{H} \neq \mathsf{T}$, then $u \notin \mathsf{H}(i)$ for all positions i. Finally, formula (3) requires that whenever $\mathsf{H} \neq \mathsf{T}$, the prefix of H corresponding to the *slice* of T (i.e., the maximal prefix of T which does not contain empty positions) is in $(\{a\}\{b\})^+$. This last condition can be satisfied iff the length of the slice of T is even. Hence, it easily follows that the TEL language of φ_{odd} is exactly $\mathcal{L}_{odd}$, and we are done. □

We now establish the main results of Sect. 5.

Theorem 6. *The following holds, where $k \geq 2$ and $\mathcal{O} \in \{U, R\}$:*

1. *$(THT(X, U))_{TEL} \perp LTL$ and $(THT_k(X, U))_{TEL} \perp LTL$;*
2. *$(THT(X, R))_{TEL} > LTL$ and $(THT_k(X, R))_{TEL} \perp LTL$;*
3. *$(THT(\mathcal{O}))_{TEL} \perp LTL$ and $(THT_{k+1}(\mathcal{O}))_{TEL} \perp LTL$;*
4. *$(THT_k(X, R))_{TEL} > (THT_k(X, R))_{LTL}$ and $(THT_{k-1})_{TEL} > (THT_{k-1})_{LTL}$;*
5. *(splittable THT)$_{TEL} > LTL$.*

Proof. In [2], it is shown that every TEL model of a $THT(X, U)$ has a finite set of non-empty positions. Since there are THT formulas whose LTL models have infinitely many non-empty positions, by Proposition 4, Properties 1 and 3 with $\mathcal{O} = U$ follow. One can trivially check that the LTL-expressible ω-language $\mathcal{L} = \emptyset\{a\}^\omega$ is not expressible in the fragment $THT(R)$ under the TEL semantics. Hence, by Proposition 4, Property 3 for the case $\mathcal{O} = R$ follows as well. For Properties 2 and 4, let $n \geq 1$ and $\mathcal{L}_n$ be the LTL-expressible ω-language consisting of the LTL interpretation $\emptyset^n \cdot \{a\} \cdot \emptyset^\omega$. One can easily check that no THT_h formula with $h < n$ can capture $\mathcal{L}_n$ under the TEL semantics. Since THT is expressively equivalent to $THT(X, R)$ under the LTL semantics and for all $h \geq 1$ and $\varphi \in THT_h(X, R)$, the set of LTL models of φ corresponds to the set of TEL models of the $THT_h(X, R)$ formula $\varphi \wedge \psi_{Tot}(P)$, by Theorem 5 and Proposition 4, Properties 2 and 4 follows. Finally, for Property 5, we exploit Proposition 4 and the fact that the set of LTL models of a THT formula φ corresponds to the set of TEL models of the splittable THT formula $\neg\neg\varphi \wedge \psi_{Tot}(P)$. □

We conclude this section by showing that TEL languages capture in a *weak sense* the full class of ω-regular languages. In fact, this weak equivalence, as formalized by the following Theorem 7, is similar to the well-known equivalence between ω-regular languages and ω-languages defined by formulas of Quantified propositional LTL (QLTL)[23], where for capturing a given ω-regular language over 2^P by a QLTL-formula, one needs to use quantification over additional propositions not in P. Intuitively, flat propositions in TEL play the role of bounded propositions in QLTL.

Theorem 7. *Let $\mathcal{L}$ be an ω-language over 2^P. Then, $\mathcal{L}$ is ω-regular iff there exists a finite set Q disjoint from P such that $\mathcal{L} \oplus Q$ is a TEL language.*

6   Conclusion

We have provided a systematic study of the expressiveness comparison between the LTL semantics and the TEL semantics for various natural THT syntactical fragments. Some interesting questions remain open: for example, we don't know whether the TEL semantics of the fragment THT(F, G, X) is able to capture full LTL. Additionally, it is well-known that the class of LTL-definable languages is algebraically robust, being, in particular, closed under all boolean operations. It is an intriguing open question whether the same holds for the class of TEL-definable languages.

References

1. Aguado, F., Pérez, G., Vidal, C.: Integrating temporal extensions of answer set programming. In: Cabalar, P., Son, T.C. (eds.) LPNMR 2013. LNCS (LNAI), vol. 8148, pp. 23–35. Springer, Heidelberg (2013). doi:10.1007/978-3-642-40564-8_3
2. Bozzelli, L., Pearce, D.: On the complexity of temporal equilibrium logic. In: Proceedings of 30th LICS, pp. 645–656. IEEE Computer Society (2015)
3. Brewka, G., Eiter, T., Truszczynski, M.: Answer set programming at a glance. Commun. ACM **54**(12), 92–103 (2011)
4. Cabalar, P., Demri, S.: Automata-based computation of temporal equilibrium models. In: Vidal, G. (ed.) LOPSTR 2011. LNCS, vol. 7225, pp. 57–72. Springer, Heidelberg (2012). doi:10.1007/978-3-642-32211-2_5
5. Cabalar, P., Diéguez, M.: STeLP– a tool for temporal answer set programming. In: Delgrande, J.P., Faber, W. (eds.) LPNMR 2011. LNCS (LNAI), vol. 6645, pp. 370–375. Springer, Heidelberg (2011). doi:10.1007/978-3-642-20895-9_43
6. Cabalar, P., Diéguez, M.: Strong equivalence of non-monotonic temporal theories. In: Proceedings of 14th KR. AAAI Press (2014)
7. Cabalar, P., Cerro, L.F., Pearce, D., Valverde, A.: A free logic for stable models with partial intensional functions. In: Fermé, E., Leite, J. (eds.) JELIA 2014. LNCS (LNAI), vol. 8761, pp. 340–354. Springer, Heidelberg (2014). doi:10.1007/978-3-319-11558-0_24
8. Cabalar, P., Pérez Vega, G.: Temporal equilibrium logic: a first approach. In: Moreno Díaz, R., Pichler, F., Quesada Arencibia, A. (eds.) EUROCAST 2007. LNCS, vol. 4739, pp. 241–248. Springer, Heidelberg (2007). doi:10.1007/978-3-540-75867-9_31
9. Calvanese, D., De Giacomo, G., Vardi, M.Y.: Reasoning about actions and planning in LTL action theories. In: Proceedings of 8th KR, pp. 593–602. Morgan Kaufmann (2002)
10. Bruijn, J., Pearce, D., Polleres, A., Valverde, A.: Quantified equilibrium logic and hybrid rules. In: Marchiori, M., Pan, J.Z., Marie, C.S. (eds.) RR 2007. LNCS, vol. 4524, pp. 58–72. Springer, Heidelberg (2007). doi:10.1007/978-3-540-72982-2_5
11. Etessami, K.: Stutter-invariant languages, ω-automata, and temporal logic. In: Halbwachs, N., Peled, D. (eds.) CAV 1999. LNCS, vol. 1633, pp. 236–248. Springer, Heidelberg (1999). doi:10.1007/3-540-48683-6_22
12. Fagin, R., Halpern, J., Vardi, M.: Reasoning About Knowledge, vol. 4. MIT Press, Cambridge (1995)

13. Ferraris, P.: Answer sets for propositional theories. In: Baral, C., Greco, G., Leone, N., Terracina, G. (eds.) LPNMR 2005. LNCS (LNAI), vol. 3662, pp. 119–131. Springer, Heidelberg (2005). doi:10.1007/11546207_10
14. Fink, M., Pearce, D.: A logical semantics for description logic programs. In: Janhunen, T., Niemelä, I. (eds.) JELIA 2010. LNCS (LNAI), vol. 6341, pp. 156–168. Springer, Heidelberg (2010). doi:10.1007/978-3-642-15675-5_15
15. Gelfond, M., Morales, A.: Encoding conformant planning in A-Prolog. In: Proceedings of DRT. LNCS. Springer (2004)
16. Giordano, L., Martelli, A., Dupré, D.T.: Reasoning about actions with temporal answer sets. TPLP **13**(2), 201–225 (2013)
17. Heyting, A.: Die formalen Regeln der intuitionistischen Logik. In: Three Parts, Sitzungsberichte der preussischen Akademie der Wissenschaften, pp. 311–327 (2011). English translation of Part I in Mancosu
18. Kucera, A., Strejcek, J.: The stuttering principle revisited. Acta Informatica **41**(7–8), 415–434 (2005)
19. Pearce, D.: A new logical characterisation of stable models and answer sets. In: Dix, J., Pereira, L.M., Przymusinski, T.C. (eds.) NMELP 1996. LNCS, vol. 1216, pp. 57–70. Springer, Heidelberg (1997). doi:10.1007/BFb0023801
20. Pearce, D.: Equilibrium logic. Ann. Math. Artif. Intell. **47**(1–2), 3–41 (2006)
21. Pearce, D., Valverde, A.: Towards a first order equilibrium logic for nonmonotonic reasoning. In: Alferes, J.J., Leite, J. (eds.) JELIA 2004. LNCS (LNAI), vol. 3229, pp. 147–160. Springer, Heidelberg (2004). doi:10.1007/978-3-540-30227-8_15
22. Pnueli, A.: The temporal logic of programs. In: Proceedings of 18th FOCS, pp. 46–57. IEEE Computer Society (1977)
23. Sistla, A., Vardi, M., Wolper, P.: The complementation problem for Büchi automata with appplications to temporal logic. Theor. Comput. Sci. **49**, 217–237 (1987)
24. Wu, Z.: On the expressive power of QLTL. In: Jones, C.B., Liu, Z., Woodcock, J. (eds.) ICTAC 2007. LNCS, vol. 4711, pp. 467–481. Springer, Heidelberg (2007). doi:10.1007/978-3-540-75292-9_32

Introducing Role Defeasibility
in Description Logics

Katarina Britz[1] and Ivan Varzinczak[2(✉)]

[1] CSIR-SU CAIR, Stellenbosch University, Stellenbosch, South Africa
abritz@sun.ac.za
[2] CRIL, Univ. Artois & CNRS, 62300 Lens, France
varzinczak@cril.fr

Abstract. Accounts of preferential reasoning in Description Logics often take as point of departure the semantic notion of a preference order on objects in a domain of interpretation, which allows for the development of notions of defeasible subsumption and entailment. However, such an approach does not account for defeasible roles, interpreted as partially ordered sets of tuples. We state the case for role defeasibility and introduce a corresponding preferential semantics for a number of defeasible constructs on roles. We show that this does not negatively affect decidability or complexity of reasoning for an important class of DLs, and that existing notions of preferential reasoning can be expressed in terms of defeasible roles.

Keywords: Description Logics · Defeasible reasoning · Preferential semantics

1 Introduction

Description Logics (DLs) [2] are a family of logic-based knowledge representation formalisms with appealing computational properties and a variety of applications at the confluence of modern artificial intelligence and other areas. In this regard, endowing DLs and their associated reasoning services with the ability to cope with defeasibility is a natural step in their development. Indeed, the past two decades have witnessed the surge of many attempts to introduce non-monotonic reasoning capabilities in a DL setting. These range from preferential approaches [14,15,20,22,25,27,39,40] to circumscription-based ones [6,7,41], amongst others [3,4,23,29–31,37,38,43].

Given the special status of subsumption in DLs in particular and the historical importance of entailment in logic in general, the bulk of the effort in this direction has quite naturally been put in the definition of a proper account of defeasible subsumption and in the characterisation of appropriate notions of defeasible entailment relations. Semantically, in the latter, orderings on the class of first-order interpretations are usually considered [7,12,27,28,39], whereas in the former, a typicality ordering on the objects of the domain of interpretation is put forward [14,15,25,26].

© Springer International Publishing AG 2016
L. Michael and A. Kakas (Eds.): JELIA 2016, LNAI 10021, pp. 174–189, 2016.
DOI: 10.1007/978-3-319-48758-8_12

Here we investigate a complementary notion, namely that of relativised role defeasibility. Our motivation stems essentially from the observation that a given relationship holding between some objects may be deemed more normal than between others, and that this may be the case irrespective of whether the relevant objects are typical in one way or another. As an example, consider the role name guardianOf: 'Normal' tuples in its extension (the relation it is interpreted as) may be guardian-ward tuples where the ward is a minor and the guardian a parent or natural guardian, while an 'exceptional' tuple may be a guardian-ward tuple where the ward is an adult with an appointed legal guardian. In this example, there is nothing exceptional about either the legal guardian or the ward — the exceptionality rather lies in the nature of their relationship. The role name therefore provides a primitive context relative to which exceptionality is determined, while exceptionality is evaluated semantically by comparing tuples in the role extension.

As a semantic means to capture the nuances of normality at the level of roles as motivated above, in this work we propose placing a parameterised preference order on binary relations over the domain. Armed with the semantic constructions we shall define and study here, we will see that it becomes possible to:

- Define *plausible value restrictions* [13] of the form $\forall r.C$, as in $\forall$guardianOf.Minor, which intuitively refers to those individuals whose normal guardianship relations are of minors, whilst being, for instance, the legal guardian of a developmentally disabled adult;
- Define *plausible (qualified) number restrictions* of the form $\gtrsim nr.C$ or $\lesssim nr.C$ (or $\approx nr.C$), as in $\lesssim$ 2hasSibling.Female, referring to the individuals in at most two normal sibling relationships with sisters (but who can still have a stepsister), or even $\approx$ 1marriedTo.$\top$, which describes the individuals in one normal marriage (but who can nevertheless be in a type of wedlock with someone else);
- State *plausible role inclusions* of the form $r_1 \mathbin{\underset{\sim}{\sqsubseteq}} r_2$, as in parentOf $\mathbin{\underset{\sim}{\sqsubseteq}}$ progenitorOf, stipulating that the role of being a parent is usually (but not necessarily) that of also being the progenitor;
- State *role-typicality axioms* of the form $\star r_1 \sqsubseteq \star r_2$ and $\star r(a,b)$, where $\star$ is an extension of typicality operators [9,10,25,27] that we shall define for role names (and, more generally, for compound roles). For example, $\star$progenitorOf $\sqsubseteq \star$hasChild says that typical procreation implies typical parenthood, while the assertion $\star$hasChild(john, anne) conveys the information that the tuple (john, anne) is to be regarded as a typical one in the interpretation of role hasChild;
- State *plausible role disjointness* of the form $\star r_1 \sqcap \star r_2 \sqsubseteq \bot$, as for instance in $\star$hasSibling $\sqcap \star$marriedTo $\sqsubseteq \bot$, the meaning of which speaks for itself;
- State *plausible role characteristics*, for instance saying that role marriedTo is *normally functional* and that partOf is *usually transitive*, while still allowing for exceptions, i.e., for exceptional tuples to fail the relation's property under consideration, thereby not ruling out, in the former example, the existence of polygamous mariages.

Moreover, we shall see that, with our enriched semantics, it also becomes possible to provide an alternative account of *plausible concept subsumptions* [14, 15, 22, 26] of the form $C \mathrel{\underset{\sim}{\sqsubseteq}} D$, as for instance in Mother $\mathrel{\underset{\sim}{\sqsubseteq}} \exists$hasPartner.$\top$, of which the intuition is that, usually, mothers have a partner.

By putting all of that into place, we hope to open up an avenue for further explorations of defeasibility in Description Logics, in particular in extensions of the preferential approach therein.

In the remainder of the present paper, we take the following route: after presenting the required background on DLs (Sect. 2), we introduce the semantic construction the core of the paper builds upon (Sect. 3). We then move on by studying new defeasible constructs capturing several aspects of role defeasibility (Sect. 4). In Sect. 5, we show that the important notion of plausible concept subsumption can be embedded within our framework. We then conclude with some remarks on related work and possible strands for future investigation.

2   The Description Logic $\mathcal{ALC}$

The (concept) language of $\mathcal{ALC}$ is built upon a finite set of atomic *concept names* $\mathsf{N}_{\mathscr{C}}$, a finite set of *role names* $\mathsf{N}_{\mathscr{R}}$ and a finite set of *individual names* $\mathsf{N}_{\mathscr{I}}$ such that $\mathsf{N}_{\mathscr{C}}$, $\mathsf{N}_{\mathscr{R}}$ and $\mathsf{N}_{\mathscr{I}}$ are pairwise disjoint. With $A, B, \ldots$ we denote atomic concepts, with $r, s, \ldots$ role names, and with $a, b, \ldots$ individual names. Complex concepts are denoted with $C, D, \ldots$ and are built according to the rule:

$$C ::= \top \mid \bot \mid A \mid \neg C \mid C \sqcap C \mid C \sqcup C \mid \forall r.C \mid \exists r.C$$

With $\mathcal{L}_{\mathcal{ALC}}$ we denote the *language* of all $\mathcal{ALC}$ concepts.

The semantics of $\mathcal{L}_{\mathcal{ALC}}$ is the standard set theoretic Tarskian semantics. An *interpretation* is a structure $\mathcal{I} := \langle \Delta^{\mathcal{I}}, \cdot^{\mathcal{I}} \rangle$, where $\Delta^{\mathcal{I}}$ is a non-empty set called the *domain*, and $\cdot^{\mathcal{I}}$ is an *interpretation function* mapping concept names A to subsets $A^{\mathcal{I}}$ of $\Delta^{\mathcal{I}}$, role names r to binary relations $r^{\mathcal{I}}$ over $\Delta^{\mathcal{I}}$, and individual names a to elements of the domain $\Delta^{\mathcal{I}}$, i.e., $A^{\mathcal{I}} \subseteq \Delta^{\mathcal{I}}$, $r^{\mathcal{I}} \subseteq \Delta^{\mathcal{I}} \times \Delta^{\mathcal{I}}$, $a^{\mathcal{I}} \in \Delta^{\mathcal{I}}$.

As an example, let $\mathsf{N}_{\mathscr{C}} := \{A_1, A_2, A_3\}$, $\mathsf{N}_{\mathscr{R}} := \{r_1, r_2\}$ and $\mathsf{N}_{\mathscr{I}} := \{a_1, a_2, a_3\}$. Figure 1 depicts the DL interpretation $\mathcal{I}_1 = \langle \Delta^{\mathcal{I}_1}, \cdot^{\mathcal{I}_1} \rangle$, where $\Delta^{\mathcal{I}_1} = \{x_i \mid 1 \leq i \leq 9\}$, $A_1^{\mathcal{I}_1} = \{x_1, x_4, x_6\}$, $A_2^{\mathcal{I}_1} = \{x_3, x_5, x_9\}$, $A_3^{\mathcal{I}_1} = \{x_6, x_7, x_8\}$, $r_1^{\mathcal{I}_1} = \{(x_1, x_6), (x_4, x_8), (x_2, x_5)\}$, $r_2^{\mathcal{I}_1} = \{(x_4, x_4), (x_6, x_4), (x_5, x_8), (x_9, x_3)\}$, $a_1^{\mathcal{I}_1} = x_5$, $a_2^{\mathcal{I}_1} = x_1$, $a_3^{\mathcal{I}_1} = x_2$.

Given an interpretation $\mathcal{I} = \langle \Delta^{\mathcal{I}}, \cdot^{\mathcal{I}} \rangle$, $\cdot^{\mathcal{I}}$ is extended to interpret complex concepts of $\mathcal{L}_{\mathcal{ALC}}$ in the following way:

$$\top^{\mathcal{I}} := \Delta^{\mathcal{I}}, \quad \bot^{\mathcal{I}} := \emptyset, \quad (\neg C)^{\mathcal{I}} := \Delta^{\mathcal{I}} \setminus C^{\mathcal{I}}$$

$$(C \sqcap D)^{\mathcal{I}} := C^{\mathcal{I}} \cap D^{\mathcal{I}}, \quad (C \sqcup D)^{\mathcal{I}} := C^{\mathcal{I}} \cup D^{\mathcal{I}}$$

$$(\exists r.C)^{\mathcal{I}} := \{x \in \Delta^{\mathcal{I}} \mid r^{\mathcal{I}}(x) \cap C^{\mathcal{I}} \neq \emptyset\}, \quad (\forall r.C)^{\mathcal{I}} := \{x \in \Delta^{\mathcal{I}} \mid r^{\mathcal{I}}(x) \subseteq C^{\mathcal{I}}\}$$

As an example, in the interpretation $\mathcal{I}_1$, we have $(A_1 \sqcup A_3)^{\mathcal{I}_1} = \{x_1, x_4, x_6, x_7, x_8\}$, $(A_1 \sqcap A_3)^{\mathcal{I}} = \{x_6, x_7\}$, $(\exists r_1.A_3)^{\mathcal{I}_1} = \{x_1, x_4\}$ and $(\forall r_2.A_2)^{\mathcal{I}} = \{x_9\}$.

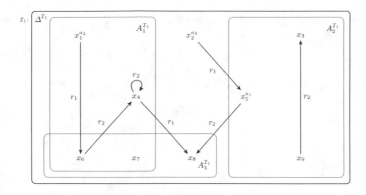

Fig. 1. An interpretation for $N_{\mathscr{C}} = \{A_1, A_2, A_3\}$, $N_{\mathscr{R}} = \{r_1, r_2\}$ and $N_{\mathscr{I}} = \{a_1, a_2, a_3\}$.

Given $C, D \in \mathcal{L}_{\mathcal{ALC}}$, $C \sqsubseteq D$ is a *subsumption statement*, read "C is subsumed by D" (or, alternatively, "D is more general than C" or "C is more specific than D"). $C \equiv D$ is an abbreviation for both $C \sqsubseteq D$ and $D \sqsubseteq C$. An $\mathcal{ALC}$ *TBox* $\mathcal{T}$ is a finite set of subsumption statements and formalises the *intensional* knowledge about a given domain of application. Given $C \in \mathcal{L}_{\mathcal{ALC}}$, $r \in N_{\mathscr{R}}$ and $a, b \in N_{\mathscr{I}}$, an *assertional statement* (*assertion*, for short) is an expression of the form $C(a)$ or $r(a, b)$. An $\mathcal{ALC}$ *ABox* $\mathcal{A}$ is a finite set of assertional statements formalising the *extensional* knowledge of the domain. We shall denote statements, both subsumption and assertional, with $\alpha, \beta, \ldots$. Given $\mathcal{T}$ and $\mathcal{A}$, with $\mathcal{K} := \mathcal{T} \cup \mathcal{A}$ we denote an $\mathcal{ALC}$ *knowledge base*.

An interpretation $\mathcal{I}$ *satisfies* a subsumption statement $C \sqsubseteq D$ (denoted $\mathcal{I} \Vdash C \sqsubseteq D$) if and only if $C^{\mathcal{I}} \subseteq D^{\mathcal{I}}$. (And then $\mathcal{I} \Vdash C \equiv D$ if and only if $C^{\mathcal{I}} = D^{\mathcal{I}}$.) In the example of Fig. 1, we have $\mathcal{I}_1 \Vdash \exists r_1.A_3 \sqsubseteq A_1$ and $\mathcal{I}_1 \not\Vdash A_1 \sqcap A_3 \sqsubseteq \forall r_2.A_2$. An interpretation $\mathcal{I}$ *satisfies* an assertion $C(a)$ (respectively, $r(a, b)$), denoted $\mathcal{I} \Vdash C(a)$ (respectively, $\mathcal{I} \Vdash r(a, b)$), if and only if $a^{\mathcal{I}} \in C^{\mathcal{I}}$ (respectively, $(a^{\mathcal{I}}, b^{\mathcal{I}}) \in r^{\mathcal{I}}$). In the above example, we have both $\mathcal{I}_1 \Vdash A_1 \sqcap \neg A_3(a_2)$ and $\mathcal{I}_1 \Vdash r_1(a_3, a_1)$, but $\mathcal{I}_1 \not\Vdash \forall r_1.A_2(a_2)$.

We say that an interpretation $\mathcal{I}$ is a *model* of a TBox $\mathcal{T}$ (denoted $\mathcal{I} \Vdash \mathcal{T}$) if and only if $\mathcal{I} \Vdash \alpha$ for every $\alpha \in \mathcal{T}$. Analogously, $\mathcal{I}$ is a model of an ABox $\mathcal{A}$ (denoted $\mathcal{I} \Vdash \mathcal{A}$) if and only if $\mathcal{I} \Vdash \alpha$ for every $\alpha \in \mathcal{A}$. We say that $\mathcal{I}$ is a model of a knowledge base $\mathcal{K} = \mathcal{T} \cup \mathcal{A}$ if and only if $\mathcal{I} \Vdash \mathcal{T}$ and $\mathcal{I} \Vdash \mathcal{A}$. A statement α is (classically) *entailed* by a knowledge base $\mathcal{K}$, denoted $\mathcal{K} \models \alpha$, if and only if every model of $\mathcal{K}$ satisfies α. If $\mathcal{K} = \emptyset$, then we have that $\mathcal{I} \Vdash \alpha$ for all interpretations $\mathcal{I}$, in which case we say α is a *validity* and denote with $\models \alpha$.

For more details on Description Logics in general and on $\mathcal{ALC}$ in particular, the reader is invited to consult the Description Logic handbook [2].

3   r-Ordered Interpretations

We now formalise the intuitive notions we briefly presented in the Introduction. Given a DL interpretation $\mathcal{I}$, we enrich it with a collection of preference relations, one for (the interpretation of) each role name in $\mathsf{N}_{\mathscr{R}}$.

Definition 1 (r-Ordered Interpretation). *An r-ordered interpretation is a tuple* $\mathcal{R} := \langle \Delta^{\mathcal{R}}, \cdot^{\mathcal{R}}, \prec^{\mathcal{R}} \rangle$ *in which* $\langle \Delta^{\mathcal{R}}, \cdot^{\mathcal{R}} \rangle$ *is a (classical) DL interpretation (see Sect. 2), and* $\prec^{\mathcal{R}} := \langle \prec_1^{\mathcal{R}}, \ldots, \prec_n^{\mathcal{R}} \rangle$, *where each* $\prec_i^{\mathcal{R}} \subseteq r_i^{\mathcal{R}} \times r_i^{\mathcal{R}}$, *for* $1 \leq i \leq n$, *is a well-founded strict partial order on* $r_i^{\mathcal{R}}$, *i.e., each* $\prec_i^{\mathcal{R}}$ *is irreflexive, transitive and every non-empty* $R \subseteq r_i^{\mathcal{R}}$ *has minimal elements w.r.t.* $\prec_i^{\mathcal{R}}$ *(see Definition 2 below).*

As an example, let $\mathsf{N}_{\mathscr{C}} := \{A_1, A_2, A_3\}$, $\mathsf{N}_{\mathscr{R}} := \{r_1, r_2\}$, $\mathsf{N}_{\mathscr{I}} := \{a_1, a_2, a_3\}$, and let the r-ordered interpretation $\mathcal{R}_1 = \langle \Delta^{\mathcal{R}_1}, \cdot^{\mathcal{R}_1}, \prec^{\mathcal{R}_1} \rangle$, where $\Delta^{\mathcal{R}_1} = \Delta^{\mathcal{I}_1}$, $\cdot^{\mathcal{R}_1} = \cdot^{\mathcal{I}_1}$, and $\prec^{\mathcal{R}_1} = \langle \prec_1^{\mathcal{R}_1}, \prec_2^{\mathcal{R}_1} \rangle$, where $\prec_1^{\mathcal{R}_1} = \{(x_4 x_8, x_2 x_5), (x_2 x_5, x_1 x_6),$ $(x_4 x_8, x_1 x_6)\}$ and $\prec_2^{\mathcal{R}_1} = \{(x_6 x_4, x_4 x_4), (x_5 x_8, x_9 x_3)\}$. (For the sake of readability, we shall henceforth sometimes write tuples of the form (x, y) as xy.) Figure 2 below depicts the r-ordered interpretation $\mathcal{R}_1$. In the picture, $\prec_1^{\mathcal{R}_1}$ and $\prec_2^{\mathcal{R}_1}$ are represented, respectively, by the dashed and the dotted arrows. (Note the direction of the $\prec^{\mathcal{R}}$-arrows, which point from more preferred to less preferred pairs of objects.) Also for the sake of readability, we shall omit the transitive $\prec^{\mathcal{R}}$-arrows.

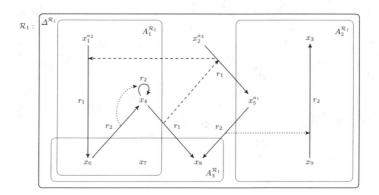

Fig. 2. An r-ordered interpretation for $\mathsf{N}_{\mathscr{C}}$, $\mathsf{N}_{\mathscr{R}}$ and $\mathsf{N}_{\mathscr{I}}$ as in Fig. 1.

Given $\mathcal{R} = \langle \Delta^{\mathcal{R}}, \cdot^{\mathcal{R}}, \prec^{\mathcal{R}} \rangle$, the intuition of $\Delta^{\mathcal{R}}$ and $\cdot^{\mathcal{R}}$ is the same as in a standard DL interpretation. The intuition underlying each of the orderings in $\prec^{\mathcal{R}}$ is that they play the role of *preference relations* (or *normality orderings*), in a sense similar to that introduced by Shoham [42] with a preference on worlds in a propositional setting and as extensively investigated by Kraus et al. [32,33] and others [11,14,25]: the pairs (x, y) that are lower down in the ordering $\prec_i^{\mathcal{R}}$ are deemed as the most normal (or typical, or expected) in the context of (the interpretation of) r_i. Technically, the difference between our definitions and those in the aforementioned work lies on the fact that our $\prec_i^{\mathcal{R}}$ are orderings on binary relations on the domain $\Delta^{\mathcal{R}}$, instead of orderings on propositional valuations or on plain objects of $\Delta^{\mathcal{R}}$.

It is worth spelling out that we do not require that pairs of objects intrinsically possess certain features that render some of them more normal than others. Rather, the intention is to provide a framework in which to express all conceivable ways in which such pairs can be ordered, in the same way that the class of all classical DL interpretations constitute a framework representing all conceivable (logically allowed) ways of representing the properties of objects and their relationships with other objects. It is up to the knowledge base at hand to impose constraints on the allowed orderings on pairs of objects in r-ordered DL interpretations in the same way as it imposes constraints on the allowed extensions of classes and roles in standard DL interpretations. (This point will become more clear from Sect. 4 onwards.)

Definition 2 (Minimality w.r.t. $\prec_i^{\mathcal{R}}$). *Let $\mathcal{R} = \langle \Delta^{\mathcal{R}}, \cdot^{\mathcal{R}}, \prec^{\mathcal{R}} \rangle$ be an r-ordered interpretation and let $R \subseteq r_i^{\mathcal{R}}$, for some $1 \leq i \leq n$. Then $\min_{\prec_i^{\mathcal{R}}} R := \{(x, y) \in R \mid$ there is no $(x', y') \in R$ such that $(x', y') \prec_i^{\mathcal{R}} (x, y)\}$, i.e., $\min_{\prec_i^{\mathcal{R}}} R$ denotes the minimal elements of R w.r.t. the preference relation $\prec_i^{\mathcal{R}}$ associated to $r_i^{\mathcal{R}}$.*

Since we assume each $\prec_i^{\mathcal{R}}$ to be a well-founded strict partial order on the respective $r_i^{\mathcal{R}}$, we are guaranteed that for every $R \subseteq r_i^{\mathcal{R}}$ such that $R \neq \emptyset$, $\min_{\prec_i^{\mathcal{R}}} R$ is well defined. (The reader familiar with the KLM approach [32] will immediately see that this implies a version of the *smoothness condition* for pairs of objects.) As an example, in Fig. 2, $\min_{\prec_1^{\mathcal{R}_1}} r_1^{\mathcal{R}_1} = \{x_4 x_8\}$.

An r-ordered interpretation $\mathcal{R}$ satisfies a (classical) subsumption statement $C \sqsubseteq D$ (denoted $\mathcal{R} \Vdash C \sqsubseteq D$) if and only if $C^{\mathcal{R}} \subseteq D^{\mathcal{R}}$. It satisfies an assertion $C(a)$ (respectively, $r(a, b)$), denoted $\mathcal{R} \Vdash C(a)$ (respectively, $\mathcal{R} \Vdash r(a, b)$), if and only if $a^{\mathcal{R}} \in C^{\mathcal{R}}$ (respectively, $(a^{\mathcal{R}}, b^{\mathcal{R}}) \in r^{\mathcal{R}}$). It is easy to see that the addition of the $\prec^{\mathcal{R}}$-component preserves the truth of all classical statements holding in the remaining structure. That is, if $\mathcal{R} = \langle \Delta^{\mathcal{R}}, \cdot^{\mathcal{R}}, \prec^{\mathcal{R}} \rangle$, then for every α, $\mathcal{R} \Vdash \alpha$ if and only if $\langle \Delta^{\mathcal{R}}, \cdot^{\mathcal{R}} \rangle \Vdash \alpha$. The role of the $\prec^{\mathcal{R}}$-components will become patent in the next section.

4 Role-Plausibility Constructs

In this section, we present the defeasible role constructs promised in the Introduction. Before doing so, we recall some distinguishing properties of general operators for defeasible reasoning, against which we shall check each of the operators to be introduced in the sequel: Given $n + 1$ partially ordered sets of objects $\langle S_i, \leq_i \rangle$, $0 \leq i \leq n$, an n-ary function $f : \Pi_{i=0}^{n-1} S_i \to S_n$ is:

- *monotone (increasing)* on S_n if the following holds:
  If $x_i \leq y_i$ for $0 \leq i < n$, then $f(x_0, \ldots, x_{n-1}) \leq f(y_0, \ldots, y_{n-1})$;
- *ampliative* with respect to an n-ary function $h : \Pi_{i=0}^{n-1} S_i \to S_n$ if:
  $h(x_1, \ldots, x_n) \leq f(x_1, \ldots, x_n)$, for all $x_i \in S_i, 0 \leq i < n$;

- *strictly ampliative* with respect to h if it is ampliative w.r.t. h, and also:
$h(x_1, \ldots, x_n) < f(x_1, \ldots, x_n)$, for some $x_i \in S_i, 0 \leq i < n$.

A function is *non-monotonic* if it is not monotone, i.e., if it fails monotonicity in at least one argument. We then observe that the concept constructor $\exists$ induces a monotone increasing function $f_\exists : \mathscr{P}(\Delta^\mathcal{I} \times \Delta^\mathcal{I}) \times \mathscr{P}(\Delta^\mathcal{I}) \longrightarrow \mathscr{P}(\Delta^\mathcal{I})$, with sets ordered by set inclusion, such that $f_\exists : \langle r^\mathcal{I}, C^\mathcal{I} \rangle \mapsto (\exists r.C)^\mathcal{I}$. Likewise, $\forall$ induces a non-monotonic function $f_\forall : \langle r^\mathcal{I}, C^\mathcal{I} \rangle \mapsto (\forall r.C)^\mathcal{I}$, which is monotone in its second argument, but not in the first. We note that strict ampliativity is a necessary condition for a concept constructor to be deemed defeasible.

In the remainder of the present section, we shall use $r_i^{\mathcal{R}|x}$ as an abbreviation for $r_i^\mathcal{R} \cap (\{x\} \times \Delta^\mathcal{R})$, i.e., the restriction of the domain of $r_i^\mathcal{R}$ to $\{x\}$.

4.1   Plausible Value Restriction

Classical value restrictions of the form $\forall r.C$ constrain objects (in its interpretation) to those that are related by r only to objects in C. This requirement can be (and, in practice, often is) too strong. For instance, consider the concept $\forall \mathsf{guardianOf.Minor}$, which we have encountered in the Introduction. An individual who has several children, but is also the legal guardian of a developmentally disabled adult would not belong to this class, even though we may want to include such an individual when referring to parents whose 'normal' guardianship role is with minors. In order to single out this case, while still being able to draw conclusions on what is typically the case about guardianship, we here make a case for *plausible* value restrictions of the form $\forall\!\!\!/\, r.C$. Intuitively, $\forall\!\!\!/\,\mathsf{guardianOf.Minor}$ should cater for the example we have just seen.

Let $\mathcal{ALC}^{\forall\!\!\!/}$ denote $\mathcal{ALC}$ extended with plausible value restrictions. We can give $\forall\!\!\!/$ a natural semantics in terms of our r-ordered interpretations as follows:

$$(\forall\!\!\!/\, r_i.C)^\mathcal{R} := \{ x \in \Delta^\mathcal{R} \mid \text{ for all } y \in \Delta^\mathcal{R}, \text{ if } (x,y) \in \min_{\prec_{r_i}^\mathcal{R}} (r_i^{\mathcal{R}|x}), \text{ then } y \in C^\mathcal{R} \}$$

Then, $\forall\!\!\!/$ induces a ternary function $f_{\forall\!\!\!/}$, with the strict partial order on the participating role as third argument, that is $f_{\forall\!\!\!/} : \langle r_i^\mathcal{R}, C^\mathcal{R}, \prec_{r_i}^\mathcal{R} \rangle \mapsto (\forall\!\!\!/\, r_i.C)^\mathcal{R}$.

Proposition 1. *The function $f_{\forall\!\!\!/}$ is non-monotonic in its first argument, monotone in its second and third arguments and is strictly ampliative w.r.t. $f_{\forall\!\!\!/}$.*

Another useful application of plausible value restrictions is in the specification of the *normal range* of a role, as in $\top \sqsubseteq \forall\!\!\!/\, r.C$ ('the range of r is normally C'). If we allow for role inverses, we can also specify the *normal domain* of a role with $\top \sqsubseteq \forall\!\!\!/\, r^-.C$ ('the domain of r is normally C').

Theorem 1. $\mathcal{ALC}^{\forall\!\!\!\!\!\vee}$ *has the finite-model property and is therefore decidable.*

The proof of Theorem 1 is via the standard technique of filtration redefined for r-ordered interpretations and making sure the resulting preference relations in the filtered model are each a strict partial order on the respective role interpretation.

Theorem 2. *In* $\mathcal{ALC}^{\forall\!\!\!\!\!\vee}$, *concept satisfiability and subsumption w.r.t. acyclic TBoxes are* PSPACE-*complete problems. Concept satisfiability and subsumption w.r.t. general TBoxes are* EXPTIME-*complete problems.*

The lower bound follows from the lower-bound result for $\mathcal{ALC}$ alone. The proof of the upper bound is along the lines of that for classical $\mathcal{ALC}$ via automata but with an extra data structure to account for the preference relations. It can be shown that the look-up at the preference relations changes neither the time complexity (the number of nodes in the search tree remains single exponential) nor the size of each branch in the depth-first search that is carried out.

4.2   Plausible Number Restriction

Next we consider qualified number restrictions, which, in the classical case, take the form $\geq nr.C$, $\leq nr.C$ or $= nr.C$, where n is a positive integer, and which allow us to specify cardinality constraints on roles with role fillers falling under a certain concept. The classical semantics of these constructs is given by:

$$(\geq nr_i.C)^{\mathcal{I}} := \{x \in \Delta^{\mathcal{I}} \mid \#\{y \in \Delta^{\mathcal{I}} \mid (x,y) \in r_i^{\mathcal{I}} \text{ and } y \in C^{\mathcal{I}}\} \geq n\}$$

$$(\leq nr_i.C)^{\mathcal{I}} := \{x \in \Delta^{\mathcal{I}} \mid \#\{y \in \Delta^{\mathcal{I}} \mid (x,y) \in r_i^{\mathcal{I}} \text{ and } y \in C^{\mathcal{I}}\} \leq n\}$$

and $= nr.C$ is seen as an abbreviation for $(\geq nr.C) \sqcap (\leq nr.C)$. The extension of $\mathcal{ALC}$ with qualified number restrictions is called $\mathcal{ALCQ}$.

It turns out such constructs, too, can be too rigid, as the following example illustrates. The concept $\leq$ 2hasSibling.Female denotes the class of people with at most two sisters and, of course, does not admit the case of individuals whose father becomes the legal guardian of a girl, thereby finding themselves with a new, unexpected sibling. In this case, we would like to be able to say that such individuals are in at most two normal sibling relationships.

To cope with cases such as this, we here introduce plausible versions of qualified number restrictions of the form $\gtrsim nr.C$, $\lesssim nr.C$ (and $\approx nr.C$). Let $\mathcal{ALCQ}^{\gtrsim}$ denote $\mathcal{ALCQ}$ extended with plausible number restrictions. These new concept constructors can be given a semantics in terms of our r-ordered interpretations in the following way:

$$(\gtrsim nr_i.C)^{\mathcal{R}} := \{x \in \Delta^{\mathcal{R}} \mid \#\{y \in \Delta^{\mathcal{R}} \mid (x,y) \in \min_{\prec_i^{\mathcal{R}}}(r_i^{\mathcal{R}|x}) \text{ and } y \in C^{\mathcal{R}}\} \geq n\}$$

$$(\lesssim nr_i.C)^{\mathcal{R}} := \{x \in \Delta^{\mathcal{R}} \mid \#\{y \in \Delta^{\mathcal{R}} \mid (x,y) \in \min_{\prec_i^{\mathcal{R}}}(r_i^{\mathcal{R}|x}) \text{ and } y \in C^{\mathcal{R}}\} \leq n\}$$

Hence, $\approx nr.C$ is just an abbreviation for $(\gtrsim nr.C) \sqcap (\lesssim nr.C)$.

With these new constructs, one can revisit the example above and define the concept $\lesssim$ 2hasSibling.Female, which is coherent in the given scenario.

Just as with $\forall$, $\gtrsim n$ and $\lesssim n$ induce ternary functions $f_{\gtrsim n} : \langle r_i^{\mathcal{R}}, C^{\mathcal{R}}, \prec_{r_i}^{\mathcal{R}} \rangle \mapsto$ $(\gtrsim nr_i.C)^{\mathcal{R}}$ and $f_{\lesssim n} : \langle r_i^{\mathcal{R}}, C^{\mathcal{R}}, \prec_{r_i}^{\mathcal{R}} \rangle \mapsto (\lesssim nr_i.C)^{\mathcal{R}}$. We then have:

Proposition 2. $f_{\gtrsim n}$ *is monotone in its first two arguments (the participating role and concept extensions) and non-monotonic in its third argument (the participating preference order).* $f_{\lesssim n}$ *is non-monotonic in its first two arguments and monotone in its third argument.*

Theorem 3. $\mathcal{ALCQ}^{\tilde{\gtrsim}}$ *has the finite-model property and is therefore decidable.*

Theorem 4. *In* $\mathcal{ALCQ}^{\tilde{\gtrsim}}$, *concept satisfiability and subsumption w.r.t. acyclic TBoxes are* PSPACE-*complete problems. Concept satisfiability and subsumption w.r.t. general TBoxes are* EXPTIME-*complete problems.*

4.3 Plausible Role Inclusion and Role Characteristics

Some expressive DLs [19] allow for the specification of (atomic) role inclusions of the form $r_i \sqsubseteq r_j$, whose semantics is given by $\mathcal{I} \Vdash r_i \sqsubseteq r_j$ if and only if $r_i^{\mathcal{I}} \subseteq r_j^{\mathcal{I}}$, capturing the intuition according to which an r_i-relationship is a special case of an r_j-one. $\mathcal{ALCHQ}$ denotes the extension of $\mathcal{ALCQ}$ with role hierarchies.

That this characterisation of role subsumption does not suffice for reasoning under uncertainty is already clear from the vast literature on non-monotonic reasoning. As a concrete example in a DL setting, consider the role inclusions guardianOf $\sqsubseteq$ parentOf and parentOf $\sqsubseteq$ progenitorOf. In the absence of a construct to account for exceptions to these inclusions, it follows that guardianOf $\sqsubseteq$ progenitorOf, a clearly undesirable consequence.

In order to cope with such cases, we here introduce plausible role inclusions of the form $r_i \mathrel{\tilde{\sqsubseteq}} r_j$, inspired by the meaning of defeasible consequence in propositional logic [32] and by defeasible concept subsumption in DLs [14], with the reading 'usually, a relationship via r_i is also an r_j-relationship.'

Let $\mathcal{AL\tilde{C}HQ}$ denote $\mathcal{ALCHQ}$ extended with plausible atomic role inclusions. Here, too, our r-ordered interpretations come in handy in providing an intuitive semantics for such a construct:

$$\mathcal{R} \Vdash r_i \mathrel{\tilde{\sqsubseteq}} r_j \text{ if and only if } \min_{\prec_i^{\mathcal{R}}} r_i^{\mathcal{R}} \subseteq r_j^{\mathcal{R}}$$

With the notion of plausible role inclusion, stating guardianOf $\tilde{\sqsubseteq}$ parentOf and parentOf $\tilde{\sqsubseteq}$ progenitorOf captures in a better way the expected intuition in the above example.

Monotonicity for role inclusions coincides with transitivity: $r_i \sqsubseteq r_j$ and $r_j \sqsubseteq r_k$ implies $r_i \sqsubseteq r_k$. That is, strengthening r_j to r_i preserves the role subsumption by r_k. Monotonicity of plausible role inclusions can be defined analogously, i.e., if $r_i \sqsubseteq r_j$ and $r_j \mathrel{\tilde{\sqsubseteq}} r_k$, then $r_i \mathrel{\tilde{\sqsubseteq}} r_k$. It then follows that $\tilde{\sqsubseteq}$, as expected, fails the monotonicity property:

Proposition 3. *Plausible atomic role inclusion in* $\mathcal{AL\tilde{C}HQ}$ *is non-monotonic.*

Theorem 5. $\mathcal{ALCHQ}$ *has the finite-model property and is therefore decidable.*

Theorem 6. *In* $\mathcal{ALCHQ}$, *concept satisfiability and subsumption w.r.t. general TBoxes are* EXPTIME-*complete problems.*

Besides role hierarchies, some DLs also allow for the expression of *role characteristics* such as functionality, transitivity, disjointness, and others, often via the special notation $\mathsf{func}(r_i)$, $\mathsf{trans}(r_i)$, $\mathsf{disj}(r_i, r_j)$, etc., of which the intuition is that "r_i is functional", "r_i is transitive", "r_i and r_j are disjoint", and so on. Semantically, this corresponds to requiring, in every interpretation $\mathcal{I}$, that $r_i^{\mathcal{I}}$ be a function, that $r_i^{\mathcal{I}}$ be a transitive relation, that $r_i^{\mathcal{I}} \cap r_j^{\mathcal{I}} = \emptyset$, etc.

It turns out that, in real-world applications, such general, universal requirements can be too strong, as we have seen in the Introduction for the roles marriedTo (functional) and partOf (transitive). In each of these cases, the property under consideration does not hold globally, but it is still interesting to be able to express that it usually holds, or that it holds at least for the typical instances of the relation. We can achieve that in our framework via defeasible versions of the above characteristic specifiers, namely $\widetilde{\mathsf{func}}(r_i)$, $\widetilde{\mathsf{trans}}(r_i)$ and $\widetilde{\mathsf{disj}}(r_i, r_j)$, of which the intuition is that, respectively, "r_i is normally functional", "r_i is normally transitive" and "r_i and r_j are normally disjoint". The semantics of such constructs could be taken as: $\min_{\prec_i^{\mathcal{R}}} r_i^{\mathcal{R}}$ is functional, $\min_{\prec_i^{\mathcal{R}}} r_i^{\mathcal{R}}$ is transitive, $\min_{\prec_i^{\mathcal{R}}} r_i^{\mathcal{R}} \cap \min_{\prec_j^{\mathcal{R}}} r_j^{\mathcal{R}} = \emptyset$.

Theorem 7. $\mathcal{ALCHQ}$ *with defeasible role characteristics has the finite-model property and is therefore decidable.*

Theorem 8. *In* $\mathcal{ALCHQ}$ *with defeasible role characteristics, concept satisfiability and subsumption w.r.t. general TBoxes are* EXPTIME-*complete problems.*

As in the classical case, it turns out that role-characteristics axioms are just syntactic sugar, since all role properties can be expressed using the constructors we have previously introduced. For instance, that a role r is usually functional can be captured via plausible qualified number restrictions (see Sect. 4.2) by stating axioms of the form $\top \sqsubseteq_{\sim} 1r.\top$ in the TBox.

An alternative characterisation of defeasible transitivity can be obtained in terms of role composition and defeasible role subsumption. This, of course, requires a generalisation of preferences on role names to *operations* on roles so that one can talk about e.g. the most preferred pairs of a compound relation. This is what we address in the remainder of the present section.

Given an r-ordered interpretation $\mathcal{R}$ and role names r_1 and r_2, together with their respective preference relations $\prec_{r_1}^{\mathcal{R}}$ and $\prec_{r_2}^{\mathcal{R}}$, the following are questions that naturally arise in the context of role composition: What is $\prec_{r_1 \circ r_2}^{\mathcal{R}}$? Can $\prec_{r_1 \circ r_2}^{\mathcal{R}}$ be defined in terms of $\prec_{r_1}^{\mathcal{R}}$ and $\prec_{r_2}^{\mathcal{R}}$? More generally, do $\prec_{r_1}^{\mathcal{R}}, \ldots, \prec_{r_n}^{\mathcal{R}}$ completely define the respective preference relation associated with any composition of $r_1, \ldots, r_n$?

Intuitively, a tuple is more plausible in a composed relation if it arises as the composition of two more preferred tuples in the component relations, and it does not also arise as the composition of two less preferred tuples. The latter condition is necessary to eliminate conflicting preferences in the composite order. Technically, it ensures that the resulting relation is a strict partial order. Formally,

$$\prec^{\mathcal{R}}_{r_1 \circ r_2} := \{(x_1 y_1, x_2 y_2) \mid \text{for some } z_1, z_2 \; [(x_1 z_1, x_2 z_2) \in \prec^{\mathcal{R}}_{r_1} \text{ and } (z_1 y_1, z_2 y_2) \in \prec^{\mathcal{R}}_{r_2}]$$
$$\text{and for no } z_1, z_2 \; [(x_2 z_2, x_1 z_1) \in \prec^{\mathcal{R}}_{r_1} \text{ and } (z_2 y_2, z_1 y_1) \in \prec^{\mathcal{R}}_{r_2}]\}.$$

As an example, a typical tuple in the relation $(\mathsf{hasChild} \circ \mathsf{hasChild})^{\mathcal{R}}$ could be a grandparent and biological grandchild.

Armed with a definition of plausible role composition, we can now provide an alternative characterisation of defeasible role transitivity: r_i is plausibly transitive if and only if $r_i \circ r_i \sqsubseteq r_i$. This definition requires only the most typical tuples in the composite relation $(r_i \circ r_i)^{\mathcal{R}}$ to be in $r_i^{\mathcal{R}}$, and is therefore not equivalent to the requirement that $\min_{\prec^{\mathcal{R}}_i} r_i^{\mathcal{R}}$ be transitive. Which of these two definitions is correct depends on what we want to model, and warrants further investigation.

4.4 Typicality of Roles

Plausible role inclusions of the form $r_i \sqsubseteq r_j$ (or, more generally, $r_1 \circ \cdots \circ r_k \sqsubseteq r_j$) carry an implicit notion of *typicality*, namely that typical r_is are r_js (or that the typical instances of $r_1 \circ \cdots \circ r_k$ are in the extension of r_j). Such a notion is implicit inasmuch as one cannot directly refer to the typical instances of r_i (or even of $r_1 \circ \cdots \circ r_k$) in the *object* language. (An analogous observation can be made about plausible concept inclusions of the form $C \sqsubseteq D$ — see Sect. 5.)

As has been argued in a propositional setting [9,10], having an explicit notion of typicality at one's disposal comes in handy from a modeling perspective, besides increasing the expressive power of the language at no extra computational cost. The modeling interest translates into the freedom to refer to typicality anywhere within a sentence and not just in the antecedent (LHS) of 'implication-like' statements [16,17], as with plausible subsumptions.

In a DL setting, this need is mainly felt when stating ABox assertions, namely in specifying that an individual is a typical instance of a class or that a pair of individuals is a typical instance of a role.

This issue has partially been addressed in the literature in that explicit notions of *concept* typicality have been introduced [5,25], where with $\mathbf{T}(C)$ or $\mathbf{N}(C)$ one can refer, in both the TBox and the ABox, to the most typical (or most normal) members of a class. To the best of our knowledge, typicality of roles has never been considered before. Therefore, here we make a case for introducing a typicality operator for roles, with which one can capture the most normal or typical instances of a *relationship*.

Let $\star$ denote a unary operator on roles of which the intuition is precisely as motivated above and whose semantics is given by:

$$(\star r_i)^{\mathcal{R}} := \min_{\prec^{\mathcal{R}}_i} r_i^{\mathcal{R}}$$

In a logic equipped with $\star$, plausible role subsumption becomes redundant, since for every r_i, r_j, $\mathcal{R} \Vdash r_i \sqsubseteq r_j$ iff $\mathcal{R} \Vdash \star r_i \sqsubseteq r_j$. A concrete example is $\star \mathsf{parentOf} \sqsubseteq \mathsf{progenitorOf}$, which we have seen in the previous section. Other examples involving the use of $\star$ are $\star$marriedTo $\sqsubseteq$ $\star$hasPartner (with typicality also in the RHS) and $\star$marriedTo(john, mary) (an explicit instantiation of the typical portion of a role).

Let $f_\star : \langle r_i^{\mathcal{R}}, \prec_i^{\mathcal{R}} \rangle \mapsto min_{\prec_i^{\mathcal{R}}} r_i^{\mathcal{R}}$ denote the function induced by $\star$.

Proposition 4. $f_\star$ *is monotone (increasing) in its first argument, monotone (decreasing) in its second argument, and non-monotonic in general.*

Theorem 9. $\mathcal{ALCHQ}$ *with role typicality has the finite-model property.*

Theorem 10. *In $\mathcal{ALCHQ}$ with role typicality, concept satisfiability and subsumption w.r.t. general TBoxes are* EXPTIME-*complete problems.*

We conclude this section with a remark on further fruitfulness of role typicality from a modeling perspective. First, in DLs also allowing for Boolean operators on roles, with a statement of the form $\star r_i \sqcap \star r_j \sqsubseteq \bot$ one can express plausible role disjointness (see Sect. 4.3). Second, role typicality may be useful in further constraining certain roles via role constructors, e.g. $\star$hasGrandChild $\sqsubseteq$ $\star$hasChild $\circ$ $\star$hasChild (typical grandparenthoods are compositions of typical parenthoods). Both cases go beyond $\mathcal{ALCHQ}$ and we shall leave for future work.

5   Embedding Plausible Concept Subsumption

As an approach to the formalisation of defeasible inheritance in DLs, Britz et al. [14] introduced the notion of *plausible concept subsumption*, which is captured by statements of the form $C \mathrel{\vcenter{\hbox{$\subset$}}\kern-0.5em\raise0.3ex\hbox{$\sim$}} D$, read "usually, C is subsumed by D". Building up on the work by Kraus et al. [32] in the propositional case, Britz et al. [12] have put forward the following list of properties that $\mathrel{\vcenter{\hbox{$\subset$}}\kern-0.5em\raise0.3ex\hbox{$\sim$}}$ ought to satisfy in order to be considered as appropriate in a non-monotonic setting:

$$(\text{Cons})\ \top \mathrel{\not\sqsubseteq\kern-0.3em\raise0.3ex\hbox{$\sim$}} \bot\quad (\text{Ref})\ C \mathrel{\vcenter{\hbox{$\subset$}}\kern-0.5em\raise0.3ex\hbox{$\sim$}} C\quad (\text{LLE})\ \frac{\models C \equiv D,\ C \mathrel{\vcenter{\hbox{$\subset$}}\kern-0.5em\raise0.3ex\hbox{$\sim$}} E}{D \mathrel{\vcenter{\hbox{$\subset$}}\kern-0.5em\raise0.3ex\hbox{$\sim$}} E}\quad (\text{And})\ \frac{C \mathrel{\vcenter{\hbox{$\subset$}}\kern-0.5em\raise0.3ex\hbox{$\sim$}} D,\ C \mathrel{\vcenter{\hbox{$\subset$}}\kern-0.5em\raise0.3ex\hbox{$\sim$}} E}{C \mathrel{\vcenter{\hbox{$\subset$}}\kern-0.5em\raise0.3ex\hbox{$\sim$}} D \sqcap E}$$

$$(\text{Or})\ \frac{C \mathrel{\vcenter{\hbox{$\subset$}}\kern-0.5em\raise0.3ex\hbox{$\sim$}} E,\ D \mathrel{\vcenter{\hbox{$\subset$}}\kern-0.5em\raise0.3ex\hbox{$\sim$}} E}{C \sqcup D \mathrel{\vcenter{\hbox{$\subset$}}\kern-0.5em\raise0.3ex\hbox{$\sim$}} E}\quad (\text{RW})\ \frac{C \mathrel{\vcenter{\hbox{$\subset$}}\kern-0.5em\raise0.3ex\hbox{$\sim$}} D,\ \models D \sqsubseteq E}{C \mathrel{\vcenter{\hbox{$\subset$}}\kern-0.5em\raise0.3ex\hbox{$\sim$}} E}\quad (\text{CM})\ \frac{C \mathrel{\vcenter{\hbox{$\subset$}}\kern-0.5em\raise0.3ex\hbox{$\sim$}} D,\ C \mathrel{\vcenter{\hbox{$\subset$}}\kern-0.5em\raise0.3ex\hbox{$\sim$}} E}{C \sqcap D \mathrel{\vcenter{\hbox{$\subset$}}\kern-0.5em\raise0.3ex\hbox{$\sim$}} E}$$

The last six properties are the obvious translations of the properties for preferential consequence relations proposed by Kraus et al. [32] in the propositional setting. They have been discussed at length in the literature for both the propositional and the DL cases [26,32,33] and we shall not do so here.

A plausible concept subsumption $\mathrel{\vcenter{\hbox{$\subset$}}\kern-0.5em\raise0.3ex\hbox{$\sim$}}$ satisfying all seven properties above is called a *preferential* subsumption. One can require $\mathrel{\vcenter{\hbox{$\subset$}}\kern-0.5em\raise0.3ex\hbox{$\sim$}}$ to satisfy other properties as well. Of particular interest is the property of rational monotonicity below:

$$(\text{RM})\ \frac{C \mathrel{\vcenter{\hbox{$\subset$}}\kern-0.5em\raise0.3ex\hbox{$\sim$}} D,\ C \mathrel{\not\sqsubseteq\kern-0.3em\raise0.3ex\hbox{$\sim$}} \neg C'}{C \sqcap C' \mathrel{\vcenter{\hbox{$\subset$}}\kern-0.5em\raise0.3ex\hbox{$\sim$}} D}$$

A plausible subsumption also satisfying (RM) is called a *rational subsumption*.

The intuition for the semantics of a statement of the form $C \mathrel{\vcenter{\hbox{$\sqsubseteq$}}\mkern-14mu\raise-0.5ex\hbox{$\approx$}} D$ is that those most typical C-objects are also D-objects. In Britz et al.'s approach, this is captured by placing a preference relation on the domain $\Delta^{\mathcal{I}}$ of every DL interpretation and evaluating $C \mathrel{\vcenter{\hbox{$\sqsubseteq$}}\mkern-14mu\raise-0.5ex\hbox{$\approx$}} D$ to true whenever the minimal C-objects are included in $D^{\mathcal{I}}$.

In what follows, we show one possible way in which plausible concept inclusions can be given a semantics within our r-ordered interpretations framework.

The starting point is to also allow for a *universal role* u and *role identity* constructs of the form $id(C)$ [19], where $C \in \mathcal{L}_{\mathcal{ALC}}$, and of which the semantics is given by

$$ u^{\mathcal{R}} := \Delta^{\mathcal{R}} \times \Delta^{\mathcal{R}} \qquad id(C)^{\mathcal{R}} := \{(x,x) \in \Delta^{\mathcal{R}} \times \Delta^{\mathcal{R}} \mid x \in C^{\mathcal{R}}\} $$

Next, one has to place an ordering $\prec_u^{\mathcal{R}}$ on the elements of $u^{\mathcal{R}}$ in the same way as for the other role interpretations. The intuition of doing so is that the most normal $id(C)$-pairs w.r.t. $\prec_u^{\mathcal{R}}$ correspond (implicitly) to the most normal C-objects, i.e., we get an ordering on the elements of $C^{\mathcal{R}}$ induced by the absolute ordering on the elements of $u^{\mathcal{R}}$. Armed with these ideas, we can provide a semantics for the notion of plausible concept inclusion as follows:

$$ \mathcal{R} \Vdash C \mathrel{\vcenter{\hbox{$\sqsubseteq$}}\mkern-14mu\raise-0.5ex\hbox{$\approx$}} D \text{ if and only if } \min_{\prec_u^{\mathcal{R}}} id(C)^{\mathcal{R}} \subseteq id(D)^{\mathcal{R}} $$

Proposition 5. $\mathrel{\vcenter{\hbox{$\sqsubseteq$}}\mkern-14mu\raise-0.5ex\hbox{$\approx$}}$ *is strictly ampliative and non-monotonic.*

Proposition 6. $\mathrel{\vcenter{\hbox{$\sqsubseteq$}}\mkern-14mu\raise-0.5ex\hbox{$\approx$}}$ *is a preferential subsumption relation.*

If we also require $\prec_u^{\mathcal{R}}$ to be a *modular* order, then the above construction delivers a rational $\mathrel{\vcenter{\hbox{$\sqsubseteq$}}\mkern-14mu\raise-0.5ex\hbox{$\approx$}}$. Previous results for Rational Closure in DLs [12] carry over to $\mathcal{ALC}$ with plausible concept inclusions as defined above.

Theorem 11. $\mathcal{ALCQ}$ *extended with plausible concept inclusions has the finite-model property and is therefore decidable.*

Theorem 12. *In $\mathcal{ALCQ}$ with plausible concept inclusions, concept satisfiability and subsumption w.r.t. general TBoxes are* EXPTIME-*complete problems.*

6   Related and Future Work

We start by observing that the operators we have introduced here do not aim at providing a formal account of the notion of *most*, as addressed in the study of generalised quantifiers [36] and, more recently, in a modal context by Veloso et al. [44] and Askounis et al. [1]. Clearly, our defeasible operators are not about degrees of truth as has been studied in fuzzy logics, nor about degrees of possibility and necessity as addressed by possibilistic logics [24]. They rather relate to and generalise the notions of defeasible modalities [17,18] and defeasible quantifiers [13] we studied previously.

In a sense, the notions we investigated here can be seen as the qualitative counterpart of possibilistic modalities [34,35]. There, each possible world w is associated with a *possibility distribution* $\pi_w : W \longrightarrow [0,1]$, the intuition of which is to capture the degree of likelihood (in terms of belief) of all possible worlds w.r.t. w. In that setting, the pairs (w, w') for which $\pi_w(w')$ is maximal correspond here to the most preferred pairs in the interpretation of a *single* role name.

In this paper, we have assumed $\mathcal{ALC}$, $\mathcal{ALCQ}$ or $\mathcal{ALCHQ}$ as the underlying DL and we have investigated individual extensions of each one with the constructors we introduced. As a next step, we shall consider different combinations of our defeasible constructs, also together with other DL operators not considered here, like inverse roles, and study the resulting computational properties.

Finally, here we have not addressed the question as to what an appropriate notion of non-monotonic entailment for the different extensions of $\mathcal{ALC}$ with defeasible operators is, especially in the presence of ABoxes. Indeed, in this paper we have contented ourselves with the standard (Tarskian) definition, which is monotonic (and therefore not suitable in some contexts). The recent extensions of the notion of Rational Closure [33] by Booth et al. [8,9], Casini et al. [21] and Giordano et al. [27,28] may provide us with a springboard with which to investigate this matter in the more expressive languages we introduced here.

Acknowledgements. This work is based on research supported in part by the National Research Foundation of South Africa (Grant Numbers 103345 and 85482).

References

1. Askounis, D., Koutras, C.D., Zikos, Y.: Knowledge Means '*All*', Belief Means '*Most*'. In: Cerro, L.F., Herzig, A., Mengin, J. (eds.) JELIA 2012. LNCS (LNAI), vol. 7519, pp. 41–53. Springer, Heidelberg (2012). doi:10.1007/978-3-642-33353-8_4
2. Baader, F., Calvanese, D., McGuinness, D., Nardi, D., Patel-Schneider, P. (eds.): The Description Logic Handbook: Theory, Implementation and Applications, 2nd edn. Cambridge University Press, Cambridge (2007)
3. Baader, F., Hollunder, B.: How to prefer more specific defaults in terminological default logic. In: Bajcsy, R. (ed.) Proceedings of the 13th International Joint Conference on Artificial Intelligence (IJCAI), pp. 669–675. Morgan Kaufmann Publishers (1993)
4. Baader, F., Hollunder, B.: Embedding defaults into terminological knowledge representation formalisms. J. Autom. Reasoning **14**(1), 149–180 (1995)
5. Bonatti, P., Faella, M., Petrova, I., Sauro, L.: A new semantics for overriding in description logics. Artif. Intell. **222**, 1–48 (2015)
6. Bonatti, P., Faella, M., Sauro, L.: Defeasible inclusions in low-complexity DLs. J. Artif. Intell. Res. **42**, 719–764 (2011)
7. Bonatti, P., Lutz, C., Wolter, F.: The complexity of circumscription in description logic. J. Artif. Intell. Res. **35**, 717–773 (2009)
8. Booth, R., Casini, G., Meyer, T., Varzinczak, I.: On the entailment problem for a logic of typicality. In: Proceedings of the 24th International Joint Conference on Artificial Intelligence (IJCAI) (2015)

9. Booth, R., Meyer, T., Varzinczak, I.: PTL: a propositional typicality logic. In: Cerro, L.F., Herzig, A., Mengin, J. (eds.) JELIA 2012. LNCS (LNAI), vol. 7519, pp. 107–119. Springer, Heidelberg (2012). doi:10.1007/978-3-642-33353-8_9

10. Booth, R., Meyer, T., Varzinczak, I.: A propositional typicality logic for extending rational consequence. In: Fermé, E., Gabbay, D., Simari, G. (eds.) Trends in Belief Revision and Argumentation Dynamics. Studies in Logic - Logic and Cognitive Systems, vol. 48, pp. 123–154. King's College Publications, London (2013)

11. Boutilier, C.: Conditional logics of normality: a modal approach. Artif. Intell. **68**(1), 87–154 (1994)

12. Britz, K., Casini, G., Meyer, T., Moodley, K., Varzinczak, I.: Ordered interpretations and entailment for defeasible description logics. Technical report, CAIR, CSIR Meraka and UKZN, South Africa (2013). http://tinyurl.com/cydd6yy

13. Britz, K., Casini, G., Meyer, T., Varzinczak, I.: Preferential role restrictions. In: Proceedings of the 26th International Workshop on Description Logics, pp. 93–106 (2013)

14. Britz, K., Heidema, J., Meyer, T.: Semantic preferential subsumption. In: Lang, J., Brewka, G. (eds.) Proceedings of the 11th International Conference on Principles of Knowledge Representation and Reasoning (KR), pp. 476–484. AAAI Press/MIT Press (2008)

15. Britz, K., Meyer, T., Varzinczak, I.: Semantic foundation for preferential description logics. In: Wang, D., Reynolds, M. (eds.) AI 2011. LNCS (LNAI), vol. 7106, pp. 491–500. Springer, Heidelberg (2011). doi:10.1007/978-3-642-25832-9_50

16. Britz, K., Varzinczak, I.: Defeasible modes of inference: a preferential perspective. In: Proceedings of the 14th International Workshop on Nonmonotonic Reasoning (NMR) (2012)

17. Britz, K., Varzinczak, I.: Defeasible modalities. In: Proceedings of the 14th Conference on Theoretical Aspects of Rationality and Knowledge (TARK), pp. 49–60 (2013)

18. Britz, K., Varzinczak, I.: Preferential modalities revisited. In: Proceedings of the 16th International Workshop on Nonmonotonic Reasoning (NMR) (2016)

19. Calvanese, D., Giacomo, G.: Expressive description logics. In: Baader, F., et al. [2], Chap. 5, pp. 193–236

20. Casini, G., Meyer, T., Moodley, K., Sattler, U., Varzinczak, I.: Introducing defeasibility into OWL ontologies. In: Arenas, M., et al. (eds.) ISWC 2015. LNCS, vol. 9367, pp. 409–426. Springer, Heidelberg (2015). doi:10.1007/978-3-319-25010-6_27

21. Casini, G., Meyer, T., Moodley, K., Varzinczak, I.: Nonmonotonic reasoning in description logics: Rational closure for the ABox. In: Proceedings of the 26th International Workshop on Description Logics. pp. 600–615 (2013)

22. Casini, G., Straccia, U.: Rational closure for defeasible description logics. In: Janhunen, T., Niemelä, I. (eds.) JELIA 2010. LNCS (LNAI), vol. 6341, pp. 77–90. Springer, Heidelberg (2010). doi:10.1007/978-3-642-15675-5_9

23. Donini, F., Nardi, D., Rosati, R.: Description logics of minimal knowledge and negation as failure. ACM Trans. Comput. Logic **3**(2), 177–225 (2002)

24. Dubois, D., Lang, J., Prade, H.: Possibilistic logic. In: Gabbay, D., Hogger, C., Robinson, J. (eds.) Handbook of Logic in Artificial Intelligence and Logic Programming, vol. 3, pp. 439–513. Oxford University Press, Oxford (1994)

25. Giordano, L., Gliozzi, V., Olivetti, N., Pozzato, G.L.: Preferential description logics. In: Dershowitz, N., Voronkov, A. (eds.) LPAR 2007. LNCS (LNAI), vol. 4790, pp. 257–272. Springer, Heidelberg (2007). doi:10.1007/978-3-540-75560-9_20

26. Giordano, L., Gliozzi, V., Olivetti, N., Pozzato, G.: $\mathcal{ALC} + T$: a preferential extension of description logics. Fundamenta Informaticae **96**(3), 341–372 (2009)

27. Giordano, L., Gliozzi, V., Olivetti, N., Pozzato, G.: A non-monotonic description logic for reasoning about typicality. Artif. Intell. **195**, 165–202 (2013)
28. Giordano, L., Gliozzi, V., Olivetti, N., Pozzato, G.: Semantic characterization of rational closure: from propositional logic to description logics. Artif. Intell. **226**, 1–33 (2015)
29. Governatori, G.: Defeasible description logics. In: Antoniou, G., Boley, H. (eds.) RuleML 2004. LNCS, vol. 3323, pp. 98–112. Springer, Heidelberg (2004). doi:10. 1007/978-3-540-30504-0_8
30. Grosof, B., Horrocks, I., Volz, R., Decker, S.: Description logic programs: combining logic programs with description logic. In: Proceedings of the 12th International Conference on World Wide Web (WWW), pp. 48–57. ACM (2003)
31. Heymans, S., Vermeir, D.: A defeasible ontology language. In: Meersman, R., Tari, Z. (eds.) OTM 2002. LNCS, vol. 2519, pp. 1033–1046. Springer, Heidelberg (2002). doi:10.1007/3-540-36124-3_66
32. Kraus, S., Lehmann, D., Magidor, M.: Nonmonotonic reasoning, preferential models and cumulative logics. Artif. Intell. **44**, 167–207 (1990)
33. Lehmann, D., Magidor, M.: What does a conditional knowledge base entail? Artif. Intell. **55**, 1–60 (1992)
34. Liau, C.J.: On the possibility theory-based semantics for logics of preference. Int. J. Approximate Reasoning **20**(2), 173–190 (1999)
35. Liau, C.J., Lin, B.P.: Possibilistic reasoning-a mini-survey and uniform semantics. Artif. Intell. **88**(1–2), 163–193 (1996)
36. Lindström, P.: First-order predicate logic with generalized quantifiers. Theoria **32**, 286–195 (1966)
37. Padgham, L., Zhang, T.: A terminological logic with defaults: a definition and an application. In: Bajcsy, R. (ed.) Proceedings of the 13th International Joint Conference on Artificial Intelligence (IJCAI), pp. 662–668. Morgan Kaufmann Publishers (1993)
38. Qi, G., Pan, J.Z., Ji, Q.: Extending description logics with uncertainty reasoning in possibilistic logic. In: Mellouli, K. (ed.) ECSQARU 2007. LNCS (LNAI), vol. 4724, pp. 828–839. Springer, Heidelberg (2007). doi:10.1007/978-3-540-75256-1_72
39. Quantz, J., Royer, V.: A preference semantics for defaults in terminological logics. In: Proceedings of the 3rd International Conference on Principles of Knowledge Representation and Reasoning (KR), pp. 294–305 (1992)
40. Quantz, J., Ryan, M.: Preferential default description logics. Technical report, TU Berlin (1993). www.tu-berlin.de/fileadmin/fg53/KIT-Reports/r110.pdf
41. Sengupta, K., Krisnadhi, A.A., Hitzler, P.: Local closed world semantics: grounded circumscription for OWL. In: Aroyo, L., Welty, C., Alani, H., Taylor, J., Bernstein, A., Kagal, L., Noy, N., Blomqvist, E. (eds.) ISWC 2011. LNCS, vol. 7031, pp. 617–632. Springer, Heidelberg (2011). doi:10.1007/978-3-642-25073-6_39
42. Shoham, Y.: Reasoning about Change: Time and Causation from the Standpoint of Artificial Intelligence. MIT Press, Massachusetts (1988)
43. Straccia, U.: Default inheritance reasoning in hybrid KL-ONE-style logics. In: Bajcsy, R. (ed.) Proceedings of the 13th International Joint Conference on Artificial Intelligence (IJCAI), pp. 676–681. Morgan Kaufmann Publishers (1993)
44. Veloso, P., Veloso, S., Viana, J., de Freitas, R., Benevides, M., Delgado, C.: On vague notions and modalities: a modular approach. Logic J. IGPL **18**(3), 381–402 (2009)

Opposition Frameworks

Cosmina Croitoru[1,2(✉)] and Kurt Mehlhorn[1]

[1] Max Planck Institut for Informatics, Saarbrücken, Germany
cosmina.croitoru@gmail.com
[2] Saarbrücken Graduate School in Computer Science, Saarland University,
Saarbrücken, Germany

Abstract. In this paper we introduce opposition frameworks, a generalization of Dung's argumentation frameworks.

While keeping the attack relation as the sole type of interaction between nodes and the abstract level of argumentation frameworks, opposition networks add more flexibility, reducing the gap between structured and abstract argumentation. A *guarded attack calculus* is developed in order to obtain proper generalizations of Dung's admissibility-based semantics. The high modeling capabilities of our new setting offer an alternative instantiation solution (of other existing argumentation frameworks) for arguments evaluation.

1 Introduction

Dung [15], in a landmark paper in the area of *Computational Argumentation*, initiated the study of the following problem:

> *If the edges of a given directed graph are seen as attacks, how can a satisfactory set of winner nodes be rationally selected and justified?*

By interpreting the nodes of such directed graphs as *arguments* and designing a *conflict-resolution* formalism to make distinction among *acceptable* and *unacceptable* arguments, Dung introduced **Argumentation Frameworks** (AFs for short) and developed an interesting *calculus of opposition*, as coined in Brewka [6]. More precisely, the acceptability of an argument is defined based on its membership in an *admissible set* of arguments satisfying certain additional properties. An admissible set of arguments is *conflict-free* (i.e., there is no attack between its members) and *defends itself against any attack*: for each attack from an argument a against one of its members there is a counter-attack from one of its members against a. This kind of rationality based on the possibility of extending a specified argument to a set of "collectively acceptable" arguments is called *extension based semantics*. The *grounded, preferred* and *stable semantics* defined by Dung (see Sect. 2) formalize different intuitions about "collective acceptance" on the basis of a given framework.

In this paper we introduce **Opposition Frameworks** (OFs for short) that generalize Dung's framework without self-attacks, by considering more fine-grained notions of conflict-freeness and admissibility.

© Springer International Publishing AG 2016
L. Michael and A. Kakas (Eds.): JELIA 2016, LNAI 10021, pp. 190–206, 2016.
DOI: 10.1007/978-3-319-48758-8_13

An OF is a labeled directed multigraph whose directed edges represent attacks between its nodes. A node is no longer an atomic argument as in AFs, but a composed object, interpreted as the *position* of an agent in a debate. The position of a node v is a finite set $g(v)$ of *facts granted* by v. Depending on the real world problem modeled, the facts can be statements, claims, pieces of evidence, locutions, issues, etc. The set $g(v)$ of facts granted by a node v has no mathematical structure associated; it is, simply, a list of facts approved by the node v, based on which v develops its attacks. Each attack a has a *source* node $s(a)$, a target node $t(a)$, and is labeled by a pair $(\gamma(a), \delta(a))$ of (disjoint) sets of facts. Here $\gamma(a) \subseteq g(s(a))$ is the *guard* of the attack a, and $\delta(a)$ is a nonempty subset of $g(t(a)) - g(s(a))$, representing the facts (granted by the node $t(a)$) that are *denied* by the source node, $s(a)$, of the attack a. So, if a node v attacks a node w via the attack a, that is $s(a) = v$ and $t(a) = w$, then the guard $\gamma(a)$ specifies the set of facts – granted by v – based on which v does not admit the facts in $\delta(a)$ – granted by w.

It follows that, in OFs, arguments are seen as ensembles formed by the facts granted by a node together with the attacks issuing from this node. To illustrate how this can arise in real world situations, let us consider the following possible political debate.

Example 1 (adapted from Wang and Luo [29]). Let us construct an OF by assigning a node for each of the 5 positions in the following debate on the set $\{f_1, \ldots, f_9\}$ of facts:

v_1 : "$\overline{\text{Reducing emissions of greenhouse gases}}^{f_1}$ is crucially for the $\overline{\text{protection of our health}}^{f_2}$ and, clearly, it is more important than $\overline{\text{developing economy}}^{f_3}$."

v_2 : "$\overline{\text{Developing economy}}^{f_3}$ will ensure $\overline{\text{creating job positions}}^{f_4}$ and it is more significant than $\overline{\text{protecting the environment}}^{f_8}$."

v_3 : "We need not to focus on $\overline{\text{developing economy}}^{f_3}$ and urgently should take measures to $\overline{\text{protect environment}}^{f_8}$, e.g., $\overline{\text{reduce emissions of greenhouse gases}}^{f_1}$, and $\overline{\text{save water}}^{f_5}$."

v_4 : "Currently it is more important to $\overline{\text{create job positions}}^{f_4}$ for $\overline{\text{increasing number of graduates}}^{f_6}$, than being concerned with $\overline{\text{reducing emissions of greenhouse gases}}^{f_1}$. It is obvious that by $\overline{\text{hiring new people}}^{f_9}$ it is not necessary to be concerned with $\overline{\text{protecting human health}}^{f_2}$."

v_5 : "Instead of $\overline{\text{creating several job positions}}^{f_4}$ in order to $\overline{\text{increase the number of graduates}}^{f_6}$, we should concentrate on $\overline{\text{protecting the environment}}^{f_8}$ to guarantee $\overline{\text{earth security}}^{f_7}$."

Graphically, in Fig. 1 below, each node is decorated with its granted set and each attack a, with source $s(a) = v_i$ and target $t(a) = v_j$, is labeled with the pair $(\gamma(a), \delta(a))$.

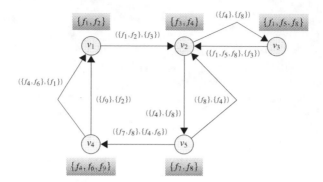

Fig. 1. OF modeling the political debate in Example 1.

Note that we have two attacks from v_4 to v_1 which differ by their labels, and this kind of multiple attacks does not exist in Dung's argumentation frameworks.

This example is considered only for illustration purpose. A software system for automatically modeling such a debate, that is to construct positions, facts and attack's labels, must use appropriate natural language processing tools, e.g., Finegan-Dollak and Radev [18], and/or specialized debating websites, e.g., Debatepedia[1], (see also Rahwan et al. [27], or Leite and Martins [20]), but it is beyond the scope of this paper.

The above example shows that an OF can model which precise part of an "argument" is in conflict with which part of another "argument", without requiring a logical language and an inference relation. Our new formalism is more abstract than the existing structured AFs and it is well suited to represent complex non-logical information.

Intuitively, a *guarded attack* shows the reason why a node attacks another one. Let a be an attack on the node w (that is, $t(a) = w$). We say that a is *harmful to* w if w can not counter-attack a: there is no attack a' from w to the source of a denying at least one fact in the guard of a ($\forall a'$ with $s(a') = w$ and $t(a') = s(a)$ we have $\delta(a') \cap \gamma(a) = \emptyset$). We develop a *guarded attack calculus* in order to extend the basic notions which underly the classical Dung's semantics, so preserving the diversity of reasoning schemes for AFs. Our new formalism is based on the graph operation of *contraction* and can be described as follows. To decide if a given node v can be *accepted*, we look at the attacks on v; if there is no attack harmful to v, then it is accepted; otherwise, we search a node w which is not in "conflict" with v (no fact denied by an attack from one is granted by the other) and denies at least one fact of the guard of an attack harmful to v; if w does not exist, then v can *not be accepted*; if w exists, we consider their *coalition* $\{v, w\}$ as a new super-node $v_{\{v,w\}}$ with $g(v_{\{v,w\}}) = g(v) \cup g(w)$, delete the nodes v and w, and replace them by the super-node $v_{\{v,w\}}$ as the source or the target of each attack from or to v and w; the decision process is continued using the super-node in the new OF. Adapting the notions of *conflict-freeness*

[1] http://dbp.idebate.org.

and *defense*, we show that there is a sequence of coalition choices for which the above outlined process ends with an accepted (super)node if and only if there is an *admissible set* of nodes containing v. Since AFs are particular OFs (see the end of Subsect. 3.1), we obtain a more intuitive and algorithmic way of handling classical admissibility argumentation semantics.

Returning to the Example 1, if we want to see the status of v_2 in this OF using the above outlined process, it is obvious that it needs to make a coalition with v_4 in order to deny a fact in the guard of the attack from v_1. The super-node $v_{\{v_2,v_4\}}$ has no harmful attack in the contracted OF, therefore v_2 is accepted. If we delete the set-labels, replace the multiple attack by a single directed edge and call the nodes arguments in the OF in Fig. 1, we obtain (the digraph of) an AF; in this AF the set of arguments $\{v_2, v_4\}$ is a *preferred* and *stable extension* (see Sect. 2). Hence the outputs of the two frameworks agree. On the other hand, the set $\{v_1, v_3, v_5\}$ is another *preferred* and *stable extension* in the AF. However, the set of nodes $\{v_1, v_3, v_5\}$ can not be considered as a "solution" in the OF in Fig. 1, since it does not (collectively) defend the node v_1 against the attack with source v_4 and labeled $(\{f_9\}, \{f_2\})$. It follows that the use of guards, on which OFs are developed, provides more accurate outputs than the dichotomy between the existence and lack of attacks, on which Dung's frameworks are based (further differences are highlighted in Subsect. 3.1 in the comments after Fig. 2).

Note the difference between our OFs and structured/deductive argumentation frameworks [1,11,19,26]: while in these logic based frameworks the internal structure of the arguments generates and explains the (inferential) nature of the attacks expressed as uniform (i.e., the same for all nodes) rules, the users of OF's are free to choose between uniform or non-uniform rules to construct the attack's labels. These labels can be automatically constructed if the content of a node (that is, its granted set of facts) is equipped with a mathematical (logical, combinatorial, algebraic, etc.) structure. The gain over the AF's instantiation approach is that our model is more general and the use of attack's labels reduces the number of "arguments" to be considered (see also the discussion after the Proposition 6 in the end of Sect. 3).

The remainder of this paper is organized as follows. In Sect. 2 we give a short introduction in Dung's abstract argumentation. In Sect. 3, we define formally OFs, show that AFs are particular OFs, extend Dung's acceptability semantics, discuss complexity issues, develop a new DPLL type acceptance algorithm, and define logical semantics for OFs. Finally, in Sect. 4 we conclude the paper and discuss future work.

2   Argumentation Frameworks

In this section we present the basic concepts used for defining classical semantics in abstract argumentation frameworks as introduced by Dung [15].

Definition 1. An *Argumentation Framework* is a digraph $AF = (A, E)$, where A is a finite and nonempty set; the vertices in A are called *arguments*, and if $(a, b) \in E$ is a directed edge, then *argument a attacks argument b*.

Definition 2. An *extension-based acceptability semantics* is a map σ assigning to each $AF = (A, E)$ a set $\sigma(AF) \subseteq 2^A$. A member $S \in \sigma(AF)$ is called a σ-*extension* in AF. If $AF = (A, E)$ is an AF, σ a semantics and $a \in A$, then a is σ-*credulously accepted* if $a \in \bigcup_{S \in \sigma(AF)} S$ and a is σ-*sceptically accepted* if $a \in \bigcap_{S \in \sigma(AF)} S$.

For $a \in A$ we denote $a^+ = \{b \in A | \ (a, b) \in E\}$ the set of all arguments *attacked* by a, and $a^- = \{b \in A | \ (b, a) \in E\}$ the set of all arguments *attacking* a. These notations can be extended to sets $S \subseteq A$: $S^+ = \bigcup_{a \in S} a^+$, and $S^- = \bigcup_{a \in S} a^-$.

The set S of arguments *defends* an argument $a \in A$ if $a^- \subseteq S^+$. The set of *all arguments defended by a set* S of arguments is denoted by $F(S)$. For $\mathbb{M} \subseteq 2^A$, $\mathbf{max}(\mathbb{M})$ ($\mathbf{min}(\mathbb{M})$) denotes the set of maximal (minimal) members of $\mathbb{M}$. The main extension-based acceptability semantics are:

Definition 3. Let $AF = (A, E)$ be an AF.

- A *conflict-free set* in AF is a set $S \subseteq A$ such that $S \cap S^+ = \emptyset$. We will denote $\mathbf{cf}(AF) = \{S \subseteq A | S$ is conflict-free set $\}$.
- An *admissible set* in AF is a set $S \in \mathbf{cf}(AF)$ with $S^- \subseteq S^+$.
- A *complete extension* in AF is a set $S \in \mathbf{cf}(AF)$ s.t. $S = F(S)$. We will denote $\mathbf{comp}(AF) = \{S \subseteq A | S$ is complete extension$\}$.
- A *preferred extension* in AF is a set $S \in \mathbf{max}(\mathbf{comp}(AF))$.
- A *grounded extension* in AF is a set $S \in \mathbf{min}(\mathbf{comp}(AF))$.
- A *stable extension* in AF is a set $S \in \mathbf{cf}(AF)$ s.t. $S^+ = A - S$.

3   Opposition Frameworks

3.1   Defining the New Framework

In this subsection, we define OFs, discuss their compatibility with Dung's structures and specify how to see AFs as OFs.

Definition 4 (Opposition Framework (OF)). *An opposition framework is a tuple $OF = (N, F, g, A, s, t, \gamma, \delta)$ where:*

- *N is a finite set of **nodes**; F is a finite set of **facts**; $g : N \to 2^F$ is a function that associates to each node $v \in N$, its **granted** set $g(v)$ of facts in F,*
- *A is a finite set of **attacks**; $s, t : A \to N$ are functions that associate to each attack $a \in A$ its **source** node $s(a)$, and its **target** node $t(a)$,*
- *$\gamma, \delta : A \to 2^F$ are functions that associate to each attack $a \in A$ its **guard** $\gamma(a) \subseteq g(s(a))$, and its **denied set of facts** $\delta(a)$, with $\delta(a) \subseteq g(t(a)) - g(s(a))$.*

In words, an OF is a labeled multi-digraph in which each directed edge (v, w) corresponds to an attack a from the node $s(a) = v$ to node $t(a) = w$, that is based on a set of facts $\gamma(a) \subseteq g(v)$ granted by v, and denies the set $\delta(a) \subseteq g(w)$ of facts granted by w. Throughout this paper we assume that the sets $g(v)$, $\gamma(a)$, $\delta(a)$ are non-empty.

The condition $\delta(a) \subseteq g(t(a)) - g(s(a))$ forbids the attack a to deny the facts granted by its source. In particular, there is no attack in A such that $s(a) = t(a)$ (there are no self-attacks). However, we can have parallel attacks: a set of attacks $A_0 \subseteq A$ with $|A_0| \geq 2$ and $s(a) = s(a')$ and $t(a) = t(a')$, for every $a, a' \in A_0$.

Graphically, each node is decorated with its granted set and each attack a with source $s(a) = v$ and target $t(a) = w$ is labeled with the pair $(\gamma(a), \delta(a))$, as depicted in Fig. 1. Let us observe that the granted sets of nodes v_1 and v_4 are $g(v_1) = \{f_1, f_2\}$ and $g(v_4) = \{f_4, f_6, f_9\}$. The two attacks ($a_1$ and a_2) from v_4 to v_1 form a multiple attack of v_4 against v_1. They differ by their labels: $(\gamma(a_1), \delta(a_1)) = (\{f_4, f_6\}, \{f_1\})$ and $(\gamma(a_2), \delta(a_2)) = (\{f_9\}, \{f_2\})$. The meaning is that the attack a_1, based on f_4 and f_6 (granted by the source node of a_1), denies f_1, one of the facts granted by the target of a_1, while the attack a_2, based on f_9, denies f_2. We will assume in the following that multiple attacks have different labels.

The granted set $g(v)$ of a node v can be interpreted as a node interface, exhibiting its pieces of evidence which can be accepted or attacked by the other nodes. The set $g(v)$ can not be replaced in the digraph representing the OF by a set of non-conflicting nodes (viewing the items in $g(v)$ as sub-arguments) due to the rule-based way the attacks are conceived. For example, in Fig. 2(i), we consider an OF having only two nodes v_1 and v_2, with $g(v_1) = \{f_1, f_2, f_3\}$ and $g(v_2) = \{f_2, f_4\}$, and a symmetric pair of attacks a_1 and a_2. In Fig. 2(ii), we transform this OF into a digraph (AF) with vertices set $\{f_1, f_2, f_3, f_4\}$ and attacks generated by the rules associated to a_1 (($\{f_2\}, \{f_1\}$) gives the attack (f_2, f_1)) and a_2 (($\{f_3\}, \{f_4\}$) gives the attack (f_3, f_4)). But then, the set $\{f_1, f_2, f_3\}$ is not conflict free, which contradicts the intuition that in the OF the set $g(v)$ granted by a node v is not conflicting.

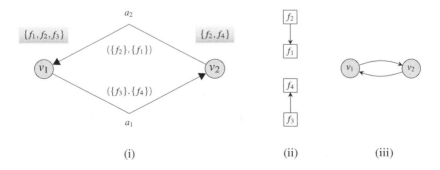

Fig. 2. Trying to model an OF as an AF.

Hence OFs offer a more general approach of modeling collective attacks as the one proposed in Nielson and Parsons [23], where sets of arguments rather than single arguments may be needed to attack another argument. On the other hand, if we view the OF in (i) simply as the AF with two arguments v_1 and v_2 attacking each other (as in Fig. 2(iii)), then each argument is credulously stable accepted (see Coste-Marquis *et al.* [12]), which is not what the OF suggests (the attack a_2 against v_1 can not be defended, because of f_2, which is not denied, and the attack a_1 against v_2 can not be defended, because of f_3). It follows that the semantics of the two models (AF and OF) differ. Hence the acceptability based semantics for OFs must be defined in an appropriate way in order to catch the intended intuition and to have stronger versions of the Dung's semantics imposed by the fined-grained environment considered in OFs.

We close this subsection by noting that any AF without self-attacks can be seen as a (trivial) OF, specified (for further use) in the following definition, and illustrated by a simple example in Fig. 3.

Definition 5 (OF associated to an AF). *Let $AF = (Arg(AF), Def(AF))$ be an argumentation framework without self-attacks. The **opposition framework** associated to AF is $OF_{AF} = (N, F, g, A, s, t, \gamma, \delta)$, where:*

- $N = F = Arg(AF)$; $g(a) = \{a\}$, $\forall a \in Arg(AF)$; $A = Def(AF)$;
- $\forall d = (a, b) \in Def(AF)$, $s(d) = a$ *and* $t(d) = b$, $\gamma(d) = \{a\}$ *and* $\delta(d) = \{b\}$.

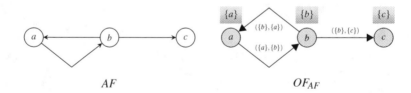

$$AF \qquad\qquad\qquad OF_{AF}$$

Fig. 3. OF associated to an AF.

3.2   Conflict-Freeness

Let $OF = (N, F, g, A, s, t, \gamma, \delta)$ be an opposition framework. For $S \subseteq N$, we denote by $\alpha^-(S)$ $(\alpha^+(S))$ the set of attacks having the target (source) in S:

$$\alpha^-(S) = \{a \in A \mid t(a) \in S\} \text{ and } \alpha^+(S) = \{a \in A \mid s(a) \in S\}.$$

We write $\alpha^+(v)$ $(\alpha^-(v))$ instead of $\alpha^+(\{v\})$ $(\alpha^-(\{v\}))$.

A **weak conflict-free (wcf)** set of nodes is any set $S \subseteq N$ such that there is no attack a with $s(a), t(a) \in S$. Clearly, singletons $\{v\}$, for $v \in N$, are wcf sets.

In AFs, wcf sets are simple called conflict-free sets, and can be conceived as collective (super)arguments. Formally, if S is a conflict-free set of arguments in an AF, we can replace it by a (super)node a_S and each attack from (to) an argument in S is replaced by an attack from (to) v_S (multiple attacks are replaced by a single attack). This graph operation (called contraction) creates no self-attacks, since S is a conflict-free set. The contraction operation of a wcf set S in an OF assigns the union of the granted sets of the members of S as the granted set of v_S, the sources (or targets) of attacks from (to) a member of S are replaced by v_S (multiple attacks are accepted). The problem that can arise is that for some new attack a with $s(a) = v_S$ we can have $\delta(a) \cap g(v_S) \neq \emptyset$.

A **strong conflict-free (scf)** set of nodes is any set $S \subseteq N$ such that $\forall a \in \alpha^+(S)$, $\delta(a) \cap g(s') = \emptyset$, for every $s' \in S$. In words, no attack with source in S denies a fact granted by a node in S. The following lemma holds.

Lemma 1. *(i) In an OF any scf set is a wcf set. (ii) If in an OF the granted sets, $g(v)$, are disjoint (i.e. $g(v) \cap g(w) = \emptyset$, for all distinct $v, w \in N$) then a set of nodes is wcf if and only if it is scf. In particular, if OF_{AF} is the OF associated to an AF AF, then a set S of arguments in AF is conflict-free if and only if it is scf in OF_{AF}.*

Scf sets can be safely used in the OF's contraction operation:

Proposition 1. *Let $OF = (N, F, g, A, s, t, \gamma, \delta)$ be an opposition framework and $S \subseteq N$ a wcf set of nodes. Let $OF|_S = (N_1, F_1, g_1, A_1, s_1, t_1, \gamma_1, \delta_1)$ be the tuple, where*

$$N_1 = (N - S) \dot{\cup} \{v_S\}, \ F_1 = F, \ A_1 = A, \ \gamma_1 = \gamma, \ \delta_1 = \delta,$$

$$g_1(v) = \begin{cases} g(v) & \text{if } v \in N - S \\ \bigcup_{w \in S} g(w) & \text{if } v = v_S \end{cases}$$

$$s_1(a) = \begin{cases} s(a) & \text{if } a \notin \alpha^+(S) \\ v_S & \text{if } a \in \alpha^+(S) \end{cases} \text{ and } t_1(a) = \begin{cases} t(a) & \text{if } a \notin \alpha^-(S) \\ v_S & \text{if } a \in \alpha^-(S) \end{cases}.$$

*Then $OF|_S$ is an OF (obtained **by contraction of** S) if and only if S is a scf set of nodes.*

Proof. Suppose that $OF|_S$ is an opposition framework. To show that S is a scf set in OF, let $a \in A$ with $s(a) \in S$. In $OF|_S$ we have $s_1(a) = v_S$ and therefore $\delta_1(a) \cap g_1(v_S) = \emptyset$. By the definition of functions δ_1 and g_1, it follows that in OF we have $\delta(a) \cap \bigcup_{w \in S} g(w) = \emptyset$, that is $\delta(a) \cap g(w) = \emptyset$, for every $w \in S$. Hence S is a scf set in OF.

Conversely, suppose that S is a scf set in OF. To show that $OF|_S$ is an OF, we have to prove that $\delta_1(a) \subseteq g_1(t_1(a)) - g_1(s_1(a)), \forall a \in A_1 = A$. By the definition of $OF|_S$, this holds trivially for every a with $s_1(a) \neq v_S$. If $s_1(a) = v_S$, then $t_1(a) \notin S$ (since S is wcf set) and, therefore, $\delta_1(a) = \delta(a)$, $t_1(a) = t(a)$, and $g_1(t_1(a)) = g(t(a))$. Because $g_1(s_1(a)) = g_1(v_S) = \bigcup_{w \in S} g(w)$ we have to prove that $\delta(a) \subseteq g(t(a)) - \bigcup_{w \in S} g(w)$. But this holds, since $s(a) \in S$ and S is a scf set (i.e., $\delta(a) \cap g(w) = \emptyset$ for every $w \in S$). $\qquad\square$

3.3 Extending Dung's Semantics

Let $OF = (N, F, g, A, s, t, \gamma, \delta)$ be an opposition framework, $S \subseteq N$ and $v \in N$.
Let us denote $g(S) = \bigcup_{s \in S} g(s)$. We say that v is **defended by** S if

- $\forall a \in \alpha^+(v)$ we have $\delta(a) \cap g(S) = \emptyset$, and
- $\forall a \in \alpha^-(v)$, $\exists a^c \in \alpha^+(S)$ such that $t(a^c) = s(a)$ and $\delta(a^c) \cap \gamma(a) \neq \emptyset$.

In words, a node v is defended by a set S of nodes if, firstly, no attack with
the source v denies a fact granted by a node in S, and, secondly, for any attack
a targeting v there is a counter-attack coming from S, targeting the source of a,
and denying at least one fact of the guard of a. In Fig. 4, the set $\{v_3\}$ defends
the node v_1, but the set $\{v_4\}$ does not defend v_1 despite of the attack of $\{v_4\}$
(against the attacker v_2 of v_1), which doesn't deny the fact f_4. Note that there
is no attack with source v_1, hence the first condition in the definition of defense
holds trivially.

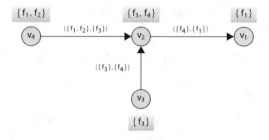

Fig. 4. $\{v_3\}$ defends v_1, but $\{v_4\}$ does not defend v_1.

The set of arguments defended by a set S is denoted by $\mathbb{D}(S)$.

An **admissible set** is any scf set $S \subseteq N$ with the property that for any
$a \in \alpha^-(S)$ there is $a^c \in \alpha^+(S)$ such that $t(a^c) = s(a)$ and $\delta(a^c) \cap \gamma(a) \neq \emptyset$. In
words, a scf set is admissible if the guard of any attack targeting a member of S
has at least one fact that is denied by an attack with source in S. The following
proposition gives some basic properties of admissible sets.

Proposition 2

(i) In an OF a set S of nodes is admissible if and only if $S \subseteq \mathbb{D}(S)$.

(ii) (Dung's Fundamental Lemma for OFs) Let $OF = (N, F, g, A, s, t, \gamma, \delta)$ be an
OF, $S \subseteq N$ an admissible set, and $u, v \in \mathbb{D}(S)$. Then
  1. $S' = S \cup \{u\}$ is an admissible set, and
  2. if $\{u, v\}$ is a scf set then $v \in \mathbb{D}(S')$.

(iii) A set S of arguments in an argumentation framework AF is admissible in
AF if and only if it is admissible in OF_{AF}.

Proof

(i) If $S \subseteq \mathbb{D}(S)$ then, by the first condition in the definition of the defense of a node by a set of nodes, it follows that S is a scf set. The second condition in the same definition shows that S is an admissible set. Conversely, if S is an admissible set and $v \in S$, since S is a scf set it follows that $\forall a \in \alpha^+(v)$ we have $\delta(a) \cap g(s') = \emptyset$, for every $s' \in S$. By the definition of an admissible set, it follows that any attack targeting v has at least one fact that is denied by an attack with source in S. Hence $v \in \mathbb{D}(S)$.

(ii) Since S is admissible, it is a scf set. From $u \in \mathbb{D}(S)$ it follows that $S' = S \cup \{u\}$ is a scf set. Any attack targeting a member of S' has at least one fact that is denied by an attack with source in S, since S is admissible and $u \in \mathbb{D}(S)$. Hence S' is an admissible set. To prove the second statement, observe that it is sufficient to prove that $S' \cup \{v\}$ is a scf set. This follows since $S \cup \{u\}$ and $S \cup \{v\}$ are scf sets and the hypothesis that $\{u, v\}$ is a scf set (note that this hypothesis is not necessary for AFs).

(iii) If S is an admissible set of arguments in AF then it is conflict-free in AF and therefore is a scf set in OF_{AF}, by Lemma 1 (ii). Furthermore in AF we have $S^- \subseteq S^+$ and, by Definition 5, any attack targeting a member of S has at least one fact that is denied by an attack with source in S. Hence, S is an admissible set in OF_{AF}. The converse implication can be proved in a similar way. □

By Proposition 2, Dung's admissibility based extensions for AFs can be extended to OFs as follows: in an OF a **complete extension** is an admissible set S satisfying $\mathbb{D}(S) = S$, a **preferred extension** is a maximal (w.r.t. set inclusion) complete extension, a **grounded extension** is a minimal (w.r.t. set inclusion) complete extension, and a **stable extension** is an admissible set S with the property that each node $v \notin S$ is the target of an attack in $\alpha^+(S)$.

To keep things simple, we will consider here a simple form of acceptance of a node in an OF, which corresponds to credulously preferred acceptance in AFs. A node v is **accepted** in an OF if there is an admissible set S in OF containing v; otherwise it is **rejected**. The node v is **inceptively accepted** if $\{v\}$ is an admissible set. Using the definition of an admissible set, Propositions 1 and 2, we can prove the following result, which is very useful from the algorithmic point of view.

Proposition 3. *A node v is accepted in an opposition framework OF if and only if there is a scf set S such that $v \in S$ and v_S is inceptively accepted in $OF|_S$.*

Since AFs are very special cases of OFs, using Proposition 2 (iii), we obtain the following result on the complexity of deciding if a node can be accepted.

Proposition 4. *Deciding if a node is accepted in an OF is an NP-complete problem.*

Proof. The hardness follows by adapting a known polynomial reduction from the satisfiability problem Dimopoulos and Torres [14] or Dunne and Bench-Capon [16] for AFs. Obviously, verifying if a guessed set contains the given node and is admissible can be done in polynomial time (in the "size" of the OF), so the decision problem is in NP.   □

3.4   A DPLL Type Acceptance Algorithm

In this subsection, we give a Davis-Putnam-Logemann-Loveland (DPLL) type (Davis *et al.* [13]) algorithm for deciding the acceptance of a node in an OF, that improves a backtrack search exhaustive algorithm by the eager use of a "unit rule" at each step in the construction of a scf set S as in Proposition 3.

Let $OF = (N, F, g, A, s, t, \gamma, \delta)$ be an OF and $v \in N$. If we denote by $\Delta(v) = \bigcup_{a \in \alpha^+(v)} \delta(a)$ the set of facts denied by the attacks out of v, then the set of *harmful attacks* to v is

$$\alpha^-_{harm}(v) = \{a \in \alpha^-(v) \mid \gamma(a) \cap \Delta(v) = \emptyset \text{ or } s(a) \notin \bigcup_{a' \in \alpha^+(v)} t(a')\}.$$

If $\alpha^-_{harm}(v) = \emptyset$ then v is inceptively accepted, otherwise we are looking for a node w to make a coalition with v in order to deny as many attacks as possible from $\alpha^-_{harm}(v)$. The coalition $\{v, w\}$ must be a scf set, therefore w must belong to the *backing* set of nodes associated to v:

$$bck(v) = \{w \in N \mid \{v, w\} \text{ is scf, } \Delta(w) \cap (\bigcup_{a \in \alpha^-_{harm}(v)} \gamma(a)) \neq \emptyset\}.$$

For each attack $a \in \alpha^-_{harm}(v)$, we denote by $nem(a)$ the set of *nemeses nodes* in $bck(v)$ which have at least one attack that denies at least one fact in the guard of a:

$$nem(a) = \{w \in bck(v) \mid \exists a' \in \alpha^+(w) \cap \alpha^-(s(a)) \text{ s.t. } \delta(a') \cap \gamma(a) \neq \emptyset\}.$$

If there is $a \in \alpha^-_{harm}(v)$ with $nem(a) = \emptyset$, then v can make no coalition in order to counterattack a, so v can not be accepted. If $nem(a)$ is a singleton, $nem(a) = \{w_0\}$, then v is *forced* to make a coalition with w_0 for denying at least one fact in $\gamma(a)$ (there is no scf set S such that $v \in S$, $w_0 \notin S$ and S counterattacks the attack a on v). This is the "unit rule" which will be followed every time when a candidate for coalition is searched.

If $|nem(a)| \geq 2$, then v must try to make coalitions with each node in $nem(a)$ to see if it can extend to a self-defending scf set.

The resulting algorithm can be described as follows:

Accept(OF, v)

Input : $OF = (N, F, g, A, s, t, \gamma, \delta)$ an OF, $v \in N$.
Output : YES if v is accepted, NO otherwise.

(ACCEPT)   **if** $\alpha^-_{harm}(v) = \emptyset$ **then return** YES.
(REJECT)   **if** $\exists a \in \alpha^-_{harm}(v)$ s.t. $nem(a) = \emptyset$ **then return** NO.
(UNIT RULE) **if** $\exists a \in \alpha^-_{harm}(v)$ s.t. $|nem(a)| = 1$ **then**
                       let $w \in N$ s.t. $nem(a) = \{w\}$;
              return Accept$(OF|_{\{v,w\}}, v_{\{v,w\}})$.
(BRANCH) $Candidates \leftarrow \bigcup_{a \in \alpha^-_{harm}(v)} nem(a)$
              while $Candidates \neq \emptyset$ **do**
                  $w \leftarrow$ a node in $Candidates$
                  if Accept$(OF|_{\{v,w\}}, v_{\{v,w\}})$
                     then return YES
                     else $Candidates \leftarrow Candidates - \{w\}$.

Proposition 5. Accept(OF, v) *returns YES if and only if there is an admissible set S in the* OF *OF such that $v \in S$.*

Proof. The proof follows from Proposition 3 and the discussion before the description of the algorithm.   □

To see the advantages of this algorithm over chronological backtracking schemes, we consider the OF associated to the AF in Fig. 5 (showing also its favorable position over similar algorithms for AFs, e.g. Nofal *et al.* [25]).

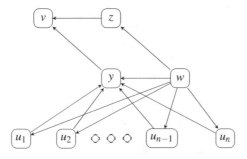

Fig. 5. No scf set $\{v\} \cup A$ is admissible, for $A \subseteq \{u_1, \ldots, u_n\}$.

Applying Accept(OF, v), the attack a with $s(a) = z$ and $t(a) = v$ is from $\alpha^-(v)$, and since $nem(a) = \{w\}$, the "unit rule" Accept$(OF|_{\{v,w\}}, v_{\{v,w\}})$ is called, which returns YES, that is v is accepted since $\{v, w\}$ is an admissible set. On the other hand, a chronological backtrack search could try any of the 2^n scf sets $\{v\} \cup A$, for $A \subseteq \{u_1, \ldots, u_n\}$, (which are not admissible sets) before the solution $\{v, w\}$ is discovered.

Note that the algorithm described can be easily modified to return the "explanation set" S in case of acceptance.

3.5   Logical Semantics

In this subsection, we characterize admissible sets in an OF by the models of a formula expressed in propositional logic (for AFs this is done by Besnard and Doutre [4]).

More precisely, if $OF = (N, F, g, A, s, t, \gamma, \delta)$ is an OF, then we consider a propositional variable x_v for each $v \in N$. We want to construct a formula Φ over variables $\{x_v | v \in N\}$ such that $S \subseteq N$ is an admissible set in OF if and only if there is a model m of Φ with $S = \{v \in N \,|\, m(x_v) = true\}$.

To characterize the scf sets, let us consider the formula $\text{AtMostOne}(x, y) = \neg(x \wedge y)$. Two nodes v and w belong to the same scf set if and only if there are no facts granted by one and denied by the other: $g(v) \cap \Delta(w) = \emptyset$ and $g(w) \cap \Delta(v) = \emptyset$. Therefore the formula

$$\Phi_1 = \bigwedge_{\substack{v, w \in N, v \neq w \\ g(v) \cap \Delta(w) \neq \emptyset}} \text{AtMostOne}(x_v, x_w)$$

has the property that if m is a model of Φ_1, then $S = \{v \in V | m(x_v) = true\}$ is a scf set, and if S is a scf set then taking $m(x_v) := true$ for $v \in S$ and $m(x_v) := false$ for $v \in N - S$, we obtain a model of Φ_1.

To characterize the admissible sets, let us consider

$$\Phi_2 = \bigwedge_{v \in V} (x_v \rightarrow \bigwedge_{a \in \alpha^-(v)} (\bigvee_{\substack{u: \exists a' \in \alpha^+(u) \text{ s.t.} \\ t(a')=s(a) \,\&\, \delta(a') \cap \gamma(a) \neq \emptyset}} x_u)).$$

If m is a model of Φ_2 and $S = \{v \in V | m(x_v) = true\}$, then each vertex v in S is either not attacked ($\alpha^-(v) = \emptyset$ and $\bigwedge_{a \in \alpha^-(v)} (\ldots)$ is $true$), or for each attack a on v at least one fact in the guard of a is denied by an attack from a vertex u in S (that is, $m(x_u) = true$ and $\exists a' \in \alpha^+(u)$ such that $t(a') = s(a)$ and $\delta(a') \cap \gamma(a) \neq \emptyset$). It follows that if m is also a model for Φ_1 then S is a scf set counterattacking each attack against it, that is S is an admissible set. Conversely, if S is an admissible set then it is easy to see that taking $m(x_v) := true$ for $v \in S$ and $m(x_v) := false$ for $v \in N - S$, we obtain a model of $\Phi_1 \wedge \Phi_2$. Hence we have the following proposition.

Proposition 6. *If m is a model of $\Phi = \Phi_1 \wedge \Phi_2$ then $S = \{v \in N | m(x_v) = true\}$ is an admissible set in OF. Conversely, if S is an admissible set in OF then m, given by $m(x_v) := true$ for $v \in S$ and $m(x_v) := false$ for $v \in N - S$, is a model of Φ.*

Proof. Let $S = \{v \in N | m(x_v) = true\}$, for some model m of $\Phi = \Phi_1 \wedge \Phi_2$. If S is not a scf set, then there are $v, w \in S$ such that $\Delta(w) \cap g(v) \neq \emptyset$. Hence $m(x_v) = m(x_w) = true$ and m does not satisfy AtMostOne(x_v, x_w). Since $\Delta(w) \cap g(v) \neq \emptyset$, it follows that AtMostOne(x_v, x_w) occurs in Φ_1. Therefore m does not satisfy Φ_1 and hence m is not a model of Φ, a contradiction. To prove that S is an admissible set, suppose that there is an attack $a \in \alpha^-(S)$ which is not counterattacked by S. If $t(a) = v$ and $s(a) = w$ then $m(x_v) = true$ and $m(x_w) = false$, since S is a scf set. Since a is not counterattacked by S, it follows that for each $u \in N$ such that there is $a' \in \alpha^+(u)$ with $t(a') = w$ and $\delta(a') \cap \gamma(a) \neq \emptyset$, we have $u \notin S$, that is, $m(x_u) = false$. We have obtained that the conjunction in Φ_2 corresponding to x_v evaluates to false under m and hence m is not a model of Φ_2, a contradiction.

Conversely, let S be an admissible set in OF, and m the assignment given by $m(x_v) = true$ if and only if $v \in S$. Then, m is a model of Φ_1 since S is a scf set. Also, m is a model of Φ_2 since for $v \notin S$ the implication $x_v \rightarrow \ldots$ evaluates to true and for $v \in S$ the same implication evaluates to true since S counterattacks any attack on v. $\qquad\square$

Example. For the OF in Fig. 4 the above Φ_1, Φ_2 are:

Φ_1 = AtMostOne(x_{v_1}, x_{v_2}) $\wedge$ AtMostOne(x_{v_2}, x_{v_3}) $\wedge$ AtMostOne(x_{v_2}, x_{v_4}) $\wedge$ AtMostOne(x_{v_3}, x_{v_4}).

Let us write $\Phi_2 = \Phi_{21} \bigwedge \Phi_{22} \bigwedge \Phi_{23} \bigwedge \Phi_{24}$, where $\Phi_{2i} = (x_{v_i} \rightarrow \ldots)$, for $i \in \{1, 2, 3, 4\}$, are the following implications: $\Phi_{21} = x_{v_1} \rightarrow x_{v_3}$, $\Phi_{22} = x_{v_2} \rightarrow false = \neg x_{v_2}$, $\Phi_{23} = x_{v_3} \rightarrow true$, $\Phi_{24} = x_{v_4} \rightarrow true$. Hence, $\Phi_2 = (x_{v_1} \rightarrow x_{v_3}) \wedge \neg x_{v_2}$. It is not difficult to see that the only models of $\Phi_1 \wedge \Phi_2$ are those obtained by setting x_v to true, for $v \in S$, where S is an admissible set of the OF: $\emptyset, \{v_3\}, \{v_4\}, \{v_1, v_3\}$.

The above proposition shows also that it is not possible to simulate an OF with the set of facts F, by considering an argumentation framework $AF = (A, E)$ with $A \subseteq 2^F$. Indeed, as $\Phi = \Phi_1 \wedge \Phi_2$ shows, we have to consider additional constraints to bind the subsets of F (nodes in AF) corresponding to the guards of the attacks issuing from each node in OF. In structured (logical) argumentation this is done by considering an argument together with all its sub-arguments, but this is not practical for most of OFs.

4   Discussion

In this paper we introduced a new generalization of Dung's argumentation framework which is conceptually different from other generalized abstract argumentation frameworks, see Brewka *et al.* [7], or Modgil [21]. More precisely, for the first time, it formally exploits the link that exists between "attacks" and "node's positions" capturing some high-level intuition, not addressed by other proposals. The main idea is to keep the abstract level of the original structures, its simplicity and intuitive approach but, at the same time, to increase their modeling capabilities. The "nodes" of our OFs have a minimal **content** expressed as finite non-empty sets of facts (the node's position), which are used to relate the "attacks" between two nodes to their positions. This gives a new perspective on the "consistent sets of nodes" which goes beyond the usual conflict-freeness (which is responsible for some rationality violations observed in the instantiation-based argumentation, Caminada and Amgoud [11], Amgoud [1]). More precisely, in our strong conflict-free sets we forbid not only the attacks between their members but also require that the outside attacks are not in contradiction with their members positions. Unfortunately, this does not prevent that (when our OFs are used as instantiation destination of logical structured argumentation frameworks) nodes with mutually consistent positions to be globally contradictory. This happens because the attack relation is binary.

We introduced a simple recursive definition of acceptance: a node (the position expressed by a node) is accepted in an OF if either it can counterattack all attacks targeting it or there is another "compatible" node such that in the OF obtained by "contracting" these two nodes in a single "supernode" this supernode is accepted. Note that this type of acceptance is different from that considered in *abstract dialectical frameworks* Brewka and Woltran [8], or *GRaph-based Argument Processing with Patterns of Acceptance* Brewka and Woltran [9], where the acceptance of a node is a function defined on the set of its parents (that is the nodes having a directed edge to it). Also our approach is conceptually different from proof procedures, see Modgil and Caminada [22]. Technically, using "guarded attacks" and a suitable graph operation of contraction, we proved that this type of acceptance is compatible in the particular case of AFs with Dung's admissibility-based semantics, showing that it is actually a proper generalization of the Dung semantics. Hence, if we use OFs instead of AFs as a target system to evaluate arguments in structured argumentation frameworks, then we obtain the same results if the OF_{AF} (see Definition 5) is considered for reusability reasons. However, a more fine-grained generation of the target OF – by explicitly devising rules of attacks (via their guards), which are non-uniform (depend on the source/target node) – may be used to obtain improved modeling. We note also that in our guarded attack calculus, the attacks on the attacks Villata *et al.* [28]) are implicitly considered. The use of the set of attacks ($\alpha^-(v)$ in OFs) instead of the set of parents (v^- in AFs or ADFs) in the study of the acceptability of a node v simplifies the description of acceptability algorithms. A novel DPLL type backtracking acceptance algorithm is described. Some improvements can be further obtained by using *abstract* DPLL *with learning*, Nieuwenhuis *et al.* [24] (see also Brochenin *et al.* [10]). The idea is to add dummy facts to nodes in order to learn that some (set of) nodes are not useful in finding a successful coalition for the acceptance of a given node v.

The characterization of admissible sets in an OF by the models of a formula expressed in propositional logic shows a lazy way to map an OF to an AF (via naive transformations of this formula) in a manner preserving semantic properties of the first one. The study of the efficiency of such a mapping (similar to that initiated by Brewka *et al.* [8] for ADFs) is an interesting future research direction.

There are a number of ways to extend this work. One future direction consists of extending the *guarded attack calculus* by replacing the simple attack labels, $(\gamma(a), \delta(a))$, with more involved logical constraints. Also, moving to temporal (modal) logic for the interpretation of *harmful* attacks represents an interesting future extension. Another compelling future direction opened by the multidigraph approach of this paper is to use some other graph operations together with a minimal (logical or combinatorial) structure on the sets $g(v)$ in order to improve the modeling capabilities of OFs. For example, adding minimal (logical or combinatorial) structure on the sets $g(v)$ of facts granted by a node v and suitable graph operations of contraction or expansion, it is possible to consider hierarchical structures in which the nodes are OFs (or AFs) and the guarded attacks as explicated discordances between the outputs of their source and target (sub)structures. AFs have been generalized (see, e.g., Bench-Capon [3], Bourguet *et al.* [5], Dunne *et al.* [17]) by adding weights to arguments or attacks in order to increase their modeling capacity. We can consider a similar extension for OFs, by providing the facts and attacks with weights, called *vitality* for facts, and *strength* for attacks. The facts effectively denied by an attack a are those facts in $\delta(a)$ having a vitality smaller than the strength of the attack a. In this way, an weighted OF could be used to represent families of OFs. Finally, we intend to study how the set of accepted nodes in a given OF changes, when the sets of granted facts of some nodes are restricted or expanded, modeling the usual "what if ...?" questions in (political) practice, aiming to use our OFs in argumentative decision-making systems (see, e.g., Baroni *et al.* [2]).

References

1. Amgoud, L.: Postulates for logic-based argumentation systems. Int. J. Approximate Reasoning **55**, 2028–2048 (2014)
2. Baroni, P., Romano, M., Toni, F., Aurisicchio, M., Bertanza, G.: Automatic evaluation of design alternatives with quantitative argumentation. Argum. Comput. **6**, 24–49 (2015)
3. Bench-Capon, T.: Persuasion in practical argument using value-based argumentation frameworks. J. Logic Comput. **13**, 429–448 (2003)
4. Besnard, P., Doutre, S.: Checking the acceptability of a set of arguments. In: Proceedings of NMR, pp. 59–64 (2004)
5. Bourguet, J.-R., Amgoud, L., Thomopoulos, R.: Towards a unified model of preference-based argumentation. In: Link, S., Prade, H. (eds.) FoIKS 2010. LNCS, vol. 5956, pp. 326–344. Springer, Heidelberg (2010). doi:10.1007/978-3-642-11829-6_21
6. Brewka, G.: Nonmonotonic tools for argumentation. In: Janhunen, T., Niemelä, I. (eds.) JELIA 2010. LNCS (LNAI), vol. 6341, pp. 1–6. Springer, Heidelberg (2010). doi:10.1007/978-3-642-15675-5_1
7. Brewka, G., Polberg, S., Woltran, S.: Generalizations of dung frameworks and their role in formal argumentation. IEEE Intell. Syst. **29**, 30 (2014)
8. Brewka, G., Woltran, S.: Abstract dialectical frameworks. In: Proceedings of KR 2010, pp. 102–111 (2010)
9. Brewka, G., Woltran, S.: GRAPPA: a semantic framework for graph-based argument processing. In: Proceedings of ECAI 2014, pp. 153–158 (2014)
10. Brochenin, R., Linsbichler, B., Wallner, J.P., Woltran, S.: Abstract solvers for dung's argumentation frameworks. In: Proceedings of TAFA (2015)

11. Caminada, M., Amgoud, L.: On the evaluation of argumentation formalisms. Artif. Intell. **171**, 286–310 (2007)
12. Coste-Marquis, S., Devred, C., Marquis, P.: Symmetric argumentation frameworks. In: Godo, L. (ed.) ECSQARU 2005. LNCS (LNAI), vol. 3571, pp. 317–328. Springer, Heidelberg (2005). doi:10.1007/11518655_28
13. Davis, M., Logemann, G., Loveland, D.V.: A machine program for theorem-proving. Commun. ACM **5**, 394–397 (1962)
14. Dimopoulos, Y., Torres, A.: Graph theoretical structures in logic programs and default theories. Theor. Comput. Sci. **170**, 209–244 (1996)
15. Dung, P.M.: On the acceptability of arguments and its fundamental role in non-monotonic reasoning, logic programming and n-person games. Artif. Intell. **77**, 321–357 (1995)
16. Dunne, P., Bench-Capon, T.: Coherence in finite argument systems. Artif. Intell. **141**, 187–203 (2002)
17. Dunne, P.E., Hunter, A., McBurney, P., Parsons, S., Wooldridge, M.: Weighted argument systems: basic definitions, algorithms, and complexity results. Artif. Intell. **175**, 457–486 (2011)
18. Finegan-Dollak, C., Radev, D.R.: Sentence simplification, compression, and disaggregation for summarization of sophisticated documents. J. Assoc. Inf. Sci. Technol. **67**, 2437 (2015)
19. Hunter, A., Gorogiannis, N.: Instantiating abstract argumentation with classical logic arguments: postulates and properties. Artif. Intell. **175**, 1479–1497 (2011)
20. Leite, J., Martins, J.: Social abstract argumentation. In: Proceedings of IJCAI (2011)
21. Modgil, S.: Revisiting abstract argumentation frameworks. In: Black, E., Modgil, S., Oren, N. (eds.) TAFA 2013. LNCS (LNAI), vol. 8306, pp. 1–15. Springer, Heidelberg (2014). doi:10.1007/978-3-642-54373-9_1
22. Modgil, S., Caminada, M.: Proof theories and algorithms for abstract argumentation frameworks. In: Simari, G., Rahwan, I. (eds.) Argumentation in Artificial Intelligence, pp. 105–129. Springer, Heidelberg (2009). doi:10.1007/978-0-387-98197-0_6
23. Nielson, S., Parsons, S.: A generalization of dung's abstract framework for argumentation: arguing with sets of attacking arguments. In: Proceedings of ArgMAS 2006, pp. 54–73 (2006)
24. Nieuwenhuis, R., Oliveras, A., Tinelli, C.: Solving SAT and SAT modulo theories: from an abstract Davis-Putnam-Logemann-Loveland procedure to DPLL(T). J. ACM **53**, 937–977 (2006)
25. Nofal, S., Atkinson, K., Dunne, P.: Algorithms for decision problems in argument systems under preferred semantics. Artif. Intell. **207**, 23–51 (2014)
26. Prakken, H.: An abstract framework for argumentation with structured arguments. Argum. Comput. **1**, 93–124 (2010)
27. Rahwan, I., Zablith, F., Reed, C.: Laying the foundations for a world wide argument web. Artif. Intell. **171**, 897–921 (2007)
28. Villata, S., Boella, G., van der Torre, L.: Attack semantics for abstract argumentation. In: Proceedings of IJCAI 2011, pp. 406–413 (2011)
29. Wang, B., Luo, G.: Extend argumentation frameworks based on degree of attack. In: Proceedings of the 9th IEEE International Conference on Cognitive Informatics, ICCI 2010, pp. 771–776 (2010)

Prompt Interval Temporal Logic

Dario Della Monica[1]([✉]), Angelo Montanari[2], Aniello Murano[1],
and Pietro Sala[3]

[1] Università degli Studi di Napoli "Federico II", Napoli, Italy
dario.dellamonica@unina.it, murano@na.infn.it
[2] University of Udine, Udine, Italy
angelo.montanari@uniud.it
[3] University of Verona, Verona, Italy
pietro.sala@univr.it

Abstract. Interval temporal logics are expressive formalisms for temporal representation and reasoning, which use time intervals as primitive temporal entities. They have been extensively studied for the past two decades and successfully applied in AI and computer science. Unfortunately, they lack the ability of expressing promptness conditions, as it happens with the commonly-used temporal logics, e.g., LTL: whenever we deal with a liveness request, such as "something good eventually happens", there is no way to impose a bound on the delay with which it is fulfilled. In the last years, such an issue has been addressed in automata theory, game theory, and temporal logic. In this paper, we approach it in the interval temporal logic setting. First, we introduce PROMPT-PNL, a prompt extension of the well-studied interval temporal logic PNL, and we prove the undecidability of its satisfiability problem; then, we show how to recover decidability (NEXPTIME-completeness) by imposing a natural syntactic restriction on it.

1 Introduction

Interval temporal logics provide a powerful framework suitable for reasoning about time. Unlike classic temporal logics, such as Linear Temporal Logic (LTL) [21] and the like, they use time intervals, instead of time points, as primitive temporal entities. Such a distinctive feature turns out to be very useful in various Computer Science and AI application domains, ranging from hardware and real-time system verification to natural language processing, from constraint satisfaction to planning [1,2,10,20,22,23]. As concrete applications, we mention TERENCE [14], an adaptive learning system for poor comprehenders and their educators (based on *Allen's interval algebra* IA [1]), and RISMA [17], an algorithm to analyze behavior and performance of real-time data systems (based on Halpern and Shoham's *modal logic of Allen's relations* HS [15]).

A fundamental class of properties that can be expressed in (both interval- and point-based) temporal logics is that of *liveness* properties, which allow one to state that something "good" will eventually happen. However, a limitation that is common to most temporal logics is the lack of support for *promptness*: it is

© Springer International Publishing AG 2016
L. Michael and A. Kakas (Eds.): JELIA 2016, LNAI 10021, pp. 207–222, 2016.
DOI: 10.1007/978-3-319-48758-8_14

not possible to bound the delay with which a liveness request is fulfilled, despite the fact that this is desirable for many practical applications (see [16] for a convincing argument). To overcome such a shortcoming, a whole body of work has been recently devoted to the study of promptness. In [4,16], the authors extend LTL with the ability of bounding the delay with which a temporal request is satisfied. In [3], the use of prompt accepting conditions in the context of ω-regular automata is explored by introducing *prompt-Büchi automata*, whose accepting condition imposes the existence of a bound on the number of non-accepting states in between two consecutive occurrences of accepting ones. Prompt extensions of LTL have also been investigated outside the realm of closed systems. Two-player turn-based games with perfect information have been explored in the prompt LTL setting in [24]. In [9], the authors lift the prompt semantics to ω-regular games, under the parity winning condition, by introducing *finitary parity* games. They make use of the concept of *distance* between positions in a play that refers to the number of edges traversed in the game arena; the classical parity winning condition is then reformulated to take into consideration only those states occurring with a bounded distance. Such an idea has been generalised to deal with more involved prompt parity conditions [13,19]. In the field of formal languages, promptness comes into play in [6], where ωB-regular languages and their automata counterpart, known as ωB-automata, are studied. Intuitively, ωB-regular languages extend ω-regular ones with the ability of bounding the distance between occurrences of sub-expressions in consecutive ω-iterations, within each word of the language. Finally, an extension of alternating-time epistemic temporal logic with prompt-eventuality has been recently investigated in [5].

In this paper, we show that interval temporal logics can be successfully provided with a support for prompt-liveness specifications by lifting the work done in [4,16] to the interval-based setting.

In [4], the language of LTL is enriched with *parameterized* versions of temporal modalities F (*eventually*) and U (*until*), as well as of the dual modalities G (*globally*) and R (*release*). The resulting logic, called PLTL, features the following parameterized modalities: $F_{\leq x}$, $F_{>y}$, $G_{\leq y}$, $G_{>x}$, $U_{\leq x}$, $U_{>y}$, $R_{\leq y}$, and $R_{>x}$, where $x \in X$, $y \in Y$, and X and Y are two disjoint sets of *bounding variables*. Intuitively, a formula $F_{\leq x}\phi$ is true if ϕ is satisfied within x time units, according to the valuation of x (the other parameterized modalities have an analogous interpretation). Thus, PLTL models are LTL models, i.e., words over the powerset of the set of atomic propositions, enriched with a valuation for the bounding variables in $X \cup Y$. The satisfiability problem for PLTL is PSPACE-complete, as for LTL. The assumption that X and Y are disjoint is crucial in retaining decidability. In [16], the authors introduce the logic PROMPT-LTL, which restricts PLTL in three ways: (*i*) a parameterized version is introduced for the modality F only (parameterized versions of modalities G, U, and R are not included); (*ii*) only upper bounds appear in parameterized modalities, i.e., no subscript of the form $_{>x}$ occurs; (*iii*) there is only one bounding variable. The restriction imposed by PROMPT-LTL is less strong than it looks like: as shown in [4], operator $F_{\leq x}$, along with the classic LTL constructs, is enough to define operators $G_{>x}$,

$U_{\leq x}$, $R_{>x}$ (i.e., all the operators involving in their subscript variables in X). As PROMPT-LTL enriches LTL with the ability of limiting the amount of time a fulfillment of an existential request (corresponding to a liveness property) can be delayed, it can be thought of as an extension of LTL with *prompt liveness*. In [16], it is shown that reasoning about PROMPT-LTL is not harder than reasoning about LTL, with respect to a series of basic problems, including satisfiability (PSPACE-complete).

In the present paper, we show how to extend the logic PNL of temporal neighborhood (a well-known fragment of HS whose satisfiability problem is NEXPTIME-complete [8]), with the ability of expressing prompt-liveness properties. Following the approach of [16], we introduce 'prompt' versions (i.e., upper bounds only) of all modalities of PNL. The resulting modality templates are as follows: the *prompt-right-adjacency* $\langle A_x \rangle$ and the *prompt-left-adjacency* $\langle \overline{A}_x \rangle$, capturing prompt-liveness in the future and in the past, respectively, as well as the dual modalities $[A_x]$ and $[\overline{A}_x]$. Intuitively, a modality $\langle A_x \rangle$ (for some upper bound x) forces the existence of an event starting exactly when the current one terminates and ending within an amount of time bounded above by the value of x. Similarly, $\langle \overline{A}_x \rangle$ forces the existence of an event ending exactly when the current one begins and starting at most x time units before the beginning of the current one. Modalities $[A_x]$ and $[\overline{A}_x]$ express dual properties in the standard way, namely, $[A_x]\psi$ stands for $\neg\langle A_x \rangle\neg\psi$ and $[\overline{A}_x]\psi$ stands for $\neg\langle \overline{A}_x \rangle\neg\psi$. We name the proposed logic PROMPT-PNL (Sect. 2).

We first prove that the future fragment of PROMPT-PNL (PROMPT-RPNL), involving the future modalities $\langle A \rangle$, $[A]$, $\langle A_x \rangle$, and $[A_x]$ only, is expressive enough to encode the *finite colouring problem*, known to be undecidable [18]. Undecidability of PROMPT-RPNL (and PROMPT-PNL) immediately follows (Sect. 3). Notably, unlike LTL, PNL is strictly more expressive than its future fragment RPNL (see [12]); such a separation result holds between PROMPT-PNL and PROMPT-RPNL as well. Our undecidability result hinges on the unrestricted use of bounding variables within prompt modalities, which allows one to somehow establish tight bounds for the length of intervals. We show that decidability can be recovered by using two disjoint sets of bounding variables, one for existential modalities and the other for universal ones. Formulas of the resulting logic, which we name PROMPT$\overset{d}{-}$PNL, enjoy some useful monotonicity property, i.e., the truth of a formula $\langle A_x \rangle\psi$ under a certain interpretation $\sigma(x)$ of the bounding variable x implies its truth under every interpretation σ', with $\sigma'(x) \geq \sigma(x)$. This allows us to prove a small (pseudo-)model property for PROMPT$\overset{d}{-}$PNL, from which we conclude that the satisfiability problem for PROMPT$\overset{d}{-}$PNL is NEXPTIME-complete (Sect. 4). Due to lack of space, most of the proofs are omitted (see [11] for full proofs).

2   The Logic PROMPT-PNL

Let us start with some basic notions of interval-based temporal logics. A *linear order* $\mathbb{D}$ is a pair $\langle D, < \rangle$, where D is a set, called *domain*, whose elements are referred to as *points*, and $<$ is a strict total order over D. A (strongly) *discrete* linear order is a linear order such that there are only finitely many points in between any two points. In the rest of the paper, we tacitly assume every domain to be discrete. For the sake of simplicity, we identify the domain of a linear order with the linear order itself, e.g., we write "$d \in \mathbb{D}$" instead of "$d \in D$". Let $d \in \mathbb{D}$. The *successors* (resp., *predecessors*) of d in $\mathbb{D}$ are the points $d' \in \mathbb{D}$ such that $d < d'$ (resp., $d' < d$); the *immediate successor* (resp., *immediate predecessor*) of d in $\mathbb{D}$, denoted by $\text{succ}_{\mathbb{D}}(d)$ (resp., $\text{pred}_{\mathbb{D}}(d)$), is (if any) the point $d' \in \mathbb{D}$ such that d' is a successor (resp., predecessor) of d in $\mathbb{D}$ and no point $d'' \in \mathbb{D}$ exists with $d < d'' < d'$ (resp., $d' < d'' < d$). Note that $\text{succ}_{\mathbb{D}}(d)$ (resp., $\text{pred}_{\mathbb{D}}(d)$) is defined unless d is the greatest (resp., least) element in $\mathbb{D}$. Given a linear order $\mathbb{D}$ and two points $a, b \in \mathbb{D}$, with $a < b$, we denote by $[a, b]$ an *interval* (over $\mathbb{D}$). The set of intervals over a linear order $\mathbb{D}$ is denoted by $\mathbb{I}(\mathbb{D})$. An *interval structure* (over a countable set $\mathcal{AP}$ of *atomic propositions*) is a pair $\langle \mathbb{D}, V \rangle$, where $\mathbb{D}$ is a linear order and $V : \mathbb{I}(\mathbb{D}) \to 2^{\mathcal{AP}}$ is a *valuation function*, which assigns to each interval over $\mathbb{D}$ the set of atomic proposition that are true over it. Given a linear order $\mathbb{D}$ and $a, b \in \mathbb{D}$, we denote by $\mathbb{D}^{\geq a}$ (resp., $\mathbb{D}^{>a}$, $\mathbb{D}^{\leq a}$, $\mathbb{D}^{<a}$, $\mathbb{D}^{[a,b]}$, $\mathbb{D}^{]a,b[}$, $\mathbb{D}^{[a,b[}$, $\mathbb{D}^{]a,b]}$) the set of elements $d \in \mathbb{D}$ such that $d \geq a$ (resp., $d > a$, $d \leq a$, $d < a$, $a \leq d \leq b$, $a < d < b$, $a \leq d < b$, $a < d \leq b$). For instance, we denote by $\mathbb{R}^{>0}$ the set of positive reals.

Syntax and Semantics. Let $\mathcal{AP}$ (*atomic propositions*) and X (*bounding variables*) be two countable sets. Formulas of PROMPT-PNL in negation normal form are defined as follows:

$$\varphi \ ::= \ p \ \mid \ \varphi \wedge \varphi \ \mid \ \langle A \rangle \varphi \ \mid \ \langle \overline{A} \rangle \varphi \ \mid \ \langle A_x \rangle \varphi \ \mid \ \langle \overline{A}_x \rangle \varphi$$
$$\mid \ \neg p \ \mid \ \varphi \vee \varphi \ \mid \ [A]\varphi \ \mid \ [\overline{A}]\varphi \ \mid \ [A_x]\varphi \ \mid \ [\overline{A}_x]\varphi$$

where $p \in \mathcal{AP}$ and $x \in X$. We also use other standard Boolean connectives, e.g., $\to$, and logical constants $\top$ and $\bot$, which are defined in the usual way. We denote by PROMPT-RPNL the PROMPT-PNL fragment obtained by excluding past modalities $\langle \overline{A} \rangle$, $[\overline{A}]$, $\langle \overline{A}_x \rangle$, and $[\overline{A}_x]$, and we write PROMPT-(R)PNL when we refer to both formalisms. In the following, we will take the liberty of writing PROMPT-(R)PNL formulas not in negation normal form when useful.

PROMPT-(R)PNL models are interval structures enriched with a valuation function for bounding variables in X and a metric over the underlying domain. Formally, a model for PROMPT-(R)PNL (over $\mathcal{AP}$ and X) is a quadruple $\langle \mathbb{D}, V, \sigma, \delta \rangle$, where $\langle \mathbb{D}, V \rangle$ is an interval structure ($\mathbb{D}$ is the *domain* of the model), $\sigma : X \to \mathbb{R}^{>0}$ is a *valuation function for bounding variables*, and $\delta : \mathbb{D} \times \mathbb{D} \to \mathbb{R}^{>0}$ is a *metric* over $\mathbb{D}$ (i.e., the pair $(\mathbb{D}, \delta)$ is a metric space) satisfying the additional properties: for every $d, d', d'' \in \mathbb{D}$ (*i*) if $d < d' < d''$, then $\delta(d, d'') = \delta(d, d') + \delta(d', d'')$, (*ii*) if d has infinitely many successors in $\mathbb{D}$, then the set $\{\delta(d, \bar{d}) \mid d < \bar{d}\}$ is not bounded above, and (*iii*) if d has infinitely many predecessors in $\mathbb{D}$, then the set $\{\delta(\bar{d}, d) \mid \bar{d} < d\}$ is not bounded above. For a model $M = \langle \mathbb{D}, V, \sigma, \delta \rangle$, we let $\mathbb{D}_M = \mathbb{D}$, $V_M = V$, $\sigma_M = \sigma$, and $\delta_M = \delta$, that is, $\mathbb{D}_M$, V_M, σ_M, and δ_M denote the four components of M. A PROMPT-(R)PNL model is finite (resp., infinite) if so is its domain.

The *truth value* of a `PROMPT-PNL` formula over a model and an interval in it is inductively defined as follows:

- $M, [a, b] \models p$ if and only if $p \in V_M([a, b])$, for every $p \in \mathcal{AP}$;
- $M, [a, b] \models \neg p$ if and only if $p \notin V_M([a, b])$, for every $p \in \mathcal{AP}$;
- $M, [a, b] \models \varphi_1 \wedge \varphi_2$ if and only if $M, [a, b] \models \varphi_1$ and $M, [a, b] \models \varphi_2$;
- $M, [a, b] \models \varphi_1 \vee \varphi_2$ if and only if $M, [a, b] \models \varphi_1$ or $M, [a, b] \models \varphi_2$;
- $M, [a, b] \models \langle A \rangle \varphi$ if and only if there is $c \in \mathbb{D}_M^{>b}$ such that $M, [b, c] \models \varphi$;
- $M, [a, b] \models [A] \varphi$ if and only if for all $c \in \mathbb{D}_M^{>b}$ it holds $M, [b, c] \models \varphi$;
- $M, [a, b] \models \langle \overline{A} \rangle \varphi$ if and only if there is $c \in \mathbb{D}_M^{<a}$ such that $M, [c, a] \models \varphi$;
- $M, [a, b] \models [\overline{A}] \varphi$ if and only if for all $c \in \mathbb{D}_M^{<a}$ it holds $M, [c, a] \models \varphi$;
- $M, [a, b] \models \langle A_x \rangle \varphi$ if and only if there is $c \in \mathbb{D}_M^{>b}$, with $\delta_M(b, c) \leq \sigma_M(x)$, such that $M, [b, c] \models \varphi$, for every $x \in X$;
- $M, [a, b] \models [A_x] \varphi$ if and only if for all $c \in \mathbb{D}_M^{>b}$, with $\delta_M(b, c) \leq \sigma_M(x)$, it holds $M, [b, c] \models \varphi$, for every $x \in X$;
- $M, [a, b] \models \langle \overline{A}_x \rangle \varphi$ if and only if there is $c \in \mathbb{D}_M^{<a}$, with $\delta_M(c, a) \leq \sigma_M(x)$, such that $M, [c, a] \models \varphi$, for every $x \in X$;
- $M, [a, b] \models [\overline{A}_x] \varphi$ if and only if for all $c \in \mathbb{D}_M^{<a}$, with $\delta_M(c, a) \leq \sigma_M(x)$, it holds $M, [c, a] \models \varphi$, for every $x \in X$.

The truth value of a `PROMPT-RPNL` formula is obtained, as expected, by restricting to the relevant clauses only.

In `PNL`, modalities $\langle L \rangle$ and $\langle \overline{L} \rangle$, corresponding to Allen's relations *later* and *before*, are definable as: $\langle L \rangle \varphi \equiv \langle A \rangle \langle A \rangle \varphi$ and $\langle \overline{L} \rangle \varphi \equiv \langle \overline{A} \rangle \langle \overline{A} \rangle \varphi$. Additionally, in `PROMPT-PNL` it is possible to define the 'prompt' counterparts of modalities $\langle L \rangle$ and $\langle \overline{L} \rangle$ as: $\langle L_x \rangle \varphi \equiv \langle A_x \rangle \langle A_x \rangle \varphi$ and $\langle \overline{L}_x \rangle \varphi \equiv \langle \overline{A}_x \rangle \langle \overline{A}_x \rangle \varphi$. The resulting semantic interpretation for $\langle L_x \rangle$ and $\langle \overline{L}_x \rangle$ is as follows:

- $M, [a, b] \models \langle L_x \rangle \varphi$ if and only if there is $[c, d] \in \mathbb{I}(\mathbb{D}_M)$ such that $b < c$, $\delta_M(b, c) \leq \sigma_M(x)$, $\delta_M(c, d) \leq \sigma_M(x)$, and $M, [c, d] \models \varphi$;
- $M, [a, b] \models \langle \overline{L}_x \rangle \varphi$ if and only if there is $[c, d] \in \mathbb{I}(\mathbb{D}_M)$ such that $d < a$, $\delta_M(d, a) \leq \sigma_M(x)$, $\delta_M(c, d) \leq \sigma_M(x)$, and $M, [c, d] \models \varphi$.

Intuitively, a modality $\langle L_x \rangle$, for some bounding variable x, requires the existence of an event starting and ending within a bounded amount of time after the termination of the current one (modalities $\langle \overline{L}_x \rangle$ impose an analogous constraint in the past). Obviously, only $\langle L_x \rangle$ is definable in `PROMPT-RPNL` ($\langle \overline{L}_x \rangle$ is not).

The *globally-in-the-future* modality $[G]$ is defined as $[G]\psi \equiv \psi \wedge [A]\psi \wedge [A][A]\psi$, for every `PROMPT-PNL` formula ψ; analogously the *prompt-globally-in-the-future* modality $[G_x]$ is defined as $[G_x]\psi \equiv \psi \wedge [A_x]\psi \wedge [A][A_x]\psi$, for every `PROMPT-PNL` formula ψ and $x \in X$. Given a `PROMPT-(R)PNL` model M, modalities $[G]$ and $[G_x]$ induce the sets $\mathcal{G}_M^{[a,b]} = \{[a, b]\} \cup \{[c, d] \in \mathbb{I}(\mathbb{D}_M) \mid b \leq c\}$ and $\mathcal{G}_M^{[a,b],x} = \{[a, b]\} \cup \{[c, d] \in \mathbb{I}(\mathbb{D}_M) \mid b \leq c$ and $\delta_M(c, d) \leq \sigma_M(x)\}$. We omit the subscript M when it is clear from the context. For every `PROMPT-(R)PNL` model M, $[a, b] \in \mathbb{I}(\mathbb{D}_M)$, and `PROMPT-PNL` formula ψ, it holds that $M, [a, b] \models [G]\psi$ if and only if $M, [c, d] \models \psi$ for every $[c, d] \in \mathcal{G}^{[a,b]}$ and $M, [a, b] \models [G_x]\psi$ if and only if $M, [c, d] \models \psi$ for every $[c, d] \in \mathcal{G}^{[a,b],x}$. Finally, for a model M and $[a, b] \in \mathbb{I}(\mathbb{D}_M)$, we define the *length* of $[a, b]$ (in M) as the value $\delta_M(a, b)$ and, for every $p \in \mathcal{AP}$, if $M, [a, b] \models p$, then we say that $[a, b]$ is a p-interval (in M).

The Satisfiability Problem. A PROMPT-(R)PNL formula φ is *satisfiable* if, and only if, there exist a PROMPT-(R)PNL model M and an interval $[x, y]$ in M such that $M, [x, y] \models \varphi$. Moreover, a satisfiable formula is said to be *finitely satisfiable* if there exists a finite model for it; otherwise it is *non-finitely satisfiable*. The *satisfiability* (resp., *finite satisfiability*) problem for PROMPT-(R)PNL consists in deciding whether a given PROMPT-(R)PNL formula is satisfiable (resp., finitely satisfiable).

3   Undecidability of PROMPT-RPNL

We prove the undecidability of the satisfiability problem for the logic PROMPT-RPNL (and thus for PROMPT-PNL as well), by a reduction from the *finite coloring problem* (*FCP*) [18]. An instance of FCP (aka *finite tiling problem*) is a tuple $\Delta = \langle C, H, V, c_i, c_f \rangle$, where C is a finite, non-empty set of *colours*, $H, V \subseteq C \times C$ are total binary relations over the set of colours C, and $c_i, c_f \in C$ are distinguished colours. A solution to Δ is a pair $\langle \mathcal{C}, (K, L) \rangle$, where $K, L \in \mathbb{N}$ and $\mathcal{C} : \{0, \ldots, K\} \times \{0, \ldots, L\} \to C$ is a *colouring* function such that $\mathcal{C}(0, 0) = c_i$, $\mathcal{C}(K, L) = c_f$, and, in addition,

- $(\mathcal{C}(i, j), \mathcal{C}(i + 1, j)) \in H$, for each $i < K$ and $j \leq L$ (horizontal constraint), and
- $(\mathcal{C}(i, j), \mathcal{C}(i, j + 1)) \in V$, for each $i \leq K$ and $j < L$ (vertical constraint).

FCP consists in establishing whether there are two natural numbers K and L, and a colouring of the plane $\{0, \ldots, K\} \times \{0, \ldots, L\}$ such that horizontal and vertical constraints are fulfilled, and bottom-left and top-right colours are given. CFP is undecidable [18, Proposition 7.2]. We encode CFP by means of a PROMPT-RPNL formula. The different aspects of the problem are encoded by means of (blocks of) formulas and the correctness of such partial encodings is testified by the corresponding lemmas below. Clearly, the conjunction of all these formulas is satisfiable if and only if CFP admits a solution. In what follows, we fix an interval model $M = \langle \mathbb{D}, V, \sigma, \delta \rangle$.

For every $d \in \mathbb{D}$ and $x \in X$, we define $\lfloor \sigma \rfloor_d(x) = \max\{\delta(d, d') \in \mathbb{R}^{>0} \mid d' \in \mathbb{D}^{>d} \text{ and } \delta(d, d') \leq \sigma(x)\}$. It clearly holds that $\lfloor \sigma \rfloor_d(x) \leq \sigma(x)$ and, for every $d' \in \mathbb{D}^{\geq d}$, we have that $\delta(d, d') \leq \sigma(x)$ implies $\delta(d, d') \leq \lfloor \sigma \rfloor_d(x)$. For every $x \in X$, there is exactly one point $d' \in \mathbb{D}^{\geq d}$ such that $\delta(d, d') = \lfloor \sigma \rfloor_d(x)$; we call such a point the x-*canonical successor* of d. The length of an interval $[d, d'] \in \mathbb{I}(\mathbb{D})$, where d' is the x-canonical successor of d, is said to be x-*canonical*, for every $x \in X$.

Let *succ-upperbound* be the formula $[G](\langle A \rangle \top \to \langle A_s \rangle \top)$, where $s \in X$.

Lemma 1. *If $M, [a, b] \models$ succ-upperbound for some $[a, b]$, then for every $c \in \mathbb{D}^{\geq b}$ that is not the greatest element in $\mathbb{D}$ it holds $\delta(c, \text{succ}_{\mathbb{D}}(c)) \leq \lfloor \sigma \rfloor_c(s)$. Moreover, let c' be the x-canonical successor of c. If c' is not the greatest element in $\mathbb{D}$, then $\lfloor \sigma \rfloor_c(x) + \sigma(s) > \sigma(x)$, for every $x \in X$.*

Let *less-than*(x, y) be the formula $[G](\langle A \rangle \top \rightarrow \langle A_y \rangle \mathsf{aux}_{x,y}) \wedge [G][A_x] \neg \mathsf{aux}_{x,y}$ (it is a parametric formula to be instantiated with some $x, y \in X$).

Lemma 2. *If* $M, [a, b] \models$ *less-than*(x, y) *for some* $[a, b]$, *then* $\sigma(x) < \lfloor \sigma \rfloor_c(y)$ *holds for every* $c \in \mathbb{D}^{\geq b}$, *unless* c *is the greatest element in* $\mathbb{D}$.

Let $\exists$-*last* be the conjunction of the following formulas:

$$\neg \mathsf{last} \wedge \langle A \rangle \langle A \rangle \mathsf{last} \wedge [G](\langle A \rangle \mathsf{last} \rightarrow \bigwedge_{\mathsf{p} \in \mathcal{AP}} [A](\neg \mathsf{p} \wedge [A] \neg \mathsf{p})) \tag{1}$$

$$[G](\langle A \rangle \mathsf{last} \rightarrow [A] \neg \langle A \rangle \mathsf{last}) \tag{2}$$

$$[G]((\mathsf{last} \rightarrow \langle A \rangle \mathsf{unique}) \wedge (\langle A \rangle \mathsf{unique} \rightarrow [A] \neg \langle A \rangle \mathsf{unique})) \tag{3}$$

Lemma 3. *If* $M, [a, b] \models \exists$-*last for some* $[a, b]$, *then there is exactly one* last-*interval in* $\mathcal{G}^{[a,b]}$, *say it* $[c, d]$. *Moreover, it holds* $c > b$ *and there is no* p-*interval starting in* c *or after it, for every* $\mathsf{p} \in \mathcal{AP} \setminus \{\mathsf{last}\}$.

Let $a \in \mathbb{D}$ and $[c, d] \in \mathbb{I}(\mathbb{D})$ be the unique last-interval (see Lemma 3). Given $\mathsf{p} \in \mathcal{AP}$, a p -*chain starting at* a (or, simply, p -*chain*) is a finite sequence of p-intervals $[a_0, b_0], [a_1, b_1], \ldots, [a_m, b_m]$ such that $a = a_0$, $b_m = c$, and $b_i = a_{i+1}$ for every $i \in \{0, 1, \ldots, m - 1\}$. Let *chain*$(\mathsf{p}, x)$ be the parametric formula, to be instantiated with some $\mathsf{p} \in \mathcal{AP}$ and $x \in X$, defined as the conjunction of the following ones:

$$\textit{succ-upperbound} \wedge \exists\text{-}last \tag{4}$$

$$\neg \mathsf{p} \wedge \langle A_x \rangle \mathsf{p} \wedge [G]((\mathsf{p} \wedge \neg \langle A \rangle \mathsf{last}) \rightarrow \langle A_x \rangle \mathsf{p}) \tag{5}$$

$$[G](\mathsf{p} \rightarrow \mathsf{p}_1 \vee \mathsf{p}_2) \tag{6}$$

$$[G](\langle A \rangle \mathsf{p}_i \rightarrow [A_x][A]\mathsf{p}_i^+) \qquad\qquad i \in \{1, 2\} \tag{7}$$

$$[G_x](\langle A \rangle \mathsf{p}_i^+ \rightarrow \mathsf{p}_i^-) \qquad\qquad i \in \{1, 2\} \tag{8}$$

$$[G](\mathsf{p}_i \rightarrow \neg \langle A \rangle \mathsf{p}_i^-) \qquad\qquad i \in \{1, 2\} \tag{9}$$

$$[G](\langle A \rangle \mathsf{p} \rightarrow [A_x](\neg \mathsf{p} \rightarrow [A] \neg \mathsf{p})) \tag{10}$$

Lemma 4. *If* $M, [a, b] \models$ *chain*(p, x) *for some* $[a, b]$, *then there is a finite* p-*chain starting at* b *whose intervals have* x-*canonical length. Moreover, no other* p-*interval exists in* $\mathcal{G}^{[a,b],x}$ *besides the ones in such a* p-*chain.*

We now provide an encoding of a finite plane $\{0, \ldots, K\} \times \{0, \ldots, L\}$, for some $K, L \in \mathbb{N}$. The idea is to use a u-chain whose intervals are either tile-intervals, encoding some point of the finite plane, or *-intervals, which are used as separators between rows of the plane. Let *plane* be the conjunction of the following formulas:

$$less\text{-}than(s, x) \wedge less\text{-}than(x, y) \wedge chain(\mathsf{u}, x) \wedge chain(\mathsf{row}, y) \tag{11}$$

$$[G]((\mathsf{u} \leftrightarrow * \vee \mathsf{tile}) \wedge (* \rightarrow \neg\mathsf{tile})) \tag{12}$$

$$\langle A \rangle * \wedge [G]((* \rightarrow \langle A \rangle \mathsf{tile}) \wedge (\mathsf{u} \wedge \langle A \rangle \mathsf{last} \rightarrow \mathsf{tile})) \tag{13}$$

$$[G](\langle A \rangle \mathsf{row} \rightarrow \langle A \rangle *) \tag{14}$$

$$[G](\langle A \rangle * \rightarrow [A_y](\langle A \rangle * \rightarrow \mathsf{row})) \tag{15}$$

Lemma 5. *If $M, [a, b] \models plane$ for some $[a, b]$, then there is a finite sequence of points $b = p_0^1 < p_1^1 < \ldots < p_{n_1}^1 = p_0^2 < p_1^2 < \ldots < p_{n_2}^2 = p_0^3 < \ldots < p_{n_{r-1}}^{r-1} = p_0^r < \ldots < p_{n_r}^r$, with $r \geq 1$ and $n_i > 1$ for every $i \in \{1, \ldots, r\}$ such that: (i) $[p_0^i, p_1^i]$ is a $*$-interval and its length is x-canonical, for every $i \in \{1, \ldots, r\}$; (ii) $[p_j^i, p_{j+1}^i]$ is a tile-interval and its length is x-canonical, for every $i \in \{1, \ldots, r\}$ and $j \in \{1, \ldots, n_i - 1\}$; (iii) $[p_0^i, p_0^{i+1}]$ is a row-interval and its length is y-canonical, for every $i \in \{1, \ldots, r-1\}$; (iv) $M, [p_{n_r}^r, p']$ is the unique last-interval, for some $p' > p_{n_r}^r$. Moreover, no other $*$-interval (resp., tile-interval) exists in $\mathcal{G}^{[a,b],x}$.*

The encoding of the finite plane $\{0, \ldots, K\} \times \{0, \ldots, L\}$ we have obtained so far is incomplete, the problem being that rows (row-intervals) do not necessarily contain the same number of tiles (tile-intervals). In order to overcome such a problem, we introduce below corr-intervals, which are used to link the ith tile-interval of a row to the ith tile-interval of the next row (if any) and to the ith tile-interval of the previous row (if any). This will guarantee that each row of our encoding features the same number of tiles.

Let $w\text{-}def$ be the conjunction of the following formulas:

$$less\text{-}than(x, w) \wedge less\text{-}than(w, y) \tag{16}$$

$$[A_y]\neg\langle A \rangle *\text{-aux} \wedge ((\langle A_y \rangle(\mathsf{row} \wedge \neg\langle A_x \rangle \mathsf{last}) \rightarrow \langle A \rangle \langle A \rangle *\text{-aux}) \tag{17}$$

$$\langle A_s \rangle \langle A_w \rangle([A](\neg\mathsf{last} \wedge [A]\neg\mathsf{last}) \vee \langle A \rangle *\text{-aux}) \tag{18}$$

Lemma 6. *If $M, [a, b] \models plane \wedge w\text{-}def$ for some $[a, b]$, then $\sigma(w) < \lfloor \sigma \rfloor_c(y) \leq \sigma(y) < \sigma(w) + \sigma(s)$ for every $c \in \mathbb{D}^{\geq b}$, unless c is the greatest element in $\mathbb{D}$.*

Let *correspondence* be the conjunction of the following formulas:

$$plane \wedge w\text{-}def \wedge less\text{-}than(s, z) \wedge less\text{-}than(z, x) \tag{19}$$

$$[G]((\langle A_x \rangle \mathsf{u} \rightarrow [A_z]\langle A_z \rangle(\mathsf{u}\text{-suffix} \wedge ((\langle A_x \rangle \mathsf{u} \vee \langle A \rangle \mathsf{last}))) \tag{20}$$

$$[G_s]\neg\mathsf{u}\text{-suffix} \tag{21}$$

$$[G]((\mathsf{row} \wedge \neg\langle A \rangle \mathsf{last}) \rightarrow \mathsf{corr}) \tag{22}$$

$$[G]((\langle A_x \rangle \mathsf{tile} \wedge \langle A \rangle \langle A_x \rangle *) \rightarrow \langle A_y \rangle \mathsf{corr}) \tag{23}$$

$$[G_w]\neg\mathsf{corr} \tag{24}$$

$$[G](\mathsf{corr} \rightarrow \langle A \rangle \mathsf{tile}) \tag{25}$$

$$[G](\langle A_x \rangle(\mathsf{tile} \wedge \langle A_x \rangle *) \rightarrow [A_y](\mathsf{corr} \rightarrow \langle A_x \rangle(\mathsf{tile} \wedge \langle A_x \rangle *))) \tag{26}$$

Lemma 7. *If $M, [a, b] \models$ correspondence for some $[a, b]$, then $[p_j^i, p_j^{i+1}]$ is a corr-interval, with $\sigma(w) < \delta(p_j^i, p_j^{i+1}) \leq \sigma(y)$, for every $i \in \{1, \ldots, r-1\}$ and $j \in \{0, \ldots, n_i - 1\}$. Moreover, for every $i \in \{1, \ldots, r-1\}$, it holds that $n_i = n_{i+1}$.*

Now, let $\Delta = \langle C, H, V, c_i, c_f \rangle$ be an instance of FCP and let φ_Δ be the conjunction of the following formulas:

$$correspondence \wedge \langle A_x \rangle c_i \wedge [G_x]((\text{tile} \wedge \langle A \rangle \text{last}) \to c_f) \tag{27}$$

$$[G_x](\text{tile} \leftrightarrow \bigvee_{c \in C} c) \wedge [G](\bigwedge_{c,c' \in C, c \neq c'} \neg(c \wedge c')) \tag{28}$$

$$[G](\langle A_x \rangle(\text{tile} \wedge \langle A_x \rangle \text{tile}) \to \bigvee_{(c,c') \in H} \langle A_x \rangle(c \wedge \langle A_x \rangle c')) \tag{29}$$

$$[G_x]((\langle A_x \rangle \text{tile} \wedge \langle A_y \rangle \text{corr}) \to \bigvee_{(c,c') \in V} (\langle A_x \rangle c \wedge [A_y](\text{corr} \to \langle A_x \rangle c'))) \tag{30}$$

Lemma 8. *The formula φ_Δ is satisfiable iff the CFP instance Δ has a positive answer.*

Theorem 1. *The satisfiability problem for PROMPT-RPNL, and thus the one for PROMPT-PNL, is undecidable.*

4   Decidability of PROMPT$\overset{d}{-}$PNL

In this section, we show how to restrict the use of prompt modalities to get a fragment of PROMPT-PNL with a decidable satisfiability problem.

We define PROMPT$\overset{d}{-}$PNL as the fragment of PROMPT-PNL obtained by using disjoint sets of bounding variables for existential and universal prompt modalities. Formally, let us partition the set X of bounding variables into sets $X_\Diamond$ and $X_\Box$. The syntax of PROMPT$\overset{d}{-}$PNL is defined as:

$$\varphi ::= \quad p \quad | \quad \varphi \wedge \varphi \quad | \quad \langle A \rangle \varphi \quad | \quad \langle \overline{A} \rangle \varphi \quad | \quad \langle A_x \rangle \varphi \quad | \quad \langle \overline{A}_x \rangle \varphi$$
$$| \quad \neg p \quad | \quad \varphi \vee \varphi \quad | \quad [A] \varphi \quad | \quad [\overline{A}] \varphi \quad | \quad [A_y] \varphi \quad | \quad [\overline{A}_y] \varphi$$

where $p \in \mathcal{AP}$, $x \in X_\Diamond$, and $y \in X_\Box$. Since PROMPT$\overset{d}{-}$PNL is a syntactic restriction of PROMPT-PNL, both formalisms share the same semantics. In particular, a PROMPT-PNL model is a PROMPT$\overset{d}{-}$PNL model as well. Analogously to the unrestricted case, we define PROMPT$\overset{d}{-}$RPNL as PROMPT$\overset{d}{-}$PNL devoid of past modalities $\langle \overline{A} \rangle$, $[\overline{A}]$, $\langle \overline{A}_x \rangle$, and $[\overline{A}_y]$.

PROMPT$\overset{d}{-}$PNL is not closed under negation. For any given PROMPT$\overset{d}{-}$PNL formula ψ, we inductively define $neg(\psi)$ as shown in Table 1 ($neg(\psi)$ is not necessarily a PROMPT$\overset{d}{-}$PNL formula). If ψ is a (non-prompt) PNL formula, then $neg(\psi) \equiv \neg \psi$. Moreover, we define $neg(\sim \psi)$ as ψ and thus we have that $neg(neg(\psi)) \equiv \psi$, for every PROMPT$\overset{d}{-}$PNL formula ψ.

Table 1. Definition of $neg(\psi)$, for a PROMPT^d-PNL formula ψ

ψ	$neg(\psi)$	ψ	$neg(\psi)$
p	$\neg p$	$\neg p$	p
$\psi_1 \wedge \psi_2$	$neg(\psi_1) \vee neg(\psi_2)$	$\psi_1 \vee \psi_2$	$neg(\psi_1) \wedge neg(\psi_2)$
$\langle A \rangle \psi_1$	$[A]neg(\psi_1)$	$[A]\psi_1$	$\langle A \rangle neg(\psi_1)$
$\langle \overline{A} \rangle \psi_1$	$[\overline{A}]neg(\psi_1)$	$[\overline{A}]\psi_1$	$\langle \overline{A} \rangle neg(\psi_1)$

ψ	$neg(\psi)$
$\langle A_x \rangle \psi_1$ or $\langle \overline{A}_x \rangle \psi_1$ or $[A_y]\psi_1$ or $[\overline{A}_y]\psi_1$	$\sim \psi$

A close analysis of the proof of the undecidability of PROMPT-(R)PNL reveals that the unrestricted use of bounding variables within prompt modalities allows one to somehow establish tight bounds for the length of intervals, and this ability is crucial to the encoding. We are going to show that decidability can be recovered by not allowing both existential and universal prompt quantification on the same bounding variable. Intuitively, decidability follows from the fact that, when disjoint sets of bounding variables are used within existential and universal prompt modalities, formulas enjoy a monotonicity property, which does not hold for unrestricted PROMPT-(R)PNL formulas.

Let $M = \langle \mathbb{D}, V, \sigma, \delta \rangle$ be a PROMPT-PNL model, $x \in X$, and $r \in \mathbb{R}^{>0}$. We denote by $M_{[x:=r]}$ the model $\langle \mathbb{D}, V, \sigma', \delta \rangle$, where $\sigma'(x) = r$ and $\sigma'(x') = \sigma(x')$ for every $x' \in X$ with $x' \neq x$.

Proposition 1 (monotonicity). *Let ψ be a formula of PROMPT^d-PNL, M be a model of PROMPT^d-PNL, and $[a,b]$ be an interval in M. If $M, [a,b] \models \psi$, then $M_{[x:=r]}, [a,b] \models \psi$ for all $x \in X_\Diamond$ and $r \in \mathbb{R}^{>0}$, with $r \geq \sigma_M(x)$. In a dual fashion, if $M, [a,b] \models \psi$, then $M_{[y:=r]}, [a,b] \models \psi$ for all $y \in X_\Box$ and $r \in \mathbb{R}^{>0}$, with $r \leq \sigma_M(y)$.*

Checking that the above monotonicity property holds for PROMPT^d-PNL is immediate. To see that it does not hold for PROMPT-PNL, consider the formula $\psi = [A_y]\neg p \wedge \langle A_x \rangle p \wedge [A_x]\neg q \wedge \langle A_z \rangle q$. Clearly, ψ is satisfiable and all of its models are such that the value of x is bounded below by the value of y and above by the value of z.

By Proposition 1, when studying the (finite) satisfiability problem for PROMPT^d-PNL we can assume, w.l.o.g., that $|X_\Diamond| = |X_\Box| = 1$, as every formula ψ, featuring (possibly) more than one bounding variable in $X_\Diamond$ or $X_\Box$, can be transformed into an equisatisfiable one ψ', obtained by replacing two distinguished (chosen randomly) variables $\hat{x} \in X_\Diamond$ and $\hat{y} \in X_\Box$ for every $x \in X_\Diamond$ and $y \in X_\Box$, respectively. It is not difficult to check that, due to monotonicity, ψ is (finitely) satisfiable if and only if so is ψ'. Therefore, for the remainder of the section, we set $X_\Diamond = \{x\}$ and $X_\Box = \{y\}$.

Finite Satisfiability. The finite satisfiability problem for PROMPT$\overset{d}{-}$PNL can be reduced to the one for plain PNL, known to be NEXPTIME-complete [8]. Let ψ be a formula of PROMPT$\overset{d}{-}$PNL and let $plain(\psi)$ be the PNL formula obtained from ψ by:

(i) replacing existential prompt modalities by the corresponding non-prompt versions (i.e., substituting $\langle A \rangle$ for $\langle A_x \rangle$ and $\langle \overline{A} \rangle$ for $\langle \overline{A}_x \rangle$), and

(ii) replacing all sub-formulas of the forms $[A_y]\psi$ and $[\overline{A}_y]\psi$ by the constant $\top$.

It is not difficult to show by induction on the structure of ψ that if ψ is finitely satisfiable, so is $plain(\psi)$. On the other hand, if $plain(\psi)$ is finitely satisfiable, then let $M_{plain(\psi)} = \langle \mathbb{D}, V \rangle$ be a PNL model such that $M_{plain(\psi)}, [a, b] \models plain(\psi)$ for some $[a, b] \in \mathbb{I}(\mathbb{D})$. We define $\delta(d, d') = |\{d'' \in \mathbb{D} \mid d < d'' \leq d'\}|$ for every $d, d' \in \mathbb{D}$. Since $\mathbb{D}$ is finite, both $\max_\delta = \max\{\delta(d, d') \mid d, d' \in \mathbb{D} \text{ and } d \neq d'\}$ and $\min_\delta = \min\{\delta(d, d') \mid d, d' \in \mathbb{D} \text{ and } d \neq d'\}$ are well defined, thus we can set $\sigma(x) = \max_\delta$, and $\sigma(y) = \frac{\min_\delta}{2}$. It is possible to show that $M = \langle \mathbb{D}, V, \sigma, \delta \rangle$ is such that $M, [a, b] \models \psi$. Therefore, ψ is finitely satisfiable, too.

Theorem 2. *The finite satisfiability problem for* PROMPT$\overset{d}{-}$PNL *is NEXPTIME-complete.*

In order to deal with formulas that are non-finitely satisfiable, in what follows we show how the search for an infinite model can be reduced to the search for a finite witness for it, within a finite search space. Decidability of the satisfiability problem for PROMPT$\overset{d}{-}$PNL immediately follows.

4.1 Prompt Labeled Interval Structures

In this subsection we define labeled interval structures for PROMPT$\overset{d}{-}$PNL formulas, which are, intuitively, extended models, where intervals are labeled with sets of sub-formulas (instead of sets of atomic propositions) of the considered formula. From now on, we let φ be a generic PROMPT$\overset{d}{-}$PNL formula.

Let $Sub(\varphi)$ be the set of all sub-formulas of φ and let $Sub^\neg(\varphi) = \{neg(\psi) \mid \psi \in Sub(\varphi)\}$. The *closure* of φ, denoted by $Cl(\varphi)$, is the set $Sub(\varphi) \cup Sub^\neg(\varphi) \cup \{\langle A \rangle \varphi, neg(\langle A \rangle \varphi)\}$. Clearly, $|Cl(\varphi)| \leq 2 \cdot |\varphi| + 2$ holds.

A *future temporal request* of φ is a formula in $Cl(\varphi)$ having one of the following forms: $\langle A \rangle \psi$, $neg(\langle A \rangle \psi)$, $\langle A_x \rangle \psi$, $neg(\langle A_x \rangle \psi)$, $[A_y]\psi$, $neg([A_y]\psi)$, for some ψ. Analogously, a *past temporal request* of φ is a formula in $Cl(\varphi)$ having one of the following forms: $\langle \overline{A} \rangle \psi$, $neg(\langle \overline{A} \rangle \psi)$, $\langle \overline{A}_x \rangle \psi$, $neg(\langle \overline{A}_x \rangle \psi)$, $[\overline{A}_y]\psi$, $neg([\overline{A}_y]\psi)$, for some ψ. We denote by $TR_f(\varphi)$ (resp., $TR_p(\varphi)$) the set of future (resp., past) temporal requests of φ. In addition, the set of *temporal requests* of φ, denoted by $TR(\varphi)$, is defined as $TR_f(\varphi) \cup TR_p(\varphi)$.

A *φ-atom* is a subset A of $Cl(\varphi)$ such that, for every $\psi, \psi_1, \psi_2 \in Cl(\varphi)$, (i) $\psi \in A$ if and only if $neg(\psi) \notin A$, and (ii) $\psi_1 \vee \psi_2 \in A$ if and only if $\psi_1 \in A$

or $\psi_2 \in A$. Notice that conditions (i) and (ii) imply $\psi_1 \wedge \psi_2 \in A$ if and only if $\psi_1 \in A$ and $\psi_2 \in A$. We denote the set of φ-atoms by $\mathcal{A}_\varphi$.

A *prompt φ-labeled interval structure* (pLIS$_\varphi$) is a 5-tuple $\mathbf{L} = \langle \mathbb{D}, \mathcal{L}, \delta, \mathcal{X}, \mathcal{Y} \rangle$, where $(\mathbb{D}, \delta)$ is a metric space, $\mathcal{L} : \mathbb{I}(\mathbb{D}) \to \mathcal{A}_\varphi$ is a *labeling function* (or simply *labeling*) such that $\varphi \in \mathcal{L}([a,b])$ for some $[a,b] \in \mathbb{I}(\mathbb{D})$, and $\mathcal{X}, \mathcal{Y} \in \mathbb{N}$ are the *existential* and the *universal* bound, respectively. Sometimes, for the sake of brevity, we omit the last three components of the 5-tuple and we denote a pLIS$_\varphi$ as a 2-tuple $\langle \mathbb{D}, \mathcal{L} \rangle$ instead. Moreover, given a pLIS$_\varphi$ $\mathbf{L} = \langle \mathbb{D}, \mathcal{L} \rangle$, we denote by $\mathbb{D}_\mathbf{L}$ its underlying domain $\mathbb{D}$ and by $\mathcal{L}_\mathbf{L}$ the labeling function $\mathcal{L}$. A pLIS$_\varphi$ $\mathbf{L}$ is *finite* (resp., *infinite*) if so is $\mathbb{D}_\mathbf{L}$.

Given a pLIS$_\varphi$ $\mathbf{L}$ and a point $d \in \mathbb{D}_\mathbf{L}$ we define the set of *future requests of d in $\mathbf{L}$*, denoted by f-REQ$^\mathbf{L}(d)$, as $\bigcup_{d' \in \mathbb{D}^{<d}} (\mathcal{L}_\mathbf{L}(d',d) \cap TR_f(\varphi))$, the set of *past requests of d in $\mathbf{L}$*, denoted by p-REQ$^\mathbf{L}(d)$, as $\bigcup_{d' \in \mathbb{D}^{>d}} (\mathcal{L}_\mathbf{L}(d,d') \cap TR_p(\varphi))$, and the set of *requests of d in $\mathbf{L}$*, denoted by REQ$^\mathbf{L}(d)$, as f-REQ$^\mathbf{L}(d) \cup$ p-REQ$^\mathbf{L}(d)$. We denote by REQ$_\varphi$ the class of all sets of requests, i.e., REQ$_\varphi = \{\mathcal{R} \mid \mathcal{R} =$ REQ$^\mathbf{L}(d)$ for some pLIS$_\varphi$ $\mathbf{L}$ and $d \in \mathbb{D}_\mathbf{L}\}$. We have that $|\text{REQ}_\varphi| \le 2^{|Cl(\varphi)|} \le 2^{2 \cdot |\varphi| + 2}$.

An *existential request* of φ is a temporal request of φ of one the following forms: $\langle A \rangle \psi$, $\langle \overline{A} \rangle \psi$, $\langle A_x \rangle \psi$, $\langle \overline{A}_x \rangle \psi$, $neg([A_y])\psi$, and $neg([\overline{A}_y])\psi$, for some ψ. A *universal request* of φ is a temporal request of φ that is not an existential one. Let $\mathbf{L} = \langle \mathbb{D}, \mathcal{L}, \delta, \mathcal{X}, \mathcal{Y} \rangle$ be a pLIS$_\varphi$ and $d \in \mathbb{D}$. We define $\exists$-REQ$^\mathbf{L}(d) = \{\psi \in \text{REQ}^\mathbf{L}(d) \mid \psi$ is an existential request of $\varphi\}$ and $\forall$-REQ$^\mathbf{L}(d) = \text{REQ}^\mathbf{L}(d) \setminus \exists$-REQ$^\mathbf{L}(d)$.

For $\psi \in \exists$-REQ$^\mathbf{L}(d)$, we say that ψ is *fulfilled in $(\mathbf{L}, d)$ by $d' \in \mathbb{D}$* if, and only if, one of the following holds:

- $\psi = \langle A \rangle \psi'$ for some ψ' and $\psi' \in \mathcal{L}([d,d'])$,
- $\psi = \langle \overline{A} \rangle \psi'$ for some ψ' and $\psi' \in \mathcal{L}([d',d])$,
- $\psi = \langle A_x \rangle \psi'$ for some ψ', $\psi' \in \mathcal{L}([d,d'])$, and $\delta(d,d') \le \mathcal{X}$,
- $\psi = \langle \overline{A}_x \rangle \psi'$ for some ψ', $\psi' \in \mathcal{L}([d',d])$, and $\delta(d',d) \le \mathcal{X}$,
- $\psi = neg([A_y]\psi')$ for some ψ', $neg(\psi') \in \mathcal{L}([d,d'])$, and $\delta(d,d') \le \mathcal{Y}$,
- $\psi = neg([\overline{A}_y]\psi')$ for some ψ', $neg(\psi') \in \mathcal{L}([d',d])$, and $\delta(d',d) \le \mathcal{Y}$.

ψ is *fulfilled in $(\mathbf{L}, d)$* if and only if there is d' such that ψ is fulfilled in $(\mathbf{L}, d)$ by d'.

For $\psi \in \forall$-REQ$^\mathbf{L}(d)$, we say that ψ is *fulfilled in $(\mathbf{L}, d)$* if and only if, one of the following holds:

- $\psi = [A]\psi'$ for some ψ' and $\psi' \in \mathcal{L}([d,d'])$ for every $d' \in \mathbb{D}^{>d}$,
- $\psi = [\overline{A}]\psi'$ for some ψ' and $\psi' \in \mathcal{L}([d',d])$ for every $d' \in \mathbb{D}^{<d}$,
- $\psi = [A_y]\psi'$ for some ψ' and $\psi' \in \mathcal{L}([d,d'])$ for every $d' \in \mathbb{D}^{>d}$ with $\delta(d,d') \le \mathcal{Y}$,
- $\psi = [\overline{A}_y]\psi'$ for some ψ' and $\psi' \in \mathcal{L}([d',d])$ for every $d' \in \mathbb{D}^{<d}$ with $\delta(d',d) \le \mathcal{Y}$,
- $\psi = neg(\langle A_x \rangle \psi')$ for some ψ' and $neg(\psi') \in \mathcal{L}([d,d'])$ for every $d' \in \mathbb{D}^{>d}$ with $\delta(d,d') \le \mathcal{X}$,
- $\psi = neg(\langle \overline{A}_x \rangle \psi')$ for some ψ' and $neg(\psi') \in \mathcal{L}([d',d])$ for every $d' \in \mathbb{D}^{>d}$ with $\delta(d',d) \le \mathcal{X}$.

d is $\exists$-*fulfilled in* $\mathbf{L}$ if, and only if, every $\psi \in \exists\text{-}\mathsf{REQ}^\mathbf{L}(d)$ is fulfilled; d is $\forall$-*fulfilled in* $\mathbf{L}$ if, and only if, every $\psi \in \forall\text{-}\mathsf{REQ}^\mathbf{L}(d)$ is fulfilled; d is *fulfilled in* $\mathbf{L}$ if, and only if, it is both $\exists$- and $\forall$-fulfilled in $\mathbf{L}$.

An *existentially fulfilling* (resp., *universally fulfilling, fulfilling*) pLIS_φ, aka $\exists\text{-}\mathrm{pLIS}_\varphi$ (resp., $\forall\text{-}\mathrm{pLIS}_\varphi$, $\exists\forall\text{-}\mathrm{pLIS}_\varphi$), is a pLIS_φ $\mathbf{L}$ such that every $d \in \mathbb{D}_\mathbf{L}$ is $\exists$-fulfilled (resp., $\forall$-fulfilled, fulfilled) in it.

Proposition 2. φ *is satisfiable if and only if there exists a* $\exists\forall\text{-}pLIS_\varphi$, *and it is finitely satisfiable if and only if there exists a finite* $\exists\forall\text{-}pLIS_\varphi$.

Before showing the decidability of $\mathtt{PROMPT}\overset{d}{\text{-}}\mathtt{PNL}$, we prove a result that will later come in handy. A set of requests $\mathsf{REQ}^\mathbf{L}(d)$ (for a pLIS_φ $\mathbf{L}$ and $d \in \mathbb{D}_\mathbf{L}$) is *consistent* if for each $\psi \in \mathsf{REQ}^\mathbf{L}(d)$, we have that $neg(\psi) \notin \mathsf{REQ}^\mathbf{L}(d)$; otherwise, it is *inconsistent*.

Proposition 3. *Let* $\mathbf{L}$ *be a* $pLIS_\varphi$ *and* $d \in \mathbb{D}_\mathbf{L}$. *The following properties hold, unless* $\mathsf{REQ}^\mathbf{L}(d)$ *is inconsistent:*

- *if* $\mathbb{D}^{<d} \neq \emptyset$, *then* $\mathsf{f}\text{-}\mathsf{REQ}^\mathbf{L}(d) = \mathcal{L}_\mathbf{L}(d',d) \cap TR_f(\varphi)$, *for any given* $d' \in \mathbb{D}^{<d}$, *unless* $\mathsf{f}\text{-}\mathsf{REQ}^\mathbf{L}(d)$ *is inconsistent;*
- *if* $\mathbb{D}^{>d} \neq \emptyset$, *then* $\mathsf{p}\text{-}\mathsf{REQ}^\mathbf{L}(d) = \mathcal{L}_\mathbf{L}(d,d') \cap TR_p(\varphi)$, *for any given* $d' \in \mathbb{D}^{>d}$, *unless* $\mathsf{p}\text{-}\mathsf{REQ}^\mathbf{L}(d)$ *is inconsistent.*

4.2   A Bounded Witness for Non-finitely Satisfiable Formulas

Let $\mathbf{L}$ be a pLIS_φ and $d \in \mathbb{D}_\mathbf{L}$. A set of *essentials* of d (in $\mathbf{L}$) is any minimal (with respect to set inclusion) set $E \subseteq \mathbb{D}_\mathbf{L}$ such that for every $\psi \in \exists\text{-}\mathsf{REQ}^\mathbf{L}(d)$ there is $d' \in E$ for which ψ is fulfilled in $(\mathbf{L}, d)$ by d'. We denote by $\mathcal{E}_\mathbf{L}(d)$ the class containing all sets of essentials of d in $\mathbf{L}$, i.e., $\mathcal{E}_\mathbf{L}(d) = \{E \subseteq \mathbb{D}_\mathbf{L} \mid E \text{ is a set of essentials of } d \text{ in } \mathbf{L}\}$. Intuitively, a set of essentials of d is a collection of points that jointly make d $\exists$-fulfilled in $\mathbf{L}$. Clearly $\mathcal{E}_\mathbf{L}(d) \neq \emptyset$ if and only if d is $\exists$-fulfilled in $\mathbf{L}$. We lift this concept to a higher order: a set of *essentials of essentials* (or *2nd-order essentials*) of d (in $\mathbf{L}$) is any minimal (with respect to set inclusion) set $E_2 \subseteq \mathbb{D}_\mathbf{L}$ such that (i) $E_1 \subseteq E_2$ for some $E_1 \in \mathcal{E}_\mathbf{L}(d)$ and (ii) for every $d' \in E_1$ there is $E_{d'} \in \mathcal{E}_\mathbf{L}(d')$ for which $E_{d'} \subseteq E_2$. We denote by $\mathcal{E}_\mathbf{L}^2(d)$ the class containing all sets of 2nd-order essentials of d in $\mathbf{L}$, i.e., $\mathcal{E}_\mathbf{L}^2(d) = \{E \subseteq \mathbb{D}_\mathbf{L} \mid E \text{ is a set of 2nd-order essentials of } d \text{ in } \mathbf{L}\}$.

Definition 1 (representative). *Let* $\mathbf{L}$ *be a finite* $pLIS_\varphi$ *and* $d \in \mathbb{D}_\mathbf{L}$.

If $d \notin \{\min \mathbb{D}_\mathbf{L}, \max \mathbb{D}_\mathbf{L}\}$, *then a* representative *of* d *in* $\mathbf{L}$ *is a point* $e \in \mathbb{D}_\mathbf{L}$ *such that* $\mathsf{REQ}^\mathbf{L}(d) = \mathsf{REQ}^\mathbf{L}(e)$, e *is fulfilled in* $\mathbf{L}$, *and so are points in* E_2, *for some* $E_2 \in \mathcal{E}_\mathbf{L}^2(e)$ *with* $E_2 \cap \{\min \mathbb{D}, \max \mathbb{D}\} = \emptyset$.

If $d = \min \mathbb{D}_\mathbf{L}$ *(resp.,* $d = \max \mathbb{D}_\mathbf{L}$), *then a* representative *of* d *in* $\mathbf{L}$ *is a point* $e \in \mathbb{D}_\mathbf{L}$ *that is a representative of* d' *in* $\mathbf{L}$ *for some* $d' \in \mathbb{D}_\mathbf{L}$, *with* $\mathsf{p}\text{-}\mathsf{REQ}^\mathbf{L}(d') = \mathsf{p}\text{-}\mathsf{REQ}^\mathbf{L}(d)$ *(resp.,* $\mathsf{f}\text{-}\mathsf{REQ}^\mathbf{L}(d') = \mathsf{f}\text{-}\mathsf{REQ}^\mathbf{L}(d)$).

A *convex* subset of a domain $\mathbb{D}$ is a subset $\mathbb{D}'$ of $\mathbb{D}$ such that for every $d', d'' \in \mathbb{D}'$ and $d \in \mathbb{D}$, if $d' < d < d''$, then $d \in \mathbb{D}'$. A *right-convex* (resp., *left-convex*) subset of a domain $\mathbb{D}$ is a convex subset $\mathbb{D}'$ of $\mathbb{D}$ such that $\max \mathbb{D} \in \mathbb{D}'$ (resp., $\min \mathbb{D} \in \mathbb{D}'$).

Given a pLIS_φ $\mathbf{L}$ and $\mathbb{D}' \subseteq \mathbb{D}_\mathbf{L}$, we let $\text{request-sets}^\mathbf{L}(\mathbb{D}') = \{\mathcal{R} \mid \text{REQ}^\mathbf{L}(d) = \mathcal{R} \text{ for some } d \in \mathbb{D}'\}$.

Definition 2 (left- and right-periodic pLIS_φ). *Let $\mathbf{L}$ be a finite pLIS_φ. A left-period for $\mathbf{L}$ is a left-convex subset $\mathbb{E}$ of $\mathbb{D}_\mathbf{L}$ such that, for every $d \in \mathbb{E}$, if d is not fulfilled in $\mathbf{L}$ or $d = \min \mathbb{E}$, then there is $d' \in \mathbb{E}^{>d}$ for which the following holds:*

(a) d' is a representative of d in $\mathbf{L}$;
(b) $\text{request-sets}^\mathbf{L}(\mathbb{E} \setminus \{\min \mathbb{E}\})$ is equal to $\text{request-sets}^\mathbf{L}(\mathbb{E}^{<d'} \setminus \{\min \mathbb{E}\})$, which is equal to $\text{request-sets}^\mathbf{L}(\mathbb{E}^{>d'})$, and there are $d'' \in \mathbb{E}^{<d'} \setminus \{\min \mathbb{E}\}$ and $d''' \in \mathbb{E}^{>d'}$ such that $\text{p-REQ}^\mathbf{L}(\min \mathbb{E}) = \text{p-REQ}^\mathbf{L}(d'') = \text{p-REQ}^\mathbf{L}(d''')$;
(c) every $\langle A_x \rangle \psi \in \text{f-REQ}^\mathbf{L}(d')$ is fulfilled in $(\mathbf{L}, d')$ by a point belonging to $\mathbb{E}$.

A right-period for $\mathbf{L}$ is defined symmetrically.

$\mathbf{L}$ is periodic if, and only if, there exist both a left- and a right-period for it.

Definition 3 (φ-witness). *A φ-witness is a finite, periodic $\forall$-pLIS_φ $\mathbf{L}$, such that every $d \in \mathbb{D}_\mathbf{L} \setminus (\mathbb{E} \cup \mathbb{F})$ is fulfilled in $\mathbf{L}$, where $\mathbb{E}$ and $\mathbb{F}$ are, respectively, a left- and a right-period for $\mathbf{L}$, with $\mathbb{E} \cap \mathbb{F} = \emptyset$ and $\mathbb{D}_\mathbf{L} \setminus (\mathbb{E} \cup \mathbb{F}) \neq \emptyset$.*

Lemma 9. *An infinite $\exists \forall$-pLIS_φ $\mathbf{L} = \langle \mathbb{D}, \mathcal{L}, \delta, \mathcal{X}, \mathcal{Y} \rangle$ exists if and only if a φ-witness $\mathbf{L}' = \langle \mathbb{D}', \mathcal{L}', \delta', \mathcal{X}', \mathcal{Y}' \rangle$ exists.*

Thanks to the previous lemma, we can reduce the search for an infinite model for a formula to the search for a finite witness. However, since such a finite witness can be arbitrarily large, the search space is still infinite. In what follows, we provide a bound on the size of the finite witness, thus obtaining a finite search space. Decidability of $\text{PROMPT}^d\text{-PNL}$ immediately follows.

Let $\mathcal{B}_\varphi = |\text{REQ}_\varphi| \cdot (2 \cdot |\mathcal{C}l(\varphi)|^2 + 2 \cdot |\mathcal{C}l(\varphi)|) + |\text{REQ}_\varphi| \cdot |\mathcal{C}l(\varphi)| + |\mathcal{C}l(\varphi)|$.

Lemma 10. *Let $\mathbf{L} = \langle \mathbb{D}, \mathcal{L}, \delta, \mathcal{X}, \mathcal{Y} \rangle$ be a φ-witness, $\mathbb{E}$ and $\mathbb{F}$ being, respectively, a left- and a right-period for it. If $|\mathbb{E}| > \mathcal{B}_\varphi$ (resp., $|\mathbb{F}| > \mathcal{B}_\varphi$, $|\mathbb{D} \setminus (\mathbb{E} \cup \mathbb{F})| > \mathcal{B}_\varphi$), then there is a φ-witness $\mathbf{L}' = \langle \mathbb{D}', \mathcal{L}', \delta', \mathcal{X}', \mathcal{Y}' \rangle$ with $|\mathbb{D}'| = |\mathbb{D}| - 1$.*

The *size* of a pLIS_φ $\mathbf{L}$ is the size of the underlying domain $\mathbb{D}_\mathbf{L}$. The following corollary immediately follows from the above lemma.

Corollary 1 (small model property). *A φ-witness exists if and only if there is one of size at most $3 \cdot \mathcal{B}_\varphi \leq 3 \cdot [2^{2 \cdot |\varphi| + 2} \cdot (2 \cdot (2 \cdot |\varphi| + 2)^2 + 2 \cdot (2 \cdot |\varphi| + 2)) + 2^{2 \cdot |\varphi| + 2} \cdot (2 \cdot |\varphi| + 2) + (2 \cdot |\varphi| + 2)]$.*

Theorem 3. *The satisfiability problem for $\text{PROMPT}^d\text{-PNL}$ is NEXPTIME-complete.*

5   Conclusions

In this paper, we have studied the problem of enriching the well-known propositional logic of temporal neighborhood PNL with support for prompt-liveness specifications. We first proved that the logic obtained from PNL by introducing "prompt" versions of its modalities with no restriction on the use of bounding variables, that we call PROMPT-PNL, is undecidable. Then, we showed that decidability can be recovered by introducing a partition of bounding variables into two classes, one for the existential modalities, the other for the universal ones. The satisfiability problem for the resulting logic, named PROMPT^d-PNL, is indeed NEXPTIME-complete.

The work done can be further developed in various directions.

First, we are interested in identifying the minimum number of bounding variables that suffice to make PROMPT-PNL undecidable. We believe it possible to prove that when the set of variables is small enough, e.g., when it includes two bounding variables only, the logic is still expressive enough to capture some meaningful promptness conditions and remains decidable.

We also aim at investigating the more powerful setting of *parametric* extensions of PNL. Parametric PNL can be viewed as a natural generalization of PROMPT-PNL, as *parametric modalities* allow one to express both lower and upper bounds on the delay with which a request is fulfilled (PROMPT-PNL only copes with the latter).

Last but not least, we are interested in comparing the expressiveness of the logics PROMPT-PNL and PROMPT^d-PNL with that of *metric PNL* , that is, the metric extension of PNL introduced and systematically studied in [7].

Acknowledgements. The authors acknowledge the support from the Italian GNCS project *Logics, automata, and games for auto-adaptive systems*. In addition, Dario Della Monica and Aniello Murano acknowledge the support from the POR Campania project *Strategic reasoning for multi-agent systems*.

References

1. Allen, J.F.: Maintaining knowledge about temporal intervals. Commun. ACM **26**(11), 832–843 (1983)
2. Allen, J.F.: Towards a general theory of action and time. Artif. Intell. **23**(2), 123–154 (1984)
3. Almagor, S., Hirshfeld, Y., Kupferman, O.: Promptness in ω-regular automata. In: Bouajjani, A., Chin, W.-N. (eds.) ATVA 2010. LNCS, vol. 6252, pp. 22–36. Springer, Heidelberg (2010). doi:10.1007/978-3-642-15643-4_4
4. Alur, R., Etessami, K., La Torre, S., Peled, D.: Parametric temporal logic for "model measuring". ACM Trans. Comput. Log. **2**(3), 388–407 (2001). http://doi.acm.org/10.1145/377978.377990
5. Aminof, B., Murano, A., Rubin, S., Zuleger, F.: Prompt alternating-time epistemic logics. In: Baral, C., Delgrande, J.P., Wolter, F. (eds.) Proceedings of the 15th KR, pp. 258–267. AAAI Press (2016)

6. Bojańczyk, M., Colcombet, T.: Bounds in ω-regularity. In: LICS, pp. 285–296. IEEE Computer Society (2006)
7. Bresolin, D., Della Monica, D., Goranko, V., Montanari, A., Sciavicco, G.: Metric propositional neighborhood interval logics on natural numbers. Softw. Syst. Model. (SoSyM) **12**(2), 245–264 (2013)
8. Bresolin, D., Goranko, V., Montanari, A., Sciavicco, G.: Propositional interval neighborhood logics: expressiveness, decidability, and undecidable extensions. Ann. Pure Appl. Logic **161**(3), 289–304 (2009). http://dx.doi.org/10.1016/j.apal.2009.07.003
9. Chatterjee, K., Henzinger, T.A., Horn, F.: Finitary winning in ω-regular games. ACM Trans. Comput. Logic **11**(1) (2009)
10. Della Monica, D., Goranko, V., Montanari, A., Sciavicco, G.: Interval temporal logics: a journey. Bull. Eur. Assoc. Theoret. Comput. Sci. **105**, 73–99 (2011)
11. Della Monica, D., Montanari, A., Murano, A., Sala, P.: Prompt interval temporal logic (extended version) (2016). http://wpage.unina.it/dario.dellamonica/techrep/promptPNL_ext.pdf
12. Della Monica, D., Montanari, A., Sala, P.: The importance of the past in interval temporal logics: the case of propositional neighborhood logic. In: Artikis, A., Craven, R., Kesim Çiçekli, N., Sadighi, B., Stathis, K. (eds.) Logic Programs, Norms and Action. LNCS (LNAI), vol. 7360, pp. 79–102. Springer, Heidelberg (2012). doi:10.1007/978-3-642-29414-3_6
13. Fijalkow, N., Zimmermann, M.: Cost-Parity and Cost-Streett Games. In: FSTTCS. LIPIcs, vol. 18, pp. 124–135 (2012)
14. Gennari, R., Tonelli, S., Vittorini, P.: An AI-based process for generating games from flat stories. In: Proceedings of the 33rd SGAI, pp. 337–350 (2013)
15. Halpern, J.Y., Shoham, Y.: A propositional modal logic of time intervals. J. ACM **38**(4), 935–962 (1991). http://doi.acm.org/10.1145/115234.115351
16. Kupferman, O., Piterman, N., Vardi, M.Y.: From liveness to promptness. Formal Methods Syst. Des. **34**(2), 83–103 (2009)
17. Laban, S., El-Desouky, A.: RISMA: a rule-based interval state machine algorithm for alerts generation, performance analysis and monitoring real-time data processing. In: Proceedings of the EGU General Assembly 2013. Geophysical Research Abstracts, vol. 15 (2013)
18. Lodaya, K., Parikh, R., Ramanujam, R., Thiagarajan, P.: A logical study of distributed transition systems. Inf. Comput. **119**(1), 91–118 (1995). http://www.sciencedirect.com/science/article/pii/S0890540185710784
19. Mogavero, F., Murano, A., Sorrentino, L.: On promptness in parity games. In: McMillan, K., Middeldorp, A., Voronkov, A. (eds.) LPAR 2013. LNCS, vol. 8312, pp. 601–618. Springer, Heidelberg (2013). doi:10.1007/978-3-642-45221-5_40
20. Moszkowski, B.: Reasoning about digital circuits. Technical report. stan-cs-83-970, Dept. of Computer Science, Stanford University, Stanford, CA (1983)
21. Pnueli, A.: The temporal logic of programs. In: Proceedings of the 18th Annual Symposium on Foundations of Computer Science (FOCS), pp. 46–57. IEEE Computer Society (1977)
22. Pratt-Hartmann, I.: Temporal prepositions and their logic. Artif. Intell. **166**(1–2), 1–36 (2005)
23. Zhou, C., Hansen, M.R.: Duration calculus: a formal approach to real-time systems. EATCS Monographs in Theoretical Computer Science. Springer, Heidelberg (2004)
24. Zimmermann, M.: Optimal bounds in parametric LTL games. Theor. Comput. Sci. **493**, 30–45 (2013). http://dx.doi.org/10.1016/j.tcs.2012.07.039

Exploiting Contextual Knowledge for Hybrid Classification of Visual Objects

Thomas Eiter and Tobias Kaminski$^{(\boxtimes)}$

Institute of Information Systems, TU Wien, Vienna, Austria
{eiter,kaminski}@kr.tuwien.ac.at

Abstract. We consider the problem of classifying visual objects in a scene by exploiting the semantic context. For this task, we define hybrid classifiers (HC) that combine local classifiers with context constraints, and can be applied to collective classification problems (CCPs) in general. Context constraints are represented by weighted ASP constraints using object relations. To integrate probabilistic information provided by the classifier and the context, we embed our encoding in the formalism LP^{MLN}, and show that an optimal labeling can be efficiently obtained from the corresponding LP^{MLN} program by employing an ordinary ASP solver. Moreover, we describe a methodology for constructing an HC for a CCP, and present experimental results of applying an HC for object classification in indoor and outdoor scenes, which exhibit significant improvements in terms of accuracy compared to using only a local classifier.

1 Introduction

For several decades, AI research has devoted huge efforts to automate logical reasoning in *knowledge representation and reasoning* (*KRR*) and to develop methods for statistical learning and inference in *machine learning* (*ML*). While these areas are rather mature, it became evident that many real-world domains require both logical and statistical reasoning as they comprise complex relational as well as uncertain information. Consequently, *statistical relational learning* (*SRL*) has gained momentum, and many approaches which combine statistical and logical methods have been developed (see [9] for an overview).

One of the basic tasks in SRL is *collective classification*, which is simultaneously finding correct labels for a number of interrelated objects; this has applications in many concrete domains, e.g. classification of interlinked documents, part-of-speech tagging and optical character recognition [21]. A further such application is to predict the labels (i.e., class memberships) of objects in a complex visual scene that contains many objects of different classes. Even if advanced and robust algorithms for object recognition have been developed, e.g. *SIFT* descriptors [12] and the *bag of keypoints* approach [4], they may fail

This research has been supported by the Austrian Science Fund (FWF) projects P27730 and W1255-N23.

© Springer International Publishing AG 2016
L. Michael and A. Kakas (Eds.): JELIA 2016, LNAI 10021, pp. 223–239, 2016.
DOI: 10.1007/978-3-319-48758-8_15

Fig. 1. Objects in a scene with predicted labels (from the LabelMe dataset [19])

unavoidably and yield ambiguous results due to few training data, noisy inputs, or inherent ambiguity of visual appearance (e.g. a lemon and a tennis ball might be indistinguishable in a low resolution image [16]). It is then still possible to draw on further information from the scene in which an object occurs to disambiguate its label. For an example, consider the street scene in Fig. 1, where object 2 is wrongly labeled as 'building' in the center image. This misclassification could be resolved by considering all object labels simultaneously, drawing on background knowledge that wheels normally appear at the bottom of a car; thus, the probability for labeling object 2 as 'car' increases.

In KRR, a natural approach to formalize admissible labelings of objects respecting their interrelations would consist in imposing logical constraints on labelings and using constraint programming techniques to compute 'possible worlds' represented by complete labelings. While this approach yields all consistent labelings, it neglects (hidden) features of the concrete classification problem. Hence, it is desirable to combine constraints over label assignments with the output of a probabilistic classifier processing (low-level) object features. A naive such combination is to use a ranking over all labels for each object induced by the probability distributions given by a classifier, and to compute the labeling that maximizes the rank of the assigned labels while satisfying all constraints. However, in real-world domains this approach turns out to be too restrictive. First, real data necessarily has exceptions that cannot all be modeled, which may prevent that a consistent solution is found; second, this approach retains no information about the metric distance between label probabilities, which is essential for deciding whether a label should be changed to a less likely one in order to satisfy some constraint.

In this paper, we bridge the gap between combinatorial and probabilistic object classification by encoding the context of a concrete *collective classification problem* (*CCP*) in a set of *answer set programming* (*ASP*) rules and constraints that we assign a probabilistic semantics. Using ASP to formalize context knowledge, we can combine multiple context relations in even complex constraints and utilize *closed world reasoning* to express e.g. that objects not containing car parts should not be labeled as cars.

Our main contributions are briefly summarized as follows.

(1) We define a general framework for solving CCPs that combines a generic local classifier and context constraints into a *hybrid classifier*, which is given semantics via an embedding into LP^{MLN} [10]. We then show how solutions can be obtained efficiently with a backtranslation from LP^{MLN} into classical answer set programs with weak constraints [2], and by leveraging combinatorial optimization capabilities of state-of-the-art ASP solvers.
(2) We describe a methodology for constructing a hybrid classifier for a specific domain by designing and tuning a context encoding. To the best of our knowledge, this has not been considered before.
(3) We examine the usefulness of our methodology with an extensive empirical evaluation in the domain of visual object classification in indoor as well as outdoor scenes. The results provide evidence that hybrid classifiers can significantly improve accuracy, provided that the local classifier works reasonably well, given the outset of few training data, noisy data or ambiguous data. Furthermore, they show that tuning and the use of a validation set are important elements for increasing accuracy gains.

Notably, in our approach knowledge representation and reasoning is a first-class citizen, while SRL approaches often rely on statistical formulations and probabilistic solving methods; this seems less geared towards combinatorial problem solving. Moreover, our encoding can be easily extended by spatial reasoning via rules over extracted facts, as well as by a component for taxonomical reasoning over label categories.

2   Preliminaries

Answer set programs with weak constraints [2] constitute the host language of our hybrid classification encoding. A *normal logic program* P is a finite set of rules of the form

$$H \leftarrow B_1, ..., B_k, \mathbf{not}\, B_{k+1}, ..., \mathbf{not}\, B_m, \qquad (1)$$

where H and all B_i are function-free first-order atoms from a classical first-order signature. Given a rule r, H is called the head of r, $B^+(r) = \{B_1, ..., B_k\}$ its *positive body* and $B^-(r) = \{B_{k+1}, ..., B_m\}$ its *negative body*. A rule without a head is called a *constraint*. The grounding P_g of P is obtained by replacing all variables by constants occurring in P in all possible ways, as usual. Stable models (or answer sets) are the minimal models of the GL-reduct (cf. [8]).

A *weak constraint* is written as follows:

$$:\sim B_1, ..., B_k, \mathbf{not}\, B_{k+1}, ..., \mathbf{not}\, B_m \,[w]. \qquad (2)$$

The weight w of a weak constraint c, denoted $weight(c)$, is either an integer constant or a variable occurring in the positive body of the constraint. A ground weak constraint has the same weight as the constraint it originates from. For a

Herbrand interpretation I and a set C of weak constraints, the violation cost of C wrt. I is $cost_I(C) = \sum_{c' \in C'} weight(c')$, where $C' \subseteq C$ are the weak constraints such that $B^+ \subseteq I$ and $B^- \cap I = \emptyset$. The answer sets of $P \cup C$ are all those answer sets I of P such that no answer set I' of P with $cost_{I'}(C) < cost_I(C)$ exists.

We assign a probabilistic semantics to our encoding by utilizing the formalism LP^{MLN} [10], which employs weighted rules for combining ASP with probabilistic graphical models based on *Markov logic networks (MLNs)* [18]. LP^{MLN} programs generalize normal logic programs by assigning a weight w to every rule r of form (1) in the program. The weight w is either a real number or α, representing the infinite weight. When grounding an LP^{MLN} program, every ground weighted rule $w : r_g$ is mapped to the same weight w as its non-ground counterpart $w : r$. A probabilistic semantics is defined for LP^{MLN} programs as follows.

Definition 1 (Unnormalized weight [10]**).** *For an LP^{MLN} program Π and a Herbrand interpretation I, the unnormalized weight of I under Π is given by*

$$
W_\Pi(I) = \begin{cases} exp\left(\sum_{w:r \in \Pi_I} w \right) & \text{if } I \in SM[\Pi], \\ 0 & \text{otherwise}, \end{cases} \tag{3}
$$

where Π_I represents all weighted rules $w : r$ in Π s.t. $I \models r$, and $SM[\Pi]$ contains all I s.t. I is a classical answer set of Π_I, omitting the weights.

In order to obtain a probability distribution over all Herbrand interpretations wrt. an LP^{MLN} program, the corresponding weights have to be normalized.

Definition 2 (Normalized weight [10]**).** *For an LP^{MLN} program Π and a Herbrand interpretation I, the normalized weight of I under Π is given by*

$$
P_\Pi(I) = \lim_{\alpha \to \infty} \frac{W_\Pi(I)}{\sum_{J \in SM[\Pi]} W_\Pi(J)}. \tag{4}
$$

Lee and Wang [10] define a (probabilistic) stable model of an LP^{MLN} program Π to be a Herbrand interpretation I s.t. $P_\Pi(I) \neq 0$.

Since our goal is to use LP^{MLN} programs for finding the global best labeling for a set of objects, i.e. the answer set encoding the label assignment with the highest probability, we do not discuss conditional probability queries here. Lee and Wang show a close relationship between ASP with weak constraints and LP^{MLN} programs, such that under certain conditions the answer set with the highest normalized probability can be computed directly by an ordinary answer set solver that exhibits optimization capabilities. The authors define a translation $\tau(P) = \Pi$ from an answer set program with weak constraints P to an LP^{MLN} program Π, and show the following correspondence.

Proposition 1 (adapted from [10]**).** *For an answer set program with weak constraints P that has an answer set, its answer sets are the Herbrand interpretations $\{I | \nexists I' : P_\Pi(I') > P_\Pi(I)\}$, where $\Pi = \tau(P)$.*

For translating an LP^{MLN} program into an answer set program with weak constraints, we apply τ^{-1}, which is only applicable to LP^{MLN} programs in which all rules are assigned the infinite weight α and only constraints of the form (2) are assigned arbitrary weights. The translation τ^{-1} works by omitting the weight of rules with non-empty head and by replacing constraints of the form $w : \leftarrow B_1, ..., B_k, \textbf{not } B_{k+1}, ..., \textbf{not } B_m$ by a rule $H \leftarrow B_1, ..., B_k, \textbf{not } B_{k+1}, ..., \textbf{not } B_m$ together with the weak constraint $:\sim \textbf{not } H [-w]$, where H is a fresh atom not occurring elsewhere.[1] Under the mentioned restrictions, Proposition 1 still holds.

3   Hybrid Classification

We aim at applying LP^{MLN} programs for simultaneously classifying all objects in a visual scene. In order to obtain a complete labeling that is as close as possible to the ground truth, we exploit two sources of probabilistic information regarding the most likely label for a given object. On the one hand, we use a *classifier* that is trained on vectors of object features and predicts the probability of each local label given the features of a single new object. On the other hand, we exploit the *relational context* defined by relations between several objects, by learning the probability of certain label combinations for sets of objects that are related in specific ways, e.g. some objects in an image may be contained in some other objects more or less frequently. In this way, the notion of the best label for some object is probabilistically constrained from two sides, and we strive for an optimal label on the basis of all probabilistic information available. We refer to our combination of local classifier and relational context as *hybrid classifier* (*HC*); notably, their classification results increasingly disagree with context elaboration, and the relational component has a richer structure than in most related approaches on collective classification.

In this section, we define an HC in form of an LP^{MLN} encoding that combines a local classifier with a set of weighted context constraints over label assignments wrt. the relational structure. We start by defining *collective classification problems* (*CCPs*) based on the definition in [21], but we generalize the neighborhood function used there to arbitrary relations between objects. First, we introduce a schema on the basis of which a group of CCPs can be defined.

Definition 3 (CCS). *A collective classification schema (CCS) is represented by a pair $S = \langle L, R \rangle$ consisting of*

- *a set $L = \{l_1, ..., l_m\}$ of possible object labels,*
- *a family $R = \{R_0, ..., R_k\}$ of sets of 0- to k-ary context relation names.*

The sets $R_i \in R$ contain names for i-ary relations between objects that can, for instance, be extracted from a scene image, e.g. a binary relation entailing all pairs of objects where the first object is contained in the second object, or a

---

[1] As the logic program rules here are more restricted than in [10], we adapt the translation defined there. Real-valued weights can be approximated by integers in weak constraints.

ternary relation stating that an object is located in-between two other objects. The set L contains possible object labels, e.g. 'car' and 'tree' for objects in a street scene.

A CCS is instantiated by a CCP, by fixing the set of objects that need to be classified together with their local object features as well as the concrete relations occurring between them, as follows.

Definition 4 (CCP). *A collective classification problem (CCP) is represented by a triple* $\mathcal{C} = \langle S, O, e \rangle$ *consisting of*

- *a CCS* $S = \langle L, R \rangle$,
- *a set* $O = \{o_1, ..., o_n\}$ *of objects with associated features* $f(o_i)$ *for each* $o_i \in O$,
- *a function* $e : \bigcup_{R_i \in R} \to O^k$ *that maps each i-ary relation name to a concrete i-ary relation over objects.*

A solution for a CCP is a complete labeling *represented by a mapping* $\lambda : O \to L$, *assigning a label from L to each object in O.*

Next, we introduce *local classifiers*, where we abstract from the level of particular object features and assume a classifier that is able to return a probability distribution over all labels for each object by processing their corresponding features. Subsequently, we draw on the information provided by local classifier c for hybrid classification by integrating c with a context encoding into an HC.

Definition 5 (Local classifier). *Given a CCS* $S = \langle L, R \rangle$, *a local classifier c is a function that maps the feature vector $f(o)$ of an object o to a discrete probability distribution P_o^c over all labels in L (on the basis of their associated feature vectors).*

Due to the generality of the approach, different kinds of classifiers, e.g. *Logistic Regression* or *Neural Networks*, can be utilized to instantiate the local classifier c.

Example 1. For the scene in Fig. 1, we construct a corresponding CCP $\mathcal{C} = \langle S, O, e \rangle$ with $S = \langle \{car, building, wheel\}, \{\emptyset, \emptyset, \{contains\}\} \rangle$, $O = \{o_1, o_2\}$ (omitting 'object 3') and $e(contains) = \{\langle o1, o2 \rangle\}$. We assume that the classifier c for $\mathcal{C}$ yields, based on the object features $f(o_i)$ extracted from the image, $P_{o_1}^c(car) = 0.4$, $P_{o_1}^c(building) = 0.5$, $P_{o_1}^c(wheel) = 0.1$, $P_{o_2}^c(car) = 0.1$, $P_{o_2}^c(building) = 0.1$ and $P_{o_2}^c(wheel) = 0.8$.

In other approaches [1,6,16], relations between objects are often used to conditionalize the probability distribution of label combinations of the involved objects. As we use ASP constraints to describe the relational context, we use the relations in the sets R_i differently, i.e. to state restrictions over expected label assignments via relations that may be derived from further relations together with other supposed label assignments.

Following Richardson and Domingos [18], the weight of a context constraint in LP^{MLN} can be interpreted as the logarithm of the odds between a possible world where it is satisfied and one where it is not (called the *log odds*), other things being equal. In general, context constraints are not independent from each other, thus changing their truth value also changes the value of other constraints. However, as we consider cases with only few training data (such that the classifier output can still be improved by considering the context), it is unfeasible to learn all interactions between constraints from it. Thus, we assume *bona fide* independence of context constraints and straight use the *log odds* for the constraints calculated from the training instances as weights.

The restrictions over label assignments in terms of the relational context are formalized by a *context encoding* as follows:

Definition 6 (Context encoding). *Given a CCS $S = \langle L, R \rangle$, we use the following designated predicates:* context relation predicates $\mathcal{R} = \bigcup_{R_i \in R} R_i$ *and* helper predicates $\mathcal{H}$ *ranging over tuples of objects, and the* label assignment predicate a_label *ranging over pairs of objects and labels. A context encoding E for S is an LP^{MLN} program that consists of rules of the form*

$$\alpha : h(\overline{X}) \leftarrow b_1(\overline{X}), \ldots, b_k(\overline{X}), \mathbf{not}\, b_{k+1}(\overline{X}), \ldots, \mathbf{not}\, b_m(\overline{X}), \tag{5}$$

where $h \in \mathcal{H}$ and $b_1, \ldots, b_m \in \mathcal{R} \cup \mathcal{H} \cup \{a\_label\}$; and constraints of the form

$$w : \leftarrow b_1(\overline{X}), \ldots, b_k(\overline{X}), \mathbf{not}\, b_{k+1}(\overline{X}), \ldots, \mathbf{not}\, b_m(\overline{X}), \tag{6}$$

where $b_1, \ldots, b_m \in \mathcal{R} \cup \mathcal{H} \cup \{a\_label\}$, and w is the log odds for the constraint being satisfied given the extensions of the predicates in $\mathcal{R} \cup \mathcal{H}$ (as learned from training data).

The helper predicates in $\mathcal{H}$ are used to recursively aggregate relations and label assignments into new relations, which can be utilized to restrict permissible assignments.

Example 2 (cont'd). We define a simple context encoding E for S from Example 1, using the context relation predicate *contains* and the helper predicate *has_car_part*:

$$\alpha : has\_car\_part(X) \leftarrow contains(X, Y), a\_label(Y, wheel) \tag{7}$$

$$1.95 : \leftarrow \mathbf{not}\, a\_label(X, car), has\_car\_part(X) \tag{8}$$

The particular weight is chosen for the context constraint because we assume here that we have observed 28 cases in our training data where an object that has a car part is actually a car, and four cases where it is not, i.e. the log odds for the constraint being true given the extension of the predicate *has_car_part* are $ln(28/4) \approx 1.95$.

Taxonomic reasoning can easily be added by introducing, e.g. a rule that derives all labels representing car parts. Likewise, spatial reasoning can be implemented by inferring further relations from the given relations (e.g., an object overlaps with another object if one contains the other).

We combine a local classifier for a CCS $S = \langle L, R \rangle$ and a context encoding for S into an HC that yields a solution for a CCP $\mathcal{C} = \langle S, O, e \rangle$ as follows:

Definition 7 (Hybrid classifier encoding). *Given a CCP $\mathcal{C} = \langle S, O, e \rangle$ for a CCS $S = \langle L, R \rangle$, a local classifier c, and a context encoding E for S, the hybrid classifier (HC) for $\mathcal{C}$ is represented by an LP^{MLN} program $\Pi_{\mathcal{C}}(c, E) = E \cup A(c, O) \cup I(\mathcal{C})$ where the classifier assignment encoding $A(c, O)$ contains*

(1) the weighted facts
$\quad \alpha : label(l_i)$ *for each label $l_i \in L$,*
$\quad \alpha : clf(o_i, l_j, p)$ *for each $o_i \in O$ and $l_j \in L$, where $p = ln \left(\frac{P_{o_i}^c(l_j)}{1 - P_{o_i}^c(l_j)} \right)$,*

(2) the two guessing rules
$\quad \alpha : a\_label(O, L) \leftarrow object(O), label(L), not\ n\_a\_label(O, L),$
$\quad \alpha : n\_a\_label(O, L) \leftarrow object(O), label(L), not\ a\_label(O, L),$

(3) the unique assignment constraint
$\quad \alpha : \leftarrow \#count\{L : a\_label\_prob(X, L, P)\} \neq 1, object(X),$

(4) the weighted classifier constraint
$\quad P : \leftarrow not\ a\_label\_prob(O, L, P), clf(O, L, P)$
and the rule
$\quad \alpha : a\_label\_prob(O, L, P) \leftarrow a\_label(O, L), clf(O, L, P),$

and the CCP instance encoding $I(\mathcal{C})$ contains

(5) the weighted facts
$\quad \alpha : object(o_i)$ *for each object $o_i \in O$, and*
$\quad \alpha : r_i(o_1, \ldots, o_i)$ *for each $r_i \in R_i$ and each $\langle o_1, \ldots, o_i \rangle \in e(r_i)$.*

Here, (5) represents the input part of the HCP, while (2)–(4) are fixed; (2) and (3) ensure that each object gets exactly one label, and (4) assigns the weights by the local classifier to the separate label assignments. Again, we use the log odds between a complete label assignment where a label is assigned vs. not assigned from the local classifier as weight.

Intuitively, a solution of an HCP should minimize the violation costs of context constraints, but at the same time maximize the joint classifier probability of the label assignment. As the two optimization criteria are opposite in general, the goal is a good compromise that yields a better label assignment than the one of the local classifier. As it is not clear a priori how much influence the classifier and the context constraints should have on a solution, the probabilities returned by the local classifier in (4) could be scaled by an influence factor such that its impact on a solution can be varied for tuning an HC.

A solution for a CCP wrt. an HC is defined as follows.

Definition 8 (HC solution). *A solution for a CCP $\mathcal{C}$ provided by an HC $\Pi_{\mathcal{C}}(c, E)$ is a solution λ for $\mathcal{C}$ s.t. for some Herbrand interpretation I, no Herbrand interpretation I' with $P_{\Pi_{\mathcal{C}}(c,E)}(I') > P_{\Pi_{\mathcal{C}}(c,E)}(I)$ exists and $a\_label(o_i, l_i) \in I$ iff $\lambda(o_i) = l_i$.*

Definition 7 encodes the optimization problem by an LP^{MLN} program that can be translated into an ordinary answer set program with weak constraints, such that a solution according to Definition 8 can be extracted from any answer set (cf. Proposition 1).

Example 3 (cont'd). The LP^{MLN} program $\Pi_{\mathcal{C}}(c, E)$ representing the HC for $\mathcal{C}$, c and E as in the previous examples consists of E, with the weighted facts $\alpha : obj(o1)$, $\alpha : obj(o2)$, $\alpha : label(c)$, $\alpha : label(b)$, $\alpha : label(w)$, $\alpha : clf(o1, c, \text{-}0.41)$, $\alpha : clf(o1, b, 0)$, $\alpha : clf(o1, w, \text{-}2.2)$, $\alpha : clf(o2, c, \text{-}2.2)$, $\alpha : clf(o2, b, \text{-}2.2)$, $\alpha : clf(o2, w, 1.39)$ and $\alpha : contains(o1, o2)$ (abbreviating the labels), and (2) to (4) from Definition 7.

Without the context encoding E, the single stable model of the program with the highest normalized weight would contain $a\_label(o1, b)$ and $a\_label(o2, w)$; this does not correspond to the correct labeling of the scene shown rightmost in Fig. 1. The previous assignment would not satisfy the constraint in E. Hence, when considering E, there are three ways to satisfy it by changing the assigned labels: changing (1) the label of $o1$ to *car*; or (2) the label of $o2$ to either (2) *building* or (3) *car*. As the constraint has weight 1.95 and the label adaptations result in a weight difference of -0.41 for (1) and -3.59 for (2) and (3) for the classifier constraints, only (1) would yield an overall weight improvement. Thus, labeling o_1 as *car* and o_2 as *wheel* is the only solution for $\mathcal{C}$ via $\Pi_{\mathcal{C}}(c, E)$ according to Definition 8; this is the correct labeling of the scene.

Note that if the difference between the probability that $o2$ is a *wheel* and e.g. a *building* would be small enough, satisfying the constraint (7) in E by changing the label of $o2$ could actually result in a higher overall weight. Thus, context constraints can also decrease the accuracy of the resulting labeling, depending on the quality of the probabilities provided by the classifier.

4   Hybrid Classifier Construction

After having defined HCs abstractly above, we now describe a methodology for constructing a concrete HC for a given CCP, which we also employ in our empirical evaluation. We suggest the following strategy for obtaining a good HC, where the objective is high accuracy of the corresponding solution.

(1) *Data and local classifier preparation.* We assume that we are given a set of CCPs that are all defined over the same CCS for training the HC, together with a solution λ for each CCP representing the ground truth. Obviously, the concrete relations e are usually different in each CCP and first must be extracted from the raw data. For testing the influence of different context constraints, it is crucial to use part of the data for validation to avoid over-fitting of the designed constraint encoding. Hence, we split the initial data set into a training set, a validation set and a test set. The local classifier is trained on the associated features of all objects in the CCPs in the training set separately.

(2) *Designing the context encoding.* Although context constraints theoretically could be learned, e.g. by ILP techniques, the current approach assumes that a domain expert with background knowledge on the particular task for the HC has designed the context encoding. However, failure patterns in the output of the local classifier can be used to guide the design process. For

this purpose, the local classifier is first used to classify all objects in the validation set and a *confusion matrix* is compiled, which reveals objects that are difficult to classify for the local classifier and the pairs of labels confused most often. This way, the constraint encoding can be tailored to counter the shortcomings of the local classifier that might result from few, noisy or ambiguous data.

For a constraint c of the form (6) (see Definition 6), its weight w is computed as follows. Determine in the training set the number of ground instances where the label assignment specified by atoms in L is false (resp., true), denoted by f_c (resp., t_c), provided the context described by the atoms in $\mathcal{R} \cup \mathcal{H}$ of (6) is satisfied. If we would not fix these atoms for counting, e.g. in Example 2 for (8) each object not containing a car part would count as positive instance. However, in this case we are interested in the odds for an object being a car if it has a car part. The weight w of the constraint c is then $\ln(f_c/t_c)$.

(3) *Constraint selection and influence tuning.* After having designed the constraint encoding, the resulting HC could be evaluated already on the test set and used on new CCP instances. However, as discussed in Example 3, context constraints may also decrease the overall accuracy of the results. Hence, the constraint encoding E should be evaluated on the validation set first. As constraints may interact, in general each subset C of constraints must be tested to single out the optimal one wrt. the validation set. As there are exponentially many C, a heuristics is to assess the influence of each constraint c separately and keep it if the accuracy does not decrease if c is applied alone resp. increase if c is dropped from the set of all constraints. In addition, the validation set can be used to tune the influence of the local classifier and the context encoding on the solution, by testing different influence factors.

Example 4 (HC in visual scenes). In the context of visual object classification in scene images, a CCS $S = \langle L, R \rangle$ is created by defining the set L of possible labels for the objects in a class of scenes, e.g. 'car', 'building' and 'tree' for outdoor scenes, and 'table', 'chair' and 'shelf' for indoor scenes, and by fixing the considered set R of relations between objects. Spatial relations such as 'contains', 'intersects' and 'touches' are arguably most prevalent in visual scenes, but R may include also other relations, even relating local features of different objects, such as the binary relation 'has_same_color'.

To turn a set of scene images into a set of CCPs, the image first must be segmented into regions containing single objects. Many procedures for image segmentation exist (see e.g. the survey in [25]); we simply assume here that the image is already segmented. The visual features of the separate segments represent the input to the local classifier, which needs to be trained on a training set of segments representing objects O from training CCPs $\langle S, O, e \rangle$ and the corresponding set L of labels. The extension e of the relations R must be extracted for each CCP separately from the information provided by the scene image and its segmentation, e.g. by computing spatial relations wrt. their bounding boxes or polygon coordinates. Further, implicitly entailed spatial relations can be derived e.g. by employing a spatial reasoning calculus such as RCC8 [17].

Suppose we examine the confusion matrix for the local classifier on the validation set for indoor scenes, and we observe that doors are often misclassified as tables (their surfaces look nearly identical). We then could add a constraint c to the encoding E which states that tables are not contained in walls. We compute f_c and t_c by counting the objects in the training set contained in a wall that are non-tables resp. tables; presumably the resulting weight $\ln(f_c/t_c)$ is quite high. After having added several constraints to E, we test how removing single constraints (or sets of them) affects the accuracy on the validation set. In that, we might observe that the constraint prohibiting tables in walls actually decreases the overall accuracy, even if it is mostly satisfied on the training data. Indeed, possibly some doors are still wrongly labeled as 'table' while the correct label 'wall' of a wall is changed to an incorrect one. This might have further implications; e.g. if a constraint states that windows only occur in walls, many windows are misclassified too. This illustrates the importance of constraint selection for HC construction.

5 Evaluation

In this section, we evaluate two concrete HCs for two different sets of benchmark instances in order to empirically investigate the effect of applying context constraints. Our goal is to ascertain (Q1) whether a higher classification accuracy is achievable by employing an HC instead of a local classifier, (Q2) which influence the quality of the local classifier has on HC performance, and (Q3) which impact constraint selection and influence tuning have on the solution quality.

We expected that HCs improve the accuracy provided that the local classifier yields sufficiently many correct labels, as a basis to correct the other labels; furthermore, that the accuracy gain can be increased by tuning an HC on the validation set.

Experimental Setup. For experimentation, we implemented an HC framework in Python that enables construction and evaluation of HCs for object classification in scene images. As local classifier, we used *Logistic Regression* from the *scikit-learn* library [14], which we trained on features extracted from image segments obtained by the *bag of keypoints* approach [4], which uses vector quantization of invariant image descriptors. For creating the visual vocabulary, we employed *k-means clustering* and *Scale Invariant Feature Transform* (*SIFT*) descriptors [12]; they are suited for our purpose as they are invariant wrt. transformations, varying illumination and overlapping objects. To detect and compute SIFT descriptors, we used the *OpenCV*[2] library.

Furthermore, we used the *Shapely*[3] package for Python to calculate concrete spatial relations between object-polygons in each scene, based on the *DE-9IM*

---

[2] http://opencv.org/.

[3] https://pypi.python.org/pypi/Shapely.

Fig. 2. Example of a typical indoor and outdoor scene from the LabelMe dataset [19]

Table 1. Results for local classifier and HC with (+sel) or without (−sel) constraint selection and with (+tun) or without (−tun) influence tuning

Data set	Local classifier	HC −sel −tun	HC −sel +tun	HC +sel −tun	HC +sel +tun
(E1) validation	46.3 %	53.3 %	52.9 %	57.1 %	58.0 %
(E1) test	46.5 %	52.2 %	52.7 %	54.4 %	55.5 %
(E2) validation	59.7 %	63.3 %	67.7 %	68.8 %	70.6 %
(E2) test	58.1 %	59.6 %	69.0 %	71.0 %	73.2 %

model [23]. Moreover, for computing the optimal solution of an HC encoding, we utilized CLASP 3.1.2 and GRINGO 4.5.1 [7].

Benchmark Instances. The experiments have been conducted on two sets of scene images from the *LabelMe* dataset [19]. We used a custom segmentation obtained manually, as for testing the impact of context constraints the quality of the available segmentations as well as the user-defined labels varied considerably. The data sets used in our experiments, the segmentation data, the constraint encodings and all results are available at http://www.kr.tuwien.ac.at/research/projects/inthex/hc-experiments/.

We use (E1) a set of *indoor office scenes* and (E2) a set of *outdoor street scenes*, each containing 120 images, which we split into a training set and validation set of 30 images each, and a test set of 60 images. A typical scene from each data set is shown in Fig. 2. For both types, we defined 12 labels for the objects that occur most frequently:

- indoor: 'chair' (c), 'monitor' (mn), 'keyboard' (k), 'mouse' (ms), 'table' (t), 'book' (bk), 'shelf' (s), 'wall' (wl), 'board' (br), 'person' (p), 'door' (d) and 'window' (wi),
- outdoor: 'sign' (sg), 'person' (p), 'tree' (tr), 'window' (wi), 'door' (d), 'street' (st), 'car' (c), 'sky' (sk), 'building' (b), 'sidewalk' (si), 'wheel' (wh) and 'trunk' (trn).

Indoor scenes contain 7 to 23 objects, outdoor scenes 7 to 28. In total, (E1) contains 2046 objects, and (E2) has 2280 objects. We extracted the binary spatial relations 'contains', 'close_to', 'above', 'under', 'overlaps', 'contains_in_bottom_part'

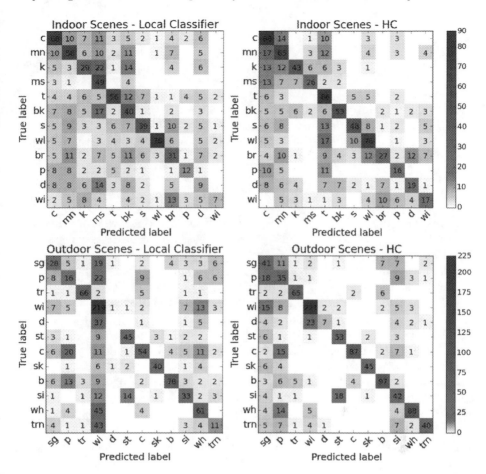

Fig. 3. Confusion matrices of local classifier and HC test results for indoor and outdoor scenes

and 'higher' from the images for use in our constraint encodings, from which we created an HC for each dataset.

Experimental Results. After training the local classifiers on all objects in the training sets, we applied them to the validation sets; for indoor scenes, the average accuracy was 46.3 % and for outdoor scenes 59.7 %. We then constructed HCs, following the methodology from Sect. 4, by setting up 20 constraints in each case and selecting a subset of 13 constraints after testing different combinations. The accuracy increased for the indoor validation set to 57.1 % and for the outdoor validation set to 69.0 %.

In addition, we tested different influence factors, viz. 0.1, 1, 10, and 100 for the classifier weights; for both data sets, factor 10 yielded the best results due to less erroneous changes of labels correctly predicted by the local classifier. This value is thus suggestive as a default for our use case, and we fixed the influence factors to these values.

We then applied the final HCs to the test sets. Overall, for indoor scenes the accuracy increased from 46.5 % to 55.5 %, and the HC was better than the local classifier on 38 scenes and worse on 11 out of 60. For outdoor scenes, the accuracy increased from 58.1 % to 73.2 %, and the HC was better than the local classifier on 57 cases and worse in 1 case. Thus (Q1), whether an HC can be better than a local classifier, has in these use cases a positive answer. The test results are summarized in Table 1.

Regarding (Q3), i.e., the impact of constraint selection and influence tuning, simply adding all 20 constraints increased the accuracy for indoor scenes from 46.5 % to 52.2 % and for outdoor scenes from 58.1 % to merely 59.6 %; this confirms that constraint selection is a crucial step in HC construction. Influence tuning also proved beneficial and helped to increase the accuracy further in both cases (cf. Table 1).

To provide more details on the effect of the context constraints on the particular labels, Fig. 3 shows the confusion matrices of the local classifiers and the final HCs wrt. both test sets. As can be seen e.g. from the rows for books and shelves in the matrix for the indoor local classifier, it misclassifies them more than half of the time. By adding a constraint that books are contained in shelves (weight 5.067) and that shelves contain books (weight 3.967), the number of correctly classified shelves increased from 56 to 86, and for books from 40 to 53. Similarly, considering the matrix for the outdoor local classifier, adding a constraint that windows are contained in buildings or in the upper parts of cars (weight 3.863) decreases wrong window classifications from 269 to 37.

As for (Q2), we artificially decreased the quality of the local classifier by training it on a gradually shrunken training set. Notably the benefit of adding context constraints decreased with the accuracy of the local classifier, and when it was below ≈35 % for indoor resp. ≈45 % for outdoor scenes, the local classifier outperformed the HC.

Finding the optimal solution for an HC encoding for a given scene by CLASP usually took just a few seconds, on a Linux machine with an 2.5 GHz Intel Core i5 CPU and 8 GB RAM. We used a timeout of 20 s, which was only reached by few instances containing many objects, and did not show to have a negative impact on the results.

6   Related Work

As context information is valuable for simultaneous classification of visual objects, many approaches—mainly in *Computer Vision*—exploit scene information and provide either a statistical summary of the image (also called *Gist*) as additional input to the classifier, or exploit relationships between particular objects in a scene (often called the *semantic context*) [15]. Rabinovich and Belongie [15] argue that by considering semantic context, stronger contextual constraints can be imposed (e.g. also spatial relations), and show empirically that they can greatly improve recognition performance. Most approaches using semantic context for label prediction employ some kind of *graphical model*, e.g. *conditional random fields* [16] or *Markov logic networks* [3,13,24] in which the mutual influence of labelings is directly encoded by conditional probabilities. Another approach that is very effective for object classification in complex scenes [1] and for collective classification in general [22] is the *iterative classification algorithm* (*ICA*) [21], which iteratively predicts and updates the label of each object based on the current labeling.

Clearly, our approach is related to approaches that consider semantic context or use graphical models. Those above are different from ours as they usually employ probabilistic inference methods such as *Markov chain Monte Carlo* and do not use combinatorial optimization techniques. In addition, often only simple relations such as the co-occurrence frequency of objects were addressed [1,16]. In contrast, we consider diverse relations between objects extracted from an image (e.g. their position, height and spatial relation to other objects) and they can be combined into more complex relations. Notably, *closed world reasoning* can directly be employed in our approach. In *Markov logic*, this is not straightforward since in the worst case an exponential number of *loop formulas* has to be computed in order to translate LP^{MLN} to Markov logic [10].

An approach similar to ours is presented in [20], where spatial context is also formalized as constraints to increase collective classification accuracy. However, *Fuzzy CSPs* and *Branch and Bound* are used instead of probabilistic semantics, and only basic relation types are considered. From a bird's eye view, our probabilistic approach achieves a higher accuracy gain with considerably less training data, but further research (requiring an implementation of [20] and suitable benchmarks) is needed for a clear picture.

7   Conclusion

In this paper, we have introduced a general framework for solving CCPs and a methodology for its application. Our tests show that classification of objects can be significantly improved by considering their semantic context. At the same time, the achievable improvement highly depends on the selected constraints and their interaction, as well as on the quality of the local classifier. If the latter labels most objects incorrectly, the context constraints intuitively lack a reasonable base for correction as wrong labels do not help to infer correct labels of other objects. Overall, we found that best HC results can be obtained when the local classifier performs reasonably well but there is still room for improvement, and when the right set of constraints is selected using a validation set.

Even though we address a specific application, our framework is applicable to a wide range of tasks. For instance, linked data (e.g. social networks or citation graphs) has been considered as a domain for collective classification [11]. Previous work in this area mostly focuses on uniform neighborhood relations, where complex reasoning over context relations is not required. However, there is much room for exploiting rich relational structures in these domains as well, similar to the ones provided by spatial relations in the visual domain, e.g., by integrating an ontology that defines a number of properties of and relations between people and utilizing, e.g., the transitive closure of the friend-of relation computed in the ASP part.

Outlook. Regarding future work, we aim to integrate our framework into the HEX formalism [5], which extends ASP with external sources and would allow us to interface an ontology reasoner and a spatial reasoning calculus, such as RCC8, directly from within our encoding. In addition, the local classifier could be implemented as an external source as well, resulting in a more modular approach. This way, the classifier could be oriented based on information derived in the ASP part. For instance, if there are two rules stating that the object attached to a car and a bicycle is a wheel, and the label 'wheel' is assigned to some object, abduction could be used to find that the object is either attached to a car or to a bicycle. Subsequently, the classifier could be queried to find the most likely explanation for discovering a wheel.

References

1. Angin, P., Bhargava, B.: A confidence ranked co-occurrence approach for accurate object recognition in highly complex scenes. J. Internet Technol. **14**(1), 13–19 (2013)
2. Buccafurri, F., Leone, N., Rullo, P.: Enhancing disjunctive datalog by constraints. IEEE Trans. Knowl. Data Eng. **12**(5), 845–860 (2000)
3. Chechetka, A., Dash, D., Philipose, M.: Relational learning for collective classification of entities in images. In: AAAI Workshops on Statistical Relational Artificial Intelligence, AAAI Workshop 2010. AAAI (2010)
4. Csurka, G., Dance, C.R., Fan, L., Willamowski, J., Bray, C.: Visual categorization with bags of keypoints. In: Workshop on Statistical Learning in Computer Vision, ECCV 2004, pp. 1–22 (2004)
5. Eiter, T., Ianni, G., Schindlauer, R., Tompits, H.: A uniform integration of higher-order reasoning and external evaluations in answer-set programming. In: International Joint Conference on Artificial Intelligence, IJCAI 2005, pp. 90–96. Professional Book Center (2005)
6. Galleguillos, C., Rabinovich, A., Belongie, S.J.: Object categorization using co-occurrence, location and appearance. In: IEEE Computer Society Conference on Computer Vision and Pattern Recognition, CVPR 2008. IEEE Computer Society (2008)
7. Gebser, M., Kaufmann, B., Kaminski, R., Ostrowski, M., Schaub, T., Schneider, M.T.: Potassco: the potsdam answer set solving collection. AI Commun. **24**(2), 107–124 (2011)
8. Gelfond, M., Lifschitz, V.: Classical negation in logic programs and disjunctive databases. New Gener. Comput. **9**(3/4), 365–386 (1991)
9. Getoor, L.: Introduction to Statistical Relational Learning. MIT Press, Cambridge (2007)
10. Lee, J., Wang, Y.: Weighted rules under the stable model semantics. In: Proceedings of the Fifteenth International Conference on Principles of Knowledge Representation and Reasoning, KR 2016, pp. 145–154. AAAI Press (2016)

11. London, B., Getoor, L.: Collective classification of network data. In: Aggarwal, C.C. (ed.) Data Classification: Algorithms and Applications, pp. 399–416. CRC Press, Boca Raton (2014)
12. Lowe, D.G.: Object recognition from local scale-invariant features. In: 7th IEEE International Conference on Computer Vision, ICCV 1999, pp. 1150–1157 (1999)
13. Marton, Z.C., Rusu, R.B., Jain, D., Klank, U., Beetz, M.: Probabilistic categorization of kitchen objects in table settings with a composite sensor. In: International Conference on Intelligent Robots and Systems, IEEE/RSJ 2009, pp. 4777–4784. IEEE (2009)
14. Pedregosa, F., Varoquaux, G., Gramfort, A., Michel, V., Thirion, B., Grisel, O., Blondel, M., Prettenhofer, P., Weiss, R., Dubourg, V., VanderPlas, J., Passos, A., Cournapeau, D., Brucher, M., Perrot, M., Duchesnay, E.: Scikit-learn: machine learning in Python. J. Mach. Learn. Res. **12**, 2825–2830 (2011)
15. Rabinovich, A., Belongie, S.J.: Scenes vs. objects: a comparative study of two approaches to context based recognition. In: IEEE Conference on Computer Vision and Pattern Recognition, CVPR Workshops 2009, pp. 92–99. IEEE Computer Society (2009)
16. Rabinovich, A., Vedaldi, A., Galleguillos, C., Wiewiora, E., Belongie, S.J.: Objects in context. In: IEEE 11th International Conference on Computer Vision, ICCV 2007, pp. 1–8. IEEE Computer Society (2007)
17. Randell, D.A., Cui, Z., Cohn, A.G.: A spatial logic based on regions and connection. In: Proceedings of the 3rd International Conference on Principles of Knowledge Representation and Reasoning, KR 1992, pp. 165–176. Morgan Kaufmann (1992)
18. Richardson, M., Domingos, P.M.: Markov logic networks. Mach. Learn. **62**(1–2), 107–136 (2006)
19. Russell, B.C., Torralba, A., Murphy, K.P., Freeman, W.T.: LabelMe: a database and web-based tool for image annotation. Int. J. Comput. Vis. **77**(1–3), 157–173 (2008)
20. Saathoff, C., Staab, S.: Exploiting spatial context in image region labelling using fuzzy constraint reasoning. In: Ninth International Workshop on Image Analysis for Multimedia Interactive Services, WIAMIS 2008, pp. 16–19. IEEE Computer Society (2008)
21. Sen, P., Namata, G., Bilgic, M., Getoor, L.: Collective classification. In: Sammut, C., Webb, G.I. (eds.) Encyclopedia of Machine Learning, pp. 189–193. Springer, US (2010)
22. Sen, P., Namata, G., Bilgic, M., Getoor, L., Gallagher, B., Eliassi-Rad, T.: Collective classification in network data. AI Mag. **29**(3), 93–106 (2008)
23. Strobl, C.: Dimensionally extended nine-intersection model (DE-9IM). In: Shekhar, S., Xiong, H. (eds.) Encyclopedia of GIS, pp. 240–245. Springer, US (2008)
24. Tran, S.D., Davis, L.S.: Event modeling and recognition using Markov logic networks. In: Forsyth, D., Torr, P., Zisserman, A. (eds.) ECCV 2008. LNCS, vol. 5303, pp. 610–623. Springer, Heidelberg (2008). doi:10.1007/978-3-540-88688-4_45
25. Zhang, H., Fritts, J.E., Goldman, S.A.: Image segmentation evaluation: a survey of unsupervised methods. Comput. Vis. Image Underst. **110**(2), 260–280 (2008)

Reasoning About Justified Belief
Based on the Fusion of Evidence

Tuan-Fang Fan[1] and Churn-Jung Liau[2(✉)]

[1] Department of Computer Science and Information Engineering,
National Penghu University of Science and Technology, Penghu 880, Taiwan
dffan@npu.edu.tw
[2] Institute of Information Science, Academia Sinica, Taipei 115, Taiwan
liaucj@iis.sinica.edu.tw

Abstract. In this paper, we propose logics for reasoning about belief and evidence. Starting from justification logic (JL) in which the reasons why a fact is believed are explicitly represented as justification terms, we explore the relationship between justified belief and fused information from different evidential sources. We argue that the expressive power of JL is inadequate for our purpose, because, while a justification formula can represent that a piece of evidence is admissible for the belief, it cannot express whether the evidence has been actually observed. Therefore, to address the issue, we propose more fine-grained JL's that can express the informational content of evidence, and the actual observation of evidence is definable in such logics. As a byproduct, we also show that the proposed logics are easily extended to accommodate dynamic evidential reasoning. Consequently, we can integrate JL and dynamic epistemic logic (DEL) paradigms in a natural way.

1 Introduction

Modal logic has been a standard approach for reasoning about knowledge and belief of intelligent agents [13,22] since the seminal work by Hintikka [18]. Because the formula $\Box\varphi$ is interpreted as "φ is believable" or "φ is knowable" in the epistemic/doxastic reading of modal logics[1], explicit justifications are not represented in the logic. By contrast, justification logics (JL) supply the missing component by adding justification terms to epistemic formulas [2,5,6,15]. The first member of the JL family is the logic of proofs (LP) proposed in [1]. Although the original purpose of LP is to formalize the Brouwer-Heyting-Kolmogorov semantics for intuitionistic logic and establish the completeness of intuitionistic logic with respect to this semantics, in a more general setting, JL has evolved

---

The work is partially supported by the Ministry of Science and Technology of Taiwan under Grants MOST 105-2410-H-346-006-MY2 and MOST 104-2221-E-001-010-MY3.

[1] For the purpose of the paper, the difference among belief, knowledge, and information is not important. Hence, hereafter, we use epistemic reasoning to denote reasoning about any kind of informational attitude for an agent.

L. Michael and A. Kakas (Eds.): JELIA 2016, LNAI 10021, pp. 240–255, 2016.
DOI: 10.1007/978-3-319-48758-8_16

into a kind of explicit epistemic logic and received much attention in computer science and AI [2,6].

Currently, the most prominent semantics of JL is based on Fitting models, which are essentially extensions of Kripke models for epistemic logic with an *admissible evidence function*, i.e., a mapping from justification terms and formulas to states that stipulates in what state the evidence is admissible for the formula. However, Fitting semantics suffers the ambiguous interpretation of a justification formula as justified belief or simply the admissibility relation between evidence and belief. The ambiguity arises mainly from the inadequate expressive power of JL. While a justification formula can represent that a piece of evidence is admissible for the belief, it cannot express whether the evidence has been actually observed. Therefore, to facilitate the more fine-grained distinction between admissible and actual evidence, we must enhance the expressive power of the JL language. To address the issue, we propose a JL that can express the informational contents of justification terms; and the fact that a piece of evidence has been actually observed is definable in such logics. Furthermore, the recent development on dynamic epistemic logic (DEL) has shown that modeling dynamics of information plays a crucial role in epistemic reasoning [8,12]. As a byproduct, we also show that the proposed logics can be extended to accommodate dynamic evidential reasoning and hence we can easily integrate JL and DEL paradigms.

The remainder of the paper is organized as follows. In Sect. 2, we review JL and its semantics. In Sect. 3, we present a detailed analysis on the ambiguity problem of JL. In Sect. 4, we propose a fine-grained JL with informational contents of evidence that is expressive enough to overcome the problem. In Sect. 5, we present an alternative fine-grained JL that can differentiate the distinction between direct and indirect observations of evidences with the same informational contents. In Sect. 6, we extend the proposed logics to their dynamic versions. Section 7 contains the comparison with related work. In Sect. 8, we present the conclusion and indicate future research directions.

2   Preliminaries

2.1   Modal Logic

We start with a brief account of classical modal epistemic logic [11]. Let Φ denote the set of propositional symbols. Then, the formulas of the propositional modal logic are defined as follows:

$$\varphi ::= p \mid \perp \mid \varphi \rightarrow \varphi \mid \Box\varphi,$$

where $p \in \Phi$, $\perp$ is the logical constant representing *falsum* , $\rightarrow$ is the material implication, and $\Box$ is the epistemic modality. Other logical connectives such as $\top, \neg, \wedge, \vee, \equiv$ and modality $\Diamond$ are defined as abbreviations as usual. We use $\mathcal{L}_\Box$ to denote the propositional modal language.

The standard semantics of modal logic is based on Kripke model, which is a triple $\mathfrak{M} = \langle W, R, \Vdash \rangle$, where W is a set of possible worlds (states), $R \subseteq W \times W$ is a binary *accessibility relation* on W, and $\Vdash \subseteq W \times \Phi$ is a *forcing relation* between possible worlds and propositional symbols such that $w \Vdash p$ means that p is satisfied in w. As usual, for any $w \in W$, we use $R(w)$ to denote the set of worlds accessible from w, i.e., $R(w) = \{u \in W \mid (w, u) \in R\}$. The forcing relation can be extended to a relation $\Vdash_{\mathfrak{M}}$ between W and $\mathcal{L}_\square$ by the semantic rules. In addition to the standard rules for classical connectives, we have $w \Vdash_{\mathfrak{M}} \square\varphi$ iff for any u such that $(w, u) \in R$, $u \Vdash_{\mathfrak{M}} \varphi$. We usually drop the subscript and simply write $\Vdash$ for the extended forcing relation when the model $\mathfrak{M}$ is clear from the context. The definitions of semantic consequence and validity are standard. Let $\Sigma \cup \{\varphi\}$ be a set of formulas. Then, we use $\Sigma \models \varphi$ and $\models \varphi$ to denote that φ is a semantic consequence of Σ and that φ is valid respectively.

2.2   Justification Logic

To represent justifications, JL provides formal terms built up from constants and variables using various operation symbols. Constants represent justifications for commonly accepted truths—typically axioms, whereas variables denote unspecified justifications. While different variants of JL allow different operation symbols, most of them contain *application* and *sum*. Specifically, the justification terms and formulas of the basic JL are defined as follows:

$$t ::= a \mid x \mid t \cdot t \mid t + t,$$

$$\varphi ::= p \mid \bot \mid \varphi \to \varphi \mid t{:}\varphi,$$

where $p \in \Phi$, a is a justification constant, and x is a justification variable. We use $\mathcal{L}_J$ to denote the basic JL language and Tm to denote the set of all justification terms.

JL furnishes an evidence-based foundation for epistemic logic by using justification formulas $t : \varphi$ to denote "t is a justification of φ", or more strictly, "t is accepted as a justification of φ" [2]. Semantically, the formula $t : \varphi$ can be regarded as indicating that t is an admissible evidence for φ and based on the evidence, φ is believed. Thus, the model of JL is the Kripke model enriched with an additional evidence component [2,15]. This kind of model, called *Kripke-Fitting model* or simply *Fitting model*, is formally defined as a quadruple $\mathfrak{M} = \langle W, R, E, \Vdash \rangle$, where $\langle W, R, \Vdash \rangle$ is a Kripke model and E is an *admissible evidence function* such that $E(t, \varphi) \subseteq W$ for any justification term t and formula φ. Intuitively, $E(t, \varphi)$ specifies the set of possible worlds in which t is regarded as admissible evidence for φ. In this paper, we consider the basic JL in which it is required that E must satisfy the closure condition with respect to the application and sum operations:

- Application: $E(s, \varphi \to \psi) \cap E(t, \varphi) \subseteq E(s \cdot t, \psi)$;
- Sum: $E(s, \varphi) \cup E(t, \varphi) \subseteq E(s + t, \varphi)$;

The first condition states that an admissible evidence for $\varphi \to \psi$, which can be regarded as a function that transforms a justification of φ to a justification of ψ, can be applied to an admissible evidence for φ to obtain an admissible evidence for ψ. The second condition guarantees that adding a piece of new evidence does not defeat the original evidence. That is, $s + t$ is still an admissible evidence for φ whenever either s or t is an admissible evidence for φ. The forcing relation $\Vdash$ between W and the justification formula $t : \varphi$ satisfies the following condition:

- $w \Vdash t : \varphi$ iff $w \in E(t, \varphi)$ and for any u such that $(w, u) \in R$, $u \Vdash \varphi$.

We will use (F1) and (F2) to denote the conditions "$w \in E(t, \varphi)$" and "for any u such that $(w, u) \in R$, $u \Vdash \varphi$" respectively.

---

1. **Axioms:**
   (a) **Prop:** The standard set of axioms for classical propositional logic
   (b) **Application:**
   $$s : (\varphi \to \psi) \to (t : \varphi \to s \cdot t : \psi);$$
   (c) **Sum:** $s : \varphi \to s + t : \varphi, t : \varphi \to s + t : \varphi$
2. **Rules of Inference:**
   (a) **Modus Ponens:** from φ and $\varphi \to \psi$, infer ψ;
   (b) **Axiom Internalization Rule:** from any instance φ of the axiom schemata above and any sequence of justification constants $c_1, c_2, \ldots, c_n$, infer $c_n : c_{n-1} : \cdots c_1 : \varphi$.

Fig. 1. The axiomatic system J

The basic JL system, denoted by J, is comprised of the axioms and inference rules presented in Fig. 1. The Axiom Internalization Rule behaves like the necessitation rule in modal logic[2]. The intuition is that because an axiom φ is assumed to be justified, the formula $c_1 : \varphi$ is postulated for some justification constant c_1. In addition, because we assume that the new principle $c_1 : \varphi$ is also justified, we can postulate $c_2 : c_1 : \varphi$ for a constant c_2, etc. For the soundness of the rule, a further restriction on the admissible evidence function is needed:

- for any instance φ of the axiom schemata above and any sequence of justification constants $c_1, c_2, \ldots, c_n (n \geq 1)$, $E(c_n, c_{n-1} : \cdots c_1 : \varphi) = W$.

---

[2] An arbitrary subset of formulas of the form $c_n : c_{n-1} : \cdots c_1 : \varphi$ is called a constant specification (CS) [2]. More generally, we can replace the rule with a CS. Then, the rule corresponds to the special case of total CS in which the CS is the set of all such formulas.

3   On the Twofold Interpretation of Justification Formulas

In [1], it is claimed that the intended semantics of $t : \varphi$ in LP is "t is a proof of φ", which is exactly captured by the condition (F1) in Fitting semantics. When the justification t represents a proof in some mathematical or logical system, (F1) naturally implies condition (F2) of Fitting semantics. The fact that (F1) implies (F2) is called the principle of *justification yielding belief* (JYB) in [3] and formalized in the modular semantics introduced there. However, when LP is evolving into the more general JL for epistemic reasoning, the principle becomes less convincing because $t : \varphi$ has the following two ambiguous interpretations:

1. t is a piece of actually observed evidence for φ: then the JYB principle holds and the truth condition of $t : \varphi$ can be formalized in Fitting semantics. However, in this case, the axiom Sum seems doubtful because t being actually observed does not imply that $t + s$ has been also actually observed.
2. t is regarded as admissible or relevant evidence for φ: it means that φ will be believed once t is observed. However, it does not assert that t has been actually observed. Hence, it is possible that φ is not believed currently. In this case, the axiom Sum is valid but the JYB principle fails. Therefore, condition (F2) in Fitting semantics must be dropped.

The following running example illustrates this ambiguity.

Example 1. *Ann is a biologist who has conjectured a grand theory regarding human brain, and to confirm the theory, she forms two testable hypotheses p and q. In other words, the truth of the hypotheses will provide confirmation of the theory to a large degree. To test these hypotheses, she must design and conduct a series of experiments to observe their outcomes. Because Ann is also a good reasoner, she can envision several outcomes that will justify her hypotheses. Among the outcomes, she knows that t_1 and t_2 are good reasons for believing p and q respectively. Hence, t_1 and t_2 are regarded as potential evidence. However, because of the shortage of budget, she can only conduct the experiments to test p and after the experiments, she indeed observe the outcome t_1. Consequently, among the two pieces of evidence, only t_1 is actually observed and become actual evidence. Then, by the first interpretation, $t_1 : p$ is true but $t_1 + t_2 : p$ does not hold because according to the interpretation, $t_1 + t_2 : p$ is true only when both t_1 and t_2 are actually observed. That is, the axiom Sum is violated for the first interpretation. On the other hand, in the second interpretation, $t : \varphi$ simply means that t is potential evidence for φ no matter whether t is actually observed. Thus, both $t_1 : p$ and $t_2 : q$ are true according to the interpretation. However, while p is believed in this situation, q is not necessarily believed because t_2 is not actually observed yet. In addition, $t_1 + t_2$, which means the joint observation of t_1 and t_2, is also potential evidence for both p and q because once t_1 and t_2 are simultaneously observed, the joint evidence is a good reason for believing p and q. Therefore, the axiom Sum is indeed valid for the second interpretation.* ⊣

4   Justification Logic with Informational Contents of Evidence

The analysis in the preceding section shows that the ambiguity arises because of the inadequate expressive power of JL for reasoning about justified belief based on fusion of evidence. During the evolution from LP to JL, while the semantic meaning of justification has been extended from mathematical proof to general evidence, the syntax of the language remains unchanged and hence the expressive power is no longer adequate for explicit epistemic reasoning. Therefore, to overcome the problem, we need a more fine-grained language that can differentiate these two interpretations of justification formulas.

The key point to clarify the ambiguity is whether a piece of evidence has been actually observed. The basic idea is that evidence has some informational contents and if a piece of evidence has been observed, then its informational contents should have been assimilated into the current belief. Thus, our language must be extended with modal operators $\Box_t$ to represent the informational contents of t for each justification term t. In addition, we have a special constant ϵ and a corresponding epistemic operator $\Box_\epsilon$ that represent the agent's belief based on the accumulation of evidence so far. To represent the fusion of the agent's belief and evidence, we employ the Boolean modal logic (BML) encompassing union, intersection and complement of modalities [16]. Moreover, we need a relational symbol to compare the relative strength of informational contents between different justification terms or between ϵ and justification terms.

To implement these ideas, we present a JL with informational contents of evidence (JL-ICE). For the language of JL-ICE, the definition of justification terms remains the same as that of JL and the formation rules of Boolean modality expressions and formulas are as follows:

$$\alpha ::= \epsilon \mid t \mid \mathbf{1} \mid \overline{\alpha} \mid \alpha \cap \alpha \mid \alpha \cup \alpha$$

$$\varphi ::= p \mid \bot \mid \varphi \to \varphi \mid t\!:\!\varphi \mid \Box_\alpha \varphi \mid \sigma \lesssim \sigma,$$

where $p \in \Phi$, $t \in \mathsf{Tm}$ is a justification term, and σ is a *pseudo-justification term* (or simply *pseudo-term*), which is defined as a finite conjunction of justification terms or ϵ, i.e. a special kind of Boolean modality expression $t_1 \cap t_2 \cap \cdots \cap t_k$, where each $t_i (1 \le i \le k)$ is either a justification term or ϵ. The resultant language is denoted by $\mathcal{L}_J^{ice}$. We abbreviate $\overline{\mathbf{1}}$ as $\mathbf{0}$, $\sigma_1 \lesssim \sigma_2 \wedge \sigma_2 \lesssim \sigma_1$ as $\sigma_1 \sim \sigma_2$, and $\Box_\alpha \varphi \wedge \Box_{\overline{\alpha}} \neg \varphi$ as $\boxdot_\alpha \varphi$. Also, as usual, $\Diamond_\alpha \varphi$ is the abbreviation of $\neg \Box_\alpha \neg \varphi$. Let Tm^+ and Bn denote the set of pseudo-terms and the set of Boolean modality expressions respectively. Then, by definition, we have $\mathsf{Tm} \subset \mathsf{Tm}^+ \subset \mathsf{Bn}$. Because we regard Bn as a Boolean algebra that is the closure of atomic terms in $\mathsf{Tm} \cup \{\epsilon\}$ with respect to the algebraic operations $\cap, \cup$, and $^-$, we identify expressions that are equal under the Boolean equational theory. For example, $\overline{\overline{t}}$ is regarded as identical to t.

In the logical language, a pseudo-term σ denotes the accumulation of evidence and belief terms appearing in σ and $\Box_\sigma$ represents its informational contents.

Intuitively, $\Box_\epsilon\varphi$ means that the agent (implicitly) believes φ or has the information φ based on the fusion of evidence observed so far; and $\Box_t\varphi$ means that the informational contents of t implies φ. Metaphorically, t can also be regarded as a virtual agent so that $\Box_t\varphi$ means that the virtual agent t believes φ. Therefore, $\Box_\sigma$ is simply the distributed knowledge operator defined in [13] to denote the belief fusion of an agent group σ. Furthermore, the formula $\sigma_1 \lesssim \sigma_2$ means that the informational content of σ_1 is at least as informative as that of σ_2[3]. To characterize $\sigma_1 \lesssim \sigma_2$ in terms of modal operator, we need $\boxdot_\alpha\varphi$ to denote that the *exact* informational content of α is φ (see the axiom CIC2 below). As we need both the intersection and complement of modalities for denoting information fusion and exact information, the whole Boolean algebra of modalities is available in the language due to De Morgan law and the law of excluded middle.

The rich language facilitates the expression of the fact that the evidence t has been actually observed as the formula $\epsilon \lesssim t$, i.e. the informational contents of t have been assimilated into the current belief represented by ϵ. In the language, the justification formula $t : \varphi$ is reserved for representing the admissibility of t with respect to φ. That is, $t : \varphi$ means that t is potential evidence for believing φ. Then, we can abbreviate $(t : \varphi) \wedge (\epsilon \lesssim t)$ as $t \curvearrowright \varphi$ which intuitively means that φ is a belief justified by the actual observation of t. Note that we cannot simplemindedly define "t being actual evidence for φ" as $t : \varphi \wedge \Box_\epsilon\varphi$ because there may exist multiple pieces of potential evidence with different informational contents for the same formula φ. Hence, only one of them being actualized (so that $\Box_\epsilon\varphi$ is true) does not imply that all of them are actually observed.

For the semantics of JL-ICE, its Kripke-Fitting model is defined as a tuple $\mathfrak{M} = \langle W, R_\epsilon, (R_t)_{t\in\mathsf{Tm}}, E, \Vdash \rangle$, where $\langle W, R_\epsilon, E, \Vdash \rangle$ is a Fitting model of JL, and $R_t \subseteq W \times W$ is a binary relation for each justification term t such that the coherence condition $R_{s+t} = R_{s\cdot t} = R_s \cap R_t$ is satisfied. At first glance, it seems odd that the accessibility relations for R_{s+t} and $R_{s\cdot t}$ are the same while $s+t$ and $s\cdot t$ are different terms. However, from the perspective of informational contents, $s + t$ and $s \cdot t$ both stand for the fusion of informational contents of s and t. In other words, $s+t$ and $s\cdot t$ represent two different ways to combine the evidences s and t. On one hand, $s+t$ denotes the simultaneous presentation of both pieces of evidences; and on the other hand, $s \cdot t$ means that the evidence s for a rule is applied to the evidence t for the antecedent of the rule to obtain the evidence $s \cdot t$ for the consequent. Nevertheless, no matter how s and t are combined, their informational contents are exactly assimilated into the merged evidence. Hence, although $s + t$ and $s \cdot t$ have different operational meaning, the denotational meanings of their informational contents are the same. On the other hand, this does not mean that one of $\cdot$ and $+$ is redundant because they can keep track of different derivation paths of justified belief. By induction, we can define R_α for any $\alpha \in \mathsf{Bn}$ such that the following conditions are satisfied:

- $R_1 = W \times W$,
- $R_{\overline{\alpha}} = \overline{R_\alpha} = W \times W - R_\alpha$,

---

[3] Syntactically, it seems more natural to use $\sigma_1 \lesssim \sigma_2$ to denote that σ_1 is at most as informative as σ_2. However, our reading is based on the semantic viewpoint, which means that the set of accessible worlds for σ_1 is a subset of that for σ_2.

- $R_{\alpha \cap \beta} = R_\alpha \cap R_\beta$,
- $R_{\alpha \cup \beta} = R_\alpha \cup R_\beta$.

According to the definition, it can be easily seen that $R_{s+t} = R_{s \cdot t} = R_{s \cap t}$.

The forcing relation $\Vdash$ is extended to a binary relation between W and $\mathcal{L}_J^{ice}$ as follows:

- $w \Vdash t : \varphi$ iff $w \in E(t, \varphi)$,
- $w \Vdash \Box_\alpha \varphi$ iff for any u such that $(w, u) \in R_\alpha$, $u \Vdash \varphi$,
- $w \Vdash \sigma' \precsim \sigma$ iff $R_{\sigma'}(w) \subseteq R_\sigma(w)$.

Furthermore, we require that the admissible evidence function has the following connection with informational contents of evidence:

- if $w \in E(t, \varphi)$, then for any u such that $(w, u) \in R_t$, we have $u \Vdash \varphi$, i.e. $w \Vdash \Box_t \varphi$.

That is, t is regarded as admissible evidence for φ only when φ is derivable from informational contents of t.

We use $\models_{J^{ice}}$ to denote the validity and semantic consequence in JL-ICE. The validity in JL-ICE can be characterized by the Hilbert-style axiomatization J^{ice} presented in Fig. 2.

Although the semantic meaning of $t : \varphi$ in our logic is different than that in JL, the axioms and rules in J are still valid because of the closure conditions on the admissible evidence function. Axioms K and rule Nec indicate that $\Box_\alpha$ is a normal modal operator. Axiom Con is a connection axiom between justification formulas and informational content formulas. It requires that t is a good reason for φ only if φ is derivable from informational contents of t. Axioms Coh formulate the coherence condition on binary relations R_t in the Kripke-Fitting model. Axiom BML is the complete axiomatization of Boolean modal logic introduced in [16], which reflects the properties of Boolean modalities. In particular, because R_1 is the universal relation, the axioms (ii)–(iv) indicate that $\Box_1$ is an S5 modality. In addition, axiom (vi) represent a kind of monotonicity, where $\vdash_{BA}$ denotes the derivation in Boolean algebra. Hence, $\vdash_{BA} \alpha \cap \beta = \beta$ means that $\beta \leq \alpha$ according to the ordering on the Boolean algebra. Axioms CIC1 and CIC2 stipulate the comparison of informational contents. CIC1 asserts that if the informational content of σ' is richer than that of σ, then anything that can be derived from the informational contents of σ is also derivable from σ'. However, the latter is simply a necessary consequence of $\sigma' \precsim \sigma$. In general, the converse implication of CIC1 does not hold because the contingent truth of $\Box_\sigma \varphi \rightarrow \Box_{\sigma'} \varphi$ for a particular φ does not imply that the informational content of σ' is richer than that of σ. To have the sufficient condition of $\sigma' \precsim \sigma$, we must require that $\Box_\sigma \varphi \rightarrow \Box_{\sigma'} \varphi$ holds for any formula φ. However, the requirement can be represented only by an infinitary conjunction (or the universal quantifier). To address the difficulty in our finitary language, axiom CIC2 employs the $\boxdot_\sigma$ modality, which corresponds to the only-knowing operator defined in [21].

1. **The axioms and rules of system J**
2. **Axioms:**
    (a) K: $\Box_\alpha(\varphi \to \psi) \to (\Box_\alpha\varphi \to \Box_\alpha\psi)$;
    (b) Con: $t : \varphi \to \Box_t\varphi$
    (c) Coh: $s + t \sim s \cap t;\ s \cdot t \sim s \cap t$
    (d) BML:
        i. $(\Box_\alpha\varphi \wedge \Box_\beta\varphi) \to \Box_{\alpha \cup \beta}\varphi$;
        ii. $\Box_1\varphi \to \varphi$;
        iii. $\Box_1\varphi \to \Box_1\Box_1\varphi$;
        iv. $\varphi \to \Box_1 \Diamond_1 \varphi$;
        v. $\Box_0\bot$;
        vi. $\Box_\alpha\varphi \to \Box_\beta\varphi$ if $\vdash_{BA} \alpha \cap \beta = \beta$
    (e) CIC1: $\sigma' \precsim \sigma \to (\Box_\sigma\varphi \to \Box_{\sigma'}\varphi)$;
    (f) CIC2: $(\Box_{\sigma'}\varphi \wedge \Box_\sigma\varphi) \to \sigma' \precsim \sigma$;
    (g) $PO_{\precsim}$:
        i. $\sigma \precsim \sigma$;
        ii. $\sigma_1 \precsim \sigma_2 \to (\sigma_2 \precsim \sigma_3 \to \sigma_1 \precsim \sigma_3)$.
    (h) Mon: $(\sigma'_1 \precsim \sigma_1 \wedge \sigma'_2 \precsim \sigma_2) \to \sigma'_1 \cap \sigma'_2 \precsim \sigma_1 \cap \sigma_2$;
3. **Rules of inference:**
    (a) Nec: from φ infer $\Box_\alpha\varphi$;
    (b) Bool: from $\vdash_{BA} \sigma \cap \sigma' = \sigma'$ infer $\sigma' \precsim \sigma$.

Fig. 2. The axiomatic system J^{ice}

According to the semantics of Boolean modalities, $\boxdot_\sigma\varphi$ means that the informational content of σ is exactly represented by φ. Hence, $\boxdot_\sigma\varphi \wedge \boxdot_{\sigma'}\varphi$ means that the informational content of σ' implies the exact informational content of σ, i.e., $\sigma' \precsim \sigma$. More formally, $w \Vdash (\Box_{\sigma'}\varphi \wedge \boxdot_\sigma\varphi)$ iff $R_{\sigma'}(w) \subseteq |\varphi|$ and $R_\sigma(w) = |\varphi|$[4], which implies $R_{\sigma'}(w) \subseteq R_\sigma(w)$, i.e., the truth condition of $\sigma' \precsim \sigma$ in w. Axiom $PO_{\precsim}$ asserts that $\precsim$ is a pre-order (i.e., reflexive and transitive) relation. Axiom Mon means that the Boolean conjunction $\cap$ is a monotonic operation in its both arguments with respect to the information ordering $\precsim$. Finally, rule Bool requires that the information ordering respects the ordering on the Boolean algebra.

The notions of *proof* (or *derivations*) and *theoremhood* in an axiomatic system are standard. Let $\Sigma \cup \{\varphi\}$ be a subset of JL-ICE formulas. Then, we use $\Sigma \vdash_{\mathsf{Jice}} \varphi$ and $\vdash_{\mathsf{Jice}} \varphi$ to denote that φ is derivable from Σ and that φ is a theorem in J^{ice} respectively. A set Σ is *inconsistent* if $\Sigma \vdash_{\mathsf{Jice}} \bot$, otherwise, Σ is consistent. Then, we conjecture the following soundness and completeness (meta-)theorem for the system J^{ice} (in the presentation of the theorem, we omit the subscripts J^{ice} and J^{ice} from $\models_{\mathsf{Jice}}$ and $\vdash_{\mathsf{Jice}}$ respectively).

---

[4] $|\varphi| = \{u \in W \mid u \Vdash \varphi\}$ is the truth set of φ.

Theorem 1. *For any* $\Sigma \cup \{\varphi\} \subseteq \mathcal{L}_J^{ice}$, *we have* $\Sigma \vdash \varphi$ *iff* $\Sigma \models \varphi$.

Several sample theorems in J^{ice} include $t \curvearrowright \varphi \rightarrow \Box_\epsilon \varphi$, $s \curvearrowright (\varphi \rightarrow \psi) \rightarrow (t \curvearrowright \varphi \rightarrow s \cdot t \curvearrowright \psi)$, and $(s \curvearrowright \varphi \wedge t \curvearrowright \psi) \rightarrow s + t \curvearrowright \varphi$. However, $t : \varphi \rightarrow \Box_\epsilon \varphi$ and $s \curvearrowright \varphi \rightarrow s + t \curvearrowright \varphi$ are invalid.

5   Justification Logic with Direct Observations

In the JL-ICE, we do not distinguish direct or indirect observations of evidences. Therefore, if the informational contents of two pieces of evidences are the same, then the actual observation of one piece of evidence can also be regarded as the observation of the other one even though the latter is not directly observed.

Example 2. *Returning to our running example, assume that Ann, without enough budget for experiments to test q, decides to search the literature to see if there are some alternative ways to test the hypothesis. Upon reading her colleague Bob's articles, she learns that Bob ever observed outcomes s_1 and s_2 in his experiments. Although the experiments are not originally designed for testing q, Ann finds that the joint evidence s_1 and s_2 is in fact equivalent to the outcome t_2 in her intended experiments. In such case, Ann decides to accept q and it seems reasonable to say that she believes q due to the justification t_2, i.e., $t_2 \curvearrowright q$, although t_2 has not been observed directly by herself. However, if Ann simply finds that the joint evidence s_1 and s_2 can verify her hypothesis q but does not realize that the joint evidence is in fact equivalent to the outcome t_2. Then, it seems doubtful to say that she believes q due to the justification t_2, although we can say that she believes q due to the justification $s_1 + s_2$.* ⊣

From the example above, we can see that it is sometimes necessary to distinguish between different pieces of evidences with the same informational contents. To achieve this, we propose the following JL with direct observation (JL-DO). In the logic, we no longer use $\epsilon \lesssim t$ to express that the evidence t has been observed. Hence, we do not need the type of comparison formula any more. The corresponding axioms for the comparison of informational contents are then removable. Consequently, the full expressive power of BML is not necessary. This results in a reduced set of modalities.

The modalities and formulas of the JL-DO language are formed as follows:

$$\alpha ::= \epsilon \mid t \mid \alpha \cap \alpha$$

$$\varphi ::= p \mid \bot \mid \varphi \rightarrow \varphi \mid t{:}\varphi \mid \Box_\alpha \varphi \mid \mathrm{DO}(t),$$

where $p \in \Phi$ and $t \in \mathsf{Tm}$ is a justification term. In the language, the set of modalities is simply the set of pseudo-terms. We use $\mathcal{L}_J^{do}$ to denote the language. Then, we can define $t \hookrightarrow \varphi$ as the abbreviation of $t : \varphi \wedge \mathrm{DO}(t)$ to represent that φ is justified belief by the direct observation of the evidence t. For the semantics, the Kripke-Fitting model for JL-DO is defined as a tuple $\mathfrak{M} = \langle W, R_\epsilon, (R_t)_{t \in \mathsf{Tm}}, E, D, \Vdash \rangle$, which is the extension of a model for JL-ICE with a function $D : W \to 2^{\mathsf{Tm}}$ such that for each $w \in W$, $D(w)$ is closed under $\cdot$ and $+$. Intuitively, $D(w)$ means the set of evidences that have been directly observed in w. The closure condition means that, if both evidences s and t are directly observed in w, then the combined evidences $s+t$ and $s \cdot t$ are also regarded as being directly observed. In addition to the coherence conditions imposed on models for JL-ICE, we require that a JL-DO model must satisfy

$$R_\epsilon(w) \subseteq \bigcap_{t \in D(w)} R_t(w)$$

for each $w \in W$. Therefore, if a piece of evidence has been directly observed in w, then its informational contents should be assimilated into the agent's belief. However, we do not require the converse implication any longer. In other words, it is possible that $R_\epsilon(w) \subseteq R_t(w)$ for some evidence t but t is not directly observed. The semantic condition for the newly added formula is

$- \; w \Vdash \mathrm{DO}(t)$ iff $t \in D(w)$.

The axiomatic system for J^{do} is presented in Fig. 3, which is essentially a reduced set of axioms for J^{ice} with a slight modification and the addition of two new axioms Do and Cls for direct observation. Axioms and rules for system J, axioms K and Con, and rule Nec are preserved. Axiom Coh is modified to express the equivalence between formulas instead of equal informativeness between modalities, because the latter is no longer in the language. For axiom BML, only the monotonicity axiom is kept. The newly added axiom Do exactly represents the condition imposed on JL-DO models, whereas axiom Cls corresponds to the closure condition on the function D. Then, we have the soundness and completeness of J^{do} as follows (as above, we omit the subscripts J^{do} and J^{do}):

---

1. The axioms and rules of system **J**
2. Axioms:
    (a) K: $\Box_\alpha(\varphi \to \psi) \to (\Box_\alpha \varphi \to \Box_\alpha \psi)$;
    (b) Con: $t {:} \varphi \to \Box_t \varphi$;
    (c) Coh: $\Box_{s+t} \varphi \equiv \Box_{s \cap t} \varphi$; $\Box_{s \cdot t} \varphi \equiv \Box_{s \cap t} \varphi$;
    (d) BML: $\Box_\alpha \varphi \to \Box_\beta \varphi$ if $\alpha \sqsubseteq \beta$ (i.e. every term appearing in α also appears in β);
    (e) Do: $\mathrm{DO}(t) \to (\Box_t \varphi \to \Box_\epsilon \varphi)$;
    (f) Cls: $(\mathrm{DO}(s) \wedge \mathrm{DO}(t)) \to (\mathrm{DO}(s + t) \wedge \mathrm{DO}(s \cdot t))$.
3. Rule of inference:
    (a) Nec: from φ infer $\Box_\alpha \varphi$;

Fig. 3. The axiomatic system J^{do}

Theorem 2. *For any $\Sigma \cup \{\varphi\} \subseteq \mathcal{L}_J^{do}$, we have $\Sigma \vdash \varphi$ iff $\Sigma \models \varphi$.*

Several sample theorems in J^{do} include $t \hookrightarrow \varphi \rightarrow \Box_\epsilon \varphi$, $s \hookrightarrow (\varphi \rightarrow \psi) \rightarrow (t \hookrightarrow \varphi \rightarrow s \cdot t \hookrightarrow \psi)$, and $(s \hookrightarrow \varphi \wedge t \hookrightarrow \psi) \rightarrow s + t \hookrightarrow \varphi$. However, $t : \varphi \rightarrow \Box_\epsilon \varphi$ and $s \hookrightarrow \varphi \rightarrow s + t \hookrightarrow \varphi$ are invalid.

6   Dynamic Justification Logic

In our running example, we can see that Ann's belief is changed by the experimental outcome t_1. Hence, the observation of the outcome t_1 is a kind of informative or epistemic action for Ann that leads to her belief update. So far, the logics JL-ICE and JL-DO can only reason about an agent's static belief and its justification. However, modeling the dynamic change of belief and information is the theme of the dynamic epistemic logic (DEL) paradigm which has grown significantly and found a lot of applications to AI, computer science, multi-agent systems, philosophy, and cognitive science in recent years [8,12].

The operators for epistemic action correspond to a type of dynamic modality that is interpreted by transforming the models themselves rather than by the accessibility relation between worlds within a fixed model. In our systems, the dynamic modality corresponds to the observation of evidence. Therefore, the dynamic JL-ICE (DJL-ICE) and dynamic JL-DO (DJL-DO) languages are respectively the extensions of the JL-ICE and JL-DO languages with a class of dynamic modalities $[\downarrow t]$ for every $t \in \mathsf{Tm}$, and formulas of the resultant language are defined by adding formulas of the form $[\downarrow t]\varphi$ to the static languages. Formally, the formulas of the dynamic languages are defined by

$$\varphi ::= \varphi_0 \mid \bot \mid \varphi \rightarrow \varphi \mid \Box_\alpha \varphi \mid \sigma \lesssim \sigma \mid [\downarrow t]\varphi,$$

and

$$\varphi ::= \varphi_0 \mid \bot \mid \varphi \rightarrow \varphi \mid \Box_\alpha \varphi \mid \mathrm{DO}(t) \mid [\downarrow t]\varphi$$

respectively, where φ_0 denotes a formula of the static language. Note that we do not allow the occurrence of dynamic formula inside $t :$ because a dynamic formula can generally be rewritten into an equivalent static formula (see below). However, the rule for substitution of equivalents is not valid for $t : \varphi$ (i.e., $t : \varphi$ and $\varphi \equiv \psi$ do not imply $t : \psi$ in general). Hence, the occurrence of dynamic formula inside the scope of the $t :$ operator will block our derivation system. We denote the languages by $\mathcal{L}_{DJ}^{ice}$ and $\mathcal{L}_{DJ}^{do}$ respectively.

For the semantics, the model of the dynamic language is completely the same as that of the static one. The extra feature is the extended forcing relation between possible worlds and the new type of formulas. Let the static model be $\mathfrak{M} = \langle W, R_\epsilon, (R_t)_{t \in \mathsf{Tm}}, E, \Vdash \rangle$ or $\mathfrak{M} = \langle W, R_\epsilon, (R_t)_{t \in \mathsf{Tm}}, E, D, \Vdash \rangle$. Then, the relation satisfies

– $w \Vdash_{\mathfrak{M}} [\downarrow t]\varphi$ iff $w \Vdash_{\mathfrak{M}_t} \varphi$, where

$$\mathfrak{M}_t = \langle W, R'_\epsilon, (R_t)_{t \in \mathsf{Tm}}, E, \Vdash \rangle$$

or

$$\mathfrak{M}_t = \langle W, R'_\epsilon, (R_t)_{t \in \mathsf{Tm}}, E, D', \Vdash \rangle$$

is a new model such that $R'_\epsilon = R_\epsilon \cap R_t$ and $D'(w) = D(w) \cup \{t\}$ for any $w \in W$.

Reasoning about belief change in the dynamic logics can be achieved by using an axiomatic system. As in the typical case of DEL, the complete axiomatizations DJ^{ice} and DJ^{do} are comprised of a complete axiomatization for the static base language (i.e., J^{ice} and J^{do}), and on top of that, a number of *reduction axioms* that analyze effects of epistemic action. The set of reduction axioms is presented in Fig. 4, where, for every $\alpha \in \mathsf{Bn}$ (and also $\sigma \in \mathsf{Tm}^+$) and $t \in \mathsf{Tm}$, we define α_t as the simultaneous replacement of every occurrence of ϵ in α with $\epsilon \cap t$. Obviously, if ϵ does not occur in α, then $\alpha_t = \alpha$.

---

1. **Reduction axioms:**
   (a) $[\downarrow t]p \equiv p$ if $p \in \Phi$;
   (b) $[\downarrow t]\bot \equiv \bot$;
   (c) $[\downarrow t](\varphi \to \psi) \equiv ([\downarrow t]\varphi \to [\downarrow t]\psi)$;
   (d) $[\downarrow t](s : \varphi) \equiv (s : \varphi)$;
   (e) $[\downarrow t]\Box_\alpha \varphi \equiv \Box_{\alpha_t}[\downarrow t]\varphi$;
   (f) i. for DJ^{ice}: $[\downarrow t](\sigma' \precsim v) \equiv (\sigma'_t \precsim \sigma_t)$;
        ii. for DJ^{do}: $[\downarrow t]\mathrm{DO}(t) \equiv \top$ and $[\downarrow t]\mathrm{DO}(s) \equiv \mathrm{DO}(s)$ if $s \neq t$.
2. **Rule of inference:**
   (a) **DNec:** from φ infer $[\downarrow t]\varphi$

Fig. 4. Reduction axioms for DJ^{ice} and DJ^{do}

The reduction axioms describe how the dynamic modality $[\downarrow t]$ interacts with other logical operators of the static language. These axioms move each logical operator of the static language outside the scope of the dynamic modality or simply remove the dynamic modality in the cases of atomic formulas, justification formulas, informational comparison formulas, and direct observation formulas. As a side-effect, working inside out in a stepwise manner, such a "recursion equation" allows us to translate any formula from the dynamic language into an equivalent formula of the static language. Consequently, the completeness of the systems DJ^{ice} and DJ^{do} follows from the completeness of J^{ice} and J^{do} respectively.

Theorem 3. *Let $\Sigma \cup \{\varphi\}$ be a subset of formulas in the dynamic language. Then, we have $\Sigma \vdash \varphi$ iff $\Sigma \models \varphi$, where $\vdash$ and $\models$ correspond to the derivation and consequence relations in the dynamic logic respectively.*

Example 3. *Let us continue with Example 1 and consider the JL-ICE models at two moments—the model* $\mathfrak{M} = \langle W, R_\epsilon, (R_t)_{t\in\mathsf{Tm}}, E, \Vdash \rangle$ *before Ann conducts the experiments and the model* $\mathfrak{M}_{t_1} = \langle W, R'_\epsilon, (R_t)_{t\in\mathsf{Tm}}, E, \Vdash \rangle$ *after she has observed the outcome* t_1. *Obviously, an observation does not change the components* W, E, R_t's, *and* $\Vdash$. *In particular, the informational contents of each piece of evidence remain constant during the observation process*[5]. *Because we are concerned with only the two hypotheses* p *and* q, *we can assume that* W *has four possible worlds which correspond to their truth assignments, i.e.* $W = \{00, 01, 10, 11\}$. *In addition, we assume that the two hypotheses indeed hold and Ann does not have any a prior knowledge about their truth or falsehood. Thus, the actual world* $w = 11$ *and* $R_\epsilon = W \times W$. *Because* t_1 *and* t_2 *are good reasons for* p *and* q *respectively, we can reasonably set* $E(t_1, p) = E(t_2, q) = W$ *and let* $R_{t_1} = W \times \{10, 11\}$ *and* $R_{t_2} = W \times \{01, 11\}$. *For our purpose here, we do not have to completely specify the function* E. *However, we do assume that it is* minimally *closed under the closure conditions for Kripke-Fitting models. Hence, for example, we can safely assume that* $E(t_1, q) = E(t_2, p) = \emptyset$. *Then, according to dynamic semantics,* $R'_\epsilon = R_{t_1}$. *Furthermore,* $\Vdash$ *is defined according to the obvious specification of each world. For example,* $01 \Vdash q, 11 \Vdash p, 11 \Vdash p$, *etc.*

From the models above, we can list some formulas that are satisfied in $\mathfrak{M}, w$:

$$t_1 : p, t_2 : q, \neg\Box_\epsilon p, \neg\Box_\epsilon q, \Box_{t_1} p, \Box_{t_2} q, \neg(\epsilon \lesssim t_1);$$

and derive the following consequences (among others) by using the axiomatic systems and definitions:

$$t_1 + t_2 : p, [\downarrow t_1](\epsilon \lesssim t_1), [\downarrow t_1]t_1 \frown p, [\downarrow t_1]\Box_\epsilon p.$$

However, $[\downarrow t_1](t_1 + t_2)\frown p$ *is false because* $t_1 \frown p \to (t_1 + t_2)\frown p$ *is not valid.*   ⊣

7 Related Work

In recent years, logic for reasoning about evidence and belief has received much attention [7,9,10,24]. Among them, the work that is closet to ours is a very expressive logic JB proposed in [7]. In the logic, the status of evidence has a much finer distinction and a salient feature of the logic is that its evidence term t must be formed by the following formation rule

$$t ::= c_\varphi \mid t + t \mid t \cdot t,$$

where each c_φ is an evidential certificate (a canonical piece of evidence in support) of the formula φ. Hence, unlike JL and our logic in which admissibility of evidence with respect to a formula is determined by the admissible evidence function E in Kripke-Fitting models, the admissibility relation in JB, denoted by $\gg$, can be syntactically determined as the smallest relation between terms

---

[5] We ignore the quantum observation that may change the outcome of observation itself.

and formulas satisfying the following three conditions: (1) $c_\varphi \gg \varphi$; (2) if $s \gg \varphi$ and $t \gg (\varphi \to \psi)$, then $s \cdot t \gg \psi$; (3) if $s \gg \varphi$ or $t \gg \varphi$, then $s + t \gg \varphi$. In some sense, evidence c_φ is an evidential constant which explicitly encodes its informational content. However, unlike the informational content operator $\Box_c$ in our logic, the logical consequence of φ is not regarded as the informational content of c_φ. In other words, because $\Box_c$ is a normal modal operator, $\Box_c\varphi$ implies $\Box_c\psi$ for any logical consequence ψ of φ, but c_ψ and c_φ are simply regarded as two independent evidential certificates and c_φ is not necessarily an evidential certificate of ψ.

While JL regards justification terms and formulas as two sorts of syntactically separate entities and JB regards justification terms as comprised only from primitive constants representing certificates of formulas, the logic of evidence Log in [9, 10] completely abandons the notion of using a separate sort of terms to represent evidence. Consequently, although Log can express some relationship between evidence and belief, the justified belief $t\frown\varphi$ or $t\hookrightarrow\varphi$ is no longer expressible.

8 Conclusion

In this paper, we enrich JL with modalities that can represent informational contents of accumulated evidence. In the enriched languages, we can clarify the ambiguous interpretation of justification formulas. While the clarification is unnecessary when justification terms are regarded as mathematical proofs as in the case of LP, it become crucially important when LP is evolved into general JL for reasoning about explicit belief. The resultant languages are expressive enough to address the issue of the mismatch between the formal semantics and the intuitive explanation of the Sum axiom. Moreover, as a byproduct, we show that the DEL-like dynamic modalities can be easily integrated into the enriched logics and this leads to logics for dynamic evidential reasoning with justifications.

In classical JL, when both s and t are admissible evidences for φ, it is impossible that one of $s : \varphi$ and $t : \varphi$ is true and the other is false. Thus, it is implicitly assumed that all or no pieces of admissible evidence are actually observed in the logic. By contrast, our logics can represent the situation that some but not all pieces of admissible evidence for a formula has been actualized. Theoretically, the more actual observations should imply stronger belief on the formula. Hence, it is possible to extend our logics to cover reasoning about fusion of uncertain beliefs. There have been a few works on combining uncertainty reasoning with JL in recent years [4, 14, 19, 20, 23]. Along this direction, the next step on our agenda will be the fine-grained JL for reasoning about belief fusion and uncertainty. In addition, although we have provided a Hilbert-style axiomatization for JL-ICE and JL-DO, from the practical viewpoint, exploring the possibility of more efficient proof systems for the logic remains an important open question. Finally, inspired by Gettier's example [17], we would like to formulate the distinction between proper and improper justifications in our framework.

References

1. Artemov, S.: Explicit provability and constructive semantics. Bull. Symb. Logic **7**, 1–36 (2001)
2. Artemov, S.: The logic of justification. Rev. Symb. Logic **1**, 477–513 (2008)
3. Artemov, S.: The ontology of justifications in the logical setting. Stud. Logica **100**(1–2), 17–30 (2012)
4. Artemov, S.: On aggregating probabilistic evidence. In: Artemov, S., Nerode, A. (eds.) LFCS 2016. LNCS, vol. 9537, pp. 27–42. Springer, Heidelberg (2016). doi:10. 1007/978-3-319-27683-0_3
5. Artemov, S., Fitting, M.: Justification logic. In: Zalta, E. (ed.) The Stanford Encyclopedia of Philosophy, Fall 2012 edn. Stanford University, Stanford (2012)
6. Artemov, S., Nogina, E.: Introducing justification into epistemic logic. J. Logic Comput. **15**(6), 1059–1073 (2005)
7. Baltag, A., Renne, B., Smets, S.: The logic of justified belief change, soft evidence and defeasible knowledge. In: Ong, L., Queiroz, R. (eds.) WoLLIC 2012. LNCS, vol. 7456, pp. 168–190. Springer, Heidelberg (2012). doi:10.1007/978-3-642-32621-9_13
8. van Benthem, J.: Logical Dynamics of Information and Interaction. Cambridge University Press, Cambridge (2014)
9. van Benthem, J., Duque, D.F., Pacuit, E.: Evidence and plausibility in neighborhood structures. Ann. Pure Appl. Logic **165**(1), 106–133 (2014)
10. van Benthem, J., Pacuit, E.: Dynamic logics of evidence-based beliefs. Stud. Logica **99**(1), 61–92 (2011)
11. Blackburn, P., de Rijke, M., Venema, Y.: Modal Logic. Cambridge University Press, Cambridge (2001)
12. van Ditmarsch, H., van der Hoek, W., Kooi, B.: Dynamic Epistemic Logic. Springer, New York (2008)
13. Fagin, R., Halpern, J., Moses, Y., Vardi, M.: Reasoning about Knowledge. MIT Press, Cambridge (1996)
14. Fan, T., Liau, C.: A logic for reasoning about justified uncertain beliefs. In: Proceedings of the Twenty-Fourth International Joint Conference on Artificial Intelligence (IJCAI), pp. 2948–2954 (2015)
15. Fitting, M.: The logic of proofs, semantically. Ann. Pure Appl. Logic **132**(1), 1–25 (2005)
16. Gargov, G., Passy, S.: A note on boolean modal logic. In: Petrov, P. (ed.) Mathematical Logic, pp. 299–309. Springer, New York (1990)
17. Gettier, E.: Is justified true belief knowledge? Analysis **23**, 121–123 (1963)
18. Hintikka, J.: Knowledge and Belief. Cornell University Press, Ithaca (1962)
19. Kokkinis, I., Maksimovic, P., Ognjanovic, Z., Studer, T.: First steps towards probabilistic justification logic. Logic J. IGPL **23**(4), 662–687 (2015)
20. Kokkinis, I., Ognjanović, Z., Studer, T.: Probabilistic justification logic. In: Artemov, S., Nerode, A. (eds.) LFCS 2016. LNCS, vol. 9537, pp. 174–186. Springer, Heidelberg (2016). doi:10.1007/978-3-319-27683-0_13
21. Levesque, H.: All I know: a study in autoepistemic logic. Artif. Intell. **42**(2), 263–309 (1990)
22. Meyer, J.J.C., van der Hoek, W.: Epistemic Logic for AI and Computer Science. Cambridge University Press, Cambridge (1995)
23. Milnikel, R.: The logic of uncertain justifications. Ann. Pure Appl. Logic **165**, 305–315 (2014)
24. Menasché Schechter, L.: A logic of plausible justifications. In: Ong, L., Queiroz, R. (eds.) WoLLIC 2012. LNCS, vol. 7456, pp. 306–320. Springer, Heidelberg (2012). doi:10.1007/978-3-642-32621-9_23

Writing Declarative Specifications for Clauses

Martin Gebser[2], Tomi Janhunen[1(✉)], Roland Kaminski[2], Torsten Schaub[2,3],
and Shahab Tasharrofi[1]

[1] Helsinki Institute for Information Technology HIIT,
Aalto University, Espoo, Finland
Tomi.Janhunen@aalto.fi
[2] Institute for Informatics and Computational Science,
University of Potsdam, Potsdam, Germany
[3] INRIA Rennes, Bretagne Atlantique Research Centre, Rennes, France

Abstract. Modern satisfiability (SAT) solvers provide an efficient implementation of classical propositional logic. Their input language, however, is based on the conjunctive normal form (CNF) of propositional formulas. To use SAT solver technology in practice, a user must create the input clauses in one way or another. A typical approach is to write a procedural program that generates formulas on the basis of some input data relevant for the problem domain and translates them into CNF. In this paper, we propose a declarative approach where the intended clauses are specified in terms of rules in analogy to answer set programming (ASP). This allows the user to write first-order specifications for intended clauses in a schematic way by exploiting term variables. We develop a formal framework required to define the semantics of such specifications. Moreover, we provide an implementation harnessing state-of-the-art ASP grounders to accomplish the grounding step of clauses. As a result, we obtain a general-purpose clause-level grounding approach for SAT solvers. Finally, we illustrate the capabilities of our specification methodology in terms of combinatorial and application problems.

1 Introduction

Satisfiability (SAT) solvers [1] provide an efficient way to implement classical propositional logic. The conjunctive normal form (CNF) of formulas, which is based on disjunctions of literals also known as *clauses*, forms the standard input language supported by solvers. However, writing clauses directly is not very practical from the modeling perspective. This suggests the use of a more expressive language supporting the entire range of logical connectives and allowing for (universally quantified) first-order variables to write formulas in a schematic way. E.g., the following formula aims to deny occurrences of triangles in a directed graph represented by the edge/2 predicate:

$$\mathsf{edge}(X,Y) \wedge \mathsf{edge}(Y,Z) \wedge (X \neq Y) \wedge (X \neq Z) \wedge (Y \neq Z) \rightarrow \neg\mathsf{edge}(Z,X). \quad (1)$$

T. Schaub—Affiliated with Simon Fraser University, Canada, and IIIS Griffith University, Australia.

© Springer International Publishing AG 2016
L. Michael and A. Kakas (Eds.): JELIA 2016, LNAI 10021, pp. 256–271, 2016.
DOI: 10.1007/978-3-319-48758-8_17

On the one hand, variables seem crucial to achieve the flexibility required in modeling but, on the other hand, they lead to the problem of instantiating or *grounding* the variables when actual inference is performed. In the presence of facts edge(a, b), edge(b, c), and edge(c, a), the essential step is to substitute the universally quantified variables X, Y, and Z in (1) by the constants a, b, and c. While $3^3 = 27$ different substitutions are applicable, only one of them is useful for showing unsatisfiability. The theory of grounding goes back to Herbrand's seminal work, and it has been addressed in many contexts, such as first-order model generation and theorem proving (see, e.g., [2,3]) as well as AI planning (cf. [4]). The substitution of variables by constants or more generally ground terms is subject to combinatorial explosion when the underlying domain grows. To cut down the number of resulting ground instances, a variety of techniques have been proposed, including clause splitting, structural constraints, and contraction techniques to discard or simplify instances [5]. Also, by carefully analyzing variable ranges, it is possible to reduce the number of clauses or formulas generated [3,6].

The approach proposed in this paper also relies on domain information, but we suggest to use declarative specifications based on *closed world assumption* (CWA) for controlling domains. In case of (1), this means that there is no edge between any given pair of nodes, thus falsifying the implication antecedent, unless specified otherwise. We provide an implementation harnessing state-of-the-art *answer set programming* (ASP) [7] grounders for the computation of domains and variable instantiation, since they offer built-in support for CWA and a rich rule-based language to express domain knowledge.

What remains is choosing the kind of formulas to ground. While free choice among logical connectives seems desirable from the modeling perspective, translation into CNF is necessary to use SAT solvers. The classification of propositional (ground) formulas often requires the introduction of new variables, e.g., using the Tseitin transformation, to avoid exponential blow-ups, and in some cases the auxiliary variables significantly affect solver performance [8–10]. The idea of this paper is to write declarative specifications for clauses, thus enabling a user to define the input of a SAT solver directly. Following the traditional *what you see is what you get* principle, clauses in the grounder output can be traced back to the schematic specification. The trade-off is that the user has to decide about potential new variables in a formalization, but specifying such variables at the schematic level also provides more direct access than an implicit clause compilation. In fact, given the expressiveness of modeling languages supported by off-the-shelf ASP grounders [11,12], we expect that declarative specifications are easier to develop and maintain than their procedural counterparts. For one, it is possible to separate domain descriptions from logical axioms, which enables *uniform* encodings that are independent of particular instance data [13]. For another, the level of abstraction provided by first-order rules makes specifications highly *elaboration tolerant* [14].

The rest of this paper is organized as follows. The syntax and semantics of the clause specification language is defined in Sect. 2. In Sect. 3, we illustrate the proposed language on practical modeling scenarios. Section 4 presents a stream-lined implementation, interfacing the state-of-the-art ASP grounder GRINGO [15] with SAT or MaxSAT solvers, and an experimental evaluation where haplotype inference is remodeled using clause programs. Finally, we discuss related work and conclude the paper in Sect. 5.

2   Clause Programs

We begin by presenting the syntax of clause programs and then concentrate on defining their semantics. To specify clause programs in the first-order case with variables, we define *terms* as expressions built from function symbols f, also called constants in case of arity zero, or variable symbols X. The signature for predicate symbols, denoted by $\mathcal{P}$, splits into $\mathcal{P}_d$ and $\mathcal{P}_v$, i.e., *domain* predicates being minimized and those allowed to *vary* as typical in classical logic. A *first-order atom* $p(t_1, \ldots, t_n)$, or an *atom* for short, consists of an n-ary predicate symbol $p \in \mathcal{P}$ and terms $t_1, \ldots, t_n$ listed as its arguments. A *literal* is either an atom a or its negation $\neg a$.

A *clause program* P can have rules of two kinds: *domain rules* of the form (2), also known as normal rules in ASP, as well as *clause rules* of the form (3):

$$a \leftarrow c_1, \ldots, c_m, \sim d_1, \ldots, \sim d_n. \tag{2}$$

$$a_1 \vee \cdots \vee a_k \vee \neg b_1 \vee \cdots \vee \neg b_l \leftarrow c_1, \ldots, c_m, \sim d_1, \ldots, \sim d_n. \tag{3}$$

In the rules above, a, $c_1, \ldots, c_m$, and $d_1, \ldots, d_n$ are domain atoms expressed in $\mathcal{P}_d$, and the symbol $\sim$ stands for default negation. Domain rules (2) are used to specify appropriate domain relations for variable instantiation. The atoms $a_1, \ldots, a_k$ and $b_1, \ldots, b_l$ in a clause rule (3) are expressed in $\mathcal{P}_v$. The *head* $a_1 \vee \cdots \vee a_k \vee \neg b_1 \vee \cdots \vee \neg b_l$ is a schema for propositional clauses where $\vee$ and $\neg$ stand for classical disjunction and negation, respectively. The *body* $c_1, \ldots, c_m, \sim d_1, \ldots, \sim d_n$ essentially provides the conditions for creating the head clause, including the determination of variable assignments.

The semantics of clause programs is defined using Herbrand models as follows. Given a clause program P, we define its Herbrand universe $\mathrm{Hu}(P)$ and Herbrand base $\mathrm{Hb}(P)$ in the standard way. The base $\mathrm{Hb}(P)$ is partitioned into $\mathrm{Hb}_d(P)$ and $\mathrm{Hb}_v(P)$ based on the signatures $\mathcal{P}_d$ and $\mathcal{P}_v$, respectively. A (Herbrand) *interpretation* I of P is written as a subset of $\mathrm{Hb}(P)$. Moreover, we distinguish its projections $I_d = I \cap \mathrm{Hb}_d(P)$ and $I_v = I \cap \mathrm{Hb}_v(P)$. Assuming that P is variable-free or *ground*, the body of (2) or (3) is satisfied in I iff $\{c_1, \ldots, c_m\} \subseteq I_d$ and $\{d_1, \ldots, d_n\} \cap I_d = \emptyset$. The head of (2) is satisfied in I iff $a \in I_d$, while the head of (3) is satisfied in I iff $\{b_1, \ldots, b_l\} \subseteq I_v$ implies $\{a_1, \ldots, a_k\} \cap I_v \neq \emptyset$. An interpretation $I \subseteq \mathrm{Hb}(P)$ is a *model* of P iff, for every rule (2) or (3) of P, the satisfaction of the body in I implies the satisfaction of the head in I. To enforce the minimal interpretation of domain predicates, we define the *domain reduct* P^I of P with respect to I to contain a rule $a \leftarrow c_1, \ldots, c_m$ for every domain rule (2) of P such that $\{d_1, \ldots, d_n\} \cap I_d = \emptyset$. The program

P^I is a Horn theory and guaranteed to have a unique $\subseteq$-minimal model over $\mathrm{Hb_d}(P)$, the *least model* of P^I.

Definition 1. *Let P be a clause program and $\mathrm{Gnd}(P)$ the respective Herbrand instantiation of P over $\mathrm{Hu}(P)$. An interpretation $I \subseteq \mathrm{Hb}(P)$ is a domain stable model of P iff I is a model of $\mathrm{Gnd}(P)$ such that I_d is the least model of $\mathrm{Gnd}(P)^I$.*

While the abstract criteria for domain stable models are formulated in terms of the full Herbrand instantiation $\mathrm{Gnd}(P)$, the actual goal is to generate small subsets of $\mathrm{Gnd}(P)$ without affecting domain stable models. The intended way of applying Definition 1 in practice is to let an ASP grounder calculate I_d, which also determines the relevant clauses. After that, a SAT solver can be invoked to compute I_v such that $I = I_\mathrm{d} \cup I_\mathrm{v}$ is a model of $\mathrm{Gnd}(P)$. In order to use ASP grounders, we have to restrict variable occurrences in rules. A rule of the form (2) or (3) is called *safe* if all variables occurring in the head also appear in the positive conditions $c_1, \ldots, c_m$ of the body, which thereafter constrain their domains. Moreover, it is reasonable to assume that the domain part of a clause program P has a total well-founded model (cf. [16]) that can be calculated by an ASP grounder. We therefore require domain rules (2) of P to be *stratified* (cf. [17]), which confines recursive dependencies of a predicate in $\mathcal{P}_\mathrm{d}$ on itself to be purely based on $c_1, \ldots, c_m$ in the positive body parts of rules. All clause programs considered in the following are safe and their domain rules stratified. This means that rule bodies are fully evaluated during grounding, and the heads of clause rules (3) provide the input of a SAT solver, searching for (classical) models of the propositional clauses.

Example 1. Let us consider the following clause program for graph coloring:

$$\mathsf{node}(X) \leftarrow \mathsf{edge}(X, Y). \tag{4}$$
$$\mathsf{node}(Y) \leftarrow \mathsf{edge}(X, Y). \tag{5}$$
$$\mathsf{b}(X) \vee \mathsf{g}(X) \vee \mathsf{r}(X) \leftarrow \mathsf{node}(X). \tag{6}$$
$$\neg \mathsf{b}(X) \vee \neg \mathsf{b}(Y) \leftarrow \mathsf{edge}(X, Y). \tag{7}$$
$$\neg \mathsf{g}(X) \vee \neg \mathsf{g}(Y) \leftarrow \mathsf{edge}(X, Y). \tag{8}$$
$$\neg \mathsf{r}(X) \vee \neg \mathsf{r}(Y) \leftarrow \mathsf{edge}(X, Y). \tag{9}$$

The idea is that these rules are conjoined with facts representing an input graph. To this end, let us use the three facts from the context of (1). Together with the domain rules (4) and (5), such facts give rise to the following least model I_d:

$$\mathsf{edge}(a, b), \mathsf{edge}(b, c), \mathsf{edge}(c, a), \mathsf{node}(a), \mathsf{node}(b), \text{ and } \mathsf{node}(c).$$

The atoms in I_d determine the domains of variables in (6)–(9), resulting in the clauses:

$\mathsf{b}(a) \vee \mathsf{g}(a) \vee \mathsf{r}(a)$,	$\mathsf{b}(b) \vee \mathsf{g}(b) \vee \mathsf{r}(b)$,	$\mathsf{b}(c) \vee \mathsf{g}(c) \vee \mathsf{r}(c)$,
$\neg \mathsf{b}(a) \vee \neg \mathsf{b}(b)$,	$\neg \mathsf{b}(b) \vee \neg \mathsf{b}(c)$,	$\neg \mathsf{b}(c) \vee \neg \mathsf{b}(a)$,
$\neg \mathsf{g}(a) \vee \neg \mathsf{g}(b)$,	$\neg \mathsf{g}(b) \vee \neg \mathsf{g}(c)$,	$\neg \mathsf{g}(c) \vee \neg \mathsf{g}(a)$,
$\neg \mathsf{r}(a) \vee \neg \mathsf{r}(b)$,	$\neg \mathsf{r}(b) \vee \neg \mathsf{r}(c)$,	$\neg \mathsf{r}(c) \vee \neg \mathsf{r}(a)$.

These clauses can be satisfied, e.g., by letting $I_v = \{b(a), g(b), r(c)\}$, which gives rise to a domain stable model $I = I_d \cup I_v$. ∎

3   Modeling Methodology and Applications

We have above introduced the paradigm of clause programs in a simple setting where the domain part is written in *normal* ASP-style rules. Using syntactic sugar available in GRINGO, however, the compactness and flexibility of clause programs can be further enhanced. We below illustrate the practice of clause programs on several use cases.

Graph Coloring. To begin with, we generalize the program in Example 1 to n colors:

$$\mathsf{color}(1 \dots n). \tag{10}$$

$$\mathsf{node}(X; Y) \leftarrow \mathsf{edge}(X, Y). \tag{11}$$

$$\bigvee \mathsf{hc}(X, C) : \mathsf{color}(C) \leftarrow \mathsf{node}(X). \tag{12}$$

$$\neg\mathsf{hc}(X, C) \vee \neg\mathsf{hc}(Y, C) \leftarrow \mathsf{edge}(X, Y), \mathsf{color}(C). \tag{13}$$

By setting the constant n to some integer, say 3, it defines a range of colors by (10): $\mathsf{color}(1)$, $\mathsf{color}(2)$, and $\mathsf{color}(3)$. The separator ";" in the second domain rule (11) is used to specify alternative terms for which the head atom is instantiated, so that (11) amalgamates (4) and (5). Unlike (6), the clause rule (12), applying to each term X from $\mathsf{node}(X)$, is parameterized by a *conditional literal* $\mathsf{hc}(X, C)$, where instances over all terms C from $\mathsf{color}(C)$ are included in a disjunction. This enables the specification of clauses whose length depends *dynamically* on a problem instance, such as the number of colors in this case. Finally, the clause rule (13) generalizes (7)–(9).

Example 2. Based on the least model I_d from Example 1, augmented with $\mathsf{color}(1)$, $\mathsf{color}(2)$, and $\mathsf{color}(3)$, the clauses obtained from (12) and (13) are as follows:

$$
\begin{array}{lll}
\mathsf{hc}(a,1) \vee \mathsf{hc}(a,2) \vee \mathsf{hc}(a,3), & \mathsf{hc}(b,1) \vee \mathsf{hc}(b,2) \vee \mathsf{hc}(b,3), & \mathsf{hc}(c,1) \vee \mathsf{hc}(c,2) \vee \mathsf{hc}(c,3), \\
\quad \neg\mathsf{hc}(a,1) \vee \neg\mathsf{hc}(b,1), & \quad \neg\mathsf{hc}(a,2) \vee \neg\mathsf{hc}(b,2), & \quad \neg\mathsf{hc}(a,3) \vee \neg\mathsf{hc}(b,3), \\
\quad \neg\mathsf{hc}(b,1) \vee \neg\mathsf{hc}(c,1), & \quad \neg\mathsf{hc}(b,2) \vee \neg\mathsf{hc}(c,2), & \quad \neg\mathsf{hc}(b,3) \vee \neg\mathsf{hc}(c,3), \\
\quad \neg\mathsf{hc}(c,1) \vee \neg\mathsf{hc}(a,1), & \quad \neg\mathsf{hc}(c,2) \vee \neg\mathsf{hc}(a,2), & \quad \neg\mathsf{hc}(c,3) \vee \neg\mathsf{hc}(a,3).
\end{array}
$$

The clauses resemble those in Example 1, yet using the generic predicate $\mathsf{hc}(X, C)$ for node X *having color* C, rather than dedicated predicates b/1, g/1, and r/1 for blue, green, and red, respectively. Accordingly, an assignment of distinct colors to the three nodes at hand is expressed by a projection like $I_v = \{\mathsf{hc}(a,1), \mathsf{hc}(b,2), \mathsf{hc}(c,3)\}$. ∎

n-Queens. The next clause program, encoding the well-known n-queens problem, illustrates the use of built-in integer arithmetic supported by ASP grounders like GRINGO:

$$\text{coord}(1 \ldots n). \qquad \text{dir}(0, -1). \quad \text{dir}(-1, 0). \quad \text{dir}(-1, -1). \quad \text{dir}(-1, 1). \qquad (14)$$

$$\text{target}(X, Y, R, C) \leftarrow \text{coord}(X; Y; X+R; Y+C), \text{dir}(R, C). \qquad (15)$$

$$\text{attack}(X+R, Y+C, R, C) \vee \neg\text{queen}(X, Y) \leftarrow \text{target}(X, Y, R, C). \qquad (16)$$

$$\text{attack}(X+R, Y+C, R, C) \vee \neg\text{attack}(X, Y, R, C) \qquad (17)$$
$$\leftarrow \text{target}(X, Y, R, C), \text{target}(X-R, Y-C, R, C).$$

$$\neg\text{attack}(X+R, Y+C, R, C) \vee \text{queen}(X, Y) \vee \qquad (18)$$
$$\bigvee \text{attack}(X, Y, R, C) : \text{target}(X-R, Y-C, R, C) \leftarrow \text{target}(X, Y, R, C).$$

$$\neg\text{queen}(X+R, Y+C) \vee \neg\text{attack}(X+R, Y+C, R, C) \leftarrow \text{target}(X, Y, R, C). \quad (19)$$

$$\text{queen}(X, 1) \vee \bigvee \text{attack}(X, 1, 0, -1) : \text{target}(X, 2, 0, -1) \leftarrow \text{coord}(X). \qquad (20)$$

$$\text{queen}(1, Y) \vee \bigvee \text{attack}(1, Y, -1, 0) : \text{target}(2, Y, -1, 0) \leftarrow \text{coord}(Y). \qquad (21)$$

The facts in (14) provide row and column coordinates, ranging from 1 to some integer value for n, as well as the differences between the coordinates of adjacent cells in horizontal, vertical, and diagonal directions. Particular adjacent cells are indicated by the domain rule (15), where an instance of $\text{target}(X, Y, R, C)$ expresses that the cells at coordinates (X, Y) and $(X+R, Y+C)$ are adjacent. Given this, the clause rules (16)–(18) specify conditions enforcing that $\text{attack}(X+R, Y+C, R, C)$ is true iff some cell with coordinates $(X-k*R, Y-k*C)$ for $k \geq 0$ hosts a queen, represented by a corresponding instance of $\text{queen}(X, Y)$. The clauses specified by (19) then forbid a queen at $(X+R, Y+C)$ if the cell is horizontally, vertically, or diagonally attacked. Finally, the clause rules (20) and (21) express that any row or column must contain some queen, which can be checked at the first row or column position, respectively.

Example 3. For $n = 4$, the least model I_d includes the following atoms indicating horizontal attacks along the first row, obtained by instantiating X, R, and C with 1, 0, and -1 in (15): $\text{target}(1, 2, 0, -1)$, $\text{target}(1, 3, 0, -1)$, and $\text{target}(1, 4, 0, -1)$. These atoms induce nine instances of (16)–(18), whose conjunction is equivalent to formulas

$$\text{attack}(1, 1, 0, -1) \leftrightarrow \text{queen}(1, 2) \vee \text{attack}(1, 2, 0, -1),$$
$$\text{attack}(1, 2, 0, -1) \leftrightarrow \text{queen}(1, 3) \vee \text{attack}(1, 3, 0, -1),$$
$$\text{attack}(1, 3, 0, -1) \leftrightarrow \text{queen}(1, 4).$$

Clauses from (19) exclude horizontal attacks: $\neg\text{queen}(1, 1) \vee \neg\text{attack}(1, 1, 0, -1)$, $\neg\text{queen}(1, 2) \vee \neg\text{attack}(1, 2, 0, -1)$, $\neg\text{queen}(1, 3) \vee \neg\text{attack}(1, 3, 0, -1)$. ∎

Propositional Logic. Next we illustrate how the satisfiability problem of full propositional logic can be captured in a declarative way. To this end, a meta-representation of a propositional theory is needed, using function symbols (supported by ASP grounders like GRINGO) to represent Boolean connectives. For brevity, we only consider disjunction and negation here, but note that our approach easily extends to other connectives as well. We use constants for atoms, the functions or/2 and neg/1 for disjunction and negation, and the predicate sentence/1 to declare sentences in a theory. Given this, we axiomatize the satisfaction of the theory as follows:

$$\text{subformula}(F) \leftarrow \text{sentence}(F). \tag{22}$$

$$\text{subformula}(F) \leftarrow \text{subformula}(\text{neg}(F)). \tag{23}$$

$$\text{subformula}(F; G) \leftarrow \text{subformula}(\text{or}(F, G)). \tag{24}$$

$$\text{sat}(\text{neg}(F)) \vee \text{sat}(F) \leftarrow \text{subformula}(\text{neg}(F)). \tag{25}$$

$$\text{sat}(\text{or}(F, G)) \vee \neg\text{sat}(F) \leftarrow \text{subformula}(\text{or}(F, G)). \tag{26}$$

$$\text{sat}(\text{or}(F, G)) \vee \neg\text{sat}(G) \leftarrow \text{subformula}(\text{or}(F, G)). \tag{27}$$

$$\neg\text{sat}(\text{neg}(F)) \vee \neg\text{sat}(F) \leftarrow \text{subformula}(\text{neg}(F)). \tag{28}$$

$$\neg\text{sat}(\text{or}(F, G)) \vee \text{sat}(F) \vee \text{sat}(G) \leftarrow \text{subformula}(\text{or}(F, G)). \tag{29}$$

$$\text{sat}(F) \leftarrow \text{sentence}(F). \tag{30}$$

Here, the domain rules (22)–(24) derive the subformulas of the given theory, and the clause rules (25)–(29) evaluate these subformulas according to the interpretation of atoms and the semantics of propositional connectives. Finally, the clause rule (30) asserts that all sentences in the given theory must be satisfied. For instance, the sentence $\neg p \vee \neg q$ is represented by the following clauses:

$\text{sat}(\text{neg}(p)) \vee \text{sat}(p),$ $\qquad\qquad$ $\neg\text{sat}(\text{neg}(p)) \vee \neg\text{sat}(p),$
$\text{sat}(\text{neg}(q)) \vee \text{sat}(q),$ $\qquad\qquad$ $\neg\text{sat}(\text{neg}(q)) \vee \neg\text{sat}(q),$
$\text{sat}(\text{or}(\text{neg}(p), \text{neg}(q))) \vee \neg\text{sat}(\text{neg}(p)),$ $\quad$ $\text{sat}(\text{or}(\text{neg}(p), \text{neg}(q))) \vee \neg\text{sat}(\text{neg}(q)),$
$\neg\text{sat}(\text{or}(\text{neg}(p), \text{neg}(q))) \vee \text{sat}(\text{neg}(p)) \vee \text{sat}(\text{neg}(q)),$ $\quad$ $\text{sat}(\text{or}(\text{neg}(p), \text{neg}(q))).$

In summary, the above use cases illustrate how clause programs can uniformly model non-trivial combinatorial as well as application problems. The presented encodings exploit built-in integer arithmetic, aggregation operations, function symbols, and the closed world assumption of ASP in concise first-order specifications of schematic clauses. In particular, fixpoint constructions enable deriving (implicit) domains of variables from instance data, thus reducing the need for involved procedural computations.

4   Implementation

To implement the grounding of clause programs, we utilize the state-of-the-art ASP grounder GRINGO [15]. This is feasible because GRINGO (from version 2 on) supports classical literals and disjunctive rule heads as in (3). By hiding and hence omitting the domain part of a clause program P, the ground program $\text{Gnd}(P)$ is essentially a set of ground disjunctions $a_1 \vee \cdots \vee a_k \vee \neg b_1 \vee \cdots \vee \neg b_l$. From the perspective of GRINGO, the semantics of $\text{Gnd}(P)$ is based on consistent sets of classical literals, also known as *answer sets* [18], which can be viewed as minimal *hitting sets* for the disjunctions in $\text{Gnd}(P)$. For the purposes of this work, however, we re-establish the semantic connection between an atom a and its classical negation $\neg a$ by transforming disjunctions into a set $\text{Cl}(\text{Gnd}(P))$ of clauses in DIMACS format, serving as input of SAT solvers, or optionally into pseudo-Boolean constraints in OPB format. This step is implemented by a tool called SATGRND (v. 1.24), which passes the symbolic names of atoms on as comments in its output. The transformation preserves classical models and satisfiability, so that satisfying assignments of $\text{Cl}(\text{Gnd}(P))$ correspond to domain stable models of P.[1] Additionally, the file formats for satisfiability modulo theories (SMT) and mixed integer programming (MIP) are supported.

Beyond this basic transformation, SATGRND can be used to extract graph information from symbolic atom names, as exploited in the SAT modulo graphs approach [20,21]. Both in plain SAT and SAT modulo graphs, models may be subject to optimization, expressible by optimization statements in the input language of GRINGO, in which case SATGRND generates (weighted partial) MaxSAT problems in DIMACS format, or again optionally OPB format, which supports objective functions. Moreover, SATGRND permits the computation of classical models for (disjunctive) logic programs in general and is provided along with sample encodings for the use cases in the previous section.[2]

In order to compare SATGRND's declarative approach with a procedural implementation producing a solver's input, we investigated the optimization problem of haplotype inference [22,23]. The task is to compute a cardinality-minimal set H of haplotypes that explain a set G of genotypes, as given on the right.

G	1 2 3		H	1 2 3
g_1	1 1 0		h_1	1 1 0
g_2	1 2 0		h_2	1 0 0
g_3	2 1 2		h_3	0 1 1

Genotypes g_i are determined by strings of some fixed length l, consisting of the symbols '0', '1', and '2'. Haplotypes h_j are also strings of length l, yet admitting '0' and '1' only. Two (not necessarily distinct) haplotypes h_{j_1}, h_{j_2} explain a genotype g_i if, for each string position $1 \leq k \leq l$, we have that $g_i^k = 2$ implies $h_{j_1}^k \neq h_{j_2}^k$, while $h_{j_1}^k = h_{j_2}^k = g_i^k$ otherwise. In the above table, g_1 is explained by h_1, h_1, g_2 by h_1, h_2, and g_3 by h_1, h_3. Moreover, one can check that at least three haplotypes are needed to explain g_1, g_2, and g_3, so that $H = \{h_1, h_2, h_3\}$ is an optimal solution.

The tool RPOLY[3] provides a reference implementation of haplotype inference, using a generator to convert instance data into a problem representation in OPB format, which is then passed on to a pseudo-Boolean solver like MINISAT+ [24]. The pseudo-Boolean constraints produced by the generator, described in [22,23], exploit domain knowledge to achieve a compact representation: duplicated genotypes as well as isomorphic string positions in the input are conflated, and static symmetry breaking is applied to disambiguate pairs of haplotypes used to explain

---

[1] Classical models can be encoded in ASP, e.g., using choice rules and integrity constraints [19].

[2] http://research.ics.aalto.fi/software/asp/satgrnd/.

[3] http://sat.inesc-id.pt/software/rpoly/.

genotypes. For instance, the string positions 1 and 3 are isomorphic for the above genotypes $G = \{g_1, g_2, g_3\}$, given that the other column is reproduced by swapping '0' and '1' in one of the columns. In such a case, either of the isomorphic positions can be reproduced from the other, and only one representative needs to be computed by a solver. Moreover, for each genotype g_i, an arbitrary occurrence of '2' at remaining positions can be picked to statically fix one of the haplotypes explaining g_i to '0', and the other to '1' at this position. In fact, the combination of both techniques directly leads to the above haplotypes $H = \{h_1, h_2, h_3\}$, simply by applying static symmetry breaking to the occurrences of '2' at the second position of g_2 (which gives $h_1 = g_1$ and h_2 to explain g_2) and the first position of g_3, and then using the opposite symbol among '0' and '1' for aligning the '2' at the isomorphic third position of g_3 (thus reproducing h_1 along with its counterpart h_3 to explain g_3).

In general, not all occurrences of '2' can be fixed a priori, and the problem representation generated by RPOLY includes variables t_i^k to indicate whether a remaining occurrence of '2' at the k-th position of g_i is split up similar or opposite to the statically fixed '2' in the two haplotypes explaining g_i. This determines the used haplotypes, and further variables $x_{i_1, i_2}^{e_1, e_2}$ for genotypes g_{i_1}, g_{i_2} such that $i_1 < i_2$ and $e_1, e_2 \in \{0, 1\}$ are implied when any pair of some of the (at most) two haplotypes to explain g_{i_1} or g_{i_2}, respectively, is different. Finally, variables $u_{i_2}^{e_2}$, indicating haplotypes used first in explaining g_{i_2}, i.e., $x_{i_1, i_2}^{e_1, e_2}$ holds for all $i_1 < i_2$ and $e_1 \in \{0, 1\}$, are to be minimized.

We took the ideas implemented by RPOLY as basis for a corresponding encoding of haplotype inference by a clause program, (see Footnote 5) as shown in Fig. 1. A problem instance specifies genotypes like the above by facts

> gene(1), symb(1, 1, 1), symb(1, 2, 1), symb(1, 3, 0), position(1),
> gene(2), symb(2, 1, 1), symb(2, 2, 2), symb(2, 3, 0), position(2),
> gene(3), symb(3, 1, 2), symb(3, 2, 1), symb(3, 3, 2), and position(3).

Given such facts, the domain rules (31) and (32) take care of filtering duplicates, where the conditional literal $\mathsf{diff}(G_1, G_2)$ in (32) checks whether any genotype G_1 whose identifier is smaller than G_2 differs from G_2 at some string position. If so, an instance of $\mathsf{keep}(G_2)$ indicates that genotype G_2 is not a duplicate and to be explained by haplotypes. Similar to (31), the domain rules (33)–(35) derive instances of $\mathsf{dist}(K_1, K_2)$, expressing that a string position K_2 is not isomorphic to the smaller position K_1. To this end, (33) and (34) apply if '0' and '1' both occur at K_1 and K_2 in some genotype as well as either of them twice in another genotype. Moreover, (35) checks for an occurrence of '2' at either K_1 or K_2 to signal a difference between the two positions. The domain rule (36) then derives $\mathsf{pick}(K_2)$ if the conditional literal $\mathsf{dist}(K_1, K_2)$ yields that no smaller position K_1 is isomorphic to K_2. For the given problem instance, we obtain $\mathsf{keep}(1)$, $\mathsf{keep}(2)$, and $\mathsf{keep}(3)$, as none of the three genotypes is a duplicate, along with $\mathsf{keep}(1)$ and $\mathsf{keep}(2)$, since the third string position is isomorphic to the first.

The final domain rule (37) determines the number of occurrences of '2' at non-isomorphic string positions in order to perform static symmetry breaking by means of the clause rule (38). In the latter rule, we use the min aggregation

$$\mathsf{diff}(G_1, G_2) \leftarrow \mathsf{symb}(G_1, K, X), \mathsf{gene}(G_2), G_1 < G_2, {\sim}\mathsf{symb}(G_2, K, X). \tag{31}$$

$$\mathsf{keep}(G_2) \leftarrow \mathsf{gene}(G_2), \mathsf{diff}(G_1, G_2) : (\mathsf{gene}(G_1), G_1 < G_2). \tag{32}$$

$$\mathsf{flip}(K_1, K_2) \leftarrow \mathsf{symb}(G, K_1, X), \mathsf{symb}(G, K_2, 1 - X), K_1 < K_2, X < 2. \tag{33}$$

$$\mathsf{dist}(K_1, K_2) \leftarrow \mathsf{symb}(G, K_1, X), \mathsf{symb}(G, K_2, X), \mathsf{flip}(K_1, K_2), X < 2. \tag{34}$$

$$\mathsf{dist}(K_1, K_2) \leftarrow \mathsf{symb}(G, K_1, X_1), \mathsf{symb}(G, K_2, X_2), K_1 < K_2, \tag{35}$$
$$X_1/2 + X_2/2 = 1.$$

$$\mathsf{pick}(K_2) \leftarrow \mathsf{position}(K_2), \mathsf{dist}(K_1, K_2) : (\mathsf{position}(K_1), K_1 < K_2). \tag{36}$$

$$\mathsf{twos}(K, S) \leftarrow \mathsf{pick}(K), S = |\{G : (\mathsf{keep}(G), \mathsf{symb}(G, K, 2))\}|. \tag{37}$$

$$\mathsf{vary}(G, K) \leftarrow \mathsf{keep}(G), (S, K) = \min\{(T, L) : (\mathsf{twos}(L, T), \mathsf{symb}(G, L, 2))\}. \tag{38}$$

$$\neg\mathsf{same}(G_1, 0 \ldots 1, G_2, 0 \ldots 1) \leftarrow \mathsf{keep}(G_1), \mathsf{keep}(G_2), \mathsf{pick}(K), G_1 < G_2, X < 2, \tag{39}$$
$$\mathsf{symb}(G_1, K, X), \mathsf{symb}(G_2, K, 1 - X).$$

$$\neg\mathsf{same}(G_1, 0 \ldots 1, G_2, E) \vee \bigvee \mathsf{vary}(G_2, K) : E = X \vee \bigvee \neg\mathsf{vary}(G_2, K) : E \neq X \tag{40}$$
$$\leftarrow \mathsf{keep}(G_1), \mathsf{keep}(G_2), \mathsf{pick}(K), G_1 < G_2, X < 2,$$
$$\mathsf{symb}(G_1, K, X), \mathsf{symb}(G_2, K, 2), E = 0 \ldots 1.$$

$$\neg\mathsf{same}(G_1, E, G_2, 0 \ldots 1) \vee \bigvee \mathsf{vary}(G_1, K) : E = X \vee \bigvee \neg\mathsf{vary}(G_1, K) : E \neq X \tag{41}$$
$$\leftarrow \mathsf{keep}(G_1), \mathsf{keep}(G_2), \mathsf{pick}(K), G_1 < G_2, X < 2,$$
$$\mathsf{symb}(G_1, K, 2), \mathsf{symb}(G_2, K, X), E = 0 \ldots 1.$$

$$\neg\mathsf{same}(G_1, E, G_2, E) \vee \neg\mathsf{vary}(G_1, K) \vee \mathsf{vary}(G_2, K) \tag{42}$$
$$\leftarrow \mathsf{keep}(G_1), \mathsf{keep}(G_2), \mathsf{pick}(K), G_1 < G_2,$$
$$\mathsf{symb}(G_1, K, 2), \mathsf{symb}(G_2, K, 2), E = 0 \ldots 1.$$

$$\neg\mathsf{same}(G_1, E, G_2, E) \vee \mathsf{vary}(G_1, K) \vee \neg\mathsf{vary}(G_2, K) \tag{43}$$
$$\leftarrow \mathsf{keep}(G_1), \mathsf{keep}(G_2), \mathsf{pick}(K), G_1 < G_2,$$
$$\mathsf{symb}(G_1, K, 2), \mathsf{symb}(G_2, K, 2), E = 0 \ldots 1.$$

$$\neg\mathsf{same}(G_1, E, G_2, 1 - E) \vee \neg\mathsf{vary}(G_1, K) \vee \neg\mathsf{vary}(G_2, K) \tag{44}$$
$$\leftarrow \mathsf{keep}(G_1), \mathsf{keep}(G_2), \mathsf{pick}(K), G_1 < G_2,$$
$$\mathsf{symb}(G_1, K, 2), \mathsf{symb}(G_2, K, 2), E = 0 \ldots 1.$$

$$\neg\mathsf{same}(G_1, E, G_2, 1 - E) \vee \bigvee \mathsf{vary}(G_1, K) : G_1 < G_2 \vee \bigvee \mathsf{vary}(G_2, K) : G_1 < G_2 \tag{45}$$
$$\leftarrow \mathsf{keep}(G_1), \mathsf{keep}(G_2), \mathsf{pick}(K), (G_1, E) < (G_2, 1),$$
$$\mathsf{symb}(G_1, K, 2), \mathsf{symb}(G_2, K, 2), E = 0 \ldots 1.$$

$$\mathsf{used}(G_2, E_2) \vee \tag{46}$$
$$\bigvee \mathsf{same}(G_1, E_1, G_2, E_2) : (\mathsf{keep}(G_1), E_1 = 0 \ldots 1, (G_1, E_1) < (G_2, E_2))$$
$$\leftarrow \mathsf{keep}(G_2), E_2 = 0 \ldots 1.$$

$$\mathsf{minimize}\, |\{(G, E) : \mathsf{used}(G, E)\}|. \tag{47}$$

Fig. 1. A clause program encoding haplotype inference

operation of GRINGO to pick an occurrence of '2' (if there is any) in a genotype g_i such that the overall number of '2's at the respective position k is minimal. This in turn maximizes the number of '0's and '1's at position k, following the rationale that fixing such a position to '0' or '1' directly discards plenty options of sharing one of the two haplotypes used to explain g_i. The atom $\mathsf{vary}(g_i, k)$ in a unit clause expressed by (38) stands for the variable t_i^k, whose truth signals that the first haplotype explaining g_i contains '0' at position k and the second '1', while '0' and '1' are swapped when t_i^k or $\mathsf{vary}(g_i, k)$, respectively, is false.

The purpose of the clause rules (39)–(45) is to assert a literal $\neg\mathsf{same}(g_{i_1}, e_1, g_{i_2}, e_2)$ for genotypes g_{i_1}, g_{i_2} such that $i_1 \leq i_2$ and $e_1, e_2 \in \{0, 1\}$ when two of the haplotypes explaining g_{i_1} and g_{i_2} are different, so that the literals correspond to the aforementioned variables $x_{i_1, i_2}^{e_1, e_2}$. In a nutshell, rule (39) applies to haplotypes whose genotypes differ on '0' and '1' at a position, (40) and (41) align a '0' or '1' in either g_{i_1} or g_{i_2} with the interpretation of $t_{i_2}^k$ or $t_{i_1}^k$, respectively, and (42)–(45) compare $t_{i_1}^k$ and $t_{i_2}^k$ in case both g_{i_1} and g_{i_2} contain '2' at position k. Note that (45) yields $\neg\mathsf{same}(g_i, 0, g_i, 1)$ for genotypes g_i with some occurrence of '2', and all clauses have in common that they imply $\neg\mathsf{same}(g_{i_1}, e_1, g_{i_2}, e_2)$ for pairs of haplotypes that differ at some position. For instance, the facts given above along with the domain rules (37)–(37) lead to the clauses:

$\neg\mathsf{same}(1, 0, 2, 0) \vee \neg\mathsf{vary}(2, 2), \quad \neg\mathsf{same}(1, 1, 2, 0) \vee \neg\mathsf{vary}(2, 2),$

$\neg\mathsf{same}(2, 0, 3, 0) \vee \neg\mathsf{vary}(2, 2), \quad \neg\mathsf{same}(2, 0, 3, 1) \vee \neg\mathsf{vary}(2, 2),$

$\neg\mathsf{same}(1, 0, 2, 1) \vee \mathsf{vary}(2, 2), \quad \neg\mathsf{same}(1, 1, 2, 1) \vee \mathsf{vary}(2, 2), \quad \neg\mathsf{same}(2, 0, 2, 1),$

$\neg\mathsf{same}(2, 1, 3, 0) \vee \mathsf{vary}(2, 2), \quad \neg\mathsf{same}(2, 1, 3, 1) \vee \mathsf{vary}(2, 2),$

$\neg\mathsf{same}(1, 0, 3, 0) \vee \neg\mathsf{vary}(3, 1), \quad \neg\mathsf{same}(1, 1, 3, 0) \vee \neg\mathsf{vary}(3, 1),$

$\neg\mathsf{same}(2, 0, 3, 0) \vee \neg\mathsf{vary}(3, 1), \quad \neg\mathsf{same}(2, 1, 3, 0) \vee \neg\mathsf{vary}(3, 1),$

$\neg\mathsf{same}(1, 0, 3, 1) \vee \mathsf{vary}(3, 1), \quad \neg\mathsf{same}(1, 1, 3, 1) \vee \mathsf{vary}(3, 1),$

$\neg\mathsf{same}(2, 0, 3, 1) \vee \mathsf{vary}(3, 1), \quad \neg\mathsf{same}(2, 1, 3, 1) \vee \mathsf{vary}(3, 1), \quad \neg\mathsf{same}(3, 0, 3, 1).$

That is, the two haplotypes explaining g_2 or g_3, respectively, are inherently different from one another, and the unit clauses $\neg\mathsf{same}(2, 0, 2, 1)$ and $\neg\mathsf{same}(3, 0, 3, 1)$ represent the truth of $x_{2,2}^{0,1}$ and $x_{3,3}^{0,1}$. Moreover, the clauses including, e.g., $\neg\mathsf{same}(1, e, 3, 0)$ and $\neg\mathsf{same}(1, e, 3, 1)$ with $e \in \{0, 1\}$ stand for $x_{1,3}^{e,0} \vee \neg t_3^1$ and $x_{1,3}^{e,1} \vee t_3^1$, thus reflecting differences between the haplotypes for g_1 that contain '1' at position 1 and either of the two haplotypes for g_3. Also note that none of the clauses refers to '2' at the third position of g_3 or t_3^3, respectively, since the third string position is isomorphic to the first.

The last clause rule (46) implies $\mathsf{used}(g_{i_2}, e_2)$, corresponding to variables $u_{i_2}^{e_2}$ for genotypes g_{i_2} and $e_2 \in \{0, 1\}$, to indicate first uses of haplotypes. Such atoms are subject to minimization in view of the minimize statement in (47), instantiated as follows:

$\mathsf{used}(1, 0),$

$\mathsf{used}(1, 1) \vee \mathsf{same}(1, 0, 1, 1),$

$\mathsf{used}(2, 0) \vee \mathsf{same}(1, 0, 2, 0) \vee \mathsf{same}(1, 1, 2, 0),$

$\mathsf{used}(2, 1) \vee \mathsf{same}(1, 0, 2, 1) \vee \mathsf{same}(1, 1, 2, 1) \vee \mathsf{same}(2, 0, 2, 1),$

$\mathsf{used}(3, 0) \vee \mathsf{same}(1, 0, 3, 0) \vee \mathsf{same}(1, 1, 3, 0) \vee \mathsf{same}(2, 0, 3, 0) \vee \mathsf{same}(2, 1, 3, 0),$

$\mathsf{used}(3,1) \vee \mathsf{same}(1,0,3,1) \vee \mathsf{same}(1,1,3,1) \vee \mathsf{same}(2,0,3,1) \vee \mathsf{same}(2,1,3,1)$
$$\vee\ \mathsf{same}(3,0,3,1),$$

$\text{minimize } |\{(1,0) : \mathsf{used}(1,0), (1,1) : \mathsf{used}(1,1), (2,0) : \mathsf{used}(2,0),$
$$(2,1) : \mathsf{used}(2,1), (3,0) : \mathsf{used}(3,0), (3,1) : \mathsf{used}(3,1)\}|.$$

One can check that all clauses are satisfied by a domain stable model I such that

$$I_\mathrm{v} = \{\mathsf{vary}(2,2), \mathsf{vary}(3,1), \mathsf{same}(1,0,1,1), \mathsf{same}(1,0,2,1), \mathsf{same}(1,0,3,1),$$
$$\mathsf{used}(1,0), \mathsf{used}(2,0), \mathsf{used}(3,0)\}.$$

The number of distinct haplotypes, given by the predicate $\mathsf{used}/2$, is minimal, and in total there are 21 optimal models comprising the above haplotypes $H = \{h_1, h_2, h_3\}$.

In the pseudo-Boolean constraints of RPOLY as well as the encoding in Fig. 1, the variables $x_{i_1,i_2}^{e_1,e_2}$ and $u_{i_2}^{e_2}$, signaling differences between haplotypes and those to count in the objective function, are handled by implications forcing them to true. In the following, we refer to this encoding approach by "Implication". We also implemented an encoding variant, indicated by "Equivalence", where such derived variables are matched to the conditions they express and cannot vary in case a condition does not apply. The stronger assertions of "Equivalence" thus reduce combinatorics to the prize of an increased number of clauses. Moreover, [22] mentions a condition under which at least three of four haplotypes explaining two genotypes g_{i_1}, g_{i_2} must be different, which can be expressed by clauses of the form $\neg x_{i_1,i_2}^{e_1,e_2} \vee \neg x_{i_1,i_2}^{e_3,e_4}$ for $e_1, e_2, e_3, e_4 \in \{0,1\}$ such that $e_1 \neq e_3$ or $e_2 \neq e_4$. Interestingly, respective pseudo-Boolean constraints are not generated by RPOLY, while the encoding variants denoted by "Implication-LB" and "Equivalence-LB" include such clauses. The four available encoding variants can be activated easily via command-line switches of GRINGO, and the encoding extensions for enabling flexibility amount to another ten selectively used schematic clause rules (see Footnote 5).

To compare solving performance relative to input generated by RPOLY or by using clause programs and SATGRND, we ran the pseudo-Boolean solvers MIN-ISAT+ (v. 1.0) and CLASP (v. 3.1.4), the latter performing unsatisfiability-based optimization (cf. [25]), sequentially on a Linux machine equipped with Intel Xeon E5-4650 2.70 GHz processors. Instance data, out of which we selected the 63 instances such that some of the two solvers took more than ten seconds in a preliminary screening phase, was kindly provided by the authors of RPOLY. All solver runs were completed with an optimal solution, i.e., no effective time or memory limit was enforced. Table 1 provides averages over the 63 selected instances in terms of runtime and numbers of conflicts as well as constraints, the latter as reported by CLASP and MINISAT+, relative to input generated by RPOLY or SATGRND with the four encoding variants outline above. The conversion of instance data to a problem representation in OPB format, using RPOLY or SATGRND, was done offline and does thus not contribute to measured runtimes. Clearly, the procedural implementation by RPOLY is noticeably quicker than the grounding step of SATGRND, as the latter is geared for modeling flexibility rather than low-level performance.

Table 1. Experiments with CLASP and MINISAT+ on haplotype inference benchmarks

	RPOLY	Implication	Implication-LB	Equivalence	Equivalence-LB	
Runtime	182.3	**3.3**	3.5	4.7	5.5	CLASP
Conflicts	466,933	47,262	52,420	57,789	67,178	
Constraints	36,299	28,318	28,454	49,054	49,192	
Runtime	**133.6**	1789.8	1402.7	2639.1	2467.4	MINISAT+
Conflicts	863,514	6,779,058	6,441,567	6,769,964	5,866,433	
Constraints	36,859	28,500	28,638	51,003	51,142	

Considering the average runtimes of both solvers, the best highlighted in boldface, CLASP is an order of magnitude faster on input provided by SATGRND, while the opposite effect applies to MINISAT+ on input generated by RPOLY. We attribute such inverse behavior to different selections of string positions for static symmetry breaking. In our encoding in Fig. 1, we use a greedy approach aiming to reduce the resulting number of clauses: for each genotype, pick some occurrence of '2' that maximizes the number of '0's and '1's at this position. The strategy applied by RPOLY is, to our knowledge, not documented in the literature, and the apparent difference to ours can be observed on the numbers of constraints reported by CLASP and MINISAT+ in the first two columns of Table 1. In fact, there is a lot of room for different strategies, and declarative specifications by clause programs offer means for the rapid prototyping of alternative approaches.

Regarding the runtime differences between CLASP and MINISAT+, we want to stress that CLASP is a recent system, whereas MINISAT+ is not actively maintained. Hence, rather than further comparing the solvers to each other, it is more meaningful to concentrate on the effect of the encoding variants in the last three columns of Table 1, whose clauses differ from the pseudo-Boolean constraints of RPOLY. Here, we observe an expected rough doubling of size, witnessed by numbers of constraints, for the two "Equivalence" approaches. Since the size increase deteriorates runtimes and does not reduce conflicts significantly, the more relaxed approach taken by RPOLY and the "Implication" encoding is clearly the right choice. Moreover, the addition of clauses asserting necessary differences between haplotypes explaining different genotypes in "Implication-LB" (and "Equivalence-LB") modestly improves the runtime of MINISAT+ and its reported conflicts, yet not by a substantial amount. There are, however, no gains for CLASP, which again confirms the choice of RPOLY not to generate such constraints as appropriate. In summary, our practical case study demonstrates the utility of clause programs to implement a problem encoding, investigate the effect of alternative formulations, and identify parts that are critical for solving performance.

5   Discussion of Related Work and Conclusion

In this paper, we promote declarative domain specifications in contrast to procedural ones that are typical when solvers are interfaced with a programming library (see, e.g., the Python interface of Microsoft's Z3). Naturally, other declarative approaches exist. In the context of pseudo-Boolean solvers, the system PSGRND [26] can be used to ground clauses and their extensions. The domain information, however, is given by type declarations for predicates, and it is not possible to define types in terms of others. The first-order approaches of [2, 6, 27, 28] also aim to restrict variable domains recursively over the structure of first-order formulas, where the CWA is limited to predicates that are defined (inductively) in terms of those allowed to vary. The same can be stated about the methods proposed for *effectively* propositional logic [3, 5], although domain constraints are imposed. The IDP3 system [29] exploits PROLOG-style rules to express domain information, but it processes them through query answering rather than bottom-up evaluation. In [4], the grounding problem is addressed in the context of planning domain definition language (PDDL) descriptions over finite domains. While this approach explores a Datalog representation and grounding techniques similar to ASP, it is specialized to planning tasks. The interface provided by GRINGO is more general, in particular, given that domains need not be finitely bounded a priori. Last but not least, note that traditional constraint models [30, 31] can also be translated into CNF (see, e.g., [10]), yet expressing recursive domain specifications remains difficult.

Since its initial conception [32], SATGRND has been used in several lines of work: firstly as a grounder to support high-level declarative specifications for the SAT-TO-SAT solver [33], and also as a tool to convert meta-representations of quantified Boolean formulas to layers of CNFs [34]. Secondly, SATGRND has been used in [35] to support declarative solver development for knowledge representation languages. Specifically, we took advantage of SATGRND to specify and implement a solver for combined logic programs [36].

In conclusion, we suggest to utilize ASP grounders for instantiating first-order clauses involving term variables. This provides us with means to control the resulting propositional clauses in a declarative way and to avoid the implicit introduction of new Boolean variables, which is practically necessary otherwise, e.g., when translating logic programs into SAT [37]. The combination of GRINGO and SATGRND forms a general-purpose grounding tool not confined to a particular application domain. Due to the versatile and eventually Turing-complete input language of GRINGO, complex domain specifications can be written to support fine-grained instantiation of term variables. The uniform rule-based syntax makes specifications highly elaboration tolerant and independent of particular instance data. We expect that the grounding methodology introduced in this paper can be beneficial for SAT application developers in order to rapidly devise and experiment with encodings directly at clause level.

Acknowledgments. This work was funded by the Academy of Finland (251170), DFG (SCHA 550/9), as well as DAAD and the Academy of Finland (57071677 and 279121). We are grateful to João Marques-Silva and Inês Lynce for kindly providing us with the benchmark instances used in Sect. 4.

References

1. Biere, A., Heule, M., van Maaren, H., Walsh, T.: Handbook of Satisfiability. IOS Press, Amsterdam (2009)
2. Aavani, A., Wu, X.N., Tasharrofi, S., Ternovska, E., Mitchell, D.: Enfragmo: a system for modelling and solving search problems with logic. In: Bjørner, N., Voronkov, A. (eds.) LPAR 2012. LNCS, vol. 7180, pp. 15–22. Springer, Heidelberg (2012). doi:10.1007/978-3-642-28717-6_4
3. Navarro, J.A., Voronkov, A.: Proof systems for effectively propositional logic. In: Armando, A., Baumgartner, P., Dowek, G. (eds.) IJCAR 2008. LNCS (LNAI), vol. 5195, pp. 426–440. Springer, Heidelberg (2008). doi:10.1007/978-3-540-71070-7_36
4. Helmert, M.: Concise finite-domain representations for PDDL planning tasks. Artif. Intell. **173**(5–6), 503–535 (2009)
5. Schulz, S.: A comparison of different techniques for grounding near-propositional CNF formulae. In: Proceedings of FLAIRS 2002, pp. 72–76. AAAI Press (2002)
6. Wittocx, J., Mariën, M., Denecker, M.: Grounding FO and FO(ID) with bounds. J. Artif. Intell. Res. **38**, 223–269 (2010)
7. Brewka, G., Eiter, T., Truszczyński, M.: Answer set programming at a glance. Commun. ACM **54**, 92–103 (2011)
8. Asín, R., Nieuwenhuis, R., Oliveras, A., Rodríguez-Carbonell, E.: Cardinality networks: a theoretical and empirical study. Constraints **16**(2), 195–221 (2011)
9. Audemard, G., Katsirelos, G., Simon, L.: A restriction of extended resolution for clause learning SAT solvers. In: Proceedings of AAAI 2010, pp. 15–20. AAAI Press (2010)
10. Huang, J.: Universal booleanization of constraint models. In: Stuckey, P.J. (ed.) CP 2008. LNCS, vol. 5202, pp. 144–158. Springer, Heidelberg (2008). doi:10.1007/ 978-3-540-85958-1_10
11. Gebser, M., Kaminski, R., Ostrowski, M., Schaub, T., Thiele, S.: On the input language of ASP grounder gringo. In: Erdem, E., Lin, F., Schaub, T. (eds.) LPNMR 2009. LNCS (LNAI), vol. 5753, pp. 502–508. Springer, Heidelberg (2009). doi:10. 1007/978-3-642-04238-6_49
12. Leone, N., Pfeifer, G., Faber, W., Eiter, T., Gottlob, G., Perri, S., Scarcello, F.: The DLV system for knowledge representation and reasoning. ACM Trans. Comput. Logic **7**(3), 499–562 (2006)
13. Schlipf, J.: The expressive powers of the logic programming semantics. J. Comput. Syst. Sci. **51**, 64–86 (1995)
14. McCarthy, J.: Elaboration tolerance (2003). http://www-formal.stanford.edu/ jmc/elaboration.ps
15. Gebser, M., Kaminski, R., König, A., Schaub, T.: Advances in gringo series 3. In: Delgrande, J.P., Faber, W. (eds.) LPNMR 2011. LNCS (LNAI), vol. 6645, pp. 345–351. Springer, Heidelberg (2011). doi:10.1007/978-3-642-20895-9_39
16. Van Gelder, A., Ross, K., Schlipf, J.: The well-founded semantics for general logic programs. J. ACM **38**(3), 620–650 (1991)
17. Ullman, J.: Principles of Database and Knowledge-Base Systems. CS Press, New York (1988)
18. Gelfond, M., Lifschitz, V.: Classical negation in logic programs and disjunctive databases. New Gener. Comput. **9**(3–4), 365–386 (1991)
19. Simons, P., Niemelä, I., Soininen, T.: Extending and implementing the stable model semantics. Artif. Intell. **138**(1–2), 181–234 (2002)

20. Gebser, M., Janhunen, T., Rintanen, J.: Answer set programming as SAT modulo acyclicity. In: Proceedings of ECAI 2014, pp. 351–356. IOS Press (2014)
21. Gebser, M., Janhunen, T., Rintanen, J.: SAT modulo graphs: acyclicity. In: Fermé, E., Leite, J. (eds.) JELIA 2014. LNCS (LNAI), vol. 8761, pp. 137–151. Springer, Heidelberg (2014). doi:10.1007/978-3-319-11558-0_10
22. Graça, A., Marques-Silva, J., Lynce, I., Oliveira, A.L.: Efficient haplotype inference with combined CP and OR techniques. In: Perron, L., Trick, M.A. (eds.) CPAIOR 2008. LNCS, vol. 5015, pp. 308–312. Springer, Heidelberg (2008). doi:10.1007/978-3-540-68155-7_28
23. Graça, A., Marques-Silva, J., Lynce, I., Oliveira, A.L.: Efficient haplotype inference with pseudo-Boolean optimization. In: Anai, H., Horimoto, K., Kutsia, T. (eds.) AB 2007. LNCS, vol. 4545, pp. 125–139. Springer, Heidelberg (2007). doi:10.1007/978-3-540-73433-8_10
24. Eén, N., Sörensson, N.: Translating pseudo-Boolean constraints into SAT. J. Satisfiability Boolean Model. Comput. **2**, 1–26 (2006)
25. Andres, B., Kaufmann, B., Matheis, O., Schaub, T.: Unsatisfiability-based optimization in clasp. In: Technical Communications of ICLP 2012, pp. 212–221. LIPIcs (2012)
26. East, D., Iakhiaev, M., Mikitiuk, A., Truszczyński, M.: Tools for modeling and solving search problems. AI Commun. **19**(4), 301–312 (2006)
27. Blockeel, H., Bogaerts, B., Bruynooghe, M., De Cat, B., De Pooter, S., Denecker, M., Labarre, A., Ramon, J., Verwer, S.: Modeling machine learning and data mining problems with FO(.). In: Technical Communications of ICLP 2012, pp. 14–25. LIPIcs (2012)
28. Jansen, J., Dasseville, I., Devriendt, J., Janssens, G.: Experimental evaluation of a state-of-the-art grounder. In: Proceedings of PPDP 2014, pp. 249–258. ACM Press (2014)
29. Jansen, J., Jorissen, A., Janssens, G.: Compiling input* FO(.) inductive definitions into tabled prolog rules for IDP3. Theor. Pract. Logic Program. **13**(4–5), 691–704 (2013)
30. Cadoli, M., Schaerf, A.: Compiling problem specifications into SAT. Artif. Intell. **162**(1–2), 89–120 (2005)
31. Stuckey, P., Feydy, T., Schutt, A., Tack, G., Fischer, J.: The MiniZinc challenge 2008–2013. AI Mag. **35**(2), 55–60 (2014)
32. Gebser, M., Janhunen, T., Kaminski, R., Schaub, T., Tasharrofi, S.: Writing declarative specifications for clauses. In: Proceedings of GTTV (2015)
33. Janhunen, T., Tasharrofi, S., Ternovska, E.: SAT-to-SAT: declarative extension of SAT solvers with new propagators. In: Proceedings of AAAI 2016, pp. 978–984. AAAI Press (2016)
34. Bogaerts, B., Janhunen, T., Tasharrofi, S.: Solving QBF instances with nested SAT solvers. In: Proceedings of AAAI-16 Workshop on Beyond NP, pp. 307–313. AAAI Press (2016). http://www.aaai.org/ocs/index.php/WS/AAAIW16/paper/view/12603/12381
35. Bogaerts, B., Janhunen, T., Tasharrofi, S.: Declarative solver development: case studies. In: Proceedings of KR 2016, pp. 74–83. AAAI Press (2016)
36. Bogaerts, B., Janhunen, T., Tasharrofi, S.: Stable-unstable semantics: beyond NP with normal logic programs. Theory and Practice of Logic Programming (2016, to appear)
37. Janhunen, T.: Some (in)translatability results for normal logic programs and propositional theories. J. Appl. Non-Class. Logics **16**(1–2), 35–86 (2006)

Standard Sequent Calculi
for Lewis' Logics of Counterfactuals

Marianna Girlando[1]([✉]), Björn Lellmann[2],
Nicola Olivetti[1], and Gian Luca Pozzato[3]

[1] Aix Marseille Univ, CNRS, ENSAM, Université de Toulon,
LSIS UMR 7296, 13397 Marseille, France
{marianna.girlando,nicola.olivetti}@univ-amu.fr
[2] Technische Universität Wien, Vienna, Austria
lellmann@logic.at
[3] Dipartimento di Informatica, Universitá di Torino, Turin, Italy
gianluca.pozzato@unito.it

Abstract. We present new sequent calculi for Lewis' logics of counterfactuals. The calculi are based on Lewis' connective of comparative
plausibility and modularly capture almost all logics of Lewis' family.
Our calculi are standard, in the sense that each connective is handled
by a finite number of rules with a fixed and finite number of premises;
internal, meaning that a sequent denotes a formula in the language, and
analytical. We present two equivalent versions of the calculi: in the first
one, the calculi comprise simple rules; we show that for the basic case of
logic $\mathbb{V}$, the calculus allows for syntactic cut-elimination, a fundamental
proof-theoretical property. In the second version, the calculi comprise
invertible rules, they allow for terminating proof search and semantical completeness. We finally show that our calculi can simulate the only
internal (non-standard) sequent calculi previously known for these logics.

1 Introduction

In his seminal works [14], Lewis proposed a formalization of conditional logics
in order to represent a kind of hypothetical reasoning that cannot be captured
by the material implication of classical logic. His original motivation was to formalize counterfactuals, that is to say, conditionals of the form "if A were the
case then B would be the case", where A is false. Independently from counterfactuals, conditional logics have found an interest in several fields of knowledge
representation; for instance, they have been used to model belief change [10].
To this regard, a multi-agent version of Lewis' conditional logic $\mathbb{VTA}$ [2,3] has

---

B. Lellmann—Funded by the European Union's Horizon 2020 research and innova-
tion programme under the Marie Skłodowska-Curie grant agreement No 660047.
G.L. Pozzato—Partially supported by the project "ExceptionOWL", Universitá di
Torino and Compagnia di San Paolo, call 2014 "Excellent (young) PI".
M. Girlando—Partially supported by the *LabEx Archimède*, AMU.

L. Michael and A. Kakas (Eds.): JELIA 2016, LNAI 10021, pp. 272–287, 2016.
DOI: 10.1007/978-3-319-48758-8_18

been used to formalize epistemic change in a multi-agent setting, where the conditional operator expresses the "conditional beliefs" of an agent. In a different context, conditional logics have been used to reason about prototypical properties [5,8], and to provide an axiomatic foundation of non-monotonic reasoning [11], in which a conditional $A \mathbin{\Box\!\!\rightarrow} B$ is read as "in normal circumstances, if A then B".

The family of logics studied by Lewis is semantically characterized by sphere models, a particular kind of neighbourhood models introduced by Lewis himself. In Lewis' terminology, a *sphere* denotes a set of worlds; in sphere models, each world is equipped with a nested system of such spheres. From the viewpoint of the given world, inner sets represent the "most plausible worlds", while worlds belonging only to outer sets are considered as less plausible. In order to treat the conditional operator, Lewis takes as primitive the comparative plausibility connective $\preccurlyeq$: a formula $A \preccurlyeq B$ means "A is at least as plausible as B". The conditional $A \mathbin{\Box\!\!\rightarrow} B$ can be then defined as "A is impossible" or "$A \wedge \neg B$ is less plausible than $A \wedge B$". However, the latter assertion is equivalent to the simpler one "$A \wedge \neg B$ is less plausible than A"[1].

From the point of view of proof theory and automated deduction, conditional logics do not have a state of the art comparable with, say, the one of modal logics, for which there exist well-established calculi with well-understood proof-theoretical and computational properties. Calculi for some weaker conditional logics are given, e.g., in [1,18] and more recently in [15,19]. Regarding Lewis' counterfactual logics, external labelled calculi have been proposed in [9] and in [16], both based on a relational reformulation of the sphere semantics. We are interested in *internal* sequent calculi, where a sequent denotes a formula of the language. Calculi of this kind have been proposed by Gent [7] and de Swart [20], and more recently in [12,13]. They are analytical and provide a decision procedure for the respective logics; on the other hand, they comprise an infinite set of rules with a variable number of premises.

Our aim is to provide internal calculi for the whole family of Lewis' logics. We sought the calculi to display the following features: (i) they should be *standard*, i.e. each connective should be handled by a fixed finite set of rules with a fixed finite set of premises; (ii) they should be *modular*, i.e. it should be possible to obtain calculi for stronger logics adding independent rules to calculi for weaker ones; (iii) they should have good proof-theoretical properties, first they should allow a syntactic proof of cut admissibility; (iv) they should provide a decision procedure for the respective logics; finally (v) they should be of optimal complexity with respect to the known complexity of the logic. In our opinion requirement (i) is particularly important: a standard calculus could provide a self-explanatory presentation of the logic, thus a kind of proof-theoretic semantics. A first step in this direction is the calculus $\mathcal{I}_V$ presented in [17] for logic $\mathbb{V}$: it is internal and it is formulated in terms of structured sequents containing blocks encoding disjunctions of $\preccurlyeq$-formulas. The calculus provides an optimal decision procedure for $\mathbb{V}$; however, no syntactic proof of cut admissibility is known for it.

---

[1] It is worth noticing that in turn the connective $\preccurlyeq$ can be defined in terms of $\mathbin{\Box\!\!\rightarrow}$.

In this work we make a further step towards the objectives mentioned above, extending the results of [17]. We present internal, standard, cut-free calculi for most logics of the Lewis family, namely logics $\mathbb{V}$, $\mathbb{VN}$, $\mathbb{VT}$, $\mathbb{VW}$, $\mathbb{VC}$, $\mathbb{VA}$ and $\mathbb{VNA}$ (hereafter denoted by $\mathcal{L}$). Our calculi make use of a simplified block structure with respect to $\mathcal{I}_V$. We first present the calculi $\mathcal{I}_{\mathcal{L}}$, containing particularly perspicuous non-invertible rules together with explicit contraction rules. As a preliminary result we provide a syntactic proof of the admissibility of the cut rule for the basic case of logic $\mathbb{V}$, obtaining, as a by-product, a syntactic proof of completeness of the calculus. We then present the calculi $\mathcal{I}_{\mathcal{L}}^i$, an alternative version of $\mathcal{I}_{\mathcal{L}}$ with invertible rules and provably admissible contraction rules. We show that calculi $\mathcal{I}_{\mathcal{L}}^i$ are equivalent to $\mathcal{I}_{\mathcal{L}}$, and that they allow terminating proof-search; therefore they provide a decision procedure for the respective logics. Moreover, we also prove the semantic completeness of $\mathcal{I}_{\mathcal{L}}^i$ calculi for all logics of Lewis family not including the absoluteness condition. As a final result, we show that calculi $\mathcal{I}_{\mathcal{L}}$ (whence $\mathcal{I}_{\mathcal{L}}^i$) can simulate the non-standard calculi of [12,13]. This result is interesting in itself as it clarifies the relation between rather different proof-systems, and moreover it provides an alternative completeness proof of both $\mathcal{I}_{\mathcal{L}}$ and $\mathcal{I}_{\mathcal{L}}^i$ calculi, in particular for the missing cases of logics $\mathbb{VA}$ and $\mathbb{VNA}$. For the remaining logics of Lewis' family such as $\mathbb{VTA}$, $\mathbb{VWA}$, and $\mathbb{VCA}$ the issue of completeness of our calculi is open and will be dealt with in future research.

2   Preliminaries

We consider the *conditional logics* defined by Lewis in [14]. The set of *conditional formulae* is given by $\mathcal{F} ::= p \mid \bot \mid \mathcal{F} \to \mathcal{F} \mid \mathcal{F} \preccurlyeq \mathcal{F}$, where $p \in \mathcal{V}$ is a propositional variable. The other boolean connectives are defined in terms of $\bot, \to$ as usual. Intuitively, a formula $A \preccurlyeq B$ is interpreted as "A is at least as plausible as B".

As mentioned above, Lewis' counterfactual implication $\Box\!\!\to$ can be defined in terms of comparative plausibility $\preccurlyeq$ as $A \Box\!\!\to B \equiv (\bot \preccurlyeq A) \vee \neg((A \wedge \neg B) \preccurlyeq A)$.

The semantics of this logic is defined by Lewis in terms of *sphere semantics*:

Definition 1. *A* sphere model *(or* model*) is a triple $\langle W, \mathsf{SP}, [\![.]\!]\rangle$, consisting of a non-empty set W of elements, called* worlds, *a mapping $\mathsf{SP} : W \to \mathcal{P}(\mathcal{P}(W))$, and a propositional valuation $[\![.]\!] : \mathcal{V} \to \mathcal{P}(W)$. Elements of $\mathsf{SP}(x)$ are called* spheres. *We assume the following conditions: for every $\alpha \in \mathsf{SP}(w)$ we have $\alpha \neq \emptyset$, and for every $\alpha, \beta \in \mathsf{SP}(w)$ we have $\alpha \subseteq \beta$ or $\beta \subseteq \alpha$. The latter condition is called* sphere nesting.

The valuation $[\![.]\!]$ is extended to all formulae by: $[\![\bot]\!] = \emptyset$; $[\![A \to B]\!] = (W - [\![A]\!]) \cup [\![B]\!]$; $[\![A \preccurlyeq B]\!] = \{w \in W \mid$ for all $\alpha \in \mathsf{SP}(w)$. if $[\![B]\!] \cap \alpha \neq \emptyset$, then $[\![A]\!] \cap \alpha \neq \emptyset\}$. For $w \in W$ we also write $w \Vdash A$ instead of $w \in [\![A]\!]$. As for spheres, we write $\alpha \Vdash^\forall A$ meaning $\forall x \in \alpha$. $x \Vdash A$ and $\alpha \Vdash^\exists A$ meaning $\exists x \in \alpha$. $x \Vdash A^2$. Validity and satisfiability of formulae in a class of models are defined as usual. Conditional logic $\mathbb{V}$ is the set of formulae valid in all sphere models.

---

[2] Employing this notation, satisfiability of a $\preccurlyeq$-formula in a model becomes the following: $x \Vdash A \preccurlyeq B$ iff for all $\alpha \in \mathsf{SP}(x)$. $\alpha \Vdash^\forall \neg B$ or $\alpha \Vdash^\exists A$.

Extensions of $\mathbb{V}$ are semantically given by specifying additional conditions on the class of sphere models, namely:

- *normality*: for all $w \in W$ we have $\mathsf{SP}(w) \neq \emptyset$;
- *total reflexivity*: for all $w \in W$ we have $w \in \bigcup \mathsf{SP}(w)$;
- *weak centering*: normality holds and for all $\alpha \in \mathsf{SP}(w)$ we have $w \in \alpha$;
- *centering*: for all $w \in W$ we have $\{w\} \in \mathsf{SP}(w)$;
- *absoluteness*: for all $w, v \in W$ we have $\mathsf{SP}(w) = \mathsf{SP}(v)$.[3]

Extensions of $\mathbb{V}$ are denoted by concatenating the letters for these properties: $\mathbb{N}$ for normality, $\mathbb{T}$ for total reflexivity, $\mathbb{W}$ for weak centering, $\mathbb{C}$ for centering, and $\mathbb{A}$ for absoluteness. All the above logics can be characterized by axioms in a Hilbert-style system [14, Chap. 6]. The modal axioms formulated in the language with only the comparative plausibility operator are presented in Table 1 (where $\vee$ and $\wedge$ bind stronger than $\preccurlyeq$). The propositional axioms and rules are standard.

Table 1. Lewis' logics and axioms.

$$\mathsf{CPR} \frac{\vdash B \to A}{\vdash A \preccurlyeq B} \qquad \mathsf{CPA}\ (A \preccurlyeq A \vee B) \vee (B \preccurlyeq A \vee B)$$

$$\mathsf{TR}\ (A \preccurlyeq B) \wedge (B \preccurlyeq C) \to (A \preccurlyeq C) \quad \mathsf{CO}\ (A \preccurlyeq B) \vee (B \preccurlyeq A)$$

$$\mathsf{N}\ \neg(\bot \preccurlyeq \top) \qquad\qquad\qquad \mathsf{W}\ A \to (A \preccurlyeq \top)$$

$$\mathsf{T}\ (\bot \preccurlyeq \neg A) \to A \qquad\qquad \mathsf{A1}\ (A \preccurlyeq B) \to \big(\bot \preccurlyeq \neg(A \preccurlyeq B)\big)$$

$$\mathsf{C}\ (A \preccurlyeq \top) \to A \qquad\qquad \mathsf{A2}\ \neg(A \preccurlyeq B) \to \big(\bot \preccurlyeq (A \preccurlyeq B)\big)$$

$$\mathcal{A}_\mathsf{V} := \{\mathsf{CPR}, \mathsf{CPA}, \mathsf{TR}, \mathsf{CO}\}$$

$$\mathcal{A}_\mathsf{VN} := \mathcal{A}_\mathsf{V} \cup \{\mathsf{N}\} \qquad \mathcal{A}_\mathsf{VT} := \mathcal{A}_\mathsf{V} \cup \{\mathsf{N}, \mathsf{T}\} \qquad \mathcal{A}_\mathsf{VW} := \mathcal{A}_\mathsf{V} \cup \{\mathsf{N}, \mathsf{T}, \mathsf{W}\}$$

$$\mathcal{A}_\mathsf{VC} := \mathcal{A}_\mathsf{V} \cup \{\mathsf{N}, \mathsf{T}, \mathsf{W}, \mathsf{C}\} \quad \mathcal{A}_\mathsf{VA} := \mathcal{A}_\mathsf{V} \cup \{\mathsf{A1}, \mathsf{A2}\} \quad \mathcal{A}_\mathsf{VNA} := \mathcal{A}_\mathsf{V} \cup \{\mathsf{N}, \mathsf{A1}, \mathsf{A2}\}$$

3   A Sequent Calculus for Lewis' Logic and Extensions

We propose internal sequent calculi for the basic Lewis' logic $\mathbb{V}$ as well as for some extensions. Our calculi are based on a modification of the sequent format from [17]. To make contraction explicit we consider sequents based on multisets, and write Γ, Δ for multiset union and A^n for the multiset containing n copies of the formula A. The basic constituent of sequents are *blocks* of the form $[A_1, \ldots, A_m \lhd A]$, with $A_1, \ldots, A_m, A$ formulas, representing disjunctions of $\preccurlyeq$-formulas.

Definition 2. *A* block *is a tuple consisting of a multiset Σ of formulae and a single formula A, written $[\Sigma \lhd A]$. A* sequent *is a tuple $\Gamma \Rightarrow \Delta$, where Γ is a*

---

[3] Lewis' original presentation in [14] is slightly different: he did not assume the general condition on sphere models that for every $\alpha \in \mathsf{SP}(w)$: $\alpha \neq \emptyset$, and formulated normality as $\forall w \in W\ :\ \bigcup \mathsf{SP}(w) \neq \emptyset$ and weak centering as normality plus $\forall w \in W\ \alpha \in \mathsf{SP}(w)$, if $\alpha \neq \emptyset$ then $w \in \alpha$. Furthermore, note that absoluteness can be equally stated as *local absoluteness*: $\forall w \in W \forall v \in \bigcup \mathsf{SP}(w)\ \mathsf{SP}(w) = \mathsf{SP}(v)$.

multiset of conditional formulae, and Δ is a multiset of conditional formulae and blocks. The formula interpretation *of a sequent is given by (all blocks shown):*

$$\iota(\Gamma \Rightarrow \Delta', [\Sigma_1 \lhd A_1], \ldots, [\Sigma_n \lhd A_n]) := \bigwedge \Gamma \to \bigvee \Delta' \vee \bigvee_{1 \le i \le n} \bigvee_{B \in \Sigma_i} (B \preccurlyeq A_i)$$

Table 2 presents non-invertible calculi for logic $\mathbb{V}$ and its extensions, including rules for contraction both on the sequent level and inside blocks[4]. We write $[\Theta, \Sigma \lhd A]$ for $[(\Theta, \Sigma) \lhd A]$, with Θ, Σ standing for multiset union.

Table 2. The calculus $\mathcal{I}_{\mathbb{V}}$ and its extensions

$$\frac{}{\Gamma, \bot \Rightarrow \Delta} \bot_L \qquad \frac{}{\Gamma, p \Rightarrow \Delta, p} \text{ init} \qquad \frac{\Gamma, B \Rightarrow \Delta \quad \Gamma \Rightarrow \Delta, A}{\Gamma, A \to B \Rightarrow \Delta} \to_L \qquad \frac{\Gamma, A \Rightarrow \Delta, B}{\Gamma \Rightarrow \Delta, A \to B} \to_R$$

$$\frac{\Gamma \Rightarrow \Delta, [A \lhd B]}{\Gamma \Rightarrow \Delta, A \preccurlyeq B} \preccurlyeq_R \qquad \frac{\Gamma \Rightarrow \Delta, [D, \Sigma \lhd A] \quad \Gamma \Rightarrow \Delta, [\Sigma \lhd C]}{\Gamma, C \preccurlyeq D \Rightarrow \Delta, [\Sigma \lhd A]} \preccurlyeq_L$$

$$\frac{\Gamma \Rightarrow \Delta, [\Sigma_1, \Sigma_2 \lhd A] \quad \Gamma \Rightarrow \Delta, [\Sigma_1, \Sigma_2 \lhd B]}{\Gamma \Rightarrow \Delta, [\Sigma_1 \lhd A], [\Sigma_2 \lhd B]} \text{ com} \qquad \frac{A \Rightarrow \Sigma}{\Gamma \Rightarrow \Delta, [\Sigma \lhd A]} \text{ jump}$$

$$\frac{A, A, \Gamma \Rightarrow \Delta}{A, \Gamma \Rightarrow \Delta} \text{ Con}_L \qquad \frac{\Gamma \Rightarrow \Delta, A, A}{\Gamma \Rightarrow \Delta, A} \text{ Con}_R \qquad \frac{\Gamma \Rightarrow \Delta, [\Sigma \lhd A], [\Sigma \lhd A]}{\Gamma \Rightarrow \Delta, [\Sigma \lhd A]} \text{ Con}_S$$

$$\frac{\Gamma \Rightarrow \Delta, [\Sigma, A, A \lhd B]}{\Gamma \Rightarrow \Delta, [\Sigma, A \lhd B]} \text{ Con}_B \qquad \frac{\Gamma \Rightarrow \Delta, [\bot \lhd T]}{\Gamma \Rightarrow \Delta} \text{ N} \qquad \frac{\Gamma \Rightarrow \Delta, B \quad \Gamma \Rightarrow \Delta, [\bot \lhd A]}{\Gamma, A \preccurlyeq B \Rightarrow \Delta} \text{ T}$$

$$\frac{\Gamma \Rightarrow \Delta, \Sigma}{\Gamma \Rightarrow \Delta, [\Sigma \lhd A]} \text{ W} \qquad \frac{\Gamma, C \Rightarrow \Delta \quad \Gamma \Rightarrow D, \Delta}{\Gamma, C \preccurlyeq D \Rightarrow \Delta} \text{ C} \qquad \frac{\Gamma^{\preccurlyeq}, B \Rightarrow \Delta^{\preccurlyeq}, \Sigma}{\Gamma \Rightarrow \Delta, [\Sigma \lhd B]} \text{ A}$$

Here $\Gamma^{\preccurlyeq} \Rightarrow \Delta^{\preccurlyeq}$ is $\Gamma \Rightarrow \Delta$ restricted to formulae of the form $C \preccurlyeq D$ and blocks.

$$\mathcal{I}_{\mathbb{V}} := \{\bot_L, \text{init}, \to_L, \to_R, \preccurlyeq_R, \preccurlyeq_L, \text{com}, \text{jump}, \text{Con}_R, \text{Con}_L, \text{Con}_S\}$$

$$\mathcal{I}_{\mathbb{VN}} := \mathcal{I}_{\mathbb{V}} \cup \{\mathsf{N}\} \qquad \mathcal{I}_{\mathbb{VW}} := \mathcal{I}_{\mathbb{V}} \cup \{\mathsf{N}, \mathsf{T}, \mathsf{W}\} \qquad \mathcal{I}_{\mathbb{VA}} := \mathcal{I}_{\mathbb{V}} \cup \{\mathsf{A}\}$$
$$\mathcal{I}_{\mathbb{VT}} := \mathcal{I}_{\mathbb{V}} \cup \{\mathsf{N}, \mathsf{T}\} \qquad \mathcal{I}_{\mathbb{VC}} := \mathcal{I}_{\mathbb{V}} \cup \{\mathsf{N}, \mathsf{T}, \mathsf{W}, \mathsf{C}\} \qquad \mathcal{I}_{\mathbb{VNA}} := \mathcal{I}_{\mathbb{V}} \cup \{\mathsf{N}, \mathsf{A}\}$$

For notational convenience in the following we take $\mathcal{L}$ to range over the logics $\mathbb{V}, \mathbb{VN}, \mathbb{VT}, \mathbb{VW}, \mathbb{VC}, \mathbb{VA}, \mathbb{VNA}$, unless specified otherwise. As usual, given a formula $G \in \mathcal{L}$, in order to check whether G is valid we look for a derivation of $\Rightarrow G$. Given a sequent $\Gamma \Rightarrow \Delta$, we say that it is derivable, written $\mathcal{I}_{\mathcal{L}} \vdash \Gamma \Rightarrow \Delta$, if it admits a *derivation*, namely a tree where the root is $\Gamma \Rightarrow \Delta$, every leaf is an instance of axioms init or $\bot_L$, and every non-leaf node is (an instance of) the conclusion of a rule having (an instance of) the premises of the rule as children.

Given the definition of $\Box\!\!\to$ in terms of $\preccurlyeq$, rules for counterfactual implication can be explicitly stated as follows:

$$\frac{\bot \preccurlyeq A, \Gamma \Rightarrow \Delta \quad \Gamma \Rightarrow \Delta, [A \wedge \neg B \lhd A]}{A \Box\!\!\to B, \Gamma \Rightarrow \Delta} \Box\!\!\to_L \qquad \frac{(A \wedge \neg B) \preccurlyeq A, \Gamma \Rightarrow \Delta, [\bot \lhd A]}{\Gamma \Rightarrow \Delta, A \Box\!\!\to B} \Box\!\!\to_R$$

---

[4] Actually, the rules Con_S and Con_B are not needed for completeness (refer to Sect. 6); we have included them in our official formulation of the calculi for technical convenience.

Theorem 3 (Soundness). *If $\mathcal{I}_\mathcal{L} \vdash \Gamma \Rightarrow \Delta$, then $\iota(\Gamma \Rightarrow \Delta)$ is a theorem of $\mathcal{L}$.*

Example 4. To illustrate the use of the calculus we show a derivation of the characteristic axiom $(\bot \preccurlyeq \neg A) \to A$ for logic $\mathbb{VT}$ in the calculus $\mathcal{I}_{\mathbb{VW}}$ and a derivation of it in the calculus $\mathbb{VC}$ (where $\neg A = (A \to \bot)$):

$$
\cfrac{
\cfrac{
\cfrac{\overline{A \Rightarrow A, \bot, \bot}\ \text{init}}{\Rightarrow A, A \to \bot, \bot}\ {\to}_R
}{\Rightarrow A, [(A \to \bot), \bot \lhd \top]}\ \text{W} \quad
\cfrac{
\cfrac{\overline{\bot \Rightarrow \bot}\ {\bot}_L}{\Rightarrow A, [\bot \lhd \bot]}\ \text{jump}
}{}\ {\preccurlyeq}_L
}{
\cfrac{
\cfrac{\bot \preccurlyeq (A \to \bot) \Rightarrow A, [\bot \lhd \top]}{\bot \preccurlyeq (A \to \bot) \Rightarrow A}\ \text{N}
}{\Rightarrow (\bot \preccurlyeq (A \to \bot)) \to A}\ {\to}_R
}
$$

$$
\cfrac{
\cfrac{\bot \Rightarrow A}{}\ {\bot}_L \quad
\cfrac{\overline{A \Rightarrow A, \bot}\ \text{init}}{\Rightarrow A, A \to \bot}\ {\to}_R
}{\bot \preccurlyeq (A \to \bot) \Rightarrow A}\ \text{C}
$$

Therefore, rule T could be omitted in the rule sets $\mathcal{I}_{\mathbb{VW}}$ and $\mathcal{I}_{\mathbb{VC}}$.

Completeness of the calculi is shown in next section. We now provide the cut elimination proof in presence of the contraction rules (Con_L, Con_R, Con_S and Con_B). The general strategy, adapted from the hypersequent setting [4], consists of eliminating topmost applications of cut of maximal complexity by first permuting them into the left premise until we reach an occurrence of the cut formula which is principal, and then permuting them into the right one. The cut rules are:

$$
\cfrac{\Gamma \Rightarrow \Delta, A \quad A, \Sigma \Rightarrow \Pi}{\Gamma, \Sigma \Rightarrow \Delta, \Pi}\ \mathsf{cut}_1 \qquad
\cfrac{\Gamma \Rightarrow \Delta, [\Omega \lhd A] \quad \Sigma \Rightarrow \Pi, [A, \Theta \lhd B]}{\Gamma, \Sigma \Rightarrow \Delta, \Pi\,[\Omega, \Theta \lhd B]}\ \mathsf{cut}_2
$$

Definition 5. *We write $\mathcal{I}_\mathcal{L}\mathsf{Cut}$ for the calculus $\mathcal{I}_\mathcal{L}$ extended with the cut rules cut_1 and cut_2. The complexity of an application of cut_1 or cut_2 is the complexity of the cut formula, i.e., the number $|A|$ of symbols of the cut formula A. Given a derivation $\mathcal{D}$ in $\mathcal{I}_\mathcal{L}\mathsf{Cut}$, its formula cut rank $\mathsf{rk}_{\mathsf{cut}_1}(\mathcal{D})$ is the maximal complexity of an application of cut_1 in it. Analogously, its structural cut rank $\mathsf{rk}_{\mathsf{cut}_2}(\mathcal{D})$ is the maximal complexity of an application of cut_2 in it. The height of a derivation is the number of nodes of its longest branch minus one. Thus, a derivation of height 0 is an axiom. We write $\mathcal{I}_\mathcal{L} \vdash_n \Gamma \Rightarrow \Delta$ if there exists a derivation of height n in $\mathcal{I}_\mathcal{L}$ with endsequent $\Gamma \Rightarrow \Delta$. Similarly for $\mathcal{I}_\mathcal{L}\mathsf{Cut}$.*

By straightforward induction on the height of the derivation we obtain:

Lemma 6. *The weakening rules are height-preserving admissible in $\mathcal{I}_\mathcal{L}$ and $\mathcal{I}_\mathcal{L}\mathsf{Cut}$, i.e. (using the uniform notation $\mathcal{I}_\mathcal{L}(\mathsf{Cut})$ for both cases): If $\mathcal{I}_\mathcal{L}(\mathsf{Cut}) \vdash_n \Gamma \Rightarrow \Delta$, then $\mathcal{I}_\mathcal{L}(\mathsf{Cut}) \vdash_n \Gamma, \Sigma \Rightarrow \Delta, \Pi$ and if $\mathcal{I}_\mathcal{L}(\mathsf{Cut}) \vdash_n \Gamma \Rightarrow \Delta, [\Sigma \lhd A]$, then $\mathcal{I}_\mathcal{L}(\mathsf{Cut}) \vdash_n \Gamma \Rightarrow \Delta, [\Sigma, \Omega \lhd A]$. Moreover, both the formula cut rank and the structural cut rank are preserved.*

Lemma 7 (cut$_1$-reduction). *Suppose $\mathcal{I}_\mathbb{V}\mathsf{Cut} \vdash \Gamma \Rightarrow \Delta, A^n$ and $\mathcal{I}_\mathbb{V}\mathsf{Cut} \vdash A^m, \Sigma \Rightarrow \Pi$ by derivations $\mathcal{D}_1$ and $\mathcal{D}_2$ with $\mathsf{rk}_{\mathsf{cut}_1}(\mathcal{D}_1) < |A| > \mathsf{rk}_{\mathsf{cut}_1}(\mathcal{D}_2)$ and $\mathsf{rk}_{\mathsf{cut}_2}(\mathcal{D}_1) < |A| > \mathsf{rk}_{\mathsf{cut}_2}(\mathcal{D}_2)$, where A^n and A^m are n and m occurrences of A. Then there is a derivation $\mathcal{D}$ in $\mathcal{I}_\mathbb{V}\mathsf{Cut}$ of $\Gamma, \Sigma \Rightarrow \Delta, \Pi$ with $\mathsf{rk}_{\mathsf{cut}_1}(\mathcal{D}) < |A| > \mathsf{rk}_{\mathsf{cut}_2}(\mathcal{D})$.*

Proof. By induction on the sum of the heights of $\mathcal{D}_1$ and $\mathcal{D}_2$. We write R_1 and R_2 for the last rules in $\mathcal{D}_1$ resp. $\mathcal{D}_2$, and count the atom p in init and the contracted formula in the contraction rules as principal. If none of the occurrences of A is principal in R_1, we apply the induction hypothesis on the premise(s) of R_1 followed by R_1. Otherwise, if none of the occurrences of A is principal in R_2, we apply the induction hypothesis to the premise(s) of R_2 followed by R_2.

If at least one occurrence of A was principal both in R_1 and R_2, we apply the induction hypothesis to the premise(s) of R_1 and the conclusion of R_2 and vice versa to delete the occurrences of A in the context. If either of the rules was a contraction rule we are done, otherwise apply cut$_1$ or cut$_2$ on formulae of smaller complexity. The propositional cases are standard, the case where $A = C \preccurlyeq D$ is straightforward. Applying contraction rules then yields the result.   □

Lemma 8 (Shift-right).   *Suppose for* $k_1, \ldots, k_n \geq 1$ *we have* $\mathcal{I}_\forall$Cut-*derivations* $\mathcal{D}_1$ *and* $\mathcal{D}_2$ *of* $\Gamma \Rightarrow \Delta, [\Omega \lhd A]$ *and* $\Sigma \Rightarrow \Pi, \left[A^{k_1}, \Theta_1 \lhd B_1\right],$ $\ldots, \left[A^{k_n}, \Theta_n \lhd B_n\right]$ *respectively with* $\mathsf{rk}_{\mathsf{cut}_1}(\mathcal{D}_1) \leq |A| \geq \mathsf{rk}_{\mathsf{cut}_1}(\mathcal{D}_2)$ *and* $\mathsf{rk}_{\mathsf{cut}_2}(\mathcal{D}_1) < |A| > \mathsf{rk}_{\mathsf{cut}_2}(\mathcal{D}_2)$ *such that the last applied rule in* $\mathcal{D}_1$ *is* jump. *Then there is a derivation* $\mathcal{D}$ *in* $\mathcal{I}_\forall$Cut *with* $\mathsf{rk}_{\mathsf{cut}_1}(\mathcal{D}) \leq |A| > \mathsf{rk}_{\mathsf{cut}_2}(\mathcal{D})$ *of the sequent*

$$\Gamma, \Sigma \Rightarrow \Delta, \Pi, [\Omega, \Theta_1 \lhd B_1], \ldots, [\Omega, \Theta_n \lhd B_n]$$

Proof. By induction on the height of $\mathcal{D}_2$, distinguishing cases according to the last applied rule R. If R is a rule other than jump, com we apply the induction hypothesis to the premise(s) of R, followed by R if necessary. In particular, the general induction hypothesis immediately takes care of Con$_S$ and Con$_B$. If R is jump, we apply cut$_1$ several times to the occurrence of A in the premise of the application of jump in $\mathcal{D}_1$ and the occurrences of A in the premise of R, followed by applications of Con$_L$ and an application of jump. These new cuts have complexity $|A|$. If R is com, again we apply the induction hypothesis on the premises of R, but now we might need to apply weakening inside a block before applying com again.   □

Lemma 9 (cut$_2$-reduction). *Suppose we have* $\mathcal{I}_\forall$-*derivations* $\mathcal{D}_1$ *and* $\mathcal{D}_2$ *of* $\Gamma \Rightarrow \Delta, [\Omega_1 \lhd A], \ldots, [\Omega_n \lhd A]$ *and* $\Sigma \Rightarrow \Pi, [A, \Theta \lhd B]$ *with* $\mathsf{rk}_{\mathsf{cut}_1}(\mathcal{D}_1) \leq |A| \geq \mathsf{rk}_{\mathsf{cut}_1}(\mathcal{D}_2)$ *and* $\mathsf{rk}_{\mathsf{cut}_2}(\mathcal{D}_1) < |A| > \mathsf{rk}_{\mathsf{cut}_2}(\mathcal{D}_2)$. *Then there is a derivation* $\mathcal{D}$ *in* $\mathcal{I}_\forall$Cut *with* $\mathsf{rk}_{\mathsf{cut}_1}(\mathcal{D}) \leq |A| > \mathsf{rk}_{\mathsf{cut}_2}(\mathcal{D})$ *of the sequent*

$$\Gamma, \Sigma \Rightarrow \Delta, \Pi, [\Omega_1, \Theta \lhd B], \ldots, [\Omega_n, \Theta \lhd B]$$

Proof. By induction on the height of $\mathcal{D}_1$, distinguishing cases according to the last applied rule R. If none of the occurrences of A in the conclusion of R is in an active block we apply the induction hypothesis to the premise(s) of R followed by an application of R. Suppose A occurs in an active block. If R is com or $\preccurlyeq_L$ we apply the induction hypothesis on the premises, followed possibly by admissibility of Weakening (Lemma 6) and finally an application of R. If R is Con$_B$, we simply apply the induction hypothesis to its premise. If R is jump, we apply Lemma 8.   □

Theorem 10 (Cut Elimination). *If $\mathcal{I}_\mathbb{V}\mathsf{Cut} \vdash \Gamma \Rightarrow \Delta$, then $\mathcal{I}_\mathbb{V} \vdash \Gamma \Rightarrow \Delta$. In particular, there is a procedure to eliminate cuts from a derivation in $\mathcal{I}_\mathbb{V}\mathsf{Cut}$.*

Proof. We show how to convert an $\mathcal{I}_\mathbb{V}\mathsf{Cut}$-derivation $\mathcal{D}$ into a cut-free derivation with same conclusion by induction on the tuples $\langle \mathsf{rk}_{\mathsf{cut}_1}(\mathcal{D}), \#_{\mathsf{cut}_2}(\mathcal{D}), \#_{\mathsf{cut}_1}(\mathcal{D}) \rangle$ in the lexicographic ordering, where $\#_{\mathsf{cut}_1}(\mathcal{D})$ is the number of applications of cut_1 in $\mathcal{D}$ with cut formula of complexity $\max\{\mathsf{rk}_{\mathsf{cut}_1}(\mathcal{D}), \mathsf{rk}_{\mathsf{cut}_2}(\mathcal{D})\}$, and analogous for $\#_{\mathsf{cut}_2}(\mathcal{D})$ with respect to cut_2. A topmost application of cut_1 with complexity $\max\{\mathsf{rk}_{\mathsf{cut}_1}(\mathcal{D}), \mathsf{rk}_{\mathsf{cut}_2}(\mathcal{D})\}$ is eliminated using Lemma 7. A topmost application of cut_2 with complexity $\max\{\mathsf{rk}_{\mathsf{cut}_1}(\mathcal{D}), \mathsf{rk}_{\mathsf{cut}_2}(\mathcal{D})\}$ is eliminated using Lemma 9. It follows from the lemmas that in both cases the induction measure decreases. $\square$

As a consequence of the admissibility of cut, we can provide a syntactical proof of completeness of logic $\mathbb{V}$:

Corollary 11 (Completeness via cut elimination). *If a formula F is valid in $\mathbb{V}$, then there is a derivation of $\Rightarrow F$ in $\mathcal{I}_\mathbb{V}$.*

Proof. By deriving the rules and axioms of the Hilbert-calculus for $\mathbb{V}$ (Table 1) in $\mathcal{I}_\mathbb{V}\mathsf{Cut}$ and using Theorem 10. For rule CPR from $\Rightarrow B \to A$ by propositional rules and cut_1 we obtain $B \Rightarrow A$, and applications of jump and $\preccurlyeq_R$ yield $\Rightarrow A \preccurlyeq B$. $\square$

4   The Invertible Calculus

In Table 3 we present fully invertible calculi for Lewis' logics. The equivalence between $\mathcal{I}_\mathcal{L}$ and $\mathcal{I}_\mathcal{L}^i$ is proved via admissibility of weakening and contraction; furthermore, we shall use $\mathcal{I}_\mathcal{L}^i$ to semantically prove completeness of logics $\mathbb{V}$, $\mathbb{VN}$, $\mathbb{VT}$, $\mathbb{VW}$ and $\mathbb{VC}$. It can be shown that weakening is height preserving admissible in $\mathcal{I}_\mathbb{V}^i$ and its extensions, and that all the rules are invertible, with the exception of jump and A^i. Given these properties, we can prove that:

Lemma 12 (Adm. of Contraction). *1. Rules Con_L and Con_R are admissible in $\mathcal{I}_\mathcal{L}^i$; 2. Rule Con_S is admissible in $\mathcal{I}_\mathcal{L}^i$; 3. Rule Con_B is admissible in $\mathcal{I}_\mathcal{L}^i$.*

Theorem 13 (Equivalence). *For A arbitrary formula, A is derivable in the calculus $\mathcal{I}_\mathcal{L}$ iff A is derivable in the invertible calculus $\mathcal{I}_\mathcal{L}^i$.*

Proof. Both directions are proved by easy induction on the height of the derivation, modulo weakening and contraction. Note that for the [**if**] direction application of weakening is justified, since the rule is admissible in the calculus $\mathcal{I}_\mathcal{L}$, and for direction [**only if**] applications of weakening and contraction are legitimate since both rules are admissible in $\mathcal{I}_\mathcal{L}^i$. $\square$

Standard reasoning shows that the calculi $\mathcal{I}_\mathcal{L}^i$ can be used in a decision procedure for the logic $\mathcal{L}$ as follows. Since contractions and weakenings are admissible we

Table 3. The invertible calculus $\mathcal{I}_V^i$ and its extensions

$$\frac{}{\Gamma, \bot \Rightarrow \Delta} \ {}^{\bot_L} \qquad \frac{}{\Gamma, p \Rightarrow \Delta, p} \ \text{init} \qquad \frac{\Gamma, B \Rightarrow \Delta \quad \Gamma \Rightarrow \Delta, A}{\Gamma, A \to B \Rightarrow \Delta} \to_L \qquad \frac{\Gamma, A \Rightarrow \Delta, B}{\Gamma \Rightarrow \Delta, A \to B} \to_R$$

$$\frac{\Gamma \Rightarrow \Delta, [A \vartriangleleft B]}{\Gamma \Rightarrow \Delta, A \preccurlyeq B} \preccurlyeq_R \qquad \frac{\Gamma, A \preccurlyeq B \Rightarrow \Delta, [B, \Sigma \vartriangleleft C] \quad \Gamma, A \preccurlyeq B \Rightarrow \Delta, [\Sigma \vartriangleleft A], [\Sigma \vartriangleleft C]}{\Gamma, A \preccurlyeq B \Rightarrow \Delta, [\Sigma \vartriangleleft C]} \preccurlyeq_L^i$$

$$\frac{\Gamma \Rightarrow \Delta, [\Sigma_1, \Sigma_2 \vartriangleleft A], [\Sigma_2 \vartriangleleft B] \quad \Gamma \Rightarrow \Delta, [\Sigma_1 \vartriangleleft A], [\Sigma_1, \Sigma_2 \vartriangleleft B]}{\Gamma \Rightarrow \Delta, [\Sigma_1 \vartriangleleft A], [\Sigma_2 \vartriangleleft B]} \text{ com}^i$$

$$\frac{A \Rightarrow \Sigma}{\Gamma \Rightarrow \Delta, [\Sigma \vartriangleleft A]} \text{ jump} \qquad \frac{\Gamma \Rightarrow \Delta, [\bot \vartriangleleft \top]}{\Gamma \Rightarrow \Delta} \text{ N}$$

$$\frac{\Gamma, A \preccurlyeq B \Rightarrow \Delta, B \quad \Gamma, A \preccurlyeq B \Rightarrow \Delta, [\bot \vartriangleleft A]}{\Gamma, A \preccurlyeq B \Rightarrow \Delta} \text{ T}^i \qquad \frac{\Gamma \Rightarrow \Delta, [\Sigma \vartriangleleft A], \Sigma}{\Gamma \Rightarrow \Delta, [\Sigma \vartriangleleft A]} \text{ W}^i$$

$$\frac{\Gamma, A \preccurlyeq B \Rightarrow \Delta, B \quad \Gamma, A \preccurlyeq B, A \Rightarrow \Delta}{\Gamma, A \preccurlyeq B \Rightarrow \Delta} \text{ C}^i \qquad \frac{\Gamma^{\preccurlyeq}, B \Rightarrow \Delta^{\preccurlyeq}, [\Sigma \vartriangleleft B], \Sigma}{\Gamma \Rightarrow \Delta, [\Sigma \vartriangleleft B]} \text{ A}^i$$

Here $\Gamma^{\preccurlyeq} \Rightarrow \Delta^{\preccurlyeq}$ is $\Gamma \Rightarrow \Delta$ restricted to formulae of the form $C \preccurlyeq D$ and blocks.

$$\mathcal{I}_V^i := \{\bot_L, \text{init}, \to_L, \to_R, \preccurlyeq_R, \preccurlyeq_L^i, \text{com}^i, \text{jump}\}$$

$$\mathcal{I}_{VN}^i := \mathcal{I}_V^i \cup \{\text{N}\} \qquad \mathcal{I}_{VW}^i := \mathcal{I}_V^i \cup \{\text{N}, \text{T}^i, \text{W}^i\} \qquad \mathcal{I}_{VA}^i := \mathcal{I}_V^i \cup \{\text{A}^i\}$$
$$\mathcal{I}_{VT}^i := \mathcal{I}_V^i \cup \{\text{N}, \text{T}^i\} \qquad \mathcal{I}_{VC}^i := \mathcal{I}_V^i \cup \{\text{N}, \text{T}^i, \text{W}^i, \text{C}^i\} \qquad \mathcal{I}_{VNA}^i := \mathcal{I}_V^i \cup \{\text{N}, \text{A}^i\}$$

may assume that a derivation of a duplication-free sequent (containing duplicates neither of formulae nor of blocks) only contains duplication-free sequents: whenever a (backwards) application of a rule introduces a duplicate of a formula already in the sequent, it is immediately deleted in the next step using a backwards application of weakening. While officially our calculi do not contain the weakening rules, the proof of admissibility of weakening yields a procedure to transform a derivation with these rules into one without. Since all rules have the subformula property, the number of duplication-free sequents possibly relevant to a derivation of a sequent is bounded in the number of subformulae of that sequent, and hence enumerating all possible loop-free derivations of the above form yields a decision procedure for the logic. This argument is sufficient to show termination; however, it is clear that the complexity of the resulting procedure is far from the optimal PSPACE or coNP complexities of the logics [6,20].

Theorem 14. *Proof search for a sequent $\Gamma \Rightarrow \Delta$ in calculus $\mathcal{I}_{\mathcal{L}}^i$ always comes to an end in a finite number of steps.*

5 Semantic Completeness

In this section we prove the semantic completeness of $\mathcal{I}_{\mathcal{L}}^i$. In order to simplify the proof we adopt a cumulative version of rules $\to_L$, $\to_R$, $\preccurlyeq_R$ and com^i. This allows us to consider only the upper sequent of each derivation branch, instead of taking into account whole branches of the derivation.

$$\frac{\Gamma, A \to B, B \Rightarrow \Delta \quad \Gamma, A \to B \Rightarrow \Delta, B}{\Gamma, A \to B \Rightarrow \Delta} \to_L^c$$

$$\frac{\Gamma, A \Rightarrow \Delta, A \to B, B}{\Gamma \Rightarrow \Delta, A \to B} \to^c_R \qquad \frac{\Gamma \Rightarrow \Delta, A \preccurlyeq B, [A \lhd B]}{\Gamma \Rightarrow \Delta, A \preccurlyeq B} \preccurlyeq^c_R$$

$$\frac{\Gamma \Rightarrow \Delta, [\Sigma_1, \Sigma_2 \lhd A], [\Sigma_1 \lhd A], [\Sigma_2 \lhd B] \quad \Gamma \Rightarrow \Delta, [\Sigma_1, \Sigma_2 \lhd B] [\Sigma_1 \lhd A], [\Sigma_2 \lhd B]}{\Gamma \Rightarrow \Delta, [\Sigma_1 \lhd A], [\Sigma_2 \lhd B]} \; com^c$$

Definition 15. *The modal degree of a formula resp. sequent is defined as follows:* $md(\bot) = md(P) = 0$, *for* P *atomic formula;* $md(A \to B) = max(md(A), md(B))$; $md(A \preccurlyeq B) = max(md(A), md(B)) + 1$; $md([\Sigma \lhd A]) = max(md(\Sigma), md(A)) + 1$; $md(\Gamma \Rightarrow \Delta) = max\{md(G) \mid G \in \Gamma \cup \Delta, G \text{ formula or block}\}$.

Proposition 16. *All rules of* $\mathcal{I}^i_\mathbb{V}$ *preserve the modal degree: the premises of the rule have a modal degree no greater than the one of the respective conclusion.*

Observe that jump is the only rule which decreases the modal degree. Furthermore, an application of a rule is said to be *redundant* if the conclusion of the rule can be derived from one of its premises by weakening or contraction. If a sequent is derivable it has a non redundant derivation, since the redundant applications of the rules can be removed without affecting the correctness of the derivation. If an application of com^c is non redundant, then it must respect the restriction $(*)$ $\Sigma_1 \not\subseteq \Sigma_2$ and $\Sigma_2 \not\subseteq \Sigma_1$. To see this: if $(*)$ is not respected then either $\Sigma_1 \subseteq \Sigma_2$ or $\Sigma_2 \subseteq \Sigma_1$; in both cases we get a redundant application of com^c.

Definition 17. *A sequent is saturated if it has the form* $\Pi_1 \Rightarrow \Pi_2$, $[\Sigma_1 \lhd C_1], ..., [\Sigma_n \lhd C_n]$ *where* Π_1, Π_2 *are a multi-set of formulas such that* (init) $\Pi_1 \cap \Pi_2 = \emptyset$; $(\bot_L)$ $\bot \notin \Pi_1$ *and* $\top \notin \Pi_2$; $(\to^c_L)$ *if* $A \to B \in \Pi_1$ *then either* $A \in \Pi_2$ *or* $B \in \Pi_1$; $(\to^c_R)$ *if* $A \to B \in \Pi_2$ *then* $A \in \Pi_1$ *and* $B \in \Pi_2$; (com^c) *for every* $[\Sigma_i \lhd C_i]$, $[\Sigma_j \lhd C_j]$ *it holds that either* $\Sigma_i \subseteq \Sigma_j$ *or* $\Sigma_j \subseteq \Sigma_i$; $(\preccurlyeq^c_R)$ *for every* $A \preccurlyeq B \in \Pi_2$ *it holds that* $[A \lhd B] \in \{[\Sigma_1 \lhd C_1], ..., [\Sigma_n \lhd C_n]\}$; $(\preccurlyeq^i_L)$ *for every* $A \preccurlyeq B \in \Pi_1$ *and for every* $[\Sigma_i \lhd C_i]$, *where* $1 \leqslant i \leqslant n$, *it holds that either* $B \in \Sigma_i$ *or there exists* $[\Pi, \Sigma \lhd A] \in \{[\Sigma_1 \lhd C_1], ..., [\Sigma_n \lhd C_n]\}$; (N) *either* $\Gamma \Rightarrow \Delta$ *has the form* $\bot \Rightarrow \top$ *or* $[\bot \lhd \top]$ *belongs to* Δ; (T^i) *for every* $A \preccurlyeq B$ *in* Π_1, *it holds that either* $B \in \Pi_2$ *or* $[\bot \lhd A] \in \{[\Sigma_1 \lhd C_1], ..., [\Sigma_n \lhd C_n]\}$; (W^i) *for every block* $[\Sigma \lhd A]$, *it holds that* $\Sigma \subseteq \Pi_2$; (C^i) *for every* $A \preccurlyeq B$ *in* Π_1, *it holds that either* $B \in \Pi_2$ *or* $A \in \Pi_1$. *For each logic* $\mathcal{L}$, *the definition of saturated sequent takes into account only the saturation conditions of the rules of the corresponding calculus.*

All the blocks $[\Sigma_1 \lhd C_1], ..., [\Sigma_n \lhd C_n]$ of a saturated sequent can be considered as ordered with respect to set inclusion[5]. We call *static* all the rules except for jump and A^i. By *finished* sequent we mean a sequent for which every further static rule application is redundant. Note that a finished sequent is saturated.

---

[5] A quick argument: once all non redundant com^c have been applied, it holds that either $\Sigma_i \subseteq \Sigma_j$ or $\Sigma_j \subseteq \Sigma_i$; we then order the blocks: $\Sigma_1 \subseteq \Sigma_2 \subseteq ... \subseteq \Sigma_n$.

Proposition 18. *After finitely many non redundant static rule applications we reach an axiom or a finished sequent.*

Proof. Let $\Gamma \Rightarrow \Delta$ be the root sequent of a derivation. We consider any branch of a derivation (i) without applications of jump or A^i (ii) without redundant applications of rules. Observe that each rule application *must* add at least one formula or block to each premise, and the number of formulas or blocks (each one is finite in itself) that can occur within a sequent is finite. Thus the branch must be finite: if not, then it would not contain axioms and some formula or block would be added infinitely many times by eventually redundant applications of a rule. Moreover, once a rule (R) has been applied to a formula or block, the saturation condition with respect to the rule (R) and the involved formulas or blocks will be satisfied by the premises of (R). Thus the last node of the branch, if it is not an axiom, must be finished.   □

Corollary 19. *Given a sequent $\Gamma \Rightarrow \Delta$, every branch of any derivation tree starting with $\Gamma \Rightarrow \Delta$ ends in a finite number of steps with a saturated sequent of no greater modal degree than that of $\Gamma \Rightarrow \Delta$.*

Theorem 20. *If a sequent $\Gamma_0 \Rightarrow \Delta_0$ is valid, then it is derivable in $\mathcal{I}_\mathbb{V}^i$.*

Proof. We first prove completeness for $\mathcal{I}_\mathbb{V}^i$, then show how to extend the proof to $\mathcal{I}_\mathrm{VN}^i$, $\mathcal{I}_\mathrm{VT}^i$, $\mathcal{I}_\mathrm{VW}^i$, $\mathcal{I}_\mathrm{VC}^i$[6]. The proof strategy is the same in all cases, and it proceeds by induction on the modal degree of the sequent. If $md(\Gamma_0 \Rightarrow \Delta_0) = 0$, $\Gamma_0 \Rightarrow \Delta_0$ is composed only of propositional formulas, and its completeness can be proved from the completeness of sequent calculus for propositional logic. If $md(\Gamma_0 \Rightarrow \Delta_0) > 0$, by Proposition 16 and Corollary 19 we have that $\Gamma_0 \Rightarrow \Delta_0$ can be derived from a set of saturated sequents $\Gamma_k \Rightarrow \Delta_k$ of no greater modal degree. Since all the rules are invertible, except jump, and since by hypothesis $\Gamma_0 \Rightarrow \Delta_0$ is valid, also all saturated sequents $\Gamma_k \Rightarrow \Delta_k$ are valid. Thus, either (i) $\Gamma_k \Rightarrow \Delta_k$ is an axiom, or (ii) it must have been obtained by jump from a valid sequent $\Gamma_{k+1} \Rightarrow \Delta_{k+1}$. In the first case the theorem is trivially proved. We shall prove (ii): if $\Gamma_k \Rightarrow \Delta_k$ is valid and saturated, and it is not an axiom, there exists a valid sequent $\Gamma_{k+1} \Rightarrow \Delta_{k+1}$ from which $\Gamma_k \Rightarrow \Delta_k$ is obtained by jump. We shall prove the statement by contraposition. Let $\Gamma_k \Rightarrow \Delta_k$ be the saturated sequent $\Pi_1 \Rightarrow \Pi_2, [\Sigma_1 \lhd C_1], ..., [\Sigma_k \lhd C_k]$. Suppose that none of the sequents $C_1 \Rightarrow \Sigma_1, ..., C_k \Rightarrow \Sigma_k$ is valid. We prove that the sequent $\Gamma_k \Rightarrow \Delta_k$ is not valid.

By hypothesis there are models $\mathcal{M}_1, ..., \mathcal{M}_k$ which falsify the sequents $C_1 \Rightarrow \Sigma_1, ..., C_k \Rightarrow \Sigma_k$. For $1 \leqslant j \leqslant k$, let $\mathcal{M}_j = \langle W_j, \mathsf{SP}^j, [\![.]\!]_j \rangle$ and for some elements $x_j \in W_j$ let $\mathcal{M}_j, x_j \Vdash C_j$ and $\mathcal{M}_j, x_j \nVdash S$ for all $S \in \Sigma_j$. Suppose all W_j are disjoint, i.e. $W_j \cap W_{j'} = \emptyset$. From these models we build a new model $\mathcal{M} = \langle W, \mathsf{SP}, [\![.]\!] \rangle$ as follows: $W = \cup W_l \cup \{x\}$, for x new; $\mathsf{SP}(z) = \mathsf{SP}^j(z)$, if $z \in W_j$; $\mathsf{SP}(x) = \{\alpha_1, ..., \alpha_k\}$, where $\alpha_k = \{x_k\}$; $\alpha_{k-1} = \{x_k, x_{k-1}\}$, ... , $\alpha_1 =$

---

[6] The proof uses in an essential way the fact that a backwards application of jump reduces the modal degree of a sequent. Although rule A^i plays a similar role as jump, it does not reduce the modal degree when applied backwards. Thus we need another argument for handling logics including $\mathbb{A}$; this is object of further investigation.

$\{x_k, ..., x_1\}$; $[\![P]\!] = \cup [\![P]\!]_j$, for P atomic and $P \in \Pi_2$; $[\![P]\!] = \cup [\![P]\!]_j \cup \{x\}$, for P atomic and $P \in \Pi_1$. One can easily check that for E arbitrary formula or block, it holds that if $\mathcal{M}_j, x_j \Vdash E$, then $\mathcal{M}, x_j \Vdash E$, for $1 \leqslant j \leqslant k$.

To complete the proof we show that $\mathcal{M}$ falsifies each formula or block occurring in $\Gamma_k \Rightarrow \Delta_k$. Thus, we have to prove that (a) if $G \in \Gamma_k$, then $\mathcal{M}, x \Vdash G$, for G formula; (b) if $G \in \Delta_k$, then $\mathcal{M}, x \nVdash G$, for G formula; (c) if $[\Sigma_j \lhd A_j] \in \Delta_k$, then $\mathcal{M}, x \nVdash [\Sigma_j \lhd A_j]$. The proof proceeds by induction on the modal degree of formulas. The base case and the inductive step for the propositional cases are immediate. *Proof of a.* Let $G = C \preccurlyeq D$. For the saturation conditions ($\mathsf{com^c}$) and ($\preccurlyeq_L^c$), it holds that for all blocks $[\Sigma_j \lhd A_j]$ in the saturated sequent, either $D \in \Sigma_j$ or there exists in the saturated sequent a block $[\Pi, \Sigma_l \lhd C]$, for $l \leqslant j$. Consider an arbitrary sphere $\alpha_j = \{x_k, ..., x_j\}$ and the corresponding block $[\Sigma_j \lhd A_j]$. There are two cases to consider: if (i) $D \in \Sigma_j$, by construction of the model it holds that $\alpha_j \nVdash^\exists D$, i.e. $\alpha_j \Vdash^\forall \neg D$. Suppose that (ii) there exists a block $[\Pi, \Sigma_l \lhd C]$ belonging to the saturated sequent $\Gamma_k \Rightarrow \Delta_k$. By construction of the model, we have that there exists a world x_l such that $x_l \Vdash C$; thus, $\alpha_l \Vdash^\exists C$. However, since the spheres are incremental, $\alpha_l \subseteq \alpha_j$; thus, $\alpha_j \Vdash^\exists C$. We have that for α_j arbitrary block, either $\alpha_j \Vdash^\forall \neg D$ or $\alpha_j \Vdash^\exists C$; thus, $\mathcal{M}, x \Vdash C \preccurlyeq D$. *Proof of b.* Let $G = C \preccurlyeq D$. By the saturation condition ($\preccurlyeq_R^c$) there exists a block $[\Sigma_j \lhd A_j]$ belonging to $\Gamma_k \Rightarrow \Delta_k$ such that $C \in \Sigma_j$ and $D = A_j$. Let us consider $\alpha_j = \{x_k, ..., x_j\}$. We have that $C \in \Sigma_{j+1}, ..., C \in \Sigma_k$. By construction, $x_j \nVdash C$; therefore, $x_j \nVdash C, ..., x_k \nVdash C$. Furthermore, $x_j \Vdash A_j$; thus $x_j \Vdash D$. There exists $\alpha_j \in \mathsf{SP}(x)$ such that $\alpha_j \nVdash^\forall \neg D$ and $\alpha_j \nVdash^\exists C$; thus, $\mathcal{M}, x \nVdash C \preccurlyeq D$. *Proof of c.* The same as in the previous case.

We have thus proven that if $\Gamma_k \Rightarrow \Delta_k$ is valid and saturated, and it is not an axiom, then there exists a valid sequent $\Gamma_{k+1} \Rightarrow \Delta_{k+1}$ from which $\Gamma_k \Rightarrow \Delta_k$ is obtained by jump. Since $md(\Gamma_{k+1} \Rightarrow \Delta_{k+1}) < md(\Gamma_k \Rightarrow \Delta_k)$, by inductive hypothesis we have that $\Gamma_{k+1} \Rightarrow \Delta_{k+1}$ is derivable; therefore, $\Gamma_k \Rightarrow \Delta_k$ is derivable as well, by the jump rule.

Completeness of $\mathcal{I}_{\mathsf{VN}}^i$. If $md(\Gamma_0 \Rightarrow \Delta_0) = 0$, then any saturated sequent derived from it will have the form $\Gamma_k \Rightarrow \Delta_k, [\bot \lhd \top]$, where Γ_k and Δ_k are composed only of propositional formulas. If $\Gamma_k \Rightarrow \Delta_k$ is an axiom, we are done. If $\Gamma_k \Rightarrow \Delta_k$ is not an axiom, it has a propositional countermodel. Associate this countermodel to a world x, and build a model with $W = \{x\}$ and $\mathsf{SP}(x) = \{\{x\}\}$. The reader can easily check that the model satisfies N. If $md(\Gamma_0 \Rightarrow \Delta_0) > 0$, the proof proceeds in the same way as for $\mathcal{I}_{\mathsf{V}}^i$. Notice that by inductive hypothesis all the models $\mathcal{M}_i$ involved in the construction satisfy N.

Completeness of $\mathcal{I}_{\mathsf{VT}}^i$. We modify the definition of $\mathsf{SP}(x)$ in the model $\mathcal{M}$ by adding a new sphere α_0, in order to account for total reflexivity. Thus, $\mathsf{SP}(x) = \{\alpha_0, \alpha_1, \alpha_2, ..., \alpha_k\}$, where $\alpha_k = \{x_k\}$, $\alpha_{k-1} = \{x_k, x_{k-1}\}$, ..., $\alpha_1 = \{x_k, ..., x_1\}$, $\alpha_0 = \alpha_1 \cup \{x\}$. Cases (b) and (c) remain the same as in the completeness proof for $\mathcal{I}_{\mathsf{V}}^i$. As for (a), consider $\mathsf{SP}(x) = \{\alpha_0, \alpha_1, \alpha_2, ..., \alpha_k\}$. For spheres $\alpha_k, ..., \alpha_1$ (a) holds; we have to prove that also for α_0 either $\alpha_0 \Vdash^\forall \neg D$ or $\alpha_0 \Vdash^\exists C$. We know that either (i) $\alpha_1 \Vdash^\forall \neg D$ or (ii) $\alpha_1 \Vdash^\exists C$. If (i) holds, the theorem is proved, since $\alpha_0 \Vdash^\exists C$. If it holds that $(*)$ $\alpha_1 \nVdash^\forall \neg D$ then (ii) holds. By absurd, suppose $\alpha_0 \not\Vdash^\forall \neg D$; thus, $(\ast\ast)$ $x \Vdash D$ (since all the other worlds did not satisfy D). By saturation condition $(\mathsf{T^i})$, we have that either $D \in \Delta$ or $[\bot \lhd C] \in \Delta$. There are two cases to consider. If $D \in \Delta$, since $md(D) < md(C \preccurlyeq D)$, by inductive hypothesis we have $x \not\Vdash D$, against $(\ast\ast)$. If $[\bot \lhd C] \in \Delta$, there exists a block $[\Sigma_u \lhd A_u]$ in the saturated sequent $\Gamma_k \Rightarrow \Delta_k$ such that $A_u = C$. Thus, by construction $\alpha_u \Vdash^\exists C$, and $x_u \Vdash C$ for some $x_u \in \alpha_u$. By construction $x_u \in \alpha_1$; thus, $\alpha_1 \Vdash^\exists C$ against $(\ast)$. We reached a contradiction; thus, also for α_0 it holds that $\alpha_0 \Vdash^\forall \neg D$ or $\alpha_0 \Vdash^\exists C$, and $\mathcal{M}, x \Vdash C \preccurlyeq D$.

Completeness of $\mathcal{I}^i_{\mathrm{VW}}$. We modify $\mathsf{SP}(x)$ in order to account for weak centering by adding world x to each sphere, as follows: $\mathsf{SP}(x) = \{\alpha_1, \alpha_2, ..., \alpha_k\}$, where $\alpha_k = \{x_k, x\}$; $\alpha_{k-1} = \{x_k, x_{k-1}, x\}$, ..., $\alpha_1 = \{x_k, ..., x_1, x\}$. We have to prove that conditions (a), (b) and (c) hold. The proof makes an essential use of the saturation condition $(\mathsf{W^i})$, and it is omitted for space reasons.

Completeness of $\mathcal{I}^i_{\mathrm{VC}}$. For centering, we modify $\mathsf{SP}(x)$ by adding a new sphere α_{k+1}, which contains only x. Namely: $\alpha_{k+1} = \{x\}$; $\alpha_k = \{x_k, x\}$; $\alpha_{k-1} = \{x_k, x_{k-1}, x\}$,..., $\alpha_1 = \{x_k, ..., x_1, x\}$. Conditions (b) and (c) are as in the proof for $\mathcal{I}^i_{\mathrm{VW}}$; case (a) is slightly different and employs the saturation condition $(\mathsf{C^i})$. $\square$

6   Completeness via Translation

We can give quick alternative completeness proofs for the proposed calculi by simulating derivations in the corresponding sequent calculi from [12,13], shown in Table 4. The main difficulty is to simulate the rules for $\preccurlyeq$.

Table 4. The rules and rule sets for extensions of $\mathbb{V}_{\preccurlyeq}$.

$$\frac{\{B_k \Rightarrow D_1, \ldots, D_m, A_1, \ldots, A_n \mid 1 \le k \le n\} \cup \{C_k \Rightarrow D_1, \ldots, D_{k-1}, A_1, \ldots, A_n \mid 1 \le k \le m\}}{\Gamma, C_1 \preccurlyeq D_1, \ldots, C_m \preccurlyeq D_m \Rightarrow A_1 \preccurlyeq B_1, \ldots, A_n \preccurlyeq B_n, \Delta} \; R_{m,n}$$

$$\frac{\{C_k \Rightarrow D_1, \ldots, D_{k-1} \mid 1 \le k \le m\} \cup \{\Gamma \Rightarrow D_1, \ldots, D_m, \Delta\}}{\Gamma, C_1 \preccurlyeq D_1, \ldots, C_m \preccurlyeq D_m \Rightarrow \Delta} \; T_m \qquad \frac{\Gamma, C \Rightarrow \Delta \quad \Gamma \Rightarrow D, \Delta}{\Gamma, C \preccurlyeq D \Rightarrow \Delta} \; C2$$

$$\frac{\{B_k \Rightarrow D_1, \ldots, D_m, A_1, \ldots, A_n \mid 1 \le k \le n\} \cup \{\Gamma \Rightarrow D_1, \ldots, D_m, A_1, \ldots, A_n, \Delta\}}{\Gamma, C_1 \preccurlyeq D_1, \ldots, C_m \preccurlyeq D_m \Rightarrow A_1 \preccurlyeq B_1, \ldots, A_n \preccurlyeq B_n, \Delta} \; W_{m,n} \qquad \frac{\Gamma \Rightarrow A, \Delta}{\Gamma \Rightarrow A \preccurlyeq B, \Delta} \; W2$$

$$\frac{\left\{\Gamma^{\preccurlyeq}, B_k \Rightarrow D_1, \ldots, D_m, A_1, \ldots, A_n, \Delta^{\preccurlyeq} \mid 1 \le k \le n\right\} \cup \left\{\Gamma^{\preccurlyeq}, C_k \Rightarrow D_1, \ldots, D_{k-1}, A_1, \ldots, A_n, \Delta^{\preccurlyeq} \mid 1 \le k \le m\right\}}{\Gamma, C_1 \preccurlyeq D_1, \ldots, C_m \preccurlyeq D_m \Rightarrow A_1 \preccurlyeq B_1, \ldots, A_n \preccurlyeq B_n, \Delta} \; A_{m,n}$$

$\Gamma^{\preccurlyeq}$ is the restriction of Γ to formulae of the form $A \preccurlyeq B$; $\mathcal{R}_{\mathbb{V}_{\preccurlyeq}} := \{R_{m,n} \mid m \ge 0, n \ge 1\}$;

$\mathcal{R}_{\mathrm{VN}_{\preccurlyeq}} := \{R_{m,n} \mid m+n \ge 1\}$	$\mathcal{R}_{\mathrm{VC}_{\preccurlyeq}} := \mathcal{R}_{\mathbb{V}_{\preccurlyeq}} \cup \{R_{\mathrm{W2}}, R_{\mathrm{C2}}\}$
$\mathcal{R}_{\mathrm{VT}_{\preccurlyeq}} := \mathcal{R}_{\mathbb{V}_{\preccurlyeq}} \cup \{T_m \mid m \ge 1\}$	$\mathcal{R}_{\mathrm{VA}_{\preccurlyeq}} := \{A_{m,n} \mid m \ge 0, \, n \ge 1\}$
$\mathcal{R}_{\mathrm{VW}_{\preccurlyeq}} := \mathcal{R}_{\mathbb{V}_{\preccurlyeq}} \cup \{W_{m,n} \mid m+n \ge 1\}$	$\mathcal{R}_{\mathrm{VNA}_{\preccurlyeq}} := \{A_{m,n} \mid m+n \ge 1\}$

Theorem 21. *Every rule of $\mathcal{R}_{\mathcal{L}}$ is derivable in $\mathcal{I}_{\mathcal{L}} \smallsetminus \{\mathsf{Con}_S, \mathsf{Con}_B\}$. Hence $\mathcal{I}_{\mathcal{L}} \smallsetminus$ $\{\mathsf{Con}_S, \mathsf{Con}_B\}$ is cut-free complete for $\mathcal{L}$.*

Proof. We only consider the rules for $\preccurlyeq$, the remaining rules are straightforward. For the sake of readability for $k < \ell$ we abbreviate $C_k \preccurlyeq D_k, \dots, C_\ell \preccurlyeq D_\ell$ by $(C \preccurlyeq D)_k^\ell$. Similarly, we write $\mathbf{A}_k^\ell$ for $A_k, \dots, A_\ell$, and $\mathbf{D}_k^\ell$ for $D_k, \dots, D_\ell$. To simulate rule $R_{m,n}$, for every $k \leq n$ we have the following derivation:

$$
\cfrac{
\cfrac{
\cfrac{B_k \Rightarrow \mathbf{A}_1^n, \mathbf{D}_1^m}{\Gamma \Rightarrow \Delta, [\mathbf{A}_1^n, \mathbf{D}_1^m \lhd B_k]} \text{ jump }
\qquad
\cfrac{C_m \Rightarrow \mathbf{A}_1^n, \mathbf{D}_1^{m-1}}{\Gamma \Rightarrow \Delta, \left[\mathbf{A}_1^n, \mathbf{D}_1^{m-1} \lhd C_m\right]} \text{ jump }
}{\Gamma, C_m \preccurlyeq D_m \Rightarrow \Delta, \left[\mathbf{A}_1^n, \mathbf{D}_1^{m-1} \lhd B_k\right]} \preccurlyeq_L
\\[6pt]
\vdots
\\[2pt]
\cfrac{\Gamma, (C \preccurlyeq D)_2^m \Rightarrow \Delta, [\mathbf{A}_1^n, D_1 \lhd B_k]
\qquad
\cfrac{C_1 \Rightarrow \mathbf{A}_1^n}{\Gamma, (C \preccurlyeq D)_2^m \Rightarrow \Delta, [\mathbf{A}_1^n \lhd C_1]} \text{ jump }}{}
}{\Gamma, (C \preccurlyeq D)_1^m \Rightarrow \Delta, [\mathbf{A}_1^n \lhd B_k]} \preccurlyeq_L
$$

The conclusion is obtained by weakening (Lemma 6) and multiple applications of com to these sequents, followed by the derivation

$$
\cfrac{\Gamma, (C \preccurlyeq D)_1^m \Rightarrow \Delta, [A_1 \lhd B_1], \dots, [A_n \lhd B_n]}{\Gamma, C_1 \preccurlyeq D_1, \dots, C_m \preccurlyeq D_m \Rightarrow \Delta, A_1 \preccurlyeq B_1, \dots, A_n \preccurlyeq B_n} \preccurlyeq_R
$$

The simulations for the remaining rules apart from T_m are only slight modifications. For instance, to simulate $R_{m,0}$ we would have the rule N instead of the blocks of $\preccurlyeq_R$ and com at the bottom, for $W_{m,n}$ with $n \geq 1$ we replace the top leftmost application of jump by an application of W, for $W_{m,0}$ we apply N at the bottom, and for $A_{m,n}$ we replace all applications of jump by A. Rule $C2$ is simulated straightforwardly by W followed by $\preccurlyeq_R$. For rule T_m finally, we first construct for $\ell, k \geq 0$ derivations $\mathcal{D}_{\ell,\ell+k+1}$ of the sequents

$$
\Omega, (C \preccurlyeq D)_1^\ell \Rightarrow \Theta, \left[\bot, \mathbf{D}_{\ell+1}^{\ell+k}, \Sigma \lhd C_{\ell+k+1}\right]
$$

for arbitrary Ω, Θ, Σ from the premises $\{C_i \Rightarrow \mathbf{D}_1^{i-1} \mid 1 \leq i \leq \ell + k + 1\}$ as follows. The derivation $\mathcal{D}_{0,k+1}$ is straightforward using the rules of weakening (Lemma 6) and jump. The derivation $\mathcal{D}_{\ell+1,\ell+1+k+1}$ is obtained by

$$
\cfrac{
\Omega, (C \preccurlyeq D)_1^\ell \Rightarrow \Theta, \left[\bot, \mathbf{D}_{\ell+1}^{\ell+1+k}, \Sigma \lhd C_{\ell+1+k+1}\right]
\qquad
\Omega, (C \preccurlyeq D)_1^\ell \Rightarrow \Theta, \left[\bot, \mathbf{D}_{\ell+2}^{\ell+1+k}, \Sigma \lhd C_{\ell+1}\right]
}{\Omega, (C \preccurlyeq D)_1^{\ell+1} \Rightarrow \Theta, \left[\bot, \mathbf{D}_{\ell+2}^{\ell+1+k}, \Sigma \lhd C_{\ell+1+k+1}\right]} \preccurlyeq_L
$$

where the premises are derived by $\mathcal{D}_{\ell,\ell+1+k+1}$ and $\mathcal{D}_{\ell,\ell+1}$. We obtain T_m as:

$$\cfrac{\cfrac{\Gamma \Rightarrow \Delta, \boldsymbol{D}_1^m \quad \Gamma \Rightarrow \Delta, \boldsymbol{D}_2^m, [\bot \lhd C_1]}{\Gamma, C_1 \preccurlyeq D_1 \Rightarrow \Delta, \boldsymbol{D}_2^m} \ \mathsf{T} \quad \Gamma, C_1 \preccurlyeq D_1 \Rightarrow \Delta, \boldsymbol{D}_3^m, [\bot \lhd C_2]}{\Gamma, (\boldsymbol{C} \preccurlyeq \boldsymbol{D})_1^2 \Rightarrow \Delta, \boldsymbol{D}_3^m} \ \mathsf{T}$$

$$\vdots$$

$$\cfrac{\Gamma, (\boldsymbol{C} \preccurlyeq \boldsymbol{D})_1^{m-1} \Rightarrow \Delta, D_m \quad \Gamma, (\boldsymbol{C} \preccurlyeq \boldsymbol{D})_1^{m-1} \Rightarrow \Delta, [\bot \lhd C_m]}{\Gamma, (\boldsymbol{C} \preccurlyeq \boldsymbol{D})_1^m \Rightarrow \Delta} \ \mathsf{T}$$

where the premises are derived using $\mathcal{D}_{0,1}, \mathcal{D}_{1,2}, \ldots, \mathcal{D}_{m-1,m}$. Note that none of the simulations uses Con_S. □

Corollary 22. *Let* $\mathcal{L} \in \{\mathbb{V}, \mathbb{VN}, \mathbb{VT}, \mathbb{VW}, \mathbb{VA}, \mathbb{VNA}\}$. *Then the calculus* $\mathcal{I}_{\mathcal{L}}^i$ *is complete for* $\mathcal{L}$. □

7 Conclusions

We have introduced internal, standard, cut-free calculi for Lewis' logics $\mathbb{V}$, $\mathbb{VN}$, $\mathbb{VT}$, $\mathbb{VW}$, $\mathbb{VC}$, $\mathbb{VA}$ and $\mathbb{VNA}$, extending the basic ideas of the calculi proposed in [17] for the basic system $\mathbb{V}$. The same logics have been considered in [12,13], where calculi comprising an infinite set of rules with a variable number of premises are introduced, whereas the calculi we have introduced here are standard in the sense that each connective is handled by a fixed finite set of rules with a fixed finite set of premises. As far as we know, these are the first standard and internal calculi covering most, if not all, logics of the Lewis' family.

In future research we aim at extending the proof of cut elimination to extensions of $\mathbb{V}$. Moreover, we aim at providing a semantic completeness proof also for the logics with the absoluteness condition. Finally we shall study how to obtain optimal decision procedures for the respective logics based on our calculi.

References

1. Alenda, R., Olivetti, N., Pozzato, G.L.: Nested sequent calculi for normal conditional logics. J. Log. Comput. **26**(1), 7–50 (2013)
2. Baltag, A., Smets, S.: The logic of conditional doxastic actions. Texts Logic Games **4**, 9–31 (2008). Special Issue on New Perspectives on Games and Interaction
3. Board, O.: Dynamic interactive epistemology. Games Econ. Behav. **49**(1), 49–80 (2004)
4. Ciabattoni, A., Metcalfe, G., Montagna, F.: Algebraic and proof-theoretic characterizations of truth stressers for MTL and its extensions. Fuzzy Sets Syst. **161**, 369–389 (2010)
5. Delgrande, J.P.: On first-order conditional logics. Artif. Intell. **105**(1), 105–137 (1998)
6. Friedman, N., Halpern, J.Y.: On the complexity of conditional logics. In: Doyle, J., Sandewall, E., Torasso, P. (eds.) KR 1994, pp. 202–213. Morgan Kaufmann (1994)

7. Gent, I.P.: A sequent or tableaux-style system for Lewis's counterfactual logic $\mathbb{VC}$. Notre Dame J. Formal Logic **33**(3), 369–382 (1992)
8. Ginsberg, M.L.: Counterfactuals. Artif. Intell. **30**(1), 35–79 (1986)
9. Giordano, L., Gliozzi, V., Olivetti, N., Schwind, C.: Tableau calculus for preference-based conditional logics: PCL and its extensions. ACM Trans. Comput. Logic (TOCL) **10**(3), 21 (2009)
10. Grahne, G.: Updates and counterfactuals. J. Logic Comput. **8**(1), 87–117 (1998)
11. Kraus, S., Lehmann, D., Magidor, M.: Nonmonotonic reasoning, preferential models and cumulative logics. Artif. Intell. **44**(1–2), 167–207 (1990)
12. Lellmann, B.: Sequent calculi with context restrictions and applications to conditional logic. Ph.D. thesis, Imperial College London. http://hdl.handle.net/10044/1/18059
13. Lellmann, B., Pattinson, D.: Sequent Systems for Lewis' Conditional Logics. In: Cerro, L.F., Herzig, A., Mengin, J. (eds.) JELIA 2012. LNCS (LNAI), vol. 7519, pp. 320–332. Springer, Heidelberg (2012). doi:10.1007/978-3-642-33353-8_25
14. Lewis, D.: Counterfactuals. Blackwell, Oxford (1973)
15. Negri, S., Olivetti, N.: A sequent calculus for preferential conditional logic based on neighbourhood semantics. In: Nivelle, H. (ed.) TABLEAUX 2015. LNCS (LNAI), vol. 9323, pp. 115–134. Springer, Heidelberg (2015). doi:10.1007/978-3-319-24312-2_9
16. Negri, S., Sbardolini, G.: Proof analysis for Lewis counterfactuals. Rev. Symbolic Logic **9**(1), 44–75 (2016)
17. Olivetti, N., Pozzato, G.L.: A standard internal calculus for Lewis' counterfactual logics. In: Nivelle, H. (ed.) TABLEAUX 2015. LNCS (LNAI), vol. 9323, pp. 270–286. Springer, Heidelberg (2015). doi:10.1007/978-3-319-24312-2_19
18. Pattinson, D., Schröder, L.: Generic modal cut elimination applied to conditional logics. Log. Methods Comput. Sci. **7**(1: 4), 1–28 (2011)
19. Poggiolesi, F.: Natural deduction calculi and sequent calculi for counterfactual logics. Stud. Logica **104**, 1003–1036 (2016)
20. de Swart, H.C.M.: A Gentzen- or Beth-type system, a practical decision procedure and a constructive completeness proof for the counterfactual logics $\mathbb{VC}$ and $\mathbb{VCS}$. J. Symbolic Logic **48**(1), 1–20 (1983)

Incremental Computation of Deterministic Extensions for Dynamic Argumentation Frameworks

Sergio Greco and Francesco Parisi$^{(\boxtimes)}$

DIMES Department, University of Calabria, Rende, Italy
{greco,fparisi}@dimes.unical.it

Abstract. We address the problem of efficiently recomputing the extensions of abstract argumentation frameworks (AFs) which are updated by adding/deleting arguments or attacks. In particular, after identifying some properties that hold for updates of AFs under several well-known semantics, we focus on the two most popular 'deterministic' semantics (namely, *grounded* and *ideal*) and present two algorithms for their incremental computation, well-suited to dynamic applications where updates to an initial AF are frequently performed to take into account new available knowledge. We experimentally validated the proposed approach.

1 Introduction

Abstract argumentation has emerged as a central field in Artificial Intelligence [3,10,27,39,41,42]. Although the underlying idea is very simple and intuitive, most of the semantics proposed so far suffer from a high computational complexity [22,24–26,29–33]. Complexity bounds and evaluation algorithms for argumentation frameworks (AFs) have been deeply studied in the literature, but this research focused on 'static' frameworks, whereas, in practice, AFs are not static systems [4,5,19,28,37]. Typically an AF represents a temporary situation as new arguments and attacks continuously can be added/removed to take into account new available knowledge. This may change significantly the conclusions that can be derived. For instance, when a new attack is added to an AF, existing attacks may cease to apply and new attacks become applicable. Surprisingly, the definition of evaluation algorithms and the analysis of the computational complexity taking into account such dynamic aspects have been mostly neglected, whereas in these situations incremental computation techniques can greatly improve performance. Sometimes changes to the AF can make small changes to the set of conclusions, and recomputing the whole semantics from scratch can be avoided. For instance, consider the situation shown in Fig. 1: the initial AF $\mathcal{A}_0$, where h is not attacked by any other argument, is updated to AF $\mathcal{A}$ by adding attack (g, h). According to the most popular argumentation semantics, i.e. *grounded, complete, ideal, preferred, stable,* and *semi-stable* [15,20,21], the initial AF $\mathcal{A}_0$ admits the extension $E_0 = \{a, h, g, e, l, m, o\}$, whereas the extension for the updated framework $\mathcal{A}$ becomes $E = \{a, c, g, e, l, m, o\}$. As it

© Springer International Publishing AG 2016
L. Michael and A. Kakas (Eds.): JELIA 2016, LNAI 10021, pp. 288–304, 2016.
DOI: 10.1007/978-3-319-48758-8_19

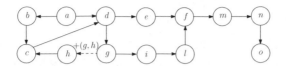

Fig. 1. AFs $\mathcal{A}_0$ and $\mathcal{A} = +(g,h)(\mathcal{A}_0)$

will be shown later, for the grounded and ideal semantics, which are deterministic, the extension E can be efficiently computed incrementally by looking only at a small part of the AF, which is "influenced by" the update operation. This part is just $\{h, c\}$ in our example, and we will show that the membership of the other arguments to E does not depend on the update operation, and thus we do not need to compute them again after performing update $+(g,h)$.

Contributions. The main contributions are as follows:

- We introduce the concept of *influenced set* consisting of the arguments whose status could change after an update. The influenced set refines the previously proposed set of *affected arguments* [4,37] and is used to compute extensions more efficiently.
- We present an incremental algorithm for recomputing the grounded extension. It is very efficient as it (iteratively) computes the status of influenced arguments only.
- We show that an argument a belongs to the ideal extension if and only if there is a *coherent winning strategy* for it and there is no coherent winning strategy for all arguments which attack (even indirectly) a.
- We present an incremental algorithm for the efficient recomputation of the ideal extensions which is based on the previously mentioned result and takes advantage of both the set of influenced arguments and the incremental algorithm for computing the grounded extensions.
- We report on experiments showing the effectiveness of our approach on both real and synthetic AFs.

2   Related Work

There have been several efforts coping with dynamics aspects of abstract argumentation. In [12,13] the principles according to which the extension does not change when the set of arguments/attacks are changed have been studied. However, this work does not consider how the extensions of an AF evolve when new arguments are added or some of the old ones are removed. [17,18] addressed the problem of revising the set of extensions of an AF, and studied how the extensions can evolve when a new argument is considered. However, they focus on adding only one argument interacting with one initial argument (i.e. an argument which is not attacked by any other argument). The work in [17,18] has been extended in [11], where the evolution of the set of extensions after performing a change operation (addition/removal of arguments/interaction) is studied.

Dynamic argumentation has been applied to decision-making of an autonomous agent in [1], where it is studied how the acceptability of arguments evolves when a new argument is added to the decision system. However, they do not compute the whole extensions and also focused on the case where only one argument is added to the system.

The division-based method, proposed in [37] and refined in [4], divides the updated framework into two parts: *affected* and *unaffected*, where only the status of affected arguments is recomputed after updates. However, the set of affected arguments consists of those that are reachable from the updated arguments, which is often larger than the set that actually needs to be considered when recomputing the extension. For the AF of Fig. 1, all the arguments in the chains originated by h turn out to be 'affected'. But we only need to recompute the status of h and c after the update. Recently, [45] introduced a matrix representation of AFs and proposed a matrix reduction that when applied to dynamic AFs resembles the division-based method proposed in [37]. In [5,9] an approach exploiting the concept of splitting of logic programs [38] was adopted to deal with dynamic argumentation. However, the technique considers weak expansions of the initial AF, where added arguments never attack previous ones. Recently, [16] studied the relationship between argumentation and logic programming [14,34,35].

[8] investigated whether and how it is possible to modify a given AF in such a way that a desired set of arguments becomes an extension, whereas [40] studied equivalence between two AFs when further information (another AF) is added to both simultaneously. [6] focused on specific expansions where new arguments and attacks may be added but the attacks among the old arguments remain unchanged, while [7] characterized update and deletion equivalence, where adding as well as deleting arguments and attacks is allowed (deletions were not considered in [6,40]).

To the best of our knowledge, this is the first paper that exploits the initial extension E_0 of an AF $\mathcal{A}_0$ not only for computing the set $\mathcal{I}(u, \mathcal{A}_0, E_0)$ of arguments influenced by an update u but also for recomputing the status of the arguments in $\mathcal{I}(u, \mathcal{A}_0, E_0)$ by applying early termination conditions. A short version of this paper appeared in [36].

3 Preliminaries

We assume the existence of a set Arg whose elements are called *arguments*. An *(abstract) argumentation framework* [20] *(AF)* is a pair $\langle A, \Sigma \rangle$, where $A \subseteq Arg$ and $\Sigma \subseteq A \times A$ is a binary relation over A whose elements are referred to as *attacks*. Essentially, an AF is a directed graph in which the arguments are represented by the nodes and the attack relation is represented by the set of directed edges. An argument is an abstract entity whose role is determined by its relationships with other arguments.

Given arguments $a, b \in A$, we say that a *attacks* b iff $(a, b) \in \Sigma$. An argument a *attacks* a set $S \subseteq A$ iff $\exists b \in S$ such that a *attacks* b. We use $S^+ = \{b \mid \exists a \in S :$

$(a, b) \in \Sigma\}$ and $S^- = \{b \mid \exists a \in S : (b, a) \in \Sigma\}$ to denote the sets of all arguments that are attacked by S and attack S, respectively. A set $S \subseteq A$ *defends* a iff $\forall b \in A$ such that b *attacks* a, there is $c \in S$ such that c *attacks* b. S is said to be (i) *conflict-free*, if there are no $a, b \in S$ such that a *attacks* b; (ii) *admissible*, if it is conflict-free and it defends all its arguments.

A semantics specifies the criteria for identifying a set of arguments considered to be "reasonable" together, called *extension*. A *complete extension* (co) is an admissible set that contains all the arguments that it defends. A complete extension S is said to be: (i) *preferred (pr)* iff it is maximal; (ii) *semi-stable (ss)* iff $S \cup S^+$ is maximal; (iii) *stable (st)* iff it attacks each argument in $A \setminus S$; (iv) *grounded (gr)* iff it is minimal; (v) *ideal (id)* iff it is contained in every preferred extension and it is maximal.

Given an AF $\mathcal{A}$ and a semantics $\mathcal{S} \in \{\text{co}, \text{pr}, \text{ss}, \text{st}, \text{gr}, \text{id}\}$, we use $\mathcal{E}_\mathcal{S}(\mathcal{A})$ to denote the set of $\mathcal{S}$-extensions of $\mathcal{A}$. All the above-mentioned semantics except the stable admit at least one extension, and the grounded and ideal admit exactly one extension [15,20,21]. Semantics gr and id are called *deterministic* or *unique status* as $|\mathcal{E}_{\text{gr}}(\mathcal{A})| = |\mathcal{E}_{\text{id}}(\mathcal{A})| = 1$. It is well-known that, for any AF $\mathcal{A}$, $\mathcal{E}_{\text{gr}}(\mathcal{A}) \subseteq \mathcal{E}_{\text{co}}(\mathcal{A})$ and $\mathcal{E}_{\text{id}}(\mathcal{A}) \subseteq \mathcal{E}_{\text{co}}(\mathcal{A})$, and $\mathcal{E}_{\text{st}}(\mathcal{A}) \subseteq \mathcal{E}_{\text{ss}}(\mathcal{A}) \subseteq \mathcal{E}_{\text{pr}}(\mathcal{A}) \subseteq \mathcal{E}_{\text{co}}(\mathcal{A})$.

Example 1. Consider the AF $\mathcal{A}_0$ shown in Fig. 2. Then, the set of admissible sets is $\{\ \emptyset,\ \{a\},\ \{d\},\ \{a, d\},\ \{b, d\}\ \}$, and $\mathcal{E}_\mathcal{S}(\mathcal{A}_0)$ with $\mathcal{S} \in \{\text{co}, \text{pr}, \text{ss}, \text{st}, \text{gr}, \text{id}\}$ is as reported in the second column of the table in Fig. 3. □

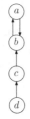

$\mathcal{S}$	$\mathcal{E}_\mathcal{S}(\mathcal{A}_0)$	$\mathcal{E}_\mathcal{S}(\mathcal{A}_1)$	$\mathcal{E}_\mathcal{S}(\mathcal{A}_2)$
co	$\{\{d\}, \{a, d\}, \{b, d\}\}$	$\{\emptyset, \{a, d\}\}$	$\{\emptyset, \{a, d\}, \{b, c\}\}$
pr	$\{\{a, d\}, \{b, d\}\}$	$\{\{a, d\}\}$	$\{\{a, d\}, \{b, c\}\}$
ss	$\{\{a, d\}, \{b, d\}\}$	$\{\{a, d\}\}$	$\{\{a, d\}, \{b, c\}\}$
st	$\{\{a, d\}, \{b, d\}\}$	$\{\{a, d\}\}$	$\{\{a, d\}, \{b, c\}\}$
gr	$\{\{d\}\}$	$\{\emptyset\}$	$\{\emptyset\}$
id	$\{\{d\}\}$	$\{\{a, d\}\}$	$\{\emptyset\}$

Fig. 2. AF $\mathcal{A}_0$ of Example 1.

Fig. 3. Sets of extensions for the AF of Example 1, and changes in the sets after performing updates $+(b, d)$ and $-(c, b)$.

The argumentation semantics can be also defined in terms of *labelling*. A labelling for an AF $\mathcal{A} = \langle A, \Sigma \rangle$ is a total function $L : A \rightarrow \{\text{IN}, \text{OUT}, \text{UN}\}$ assigning to each argument a label. $L(a) = \text{IN}$ means that argument a is accepted, $L(a) = \text{OUT}$ means that a is rejected, while $L(a) = \text{UN}$ means that a is undecided.

Let $in(L) = \{a \mid a \in A \wedge L(a) = \text{IN}\}$, $out(L) = \{a \mid a \in A \wedge L(a) = \text{OUT}\}$, and $un(L) = \{a \mid a \in A \wedge L(a) = \text{UN}\}$. In the following, we also use the triple $\langle in(L), out(L), un(L) \rangle$ to represent L. A labelling L is said to be *admissible (or legal)* if $\forall a \in in(L) \cup out(L)$ (i) if $L(a) = \text{OUT}$ then $\exists b \in A$ such that $(b, a) \in \Sigma$ and $L(b) = \text{IN}$; and (ii) if $L(a) = \text{IN}$ then $L(b) = \text{OUT}$ for all $b \in A$ such that $(b, a) \in \Sigma$. L is a complete labelling iff conditions (i) and (ii) hold for all $a \in A$.

Between complete extensions and complete labellings there is a bijective mapping defined as follows: for each extension E there is a unique labelling $L = \langle E, E^+, A \setminus (E \cup E^+) \rangle$ and for each labelling L there is a unique extension $in(L)$. We say that L is the labelling *corresponding* to E.

In the following, we say that the *status of an argument* a w.r.t. a labelling L (or its corresponding extension $in(L)$) is IN (resp., OUT, UN) iff $L(a) =$ IN (resp., $L(a) =$ OUT, $L(a) =$ UN). We will avoid to mention explicitly the labelling (or the extension) whenever it is understood.

Updates. An *update* u for an AF $\mathcal{A}_0$ consists in modifying $\mathcal{A}_0$ into an AF $\mathcal{A}$ by adding or removing arguments or attacks. *As explained below, we can focus on updates consisting of adding/deleting an attack* (a, b) *between arguments belonging to* $\mathcal{A}_0$. We use $+(a, b)$ (resp. $-(a, b)$) to denote the addition (resp. deletion) of (a, b), and $u(\mathcal{A}_0)$ to denote the application of update $u = \pm(a, b)$ to $\mathcal{A}_0$ (with $\pm$ meaning either $+$ or $-$).

Updating an AF implies that its semantics (sets of extensions or labellings) changes.

Example 2. Consider the AF $\mathcal{A}_0$ of Example 1. For each semantics $\mathcal{S}$, the set $\mathcal{E}_\mathcal{S}(\mathcal{A}_1)$ of extensions for $\mathcal{A}_1 = +(b, d)(\mathcal{A}_0)$ is reported in the third column in Fig. 3. If update $-(c, b)$ is performed on $\mathcal{A}_1$, then $\mathcal{E}_\mathcal{S}(\mathcal{A}_2)$ with $\mathcal{A}_2 = -(c, b)(\mathcal{A}_1)$ is as shown on the last column in Fig. 3.   □

Remark (general updates). It is worth noting that focusing on single attack updates of the form $u = \pm(a, b)$ is not a limitation as *multiple (attack) updates* to be performed simultaneously can be simulated by performing a single attack update to a new AF obtained by suitably modifying the initial AF $\mathcal{A}_0$. In fact, performing a set of updates $U = \{+(a_1, b_1), \ldots, +(a_n, b_n), -(a'_1, b'_1), \ldots, -(a'_m, b'_m)\}$ on $\mathcal{A}_0$ can be reduced to performing a single update $+(v, w)$ on the AF $\mathcal{A}_0^U$ which is obtained from $\mathcal{A}_0$ by (*i*) adding arguments x_i, y_i and the chain of attacks between a_i and b_i as shown in Fig. 4, for each update $+(a_i, b_i) \in U$; (*ii*) replacing each attack (a'_j, b'_j) in $\mathcal{A}_0$ with the chain of attacks between a'_j and b'_j as shown in Fig. 4, for each update $-(a'_j, b'_j) \in U$; and (*iii*) adding the new arguments v, w, w' and the attacks involving them as shown in Fig. 4. For instance, for the AF $\mathcal{A}_0$ of Example 1 and the set of updates $U = \{+(b, d), -(c, b)\}$, we obtain the AF $\mathcal{A}_0^U$ shown in Fig. 5. The formal definition of the construction above as well as proofs of equivalence ($\mathcal{A}_0$ and $\mathcal{A}_0^U$ have the same extensions under projection to the arguments of $\mathcal{A}_0$) will be provided in the extended version of this paper.

Concerning the addition (resp. deletion) of a set of isolated arguments, it is easy to see that if $\mathcal{A}$ is obtained from $\mathcal{A}_0$ through the addition (resp. deletion) of a set S of isolated arguments, then, let E_0 be an extension for $\mathcal{A}_0$, $E = E_0 \cup S$ (resp. $E = E_0 \setminus S$) is an extension for $\mathcal{A}$ that can be trivially computed. Of course, if arguments in S are not isolated, we can first delete all attacks involving arguments in S; adding an attack between an argument in $\mathcal{A}_0$ and a new argument can be simulated as well. In our experiments we have considered both single and multiple attack updates.

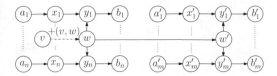

Fig. 4. Simulating multiple updates by a single one.

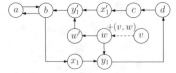

Fig. 5. $\mathcal{A}_0^U$ for $U=\{+(b,d),-(c,b)\}$.

4 Influenced Arguments

In this section, we first identify conditions ensuring that a given $\mathcal{S}$-extension continues to be an $\mathcal{S}$-extension after an update, and then introduce the *influenced set* that will be used to limit the set of arguments that needs to be recomputed after an update.

The following two propositions introduce sufficient conditions guaranteeing that a given $\mathcal{S}$-extension is still an $\mathcal{S}$-extension after performing an update.

Proposition 1. *Let $\mathcal{A}_0$ be an AF, $u = +(a,b)$ an update, $\mathcal{S}$ a semantics, $E_0 \in \mathcal{E}_\mathcal{S}(\mathcal{A}_0)$ an extension of $\mathcal{A}_0$ under semantics $\mathcal{S}$, and L_0 the labelling corresponding to E_0. Then $E_0 \in \mathcal{E}_\mathcal{S}(u(\mathcal{A}_0))$ if*

- *$\mathcal{S} \in \{co, st, gr\}$ and one of the following conditions holds:*
  - *$L_0(a) \neq$ IN and $L_0(b) \neq$ IN,*
  - *$L_0(a) =$ IN and $L_0(b) =$ OUT;*
- *$\mathcal{S} \in \{pr, ss, id\}$ and $L_0(b) =$ OUT.*

Proposition 2. *Let $\mathcal{A}_0$ be an AF, $u = -(a,b)$, $\mathcal{S} \in \{co, pr, ss, st, gr\}$, and $E_0 \in \mathcal{E}_\mathcal{S}(\mathcal{A}_0)$ an extension of $\mathcal{A}_0$ under $\mathcal{S}$. Then $E_0 \in \mathcal{E}_\mathcal{S}(u(\mathcal{A}_0))$ if one of the following conditions holds: 1) $L_0(a)=$OUT; 2) $L_0(a)=$UN and $L_0(b)=$OUT.*

Example 3. Consider the AFs $\mathcal{A}_1=+(b,d)(\mathcal{A}_0)$ and $\mathcal{A}_2=-(c,b)(\mathcal{A}_1)$, where $\mathcal{A}_0$ is the AF of Example 2. For $\mathcal{S} \in \{co, pr, ss, st\}$, extension $\{a,d\}$ of $\mathcal{A}_1$ is still an extension of $\mathcal{A}_2$ as $L_0(c)=$OUT (see Fig. 3). The grounded extension $\emptyset$ of $\mathcal{A}_1$ is still a grounded extension of $\mathcal{A}_2$, whereas the ideal extension $\{a,d\}$ of $\mathcal{A}_1$ is not the ideal extension of $\mathcal{A}_2$. $\square$

Given an AF $\mathcal{A} = \langle A, \Sigma \rangle$ and an argument $b \in A$, we denote as $Reach_\mathcal{A}(b)$ the set of arguments that are reachable from b in $\mathcal{A}$. We now introduce the *influenced set*.

Definition 1 (Influenced set). Let $\mathcal{A} = \langle A, \Sigma \rangle$ be an AF, $u = \pm(a,b)$ an update, E an extension of $\mathcal{A}$ under a given semantics $\mathcal{S}$, and let

$$- \mathcal{I}_0(u, \mathcal{A}, E) = \begin{cases} \emptyset & \text{if } E \in \mathcal{E}_\mathcal{S}(u(\mathcal{A})) \text{ [e.g., the conditions of Prop. 1/2 hold] } or \\ & \exists(z,b) \in \Sigma \text{ s.t. } z \in E \wedge z \notin Reach_\mathcal{A}(b); \\ \{b\} & otherwise; \end{cases}$$

- $\mathcal{I}_{i+1}(u, \mathcal{A}, E) = \mathcal{I}_i(u, \mathcal{A}, E) \cup \{y \mid \exists (x, y) \in \Sigma \ s.t. \ x \in \mathcal{I}_i(u, \mathcal{A}, E) \wedge \not\exists (z, y) \in \Sigma \ s.t. \ z \in E \wedge z \notin Reach_{\mathcal{A}}(b)\}$.

The *influenced set* of u w.r.t. $\mathcal{A}$ and E is $\mathcal{I}(u, \mathcal{A}, E) = \mathcal{I}_n(u, \mathcal{A}, E)$ such that $\mathcal{I}_n(u, \mathcal{A}, E) = \mathcal{I}_{n+1}(u, \mathcal{A}, E)$. □

Thus, the set of arguments that are influenced by an update of the status of b are those that can be reached from b without using any intermediate argument y whose status is known to be OUT because it is determined by an argument $z \in E$ which is not reachable from (and thus not influenced by) b.

Example 4. For the AF $\mathcal{A}_0 = \langle A_0, \Sigma_0 \rangle$ of Fig. 1, whose grounded extension is $E_0 = \{a, h, g, e, l, m, o\}$, we have that $Reach_{\mathcal{A}_0}(h) = A_0 \setminus \{a, b\}$, and the influenced set of $u = +(g, h)$ is $\mathcal{I}(u, \mathcal{A}_0, E_0) = \{h, c\}$. Note that $d \notin \mathcal{I}(u, \mathcal{A}_0, E_0)$ since it is attacked by $a \in E_0$. Thus the arguments that can be reached only using d cannot belong to $\mathcal{I}(u, \mathcal{A}_0, E_0)$ either. For $\mathcal{A} = u(\mathcal{A}_0)$, whose grounded extension is $E = \{a, c, g, e, l, m, o\}$, we have that $S = \mathcal{I}(u, \mathcal{A}, E)$ is still $\{h, c\}$. Therefore, only the status of arguments in S could change and their status can be determined by considering a restricted AF containing only arguments in $S \cup S^-$. □

Proposition 3. *Given an AF $\mathcal{A} = \langle A, \Sigma \rangle$, an update $u = \pm(a, b)$, and an extension E, the complexity of computing the influenced set of u w.r.t. $\mathcal{A}$ and E is $O(|\Sigma|)$.*

All the arguments not belonging to the influenced set of an update will still belong to an extension of the updated AF.

Theorem 1. *Let $\mathcal{A}_0$ be an AF, and $\mathcal{A} = u(\mathcal{A}_0)$ be the AF resulting from performing update $u = \pm(a, b)$ on $\mathcal{A}_0$. Let $E_0 \in \mathcal{E}_{\mathcal{S}}(\mathcal{A}_0)$ be an extension for $\mathcal{A}_0$ under any semantics $\mathcal{S} \in \{co, pr, ss, st, gr, id\}$. Let $\overline{\mathcal{I}} = Arg \setminus \mathcal{I}(u, \mathcal{A}_0, E_0)$ be the set of the arguments that are not influenced by u in $\mathcal{A}_0$ w.r.t. E_0. Then, either $\mathcal{E}_{\mathcal{S}}(\mathcal{A}) = \emptyset$ or there is an extension $E \in \mathcal{E}_{\mathcal{S}}(\mathcal{A})$ for $\mathcal{A}$ such that $(E \cap \overline{\mathcal{I}}) = (E_0 \cap \overline{\mathcal{I}})$.*

We conclude this section by introducing a refinement of Proposition 1.

Proposition 4. *Let $\mathcal{A}_0$ be an AF, $u = +(a, b)$, $\mathcal{S} \in \{co, pr, ss, st, gr\}$, and $E_0 \in \mathcal{E}_{\mathcal{S}}(\mathcal{A}_0)$ an extension of $\mathcal{A}_0$ under $\mathcal{S}$. Then $E_0 \in \mathcal{E}_{\mathcal{S}}(u(\mathcal{A}_0))$ if one of the conditions of Proposition 1 holds or all the next three conditions hold: (1) $L_0(a) = $ OUT, (2) $L_0(b) = $ IN and (3) either (i) $\mathcal{S} \in \{co, st, ss, pr\}$ or (ii) $a \notin \mathcal{I}(u, \mathcal{A}_0, E_0)$ and $\mathcal{S} = gr$.*

Example 5. Consider AFs $\mathcal{A}_0$ and $\mathcal{A}_1 = +(b, d)(\mathcal{A}_0)$ of Examples 1 and 3. For $\mathcal{S} \in \{co, pr, ss, st\}$, extension $E_0 = \{a, d\}$ for $\mathcal{A}_0$ is still an extension of the AF $\mathcal{A}_1$ as $L_0(b) = $ OUT and $L_0(d) = $ IN (see Fig. 3). However, the grounded extension $E'_0 = \{d\}$ for $\mathcal{A}_0$ is not guaranteed to be a grounded extension for $\mathcal{A}_1$ as neither Proposition 1 nor conditions (1) and 3.(ii) of Proposition 4 hold (b is UN and $b \in \mathcal{I}(+(b, d), \mathcal{A}_0, E'_0)$).

5   Recomputing Unique Status Semantics

Given an AF $\mathcal{A}_0$, a deterministic semantics $\mathcal{S} \in \{\text{gr}, \text{id}\}$, the extension E_0 for $\mathcal{A}_0$ under $\mathcal{S}$, an update u for $\mathcal{A}_0$ yielding $\mathcal{A} = u(\mathcal{A}_0)$, we address the problem of efficiently computing the $\mathcal{S}$-extension E of the updated AF $\mathcal{A}$ starting from E_0.

For any AF $\mathcal{A} = \langle A, \Sigma \rangle$ and set $S \subseteq A$ of arguments, we denote with $\Pi(S, \mathcal{A}) = \langle S, \Sigma \cap S \times S \rangle$ the subgraph of $\mathcal{A}$ induced by the nodes in S. Moreover, given two AFs $\mathcal{A}_1 = \langle A_1, \Sigma_1 \rangle$ and $\mathcal{A}_2 = \langle A_2, \Sigma_2 \rangle$, we denote as $\mathcal{A}_1 \sqcup \mathcal{A}_2 = \langle A_1 \cup A_1, \Sigma_1 \cup \Sigma_2 \rangle$ the union of the two AFs.

5.1   Grounded Semantics

Our algorithm first identifies the restricted subgraph of the given AF containing the arguments influenced by the update.

Definition 2 (Restricted AF for grounded semantics). Given an AF $\mathcal{A} = \langle A, \Sigma \rangle$, a grounded extension E for $\mathcal{A}$, and an update $u = \pm(a, b)$, the restricted AF of $\mathcal{A}$ w.r.t. E and u (denoted as $\mathcal{R}_{\text{gr}}(u, \mathcal{A}, E)$) is as follows.

- $\mathcal{R}_{\text{gr}}(u, \mathcal{A}, E)$ is empty if $\mathcal{I}(u, \mathcal{A}, E) = \emptyset$ or one of the conditions of Proposition 4 holds.
- $\mathcal{R}_{\text{gr}}(u, \mathcal{A}, E) = \Pi(\mathcal{I}(u, \mathcal{A}, E), u(\mathcal{A})) \sqcup T_1 \sqcup T_2$ where:
  - T_1 is the union of the AFs $\langle \{a, b\}, \{(a, b)\} \rangle$ s.t. (a, b) is an attack of $u(\mathcal{A})$ and $a \notin \mathcal{I}(u, \mathcal{A}, E)$, $a \in E$, and $b \in \mathcal{I}(u, \mathcal{A}, E)$;
  - $T_2 = \langle \{c \mid Check(c)\}, \{(c, c) \mid Check(c)\} \rangle$, where $Check(c)$ is true if $\exists (e, c) \in \Sigma$ such that $c \in \mathcal{I}(u, \mathcal{A}, E)$ and $e \notin \mathcal{I}(u, \mathcal{A}, E)$ and $e \notin E \cup E^+$. $\square$

Hence, AF $\mathcal{R}_{\text{gr}}(u, \mathcal{A}, E)$ contains, in addition to the subgraph of $u(\mathcal{A})$ induced by $\mathcal{I}(u, \mathcal{A}, E)$, additional nodes and edges containing needed information on the "external context", i.e. information about the status of arguments which are attacking some argument in $\mathcal{I}(u, \mathcal{A}, E)$. Specifically, if there is in $u(\mathcal{A})$ an edge from node $a \notin \mathcal{I}(u, \mathcal{A}, E)$ whose status in IN to node $b \in \mathcal{I}(u, \mathcal{A}, E)$, then we add the edge (a, b) so that, as a does not have incoming edges in $\mathcal{R}_{\text{gr}}(u, \mathcal{A}, E)$, its status is confirmed to be IN. Moreover, if there is in $u(\mathcal{A})$ an edge from a node $e \notin \mathcal{I}(u, \mathcal{A}, E)$ to $c \in \mathcal{I}(u, \mathcal{A}, E)$ such that e is UN, we add edge (c, c) to $\mathcal{R}_{\text{gr}}(u, \mathcal{A}, E)$ so that the status of c cannot be IN. Using fake arguments/attacks to represent external contexts has been exploited in a similar way in [2], where decomposability properties of argumentation semantics are studied.

Example 6. Continuing Example 4, $\mathcal{R}_{\text{gr}}(+(g, h), \mathcal{A}_0, E_0)$ consists of the subgraph induced by $\mathcal{I}(u, \mathcal{A}_0, E_0) = \{h, c\}$ as well as the edge (g, h) which is an attack towards argument $h \in \mathcal{I}(u, \mathcal{A}_0, E_0)$ coming from argument g outside $\mathcal{I}(u, \mathcal{A}_0, E_0)$ labelled as IN. Hence, $\mathcal{R}_{\text{gr}}(+(g, h), \mathcal{A}_0, E_0) = \langle A_d, \Sigma_d \rangle$ with $A_d = \{g, h, c\}$ and $\Sigma_d = \{(g, h), (h, c)\}$.

Example 7. Consider the AF $\mathcal{A}_0 = \langle\{a, b, c, d, e, f, g\}, \{(a, b), (b, a), (c, d),$ $(d, c), (a, c), (b, c), (f, c), (g, f)\}\rangle$ and the update $u = +(e, d)$. We have that (i) the grounded extension of $\mathcal{A}_0$ is $E_0 = \{g, e\}$ (i.e. arguments a, b, c, d are all labeled as UN); (ii) the influenced set is $\mathcal{I}(u, \mathcal{A}_0, E_0) = \{c, d\}$; and (iii) the restricted AF is $\mathcal{R}_{gr}(u, \mathcal{A}_0, E_0) = \langle\{c, d\}, \{(c, d), (d, c)\}\rangle \sqcup T_1 \sqcup T_2$ where $T_1 = \langle\{e, d\}, \{(e, d)\}\rangle$ and $T_2 = \langle\{c\}, \{(c, c)\}\rangle$. That is, $\mathcal{R}_{gr}(u, \mathcal{A}_0, E_0) = \langle\{c, d, e\}, \{(c, d), (d, c), (e, d), (c, c)\}\rangle$. □

Algorithm 1 first checks if the restricted AF (computed w.r.t. update $u = \pm(a, b)$) is empty (Line 3). If this is the case, then $E = E_0$. Otherwise, the status of arguments in $S = \mathcal{I}(u, \mathcal{A}_0, E_0)$ needs to be recomputed and the extension E of $u(\mathcal{A}_0)$ is constructed at Line 4 by combining the arguments in E_0 not belonging to the influenced part and the arguments returned by Function *IFP* (incremental fixpoint), which is invoked with AF $\mathcal{A}_d = \langle A_d, \Sigma_d \rangle$ (the restricted graph of $\mathcal{A}$) and starting extension $E_0 \cap A_d$ (the restriction of E_0 to A_d). Function *IFP* first computes the initial set of nodes which are labelled IN or OUT. If no argument can be labelled IN, it returns the empty set. Otherwise, it iteratively applies function G that takes as input the set of arguments S_{OUT} which have been labeled OUT so far and the subset $\Delta_{\text{OUT}} \subseteq S_{\text{OUT}}$ of arguments which have been labelled OUT in the last step, and returns the arguments $b \in \Delta_{\text{OUT}}^+$ such that for every attack $(a, b) \in \Sigma$, argument $a \in S_{\text{OUT}}$ (i.e. a is labelled OUT). Similarly to the characteristic function of an AF [20], function G infers new arguments that can be labelled IN; but it is more efficient as it only uses arguments labelled in the last step. Function G returns the set Δ_{IN} of arguments which are labeled IN at Line 5. Arguments labeled OUT are immediately derived by taking Δ_{IN}^+, that is the arguments which are attacked by some argument which has been labelled as IN (Line 6). Function G is iteratively applied until, in the last step of the **repeat** loop, all arguments derived are confirmed to be in the extension E_0 of the AF $\mathcal{A}_0$ being updated (i.e., $\Delta_{\text{IN}} \subseteq E_0$).

Example 8. Consider the AF $\mathcal{A}_0$ of Fig. 1 where $E_0 = \{a, h, g, e, l, m, o\}$ and $\mathcal{I}(u, \mathcal{A}_0, E_0) = \{h, c\}$. Algorithm 1 computes the grounded extension E of the AF $\mathcal{A} = +(g, h)(\mathcal{A}_0)$ as follows. The restricted AF $\mathcal{A}_d = \langle A_d, \Sigma_d \rangle = \mathcal{R}_{gr}(u, \mathcal{A}_0, E_0)$ is computed (at Line 2) obtaining $A_d = \{g, h, c\}$ and $\Sigma_d = \{(g, h), (h, c)\}$. As A_d is not empty, Function *IFP* with actual parameters $\mathcal{A}_d$ and $E_0 \cap A_d = \{g, h\}$ is called at Line 4. Function *IFP* first computes $S_{\text{IN}} = \Delta_{\text{IN}} = \{g\}$ and $S_{\text{OUT}} = \Delta_{\text{OUT}} = \{h\}$. Next, at the first iteration of the **repeat** loop, it is computed $\Delta_{\text{IN}} = G(\{h\}, \{h\}) = \{c\}$ (Line 5) and $\Delta_{\text{OUT}} = \emptyset$ (Line 6) as there is no argument attacked by c in $\mathcal{A}_d$. The loop is entered a second time, where Δ_{IN} stay empty and the until-condition is fulfilled. Then the function returns the set $\{g, c\}$ and E turns out to be the set $\{a, g, e, l, m, o\} \cup \{g, c\}$.

Theorem 2. *For any AF $\mathcal{A} = \langle A, \Sigma \rangle$, the complexity of computing $IFP(\mathcal{A}, E_0)$, with $E_0 \subset A$, is $O(|A| \times \bar{d}^2)$, where $\bar{d}$ is the maximum input degree of a node (i.e., the maximum number of attacks towards an argument in A).*

Algorithm 1. Incr-Grounded-Sem($\mathcal{A}_0, u, E_0$)	**Function 1.** *IFP($\mathcal{A}, E_0$)*
Input: AF $\mathcal{A}_0 = \langle A_0, \Sigma_0 \rangle$, $u = \pm(a,b)$, grounded extension E_0; **Output:** Revised grounded extension E 1: Let $S = \mathcal{I}(u, \mathcal{A}_0, E_0)$; 2: Let $\mathcal{A}_d = \langle A_d, \Sigma_d \rangle = \mathcal{R}_{\mathrm{gr}}(u, \mathcal{A}_0, E_0)$; 3: **if** $(A_d = \emptyset)$ **then** $E = E_0$; 4: **else** $E = (E_0 \setminus S) \cup IFP(\mathcal{A}_d, E_0 \cap A_d)$;	**Input:** AF $\mathcal{A} = \langle A, \Sigma \rangle$, Extension E_0; **Output:** Extension E 1: $S_{\mathrm{IN}} = \Delta_{\mathrm{IN}} = \{\, a \mid \not\exists(c,a) \in \Sigma \,\}$; 2: **if** $(S_{\mathrm{IN}} = \emptyset)$ **return** S_{IN}; 3: $S_{\mathrm{OUT}} = \Delta_{\mathrm{OUT}} = \Delta_{\mathrm{IN}}^{+}$; 4: **repeat** 5: $\Delta_{\mathrm{IN}} = G(S_{\mathrm{OUT}}, \Delta_{\mathrm{OUT}}) \setminus S_{\mathrm{IN}}$; 6: $\Delta_{\mathrm{OUT}} = \Delta_{\mathrm{IN}}^{+} \setminus S_{\mathrm{OUT}}$; 7: $S_{\mathrm{IN}} = S_{\mathrm{IN}} \cup \Delta_{\mathrm{IN}}$; 8: $S_{\mathrm{OUT}} = S_{\mathrm{OUT}} \cup \Delta_{\mathrm{OUT}}$; 9: **until** $\Delta_{\mathrm{IN}} \subseteq E_0$ 10: **if** $(\Delta_{\mathrm{IN}} = \emptyset)$ **return** S_{IN}; 11: **else return** $S_{\mathrm{IN}} \cup (E_0 \setminus (S_{\mathrm{IN}} \cup S_{\mathrm{OUT}}))$;

Theorem 3. *For any AF $\mathcal{A}_0 = \langle A_0, \Sigma_0 \rangle$ with grounded extension E_0, and $u = \pm(a,b)$, the complexity of Algorithm* Incr-Grounded-Sem($\mathcal{A}_0, u, E_0$) *is $O(|\Sigma_0| + |\mathcal{I}(u, \mathcal{A}_0, E_0)| \times \bar{d}^2)$, where $\bar{d}$ is the maximum input degree of a node.*

Theorem 4. *Given an AF $\mathcal{A}_0$, an update $u = \pm(a,b)$ for $\mathcal{A}_0$ yielding $\mathcal{A}=u(\mathcal{A}_0)$, and the grounded extension E_0 of $\mathcal{A}_0$, Algorithm 1 computes the grounded extension E of $\mathcal{A}$.*

5.2 Ideal Semantics

Before introducing the restricted AF for ideal semantics, denoted as $\mathcal{R}_{id}(u, \mathcal{A}, E)$, we define the paths, providing the information on the "context" outside the influenced set $S = \mathcal{I}(u, \mathcal{A}, E)$, that need to be added to determine the new status of arguments in S. Given an AF $\mathcal{A} = \langle A, \Sigma \rangle$ with ideal extension E and a set $S \subseteq A$, $Node(\mathcal{A}, S, E)$ (resp. $Edge(\mathcal{A}, S, E)$) denotes a set of arguments $x_1, ..., x_n$ (resp. attacks $(x_1, x_2), ..., (x_{n-1}, x_n)$) in $\mathcal{A}$ such that there is a path $x_1 ... x_n$ in $\mathcal{A}$ with $x_n \in S$, $x_1, ..., x_{n1} \notin S$ and $x_1, ..., x_{n1} \notin E \cup E^+$ (i.e., $x_1, ..., x_{n1}$ are UN). Essentially, if S is the influenced set of an update, to determine the status of nodes in S we must also consider all nodes and attacks occurring in paths (of any length) ending in S whose nodes outside S are all labeled as UN. The motivation to also consider the paths ending in S is that some of the undecided arguments occurring in these paths could be labelled IN or OUT in some preferred labelling and, therefore, together they could determine a change in the status of nodes in S.

Definition 3 (Restricted AF for ideal semantics). Given an AF $\mathcal{A} = \langle A, \Sigma \rangle$, an ideal extension E for $\mathcal{A}$ and an update $u = \pm(a,b)$, the restricted AF of $\mathcal{A}$ w.r.t. E and u (denoted as $\mathcal{R}_{\mathrm{id}}(u, \mathcal{A}, E)$) is as follows.

- $\mathcal{R}_{\mathrm{id}}(u, \mathcal{A}, E)$ is empty if $\mathcal{I}(u, \mathcal{A}, E)$ is empty.
- $\mathcal{R}_{\mathrm{id}}(u, \mathcal{A}, E) = \Pi(\mathcal{I}(u, \mathcal{A}, E), u(\mathcal{A})) \sqcup T_1 \sqcup T_2$ where, let $S = \mathcal{I}(u, \mathcal{A}, E)$:
  - T_1 is the union of the AFs $\langle \{a, b\}, \{(a, b)\} \rangle$ s.t. (a, b) is an attack of $u(\mathcal{A})$ and $a \notin \mathcal{I}(u, \mathcal{A}, E)$, $a \in E$, and $b \in \mathcal{I}(u, \mathcal{A}, E)$;
  - T_2 is the union of the AFs $\langle Node(\mathcal{A}, S, E), Edge(\mathcal{A}, S, E) \rangle$. $\square$

Example 9. Continuing Example 7 we have that (*i*) the ideal extension of $\mathcal{A}$ is $E_0' = \{g, e, d\}$ (i.e. arguments a and b are both labeled as UN); and (*ii*) the restricted AF is $\mathcal{R}_{id}(u, \mathcal{A}_0, E_0') = \langle \{c, d\}, \{(c, d), (d, c)\} \rangle \sqcup T_1 \sqcup T_2$ where $T_1 = \langle \{e, d\}, \{(e, d)\} \rangle$ and $T_2 = \langle \{a, b, c\}, \{(a, b), (b, c), (b, a), (a, c)\} \rangle$. That is, $\mathcal{R}_{id}(u, \mathcal{A}_0, E_0') = \langle \{a, b, c, d, e\}, \{(a, b), (b, a), (c, d), (d, c), (a, c), (b, c), (e, d)\} \rangle$. ☐

Once identified the restricted AF, our algorithm for computing the ideal extension uses the novel concept of *coherent winning strategy* (CWS) that we introduce below after briefly recalling *Two Party Immediate Response Disputes* [23, 44].

In a *dispute* two players, *proponent* (*PRO*) and *opponent* (*OPP*), move arguments to each other. A dispute for an argument a_1 is a sequence of arguments $d = a_1, \ldots, a_n$ where a_1 is moved by *PRO* and consecutive arguments a_i, a_{i+1} in d are such that $(a_{i+1}, a_i) \in \Sigma$ and are moved by different players. A dispute is *legal* iff *i*) *OPP* never uses the same argument twice, and *ii*) *PRO* never uses a self-attacking argument or an argument attacking one previously used by him.

Given an AF $\mathcal{A} = \langle A, \Sigma \rangle$ and an argument $a \in A$, the *dispute tree* $T(a, \mathcal{A})$ for $\mathcal{A}$ is the maximal tree whose root is a and whose branches (disputes) are legal disputes for a. For any subtree t of $T(a, \mathcal{A})$, we denote by $PRO(t)$ (resp. $OPP(t)$) the set of arguments moved by *PRO* (resp., *OPP*) occurring in t. Moreover, $ST(a, \mathcal{A})$ denotes the set of subtrees w derived from $T(a, \mathcal{A})$ by pruning branches in such a way that each node in $OPP(w)$ has only one child node (the set of child nodes of any node in $PRO(w)$ remains the same).

Definition 4 (Coherent Winning Strategy (CWS)). Let $\mathcal{A} = \langle A, \Sigma \rangle$ and $a \in A$. A subtree $w \in ST(a, \mathcal{A})$ is a *winning strategy* for a iff all leaf nodes of w belong to $PRO(T(a, \mathcal{A}))$. w is said to be *coherent* w.r.t. $E \subseteq A$ iff (*i*) $PRO(w) \cap E^+ = \emptyset$ and (*ii*) $OPP(w) \cap E = \emptyset$. The set of CWSs for a in $\mathcal{A}$ w.r.t. E is denoted as $\mathcal{CW}(a, \mathcal{A}, E)$. ☐

Checking whether an argument belongs to the ideal extension of an updated AF can be accomplished using CSWs.

Theorem 5. *Let $\mathcal{A}_0 = \langle A_0, \Sigma_0 \rangle$, E_0 the ideal extension of $\mathcal{A}_0$, $u = \pm(a, b)$, $S = \mathcal{I}(u, \mathcal{A}_0, E_0)$, and $\mathcal{A} = u(\mathcal{A}_0)$. Then, the ideal extension E of $\mathcal{A}$ contains argument c iff there is a CWS $w \in \mathcal{CW}(c, \mathcal{R}_{id}(u, \mathcal{A}_0, E_0), E_0 \setminus S)$ such that $\forall c' \in OPP(w)$, $\not\exists$ CWS $w' \in \mathcal{CW}(c', \mathcal{R}_{id}(u, \mathcal{A}_0, E_0), E_0 \setminus S)$.*

A CWS $w \in \mathcal{CW}(c, \mathcal{A}, E)$ is *successful* if it satisfies the condition of Theorem 5.

Corollary 1. *Let $\mathcal{A}_0 = \langle A_0, \Sigma_0 \rangle$, E_0 the ideal extension of $\mathcal{A}_0$, and $u = \pm(a, b)$ an update. Then, $PRO(w) \subseteq E$ where E is the ideal extension of $\mathcal{A} = u(\mathcal{A}_0)$ and w is a successful CWS in $\mathcal{CW}(c, \mathcal{R}_{id}(u, \mathcal{A}_0, E_0), E_0 \setminus \mathcal{I}(u, \mathcal{A}, E_0))$.*

Algorithm 2. Incr-Ideal-Sem$(\mathcal{A}_0, u, E_0)$

Input: AF $\mathcal{A}_0 = \langle A_0, \Sigma_0 \rangle$, $u = \pm(a, b)$, Ideal
extension E_0;
Output: Revised ideal extension E;
1: Let $\mathcal{A} = u(\mathcal{A}_0)$;
2: $S = \mathcal{I}(u, \mathcal{A}_0, E_0)$;
3: $E = E_0 \setminus S$;
4: **if** $(S = \emptyset)$ **then return**
5: **while** $(S \neq \emptyset)$ **do**
6:     $\mathcal{A}_d = \langle A_d, \Sigma_d \rangle = \mathcal{R}_{gr}(u, \mathcal{A}_0, E)$;
7:     $\Delta_{\mathrm{IN}} = IFP(\mathcal{A}_d, E \cap A_d)$;
8:     $S = S \setminus (\Delta_{\mathrm{IN}} \cup \Delta_{\mathrm{IN}}^+)$;
9:     $E = E \cup \Delta_{\mathrm{IN}}$;
10:    $\mathcal{A}_d = \mathcal{R}_{id}(u, \mathcal{A}_0, E)$;
11:    Select an argument $c \in S$;
12:    **if** $\exists$ successful CWS $w \in \mathcal{CW}(c, \mathcal{A}_d, E)$
       then
13:        $\Delta_{\mathrm{IN}} = PRO(w)$;
14:        $S = S \setminus (\Delta_{\mathrm{IN}} \cup \Delta_{\mathrm{IN}}^+)$;
15:        $E = E \cup \Delta_{\mathrm{IN}}$;
16:    **else** $S = S \setminus \{c\}$;

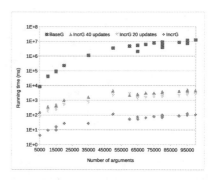

Fig. 6. Run times (ms) of *BaseG*
and *IncrG* for 1, 20, and 40 updates
over **REAL**.

Algorithm 2 computes the ideal extension E of an updated AF $\mathcal{A} = u(\mathcal{A}_0)$
using the ideal extension E_0 of AF $\mathcal{A}_0$. It starts by identifying the set S of arguments whose status need to be recomputed (Line 2) and the starting extension
that will be iteratively incremented to obtain the ideal extension (Line 3). It
first checks if the influenced set is empty (Line 4); in such a case $E = E_0$ and
then it stops. If this is not the case, it iterates to reach a fixpoint. At each step it
first computes the grounded semantics (lines 6–9) and next search for a CWS for
some unlabelled argument (lines 10–16). More specifically, before computing the
grounded semantics (Line 7), the (restricted) AF is computed using $\mathcal{R}_{gr}$ (Line
6). Using the result of Function IFP, extension E and the set S of unlabelled
arguments are updated at lines 8-9 by including in the current ideal extension E
all the arguments belonging to the grounded extension Δ_{IN} and removing from
S all new arguments that have been decided. Analogously, before searching for
a successful CWS (Line 12), the restricted AF is computed using $\mathcal{R}_{id}$ (Line 10).
Finally, the existence of a successful CWS w is exploited for updating extension
E and the set S of unlabelled arguments (lines 14–16).

Theorem 6. *Given an AF $\mathcal{A}_0$ whose ideal extension is E_0, and an update $u = \pm(a, b)$ such that $u(\mathcal{A}_0) = \mathcal{A}$, Algorithm 2 computes the ideal extension E of $\mathcal{A}$.*

6   Experiments

We implemented a prototype for incremental computation of argumentation
semantics using the Java argumentation libraries provided by the *Tweety*
project [43].

Datasets. For the experiments on the grounded semantics, we used two datasets
provided as benchmarks at ICCMA (http://argumentationcompetition.org):

(i) REAL consists of 19 AFs $\langle A_0, \Sigma_0 \rangle$ with $|A_0| \in [5K, 100K]$ and $|\Sigma_0| \in [7K, 143K]$; (ii) SYN1 consists of 24 AFs $\langle A_0, \Sigma_0 \rangle$ with $|A_0| \in [1K, 4K]$ and $|\Sigma_0| \in [14K, 172K]$. The AFs in the two datasets have a different structure: on average, $|Reach_{\mathcal{A}_0}(a)|$ is around 2200 for arguments a in SYN1, while it is about 10 for REAL; moreover, the average number of attacks per argument for REAL is 1.5 while it is 26 for SYN1.

For the experiments on the ideal semantics, we built dataset SYN2 that consists of AFs whose size is smaller than those in REAL and SYN1 because computing the initial ideal extension for the datasets above is prohibitive due to its exponential complexity (specifically, computing the ideal extension is $FP_{||}^{NP}$-hard [22]). SYN2 consists of 20 AFs for each of the number of arguments in $\{50, 75, \ldots, 175\}$. Each AF in SYN2 was obtained by first generating its arguments and then adding for each argument on average 2 attacks toward arguments in the AF being generated. Finally, for each argument not yet connected, an attack from or to this argument from the others was added.

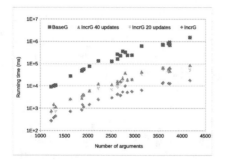   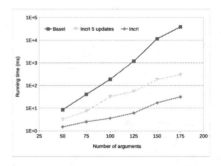

Fig. 7. Run times (ms) of *BaseG* and *IncrG* for 1, 20, and 40 updates over SYN1.

Fig. 8. Run times (ms) of *BaseI* and *IncrI* for 1 and 5 updates over SYN2

Algorithms. For each AF $\mathcal{A}_0 = \langle A_0, \Sigma_0 \rangle$ in each dataset, we first computed the grounded (resp. ideal) extension E_0. Then, when considering a single update, we randomly selected an update u of the form $+(a, b)$ (with $a, b \in A_0$ and $(a, b) \notin \Sigma_0$) or $-(a, b)$ (with $(a, b) \in \Sigma_0$). For the case of multiple updates, we randomly generated a set U of updates of the above form. Next, we executed the following algorithms:

– *BaseG* and *BaseI* which compute, respectively, the grounded and ideal semantics E of the updated AF $u(\mathcal{A}_0)$ from scratch (these algorithms were also used to compute the initial extension E_0 which is taken as input by the incremental algorithms). *BaseG* finds the fixpoint of the characteristic function of an AF as implemented in the libraries of *Tweety* [43], while *BaseI* uses the algorithm implemented by Dung-O-Matic engine (http://www.arg-tech.org/index.php/projects/dung-o-matic).

- *Incr-Grounded-Sem* and *Incr-Ideal-Sem* (**IncrG** and **IncrI** for short) which incrementally compute the grounded and ideal extension E by implementing Algorithms 1 and 2, respectively.

The construction of Fig. 4 was used for computing extensions of AFs updated by a set U of updates (multiple updates) by the incremental algorithms *IncrG* and *IncrI*.

Results. Figures 6 and 7 report the run times (log scale) of *BaseG* and *IncrG* for computing the grounded extensions of the updated AFs versus the number of arguments over REAL and SYN1, respectively. The figures also report the run times of *IncrG* for computing the grounded extensions after performing 20 and 40 updates, where for multiple updates the restricted AF and the starting extension also take into account arguments and attacks added to the construction of Fig. 4. The experiments also showed that, on average, the size of the influenced set w.r.t. that of the input AF for REAL (resp. SYN1) is about 0.01 % (resp. 1 %) for single update, 0.1 % (resp. 9 %) for 20 updates, and 0.5 % (resp. 15 %) for 40 updates. Figure 8 reports the run times (log scale) of *BaseI* and *IncrI* for computing the ideal extensions after performing one and five updates versus the number of arguments over SYN2. The experiments showed that the size of the influenced set w.r.t. that of the input AF for SYN2 is 6 % for single update and 43 % for 5 updates.

From these results, we can draw the following conclusions:

- The time needed by our algorithms for incrementally computing the grounded and ideal extensions is orders of magnitude better than the time needed to recompute the whole extension from scratch. This holds even in the case of multiple updates where there is an overload due to the construction of Fig. 4.
- While the improvement obtained for the grounded semantics is almost constant w.r.t. the size of the input AFs, the improvement obtained for the ideal semantics increases with the size of the input AFs. In fact, since computing the ideal semantics is exponential in the size of the input AF, the improvement derived from considering the restricted AF is exponential in the size of the restriction (arguments and attacks in the input AF not occurring in the restricted AF).
- The definition of influenced set substantially restricts the portion of the AF to be analysed for recomputing the semantics of an AF after performing an update. It is worth noting that this means that even using *any non-incremental* algorithm taking as input the restricted AF would result in a performance improvement, since the size of the input data to be processed would be significantly smaller.

The experiments also showed the trade-off between applying a number n of updates by using the construction of Fig. 4 (i.e., multiple updates) and performing a sequence of n single updates by running n times the incremental algorithms: the former approach is preferable for more than 20 (resp., 5) updates for REAL (resp. SYN1) under the grounded semantics, while under the ideal semantics it is preferable for less than 7 updates, on average. In fact, the overhead due to the construction of Fig. 4 is relatively small and turns to be more and more convenient for a sizeable set of updates under the grounded semantics. However, it increases with the size of the input AF and becomes relatively large for (the smaller dataset) SYN2 under the ideal semantics, making the approach based on performing sequence of single updates more suitable in this case.

7   Conclusion and Future Work

We presented two incremental algorithms for computing deterministic extensions of updated AFs. The algorithms exploit the initial extension of an AF for computing the set of arguments influenced by an update, and for detecting early termination conditions during the recomputation of the status of the arguments. Although our presentation focused on adding/removing one attack, our technique can be used in the case of general updates. The experiments, conducted considering also multiple updates, showed that the incremental computation outperforms that of the base (non-incremental) computation. The experiments also showed that our definition of influenced set drastically restricts the portion of the AF to be analysed for recomputing the semantics after an update.

Our current research is concentrated on the application of the techniques developed in this paper to other (multiple status) semantics. In this regard, there are two interesting aspects that deserve more investigation. First, the identification of restricted AFs for these semantics would enable the use of existing (non-incremental) algorithms taking as input a smaller AF for computing extensions. Second, we envisage the definition of incremental algorithms that make use of initial extensions for computing extensions after updates for multiple status semantics where we need to deal with the additional issue that extensions can be split/merged after an update.

References

1. Amgoud, L., Vesic, S.: Revising option status in argument-based decision systems. J. Log. Comput. **22**(5), 1019–1058 (2012)
2. Baroni, P., Boella, G., Cerutti, F., Giacomin, M., van der Torre, L.W.N., Villata, S.: On the input/output behavior of argumentation frameworks. Artif. Intell. **217**, 144–197 (2014)
3. Baroni, P., Caminada, M., Giacomin, M.: An introduction to argumentation semantics. Knowl. Eng. Rev. **26**(4), 365–410 (2011)
4. Baroni, P., Giacomin, M., Liao, B.: On topology-related properties of abstract argumentation semantics. a correction and extension to dynamics of argumentation systems: A division-based method. Artif. Intell. **212**, 104–115 (2014)
5. Baumann, R.: Splitting an argumentation framework. In: Proceedings of International Conference on Logic Programming and Nonmonotonic Reasoning (LPNMR), pp. 40–53 (2011)
6. Baumann, R.: Normal and strong expansion equivalence for argumentation frameworks. Artif. Intell. **193**, 18–44 (2012)

7. Baumann, R.: Context-free and context-sensitive kernels: update and deletion equivalence in abstract argumentation. In: Proceedings of ECAI, pp. 63–68 (2014)
8. Baumann, R., Brewka, G.: Expanding argumentation frameworks: enforcing and monotonicity results. In: Proceedings of COMMA, pp. 75–86 (2010)
9. Baumann, R., Brewka, G., Dvořák, W., Woltran, S.: Parameterized splitting: a simple modification-based approach. In: Correct Reasoning - Essays on Logic-Based AI in Honour of Vladimir Lifschitz, pp. 57–71 (2012)
10. Bench-Capon, T.J.M., Dunne, P.E.: Argumentation in artificial intelligence. Artif. Intell. **171**(1015), 619–641 (2007)
11. Bisquert, P., Cayrol, C., de Saint-Cyr, F.D., Lagasquie-Schiex, M.: Characterizing change in abstract argumentation systems. Trends Belief Revision Argum. Dyn. **48**, 75–102 (2013)
12. Boella, G., Kaci, S., van der Torre, L.W.N.: Dynamics in argumentation with single extensions: abstraction principles and the grounded extension. In: Proceedings of ECSQARU, pp. 107–118 (2009)
13. Boella, G., Kaci, S., van der Torre, L.W.N.: Dynamics in argumentation with single extensions: attack refinement and the grounded extension. In: Proceedings of ArgMAS, pp. 150–159 (2009)
14. Calautti, M., Greco, S., Trubitsyna, I.: Detecting decidable classes of finitely ground logic programs with function symbols. In: 15th International Symposium on Principles and Practice of Declarative Programming, PPDP 2013, Madrid, Spain, 16–18 September 2013, pp. 239–250 (2013)
15. Caminada, M.: Semi-stable semantics. In: Proceedings of COMMA, pp. 121–130 (2006)
16. Caminada, M., Sá, S., Alcântara, J., Dvořák, W.: On the equivalence between logic programming semantics and argumentation semantics. Int. J. Approx. Reason. **58**, 87–111 (2015)
17. Cayrol, C., de Saint-Cyr, F.D., Lagasquie-Schiex, M.: Revision of an argumentation system. In: Proceedings of KR, pp. 124–134 (2008)
18. Cayrol, C., de Saint-Cyr, F.D., Lagasquie-Schiex, M.: Change in abstract argumentation frameworks: adding an argument. J. Artif. Intell. Res. **38**, 49–84 (2010)
19. Charwat, G., Dvořák, W., Gaggl, S.A., Wallner, J.P., Woltran, S.: Methods for solving reasoning problems in abstract argumentation - a survey. Artif. Intell. **220**, 28–63 (2015)
20. Dung, P.M.: On the acceptability of arguments and its fundamental role in non-monotonic reasoning, logic programming and n-person games. Artif. Intell. **77**(2), 321–358 (1995)
21. Dung, P.M., Mancarella, P., Toni, F.: Computing ideal sceptical argumentation. Artif. Intell. **171**(10–15), 642–674 (2007)
22. Dunne, P.E.: The computational complexity of ideal semantics. Artif. Intell. **173**(18), 1559–1591 (2009)
23. Dunne, P.E., Bench-Capon, T.J.M.: Two party immediate response disputes: properties and efficiency. Artif. Intell. **149**(2), 221–250 (2003)
24. Dunne, P.E., Wooldridge, M.: Complexity of abstract argumentation. In: Argumentation in Artificial Intelligence, pp. 85–104 (2009)
25. Dvořák, W., Pichler, R., Woltran, S.: Towards fixed-parameter tractable algorithms for argumentation. In: Proceedings of KR (2010)
26. Dvořák, W., Woltran, S.: Complexity of semi-stable and stage semantics in argumentation frameworks. Inf. Process. Lett. **110**(11), 425–430 (2010)

27. Eiter, T., Strass, H., Truszczyński, M., Woltran, S. (eds.): Advances in Knowledge Representation, Logic Programming, and Abstract Argumentation. LNCS (LNAI), vol. 9060. Springer, Heidelberg (2015)

28. Falappa, M.A., Garcia, A.J., Kern-Isberner, G., Simari, G.R.: On the evolving relation between belief revision and argumentation. Knowl. Eng. Rev. **26**(1), 35–43 (2011)

29. Fazzinga, B., Flesca, S., Parisi, F.: Efficiently estimating the probability of extensions in abstract argumentation. In: Proceedings of SUM, pp. 106–119 (2013)

30. Fazzinga, B., Flesca, S., Parisi, F.: On the complexity of probabilistic abstract argumentation. In: Proceedings of IJCAI, pp. 898–904 (2013)

31. Fazzinga, B., Flesca, S., Parisi, F.: On the complexity of probabilistic abstract argumentation frameworks. ACM Trans. Comput. Log. **16**(3), 22 (2015)

32. Fazzinga, B., Flesca, S., Parisi, F.: On efficiently estimating the probability of extensions in abstract argumentation frameworks. Int. J. Approx. Reason. **69**, 106–132 (2016)

33. Fazzinga, B., Flesca, S., Parisi, F., Pietramala, A.: PARTY: a mobile system for efficiently assessing the probability of extensions in a debate. In: Proceedings of DEXA, pp. 220–235 (2015)

34. Greco, S., Molinaro, C., Trubitsyna, I.: Logic programming with function symbols: checking termination of bottom-up evaluation through program adornments. TPLP **13**(4–5), 737–752 (2013)

35. Greco, S., Molinaro, C., Trubitsyna, I., Zumpano, E.: NP datalog: a logic language for expressing search and optimization problems. TPLP **10**(2), 125–166 (2010)

36. Greco, S., Parisi, F.: Efficient computation of deterministic extensions for dynamic abstract argumentation frameworks. In: Proceedings of ECAI, pp. 1668–1669 (2016)

37. Liao, B.S., Jin, L., Koons, R.C.: Dynamics of argumentation systems: a division-based method. Artif. Intell. **175**(11), 1790–1814 (2011)

38. Lifschitz, V., Turner, H.: Splitting a logic program. In: Proceedings of ICLP, pp. 23–37 (1994)

39. Modgil, S., Prakken, H.: Revisiting preferences and argumentation. In: Proceedings of IJCAI, pp. 1021–1026 (2011)

40. Oikarinen, E., Woltran, S.: Characterizing strong equivalence for argumentation frameworks. Artif. Intell. **175**(14–15), 1985–2009 (2011)

41. Pollock, J.L.: Perceiving and reasoning about a changing world. Comput. Intell. **14**(4), 498–562 (1998)

42. Rahwan, I., Simari, G.R.: Argumentation in Artificial Intelligence. Springer, New York (2009)

43. Thimm, M.: Tweety: a comprehensive collection of java libraries for logical aspects of artificial intelligence and knowledge representation. In: Proceedings of KR (2014)

44. Vreeswijk, G., Prakken, H.: Credulous and sceptical argument games for preferred semantics. In: Proceedings of JELIA, pp. 239–253 (2000)

45. Xu, Y., Cayrol, C.: The matrix approach for abstract argumentation frameworks. In: Proceedings of International TAFA Workshop, pp. 243–259 (2015)

Revising Possibilistic Knowledge Bases via Compatibility Degrees

Yifan Jin[⊠], Kewen Wang, Zhe Wang, and Zhiqiang Zhuang

Griffith University, 170 Kessels Rd, Nathan, QLD 4111, Australia
yifan.jin@griffithuni.edu.au, {k.wang,zhe.wang,z.zhuang}@griffith.edu.au

Abstract. Possibilistic logic is a weighted logic for dealing with incomplete and uncertain information by assigning weights to propositional formulas. A possibilistic knowledge base (KB) is a finite set of such formulas. The problem of revising a possibilistic KB by possibilistic formula is not new. However, existing approaches are limited in two ways. Firstly, they suffer from the so-called drowning effect. Secondly, they handle certain and uncertain formulas separately and most only handle certain inputs. In this paper, we propose a unified approach that caters for revision by both certain and uncertain inputs and relieves the drowning effect. The approach is based on a refined inconsistency degree function called compatibility degree which provides a unifying framework (called cd-revision) for defining specific revision operators for possibilistic KBs. Our definition leads to an algorithm for computing the result of the proposed revision. The revision operators defined in cd-revision possess some desirable properties including those from classic belief revision and some others that are specific to possibilistic revision. We also show that several major revision operators for possibilistic, stratified and prioritised KBs can be embedded in cd-revision.

1 Introduction

The area of *belief revision* deals with incorporating new information into a knowledge base (KB) while preserving its consistency. A set of postulates is given in [1] for characterizing the intuitions behind rational belief revision.

Possibilistic logic is a weighted logic for dealing with incomplete and uncertain information. A possibilistic KB is a set of *weighted formulas*, denoted as (ϕ, α), where ϕ is a classical formula and α a number that represents how certain we are about the truth of ϕ. Belief revision for possibilistic KBs has been studied in for example [7,12]. Syntactically, the approaches come down to adding a formula to a belief base at a certain prescribed level. The problem is non-trivial as we have to keep the prescribed priority of the added formula in the KB.

After revising a possibilistic KB by a weighted formula (ϕ, α), we expect that ϕ is believed to a degree of certainty α in the revised KB. There are two views of this certainty in the literature. One sees it as enforcing a constraint [7]. Another is by taking it into account only if it leads to a strengthening of the certainty [12]. The two views have been extended in [5,6] to form a series of belief revision

© Springer International Publishing AG 2016
L. Michael and A. Kakas (Eds.): JELIA 2016, LNAI 10021, pp. 305–319, 2016.
DOI: 10.1007/978-3-319-48758-8_20

operators. However, many of them suffer from the so called "drowning effect". That is, after revising a KB, formulas with weights lower than a certain degree of the KB are either totally neglected or heavily modified. Consider the possibilistic KB $\{(\neg rainy \rightarrow go\_outing, 0.9), (rainy \vee windy, 0.8), (\neg go\_outing, 0.8)\}$, which says it is quite possible that (1) if it does not rain then we will go outing, (2) it will be rainy or windy, and (3) we will not go outing. When revising the KB by the fact that it is not rainy, i.e., $(\neg rainy, 1)$, methods in [5,6] will discard $(rainy \vee windy, 0.8)$, even though this formula has nothing to do with the inconsistency. The problem gets worse if the inconsistency degree is high. Many efforts have been made to deal with this problem [4,8,17–19]. Some does it by restricting the input to be certain ones (i.e., formulas with weight 1) and some are based on semantic approaches.

Our goal is to establish a unified belief revision function that deals with both certain and uncertain inputs and at the same time avoids the drowning effect as much as possible. The function adapts the view of seeing (ϕ, α) as a constraint, which means that the formula ϕ should be believed to a degree of certainty α exactly. In this respect, [7,18] are closely related to ours. The revision operators in both [7,18] are based on possibility distributions. The former is defined for arbitrary possibilistic formulas (ϕ, α) $(0 < \alpha \leq 1)$ while the latter is defined for certain inputs $(\phi, 1)$. In addition, a syntactic approach based on inconsistency only is also provided in [7], which is sound and complete with respect to their semantic revision.

We first propose a syntactic characterization for inconsistency of possibilistic KBs, called *compatibility degree*, which measures the inconsistency for each collection of formulas. Based on the characterization, we establish a framework for defining revision in possibilistic logic, called to as *compatibility degree based revision* or simply *cd-revision*. cd-revision satisfies major postulates for classic belief revision. An algorithm is developed for the proposed revision. Significantly, the revision framework is general enough to subsume many earlier approaches [5,7,18] thus providing a unifying framework for possibilistic logic belief revision.

The rest of this paper is organized as follows. We first introduce possibilistic logic in Sect. 2. We then define the notion of compatibility degree in possibilistic logic in Sect. 3. In Sect. 5, we define our revision framework as well as a related algorithm based on compatibility level. Section 6 is devoted to the logical properties of our revision approach. Finally we discuss how our methods are related to previous work in Sect. 7 and give conclusion in Sect. 8.

2   Possibilistic Logic

We work with propositional possibilistic logic [10], which is built on classical propositional logic. A formula in possibilistic logic is of the form (ϕ, α) where ϕ is a propositional formula and $\alpha \in (0, 1]$ is the *weight* of ϕ. Intuitively, (ϕ, α) expresses that ϕ is certain at least to the degree of α. Such formulas are referred to as possiblistic formulas. A possibilistic KB is a finite set of possibilistic formulas. Each possibilistic KB K can be transformed into an equivalent possibilistic

KB K' in clausal form where for each ϕ in K' is a clause (i.e., a disjunction of possibly negated atoms). For simplicity, in what follows we assume w.l.o.g. that each possibilistic KB is in clausal form. We define the classical projection of a possibilistic KB K as the KB $K^* = \{\phi \mid (\phi, \alpha) \in K\}$. We use $\models$ to represent classical entailment.

The semantics of possibilistic logic is based on the notion of *possibility distributions*. A possibility distribution π is a mapping from all interpretations to the interval $[0, 1]$. For an interpretation I, $\pi(I)$ represents the degree of compatibility of I with the real world. Such that, $\pi(I) = 0$ means that I is impossible to be the real world; $\pi(I) = 1$ means that nothing prevent I from being the real world; and $0 < \pi(I) < 1$ means that I is somewhat possible to be the real world.

A possibility distribution π *satisfies* a possibilistic KB K if $\pi(I) \leq \pi_K(I)$ for all I, where π_K is obtained as follows

$$\pi_K(I) = \begin{cases} 1, & \text{if } I \models \phi \text{ for every } (\phi, \alpha) \in K \\ 1 - max\{\alpha \mid (\phi, \alpha) \in K \text{ and } I \nvDash \phi\}, & \text{otherwise} \end{cases}$$

π_K is in fact the least specific possibility distribution satisfying K [10].

From π_K, two dual measures can be determined for a propositional formula ϕ. The *necessity degree* of ϕ denoted as $N(\phi)$ is defined as $N(\phi) = 1 - max\{\pi_K(I) \mid I \models \neg\phi\}$; and the *possibility degree* of ϕ denoted as $\Pi(\phi)$ is defined as $\Pi(\phi) = 1 - N(\neg\phi)$. Intuitively, the possibility degree says to what extent ϕ is consistent with K and the necessity degree says to what extend ϕ is entailed by K. We refer the readers to [10] for further details.

A possibilistic KB K is consistent if K^* is *consistent*, and inconsistent as otherwise. The inconsistency degree of K is defined as

$$Inc(K) = 1 - max\{\pi_K(I) \mid I \in \Omega\}.$$

The inconsistency degree indicates to what extent K is consistent, which can be seen from the fact that $K_{>Inc(K)} = \{(\phi_i, \alpha_i) \mid (\phi_i, \alpha_i) \in K, \alpha_i > Inc(K)\}$ is consistent whereas for any $\alpha \leq Inc(K)$, $K_{>Inc(K)} \subset K_{\geq\alpha} \subseteq K$ is inconsistent.

Given a possibilistic KB K, a propositional formula ϕ is a *plausible consequence* of K, denoted $K \models_p \phi$, if $K^*_{>Inc(K)} \models \phi$. For simplicity, we also say K entails ϕ. A possibilistic formula (ϕ, α) is a *consequence* of K, denoted $K \models (\phi, \alpha)$, if $\alpha > Inc(K)$ and $K^*_{\geq\alpha} \models \phi$. Moreover, ϕ is a *consequence* of K to a degree α, denoted $K \models_\pi (\phi, \alpha)$, if $K \models (\phi, \alpha)$ and $\forall \beta > \alpha$, $K \nvDash (\phi, \beta)$.

3   Compatibility Degree

To avoid the "drowning effect", we introduce a degree that can characterise the consistency of all subsets of a possibilistic KB. Inspired by [2,3], we define the following degree function called *compatibility degree*.

Definition 1. *Given a possibilistic KB K, the compatibility degree $C_K : 2^K \mapsto [0, 1]$ is such that for each $K' \subseteq K$,*

$$C_K(K') = \begin{cases} 1 - max\{\alpha \mid (\phi, \alpha) \in K \setminus K'\} & \text{if } K'^* \text{ is consistent} \\ 0 & \text{otherwise} \end{cases}$$

Intuitively, only a consistent subset K' of K has a positive compatibility degree and the degree is higher (closer to 1) if K' contains formulas (from K) with higher certainty. When the background KB K is clear, we will omit the subscript.

Example 1. *Let* $K = \{(p \vee r, 0.9), (p \vee \neg q, 0.8), (\neg r, 0.8)\}$. *Consider the following sub-KB:* $K_1 = \{(p \vee r, 0.9)\}$, $K_2 = \{(p \vee \neg q, 0.8)\}$, $K_3 = \{(p \vee r, 0.9), (p \vee \neg q, 0.8)\}$, $K_4 = K$. *We have* $C_K(K_1) = 0.2$, $C_K(K_2) = 0.1$, $C_K(K_3) = 0.2$ *and* $C_K(K_4) = 1$.

It is easy to see that the compatibility degree is monotonically non-decreasing.

Lemma 1. *Given a possibilistic KB* K, *if* K' *and* K'' *are consistent and* $K'' \subseteq K' \subseteq K$, *then* $C_K(K'') \leq C_K(K')$.

Proof. If $K'' \subseteq K' \subseteq K$ then we have $K \setminus K' \subseteq K \setminus K''$ Thus $max\{\alpha \mid (\phi, \alpha) \in K \setminus K'\} \leq max\{\alpha \mid (\phi, \alpha) \in K \setminus K''\}$. As a result, $C_K(K'') = 1 - max\{\alpha \mid (\phi, \alpha) \in K \setminus K''\} \leq C_K(K') = 1 - max\{\alpha \mid (\phi, \alpha) \in K \setminus K'\}$. ∎

While the compatibility degree is defined syntactically, it is able to characterise the semantics of possibilistic logic. The following proposition shows that the least specific possibility distribution satisfying K can be characterised by the compatibility degree function.

Proposition 1. *Let* K *be a possibilistic KB. For every interpretation* I *the least specific possibility distribution w.r.t.* I *corresponds to the compatibility degree of some subset* K' *of* K, *such that* $\pi_K(I) = C_K(K')$.

Proof. Given an interpretation I, let $K' = \{(\phi, \alpha) \mid (\phi, \alpha) \in K$ and $I \models \phi\}$ and for each formula $(\phi, \alpha) \in K \setminus K'$ we require $I \not\models \phi$. Thus, $\pi_K(I) = 1 - max\{\alpha \mid (\phi, \alpha) \in K$ and $I \not\models \phi)\} = 1 - max\{\alpha \mid (\phi, \alpha) \in K \setminus K'\} = C_K(K')$. ∎

A corallary of Proposition 1 is that the necessity degree and inconsistency degree can both be characterised by the compatibility degree.

Corollary 1. *Let* K *be a possibilistic KB,* I *be an interpretation and* ϕ *be a propositional formula. Then the following three statements hold:*

1. $\pi_K(I) \geq C_K(K')$ *for each* I *and* K' *such that* $K' \subseteq K$ *and* $I \models K'^*$.
2. $N(\phi) = 1 - max\{C_K(K') \mid K' \subseteq K$ *and* $K'^* \not\models \phi\}$.
3. $Inc(K) = 1 - max\{C_K(K') \mid K' \subseteq K\}$.

4   Revision Based on Compatibility Degrees

In this section, we study the problem of revising a possibilistic KB K by a possibilistic formula (μ, α). As usual, we assume K is consistent. Similar to classic belief revision, when (μ, α) is added to K, the union $K \cup \{(\mu, \alpha)\}$ can be inconsistent and thus we need to obtain a new KB K' such that $K' \cup \{(\mu, \alpha)\}$

is consistent and K' is as close to K as possible. The basic idea of our approach is to find subsets of K that are consistent with (μ, α) and have the maximum compatibility degree. To formalise this idea, we first propose a unified revision method based on compatibility degree. This method can be applied to both the cases of $\alpha = 1$ (i.e., revision by certain information) and $\alpha < 1$ (i.e., revision by uncertain information). Then we give the details of our revision for the two cases.

4.1 Definition of Possibilistic Revision

Our revision operator is based on a selection function. A selection function γ maps each collection of classical KBs $\mathcal{S}$ to a subset of $\mathcal{S}$ such that $\gamma(\mathcal{S})$ is non-empty whenever $\mathcal{S}$ is so. Two concrete selection functions are γ_{max}, which maps a set of classical KBs to the set of its maximal elements $w.r.t.$ subset relation, and γ_{min}, which maps a set of classical KBs to the set of its minimal elements $w.r.t.$ subset relation. For instance, let $\mathcal{S} = \{\{\varphi\}, \{\psi\}, \{\varphi, \psi\}\}$, then $\gamma_{max}(\mathcal{S}) = \{\{\varphi, \psi\}\}$ and $\gamma_{min}(\mathcal{S}) = \{\{\varphi\}, \{\psi\}\}$.

When revising possibilistic KB K with a possibilistic formula (μ, α) $(0 < \alpha \leq 1)$, we have three possible cases.

Case 1, $K^* \not\models \mu$ and $K^* \not\models \neg\mu$. This case is trivial since K does not contain any information about μ. Then the revision result is simply $K \cup \{(\mu, \alpha)\}$.

Case 2, $K^* \models \neg\mu$, that is, K^* is inconsistent with μ. In this case, we need to select subsets of K that are consistent with μ and have the maximum compatibility degree, so as to preserve as many formulas from K with high certainty as possible.

Case 3, $K^* \models \mu$, then μ is believed to a degree β in K and it is possible that $\beta > \alpha$. In this case, adding (μ, α) to K can not guarantee μ to have a certainty degree α. We need to first identify subsets K' of K that do not entail μ and have the maximum compatibility degree (which is again to preserve as many formulas from K with their initial certainty as possible), and then adjust the weights of the remaining formulas in K (not in K') according to α.

Before defining our revision, we need to introduce some preparatory notations. For a possibilistic KB K and a propositional formula ϕ, let $c(K, \phi) = max\{C(K') \mid K' \subseteq K, K'^* \not\models \phi\}$ and $\mathcal{S}(K, \phi) = \{K' \subseteq K \mid C(K') = c(K, \phi), K'^* \not\models \phi\}$. We are also interested in the set $\mathcal{S}(K, \neg\mu)$ and $\mathcal{S}(K, \mu)$. The first set is the set of subsets K' of K that are consistent with μ (i.e., $K'^* \not\models \neg\mu$) and with the maximum compatibility degree $c(K, \neg\mu)$, and the second is the set of subsets K' of K that do not entail μ (i.e., $K'^* \not\models \mu$) with the maximum compatibility degree $c(K, \mu)$.

As we use a selection function to determine the result of revision, forming the multiple subsets of K amy be returned, resulting in multiple candidates for revision results. A common practice to handle multiple candidates in classic belief revision is to intersect them. To avoid lost of information, we define the intersection of multiple possibilistic KBs as the intersection of their logical closures.

Given a possibilistic logic KB K, its logical consequences are the possibilistic formulas obtained by exhaustively applying the following inference rules [11]:

$$(\phi, \alpha), (\neg\phi \vee \psi, \beta) \vdash (\psi, min\{\alpha, \beta\})$$
$$(\phi, \alpha) \vdash (\phi, \beta) \text{ if } \beta \leq \alpha.$$

In theory, the second inference rule will lead to an infinite number of possibilistic formulas. In practice, however, for each propositional formula ϕ in K, we keep only the possibilistic formula (ϕ, α) that has the maximum weight α for ϕ. That is, if $\alpha_1 > \alpha_2$, then (ϕ, α_2) is omitted. In this way, the set of consequences of (ϕ, α) has a finite representation although it is essentially infinite.

Without loss of generality, in what follows, we assume K is logically closed, that is, K contains all of its logical consequences.

Now we are ready to give our compatibility degree-based framework cd-revision, for revising a possibilistic KB by a possibilistic formula.

Definition 2. *Let K be a possibilistic KB, (μ, α) be a possibilistic formula, and γ a selection function. The result of revising K by (μ, α), denoted as $K \circ (\mu, \alpha)$, is*

- $\bigcap \gamma(\mathcal{S}(K, \neg\mu)) \cup \{(\mu, \alpha)\}$*, if $K^* \nvDash \mu$; and*
- $\bigcap \{K' \cup \tilde{K}' \mid K' \in \gamma(\mathcal{S}(K, \mu))\} \cup \{(\mu, \alpha)\}$ *where $\tilde{K}' = \{(\phi, \beta') \mid (\phi, \beta) \in K \setminus K', \beta' = min(\alpha, \beta)\}$, otherwise.*

Note that cases 1 and 2 correspond to the first item, while case 3 corresponds to the second item in which $\tilde{K}'$ is obtained by revising the weights of certain formulas so that $K \circ (\mu, \alpha) \models_\pi (\mu, \alpha)$ holds. The basic idea of the possibilistic revision is similar to classical revision, that is, the revision of possibilistic K by (μ, α) is defined in terms of a generalised notion of "maximal subsets of K that are consistent with (μ, α)". However, the problem of possibilistic revision is more complex than classical revision in that we need to take care of weights of formulas while resolving inconsistency.

Existing approaches to possibilistic revision provide different definitions for the case when the new information (ϕ, α) is certain $(\alpha = 1)$ and when it is uncertain $(\alpha < 1)$. Definition 2 provides a unifying revision framework for both cases. In the following two subsections, we will discuss in detail the properties of our cd-revision in the two cases, and provide some further discussions on the definition of cd-revision as well as some examples.

4.2   Revision by Certain Information

When the new information (μ, α) is certain, i.e., $\alpha = 1$, case 3 (Sect. 4.1) does not occur. Thus, we have from Definition 2: $K \circ (\mu, 1) = \bigcap \gamma(\mathcal{S}(K, \neg\mu)) \cup \{(\mu, 1)\}$.

The next proposition shows that $c(K, \neg\mu)$ can be obtained from the inconsistency degree of the union of K and $\{(\mu, 1)\}$. It will be useful for computing the revision $K \circ (\mu, 1)$. The following proposition shows that the maximal compatibility in this case can be obtained via inconsistency degree.

Proposition 2. *Given a possibilistic KB K and a propositional formula ϕ, then*
$c(K, \phi) = 1 - Inc(K \cup \{(\neg\phi, 1)\}) = N(\phi)$.

The following example shows that cd-revision is able to avoid the "drowning effect" occurring in some existing approaches to revision by certain information [5,7].

Example 2. *Let $K = \{(p \vee r, 0.9), (p \vee \neg q, 0.8), (\neg r, 0.8)\}$ and $\mu = \neg p$. We have $c(K, \neg\mu) = 0.2$ and $S(K, \neg\mu) = \{\{(p \vee r, 0.9), (p \vee \neg q, 0.8)\}, \{(p \vee r, 0.9)\}\}$. Taking the selection function γ_{max}, the result of revising K by $(\mu, 1)$ is $K \circ (\neg p, 1) = \{(p \vee r, 0.9), (p \vee \neg q, 0.8), (\neg p, 1)\}$.*
On the other hand, both approaches in [5, 7] suffer from the drowning effect since they discard $(p \vee \neg q, 0.8)$.

The following result relates the necessity degree of a formula in the result of revision to those of the same formula in the selected subsets of K.

Proposition 3. *Let K be a possibilistic KB, μ and ϕ be two propositional formulas.*
Then the necessity degree of ϕ w.r.t. $K \circ (\mu, 1)$ is $N(\phi) = min\{N'(\phi) \mid K' \in \gamma(S(K, \neg\mu))$ and $N'(\phi)$ is the necessity degree of ϕ w.r.t.$K'\}$.

Proof. Suppose two knowledge bases K' and K'' are elements of $\gamma(S(K, \neg\mu))$. Let $K' \models_\pi (\phi, \alpha)$, $K'' \models_\pi (\phi, \beta)$, and $\alpha \geq \beta$. Following the inference rules above, we have $(\phi, \alpha) \models (\phi, \beta)$. Therefore, $N(\phi) = min\{N'(\phi) \mid K' \in \gamma(S(K, \neg\mu))$ and $N'(\phi)$ is the necessity degree of ϕ w.r.t.$K'\}$. ∎

By the above proposition, it is easy to see the following corollary, which relates the possibility distribution to those of the selected subsets of K.

Corollary 2. *Let K be a possibilistic KB, μ be a propositional formula and π be the most specific possibility distribution of $K \circ (\mu, 1)$. Then, for each interpretation I, $\pi(I) = max\{\pi'_{K'}(I) \mid K' \in \gamma(S(K, \neg\mu))\}$ where $\pi'_{K'}$ is the least specific possibility distribution of K'.*

4.3   Revision by Uncertain Information

When the new information (μ, α) is uncertain, i.e., $0 < \alpha < 1$, in contrast to the case of revision by certain information, we need to take care of formula weights as well as inconsistency. In particular, the necessity degree of μ in the result of revision must be $N(\mu) = \alpha$. This difference is reflected in case 3 in Sect. 4.1 and the second item of Definition 2. In this subsection, we will focus on this case, i.e., when the initial KB entails μ.

Given the selection function, in this case, the result of revision is determined by the set $S(K, \mu)$, which consists of the subsets of K that do not entail μ and is in turn determined by the maximum compatibility degree $c(K, \mu)$. As shown in Proposition 2, $c(K, \mu) = 1 - Inc(K \cup \{(\neg\mu, 1)\})$.

Existing approaches [5,7] also suffer from the drowning effect when revising a possibilistic KB K by uncertain information (μ, α), especially when K entails μ. In this case all formulas in K with weight less or equal to $c(K, \mu)$ would be changed. Such changes are often unnecessary and can be avoided by cd-revision, as shown in the following example.

Example 3. *Let* $K = \{(p \vee \neg r, 0.9), (r, 0.8), (a, 0.8)\}$ *and* $\mu = p$. *We have* $c(K, \mu) = 0.2$ *and* $\mathcal{S}(K, \mu) = \{\{(p \vee \neg r, 0.9), (a, 0.8)\}, \{(p \vee \neg r, 0.9)\}\}$. *Taking the selection function* γ_{max}, *the result of revising* K *by* $(p, 0, 9)$ *is* $K \circ (p, 0.9) = \{(p, 0.9), (p \vee \neg r, 0.9), (r, 0.8), (a, 0.8)\}$, *where all the initial weights are preserved. The result of revising* K *by* $(p, 0, 3)$ *is* $K \circ (p, 0.3) = \{(p, 0.3), (p \vee \neg r, 0.9), (r, 0.3), (a, 0.8)\}$, *where only initial formula* $(r, 0.8)$ *is changed to* $(r, 0.3)$. *This is because only* r *is relevant to the necessity degree of* p.

However, methods in [7] will also change the weight of a *to 0.3, which is unnecessary.*

5   Revision Algorithm

In this section, we present an algorithm for our revision approach with a specific selection function γ_{max}. For the case where the initial possibilistic KB K does not entail μ (i.e., the first item in Definition 2), the revision operator behaves in a similar way as classic belief revision and hence can be computed by adapting algorithms for classic belief revision. The interesting and challenging case is when K does entail μ (i.e., the second item in Definition 2).

The algorithm manages a set $\mathcal{S}$ of subsets of K such that each subset does not entail μ if K^* entails μ or does not entail $\neg \mu$ when K^* does not entail μ. Initially, $\mathcal{S}$ contains only the empty set (line 1); then the algorithm incrementally extends the sets in $\mathcal{S}$ till each set has the maximum compatibility degree. This is achieved by first dividing the formulas in K into m tiers according to their weights (lines 2 and 4), then attempting to add the formulas (in decreasing order of their weights) to the sets S in $\mathcal{S}$, as long as the extended set $S \cup T$ does not entail μ if K^* entails μ (lines 6–7), or as long as the extended set $S \cup T$ does not entail $\neg \mu$ if K^* does not entail μ. Finally, $\mathcal{S}$ consists of all the subsets of K that does not entail μ if K^* entails μ or does not entail $\neg \mu$ if K^* does not entail μ. The sets in $\mathcal{S}$ will have the maximum compatibility degree, that is $\mathcal{S}(K, \mu)$ in Sect. 4.1. The rest of the algorithm (lines 12–16) implements the second item of Definition 2 and returns the result of revision respectively.

Example 4. *(Example 3 cont.) To revise* K *by* $(p, 0.3)$, *Algorithm 1 first divides the formulas in* K *into two tiers* $T_1 = \{(p \vee \neg r, 0.9)\}$ *and* $T_2 = \{(r, 0.8), (a, 0.8)\}$. *For* $i = 1$ *and* $S = \emptyset$, *it computes in line 7* $T_S = \{\{(p \vee \neg r, 0.9)\}\}$, *and adds it to* $\mathcal{S}$ *in line 10. As a result, the new* $\mathcal{S} = \{\{(p \vee \neg r, 0.9)\}\}$. *For* $i = 2$ *and* $S = \{(p \vee \neg r, 0.9)\}$, $T_S = \{\{(a, 0.8)\}\}$, *and* $\mathcal{S} = \{\{(p \vee \neg r, 0.9), (a, 0.8)\}\}$. *After this, the algorithm takes (line 12)* $S = \{(p \vee \neg r, 0.9), (a, 0.8)\}$ *and* $D_S = \{(r, 0.8)\}$, *and modifies (lines 14–15)* D_S *to* $D'_S = \{(r, 0.3)\}$. *Finally, the KB* $\{(p, 0.3), (p \vee \neg r, 0.9), (a, 0.8), (r, 0.3)\}$ *is returned, which is the revision result defined in Definition 2.*

Algorithm 1. Computing the result of revision

Input: A possibilistic KB K and a possibilistic formula (μ, α)
Output: $K \circ (\mu, \alpha)$
1: initially, assign $\mathcal{S} := \{\emptyset\}$ and $i := 1$
2: let $l_1 > l_2 > \cdots > l_m > 0$ be the sequence of all the distinct weights in K
3: **while** $i \leq m$ **do**
4:      $T_i := \{(\phi, \beta) \in K \mid \beta = l_i\}$
5:      **for all** $S \in \mathcal{S}$ **do**
6:          **if** $K^* \models \mu$ **then**
7:              $\mathcal{T}_S := \{T \subseteq T_i \mid T^* \cup S^* \not\models \mu, \text{ and } T'^* \cup S^* \models \mu \text{ for all } T' s.t. \, T \subset T' \subseteq T_i\}$
8:          **else**
9:              $\mathcal{T}_S := \{T \subseteq T_i \mid T^* \cup S^* \not\models \neg\mu, \text{ and } T'^* \cup S^* \models \neg\mu \text{ for all } T' s.t. \, T \subset T' \subseteq T_i\}$
10:      $\mathcal{S} := \{S \cup T \mid S \in \mathcal{S}, T \in \mathcal{T}_S\}$
11:      $i := i + 1$
12: **if** $K^* \models \mu$ **then**
13:      **for all** $S \in \mathcal{S}$ and $D_S = K \setminus S$ **do**
14:          **for all** $(\phi, \beta) \in D_S$ **do**
15:              **if** $\beta > \alpha$ **then** $D_S := D_S \setminus \{(\phi, \beta)\} \cup \{(\phi, \alpha)\}$
16:      **return** $\bigcap \{S \cup D_S \mid S \in \mathcal{S}\} \cup \{(\mu, \alpha)\}$
17: **else**
18:      **return** $\bigcap \{S \mid S \in \mathcal{S}\} \cup \{(\mu, \alpha)\}$

When revising K by (μ, α) in the case that K^* entails μ, the revision amounts to adjusting the weights of some formulas in K to α and adding (μ, α) to K. Algorithm 1 searches for the formulas in K whose weights need to be adjusted according to the definition of revision, that is, by computing $\gamma_{max}(\mathcal{S}(K, \mu))$ and checking the complements of the sets in $\gamma_{max}(\mathcal{S}(K, \mu))$. The following result shows that Algorithm 1 correctly computes the revision.

Proposition 4. *Let K be a possibilistic KB, (μ, α) be a formula and γ_{max} be the selection function. Then, Algorithm 1 returns $K \circ (\mu, \alpha)$.*

Proof. Let us consider the case such that $K^* \models \mu$. This could be proved by induction. For all formulas in K such that $l_1 > l_2 > \cdots > l_m > 0$ is the sequence of all the distinct weights in K. First consider when $m = 1$. In this case, $\gamma_{max}(\mathcal{S}(K, \mu))$ select all maximal subset of K such that its classical projection does not entail μ, this equals to $\mathcal{S}$ in Algorithm 1. Thus the result holds.

Now assume when $m = n$ the result holds, then for $m = n + 1$, if $K' = \{(\phi_i, \alpha_i) \mid \alpha_i \in \{l_1, \ldots, l_n\}\} \not\models \mu$ then $\gamma_{max}(\mathcal{S}(K, \mu))$ in Definition 2 contains K' and maximal subsets of $\{(\phi_i, \alpha_i) \mid \alpha_i = l_{n+1}\}$ which does not entail μ, this coincide with $\mathcal{S}$ in Algorithm 1. Next, if $K' = \{(\phi_i, \alpha_i) \mid \alpha_i \in \{l_1, \ldots, l_n\}\} \models \mu$, by induction, we have for all previous n layers, $\gamma_{max}(\mathcal{S}(K, \mu))$ and $\mathcal{S}$ in Algorithm 1 are equal. Moreover, adding formulas in the $n + 1$ level to sets in $\gamma_{max}(\mathcal{S}(K, \mu))$ will not change its compatibility degree since $l_{n+1} < l_n$. Thus the result holds for $m = n + 1$. ∎

It is also possible to slightly change lines 7 and 9 in this algorithm to handle other selection functions. For example, let $\mathcal{T}_S := \{T \subseteq T_i \mid T^* \cup S^* \not\models \mu$ and $T'^* \cup S^* \models \mu$ for all $T's.t.\ |T| < |T'|$ and $T' \subseteq T_i\}$, and this corresponds to cardinality-maximal selection function.

According to the algorithm, if there are m distinct weights in K, we need to apply line 7 or 9 m times. Suppose we use γ_{max} as selection function, then the complexity of this algorithm is not much harder than that of full meet base revision operator in [17]. That is, it needs at most $[\mathcal{O}(\log n)]$ calls to a NP oracle to generate a revised base.

6   Properties of the Proposed Possibilistic Revision

In this section, we present some logical properties of our possibilistic revision. We first adapt the well know KM postulates to revision of possibilistic revision and show that they are satisfied by our cd-revision (for both certain and uncertain information). Then we study properties that characterise the change of formula weights in possibilistic revision.

AGM postulates are commonly accepted as the best set of postulates for capturing the intuition behind rational belief revision. A reformulation of these postulates is given in [14], which are often referred to as the *KM postulates*.

The KM postulates have been adapted for belief revision in [15,18], however the adapted postulates are either only defined for revision by certain information, or only take into account uncertainty input if it leads to stronger certainty. Here, we further generalise the postulates for revision by both certain and uncertain information.

Proposition 5. *Let $\circ$ be the cd-revision operator defined by the selection function γ_{max}. Then the following statements hold:*

(R1) $K \circ (\mu, \alpha) \models_\pi (\mu, \alpha)$.

(R2) *If μ is consistent, then $K \circ (\mu, \alpha)$ is consistent.*

(R3) *If $\mu_1 \equiv \mu_2$ then $K \circ (\mu_1, \alpha) \equiv K \circ (\mu_2, \alpha)$.*

(R4) $((K \circ (\mu, \alpha)) \cup (\phi, \beta))^* \models (K \circ (\mu \wedge \phi, min(\alpha, \beta)))^*$.

(R5) *If $(K \circ (\mu, \alpha))^* \models \phi$ and $(K \circ (\phi, \beta))^* \models \mu$, then $(K \circ (\mu, \alpha))^* \equiv (K \circ (\phi, \beta))^*$.*

(R6) $(K \circ (\mu, \alpha))^* \cup (K \circ (\phi, \beta))^* \models^* (K \circ (\mu \vee \phi, max(\alpha, \beta)))^*$.

The (R1) says the new information is firmly believed "as is", that is, the necessity degree of the new formula μ will keep the same after revision. In this way, we are seeing the new information as a constraint. (R2) says the revision result will be consistent. Notice we do not have $K \circ (\mu, \alpha) \equiv K \cup \{(\mu, \alpha)\}$ if $K \cup \{(\mu, \alpha)\}$ is consistent in general. This is due to the fact that formula weights in K can be changed during revision. However, we do have a modified version of the postulate in place: $K \circ (\mu, \alpha) \equiv K \cup \{(\mu, \alpha)\}$ if $K \cup \{(\mu, \alpha)\}$ is consistent and $N(\mu) \leq \alpha$ in K. (R3) is a weakening version of the syntactic independent postulate. (R4) − (R6) are natural variants of KM postulates in possibilistic revision.

In the case when $K^* \models \neg\mu$, the correctness of these postulates have been shown in [18]. In addition, for $K^* \models \mu$, the cd-revision operator will only change the weights, not the the classic formulas. Thus the postulates still hold. However, as the problem of drowning effect is our focus, we are more interested in the formula necessity degree changes before and after revision. We now consider the logical properties of cd-revision that characterise the change of formula necessity degrees (as well as formula change).

First, we consider the case when $K^* \models \neg\mu$. Recall that the inconsistency degree $Inc(K \cup \{\mu, \alpha\})$ can be defined in terms of compatibility degree as shown in Corollary 1. Thus, we have the following proposition.

Proposition 6. *Let $\circ$ be the cd-revision operator defined by the selection function γ_{max}. If $K^* \models \neg\mu$. Then the following statements hold:*

$(R7-)$ *If $K \models_\pi (\phi, \beta)$, $\beta \leq Inc(K \cup \{\mu, \alpha\})$ and $((K \circ (\mu, \alpha))_{\geq\beta})^* \models \phi$, then $K \circ (\mu, \alpha) \models_\pi (\phi, \beta)$.*
$(R7+)$ *If $K \models_\pi (\phi, \beta)$, $\beta > Inc(K \cup \{\mu, \alpha\})$, then $K \circ (\mu, \alpha) \models_\pi (\phi, \beta)$.*

$(R7-)$ and $(R7+)$ characterise the change of necessity degrees in possibilistic revision in case when $K^* \models \neg\mu$. Specifically, $(R7-)$ says if a formula ϕ can be entailed before and after revision, and its necessity degree is lower or equal to the inconsistency degree, then its necessity degree will not be changed after revision. This is an advantage compared to existing revision methods that suffer from the drowning effect. In those methods, all formulas with necessity degree lower than or equal to $Inc(K)$ will be removed. $(R7+)$ says if a formula ϕ can be entailed before revision, and its necessity degree is higher than the inconsistency degree, then its necessity degree will not change after revision.

Now we consider the case where $K^* \models \mu$, in this case, we have.

Proposition 7. *Let $\circ$ be the cd-revision operator defined by the selection function γ_{max}. If $K^* \models \mu$, then the following statements hold:*

$(R8-)$ *If $K \models_\pi (\phi, \beta), \beta \leq \alpha$, then $K \circ (\mu, \alpha) \models_\pi (\phi, \beta)$.*
$(R8+)$ *If $K \models_\pi (\phi, \beta), \beta > \alpha$, then $K \circ (\mu, \alpha) \models (\phi, \alpha)$.*

$(R8-)$ and $(R8+)$ characterise the necessity degree changes before and after revision if $K^* \models \mu$. Specifically, $(R8-)$ states that if a formula ϕ's necessity degree is lower than or equal to the weight of the revision formula μ, then its necessity degree will not be changed. On the contrary, $(R8+)$ states that if a formula's necessity degree is higher than the weight of the revision formula μ before revision, then its necessity degree might be lower after revision. Note that we use $\models$ instead of $\models_\pi$. This is because not all formulas with higher necessity degree than α will be lowered to α, compared to existing revision methods where all necessity degrees of such formulas will be lowered to α, our cd-revision operator is more fine-grained.

7   Relation to Other Possibilistic Revisions

As explained previously, our possibilistic revision is a generalisation of classic belief revision if each propositional formula ϕ is regarded as a possibilistic formula with weight 1, i.e., $(\phi, 1)$. In this section, we show that the approaches to possibilistic revision in [7,18] can be also embedded in our compatibility degree based framework.

Firstly, we show that compatibility degree based revision of a possibilistic KB by a certain formula is expressible in possibilistic logic.

We first present the following lemma which states that γ_{min} can always return a unique (minimum) element.

Lemma 2. *Let K be a possibilistic KB and $(\mu, 1)$ be a certain formula. Then the set $\mathcal{S}(K, \neg\mu)$ always has a (unique) minimum element.*

Proof. Let $K_0 = \{(\phi, \alpha) \mid (\phi, \alpha) \in K, \alpha > 1 - c(K, \neg\mu)\}$. Then $C(K_0) = c(K, \neg\mu)$. Also, $K_0^* \not\models \neg\mu$. Thus, $K_0 \in \mathcal{S}(K, \neg\mu)$.

On the other hand, if $K' \in \mathcal{S}(K, \neg\mu)$, then $C(K') = c(K, \neg\mu)$, which implies that every formula whose weight is strictly greater than $1 - c(K, \neg\mu)$ must be in K'. That is, $K_0 \subseteq K'$ and thus K_0 is the minimum element of $\mathcal{S}(K, \neg\mu)$.   ∎

In [7] a revision operator is defined for both certain input and uncertain input. For convenience, we name it as b-revision. We will show that their revision for certain input is equivalent to ours. Example 3 demonstrates that b-revision for uncertain inputs is different from our cd-revision in general. However, we will also show that b-revision can be characterised using our compatibility degree based approach.

Proposition 8. *Let K be a possibilistic KB and $(\mu, 1)$ be a possibilistic formula. If the selection function is γ_{min}, then the compatibility degree based revision of K by $(\mu, 1)$ coincides with the revision in [7].*

Proposition 9. *Let K be a possibilistic logic KB K and (μ, α) be a possibilistic formula with (μ, α) such that K^* is inconsistent with $\neg\mu$. Set $S = \gamma_{min}(\mathcal{S}(K, \mu))$ and define $K \odot (\mu, \alpha) = \{(\mu, \alpha)\} \cup S \cup \{(\phi \vee \neg\mu, \alpha) \mid (\phi, \alpha) \in K \setminus S)\}$. Then $K \odot (\mu, \alpha)$ coincides with b-revision.*

This result follows directly from Corollary 1 and Lemma 2.

A syntactic revision operator for possibilistic revision by certain information (abbreviated q-revision) is proposed by Qi in [18]. We show that q-revision can also be embedded in our compatibility degree based approach.

Proposition 10. *Let K be a possibilistic KB, $(\mu, 1)$ be a certain formula and the selection function be γ_{max}. Then q-revision coincides with cd-revision.*

The above result implies that the syntactical algorithm (Algorithm 2) in [18] computes our cd-revision. So, cd-revision is actually a semantic counterpart of q-revision.

Moreover, some revision methods developed for other prioritized/stratified KBs can also be embedded in our cd-revision framework by using different selection functions. We note that each stratified knowledge base $K_S = (K_1, K_2, \ldots, K_m)$ be expressed as a possibilistic logic base $K = (K'_1, K'_2, \ldots, K'_m)$ where $K'_i = \{(\phi, \alpha) \mid \phi \in K_i, \alpha = l_i\}$ and $l_1 > l_2 > \cdots > l_m > 0$ is a sequence of distinct weights.

In [9,16], the authors introduced the discrimin revision operator $\circ_{discrimin}$ for stratified KBs. In Definition 2 in Sect. 4, by choosing the selection function as γ_{max}, we can define a cd-revision operator $\circ_m$ as $K \circ_m (\mu, 1) = \cap\{K' \cup \{(\mu, 1)\} \mid K' \in \gamma_{max}(\mathcal{S}(K, \neg\mu))\}$. Then we have the following proposition.

Proposition 11. *Let K_S be a stratified knowledge base, K be its associated possibilistic logic, and $\circ_{discrimin}$ be the discrimin revision operator. Then $K_S \circ_{discrimin} \mu = (K \circ_m (\mu, 1))^*$.*

Aside from selection function γ_{max}, it is possible to use cardinality-maximal selection function γ_{cmax}. Thus we are able to define another cd-revision operator $\circ_{cm}$ as $K \circ_{cm} (\mu, 1) = \cap\{K' \cup \{(\mu, 1)\} \mid K' \in \gamma_{cmax}(\mathcal{S}(K, \neg\mu))\}$. It is interesting to observe that this cd-revision operator is essentially the lex-preferred revision operator $\circ_{leximin}$ for stratified knowledge bases in [4].

Proposition 12. *Let K_S be a stratified knowledge base, K be its associated possibilistic logic, and $\circ_{leximin}$ be the lex-preferred revision operator. Then $K_S \circ_{leximin} \mu = (K \circ_{cm} (\mu, 1))^*$.*

The above results show that several major revision operator for certain inputs in stratified/prioritised knowledge bases can be seen as special cases or variations of cd-revision in possibilistic logic.

In addition, there are some other methods for revising stratified/prioritised KBs such as [4,9]. These revisions are quite different from ours in that they aim to provide a more fine-grained result for belief revision in propositional logic. Thus, in their approaches, the preference/stratification information is used only for better resolving inconsistency. For this reason, the result of their revision is still a KB in propositional logic, while possibilistic revisions including the proposed cd-revsiion, b-revision and q-revision require the revision result is a possibilistic KB.

8   Conclusion

In this paper, we have proposed the notion of compatibility degrees for better characterising or as an alternative measure for the inconsistency degree of a possibilistic KB. Based on this notion, we have developed a novel syntactic approach to revision in possibilistic logic, which serves as a unifying framework for defining possibilistic revision by both certain and uncertain new information. Significantly, our approach is able to lessen the undesired drowning effect. We have shown that our cd-revision satisfies major postulates adapted from classic belief revision. We have also developed a sound and complete algorithm for computing the results of revision. Finally, we have shown that our approach subsumes two major approaches for possibilistic revision.

As an on-going work, we are looking into establishing representation theorem for cd-revision framework. This is not straightforward, as possibilistic logic with disjunction is not a straightforward extension of possibilistic logic [13], and disjunction among possibilistic KBs may be required in establishing the representation theorem. To this end, we might need to consider alternate postulates or methods other than intersection of candidates. Also, when revised by uncertain input, degrees for formulas in a KB can decrease. This kind of change is more like contraction than revision. Therefore, comparing this approach with contraction operators in belief revision is also interesting. Moreover, a more detailed analysis about different selection functions and their properties is also desired. Finally, our current algorithm implements the definition in a direct manner, thus optimised search methods for identifying formulas whose weights need to be adjusted can improve efficiency of the algorithm.

Acknowledgement. We would like to thank three anonymous referees for their constructive comments. This work was supported by Australian Research Council (ARC) under grant DP130102302.

References

1. Alchourrón, C., Gärdenfors, P., Makinson, D.: On the logic of theory change: partial meet contraction and revision functions. J. Symb. Log. **50**(2), 510–530 (1985)
2. Bauters, K., Schockaert, S., Cock, M., Vermeir, D.: Possible and necessary answer sets of possibilistic answer set programs. In: Proceedings of the 24th International Conference on Tools with Artificial Intelligence, ICTAI, pp. 836–843 (2012)
3. Bauters, K., Schockaert, S., Cock, M., Vermeir, D.: Semantics for possibilistic answer set programs: uncertain rules versus rules with uncertain conclusions. Int. J. Approx. Reason. **55**(2), 739–761 (2014)
4. Benferhat, S., Cayrol, C., Dubois, D., Lang, J., Prade, H.: Inconsistency management and prioritized syntax-based entailment. IJCAI **93**, 640–645 (1993)
5. Benferhat, S., da Costa Pereira, C., Tettamanzi, A.: Hybrid possibilistic conditioning for revision under weighted inputs. In: 20th European Conference on Artificial Intelligence, pp. 151–156 (2012)
6. Benferhat, S., da Costa Pereira, C., Tettamanzi, A.: Syntactic computation of hybrid possibilistic conditioning under uncertain inputs. In: Proceedings of the Twenty-Third international joint conference on Artificial Intelligence, pp. 739–745 (2013)
7. Benferhat, S., Dubois, D., Prade, H., Williams, M.: A practical approach to revising prioritized knowledge bases. Stud. Logica **70**(1), 105–130 (2002)
8. Benferhat, S., Dubois, D., Prade, H., Williams, M.: A framework for iterated belief revision using possibilistic counterparts to jeffrey's rule. Fundamenta Informaticae **99**(2), 147 (2010)
9. Brewka, G.: Preferred subtheories: an extended logical framework for default reasoning. IJCAI **89**, 1043–1048 (1989)
10. Dubois, D., Lang, J., Prade, H.: Possibilistic logic (1994)

11. Dubois, D., Lang, J., Prade, H.: Possibilistic logic. In: Gabbay, D.M., et al. (eds.) Handbook of Logic in Artificial Intelligence and Logic Programming, vol. 3, pp. 439–513. Oxford University Press, New York (1997)
12. Dubois, D., Prade, H.: A synthetic view of belief revision with uncertain inputs in the framework of possibility theory. Int. J. Approx. Reason. **17**, 295–324 (1997)
13. Dubois, D., Prade, H.: Generalized Possibilistic Logic, pp. 428–432. Springer, Berlin (2011)
14. Katsuno, H., Mendelzon, A.: Propositional knowledge base revision and minimal change. Artif. Intell. **52**(3), 263–294 (1992)
15. Ma, J., Liu, W.: A framework for managing uncertain inputs: an axiomization of rewarding. Int. J. Approx. Reason. **52**(7), 917–934 (2011)
16. Nebel, B.: Belief revision and default reasoning: syntax-based approaches. In: KR, pp. 417–428 (1991)
17. Nebel, B.: How hard is it to revise a belief base? In: Dubois, D., Prade, H. (eds.) Handbook of Defeasible Reasoning and Uncertainty Management Systems. Springer, Netherlands (1998)
18. Qi, G.: A semantic approach for iterated revision in possibilistic logic. In: Proceedings of the 23rd AAAI Conference on Artificial Intelligence, pp. 523–528 (2008)
19. Qi, G., Wang, K.: Conflict-based belief revision operators in possibilistic logic. In: AAAI (2012)

Proving Craig and Lyndon Interpolation Using Labelled Sequent Calculi

Roman Kuznets[✉]

Institut für Computersprachen, TU Wien, Vienna, Austria
roman@logic.at

Abstract. Interpolation is a fundamental logical property with applications in mathematics, computer science, and artificial intelligence. In this paper, we develop a general method of translating a semantic description of modal logics via Kripke models into a constructive proof of the Lyndon interpolation property (LIP) via labelled sequents. Using this method we demonstrate that all frame conditions representable as Horn formulas imply the LIP and that all 15 logics of the modal cube, as well as the infinite family of transitive Geach logics, enjoy the LIP.

Keywords: Craig interpolation · Lyndon interpolation · Labelled sequents · Modal logic · Geach formulas

1 Introduction

Interpolation is a fundamental logical property with applications in mathematics, computer science, and artificial intelligence. For instance, *uniform interpolation* is related to *variable forgetting*. The Craig Interpolation Property (CIP) states that, for any valid fact $A \rightarrow B$ of the logic, there must exist an *interpolant C* in the common language of A and B such that both $A \rightarrow C$ and $C \rightarrow B$ are valid. The CIP is used, e.g., to prove correctness of algorithms for reasoning about knowledge bases with overlap in content [1]. The Lyndon Interpolation Property (LIP) strengthens the CIP by requiring that not just *propositional atoms* in C but their *literals*, i.e., polarized propositional atoms, be common to A and B. The LIP and CIP are known to imply the Beth definability property, which can be applied to rewritings in description logics [4], commonly used in knowledge representation [18].

In this paper, we develop a general method of translating a semantic description of a modal logic (with classical propositional background) via Kripke models into a constructive proof of the LIP. Hence, the *common language* is to be understood as common literals. While we formulate our results for the LIP, they are directly applicable to the weaker CIP too. The proof-theoretic method of proving the LIP is to construct an interpolant by induction on a derivation of

This material is based upon work supported by the Austrian Science Fund (FWF) Lise Meitner Grant M 1770-N25.

L. Michael and A. Kakas (Eds.): JELIA 2016, LNAI 10021, pp. 320–335, 2016.
DOI: 10.1007/978-3-319-48758-8_21

(a representation of) $A \to B$ in a suitable analytic sequent calculus. The method is modular: if the sequent system is strengthened by an extra rule, only this additional rule needs to be checked to extend the LIP to the resulting stronger logic.

Until recently, a major weakness of the method was the limited expressivity of analytic sequent calculi. Recent advances extended the reach of the method to nested sequents ([6]) and hypersequents ([12]). These results were unified and generalized to a wide range of *internal* sequent-like formalisms in [13]. In this paper, we develop a similar method for the *external* formalism of labelled sequents[1], which is strictly more expressive [8] and was just recently shown in [5] to capture all modal logics complete w.r.t. first-order definable frame conditions. Moreover, labelled sequent rules can be effectively generated from these frame conditions. In this paper, we harness this strength by outlining sufficient criteria on the frame conditions to guarantee the LIP. We also provide an algorithm for constructing an interpolant.

The paper is structured as follows. In Sect. 2, we describe the formalism of labelled sequents (closely following [16]) and outline the method of proving the LIP using labelled sequents. In Sect. 3, we show how to construct an interpolant for all the labelled rules of the basic normal modal logic K. In Sect. 4, we prove that all logics complete w.r.t. quantifier-free Horn formulas enjoy the LIP and argue that the restriction to Horn clauses is essential. We also extend these results to labelled sequents with equality atoms. In Sect. 5, we extend the method to several common types of Horn-like geometric rules and apply our findings to the infinite family of Geach logics. Section 6 contains related work, a summary of our results, and a discussion of future research.

2   Interpolation for Labelled Sequent Calculi

Definition 1 (Labelled sequent). *A labelled sequent, from now on a sequent, is an object $\Gamma \Rightarrow \Delta$ with Γ and Δ being multisets[2] of labelled formulas $\mathsf{w} : A$ and relational atoms $\mathsf{w}R\mathsf{o}$, where w and o are labels from a fixed countable set Lab and A is a modal formula in negation normal form (NNF)[3].*

Definition 2 (Kripke model). *A Kripke frame is (W, R) where $W \neq \varnothing$ and $R \subseteq W \times W$. A Kripke model $\mathcal{M}$ is (W, R, V) where $V : \mathsf{Prop} \to 2^W$ is a function on the set Prop of propositional atoms. The satisfaction relation between $w \in W$ and modal formulas is defined recursively: $\mathcal{M}, w \Vdash P$ iff $w \in V(P)$; $\mathcal{M}, w \Vdash \overline{P}$ iff $w \notin V(P)$; $\wedge$ and $\vee$ behave classically; $\mathcal{M}, w \Vdash \square A$ iff $\mathcal{M}, u \Vdash A$ whenever wRu; $\mathcal{M}, w \Vdash \Diamond A$ iff $\mathcal{M}, u \Vdash A$ for some u such that wRu.*

---

[1] Unlike internal formalisms, external ones cannot generally be translated into formulas, typically because of the essential use of semantic elements, e.g., Kripke worlds.

[2] The method also works for sequence- and set-based sequents.

[3] NNF is used here to simplify the notation rather than out of necessity and means that negation is restricted to propositional atoms, creating two literals P and $\overline{P}$ for each atom. Primary connectives are $\wedge$, $\vee$, $\square$, and $\Diamond$. Negation $\overline{A}$ is a function of a formula A defined via De Morgan laws. $A \to B := \overline{A} \vee B$.

Table 1. Initial sequents

$$\mathsf{w}:P, \Gamma \Rightarrow \Delta, \mathsf{w}:P \qquad \mathsf{w}:\overline{P}, \Gamma \Rightarrow \Delta, \mathsf{w}:\overline{P} \qquad \mathsf{w}:\bot, \Gamma \Rightarrow \Delta$$
$$\mathsf{w}:P, \mathsf{w}:\overline{P}, \Gamma \Rightarrow \Delta \qquad \Gamma \Rightarrow \Delta, \mathsf{w}:P, \mathsf{w}:\overline{P} \qquad \Gamma \Rightarrow \Delta, \mathsf{w}:\top$$

Table 2. Propositional rules for NNF

$$\frac{\mathsf{w}:A, \mathsf{w}:B, \Gamma \Rightarrow \Delta}{\mathsf{w}:A \wedge B, \Gamma \Rightarrow \Delta} L\wedge \qquad \frac{\Gamma \Rightarrow \Delta, \mathsf{w}:A \quad \Gamma \Rightarrow \Delta, \mathsf{w}:B}{\Gamma \Rightarrow \Delta, \mathsf{w}:A \wedge B} R\wedge$$

$$\frac{\mathsf{w}:A, \Gamma \Rightarrow \Delta \quad \mathsf{w}:B, \Gamma \Rightarrow \Delta}{\mathsf{w}:A \vee B, \Gamma \Rightarrow \Delta} L\vee \qquad \frac{\Gamma \Rightarrow \Delta, \mathsf{w}:A, \mathsf{w}:B}{\Gamma \Rightarrow \Delta, \mathsf{w}:A \vee B} R\vee$$

Definition 3 (Labelled semantics). *An interpretation into a Kripke model* $\mathcal{M} = (W, R, V)$ *is a map* $[\![\cdot]\!] : \mathsf{Lab} \to W$ *from labels to worlds.* $\vDash [\![\Gamma \Rightarrow \Delta]\!]$, *if the following holds: if* $\mathcal{M}, [\![\mathsf{w}]\!] \Vdash A$ *for each* $\mathsf{w} : A \in \Gamma$ *and* $[\![\mathsf{w}]\!] R [\![\mathsf{o}]\!]$ *for each* $\mathsf{w}R\mathsf{o} \in \Gamma$, *then* $\mathcal{M}, [\![\mathsf{u}]\!] \Vdash B$ *for some* $\mathsf{u} : B \in \Delta$. *A sequent* $\Gamma \Rightarrow \Delta$ *is valid in a class* $\mathcal{C}_\mathsf{L}$ *of Kripke models, written* $\mathcal{C}_\mathsf{L} \vDash \Gamma \Rightarrow \Delta$, *if* $\vDash [\![\Gamma \Rightarrow \Delta]\!]$ *for each* $\mathcal{M} \in \mathcal{C}_\mathsf{L}$ *and each interpretation* $[\![\cdot]\!]$ *into* $\mathcal{M}$.

The rules of the calculus **SK** for the basic normal modal logic K can be found in Tables 1, 2 and 3 (this calculus is a trivial modification of the calculus **G3K** from [16, Table 11.5] for the NNF language). As is standard, we omit initial sequents $\mathsf{w}R\mathsf{o}, \Gamma \Rightarrow \Delta, \mathsf{w}R\mathsf{o}$, which do not affect completeness because the satisfaction relation ignores relational atoms in the consequent. Unless stated otherwise, from now on $\mathcal{C}_\mathsf{L}$ stands for an arbitrary class of Kripke models.

We replace a formula-level interpolation statement with a sequent-level Component wise Interpolation Property (CWIP). While the concept of the CWIP for (labelled) sequents is the same as for nested sequents and hypersequents, the labelled notation facilitates a much simpler presentation. Interpolants are objects of the following type:

Definition 4 (Multiformula). *The grammar*

$$\mho ::= \mathsf{w} : C \mid (\mho \mathbin{\textcircled{\wedge}} \mho) \mid (\mho \mathbin{\textcircled{\vee}} \mho)$$

defines multiformulas, *where* $\mathsf{w} : C$ *is a labelled formula. For an interpretation* $[\![\cdot]\!]$ *into a model* $\mathcal{M}$, *we say*

1. $\vDash [\![\mathsf{w} : C]\!]$ *iff* $\mathcal{M}, [\![\mathsf{w}]\!] \Vdash C$;
2. $\vDash [\![\mho_1 \mathbin{\textcircled{\vee}} \mho_2]\!]$ *iff* $\vDash [\![\mho_i]\!]$ *for some* $i = 1, 2$;
3. $\vDash [\![\mho_1 \mathbin{\textcircled{\wedge}} \mho_2]\!]$ *iff* $\vDash [\![\mho_i]\!]$ *for each* $i = 1, 2$.

Thus, the external $\textcircled{\wedge}$ *and* $\textcircled{\vee}$ *on multiformulas correspond to* $\wedge$ *and* $\vee$ *on formulas.*

Table 3. Modal rules. For $L\Diamond$ and $R\Box$, the eigenvariable o does not occur in the conclusion

$$\frac{\mathsf{o}:A,\mathsf{w}:\Box A,\mathsf{wRo},\Gamma\Rightarrow\Delta}{\mathsf{w}:\Box A,\mathsf{wRo},\Gamma\Rightarrow\Delta}\,L\Box \qquad\qquad \frac{\mathsf{wRo},\Gamma\Rightarrow\Delta,\mathsf{o}:A}{\Gamma\Rightarrow\Delta,\mathsf{w}:\Box A}\,R\Box$$

$$\frac{\mathsf{wRo},\mathsf{o}:A,\Gamma\Rightarrow\Delta}{\mathsf{w}:\Diamond A,\Gamma\Rightarrow\Delta}\,L\Diamond \qquad\qquad \frac{\mathsf{wRo},\Gamma\Rightarrow\Delta,\mathsf{w}:\Diamond A,\mathsf{o}:A}{\mathsf{wRo},\Gamma\Rightarrow\Delta,\mathsf{w}:\Diamond A}\,R\Diamond$$

Table 4. Interpolating initial sequents

$$\mathsf{w}:P,\Gamma\xRightarrow{\mathsf{w}:P}\Delta,\mathsf{w}:P \qquad \mathsf{w}:\overline{P},\Gamma\xRightarrow{\mathsf{w}:\overline{P}}\Delta,\mathsf{w}:\overline{P} \qquad \mathsf{w}:\bot,\Gamma\xRightarrow{\mathsf{w}:\bot}\Delta$$

$$\mathsf{w}:P,\mathsf{w}:\overline{P},\Gamma\xRightarrow{\mathsf{w}:\bot}\Delta \qquad \Gamma\xRightarrow{\mathsf{w}:\top}\Delta,\mathsf{w}:P,\mathsf{w}:\overline{P} \qquad \Gamma\xRightarrow{\mathsf{w}:\top}\Delta,\mathsf{w}:\top$$

Definition 5 (Ant$_f$, Con$_f$, Ant$_r$). *For an interpretation $[\![\cdot]\!]$ into a model $\mathcal{M}$ and a multiset Γ of labelled formulas and relational atoms, we write*

$\vDash [\![\mathsf{Ant}_f(\Gamma)]\!]$ *iff* $\mathcal{M},[\![\mathsf{w}]\!]\Vdash A$ *for each* $\mathsf{w}:A\in\Gamma$,

$\vDash [\![\mathsf{Ant}_r(\Gamma)]\!]$ *iff* $[\![\mathsf{w}]\!]\,R\,[\![\mathsf{o}]\!]$ *for each* $\mathsf{wRo}\in\Gamma$, *and*

$\vDash [\![\mathsf{Con}_f(\Gamma)]\!]$ *iff* $\mathcal{M},[\![\mathsf{w}]\!]\Vdash A$ *for some* $\mathsf{w}:A\in\Gamma$.

Definition 6 (CWIP). *A multiformula $\mho$ is a $\mathcal{C}_L$-interpolant of $\Gamma\Rightarrow\Delta$, written $\Gamma\xRightarrow{\mho}\Delta$, if all of the following conditions hold:*

1. *each label w occurring in $\mho$ occurs in Γ or in a labelled formula from Δ;*
2. *each literal P or $\overline{P}$ occurring in $\mho$ occurs in both Γ and Δ;*
3. *for any interpretation $[\![\cdot]\!]$ into a model $\mathcal{M}\in\mathcal{C}_L$ with $\vDash [\![\mathsf{Ant}_r(\Gamma)]\!]$:*

$$\vDash [\![\mathsf{Ant}_f(\Gamma)]\!] \qquad\qquad implies \qquad \vDash [\![\mho]\!], \qquad\qquad (1)$$

$$\vDash [\![\mho]\!] \qquad\qquad implies \qquad \vDash [\![\mathsf{Con}_f(\Delta)]\!]. \qquad\qquad (2)$$

A calculus **SL** *has the CWIP w.r.t. $\mathcal{C}_L$ iff every* **SL**-*derivable sequent has a $\mathcal{C}_L$-interpolant.*

The modularity of the proof-theoretic method follows from the trivial.

Fact 7. *If $\mho$ is a $\mathcal{C}_L$-interpolant of $\Gamma\Rightarrow\Delta$, it is also a $\mathcal{C}'_L$-interpolant of the same sequent w.r.t. any class $\mathcal{C}'_L\subseteq\mathcal{C}_L$.*

Definition 8 (Duality). *We say that a labelled calculus* **SL** *has the* duality *property whenever*

$$\mathbf{SL}\vdash \mathsf{w}:A,\Gamma\Rightarrow\Delta \qquad iff \qquad \mathbf{SL}\vdash\Gamma\Rightarrow\Delta,\mathsf{w}:\overline{A}.$$

Theorem 9 (Reducing LIP to CWIP). *Let* **SL** *be a labelled calculus for a logic L such that* **SL** *has the duality property and invertible rule $R\lor$ and such that both L and* **SL** *are sound and complete (adequate) w.r.t. $\mathcal{C}_L$. If* **SL** *has the CWIP w.r.t. $\mathcal{C}_L$, then L has the LIP.*

Proof. Assume that **SL** satisfies the CWIP and $\mathsf{L} \vdash A \rightarrow B$. Then $\mathcal{C}_\mathsf{L} \vDash A \rightarrow B$ by soundness of L and **SL** $\vdash \Rightarrow$ w : $\overline{A} \vee B$ by completeness of **SL**. **SL** $\vdash \Rightarrow$ w : $\overline{A}$, w : B by invertibility of $R\vee$ and **SL** $\vdash$ w : $A \Rightarrow$ w : B by duality. By CWIP, w : $A \stackrel{\mho}{\Rightarrow}$ w : B for some $\mho$ that has only w as a label. It is easy to see that w : $A \xrightarrow{\text{w}:C}$ w : B for C obtained from $\mho$ by omitting all labels and replacing $\oslash$ and $\otimes$ with $\wedge$ and $\vee$ respectively. It immediately follows that C is a Lyndon interpolant of $A \rightarrow B$. $\square$

Remark 10. Only a derivation of w : $A \Rightarrow$ w : B is needed for the reduction. Since relational atoms cannot occur in the consequents in such derivations, from now on we allow only labelled formulas in consequents.

3   Interpolation Basis: Basic Normal Modal Logic K

The modularity of the proof-theoretic method means that each sequent rule can be treated separately as long as the logic and its labelled calculus satisfy the conditions of Theorem 9. As all labelled calculi we consider extend **SK** for the basic normal modal logic K, we start by describing interpolant transformations for all rules of **SK**. Table 4 presents interpolants for all initial sequents from Table 1. Since many single-premise rules require no change in the interpolant, we describe a sufficient condition for this to happen:

Definition 11 (Local rules). *A rule*

$$\frac{\Gamma_p \Rightarrow \Delta_p}{\Gamma_c \Rightarrow \Delta_c} \; \mathsf{r}$$

is called $\mathcal{C}_\mathsf{L}$-local if

1. *each label from the premise occurs in the conclusion;*
2. *each literal from Γ_p (from Δ_p) occurs in Γ_c (in Δ_c);*
3. *for any interpretation $\llbracket \cdot \rrbracket$ into any $\mathcal{M} \in \mathcal{C}_\mathsf{L}$,*
    (a) $\vDash \llbracket \mathsf{Ant_r}(\Gamma_c) \rrbracket$ *implies* $\vDash \llbracket \mathsf{Ant_r}(\Gamma_p) \rrbracket$;
    (b) $\vDash \llbracket \mathsf{Ant_r}(\Gamma_c) \rrbracket$ *and* $\vDash \llbracket \mathsf{Ant_f}(\Gamma_c) \rrbracket$ *imply* $\vDash \llbracket \mathsf{Ant_f}(\Gamma_p) \rrbracket$;
    (c) $\vDash \llbracket \mathsf{Ant_r}(\Gamma_c) \rrbracket$ *and* $\vDash \llbracket \mathsf{Con_f}(\Delta_p) \rrbracket$ *imply* $\vDash \llbracket \mathsf{Con_f}(\Delta_c) \rrbracket$.

Example 12. The rules $L\wedge$ and $R\vee$ from Table 2 and $L\square$ and $R\Diamond$ from Table 3 are $\mathcal{C}_\mathsf{L}$-local for any $\mathcal{C}_\mathsf{L}$.

Lemma 13 (Local).   *Given a $\mathcal{C}_\mathsf{L}$-local rule, each $\mathcal{C}_\mathsf{L}$-interpolant of the rule's premise $\Gamma_p \Rightarrow \Delta_p$ is also a $\mathcal{C}_\mathsf{L}$-interpolant of its conclusion $\Gamma_c \Rightarrow \Delta_c$.*

Proof. Let $\mho$ be a $\mathcal{C}_\mathsf{L}$-interpolant of $\Gamma_p \Rightarrow \Delta_p$. The conditions on labels and on common literals for $\Gamma_c \Rightarrow \Delta_c$ are inherited from the premise by the definition of local rules. Consider an interpretation $\llbracket \cdot \rrbracket$ into an $\mathcal{M} \in \mathcal{C}_\mathsf{L}$ with $\vDash \llbracket \mathsf{Ant_r}(\Gamma_c) \rrbracket$. Then $\vDash \llbracket \mathsf{Ant_r}(\Gamma_p) \rrbracket$. If $\vDash \llbracket \mathsf{Ant_f}(\Gamma_c) \rrbracket$, then $\vDash \llbracket \mathsf{Ant_f}(\Gamma_p) \rrbracket$, and, hence, $\vDash \llbracket \mho \rrbracket$. If $\vDash \llbracket \mho \rrbracket$, then $\vDash \llbracket \mathsf{Con_f}(\Delta_p) \rrbracket$, and, hence, $\vDash \llbracket \mathsf{Con_f}(\Delta_c) \rrbracket$. $\square$

Lemma 14 ($R\wedge$, $L\vee$)

1. *If $\mho_1$ and $\mho_2$ are $\mathcal{C}_\mathsf{L}$-interpolants of the premises of the rule $R\wedge$, then $\mho_1 \otimes \mho_2$ is a $\mathcal{C}_\mathsf{L}$-interpolant of its conclusion.*
2. *If $\mho_1$ and $\mho_2$ are $\mathcal{C}_\mathsf{L}$-interpolants of the premises of the rule $L\vee$, then $\mho_1 \varotimes \mho_2$ is a $\mathcal{C}_\mathsf{L}$-interpolant of its conclusion.*

Proof. Similar to that of Lemma 13. □

Lemma 15 ($L\Diamond$, $R\Box$). *Let $\mathsf{o} \neq \mathsf{w}$ and o occur in neither Γ nor Δ. If*

$$\mho_p = \bigvee_{i=1}^{n} \left(\bigwedge_{j=1}^{m_i} \mathsf{w}_{ij} : D_{ij} \ \otimes \bigwedge_{k=1}^{l_i} \mathsf{o} : C_{ik} \right)$$

is a $\mathcal{C}_\mathsf{L}$-interpolant of the $L\Diamond$'s premise $\mathsf{w}R\mathsf{o}, \mathsf{o} : A, \Gamma \Rightarrow \Delta$, then

$$\mho_c = \bigvee_{i=1}^{n} \left(\bigwedge_{j=1}^{m_i} \mathsf{w}_{ij} : D_{ij} \ \otimes \ \mathsf{w} : \left(\Diamond \bigwedge_{k=1}^{l_i} C_{ik} \right) \right)$$

is a $\mathcal{C}_\mathsf{L}$-interpolant of its conclusion $\mathsf{w} : \Diamond A, \Gamma \Rightarrow \Delta$. If

$$\mho_p = \bigwedge_{i=1}^{n} \left(\bigvee_{j=1}^{m_i} \mathsf{w}_{ij} : D_{ij} \ \varotimes \bigvee_{k=1}^{l_i} \mathsf{o} : C_{ik} \right)$$

is a $\mathcal{C}_\mathsf{L}$-interpolant of the $R\Box$'s premise $\mathsf{w}R\mathsf{o}, \Gamma \Rightarrow \Delta, \mathsf{o} : A$, then

$$\mho_c = \bigwedge_{i=1}^{n} \left(\bigvee_{j=1}^{m_i} \mathsf{w}_{ij} : D_{ij} \ \varotimes \ \mathsf{w} : \left(\Box \bigvee_{k=1}^{l_i} C_{ik} \right) \right)$$

is a $\mathcal{C}_\mathsf{L}$-interpolant of its conclusion $\Gamma \Rightarrow \Delta, \mathsf{w} : \Box A$.
W.l.o.g. $\mho_p$ is assumed to be in DNF or CNF respectively, which is achieved by the standard conversion method applied to $\varotimes$ and $\otimes$.

Definition 16. *Given an interpretation $\llbracket \cdot \rrbracket$ into a model $\mathcal{M} = (W, R, V)$, a sequence of distinct labels $\mathbf{o} = \mathsf{o}_1, \dots, \mathsf{o}_n$ from Lab, and a sequence of worlds $\mathbf{u} = u_1, \dots, u_n$ from W, a new interpretation $\llbracket \cdot \rrbracket_{\mathbf{o}}^{\mathbf{u}}$ into $\mathcal{M}$ is defined as follows:*

$$\llbracket \mathsf{o}_i \rrbracket_{\mathbf{o}}^{\mathbf{u}} := u_i \ , \qquad \llbracket \mathsf{w} \rrbracket_{\mathbf{o}}^{\mathbf{u}} := \llbracket \mathsf{w} \rrbracket \ \ if \ \mathsf{w} \notin \{\mathsf{o}_1, \dots, \mathsf{o}_n\}.$$

Proof (of Lemma 15). The proofs for the two rules are similar. We give the one for $L\Diamond$. The label and common literal conditions are clearly satisfied. Consider any interpretation $\llbracket \cdot \rrbracket$ into an $\mathcal{M} = (W, R, V) \in \mathcal{C}_\mathsf{L}$ such that $\vDash \llbracket \mathsf{Ant}_r(\mathsf{w} : \Diamond A, \Gamma) \rrbracket$.

Assume $\vDash \llbracket \mathsf{Ant}_f(\mathsf{w} : \Diamond A, \Gamma) \rrbracket$. Since $\mathcal{M}, \llbracket \mathsf{w} \rrbracket \Vdash \Diamond A$, there is $u \in W$ such that $\llbracket \mathsf{w} \rrbracket \, Ru$ and $\mathcal{M}, u \Vdash A$. Clearly, $\vDash \llbracket \mathsf{Ant}_r(\mathsf{w}R\mathsf{o}, \mathsf{o} : A, \Gamma) \rrbracket_{\mathsf{o}}^{u}$ because o does not occur in Γ. Since $\vDash \llbracket \mathsf{Ant}_f(\mathsf{w}R\mathsf{o}, \mathsf{o} : A, \Gamma) \rrbracket_{\mathsf{o}}^{u}$, for some disjunct $1 \leq i \leq n$ of $\mho_p$

$$\vDash \left\llbracket \bigwedge_{j=1}^{m_i} \mathsf{w}_{ij} : D_{ij} \ \otimes \bigwedge_{k=1}^{l_i} \mathsf{o} : C_{ik} \right\rrbracket_{\mathsf{o}}^{u} , \tag{3}$$

in particular, $\mathcal{M}, u \Vdash C_{ik}$ for all $k = 1, \ldots, l_i$. Given that $[\![\mathsf{w}]\!] \, Ru$, we see that $\mathcal{M}, [\![\mathsf{w}]\!] \Vdash \Diamond \wedge_{k=1}^{l_i} C_{ik}$.[4] Thus, $\vDash \left[\!\!\left[\oslash_{j=1}^{m_i} \mathsf{w}_{ij} : D_{ij} \, \oslash \, \mathsf{w} : \left(\Diamond \wedge_{k=1}^{l_i} C_{ik} \right) \right]\!\!\right]_{\mathsf{o}}^{u}$. Further, given that neither w nor any of w_{ij} is o, we have $\vDash [\![\mho_c]\!]$, which completes the proof of (1) for the conclusion of $L\Diamond$.

Assume now that $\vDash [\![\mho_c]\!]$. Then $\vDash \left[\!\!\left[\oslash_{j=1}^{m_i} \mathsf{w}_{ij} : D_{ij} \, \oslash \, \mathsf{w} : \left(\Diamond \wedge_{k=1}^{l_i} C_{ik} \right) \right]\!\!\right]$ for some disjunct $1 \leq i \leq n$ of $\mho_c$. In particular, $\mathcal{M}, [\![\mathsf{w}]\!] \Vdash \Diamond \wedge_{k=1}^{l_i} C_{ik}$. Thus, there is $u \in W$ such that $[\![\mathsf{w}]\!] \, Ru$ and $\mathcal{M}, u \Vdash C_{ik}$ for all $k = 1, \ldots, l_i$. Again we have $\vDash [\![\mathsf{Ant_r}(\mathsf{wRo}, \mathsf{o} : A, \Gamma)]\!]_{\mathsf{o}}^{u}$ and (3) holds for one of disjuncts of $\mho_p$. It follows that $\vDash [\![\mathsf{Con_f}(\Delta)]\!]_{\mathsf{o}}^{u}$ and, since o does not occur in Δ, also $\vDash [\![\mathsf{Con_f}(\Delta)]\!]$. $\qquad\square$

Corollary 17. K *enjoys the LIP.*

Proof. The CWIP for **SK** w.r.t. to the class $\mathcal{K}$ of all Kripke models follows from Table 4 and Lemmas 13–15. Adequacy of K w.r.t. $\mathcal{K}$ is due to Kripke [11]. Invertibility of all rules of **SK** including $R\vee$ is proved in [16]. The height-preserving duality property is proved by induction on the derivation depth. $\qquad\square$

4   Mathematical Rules with or without Equality Atoms

Now that the minimal modal logic having Kripke semantics is dealt with, we start considering frame conditions that preserve the LIP. In this section, we explore the exact scope of our method for quantifier-free frame conditions, which generate *mathematical* rules [16]. As noted in [16, Proposition 6.8], any quantifier-free property of Kripke frames can be represented as $P_1 \wedge \ldots \wedge P_m \rightarrow Q_1 \vee \ldots \vee Q_n$ where P_i and Q_j are relational atoms. It is, however, clear that the case of $n \geq 2$ cannot be generally treated by our or, indeed, any other method. The logic S4.3 of transitive, reflexive, and connected frames does not enjoy even Craig interpolation [14]. Later, we successfully deal with reflexivity and transitivity, hence, it is *connectedness* ($wRo \wedge wRu \rightarrow oRu \vee uRo$) that is to blame for the breakdown of interpolation. Thus, we concentrate on the cases of $n \leq 1$, or Horn clauses. For $n = 0$, restricting a class $\mathcal{C}_\mathsf{L}$ by a frame condition $w_1 Ru_1 \wedge \ldots \wedge w_m Ru_m \rightarrow \bot$ corresponds to adding initial sequents $\mathsf{w}_1 \mathsf{Ru}_1, \ldots, \mathsf{w}_m \mathsf{Ru}_m, \Gamma \Rightarrow \Delta$ to the labelled calculus (for some 1–1 onto map of metavariables $w_1, u_1, \ldots, w_m, u_m$ onto labels $\mathsf{w}_1, \mathsf{u}_1, \ldots, \mathsf{w}_m, \mathsf{u}_m$. In particular, the adequacy of the labelled calculus is preserved [16].

Lemma 18. *If all frames in $\mathcal{C}_\mathsf{L}$ satisfy*

$$w_1 Ru_1 \wedge \ldots \wedge w_m Ru_m \rightarrow \bot,$$

then $\mathsf{w}_1 : \bot$ is a $\mathcal{C}_\mathsf{L}$-interpolant of $\mathsf{w}_1 \mathsf{Ru}_1, \ldots, \mathsf{w}_m \mathsf{Ru}_m, \Gamma \Rightarrow \Delta$.

Proof. Similar to initial sequents $\mathsf{w} : \bot, \Gamma \Rightarrow \Delta$ for **SK**. $\qquad\square$

---

[4] It also holds for $l_i = 0$: the empty conjunction is $\top$ and $\mathcal{M}, [\![\mathsf{w}]\!] \Vdash \Diamond\top$.

Table 5. Common Horn frame conditions

Reflexivity	Transitivity		
wRw	$wRo \wedge oRr \to wRr$		
$\dfrac{\mathsf{wRw}, \Gamma \Rightarrow \Delta}{\Gamma \Rightarrow \Delta}\ Ref^\dagger$	$\dfrac{\mathsf{wRr}, \mathsf{wRo}, \mathsf{oRr}, \Gamma \Rightarrow \Delta}{\mathsf{wRo}, \mathsf{oRr}, \Gamma \Rightarrow \Delta}\ Trans$		$\dfrac{\mathsf{wRw}, \mathsf{wRw}, \Gamma \Rightarrow \Delta}{\mathsf{wRw}, \Gamma \Rightarrow \Delta}\ Trans^*$
Symmetry	Euclideanness		
$wRo \to oRw$	$wRo \wedge wRr \to oRr$		
$\dfrac{\mathsf{oRw}, \mathsf{wRo}, \Gamma \Rightarrow \Delta}{\mathsf{wRo}, \Gamma \Rightarrow \Delta}\ Sym$	$\dfrac{\mathsf{oRr}, \mathsf{wRo}, \mathsf{wRr}, \Gamma \Rightarrow \Delta}{\mathsf{wRo}, \mathsf{wRr}, \Gamma \Rightarrow \Delta}\ Eucl$		$\dfrac{\mathsf{oRo}, \mathsf{wRo}, \Gamma \Rightarrow \Delta}{\mathsf{wRo}, \Gamma \Rightarrow \Delta}\ Eucl^*$

Definition 19. *A labelled rule has the* subterm property *if each label from each premise, except for* eigenvariables, *occurs in the conclusion. Restricting a rule* r *to those instances that have the subterm property yields the rule* r†.

It was shown in [16, Theorem 11.27 and Corolloray 11.29] that restricting a class of frames by a Horn clause $w_1 R u_1 \wedge \ldots \wedge w_m R u_m \to v R z$ for $n = 1$ corresponds to adding to the labelled calculus both

- the rule

$$\frac{\mathsf{vRz}, \mathsf{w_1 Ru_1}, \ldots, \mathsf{w_m Ru_m}, \Gamma \Rightarrow \Delta}{\mathsf{w_1 Ru_1}, \ldots, \mathsf{w_m Ru_m}, \Gamma \Rightarrow \Delta}\ Math^\dagger \qquad (4)$$

with the subterm property, i.e., restricted to instances with both v and z occurring in the conclusion, and
- rules obtained from it by the *closure condition*, i.e., by contracting identical relational atoms $\mathsf{w_i Ru_i}$ and $\mathsf{w_j Ru_j}$ from the conclusion in both premise and conclusion for those instances of the rule that contain such identical atoms.

Example 20. Common examples of such Horn restrictions and their corresponding rules can be found in Table 5. Rules *Trans** and *Eucl** are added due to the closure condition and correspond to wRo = oRr in *Trans* and wRo = wRr in *Eucl* respectively. Note that all rules but *Ref* already have the subterm property.

Lemma 21. *An interpolant transformation for a rule* r *is also applicable for the rules* r* *obtained from* r *by the closure condition. More precisely, applying the interpolant transformation for* r *to an interpolant for the premise of a rule* r* *yields an interpolant for the conclusion of* r*.

Proof. This observation follows from the fact that the definition of component-wise interpolant is not sensitive to the multiplicities of relational atoms.   □

Thus, from now on we consider r*-variants obtained from r by the closure condition to be "instances" of r and do not mention them explicitly.

Table 6. Rules for equality atoms († means the subterm property restriction)

$$\frac{\mathsf{w} = \mathsf{w}, \Gamma \Rightarrow \Delta}{\Gamma \Rightarrow \Delta} \dagger \qquad \frac{\mathsf{o}R\mathsf{r}, \mathsf{w} = \mathsf{o}, \mathsf{w}R\mathsf{r}, \Gamma \Rightarrow \Delta}{\mathsf{w} = \mathsf{o}, \mathsf{w}R\mathsf{r}, \Gamma \Rightarrow \Delta} \qquad \frac{\mathsf{w}R\mathsf{r}, \mathsf{o} = \mathsf{r}, \mathsf{w}R\mathsf{o}, \Gamma \Rightarrow \Delta}{\mathsf{o} = \mathsf{r}, \mathsf{w}R\mathsf{o}, \Gamma \Rightarrow \Delta}$$

$$\frac{\mathsf{o} = \mathsf{r}, \mathsf{w} = \mathsf{o}, \mathsf{w} = \mathsf{r}, \Gamma \Rightarrow \Delta}{\mathsf{w} = \mathsf{o}, \mathsf{w} = \mathsf{r}, \Gamma \Rightarrow \Delta} \qquad \frac{\mathsf{o}{:}A, \mathsf{w} = \mathsf{o}, \mathsf{w}{:}A, \Gamma \Rightarrow \Delta}{\mathsf{w} = \mathsf{o}, \mathsf{w}{:}A, \Gamma \Rightarrow \Delta}$$

Lemma 22 (Horn). *If all frames in $\mathcal{C}_\mathsf{L}$ satisfy*

$$w_1 R u_1 \wedge \ldots \wedge w_m R u_m \to v R z,$$

then a $\mathcal{C}_\mathsf{L}$-interpolant of the premise of (4) is a $\mathcal{C}_\mathsf{L}$-interpolant of its conclusion.

Proof. This follows from Lemma 13 as (4) (and all its contracted versions) is $\mathcal{C}_\mathsf{L}$-local, e.g., the locality condition 1. follows from the subterm property. □

The formalism of labelled sequents can be enriched with equality atoms $\mathsf{w} = \mathsf{o}$ and the rules in Table 6 without affecting the adequacy results ([16, Sect. 11.6]). Equality atoms can be treated the same way as relational atoms, e.g., $\vDash [\![\mathsf{Ant}_\mathsf{r}\Gamma]\!]$ now means that $[\![\mathsf{w}]\!]\, R\, [\![\mathsf{o}]\!]$ for each $\mathsf{w}R\mathsf{o} \in \Gamma$ and $[\![\mathsf{w}]\!] = [\![\mathsf{o}]\!]$ for each $\mathsf{w} = \mathsf{o} \in \Gamma$. It follows from the definition of local rules that

Lemma 23. *All rules from Table 6 are $\mathcal{C}_\mathsf{L}$-local for any $\mathcal{C}_\mathsf{L}$.*

Further, it is easy to see that the proof of Lemma 13 directly applies also to labelled calculi with equality. Using the same construction of labelled rules from Horn clauses as $Math^\dagger$ in the previous section and assuming w.l.o.g. that no equality atoms occur among P_i, we can prove that such rules with the subterm property are still $\mathcal{C}_\mathsf{L}$-local in the presence of equality atoms:

Lemma 24. *If all frames in $\mathcal{C}_\mathsf{L}$ satisfy*

$$w_1 R u_1 \wedge \ldots \wedge w_m R u_m \to v = z,$$

then a $\mathcal{C}_\mathsf{L}$-interpolant of the premise of (4) with $\mathsf{v} = \mathsf{z}$ instead of $\mathsf{v}R\mathsf{z}$ is also a $\mathcal{C}_\mathsf{L}$-interpolant of its conclusion.

5   Geometric Rules

Dyckhoff and Negri [5] showed how to geometrize any first-order frame condition. Once again, we restrict our attention to single-conclusion canonical geometric implications

$$w_1 R o_1 \wedge \ldots \wedge w_m R o_m \to \exists y_1 \ldots \exists y_k \big(Q_1(\boldsymbol{y}) \wedge \ldots \wedge Q_l(\boldsymbol{y})\big),$$

where $y_j \notin \{w_1, o_1, \ldots, w_m, o_m\}$ for any pairwise distinct $y_1, \ldots, y_k = \boldsymbol{y}$ and, w.l.o.g., $Q_i(\boldsymbol{y})$ are relational atoms. They correspond to the rules

$$\frac{Q_1(\mathbf{y}), \ldots, Q_l(\mathbf{y}), \mathsf{w}_1\mathsf{Ro}_1, \ldots, \mathsf{w}_m\mathsf{Ro}_m, \Gamma \Rightarrow \Delta}{\mathsf{w}_1\mathsf{Ro}_1, \ldots, \mathsf{w}_m\mathsf{Ro}_m, \Gamma \Rightarrow \Delta} \; Geom^\dagger \tag{5}$$

where the eigenvariables $y_1, \ldots, y_k = \mathbf{y}$ do not occur in the conclusion. We consider first a subset of such rules that we call *telescopic*.

5.1 Telescopic Rules

Definition 25 (Telescopic). Telescopic *frame conditions have the form*

$$\bigwedge_{i=1}^{m} w_i R o_i \quad \rightarrow \quad \exists y_1 \ldots \exists y_k \big(x R y_1 \wedge y_1 R y_2 \wedge \ldots \wedge y_{k-1} R y_k \big) \tag{6}$$

where $\{y_1, \ldots, y_k\} \cap \{x, w_1, o_1, \ldots, w_m, o_m\} = \varnothing$.

Corresponding rules $\dfrac{\mathsf{x}\mathsf{Ry}_1, \mathsf{y}_1\mathsf{Ry}_2, \ldots, \mathsf{y}_{k-1}\mathsf{Ry}_k, \mathsf{w}_1\mathsf{Ro}_1, \ldots, \mathsf{w}_m\mathsf{Ro}_m, \Gamma \Rightarrow \Delta}{\mathsf{w}_1\mathsf{Ro}_1, \ldots, \mathsf{w}_m\mathsf{Ro}_m, \Gamma \Rightarrow \Delta} \; Tele^\dagger$
have x occurring in the conclusion and pairwise distinct eigenvariables $y_1, \ldots, y_k$ (and may generate contracted versions by the closure condition).

Lemma 26. *Let all frames in a class* $\mathcal{C}_{\mathsf{L}}$ *satisfy* (6). *For any* $\mathcal{C}_{\mathsf{L}}$*-interpolant*[5]

$$\mho_p = \bigvee_{i=1}^{n} \left(\bigwedge_{b=1}^{m_i} \mathsf{u}_{ib} : D_{ib} \; \oslash \; \bigwedge_{j=1}^{k} \mathsf{y}_j : C_{ij} \right)$$

of the the premise of $Tele^\dagger$, *we have that*

$$\mho_c = \bigvee_{i=1}^{n} \left(\bigwedge_{b=1}^{m_i} \mathsf{u}_{ib} : D_{ib} \; \oslash \; \mathsf{x} : \mathbb{T}_i \right)$$

is a $\mathcal{C}_{\mathsf{L}}$*-interpolant of the rule's conclusion, where*

$$\mathbb{T}_i := \Diamond(C_{i,1} \wedge \Diamond(C_{i,2} \wedge \Diamond(\ldots \wedge \Diamond(C_{i,k-1} \wedge \Diamond C_{ik}) \ldots))).$$

Proof. Let us abbreviate the premise and conclusion sequents as $\Gamma_p \Rightarrow \Delta$ and $\Gamma_c \Rightarrow \Delta$ respectively. The common literal condition is clearly preserved. Eigenvariables y_j occur neither in $\Gamma_c \Rightarrow \Delta$ nor in $\mho_c$. Consider an interpretation $[\![\cdot]\!]$ into a model $\mathcal{M} = (W, R, V) \in \mathcal{C}_{\mathsf{L}}$ such that $\vDash [\![\mathsf{Ant}_r(\Gamma_c)]\!]$.

---

[5] For each eigenvariable y_j we have collected all formulas labelled with y_j within each disjunct into one labelled formula by transforming $\mathsf{v} : A \oslash \mathsf{v} : B$ into $\mathsf{v} : (A \wedge B)$ if more than one formula has this label or by adding $\mathsf{y}_j : \top$ if no formula has.

Assume $\vDash [\![\mathsf{Ant}_f(\Gamma_c)]\!]$. Since $[\![\mathsf{w}_l]\!] R [\![\mathsf{o}_l]\!]$ for all l, by (6) there are $\mathsf{y}_j \in W$ such that $[\![\mathsf{x}]\!] R y_1 R \ldots R y_{k-1} R y_k$. Since y_j does not occur in $\Gamma_c \Rightarrow \Delta$, it follows that $\vDash [\![\mathsf{Ant}_r(\Gamma_p)]\!]_{\mathbf{y}}^{\mathbf{y}}$ and $\vDash [\![\mathsf{Ant}_f(\Gamma_p)]\!]_{\mathbf{y}}^{\mathbf{y}}$. Thus, for some disjunct $1 \leq i \leq n$ of $\mho_p$,

$$\vDash \left[\!\!\left[\bigotimes_{b=1}^{m_i} \mathsf{u}_{ib} : D_{ib} \ \oslash \ \bigotimes_{j=1}^{k} \mathsf{y}_j : C_{ij} \right]\!\!\right]_{\mathbf{y}}^{\mathbf{y}}, \tag{7}$$

in particular, $\mathcal{M}, y_j \Vdash C_{ij}$ for all $j = 1, \ldots, k$ for this i. It is easy to show by induction that $\mathcal{M}, y_j \Vdash C_{ij} \wedge \Diamond(C_{i,j+1} \wedge \Diamond(\ldots \wedge \Diamond(C_{i,k-1} \wedge \Diamond C_{ik}) \ldots))$ culminating in $\mathcal{M}, [\![\mathsf{x}]\!] \Vdash \mathbb{T}_i$. Since neither of u_{ib} coincides with any of y_j, it follows that $\vDash [\![\mho_c]\!]$.

Assume now that $\vDash [\![\mho_c]\!]$. Then $\vDash [\![\oslash_{b=1}^{m_i} \mathsf{u}_{ib} : D_{ib} \ \oslash \ \mathsf{x} : \mathbb{T}_i]\!]$ holds for some $1 \leq i \leq n$. In particular, $\mathcal{M}, [\![\mathsf{x}]\!] \Vdash \mathbb{T}_i$. Thus, there exist worlds $y_j \in W$ such that $[\![\mathsf{x}]\!] R y_1 R y_2 R \ldots R y_{k-1} R y_k$ and $\mathcal{M}, y_j \Vdash C_{ij}$ for all $j = 1, \ldots, k$. Again, $\vDash [\![\mathsf{Ant}_r(\Gamma_p)]\!]_{\mathbf{y}}^{\mathbf{y}}$ and, hence, (7) holds for some disjunct of $\mho_p$. It follows that $\vDash [\![\mathsf{Conf}(\Delta)]\!]_{\mathbf{y}}^{\mathbf{y}}$. Since none of y_j occurs in Δ, we have $\vDash [\![\mathsf{Conf}(\Delta)]\!]$. $\qquad\square$

Example 27. The simplest and most familiar example of a telescopic frame condition is *seriality*: $\exists y(xRy)$. The corresponding rule is $\dfrac{x R y, \Gamma \Rightarrow \Delta}{\Gamma \Rightarrow \Delta} \ Ser^\dagger$ where x occurs in the conclusion and the eigenvariable y doesn't. Thus, for any class $\mathcal{C}_{\mathsf{L}}$ whose models have serial frames, if $\oslash_{i=1}^{n} (\oslash_{b=1}^{m_i} \mathsf{u}_{ib} : D_{ib} \ \oslash \ \mathsf{y} : C_i)$ is a $\mathcal{C}_{\mathsf{L}}$-interpolant of $xRy, \Gamma \Rightarrow \Delta$, then $\oslash_{i=1}^{n} (\oslash_{b=1}^{m_i} \mathsf{u}_{ib} : D_{ib} \ \oslash \ \mathsf{x} : \Diamond C_i)$ is a $\mathcal{C}_{\mathsf{L}}$-interpolant of $\Gamma \Rightarrow \Delta$, where x occurs in Γ or Δ, y does not, and y does not coincide with any of u_{ib}. This is essentially the same transformation as used for $L\Diamond$.

5.2   Non-telescopic Geometric Rules

While $\Diamond$ helps describe one accessible world, more complex configurations of eigenvariables are hard to describe by modal formulas. Consider *convergence* $wRo_1 \wedge wRo_2 \rightarrow \exists y(o_1 Ry \wedge o_2 Ry)$, a single-conclusion canonical geometric implication that cannot be handled using Lemma 26. It is not clear which formulas are to be true at w, o, o_1, and o_2 in order to ensure that the interpolant information from the conclusion can be lifted to the premise. For instance, for the case of convergence, $\mathsf{o}_i : \Diamond C$ only describes a world satisfying C and accessible from $[\![\mathsf{o}_i]\!]$. It is not clear how to pinpoint a world satisfying C and simultaneously accessible from $[\![\mathsf{o}_1]\!]$ and $[\![\mathsf{o}_2]\!]$. Indeed, $\mathsf{o}_1 : \Diamond C \oslash \mathsf{o}_2 : \Diamond C$ only implies that each of the two worlds has an accessible world, o_1' and o_2' respectively, satisfying C but cannot guarantee that $o_1' = o_2'$. To overcome this difficulty, we use a convergence-like property to find a third C-world y accessible from both o_1' and o_2' and a transitivity-like property to ensure that y is directly accessible from both original worlds $[\![\mathsf{o}_1]\!]$ and $[\![\mathsf{o}_2]\!]$.

In this section, we outline general conditions and an interpolant transformation that enable us to carry the interpolation proof beyond geometric rules whose eigenvariables form disjoint telescopes. While the conditions themselves are a bit technical, they can be viewed as weakened forms of transitivity and convergence adapted to the particulars of a given sequent rule. As a result, both density and convergence become amenable to our method in presence of some additional frame properties.

W.l.o.g. we assume that each $Q_j(\boldsymbol{y})$ is a relational atom containing an occurrence of one of y_j's because eigenvariable-free conjuncts can be pulled out and handled using Lemma 22. We demonstrate interpolation for frame conditions

$$\bigwedge_{i=1}^{m} w_i Ro_i \quad \rightarrow \quad \exists y_1 \ldots \exists y_k \bigwedge_{j=1}^{l} x_j Re_j, \tag{8}$$

where each $x_j Re_j$ contains a y_i and each y_i occurs among x_j's and e_j's. The corresponding rule is $\dfrac{x_1 Re_1, \ldots, x_l Re_l, w_1 Ro_1, \ldots, w_m Ro_m, \Gamma \Rightarrow \Delta}{w_1 Ro_1, \ldots, w_m Ro_m, \Gamma \Rightarrow \Delta}$ GI† with eigenvariables $y_1, \ldots, y_k$ where each x_j and e_j that is not an eigenvariable must occur in the conclusion sequent.

Definition 28 (Conmap and premap). *An interpretation $[\![\cdot]\!]$ into $\mathcal{M}$ is called an* r-conmap *(an* r-premap*) for a rule* $\dfrac{\Gamma_p \Rightarrow \Delta_p}{\Gamma_c \Rightarrow \Delta_c}$ r *if* $\vDash [\![\mathsf{Ant}_r(\Gamma_c)]\!]$ $(\vDash [\![\mathsf{Ant}_r(\Gamma_p)]\!])$.

Lemma 29. *If $\mathcal{M}$ is a model satisfying (8), any GI†-conmap $[\![\cdot]\!]$ into $\mathcal{M}$ can be modified into a GI†-premap $[\![\cdot]\!]_{\boldsymbol{y}}^{\boldsymbol{y}}$ into $\mathcal{M}$.*

Proof. It immediately follows from (8). □

Definition 30 (Interpolable rule). *Let all frames of a class $\mathcal{C}_\mathsf{L}$ satisfy (8). A rule GI† is $\mathcal{C}_\mathsf{L}$-interpolable for an order $\langle y_1, \ldots, y_k \rangle$ on its eigenvariables if a parent function* par $:$ Lab $\to$ Lab *exists satisfying the following three properties:*

– *for each y_j, there is i such that* par$(y_j) Ry_j = x_i Re_i$ *where x_i must either occur in the conclusion of GI† or be $y_{j'}$ for some $j' < j$;*   (connectedness)

given any model $\mathcal{M} = (W, R, V) \in \mathcal{C}_\mathsf{L}$, any GI†-conmap $[\![\cdot]\!]$ into $\mathcal{M}$ and any GI†-premap $[\![\cdot]\!]_{y_1, \ldots, y_k}^{y_1, \ldots, y_k}$ into $\mathcal{M}$, for each $j = 1, \ldots, k$

– *if $y_j Ry_j'$, there is a GI†-premap $[\![\cdot]\!]_{y_1, \ldots, y_{j-1}, y_j, \ldots y_k}^{y_1, \ldots, y_{j-1}, y_j', \ldots, y_k'}$ into $\mathcal{M}$;*   (pushability)
– *if $[\![$par$(y_j)]\!]_{y_1, \ldots, y_k}^{y_1, \ldots, y_k} Rz_l$ for all $1 \le l \le s$, there exists y_j' such that $z_l Ry_j'$ for all $1 \le l \le s$ and a GI†-premap $[\![\cdot]\!]_{y_1, \ldots, y_{j-1}, y_j, \ldots y_k}^{y_1, \ldots, y_{j-1}, y_j', \ldots, y_k'}$ into $\mathcal{M}$.*   (conjoinability)

Definition 31 (Geach properties). *The Scott–Lemmon generalizations of the Geach convergence axiom are known to correspond to the $hijk$-convergence properties $wR^h v \wedge wR^j u \to \exists y (vR^i y \wedge uR^k y)$ [7, Sect. 9]. We only consider the cases of $h, i, j, k \ge 1$. Each $hijk$-convergence property can be written as a canonical geometric implication:*

$$wRv_1 \wedge \ldots \wedge v_{h-1} Rv \quad \wedge \quad wRu_1 \wedge \ldots \wedge u_{j-1} Ru \quad \rightarrow$$
$$\exists z_1 \ldots \exists z_{i-1} \exists y_1 \ldots \exists y_{k-1} \exists y (vRz_1 \wedge \ldots \wedge z_{i-1} Ry \wedge uRy_1 \wedge \ldots \wedge y_{k-1} Ry). \tag{9}$$

It is tedious but not hard to prove the following two lemmas:

Lemma 32. *If all frames in $\mathcal{C}_L$ are hijk-convergent and transitive (shift-transitive if $h, j \geq 2$), then $\mathsf{GI}^\dagger$ for the case of (8) being the hijk-convergence property (9) is $\mathcal{C}_L$-interpolable for the order $\langle z_1, \ldots, z_{i-1}, y_1, \ldots, y_{k-1}, y \rangle$.*

Lemma 33. *Let $m < n$ and all frames in $\mathcal{C}_L$ be transitive, Euclidean, and (n, m)-transitive, i.e., satisfy $wR^m x \rightarrow wR^n x$. Then taking the frame condition (8) to be $wRv_1 \wedge \ldots \wedge v_{m-1}Rx \rightarrow \exists y_1 \ldots \exists y_{n-1}(wRy_1 \wedge \ldots \wedge y_{n-1}Rx)$, the rule $\mathsf{GI}^\dagger$ is $\mathcal{C}_L$-interpolable for the order $\langle y_1, \ldots, y_{n-1} \rangle$.*

Definition 34 (Transformation for interpolable rules). *For*

$$\mho = \bigwedge_{r=1}^{s} \bigvee_{b=1}^{t_r} \mathsf{v}_{rb} : D_{rb}$$

in CNF and arbitrary labels y and x such that $\mathsf{y} \neq \mathsf{x}$,

$$\mathsf{rem}\,(\mathsf{y}, \mathsf{x}, \mho) := \bigwedge_{r=1}^{s} \left(\mathsf{x} : \Diamond\Box \bigvee_{\mathsf{v}_{rb}=\mathsf{y}} D_{rb} \quad \varnothing \quad \bigvee_{\mathsf{v}_{rb} \neq \mathsf{y}} \mathsf{v}_{rb} : D_{rb} \right).$$

It is clear that y does not occur in $\mathsf{rem}(\mathsf{y}, \mathsf{x}, \mho)$. Let a rule $\mathsf{GI}^\dagger$ be $\mathcal{C}_L$-interpolable for the order $\langle y_1, \ldots, y_k \rangle = \mathbf{y}$ and parent function par. For each $j = 0, \ldots, k$,

$$\mathsf{rem}_j(\mathbf{y}, \mathsf{GI}^\dagger, \mho) := \begin{cases} \mho & \text{if } j = k, \\ \mathsf{rem}(\mathsf{y}_{j+1}, \mathsf{par}(\mathsf{y}_{j+1}), \mathsf{rem}_{j+1}(\mathbf{y}, \mathsf{GI}^\dagger, \mho)) & \text{if } j \leq k-1. \end{cases} \quad (10)$$

Note that $\mathsf{rem}_j(\mathbf{y}, \mathsf{GI}^\dagger, \mho)$ is in CNF and $y_{j+1}, \ldots, y_k$ don't occur in it. Finally, $\mathsf{rem}(\mathbf{y}, \mathsf{GI}^\dagger, \mho) := \mathsf{rem}_0(\mathbf{y}, \mathsf{GI}^\dagger, \mho)$ and contains no eigenvariables of $\mathsf{GI}^\dagger$.

Lemma 35. *Let $\mathcal{C}_L$ satisfy (8) and $\mathsf{GI}^\dagger$ be $\mathcal{C}_L$-interpolable for the order $\mathbf{y} = \langle y_1, \ldots, y_k \rangle$ and a parent function par. Then for any $\mathcal{C}_L$-interpolant $\mho$ of the premise of $\mathsf{GI}^\dagger$ in CNF, $\mathsf{rem}(\mathbf{y}, \mathsf{GI}^\dagger, \mho)$ is a $\mathcal{C}_L$-interpolant of the conclusion of $\mathsf{GI}^\dagger$.*

Proof. Let $\Gamma_p \Rightarrow \Delta$ and $\Gamma_c \Rightarrow \Delta$ be the premise and conclusion of $\mathsf{GI}^\dagger$. Let $\Gamma_p \overset{\mho}{\Rightarrow} \Delta$ for some $\mho$ in CNF, let $\mathcal{M} \in \mathcal{C}_L$, and let $\llbracket \cdot \rrbracket$ be a $\mathsf{GI}^\dagger$-conmap into $\mathcal{M}$. The label and common language conditions are satisfied because of the subterm property and the absence of eigenvariables in $\mathsf{rem}(\mathbf{y}, \mathsf{GI}^\dagger, \mho)$ and because no labelled formula is changed by $\mathsf{GI}^\dagger$ and $\mathsf{rem}(\mathbf{y}, \mathsf{GI}^\dagger, \mho)$ has the same literals as $\mho$ respectively.

Given $\models \llbracket \mathsf{Ant}_f(\Gamma_c) \rrbracket$, let us show $\models \llbracket \mathsf{rem}(\mathbf{y}, \mathsf{GI}^\dagger, \mho) \rrbracket$. We abbreviate $\mho_j := \mathsf{rem}_j(\mathbf{y}, \mathsf{GI}^\dagger, \mho)$. It can be proved by induction on $j = k, \ldots, 0$ that $\models \llbracket \mho_j \rrbracket_{y_1, \ldots, y_j}^{y_1, \ldots, y_j}$ for any $\mathsf{GI}^\dagger$-premap $\llbracket \cdot \rrbracket_{\mathbf{y}}^{\mathbf{y}}$ into $\mathcal{M}$. In particular, $\models \llbracket \mho_0 \rrbracket$ for any $\mathsf{GI}^\dagger$-premap $\llbracket \cdot \rrbracket_{\mathbf{y}}^{\mathbf{y}}$ into $\mathcal{M}$. It remains to note that such premaps exist by Lemma 29 and that $\mho_0 = \mathsf{rem}(\mathbf{y}, \mathsf{GI}^\dagger, \mho)$. This completes the proof of (1).

Given $\vDash \left[\!\left[\mathsf{rem}(\mathbf{y}, \mathsf{GI}^\dagger, \mho)\right]\!\right]$, let us show $\vDash \left[\!\left[\mathsf{Con}_\mathsf{f}(\Delta)\right]\!\right]$. We can prove by induction on $j = 0, \ldots, k$ that there is a $\mathsf{GI}^\dagger$-premap $\left[\!\left[\cdot\right]\!\right]_{y_1,\ldots,y_j,y_{j+1},\ldots,y_k}^{y_1^1,\ldots,y_j^j,y_{j+1}^j,\ldots,y_k^j}$ into $\mathcal{M}$ such that $\vDash \left[\!\left[\mho_j\right]\!\right]_{y_1,\ldots,y_j}^{y_1^1,\ldots,y_j^j}$. In particular, since $\mho = \mho_k$, we have $\vDash \left[\!\left[\mho\right]\!\right]_{\mathbf{y}}^{\boldsymbol{y}}$ for $\boldsymbol{y} = y_1^1, \ldots, y_k^k$. Since $\Gamma_p \overset{\mho}{\Rightarrow} \Delta$, it follows that $\vDash \left[\!\left[\mathsf{Con}_\mathsf{f}(\Delta)\right]\!\right]_{\mathbf{y}}^{\boldsymbol{y}}$. But Δ contains no eigenvariables. Hence, $\vDash \left[\!\left[\mathsf{Con}_\mathsf{f}(\Delta)\right]\!\right]$. This completes the proof of (2). $\qquad\square$

Corollary 36. *Modal logics complete w.r.t. Kripke models defined via*

- *Horn properties, including reflexivity, transitivity, symmetry, Euclideanness, $(1, n)$-transitivity, and functionality, as well as the shift versions thereof,*
- *telescopic properties, including seriality, and*
- *properties generating interpolable rules, including $hijk$-convergence with $h, i, j, k \geq 1$ (in presence of transitivity or, for $h, j \geq 2$, shift transitivity); density (in presence of transitivity and Euclideanness); (n, m)-transitivity for $m < n$ (in presence of transitivity and Euclideanness)*

enjoy LIP. In particular, logics with LIP proved using labelled sequents include all 15 logics of the so-called modal cube from [7, Sect. 8], K4.2, S4.2, and $\mathsf{K4}_{1,n}$, as well as the infinite family of non-degenerate Geach logics over K4 and almost the full family of Geach logics over K5 (due to the shift transitivity of the latter).

6 Related Work, Conclusion, and Future Work

The body of work on interpolation is so great and so varied that it is hopeless to try giving even a restricted overview of the field. While this is the first result on proving interpolation using labelled sequent calculi, there were several recent advances in other proof formalisms. Brotherston and Goré [3] developed a method of using display calculi for proving interpolation for displayable substructural logics. Bílková [2] and Herzig and Mengin [9] used nested sequent calculi and resolution respectively to show the stronger and, consequently, rarer uniform interpolation. Pattinson [17] provided a blanket proof of uniform interpolation for the somewhat restricted class of rank-1 modal logics. Iemhoff [10] connected the existence of ordinary sequent calculi to the property of uniform interpolation, which can be used to show the absence of such sequent calculi, but can only prove uniform interpolation for logics with sequent systems.

By using a non-constructive method based on duality theory, Marx proved a similar but slightly weaker result than ours [15, Corollary B.4.1]: a non-constructive proof of Craig interpolation for logics defined by frame conditions given by universal Horn sentences, compared to our constructive proof of Lyndon interpolation for the same logics. It would be interesting to compare the semantic restrictions of his method with those of our method. Perhaps, a more exact upper bound and a better description of both methods' applicability area(s) can be obtained by such comparative analysis.

We developed a constructive and modular method of proving the Lyndon (and Craig) Interpolation Property for modal logics by using labelled sequent calculi. The method is sufficient to establish the LIP for all frame conditions described by quantifier-free Horn formulas. For geometric formulas, the method generally requires additional conditions similar to transitivity and convergence in nature, but is still sufficient to tackle an infinite family of standard modal logics.

Many questions remain open. The extension to multimodal logics and to first-order languages is long overdue. Intuitionistic systems have so far evaded this method. Logics like GL can be captured by labelled sequents even though they are not first-order definable. Thus, our method should extend to them too.

Acknowledgments. I am grateful to M. Fitting, whose idea started this interpolation project. I thank S. Negri for encouragement, V. Sikimić for procuring a source not available online, Y. Venema and M. Marx for valuable information on the nonconstructive method. I am deeply indebted to B. Lellmann, who is always ready to listen and has provided many inspiring suggestions for improving this paper. I thank the anonymous reviewers for the suggestions on terminology.

References

1. Amir, E., McIlraith, S.: Partition-based logical reasoning for first-order and propositional theories. Artif. Intell. **162**(1–2), 49–88 (2005)
2. Bílková, M.: A note on uniform interpolation proofs in modal deep inference calculi. In: Bezhanishvili, N., Löbner, S., Schwabe, K., Spada, L. (eds.) TbiLLC 2009. LNCS (LNAI), vol. 6618, pp. 30–45. Springer, Heidelberg (2011). doi:10.1007/978-3-642-22303-7_3
3. Brotherston, J., Goré, R.: Craig interpolation in displayable logics. In: Brünnler, K., Metcalfe, G. (eds.) TABLEAUX 2011. LNCS (LNAI), vol. 6793, pp. 88–103. Springer, Heidelberg (2011). doi:10.1007/978-3-642-22119-4_9
4. ten Cate, B., Franconi, E., Seylan, İ.: Beth definability in expressive description logics. J. Arti. Intell. Res. **48**(1), 347–414 (2013)
5. Dyckhoff, R., Negri, S.: Geometrisation of first-order logic. Bull. Symbolic Logic **21**(2), 123–163 (2015)
6. Fitting, M., Kuznets, R.: Modal interpolation via nested sequents. Ann. Pure Appl. Logic **166**(3), 274–305 (2015)
7. Garson, J.: Modal logic. In: Zalta, E.N., (ed.) The Stanford Encyclopedia of Philosophy (2016). http://plato.stanford.edu/entries/logic-modal/
8. Goré, R., Ramanayake, R.: Labelled tree sequents, tree hypersequents and nested (deep) sequents. In: Bolander, T., Braüner, T., Ghilardi, S., Moss, L. (eds.) Advances in Modal Logic, vol. 9, pp. 279–299. College Publications (2012)
9. Herzig, A., Mengin, J.: Uniform interpolation by resolution in modal logic. In: Hölldobler, S., Lutz, C., Wansing, H. (eds.) JELIA 2008. LNCS (LNAI), vol. 5293, pp. 219–231. Springer, Heidelberg (2008). doi:10.1007/978-3-540-87803-2_19
10. Iemhoff, R.: Uniform interpolation and sequent calculi in modal logic. Preprint 325, Logic Group Preprint Series (2015)
11. Kripke, S.A.: Semantical analysis of modal logic I: normal modal propositional calculi. Z. Math. Logik Grundlagen Math. **9**(5–6), 67–96 (1963)
12. Kuznets, R.: Craig interpolation via hypersequents. In: Probst, D., Schuster, P. (eds.) Concepts of Proof in Mathematics, Philosophy, and Computer Science. Ontos Mathematical Logic, vol. 6, pp. 193–214. De Gruyter, Berlin (2016)

13. Kuznets, R.: Interpolation method for multicomponent sequent calculi. In: Artemov, S., Nerode, A. (eds.) LFCS 2016. LNCS, vol. 9537, pp. 202–218. Springer, Heidelberg (2016). doi:10.1007/978-3-319-27683-0_15

14. Maksimova, L.L.: Absence of the interpolation property in the consistent normal modal extensions of the Dummett logic. Algebra Logic **21**(6), 460–463 (1982)

15. Marx, M., Venema, Y.: Multi-dimensional Modal Logic. Applied Logic Series, vol. 4. Springer, Heidelberg (1997)

16. Negri, S., von Plato, J.: Proof Analysis: A Contribution to Hilbert's Last Problem. Cambridge University Press, Cambridge (2011)

17. Pattinson, D.: The logic of exact covers: completeness and uniform interpolation. In: 2013 28th Annual ACM/IEEE Symposium on Logic in Computer Science, pp. 418–427. IEEE (2013)

18. Thomason, R.: Logic and artificial intelligence. In: Zalta, E.N. (ed.) The Stanford Encyclopedia of Philosophy (2014). http://plato.stanford.edu/entries/logic-ai/

Efficient Reasoning for Inconsistent Horn Formulae

Joao Marques-Silva[1]([✉]), Alexey Ignatiev[1,4], Carlos Mencía[2],
and Rafael Peñaloza[3]

[1] University of Lisbon, Lisbon, Portugal
{jpms,aignatiev}@ciencias.ulisboa.pt
[2] University of Oviedo, Oviedo, Spain
cmencia@gmail.com
[3] Free University of Bozen-Bolzano, Bolzano, Italy
rafael.penaloza@unibz.it
[4] ISDCT SB RAS, Irkutsk, Russia

Abstract. Horn formulae are widely used in different settings that include logic programming, answer set programming, description logics, deductive databases, and system verification, among many others. One concrete example is concept subsumption in lightweight description logics, which can be reduced to inference in propositional Horn formulae. Some problems require one to reason with inconsistent Horn formulae. This is the case when providing minimal explanations of inconsistency. This paper proposes efficient algorithms for a number of decision, function and enumeration problems related with inconsistent Horn formulae. Concretely, the paper develops efficient algorithms for finding and enumerating minimal unsatisfiable subsets (MUSes), minimal correction subsets (MCSes), but also for computing the lean kernel. The paper also shows the practical importance of some of the proposed algorithms.

1 Introduction

Horn formulae have been studied since at least the middle of the past century [18,19]. More recently, Horn formulae have been used in a number of different settings, which include logic programming, answer set programming and deductive databases, but also description logics. In addition, there is a growing interest on Horn formula reasoning in formal methods [12,13]. In the area of description logics, there is a tight relationship between description logic reasoning and Horn formulae. This is true for lightweight description logics [2,3,5,23,32,42,44,46], but there exists recent work suggesting the wider application of Horn formulae to (non-lightweight) description logic reasoning [9].

It is well-known that the decision problem for Horn formulae is in P [18], with linear-time algorithms known since the 80s [16,20,37]. Nevertheless, other decision, function and enumeration problems are of interest when reasoning about Horn formulae, which find immediate application in other settings, that include description logics. Moreover, related problems on Horn formulae have

© Springer International Publishing AG 2016
L. Michael and A. Kakas (Eds.): JELIA 2016, LNAI 10021, pp. 336–352, 2016.
DOI: 10.1007/978-3-319-48758-8_22

been studied earlier in other contexts [17,31]. This paper extends earlier work on developing efficient algorithms for reasoning about Horn formulae [3,5,42]. Concretely, the paper investigates the complexity of finding and enumerating MUSes, MCSes, but also the complexity of computing the lean kernel [24–27]. The paper also studies MUS and MCS membership and related problems. In addition, the paper also investigates the practical significance of some of these new algorithms.

The paper is organized as follows. Section 2 introduces the notation used throughout the paper. Section 3 revisits the well-known linear time unit resolution (LTUR) algorithm, and proposes two algorithms used extensively in the remainder of the paper. Section 4 develops the main results in the paper. The practical significance of the work is briefly addressed in Section 5, before concluding in Section 6.

2   Preliminaries

This section introduces the notation and definitions used throughout the paper. We assume that the reader is familiar with the basic notions of propositional logic (see e.g. [11]). CNF formulae are defined over a finite set of propositional variables. A literal is a variable or its complement. A *clause* is a disjunction of literals, also interpreted as a set of literals. A *CNF formula* $\mathcal{F}$ is a finite conjunction of clauses, also interpreted as a finite set of clauses. In some settings, it is convenient to view a CNF formula as a multiset of clauses, where the same clause can appear more than once. The set of variables associated with a CNF formula $\mathcal{F}$ is denoted by $\mathrm{var}(\mathcal{F})$. We often use $X \triangleq \mathrm{var}(\mathcal{F})$, with $n \triangleq |X|$. $m \triangleq |\mathcal{F}|$ represents the number of clauses in the formula, and the number of literal occurrences in $\mathcal{F}$ is represented by $||\mathcal{F}||$. An *assignment* is a mapping from X from $\{0,1\}$, and total assignments are assumed throughout. Moreover, the semantics of propositional logic is assumed. For a formula $\mathcal{F}$, we write $\mathcal{F} \nvDash \bot$ (resp. $\mathcal{F} \vDash \bot$) to express that $\mathcal{F}$ is satisfiable (resp. unsatisfiable).

In this paper we focus on Horn formulae. Intuitively, Horn formulae are sets of implications of the form $A_1 \wedge A_2 \wedge \ldots \wedge A_{k_j} \rightarrow I_j$, where all A_r are positive literals defined over the variables in X, and I_j is either a positive literal or $\bot$. Formally, a Horn formula $\mathcal{F}$ is a CNF formula where each clause contains at most one positive literal. Clauses without a positive literal are called *goal* clauses, and those with a positive literal are called *definite*. Given a (Horn) clause $c \in \mathcal{F}$, $P(c)$ denotes the set of variables appearing positively in c. For Horn clauses, $P(c)$ always contains at most one element. Likewise, $N(c)$ denotes the set of variables appearing negatively in c. We apply a similar notation for variables v. In this case, $N(v)$ (resp. $P(v)$) denotes the set of clauses where v occurs as a negative (resp. positive) literal.

We are interested in inconsistent formulae $\mathcal{F}$, i.e. $\mathcal{F} \vDash \bot$, such that some clauses in $\mathcal{F}$ can be *relaxed* (i.e. allowed not to be satisfied) to restore consistency, whereas others cannot. Thus, we assume that $\mathcal{F}$ is partitioned into two subformulae $\mathcal{F} = \mathcal{B} \cup \mathcal{R}$, where $\mathcal{R}$ contains the *relaxable* clauses, and $\mathcal{B}$ contains the *non-relaxable* clauses. $\mathcal{B}$ can be viewed as background knowledge, which must always be kept. As we will see in this paper, allowing $\mathcal{B} \neq \emptyset$ can affect the computational complexity and the runtime behavior of the tasks that we consider.

Given an inconsistent CNF formula $\mathcal{F}$, we are interested in detecting the clauses that are responsible for unsatisfiability among those that can be relaxed, as defined next.

Definition 1 (Minimal Unsatisfiable Subset (MUS)). *Let $\mathcal{F} = \mathcal{B} \cup \mathcal{R}$ denote an inconsistent set of clauses ($\mathcal{F} \vDash \bot$). $\mathcal{M} \subseteq \mathcal{R}$ is a* Minimal Unsatisfiable Subset *(MUS) iff $\mathcal{B} \cup \mathcal{M} \vDash \bot$ and $\forall_{\mathcal{M'} \subsetneq \mathcal{M}}, \mathcal{B} \cup \mathcal{M'} \nvDash \bot$. $\bigcup \mathrm{MU}(\mathcal{F})$ denotes the union of all MUSes.*

Informally, an MUS provides the minimal information that needs to be added to the background knowledge $\mathcal{B}$ to obtain an inconsistency; thus, it explains the causes for this inconsistency. Alternatively, one might be interested in correcting the formula, removing some clauses to achieve consistency.

Definition 2 (MCS, MSS). *Let $\mathcal{F} = \mathcal{B} \cup \mathcal{R}$ denote an inconsistent set of clauses ($\mathcal{F} \vDash \bot$). $\mathcal{C} \subseteq \mathcal{R}$ is a* Minimal Correction Subset *(MCS) iff $\mathcal{B} \cup \mathcal{R} \setminus \mathcal{C} \nvDash \bot$ and $\forall_{\mathcal{C'} \subsetneq \mathcal{C}}, \mathcal{B} \cup \mathcal{R} \setminus \mathcal{C'} \vDash \bot$. We use $\bigcup \mathrm{MC}(\mathcal{F})$ to denote the union of all MCSes. $\mathcal{S} \subseteq \mathcal{R}$ is a* Maximal Satisfiable Subset *(MSS) iff $\mathcal{B} \cup \mathcal{S} \nvDash \bot$ and $\forall_{\mathcal{S'} \supsetneq \mathcal{S}}, \mathcal{B} \cup \mathcal{S'} \vDash \bot$.*

It is well known that there is a close connection between MUSes, MCSes, and MSSes. Indeed, it is easy to see that a set $\mathcal{C}$ is an MCS iff $\mathcal{R} \setminus \mathcal{C}$ is an MSS. Moreover, there exists a minimal hitting set duality between MUSes and MCSes [43]. In particular this means that $\bigcup \mathrm{MU}(\mathcal{F}) = \bigcup \mathrm{MC}(\mathcal{F})$.

The lean kernel [24–27] represents an (easier to compute) over-approximation of $\bigcup \mathrm{MU}(\mathcal{F})$, containing all clauses that can be included in a resolution refutation of $\mathcal{F}$, with $\mathcal{F} \vDash \bot$. The lean kernel of a CNF formula is tightly related with the maximum autarky of the formula, one being the complement of the other [24–27]. Computation of the lean kernel for Horn formulae is analyzed in Section 4.3.

For arbitrary CNF formulae, there exists recent work on extracting MUSes [7,10], and on extracting MCSes [6,33,35,36]. The complexity of extracting MUSes for Horn formulae has also been studied in the context of so-called axiom pinpointing for light-weight description logics [5,41,42]. In particular, it has been shown that axiom pinpointing for the $\mathcal{EL}$ family of description logics [4,5] can be reduced to the problem of computing MUSes of a Horn formula with $\mathcal{B} \neq \emptyset$ (see [2,3,44] for details).

We also assume that the reader is familiar with the basic notions of computational complexity; for details, see [22,39,40]. Throughout the paper, the following abbreviations are used. For decision problems [39], NPC stands for NP-complete, and P^{NP} (or Δ_2^{p}) denotes the class of problems that can be decided with a polynomial number of calls (on the problem representation) to an NP oracle. Similarly, $\mathrm{P}^{\mathrm{NP}}[\log]$ denotes the class of problems that can be decided with a logarithmic number of calls to an NP oracle (where n denotes the size of the problem instance). For enumeration problems [22], OP stands for *output polynomial* and PD stands for *polynomial delay*, denoting respectively algorithms that run in time polynomial on the size of the input and already computed solutions (i.e. the output), and algorithms that compute each solution in time polynomial solely on the size of the input. Finally, for function (or search problems), the notation used for characterizing the complexity of decision problems is prefixed with F [39]. For example, $\mathrm{FP}^{\mathrm{NP}}$ denotes the class of function problems solved with a polynomial number of calls to an NP oracle. Similarly, $\mathrm{FP}^{\mathrm{NP}}[\mathsf{log}]$ (respectively $\mathrm{FP}^{\mathrm{NP}}[\mathsf{wit,log}]$) denotes the class of function problems solved with a logarithmic number of calls to an NP oracle (respectively to a witness producing NP oracle [14]).

3   Basic LTUR and Saturation

It is well-known that consistency of Horn formulae can be decided in linear time on the size of the formula [16,20,37]. A simple algorithm that achieves this linear-time behavior on the number of literals appearing in the formula, is known as *linear time unit resolution* (LTUR) [37]. Motivated by the different uses in the remainder of the paper, a possible implementation is analyzed next. In addition, we also introduce an extension of LTUR that saturates the application of unit propagation rules, without affecting the linear-time behavior. We then show how the result of this saturation can be used to trace the causes of all consequences derived by LTUR.

3.1   Linear Time Unit Resolution

LTUR can be viewed as one-sided unit propagation, in the sense that only variables assigned value 1 are propagated. The algorithm starts with all variables assigned value 0, and repeatedly flips variables to 1, one at a time. Let $\eta : \mathcal{F} \to \mathbb{N}_0$ associate a counter with each clause, representing the number of negative literals *not* assigned value 0. Given an assignment, a goal clause $c \in \mathcal{F}$ is falsified if $\eta(c) = 0$. Similarly, a definite clause $c \in \mathcal{F}$ is unit and requires the sole positive literal to be assigned value 1 when $\eta(c) = 0$. LTUR maintains the η counters, propagates assignments due to unit definite clauses and terminates either when a falsified goal clause is identified or when no more definite clauses require that their sole positive literal be assigned value 1. The procedure starts with unit positive clauses c_r for which $\eta(c_r) = 0$. Clearly, a Horn formula without unit positive clauses is trivially satisfied. In the following, $\gamma : \mathcal{F} \to \{0,1\}$ denotes whether a clause $c \in \mathcal{F}$ is a goal clause, in which case $\gamma(c) = 1$. Finally, $\alpha : \mathrm{var}(\mathcal{F}) \to 2^{\mathcal{F}}$ is a function that assigns to each variable v a set of clauses $\alpha(v)$ that are deemed responsible for assigning value 1 to v. If the value of v is not determined to be 1, then $\alpha(v) = \emptyset$. As is standard in CDCL SAT solving [11], $\alpha(v)$ will be referred to as the *antecedent* (set) of v. The organization of LTUR is summarized in Algorithm 1. The initialization step sets the initial values of the η counters, the α values, and the value of the γ flag. Q is initialized with the variables in the unit positive clauses. For every $v \in Q$, $\alpha(v)$ contains the unit clause v. For all other variables, the value of α is $\emptyset$. Clearly, this initialization runs in time linear

Function LTUR($\mathcal{F}$)

    Input   : $\mathcal{F}$: input Horn formula

    Output: falsified clause, if any; α: antecedents

1    $(Q, \eta, \gamma, \alpha) \leftarrow$ Initialize($\mathcal{F}$)

2   **while** $Q \neq \emptyset$ **do**   // Q: queue of variables assigned 1

3        $v_j \leftarrow$ ExtractFirstVariable(Q)

4   **foreach** $c_i \in N(v_j)$ **do**

5            $\eta(c_i) \leftarrow \eta(c_i) - 1$

6   **if** $\eta(c_i) = 0$ **then**

7   **if** $\gamma(c_i)$ **then return** $(\{c_i\}, \alpha)$

8                $v_r \leftarrow$ PickVariable($P(c_i)$)

9   **if** $\alpha(v_r) = \emptyset$ **then**

10   AppendToQueue(Q, v_r)

11                    $\alpha(v_r) \leftarrow \{c_i\}$

12   **return** $(\emptyset, \alpha)$

Algorithm 1. The LTUR algorithm

on the number of literals. The main loop analyzes the variables assigned value 1 in order. Notice that a variable v is assigned value 1 iff $\alpha(v) \neq \emptyset$. For each variable $v \in Q$, the counter η of the clauses where v occurs as a negative literal is decreased. If the $\eta(c) = 0$ for some clause c, then either the formula is inconsistent, if c is a goal clause, or the positive literal of c is assigned value 1 and added to Q. The operation of LTUR is such that $|\alpha(v)| \leq 1$ for $v \in \text{var}(\mathcal{F})$. It is easy to see that LTUR runs in linear time on the number of literals of $\mathcal{F}$ [37]: each variable v is analyzed only once, since v is added to the queue Q only if $\alpha(v) = \emptyset$, and after being added to Q, $\alpha(v) \neq \emptyset$ and $\alpha(v)$ will not be set to $\emptyset$ again. Thus, v will not be added to Q more than once. For each variable v, its clauses are analyzed at most once, in case v was added to Q. Thus, the number of times literals are analyzed during the execution of LTUR is $\mathcal{O}(\|\mathcal{F}\|)$.

It is often convenient to run LTUR incrementally. Given $\mathcal{F} = \mathcal{R} \cup \mathcal{B}$, one can add a unit positive clause at a time, and run LTUR while consistency is preserved. If no inconsistency is identified for any of the unit positive clauses, the total run time is $\mathcal{O}(\|\mathcal{F}\|)$. In contrast, if inconsistency is identified for some unit positive clause, consistency may be recovered by undoing only the last sequence of variables assigned value 1. Incremental LTUR plays an important role in the algorithms described in Sect. 4, concretely for MUS and MCS extraction.

3.2 LTUR Saturation

We will often resort to a modified version of LTUR, which we call LTUR *saturation* (LTURs). LTURs also runs in linear time on the number of literals, but exhibits properties that are relevant when analyzing inconsistent Horn formulae. The basic idea is *not* to terminate the execution of LTUR when a falsified goal clause is identified. Instead, the falsified clause is recorded, and the one-sided unit propagation of LTUR continues to be executed. The procedure only

Function LTURs($\mathcal{F}$)

    Input : $\mathcal{F}$: input Horn formula

    Output: $\mathcal{U}$: falsified clauses; α: antecedent sets

1    $(Q, \eta, \gamma, \alpha, \mathcal{U}) \leftarrow$ Initialize($\mathcal{F}$)

2   **while** $Q \neq \emptyset$ **do**   // Q: queue of variables assigned 1

3        $v_j \leftarrow$ ExtractFirstVariable(Q)

4   **foreach** $c_i \in N(v_j)$ **do**

5            $\eta(c_i) \leftarrow \eta(c_i) - 1$

6   **if** $\eta(c_i) = 0$ **then**

7   **if** $\gamma(c_i)$ **then**

8                    $\mathcal{U} \leftarrow \mathcal{U} \cup \{c_i\}$

9   **else**

10                  $v_r \leftarrow$ PickVariable($P(c_i)$)

11   **if** $\alpha(v_r) = \emptyset$ **then**

12   AppendToQueue(Q, v_r)

13                  $\alpha(v_r) \leftarrow \alpha(v_r) \cup \{c_i\}$

14   **return** $(\mathcal{U}, \alpha)$

Algorithm 2. The LTURs algorithm

terminates when Q is empty. Besides $\mathcal{U}$, in this case the value of $\alpha(v)$ is updated with any clause that can serve to determining the assignment of v to value 1.

Algorithm 2 summarizes the main steps of LTURs. When compared with LTUR, the main difference is the set $\mathcal{U}$, initially set to $\emptyset$, and to which the falsified clauses are added to. Using the same arguments presented in Sect. 3.1, it can be shown that LTURs also runs in time $\mathcal{O}(||\mathcal{F}||)$.

3.3 Tracing Antecedents

Another important step when analyzing inconsistent Horn formulae is to trace antecedents. Algorithm 3 describes an approach for tracing that is based on

Function TraceClauses($\mathcal{U}, \alpha$)

    Input : $\mathcal{U}$: falsified clause(s); α: antecedents

    Output: $\mathcal{M}$: traced clauses from $\mathcal{F}$, given $\mathcal{U}$ and α

1    $(S, \mathcal{M}, \phi) \leftarrow$ Initialize($\mathcal{U}$)

2   **while not** Empty(S) **do**

3        $c_i \leftarrow$ PopClause(S)

4   **foreach** $v_r \in N(c_i)$ **do**

5   **foreach** $c_a \in \alpha(v_r)$ **do**

6   **if** $\phi(c_a) = 0$ **then**

7                  $\phi(c_a) \leftarrow 1$

8   PushClause(S, c_a)

9                  $\mathcal{M} \leftarrow \mathcal{M} \cup \{c_a\}$

10   **return** $\mathcal{M}$

Algorithm 3. Tracing antecedents

knowing at least one antecedent for each variable assigned 1. Thus, this method can be used after running LTUR or LTURs. In the algorithm, ϕ is used as a flag to ensure each clause is traced at most once. The stack S is initialized with the clauses in $\mathcal{U}$. Algorithm 3 implements a depth-first traversal of the graph induced by the antecedent sets, starting from the clauses in $\mathcal{U}$. Hence, the algorithm runs in $\mathcal{O}(\|\mathcal{F}\|)$ time.

4   Efficient Reasoning for Inconsistent Horn Formulae

In this section we analyze a number of computational problems related with the analysis of inconsistent Horn formulae. The main results obtained are summarized in Table 1. Some of the results, depicted with slanted text, are adapted from the literature. We briefly recall these results before presenting our contributions.

An algorithm for enumerating all MUSes of an inconsistent Horn formula without background knowledge can be obtained through a straightforward modification of the method presented in [42]. In the presence of background knowledge (that is, when $\mathcal{B} \neq \emptyset$), it was shown in [5, Theorem 4] that no output polynomial algorithm exists for enumerating all MUSes (unless P = NP). A similar approach was used to prove that MCSes for formulae with background knowledge cannot be enumerated in output polynomial time in [41, Theorem 6.15], unless P = NP. In [42, Theorems 17 and 18] is was also shown that deciding MUS membership for a clause is NP-complete. A simple algorithm for finding one MUS requires one inconsistency check for every relaxable clause in the formula [8,15]. The linear runtime of LTUR [16,37] guarantees that one MUS can be computed in quadratic time. This upper bound was further refined to $\mathcal{O}(|\mathcal{M}| \cdot \|\mathcal{F}\|)$, where $\mathcal{M}$ is the size of the largest MUS, in [3]. In the following we provide more details on these results, and prove the remaining claims from Table 1.

Table 1. Summary of results

$\mathcal{B}$?	1 MUS	MUS Enum	1 MCS	MCS Enum	Lean Kernel	$\in$ MUS	$\in$ MCS	$\bigcup$ MU, $\bigcup$ MC
$\mathcal{B} = \emptyset$	linear	*PD*	linear	*PD*	linear	*NPC*	*NPC*	FP^{NP}[wit,log]
$\mathcal{B} \neq \emptyset$	*poly*	*not OP*	poly	*not OP*	linear	*NPC*	*NPC*	FP^{NP}[wit,log]

4.1   MUS Extraction and Enumeration

We first focus on the problems related to extracting and enumerating MUSes. As mentioned already, to compute one MUS one can simply perform a linear number of inconsistency tests—one for each clause in $\mathcal{R}$. This yields an overall quadratic behaviour. As we show next, in the absence of background knowledge, one MUS can be extracted in linear time.

Proposition 1 (MUS Extraction, $\mathcal{B} = \emptyset$). *Let* $\mathcal{F} \models \perp$, *with* $\mathcal{B} = \emptyset$. *One MUS of* $\mathcal{F}$ *can be computed in time* $\mathcal{O}(\|\mathcal{F}\|)$.

Proof. Horn formulae are decided by LTUR, that implements (one-sided) unit propagation and runs in $\mathcal{O}(||\mathcal{F}||)$. It is well-known that unsatisfiable subsets computed with unit propagation are MUSes [29, Proposition 1]. Thus, tracing antecedents, starting from the falsified goal clause $c \in \mathcal{F}$ returned by LTUR, yields an MUS of $\mathcal{F}$. Algorithm 3 illustrates an implementation of clause tracing that runs in $\mathcal{O}(||\mathcal{F}||)$. Overall, both LTUR and clause tracing are run once. Hence, an MUS is extracted in time $\mathcal{O}(||\mathcal{F}||)$.   □

One important observation is that the polynomial delay enumeration algorithm presented in [42] uses an arbitrary polynomial-time MUS extraction algorithm as a black-box. Thus, the linear time extraction method presented above can be exploited to enumerate all MUSes more efficiently.

When the formula $\mathcal{F}$ contains background knowledge, MUS extraction becomes more expensive. As shown recently in [3] through an insertion-based algorithm, in this case an MUS can be computed in $\mathcal{O}(|\mathcal{M}| \cdot ||\mathcal{F}||)$ time, where $\mathcal{M}$ is the size of the largest MUS. This is achieved by running LTUR incrementally, allowing the run time of successive consistent runs of LTUR to amortize to $||\mathcal{F}||$. Unfortunately, background knowledge has a more important effect on the enumeration problem. Indeed, as shown in [5], if $\mathcal{B} \neq \emptyset$, it is impossible to enumerate all MUSes in output polynomial time, unless P = NP.

4.2   MCS Extraction and Enumeration

A simple algorithm for computing one MCS consists in running LTUR first over all the clauses in $\mathcal{B}$, and then incrementally adding each clause c in $\mathcal{R} = \mathcal{F} \setminus \mathcal{B}$ to the execution of LTUR. As soon as LTUR detects an inconsistency, the latest clause c inserted is known to belong to an MCS and is added to a set $\mathcal{C}$; this clause is retracted, and the process continues. When all clauses have been tested, $\mathcal{C}$ contains an MCS, and its complement is an MSS. Overall, by running LTUR incrementally, the consistent calls to LTUR amortize to $||\mathcal{F}||$. For the inconsistent calls to LTUR, i.e. those producing clauses added to $\mathcal{C}$, one needs to undo the incremental run of LTUR, which in the worst-case runs in $||\mathcal{F}||$. This process needs to be executed once for each clause in $\mathcal{C}$. Taking into account that the (amortized) running time of LTUR is $\mathcal{O}(||\mathcal{F}||)$, an MCS can be computed in time $\mathcal{O}(|\mathcal{C}| \cdot ||\mathcal{F}||)$, where $\mathcal{C}$ is the size of the largest MCS in $\mathcal{F}$.

As it was the case for MUSes, the MCS extraction procedure can be improved to run in linear time in the case where $\mathcal{B} = \emptyset$. Consider again the execution of LTURs (see Algorithm 2). Since $\mathcal{B} = \emptyset$, any clause can be included in an MCS. This observation yields the following result.

Proposition 2. *Given $\mathcal{F}$, with $\mathcal{F} \vDash \bot$, the set $\mathcal{U}$ computed by LTURs is an MCS of $\mathcal{F}$.*

Proof. First, we show that $\mathcal{U}$ is a correction set. Observe that $\mathcal{U}$ is composed of goal clauses. Goal clauses do not serve to propagate other variables to value 1 and do not serve to prevent variables from being assigned value 1 when running LTURs. Thus, removing these clauses will not elicit further propagation

Function $\mathrm{MCSEnum}(\mathcal{F}, \tau)$

    Global : $\mathbb{M}$: MCS register

    Input   : $\mathcal{F}$: input Horn formula; τ: clause tags

1     $(\mathcal{U}, \alpha) \leftarrow \mathtt{LTURs}(\mathcal{F})$ // Use LTUR saturation to find MCS candidate

2   **if** $\mathcal{U} = \emptyset$ **then return**

3     $(\mathcal{C}, \mathcal{V}) \leftarrow \mathtt{PickVariables}(\mathcal{U})$ // $\mathcal{V}$: variables of negative literals in $\mathcal{U}$

4   **if** $\mathtt{MCSRegistered}(\mathcal{C}, \mathbb{M})$ **then return**

5     $\mathtt{RegisterMCS}(\mathcal{C}, \mathbb{M})$ // Record computed MCS in MCS register

6   **foreach** $v \in \mathcal{V}$ **do**

7          $\mathcal{W} \leftarrow \mathtt{DropClauses}(\mathcal{F}, \neg v)$ // Drop clauses with literal $\neg v$

              // Next, drop literal v in clauses of $\mathcal{W}$ and tag clauses

8          $(\mathcal{W}, \tau) \leftarrow \mathtt{DropLitsTagCls}(\mathcal{W}, \tau, v)$

9          $\mathrm{MCSEnum}(\mathcal{W}, \tau)$ // Recursive call of MCS enumeration

Algorithm 4. MCS enumeration with polynomial delay

of variables to value 1. Since these are the only falsified clauses, if the clauses in $\mathcal{U}$ are removed, what remains is satisfiable; hence $\mathcal{U}$ is a correction set. To show that $\mathcal{U}$ is minimal, observe that if any clause in $\mathcal{U}$ is not removed, then it will remain unsatisfied, again because removing clauses in $\mathcal{U}$ does not alter the variables assigned value 1. Thus, $\mathcal{U}$ is a correction set for $\mathcal{F}$ and it is minimal, and so it is an MCS for $\mathcal{F}$. $\square$

Corollary 1. *LTURs computes an MCS in linear time on the number of literals.*

In different settings, enumeration of MUSes and MCSes is paramount [5,42,44]. We can use the linear time algorithm for MCS extraction to develop a polynomial delay algorithm for enumerating MCSes of a Horn formula when $\mathcal{B} = \emptyset$. We know how to compute one MCS in linear time, by applying LTURs and falsifying goal clauses. The question is then how to iterate the computation of MCSes. The approach we follow is to transform the formula, so that different sets of falsified goal clauses are obtained. Given a goal clause c with a negative literal ℓ on variable v, the transformation is to remove the clauses with literal $\neg v$, and remove the literal v from each clause c' containing that literal. The resulting clause $c_r = c' \setminus \{v\}$ becomes a goal clause. The newly created goal clause is *tagged* with the variable v. As the formula is transformed, $\tau(c)$ indicates whether c is tagged, taking value $\perp$ if not, or being assigned some variable otherwise. As a result, when LTURs is used to find a set of falsified goal clauses, the computed MCSes must also account for the set of tags associated with these falsified goal clauses.

Algorithm 4 summarizes the main steps of the MCS enumeration algorithm with polynomial delay. At each step, LTURs is used to find a set of falsified *goal* clauses which, together with the tag associated with each falsified goal clause (if any), represents an MCS for $\mathcal{F}$. $\mathcal{V}$ represents the negative literals in falsified goal clauses, and will be used to create additional subproblems. In contrast, $\mathcal{C}$ represents the literals in $\mathcal{V}$ and also includes the variables in the tags of the falsified goal clauses. If the computed MCS has already been seen before, then

Table 2. MCS enumeration example

Formula $\mathcal{F}$	Depth	False clauses	MCS	Literals	Picked literal
$\mathcal{F}_1 \triangleq \{(x_1),(\neg x_1),(x_2),(\neg x_2)\}$	0	$\{(\neg x_1),(\neg x_2)\}$	$\{(\neg x_1),(\neg x_2)\}$	$\{x_1,x_2\}$	x_1
$\mathcal{F}_2 \triangleq \{(),(x_2),(\neg x_2)\}$	1	$\{(),(\neg x_2)\}$	$\{(x_1),(\neg x_2)\}$	$\{x_2\}$	x_2
$\mathcal{F}_3 \triangleq \{(),()\}$	2	$\{(),()\}$	$\{(x_1),(x_2)\}$	$\emptyset$	$-$
$\mathcal{F}_1$	0	$-$	$-$	$\{x_1,x_2\}$	x_2
$\mathcal{F}_4 \triangleq \{(x_1),(\neg x_1),()\}$	1	$\{(\neg x_1),()\}$	$\{(\neg x_1),(x_2)\}$	$\{x_1\}$	x_1
$\mathcal{F}_5 \triangleq \{(),()\}$	2	$\{(),()\}$	$\{(x_1),(x_2)\}$	$\emptyset$	$-$

the algorithm returns without further action. Otherwise, the MCS has not been computed before, and it is recorded in a global register of MCSes M. This MCS is then used to generate a number of modified formulas, from which additional MCSes of the original $\mathcal{F}$ can be computed. Observe that line 7 and line 8 in Algorithm 4 can be viewed as *forcing* some variable to be assigned value 0, hence blocking the one-sided unit propagation of LTUR.

Example 1. Consider the formula: $\mathcal{F} \triangleq \{(x_1),(\neg x_1),(x_2),(\neg x_2)\}$. Table 2 summarizes the execution of Algorithm 4. For each recursion depth (0, 1 or 2), the literal picked is the literal selected in line 6 of Algorithm 4. Given the falsified clauses identified by LTURs, the actual MCS is obtained from these clauses, each augmented with its own tagging literal, if any.

Proposition 3. *Algorithm 4 is sound and complete; i.e., it computes all MCSes.*

Proof (Sketch). Algorithm 4 iterates the enumeration of MCSes by selecting some variable v assigned value 1 by LTURs (see line 6), and then changing the formula such that the variable is removed. This step corresponds to replacing the variable v with value 0, or alternatively by forcing v to be assigned value 0. This process changes the set of falsified clauses. These observations enable us to prove soundness and completeness.

Soundness. The proof is by induction on i, the number of variables forced to be assigned value 0 in, which uniquely identify each MCS. For the base case ($i = 1$), consider the MCS associated with no variables yet forced to be assigned value 0. Force some 1-valued variable in the MCS to be assigned value 0. Re-run LTURs. The set of falsified clauses is an MCS, provided we augment the falsified goal clauses with their tag variable. For the inductive step, suppose we have i variables forced to be assigned value 0 and some current MCS. Force some other 1-valued variable in the MCS to be assigned value 0. Run LTURs. Again, the set of falsified clauses is an MCS.

Completeness. Consider the operation of moving from one MCS to another, obtained from assigning some variables to value 0. This consists in reverting some unit propagation step, where a variable was assigned value 1 and is now forced to be assigned value 0. The algorithm reverts unit propagation steps in order, creating a search tree. Each node in this search tree represents one MCS and is expanded into k children. Each child node is associated with one of the 1-valued literals in the MCS to be forced to be assigned value 0. Thus, Algorithm 4 will enumerate all subsets of variables assigned value 1, which lead to a conflict being identified, and so all MCSes are enumerated.   □

Proposition 4. *Algorithm 4 enumerates the MCSes of an inconsistent Horn formula $\mathcal{F}$ with polynomial delay.*

Proof (Sketch). At each iteration, Algorithm 4 runs LTURs in linear time, and transforms the current working formula, also a linear time operation, once for each literal in the target set of literals. The algorithm must check whether the MCS has already been computed, which can be done in time logarithmic on the number of MCSes stored in the MCS registry, e.g. by representing the registry with a balanced search tree. The additional work done by Algorithm 4 in between computed MCSes is polynomial on the formula size. The iterations that do not produce an MCS are bounded by a polynomial as follows. An MCS can be repeated from a recursive call, but only after one new MCS is computed. Each new MCS can recursively call Algorithm 4 $\mathcal{O}(|\mathcal{F}|)$ times, in the worst-case each call leading to an MCS not being computed. Thus, the overall cost of recursive calls to Algorithm 4 leading to an MCS not being computed is polynomial. Therefore, Algorithm 4 computes MCSes of an inconsistent Horn formula with polynomial delay.   □

4.3   Finding the Lean Kernel

The lean kernel is the set of all clauses that can be used in some resolution refutation of a propositional formula, and has been shown to be tightly related with the concept of maximum autarky [24–26]. Autarkies were proposed in the mid 80s [38] with the purpose of devising an algorithm for satisfiability requiring less than 2^n steps. Later work revealed the importance of autarkies when analyzing inconsistent formulas [24,25,27,34]. Indeed, the lean kernel represents an over-approximation of $\bigcup \mathsf{MU}$ [24–27], that is in general easier to compute for arbitrary CNF formulae. As shown in this section, the same holds true for Horn formulae.

Example 2. Consider the Horn formula: $\mathcal{F} \triangleq \{(a), (\neg a \vee b), (\neg b \vee x), (\neg x \vee b), (\neg b \vee c), (\neg c), (\neg b \vee d)\}$. It is easy to see that the lean kernel of $\mathcal{F}$ is: $\mathcal{K} \triangleq \{(a), (\neg a \vee b), (\neg b \vee x), (\neg x \vee b), (\neg b \vee c), (\neg c)\}$. Indeed, there exists a resolution proof that resolves on x once and on b twice in addition to resolving on a and c. On the other hand, $\mathcal{F}$ has only one MUS, and hence $\bigcup \mathsf{MU}$ is given by: $\mathcal{U} \triangleq \{(a), (\neg a \vee b), (\neg b \vee c), (\neg c)\}$.

The most efficient practical algorithms for computing the maximum autarky, and by extension the lean kernel, exploit intrinsic properties of maximum autarkies and reduce the problem to computing one MCS [34]. Other recently proposed algorithms require asymptotically fewer calls in the worst case [28].

Function LEANKERNEL($\mathcal{F}$)
  Input : $\mathcal{F}$: input Horn formula
  Output: $\mathcal{K}$: lean kernel of $\mathcal{F}$
1    $(\mathcal{U}, \alpha) \leftarrow$ LTURs($\mathcal{F}$)   // See Algorithm 2
2    $\mathcal{K} \leftarrow$ TraceAntecedents($\mathcal{U}, \alpha$)   // See Algorithm 3
3   **return** $\mathcal{K}$

Algorithm 5. Computing the Lean Kernel

The reduction of maximum autarky to the problem of computing one MCS involves calling a SAT solver on an arbitrary CNF formula a logarithmic number of times, in the worst-case. In contrast, it is possible to obtain a polynomial (non-linear) time algorithm by exploiting LTUR [37] and the maximum autarky extraction algorithm based on the iterative removal of resolution refutations [26]. This simple polynomial time algorithm can be further refined to achieve a linear time runtime behavior for computing the lean kernel for Horn formulae, even in the presence of background knowledge, as shown next.

Algorithm 5 exploits LTUR saturation for computing a set of clauses $\mathcal{K}$ that corresponds to the lean kernel. The algorithm simply traverses all possible antecedents, starting from the falsified clauses until the unit positive clauses are reached. The set of all traced clauses corresponds to the lean kernel, as they are all clauses that can appear in a resolution refutation, by construction (see Proposition 5). Notice that the correctness of this algorithm does not depend on the presence or absence of background knowledge. Thus, the lean kernel can be computed in linear time also for formulas with $\mathcal{B} \neq \emptyset$.

Example 3. Consider again the formula $\mathcal{F}$ from Example 2. After applying LTURs to $\mathcal{F}$, we obtain the antecedent sets of all activated variables. Observe that, among others, $(\neg b \vee x)$ and $(\neg x \vee b)$ are antecedents of x and b, respectively. After tracing the antecedents of the falsified clauses, we obtain the set of clauses $\mathcal{U}$.

Proposition 5. *Algorithm 5 computes the lean kernel of the input Horn formula $\mathcal{F}$.*

Proof. Recall that LTURs only assigns the value 1 to a variable v when this is necessary to satisfy some clause in $\mathcal{F}$. In order to trace the causes for inconsistency, all such clauses are stored by LTURs as antecedents for the variable activation. Thus, for every clause c in $\alpha(v)$ there exists a proof derivation for the assignment of 1 to v that uses this clause c. Thus all the traced clauses from $\mathcal{F}$ given the falsified clauses and α appear in some resolution refutation of $\mathcal{F}$; that is, they belong to the lean kernel.

Conversely, notice that resolving two Horn clauses yields a new Horn clause. Moreover, the number of variables in a clause can only be reduced by resolving with a clause containing only a single (positive) variable. Thus, every resolution refutation of $\mathcal{F}$ can be transformed into a sequence of steps of LTUR leading to a conflict, with the resolving clauses appearing as antecedents for each activation.

In particular, all clauses in the lean kernel are found while tracing antecedents of falsified clauses.   □

4.4   MUS and MCS Membership

As stated already, the lean kernel is an over-approximation of $\bigcup\text{MU}$ [25] that can be computed in linear time. In contrast, finding the precise set $\bigcup\text{MU}$ is significantly harder. In fact, deciding whether a given clause c belongs to $\bigcup\text{MU}$ is NP-complete, even if $\mathcal{B} = \emptyset$.

Definition 3 (MUS/MCS Membership). *Let $\mathcal{F}$ be a formula and $c \in \mathcal{F} \setminus \mathcal{B}$. The* MUS *membership problem is to decide whether there exists an MUS $\mathcal{M}$ of $\mathcal{F}$ such that $c \in \mathcal{M}$. The* MCS *membership problem is to decide whether there exists an MCS $\mathcal{C}$ of $\mathcal{F}$ such that $c \in \mathcal{C}$.*

It was previously shown that MUS membership is a computationally hard problem. Indeed, for Horn formulae this problem is already NP-complete [42, Theorems 17 and 18], and for arbitrary CNF formulae, its complexity increases to Σ_2^p-complete [30].

Interestingly, the hitting set duality between MUSes and MCSes [43] implies that a clause is in some MCS if and only if it is in some MUS. In other words, the identity $\bigcup\text{MU}(\mathcal{F}) = \bigcup\text{MC}(\mathcal{F})$ holds. From this fact, it automatically follows that MCS membership is also NP-complete [41, Theorem 6.5].

Proposition 6. *The MCS membership problem is NP-complete.*

Through the non-deterministic algorithm that decides MUS membership, it is then possible to prove, using the techniques from [21] that $\bigcup\text{MU}$ can be computed through logarithmically many calls to a witness oracle.

Proposition 7. $\bigcup\text{MU}(\mathcal{F})$ *is in* $\text{FP}^{\text{NP}}[\text{wit,log}]$.

Proof (Sketch). Notice first that $\bigcup\text{MU}(\mathcal{F})$ can be computed through a linear number of parallel queries to an NP oracle. More precisely, for every clause c in $\mathcal{F}$ we decide the MUS membership problem for c. As shown in [21, Remark 4], these parallel queries can be replaced by a logarithmic number of calls to a witness oracle. It then follows that $\bigcup\text{MU}(\mathcal{F})$ is in $\text{FP}^{\text{NP}}[\text{wit,log}]$.   □

Remark 1. Since $\bigcup\text{MU}(\mathcal{F}) = \bigcup\text{MC}(\mathcal{F})$, then $\bigcup\text{MC}(\mathcal{F})$ is also in $\text{FP}^{\text{NP}}[\text{wit,log}]$.

5   Experimental Results

To illustrate the importance of the algorithms developed in Sect. 4, we investigate the size of the lean kernel (see Algorithm 5) for 1000 unsatisfiable Horn formulae that encode axiom pinpointing problems in the description logic $\mathcal{EL}^+$ using the encoding from [44–46]. These instances were used in [3] as benchmarks for enumerating MUSes of Horn formulae (with $\mathcal{B} \neq \emptyset$). There are two

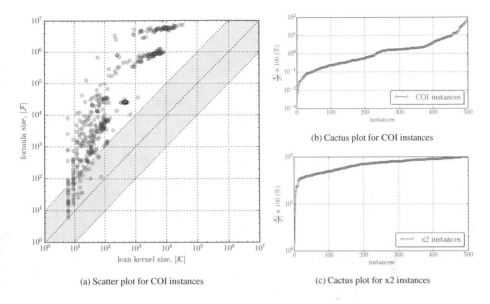

(a) Scatter plot for COI instances   (c) Cactus plot for x2 instances

Fig. 1. Formula reductions for COI and x2 instances

kinds of instances that correspond to two different reduction techniques proposed in [45, 46], namely COI and the more effective x2 optimization. The experiments include 500 instances of each kind. Earlier work [3, 45, 46] showed that the size of the formulae has a great impact in the efficiency of MUS enumeration, being the COI instances (much) harder to solve than the x2 instances.

We computed the lean kernel of each of the 1000 test formulae and compared the size of the result with the size of the original formula. The results of these comparisons are depicted in Fig. 1. The scatter plot in Fig. 1a summarizes the formulae reductions for the COI instances. The cactus plots summarize the formulae reductions for the COI and x2 instances, respectively. As can be observed, for the COI instances with more than 100 clauses, the size of the lean kernel (i.e. an over-approximation of the clauses that are relevant for computing MUSes and MCSes) is often around 1% (or less) of the original formula. Figure 1b confirms that for around 50% of the instances, the lean kernel size is less than 1% of the original problem instance size. In other words, the lean kernel is at least two orders of magnitude smaller than the input formula in most of these cases. In practical terms, this means that for many of the Horn formulae used for axiom pinpointing in the recent past based on COI reduction, around more than 99% of the clauses are irrelevant for the computation of MUSes and MCSes. The results obtained for the x2 instances (Fig. 1c) are not as dramatic. This was expected as the x2 reduction is more effective in removing irrelevant clauses from the formula. However, even in this case the lean kernel is strictly smaller than the input formula in all but 19 instances. From these 19 instances, one has 25 clauses, and all others contain 6 clauses; thus, it is not surprising that no reduction was achieved through the lean kernel. Interestingly, about half of the instances observed a reduction of over 20 %, and in some extreme cases the size of the formula was reduced in more than 90 %. To the best of our knowledge, these are the first practical problem instances for which the size of the maximum autarky (i.e., the complement of the lean kernel) is non-negligible.

6   Conclusions

We have developed several new results related to reasoning about inconsistent Horn formulae. These results complement earlier work [3,5,42], and find application in a number of settings, including axiom pinpointing of lightweight description logics. In particular, we presented a polynomial delay algorithm for enumerating all MCSes, and a linear-time method for computing the lean kernel of a formula.

We illustrate the relevance of our work by analyzing Horn formulae that encode axiom pinpointing problems in the description logic $\mathcal{EL}^+$. The experimental results show that commonly used Horn formulae [2,3,44] contain a very large proportion of irrelevant clauses, i.e. clauses that do not interfere with consistency. With the exception of a few outliers related with very small formulae, most formulae have around 99 % of irrelevant clauses, which can be identified with a linear time algorithm. From a practical perspective, a natural step is to exploit the linear time lean kernel identification in state of the art axiom pinpointing tools [1–3,32] and other problems where MUS enumeration and membership are important.

References

1. Arif, M.F., Mencía, C., Ignatiev, A., Manthey, N., Peñaloza, R., Marques-Silva, J.: BEACON: an efficient SAT-based tool for debugging $\mathcal{EL}^+$ ontologies. In: Creignou, N., Le Berre, D. (eds.) SAT 2016. LNCS, vol. 9710, pp. 521–530. Springer, Heidelberg (2016). doi:10.1007/978-3-319-40970-2_32
2. Arif, M.F., Mencía, C., Marques-Silva, J.: Efficient axiom pinpointing with EL2MCS. In: Hölldobler, S., Krötzsch, M., Peñaloza, R., Rudolph, S. (eds.) KI 2015. LNCS (LNAI), vol. 9324, pp. 225–233. Springer, Heidelberg (2015). doi:10.1007/978-3-319-24489-1_17
3. Arif, M.F., Mencía, C., Marques-Silva, J.: Efficient MUS enumeration of horn formulae with applications to axiom pinpointing. In: Heule, M., Weaver, S. (eds.) SAT 2015. LNCS, vol. 9340, pp. 324–342. Springer, Heidelberg (2015). doi:10.1007/978-3-319-24318-4_24
4. Baader, F., Brandt, S., Lutz, C.: Pushing the $\mathcal{EL}$ envelope. In: IJCAI, pp. 364–369 (2005)
5. Baader, F., Peñaloza, R., Suntisrivaraporn, B.: Pinpointing in the description logic $\mathcal{EL}^+$. In: Hertzberg, J., Beetz, M., Englert, R. (eds.) KI 2007. LNCS (LNAI), vol. 4667, pp. 52–67. Springer, Heidelberg (2007). doi:10.1007/978-3-540-74565-5_7
6. Bacchus, F., Davies, J., Tsimpoukelli, M., Katsirelos, G.: Relaxation search: a simple way of managing optional clauses. In: AAAI, pp. 835–841 (2014)

7. Bacchus, F., Katsirelos, G.: Using minimal correction sets to more efficiently compute minimal unsatisfiable sets. In: Kroening, D., Păsăreanu, C.S. (eds.) CAV 2015. LNCS, vol. 9207, pp. 70–86. Springer, Heidelberg (2015). doi:10.1007/978-3-319-21668-3_5

8. Bakker, R.R., Dikker, F., Tempelman, F., Wognum, P.M.: Diagnosing and solving over-determined constraint satisfaction problems. In: IJCAI, pp. 276–281 (1993)

9. Bate, A., Motik, B., Grau, B.C., Simancik, F., Horrocks, I.: Extending consequence-based reasoning to SRIQ. In: KR, pp. 187–196 (2016)

10. Belov, A., Lynce, I., Marques-Silva, J.: Towards efficient MUS extraction. AI Commun. 25(2), 97–116 (2012)

11. Biere, A., Heule, M., van Maaren, H., Walsh, T. (eds.): Handbook of Satisfiability. Frontiers in Artificial Intelligence and Applications, vol. 185. IOS Press, Amsterdam (2009)

12. Bjørner, N., Fioravanti, F., Rybalchenko, A., Senni, V. (eds.) Proceedings First Workshop on Horn Clauses for Verification and Synthesis, HCVS 2014, Vienna, Austria, 17 July 2014. EPTCS, vol. 169 (2014)

13. Bjørner, N., Gurfinkel, A., McMillan, K., Rybalchenko, A.: Horn clause solvers for program verification. In: Beklemishev, L.D., Blass, A., Dershowitz, N., Finkbeiner, B., Schulte, W. (eds.) Fields of Logic and Computation II: Essays Dedicated to Yuri Gurevich on the Occasion of his 75th Birthday. LNCS, vol. 9300, pp. 24–51. Springer, Heidelberg (2015). doi:10.1007/978-3-319-23534-9_2

14. Buss, S.R., Krajíček, J., Takeuti, G.: Provably total functions in the bounded arithmetic theories R_3^i, U_2^i, and V_2^i. In: Clote, P., Krajíček, J. (eds.) Arithmetic, Proof Theory, and Computational Complexity, pp. 116–161. OUP (1995)

15. Chinneck, J.W., Dravnieks, E.W.: Locating minimal infeasible constraint sets in linear programs. INFORMS J. Comput. 3(2), 157–168 (1991)

16. Dowling, W.F., Gallier, J.H.: Linear-time algorithms for testing the satisfiability of propositional Horn formulae. J. Log. Program. 1(3), 267–284 (1984)

17. Eiter, T., Gottlob, G.: The complexity of logic-based abduction. J. ACM 42(1), 3–42 (1995)

18. Henschen, L.J., Wos, L.: Unit refutations and Horn sets. J. ACM 21(4), 590–605 (1974)

19. Horn, A.: On sentences which are true of direct unions of algebras. J. Symb. Log. 16(1), 14–21 (1951)

20. Itai, A., Makowsky, J.A.: Unification as a complexity measure for logic programming. J. Log. Program. 4(2), 105–117 (1987)

21. Janota, M., Marques-Silva, J.: On the query complexity of selecting minimal sets for monotone predicates. Artif. Intell. 233, 73–83 (2016)

22. Johnson, D.S., Papadimitriou, C.H., Yannakakis, M.: On generating all maximal independent sets. Inf. Process. Lett. 27(3), 119–123 (1988)

23. Kazakov, Y., Krötzsch, M., Simancik, F.: The incredible ELK - from polynomial procedures to efficient reasoning with ontologies. J. Autom. Reasoning 53(1), 1–61 (2014)

24. Kleine Büning, H., Kullmann, O.: Minimal unsatisfiability and autarkies. In: Biere, A., et al. [11], pp. 339–401

25. Kullmann, O.: Investigations on autark assignments. Discrete Appl. Math. 107 (1–3), 99–137 (2000)

26. Kullmann, O.: On the use of autarkies for satisfiability decision. Electron. Notes Discrete Math. 9, 231–253 (2001)

27. Kullmann, O., Lynce, I., Marques-Silva, J.: Categorisation of clauses in conjunctive normal forms: minimally unsatisfiable sub-clause-sets and the lean kernel. In: Biere, A., Gomes, C.P. (eds.) SAT 2006. LNCS, vol. 4121, pp. 22–35. Springer, Heidelberg (2006). doi:10.1007/11814948_4

28. Kullmann, O., Marques-Silva, J.: Computing maximal autarkies with few and simple oracle queries. In: Heule, M., Weaver, S. (eds.) SAT 2015. LNCS, vol. 9340, pp. 138–155. Springer, Heidelberg (2015). doi:10.1007/978-3-319-24318-4_11

29. Li, C.M., Manyà, F., Mohamedou, N.O., Planes, J.: Resolution-based lower bounds in MaxSAT. Constraints 15(4), 456–484 (2010)

30. Liberatore, P.: Redundancy in logic I: CNF propositional formulae. Artif. Intell. 163(2), 203–232 (2005)

31. Liberatore, P.: Redundancy in logic II: 2CNF and Horn propositional formulae. Artif. Intell. 172(2–3), 265–299 (2008)

32. Manthey, N., Peñaloza, R., Rudolph, S.: Efficient axiom pinpointing in $\mathcal{EL}$ using SAT technology. In: DL (2016)

33. Marques-Silva, J., Heras, F., Janota, M., Previti, A., Belov, A.: On computing minimal correction subsets. In: IJCAI, pp. 615–622 (2013)

34. Marques-Silva, J., Ignatiev, A., Morgado, A., Manquinho, V.M., Lynce, I.: Efficient autarkies. In: ECAI, pp. 603–608 (2014)

35. Mencía, C., Ignatiev, A., Previti, A., Marques-Silva, J.: MCS extraction with sublinear oracle queries. In: Creignou, N., Le Berre, D. (eds.) SAT 2016. LNCS, vol. 9710, pp. 342–360. Springer, Heidelberg (2016). doi:10.1007/978-3-319-40970-2_21

36. Mencía, C., Previti, A., Marques-Silva, J.: Literal-based MCS extraction. In: IJCAI, pp. 1973–1979 (2015)

37. Minoux, M.: LTUR: a simplified linear-time unit resolution algorithm for Horn formulae and computer implementation. Inf. Process. Lett. 29(1), 1–12 (1988)

38. Monien, B., Speckenmeyer, E.: Solving satisfiability in less than 2^n steps. Discrete Appl. Math. 10(3), 287–295 (1985)

39. Papadimitriou, C.H.: Computational Complexity. Addison Wesley, Redwood City (1993)

40. Papadimitriou, C.H.: NP-completeness: a retrospective. In: Degano, P., Gorrieri, R., Marchetti-Spaccamela, A. (eds.) ICALP 1997. LNCS, vol. 1256, pp. 2–6. Springer, Heidelberg (1997). doi:10.1007/3-540-63165-8_160

41. Peñaloza, R.: Axiom-pinpointing in description logics and beyond. Ph.D. thesis, Dresden University of Technology, Germany (2009)

42. Peñaloza, R., Sertkaya, B.: On the complexity of axiom pinpointing in the $\mathcal{EL}$ family of description logics. In: KR (2010)

43. Reiter, R.: A theory of diagnosis from first principles. Artif. Intell. 32(1), 57–95 (1987)

44. Sebastiani, R., Vescovi, M.: Axiom pinpointing in lightweight description logics via Horn-SAT encoding and conflict analysis. In: Schmidt, R.A. (ed.) CADE 2009. LNCS (LNAI), vol. 5663, pp. 84–99. Springer, Heidelberg (2009). doi:10.1007/978-3-642-02959-2_6

45. Sebastiani, R., Vescovi, M.: Axiom pinpointing in large $\mathcal{EL}^+$ ontologies via SAT and SMT techniques. Technical report DISI-15-010, DISI, University of Trento, Italy. http://disi.unitn.it/~rseba/elsat/elsat_techrep.pdf

46. Vescovi, M.: Exploiting SAT and SMT techniques for automated reasoning and ontology manipulation in description logics. Ph.D. thesis, University of Trento (2011)

Information Flow Under Budget Constraints

Pavel Naumov[1(✉)] and Jia Tao[2]

[1] Vassar College, Poughkeepsie, NY, USA
pgn2@cornell.edu
[2] The College of New Jersey, Ewing, NJ, USA
taoj@tcnj.edu

Abstract. Although first proposed in the database theory as properties of functional dependencies between attributes, Armstrong's axioms capture general principles of information flow by describing properties of dependencies between sets of pieces of information. This paper generalizes Armstrong's axioms to a setting in which there is a cost associated with information. The proposed logical system captures general principles of dependencies between pieces of information constrained by a given budget.

1 Introduction

1.1 Functional Dependency

Armstrong [4] introduced a system of three axioms describing the properties of functional dependencies between sets of attributes in a database. The applicability of these axioms goes far beyond the domain of databases. They capture the properties of functional dependency between any two sets of pieces of information. To describe this setting informally, one can think of an agent that has knowledge of some of the pieces of information and is interested in uncovering some other pieces. For example, knowing a cyphertext c and the decryption key k, one can determine the plain text message m. We write this as $c, k \rhd m$. Yet, one cannot determine the original message from the cyphertext alone without the encryption key, and thus, $\neg(c \rhd m)$. Keeping the intended epistemic interpretation in mind, we refer to the pieces of information as *secrets*.

The property $c, k \rhd m$ is valid when secrets c, k, and m are a cyphertext, a decryption key, and the corresponding plain text message. However, it may not be valid under some other interpretation of these secrets. Armstrong's axioms capture the most general properties of functional dependencies that are valid in all settings. These axioms are:

(A1) *Reflexivity:* $A \rhd B$, if $B \subseteq A$,
(A2) *Augmentation:* $A \rhd B \to A, C \rhd B, C$,
(A3) *Transitivity:* $A \rhd B \to (B \rhd C \to A \rhd C)$,

where A, B denotes the union of sets of secrets A and B, and $\varphi \to \psi$ denotes the logical implication. Armstrong [4] proved the soundness and the completeness of this logical system with respect to a database semantics.

© Springer International Publishing AG 2016
L. Michael and A. Kakas (Eds.): JELIA 2016, LNAI 10021, pp. 353–368, 2016.
DOI: 10.1007/978-3-319-48758-8_23

The above axioms became known in database literature as Armstrong's axioms, see Garcia-Molina, Ullman, and Widom [8, p. 81]. Beeri, Fagin, and Howard [5] suggested a variation of Armstrong's axioms that describes properties of multi-valued dependency. Hartmann, Link, and Schewe [10] investigated a "weak" version of functional dependency. Väänänen [18] proposed a first order version of these principles. Naumov and Nicholls [14] developed a similar set of axioms for what they called the *rationally* functional dependency.

1.2   Approximate Dependency

There have been two different approaches to extending Armstrong's axioms to handle approximate reasoning. Bělohlávek and Vychodil [6] described a complete logical system that formally captures the relation *approximate values of secrets in set A functionally determine approximate values of secrets in set B*. In his upcoming work [19], Väänänen considered the relation *secrets in set A determine secrets in set B with exception of p fraction of possible combinations of values of all secrets*. We denote this relation by $A \vartriangleright_p B$. For example, $A \vartriangleright_{0.05} B$ means that secrets in set A determine secrets in set B in all but 5% of the possible combinations. Väänänen [19] proposed a complete axiomatic system for this relation, consisting of the following principles for all real numbers $p, q \in [0, 1]$:

1. Reflexivity: $A \vartriangleright_0 B$, where $B \subseteq A$,
2. Totality: $A \vartriangleright_1 B$,
3. Weakening: $A \vartriangleright_p C, D \to A, B \vartriangleright_p C$,
4. Augmentation: $A \vartriangleright_p B \to A, C \vartriangleright_p B, C$,
5. Transitivity: $A \vartriangleright_p B \to (B \vartriangleright_q C \to A \vartriangleright_{p+q} C)$, where $p + q \leq 1$,
6. Monotonicity: $A \vartriangleright_p B \to A \vartriangleright_q B$, where $p \leq q$.

Note that Väänänen's relation $A \vartriangleright_p B$, when $p = 0$, is exactly the original Armstrong's functional dependency relation. In the case of an arbitrary p, relation $A \vartriangleright_p B$ could be considered as a "weaker" form of functional dependency, which might hold even in the cases where the functional dependency does not hold.

1.3   Budget-Constrained Dependency

In this paper we propose another interpretation of atomic predicate $A \vartriangleright_p B$ that we call *the budget-constrained dependency*. Just like Väänänen's approximate dependency, the budget-constrained dependency is a weaker form of the original Armstrong's functional dependency relation. Intuitively, $A \vartriangleright_p B$ means that *an agent who already knows secrets in set A can recover secrets in set B at cost no more than p*. More formally, we assume that a non-negative cost is assigned to each secret and that $A \vartriangleright_p B$ means that there is a way to add several secrets with the total cost no more than p to set A in such a way that the extended set of secrets functionally determines all secrets in set B.

One example of such a setting is fees associated with information access: criminal background check fees, court records obtaining fees, etc. Another example is geological explorations, where learning about deposits of mineral resources often requires costly drilling. Although it is convenient to think about a budget constraint as a financial one, a budget constraint can also refer to a limit on time, space, or some other resource.

In this paper we introduce a sound and complete logical system for the budget-constrained dependency which is based on the following three principles that generalize Armstrong's axioms:

1. *Reflexivity:* $A \rhd_p B$, if $B \subseteq A$,
2. *Augmentation:* $A \rhd_p B \to A, C \rhd_p B, C$,
3. *Transitivity:* $A \rhd_p B \to (B \rhd_q C \to A \rhd_{p+q} C)$.

1.4   Functional vs. Budget-Constrained Dependencies

Armstrong's axioms of functional dependency as well as our axioms of budget-constrained functional dependency can be formulated into two different ways using languages with different expressive power.

One approach is to allow only statements in our language that have the form $A \rhd_p B$ and not allow Boolean combinations of such statements. In this case, Armstrong's axioms should be stated as inference rules that allow to derive statements of the form $A \rhd_p B$ from other statements of the same form.

The other approach is to include Boolean connectives into the language. In this case, statements of the form $A \rhd_p B$ become atomic statements in the language. Then, Armstrong's axioms can be stated as actual axioms that would be used in the logical system along with the propositional tautologies and Modus Ponens inference rule.

The second approach clearly yields a more expressive language. While the proofs of the completeness of original Armstrong's axioms of functional dependency are surprisingly similar for these two cases, the situation is different when it comes to budget-constrained dependency. The more expressive language requires a significantly more sophisticated argument to prove the completeness theorem. In this paper we only consider the more expressive language. In the rest of this section we look at several examples to compare challenges raised by the proofs of the completeness for Armstrong's functional dependency and our budget-constrained dependency.

As the first example, consider the formula $a \rhd b \to b \rhd a$ in the language without budget constraints. To construct a counterexample for this formula we need to describe a model in which secret a functionally determines secret b but not vice versa. Informally, to construct this model, imagine a and b to be two paper folders. Let folder a contain copies of two different (and unrelated to each other) documents: X and Y, and let folder b contain only a copy of document Y. In this case, an agent can recover the content of folder b based on folder a but not vice versa.

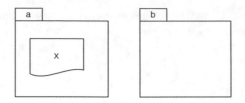

Fig. 1. Formula $a \triangleright b$ is true, but formula $b \triangleright a$ is false.

There is even a simpler counterexample for formula $a \triangleright b \rightarrow b \triangleright a$. Namely, consider a model in which folder a stores a copy of document X and folder b is empty, see Fig. 1. In this model, based on the content of folder a one can vacuously recover the content of empty folder b. At the same time, based on the content of empty folder b one cannot recover the content of folder a. Thus, in this model formula $a \triangleright b \rightarrow b \triangleright a$ is false.

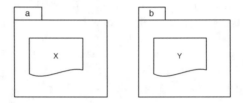

Fig. 2. Formulas $a \triangleright b$ and $b \triangleright a$ are both false.

Now consider formula $a \triangleright b \vee b \triangleright a$. To construct its counterexample, one can consider a model in which folders a and b containing copies of two different (and unrelated to each other) documents X and Y respectively, see Fig. 2.

To construct counterexamples for more complicated formulas, one can consider models with multiple folders containing copies of multiple documents. An example of such a model is depicted in Fig. 3. In this model $a, b \triangleright c$ is true because anyone with access to folders a and b knows the content of folder c. The folder/document model informally described here is sufficiently general to create a counterexample for each formula unprovable from Armstrong's axioms.

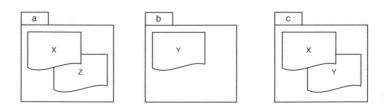

Fig. 3. Formula $a, b \triangleright c$ is true.

In fact, the original Armstrong's proof of the completeness for his rule-based system and the proof of the completeness for the corresponding axiom-based system [11] could be viewed as formalizations of this folder/document construction.

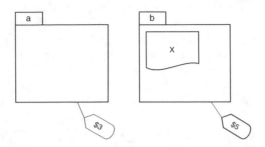

Fig. 4. Formula $a \rhd_4 b$ is false.

The situation becomes significantly more complicated once the cost of information is added to the language. Let us start with a very simple example. If we want to construct a counterexample for formula $a \rhd_4 b$, then we can consider a model depicted in Fig. 4 with two folders: a and b, priced at \$3 and \$5, respectively. The first folder is empty and the second contains a copy of the document X. It is clear that in this model anyone who knows the content of folder a still needs to spend \$5 to learn the content of folder b. Thus, budget-constrained dependency $a \rhd_p b$ is not satisfied in this model for each $p < 5$.

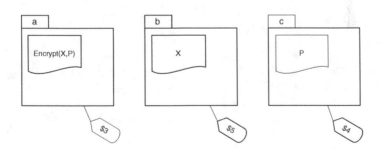

Fig. 5. Formula $a \rhd_4 b \to \varnothing \rhd_4 b$ is false.

Let us now consider a more interesting example. Suppose that we want to construct a counterexample for the formula $a \rhd_4 b \to \varnothing \rhd_4 b$. That is, we want to construct a model where anyone who knows the content of folder a can reconstruct the content of folder b after spending at most \$4. Yet, the same cannot be done without access to folder a. To construct such a model we use the cryptographic tool called one-time encryption pad[1]. Our model consists of three folders a, b, and c priced at \$3, \$5, and \$4, respectively, see Fig. 5. Let folder b contain a copy of a document X, folder c contain an encryption pad P, and folder a contain the encrypted version of the document. In this model, $\varnothing \rhd_4 b$ is false because \$4 buys either access to the encryption pad in folder c or access to the encrypted text in folder a, but not both. However, formula $a \rhd_4 b$ is true in the same model because anyone who knows encrypted text $Encrypt(X, P)$ can spend \$4 on pad P, decode message X, and thus, learn the content of folder b.

The one-time pad encryption is known in cryptography as a symmetric-key algorithm because the same key (i.e. the one-time pad) could be used to encrypt and to decrypt the text. As a result, in the model depicted in Fig. 5, not only formula $a \rhd_4 b$ is true, but formula $b \rhd_4 a$ is true as well.

For the next example, we construct a counterexample for formula

$$a \rhd_4 b \to (\varnothing \rhd_4 b \lor b \rhd_4 a).$$

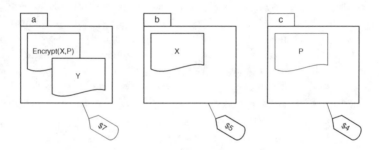

Fig. 6. Formula $a \rhd_4 b \to (\varnothing \rhd_4 b \lor b \rhd_4 a)$ is false.

This is an easier task than one might think because one just needs to modify the previous model by adding to the folder a some extra document not related to the document X and to raise the price of this folder, see Fig. 6. This guarantees that the only way to learn all the content of folder a is to buy folder a directly.

The situation becomes much more complicated if we want (i) the value of secret a to be recoverable from the value of secret b and (ii) the value of secret b to be recoverable from the value of secret a, but at a different price. For instance, if we want to construct a counterexample for the following formula:

$$a \rhd_1 b \land b \rhd_5 a \to (\varnothing \rhd_5 a \lor \varnothing \rhd_1 b \lor b \rhd_4 a). \tag{1}$$

At first glance, this goal could be achieved using asymmetric key cryptography, commonly used in the public-key encryption. For instance, suppose that folder

---

[1] The one-time encryption pad is not the only way to construct a counterexample for formula $a \rhd_4 b \to \varnothing \rhd_4 b$. We introduce one-time pads to prepare readers for the general proof of the completeness presented later in this paper.

a contains a document X and folder b contains the same document encrypted with an encryption key k_e, see Fig. 7. To obtain the content of folder b based on the content of folder a, one only needs to know the encryption key k_e. To restore the content of folder a based on folder b one needs to know the value of the decryption[2] key k_d. If the encryption key and the decryption key are priced at \$1 and \$5 respectively, the formula $b \rhd_4 a$ is not satisfied from the cryptographic point of view. Since folders a and b are priced in this model at \$100 each, formulas $\varnothing \rhd_5 a$ and $\varnothing \rhd_1 b$ are not satisfied either. Thus, the entire formula (1) is not satisfied from the cryptographic point of view.

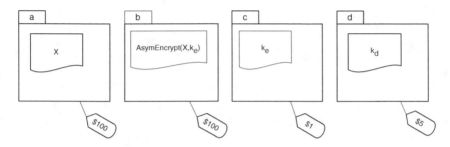

Fig. 7. Formula $a \rhd_1 b \wedge b \rhd_5 a \rightarrow (\varnothing \rhd_5 a \vee \varnothing \rhd_1 b \vee b \rhd_4 a)$ is false.

Note, however, that cryptographic asymmetric-key algorithms are only polynomial time secure and the proof of polynomial time security requires an appropriate computational hardness assumption [13, Chap. 2]. In other words, in public-key cryptography, the encrypted text can be decrypted using only the public encryption key if one has exponential time for the decryption. Neither Armstrong's [4] definition of functional dependency nor our definition of budget-constrained functional dependency, given in Definition 6 below, assumes any upper bound on the computability of the functional dependency. From our point of view, one would be able to eventually restore the content of folder a based on folder b by spending \$1 on the content of folder c. Thus, in the above setting, without polynomial restriction on computability, not only formula $b \rhd_4 a$ is true, but formula $b \rhd_1 a$ is true as well.

Figure 8 shows a counterexample for statement (1) that uses non-computable functional dependency. Assume that folders a and b contain copies of unrelated documents X and Y, folder c contains an infinite supply of one-time encryption pads $P_1, P_2, P_3, \ldots$ and folder d contains another infinite set of one-time encryption pads $Q_1, Q_2, Q_3, \ldots$. First, encrypt document Y with one-time pad P_1 and place a copy of the resulting cyphertext $Encrypt(Y, P_1)$ into folder a. Next, encrypt $Encrypt(Y, P_1)$ with pad Q_2 and place a copy of the

---

[2] In public-key cryptography, an encryption key is known as the public key and a decryption key as the private key. We do not use these terms here because in our setting neither of the keys is public in the sense that both of them have associated costs.

resulting cyphertext $Encrypt(Encrypt(Y, P_1), Q_2)$ into folder b. Then, use pad P_3 to encrypt $Encrypt(Encrypt(Y, P_1), Q_2)$ and place a copy of the resulting cyphertext $Encrypt(Encrypt(Encrypt(Y, P_1), Q_2), P_3)$ into folder a, and so on ad infinitum. Perform similar steps with the document X, as shown in Fig. 8.

To show that the model depicted in Fig. 8 is a counterexample for formula (1), we need to prove that both formulas $a \triangleright_1 b$ and $b \triangleright_5 a$ are satisfied in this model and each of the formulas $\varnothing \triangleright_5 a$, $\varnothing \triangleright_1 b$, and $b \triangleright_4 a$ is not satisfied. First, notice that formula $a \triangleright_1 b$ is satisfied because folder a contains all documents in folder b encrypted with one-time pads $P_1, P_2, \ldots$ and that all these pads could be acquired for \$1 by buying folder c. Second, formula $b \triangleright_5 a$ is satisfied for a similar reason using pads $Q_1, Q_2, \ldots$. Third, formula $\varnothing \triangleright_5 a$ is not satisfied because for \$5 one can only buy either folder c or folder d, both containing only one-time pads. In the absence of folder b, one-time encryption pads can not be used to recover document X stored in folder a. Formula $\varnothing \triangleright_1 b$ is not satisfied for a similar reason. Finally, $b \triangleright_4 a$ is not satisfied because \$4 is not enough to buy the content of folder d. This amount of money can only be used to buy pads $P_1, P_2, \ldots$ in folder c. Knowing the content of folder b and one-time pads $P_1, P_2, \ldots$, one can not recover document X contained in folder a. The counterexample described above produces non-computable functional dependency because the number of folders is infinite.

In the full version [15] of this paper we prove the completeness of our logical system. At the core of this proof is a generalized version of the construction presented in Fig. 8.

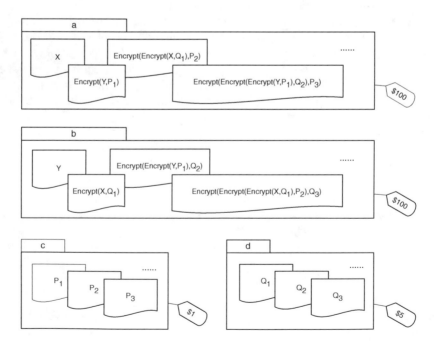

Fig. 8. Formula $a \triangleright_1 b \wedge b \triangleright_5 a \rightarrow (\varnothing \triangleright_5 a \vee \varnothing \triangleright_1 b \vee b \triangleright_4 a)$ is false.

As we have seen in the examples above, the complexity of constructing counterexamples arises from the formulas that contain disjunctions in the conclusions. Such formulas cannot be expressed in the logical systems that have no Boolean connectives and express Armstrong's axioms as inference rules. Although we did not work out the details, we believe that, in the case of such a less expressive logical system, the proof of the completeness presented in the full version [15] of this paper could be significantly simplified.

1.5   Related Literature

The axiomatic system proposed in this paper is related to other logical systems for reasoning about bounded resources. The classical logical system for reasoning about resources is the linear logic of Girard [9]. Alechina and Logan [1] presented a family of logical systems for reasoning about beliefs of a perfect reasoner that can only derive consequences of her beliefs after some time delay. This approach has been further developed into the multi-agent Timed Reasoning Logic in [3]. Bulling and Farwer [7] proposed Resource-Bounded Tree Logics for reasoning about resource-bounded computations and obtained preliminary results on the complexity and decidability of model checking for these logics. Alechina, Logan, Nga, and Rakib [2] incorporated resource requirements into Coalition logic and gave a sound and complete axiomatization of the resulting system. Another logical system for reasoning about knowledge under bounded resources was proposed by Jamroga and Tabatabaei [12]. Their paper focuses on the expressive power of the language of the system and the model checking algorithm. Naumov and Tao introduced sound and complete modal logics for reasoning about budget-constrained knowledge [16] and cost of privacy [17]. Unlike our current system all of the above logics do not provide a language for expressing functional dependencies.

1.6   Outline

The rest of the paper is organized as follows. In Sect. 2 we formally define the language of our logical system and its informational semantics. In Sect. 3 we list the axioms of the system that have already been discussed in the introduction. In Sect. 4 we give several examples of formal proofs in our logical system. In Sect. 5 we prove the soundness of our axioms with respect to the informational semantics. Section 6 states the completeness theorem. The proof of the completeness theorem can be found in the full version of this paper [15].

2   Syntax and Semantics

In this section we introduce the language of our system and formally describe its intended semantics that we call *informational semantics*.

Definition 1. *For any set of "secrets" S, let language $\Phi(S)$ be the minimum set of formulas such that*

1. $A \rhd_p B \in \Phi(\mathcal{S})$ for all finite sets $A, B \subseteq \mathcal{S}$ and all real numbers $p \geq 0$,
2. if $\varphi \in \Phi(\mathcal{S})$, then $\neg\varphi \in \Phi(\mathcal{S})$,
3. if $\varphi, \psi \in \Phi(\mathcal{S})$, then $\varphi \to \psi \in \Phi(\mathcal{S})$.

Next, we introduce the formal informational semantics of our logical system. The only significant difference between our semantics and the one used by Armstrong [4] is the costs function $\|\cdot\|$ that assigns a non-negative cost to each secret. Note that we assume that the cost is assigned to a secret, not to its value. For example, if we assign a certain cost to a folder with documents, then this cost is uniform and does not depend on the content of the documents in this folder.

Definition 2. *An informational model is a tuple* $\langle \mathcal{S}, \{D_a\}_{a \in \mathcal{S}}, \|\cdot\|, \mathcal{L}\rangle$, *where*

1. $\mathcal{S}$ *is an arbitrary set of "secrets",*
2. D_a *is a set representing the domain of secret* $a \in \mathcal{S}$,
3. $\|\cdot\|$ *is a cost function that maps each secret* $a \in \mathcal{S}$ *into a non-negative real number or infinity* $+\infty$,
4. $\mathcal{L} \subseteq \prod_{a \in \mathcal{S}} D_a$ *is the set of vectors of values of secrets that satisfy the constraints imposed by the informational model.*

Note that we allow infinite attribute costs in our semantics captured in Definition 2 to include the possibility of attributes that cannot be bought. For the same reason, we do *not* allow infinite costs in our syntax given in Definition 1. In the example depicted in Fig. 8, folders are secrets and the information stored in the documents contained in a folder is a value of such a secret. The set of all possible values of a secret is its domain. The cost of different secrets is specified explicitly in Fig. 8. Note that there is a certain dependency between the plaintext, one-time encryption pads, and the cyphertext. In other words, not all combinations of values of different secrets are possible. The set $\mathcal{L}$ is the set of all possible combinations of these values.

We allow the cost $\|a\|$ of a secret a to be infinity. Informally, one can interpret this as secret a not being available for purchase at any cost. If all secrets are available for sale, then we say that the informational model is *finite cost*.

As an example, the setting described in Fig. 4 could be formally captured in informational model $I_0 = \langle \{a, b\}, \{D_x\}_{x \in \{a,b\}}, \|\cdot\|, \mathcal{L}\rangle$, where the domain (range of values) D_a of the empty folder a is a single element set: $\{null\}$, the domain D_b of secret b is the set of all, say binary, strings $\{0,1\}^*$, cost $\|a\|$ of secret a is 3, cost $\|b\|$ of secret b is 5, and set of vectors $\mathcal{L}$ is the set of all pairs in set $D_a \times D_b = \{\langle null, s\rangle \mid s \in \{0,1\}^*\}$.

Definition 3. *Informational model* $\langle \mathcal{S}, \{D_a\}_{a \in \mathcal{S}}, \|\cdot\|, \mathcal{L}\rangle$ *is finite cost if* $\|a\| < +\infty$ *for each* $a \in \mathcal{S}$.

For example, informational model I_0 for the setting described in Fig. 4 is a finite cost model, because $\|a\| = 3 < \infty$ and $\|b\| = 5 < \infty$.

Definition 4. *For any vector $\ell_1 = \langle f_a^1 \rangle_{a \in \mathcal{S}} \in \mathcal{L}$, any vector $\ell_2 = \langle f_a^2 \rangle_{a \in \mathcal{S}} \in \mathcal{L}$, and any set $A \subseteq \mathcal{S}$, let $\ell_1 =_A \ell_2$ if $f_a^1 = f_a^2$ for each secret $a \in A$.*

For example, $\langle null, 01 \rangle =_{\{a\}} \langle null, 1011 \rangle$ and $\langle null, 01 \rangle \neq_{\{a,b\}} \langle null, 1011 \rangle$ for model I_0.

Definition 5. *For each finite set $A \subseteq \mathcal{S}$, let $\|A\| = \sum_{a \in A} \|a\|$.*

Thus, $\|\{a, b\}\| = \|a\| + \|b\| = 3 + 5 = 8$ for model I_0.

The next definition is the key definition of this section. It specifies the formal semantics of our logical system. Item 1 of this definition provides the exact meaning of the budget-constrained dependency. In this definition and throughout the rest of the paper, by A, B we denote the union of sets A and B.

Definition 6. *For each informational model $I = \langle \mathcal{S}, \{D_a\}_{a \in \mathcal{S}}, \|\cdot\|, \mathcal{L} \rangle$ and each formula $\varphi \in \Phi(\mathcal{S})$, the satisfiability relation $I \vDash \varphi$ is defined as follows:*

1. *$I \vDash A \rhd_p B$ when there is a finite set $C \subseteq \mathcal{S}$ such that $\|C\| \leq p$ and for each pair of vectors $\ell_1, \ell_2 \in \mathcal{L}$, if $\ell_1 =_{A,C} \ell_2$, then $\ell_1 =_B \ell_2$,*
2. *$I \vDash \neg \psi$ if $I \nvDash \psi$,*
3. *$I \vDash \psi \to \chi$ if $I \nvDash \psi$ or $I \vDash \chi$.*

Then, $I_0 \Vdash \varnothing \rhd_0 a$ because $\ell_1 =_a \ell_2$ for any two vectors $\ell_1, \ell_2 \in \{nill\} \times \{0,1\}^*$.

3   Axioms

For any set of secrets $\mathcal{S}$, our logical system, in addition to the propositional tautologies in language $\Phi(\mathcal{S})$ and the Modus Ponens inference rule, contains the following axioms:

1. Reflexivity: $A \rhd_p B$, where $B \subseteq A$,
2. Augmentation: $A \rhd_p B \to A, C \rhd_p B, C$,
3. Transitivity: $A \rhd_p B \to (B \rhd_q C \to A \rhd_{p+q} C)$.

We write $\vdash \varphi$ if formula φ is derivable in our system. Also, we write $X \vdash \varphi$ if formula φ is derivable in our system extended by the set of additional axioms X.

4   Examples of Proofs

We prove the soundness of our logical system in the next section. Here we provide several examples of formal proofs in this system. We start by showing that Väänänen's Weakening and Monotonicity axioms [19] are derivable in our system.

Proposition 1 (Weakening). $\vdash A \rhd_p C, D \to A, B \rhd_p C$.

Proof. By Augmentation axiom,

$$\vdash A \rhd_p C, D \to A, B \rhd_p B, C, D. \tag{2}$$

By Reflexivity axiom,

$$\vdash B, C, D \rhd_0 C. \tag{3}$$

By Transitivity axiom,

$$A, B \rhd_p B, C, D \to (B, C, D \rhd_0 C \to A, B \rhd_p C). \tag{4}$$

Finally, from (2), (3), and (4), by the laws of propositional logic,

$$\vdash A \rhd_p C, D \to A, B \rhd_p C.$$

$\square$

Proposition 2 (Monotonicity). $\vdash A \rhd_p B \to A \rhd_q B$, *where* $p \le q$.

Proof. By Reflexivity axiom,

$$\vdash B \rhd_{q-p} B. \tag{5}$$

By Transitivity axiom,

$$\vdash A \rhd_p B \to (B \rhd_{q-p} B \to A \rhd_q B). \tag{6}$$

Finally, from (5) and (6), by the laws of propositional logic,

$$\vdash A \rhd_p B \to A \rhd_q B.$$

$\square$

As our last example, we prove a generalized version of Augmentation axiom.

Proposition 3. $\vdash A \rhd_p B \to (C \rhd_q D \to A, C \rhd_{p+q} B, D)$.

Proof. By Augmentation axiom,

$$\vdash A \rhd_p B \to A, C \rhd_p B, C \tag{7}$$

and

$$\vdash C \rhd_q D \to B, C \rhd_q B, D. \tag{8}$$

At the same time, by Transitivity axiom,

$$\vdash A, C \rhd_p B, C \to (B, C \rhd_q B, D \to A, C \rhd_{p+q} B, D). \tag{9}$$

Finally, from (7), (8), and (9), by the laws of propositional logic,

$$\vdash A \rhd_p B \to (C \rhd_q D \to A, C \rhd_{p+q} B, D).$$

$\square$

5   Soundness

In this section we prove the soundness of our logical system.

Theorem 1. *If $\varphi \in \Phi(\mathcal{S})$ and $\vdash \varphi$, then $I \vDash \varphi$ for each informational model $I = \langle \mathcal{S}, \{D_a\}_{a \in \mathcal{S}}, \|\cdot\|, \mathcal{L} \rangle$.*

The soundness of propositional tautologies and the Modus Ponens inference rule follows from Definition 6 in the standard way. Below we prove the soundness of the remaining axioms as separate lemmas.

Lemma 1. *For all finite sets $A, B \subseteq \mathcal{S}$, if $B \subseteq A$, then $I \vDash A \rhd_p B$.*

Proof. Let $C = \varnothing$. Thus, $\|C\| = \|\varnothing\| = 0 \leq p$. Consider any two vectors $\ell_1, \ell_2 \in \mathcal{L}$ such that $\ell_1 =_{A,C} \ell_2$. It suffices to show that $\ell_1 =_B \ell_2$, which is true due to Definition 4 and the assumption $B \subseteq A$. □

Lemma 2. *For all finite sets $A, B, C \subseteq \mathcal{S}$, if $I \vDash A \rhd_p B$, then $I \vDash A, C \rhd_p B, C$.*

Proof. By Definition 6, assumption $I \vDash A \rhd_p B$ implies that there is a set $D \subseteq \mathcal{S}$ such that (i) $\|D\| \leq p$ and (ii) for each $\ell_1, \ell_2 \in \mathcal{L}$, if $\ell_1 =_{A,D} \ell_2$, then $\ell_1 =_B \ell_2$.

Consider now $\ell_1, \ell_2 \in \mathcal{L}$ such that $\ell_1 =_{A,C,D} \ell_2$. It suffices to show that $\ell_1 =_{B,C} \ell_2$. Note that assumption $\ell_1 =_{A,C,D} \ell_2$ implies that $\ell_1 =_{A,D} \ell_2$ and $\ell_1 =_C \ell_2$ by Definition 4. Due to condition (ii) above, the former implies that $\ell_1 =_B \ell_2$. Finally, statements $\ell_1 =_B \ell_2$ and $\ell_1 =_C \ell_2$ together imply that $\ell_1 =_{B,C} \ell_2$. □

Lemma 3. *For all finite sets $A, B, C \subseteq \mathcal{S}$, if $I \vDash A \rhd_p B$ and $I \vDash B \rhd_q C$, then $I \vDash A \rhd_{p+q} C$.*

Proof. By Definition 6, assumption $I \vDash A \rhd_p B$ implies that there is $D_1 \subseteq \mathcal{S}$ such that (i) $\|D_1\| \leq p$ and (ii) for each $\ell_1, \ell_2 \in \mathcal{L}$, if $\ell_1 =_{A,D_1} \ell_2$, then $\ell_1 =_B \ell_2$.

Similarly, assumption $I \vDash B \rhd_q C$ implies that there is $D_2 \subseteq \mathcal{S}$ such that (iii) $\|D_2\| \leq q$ and (iv) for each $\ell_1, \ell_2 \in \mathcal{L}$, if $\ell_1 =_{B,D_2} \ell_2$, then $\ell_1 =_C \ell_2$.

Let $D = D_1, D_2$. By Definition 5, $\|D\| \leq \|D_1\| + \|D_2\|$. Taking into account statements (i) and (iii) above, we conclude that $\|D\| \leq p + q$. Consider any two vectors $\ell_1, \ell_2 \in \mathcal{L}$ such that $\ell_1 =_{A,D} \ell_2$. It suffices to show that $\ell_1 =_C \ell_2$. Indeed, by Definition 4, assumption $\ell_1 =_{A,D} \ell_2$ implies that $\ell_1 =_{A,D_1} \ell_2$. Hence, $\ell_1 =_B \ell_2$ due to condition (ii). At the same time, assumption $\ell_1 =_{A,D} \ell_2$ also implies that $\ell_1 =_{D_2} \ell_2$ by Definition 4. Thus, $\ell_1 =_{B,D_2} \ell_2$ by Definition 4. Therefore, $\ell_1 =_C \ell_2$ due to condition (iv). □

This concludes the proof of Theorem 1.

6   On the Completeness Theorem

The main result of this paper is a completeness theorem for our logical system with respect to the informational semantics. The completeness could be stated in different non-equivalent forms that we discuss and compare in this section.

Informally, a completeness theorem states that if a formula φ is not provable in our system, then there is an informational model I such that $I \nVDash \varphi$. To state the theorem formally, we need to decide if model I must use only secrets explicitly mentioned in formula φ or a set of secrets of model I could be a superset of the set of secrets used in formula φ.

This distinction applies not only to our system, but to other logical systems as well. For example, formulas in first order logic can have constants. When we prove the completeness of the first order logic, we allow universes that have more elements than the number of constants. This is significant because, for example, formula

$$\forall x(c_1 = c_2 \lor x = c_1 \lor x = c_2) \tag{10}$$

is not provable in the first order logic, but it is true in any model with a universe consisting of only elements that are interpretations of c_1 and c_2. Thus, to construct a counterexample for this formula one needs to consider first order models with more than two elements in the universe.

The situation with our logical system is similar. To prove the completeness of the system we often need to introduce additional secrets not explicitly mentioned in the formula. An analog of formula (10) is, for example, formula

$$\neg(a \rhd_1 b) \to (\neg(b \rhd_1 a) \to \neg(\varnothing \rhd_2 a, b)). \tag{11}$$

This formula is true in any informational model that has only two secrets explicitly mentioned in the formula: secret a and secret b. Indeed, the assumption $\neg(a \rhd_1 b)$ implies that costs of secret b is more than 1. Similarly, assumption $\neg(b \rhd_1 a)$ implies that costs of secret a is more than 1. So, given a budget of only 2, one can buy at most one of secrets a and b. Without loss of generality, assume that secret a is bought. After that purchase, the amount left is less than 1. Per assumption $\neg(a \rhd_1 b)$, the value of b is not attainable on this budget.

At the same time, formula (11) is not true in the information model that has three secrets: a, b, and c, all priced at 1.5, where values of a and b are unrelated and c is pair $\langle a, b \rangle$. One can think about this example as a formalization of "buy one, get one free" marketing.

In this paper we study the most general logical principles of budget-constrained dependency. Thus, we do not include principles like formula (11), that are true only for a specific set of secrets. In other words, when constructing a counterexample for the completeness theorem, we allow additional secrets that are not explicitly mentioned in the original formula. The completeness theorem is stated below.

Theorem 2. *For each formula $\varphi \in \Phi(\mathcal{S})$, if $\nvdash \varphi$, then there is a finite informational model $I = \langle \mathcal{S}, \{D_a\}_{a \in \mathcal{S}}, \| \cdot \|, \mathcal{L} \rangle$ such that $I \nVDash \varphi$.*

The proof of this theorem can be found in the full version of this paper [15].

7   Conclusion

In this paper we have introduced a notion of budget-constrained dependency that generalizes the notion of functional dependency previously studied by Armstrong [4]. We propose a sound and complete axiomatization that captures the properties of the budget-constrained dependency. Although the axioms of our system are generalizations of Armstrong's original axioms, the proof of the completeness for our system is significantly more complicated than Armstrong's counterpart.

References

1. Alechina, N., Logan, B.: Ascribing beliefs to resource bounded agents. In: Proceedings of the First International Joint Conference on Autonomous Agents and Multi-Agent Systems (AAMAS 2002), vol. 2, pp. 881–888. ACM Press, Bologna, July 2002
2. Alechina, N., Logan, B., Nga, N.H., Rakib, A.: Logic for coalitions with bounded resources. J. Logic Comput. **21**(6), 907–937 (2011)
3. Alechina, N., Logan, B., Whitsey, M.: A complete and decidable logic for resource-bounded agents. In: Jennings, N.R., Sierra, C., Sonenberg, L., Tambe, M. (eds.) Proceedings of the Third International Joint Conference on Autonomous Agents and Multi-Agent Systems (AAMAS 2004), pp. 606–613. ACM Press, New York (2004)
4. Armstrong, W.W.: Dependency structures of data base relationships. In: Information Processing, Proceedings of IFIP Congress, Stockholm, 1974, vol. 74, pp. 580–583. North-Holland, Amsterdam (1974)
5. Beeri, C., Fagin, R., Howard, J.H.: A complete axiomatization for functional and multivalued dependencies in database relations. In: Proceedings of the 1977 ACM SIGMOD International Conference on Management of Data, SIGMOD 1977, pp. 47–61. ACM, New York (1977)
6. Bělohlávek, R., Vychodil, V.: Data tables with similarity relations: functional dependencies, complete rules and non-redundant bases. In: Lee, M., Tan, K.-L., Wuwongse, V. (eds.) DASFAA 2006. LNCS, vol. 3882, pp. 644–658. Springer, Heidelberg (2006). doi:10.1007/11733836_45
7. Bulling, N., Farwer, B.: Expressing properties of resource-bounded systems: the logics RTL* and RTL. In: Dix, J., Fisher, M., Novák, P. (eds.) CLIMA 2009. LNCS (LNAI), vol. 6214, pp. 22–45. Springer, Heidelberg (2010). doi:10.1007/978-3-642-16867-3_2
8. Garcia-Molina, H., Ullman, J., Widom, J.: Database Systems: The Complete Book, 2nd edn. Prentice-Hall, Upper Saddle River (2009)
9. Girard, J.Y.: Linear logic. Theoret. Comput. Sci. **50**, 1–102 (1987)
10. Hartmann, S., Link, S., Schewe, K.-D.: Weak functional dependencies in higher-order datamodels. In: Seipel, D., Turull-Torres, J.M. (eds.) FoIKS 2004. LNCS, vol. 2942, pp. 116–133. Springer, Heidelberg (2004). doi:10.1007/978-3-540-24627-5_9
11. Heckle, Z., Naumov, P.: Common knowledge semantics of Armstrong's axioms. In: Kohlenbach, U., Barceló, P., Queiroz, R. (eds.) WoLLIC 2014. LNCS, vol. 8652, pp. 181–194. Springer, Heidelberg (2014). doi:10.1007/978-3-662-44145-9_13

12. Jamroga, W., Tabatabaei, M.: Accumulative knowledge under bounded resources. In: Leite, J., Son, T.C., Torroni, P., Torre, L., Woltran, S. (eds.) CLIMA 2013. LNCS (LNAI), vol. 8143, pp. 206–222. Springer, Heidelberg (2013). doi:10.1007/978-3-642-40624-9_13
13. Katz, J.: Digital Signatures. Springer Science & Business Media, New York (2010)
14. Naumov, P., Nicholls, B.: Rationally functional dependence. J. Philos. Logic **43**(2–3), 603–616 (2014)
15. Naumov, P., Tao, J.: The budget-constrained functional dependency. arXiv preprint arXiv:1507.05964 (2015)
16. Naumov, P., Tao, J.: Budget-constrained knowledge in multiagent systems. In: Proceedings of the 2015 International Conference on Autonomous Agents and Multiagent Systems, pp. 219–226. International Foundation for Autonomous Agents and Multiagent Systems (2015)
17. Naumov, P., Tao, J.: Price of privacy. In: 12th Conference on Logic and the Foundations of Game and Decision Theory (LOFT), Maastricht, the Netherlands (2016)
18. Väänänen, J.: Dependence Logic: A New Approach To Independence Friendly Logic, vol. 70. Cambridge University Press, New York (2007)
19. Väänänen, J.: The logic of approximate dependence. arXiv preprint arXiv:1408.4437 (2014)

A Tool for Probabilistic Reasoning Based on Logic Programming and First-Order Theories Under Stable Model Semantics

Matthias Nickles[1,2]([✉])

[1] INSIGHT Centre for Data Analytics, Galway, Ireland
matthias.nickles@deri.org
[2] Discipline of Information Technology, National University of Ireland,
Galway, Ireland

Abstract. This System Description paper describes the software framework PrASP ("Probabilistic Answer Set Programming"). PrASP is both an uncertainty reasoning and machine learning software and a probabilistic logic programming language based on Answer Set Programming (ASP). Besides serving as a research software platform for non-monotonic (inductive) probabilistic logic programming, our framework mainly targets applications in the area of uncertainty stream reasoning. PrASP programs can consist of ASP (AnsProlog) as well as First-Order Logic formulas (with stable model semantics), annotated with conditional or unconditional probabilities or probability intervals. A number of alternative inference algorithms allow to attune the system to different task characteristics (e.g., whether or not independence assumptions can be made).

Keywords: Artificial intelligence · Answer set programming · Probabilistic logic programming · Statistical-relational learning · SAT

1 Introduction

With this System Description paper we present the software and probabilistic logic programming language PrASP (Probabilistic Answer Set Programming)[1]. In contrast to previous publications on PrASP, we mainly focus on PrASP as a software tool for probabilistic reasoning in this work.

PrASP is both a probabilistic logic programming language and an inference tool for probabilistic inference and inductive weight learning based on *Answer Set Programming* (ASP). Reasoning in the presence of uncertainty and relational structures such as social networks or Linked Data is an important aspect of knowledge discovery and representation for the Web, the Internet Of Things, and other heterogeneous and complex domains. Probabilistic logic programing, and the ability to learn probabilistic logic programs from data, can provide an

---

[1] http://ubuntu1.it.nuigalway.ie:8977/PrASP_WebInterface/static/ABOUT.html

© Springer International Publishing AG 2016
L. Michael and A. Kakas (Eds.): JELIA 2016, LNAI 10021, pp. 369–384, 2016.
DOI: 10.1007/978-3-319-48758-8_24

attractive approach to uncertainty reasoning and statistical relational learning, since it combines the deduction power and declarative nature of logic programming (including the ability to work with inductive definitions) with probabilistic inference abilities traditionally known from graphical models, such as Bayesian and Markov networks. ASP, which has been gaining an increasing amount of interest in recent years as a declarative problem solving and knowledge representation approach, adds a fully declarative approach to logic programming (contrasting, e.g., Prolog), reasoning with incomplete information, preferences and defaults, and a powerful semantics of negation-as-failure to this picture.

We build upon existing approaches in the area of probabilistic (inductive) logic programming and an approach to FOL-syntax formulas with stable model-semantics [1], in order to provide a new ASP-based probabilistic logic programming language and inference tool which combines the benefits of non-monotonic reasoning using state-of-the-art ASP solvers with probabilistic inference and machine learning. Over (non-probabilistic) ASP as well as existing probabilistic approaches to ASP, PrASP provides an expressive unified syntax (including the possibility to annotate arbitrary ground or non-ground ASP as well as FOL formulas with point or interval (i.e., imprecise) and conditional as well as non-conditional probabilities) in combination with a hybrid set of inference approaches: in addition to precise inference algorithms for obtaining probability intervals, PrASP includes specialized, more scalable inference algorithms for cases where certain optional assumptions hold (in particular mutual independence of events) or where a maximum entropy solution is desired.

Envisaged application areas generally include fields where non-monotonic reasoning about dynamic information (in particular data streams) shall be combined with uncertainty reasoning and prediction, for example:

– Uncertainty reasoning about data streams. Various real-world applications involve data streams (e.g., messaging events, web searches and other information streams on the Internet, or sensor data streams). Stream reasoning allows for reasoning about such data streams in a reactive, incremental manner, making it an ideal application for non-monotonic approaches. However, in some scenarios (in particular with streams of sensor data), stream data is prone to inconsistencies and noise (stemming from inaccurate data sources such as sensors), which makes them a use case for uncertainty reasoning.
– Prediction of facts and rule learning. While this is not specific to probabilistic (inductive) non-monotonic reasoning, we expect synergies by combining logical approaches such as reasoning with default assumptions with machine learning approaches, as it is realized in PrASP in form of weight learning from (possibly noisy) examples.

The remainder of this paper is organized as follows: after describing related works in the next section, Sect. 3 presents the formal language and semantics of PrASP. Section 4 provides an overview of technical aspects of the implementation (including information about where PrASP and its user manual can be downloaded). Section 6 briefly outlines how PrASP can be used for stream reasoning, and Sect. 7 concludes.

2   Related Works

Approaches related to PrASP include, e.g., [2–10] which support probabilistic inference based on monotonic reasoning and [11–14] which are based on non-monotonic logic programming. Like P-log [12], our approach computes probability distributions over answer sets (that is, possible worlds are identified with answer sets). However, P-log as well as [13] do not allow for annotating arbitrary formulas (including FOL formulas) with probabilities. [6] is a recent approach to probabilistic logic programming which combines Markov Logic Network (MLN)-style rules with stable model semantics, with the benefits of being robust against inconsistencies and allowing for inductive definitions (something mere MLN does not). [14] allows to associate probabilities with abducibles (only) and to learn both rules and probabilistic weights from given data (in form of literals). Again, PrASP does not impose such restrictions on probabilistic annotations or example data. On the other hand, PrASP cannot make use of abduction for learning. Various less closely related approaches to probabilistic reasoning exist (either not based on logic programming at all, or not in the realm of non-monotonic logic programming): Stochastic Logic Programs (SLP) [3] are an influential approach where sets of rules in form of range-restricted clauses can be labeled with probabilities. Parameter learning for SLPs is approached in [4] using the EM-algorithm. Approaches which combine concepts from Bayesian network theory with relational modeling and learning are, e.g., [5,7]. Probabilistic Relational Models (PRM) [5] can be seen as relational counterparts to Bayesian networks. In contrast to these, our approach does not directly relate to graphical models such as Bayesian or Markov Networks but works on arbitrary possible worlds which are generated by ASP solvers in form of stable models (answer sets). ProbLog [8] allows for probabilistic facts, Annotated Disjunctions [15] and definite clauses, and approaches to probabilistic rule and parameter learning (from interpretations). ProbLog builds upon the influential Distribution Semantics approach [16], which is also used by other influential approaches, such as PRISM [2] and Independent Choice Logic (ICL) [9]. Another important approach outside the area of ASP are Markov Logic Networks (MLN) [10]. A Markov Logic Network consists of first-order formulas annotated with weights (which are, in contrast to PrASP, not in general probabilities). MLNs are used as templates for the construction of Markov networks. The (ground) Markov network generated from the MLN then determines a probability distribution over possible worlds, with inference performed using weighted SAT solving (which is related to but different from ASP). MLNs are syntactically roughly similar to the logic programs in our framework (where weighted formulas can also be seen as soft or hard constraints for possible worlds).

3   Syntax and Semantics

In this section, we describe the formal language and its semantics. Compared to [17], the syntax of PrASP programs has been extended (in particular by allowing interval and non-ground weights) and a variety of approximate inference algorithms have been added (see next section) to the default inference approach which is described below and which still underlies the formal semantics of PrASP programs.

PrASP (now seen as a formal language) is a Nilsson-style [18] probabilistic logic language and despite of its support for non-ground formulas and even FOL syntax essentially of propositional nature [19]. In contrast to most approaches to PLP, it is not based on (but influenced by) Distribution Semantics (DS) [16,20]. A PrASP program (called *background knowledge*) consists of a finite set of *PrASP formulas*. The software tool PrASP uses a PrASP program to compute the probabilities of another set of formulas, the so-called *query formulas*. The precise syntax of formulas depends on the external ASP grounder being employed by PrASP- in principle, any ASP grounder can be used. The current implementation has been tested with Gringo/Clingo 3 and 4 (http://potassco.sourceforge. net). Using Gringo/Clingo 4 and the internal FOL→ASP converter, each PrASP formula can be either in ASP-Core 2 syntax or in FOL syntax, more concretely a variant of F2LP syntax [1]. The full description of ASP-Core 2 syntax would go far beyond the scope of this paper, so we restrict ourselves here to the following simplified definition of ASP/FOL formulas which covers disjunctive programs as well as programs with F2LP-style FOL formulas: a *non-weighted formula* is an *ASP-style-rule* or a *FOL-style-rule*. An *ASP-style-* (disjunctive logic program) rule is an expression of the form

$$L_1|...|L_k|not\ L_{k+1}|...|not\ L_l\ :-\ L_{l+1}, ..., L_m, not\ L_{m+1}, ..., not\ L_n.$$

where *not* denotes default negation, | denotes disjunction and the L_i are literals, $0 \le k \le l \le m \le n$. A *literal* is an atom or has the form *not a* or $-a$ where a is an atom. $-$ denotes strong negation. An atom is an expression of the form p or $p(t_1, ..., t_n)$ where the t_i are terms, $n \ge 1$ and p is a predicate symbol. (ASP "specialties" such as choice constructs can be seen as syntactic sugar which we omit here). As usual in ASP, variable names start with upper-case letters whereas predicate names start with lower-case letters.

A *FOL-style-rule* has the form $F \leftarrow G$. where F and G are first-order formulas over the following symbols: & (denoting conjunction), | (as before), $\rightarrow$ (implication), *not* (as before), $-$ (as before), $![X_1, ..., X_n, d_1(X_1), ..., d_n(X_n)] : H$ denoting $\forall X_1, d_1(X_1), ..., X_n, d_n(X_n) : H$ (the d_i are called *domain predicates*, as they specify the domain of variable X_i), and $?[X_1, ..., X_n, d_1(X_1), ..., d_n(X_n)] : H$ denoting $\exists X_1, d_1(X_1), ..., X_n, d_n(X_n) : H$. H is a first-order formula. As usual, brackets can be used to enforce precedence (omitted here). FOL-style rules are understood to have a stable model (i.e., answer set) semantics as specified in [1]. Φ is the set of all predicate and term symbols as specified above.

A PrASP program (background knowledge) is a non-empty finite set $\Lambda = \{[l_i; u_i]f_i\} \cup \{[l_i; u_i|c_i]f_i\} \cup \{indep(\{f_1^i, ..., f_n^i\})\}$ of annotated non-weighted formulas (each concluded by a dot) and optional independence constraints (PrASP does not require an independence assumption but some of its inference algorithms can make use of declared or automatically discovered probabilistic independence. Alternatively, independence could be encoded indirectly by means of conditional probabilities). The $[l_i; u_i | c_i]$ and $[l_i; u_i]$ are called *weights* or *annotations* of the respective formulas. $[l; u]f$ asserts that the imprecise probability of f is within interval $[l, u]$ (i.e., $l \leq Pr(f) \leq u$) whereas $[l; u | c]f$ states that the probability of f conditioned on formula c is within interval $[l, u]$ ($l \leq Pr(f|c) \leq u$).

Formulas can be non-ground (including existentially or universally quantified variables in FOL formulas). For the purpose of this paper, weights need to be ground (real numbers), however, the prototype implementation also allows for certain non-ground weights. An independence constraint $indep(\{f_1^i, ..., f_n^i\})$ specifies that the set of formulas $\{f_1^i, ..., f_n^i\}$ is mutually independent in the probabilistic sense. Independence can also be discovered by PrASP by analyzing the background knowledge or expressed using conditional probabilities, but this is computationally more costly.

If the weight of a formula is omitted, $[1; 1]$ is assumed. Point probability weights $[p]$ are translated into weights of the form $[p; p]$ (analogously for conditional probabilities). Weighted formulas can intuitively be seen as constraints which specify which possible worlds (in the form of answer sets) are indeed possible, and with which probability. $w(f)$ denotes the weight of formula f. The f_i and c_i are formulas either in FOL syntax and supported by means of the transformation of FOL into ASP syntax described in [1]) or plain AnsProlog syntax, e.g., `[0.5] win :- coin(heads)`. Informally, every FOL formula or program with FOL formulas results in a finite set of ASP formulas.

The semantics of PrASP is defined in terms of probability distributions over possible worlds which are identified with answer sets (models) - an assumption inspired by P-Log [12]. Let $M = (D, \Theta, \pi, \mu)$ be a probability structure where D is a finite discrete domain of objects, Θ is a non-empty set of possible worlds, π is a function which assigns to the symbols in Φ predicates, functions and objects over/from D, and $\mu = (\mu^l, \mu^u)$ is a discrete probability function over Θ, a PrASP program and a query formula, as defined further below.

Each possible world is a Herbrand interpretation over Φ. Since we use answer sets as possible worlds, we define $\Gamma(a)$ to be the set of all answer sets of a (disjunctive) answer set program a.

We define a (non-probabilistic) satisfaction relation of possible worlds and unannotated programs as follows: let Λ^- be is an unannotated program and lp a transformation which transforms such a program (which might contain formulas in first-order logic syntax as well as formulas in ASP syntax) into a disjunctive program.

We define $(M, \theta) \vDash_\Theta \Lambda^-: \Leftrightarrow \theta \in \Gamma(lp(\Lambda^-))$ and $\theta \in \Theta$. For a disjunctive program ψ, we define $(M, \theta) \vDash_\Theta \psi: \Leftrightarrow \theta \in \Gamma(\psi)$ and $\theta \in \Theta$. Note that there is no need to distinguish between brave and cautious ASP inference in PrASP - inference of queries is performed by summing over possible world probabilities, as explained further below.

Probabilistic inference is defined based on a probability distribution over a finite set of possible worlds in form of answer sets (stable models) of the *spanning program* [17] $\rho(\Lambda)$ of PrASP program Λ. Informally, the spanning program $\rho(\Lambda)$

of a PrASP program Λ is a non-probabilistic disjunctive program[2] generated from Λ by removing all weights and transforming each formerly weighted formula f in Λ into a disjunctive *spanning formula*, as follows: If f is in FOL syntax, its spanning formula is the disjunction $f|not(f)$ (where as before *not* stands for default negation). If f is in ASP syntax (under stable model semantics), rules are interpreted as their FOL equivalent (i.e., with $:-$ representing implication $\leftarrow$, etc.) and the spanning formula is also $f|not(f)$. If f is an atom, the spanning formula can be expressed as a so-called *choice rule* which is equivalent to `f :- not not f` (or `f :- {not f}0` in Lparse/Gringo 3 syntax). Such rules (or more basic: disjunctions) stemming from weighted formulas are the main vehicle for expressing unweighted uncertainty in PrASP. We assume that all predicates which occur in Λ are defined (they occur in the head of at least one rule). After transforming each weighted formula into its spanning formula, the resulting FOL program under stable model semantics is transformed into ASP syntax which results in the spanning program from which in the next step the possible worlds are generated in form of the spanning program's answer sets.

Remark: alternatively, our software system can be instructed to use strong (classical) negation for modeling "opposite beliefs" $Pr(\neg\phi) = 1 - Pr(\phi)$. With the default settings, default negation (negation-as-failure) is used, i.e., $Pr(not\ \phi) = 1 - Pr(\phi)$.

To do groundwork for the computation of a probability distribution over possible worlds (answer sets) Θ from a given PrASP program Λ, we define a (non-probabilistic) satisfaction relation of possible worlds and unannotated formulas:

Let ϕ be a PrASP formula (without weight) and θ be a possible world. Furthermore, let $(M,\theta) \vDash_\Lambda \phi$ iff $(M,\theta) \vDash_\Theta \rho(\Lambda) \cup lp(\phi)$ *and* $\Theta = \Gamma(\rho(\Lambda))$ (we say formula ϕ is *true in possible world* θ). Sometimes we will just write $\theta \vDash_\Lambda \phi$ if M is given by the context. We abbreviate $(M,\theta) \vDash_\Lambda \phi$ as $\theta \vDash_\Lambda \phi$.

We can now define the *minimizing* parameterized probability distribution $\mu^l(\Lambda,\Theta,q)$ over the set $\Theta = \{\theta_1,...,\theta_m\} = \Gamma(\rho(\Lambda))$ of answer sets (possible worlds) of a PrASP program $\Lambda = \{([p_i]f_i, i = 1..n)\} \cup \{([p_i|c_i]f_i^c)\} \cup \{indep(\{f_1^i,...,f_k^i\})\}$ and a query formula q as $\{\theta_i \mapsto Pr(\theta_i) : \theta_i \in \Theta\}$ where $(Pr(\theta_1),...,Pr(\theta_m))$ is any solution of the following system of linear *constraints* (the inequalities and equalities 1–6 below) such that $Pr^l(q) = \sum_{\theta_i\in\Theta:\theta_i\vDash_\Lambda q} Pr(\theta_i)$ is minimal. Analogously, μ^u denotes a probability distribution over answer sets such that the $Pr(\theta_1),...,Pr(\theta_m)$ maximize $Pr^u(q) = \sum_{\theta_i\in\Theta:\theta_i\vDash_\Lambda q} Pr(\theta_i)$.

$$l(f_1) \leq \sum_{\theta_i\in\Theta:\theta_i\vDash_\Lambda f_1} Pr(\theta_i) \leq u(f_1) \quad \cdots \quad l(f_n) \leq \sum_{\theta_i\in\Theta:\theta_i\vDash_\Lambda f_n} Pr(\theta_i) \leq u(f_n) \tag{1}$$

$$\sum_{\theta_i\in\Theta} \theta_i = 1 \tag{2}$$

$$\forall\theta_i \in \Theta : 0 \leq Pr(\theta_i) \leq 1 \tag{3}$$

---

[2] PrASP's default ASP grounder/solver Clingo also allows for function symbols, but for simplicity we ignore functions in the rest of this section.

At this, $l(f_i)$ and $u(f_i)$ denote the lower and upper endpoints of the probability interval (imprecise probability) of unconditional formula f_i (analogous for interval endpoints $l(f_i^c|c_i)$ and $u(f_i^c|c_i)$ of conditional probabilities).

In addition, any *indep*-declaration $indep(F^i)$ in the program induces for every subset $\{f_1^i, ..., f_r^i\} \subseteq F^i$, $r > 1$ further constraints of the following form:

$$\prod_{f_{k=1..r}^i} l(f_k^i) \leq \sum_{\theta_j \in \Theta : \theta_j \models_\Lambda \bigwedge f_{k=1..r}^i} Pr(\theta_j) \leq \prod_{f_{k=\{1..r\}}^i} u(f_k^i) \qquad (4)$$

In the case of point (i.e., precise) probabilities, these encode

$Pr(\bigwedge_{k=1..r} f_k^i) = \prod_{k=1..r} Pr(f_k^i)$.

Furthermore, any conditional probability formula $[p_i|c_i]f_i^c$ in the program induces constraints for ensuring $l(f_i^c|c_i) \leq Pr(f_i^c|c_i) \leq u(f_i^c|c_i)$ (with $p_i = [l(f_i^c|c_i); u(f_i^c|c_i)]$), namely

$$\sum_{\theta_j \in \Theta} Pr(\theta_j)\nu(\theta_j, f_i^c \wedge c_i) + \sum_{\theta_j \in \Theta} -l(f_i^c|c_i)Pr(\theta_j)\nu(\theta_j, c_i) > 0 \qquad (5)$$

$$\sum_{\theta_j \in \Theta} Pr(\theta_j)\nu(\theta_j, f_i^c \wedge c_i) + \sum_{\theta_j \in \Theta} -u(f_i^c|c_i)Pr(\theta_j)\nu(\theta_j, c_i) < 0 \qquad (6)$$

At this, we define $\nu(\theta, f) = \begin{cases} 1, & \text{if } \theta \models_\Lambda f \\ 0, & \text{otherwise} \end{cases}$

For small systems, PrASP can compute minimizing and maximizing probability distributions directly using the (in)equalities above using a straightforward linear programming (linear optimization) task, resulting in interval probabilities as query results. Even more simple, if there are no probability intervals (and where the system above therefore becomes a system of linear equations), one or more candidate solution distributions can be found by PrASP using a Non-Negative Least Squares (NNLS) approach, optionally with a subsequent search for a distribution with maximum entropy. However, for obvious reasons (with these approaches, we need to compute *all* answer sets and the width of the linear system is identical to the number of answer sets), we need to use other inference approaches for other but very small systems, as described in the next section. Therefore the system of equations and inequalities above serves mainly as a vehicle to define the formal semantics of PrASP programs and queries, whereas its practical use is quite limited.

Finally, marginal inference results are obtained as follows: the result of a query of form [?] q is defined as the interval $[Pr^l(q), Pr^u(q)]$ and the result of conditional queries of form [?|c] f (which stands for $Pr(f|c)$, where c is some evidence) is computed using $Pr(f \wedge c)/Pr(c)$.
Example (using ASP-style rules only):

```
coin(1..5).
[0.4;0.6] coin_out(1,heads).
[[0.5]] coin_out(N,heads) :- coin(N), N != 1.
```

```
1{coin_out(N,heads); coin_out(N,tails)}1 :- coin(N).
n_win :- coin_out(N,tails), coin(N).
win :- not n_win.
[0.8|win] happy.
:- happy, not win.
```

The line starting with [[0.5]]... is syntactic sugar for a set of *ground* weighted rules where variable N is instantiated with all its possible values (i.e., [0.5] coin_out(2,heads) :- coin(2), 2 != 1 and [0.5] coin_out(3,heads) :- coin(3), 3 != 1). It would also be possible to use [0.5] as annotation of this rule, in which case the weight 0.5 would specify the probability of the entire non-ground formula instead.
1{coin_out(N,heads); coin_out(N,tails)}1 (Gringo4 AnsProlog syntax) denotes that a coin comes up with either heads or tails but not both.
[0.8|win] happy represents the conditional probability $Pr(happy|win) = 0.8$.

Besides ASP syntax, PrASP also understands formulas in FOL syntax. E.g., the following represents a formula with a universal quantifier. ![X,coin(X)] expresses that variable X ranges over all coins in the subformula after ":":
![X,coin(X)]: not coin_out(X,heads) <-> coin_out(X,tails).

Like ASP formulas, FOL formulas can optionally be annotated with probabilities or probability intervals, and they can also be used as conditions in conditional probabilities. Additionally, *Annotated Disjunctions* [15] can be used as syntactic sugar for regular PrASP formulas (not covered in this paper, for lack of space).

Our system accepts query formulas in various formats, including [?] a, which ask PrASP for the marginal probability of a and [?|b] a which computes the conditional probability $Pr(a|b)$. E.g., query [?|coin_out(2,tails)] happy results in [0;0]. Query formulas can be in FOL syntax - for example,
[?] coin_out(1,heads) & coin_out(2,heads) & coin_out(3,heads)
results in probability 0.15 (the & denoting conjunction).

Another small example shows how PrASP's syntax can be used to model the famous *Monty Hall problem*[3] in concise form:

```
[[0.333333]] c(1..3).
[[[0.333333|x1]]] c(1..3).
[0.5|2{c(1);x1}2] h3.
[1|2{c(2);x1}2] h3.
[0|2{c(3);x1}2] h3.
[.] x1.
```

c(i) stands for "The car is behind door i", x1 represents "contestant initially selected door 1" and h3 stands for "Monty opened door 3". Formula [[[0.333333|x1]]] c(1..3) represents three conditional probabilities $Pr(c(i)|x1) = 0.33333, i = 0..3$. Query [?|2{h3;x1}2] c(2) results in the probability 0.66666 that the candidate wins if she switches from door 1 to door 2. The m{11;12;...}n are so-called ASP *aggregates* which are true if between m

---

[3] https://en.wikipedia.org/wiki/Monty_Hall_problem

and n of the literals 11, 12, ... are true (so in the example above we could have likewise used FOL formulas of the form c(i) & x1). [.] x1 is an abbrevation of x1 | not x1.

Further examples can be found and run online using PrASP's Web Interface: http://ubuntu1.it.nuigalway.ie:8977/PrASP_WebInterface/static/ABOUT.html

4   Probabilistic Inference Approaches

PrASP (now seen as a software system) contains a variety of exact and approximate sampling and deductive as well as inductive inference algorithms. Using command line options, the user selects a *pipeline* of alternative simplification, sampling and inference or learning steps (depending on the nature of the respective problem). E.g., the user might chose to sample possible worlds using uniform sampling and to pass on the resulting models to a simulated annealing algorithm which computes a probability distribution over the sampled possible worlds. Finally, this distribution is used to compute the probabilities of the query formulas.

Figure 1 shows the inference pipeline (configurable using command line arguments). The user provides a knowledge base (called *background knowledge*) in form of a PrASP program file (top of the figure), consisting of annotated (i.e., probabilistic) and/or unannotated formulas. At this, formulas in ASP syntax (AnsProlog) can be freely mixed with FOL formulas. After an initial preprocessing step ("Preprocessing (1)") in order to resolve macro definitions and grounding of formulas annotated with weights within double-square brackets (see previous section), PrASP generates the spanning program, as described before. Afterwards, it can optionally apply various simplifications ("Preprocessing (2)"), in particular a simplification step found in many PILPs (such as in MLN), namely removal of all parts of the program which do not influence query results (command line option --mod1). The following step is called *initial sampling*. It either computes possible worlds in form of all answer sets of the spanning program or it samples a subset of these, in order to make inference tractable (as PrASP in its current version does not apply lifted inference but works, being based on ASP, basically on the propositional level, such as MLN or ProbLog). Various sampling algorithms are at choice, depending on the structure of the background knowledge. If the initial sampling step is not already sufficient to provide a probability distribution over possible worlds (which is the case if all weighted formulas are mutually independent, see below), the next step applies one of several solving algorithms, including the "vanilla" linear programming approach described in the previous section. The outcome is a probability distribution over possible worlds from which in the final step the point or interval probability of each [?]-annotated formula in the query file is computed. A large number of options can be used to configure each of these steps - please refer to the user manual linked in the next section for details.

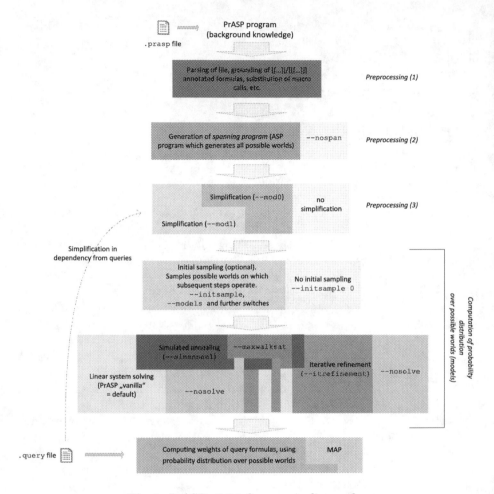

Fig. 1. PrASP v0.9 inference pipeline paths

Inference algorithms available in PrASP version 0.9.3:

Linear programming or Non-Negative Least Squares: Solution of the linear (in)equalities system as described before. With linear programming, we obtain probability intervals as query results. Very fast and precise for very small systems, intractable otherwise.

Various sampling algorithms ("initial sampling"): This step can sometimes directly compute a probability distribution over possible worlds which complies with the constraints expressed in the PrASP program, or which provides a good starting point for further solution search. If there are mutually independent probabilistic facts, initial sampling can obtain a multiset of possible worlds where the frequency of each possible world reflects the probability of such a fact (queries can then be solved merely by counting those possible worlds in which the query holds, with an additional normalization step).

Parallel simulated annealing: Can be used in combination with an initial sampling stage. This approach performs simulated annealing for inference problems where no assumptions can be made about independence or other properties of the program (except consistency). This algorithm is described in [21].

Iterative refinement: An adaptation of the algorithm described in [22] which reaches minimal Kullback–Leibler divergence to the uniform distribution (i.e., maximum entropy) given the full set of possible worlds. A brief description is provided further below.

Direct counting: Weights are transformed into unweighted ASP formulas and queries are then solved by mere counting of models (of the query) in a multiset of models (please see [17] for details). This approach essentially requires only disjunctions and choice constructs to express probabilistic uncertainty.

Induction (parameter learning): Weights of given formulas (the hypotheses) are learned from examples (facts). Please see [21] for details.

Initial evaluation results with a variant of the well-known "smokers network" task [21] indicate that PrASP inference is, for this task, competitive with a standard Markov Logic Network implementation but slower than ProbLog2 (whose syntax, however, is significantly restricted compared to PrASP and which makes strong assumptions about formula independence).

For lack of space, we present only one of the aforementioned inference algorithm here:

Algorithm 1 - called *Iterative Refinement*[4] - is based on the entropy maximizing inference approach introduced in [22] which makes use of the Kuhn-Tucker theorem, with the difference that PrASP optionally provides only a sampled subset of all models as input to the algorithms, in order to allow for (faster) approximation results. The algorithm either starts, as in [22], from the uniform distribution over the possible worlds delivered by the initial sampling step (with duplicates removed), or from the (possibly non-uniform) probability distribution obtained by the initial sampling step with duplicates retained. In the former case, the algorithm guarantees that the Kullback-Leibler divergence to the uniform distribution is minimal (and thus the final distribution's entropy is maximal). However, entropy is relative to the number of models sampled by initial sampling - if initial sampling provides only a true subset of all models of the spanning program (a concept which does not appear in [22]), entropy will also be lower compared to using the full set of possible worlds as input for iterative refinement as in [22]. In the latter case (retaining of duplicates), the counts of worlds within the multiset of possible worlds specifies the possible world probabilities which are then iteratively refined.

PrASP can also be used as an inductive logic programming tool for learning the weights of given hypotheses (PrASP formulas) from learning examples (facts or rules), however, for lack of space we refer the reader to [21] for details.

---

[4] Not related to the Iterative Refinement method in linear systems solving.

Algorithm 1. The algorithm (based on the algorithm presented in [22]) uses *initSamples* as a multiset; the original form of this algorithm without multiple instances of the same possible world is obtained by using *initSamples* as a set. We show a somewhat simplified variant for point probabilities (as opposed to probability intervals).

Require: *maxIterations*, ϵ, *initSamples*, Λ (a PrASP program), set of uncertain conditional probability formulas with (point) weights $ufw = \{(uf_i^f, uf_i^c, w_i) : [w_i|uf_i^c]uf_i^f \in \Lambda \wedge w_i < 1\}$ (the non-conditional case can simply be obtained with $uf_i^c = true$), convergence threshold ϵ

1: $Pr^0(pw_i) = \frac{frq(pw_i)}{|initSamples|} \Leftrightarrow initSamples = (pw, frq)$ ▷ $frq(pw_i)$ is the count of answer set (possible world) pw_i within multiset *initSamples*

2: $k \leftarrow 1$

3: **repeat**

4:      **for** $(uf_i^f, uf_i^c, w_i) \in uf$ **do**

5:          **for** $pw_i \in initSamples$ **do**

6:              $Pr^{k-1}(\phi) \leftarrow \sum_{\{pw_i \in initSamples : pw_i \models_\Lambda \phi\}} Pr^{k-1}(pw_i)$

7:                  for all $\phi \in \{uf_i^c \wedge uf_i^f, uf_i^c \wedge \neg uf_i^f, \neg uf_i^c\}$

8:              $b \leftarrow Pr^{k-1}(uf_i^c \wedge uf_i^f)^{w_i} Pr^{k-1}(uf_i^c \wedge \neg uf_i^f)^{1-w_i}$

9:              $a \leftarrow \dfrac{b}{b + Pr^{k-1}(\neg uf_i^c)w_i^{w_i}(1-w_i)^{1-w_i}}$

10:          $Pr^k(pw_i) = \begin{cases} Pr^{k-1}(pw_i)\frac{1-a}{Pr^{k-1}(\neg uf_i^c)} & \text{if } pw_i \models_\Lambda \neg uf_i^c \\ Pr^{k-1}(pw_i)\frac{(1-w_i)a}{Pr^{k-1}(uf_i^c \wedge \neg uf_i^f)} & \text{if } pw_i \models_\Lambda uf_i^c \wedge \neg uf_i^f \\ Pr^{k-1}(pw_i)\frac{w_i a}{Pr^{k-1}(uf_i^c \wedge uf_i^f)} & \text{if } pw_i \models_\Lambda uf_i^c \wedge uf_i^f \end{cases}$

11:          **end for**

12:      **end for**

13:      $d \leftarrow \sqrt{\sum_{pw_i \in initSamples} (Pr^k(pw_i) - Pr^{k-1}(pw_i))^2}$

14:      $k \leftarrow k + 1$

15: **until** $k > maxIterations \vee d \leq \epsilon$

Ensure: $\{Pr^k(pw_i)\} = \mu_{approx}(\Lambda)$ approximates the probability distribution $\mu(\Lambda) = Pr(\Gamma(\rho(\Lambda)))$ over the set $\Gamma(\rho(\Lambda))$ of possible worlds. $\mu(\Lambda)$ is as defined in the prvious Section. $Pr^k, Pr^{k+1}, \dots$ converges to the probability distribution with maximum entropy among all distributions over $\{pw_i\}$ where the constraints imposed by the formula weights hold, *provided Pr^0 is the uniform distribution* [22].

---

5   Implementation

The current version of PrASP is in beta state, but it already supports all features described so far (and additionally a few more experimental features which are described in the user manual - please see below).

PrASP can be tried out online using a web interface or downloaded, both from the following link:

http://ubuntu1.it.nuigalway.ie:8977/PrASP_WebInterface/static/ABOUT.html

Please note that the online version of PrASP typically works slower compared to a local installation of PrASP.

The link above also provides a comprehensive user manual with further examples.

PrASP is written in Scala and therefore requires a recent Java Runtime Environment (Java 8). The downloadable version works with Linux, MacOS X and Windows. Clingo and Gringo 4 (or higher) should be installed, as support for other ASP systems (in particular DLV) is still experimental. Due to the relatively high degree of parallelization of statistical inference and learning tasks, PrASP strongly profits from a large number of processor cores.

Requirements for further external tools depend on the inference and learning setup: PrASP contains its own Scala-written FOL→ASP converter (using the algorithm introduced in [1]) but it can optionally also use the *F2LP* tool [1] (which needs to be downloaded and installed separately). For cases where the internal equation solver is unable to compute a representative set of probability distributions, PrASP can optionally employ the SMT solver CVC4 (a form of constraint programming tool, conceptually closely related to ASP and SAT solving) in order to compute further solutions using a set of linear inequalities (relaxed forms of the original system of linear equations). Furthermore, PrASP can optionally make use of native (NN)LS solver libraries for the CPU and the GPU (if a CUDA-conforming GPU is present).

6   Uncertainty Stream Reasoning with PrASP

A major envisaged application area of PrASP is uncertainty stream reasoning. For that purpose, PrASP contains preliminary support for acting as a reasoning and relational machine learning server fed by a data stream from a local or remote host on the Internet. Clients send a stream of data in RDF or PrASP syntax to PrASP (the reasoning server). PrASP uses this data either as incrementally provided beliefs (adding to the background knowledge) or as learning examples for parameter learning.

Currently there are two clients: (1) a *console client*, where the stream data is entered manually in the console in ASP/PrASP syntax (mainly for testing and debugging purposes) and (2) an *RDF/SPARQL streaming client* (*PrASP CQELS client*) which uses the linked data stream processing engine CQELS for the preprocessing of RDF streams. More precisely, PrASP uses results of CQELS queries as incremenally provided updates to its knowledge base and/or as learning examples.

With the console client, the users enters new uncertain (probabilistic) or certain beliefs in order to incrementally add them to PrASP's background knowledge, or retracts existing belief. Analogously, the user can add/retract learning examples. PrASP responds with updates of the results of specified queries or updates of the weights of given hypotheses. The console client can be seen as a basic REPL for PrASP, although for trying out PrASP, the Web Interface (see Sect. 5) might be better suitable.

The RDF streaming client (also called PrASP CQELS client) works similarly, however, the data stream (a stream of RDF triples) is preprocessed here by a

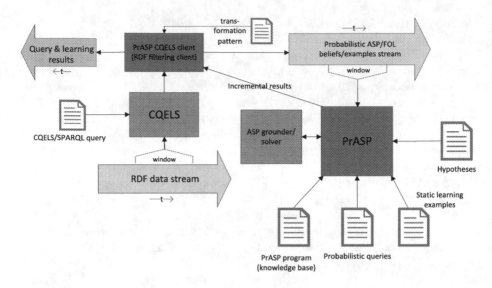

Fig. 2. PrASP stream reasoning overview

RDF stream processing engine (CQELS) whose output is translated into PrASP facts which are then used as incrementally provided belief or learning examples in the same way as with the console client. Apart from the data stream source, the user needs to specify an extended CQELS query (which is itself an extension of the SPARQL query format). This query also comprises a pattern for translating CQELS results into PrASP syntax.

Figure 2 shows the architecture of PrASP's RDF stream processing extension. An extensive example and further details are provided in the user manual (under the link in the previous section) and in [23]. For how to setup and use the extension, please refer to the user manual (see link in Sect. 5).

7　Conclusion

With this paper, we have presented a new software framework for probabilistic (inductive) logic programming based on Answer Set Programming. A strength of PrASP over related approaches is that it imposes virtually no restrictions in terms of syntax of probabilistic knowledge, queries, learning examples and hypotheses, while keeping a fundamentally simple approach to uncertainty based on the notion of spanning programs (see Sect. 3) and linear constraints implemented using various alternative approximation inference algorithms. Ongoing work is mainly focusing on the addition of further inference and sampling algorithms with improved performance characteristics. In particular, we are investigating a new, faster approach based on lifted inference which exploits symmetries discovered in the background knowledge. Aspects of future work are an empirical evaluation with real-world application scenarios (in particular in the area of probabilistic stream reasoning) and the investigation of viable, scalable approaches to structure learning (that is, the induction of new formulas from examples instead of "just" learning the weights of given hypotheses as in the current version of our software).

References

1. Lee, J., Palla, R.: System F2LP – computing answer sets of first-order formulas. In: Erdem, E., Lin, F., Schaub, T. (eds.) LPNMR 2009. LNCS (LNAI), vol. 5753, pp. 515–521. Springer, Heidelberg (2009). doi:10.1007/978-3-642-04238-6_51
2. Sato, T., Kameya, Y.: Prism: a language for symbolic-statistical modeling. In: Proceedings of the 15th International Joint Conference on Artificial Intelligence, IJCAI 1997, pp. 1330–1335 (1997)
3. Muggleton, S.: Learning stochastic logic programs. In: Electronic Transactions in Artificial Intelligence (2000)
4. Cussens, J.: Parameter estimation in stochastic logic programs. Mach. Learn. **44**, 245–271 (2000)
5. Friedman, N., Getoor, L., Koller, D., Pfeffer, A.: Learning probabilistic relational models. In: IJCAI, pp. 1300–1309. Springer (1999)
6. Lee, J., Meng, Y., Wang, Y.: Markov logic style weighted rules under the stable model semantics. In: ICLP 2015 (Technical Communications), vol. 1433, (2015)
7. Kersting, K., Raedt, L.D.: Bayesian logic programs. In: Proceedings of the 10th International Conference on Inductive Logic Programming (2000)
8. Raedt, L.D., Kimmig, A., Toivonen, H.: Problog: a probabilistic prolog and its application in link discovery. In: IJCAI, pp. 2462–2467 (2007)
9. Poole, D.: The independent choice logic for modelling multiple agents under uncertainty. Artif. Intell. **94**, 7–56 (1997)
10. Richardson, M., Domingos, P.: Markov logic networks. Mach. Learn. **62**, 107–136 (2006)
11. Ng, R.T., Subrahmanian, V.S.: Stable semantics for probabilistic deductive databases. Inf. Comput. **110**, 42–83 (1994)
12. Baral, C., Gelfond, M., Rushton, N.: Probabilistic reasoning with answer sets. Theory Pract. Log. Program. **9**, 57–144 (2009)
13. Saad, E., Pontelli, E.: Hybrid probabilistic logic programs with non-monotonic negation. In: Gabbrielli, M., Gupta, G. (eds.) ICLP 2005. LNCS, vol. 3668, pp. 204–220. Springer, Heidelberg (2005). doi:10.1007/11562931_17
14. Corapi, D., Sykes, D., Inoue, K., Russo, A.: Probabilistic rule learning in non-monotonic domains. In: Leite, J., Torroni, P., Ågotnes, T., Boella, G., Torre, L. (eds.) CLIMA 2011. LNCS (LNAI), vol. 6814, pp. 243–258. Springer, Heidelberg (2011). doi:10.1007/978-3-642-22359-4_17
15. Vennekens, J., Verbaeten, S., Bruynooghe, M.: Logic programs with annotated disjunctions. In: Demoen, B., Lifschitz, V. (eds.) ICLP 2004. LNCS, vol. 3132, pp. 431–445. Springer, Heidelberg (2004). doi:10.1007/978-3-540-27775-0_30
16. Sato, T.: A statistical learning method for logic programs with distribution semantics. In: International Conference on Logic Programming, pp. 715–729 (1995)
17. Nickles, M., Mileo, A.: Probabilistic inductive logic programming based on answer set programming. In: 15th International Workshop on Non-Monotonic Reasoning (NMR 2014) (2014)
18. Nilsson, N.J.: Probabilistic logic. Artif. Intell. **28**(1), 71–87 (1986)

19. de Bona, G., Cozman, F.G., Finger, M.: Towards classifying propositional probabilistic logics. J. Appl. Logic **12**(3), 349–368 (2014)
20. Riguzzi, F., Swift, T.: Probabilistic logic programming under the distribution semantics. In: Kifer, M., Liu, Y.A. (eds.) Declarative Logic Programming: Theory, Systems, and Applications, LNCS. Springer (2016)
21. Nickles, M., Mileo, A.: A hybrid approach to inference in probabilistic nonmonotonic logic programming. In: 2015 Probabilistic Logic Programming (PLP 2015), CEUR (2015)
22. Rödder, W., Meyer, C.: Coherent knowledge processing at maximum entropy by SPIRIT. In: Proceedings of the 12th Conference on Uncertainty in Artificial Intelligence (UAI 1996) (1996)
23. Nickles, M., Mileo, A.: Web stream reasoning using probabilistic answer set programming. In: Proceedings of Web Reasoning and Rule Systems - 8th International Conference (RR 2014) (2014)

Pakota: A System for Enforcement
in Abstract Argumentation

Andreas Niskanen[✉], Johannes P. Wallner, and Matti Järvisalo

Helsinki Institute for Information Technology HIIT, Department of Computer Science,
University of Helsinki, Helsinki, Finland
{andreas.niskanen,matti.jarvisalo}@helsinki.fi

Abstract. In this paper we describe Pakota, a system implementation that allows for solving enforcement problems over argumentation frameworks. Via harnessing Boolean satisfiability (SAT) and maximum satisfiability (MaxSAT) solvers, Pakota implements algorithms for extension and status enforcement under various central AF semantics, covering a range of NP-complete—via direct MaxSAT encodings—and Σ_2^P-complete—via MaxSAT-based counterexample-guided abstraction refinement—enforcement problems. We overview the algorithmic approaches implemented in Pakota, and describe in detail the system architecture, features, interfaces, and usage of the system. Furthermore, we present an empirical evaluation on the impact of the choice of MaxSAT solvers on the scalability of the system, and also provide benchmark generators for extension and status enforcement.

1 Introduction

Argumentation is a core area of modern artificial intelligence research, with strong connections to knowledge representation and classical and non-monotonic logics. Argumentation frameworks (AFs) [23], a central graph-based knowledge representation formalism, provide a formal basis for abstract argumentation.

Motivated also by practical applications, AFs under various semantics give rise to important—and often computationally very hard—reasoning problems over AFs. This includes what we refer to as *static* (or *non-dynamic*) AF reasoning tasks, such as the much studied problems of skeptical and credulous acceptance of arguments. Static AF reasoning tasks have been extensively studied, to the point that today several systems implementing static AF reasoning [13,14,24,26,30,31,33] are available. Most often these systems are based on declarative approaches, using propositional satisfiability (SAT) solver technology or extensions thereof for solving the core reasoning task at hand [13,14,24,26]. However, argumentation is intrinsically a dynamic process, and hence understanding and reasoning about the dynamics of AFs is a central and recent direction of research [8–10,12,18,19,21,22,29,34]. In contrast to static AF reasoning problems, few system implementations are currently available for reasoning about different aspects of AF dynamics [17,29,34].

Work funded by Academy of Finland, grants 251170 COIN, 276412, and 284591; and Research Funds of the University of Helsinki.

© Springer International Publishing AG 2016
L. Michael and A. Kakas (Eds.): JELIA 2016, LNAI 10021, pp. 385–400, 2016.
DOI: 10.1007/978-3-319-48758-8_25

In this paper, we describe in detail Pakota, a system for optimal *extension enforcement* [8,12,17,34] and *status enforcement* [29], two recently proposed hard computational problems dealing with dynamics (in connection to belief change) in abstract argumentation. In short, enforcement deals with the question of how a given AF should be revised (changed) in order for it to support (in terms of, e.g., skeptical or credulous acceptance) specific arguments.

Pakota implements algorithms for solving *optimally*—in terms of structural modifications to a given AF—various variants of NP-complete and Σ_2^P-complete extension and status enforcement problems under various AF semantics, being the first system for optimal enforcement in its generality. Pakota is based on NP-encoding enforcement problems using the Boolean optimization paradigm of maximum satisfiability (MaxSAT), and further implements *counterexample-guided abstraction refinement* (CEGAR) [15,16] algorithms based on SAT and MaxSAT solvers for Σ_2^P-complete enforcement.

2   Enforcement in Abstract Argumentation

We start by reviewing argumentation frameworks and their semantics [7,23], and the extension enforcement and status enforcement problems central to this work.

2.1   Argumentation Frameworks

Definition 1. *An* argumentation framework (AF) *is a pair* $F = (A, R)$, *where A is a finite set of arguments and $R \subseteq A \times A$ is the attack relation. The pair* $(a, b) \in R$ *means that a attacks b. An argument* $a \in A$ *is* defended *(in F) by a set* $S \subseteq A$ *if, for each* $b \in A$ *such that* $(b, a) \in R$, *there exists a* $c \in S$ *such that* $(c, b) \in R$.

Semantics for AFs are defined by functions σ which assign to each AF $F = (A, R)$ a set $\sigma(F) \subseteq 2^A$ of extensions. We consider for σ the functions *stb*, *adm*, *com* and *prf*, which stand for stable, admissible, complete and preferred, respectively.

Definition 2. *Given an AF* $F = (A, R)$, *the* characteristic function $\mathcal{F}_F : 2^A \to 2^A$ *of F is* $\mathcal{F}_F(S) = \{a \in A \mid a \text{ is defended by } S\}$. *Moreover, for a set* $S \subseteq A$, *the* range *of S is* $S_R^+ = S \cup \{a \in A \mid (b, a) \in R, b \in S\}$.

Definition 3. *Let* $F = (A, R)$ *be an AF. A set* $S \subseteq A$ *is* conflict-free *(in F), if there are no* $a, b \in S$ *such that* $(a, b) \in R$. *We denote the collection of conflict-free sets of F by* $cf(F)$. *For a conflict-free set* $S \in cf(F)$, *it holds that*

- $S \in stb(F)$ *iff* $S_R^+ = A$;
- $S \in adm(F)$ *iff* $S \subseteq \mathcal{F}_F(S)$;
- $S \in com(F)$ *iff* $S = \mathcal{F}_F(S)$;
- $S \in prf(F)$ *iff* $S \in adm(F)$ *and there is no* $T \in adm(F)$ *with* $S \subset T$;

We use "σ-extension" to refer to an extension under a semantics $\sigma \in \{stb, adm, com, prf\}$.

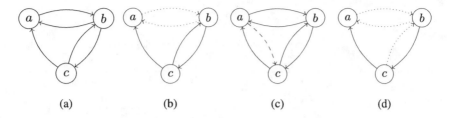

Fig. 1. An argumentation framework (a); enforcing $\{a, b\}$ to be a stable extension (b); credulous (c) and skeptical (d) status enforcement of $P = \{a, b\}$, $N = \emptyset$ under stable semantics

Example 1. As an example AF, consider $F = (A, R)$ with three arguments, $A = \{a, b, c\}$, and attacks $R = \{(a, b), (b, a), (b, c), (c, b), (c, a)\}$, with a graphical illustration shown in Fig. 1(a). This AF has the following stable extensions which, in this particular case, coincide with the preferred extensions: $stb(F) = \{\{b\}, \{c\}\}$.

When comparing attack structures of two AFs $F = (A, R)$ and $F' = (A, R')$ with the same set of arguments, we make use of the cardinality of the symmetric difference of the attack relations defined by $|R \Delta R'| = |R \setminus R'| + |R' \setminus R|$.

2.2 Extension Enforcement

We continue by recalling the problem of extension enforcement [8, 17, 34], where we are given an AF $F = (A, R)$ and a subset $T \subseteq A$ of its arguments, and the goal is to modify the attack structure R such that T becomes (a subset of) an extension under the semantics σ in the modified AF $F' = (A, R')$.

Strict enforcement requires that the given set T of arguments has to be exactly a σ-extension. In *non-strict* enforcement, T is required to be a subset of some σ-extension. We denote the set of attack structures that strictly enforce T under σ for F by

$$enf(s, F, T, \sigma) = \{R' \mid F' = (A, R'), \ T \in \sigma(F')\},$$

and by $enf(ns, F, T, \sigma) = \{R' \mid F' = (A, R'), \exists T' \in \sigma(F') : T' \supseteq T\}$

for non-strict enforcement. The number of changes of an enforcement is the size of the symmetric difference of the attack structures R and R'. From the computational perspective, we view extension enforcement as an optimization problem, seeking to minimize the number of changes to the attack structure.

Extension enforcement ($x \in \{s, ns\}$)
Input: AF $F = (A, R)$, $T \subseteq A$, semantics σ.
Task: Find an AF $F^* = (A, R^*)$ with

$$R^* \in \underset{R' \in enf(x, F, T, \sigma)}{\arg\min} \ |R \Delta R'|.$$

Table 1. Complexity of extension and status enforcement.

σ	Extension enf.		Status enf. ($N = \emptyset$)		Status enf. (unrestr. case)	
	Strict	Non-strict	Credulous	Skeptical	Credulous	Skeptical
Conflict-free	in P	in P	in P	trivial	in P	trivial
Admissible	in P	NP-c	NP-c	trivial	Σ_2^P-c	trivial
Stable	in P	NP-c	NP-c	Σ_2^P-c	Σ_2^P-c	Σ_2^P-c
Complete	NP-c	NP-c	NP-c	NP-c	Σ_2^P-c	NP-c
Preferred	Σ_2^P-c	NP-c	NP-c	in Σ_3^P	Σ_2^P-c	in Σ_3^P

Example 2. Consider AF F from Example 1 (shown in Fig. 1(a)). For enforcing set $\{a, b\}$ to be a stable extension, an optimal solution AF is shown in Fig. 1(b) where the mutual attacks between a and b are removed. In this modified AF both $\{a, b\}$ and $\{c\}$ are stable extensions.

In the corresponding decision problem we are given in addition an integer $k \geq 0$ and are asked whether it is possible to enforce T with $|R \Delta R'| \leq k$. We recall the computational complexity results from [34] for this decision problem in Table 1. Note that non-strict extension enforcement under admissible, complete, and preferred semantics coincide; thus it suffices to implement an algorithm for one of these problems to cover all three.

2.3   Status Enforcement

In the status enforcement problem [29] we are given an AF $F = (A, R)$ and two disjoint subsets $P, N \subseteq 2^A$, $P \cap N = \emptyset$. The goal is to enforce the arguments in P *positively* and arguments in N *negatively*, i.e., to modify the attack structure R so that all arguments in P are credulously or skeptically accepted and all arguments in N are not accepted in the modified AF $F' = (A, R')$.

For *credulous status enforcement*, we denote the set of attack structures that enforce (P, N) under σ for F by

$$cr(F, P, N, \sigma) = \{R' \mid F' = (A, R'), P \subseteq \bigcup \sigma(F'), N \cap \bigcup \sigma(F') = \emptyset\},$$

and, for *skeptical status enforcement*,

$$sk(F, P, N, \sigma) = \{R' \mid F' = (A, R'), P \subseteq \bigcap \sigma(F'), N \cap \bigcap \sigma(F') = \emptyset\}.$$

For $\sigma = stb$ we additionally require for skeptical status enforcement that a solution AF F' has at least one stable extension. Like extension enforcement, we view status enforcement as an optimization problem, where the goal is to minimize the cardinality of the symmetric difference of the original and the modified attack structures R and R'.

> **Optimal Credulous Status Enforcement**
> Input: AF $F = (A, R)$, $P, N \subseteq A$, semantics σ.
> Task: Find an AF $F^* = (A, R^*)$ with
>
> $$R^* \in \underset{R' \in cr(F, P, N, \sigma)}{\arg\min} \ |R \Delta R'|.$$

> **Optimal Skeptical Status Enforcement**
> Input: AF $F = (A, R)$, $P, N \subseteq A$, semantics σ.
> Task: Find an AF $F^* = (A, R^*)$ with
>
> $$R^* \in \underset{R' \in sk(F, P, N, \sigma)}{\arg\min} \ |R \Delta R'|.$$

Example 3. For the AF from Example 1, we see in Fig. 1(c) credulous and (d) skeptical status enforcement for $P = \{a, b\}$, $N = \emptyset$ under the stable semantics. In the modified AF shown in Fig. 1(c) we have added an attack from a to c, which results in an AF where $\{a\}$, $\{b\}$, and $\{c\}$ are all stable extensions. In the AF shown in Fig. 1(d) we have removed the mutual attacks between a and b, and removed the attack from c to b. This results in $\{a, b\}$ being the unique stable extension of this modified AF.

The decision problem corresponding to status enforcement is the following: given an AF $F = (A, R)$, positive and negative sets $P, N \subseteq A$ of argument statuses, a semantics σ, and an integer $k \geq 0$, can the statuses in P and N be enforced under σ with at most k modifications to the attack structure R. The computational complexity of the decision problem was established in [29]; Table 1 provides an overview. Note that credulous status enforcement under the admissible, complete, and preferred semantics coincide [29].

3   Maximum Satisfiability

For solving variants of extension and status enforcement problems, Pakota employs constraint optimization encodings using (partial) maximum satisfiability (MaxSAT for short) as the underlying declarative language. In MaxSAT, for each variable x, we have two literals, x and $\neg x$. A clause is a disjunction ($\vee$) of literals. A truth assignment is a function from variables to $\{0, 1\}$. A clause c is satisfied by a truth assignment τ, $\tau(c) = 1$, if $\tau(x) = 1$ for a literal x in c or $\tau(x) = 0$ for a literal $\neg x$ in c; otherwise τ does not satisfy c, $\tau(c) = 0$. An instance $\varphi = (\varphi_h, \varphi_s)$ of the MaxSAT problem consists of a set φ_h of *hard* clauses, and a set φ_s of *soft* clauses. Any truth assignment τ which satisfies each hard clause is a *solution* to φ. The *cost* of a solution is defined by $\text{COST}(\varphi, \tau) = \sum_{c \in \varphi_s} (1 - \tau(c))$, which is the number of soft clauses not satisfied by τ. A solution τ is *optimal* for φ if $\text{COST}(\varphi, \tau) \leq \text{COST}(\varphi, \tau')$ for all solutions τ' to φ. The output of a MaxSAT solver is an optimal solution to φ.

4   Pakota

The Pakota system is implemented in the C++ programming language. The source code is available at http://www.cs.helsinki.fi/group/coreo/pakota/ under the MIT license. In what follows, we describe the main components and system architecture of the system (Sect. 4.1) and main features of Pakota (Sect. 4.2), detail the implemented algorithms (Sect. 4.3), input and output specifications (Sect. 4.4), and usage (Sect. 4.5).

4.1   System Architecture

The system architecture of Pakota is shown in Fig. 2. Pakota accepts input for the extension enforcement problem and for the credulous and skeptical status enforcement problem in the so-called APX format (see Sect. 4.4), which is parsed into an enforcement instance. The algorithms implemented in Pakota that solve the given enforcement instance form the main component of the system and are described in Sect. 4.3, employing a MaxSAT solver, or, for problem variants beyond NP, interacting MaxSAT and SAT solvers. Pakota offers a generic MaxSAT interface for plugging in the MaxSAT solver of choice and already includes MaxSAT solvers Open-WBO [27] (version 1.3.1) and LMHS [32] (version 2015.11), and the SAT solvers MiniSAT [25] (version 2.2.0, included with LMHS) and Glucose [4–6] (version 3.0, included with Open-WBO). We detail usage of the MaxSAT interface in Sect. 4.2.

The implemented algorithms for the enforcement problems can be classified according to whether they solve an NP problem or a second-level problem. For the former, the enforcement instance is encoded in a MaxSAT instance and the solution given by

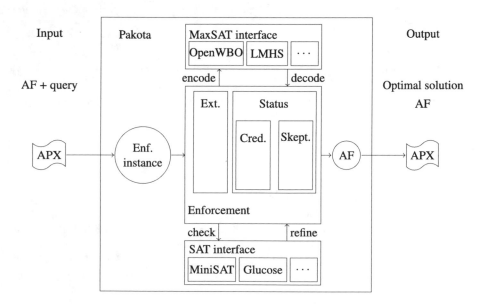

Fig. 2. System architecture of Pakota

a MaxSAT solver is decoded to construct a solution AF to the enforcement problem, again in the APX format. In the case that the given task is a second-level problem, the algorithms implement a counterexample-guided abstraction refinement procedure, thereby iteratively querying the MaxSAT solver to construct candidate solutions and checking whether the candidate is indeed a solution to the enforcement problem via a SAT solver. In case the candidate is a solution, the decoded AF is returned in the APX format. Otherwise, i.e., in case the candidate is a non-solution, the current MaxSAT encoding is iteratively refined until an actual optimal solution is found.

4.2 Features

Supported Semantics and Reasoning Modes. An overview of the semantics and reasoning modes currently supported by Pakota is given in Table 2. Implementation of different parameter choices are discussed in more detail in Sect. 4.3.

MaxSAT and SAT Solver Interfaces. Essentially any MaxSAT solver whose source code is available can be plugged into the system. This is enabled in Pakota by offering two interfaces, `MaxSATSolver.h` and `SATSolver.h`. By creating new classes that implement these interfaces and defining the pure virtual functions declared in them, one can compile and link these to the Pakota system, which will then use the corresponding MaxSAT and SAT solvers for solving the enforcement problems. As an implementation-level detail, note that, if the MaxSAT solver uses a SAT solver internally, which is usually the case, an easy solution to potential naming conflicts is to use the same SAT solver as the SAT solver in CEGAR procedures within Pakota. The source code of Pakota already includes implementations of these interfaces for two different MaxSAT solvers, Open-WBO [27] and LMHS [32], allowing the use of these solvers simply by editing the `MAXSAT_SOLVER` parameter in the included Makefile before compiling.

MaxSAT and IP Encodings. In addition to directly solving extension and status enforcement instances, Pakota can for the NP variants of the problems output the internal MaxSAT encodings both in the standard WCNF MaxSAT input format as well as integer programs (IPs) in the standard LP format (applying the standard textbook encoding of MaxSAT as IP [3]). The latter option allows for calling state-of-the-art IP solvers, such as CPLEX or Gurobi, on the encodings.

4.3 Algorithms

Depending on the inherent complexity of the problems, Pakota solves the extension or status enforcement problem at hand by either encoding the problem in MaxSAT (NP-complete problems), or within a counterexample-guided abstraction refinement (CEGAR) scheme utilizing a MaxSAT solver in an iterative or incremental fashion (problems complete for the second level of polynomial hierarchy). Table 2 provides details, depending on the chosen parameters and semantics, for each problem variant, whether it is solved via direct encoding to MaxSAT (detailed in Fig. 3) or via a MaxSAT-based CEGAR algorithm (detailed as Algorithms 1 and 2).

Table 2. Extension and status enforcement problems currently supported by Pakota.

Problem	Parameters	Semantics	Encoding/Algorithm
Extension enforcement	ns	adm, com, prf	$\text{EXT}(ns, F, T, adm)$
Extension enforcement	ns	stb	$\text{EXT}(ns, F, T, stb)$
Extension enforcement	s	adm	$\text{EXT}(s, F, T, adm)$
Extension enforcement	s	com	$\text{EXT}(s, F, T, com)$
Extension enforcement	s	stb	$\text{EXT}(s, F, T, stb)$
Extension enforcement	s	prf	Algorithm 1
Status enforcement	$cr, N = \emptyset$	adm, com, prf	$\text{STAT}(cr, A, P, \emptyset, adm)$
Status enforcement	$cr, N = \emptyset$	stb	$\text{STAT}(cr, A, P, \emptyset, stb)$
Status enforcement	cr	adm, com, prf	Algorithm 2
Status enforcement	cr	stb	Algorithm 2
Status enforcement	sk	adm	Trivial
Status enforcement	sk	stb	Algorithm 2

Encoding NP Enforcement in MaxSAT. Let $F = (A, R)$ be an AF. We utilize Boolean variables x_a and x_a^p for $a, p \in A$, and variables $r_{a,b}$ for $a, b \in A$. The intended meaning of these variables is that if x_a (x_a^p) is assigned true in an assignment then a is contained in a σ-extension in a specific AF. The AF we are referring to is either directly encoded in the formula or encoded via a truth assignment on variables $r_{a,b}$, i.e., if $r_{a,b}$ is assigned true, then there is an attack from a to b. For all considered problems, soft clauses are defined by $\varphi_s(F) = \bigwedge_{a,b \in A} r'_{a,b}$, where $r'_{a,b}$ is $r_{a,b}$ if $(a, b) \in R$, and $\neg r_{a,b}$ if $(a, b) \notin R$. Violating a soft clause corresponds to an attack being removed or added, and incurs an associated unit cost.

Hard clauses are problem dependent. The complete list of encodings used in Pakota is provided in Fig. 3. In particular, EXT refers to encodings for extension enforcement for strict (s) and non-strict (ns) modes. The other parameters are an AF $F = (A, R)$, a semantics $\sigma \in \{adm, com, stb, prf\}$, and $T \subseteq A$. For encoding the semantics, we adapt Boolean formulas from [11], originally presented for static AF reasoning problems. We also note that [17] apply similar encodings to ours in an integer programming based approach to the specific case of extension enforcement under admissible semantics.

Figure 2 shows for each NP-complete extension enforcement problem the corresponding MaxSAT encoding for which it holds that an optimal MaxSAT solution directly corresponds to an optimal solution for the extension enforcement problem. For instance, to optimally solve non-strict extension enforcement under the admissible semantics, we encode the input AF and set of arguments to be enforced via formula $\text{EXT}(ns, F, T, adm)$ and subsequently call $\text{MAXSAT}(\text{EXT}(ns, F, T, adm), \varphi_s(F))$ to compute an optimal MaxSAT solution (c, τ), with cost c and assignment τ, from which we can infer an optimal solution to the corresponding problem by extracting a new AF $F' = (A, R')$ with $R' = \{(a, b) \mid \tau(r_{a,b}) = 1\}$.

For the NP-complete status enforcement problems of credulous status enforcement under the admissible and stable semantics with empty negative set $N = \emptyset$, we implemented an analogous procedure. For the input to this problem, i.e., AF $F = (A, R)$ and positive set $P \subseteq A$, we give the MaxSAT solver the encoding $\text{STAT}(cr, A, P, \emptyset, \sigma)$, with $\sigma \in \{adm, stb\}$. From an optimal MaxSAT solution we can infer an optimal solution to the status enforcement problem similarly as for extension enforcement by generating a new AF $F' = (A, R')$ with $R' = \{(a, b) \mid \tau(r_{a,b}) = 1\}$.

The remaining encodings in Fig. 3 are used in our CEGAR algorithms for the second-level complete problems.

Counterexample-guided Abstraction Refinement. Pakota implements the second-level complete problems arising in status enforcement and extension enforcement by a counterexample-guided abstraction refinement (CEGAR) approach. Concretely, we let a MaxSAT solver compute a candidate solution from an NP abstraction of the second-level complete problem, and subsequently check whether the candidate is a solution with a SAT solver. In case a solution is found, i.e., the SAT solver reports unsatisfiability, we extract from the MaxSAT solution an optimal solution to the enforcement problem. Otherwise, we call the MaxSAT solver again on a refined formula which includes further hard clauses extracted from the counterexample delivered by the SAT solver.

The CEGAR algorithms implemented in Pakota are shown in Algorithm 1 for extension enforcement, and in Algorithm 2 for status enforcement. We describe the algorithm for extension enforcement, as the CEGAR algorithm for status enforcement is similar (the main difference lies in the used formulas).

For extension enforcement, we implemented the second-level complete problem of strict extension enforcement under the preferred semantics as shown in Algorithm 1. Given an AF $F = (A, R)$, a set $T \subseteq A$ to enforce, we define the initial hard clauses φ_h to be the same as for the NP-complete strict extension enforcement problem under the complete semantics. In the while-loop, we call the MaxSAT solver on this set of hard clauses augmented with the same soft clauses, $\varphi_s(F)$, as for the NP-complete variants. From an optimal solution τ delivered by the MaxSAT solver, we check whether this candidate is a solution to strict extension enforcement under the preferred semantics using the formula $\text{CHECK}(\tau)$ (see Fig. 3). If the SAT solver reports unsatisfiability of this formula, we terminate and return the AF encoded in τ. Otherwise we refine, i.e., increment, the hard clauses by $\text{REFINE}(\tau)$ (see again Fig. 3 for details).

For status enforcement we implemented Algorithm 2. For a given input to the second-level complete problems for status enforcement we consider here, i.e., credulous status enforcement under the admissible and stable semantics, and skeptical status enforcement under the stable semantics, this algorithm computes an optimal solution AF. The input for this problem consists of an AF $F = (A, R)$ and sets $P, N \subseteq A$.

$$\text{EXT}(ns, F, T, adm) = \bigwedge_{a \in T} x_a \wedge \bigwedge_{a,b \in A} \left((r_{a,b} \rightarrow (\neg x_a \vee \neg x_b)) \wedge \left((x_a \wedge r_{b,a}) \rightarrow \bigvee_{c \in A} (x_c \wedge r_{c,b}) \right) \right)$$

$$\text{EXT}(ns, F, T, stb) = \bigwedge_{a \in T} x_a \wedge \bigwedge_{a,b \in A} (r_{a,b} \rightarrow (\neg x_a \vee \neg x_b)) \wedge \bigwedge_{a \in A} \left(\neg x_a \rightarrow \bigvee_{b \in A} (x_b \wedge r_{b,a}) \right)$$

$$\text{EXT}(s, F, T, adm) = \bigwedge_{a,b \in T} \neg r_{a,b} \wedge \bigwedge_{a \in T} \bigwedge_{b \in A \backslash T} \left(r_{b,a} \rightarrow \bigvee_{c \in T} r_{c,b} \right)$$

$$\text{EXT}(s, F, T, com) = \bigwedge_{a,b \in T} \neg r_{a,b} \wedge \bigwedge_{a \in T} \bigwedge_{b \in A \backslash T} \left(r_{b,a} \rightarrow \bigvee_{c \in T} r_{c,b} \right) \wedge \bigwedge_{a \in A \backslash T} \bigvee_{b \in A} \left(r_{b,a} \wedge \bigwedge_{c \in T} \neg r_{c,b} \right)$$

$$\text{EXT}(s, F, T, stb) = \bigwedge_{a,b \in T} \neg r_{a,b} \wedge \bigwedge_{a \in A \backslash T} \bigvee_{b \in T} r_{b,a}$$

$$\text{CHECK}(\tau) = \bigwedge_{\tau(r_{a,b})=1} (\neg x_a \vee \neg x_b) \wedge \bigwedge_{\tau(r_{b,a})=1} \left(x_a \rightarrow \bigvee_{\tau(r_{c,b})=1} x_c \right) \wedge \bigwedge_{\tau(x_a)=1} x_a \wedge \bigvee_{\tau(x_a)=0} x_a$$

$$\psi(A) = \bigwedge_{a,b \in A} (r_{a,b} \rightarrow (\neg x_a^p \vee \neg x_b^p))$$

$$\text{STAT}(cr, A, P, N, adm) = \bigwedge_{p \in P} \left(\psi(A) \wedge \bigwedge_{a,b \in A} \left((x_a^p \wedge r_{b,a}) \rightarrow \bigvee_{c \in A} (x_c^p \wedge r_{c,b}) \right) \wedge x_p^p \wedge \bigwedge_{n \in N} \neg x_n^p \right)$$

$$\text{STAT}(cr, A, P, N, stb) = \bigwedge_{p \in P} \left(\psi(A) \wedge \bigwedge_{a \in A} \left(\neg x_a^p \rightarrow \bigvee_{b \in A} (x_b^p \wedge r_{b,a}) \right) \wedge x_p^p \wedge \bigwedge_{n \in N} \neg x_n^p \right)$$

$$\text{STAT}(sk, A, P, N, stb) = \bigwedge_{n \in N} \left(\psi(A) \wedge \bigwedge_{a \in A} \left(\neg x_a^p \rightarrow \bigvee_{b \in A} (x_b^p \wedge r_{b,a}) \right) \wedge \neg x_n^n \wedge \bigwedge_{p \in P} x_p^n \right)$$

$$\text{CHECK}(cr, A, \tau, P, N, adm) = \bigwedge_{\tau(r_{a,b})=1} (\neg x_a \vee \neg x_b) \wedge \bigwedge_{\tau(r_{b,a})=1} \left(x_a \rightarrow \bigvee_{\tau(r_{c,b})=1} x_c \right) \wedge \bigvee_{n \in N} x_n$$

$$\text{CHECK}(cr, A, \tau, P, N, stb) = \bigwedge_{\tau(r_{a,b})=1} (\neg x_a \vee \neg x_b) \wedge \bigwedge_{a \in A} \left(\neg x_a \rightarrow \bigvee_{\tau(r_{b,a})=1} x_b \right) \wedge \bigvee_{n \in N} x_n$$

$$\text{CHECK}(sk, A, \tau, P, N, stb) = \bigwedge_{\tau(r_{a,b})=1} (\neg x_a \vee \neg x_b) \wedge \bigwedge_{a \in A} \left(\neg x_a \rightarrow \bigvee_{\tau(r_{b,a})=1} x_b \right) \wedge \bigvee_{p \in P} \neg x_p$$

$$\text{REFINE}(\tau) = \neg \left(\bigwedge_{\tau(r_{a,b})=1} r_{a,b} \wedge \bigwedge_{\tau(r_{a,b})=0} \neg r_{a,b} \right)$$

Fig. 3. Encoding extension and status enforcement

Algorithm 1. Extension enforcement
1: $\varphi_h \leftarrow \text{EXT}(s, F, T, com)$
2: **while** true **do**
3: $\quad (c, \tau) \leftarrow \text{MAXSAT}(\varphi_h, \varphi_s(F))$
4: $\quad r \leftarrow \text{SAT}(\text{CHECK}(\tau))$
5: $\quad$ **if** $r = unsat$ **then** return (c, τ)
6: $\quad$ **else** $\varphi_h \leftarrow \varphi_h \wedge \text{REFINE}(\tau)$

Algorithm 2. Status enforcement
1: $\varphi_h \leftarrow \text{STAT}(M, A, P, N, \sigma)$
2: **while** true **do**
3: $\quad (c, \tau) \leftarrow \text{MAXSAT}(\varphi_h, \varphi_s(F))$
4: $\quad r \leftarrow \text{SAT}(\text{CHECK}(M, A, \tau, P, N, \sigma))$
5: $\quad$ **if** $r = unsat$ **then** return (c, τ)
6: $\quad$ **else** $\varphi_h \leftarrow \varphi_h \wedge \text{REFINE}(\tau)$

4.4   Input Format

For extension enforcement, the input AF and enforcement request are specified using the following predicates, extending the APX format for specifying AFs.

arg(X): X is an argument
att(X,Y): there is an attack from X to Y
enf(X): enforce argument X

Example 4. The enforcement of argument a for the AF in Fig. 4(a) is specified in the Pakota input format as shown in Fig. 4(b). On this input, Pakota may return the output shown in Fig. 4(c), i.e., the AF in Fig. 4(d).

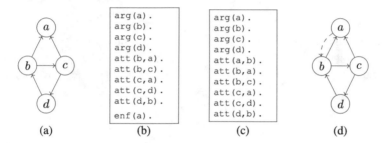

(a)   (b)   (c)   (d)

Fig. 4. Example of Pakota input and output formats

As in extension enforcement, for status enforcement the AF is represented using the `arg` and `att` predicates. The arguments to be positively and negatively enforced are represented via the pos and neg predicates, respectively. For example, `pos(a)`. enforces argument a positively. The reasoning mode between credulous and skeptical is chosen from the command line.

4.5   Usage and Options

After compilation, the Pakota system is used from the command line with

$$\text{./pakota <file> <mode> <sem> [options]}$$

The command line arguments enabling the choice of AF semantics and reasoning mode are the following.

```
<file>      : Input filename for enforcement instance in apx format.
<mode>      : Enforcement variant: mode={strict|non-strict|cred|skept}
    strict      : strict extension enforcement
    non-strict  : non-strict extension enforcement
    cred        : credulous status enforcement
    skept       : skeptical status enforcement
<sem>       : Argumentation semantics. sem={adm|com|stb|prf}
    adm         : admissible
    com         : complete
    stb         : stable
    prf         : preferred
```

Furthermore, command line options -h (for help message), -v (for version number), -o (for specifying output to file) and -t (for outputting NP-encodings in WCNF and LP formats) are available.

4.6 Benchmarks and Generators

The Pakota webpage also offers sets of benchmarks for both extension enforcement and status enforcement in the Pakota input format. Furthermore, we provide via the webpage our benchmark generator software, AfGen and EnfGen, which we used to generate the benchmark sets. The AF generator AfGen forms argumentation frameworks in APX format implementing the Erdős-Rényi random digraph model. The generator is called as

$$\text{./afgen <args> <prob>}$$

where parameters <args> and <prob> specify the number of arguments and the probability of an attack in the output AF. The generator forms an argumentation framework with arguments $1, \ldots, $ <args>, including an attack between each pair of arguments independently with probability <prob>.

The enforcement instance generator EnfGen takes as input an AF in APX format, and produces an enforcement instance. It is called as

$$\text{./enfgen <file> <mode> <enfs>}$$

where <file> is the input AF and <mode> is either ext or status, corresponding to extension and status enforcement, respectively. In case of extension enforcement, <enfs> is an integer stating the number of arguments to be enforced, and for status enforcement, <enfs> is a pair of integers, corresponding to the number of positively and negatively enforced arguments. The generator reads the arguments from the AF and samples the enforced arguments uniformly at random without replacement.

5   Performance Overview

We empirically evaluate the impact of the choice of the underlying MaxSAT solver on the performance of Pakota on various NP-complete and Σ_2^P-complete variants of extension and status enforcement. This complements the scalability experiments using only a single solver presented in [29,34], as well as the comparison presented in [34] with the IP-based approach to extension enforcement under admissible semantics described in [17]. For the NP problems, we used five state-of-the-art MaxSAT solvers: MaxHS [20], Maxino [1], MSCG [28], Open-WBO [27], and WPM [2], using the newest MaxSAT Evaluation 2015 versions, as well as the commercial IBM CPLEX integer programming solver (version 12.6). For CEGAR, we compare the performance of Open-WBO and LMHS [32] as the underlying MaxSAT solvers, as supported by Pakota. The experiments were run on 2.83-GHz Intel Xeon E5440 quad-core machines with 32-GB RAM and Debian GNU/Linux 8 using a timeout of 900 seconds per instance.

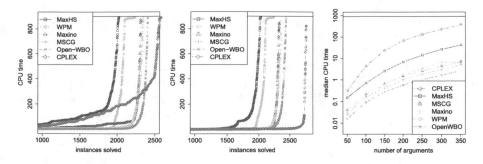

Fig. 5. MaxSAT solver comparison on NP-complete extension enforcement. Left: non-strict admissible; middle: non-strict stable; right: strict complete

We generated the benchmarks using our AfGen and EnfGen generators. For extension enforcement, for each number of arguments $|A| \in \{25, 50, \dots\}$ and each edge probability $p \in \{0.05, 0.1, 0.2, 0.3\}$, we generated five AFs. For each AF, we generated five enforcement instances with $|T|$ enforced arguments, for each $|T|/|A| \in \{0.05, 0.1, 0.2, 0.3\}$. We thus obtained 400 instances for each $|A|$. For status enforcement, for each $|A| \in \{20, 40, \dots, 200\}$ and $p \in \{0.05, 0.1, \dots, 0.35\}$, we generated 10 AFs. For each AF, we generated an enforcement instance containing $(|P|, |N|) \in \{(1,0), (2,0) \dots, (5,0), (5,1), (2,2), (1,5)\}$ positively and negatively enforced arguments. This gave a total of 560 status enforcement instances for each $|A|$.

An overview of the results, comparing the different underlying MaxSAT solvers, is provided in Fig. 5 (NP-complete extension enforcement), Fig. 6 (NP-complete status enforcement), and Fig. 7 (CEGAR for extension and status enforcement). Fig. 5 left and middle show the number of instances solved (x-axis) by different MaxSAT solvers under different per-instance timeouts (y-axis) for non-strict extension enforcement under the admissible (left) and stable semantics (middle). Interestingly, in both cases CPLEX performs well (although on admissible, on a majority of the instances is solved faster by most of the other solvers).

On strict extension enforcement under the complete semantics (Fig. 5 right), the median runtimes for CPLEX scale noticeably worse than for the rest of the solvers wrt the number of arguments. However, here we note that only CPLEX and Maxino were able to solve all instances; thus Maxino turned out to be clearly the best solver on strict complete. Fig. 6 provides an overview for credulous status enforcement under the admissible semantics. Here we observe that the so-called core-guided MaxSAT solvers perform the best, while the SAT-IP hybrid solver MaxHS—

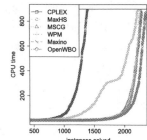

Fig. 6. NP-complete credulous status enforcement under admissible

typically competitive mainly on weighted MaxSAT instances—performs the worst. We also observed similar performance under the stable semantics. Overall, for the NP-complete enforcement problems, CPLEX and Maxino tend to provide the best choice of solvers, but the choice of the single best solver tends to depend on the problem variant (strict/non-strict, semantics).

Turning to the Σ_2^P-complete enforcement problems Fig. 7 gives an overview of the performance of Open-WBO and LMHS within our CEGAR procedures for strict extension enforcement under the preferred semantics (left), and credulous (middle) and skeptical (right) status enforcement under the stable semantics. Evidently, on these instances generated with our EnfGen, out of the two solvers Open-WBO provides the best MaxSAT solver for the CEGAR procedures.

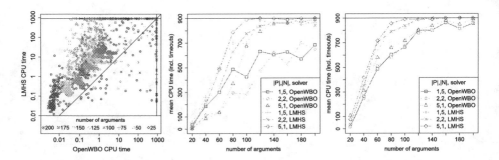

Fig. 7. MaxSAT solver comparison within CEGAR. Left: strict extension enforcement under preferred; credulous (middle) and skeptical (right) status enforcement under stable

6   Conclusions

The Pakota system is a first system implementation in its generality for solving NP-complete and Σ_2^P-complete problem instances of extension enforcement and status enforcement—two related problems motivated by the study of dynamic aspects of argumentation frameworks. We provided a detailed overview of the Pakota system— available in open source—including the input-output format, system design, functionality, details on the underlying MaxSAT encodings and MaxSAT-based CEGAR algorithms implemented in Pakota, and its API allowing for plugging in different SAT and MaxSAT solvers used as core search engines. We also provided a detailed evaluation of the impact of the choice of MaxSAT solvers (including the use of the state-of-the-art integer programming system CPLEX) on the performance of Pakota on various variants of extension and status enforcement problems. In addition to Pakota, we also provide open-source benchmark generators for extension and status enforcement for the use of the research community at large through the Pakota system webpage. Future work on Pakota includes extensions to support further central AF semantics, including grounded, semi-stable, and stage.

References

1. Alviano, M., Dodaro, C., Ricca, F.: A MaxSAT algorithm using cardinality constraints of bounded size. In: Proceedings of IJCAI, pp. 2677–2683. AAAI Press/IJCAI (2015)
2. Ansótegui, C., Didier, F., Gabàs, J.: Exploiting the structure of unsatisfiable cores in MaxSAT. In: Proceedings of the IJCAI, pp. 283–289. AAAI Press/IJCAI (2015)
3. Ansótegui, C., Gabàs, J.: Solving (weighted) partial MaxSAT with ILP. In: Gomes, E., Sellmann, M. (eds.) CPAIOR 2013. LNCS, vol. 7874, pp. 403–409. Springer, Heidelberg (2013)
4. Audemard, G., Simon, L.: Predicting learnt clauses quality in modern SAT solvers. In: Proceedings of IJCAI, pp. 399–404. AAAI Press/IJCAI (2009)
5. Audemard, G., Simon, L.: GLUCOSE 2.1: aggressive - but reactive - clause database management, dynamic restarts. In: Pragmatics of SAT (Workshop of SAT 2012) (2012)
6. Audemard, G., Simon, L.: Refining restarts strategies for SAT and UNSAT. In: Milano, M. (ed.) CP 2012. LNCS, vol. 7514, pp. 118–126. Springer, Heidelberg (2012)
7. Baroni, P., Caminada, M., Giacomin, M.: An introduction to argumentation semantics. Knowl. Eng. Rev. **26**(4), 365–410 (2011)
8. Baumann, R.: What does it take to enforce an argument? minimal change in abstract argumentation. In: Proceedings of ECAI. Frontiers in Artificial Intelligence and Applications, vol. 242, pp. 127–132. IOS Press (2012)
9. Baumann, R.: Normal and strong expansion equivalence for argumentation frameworks. Artif. Intell. **193**, 18–44 (2012)
10. Baumann, R., Brewka, G.: AGM meets abstract argumentation: Expansion and revision for Dung frameworks. In: Proceedings of IJCAI, pp. 2734–2740. AAAI Press/IJCAI (2015)
11. Besnard, P., Doutre, S.: Checking the acceptability of a set of arguments. In: Proceedings of NMR, pp. 59–64 (2004)
12. Bisquert, P., Cayrol, C., Saint-Cyr, F.D., Lagasquie-Schiex, M.-C.: Enforcement in argumentation is a kind of update. In: Liu, W., Subrahmanian, V.S., Wijsen, J. (eds.) SUM 2013. LNCS (LNAI), vol. 8078, pp. 30–43. Springer, Heidelberg (2013). doi:10.1007/978-3-642-40381-1_3
13. Cerutti, F., Dunne, P.E., Giacomin, M., Vallati, M.: Computing preferred extensions in abstract argumentation: A SAT-based approach. In: Black, E., Modgil, S., Oren, N. (eds.) TAFA 2013. LNCS (LNAI), vol. 8306, pp. 176–193. Springer, Heidelberg (2014). doi:10.1007/978-3-642-54373-9_12
14. Cerutti, F., Giacomin, M., Vallati, M.: ArgSemSAT: Solving argumentation problems using SAT. In: Proceedings of COMMA. Frontiers in Artificial Intelligence and Applications, vol. 266, pp. 455–456. IOS Press (2014)
15. Clarke, E.M., Grumberg, O., Jha, S., Lu, Y., Veith, H.: Counterexample-guided abstraction refinement for symbolic model checking. J. ACM **50**(5), 752–794 (2003)
16. Clarke, E.M., Gupta, A., Strichman, O.: SAT-based counterexample-guided abstraction refinement. IEEE Trans. Comput.-Aided Des. Integr. Circ. Syst. **23**(7), 1113–1123 (2004)
17. Coste-Marquis, S., Konieczny, S., Mailly, J., Marquis, P.: Extension enforcement in abstract argumentation as an optimization problem. In: Proceedings of IJCAI, pp. 2876–2882. AAAI Press (2015)
18. Coste-Marquis, S., Konieczny, S., Mailly, J., Marquis, P.: On the revision of argumentation systems: Minimal change of arguments statuses. In: Proceedings of KR, pp. 52–61. AAAI Press (2014)
19. Coste-Marquis, S., Konieczny, S., Mailly, J.-G., Marquis, P.: A translation-based approach for revision of argumentation frameworks. In: Fermé, E., Leite, J. (eds.) JELIA 2014. LNCS (LNAI), vol. 8761, pp. 397–411. Springer, Heidelberg (2014). doi:10.1007/978-3-319-11558-0_28

20. Davies, J., Bacchus, F.: Exploiting the power of MIP solvers in MAXSAT. In: Järvisalo, M., Van Gelder, A. (eds.) SAT 2013. LNCS, vol. 7962, pp. 166–181. Springer, Heidelberg (2013). doi:10.1007/978-3-642-39071-5_13

21. Delobelle, J., Konieczny, S., Vesic, S.: On the aggregation of argumentation frameworks. In: Proceedings of IJCAI, pp. 2911–2917. AAAI Press/IJCAI (2015)

22. Diller, M., Haret, A., Linsbichler, T., Rümmele, S., Woltran, S.: An extension-based approach to belief revision in abstract argumentation. In: Proceedings of IJCAI, pp. 2926–2932. AAAI Press/IJCAI (2015)

23. Dung, P.: On the acceptability of arguments and its fundamental role in nonmonotonic reasoning, logic programming and n-person games. Artif. Intell. **77**(2), 321–358 (1995)

24. Dvořák, W., Järvisalo, M., Wallner, J.P., Woltran, S.: Complexity-sensitive decision procedures for abstract argumentation. Artif. Intell. **206**, 53–78 (2014)

25. Eén, N., Sörensson, N.: An extensible SAT-solver. In: Giunchiglia, E., Tacchella, A. (eds.) SAT 2003. LNCS, vol. 2919, pp. 502–518. Springer, Heidelberg (2004). doi:10.1007/978-3-540-24605-3_37

26. Egly, U., Gaggl, S.A., Woltran, S.: Answer-set programming encodings for argumentation frameworks. Argum. Comput. **1**(2), 147–177 (2010)

27. Martins, R., Manquinho, V., Lynce, I.: Open-WBO: A modular MaxSAT solver. In: Sinz, C., Egly, U. (eds.) SAT 2014. LNCS, vol. 8561, pp. 438–445. Springer, Heidelberg (2014). doi:10.1007/978-3-319-09284-3_33

28. Morgado, A., Ignatiev, A., Marques-Silva, J.: MSCG: Robust core-guided MaxSAT solving. J. Satisf., Bool. Model. Comput. **9**, 129–134 (2015)

29. Niskanen, A., Wallner, J.P., Järvisalo, M.: Optimal status enforcement in abstract argumentation. In: Proceedings of IJCAI. AAAI Press/IJCAI (2016)

30. Nofal, S., Atkinson, K., Dunne, P.E.: Algorithms for decision problems in argument systems under preferred semantics. Artif. Intell. **207**, 23–51 (2014)

31. Nofal, S., Atkinson, K., Dunne, P.E.: Looking-ahead in backtracking algorithms for abstract argumentation. Int. J. Approx. Reason. **78**, 265–282 (2016)

32. Saikko, P., Berg, J., Järvisalo, M.: LMHS: A SAT-IP hybrid MaxSAT solver. In: Creignou, N., Le Berre, D. (eds.) SAT 2016. LNCS, vol. 9710, pp. 539–546. Springer, Heidelberg (2016). doi:10.1007/978-3-319-40970-2_34

33. Thimm, M., Villata, S., Cerutti, F., Oren, N., Strass, H., Vallati, M.: Summary report of the first international competition on computational models of argumentation. AI Mag. **37**(1), 102 (2016)

34. Wallner, J.P., Niskanen, A., Järvisalo, M.: Complexity results and algorithms for extension enforcement in abstract argumentation. In: Proceedings of the AAAI, pp. 1088–1094. AAAI Press (2016)

Kinetic Consistency and Relevance in Belief Revision

Pavlos Peppas[1,2]([✉]) and Mary-Anne Williams[2]

[1] Department of Business Administration, University of Patras, Patras, Greece
pavlos@upatras.gr
[2] QCIS, Faculty of Engineering and IT, University of Technology Sydney, Ultimo, Australia

Abstract. A critical aspect of rational belief revision that has been neglected by the classical AGM framework is what we call the *principle of kinetic consistency*. Loosely speaking, this principle dictates that the revision policies employed by a rational agent at different belief sets, are not independent, but ought to be related in a certain way. We formalise kinetic consistency axiomatically and semantically, and we establish a representation result explicitly connecting the two. We then combine the postulates for kinetic consistency, with Parikh's postulate for relevant change, and add them to the classical AGM postulates for revision; we call this augmented set the *extended AGM postulates*. We prove the consistency and demonstrate the scope of the extended AGM postulates by showing that a whole new class of concrete revision operators introduced hererin, called *PD operators*, satisfies all extended AGM postulates. PD operators are of interest in their own right as they are natural generalisations of Dalal's revision operator. We conclude the paper with some examples illustrating the strength of the extended AGM postulates, even for iterated revision scenarios.

1 Introduction

The classical AGM postulates for belief revision, named (K*1) - (K*8), [1], although immensely successful, [10], have left certain crucial aspects of the revision process unattended. One of them is the notion of *relevant change* discussed by Parikh in [9]. Parikh argues that during belief revision a rational agent does not change her entire belief corpus, but only the portion of it that is relevant to the new information. This intuition is formally captured by means of a new postulate called herein (wP).

Another aspect of rational belief revision, that surprisingly has received little attention in the literature, if any, is what we call the *principle of kinetic consistency*. Loosely speaking, this principle dictates that the revision policies of a rational agent over *different* theories, are not independent, but ought to be related in a certain way.

Our aim in this paper is, firstly, to formally capture the principle of kinetic consistency, and secondly, to investigate the implications of combining the AGM postulates for revision, together with the postulates for kinetic consistency and Parikh's postulate for relevant change; we call this combination the *extended AGM postulates*.

More precisely, in the first part of the paper we discuss the intuition behind the principle of kinetic consistency and we formulate two new postulates, named (KC1) - (KC2), to encode it. We also characterise kinetic consistency semantically and a representation result is provided connecting the new postulates with the semantic characterization.

© Springer International Publishing AG 2016
L. Michael and A. Kakas (Eds.): JELIA 2016, LNAI 10021, pp. 401–414, 2016.
DOI: 10.1007/978-3-319-48758-8_26

We then proceed to investigate the extended AGM postulates; i.e., the postulates (K*1) - (K*8), (wP), and (KC1) - (KC2). A by-product of our investigation is the introduction of a whole new class of concrete revision operators, called *parametrised difference revision operators*, or *PD operators* for short, that are of interest in their own right. PD operators are natural generalisations of Dalal's revision operator, with a much greater range of applicability.

We prove that every PD operator satisfies all extended AGM postulates. This result not only establishes the consistency of the extended AGM postulates but also sheds light into the scope and nature of the revision functions satisfying these postulates. The latter is an important contribution since hitherto it was clear how many, and what kind, of classical AGM revision functions survive the addition of postulate (wP) (let alone the addition of (wP) *and* (KC1)-(KC2)).[1]

We conclude the paper by illustrating the strength of the extended AGM postulates in a number of examples that are out of reach for vanilla AGM. These include (some) *iterated revision* scenarios, [12].

The paper is structured as follows. In the next section we introduce the necessary notation and terminology. Section 3 gives a brief overview of the AGM framework. In Sect. 4 we introduce and formalise the kinetic consistency principle; we also provide a representation result connecting the new postulates and semantics. Section 5 provides a brief review of relevant change. In Sect. 6 we introduce the class of PD operators and we prove that they all satisfy the extended AGM postulates. Section 7 lists a number of examples that demonstrate the strength of the extended AGM postulates. The last section contains some concluding remarks.

2   Preliminaries

Throughout this article we shall be working with a propositional language L built over *finitely many* propositional variables. The finite, nonempty set of all propositional variables is denoted by P. A literal is a variable in P or the negation of a variable. For a variable $q \in P$ we shall often write $\bar{q}$ instead of $\neg q$. The set of all interpretations over P is denoted $\mathbb{M}$. Interpretations will also be called possible worlds. We will often identify a possible world with the set (or sequence) of literals it satisfies. Moreover, we will sometimes abuse notation and use a possible world as a sentence, namely, the conjunction of all the literals it satisfies; for example, for possible worlds w, r, we may write $\neg w$ or $w \lor r$.

For a set of sentences Γ of L, we denote by $Cn(\Gamma)$ the set of all logical consequences of Γ, i.e., $Cn(\Gamma) = \{\varphi \in L : \Gamma \models \varphi\}$. A theory K of L is any set of sentences of L closed under $\models$, i.e., $K = Cn(K)$. We shall denote the set of all theories of L by $\mathbb{T}$. The set of all *consistent* theories of L is denoted by $\mathbb{K}$. A theory K of L is complete iff for all sentences $\varphi \in L$, $\varphi \in K$ or $\neg\varphi \in K$.

For a set of sentences Γ of L, $[\Gamma]$ denotes the set of all possible worlds that satisfy Γ. Often we shall use the notation $[\varphi]$ for a sentence $\varphi \in L$, as an abbreviation of $[\{\varphi\}]$. For a theory K and a set of sentences Γ of L, we shall denote by $K + \Gamma$ the closure under $\models$

---

[1] In fact in [9], Parikh conjectured that *no* classical AGM revision function survives (wP). This was later refuted in [11].

of $K \cup \Gamma$, i.e., $K + \Gamma = Cn(K \cup \Gamma)$. For a sentence $\varphi \in L$, we shall often write $K + \varphi$ as an abbreviation of $K + \{\varphi\}$. For any two sentences φ, ψ, we shall write $\varphi \equiv \psi$ as an abbreviation of $Cn(\varphi) = Cn(\psi)$.

3 The AGM Framework

In the AGM framework, [1], an agent's belief set is modelled as a theory of L. Epistemic input is represented as a logical sentence of L, and the process of belief revision is modelled as a function $*$ mapping a theory K and a sentence φ to a new theory $K * \varphi$.

An *AGM revision function*, [1], or revision function for short, is any function $* :$ $\mathbb{T} \times L \mapsto \mathbb{T}$ that satisfies certain constraints known as the *AGM postulates for revision*. There are eight such postulates, numbered (K*1) - (K*8). They are widely considered to have captured the essence of the revision process:

$(K * 1)$ $K * \varphi$ is a theory of L.
$(K * 2)$ $\varphi \in K * \varphi$.
$(K * 3)$ $K * \varphi \subseteq K + \varphi$.
$(K * 4)$ If $\neg\varphi \notin K$ then $K + \varphi \subseteq K * \varphi$.
$(K * 5)$ If φ is consistent then $K * \varphi$ is also consistent.
$(K * 6)$ If $\varphi \equiv \psi$ then $K * \varphi = K * \psi$.
$(K * 7)$ $K * (\varphi \wedge \psi) \subseteq (K * \varphi) + \psi$.
$(K * 8)$ If $\neg\psi \notin K * \varphi$ then $(K * \varphi) + \psi \subseteq K * (\varphi \wedge \psi)$.

In addition to the postulates, a constructive model for revision functions based on possible worlds was proposed in [4]. Katsuno and Mendelzon, [6], subsequently simplified this model by constraining it to propositional logic over finite variables. In particular, to every belief set K, Katsuno and Mendelzon assign a *total preorder* $\leqslant_K$ over the set of possible worlds $\mathbb{M}$.[2] We recall that a preorder $\leqslant_K$ over $\mathbb{M}$, is any binary relation in $\mathbb{M}$ that is reflexive and transitive. The preorder is total iff for all $w, w' \in \mathbb{M}$, $w \leqslant_K w'$ or $w' \leqslant w$ (we shall be using infix notation throughout this paper). As usual, $<_K$ denotes the strict part of $\leqslant_K$; i.e., $w <_K w'$ iff $w \leqslant_K w'$ and $w' \not\leqslant_K w$. Moreover, we shall write $w \approx_K w'$ iff $w \leqslant_K w'$ and $w' \leqslant_K w$.

The preorder $\leqslant_K$ is assumed to satisfy the following constraints:

(i)   If $w_1, w_2 \in [K]$, then $w_1 \approx_K w_2$.
(ii)   If $w_1 \in [K]$ and $w_2 \notin [K]$, then $w_1 <_K w_2$.

For any theory K and total preorder $\leqslant_K$ over $\mathbb{M}$, we shall say that $\leqslant_K$ is *faithful to* K iff it satisfies the constraints (i) - (ii) above.

When $\leqslant$ appears without a subscript, it represents a *function*, mapping a theory K to a total preorder $\leqslant_K$ over $\mathbb{M}$. If for all $K \in \mathbb{K}$, the preorder $\leqslant_K$ is faithful to K, then the function $\leqslant$ is called a *faithful assignment*.

---

[2] To be precise, Katsuno and Mendelzon represent an agent's beliefs by a *sentence* rather than a theory. Hence they assign preorders to sentences rather than to theories. We use theories in order to adhere more closely to the original AGM approach. Since we deal only with languages built over finitely many variables, the difference is immaterial.

Intuitively, $\leqslant_K$ represents comparative plausibility: $w \leqslant_K w'$ iff given the agent's current beliefs K, w is at least as plausible as w'. Based on this reading, Katsuno and Mendelzon define $K * \varphi$ as follows:

$(\leqslant*)$ $[K * \varphi] = min([\varphi], \leqslant_K)$.

In the above definition, $min(S, \leqslant_K)$ is the set of *minimal* elements of the set S with respect to $\leqslant_K$; i.e., $min(S, \leqslant_K) = \{w \in S : \text{for all } w' \in S, \text{if } w' \leqslant_K w, \text{then } w \leqslant_K w'\}$. Katsuno and Mendelzon proved the following representation theorem:

Theorem 1 [6]. *A revision operator * satisfies postulates (K*1) - (K*8) iff there exists a faithful assignment $\leqslant$ such that ($\leqslant*$) holds for every $K \in \mathbb{T}$ and $\varphi \in L$.*

For ease of presentation, in the rest of the paper we shall focus only on revision of *consistent* theories by *consistent* input. Hence from now, unless explicitly stated otherwise, we assume that the initial belief set K is a consistent theory, and that the epistemic input φ is a consistent sentence.

4 Kinetic Consistency

Consider a rational agent whose current belief set is K and who uses the revision function $*$ to respond to new information. We stress that $*$ is defined as a *binary function* in the AGM framework; $* : \mathbb{T} \times L \mapsto \mathbb{T}$. Hence, in view of Theorem 1, the agent is equipped with faithful preorders, not just for K, but *for every other theory as well*. Through these preorders, the agent is able to answer hypothetical questions like "would ψ be true after revision by ϕ, had the initial belief set been H instead of K?"

Should the faithful preorders assigned to different theories be related? Or does every collection $\{\leqslant_H\}_{H \in \mathbb{T}}$ of faithful preorders correspond to a rational revision policy? The AGM postulates support the latter view, since they place no constraints on the preorders assigned to different theories. This is too liberal for a wide range of applications where there needs to be some kind of *consistency* in the epistemic choices that a rational agent makes across different belief sets.

Consider for example two different consistent complete theories K and H. Then for some distinct worlds w_1, w_2, $[K] = \{w_1\}$ and $[H] = \{w_2\}$. Let r, r' be another two distinct worlds, different from w_1, w_2. Moreover assume that from the perspective of w_1 as well as from the perspective of w_2, r is at least as plausible as r'; in symbols, $r \leqslant_K r'$ and $r \leqslant_H r'$. Consider now the preorder $\leqslant_{K \cap H}$ assigned to the theory $K \cap H$. As far as the agent knows at $K \cap H$, the real world can be either w_1 or w_2. Since in both cases r is at least as plausible as r', we argue that it is unreasonable to reverse their plausibility at $K \cap H$. This is the main intuition for what we call the *principle of kinetic consistency*.

Generalising this simple intuition to arbitrary consistent theories K, H leads us to the following constraints:

(KS1)   If $r \leqslant_K r'$ and $r \leqslant_H r'$, then $r \leqslant_{K \cap H} r'$.
(KS2)   If $r <_K r'$ and $r <_H r'$, then $r <_{K \cap H} r'$.

The two constraints deal with different cases of the same intuitive idea: since the preorders assigned to K and H encode (part of) the revision strategy of a *single agent*, then if $\leqslant_K$ and $\leqslant_H$ agree on the relative plausibility of two worlds r, r', then $\leqslant_{K \cap H}$ should also agree. This is because $[K \cap H] = [K] \cup [H]$, and since the view that, say, r is more plausible than r', has prevailed among the K-worlds and moreover it has also prevailed among the H-worlds, it would be unreasonable to have a reversal of this perception when the K-worlds and the H-worlds are grouped together in $[K \cap H]$.

Depending on the class of scenarios under investigation, additional constraints between faithful preorders may be required. However, (KS1) - (KS2) are the *core* domain-independent constraints for kinetic consistency.

The postulates corresponding to the above constraints are listed below:

(KC1)   If $T * (\varphi \vee \psi) \cup H * (\varphi \vee \psi) \not\vDash \neg\varphi$, then $\neg\varphi \notin (T \cap H) * (\varphi \vee \psi)$.

(KC2)   If $\neg\psi \in T * (\varphi \vee \psi)$, $\neg\psi \in H * (\varphi \vee \psi)$, and $T * (\varphi \vee \psi) \cup H * (\varphi \vee \psi)$ is consistent, then $\neg\psi \in (T \cap H) * (\varphi \vee \psi)$.

Theorem 2. *Let $*$ be an AGM revision function and $\leqslant$ a faithful assignment corresponding to $*$ via $(\leqslant *)$. Then $*$ satisfies (KC1) - (KC2) iff $\leqslant$ satisfies (KS1) - (KS2) respectively.*

Proof

($\Rightarrow$)

Assume that $*$ satisfies (KC1). We show that $\leqslant$ satisfies (KS1). Let T, H be any two theories of L and $w, w' \in \mathbb{M}$ any two worlds such that $w \leqslant_T w'$ and $w \leqslant_H w'$. Clearly then $w \in min([w \vee w'], \leqslant_T)$, and $w \in min([w \vee w'], \leqslant_H)$. Hence by $(\leqslant *)$, $w \in [T * (w \vee w')] \cap [H * (w \vee w')]$, and therefore $T * (w \vee w') \cup H * (w \vee w') \not\vDash \neg w$. Consequently, from (KC1), $\neg w \notin (T \cap H) * (w \vee w')$. This again entails that $w \leqslant_{T \cap H} w'$. Hence (KS1) is satisfied.

Assume that $*$ satisfies (KC2). We show that $\leqslant$ satisfies (KS2). Let T, H be any two theories of L and $w, w' \in \mathbb{M}$ any two worlds such that $w <_T w'$ and $w <_H w'$. Then clearly, $w \neq w'$ and moreover, $min([w \vee w'], \leqslant_T) = min([w \vee w'], \leqslant_H) = \{w\}$. Hence, $T * (w \vee w')$ is consistent with $H * (w \vee w')$. Moreover, $\neg w' \in T * (w \vee w')$ and $\neg w' \in H * (w \vee w')$. Therefore by (KC2), $\neg w' \in (T \cap H) * (w \vee w')$. This again entails that $w <_{T \cap H} w'$. Hence (KS2) is satisfied.

($\Leftarrow$)

Assume that $\leqslant$ satisfies (KS1). We show that $*$ satisfies (KC1). Let T, H be any two theories of L and $\varphi, \psi \in L$ any two sentences such that $T * (\varphi \vee \psi) \cup H * (\varphi \vee \psi) \not\vDash \neg\varphi$. Then there is a world $w \in [T * (\varphi \vee \psi)] \cap [H * (\varphi \vee \psi)]$ such that $w \vDash \varphi$. From $w \in [T * (\varphi \vee \psi)]$ we derive that $w \leqslant_T w'$ for all $w' \in [\varphi \vee \psi]$. Similarly, from $w \in [H * (\varphi \vee \psi)]$ it follows that $w \leqslant_H w'$ for all $w' \in [\varphi \vee \psi]$. Hence from (KS1), $w \leqslant_{T \cap H} w'$ for all $w' \in [\varphi \vee \psi]$. This again entails that $w \in [(T \cap H) * (\varphi \vee \psi)]$, and since $w \vDash \varphi$, we derive that $\neg\varphi \notin (T \cap H) * (\varphi \vee \psi)$.

Assume that $\leqslant$ satisfies (KS2). We show that $*$ satisfies (KC2). Let T, H be any two theories of L and $\varphi, \psi \in L$ any two sentences such that $\neg\psi \in T * (\varphi \vee \psi)$, $\neg\psi \in H * (\varphi \vee \psi)$, and $T * (\varphi \vee \psi)$ is consistent with $H * (\varphi \vee \psi)$. If ψ is inconsistent, then by (K*1) we immediately derive that $\neg\psi \in (T \cap H) * (\varphi \vee \psi)$ as desired. Assume therefore that ψ is consistent. Since $T * (\varphi \vee \psi)$ is consistent with $H * (\varphi \vee \psi)$, there exists a world $w \in [T * (\varphi \vee \psi)] \cap [H * (\varphi \vee \psi)]$. Moreover, from $\neg\psi \in T * (\varphi \vee \psi)$ and (K*2) we derive that $\varphi \in T * (\varphi \vee \psi)$. Consequently, $w \models \varphi$ and $w \models \neg\psi$. From $w \in [T * (\varphi \vee \psi)]$ and $\neg\psi \in T * (\varphi \vee \psi)$ it follows that $w <_T w'$ for all $w' \in [\psi]$. Similarly, from $w \in [H * (\varphi \vee \psi)]$ and $\neg\psi \in H * (\varphi \vee \psi)$ it follows that $w <_H w'$ for all $w' \in [\psi]$. Hence by (KS2), $w <_{T \cap H} w'$, for all $w' \in [\psi]$. Therefore, since $w \models \varphi$, $\neg\psi \in (T \cap H) * (\varphi \vee \psi)$. Hence (KC2) is satisfied. □

5 Relevant Change

As already mentioned, relevant change is also not properly addressed in the classical AGM framework. In this section we briefly review recent work on the subject; in the following section relevant change will be combined with kinetic consistency.

Relevant change was studied by Parikh in [9], where a new postulate for it was introduced, called (P). Postulate (P) was further analysed in [11] and two different interpretations of it were identified, called the *weak* and the *strong* version of (P). The weak version of postulate (P), which we denote (wP), is much more general and intuitive, and it is this version we shall use herein.

Before presenting (wP) we need some more notation: for any sentence x, L_x denotes the (unique) smallest language in which x can be expressed. Moreover, $\overline{L_x}$ denotes the complement language, that is the language built from the propositional variables that do not appear in L_x. With this additional notation we can now present (wP):

(wP)   If $K = Cn(\{x, y\})$, $L_x \cap L_y = \emptyset$, and $\varphi \in L_x$, then $(K * \varphi) \cap \overline{L_x} = K \cap \overline{L_x}$.

Postulate (wP) essentially says the following. Suppose that the initial belief set K is divided into two disjoint compartments x, y, in the sense that the minimal languages in which the two sentences x and y can be expressed, do not share any propositional variable. If the epistemic input φ happens to be expressible solely within the language of the first compartment, then the second compartment remains unaffected by the revision of K by φ, since arguably, it is not relevant to the epistemic input.

In [11], (wP) was characterised semantically in terms of constrains over faithful preorders. This semantic characterisation of (wP) will be used later in the proof of Theorem 4 and is therefore presented below. First however we need some additional terminology and notation.

The *difference* between two possible worlds w, r, denoted $Diff(w, r)$, is defined to be the set of variables over which the two worlds disagree. Formally, $Diff(w, r) = \{q \in P : w \models q$ and $r \models \neg q\} \cup \{q \in P : w \models \neg q$ and $r \models q\}$.

The definition of $Diff$ can be extended to include the difference between a *theory* K and a world r, [11]. For this however we need some more notation: for any nonempty set of propositional variables $S \subseteq P$, by L^S we denote the propositional language built from the variables in S.

Consider now a consistent theory K, and let $Q = \{Q_1, \ldots, Q_n\}$ be a partition of P; i.e., $\bigcup Q = P$, $Q_i \neq \emptyset$, and $Q_i \cap Q_j = \emptyset$, for all $1 \leq i \neq j \leq n$. We say that $Q = \{Q_1, \ldots, Q_n\}$ is a *K-splitting* iff there exist sentences $\phi_1 \in L^{Q_1}, \ldots, \phi_n \in L^{Q_n}$, such that

$K = Cn(\{\phi_1, \ldots, \phi_n\})$. Parikh has shown in [9] that for every theory K there is a unique *finest K-splitting*, i.e., one which refines every other K-splitting.[3]

We can now define the difference between an arbitrary consistent theory K and a world r using the finest splitting of K, call it F, as follows: $Diff(K, r) = \bigcup\{F_i \in F :$ for some $\phi \in L^{F_i}, K \models \phi$ and $r \models \neg\phi\}$ (see [11] for a detailed discussion on this definition). With the extended definition of *Diff*, it was shown in [11] that (wP) can be semantically characterised by the following two constraints:

(Q1)   If $Diff(K, r) \subset Diff(K, r')$ and $Diff(r, r') \cap Diff(K, r) = \varnothing$, then $r < r'$.
(Q2)   If $Diff(K, r) = Diff(K, r')$ and $Diff(r, r') \cap Diff(K, r) = \varnothing$, then $r \approx r'$.

Theorem 3 [11]. *Let $*$ be a revision function satisfying (K*1) - (K*8), K a consistent theory, and $\leqslant_K$ a preorder faithful to K, that corresponds to $*$ at K by means of $(\leqslant*)$. Then $*$ satisfies (wP) at K iff $\leqslant_K$ satisfies (Q1) - (Q2).*

It was furthermore shown in [11] that (wP) is consistent with the AGM postulates (K*1) - (K*8). Our next aim herein is to show that (KC1) - (KC2) can also be added consistently to (K*1) - (K*8) and (wP). This is the subject of the next section.

6   Parametrised Difference Operators

To prove the consistency of the extended AGM postulates it suffices to show that there is at least one concrete revision function that satisfies them all. A good candidate would be Dalal's revision operator, [2], since it is already known to satisfy (K*1) - (K*8) and (wP), [11].

Yet consistency would be all that such a result would demonstrate; the *scope* of the extended AGM postulates would still be undetermined. We will therefore prove something stronger. We shall introduce a whole new class of revision operators, called *parametrised difference operators*, or PD operators for short, and show that each one of them satisfies (K*1) - (K*8), (wP), and (KC1) - (KC2). By doing so, we would not only prove the consistency of the extended AGM postulates, but we will also shed light to the scope and nature of the revision functions satisfying these postulates. This is important, since up to now it is not known how restrictive the addition of (wP) to (K*1) - (K*8) might be.

The PD operators are natural generalizations of Dalal's operator, so we will look at Dalal's operator first.

Dalal defines his operator, which we denote $\square$, as the function induced by means of $(\leqslant*)$, from the following preorders (one for each theory K):

$r \sqsubseteq_K r'$ *iff*   there is a $w \in [K]$ such that for all $w' \in [K]$, $|Diff(w, r)| \leqslant |Diff(w', r')|$

---

[3] A partition Q' refines another partition Q, iff for every $Q'_i \in Q'$ there is $Q_j \in Q$, such that $Q'_i \subseteq Q_j$.

Let us examine the above definition in more details through an example. Consider a language L built from only three variables a, b, c, and suppose that K is the theory $K = Cn(\{a, b, c\})$. Then the preorder that Dalal attaches to K is the following:

$$
abc \;\sqsubset_K\;
\begin{matrix} a b \overline{c} \\ a \overline{b} c \\ \overline{a} b c \end{matrix}
\;\sqsubset_K\;
\begin{matrix} \overline{a} \overline{b} c \\ \overline{a} b \overline{c} \\ a \overline{b} \overline{c} \end{matrix}
\;\sqsubset_K\; \overline{a} \overline{b} \overline{c}
$$

According to Dalal, the plausibility of a world r is determined by the number of propositional variables on which r differs from the initial world abc. A silent assumption in Dalal's approach is that *all variables have the same epistemic value*; hence for example, a change in the variable a is assumed to be as plausible (or implausible) as a change in variable b. In many scenarios though this is not true. Suppose for example that K describes our beliefs about a circuit consisting of a multiplier and two adders. Variable a represents the fact that "adder1 is working", variable b that "adder2 is working", and variable c that "the multiplier is working". Given that multipliers are less reliable than adders, if we observe that the circuit is malfunctioning, it is plausible to put the blame on the multiplier rather than on one of the adders (this is a modified version of an example in [3]). In other worlds, a change in a or b is less plausible than a change in c. We can represent this with a preorder $\trianglelefteq$ over variables, were variables appearing latter in the preorder are *more resistant to change* than the ones appearing earlier: $c \trianglelefteq a$, $c \trianglelefteq b, a \trianglelefteq b, b \trianglelefteq a, a \trianglelefteq a, b \trianglelefteq b$, and $c \trianglelefteq c$.

Given $\trianglelefteq$ we can now refine Dalal's preorder in a way that takes into account the difference in epistemic value between the three propositional variables. The resulting preorder is denoted $\sqsubseteq_K^{\trianglelefteq}$ (with $\sqsubset_K^{\trianglelefteq}$ denoting its strict part), and it is shown below:

$$
abc \;\sqsubset_K^{\trianglelefteq}\; a \overline{b} \overline{c} \;\sqsubset_K^{\trianglelefteq}\;
\begin{matrix} \overline{a} b c \\ \overline{a} b c \end{matrix}
\;\sqsubset_K^{\trianglelefteq}\;
\begin{matrix} \overline{a} b \overline{c} \\ a \overline{b} \overline{c} \end{matrix}
\;\sqsubset_K^{\trianglelefteq}\; \overline{a} b c \;\sqsubset_K^{\trianglelefteq}\; \overline{a} \overline{b} \overline{c}
$$

Observe that according to $\sqsubseteq_K^{\trianglelefteq}$, $a \overline{b} c$ is more plausible than $\overline{a} b c$, although both worlds differ in only one variables from the initial world abc. This is because, according to $\trianglelefteq$, a change in a induces greater epistemic loss than a change in c. For similar reasons, $a \overline{b} \overline{c}$ is more plausible than $\overline{a} b \overline{c}$, although both worlds differ in two variables from abc.

The example above illustrates the basic idea in our generalisation of Dalal's approach with PD preorders. Given a user-defined preorder $\trianglelefteq$, the comparative plausibility of any two worlds r and r' relative to an initial belief set K, is determined, firstly, by the number of switches in the sign of variables that are needed to take us from a K-world to r and to r' respectively. If the number of necessary switches for r is smaller than the number of necessary switches for r', then r is defined to be strictly more plausible that r'. This first step is identical to Dalal's definition. The differentiation appears when the two worlds r and r' require the *same* number of switches: Dalal defines them to be equally plausible, whereas we take into account $\trianglelefteq$ to order them. More precisely, we define r to be more plausible than r' if the set of variables that need to be switched to reach r from K, *lexicographically proceeds* (with respect to $\trianglelefteq$) the set of variables that need to be switched to reach r' from K. Below we present this more formally.

Let $\trianglelefteq$ be any total preorder over P (the set of propositional variables). For a set of propositional variables S and a variable $q \in P$, by S_q we denote the set $S_q = \{x \in S : x \trianglelefteq q\}$. We can now extend the definition of $\trianglelefteq$ to *sets* of propositional variables. In particular, for any two sets of propositional variables $S, S' \subseteq P$, we define $S \trianglelefteq S'$ iff one of the following three conditions holds:

(a) $|S| < |S'|$.
(b) $|S| = |S'|$, and for all $q \in P$, $|S_q| = |S'_q|$.
(c) $|S| = |S'|$, and for some $q \in P$, $|S_q| > |S'_q|$, and for all $p \lhd q$, $|S_p| = |S'_p|$

In the above definition, condition (b) states that S and S' are lexicographically indistinguishable with respect to $\trianglelefteq$, whereas (c) states that S lexicographically proceeds S' (wrt $\trianglelefteq$). It is not hard to verify that $\trianglelefteq$ is a total preorder over 2^P; moreover the empty set precedes every other set with respect to $\trianglelefteq$.

We can now define the *PD preorder* $\sqsubseteq_K^{\trianglelefteq}$ over $\mathbb{M}$, induced from $\trianglelefteq$ and associated to a theory K, as follows:

$$r \sqsubseteq_K^{\trianglelefteq} r' \text{ iff there is a } w \in [K] \text{ such that for all } w' \in [K], \mathit{Diff}(w, r) \trianglelefteq \mathit{Diff}(w', r').$$

Observe that when $\trianglelefteq = P \times P$, then $\sqsubseteq_K^{\trianglelefteq}$ reduces to Dalal's preorder $\sqsubseteq_K$. In what follows we will prove that, for any total preorder $\trianglelefteq$ over P, the revision function induced by the PD preorders $\{\sqsubseteq_K^{\trianglelefteq}\}_{K \in \mathbb{K}}$ satisfies all the extended AGM postulates. To this aim we recall the following lemma from [9]:

Lemma A [9]. *Let K be a theory and $\{Q_1, \ldots, Q_n\}$ a partition of P. If $\{Q_1, \ldots, Q_n\}$ is a K-splitting, then for any $r_1, \ldots, r_n \in [K]$, $Mix(r_1, \ldots, r_n; Q_1, \ldots, Q_n)$ belongs to $[K]$. Conversely, if $Mix(r_1, \ldots, r_n; Q_1, \ldots, Q_n)$ belongs to $[K]$ for all $r_1, \ldots, r_n \in [K]$, then $\{Q_1, \ldots, Q_n\}$ is a K − splitting.*

In the lemma above, $Mix(r_1, \ldots, r_n; Q_1, \ldots, Q_n)$ denotes the unique world r that agrees with r_1 on the variables in Q_1, with r_2 on the variables in Q_2, ..., and with r_n on the variables in Q_n.

We can now prove the theorem alluded earlier.

Theorem 4. *Let $\trianglelefteq$ be a total preorder over P and $*$ the revision function induced from the family of PD preorders $\{\sqsubseteq_K^{\trianglelefteq}\}_{K \in \mathbb{K}}$. Then $*$ satisfies (K*1) - (K*8), (wP), and (KC1) - (KC2).*

Proof. To prove that $*$ satisfies (K*1) - (K*8), it suffices to show that for any consistent theory K, $\sqsubseteq_K^{\trianglelefteq}$ is a total preorder and moreover that it is faithful to K.

For reflexivity, let r be any possible world. Define Q to be the set $Q = \{\mathit{Diff}(z, r) : z \in [K]\}$. Since K is consistent, $Q \neq \emptyset$. Let $\mathit{Diff}(w, r)$ be a minimal element of Q with respect to $\trianglelefteq$.[4] Clearly then, $w \in [K]$ and $\mathit{Diff}(w, r) \trianglelefteq \mathit{Diff}(w', r)$, for all $w' \in [K]$. Hence $r \sqsubseteq_K^{\trianglelefteq} r$ as desired.

For transitivity, let r, r', r'' be any three worlds such that $r \sqsubseteq_K^{\trianglelefteq} r' \sqsubseteq_K^{\trianglelefteq} r''$. From $r' \sqsubseteq_K^{\trianglelefteq} r''$ we derive that there is a world $w' \in [K]$ such that $\mathit{Diff}(w', r') \trianglelefteq \mathit{Diff}(w'', r'')$,

---

[4] Since $\trianglelefteq$ is a total preorder and $[K]$ is finite (because P is assumed to be finite), such a minimal element always exists.

for all $w'' \in [K]$. Moreover, from $r \sqsubseteq_K^{\leq} r'$ it follows that there is a $w \in [K]$ such that $Diff(w, r) \lhd Diff(w', r')$. Hence, since $\lhd$ is transitive, $Diff(w, r) \lhd Diff(w'', r'')$, for all $w'' \in [K]$. Consequently, $r \sqsubseteq_K^{\leq} r''$, and therefore $\sqsubseteq_K^{\leq}$ is transitive.

For totality, let r, r' be any two worlds and assume that $r' \not\sqsubseteq_K^{\leq} r$. Let Q be the set $Q = \{Diff(z, r) : z \in [K]\}$. Since K is consistent, $Q \neq \varnothing$. Let $Diff(w, r)$ be a minimal element of Q with respect to $\lhd$. Then $w \in [K]$ and $Diff(w, r) \lhd Diff(z, r)$, for all $z \in [K]$. Next consider any world $w' \in [K]$. From $r' \not\sqsubseteq_K^{\leq} r$, it follows that there is a $z \in [K]$ such that $Diff(w', r') \not\lhd Diff(z, r)$, and consequently, since $\lhd$ is a *total* preorder, $Diff(z, r) \lhd Diff(w', r')$. On the other hand, by the definition of w, $Diff(w, r) \lhd Diff(z, r)$. Consequently, by the transitivity of $\lhd$, $Diff(w, r) \lhd Diff(w', r')$. Since w' was chosen arbitrarily, it follows that $r \sqsubseteq_K^{\leq} r'$, and therefore $\sqsubseteq_K^{\leq}$ is total.

Next we show that $\sqsubseteq_K^{\leq}$ is faithful to K. Let r, r' be any two worlds. Moreover assume that $r \in [K]$. Clearly, $Diff(r, r) = \varnothing$ and consequently, $Diff(r, r) \lhd Diff(w', r')$ for all $w' \in [K]$; thus, since $r \in [K]$, $r \sqsubseteq_K^{\leq} r'$. This clearly entails the first condition for faithfulness. For the second condition, assume that r, r' are two worlds such that $r \in [K]$ and $r' \notin [K]$. Then $Diff(r, r) = \varnothing$ and $Diff(w', r) \neq \varnothing$ for all $w' \in [K]$. Hence, for all $w' \in [K]$, $|Diff(r, r)| < |Diff(w'r')|$, which again entails $r \sqsubseteq_K^{\leq} r'$ as desired.

We have thus shown that $\sqsubseteq_K^{\leq}$ is a total preorder that is faithful to K. By Theorem 1 it then follows that the induced revision function $*$ satisfies (K*1) - (K*8).

For (KC1), consider two arbitrary consistent theories K, H. It suffices to show that (KS1) is satisfied. Let r, r' be any two worlds such that $r \sqsubseteq_K^{\leq} r'$ and $r \sqsubseteq_H^{\leq} r'$. From $r \sqsubseteq_K^{\leq} r'$ it follows that there is a $w_1 \in [K]$ such that $Diff(w_1, r) \lhd Diff(w', r')$, for all $w' \in [K]$. Similarly, form $r \sqsubseteq_H^{\leq} r'$ it follows that there is a $w_2 \in [H]$ such that $Diff(w_2, r) \lhd Diff(w'', r')$, for all $w'' \in [H]$. Since $\lhd$ is total, $Diff(w_1, r) \lhd Diff(w_2, r)$ or $Diff(w_2, r) \lhd Diff(w_1, r)$. We assume without loss of generality that $Diff(w_1, r) \lhd Diff(w_2, r)$. Then from the transitivity of $\lhd$ we derive that $Diff(w_1, r) \lhd Diff(z, r')$, for all $z \in [K] \cup [H]$. Given that $[K] \cup [H] = [K \cap H]$, we then derive that $r \sqsubseteq_{K \cap H}^{\leq} r'$ as desired.

For (KC2), consider two arbitrary consistent theories K, H. It suffices to show that (KS2) is satisfied. This is done with a totally symmetric argument as the one above. In particular, let r, r' be two worlds such that $r \sqsubseteq_K^{\leq} r'$ and $r \sqsubseteq_H^{\leq} r'$. From $r \sqsubseteq_K^{\leq} r'$ it follows that there is a $w_1 \in [K]$ such that $Diff(w_1, r) \lhd Diff(w', r')$, for all $w' \in [K]$. Similarly, form $r \sqsubseteq_H^{\leq} r'$ it follows that there is a $w_2 \in [H]$ such that $Diff(w_2, r) \lhd Diff(w'', r')$, for all $w'' \in [H]$. Since $\lhd$ is total, $Diff(w_1, r) \lhd Diff(w_2, r)$ or $Diff(w_2, r) \lhd Diff(w_1, r)$. We assume without loss of generality that $Diff(w_1, r) \lhd Diff(w_2, r)$. Then from the transitivity of $\lhd$ we derive that $Diff(w_1, r) \lhd Diff(z, r')$, for all $z \in [K] \cup [H]$. Given that $[K] \cup [H] = [K \cap H]$, we then derive that $r \sqsubseteq_{K \cap H}^{\leq} r'$ as desired.

Finally for (wP), we shall prove instead that conditions (Q1) and (Q2) are satisfied. The proof of (Q1) follows that same line of reasoning used in the proof of Theorem 7 in [11]; the proof of (Q2) is somewhat different.

Starting with condition (Q1), let K be a consistent theory and let r, r' be any two possible worlds such that $Diff(K, r) \subset Diff(K, r')$ and $Diff(r, r') \cap Diff(K, r) = \varnothing$. Then clearly, $P - Diff(K, r) \neq \varnothing$. Let u be a world in K that agrees with r on all variables in

$P - Diff(K, r)$. [5] Moreover, let z be a K-world that differs in the least number of variables from r when restricted to $Diff(K, r)$; i.e., $|Diff(z, r) \cap Diff(K, r)| \leqslant |Diff(z', r) \cap Diff(K, r)|$ for all $z' \in [K]$. Define w to be the world that agrees with z on the variables in $Diff(K, r)$ and agrees with u on the remaining variables. Clearly, $Diff(w, r) \subseteq Diff(K, r)$. Moreover, by the definition of $Diff$, $\{Diff(K, r), P - Diff(K, r)\}$ is a K-splitting, and consequently from Lemma A and the fact that $z, u \in [K]$, we derive that $w \in [K]$.

Consider now any world $w' \in [K]$. Since $Diff(K, r) \subset Diff(K, r')$, there is at least one sentence x, built entirely from variables in $P - Diff(K, r)$, such that $K \models x$ and $r' \models \neg x$. Hence from $w' \in [K]$, we derive that $Diff(w', r') \cap (P - Diff(K, r)) \neq \emptyset$ and consequently, $|Diff(w', r') \cap (P - Diff(K, r))| > 0$. Moreover, since r and r' agree on the variables in $Diff(K, r)$ it follows that $|Diff(w', r') \cap Diff(K, r))| = |Diff(w', r) \cap Diff(K, r))|$. Consequently, $|Diff(w', r')| = |Diff(w', r') \cap Diff(K, r))| + |Diff(w', r') \cap (P - Diff(K, r))| > |Diff(w', r') \cap Diff(K, r))| = |Diff(w', r) \cap Diff(K, r))| \geq |Diff(z, r) \cap Diff(K, r))| = |Diff(w, r) \cap Diff(K, r))| = |Diff(w, r)|$. Hence we have shown that $|Diff(w, r)| < |Diff(w', r')|$ for all $w' \in [K]$. This again entails that $r \sqsubset_K^\trianglelefteq r'$ as desired.

For (Q2), let K be a consistent theory and let r, r' be any two possible worlds such that $Diff(K, r) = Diff(K, r')$ and $Diff(r, r') \cap Diff(K, r) = \emptyset$. If $Diff(K, r) = P$ then $r = r'$ and (Q2) trivially holds. Moreover, if $Diff(K, r) = \emptyset$, then $r, r' \in [K]$ and therefore (Q2) follows from the fact that $\sqsubseteq_K^\trianglelefteq$ is faithful to K. Assume therefore that $\emptyset \neq Diff(K, r) \subset P$.

Let Q be the set, $Q = \{Diff(z, r) : z \in [K]\}$ and let $Diff(w, r)$ be a minimal element of Q with respect to $\trianglelefteq$. Then, $w \in [K]$ and for all $z \in [K]$, $Diff(w, r) \trianglelefteq Diff(z, r)$.

Next we show that $Diff(w, r) \subseteq Diff(K, r)$. Assume on the contrary that $Diff(w, r) \cap (P - Diff(K, r)) \neq \emptyset$. Since r does not differ from K in any variables in $P - Diff(K, r)$, we derive that there is a $u \in [K]$ that agrees with r on all variables in $P - Diff(K, r)$ (see Footnote 5). Define z to be the world that agrees with w on the variables in $Diff(K, r)$ and agrees with u on the remaining variables. Then $Diff(z, r) \subset Diff(w, r)$ and moreover, since $\{Diff(K, r), P - Diff(K, r)\}$ is a K-splitting, by Lemma A, $z \in [K]$. This however contradicts our assumption that $Diff(w, r)$ is $\trianglelefteq$-minimal in Q. Hence we have shown that $Diff(w, r) \subseteq Diff(K, r)$; i.e., w agrees with r over all variables in $P - Diff(K, r)$.

Now pick a world $w' \in [K]$ such that $Diff(w', r')$ is $\trianglelefteq$-minimal in the set $Q' = \{Diff(z', r') : z' \in [K]\}$. By a similar argument as the one above, we derive that $Diff(w', r') \subseteq Diff(K, r)$.

Next we show that $Diff(w, r) \trianglelefteq Diff(w', r')$. Assume towards contradiction that $Diff(w', r') \lhd Diff(w, r)$. Define z to be the world that agrees with w' over the variables in $Diff(K, r)$, and it agrees with w over all remaining variables. By Lemma A, $z \in [K]$. Moreover by construction, $Diff(z, r) \subseteq Diff(K, r)$. Hence, since r and r' agree over the variables in $Diff(K, r)$, and so do z and w', we derive that $Diff(z, r) = Diff(w', r')$. From $Diff(w', r') \lhd Diff(w, r)$ we then derive that $Diff(z, r) \lhd Diff(w, r)$. This of course contradicts our initial assumption that $Diff(w, r)$ is $\trianglelefteq$-minimal in $\{Diff(z', r) : z' \in [K]\}$.

---

[5] To see that such a world indeed exists, consider the sentence φ defined as the conjunction of all literals in r that are built from variables in $P - Diff(K, r)$. Clearly then, $r \models \psi$. Moreover, $\neg \psi \notin K$, for otherwise $Diff(K, r)$ would include variables from $P - Diff(K, r)$, which is of course a contradiction. Hence there is a $u \in [K]$ such that $u \models \psi$. By the construction of ψ it follows that u agrees with r on all variables outside $Diff(K, r)$.

Thus we have shown that $Diff(w, r) \lhd Diff(w', r')$. Since $Diff(w', r')$ is $\lhd$-minimal in $\{Diff(z', r') : z' \in [K]\}$ we derive that $Diff(w, r) \lhd Diff(z', r')$, for all $z' \in [K]$. Consequently, $r \sqsubseteq_K^\lhd r'$.

By a totally symmetric argument we also derive that $r' \sqsubseteq_K^\lhd r$, thus proving (Q2). □

7   Examples

The extended AGM postulates are clearly stronger than the original ones. In [9], Parikh has already demonstrated the benefits of adding (wP) to (K*1) - (K*8). In this section we provide further examples in support of the extended AGM postulates.

Yet instead of following the path set by Parikh, we choose a different direction which better illustrates the diversity of the implications of adding (wP) and (KC1) - (KC2) to the classical AGM postulates. In particular, the first two examples below, introduced in [5,7] respectively, relate to *iterated revision* scenarios, [12], which are known to be out of reach for vanilla AGM. It is shown below that the extended AGM postulates, although not specifically designed to deal with iteration, are nevertheless strong enough to produce the desired conclusions in these examples.

Example 1 [7]. "Consider a circuit containing an adder and a multiplier. In this example, we have two atomic propositions, *adder_ok* and *multiplier_ok*, denoting respectively the fact that the adder and the multiplier are working. We have initially no information about this circuit ($\Psi \equiv \top$) and we learn that the adder and the multiplier are working ($\mu = adder\_ok \wedge multiplier\_ok$). Then someone tells us that the adder is not working ($\alpha = \neg adder\_ok$). There is, then, no reason to "forget" that the multiplier is working."

The extended AGM postulates turn the right results: since initially $\Psi = Cn(\emptyset)$, μ is consistent with Ψ, and therefore $\Psi * \mu = Cn(\{adder\_ok, multiplier\_ok\})$; (wP) then entails that $\Psi * \mu * \alpha = Cn(\{\neg adder\_ok, multiplier\_ok\})$ as desired.

Example 2 [5]. "We encounter a strange new animal and it appears to be a bird, so we believe the animal is a bird. As it comes closer to our hiding place, we see clearly that the animal is red, so we believe that it is a red bird. To remove further doubts about the animal's birdhood, we call in a bird expert who takes it for examination and concludes that it is not really a bird but some sort of mammal. The question now is whether we should still believe that the animal is red."

Once again the extended AGM postulates deliver the anticipated results. Let us denote by a the proposition "the animal is red" and by b the proposition "the animal is a bird". Our initial belief set is $K = Cn(\{b\})$. Since a is consistent with K it follows that $K * a = Cn(\{a, b\})$. Hence (wP) entails that $K * a * \neg b = Cn(\{a, \neg b\})$ as desired.

It should be noted that, not only classical AGM, but even Darwiche and Pearl's iterated revision approach, [3], has trouble dealing such examples (see [5,7,8] for details).

In Examples 1 and 2, the addition of (wP) alone to (K*1) - (K*8), suffices to produce the desired results. The last example is new and requires the full strength of the extended AGM postulates.

Example 3. A circuit consists of a multiplier and two adders. Let us denote by m the proposition "the multiplier is working", and by a_1, a_2 the propositions "the first adder is working" and "the second adder is working" respectively. After performing some tests on the circuit, we discover that the multiplier or adder 1 is malfunctioning; in symbols, $\neg m \lor \neg a_1$. Suppose that our initial belief set is $Cn(\{m, a_1, a_2\})$. Since it is known that multipliers are less reliable than adders, we end up with the belief set $Cn(\{\overline{m}, a_1, a_2\})$. For the same reason, if our initial belief set was $Cn(\{m, a_1, \overline{a_2}\})$, then $\neg m \lor \neg a_1$ would have taken us to $Cn(\{\overline{m}, a_1, \overline{a_2}\})$. What would then be our response to $\neg m \lor \neg a_1$ had our initial belief set been $Cn(\{m, a_1\})$? Given our past preference to adder 1 over the multiplier (regardless of the status of adder 2), we argue that it is reasonable to once again put the blame on the multiplier. Moreover, since adder 2 is independent from the other two components, our beliefs about adder 2 should not be effected. Indeed from (KC2) (or rather (KS2)) and (wP) we derive that the resulting belief set is indeed $Cn(\{\overline{m}, a_1\})$ as desired.

8   Conclusion

There are three main contributions in this paper. Firstly, we identified and formalised an aspect of rational belief revision that has been neglected in the classical AGM framework. We call it the *principle of kinetic consistency*. We modelled this principle axiomatically and semantically and proved a representation result connecting the two.

Secondly, we investigated the model that results from combining the AGM postulates for revision (K*1) - (K*8), with the postulates for kinetic consistency (KC1) - (KC2), and Parikh's postulate (wP) for relevant change. The extended AGM postulates were shown to be consistent and their strength was demonstrated in a number of examples that are out of reach for vanilla AGM.

Thirdly, we introduced a whole new class of concrete revision operators, called *PD operators* that are natural generalisations of Dalal's revision operator. We proved that every PD operator satisfies all extended AGM postulates. This result not only established the consistency of the extended AGM postulates, but also sheds light into the nature and scope of the revision functions satisfying these postulates.

We conclude with a note on future work. Firstly, we intend to examine more thoroughly the relationship revealed by the examples of the previous section, between the extended AGM postulates and iterated revision. Secondly, in future work we will investigate the possibility for an axiomatic characterisation of PD operators. Theorem 4 shows that all PD operators satisfy the extended AGM postulates; the converse however may not be true. If so, new axioms need to be formulated to characterise parametrised difference revision.

Acknowledgements. We are grateful to Fanis Aravanis and to the anonymous reviewers for valuable comments on this work.

References

1. Alchourron, C., Gardenfors, P., Makinson, D.: On the logic of theory change: partial meet functions for contraction and revision. J. Symbol. Logic **50**, 510–530 (1985)
2. Dalal, M.: Investigations into theory of knowledge base revision: preliminary report. In: Proceedings of 7th National Conference of the American Association for Artificial Intelligence (AAAI 1988), pp. 475–479 (1988)
3. Darwiche, A., Pearl, J.: On the logic of iterated belief revision. Artif. Intell. **89**, 1–29 (1997)
4. Grove, A.: Two modellings for theory change. J. Philos. Logic **17**, 157–170 (1988)
5. Jin, Y., Thielscher, M.: Iterated belief revision, revised. Artif. Intell. **171**, 1–18 (2007)
6. Katsuno, H., Mendelzon, A.: Propositional knowledge base revision and minimal change. Artif. Intell. **52**(3), 263–294 (1991)
7. Konieczny, S., Perez, R.P.: A framework for iterated revision. J. Appl. Non-Classical Logics **10**, 339–367 (2000)
8. Nayak, A., Pagnucco, M., Peppas, P.: Dynamic belief revision operators. Artif. Intell. **146**, 193–228 (2003)
9. Parikh, R.: Beliefs, belief revision, and splitting languages. In: Logic, Language, and Computation - CSLI Lecture Notes, vol. 2, pp. 266–278. CSLI Publications (1999)
10. Peppas, P.: Belief revision. In: van Harmelen, F., Lifschitz, V., Porter, B. (eds.) Handbook of Knowledge Representation, pp. 317–359. Elsevier Science (2008)
11. Peppas, P., Williams, M.-A., Chopra, S., Foo, N.: Relevance in belief revision. Artif. Intell. **229**, 126–138 (2015)
12. Peppas, P.: A panorama of iterated revision. In: Ove Hansson, S. (ed.) David Makinson on Classical Methods for Non-Classical Problems. Outstanding Contributions to Logic, pp. 71–94. Springer, Netherlands (2014)

DRAT Proofs for XOR Reasoning

Tobias Philipp[1]([⊠]) and Adrián Rebola-Pardo[2]

[1] International Center for Computational Logic,
Technische Universität Dresden, 01062 Dresden, Germany
tobias.philipp@tu-dresden.de
[2] TU Wien, Wien, Austria
arebolap@forsyte.tuwien.ac.at

Abstract. Unsatisfiability proofs in the DRAT format became the *de facto* standard to increase the reliability of contemporary SAT solvers. We consider the problem of generating proofs for the XOR reasoning component in SAT solvers and propose two methods: direct translation transforms every XOR constraint addition inference into a DRAT proof, whereas T-translation avoids the exponential blow-up in direct translations by using fresh variables. T-translation produces DRAT proofs from Gaussian elimination records that are polynomial in the size of the input CNF formula. Experiments show that a combination of both approaches with a simple prediction method outperforms the BDD-based method.

1 Introduction

The satisfiability problem (SAT) is a paramount problem in computer science and artificial intelligence. Modern SAT solvers based on the DPLL algorithm [10] use many advanced techniques such as *clause learning* [27], *clause removal* [2,12], *formula simplifications* [11,19] and specialized reasoning procedures such as XOR reasoning [20,21,29,31]. These improvements led to a spectacular performance of conflict-driven satisfiability solvers. However, even intensively-tested systems contain bugs [7,24], and today, unsatisfiability proofs in the DRAT proof format [32] are the *de facto* standard in the SAT community. In fact, DRAT format proof generation is a requirement in the main track of the SAT competition 2016. Recently, the DRAT format received media attention because SAT solvers solved the Pythagorean Triples Problem and its 200 TB proof was expressed in this format [17].

XOR constraints frequently arise in applications such as logical cryptanalysis [9] and pseudo-Boolean encodings [13]; 71 % of instances in the application track of the SAT Competition 2014 contain XOR constraints. Gaussian elimination can be used as an efficient reasoning procedure over XOR constraints [31]. Currently, none of the state-of-the-art SAT solvers, like Lingeling [5], Riss [23]

A. Rebola-Pardo—Supported by the LogiCS doctoral program W1255-N23 of the Austrian Science Fund (FWF), and by the Vienna Science and Technology Fund (WWTF) through grant VRG11-005.

© Springer International Publishing AG 2016
L. Michael and A. Kakas (Eds.): JELIA 2016, LNAI 10021, pp. 415–429, 2016.
DOI: 10.1007/978-3-319-48758-8_27

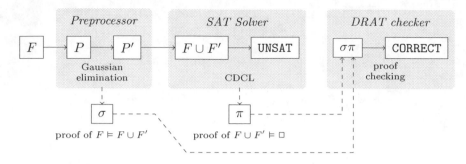

Fig. 1. Certificate-based approach for XOR reasoning: F is the input formula, P an XOR formula which is simplified to P'; F' represents the encoding as a CNF formula of P', which is then refuted. DRAT proofs π and σ are generated from Gaussian elimination preprocessing and CDCL execution. Together, they provide a full unsatisfiability certificate for F.

and `CryptoMiniSAT` [30], are able to produce proofs for XOR reasoning. Inability to produce unsatisfiability proofs for XOR reasoning can seriously hinder the performance of SAT solvers when certificate generation is required, since XOR reasoning must then be disabled. This makes the solver much less efficient for some problems, e.g. in cryptography.

The problem we address here is to generate DRAT proofs in XOR reasoning, stated as an open problem in [16,28]. As shown in Fig. 1, SAT solvers with XOR reasoning modules [29,31] detect XOR constraints P in the input formula F and apply Gaussian elimination to find small (unary and binary in `CoProcessor`), implied XOR constraints P', which are then encoded back to the formula as F'. A standard CDCL-driven SAT solver solves the new formula, producing a DRAT refutation π for $F \cup F'$. Still, the DRAT refutation does not include a witness that the XOR detection and reasoning procedure in the SAT solver was correct. To obtain a full unsatisfiability proof of F, a DRAT proof σ of $F \cup F'$ from F is needed. In this paper, we discuss how to generate such a DRAT proof.

Sinz and Biere proposed a BDD-based approach [28] which can be modified to express DRAT proofs for XOR reasoning. Heule et al. have shown that *symmetry breaking* [1] can be expressed in DRAT [15]. Although these techniques could be covered by allowing additional inference rules in the proof system, novel efficient methods for proof checking would need to be developed. Hence, verification of proof checkers would become much more costly; by generating DRAT proofs verification is avoided, since the proof itself is a certificate of correctness. Furthermore, the obtained DRAT proof is a refutation of the original clauses, so the XOR constraint detection algorithm needs not be verified.

Our Contributions.

1. We present *direct translations* which are based on DP-like variable elimination, and *T-translations* that avoid the exponential blow up by introducing

Tseitin variables. Moreover, we describe how one can adapt the BDD-based approach [28] to handle XOR constraints.

2. We prove that T-translations are polynomial in the size of the input formula, when Gaussian elimination was used, whereas the direct translation is an exponential proof in general.

3. Experiments show that the T-translation is practical as it produces proofs of reasonable size for the problems in the SAT Competition 2014. Moreover, the direct and the T-translation outperform the BDD-based approach.

2   Background

2.1   Propositional Logic and XOR Constraints

We consider a totally ordered, countably infinite set of *propositional variables*. A *literal* L is either a variable A or its *negation* $\neg A$. The *complement* of a literal L is denoted by $\overline{L}$. A *clause* is a finite disjunction of literals $(L_1 \vee \cdots \vee L_n)$. *XOR constraints* are expressions of the form $[A_1, \ldots, A_n]^k$, where A_i is a variable for every $1 \leq i \leq n$, and $k \in \{0, 1\}$. A finite set of clauses (XOR constraints, resp.) F is called a *CNF formula* (*XOR formula*, resp.).

Semantics are given by *interpretations* that map formulas to truth values: the interpretation I satisfies a clause $C = (L_1 \vee \cdots \vee L_n)$, if I satisfies some literal among $L_1, \ldots, L_n$; it satisfies an XOR constraint $X = [A_1, \ldots, A_n]^k$ if the number of the variables A_i satisfied by I has the parity of k (i.e. odd if $k = 1$ and even if $k = 0$); and it satisfies a formula F if I satisfies all elements of F. We follow the usual notion of semantic equivalence.

We assume that clauses and XOR constraints are normalized: a literal may appear only once in a clause, and a variable at most once in an XOR constraint. The normal form can be obtained by removing duplicated literals in CNF clauses as well as pairs of occurrences of the same variable in XOR constraints. Observe that these operations preserve semantic equivalence, e.g. $[p, q, r, r, q]^0$ is semantically equivalent to $[p]^0$. Consider two XOR constraints

$$X = [A_1, \ldots, A_n, B_1, \ldots, B_p]^k \qquad Y = [A_1, \ldots, A_n, B_1', \ldots, B_q']^l$$

where the A_i, B_i and B_i' are pairwise distinct variables. The *addition* of X and Y, denoted by $X \bigtriangleup Y$, is $[B_1, \ldots, B_p, B_1', \ldots, B_q']^{k \oplus l}$ where $\oplus$ represents the binary XOR operation. The *resolvent of clauses* C *and* D *upon* L is the clause obtained by removing L from C, and $\overline{L}$ from D, and afterwards combining them disjunctively. A *tautology* is a clause containing a complementary pair of literals.

2.2   Gaussian Elimination-Based XOR Reasoning in SAT Solvers

Contemporary SAT solvers such as `CryptoMiniSAT` detect XOR constraints in their direct encoding in the input formula [18]. The *direct encoding* [14] $\mathcal{D}(X)$ of an XOR constraint $X = [A_1, \ldots, A_n]^k$ is the CNF formula that contains all clauses of the form $(L_1 \vee \cdots \vee L_n)$, where the L_i are either A_i or $\neg A_i$, and the number of negated literals L_i is not equal to k modulo 2. The direct encoding of an XOR constraint is the unique CNF formula semantically equivalent to it.

$$\frac{X \qquad Y}{X \triangle Y}\text{add} \qquad \frac{}{[A, B_1, \ldots, B_n]^k}\text{def}$$

Fig. 2. XOR proof system inference rules: addition (left) and XOR definition (right), where A is a fresh variable and $k \in \{0, 1\}$

Example 1 (Direct Encoding). Let $X = [p, q, r]^0$, $Y = [p, q, s]^1$ and $Z = [r, s]^1$. Their direct encodings are:

$$\mathcal{D}(X) = \{(\neg p \vee \neg q \vee \neg r), (\neg p \vee q \vee r), (p \vee \neg q \vee r), (p \vee q \vee \neg r)\}$$
$$\mathcal{D}(Y) = \{(p \vee q \vee s), (p \vee \neg q \vee \neg s), (\neg p \vee q \vee \neg s), (\neg p \vee \neg q \vee s)\}$$
$$\mathcal{D}(Z) = \{(r \vee s), (\neg r \vee \neg s)\}$$

Note that $\mathcal{D}([]^0)$ is the empty formula, while $\mathcal{D}([]^1)$ is the unsatisfiable singleton formula consisting of the empty clause. □

For an XOR formula P, we define $\mathcal{D}(P)$ as the union of the direct encodings of XOR constraints in P. We formalize XOR reasoning as a proof system with two inference rules, given in Fig. 2. An XOR proof of an XOR formula Q from a formula P is a proof using only additions and XOR definitions, where all premises are in P and all XOR constraints in Q are either in P or occurring along the proof. Note that the addition rule subsumes Gaussian elimination steps [29], and therefore XOR proofs subsumes Gaussian elimination procedures.

Example 2. Consider the XOR formula $P = \{[p, q, r]^0, [p, q]^1\}$. We obtain the following XOR proofs of $[r]^1$, with and without the use of a single XOR definition:

$$\frac{\dfrac{\overline{[x, p, q]^0}\text{def} \qquad [p, q, r]^0}{[x, r]^0}\text{add}}{[r]^1} \qquad \frac{\dfrac{\overline{[x, p, q]^0}\text{def} \qquad [p, q]^1}{[x]^1}\text{add}}{[r]^1}\text{add} \qquad \frac{[p, q, r]^0 \qquad [p, q]^1}{[r]^1}\text{add}$$

□

2.3 DRAT Proofs

The DRAT (Deletion Resolution Asymmetric Tautology) format [32] is based on the notion of asymmetric literal addition [19]. Given a CNF formula F and a clause C, the set $\mathrm{AL}(\mathrm{F}, \mathrm{C})$ contains all literals L such that, for literals $L_1, \ldots, L_n$ occurring in C, the clause $(L_1 \vee \ldots \vee L_n \vee \overline{L})$ belongs to F. We define the *asymmetric literal addition* function ALA_F that maps a clause C to the clause $\mathrm{ALA}_F(C) = C \vee \bigvee_{L \in \mathrm{AL}(\mathrm{F},\mathrm{C})} L$. We consider the repeated application of ALA_F:

$$\mathrm{ALA}_F(C) \uparrow 0 = C \qquad \mathrm{ALA}_F(C) \uparrow n + 1 = \mathrm{ALA}_F(\mathrm{ALA}_F(C) \uparrow n)$$

A clause C is an *asymmetric tautology* (AT) w.r.t. F if, for some $n \geq 0$, $\mathrm{ALA}_F(C) \uparrow n$ is a tautology. Asymmetric tautologies can also be characterized in terms of unit propagation, i.e. $(L_1 \vee \ldots \vee L_n)$ is AT w.r.t. F if and only if unit propagation in $F \wedge \neg L_1 \wedge \ldots \wedge \neg L_n$ detects an inconsistency [3]. A clause C is a *resolution asymmetric tautology* (RAT) [19] upon L w.r.t. F if the resolvent of C and D upon L is an AT w.r.t. F for all clauses $D \in F$ with $\overline{L} \in D$.

Example 3. Consider the formula $F = \{(p \vee q), (p \vee \neg q \vee r), (\neg q \vee \neg r)\}$ Then, the application of asymmetric literal addition for p shows that the unit clause p is an AT in F, while the unit clause q is not an AT:

$$\begin{aligned}
\mathrm{ALA}_F(p) \uparrow 1 &= (p \vee \neg q) & \mathrm{ALA}_F(q) \uparrow 1 &= (q \vee \neg p) \\
\mathrm{ALA}_F(p) \uparrow 2 &= (p \vee \neg q \vee \neg r \vee r) & \mathrm{ALA}_F(q) \uparrow 2 &= \mathrm{ALA}_F(q) \uparrow 1 \\
\mathrm{ALA}_F(p) \uparrow 3 &= (p \vee \neg q \vee \neg r \vee r \vee q) & & \\
\mathrm{ALA}_F(p) \uparrow 4 &= \mathrm{ALA}_F(p) \uparrow 3 & &
\end{aligned}$$

Moreover, the unit clause $\neg q$ is a RAT, since it can only be resolved with $(p \vee q)$, yielding p which is an AT. □

Introduction of asymmetric tautologies to a formula preserves semantic equivalence, while introduction of resolution asymmetric tautologies to a formula preserves satisfiability [19]. A *DRAT proof* in a formula F is then a sequence of clauses such that every clause is either AT or RAT with respect to the formula F together with the preceding clauses. In the following we will use the fact that resolvents of C and D are asymmetric tautologies in $\{C, D\}$ [19]. This allows to regard any resolution proof using resolution inferences of the form

$$\frac{C \vee L \qquad D \vee \overline{L}}{C \vee D}\text{res}$$

as a DRAT proof by traversing the proof tree in a breadth-first top-down manner.

3   Variable-Elimination-Based Approach

In this section we present the *direct translation*, a method to construct DRAT proofs from XOR proofs based on the direct encoding of XOR constraints. Each inference in the XOR proof system is translated to a DRAT proof; concatenation of partial translations is the direct translation of an XOR proof into a DRAT proof. In the following, we give translations for the two inference rules in XOR reasoning, namely additions and XOR definitions. In general, the direct encoding of an addition is not a DRAT proof from the direct encoding of its premises:

Example 4. Consider the XOR constraints $[p, q]^0$ and $[p, q]^1$. By addition we obtain $[]^1$, whose direct encoding only contains the empty clause. However, the empty clause is not a RAT in the direct encoding of the premises, given by $\mathcal{D}([p, q]^0) \cup \mathcal{D}([p, q]^1) = \{(\neg p \vee q), (p \vee \neg q), (\neg p \vee \neg q), (p \vee q)\}$ □

In fact, the problem arises when two or more variables are eliminated by addition. We propose to eliminate the variables stepwise. Consider XOR constraints X, Y and $Z = X \triangle Y$ defining a general addition inference of the form:

$$[A_1, \ldots, A_n, B_1, \ldots, B_p]^k \triangle [A_1, \ldots, A_n, B_1', \ldots, B_q']^l = [B_1, \ldots, B_p, B_1', \ldots, B_q']^{k \oplus l}$$

The proof is constructed in a bottom-up fashion: starting from each clause C in $\mathcal{D}(Z)$, a resolution proof of C from $\mathcal{D}(X) \cup \mathcal{D}(Y)$ is generated. We know that C is a clause of the form $C = (L_1 \vee \cdots \vee L_p \vee L'_1 \vee \cdots \vee L'_q)$, where literals L_i are either B_i or $\neg B_i$, and similarly for L'_i.

C can be obtained by resolving the two clauses $C \vee A_1$ and $C \vee \neg A_1$ upon A_1. These clauses contain the literals corresponding to all the B_i, B'_i as well as to A_1. In general, we can consider a clause C' of the form $C \vee K_1 \vee \cdots \vee K_j$, where the literals K_i are either A_i or $\neg A_i$. C' can be further obtained as the resolvent of $(C \vee K_1 \vee \cdots \vee K_j \vee A_{j+1})$ and $(C \vee K_1 \vee \cdots \vee K_j \vee \neg A_{j+1})$. Generating these resolution steps recursively gives a resolution proof, where clauses in level j are of the form $C \vee K_1 \vee \cdots \vee K_j$.

$$\cfrac{\cfrac{\ddots \quad \cdot^{\cdot^{\cdot}}}{C \vee A_1 \vee A_2}\text{res} \quad \cfrac{\ddots \quad \cdot^{\cdot^{\cdot}}}{C \vee A_1 \vee \neg A_2}\text{res}}{C \vee A_1}\text{res} \quad \cfrac{\cfrac{\ddots \quad \cdot^{\cdot^{\cdot}}}{C \vee \neg A_1 \vee A_2}\text{res} \quad \cfrac{\ddots \quad \cdot^{\cdot^{\cdot}}}{C \vee \neg A_1 \vee \neg A_2}\text{res}}{C \vee \neg A_1}\text{res}$$
$$\overline{\hspace{6cm} C \hspace{6cm}}\text{res}$$

Clauses in the $(n-1)$-th level are of the form $C \vee K_1 \vee \cdots \vee K_{n-1}$. Such clauses can be guaranteed to be AT in the CNF formula $\mathcal{D}(X) \cup \mathcal{D}(Y)$. Let $\mathcal{P}(X,Y)$ be the sequence of clauses obtained from traversing the above proof tree in breadth-first, top-down manner. Then, $\mathcal{P}(X,Y)$ is a DRAT proof of the $\mathcal{D}(X \triangle Y)$ from $\mathcal{D}(X) \cup \mathcal{D}(Y)$.

On the other hand, translation of XOR definitions is straightforward. If the XOR constraint X contains a variable that does not occur in F, and $\mathcal{D}(X) = \{C_1, \ldots, C_n\}$, then $(C_1, \ldots, C_n)$ is a DRAT proof of $\mathcal{D}(X)$ from F.

The direct translation of an XOR proof is then given by the concatenation of such partial translations of the addition and XOR definition inferences along the XOR proof.

4   T-Translation of XOR Proofs

In this section we introduce *T-translations* that avoid the exponential blow-up in the proof length by expressing single XOR constraints as conjunction of several XOR constraints of fixed size. We assume from now on that variables in XOR constraints are sorted. The *natural splitting* [14] of $X = [A_1, \ldots, A_n]^k$, denoted by $\mathcal{S}(X)$, is $\{X\}$ if $|X| \leq 3$, and otherwise the set containing the following XOR constraints:

$$\overbrace{[A_1, A_2, s_0]^0 \, [s_0, A_3, s_1]^0 \, \ldots \, [s_{n-4}, A_{n-2}, s_{n-3}]^0}^{\text{splitting matrix}} \quad \overbrace{[s_{n-3}, A_{n-1}, A_n]^k}^{\text{independent constraint}} \tag{1}$$

where the s_i are fresh variables. The set of XOR constraints in the left is called the *splitting matrix* of X, denoted by $\hat{\mathcal{S}}(X)$. The rightmost XOR constraint is called the *independent constraint* of X, denoted by $\mathcal{I}_X$; in the case when $|X| \leq 3$ we define $\hat{\mathcal{S}}(X) = \emptyset$ and $\mathcal{I}_X = X$.

Example 5. We show three XOR constraints with their respective splittings, where the x_i, z_i are fresh variables. Each independent constraint is underlined.

$$X = [p_1, p_2, p_3, p_4, p_5]^1 \qquad \mathcal{S}(X) = \{[p_1, p_2, x_0]^0, [x_0, p_3, x_1]^0, \underline{[x_1, p_4, p_5]^1}\}$$
$$Y = [p_4, p_5, p_6]^0 \qquad \mathcal{S}(Y) = \{\underline{[p_4, p_5, p_6]^0}\}$$
$$Z = [p_1, p_2, p_3, p_6]^1 \qquad \mathcal{S}(Y) = \{[p_1, p_2, z_0]^0, \underline{[z_0, p_3, p_6]^1}\} \qquad \Box$$

The *linear encoding* of X, is $\mathcal{L}(X) = \mathcal{D}(\mathcal{S}(X))$, i.e. the direct encoding of the splitting. Notice that the linear encoding is equivalent w.r.t. satisfiability to the direct encoding of the XOR constraint itself, and has polynomial size. Given an XOR proof of an XOR formula Q from an XOR formula P, its *T-translation* is a DRAT proof of $\mathcal{D}(Q)$ from $\mathcal{D}(P)$ constructed as follows:

1. Obtain a *splitter* XOR proof of $\mathcal{S}(P)$ from P; its direct translation, called the *prefix proof*, is a DRAT proof of $\mathcal{L}(P)$ from $\mathcal{D}(P)$.
2. Generate an *intermediate* XOR proof of $\mathcal{S}(Q)$ from $\mathcal{S}(P)$; its direct translation, called the *lift proof*, is a DRAT proof of $\mathcal{L}(Q)$ from $\mathcal{L}(P)$.
3. Derive $\mathcal{D}(Q)$ from $\mathcal{L}(Q)$ through the *suffix proof*; the concatenation of prefix, lift and suffix is a proof of $\mathcal{D}(Q)$ from $\mathcal{D}(P)$.

4.1   Prefix Proof – Towards the Splitted Representation

In general, given the direct encoding of the splitted XOR constraint $\mathcal{L}(X) = \mathcal{D}(\mathcal{S}(X)) = \{C_1, \ldots, C_n\}$, the sequence $(C_1, \ldots, C_n)$ is not a DRAT proof from $\mathcal{D}(X)$. We therefore propose to generate a *splitter* XOR proof of $\mathcal{S}(X)$ from an XOR constraint X; applying the direct translation to this splitter yields a DRAT proof of $\mathcal{L}(X)$ from $\mathcal{D}(X)$ as follows.

Consider $X = [A_1, \ldots, A_n]^k$. Observe that $X = \triangle_{Y \in \mathcal{S}(X)} Y$. Hence, we can conclude that $\mathcal{I}_X = X \triangle (\triangle_{Y \in \hat{\mathcal{S}}(X)} Y)$. The procedure to construct the splitter of X consists on, firstly, introducing all XOR constraints in $\hat{\mathcal{S}}(X)$ as XOR definitions, which is possible as long as this is done in the order shown in (1). Secondly, the missing constraint $\mathcal{I}_X$ can be derived by, starting with X, iteratively applying addition inferences with all constraints from $\hat{\mathcal{S}}(X)$. Furthermore, provided this operation is performed in the order from (1), we are able to guarantee that this process never involves an XOR constraint larger than X, which is essential to bound the length of the obtained DRAT proof.

Example 6. Consider again the constraints in Example 5. Since the splitting of Y is $\{Y\}$, its splitter is the empty proof. The splitter of X is given by:

$$\cfrac{[p_1, p_2, p_3, p_4, p_5]^1 \qquad \cfrac{}{[p_1, p_2, x_0]^0}\ \text{def}}{\cfrac{[x_0, p_3, p_4, p_5]^1}{[x_1, p_4, p_5]^1}}\ \text{add} \qquad \cfrac{}{[x_0, p_3, x_1]^0}\ \text{def}\ \text{add} \qquad \Box$$

Applying direct translation results in a DRAT proof of $\mathcal{L}(X)$ from $\mathcal{D}(X)$, which we refer to as the *prefix* proof. In the case the aforementioned orders are used, the obtained proof is polynomial in the size of the input CNF formula.

4.2   Lifted Proof

We generate now an *intermediate* XOR proof of $\mathcal{S}(Q)$ from $\mathcal{S}(P)$; its direct translation will be the *lift* DRAT proof. It suffices to give proofs of $\mathcal{S}(Z)$ from $\mathcal{S}(X) \cup \mathcal{S}(Y)$ for every addition inference $Z = X \bigtriangleup Y$; the intermediate XOR proof is the concatenation of such proofs for every addition inference along the original XOR proof. Assume that the XOR constraints X, Y, Z contain exactly the variables $A_1 < \cdots < A_n$.

Similarly to the prefix proof, XOR constraints in the matrix $\hat{\mathcal{S}}(Z)$ can be introduced in the same order as in (1) as XOR definitions. The rest of the proof is directed towards deriving the independent XOR constraint $\mathcal{I}_Z$ by addition. It is possible to show that:

$$\mathcal{I}_Z = (\bigtriangleup_{X' \in \mathcal{S}(X)} X') \bigtriangleup (\bigtriangleup_{Y' \in \mathcal{S}(Y)} Y') \bigtriangleup (\bigtriangleup_{Z' \in \hat{\mathcal{S}}(Z)} Z')$$

As before, the result holds regardless of the order on which addition inferences are applied. However, it is possible to choose an order which produces intermediate XOR constraints of size bounded by 5, which is needed to avoid an exponential blow-up. This is attained by first adding the XOR constraints containing the literal A_1, afterwards adding those containing A_2, and so on.

Example 7. Consider X, Y and $Z = X \bigtriangleup Y$ as in Example 5. Then, one can derive $\mathcal{S}(Z)$ from $\mathcal{S}(X) \cup \mathcal{S}(Y)$ as follows:

$$\cfrac{\cfrac{\cfrac{\cfrac{\cfrac{[p_1,p_2,x_0]^0 \quad \overline{[p_1,p_2,z_0]^0}^{\text{def}}}{[x_0,z_0]^0} \quad [x_0,p_3,x_1]^0}{[x_1,z_0,p_3]^0} \quad [x_1,p_4,p_5]^1}{[z_0,p_3,p_4,p_5]^1} \quad [p_4,p_5,p_6]^0}{[z_0,p_3,p_6]^1}}{}$$

The only XOR constraint in the matrix of Z has been introduced by XOR definition on z_0. To derive the independent constraint $[z_0, p_3, p_6]^1$, we have first used up the XOR constraints containing p_1, then the remaining ones containing p_2 (in this case, none), then the remaining ones containing p_3 and so forth. □

The *lift* proof is a DRAT proof of $\mathcal{L}(Q)$ from $\mathcal{L}(P)$ obtained by applying the direct translation to the intermediate translation described above for every addition inference along the original XOR proof.

4.3   Suffix Proof – Towards the Direct Encoding

Suffix proofs are generated by listing all clauses in the direct encoding of X, since every such clause is an AT w.r.t. $\mathcal{L}(X)$. Once the three parts of the proof have been generated, the T-translation consists of their concatenation.

Theorem 8 (Main Theorem). *Let P, Q be XOR formulae, and π be an XOR proof of Q from P. Consider the prefix π_p, lift π_l and suffix π_s obtained from P, π and Q respectively. Then, $\pi_p \pi_l \pi_s$ is a DRAT proof of $\mathcal{D}(Q)$ from $\mathcal{D}(P)$.*

Proof. See [25, Corollary 7.30]. □

5   Proof Generation Using BDDs

An alternative to the proposed method consists in expressing XOR constraint
addition as an operation over binary decision diagrams (BDDs) [8]. A DRAT
proof can then be generated using a method proposed by Sinz and Biere [28].

Let us consider two XOR constraints X and Y, and assume we have computed
their BDDs B_X and B_Y. The binary Boolean function f is defined by $f(x, y) = 1$
if and only if $x = y$. Then, as shown by Fig. 3, the BDD of the XOR constraint
$X \triangle Y$ can be computed by applying the binary Boolean function f to B_X and
B_Y using a well-known algorithm to apply Boolean functions to BDDs [8].

Sinz and Biere [28] propose a proof method for BDD operations as extended
resolution proofs. In particular, for the encoding of a BDD B as a CNF formula
$\mathcal{E}(B)$ described in [28], a method to derive $\mathcal{E}(B_1 \wedge B_2)$ from $\mathcal{E}(B_1) \cup \mathcal{E}(B_2)$ by
an extended resolution proof is proposed. Due to space constraints, we do not
discuss this method in detail; it can however be adapted to our problem:

- By performing minor changes in the case where the operated BDDs are leaves,
  it is possible to extend the method so that BDDs are operated with the aforementioned Boolean function f instead of $\wedge$. This outlines another method to
  lift an XOR proof into an extended resolution proof.
- Extended resolution proofs can be easily transformed into DRAT proofs [19].
- Given a clause C and its BDD encoding B_C, clauses in $\mathcal{E}(B_C)$ can be derived
  by simply enumerating them. The encoding $\mathcal{E}(B_X)$ of the BDD of an XOR
  constraint X is derived by conjoining all the clauses in $\mathcal{D}(X)$ as BDDs, and
  then lifting this operation into a DRAT proof as above.
- In an analogous way to the T-translation suffix, clauses in the direct encoding
  of an XOR constraint X can be derived as asymmetric tautologies in $\mathcal{E}(B_X)$.

Example 9. Consider XOR constraints X and Y with direct encodings:

$$\mathcal{D}(X) = \{C_1, C_2\} \quad \mathcal{D}(Y) = \{C_3, C_4\} \quad \mathcal{D}(X \triangle Y) = \{D_1, D_2, D_3, D_4\}$$

The encodings of the BDDs corresponding to clauses C_i can be derived by enumerating the clauses in $\mathcal{E}(C_i)$. Now, since X is semantically equivalent to $C_1 \wedge C_2$

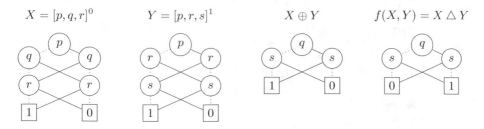

Fig. 3. BDD representation of two XOR constraints X, Y, as well as of $X \oplus Y$ and
$f(X, Y)$. A dotted (solid) line from variable A indicates the BDD after assigning A to
false (true, resp.). The correct BDD for the XOR constraint $X \triangle Y$ is that of $f(X, Y)$.

and ROBDDs are canonical [8], we have that $B_X = B_{C_1} \wedge B_{C_2}$. Applying the method from [28] yields a DRAT proof of $\mathcal{E}(B_X)$ from $\mathcal{E}(B_{C_1}) \cup \mathcal{E}(B_{C_2})$; and analogously for Y. Our variation in this method replacing $\wedge$ by f can then provide a DRAT proof of $\mathcal{E}(B_{X \triangle Y})$ from $\mathcal{E}(B_X) \cup \mathcal{E}(B_Y)$. The direct encoding of $X \triangle Y$ can be derived from $\mathcal{E}(B_{X \triangle Y})$ by introducing every clause as an AT.

$$
\left.
\begin{array}{l}
\left.
\begin{array}{l}
C_1 \rightsquigarrow \mathcal{E}(B_{C_1}) \\
C_2 \rightsquigarrow \mathcal{E}(B_{C_2})
\end{array}
\right] \wedge\; \mathcal{E}(B_{C_1 \wedge C_2}) = \mathcal{E}(B_X) \\[2ex]
\left.
\begin{array}{l}
C_3 \rightsquigarrow \mathcal{E}(B_{C_2}) \\
C_4 \rightsquigarrow \mathcal{E}(B_{C_2})
\end{array}
\right] \wedge\; \mathcal{E}(B_{C_3 \wedge C_4}) = \mathcal{E}(B_Y)
\end{array}
\right] f\; \mathcal{E}(B_{X \triangle Y}) \rightsquigarrow \{D_1,\dots,D_4\} = \mathcal{D}(X \triangle Y)
$$

$\square$

6   Length Analysis of the Constructed DRAT Proofs

Table 1 presents the exact length measures of direct translations. Translation of addition inferences is exponential on the u measure, which is the motivation behind T-translations: by bounding the maximum size of intermediate XOR constraints, we are able to asymptotically reduce the size of the lift translation.

In order to relate the number of variables occurring in the input formula to the size of the input formula, we assume that the XOR proof was obtained by Gaussian elimination, which is a safe assumption in all practical cases. In particular, we consider an XOR proof of an XOR formula Q from an XOR formula P of size n^2, where n is the number of variables in P.

Theorem 10. *If Gaussian elimination was used to obtain an XOR proof π of Q from P, then the length of the DRAT proof obtained from π by T-translation is bounded by $O((|\mathcal{D}(P)| + |\mathcal{D}(Q)|)^3)$.*

Proof. See [25, Theorem 8.2] for a proof for a regularized version of the T-translation. The proof can easily be adapted to the setting explained here. Observe this is a very loose bound, since the cubic exponent only applies to the involved XOR constraints in every inference. $\square$

Table 1. Above, (exact) proof lengths of direct translations for each inference in the input XOR proof. Below, proof length bounds for each T-translation part. We use the following measures: $l(X) = |X^*|$, $u(X,Y) = |X^* \cup Y^*|$ and $d(X,Y) = |(X \triangle Y)^*|$ where $X^* = \{A_1,\dots,A_n\}$ for an XOR constraint $X = [A_1,\dots,A_n]^k$.

Translation	Length
Direct addition $Z = X \triangle Y$	$2^{u(X,Y)-1} - 2^{d(X,Y)-1}$ if $d(X,Y) > 0$, $2^{u(X,Y)-1}$ if $d(X,Y) = 0$
Direct XOR definition X	$2^{l(X)-1}$ if $l(X) > 0$, and 1 if $l(X) = 0$
Prefix proof of XOR constraint X	$4(l(X) - 4) + 3 \cdot 2^{l(X)-1}$
Lifted proof of addition $Z = X \triangle Y$	$36u(X,Y)$
Suffix proof of XOR constraint X	$5 \cdot 2^{l(X)-1}$

Note that the size of the suffix subproof can be ignored if simplified XOR constraints are introduced back in the SAT solver with the linear encoding. T-translations are then polynomial in the size of the input CNF formula. This bound does not contradict the exponential bounds for prefix and suffix proofs: the size of XOR constraints is logarithmic in the usual measure of a proof generation method, which is the size of the input CNF formula, in our case $\mathcal{D}(P)$. This bound allows us to show a complexity gap between direct and T-translations. While the T-translation has polynomial length in the size of the input formula, this is not true in general for the direct translation. The following example shows a family of XOR proofs whose direct translation is of exponential length on the size of the input CNF formula.

Example 11. Consider XOR constraints $X_k = [p_{k-1}, p_{k+1}, q_{k+1}]^0$ and $Y_k = [p_k, p_{k+1}, q_1, \ldots, q_{k+1}]^0$ for $k \geq 0$, and the XOR formula $P_k = \{Y_0, X_1, \ldots, X_k\}$. A family of XOR proofs is given by $\varphi_k = Y_1, \ldots, Y_k$, where the i-th XOR constraint is obtained by the addition $Y_i = Y_{i-1} \triangle X_i$; these correspond to records of Gaussian elimination over P_k. Note that all premises in P_k are of length 3, so the size of $\mathcal{D}(P_k)$ is $4(k+1)$. However, the i-th addition has measures $u(Y_{i-1}, X_i) = i + 4$ and $d(Y_{i-1}, X_i) = i + 3$. Thus, the direct translation of the i-th addition is of length 2^{i+2}, totaling to translation length $2^{O(k)}$ for φ_k.   □

7   Experimental Evaluation

We implemented the three approaches for proof generation in the Scala programming language. Our algorithms for BDD manipulation are described in [6], and we based our implementation in the one released by J.C. Filliâtre[1]. We ran experiments over the instances of the application track of the SAT Competition 2014 and obtained XOR proofs from the preprocessor `CoProcessor` [22]. 210 out of 300 instances yielded nonempty XOR proofs, which constituted our benchmarks. The average length of these benchmarks was 36,000 XOR constraints, with some instances up to 10 times longer; benchmarks contain XOR constraints averaging 3.47 in size. For each benchmark we computed DRAT proofs using the direct translation, the T-translation, and the BDD-based approach. The experiments were run on an 2-core 3.5 GHz AMD Opteron machine with 192 GB RAM. A 5 min timeout was set, and proofs were generated in memory but not stored in disk. Figures 4a, b and c compare these lengths.

Our results show that the BDD-based approach performs consistently worse than both direct and T-translations. In particular, it times out on 15% of the benchmarks, compared to 13% for direct translations and none for T-translations; all terminating instances for the BDD-based approach terminate for direct and T-translation, as shown by Figs. 4a and b.

Comparison between direct and T-translation is more complex, partly due to timeouts for direct translations. Given the sheer size of some direct translations, they would have been impossible to generate within any reasonable time.

---

[1] https://github.com/zhihan/bdd-scala.

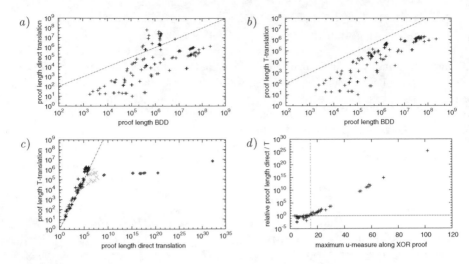

Fig. 4. Graphs (a), (b), (c) compare the three different forms of proof construction: the direct translation, the T-translation, and the BDD-based approach. The gray line indicates equal length. In Graph (c), green points correspond to the instances where BDD-based generation yields shorter proofs than direct translation; black points are the instances where the converse holds; and purple points are those where direct translation times out, where length was computed using Table 1. Graph (d) compares relative length of direct translations w.r.t. T-translations to the maximum value of the u-measure along the input XOR proof. Gray line indicates equal length of direct and T-translations; the proposed threshold value of 15 is indicated by a red dashed line. (Color figure online)

A length comparison is nevertheless possible, since direct translation length can be predicted by using the results from Table 1. Figure 4c shows these results, where predicted data is provided where the direct translation times out. Direct translations are strictly shorter than T-translations on 46 % of the instances. Moreover, whereas in some cases direct translation yields up to 300 times shorter proofs, in some other instances direct translation produces proofs 25 orders of magnitude larger than T-translation, which is consistent with our theoretical analysis in Sect. 6. Furthermore, Fig. 4c shows that, whenever T-translation is outperformed by direct translation, then so is the BDD-based approach. This suggests that the latter should not be considered for proof generation.

Further data are presented in Fig. 4d, showing a tight relation between the maximum u measure (defined in Table 1) along the input XOR proof and a length comparison of direct and T-translations. In particular, we find that T-translation outperforms direct translation in proof size whenever the former measure is larger than 15. The obtained data suggest an approach for proof generation by computing the maximum u measure in the input, and then comparing it to a threshold value of 15 to decide for the direct encoding or the linear encoding.

The particular order on which clauses in $\mathcal{D}(X)$ are conjoined to construct the BDD of the XOR constraint X does not have a significant influence on the

Table 2. Sizes of generated prefixes with the BDD-based method and with T-translation. BDD prefixes were generated by conjoining BDDs in random orders, for a sample of size 30; minimum and maximum recorded prefix lengths are shown.

Size of XOR constraint	3	5	7	9	11	13
Minimum length of BDD prefix	209	1704	15436	151855	1633456	19384645
Maximum length of BDD prefix	216	1879	16507	156914	1668015	19523431
Length of T-translation prefix	0	44	196	780	3092	12316

length of the prefix, as shown in Table 2. In particular, data suggests an average difference of around 4 % between the minimum and the maximum BDD-based prefix length, and in all cases a worse behaviour than the T-translation prefix.

8 Conclusion

Contemporary SAT solvers employ XOR reasoning techniques to efficiently solve the propositional satisfiability problem. It was an open problem [16,28] to efficiently express XOR reasoning in terms of the DRAT format. We have adapted a known BDD-based approach [28] to generate such proofs, although this method is resource-intensive and generated proofs are very long. We propose two alternatives: direct translation transforms every XOR step into a DRAT proof, whereas T-translation avoids the exponential blow-up of the direct translation by first generating a new XOR proof using Tseitin variables, and afterwards applying the direct translation. For XOR proofs produced by Gaussian elimination, T-translations are polynomial in the size of the input CNF formula. Experiments have shown that direct and T-translations outperform the BDD-based approach. The direct encoding sometimes generates proofs of enormous size; however, it is possible to predict instances where this happens, so that T-translation is applied instead. Our approach allows efficient XOR reasoning when certificates of correctness are needed, producing unsatisfiability proofs of adequate size.

In the future, we plan to implement both translations in `CoProcessor` and apply similar ideas to obtain proofs for cardinality resolution [26], as suggested in [16]. Another interesting problem is adapting the presented approaches to SAT solvers where XOR reasoning takes place within the CDCL procedure [20,21].

Acknowledgements. We would like to thank an anonymous reviewer who pointed out that the BDD-based approach could be used as a baseline.

References

1. Aloul, F.A., Ramani, A., Markov, I.L., Sakallah, K.A.: Solving difficult SAT instances in the presence of symmetry. In: DAC 2002, pp. 731–736. ACM (2002)
2. Audemard, G., Simon, L.: Predicting learnt clauses quality in modern SAT solvers. In: Boutilier, C. (ed.) IJCAI 2009, pp. 399–404. Morgan Kaufmann Publishers Inc., Pasadena (2009)

3. Beame, P., Kautz, H., Sabharwal, A.: Towards understanding and harnessing the potential of clause learning. J. Artif. Intell. Res. **22**(1), 319–351 (2004)
4. Belov, A., Diepold, D., Heule, M.J., Järvisalo, M. (eds.): Proceedings of SAT Competition 2014, Department of Computer Science Series of Publications B, vol. B-2014-2. University of Helsinki, Helsinki (2014)
5. Biere, A.: Yet another local search solver and lingeling and friends entering the SAT competition 2014. In: Belov et al. [4], pp. 39–40
6. Brace, K.S., Rudell, R.L., Bryant, R.E.: Efficient implementation of a BDD package. In: DAC, pp. 40–45 (1990)
7. Brummayer, R., Biere, A.: Fuzzing and delta-debugging SMT solvers. In: Workshop SMT 2010, pp. 1–5. ACM (2009)
8. Bryant, R.E.: Graph-based algorithms for Boolean function manipulation. IEEE Trans. Comput. **35**(8), 677–691 (1986)
9. Courtois, N.T., Bard, G.V.: Algebraic cryptanalysis of the data encryption standard. In: Galbraith, S.D. (ed.) Cryptography and Coding 2007. LNCS, vol. 4887, pp. 152–169. Springer, Heidelberg (2007). doi:10.1007/978-3-540-77272-9_10
10. Davis, M., Logemann, G., Loveland, D.: A machine program for theorem-proving. Commun. ACM **5**(7), 394–397 (1962)
11. Eén, N., Biere, A.: Effective preprocessing in SAT through variable and clause elimination. In: Bacchus, F., Walsh, T. (eds.) SAT 2005. LNCS, vol. 3569, pp. 61–75. Springer, Heidelberg (2005). doi:10.1007/11499107_5
12. Eén, N., Sörensson, N.: An extensible SAT-solver. In: Giunchiglia, E., Tacchella, A. (eds.) SAT 2003. LNCS, vol. 2919, pp. 502–518. Springer, Heidelberg (2004). doi:10.1007/978-3-540-24605-3_37
13. Eén, N., Sörensson, N.: Translating pseudo-Boolean constraints into SAT. J. Satisf. Boolean Model. Comput. **2**, 1–26 (2006)
14. Gwynne, M., Kullmann, O.: On SAT representations of XOR constraints. In: Dediu, A.-H., Martín-Vide, C., Sierra-Rodríguez, J.-L., Truthe, B. (eds.) LATA 2014. LNCS, vol. 8370, pp. 409–420. Springer, Heidelberg (2014). doi:10.1007/978-3-319-04921-2_33
15. Heule, M.J.H., Hunt, W.A., Wetzler, N.: Expressing symmetry breaking in DRAT proofs. In: Felty, A.P., Middeldorp, A. (eds.) CADE 2015. LNCS (LNAI), vol. 9195, pp. 591–606. Springer, Heidelberg (2015). doi:10.1007/978-3-319-21401-6_40
16. Heule, M.J.H., Biere, A.: Proofs for satisfiability problems. In: All About Proofs, Proofs for All (2015)
17. Heule, M.J.H., Kullmann, O., Marek, V.W.: Solving and verifying the Boolean Pythagorean Triples problem via cube-and-conquer. CoRR abs/1605.00723 (2016)
18. Heule, M.: March. Towards a lookahead SAT solver for general purposes. Master's thesis (2004)
19. Järvisalo, M., Heule, M.J.H., Biere, A.: Inprocessing rules. In: Gramlich, B., Miller, D., Sattler, U. (eds.) IJCAR 2012. LNCS (LNAI), vol. 7364, pp. 355–370. Springer, Heidelberg (2012). doi:10.1007/978-3-642-31365-3_28
20. Laitinen, T.: Extending SAT solver with parity reasoning. Ph.D. thesis (2014)
21. Laitinen, T., Junttila, T., Niemelä, I.: Classifying and propagating parity constraints. In: Milano, M. (ed.) CP 2012. LNCS, vol. 7514, pp. 357–372. Springer, Heidelberg (2012). doi:10.1007/978-3-642-33558-7_28
22. Manthey, N.: Coprocessor 2.0 – a flexible CNF simplifier. In: Cimatti, A., Sebastiani, R. (eds.) SAT 2012. LNCS, vol. 7317, pp. 436–441. Springer, Heidelberg (2012). doi:10.1007/978-3-642-31612-8_34
23. Manthey, N.: Riss 4.27. In: Belov et al. [4], pp. 65–67

24. Manthey, N., Lindauer, M.: SpyBug: automated bug detection in the configuration space of SAT solvers. In: Creignou, N., Le Berre, D. (eds.) SAT 2016. LNCS, vol. 9710, pp. 554–561. Springer, Heidelberg (2016). doi:10.1007/978-3-319-40970-2_36

25. Rebola-Pardo, A.: Unsatisfiability proofs in SAT solving with parity reasoning. Master thesis, Technische Universität Dresden, Informatik Fakultät (2015)

26. Roussel, O., Manquinho, V.M.: Pseudo-Boolean and cardinality constraints. In: Handbook of Satisfiability, Frontiers in Artificial Intelligence and Applications, vol. 185, pp. 695–733. IOS Press (2009)

27. Silva, J.P.M., Sakallah, K.A.: GRASP - a new search algorithm for satisfiability. In: ICCAD 1996, pp. 220–227. IEEE Computer Society, Washington (1996)

28. Sinz, C., Biere, A.: Extended resolution proofs for conjoining BDDs. In: Grigoriev, D., Harrison, J., Hirsch, E.A. (eds.) CSR 2006. LNCS, vol. 3967, pp. 600–611. Springer, Heidelberg (2006). doi:10.1007/11753728_60

29. Soos, M.: Enhanced Gaussian elimination in DPLL-based SAT solvers. In: POS 2010 (2010)

30. Soos, M.: Cryptominisat v4. In: Belov et al. [4], pp. 23–34

31. Soos, M., Nohl, K., Castelluccia, C.: Extending SAT solvers to cryptographic problems. In: Kullmann, O. (ed.) SAT 2009. LNCS, vol. 5584, pp. 244–257. Springer, Heidelberg (2009). doi:10.1007/978-3-642-02777-2_24

32. Wetzler, N., Heule, M.J.H., Hunt, W.A.: DRAT-trim: efficient checking and trimming using expressive clausal proofs. In: Sinz, C., Egly, U. (eds.) SAT 2014. LNCS, vol. 8561, pp. 422–429. Springer, Heidelberg (2014). doi:10.1007/978-3-319-09284-3_31

Understanding the Abstract Dialectical Framework

Sylwia Polberg[(⊠)]

University College London, Gower Street 66–72, London WC1E 6EA, UK
sylwia.polberg@gmail.com

Abstract. Among the most general structures extending the framework by Dung are the abstract dialectical frameworks (ADFs). They come equipped with various types of semantics, with the most prominent – the labeling–based one – being analyzed in the context of computational complexity, instantiations and software support. This makes the abstract dialectical frameworks valuable tools for argumentation. However, there are fewer results available concerning the relation between the ADFs and other argumentation frameworks. In this paper we would like to address this issue by introducing a number of translations from various formalisms into ADFs. The results of our study show the similarities and differences between them, thus promoting the use and understanding of ADFs. Moreover, our analysis also proves their capability to model many of the existing frameworks, including those that go beyond the attack relation. Finally, translations allow other structures to benefit from the research on ADFs in general and from the existing software in particular.

1 Introduction

Argumentation has become an influential subfield of AI [1]. Within this domain, we distinguish the abstract argumentation, at the heart of which lies Dung's framework (AF) [2]. A number of its generalizations has been proposed [3], including the abstract dialectical framework (ADF) [4]. ADFs come equipped with various types of semantics [5–8], the most prominent of which – the labeling–based one – is analyzed in the context of computational complexity [9], instantiations [10] and software support [11]. This makes ADFs valuable tools for argumentation. Unfortunately, their unusual structure can be a deterrent against their more widespread use. Moreover, at the first glance it is also difficult to say what is the relation between the ADFs and the other argumentation frameworks, in particular those that can express support [12–14].

The author is a member of the Vienna PhD School of Informatics. This research was funded by project I1102 supported by the Austrian Science Fund FWF. The author is currently supported by EPSRC Project EP/N008294/1 "Framework for Computational Persuasion".

© Springer International Publishing AG 2016
L. Michael and A. Kakas (Eds.): JELIA 2016, LNAI 10021, pp. 430–446, 2016.
DOI: 10.1007/978-3-319-48758-8_28

In this paper we would like to tackle these issues by introducing a number of translations from various formalisms into the ADFs. This includes the Dung's framework [2], the Nielsen's and Parson's framework with joint attacks [15], the extended argumentation framework [16] and the argumentation framework with necessities [13]. The results of our study show the similarities and differences between ADFs and other argumentation formalisms, thus promoting the use and understanding of ADFs. Moreover, our analysis also proves their capability to model many of the existing frameworks, including those that go beyond the attack relation. Furthermore, a wider range of extended argumentation frameworks can be translated into ADFs than into AFs [17].

This paper is structured as follows. In Sects. 2 and 3 we recall the aforementioned argumentation frameworks. We also provide a discussion on certain design differences between the ADFs and the other structures. In Sect. 5 we present our translations. We close the paper with final remarks and comments on shifting other frameworks to ADFs.

2 Argumentation Frameworks

In this section we will recall the relevant argumentation frameworks and their extension–based semantics. Despite the various structural differences between the frameworks, their semantics tend to follow the design patterns established by Dung [2]. We can obtain most of them by combining conflict–freeness, acceptability and various ways to maximize or minimize the extensions. Thus, many frameworks tend to redefine these "building blocks", and then reuse the original (or similar) definitions from [2]. Therefore, when recalling the relevant structures in this section, we will mostly provide only the necessary notions. Throughout this work, we will be focusing on finite structures.

2.1 Dung's Argumentation Framework

Let us start with the famous Dung's framework [2], which is based on binary attack.

Definition 1. *A **Dung's abstract argumentation framework** (AF) is a pair $F = (A, R)$, where A is a set of **arguments** and $R \subseteq A \times A$ is the **attack** relation.*

Definition 2. *Let $F = (A, R)$ be a Dung's framework and $X \subseteq A$ a set of arguments.*

- *the **attacker set** of X is $X^- = \{a \mid \exists b \in X, aRb\}$.*
- *the **discarded set** of X is $X^+ = \{a \mid \exists b \in X, bRa\}$.*
- *X **defends**[1] an argument $a \in A$ iff every argument $b \in A$ that attacks a is in X^+.*
- *X is **conflict–free** in F iff there are no $a, b \in X$ s.t. a attacks b.*

---

[1] Defense is often substituted with acceptability, i.e. X defends a iff a is acceptable w.r.t. X.

Definition 3. *Let $F = (A, R)$ be an AF. A set $X \subseteq A$ is:*

- *admissible in F iff it is conflict–free in F and defends in F all of its members.*
- *preferred in F iff it is maximal w.r.t. $\subseteq$ admissible in F.*
- *complete in F iff it is admissible and every $a \in A$ that is defended by X, is in X.*
- *grounded in F iff it is the least fixed point of the characteristic operator $\mathcal{F}_F : 2^A \rightarrow 2^A$ defined as $\mathcal{F}_F(X) = \{a \mid a \text{ is defended by } X \text{ in } F\}$.*
- *stable in F iff it is conflict–free in F and $A \setminus X = X^+$.*

Different types of semantics can be related to each other in a number of ways [2], however, it is usually the following properties that will hold:

Theorem 1. *Let $F = (A, R)$ be an AF. The following holds:*

1. *Every stable extension of F is also preferred, but not vice versa.*
2. *Every preferred extension of F is also complete, but not vice versa.*
3. *The grounded extension of F is the least w.r.t. $\subseteq$ complete extension of F.*

2.2   Framework with Sets of Attacking Arguments

In some cases, a single argument might not be enough to carry out an attack on another argument. For example, all of the means, motive, opportunity and evidence might be required to prove guilt. In order to grasp such problems, a framework with group conflict was developed [15]. The semantics of SETAFs are almost identical to the AF ones. Given a set $X \subseteq A$, the attacks will now be carried out not by single arguments in X, but its subsets. Thus, in the interest of space, we will not formally give their definitions.

Definition 4. *A **framework with sets of attacking arguments** (SETAF) is a pair $SF = (A, R)$, where A is the set of **arguments** and $R \subseteq (2^A \setminus \emptyset) \times A$ is the **attack** relation.*

Example 1. Let us consider the SETAF $SF = (A, R)$, where $A = \{a, b, c, d, e\}$ and $R = \{(\{a\}, c), (\{b\}, a), (\{b\}, b), (\{c\}, d), (\{e\}, a), (\{b, d\}, e)\}$. The only admissible extensions are $\emptyset$ and $\{c, e\}$; both of them are complete. $\{c, e\}$ is the preferred extension, while $\emptyset$ is grounded. Because of b, this particular framework has no stable extensions.

2.3   Extended Argumentation Framework with Collective Attacks

The extended argumentation framework with collective defense attacks [16] is an improvement of the framework studied in [17,18]. It introduces the notion of defense attacks, which occur between sets of arguments and binary conflicts. They can "override" a given attack due to e.g. the target's importance, which is a common approach in the preference–based argumentation [19,20,24]. The added value of defense attacks is the fact that the arguments carrying them out can also be attacked and questioned.

Definition 5. *An **extended argumentation framework with collective defense attacks** (EAFC) is a tuple $EFC = (A, R, D)$, where A is a set of **arguments**, $R \subseteq A \times A$ is a set of **attacks** and $D \subseteq (2^A \setminus \emptyset) \times R$ is the set of **collective defense attacks**.*

We can observe that a given attack can be successful (referred to as a defeat) or not, depending on the presence of suitable defense attacks. The defense has to include not just defending the arguments, but also a form of "protection" of the important defeats:

Definition 6. *Let $EFC = (A, R, D)$ be an EAFC and $X \subseteq A$ a set of arguments.*

- *an argument a **defeats**$_X$ an argument b in EFC w.r.t. X iff $(a, b) \in R$ and there is no $C \subseteq X$ s.t. $(C, (a, b)) \in D$.*
- *a set of pairs $R_X = \{(x_1, y_1), ..., (x_n, y_n)\}$ s.t. x_i defeats$_X$ y_i in EFC and for $i = 1...n$, $x_i \in X$, is a **reinstatement set** on X for a defeat$_X$ by argument a on argument b iff $(a, b) \in R_X$ and for every pair $(x, y) \in R_X$ and set of arguments $C \subseteq A$ s.t. $(C, (x, y)) \in D$, there is a pair $(x', y') \in R_X$ for some $y' \in C$.*
- *the **discarded set** of X is $X^+ = \{a \mid \exists b \in X$ s.t. b defeats$_X$ a and there is a reinstatement set on X for this defeat$_X\}$.*
- *X **defends** and argument $a \in A$ in EFC iff every argument $b \in A$ s.t. b defeats$_X$ a in EFC is in X^+.*
- *$X \subseteq A$ is **conflict–free** in EFC iff there are no $a, b \in X$ s.t. a defeats$_X$ b in EFC.*

With the exception of the grounded semantics, all extensions are defined in the same way as in Definition 3. Unfortunately, despite these similarities, Theorem 1 cannot be entirely extended to EAFCs. Finally, within EAFCs we can distinguish the bounded hierarchical subclass, enforcing certain restrictions on the attacks and defense attacks.

Definition 7. *Let $EFC = (A, R, D)$ be a finitiary[2] EAFC, $X \subseteq A$ a set of arguments and 2^{CF} the set of all conflict–free sets of EFC. The **characteristic function** $\mathcal{F}_{EFC} : 2^{CF} \to 2^A$ of EFC is defined as $\mathcal{F}_{EFC}(X) = \{a \mid a$ is defended by X in $EFC\}$. We define a sequence of subsets of A s.t. $\mathcal{F}_{EFC}^0 = \emptyset$ and $\mathcal{F}_{EFC}^{i+1} = \mathcal{F}_{EFC}(\mathcal{F}_{EFC}^i)$. The **grounded** extension of EFC is $\bigcup_{i=0}^{\infty}(\mathcal{F}_{EFC}^i)$.*

Theorem 2. *Let $EFC = (A, R, D)$ be a finitary EAFC. The following holds:*

1. *Every preferred extension is complete, but not vice versa.*
2. *Every stable extension is complete, but not vice versa.*
3. *The grounded extension is a minimal w.r.t. $\subseteq$ complete extension.*

---

[2] An EAFC is finitiary if for every argument and attack, the collection of its (defense) attackers is finite.

Definition 8. *An EAFC $EFC = (A, R, D)$ is **bounded hierarchical** iff there exists a partition $\delta_H = (((A_1, R_1), D_1), ..., ((A_n, R_n), D_n))$ s.t. $D_n = \emptyset$, $A = \bigcup_{i=1}^{n} A_i$, $R = \bigcup_{i=1}^{n} R_i$, $D = \bigcup_{i=1}^{n} D_i$, for every $i = 1...n$ (A_i, R_i) is a Dung's framework, and $(c, (a, b)) \in D_i$ implies $(a, b) \in R_i$, $c \subseteq A_{i+1}$.*

Example 2 [21]. Let $EFC = (\{a, b, c, d, e, f, g\}, \{(a, b), (d, c), (b, e), (e, f), (f, g)\}, \{(\{b\}, (d, c)), (\{c\}, (a, b))\})$ be an EAFC. Let us look at some of its conflict–free extensions. We can see that $\{a, b\}$ and $\{c, d\}$ are not conflict–free. However, both $\{a, b, c\}$ and $\{b, c, d\}$ are, due to the presence of defense attackers. Additionally, also $\{a, b, c, d\}$, $\{a, d, e, g\}$ and $\{b, c, a, d, f\}$ are conflict–free. The admissible extensions of EFC include $\emptyset$, $\{a\}$, $\{d\}$, $\{a, d\}$, $\{b, c\}$, $\{a, b, c\}$, $\{b, c, d\}$, $\{a, d, e\}$, $\{b, c, f\}$, $\{a, b, c, f\}$, $\{b, c, d, f\}$, $\{a, d, e, g\}$, $\{a, b, c, d\}$ and $\{a, b, c, d, f\}$. We can observe that the set $X = \{b, c\}$ is admissible. Neither a nor d defeat$_X$ any of its elements, and thus there is nothing to defend from. The set $\{a, d, e\}$ is admissible since the defeat of b by a has a reinstatement set $\{(d, c), (a, b)\}$. Although its behavior appears cyclic, it suffices for defense. The sets $\{a, d, e, g\}$ and $\{a, b, c, d, f\}$ are complete. We can observe they are incomparable and do not follow the typical semi–lattice structure of complete extensions. The grounded extension is $\{a, d, e, g\}$; it is minimal, but not the least complete extension. Both $\{a, d, e, g\}$ and $\{a, d, b, c, d, f\}$ are stable and preferred.

2.4 Argumentation Framework with Necessities

Various types of support have been studied in abstract argumentation [12–14]. Due to limited space, we will focus on the necessary support, though based on the research in [12,14] our results can be extended to other relations as well. We say that a set of arguments X *necessarily supports* b if we need to assume at least one element of X in order to accept b. Using this relation has certain important implications. First of all, argument's supporters need to be present in an extension. Secondly, an argument can be now indirectly attacked by the means of its supporters, i.e. we can "discard" an argument not just by providing a direct conflict, but also by cutting off its support. Finally, a certain notion of a validity of an argument is introduced, stemming from its participation in support cycles. It affects the acceptance and attack capabilities of an argument. Let us now recall the framework with necessities [13]:

Definition 9. *An **abstract argumentation framework with necessities** (AFN) is a tuple $FN = (A, R, N)$ where A is a set of **arguments**, $R \subseteq A \times A$ represents the **attack** relation and $N \subseteq (2^A \setminus \emptyset) \times A$ represents the **necessity** relation.*

The acyclicity restrictions are defined through the powerful sequences and the related coherent sets. By joining conflict–freeness and coherence, we obtain a new semantics which replaces conflict–freeness as the basis of stable and admissible extensions. The remaining notions are defined similarly as in Definition 3 and satisfy Theorem 1.

Definition 10. *Let $FN = (A, R, N)$ be an AFN and $X \subseteq A$ a set of arguments. An argument $a \in A$ is **powerful** in X iff $a \in X$ and there is a sequence $a_0, ..., a_k$ of elements of X s.t. : (i) $a_k = a$ (ii) there is no $B \subseteq A$ s.t. BNa_0 (iii) for $1 \leq i \leq k$: for each $B \subseteq A$ s.t. BNa_i, it holds that $B \cap \{a_0, ..., a_{i-1}\} \neq \emptyset$. A set of arguments $X \subseteq A$ is **coherent** in FN iff each $a \in X$ is powerful in X.*

Definition 11. *Let $FN = (A, R, N)$ be an AFN and $X \subseteq A$ a set of arguments.*

- *the **discarded** set of X in FN is defined as $X^{att} = \{a \mid$ for every coherent $C \subseteq A$ s.t. $a \in C$, $\exists c \in C, e \in X$ s.t. $eRc\}$[3].*
- *X **defends** an argument $a \in A$ in FN iff $X \cup \{a\}$ is coherent and for each $b \in A$, if bRa then $b \in X^{att}$.*
- *X is **conflict–free** in FN iff there are no $a, b \in X$ s.t. a attacks b.*

Definition 12. *Let $FN = (A, R, N)$ be an AFN. A set of arguments $X \subseteq A$ is:*

- ***strongly coherent** in FN iff it is conflict–free and coherent in FN*
- ***admissible** in FN iff it is strongly coherent and defends all of its arguments in FN.*
- ***stable** in FN iff it is strongly coherent in FN and $X^{att} = A \setminus X$.*

Example 3. Let $(\{a, b, c, d, e, f\}, \{(a, e), (d, b), (e, c), (f, d)\}, \{(\{b, c\}, a), (\{f\}, f)\})$ be an AFN. Its coherent sets include $\emptyset$, $\{a, b\}$, $\{a, c\}$, $\{b\}$, $\{c\}$, $\{d\}$, $\{e\}$ and any of their combinations. In total, we have six admissible extensions. $\emptyset$ is trivially admissible. So is $\{d\}$ due to the fact that f does not possess a powerful sequence in FN. However, $\{e\}$ is not admissible; it does not attack one of the coherent sets of a, namely $\{a, b\}$. Fortunately, $\{d, e\}$ is already admissible. We can observe that b can never be defended and will not appear in an admissible set. The last two admissible sets are $\{a, c\}$ and $\{a, c, d\}$. The extensions $\{d\}$, $\{d, e\}$ and $\{a, c, d\}$ are complete, with the first one being grounded and the latter two preferred. In this case, both $\{d, e\}$ and $\{a, c, d\}$ are stable.

3 Abstract Dialectical Frameworks

Abstract dialectical frameworks have been defined in [4] and further studied in [5–10]. Their main goal was to be able to express a wide range relations and try to avoid the need of introducing a new relation set each time it is needed. This is achieved by the means of acceptance conditions, which define when an argument can be accepted or rejected. They can be defined either as total functions over the parents of an argument [4] or as propositional formulas over them.

Definition 13. *An **abstract dialectical framework** (ADF) is a tuple $DF = (A, L, C)$, where A is a set of **arguments**, $L \subseteq A \times A$ is a set of **links** and $C = \{C_a\}_{a \in A}$ is a set of **acceptance conditions**, one condition per each argument. An acceptance condition is a total function $C_a : 2^{par(a)} \to \{in, out\}$, where $par(a) = \{p \in A \mid (p, a) \in L\}$ is the set of **parents** of an argument a.*

---

[3] Please note that we do not denote the AFN discarded set with X^+ as in the previous cases in order not to confuse it with the notion of the deactivated set from [13], which is less restrictive.

Due to the fact that the set of links can be inferred from the conditions, we will write simply (A, C) to denote an ADF. The basic "building blocks" of the extension–based ADF semantics from [7,8] are the decisively *in* interpretations and various types of evaluations we derive from them. A two–valued interpretation is simply a mapping that assigns truth values $\{\mathbf{t}, \mathbf{f}\}$ to (a subset of) arguments. For an interpretation v, v^x is the set of elements mapped to $x \in \{\mathbf{t}, \mathbf{f}\}$ by v. A decisive interpretation v for an argument $a \in A$ represents an assignment for a set of arguments $X \subseteq A$ s.t. independently of the status of the arguments in $A \setminus X$, the outcome of the condition of a stays the same.

Definition 14. *Let A be a collection of elements, $X \subseteq A$ its subset and v a two–valued interpretation defined on X. A **completion** of v to a set Z where $X \subseteq Z \subseteq A$, is an interpretation v' defined on Z in a way that $\forall a \in X \ v(a) = v'(a)$. v' is a $\mathbf{t}/\mathbf{f}$ completion of v iff all arguments in $Z \setminus X$ are mapped respectively to $\mathbf{t}/\mathbf{f}$.*

Definition 15. *Let $DF = (A, L, C)$ be an ADF, $X \subseteq A$ a set of arguments and v a two–valued interpretation defined on X. v is **decisive** for an argument $s \in A$ iff for any two completions $v_{par(s)}$ and $v'_{par(s)}$ of v to $X \cup par(s)$, it holds that $v_{par(s)}(C_s) = v'_{par(s)}(C_s)$. s is **decisively out/in** w.r.t. v if v is decisive and all of its completions evaluate C_s to respectively out, in.*

From now on we will focus on the minimal interpretations, i.e. those in which both $v^{\mathbf{t}}$ and $v^{\mathbf{f}}$ are minimal w.r.t. $\subseteq$. By $min\_dec(x, s)$ we denote the set of minimal two–valued interpretations that are decisively x for s, where s is an argument and $x \in \{in, out\}$. From the positive parts of a decisively *in* interpretation for a we can extract arguments required for the acceptance of a. With this information, we can define various types of evaluations, not unlike the powerful sequences in AFNs. However, due to the fact that ADFs are more expressive than AFNs, it is also the $\mathbf{f}$ parts of the used interpretations that need to be stored [7,8]:

Definition 16. *Let $DF = (A, L, C)$ be an ADF and $X \subseteq A$ a set of arguments. A **positive dependency function** (pd–function) on X is a function pd_X^{DF} assigning every argument $a \in X$ an interpretation $v \in min\_dec(in, a)$ s.t. $v^t \subseteq X$, or $\mathcal{N}$ for null iff no such v can be found. pd_X^{DF} is **sound** on X iff for no $a \in X$, $pd_X^{DF}(a) = \mathcal{N}$. pd_X^{DF} is **maximally sound** on X iff it is sound on $X' \subseteq X$ and there is no other sound function pd'^{DF}_X on X'' s.t. $\forall a \in X'$, $pd_X^{DF}(a) = pd'^{DF}_X(a)$, where $X' \subset X'' \subseteq X$.*

Definition 17. *Let $DF = (A, L, C)$ be an ADF, $S \subseteq A$ and pd_X^{DF} a maximally sound pd–function of S defined over $X \subseteq S$. A **partially acyclic positive dependency evaluation** based on pd_X^{DF} for an argument $x \in X$ is a triple $(F, (a_0, ..., a_n), B)$, where $F \cap \{a_0, ..., a_n\} = \emptyset$, $(a_0, ..., a_n)$ is a sequence of distinct elements of X satisfying the following requirements:*

– *if the sequence is non–empty, then $a_n = x$; otherwise, $x \in F$*
– *$\forall_{i=1}^{n}, pd_X^{DF}(a_i)^{\mathbf{t}} \subseteq F \cup \{a_0, ..., a_{i-1}\}, pd_X^{DF}(a_0)^{\mathbf{t}} \subseteq F$*

– $\forall a \in F$, $pd_X^{DF}(a)^{\mathbf{t}} \subseteq F$

– $\forall a \in F$, $\exists b \in F$ s.t. $a \in pd_X^{DF}(b)$.

Finally, $B = \bigcup_{a \in F} pd_X^{DF}(a)^{\mathbf{f}} \cup \bigcup_{i=0}^{n} pd_X^{DF}(a_i)^{\mathbf{f}}$. We refer to F as the **pd–set**, to $(a_0, ..., a_n)$ as the **pd–sequence** and to B as the **blocking set** of the evaluation. A partially acyclic evaluation $(F, (a_0, ..., a_n), B)$ for an argument $x \in X$ is an **acyclic positive dependency evaluation** for x iff $F = \emptyset$.

We will use the shortened notation $((a_0, ..., a_n), B)$ for the acyclic evaluations. There are two ways we can "attack" an evaluation. Either we accept an argument that needs to be rejected (i.e. it is in the blocking set), or we are able to discard one that needs to be accepted (i.e. is in the pd–sequence or the pd–set). We will be mostly concerned with the first type. We can now define various discarded sets in ADFs[4]:

Definition 18. Let $DF = (A, L, C)$ be an ADF and $X \subseteq A$ a set of arguments. The **standard discarded** set of X is $X^+ = \{a \in A \mid$ for every partially acyclic evaluation (F, G, B) for a, $B \cap X \neq \emptyset\}$. The **partially acyclic discarded** set of X is $X^{p+} = \{a \in A \mid$ there is no partially acyclic evaluation (F', G', B') for a s.t. $F' \subseteq X$ and $B' \cap X = \emptyset\}$. The **acyclic discarded** set of X is $X^{a+} = \{a \in A \mid$ for every pd–acyclic evaluation (F, B) for a, $B \cap X \neq \emptyset\}$.

Given a set of arguments X and its discarded set S, we can build a special interpretation – called **range** – with which we can check for decisiveness. The range can be constructed by assigning $\mathbf{t}$ to arguments in X and $\mathbf{f}$ to those in $S \backslash X$. Under certain conditions X and S are disjoint, which brings us to the conflict–free semantics:

Definition 19. Let $DF = (A, L, C)$ be an ADF. A set $X \subseteq A$ is a **conflict–free extension** of DF if for all $s \in X$ we have $C_s(X \cap par(s)) = in$. X is a **pd–acyclic conflict–free extension** of DF iff every $a \in X$ has an acyclic evaluation (F, B) on X s.t. $B \cap X = \emptyset$.

Lemma 1. Let $DF = (A, L, C)$ be an ADF and $X \subseteq A$ a set of arguments. If X is conflict–free in DF, then $X \cap X^+ = \emptyset$ and $X \cap X^{p+} = \emptyset$. Moreover, it holds that $X^+ \subseteq X^{p+} \subseteq X^{a+}$. If X is pd–acyclic conflict–free, then $X \cap X^{a+} = \emptyset$ and $X^{p+} = X^{a+}$.

By combining a given type of a discarded set and a given type of conflict–freeness, we have developed various families of extension–based semantics [7,8]. We have classified them into the four main types and used an xy–prefixing system to denote them. In the context of this work, three of the families will be relevant. We will now recall their definitions and refer the readers to [8] for proofs and further explanations.

---

[4] The presented definitions are generalizations of the ones from [7,8].

Definition 20. *Let $DF = (A, L, C)$ be an ADF. Let $X \subseteq A$ be a set of arguments and v_X, v_X^a and v_X^p its standard, acyclic and partially acyclic ranges.*

*If X is conflict–free and every $e \in X$ is decisively in w.r.t. v_X (v_X^p), then X is **cc–admissible (ca₂–admissible)** in DF. If X is pd–acyclic conflict–free and every $e \in X$ is decisively in w.r.t. v_X^a, then X is **aa–admissible** in DF.*

*If X is cc–admissible (ca₂–admissible, aa–admissible) and every argument $e \in A$ decisively in w.r.t. v_X (v_X^p, v_X^a) is in X, then X is **cc–complete** (**ca₂–complete, aa–complete**) in DF. If X is maximal w.r.t. set inclusion xy–admissible extension, where $x, y \in \{a, c\}$, then it is an **xy–preferred** extensions of DF.*

*If X is conflict–free and for every $a \in A \setminus X$, $C_a(X \cap par(a)) = out$, then X is a **model** of DF. If X is pd–acyclic conflict–free and $X^{a+} = A \setminus X$, then X is a **stable** extension of DF.*

*If X is the least w.r.t. $\subseteq$ cc–complete extension, then it is the **grounded** extension of DF. If X is the least w.r.t. $\subseteq$ aa–complete extension, then it is the **acyclic grounded** extension of DF.*

Finally, we can define the two important ADF subclasses. The bipolar ADFs consist only of links that are supporting or attacking. This class is particularly valuable due to its computational complexity properties [9]. The other subclass, referred to as AADF$^+$, consists of ADFs in which our semantics classification collapses. By this we understand that e.g. every cc–complete extension is aa–complete and vice versa. Moreover, this class provides a more precise correspondence between the extension and labeling–based semantics for ADFs [8]. This means that for these frameworks, we can use the DIAMOND software [11] and other results for the labeling–based semantics [9,10].

Definition 21. *Let $DF = (A, L, C)$ be an ADF. A link $(r, s) \in L$ is: (i) supporting iff for no $R \subseteq par(s)$ we have that $C_s(R) = in$ and $C_s(R \cup \{r\}) = out$ (ii) attacking iff for no $R \subseteq par(s)$ we have that $C_s(R) = out$ and $C_s(R \cup \{r\}) = in$. DF is a **bipolar** ADF (BADF) iff it contains only links that are supporting or attacking. DF is a **positive dependency acyclic** ADF (AADF$^+$) iff every partially acyclic evaluation (F, G, B) of DF is acyclic.*

Theorem 3. *Let $DF = (A, L, C)$ be an AADF$^+$. The following holds:*

- *Every conflict–free extension of DF is pd–acyclic conflict–free in DF.*
- *Every model of DF is stable in DF.*
- *The aa/cc/ca₂–admissible extensions of DF coincide.*
- *The aa/cc/ca₂–complete extensions of DF coincide.*
- *The aa/cc/ca₂–preferred extensions of DF coincide.*
- *The grounded and acyclic grounded extensions of DF coincide.*

Example 4. Let us consider the framework is $DF = (\{a, b, c, d, e, f, g\}, \{C_a : \top, C_b : \neg a \vee c, C_c : \neg d \vee b, C_d : \top, C_e : \neg b, C_f : \neg e, C_g : \neg f\})$. We can observe that both a and d have trivial acyclic evaluations $((a), \emptyset)$ and $((d), \emptyset)$. For e, f and g we can construct $((e), \{b\})$, $((f), \{e\})$ and $((g), \{f\})$. The situation only gets complicated with b and c; we have the acyclic evaluations $((b), \{a\})$, $((c, b), \{d\})$, $((c), \{d\})$, $((b, c), \{a\})$ and the partially acyclic one $(\{b, c\}, \emptyset)$. We can observe that $\emptyset$ is an admissible extension of any type; all of its discarded sets are empty. Decisively in w.r.t. its ranges are thus a and d. The set $\{a, d\}$ is again admissible. Its standard discarded set is $\emptyset$, however, the acyclic and partially acyclic ones are $\{b, c\}$. Therefore, $\{a, d\}$ is only cc–complete. Discarding b leads to the acceptance of e and g. Hence, $\{a, d, e, g\}$ is an aa– and ca$_2$–complete extension, though it does not even qualify as a cc–admissible set. We can now consider the set $\{a, b, c, d\}$. It is conflict–free, but not pd–acyclic conflict–free. Its standard and partially acyclic discarded set is $\{e\}$, which means that f can be accepted. Hence, $\{a, b, c, d, f\}$ is cc and ca$_2$–complete. Thus, in total we obtain two cc–complete, one aa–complete and two ca$_2$–complete sets. Our grounded and acyclic grounded extensions are $\{a, d\}$ and $\{a, d, e, g\}$ respectively. The latter set is also the only stable extension of our framework. However, both $\{a, d, e, g\}$ and $\{a, b, c, d, f\}$ are models.

4   Conceptual Differences Between ADFs and Other Frameworks

The more direct descendants of the Dung's framework explicitly state "this is a supporter", "this is an attacker" and so on. Thus, in order to know if a given argument can be accepted along with the other arguments, i.e. whether it is attacked, defeated or receives sufficient support, we need to go through all the relations it is a target of. In contrast, the acceptance conditions "zoom out" from singular relations. They tell us whether the argument can be accepted or not w.r.t. a given set of arguments in a straightforward manner. The focus is put on what would usually be seen as a target of a relation, while in other frameworks the attention is on the relation source. As a consequence, in order to say if a parent of an argument is its supporter, attacker or none of these, we need analyze the condition further, as seen in e.g. Definition 21. This is also one of the reasons why finding support cycles in ADFs is more difficult than in other support frameworks. Finally, since the role of parent is derived from how it affects the behavior of an argument, not whether it is in e.g. the support relation N, an attacker or a supporter in a given framework may not have the same role in the corresponding ADF:

Example 5. Let $(\{a, b, c\}, \{(b, a), (a, c)\}, \{(\{b\}, a)\})$ be an AFN, where the argument a is at the same time supported and attacked by b. In a certain sense, the (a, b) relation is difficult to classify as positive or negative. Although a cannot be accepted, it is still a valid attacker that one needs to defend from. In the ADF setting, the acceptance condition of a is unsatisfiable – whether we include or exclude b, we always reject a. It can also be seen as a $b \wedge \neg b$ formula. a does not possess any type of an evaluation and will always end up in any type of a discarded set. This also means that we do not have to "defend" from it. In this particular example, the set $\{c\}$ would not be considered admissible in our

AFN, but it would be considered an admissible extension of any type in the ADF $(\{a, b, c\}, \{C_a = b \wedge \neg b, C_b = \top, C_c = \neg a\})$.

Thus, there is an important difference between the design of ADFs and other argumentation frameworks. If we were to represent the situation as a propositional formula, it is like comparing an atom based and a literal based evaluation. The same issue arises when we consider standard and ultimate versions of logic programming semantics, as already noted in [5]. This means that if we want to translate e.g. an AFN into an ADF while still preserving the behavior of the semantics, we need to make sure that no argument is at the same time an attacker and a supporter of the same argument. A similar issue also appears in the extended argumentation frameworks. The defense attack is a type of a positive, indirect relation towards the "defended" argument. The difference is that while in the first case it is also a negative relation towards the argument carrying out the attack, in the latter the attacker and the defense attacker might be unrelated. It is not unlike what is informally referred to as the "overpowering support" in ADFs. A typical example is a condition of the form $C_a = \neg b \vee c$, where b has the power to *out* the condition unless c is present. Therefore, defense attackers from EAFC become directly related to the arguments they "protect" in ADFs, which can lead to inconsistencies.

Definition 22. *Let $FN = (A, R, N)$ be an AFN and a an argument in A. By $N(a) = \{b \mid \exists B \subseteq A \text{ s.t. } b \in B, BNa\}$ and $R(a) = \{b \mid bRa\}$ we denote the sets of arguments supporting and attacking a. Then a is **strongly consistent** iff $N(a) \cap R(a) = \emptyset$. FN is strongly consistent iff all of its arguments are strongly consistent.*

*Let $EFC = (A, R, D)$ be an EAFC. EFC is **strongly consistent** iff there are no $x, y, z \in A$ and $X \subseteq A$ s.t. $(x, y) \in R$, $x \in X$ and $(X, (z, y)) \in D$.*

Any AFN can be made strongly consistent with the help of no more than $|A|$ arguments. We basically introduce extra arguments, that we call "bypasses", that take over the support links leading to inconsistency and connect them to the original sources of these relations. For example, the AFN $(\{a, b\}, \{(a, b)\}, \{(\{a\}, b)\})$ is extended to $(\{a, a', b\}, \{(a, b)\}, \{(\{a\}, a'), (\{a'\}, b)\})$. The auxiliary arguments then need to be removed from the extensions. We can also turn them into self–attackers, which addresses the removal issue, but it also affects the stable semantics. Similar techniques can be used in the translations for EAFCs. Unfortunately, due to the space restrictions, we cannot focus on this approach here.

Please note that this analysis does not in any way imply that a given (a, b) link is assigned a single permanent "role" in ADFs, such as "attack" or "support". The framework is flexible and a link can be positive on one occasion an negative on another. A more accurate description is that a link (or its source) should have a defined role "at a point", i.e. w.r.t. a given set of arguments. ADFs ensure consistency, not constancy.

5   Translations

In this section we will show how to translate the recalled frameworks to ADFs. We will provide both functional and propositional acceptance conditions. For the latter, we would like to introduce the following notations. For a set of arguments $X = \{x_1, ..., x_n\}$, we will abbreviate the formula $x_1 \wedge ... \wedge x_n$ with $\bigwedge X$ and $\neg x_1 \wedge ... \wedge \neg x_n$ with $\bigwedge \neg X$. Similarly, $x_1 \vee ... \vee x_n$ and $\neg x_1 \vee ... \vee \neg x_n$ will be shortened to $\bigvee X$ and $\bigvee \neg X$.

5.1   Translating SETAFs and AFs into ADFs

A straightforward translation from AFs to ADFs has already been introduced in [6]. Let $a \in A$ be an argument and $\{a\}^- = \{x_1, .., x_n\}$ its attacker set in an AF. Whenever any of $x_i's$ is present, a cannot be accepted. Only when all of them are absent, we can assume a. The SETAF translation is quite similar. Let $\{a\}^- = \{X_1, ..., X_n\}$ be the collection of all sets that attack an argument a, i.e. sets s.t. $X_i Ra$. Only the presence of all members of any X_i, not just some of them, renders a unacceptable. Therefore given any set of arguments that does not fully include at least one attacking set, the acceptance condition of a is in. This brings us to the following two translations:

Translation 1. *Let $F = (A, R)$ be a Dung's framework. The ADF correspond-ing to F is $DF^F = (A, R, C)$, where $C = \{C_a\}_{a \in A}$ and every C_a is as follows:*

- *Functional form: $C_a(\emptyset) = in$ and for all nonempty $B \subseteq \{a\}^-$, $C_a(B) = out$.*
- *Propositional form: $C_a = \bigwedge \neg \{a\}^-$. In case $\{a\}^-$ is empty, $C_a = \top$.*

Translation 2. *Let $SF = (A, R)$ be a SETAF. The ADF corresponding to SF is $DF^{SF} = (A, L, C)$, where $L = \{(x, y) \mid \exists B \subseteq A, x \in B \text{ s.t. } BRy\}$, $C = \{C_a\}_{a \in A}$ and every C_a is created in the following way:*

- *Functional form: for every $B \subseteq \bigcup \{a\}^-$, if $\exists X_i \in \{a\}^-$ s.t. $X_i \subseteq B$, then $C_a(B) = out$; otherwise, $C_a(B) = in$.*
- *Propositional form: $C_a = \bigvee \neg X_1 \wedge ... \wedge \bigvee \neg X_n$. If $\{a\}^-$ is empty, $C_a = \top$.*

Neither AFs nor SETAFs rely on any form of support. Therefore, their asso-ciated ADFs are both AADF$^+$s and BADFs. Consequently, our semantics clas-sification collapses and it does not matter which type of ADF semantics we work with.

Theorem 4. *Let $SF = (A, R)$ be a SETAF or AF and $DF^{SF} = (A, L, C)$ its corresponding ADF. Then DF^{SF} is an AADF$^+$ and a BADF.*

Theorem 5. *Let $SF = (A, R)$ be a SETAF or AF and $DF^{SF} = (A, L, C)$ its corresponding ADF. A set of arguments $X \subseteq A$ is a conflict–free extensions of SF iff it is (pd–acyclic) conflict–free in DF^F. $X \subseteq A$ is a stable extensions of SF iff it is (stable) model of DF^F. $X \subseteq A$ is a grounded extensions of SF iff it is (acyclic) grounded in DF^F. $X \subseteq A$ is a σ–extensions of SF, where $\sigma \in \{admissible, preferred, complete\}$ iff it is an xy–σ–extension of DF^F for $x, y \in \{a, c\}$.*

Example 6. Let us continue Example 1. The ADF associated with SF is $DF^{SF} = (\{a,b,c,d,e\}, \{C_a : \neg a \wedge \neg e, C_b : \neg b, C_c : \neg a, C_d : \neg c, C_e : \neg b \vee \neg d\})$. $\emptyset$ is an admissible extension of any type; its discarded set is also empty. We can observe that $\{c,e\}$ is conflict–free in DF^{SF}. Its discarded set is $\{a,d\}$, thus making the set admissible in DF^{SF}. No other argument is decisively *in* w.r.t. the produced ranges and thus both sets are also complete. This makes $\emptyset$ the grounded and $\{c,e\}$ the preferred extension. Since b is not contained in any discarded set, DF^{SF} has no stable or model extensions.

5.2   Translating EAFCs into ADFs

We can now focus on translating EAFCs into ADFs. Let us assume we have an attack (b,a) that is defense attacked by sets $\{c,d\}$ and $\{e\}$. We can observe that a is rejected only if b is present and none of the defense attacking sets is fully present. On the other hand, if b is not there or either $\{c,d\}$ or $\{e\}$ are accepted, then the requirements for a are satisfied. Therefore, for a given EAFC, we can create an ADF in the following way:

Translation 3. *Let $EFC = (A, R, D)$ be a strongly consistent EAFC. Its corresponding ADF is $DF^{EFC} = (A, L, C)$, where $L = \{(a,b) \mid aRb \text{ or } \exists c \in A, X \subseteq A \text{ s.t. } a \in X, (X, (c,b)) \in D\}$, $C = \{C_a \mid a \in A\}$ and every C_a is as follows:*

- *Functional form: for every set $B \subseteq par(a)$, if $\exists x \in B$ s.t. $(x,a) \in R$ and $\not\exists B' \subseteq B$ s.t. $(B', (x,a)) \in D$, then $C_a(B) = out$; otherwise, $C_a(B) = in$*
- *Propositional form: if $\{a\}^- = \emptyset$, then $C_a = \top$; otherwise, $C_a = \bigwedge_{b \in A, (b,a) \in R} att_a^b$, where $att_a^b = \neg b \vee (\bigwedge B_1 \vee ... \wedge B_m)$ and $D_{b,a} = \{B_1, ..., B_m\}$ is the collection of all sets $B_i \subseteq A$ s.t. $(B, (b,a)) \in D$. If $D_{b,a}$ is empty, then $att_a^b = \neg b$.*

Although EAFCs are more advanced than e.g. AFs, their associated ADFs are still bipolar. However, only in the case of bounded hierarchical EAFCs they are also AADF$^+$s. The EAFC semantics are now connected to the ca$_2$–semantics family. Since the ADF associated with the framework from Example 2 is precisely the one we have considered in Example 4; we refer the reader there for further details.

Theorem 6. *Let $EFC = (A, R, D)$ be a strongly consistent EAFC and $DF^{EFC} = (A, L, C)$ its corresponding ADF. DF^{EFC} is a BADF. If EFC is bounded hierarchical, then DF^{EFC} is an AADF$^+$.*

Theorem 7. *Let EFC be a strongly consistent EAFC and $DF^{EFC} = (A, L, C)$ its corresponding ADF. A set of arguments $X \subseteq A$ is a conflict–free extension of EFC iff it is conflict–free in DF^{EFC}. X is a stable extension of EFC iff it is a model of DF^{EFC}. X is a grounded extension of EFC iff it is the acyclic grounded extension of DF^{EFC}. Finally, X is a σ–extension of EFC, where $\sigma \in \{admissible, complete, preferred\}$, iff it is a ca$_2$–$\sigma$–extension of DF^{EFC}.*

5.3   Translating AFNs into ADFs

In order to accept an AFN argument, two conditions need to be met. First of all, just like in AFs, the attackers of a given argument need to be absent. However, in addition, at least one member of every supporting set needs to be present. This gives us a description of an acceptance condition; the acyclicity will be handled by the appropriate semantics.

Translation 4. *Let $FN = (A, R, N)$ be a strongly consistent AFN. The corresponding ADF is $DF^{FN} = (A, L, C)$, where $L = \{(x, y) \mid (x, y) \in R$ or $\exists B \subseteq A, x \in B$ s.t. $BNy\}$, $C = \{C_a \mid a \in A\}$ and every C_a is as follows:*

– *Functional form: for every $P' \subseteq par(a)$, if $\exists p \in P'$ s.t. pRa or $\exists Z \subseteq A$ s.t.
  ZNa and $Z \cap P' = \emptyset$, then $C_a(P') = out$; otherwise, $C_a(P') = in$.*
– *Propositional form: $C_a = att_a \cap sup_a$, where:*
  • *$att_a = \bigwedge \neg\{a\}^-$ or $att_a = \top$ if $\{a\}^- = \emptyset$*
  • *$sup_a = (\bigvee Z_1 \wedge ... \wedge \bigvee Z_m)$, where $Z_1, ..., Z_m$ are all subsets of A s.t. Z_iNa,
    or $sup_a = \top$ if no such set exists*

The produced ADFs are still bipolar. However, whether a given ADF is an $AADF^+$ or not, depends on the support relation in the source AFN.

Theorem 8. *Let $FN = (A, R, N)$ be a strongly consistent AFN and $DF^{FN} = (A, L, C)$ its corresponding ADF. Then DF^{FN} is a BADF.*

The AFN semantics are built around the notion of coherence, which requires all relevant arguments to be (support–wise) derived in an acyclic manner. Thus, not surprisingly, it is the aa–family of ADF semantics that will be associated with the AFN semantics. In particular, we can relate powerful sequences to the acyclic evaluations. This also allows us to draw the connection between the acyclic discarded set in ADFs and the discarded set X^{att} in AFNs. Hence, there is a correspondence between the defense in AFNs and being decisively *in* w.r.t. a given interpretation in ADFs. This in turns tells us the relation between the extensions of AFNs and ADFs:

Lemma 2. *Let $FN = (A, R, N)$ be a strongly consistent AFN and $DF^{FN} = (A, L, C)$ its corresponding ADF. For a given powerful sequence for an argument $a \in A$ we can construct an associated pd–acyclic evaluation and vice versa.*

Theorem 9. *Let $FN = (A, R, N)$ be a strongly consistent AFN, $DF^{FN} = (A, L, C)$ its corresponding ADF. X is strongly coherent in FN iff it is pd–acyclic conflict–free in DF^{FN}. X is a σ–extension of FN, where $\sigma \in \{admissible, complete, preferred\}$ iff it is an aa–σ–extension of DF^{FN}. X is stable in FN iff it is stable in DF^{FN}. X is grounded in FN iff it is acyclic grounded in DF^{FN}.*

Example 7. Let us continue Example 3. The ADF associated with our AFN is $(\{a, b, c, d, e, f\}, \{C_a : b \vee c, C_b : \neg d, C_c : \neg e, C_d : \neg f, C_e : \neg a, C_f : f\})$. $\emptyset$ is trivially aa–admissible. Its acyclic discarded set is $\{f\}$, thus making d decisively *in*. Hence, $\emptyset$ is not aa–complete. The set $\{d\}$ discards f and b. This is not enough to accept any other argument. Hence, it is both aa–admissible and aa–complete. The set $\{e\}$ is pd–acyclic conflict–free, but not aa–admissible (it discards f and c). However, $\{d, e\}$ is aa–admissible (discarded set is $\{a, b, f, c\}$) and aa–complete. We can also show that $\{a, c, d\}$ is aa–admissible and aa–complete (discarded set is $\{b, f, e\}$). Therefore, $\{d\}$ is the acyclic grounded extension, while $\{d, e\}$ and $\{a, c, d\}$ are aa–preferred and stable.

6   Conclusions and Final Remarks

In this paper we have presented a number of translations from different argumentation frameworks to ADFs. We could have observed that for every structure, we have found a family of the extension–based ADF semantics which followed similar principles and thus were able to retrieve exactly the extensions of the framework we were translating. We have also identified to which ADF subclass a given translation–produced framework belongs, so that the results from [9–11] can be exploited. Our results also show the differences between ADFs and other formalisms; in particular, we had to introduce consistency constraints in order to perform a translation. Nevertheless, this shortcoming can be addressed by the introduction of linearly many new arguments that take over the support relation. Unfortunately, due to the space constraints we did not describe the bypass method in detail. For the same reasons, we could not have presented certain translations. In particular, we have omitted the approach for evidential argumentation systems [14, 22]. However, based on the SETAF and AFN methods and the results from [14], this approach can be easily extrapolated. We hope we will manage to present these results in the extended version of this work.

In establishing the connections between the semantics of argumentation frameworks and ADFs, we have focused on the extension–based family. Nevertheless, the labeling–based approach is also a prominent one, and at least in the case of ADFs, better studied. However, as analyzed in [8], the usual relation between extensions and labelings that is found e.g. in the Dung's framework, does not hold for the dialectical framework. Due to the specialized nature the semantics we have presented here, all of the available approaches can sometimes produce different results when faced with support cycles. This means that the labeling–based method can give us complete, preferred or grounded interpretations that do not necessarily correspond to the complete, preferred or grounded extensions of arbitrary AFNs and EAFCs. This can be addressed by limiting ourselves to those frameworks that are associated with AADF$^+$s. Therefore, although the approaches for AFs and SETAFs can be used without any modifications, we would have to distinguish a support acyclic subclass of AFNs and work only with bounded hierarchical EAFCs. Consequently, we have decided to focus on the extension–based semantics for ADFs which can be used without such restrictions.

Our research falls into the area of framework intertranslatability [12, 14, 17, 22, 23]. However, in this case we are moving from less to more complex structures, not the other way around. Moreover, the fact that we are working with ADFs means that the currently established methods are not particularly applicable. To the best of our knowledge, our work is the first one to focus on analyzing the relations between ADFs and other argumentation frameworks.

References

1. Rahwan, I., Simari, G.R.: Argumentation in Artificial Intelligence, 1st edn. Springer, New York (2009)
2. Dung, P.M.: On the acceptability of arguments and its fundamental role in non-monotonic reasoning, logic programming and n-person games. Artif. Intell. **77**, 321–357 (1995)
3. Brewka, G., Polberg, S., Woltran, S.: Generalizations of Dung frameworks and their role in formal argumentation. IEEE Intell. Syst. **29**, 30–38 (2014)
4. Brewka, G., Woltran, S.: Abstract dialectical frameworks. In: Proceedings of KR 2010, pp. 102–111. AAAI Press (2010)
5. Strass, H.: Approximating operators and semantics for abstract dialectical frameworks. Artif. Intell. **205**, 39–70 (2013)
6. Brewka, G., Ellmauthaler, S., Strass, H., Wallner, J.P., Woltran, S.: Abstract dialectical frameworks revisited. In: Proceedings of IJCAI 2013, pp. 803–809. AAAI Press (2013)
7. Polberg, S.: Extension-based semantics of abstract dialectical frameworks. In: Proceedings of STAIRS 2014. FAIA, vol. 264, pp. 240–249. IOS Press (2014)
8. Polberg, S.: Revisiting extension-based semantics of abstract dialectical frameworks. Technical report DBAI-TR-2015-88, Institute for Information Systems, Technical University of Vienna (2015)
9. Strass, H., Wallner, J.P.: Analyzing the computational complexity of abstract dialectical frameworks via approximation fixpoint theory. In: Proceedings of KR 2014, Vienna, Austria, pp. 101–110. AAAI Press (2014)
10. Strass, H.: Instantiating knowledge bases in abstract dialectical frameworks. In: Leite, J., Son, T.C., Torroni, P., van der Torre, L., Woltran, S. (eds.) CLIMA XIV 2013. LNCS, vol. 8143, pp. 86–101. Springer, Heidelberg (2013)
11. Ellmauthaler, S., Strass, H.: The DIAMOND system for computing with abstract dialectical frameworks. In: Proceedings of COMMA 2014. FAIA, vol. 266, pp. 233–240. IOS Press (2014)
12. Cayrol, C., Lagasquie-Schiex, M.C.: Bipolarity in argumentation graphs: towards a better understanding. Int. J. Approx. Reasoning **54**, 876–899 (2013)
13. Nouioua, F.: AFs with necessities: further semantics and labelling characterization. In: Liu, W., Subrahmanian, V.S., Wijsen, J. (eds.) SUM 2013. LNCS, vol. 8078, pp. 120–133. Springer, Heidelberg (2013)
14. Polberg, S., Oren, N.: Revisiting support in abstract argumentation systems. In: Proceedings of COMMA 2014. FAIA, vol. 266, pp. 369–376. IOS Press (2014)
15. Nielsen, S.H., Parsons, S.: A generalization of Dung's abstract framework for argumentation: arguing with sets of attacking arguments. In: Maudet, N., Parsons, S., Rahwan, I. (eds.) ArgMAS 2006. LNCS (LNAI), vol. 4766, pp. 54–73. Springer, Heidelberg (2007)
16. Modgil, S., Prakken, H.: Reasoning about preferences in structured extended argumentation frameworks. In: Proceedings of COMMA 2010, pp. 347–358 (2010)
17. Modgil, S., Bench-Capon, T.J.M.: Metalevel argumentation. J. Log. Comput. **21**, 959–1003 (2011)

18. Modgil, S.: Revisiting abstract argumentation frameworks. In: Black, E., Modgil, S., Oren, N. (eds.) TAFA 2013. LNCS, vol. 8306, pp. 1–15. Springer, Heidelberg (2014)
19. Bench-Capon, T.J.M.: Persuasion in practical argument using value-based argumentation frameworks. J. Log. Comput. **13**, 429–448 (2003)
20. Amgoud, L., Vesic, S.: A new approach for preference-based argumentation frameworks. Ann. Math. Artif. Intell. **63**, 149–183 (2011)
21. Modgil, S.: Reasoning about preferences in argumentation frameworks. Artif. Intell. **173**, 901–934 (2009)
22. Oren, N., Reed, C., Luck, M.: Moving between argumentation frameworks. In: Proceedings of COMMA 2010, Amsterdam, The Netherlands, pp. 379–390. IOS Press (2010)
23. Boella, G., Gabbay, D.M., van der Torre, L., Villata, S.: Meta-argumentation modelling I: methodology and techniques. Stud. Logica. **93**, 297–355 (2009)
24. Amgoud, L., Cayrol, C.: A reasoning model based on the production of acceptable arguments. Ann. Math. Artif. Intell. **34**(1–3), 197–215 (2002). http://dblp.uni-trier.de

Extensional Semantics for Higher-Order Logic Programs with Negation

Panos Rondogiannis[✉] and Ioanna Symeonidou

Department of Informatics and Telecommunications,
National and Kapodistrian University of Athens, Athens, Greece
prondo@di.uoa.gr, i.symeonidou@di.uoa.gr

Abstract. We develop an extensional semantics for higher-order logic programs with negation, generalizing the technique that was introduced in [2,3] for positive higher-order programs. In this way we provide an alternative extensional semantics for higher-order logic programs with negation to the one proposed in [6]. As an immediate useful consequence of our developments, we define for the language we consider the notions of *stratification* and *local stratification*, which generalize the familiar such notions from classical logic programming. We demonstrate that for stratified and locally stratified higher-order logic programs, the proposed semantics never assigns the *unknown* truth value.

1 Introduction

Research results developed in [2,3,7,13,17] have explored the possibility of designing higher-order logic programming languages with purely *extensional semantics*. The key idea behind this line of research is that if we appropriately restrict the syntax of higher-order logic programming, then we can get languages that are simple both from a semantic as-well-as from a proof-theoretic point of view. For such languages, we can show that program predicates essentially denote sets and therefore one can use standard extensional set theory in order to understand the meaning of programs and reason about them. A main difference between the extensional and the more traditional *intensional* approaches [9,15] is that the latter have richer syntax and expressive capabilities but a non-extensional semantics.

There exist at present two main extensional semantic approaches for capturing the meaning of positive (i.e., negationless) higher-order logic programs. The first approach, developed in [7,13,17], uses classical domain-theoretic tools. The second approach, developed in [2,3], builds on a fixed-point construction on the ground instantiation of the source program. Despite their different philosophies, these two approaches have recently been shown to agree [8] for a broad and useful class of programs. This fact suggests that the two aforementioned techniques can be employed as useful alternatives for the further development of higher-order logic programming.

L. Michael and A. Kakas (Eds.): JELIA 2016, LNAI 10021, pp. 447–462, 2016.
DOI: 10.1007/978-3-319-48758-8_29

A natural question that arises is whether one can still obtain an extensional semantics if negation is added to programs. This question was recently undertaken in [6], where it was demonstrated that the domain-theoretic results obtained for positive logic programs in [7,13,17], can be extended to apply to programs with negation. More specifically, as demonstrated in [6], every higher-order logic program with negation has a distinguished extensional model constructed over a logic with an infinite number of truth values. It is therefore natural to wonder whether the alternative extensional technique introduced in [2,3], can also be extended to higher-order logic programs with negation. It is exactly this question that we answer affirmatively. This brings us to the following contributions of the present paper:

- We extend the technique of [2,3] to the class of higher-order logic programs with negation. In this way we demonstrate that Bezem's approach is more widely applicable than possibly initially anticipated.
- The extensional semantics we propose appears to be simpler compared to [6] because it relies on the ground instantiation of the higher-order program and does not require the rather involved domain-theoretic constructions of [6]. However, each technique has its merits and we believe that both will prove to be useful tools in the further study of higher-order logic programming.
- As a case study of the applicability of the new semantics, we define the notions of *stratification* and *local stratification* for higher-order logic programs with negation and demonstrate that for such programs the proposed semantics never assigns the *unknown* truth value. It is worth noting that such a result under the semantics of [6] has not yet been obtained.

The rest of the paper is organized as follows. Section 2 presents in an intuitive way the semantics that will be developed in this paper. Section 3 contains background material on the infinite-valued semantics that will be the basis of our construction. Section 4 introduces the syntax and Sect. 5 the semantics of our source language. Section 6 demonstrates that the proposed semantics is extensional. In Sect. 7 the notions of *stratification* and *local stratification* are introduced. Section 8 concludes the paper with pointers to future work.

2   An Intuitive Overview of the Proposed Approach

In this paper we consider the technique for positive higher-order logic programs proposed in [2,3], and we extend it in order to apply to programs with negation in clause bodies. Given a positive higher-order logic program, the starting idea behind Bezem's approach is to take its "ground instantiation", in which we replace variables with terms created using only predicate and individual constants that appear in the program. For example, the table below depicts (in the right) the ground instantiation of a higher-order program (in the left); we use ad-hoc Prolog-like syntax:

```
q(a).                    q(a).
q(b).                    q(b).
p(Q):-Q(a).              p(q):-q(a).
id(R)(X):-R(X).          id(q)(a):-q(a).
                         p(id(q)):-id(q)(a).
                         id(id(q))(a):-id(q)(a).
                             ...
```

One can now treat the new program as an infinite propositional one (i.e., each ground atom can be seen as a propositional one). This implies that we can use the standard least fixed-point construction of classical logic programming (see for example [14]) in order to compute the set of atoms that should be taken as "true". In our example, the least fixed-point will contain atoms such as q(a), q(b), p(q), id(q)(a), p(id(q)), and so on.

The main contribution of Bezem's work was that he established that the least fixed-point semantics of the ground instantiation of every positive higher-order logic program of the language considered in [2,3], is *extensional* in a sense that can be intuitively explained as follows. It is obvious in the above example that q and id(q) are equal since they are both true of only the constant a. Therefore, we would expect that (for example) if p(q) is true then p(id(q)) is also true, because q and id(q) should be considered as interchangeable. This property of "interchangeability" is formally defined in [2,3] and it is demonstrated that it holds in the least fixed-point of the immediate consequence operator of the ground instantiation of every program.

The key idea behind extending Bezem's semantics in order to apply to higher-order logic programs with negation, is straightforward to state: given such a program, we first take its ground instantiation. The resulting program is a (possibly infinite) propositional program with negation, and therefore we can compute its semantics in any standard way that exists for obtaining the meaning of such programs. For example, one could use the well-founded semantics (or the stable model semantics), and then proceed to show that the well-founded model (respectively, each stable model) is extensional in the sense of [2,3]. Instead of using the well-founded or the stable model semantics, we have chosen to use a relatively recent proposal for assigning meaning to classical logic programs with negation, namely the infinite-valued semantics [16]. As it has been demonstrated in [16], the infinite-valued semantics is compatible with the well-founded: if we collapse the infinite-valued model to three truth values, we get the well-founded one. There are two main reasons for choosing to proceed with the infinite-valued approach:

- An extension of the infinite-valued approach was used in [6] to give the first extensional semantics for higher-order logic programs with negation. By developing our present approach using the same underlying logic, we facilitate the future comparison between the two approaches.
- As it was recently demonstrated in [5,11], the infinite-valued approach satisfies all identities of *iteration theories* [4], while the well-founded semantics does not. Since iteration theories (intuitively) provide an abstract framework

for the comparison of various semantic approaches for languages that involve recursion, the results just mentioned give an extra incentive for the further study and use of the infinite-valued approach.

We demonstrate that the infinite-valued semantics of the ground instantiation of every higher-order logic program with negation, is extensional. In this way we extend the results of [2,3] which applied only to positive programs. The proof of extensionality is quite intricate and is performed by a tedious induction on the approximations of the minimum infinite-valued model. As an immediate application of our result, we show how one can define the notions of *stratification* and *local stratification* for higher-order logic programs with negation.

It is left as an open problem whether one can extend Bezem's technique in order to get extensional models under the well-founded or the stable-model semantics. More discussion on this issue will be given in the concluding section.

3   The Infinite-Valued Semantics

In this section we give an overview of the infinite-valued approach of [16]. As in [16], we consider (possibly countably infinite) propositional programs, consisting of clauses of the form $p \leftarrow L_1, \ldots, L_n$, where each L_i is either a propositional variable or the negation of a propositional variable. The key idea of the infinite-valued approach is that, in order to give a logical semantics to negation-as-failure and to distinguish it from ordinary negation, one needs to extend the domain of truth values. For example, consider the program:

$$p \leftarrow$$
$$r \leftarrow \sim p$$
$$s \leftarrow \sim q$$

According to negation-as-failure, both p and s receive the value *True*. However, p seems "truer" than s because there is a rule which says so, whereas s is true only because we are never obliged to make q true. In a sense, s is true only by default. For this reason, it was proposed in [16] to introduce a "default" truth value T_1 just below the "real" true T_0, and (by symmetry) a weaker false value F_1 just above ("not as false as") the real false F_0. Then, negation-as-failure is a combination of ordinary negation with a weakening. Thus $\sim F_0 = T_1$ and $\sim T_0 = F_1$. Since negations can be iterated, the new truth domain has a sequence $\ldots, T_3, T_2, T_1$ of weaker and weaker truth values below T_0 but above the neutral value 0; and a mirror image sequence $F_1, F_2, F_3, \ldots$ above F_0 and below 0. Since our propositional programs are possibly countably infinite, we need a T_α and a F_α for every countable ordinal α. Then the truth domain V is shaped as follows:

$$F_0 < F_1 < \cdots < F_\omega < \cdots < F_\alpha < \cdots < 0 < \cdots < T_\alpha < \cdots < T_\omega < \cdots < T_1 < T_0$$

and the notion of "Herbrand interpretation of a program" can be generalized:

Definition 1. *An (infinite-valued) interpretation I of a propositional program* P *is a function from the Herbrand Base* B_P *of* P *to the set V of truth values.*

We will use $\emptyset$ to denote the interpretation that assigns the F_0 value to all atoms of a program. If $v \in V$ is a truth value, we will use $I \parallel v$ to denote the set of atoms which are assigned the value v by I. In order to define the notion of "model", we need the following definitions:

Definition 2. *Let I be an interpretation of a given propositional program* P. *For every negative literal* $\sim$p *appearing in* P *we extend I as follows:*

$$I(\sim p) = \begin{cases} T_{\alpha+1}, \ if \ I(p) = F_\alpha \\ F_{\alpha+1}, \ if \ I(p) = T_\alpha \\ 0, \qquad if \ I(p) = 0 \end{cases}$$

Moreover, for every conjunction of literals $L_1, \ldots, L_n$ *appearing as the body of a clause in* P, *we extend I by* $I(L_1, \ldots, L_n) = min\{I(L_1), \ldots, I(L_n)\}$.

Definition 3. *Let* P *be a propositional program and I an interpretation of* P. *Then, I satisfies a clause* $p \leftarrow L_1, \ldots, L_n$ *of* P *if* $I(p) \geq I(L_1, \ldots, L_n)$. *Moreover, I is a* model *of* P *if I satisfies all clauses of* P.

As it is demonstrated in [16], every program has a *minimum* infinite-valued model under an ordering relation $\sqsubseteq$, which compares interpretations in a stage-by-stage manner. To formally state this result, the following definitions are necessary:

Definition 4. *The* order *of a truth value is defined as follows:* $order(T_\alpha) = \alpha$, $order(F_\alpha) = \alpha$ *and* $order(0) = +\infty$.

Definition 5. *Let I and J be interpretations of a given propositional program* P *and α be a countable ordinal. We write* $I =_\alpha J$, *if for all $\beta \leq \alpha$,* $I \parallel T_\beta = J \parallel T_\beta$ *and* $I \parallel F_\beta = J \parallel F_\beta$. *We write* $I \sqsubseteq_\alpha J$, *if for all $\beta < \alpha$,* $I =_\beta J$ *and, moreover,* $I \parallel T_\alpha \subseteq J \parallel T_\alpha$ *and* $I \parallel F_\alpha \supseteq J \parallel F_\alpha$. *We write* $I \sqsubset_\alpha J$, *if* $I \sqsubseteq_\alpha J$ *but* $I =_\alpha J$ *does not hold.*

Definition 6. *Let I and J be interpretations of a given propositional program* P. *We write* $I \sqsubset J$, *if there exists a countable ordinal α such that* $I \sqsubset_\alpha J$. *We write* $I \sqsubseteq J$ *if either* $I = J$ *or* $I \sqsubset J$.

It is easy to see [16] that $\sqsubseteq$ is a partial order, $\sqsubseteq_\alpha$ is a preorder, and $=_\alpha$ is an equivalence relation. As in the case of positive programs, the minimum Herbrand model of a program P coincides with the least fixed-point of an operator T_P:

Definition 7. *Let* P *be a propositional program and let I be an interpretation of* P. *The* immediate consequence operator T_P *of* P *is defined as follows:*

$$T_P(I)(p) = lub\{I(L_1, \ldots, L_n) \mid p \leftarrow L_1, \ldots, L_n \in P\}$$

The least fixed-point M_P of T_P is constructed as follows. We start with $\emptyset$, namely the interpretation that assigns to every atom of P the value F_0. We iterate T_P on $\emptyset$ until the set of atoms having a F_0 value and the set of atoms having a T_0 value, stabilize. Then we reset the values of all remaining atoms to F_1. The procedure is repeated until the F_1 and T_1 values stabilize, and we reset the remaining atoms to F_2, and so on. It is shown in [16] that there exists a countable ordinal δ for which this process will not produce any new atoms having F_δ or T_δ values. At this point we reset all remaining atoms to 0. The following definitions formalize this process.

Definition 8. *Let* P *be a propositional program and let* I *be an interpretation of* P. *We define the interpretation* $T^\omega_{\mathsf{P},\alpha}(I)$ *as follows:*

$$T^\omega_{\mathsf{P},\alpha}(I)(\mathsf{p}) = \begin{cases} I(\mathsf{p}), & if\ order(I(\mathsf{p})) < \alpha \\ T_\alpha, & if\ \mathsf{p} \in \bigcup_{n<\omega}(T^n_\mathsf{P}(I)\ \|\ T_\alpha) \\ F_\alpha, & if\ \mathsf{p} \in \bigcap_{n<\omega}(T^n_\mathsf{P}(I)\ \|\ F_\alpha) \\ F_{\alpha+1}, & otherwise \end{cases}$$

Definition 9. *Let* P *be a propositional program. For each countable ordinal* α, *let* $M_\alpha = T^\omega_{\mathsf{P},\alpha}(I_\alpha)$ *where* $I_0 = \emptyset$, $I_\alpha = M_{\alpha-1}$ *if* α *is a successor ordinal, and*

$$I_\alpha(\mathsf{p}) = \begin{cases} M_\beta(\mathsf{p}), & if\ order(M_\beta(\mathsf{p})) = \beta\ for\ some\ \beta < \alpha \\ F_\alpha, & otherwise \end{cases}$$

if α *is a limit ordinal. The* $M_0, M_1, \ldots, M_\alpha, \ldots$ *are called the* approximations *to the minimum model of* P.

In [16] it is shown that the above sequence of approximations is well-defined. We will make use of the following lemma from [16]:

Lemma 1. *Let* P *be a propositional program and let* α *be a countable ordinal. For all* $n < \omega$, $T^n_\mathsf{P}(I_\alpha) \sqsubseteq_\alpha M_\alpha$.

The following lemma from [16] states that there exists a certain ordinal, after which new approximations do not introduce new truth values:

Lemma 2. *Let* P *be a propositional program. Then, there exists a countable ordinal* δ, *called the* depth *of* P, *such that:*

1. *for all countable ordinals* $\gamma \geq \delta$, $M_\gamma\ \|\ T_\gamma = \emptyset$ *and* $M_\gamma\ \|\ F_\gamma = \emptyset$
2. *for all* $\beta < \delta$, $M_\beta\ \|\ T_\beta \neq \emptyset$ *or* $M_\beta\ \|\ F_\beta \neq \emptyset$.

We can now define the following interpretation M_P of a given program P:

$$M_\mathsf{P}(\mathsf{p}) = \begin{cases} M_\delta(\mathsf{p}), & if\ order(M_\delta(\mathsf{p})) < \delta \\ 0, & otherwise \end{cases}$$

The following two theorems from [16], establish important properties of M_P:

Theorem 1. *The infinite-valued interpretation M_P is a model of* P. *Moreover, it is the least (with respect to $\sqsubseteq$) among all infinite-valued models of* P.

Theorem 2. *The interpretation N_P obtained by collapsing all true values of M_P to* True *and all false values to* False, *coincides with the well-founded model of* P.

The next lemma states a fact already implied earlier, namely that new approximations do not affect the sets of atoms stabilized by the preceding ones.

Lemma 3. *Let* P *be a propositional program and let α be a countable ordinal. For all countable ordinals $\beta > \alpha$, $M_\alpha =_\alpha M_\beta$. Moreover, $M_\alpha =_\alpha M_P$.*

4   The Syntax of $\mathcal{H}$

In this section we define the syntax of the language $\mathcal{H}$ that we use throughout the paper. $\mathcal{H}$ is based on a simple type system with two base types: o, the boolean domain, and ι, the domain of data objects. The composite types are partitioned into three classes: functional (assigned to function symbols), predicate (assigned to predicate symbols) and argument (assigned to parameters of predicates).

Definition 10. *A type can either be* functional, predicate, *or* argument, *denoted by σ, π and ρ respectively and defined as:*

$$\sigma := \iota \mid (\iota \to \sigma)$$
$$\pi := o \mid (\rho \to \pi)$$
$$\rho := \iota \mid \pi$$

We will use τ to denote an arbitrary type (either functional, predicate or argument one). As usual, the binary operator $\to$ is right-associative. A functional type that is different than ι will often be written in the form $\iota^n \to \iota$, $n \geq 1$. Moreover, it can be easily seen that every predicate type π can be written in the form $\rho_1 \to \cdots \to \rho_n \to o$, $n \geq 0$ (for $n = 0$ we assume that $\pi = o$). We proceed by defining the syntax of $\mathcal{H}$:

Definition 11. *The alphabet of $\mathcal{H}$ consists of the following:*

1. *Predicate variables of every predicate type π (denoted by capital letters such as* Q, R, S, . . .*).*
2. *Individual variables of type ι (denoted by capital letters such as* X, Y, Z, . . .*).*
3. *Predicate constants of every predicate type π (denoted by lowercase letters such as* p, q, r, . . .*).*
4. *Individual constants of type ι (denoted by lowercase letters such as* a, b, c, . . .*).*
5. *Function symbols of every functional type $\sigma \neq \iota$ (denoted by lowercase letters such as* f, g, h, . . .*).*

6. *The inverse implication constant* ←, *the negation constant* ∼, *the comma, the left and right parentheses, and the equality constant* ≈ *for comparing terms of type* ι.

Arbitrary variables will be usually denoted by V and its subscripted versions.

Definition 12. *The set of* terms *of* $\mathcal{H}$ *is defined as follows:*

- *Every predicate variable (respectively, predicate constant) of type* π *is a term of type* π; *every individual variable (respectively, individual constant) of type* ι *is a term of type* ι;
- *if* f *is an n-ary function symbol and* $\mathsf{E}_1, \ldots, \mathsf{E}_n$ *are terms of type* ι *then* $(\mathsf{f}\ \mathsf{E}_1 \cdots \mathsf{E}_n)$ *is a term of type* ι;
- *if* E_1 *is a term of type* $\rho \to \pi$ *and* E_2 *a term of type* ρ *then* $(\mathsf{E}_1\ \mathsf{E}_2)$ *is a term of type* π.

Definition 13. *The set of* expressions *of* $\mathcal{H}$ *is defined as follows:*

- *A term of type* ρ *is an expression of type* ρ;
- *if* E *is a term of type* o *then* $(\sim\mathsf{E})$ *is an expression of type* o;
- *if* E_1 *and* E_2 *are terms of type* ι, *then* $(\mathsf{E}_1 \approx \mathsf{E}_2)$ *is an expression of type* o.

We write $vars(\mathsf{E})$ to denote the set of all the variables in E. Expressions (respectively, terms) that have no variables will often be referred to as *ground expressions* (respectively, *ground terms*). We will omit parentheses when no confusion arises. To denote that an expression E has type ρ we will often write $\mathsf{E} : \rho$. Expressions of type o that do not contain negation will often be referred to as *atoms* or *positive literals*, while expressions of the form $(\sim\mathsf{E})$ will be called *negative literals*. A *literal* is either a positive literal or a negative literal.

Definition 14. *A* clause *of* $\mathcal{H}$ *is a formula* $\mathsf{p}\ \mathsf{V}_1, \ldots, \mathsf{V}_n \leftarrow \mathsf{L}_1, \ldots, \mathsf{L}_m$, *where* p *is a predicate constant,* $\mathsf{V}_1, \ldots, \mathsf{V}_n$ *are distinct variables,* $\mathsf{p}\ \mathsf{V}_1, \ldots, \mathsf{V}_n$ *is a term of type* o *and* $\mathsf{L}_1, \ldots, \mathsf{L}_m$ *are literals. The term* $\mathsf{p}\ \mathsf{V}_1, \ldots, \mathsf{V}_n$ *is the* head *of the clause and the conjunction* $\mathsf{L}_1, \ldots, \mathsf{L}_m$ *is its* body. *A program* P *of* $\mathcal{H}$ *is a finite set of clauses.*

Example 1. The program below defines the subset relation over unary predicates:

$$\text{subset S1 S2 :- } \sim(\text{nonsubset S1 S2}).$$
$$\text{nonsubset S1 S2 :- S1 X,} \sim(\text{S2 X}).$$

Given unary predicates p and q, subset p q is true iff p is a subset of q.   □

In the following, we will often talk about the "ground instantiation of a program". This notion is formally defined below.

Definition 15. *A substitution* θ *is a finite set of the form* $\{\mathsf{V}_1/\mathsf{E}_1, \ldots, \mathsf{V}_n/\mathsf{E}_n\}$ *where the* V_i's *are different variables and each* E_i *is a term having the same type as* V_i. *We write* $dom(\theta)$ *to denote the domain* $\{\mathsf{V}_1, \ldots, \mathsf{V}_n\}$ *of* θ. *If all the expressions* $\mathsf{E}_1, \ldots, \mathsf{E}_n$ *are ground terms,* θ *is called a* ground substitution.

We can now define the application of a substitution to an expression.

Definition 16. *Let θ be a substitution and E be an expression. Then, $E\theta$ is an expression obtained from E as follows:*

- $E\theta = E$ *if E is a predicate constant or individual constant;*
- $V\theta = \theta(V)$ *if $V \in dom(\theta)$; otherwise, $V\theta = V$;*
- $(f\ E_1 \cdots E_n)\theta = (f\ E_1\theta \cdots E_n\theta)$;
- $(E_1\ E_2)\theta = (E_1\theta\ E_2\theta)$;
- $(\sim E)\theta = (\sim E\theta)$;
- $(E_1 \approx E_2)\theta = (E_1\theta \approx E_2\theta)$.

If θ is a ground substitution such that $vars(E) \subseteq dom(\theta)$, then the ground expression $E\theta$ is called a ground instance *of E.*

Definition 17. *Let P be a program. A ground instance of a clause $p\ V_1 \cdots V_n \leftarrow L_1, \ldots, L_m$ of P is a formula $(p\ V_1 \cdots V_n)\theta \leftarrow L_1\theta, \ldots, L_m\theta$, where θ is a ground substitution whose domain is the set of all variables that appear in the clause, such that for every $V \in dom(\theta)$ with $V : \rho$, $\theta(V)$ is a ground expression of type ρ that has been formed with predicate constants, function symbols, and individual constants that appear in P. The* ground instantiation *of a program P, denoted by $Gr(P)$, is the (possibly infinite) set that contains all the ground instances of the clauses of P.*

5   The Semantics of $\mathcal{H}$

In this section we develop the semantics of $\mathcal{H}$. Our developments generalize the semantics of [2,3] for positive higher-order logic programs to programs with negation. Notice that the semantics of [2,3] is based on classical two-valued logic, while ours on the infinite-valued logic of Sect. 3.

In order to interpret the programs of $\mathcal{H}$, we need to specify the semantic domains in which the expressions of each type τ are assigned their meanings. The following definition implies that the expressions of predicate types should be understood as representing functions.

Definition 18. *A functional type structure $\mathcal{S}$ for $\mathcal{H}$ consists of two non-empty sets D and A together with an assignment $[\![\tau]\!]$ to each type τ of $\mathcal{H}$, so that the following are satisfied:*

- $[\![\iota]\!] = D$;
- $[\![\iota^n \to \iota]\!] = D^n \to D$;
- $[\![o]\!] = A$;
- $[\![\rho \to \pi]\!] \subseteq [\![\rho]\!] \to [\![\pi]\!]$.

Given a functional type structure $\mathcal{S}$, any function $v : [\![o]\!] \to V$ will be called an *infinite-valued valuation function* (or simply *valuation function*) for $\mathcal{S}$.

Definition 19. *For a program* P, *we define the* Herbrand universe *for every argument type* ρ, *denoted by* $U_{P,\rho}$ *to be the set of all ground terms of type* ρ, *that can be formed out of the individual constants, function symbols and predicate constants in the program.*

When studying the semantics of a program P, it is customary to restrict attention to the Herbrand universe and Herbrand base of the program, instead of the entirety of the language. Following [2,3], we take D and A in Definition 18 to be equal to $U_{P,\iota}$ and $U_{P,o}$ respectively. Then, each element of $U_{P,\rho\to\pi}$ can itself be perceived as a function mapping elements of $[\![\rho]\!]$ to elements of $[\![\pi]\!]$, through syntactic application mapping. That is, $E \in U_{P,\rho\to\pi}$ can be viewed as the function mapping each $E' \in U_{P,\rho}$ to the expression $E\,E' \in U_{P,\pi}$.

Definition 20. *A* Herbrand interpretation I *of a program* P *consists of*

1. *a functional type structure* $\mathcal{S}_I$, *such that* $D = U_{P,\iota}$, $A = U_{P,o}$ *and* $[\![\rho \to \pi]\!] = U_{P,\rho\to\pi}$ *for every predicate type* $\rho \to \pi$;
2. *an assignment to each individual constant* c *in* P, *of the element* $I(\mathsf{c}) = \mathsf{c}$; *to each predicate constant* p *in* P, *of the element* $I(\mathsf{p}) = \mathsf{p}$; *to each function symbol* f *in* P, *of the element* $I(\mathsf{f}) = \mathsf{f}$;
3. *a valuation function for* $\mathcal{S}_I$, $v_I(\cdot)$, *assigning to each element of* $U_{P,o}$ *an element in* V.

We call $v_I(\cdot)$ the *valuation function of* I and omit the reference to $\mathcal{S}_I$, since the latter is common to all Herbrand interpretations of a program. In fact, individual Herbrand interpretations are only set apart by their valuation functions.

Definition 21. *A* Herbrand state *(or simply* state*)* s *of a program* P *is a function that assigns to each variable* V *of type* ρ *an element of* $U_{P,\rho}$.

Given a Herbrand interpretation I and state s, we can define the semantics of expressions with respect to I and s.

Definition 22. *Let* P *be a program,* I *be a Herbrand interpretation of* P *and* s *be a Herbrand state. Then the semantics of expressions with respect to* I *and* s *is defined as follows:*

- $[\![\mathsf{c}]\!]_s(I) = I(\mathsf{c})$, *for every individual constant* c;
- $[\![\mathsf{p}]\!]_s(I) = I(\mathsf{p})$, *for every predicate constant* p;
- $[\![V]\!]_s(I) = s(V)$, *for every variable* V;
- $[\![(\mathsf{f}\,E_1, \cdots E_n)]\!]_s(I) = (\mathsf{f}\,[\![E_1]\!]_s(I) \cdots [\![E_n]\!]_s(I))$, *for every function symbol* $\mathsf{f} : \iota^n \to \iota$;
- $[\![(E_1\,E_2)]\!]_s(I) = ([\![E_1]\!]_s(I)\,[\![E_2]\!]_s(I))$;
- $[\![(E_1 \approx E_2)]\!]_s(I) = ([\![E_1]\!]_s(I) \approx [\![E_2]\!]_s(I))$;
- $[\![(\sim E)]\!]_s(I) = (\sim[\![E]\!]_s(I))$.

Since we are dealing with Herbrand interpretations, it is easy to see that for every Herbrand state s and ground expression E, we have $[\![E]\!]_s(I) = E$. Therefore, if E is a ground atom, we can write $v_I(E)$ instead of $v_I([\![E]\!]_s(I))$. Stretching this abuse of notation a little further, we can extend a valuation function to assign truth values to ground *formulas*:

Definition 23. *Let* P *be a program and* I *be a Herbrand interpretation of* P. *Then the truth value of ground formulas with respect to* I *is defined as follows:*

$$- v_I((\mathsf{E}_1 \approx \mathsf{E}_2)) = \begin{cases} F_0, & \text{if } \mathsf{E}_1 \neq \mathsf{E}_2 \\ T_0, & \text{if } \mathsf{E}_1 = \mathsf{E}_2 \end{cases};$$

$$- v_I(\sim\!\mathsf{A}) = \begin{cases} F_{\alpha+1}, & \text{if } v_I(\mathsf{A}) = T_\alpha \\ 0, & \text{if } v_I(\mathsf{A}) = 0 \\ T_{\alpha+1}, & \text{if } v_I(\mathsf{A}) = F_\alpha \end{cases};$$

$$- v_I(\mathsf{L}_1, \cdots, \mathsf{L}_n) = min\{v_I(\mathsf{L}_1), \ldots, v_I(\mathsf{L}_n)\}.$$

Based on the above definition, we can define the concept of Herbrand models for our higher-order programs in the same way as in classical logic programming.

Definition 24. *Let* P *be a program and* I *be a Herbrand interpretation of* P. *We say* I *is a* model *of* P *if* $v_I([\![\mathsf{A}]\!]_s(I)) \geq v_I([\![\mathsf{L}_1]\!]_s(I), \cdots, [\![\mathsf{L}_m]\!]_s(I))$ *holds for every clause* $\mathsf{A} \leftarrow \mathsf{L}_1, \cdots, \mathsf{L}_m$ *and every Herbrand state* s *of* P.

Bezem's semantics is based on the observation that, given a positive higher-order program, we can use the minimum model semantics of its ground instantiation as a (two-valued) valuation function defining a Herbrand interpretation for the initial program itself. We use the same idea for $\mathcal{H}$ programs; the only difference is that we employ the infinite-valued model of the ground instantiation of the program as the valuation function.

Definition 25. *Let* P *be a program. Also, let* $\mathsf{Gr}(\mathsf{P})$ *be the ground instantiation of* P *and let* $M_{\mathsf{Gr}(\mathsf{P})}$ *be the infinite-valued model of* $\mathsf{Gr}(\mathsf{P})$. *We define* $\mathcal{M}_\mathsf{P}$ *to be the Herbrand interpretation of* P *such that* $v_{\mathcal{M}_\mathsf{P}}(\mathsf{A}) = M_{\mathsf{Gr}(\mathsf{P})}(\mathsf{A})$ *for every* $\mathsf{A} \in U_{\mathsf{P},o}$.

We adopt the notation $I \parallel v$ from Sect. 3, to signify the set of atoms which are assigned a certain truth value $v \in V$ by a Herbrand interpretation I; that is, $I \parallel v = \{\mathsf{A} \mid \mathsf{A} \in U_{\mathsf{P},o} \text{ and } v_I(\mathsf{A}) = v\}$. Then the relations $\sqsubseteq_\alpha, \sqsubset_\alpha, =_\alpha, \sqsubseteq$ and $\sqsubset$ on Herbrand interpretations of a higher-order program can be defined in exactly the same manner as in the first-order case.

The next theorem verifies that our semantics is well-defined, in the sense that the interpretation we chose as the meaning of a program P is indeed a model of P. In fact it is its minimum, with respect to $\sqsubseteq$, model.

Theorem 3. $\mathcal{M}_\mathsf{P}$ *is the minimum (with respect to* $\sqsubseteq$*) Herbrand model of* P.

The proof of the theorem is relatively straightforward and is omitted due to space limitations.

6   Extensionality of the Proposed Semantics

In this section we show that the infinite-valued model we defined in the previous section enjoys the extensionality property, as this was defined in [2].

Definition 26. *Let S be a functional type structure and v be a valuation function for S. For every type τ we define the relations $\cong_{v,\tau}$ on $[\![\tau]\!]$ as follows: Let $d_1, d_2 \in [\![\tau]\!]$; then $d_1 \cong_{v,\tau} d_2$ if and only if*

1. $\tau = \iota^n \to \iota$, $n \geq 0$, and $d_1 = d_2$, or
2. $\tau = o$ and $v(d_1) = v(d_2)$, or
3. $\tau = \rho \to \pi$ and $d_1\, e_1 \cong_{v,\pi} d_2\, e_2$ for all $e_1, e_2 \in [\![\rho]\!]$, such that $e_1 \cong_{v,\rho} e_2$.

Generally, it is not guaranteed that such relations will be equivalence relations; rather they are partial equivalences. However, we are going to see that the minimum model of a program defines true equivalence relations for all types τ.

Definition 27. *Let P be a program and let I be a Herbrand interpretation of P. We say I is extensional if for all types τ the relations $\cong_{v_I,\tau}$ are reflexive, i.e. for all $E \in [\![\tau]\!]$, it holds that $E \cong_{v_I,\tau} E$.*

Theorem 4 (Extensionality). $\mathcal{M}_P$ *is extensional.*

Proof. Since the valuation function of $\mathcal{M}_P$ is $M_{\mathsf{Gr}(P)}$, effectively we need to show that $E \cong_{M_{\mathsf{Gr}(P)},\tau} E$, for every type τ and every $E \in [\![\tau]\!]$. We perform an induction on the structure of τ. For the base types ι and o the statement holds by definition, as it also does for functional types $\iota^n \to \iota$. So, for the induction step, we prove the statement for a predicate type τ, assuming that it holds for all types simpler than τ. Let A be any atom of the following form: A is headed by a predicate constant and all variables in $vars(A)$ are of types simpler than τ. Let θ, θ' be ground substitutions, such that $vars(A) \subseteq dom(\theta), dom(\theta')$ and $\theta(V) \cong_{M_{\mathsf{Gr}(P)},\rho} \theta'(V)$ for any $V : \rho$ in $vars(A)$. Then it suffices to show the following two properties, for all ordinals α: Property $P_1(\alpha)$ states that if $M_\alpha(A\theta) = T_\alpha$ then $M_{\mathsf{Gr}(P)}(A\theta') = T_\alpha$; property $P_2(\alpha)$ states that if $M_\alpha(A\theta) = F_\alpha$ then $M_{\mathsf{Gr}(P)}(A\theta') = F_\alpha$.

To see why proving the above properties is enough to establish that $E \cong_{M_{\mathsf{Gr}(P)},\tau} E$, observe the following: first of all, if τ is of the form $\rho_1 \to \cdots \to \rho_m \to o$ and $V_1 : \rho_1, \ldots, V_m : \rho_m$ are variables, then $E\, V_1 \cdots V_m$ is an atom of the form described above. Also, by Lemma 3 we have that $M_{\mathsf{Gr}(P)}(E\, \theta(V_1) \cdots \theta(V_m)) = T_\alpha$ iff $M_\alpha(E\, \theta(V_1) \cdots \theta(V_m)) = T_\alpha$. If $P_1(\alpha)$ holds, the latter implies that $M_{\mathsf{Gr}(P)}(E\, \theta'(V_1) \cdots \theta'(V_m)) = T_\alpha$. Because the relations $\cong_{M_{\mathsf{Gr}(P)},\rho_i}$ are symmetric, θ and θ' are interchangeable. Therefore the same argument can be used to infer the reverse implication, i.e. $M_{\mathsf{Gr}(P)}(E\, \theta'(V_1) \cdots \theta'(V_m)) = T_\alpha \Rightarrow M_{\mathsf{Gr}(P)}(E\, \theta(V_1) \cdots \theta(V_m)) = T_\alpha$, and thus an equivalence. If $P_2(\alpha)$ holds, the analogous equivalence can be shown for the value F_α, in the same way. Finally, the equivalence for the 0 value follows by a simple elimination argument.

We will proceed by a second induction on α. For the **second induction basis**, we have $M_0 = T^\omega_{\mathsf{Gr}(P),0}(\emptyset)$. Observe that $T^\omega_{\mathsf{Gr}(P),0}(\emptyset)(A\theta)$ will evaluate to T_0 iff there exists some $n < \omega$ for which $T^n_{\mathsf{Gr}(P)}(\emptyset)(A\theta) = T_0$. On the other hand, it will evaluate to F_0 iff there does not exist a $n < \omega$ for which $T^n_{\mathsf{Gr}(P)}(\emptyset)(A\theta) \neq F_0$. Therefore, in order to prove $P_1(0)$ and $P_2(0)$, we first need to perform a third induction on n and prove the following two properties: Property $P_1'(0, n)$, stating that if $T^n_{\mathsf{Gr}(P)}(\emptyset)(A\theta) = T_0$ then $M_{\mathsf{Gr}(P)}(A\theta') = T_0$; and property $P_2'(0, n)$, stating that if $T_{\mathsf{Gr}(\mathsf{P})}^n(\emptyset)(\mathsf{A}\theta) > F_0$ then $M_{\mathsf{Gr}(\mathsf{P})}(\mathsf{A}\theta') > F_0$. The **third induction basis** case is trivial. For the **third induction step**, first we show $P_1'(0, n+1)$. If $T_{\mathsf{Gr}(\mathsf{P})}^{n+1}(\emptyset)(\mathsf{A}\theta) = T_0$, then there exists a clause $\mathsf{A}\theta \leftarrow \mathsf{L}_1, \ldots, \mathsf{L}_k$ in $\mathsf{Gr}(\mathsf{P})$ such that for each $i \leq k$, $T_{\mathsf{Gr}(\mathsf{P})}^n(\emptyset)(\mathsf{L}_i) = T_0$. This implies that each L_i is a positive literal, since a negative one cannot be assigned the value T_0 in any interpretation. This clause is a ground instance of a clause $\mathsf{p}\,\mathsf{V}_1 \cdots \mathsf{V}_m \leftarrow \mathsf{B}_1, \ldots, \mathsf{B}_k$ in the higher-order program and there exists a substitution θ'', such that $(\mathsf{p}\,\mathsf{V}_1 \cdots \mathsf{V}_m)\theta'' = \mathsf{A}$ and, for any variable $\mathsf{V} \notin \{\mathsf{V}_1, \ldots, \mathsf{V}_m\}$ appearing in the body of the clause, $\theta''(\mathsf{V})$ is an appropriate ground term, so that $\mathsf{L}_i = \mathsf{B}_i\theta''\theta$ for all $i \leq k$. Observe that the variables appearing in the clause $(\mathsf{p}\,\mathsf{V}_1 \cdots \mathsf{V}_m)\theta'' \leftarrow \mathsf{B}_1\theta'', \ldots, \mathsf{B}_k\theta''$ are exactly the variables appearing in A and they are all of types simpler than τ. Also, the clause $\mathsf{A}\theta' \leftarrow \mathsf{B}_1\theta''\theta', \ldots, \mathsf{B}_k\theta''\theta'$ is in $\mathsf{Gr}(\mathsf{P})$ and for each $i \leq k$, $M_{\mathsf{Gr}(\mathsf{P})}(\mathsf{B}_i\theta''\theta') = T_0$ can be shown to follow from $T_{\mathsf{Gr}(\mathsf{P})}^n(\emptyset)(\mathsf{L}_i) = T_0$, by examining all possible forms each $\mathsf{B}_i\theta''$, $i \leq k$, may take. Therefore $M_{\mathsf{Gr}(\mathsf{P})}(\mathsf{A}\theta') = T_0$ must also hold. Property $P_2'(0, n+1)$ can be shown using very similar arguments. We can now use these two properties in order to show $P_1(0)$ and $P_2(0)$. By definition, if $M_0(\mathsf{A}\theta) = T_{\mathsf{Gr}(\mathsf{P}),0}^\omega(\emptyset)(\mathsf{A}\theta) = T_0$, then there exists some $n < \omega$ such that $T_{\mathsf{Gr}(\mathsf{P})}^n(\emptyset)(\mathsf{A}\theta) = T_0$. Applying $P_1'(0, n)$ to $\mathsf{A}\theta$ we immediately conclude that $M_{\mathsf{Gr}(\mathsf{P})}(\mathsf{A}\theta') = T_0$, which establishes property $P_1(0)$. Now let $M_0(\mathsf{A}\theta) = F_0$ and assume $M_{\mathsf{Gr}(\mathsf{P})}(\mathsf{A}\theta') \neq F_0$. By Lemma 3, the latter can only hold if $M_0(\mathsf{A}\theta') = T_{\mathsf{Gr}(\mathsf{P}),0}^\omega(\emptyset)(\mathsf{A}\theta') \neq F_0$ and this, in turn, means that there exists at least one $n < \omega$ such that $T_{\mathsf{Gr}(\mathsf{P})}^n(\emptyset)(\mathsf{A}\theta') > F_0$. Then, reversing the roles of θ and θ', we can apply property $P_2'(0, n)$ to $\mathsf{A}\theta'$ and conclude that $M_{\mathsf{Gr}(\mathsf{P})}(\mathsf{A}\theta) > F_0$, which, again by Lemma 3, contradicts $M_0(\mathsf{A}\theta) = F_0$. Therefore it must be $M_{\mathsf{Gr}(\mathsf{P})}(\mathsf{A}\theta') = F_0$. For the **second induction step**, it remains to prove properties $P_1(\alpha)$ and $P_2(\alpha)$ for an arbitrary countable ordinal α. Again, the proof follows arguments very similar to the ones used in the basis case and is omitted due to space limitations. □

7 Stratified and Locally Stratified Programs

In this section we define the notions of *stratified* and *locally stratified* programs and argue that atoms of such programs never obtain the truth value 0 under the proposed semantics. The notion of local stratification is a straightforward generalization of the corresponding notion for classical (first-order) logic programs. However, the notion of stratification is a genuine extension of the corresponding notion for first-order programs.

Definition 28. *A program* P *is called* locally stratified *if and only if it is possible to decompose the Herbrand base* $U_{\mathsf{P},o}$ *of* P *into disjoint sets (called* strata*)* $S_1, S_2, \ldots, S_\alpha, \ldots, \alpha < \gamma$, *where* γ *is a countable ordinal, such that for every clause* $\mathsf{H} \leftarrow \mathsf{A}_1, \ldots, \mathsf{A}_m, \sim\mathsf{B}_1, \ldots, \sim\mathsf{B}_n$ *in* $\mathsf{Gr}(\mathsf{P})$, *we have that for every* $i \leq m$, $stratum(\mathsf{A}_i) \leq stratum(\mathsf{H})$ *and for every* $i \leq n$, $stratum(\mathsf{B}_i) < stratum(\mathsf{H})$, *where* $stratum(\mathsf{C}) = \beta$, *if the atom* $\mathsf{C} \in U_{\mathsf{P},o}$ *belongs to* S_β, *and* $stratum(\mathsf{C}) = 0$, *if* $\mathsf{C} \notin U_{\mathsf{P},o}$ *and is of the form* $(\mathsf{E}_1 \approx \mathsf{E}_2)$.

All atoms in the minimum Herbrand model of a locally stratified program have non-zero values:

Lemma 4. *Let* P *be a locally stratified logic program. Then, for every atom* A $\in U_{P,o}$ *it holds* $\mathcal{M}_P(A) \neq 0$.

Proof. Theorem 2 implies that the infinite-valued model $M_{Gr(P)}$ of the ground instantiation of P assigns the truth value 0 to an atom iff the same atom is assigned this value by the well-founded model. It is trivial to see that P is a locally stratified higher-order program (in the sense of Definition 28) iff its ground instantiation is a locally stratified propositional program. Recall that the well-founded model of a locally stratified first-order program does not assign the truth value 0 to any atom [12], so neither does $M_{Gr(P)}$ or $\mathcal{M}_P$. $\square$

Since Definition 28 generalizes the corresponding one for classical logic programs, the undecidability result [10] for detecting whether a given program is locally stratified, extends directly to the higher-order case.

Lemma 5. *The problem of determining whether a given logic program* P *is locally stratified, is undecidable.*

However, there exists a notion of stratification for higher-order logic programs that is decidable and has as a special case the stratification for classical logic programs [1]. In the following definition, a predicate type π is understood to be *greater than* a second predicate type π', if π is of the form $\rho_1 \rightarrow \cdots \rightarrow \rho_n \rightarrow \pi'$, where $n \geq 1$.

Definition 29. *A program* P *is called* stratified *if and only if it is possible to decompose the set of all predicate constants that appear in* P *into a finite number* r *of disjoint sets (called* strata*)* $S_1, S_2, \ldots, S_r$, *such that for every clause* H $\leftarrow$ $A_1, \ldots, A_m, \sim B_1, \ldots, \sim B_n$ *in* P, *where the predicate constant of* H *is* p, *we have:*

1. *for every* $i \leq m$, *if* A_i *is a term that starts with a predicate constant* q, *then* $stratum(q) \leq stratum(p)$;
2. *for every* $i \leq m$, *if* A_i *is a term that starts with a predicate variable* Q, *then for all predicate constants* q *that appear in* P *such that the type of* q *is greater than or equal to the type of* Q, *it holds* $stratum(q) \leq stratum(p)$;
3. *for every* $i \leq n$, *if* B_i *starts with a predicate constant* q, *then* $stratum(q) < stratum(p)$;
4. *for every* $i \leq n$, *if* B_i *starts with a predicate variable* Q, *then for all predicate constants* q *that appear in* P *such that the type of* q *is greater than or equal to the type of* Q, *it holds* $stratum(q) < stratum(p)$;

where $stratum(r) = i$ *if the predicate symbol* r *belongs to* S_i.

Example 2. It is straightforward to see that the program:

$$p \; Q:-\sim(Q \; a).$$
$$q \; X:-(X \approx a).$$

is stratified. However, it can easily be checked that the program:

$$p\ Q:-\sim(Q\ a).$$
$$q\ X\ Y:-(X \approx a),(Y \approx a),p\ (q\ a).$$

is not stratified nor locally stratified, because if the term $q\ a$ is substituted for Q we get a circularity through negation. Notice that the type of q is $\iota \to \iota \to o$ and it is greater than the type of Q which is $\iota \to o$.   □

Since the set of predicate constants that appear in a program P is finite, and since the number of predicate constants of the program that have a greater or equal type than a given type is also finite, it follows that checking whether a given program is stratified, is decidable. Moreover, we have the following theorem:

Theorem 5. *If* P *is stratified then it is locally stratified.*

Proof. Consider a decomposition $S_1, \ldots, S_r$ of the set of predicate constants of P. This defines a decomposition $S'_1, \ldots, S'_r$ of the Herbrand base of P, as follows:

$$S'_i = \{A \in U_{P,o} \mid \text{the leftmost predicate constant of } A \text{ belongs to } S_i\}$$

It is easy to check that $S'_1, \ldots, S'_r$ corresponds to a local stratification of $U_{P,o}$.□

8   Future Work

We have defined a novel extensional semantics for higher-order logic programs with negation based on the infinite-valued logic of [16], and used it in order to define notions of stratification for such programs. We conjecture that one can define extensional semantics based on the well-founded and the stable-model approaches. Notice that despite the fact that the minimum infinite-valued model of a program collapses to the well-founded one (Theorem 2), this fact can not be used directly in order to argue about the possible extensionality of a semantics that will be based on the well-founded approach. It seems that a novel proof must be devised for this case, and we are currently investigating this issue.

References

1. Apt, K.R., Blair, H.A., Walker, A.: Towards a theory of declarative knowledge. In: Minker, J. (ed.) Foundations of Deductive Databases and Logic Programming, pp. 89–148. Morgan Kaufmann (1988)
2. Bezem, M.: Extensionality of simply typed logic programs. In: Schreye, D.D. (ed.) Logic Programming: The 1999 International Conference, Las Cruces, 29 November–4 December 1999, pp. 395–410. MIT Press (1999)
3. Bezem, M.: An improved extensionality criterion for higher-order logic programs. In: Fribourg, L. (ed.) CSL 2001 and EACSL 2001. LNCS, vol. 2142, pp. 203–216. Springer, Heidelberg (2001). doi:10.1007/3-540-44802-0_15

4. Bloom, S.L., Ésik, Z.: Iteration Theories - The Equational Logic of Iterative Processes. EATCS Monographs on Theoretical Computer Science. Springer, Heidelberg (1993)
5. Carayol, A., Ésik, Z.: An analysis of the equational properties of the well-founded fixed point. In: Baral, C., Delgrande, J.P., Wolter, F. (eds.) Principles of Knowledge Representation and Reasoning: Proceedings of the Fifteenth International Conference, KR 2016, Cape Town, 25–29 April 2016, pp. 533–536. AAAI Press (2016)
6. Charalambidis, A., Ésik, Z., Rondogiannis, P.: Minimum model semantics for extensional higher-order logic programming with negation. TPLP **14**(4–5), 725–737 (2014)
7. Charalambidis, A., Handjopoulos, K., Rondogiannis, P., Wadge, W.W.: Extensional higher-order logic programming. ACM Trans. Comput. Log. **14**(3), 21 (2013)
8. Charalambidis, A., Rondogiannis, P., Symeonidou, I.: Equivalence of two fixed-point semantics for definitional higher-order logic programs. In: Matthes, R., Mio, M. (eds.) Proceedings Tenth International Workshop on Fixed Points in Computer Science, FICS 2015, Berlin, 11–12 September 2015. EPTCS, vol. 191, pp. 18–32 (2015)
9. Chen, W., Kifer, M., Warren, D.S.: HILOG: a foundation for higher-order logic programming. J. Log. Program. **15**(3), 187–230 (1993)
10. Cholak, P., Blair, H.A.: The complexity of local stratification. Fundam. Inform. **21**(4), 333–344 (1994)
11. Ésik, Z.: Equational properties of stratified least fixed points (extended abstract). In: de Paiva, V., de Queiroz, R., Moss, L.S., Leivant, D., de Oliveira, A. (eds.) WoLLIC 2015. LNCS, vol. 9160, pp. 174–188. Springer, Heidelberg (2015). doi:10.1007/978-3-662-47709-0_13
12. Gelder, A.V., Ross, K.A., Schlipf, J.S.: The well-founded semantics for general logic programs. J. ACM **38**(3), 620–650 (1991)
13. Kountouriotis, V., Rondogiannis, P., Wadge, W.W.: Extensional higher-order datalog. In: Short Paper Proceedings of the 12th International Conference on Logic for Programming, Artificial Intelligence and Reasoning (LPAR), pp. 1–5, December 2005
14. Lloyd, J.W.: Foundations of Logic Programming. Springer, Heidelberg (1987)
15. Miller, D., Nadathur, G.: Programming with Higher-Order Logic, 1st edn. Cambridge University Press, New York (2012)
16. Rondogiannis, P., Wadge, W.W.: Minimum model semantics for logic programs with negation-as-failure. ACM Trans. Comput. Log. **6**(2), 441–467 (2005)
17. Wadge, W.W.: Higher-order horn logic programming. In: Saraswat, V.A., Ueda, K. (eds.) Proceedings of the 1991 International Symposium on Logic Programming, San Diego, 28 October–1 November 1991, pp. 289–303. MIT Press (1991)

Reactive Policies with Planning
for Action Languages

Zeynep G. Saribatur$^{(\boxtimes)}$ and Thomas Eiter

Technische Universität Wien, Vienna, Austria
{zeynep,eiter}@kr.tuwien.ac.at

Abstract. Action languages are an important family of formalisms to represent action domains in a declarative manner and to reason about them. For this reason, the behavior of an agent in an environment may be governed by policies which take such action domain descriptions into account. In this paper, we describe a formal semantics for describing policies that express a reactive behavior for an agent, and connect our framework with the representation power of action languages. In this framework, we mitigate the large state spaces by employing the notion of indistinguishability, and combine components that are efficient for describing reactivity such as target establishment and (online) planning. Our representation allows one to analyze the flow of executing the given reactive policy, and lays foundations for verifying properties of policies. Additionally, the flexibility of the representation opens a range of possibilities for designing behaviors.

1 Introduction

Reactive agents are a particular type of autonomous agents that are able to interact with the environment. They can perceive the current state of the world and figure out their next actions by consulting a given policy and their knowledge base, which describes their capabilities and represents the world's model. After executing these actions, they are able to observe the outcomes and reiterate the process. As such agents become more common in our lives, the issue of verifying that they behave as intended becomes increasingly important. It would be highly costly, time consuming and sometimes even fatal to realize on runtime that following a given policy does not provide the desired results.

For example, in search scenarios, an agent needs to find a missing person in unknown environments. A naive approach is to search for a plan that achieves the main goal, which easily becomes troublesome, since the planner needs to consider all possibilities to find a plan that guarantees finding the person. Alternatively, a reactive policy can be described for the agent (e.g., "move to the farthest visible point") that determines its course of actions and guides the agent in the environment towards the main goal, while the agent gains information

---

This work has been supported by Austrian Science Fund (FWF) project W1255-N23.

L. Michael and A. Kakas (Eds.): JELIA 2016, LNAI 10021, pp. 463–480, 2016.
DOI: 10.1007/978-3-319-48758-8_30

(e.g., obstacle locations) through its sensors on the way. Then, one can check whether this policy works or not. Verifying beforehand whether the designed policy satisfies the desired goal (e.g., can the agent always find the person?), in all possible instances of the environment is nontrivial.

As action languages [18] are a convenient tool to describe dynamic systems, one can use them in representing reactive agents and defining reactive policies. However, the shortage of representations of reactive policies using action languages with formal semantics prevents us from verifying such policies before putting them into use. We thus aim for a general model that allows for verifying the reactive behavior of agents. In that model, we want to use the representation power of the transition systems described by action languages and combine components that are efficient for describing reactivity.

We consider in this paper agents with a reactive behavior that decide their course of actions by determining targets as stepping stones to achieve during their interaction with the environment. Such agents come with an (online) planning capability that computes plans to reach the targets. This method matches the observe-think-act cycle in [20], but involves a planner that considers targets. The flexibility in the two components—target development and external planning—allows for a range of possibilities for designing behaviors. For example, one can use HEX [15] to describe a program that determines a target given the current agent state, and finds a suitable plan and execution schedule. ACTHEX programs [17], in particular, are a tool to define such reactive behaviors by allowing iterative program evaluation. Specifically, we make the following contributions:

(1) We introduce a novel framework for describing the semantics of a policy that follows a reactive behavior, by integrating components of target establishment and online planning. Our aim is not synthesis, but to lay foundations for verification of behaviors of (human-designed) reactive policies. The outsourced planning might also lend itself for modular, hierarchic planning, where macro actions (as targets) are turned into a plan of micro actions. Furthermore, outsourced planning may also be exploited to abstract from correct sub-behaviors (e.g., going always to the farthest point).

(2) We employ the notion of indistinguishable states and cluster states to reduce the large state spaces by omitting information irrelevant to the agent's behavior.

(3) We discuss complexity issues regarding the representation and show that verifying policy correctness over this framework is in PSPACE (with matching hardness instances).

(4) We connect the framework with action languages and discuss possibilities for policy formulation. In particular, we consider the action language C [19] for an application.

We proceed as follows. After some preliminaries in Sect. 2, we present a running example in Sect. 3. In Section 4, we introduce the general framework for modeling policies. Then, in Sect. 5, we show the relation with action languages. After some discussion and considering related work in Sect. 6, we conclude in Sect. 7

with issues for ongoing and future work. Throughout the paper, we consider (a fragment of) the action language $\mathcal{C}$ as a particular application, and provide example formulations.

2 Preliminaries

We define state transition systems as follows.

Definition 1. An *(original) transition system* is a tuple $\mathcal{T} = \langle S, S_0, \mathcal{A}, \Phi \rangle$ where

- S is the finite set of states,
- $S_0 \subseteq S$ is the (finite) set of possible initial states,
- $\mathcal{A}$ is the finite set of possible actions, and
- $\Phi : S \times \mathcal{A} \to 2^S$ is the transition function, which returns the set of possible successor states after applying a possible action in the current state.

For any states $s, s' \in S$, we say that there is a *trajectory* between s and s', denoted by $s \to^\sigma s'$ for some action sequence $\sigma = \langle a_1, \ldots, a_n \rangle$ where $n \geq 0$, if there exist $s_0, \ldots, s_n \in S$ such that $s = s_0, s' = s_n$ and $s_{i+1} \in \Phi(s_i, a_{i+1})$ for all $0 \leq i < n$.

If knowing the actions taken in the transitions is not necessary, then one can *project away* the actions and consider the transition function as $\Phi : S \to 2^S$, which returns the set of successor states after applying some action.

Action Languages. Rooted in the work in knowledge representation, action languages [18] describe a particular type of transition systems that are based on action signatures. An *action signature* consists of a set $\mathbf{V}$ of value names, a set $\mathbf{F}$ of fluent names and a set $\mathbf{A}$ of action names. Any *fluent* has a *value* in any *state of the world*.

A transition system of an action signature $\langle \mathbf{V}, \mathbf{F}, \mathbf{A} \rangle$ is similar to Definition 1, where $\mathcal{A} = \mathbf{A}$ and $\Phi \subseteq S \times \mathbf{A} \times S$ is the transition relation. In addition, we have a value function $V : \mathbf{F} \times S \to \mathbf{V}$, where $V(P, s)$ shows the *value of P in state s*. A transition system can be thought as a labeled directed graph, where a state s is represented by a vertex labeled with $P \to V(P, s)$, that gives the value of the fluents. Every triple $\langle s, a, s' \rangle \in \Phi$ is represented by an edge leading from a state s to s' and labeled by a.

An action a is *executable* at a state s, if there is at least one state s' such that $\langle s, a, s' \rangle \in R$ and a is *deterministic* at state s, if there is at most one such state. Concurrent execution of actions can be defined by considering transitions $\langle s, A, s' \rangle$ with a set $A \subseteq \mathbf{A}$ of actions, where each action $a \in A$ is executable at s. Here we confine to *propositional* action signatures, which have truth values as value names, $\mathbf{V} = \{\mathsf{f}, \mathsf{t}\}$.

The transition system allows one to answer queries about the domain description. For example, one can find a plan to reach a goal state from an initial state, by searching for a path between the respective vertices. The properties about the paths can be expressed using an action query language.

The action language $\mathcal{C}$ [19] is based on *causality*, where one distinguishes the cases that a fact "holds" and that it is "caused". Its syntax consists of static and dynamic laws of the form

caused F **if** G,
caused F **if** G **after** U

respectively, where F and G are formulas of fluents, and U is a formula containing fluents and elementary actions. For details, see [18,19]. We focus on a fragment of the language $\mathcal{C}$ where the heads of the static and dynamic laws only consist of literals. This restriction on the laws reduces the cost of evaluating the transitions to polynomial time.

3 Running Example: Search Scenarios

Consider a memoryless agent that can sense horizontally and vertically, in an unknown $n \times n$ grid cell environment with obstacles, where a missing person needs to be found. Suppose we are given a policy of "always go to the farthest reachable point in visible distance (until a person is found)". Following this policy, the agent would determine a *target* (i.e., the farthest point) at its current state, compute the course of actions to reach the target, execute it and observe the outcomes.

Target determination at the states according to the given policy can be done using a logic program as shown below.

$$
\begin{aligned}
targetCell(X1, Y1) &\leftarrow farthest(X, Y, X1, Y1), robotAt(X, Y), \\
&\qquad\qquad\qquad\qquad\qquad\qquad not\; personDetected. \\
personDetected &\leftarrow personDetected(X, Y). \\
targetPerson(X, Y) &\leftarrow personDetected(X, Y). \\
personFound &\leftarrow personDetected(X, Y), robotAt(X, Y).
\end{aligned}
\tag{1}
$$

The target of a state can be computed through joint evaluation of these rules over the state with the *known/observed* fluents about the agent's location and the reachable points. The target can either be moving to the farthest cell, $targetCell(X1, Y1)$, if the person is not detected, or moving to the cell of the person, $targetPerson(X, Y)$, if the person is detected. Then, an outsourced planner can be used to determine the course of actions from the agent's current location to the target location.

Given such a policy, it needs to be checked whether or not the agent can always find the person, in all instances of the environment. Note that we assume that the obstacles are always placed in a way that the person is reachable.

Figures 1(a) to (c) show some instances for $n = 3$ to demonstrate that the given policy might not always work. Firstly, notice that these initial states provide the same observations for the agent, which is shown in Fig. 1(d), since it can only observe horizontally and vertically. In these states, the agent only sees that the first column is clear of obstacles, and the first row has one obstacle. Since the

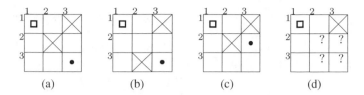

Fig. 1. (a)–(c): Possible instances of a search scenario in a grid-cell environment, (d): Agent's observation in the instances, □:agent, •:person, ×:obstacle, ?:unknown

rest of the environment can not be observed, these states are *indistinguishable* to the agent.

The farthest reachable point in these states is (3,1), which is determined as the target. Then the policy computes the course of actions to reach this target. Clearly, in Fig. 1(a) the person will be found when moved to (3,1). However, in Fig. 1(b) after reaching (3,1), the agent/policy will decide to move to (1,1) again, which results in a loop. Also, in Fig. 1(c), after reaching (3,1), the agent/policy can either choose to move to (3,3) (which results in seeing the person), or to move back to (1,1). So there is a possibility for the agent to go in a loop. Hence, the policy does not work for the last two instances.

4   Modeling Policies in Transition Systems

We consider a general notion of a policy, that guides the agent by setting up targets and determining the course of actions to bring about these targets, and describe how such a policy can be represented with transition systems.

Definition 2. A *policy* is a function $\mathcal{P}_{g_\infty,KB} : S \rightarrow 2^\Sigma$ that outputs the set of courses of actions, i.e., plans, given the current state, where Σ is the set of plans, while considering the main goal and the knowledge base, which is the formal representation of the world's model with a transition system view.

We define a transition system that shows the policy execution, while also employing the notion of *indistinguishability* to do state clustering. The determination of targets for a given state is done by a *target component*, while the (higher level) transition between states is determined by the course of actions computed by a *(online) planner component*.

Having a classification on states and defining higher level transitions helps in reducing the state space/the number of transitions. Furthermore, it aids in abstraction and allows one to emulate a modular hierarchic approach, in which a higher level (macro) action, expressed by a target, is realized by a sequence of (micro) actions that is compiled by the external planner, which may use different ways (planning on the fly, using scripts etc.)

4.1   State Profiles According to the Policy

Large state spaces are a major issue for the (original) transition system when dealing with large environments. However, depending on the agent's designed behavior, and its determination of its course of actions at a state, some information in the state may not be necessary, relevant or even observable. In this sense, the states that contain different facts about such information can be seen as *indistinguishable* to the agent. Such indistinguishable states can be clustered into one with respect to the *profiles* they provide and only the relevant information to the agent/policy can be kept.

Definition 3. A *profile scheme* is a tuple $p = \langle a_1, .., a_n \rangle$ of attributes a_i that can take values from a set V_i; a *(concrete) profile* is a tuple $\langle v_1, ..., v_n \rangle$ of values.

Note that the agent has the capability to gain knowledge, and this knowledge can eventually become relevant to the policy. So it would be useful to keep such potentially relevant knowledge in the states to pass on to the successor states even though this knowledge might not be currently relevant to the policy. Therefore the profile scheme consists of all attributes that may be relevant to the policy. A profile at a state consists of values of attributes that are partitioned as *currently relevant, irrelevant* and *not yet observed*, depending on the observability of the environment and the policy. Currently relevant attributes at a state can be regarded as the *active profile*.

Example 1. Reconsider Fig. 1. Due to partial observability, the agent is unable to distinguish its state, and the policy does not consider the unobservable parts. The agent's observation, "*robotAt*(1, 1), *obstacleAt*(1, 3), *reachable*(1, 2), *reachable*(2, 1), *reachable*(3, 1)" that is *currently relevant* and the rest of the environment that is *not yet observed*, is viewed as a profile, and the states with this profile can be clustered in one group (Fig. 1(d)).

The profile of a state is determined by evaluating a set of formulas that yield the attribute values. We consider a *classification function*, $h : S \rightarrow \Omega_h$, where Ω_h is the set of possible state clusters with respect to the profiles. For partially observable environments, same observations yield the same profile. However, in fully observable environments, observability is not of concern. One needs to check the policy to determine profiles.

Definition 4. An *equalized state* relative to the classification function h is a state $\hat{s} \in \Omega_h$.

The term *equalized* comes from the fact that the states in the same cluster are considered as the same, i.e., equal. We abuse the notation $s \in \hat{s}$ when talking about a state s that is clustered into an equalized state $\hat{s}$, and identify $\hat{s}$ with its pre-image (i.e., the set of states that are mapped to $\hat{s}$ according to h).

4.2   Transition Systems According to the Policy

We now define the notion of a transition system that is able to represent the evaluation of the policy on the state clusters.

Given a set of equalized states $\widehat{S}$, for an equalized state $\hat{s} \in \widehat{S}$, the policy $P_{g_\infty, KB}$ uses a *target function* $\mathcal{B}(\hat{s})$ to determine a target g_B from a *set of possible* targets, G_B, and then an *outsourced planner* $Reach(\hat{s}, g_B)$ to compute a plan to reach the target from the current equalized state, i.e., $P_{g_\infty, KB}(\hat{s}) = \{\sigma \mid \sigma \in Reach(\hat{s}, g_B), g_B \in \mathcal{B}(\hat{s})\}$.

Definition 5. *Reach* is an outsourced function that returns a set of plans needed to reach a state that meets the target condition g_B from the current equalized state $\hat{s} \in \widehat{S}$:

$$Reach(\hat{s}, g_B) \subseteq \{\sigma \mid \forall \hat{s}' \in Res(\hat{s}, \sigma) : \hat{s}' \models g_B\}$$

where $\hat{s} \models g_B \Leftrightarrow \forall s \in \hat{s} : s \models g_B$, and *Res* gives the resulting states of executing a sequence of actions at a state $\hat{s}$: $Res(\hat{s}, \langle\rangle) = \{\hat{s}\}$, and

$$Res(\hat{s}, \langle a_1, \ldots, a_n \rangle) = \begin{cases} \bigcup_{\hat{s}' \in \hat{\Phi}(\hat{s}, a_1)} Res(\hat{s}', \langle a_2, \ldots, a_n \rangle) & \hat{\Phi}(\hat{s}, a_1) \neq \emptyset \\ \{\hat{s}_{err}\} & \hat{\Phi}(\hat{s}, a_1) = \emptyset \end{cases}$$

for $n \geq 1$. Here $\hat{s}_{err}$ is an artifact state that does not satisfy any target, and $\hat{\Phi}$ is a transition relation of executing an action at a state $\hat{s}$:

$$\hat{\Phi}(\hat{s}, a) = \{\hat{s}' \mid \exists s' \in \hat{s}' \ \exists s \in \hat{s} : s' \in \Phi(s, a)\}.$$

The transition system that represents the policy evaluation is defined over the original transition system by taking into account the classification function and the policy.

Definition 6. An *equalized (higher level) transition system* $\mathcal{T}_{h, P_{g_\infty, KB}}$, with respect to the classification function h and the policy $P_{g_\infty, KB}$, is defined as $\mathcal{T}_{h, P_{g_\infty, KB}} = \langle \widehat{S}, \widehat{S}_0, \Sigma, G_B, \mathcal{B}, \Phi_B \rangle$, where

- $\widehat{S}$ is the finite set of equalized states;
- $\widehat{S}_0 \subseteq \widehat{S}$ is the finite set of initial equalized states, where $\hat{s} \in \widehat{S}_0$ if there is some $s_i \in \hat{s}$ such that $s_i \in S_0$ holds;
- Σ is the set of possible plans $\sigma = \langle a_1, a_2, \ldots, a_n \rangle$ where $a_i \in \mathcal{A}$, for all $i, 1 \leq i \leq n$.
- G_B is the finite set of possible *targets* relative to the behavior, where a target can be satisfied by more than one equalized state;
- $\mathcal{B} : \widehat{S} \to 2^{G_B}$, is the *target function* that returns the possible targets to achieve from the current equalized state, according to the policy;
- $\Phi_B : \widehat{S} \times \Sigma \to 2^{\widehat{S}}$ is the transition function according to the policy, called the *policy execution function*, where

$$\Phi_B(\hat{s}, \sigma) = \{\hat{s}' \mid \hat{s}' \in Res(\hat{s}, \sigma), \sigma \in Reach(\hat{s}, g_B), g_B \in \mathcal{B}(\hat{s})\};$$

it returns the possible resulting equalized states after applying the plan determined by the policy in the current equalized state.

The target function gets the equalized state as input and produces the possible targets to achieve. These targets may be expressed as formulas over the states

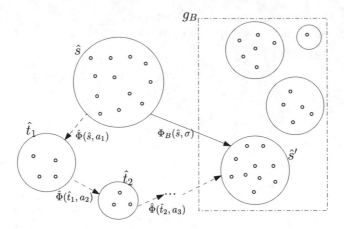

Fig. 2. A transition in the equalized transition system

(in particular, of states that are represented by fluents or state variables), or in some other representation. The aim is to intend to reach a state that satisfies the conditions of the target.

The equalized transition system $\langle \widehat{S}, \widehat{S}_0, \Sigma, \Phi_B \rangle$ can be viewed as a transition system $\langle S, S_0, \mathcal{A}, \Phi \rangle$ with an infinite set of actions. Additionally, it contains auxiliary definitions $\langle G_B, \mathcal{B} \rangle$ that are used in defining the policy.

Figure 2 demonstrates a transition in the equalized transition system. Depending on the current state, $\hat{s}$, a plan σ can be executed if it is returned by *Reach* to reach the target g_B that is determined by the policy. There may be more than one equalized state satisfying g_B, and the policy execution function $\Phi_B(\hat{s}, \sigma)$ executes σ and finds a transition into one of these states, $\hat{s}'$. In our case, the actions taken in the transitions are not of concern. Therefore, we project away the knowledge of the executed action sequences, and only consider $\Phi_B : \widehat{S} \rightarrow 2^{\widehat{S}}$. Thus, the transition Φ_B becomes a big jump between states, where the actions taken and the states passed in between are omitted.

Example 2. Figure 3 shows a part of the equalized transition system constructed according to the policy. The indistinguishable states due to partial observability are clustered into one. The policy is applied according to current observations, and the possible successor states are shown. The policy is targeting the farthest reachable point, which for $\hat{s}_1$ is (3,1). Since the agent gains knowledge about the environment while moving, there are several possibilities for the resulting state that satisfy the target $g_B = robotAt(3,1)$.

Notice that we assume that the outsourced *Reach* function is able to return conformant plans that guarantee to reach a state that satisfies the determined targets. For practical reasons, we consider *Reach* to be able to return a subset of all conformant plans. The maximal possible *Reach*, where we have equality, is denoted with $Reach_0$.

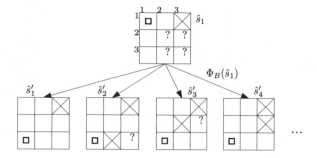

Fig. 3. Parts of an equalized transition system

Consider the case of uncertainty, where the agent requires to do some action, e.g., *checkDoor*, to gain further knowledge about its state. The target function can be modified to return dummy fluents as targets to ensure that the action is made, e.g., *doorIsChecked*, and given this target, the *Reach* function can return the desired action as the plan. The nondeterminism of the environment is modeled through the possible outcomes of *Res*.

Our generic definition allows for the possibility of representing well-known concepts like purely reactive systems or conformant planning. Reactive systems can be represented with the policy "pick some action", which models systems that immediately react to the environment without reasoning. As for conformant planning, one can set the target as the main goal. Then, *Reach* would have the difficult task of finding a plan that guarantees reaching the main goal. If however, such a plan is available, then we have the following.

Proposition 1. *Let $P = \langle a_1, \ldots, a_n \rangle$, $n \geq 1$, be a conformant plan that reaches a goal state g from the initial states $s_{01}, \ldots, s_{0r}$ in the original transition system. The plan P can be polynomially expressed in an equalized transition system.*

Proof (Sketch). One can mimic the plan by modifying the targets G_B and the target function B in a way that at each point in time the next action in the plan is returned by *Reach*, and the corresponding transition is made. For that, one needs to record information in the states and keep track of the targets. ⊓⊔

4.3   Complexity Issues

As the function *Reach* is outsourced, we rely on an implementation that returns conformant plans to achieve transitions in the equalized transition systems. This raises the issue whether a given such implementation is suitable, and leads to the question of soundness (only correct plans are output) and completeness (some plan will be output, if one exists). We next assess how expensive it is to test this, under some assumptions about the representation and computational properties of (equalized) transition systems, which will then also be used for assessing the cost of policy checking.

Assumptions. We assume that given a state $s \in S$ which is implicitly given using a binary encoding, the cost of evaluating the classification $h(s)$, the (original) transition $\Phi(s, a)$ for some action a, and recognizing the initial state, say with $\Phi_{init}(s)$, is polynomial. The cost could also be in NP, if projective (i.e., existentially quantified) variables are allowed. Furthermore, we assume that the size of the representation of a "target" in G_B is polynomial in size of the state, so that given a string, one can check in polynomial time if it is a correct target description g_B. This test can also be relaxed to be in NP by allowing projective variables.

Given these assumptions, we have the following two results on the cost of checking whether a given implementation of *Reach* is sound and complete; we assume here that testing whether $\sigma \in Reach(\hat{s}, g_B)$ is feasible in Π_2^p (i.e., it is no worse than a naive guess and check algorithm that verifies conformant plans).

Theorem 1 (Soundness of *Reach***).** *Let* $T_h = \langle \widehat{S}, \widehat{S}_0, G_B, \mathcal{B}, \Phi_\mathcal{B} \rangle$ *be a transition system w.r.t. a classification function* h. *Checking whether every transition found by the policy execution function* $\Phi_\mathcal{B}$ *induced by a given implementation Reach is correct is in* Π_3^p.

The result for soundness of *Reach*[1] is complemented with another result for completeness with respect to short (polynomial size) conformant plans that it returns.

Theorem 2 (Completeness of *Reach***).** *Let* $T_h = \langle \widehat{S}, \widehat{S}_0, G_B, \mathcal{B}, \Phi_\mathcal{B} \rangle$ *be a transition system w.r.t. a classification function* h. *Deciding whether for a given implementation Reach,* Φ_B *fulfills* $\hat{s}' \in \Phi_B(\hat{s})$ *whenever a short conformant plan from* $\hat{s}$ *to some* $g_B \in \mathcal{B}(\hat{s})$ *exists and* $\hat{s}'$ *is the resulting state after the execution of the plan in* T_h, *is in* Π_4^p.

The complexities drop if checking the output of *Reach* is lower (e.g., it drops to Π_2^p for soundness and to Π_3^p for completeness, if output checking is in co-NP).

Throughout the paper we assume that *Reach* is complete. We also restrict the plans σ that are returned by *Reach* to have polynomial size. This constraint would not allow for exponentially long conformant plans (even if they exist). Thus, the agent is forced to develop targets that it can reach in polynomially many steps. Informally, this does not limit the capability of the agent in general. The "long" conformant plans can be split into short plans with a modified policy and by encoding specific targets into the states, such that at each state, one chooses the next action with respect to the conformant plan. The targets can be encoded to give the stage of the plan execution so that the respective action is taken, or they can be encoded to assign the latest action in the conformant plan that is done from the current state.

The main goal that the policy is aiming for, denoted by g_∞, can be expressed as a formula that should be satisfied at a state. Note that the policy could be easily modified to stop or to loop in any state $\hat{s}$ that satisfies the goal.

---

[1] Proof sketches of this and further results are in the extended version at http://goo.gl/FXktqP.

Definition 7. The policy *works* w.r.t. the main goal g_∞, if for each run $\hat{s}_0, \hat{s}_1, \ldots$ such that $\hat{s}_0 \in \widehat{S}_0$ and $\hat{s}_{i+1} \in \Phi_B(\hat{s}_i)$, for all $i \geq 0$, there is some $j \geq 0$ such that $\hat{s}_j \models g_\infty$.

One can also make use of temporal operators, and define g_∞ by a temporal formula (e.g., $\mathbf{AF}(personFound)$) and then check whether the initial states in $\widehat{S}_0$ satisfy the formula.

Under the assumptions from above, we obtain the following.

Theorem 3. *The problem of determining whether the policy works is in* PSPACE.

In the proof of Theorem 3, for a counterexample, a run of at most exponential length from some initial state in which the main goal is not satisfied can be nondeterministically built in polynomial space.

Note that in this formulation, we have tacitly assumed that the main goal can be established in the original system, thus at least some trajectory from some initial state to a state fulfilling the goal exists. In a more refined version, we could define the working of a policy relative to the fact that some abstract plan would exist that makes g_∞ true; naturally, this may impact the complexity of the policy checking.

The results in Theorems 1–3 are all complemented by lower bounds for realistic parameter instantiations (notably, for action languages such as fragments of $\mathcal{C}$).

4.4   Constraining Equalization

The definition of $\hat{\Phi}$ allows for certain transitions that do not have corresponding concrete transitions in the original transition system. However, the aim of defining such an equalized transition system is not to introduce new features, but to keep the structure of the original transition system and discard the unnecessary parts with respect to the policy. Therefore, one needs to give further restrictions on the transitions.

Let us consider the following condition.

$$\hat{s}' \in \hat{\Phi}(\hat{s}, a) \Leftrightarrow \forall s' \in \hat{s}', \ \exists s \in \hat{s} : \ s' \in \Phi(s, a) \tag{2}$$

This condition ensures that a transition between two states $\hat{s}_1, \hat{s}_2$ in the equalized transition system represents that any state in $\hat{s}_2$ has a transition from some state in $\hat{s}_1$. An equalization is called *proper* if condition (2) is satisfied.

Theorem 4. *Let* $\mathcal{T}_h = \langle \widehat{S}, \widehat{S}_0, G_B, \mathcal{B}, \Phi_{\mathcal{B}} \rangle$ *be a transition system w.r.t. a classification function* h. *Let* $\hat{\Phi}$ *be the transition function that the policy execution function* $\Phi_{\mathcal{B}}$ *is based on. The problem of checking whether* $\hat{\Phi}$ *is proper is in* Π_2^p.

This result is also complemented by a lower bound similar to the results in Theorems 1–3.

The following proposition shows that the policy execution function is sound.

Proposition 2 (Soundness). *Let* $\mathcal{T}_h = \langle \widehat{S}, \widehat{S}_0, G_B, \mathcal{B}, \Phi_\mathcal{B} \rangle$ *be a transition system w.r.t. a classification function* h. *Let* $\hat{s}_1, \hat{s}_2 \in \widehat{S}$ *be equalized states that are reachable[2] from some initial states, and* $\hat{s}_2 \in \Phi_\mathcal{B}(\hat{s}_1)$. *For any concrete state* $s_2 \in \hat{s}_2$, *assuming* (2), *there is a concrete state* $s_1 \in \hat{s}_1$ *such that* $s_1 \to^\sigma s_2$ *for some action sequence* σ, *in* $\mathcal{T}$.

Proof of Proposition 2 is based on the possibility of backwards tracking with any of the plans σ executed to reach $\hat{s}_2$ from $\hat{s}_1$.

Thus, we obtain the following corollary, with the requirement of only having initial states clustered into the equalized initial states (i.e., no "non-initial" state is mapped to an initial equalized state). Technically, it should hold that $\forall s \in S_0 : h^{-1}(h(s)) \subseteq S_0$.

Corollary 1. *If there is a trajectory in the equalized transition system with initial state clustering from an equalized initial state* $\hat{s}_0$ *to* g_∞, *then for any* $g \in g_\infty$ *a trajectory can be found in the original transition system from some concrete initial state* $s_0 \in \hat{s}_0$.

Our aim is to analyze the reactive policy through the equalized transition system. If the policy does not work as expected, there will be trajectories showing the failure. Knowing that any such trajectory found in the equalized transition system exists in the original transition system is enough to conclude that the policy indeed does not work.

Current assumptions can not avoid the case where a plan σ returned by *Reach* on the equalized transition system does not have a corresponding trajectory from some initial state in the original transition system. Therefore, we consider as an additional condition

$$\hat{s}' \in \hat{\Phi}(\hat{s}, a) \Leftrightarrow \forall s \in \hat{s}, \, \exists s' \in \hat{s}' : s' \in \Phi(s, a) \tag{3}$$

that strengthens the properness condition (2). Under this condition, every plan returned by *Reach* can be successfully executed from any initial state in the original transition system $\mathcal{T}$. However, still we may lose trajectories of $\mathcal{T}$ as clustering the states might restrain conformant plans; for this, also stronger conditions like exact approximation [8], $\hat{s}' \in \hat{\Phi}(\hat{s}, a) \Leftrightarrow \forall s \in \hat{s}, \, \forall s' \in \hat{s}' : s' \in \Phi(s, a)$, is not enough. One would need to modify the target determination, i.e., the set of targets G_B and the function $\mathcal{B}$.

5   Bridging to Action Languages

We now describe how our representation of the behavior of the policy can fit into action languages. Given a domain description defined by an action language and its respective (original) transition system, we now show how to model a reactive policy and how to construct the corresponding equalized transition system.

---

[2] For a formal definition of reachability, see the extended version at http://goo.gl/FXktqP.

Classifying the State Space. The approach to classify the (original) state space relies on defining a function that classifies the states. There are at least two kinds of such classification; one can classify the states depending on the observed values of the fluents, or introduce a new set of fluents and classify the states depending on their values:

Type 1: Extend the set of truth values by $\mathbf{V'} = \mathbf{V} \cup \{u\}$, where u denotes the value to be *unknown*. Consider an *observability relation* $\mathcal{O} : \mathbf{F} \times S \to \mathbf{V'}$ which returns how the fluents' values are observed at the states. Then, consider a set of clusters, $\widehat{S}$, where a cluster $\hat{s}_i \in \widehat{S}$ contains all the states $s \in S$ that have the same observed values, i.e., $\widehat{S} = \{ \hat{s} \mid \forall d, e \in S,\ d, e \in \hat{s} \iff \forall p \in \mathbf{F} : \mathcal{O}(p,d)=\mathcal{O}(p,e) \}$. The value function for the clusters is $\widehat{V} : \mathbf{F} \times \widehat{S} \to \mathbf{V'}$.

Type 2: Consider a set of (auxiliary) fluent names $\mathbf{F}_a$, where each fluent $p \in \mathbf{F}_a$ is *related* with some fluents of $\mathbf{F}$. The relation can be shown with a mapping $\Delta : 2^{\mathbf{F} \times \mathbf{V}} \to \mathbf{F}_a \times \mathbf{V}$. Then, consider a new set of clusters, $\widehat{S}$, where a cluster $\hat{s}_i \in \widehat{S}$ contains all the states $s \in S$ that give the same values for all $p \in \mathbf{F}_a$, i.e., $\widehat{S} = \{ \hat{s} \mid \forall d, e \in S,\ d, e \in \hat{s} \iff \forall p \in \mathbf{F}_a : V(p,d)=V(p,e) \}$. The value function for the clusters is $\widehat{V} : \mathbf{F}_a \times \widehat{S} \to \mathbf{V}$.

We can consider the states in the same classification to have the same *profile*, and the classification function h as a membership function that assigns the states into groups.

Remarks.

(1) In Type 1, introducing the value *unknown* allows for describing sensing actions and knowing a fluent's true value later. Also, one needs to impose constraints; e.g., a fluent related to a grid cell can not be unknown while the robot can observe it.

(2) In Type 2, one needs to modify the action descriptions according to the newly defined fluents and define *abstract actions*. However, this is not necessary in Type 1, assuming that the action descriptions only use fluents that have *known* values.

Example 3. In $\mathcal{C}$, we introduce unknown values by auxiliary fluents as follows.

caused $uReachable(X,Y)$ **if** *not* $reachable(X,Y) \land$ *not* $\neg reachable(X,Y)$.

i.e. if it is not known that a grid cell is reachable or not, then the fluent *uReachable* becomes true. Additional rules are added to express that it becomes false otherwise.

Defining a Target Language. A policy is defined through a *target language* which figures out the targets and helps in determining the course of actions. The target determination formulas, denoted as a set of formulas $\mathcal{F}_\mathcal{B}(\widehat{\mathbf{F}})$, is constructed over $\widehat{\mathbf{F}}$, the set of fluents that the equalized transition system is built upon. The possible targets that can be determined via the evaluation of $\mathcal{F}_\mathcal{B}(\widehat{\mathbf{F}})$ are denoted as a set $\mathcal{F}_{G_B}(\widehat{\mathbf{F}})$.

Example 4. $\mathcal{F}_{\mathcal{B}}(\widehat{\mathbf{F}})$ corresponds to the set of causal laws in (1) and $\mathcal{F}_{G_B}(\widehat{\mathbf{F}})$ consists of all atoms $targetCell(X, Y)$ and $targetPerson(X, Y)$ for $1 \leq X \leq n, 1 \leq Y \leq n$.

Notice that the separation of formulas $\mathcal{F}_{\mathcal{B}}(\widehat{\mathbf{F}})$ and the targets $\mathcal{F}_{G_B}(\widehat{\mathbf{F}})$ is to allow for outsourced planners that understand simple target formulas. These planners need no knowledge to find plans. However, if one is able to use planners that are powerful enough, then the target language can be given as input to the planner, so that the planner determines the target and finds the corresponding plan.

Transition Between States. The transitions in the (projected) equalized transition system can be denoted with $\widehat{R} \subseteq \widehat{S} \times \widehat{S}$, where $\widehat{R}$ corresponds to the projection of the policy execution function Φ_B that uses (a) the target language to determine targets, (b) an outsourced planner (corresponding to the function *Reach*) to find conformant plans and (c) the computation of executing the plans (corresponding to the function *Res*). Thus, $\widehat{R}$ shows the resulting states after applying the policy.

Equalized Transition System over Action Language $\mathcal{C}$. The equalized transition system $\langle \widehat{S}, \widehat{V}, \widehat{R} \rangle$ that describes a policy is defined as follows:

(i) $\widehat{S}$ is the set of all interpretations of $\widehat{\mathbf{F}}$ such that, $\hat{s}$ satisfies every static law in $\mathcal{F}_{\mathcal{B}}(\widehat{\mathbf{F}})$.

(ii) $\widehat{V}(P, \hat{s}) = \hat{s}(P)$, where $P \in \widehat{\mathbf{F}}$,

(iii) $\widehat{R} \subseteq \widehat{S} \times \widehat{S}$ is the set of all $\langle \hat{s}, \hat{s}' \rangle$ such that
   (a) for every $s' \in \hat{s}'$ there is a trajectory from some $s \in \hat{s}$ of the form $s, A_1, s_1, \ldots, A_n, s'$ in the original transition system;
   (b) for static laws $f_1, f_2, \ldots, f_m \in \mathcal{F}_{\mathcal{B}}(\widehat{\mathbf{F}})$ for which $\hat{s}$ satisfies the body, it holds that $\hat{s}' \models g$ for some $g \in \mathcal{M}(f_1, \ldots, f_m)$, where $\mathcal{M}$ is a mapping $\mathcal{M} : 2^{\mathcal{F}_{\mathcal{B}}(\widehat{\mathbf{F}})} \to 2^{\mathcal{F}_{G_B}(\widehat{\mathbf{F}})}$, that gives the relation between the formulas and the targets.

Notice that $\widehat{R}$ in (iii) has no prescription of (a) how a trajectory is computed or (b) how a target is determined. This makes the implementation of these components flexible.

By focusing on a fragment of $\mathcal{C}$, we match the above conditions on complexity. Furthermore, by well-known results on the complexity of action language $\mathcal{C}$ [14, 27], the results in Theorems 1–4 can be turned into completeness results already for this fragment. Other languages can be similarly used to describe the equalized transition system, as long as they are powerful enough to express the concepts in the previous section.

6   Discussion

The notions of profiles and state clustering help in reducing the state space by omitting irrelevant information. This also comes in handy when dealing with partial observability, since it omits the unobservable information that is irrelevant to the policy.

In the equalized transition system, the trajectories from the initial states correspond to the policy execution, where one can check and verify properties of the policy. The properness condition ensures that any counterexample found in the equalized transition system stating a failure of the policy has a concrete trajectory in the original transition system. This way, the shortcomings of the policy can be detected, and thus improved.

For target language definitions, we can use other formalisms with different expressiveness capabilities, e.g., answer set programming. Target descriptions can be made more complex by considering formulas. In particular, target formulas with disjunctions would express nondeterminism in the environment that affects the target determination. Handling this within the framework requires further study.

It is also possible to use other plans, e.g., short conditional plans, in the planner component. Furthermore, this component can be extended by considering a plan library of precomputed plans. This offline planning component can provide the frequently used plans and reduce the calls to the online planner.

6.1   Related Work

There are works being conducted on the verification of GOLOG programs [22], a family of high-level action programming languages defined on top of action theories expressed in the situation calculus. The method of verifying properties of non-terminal processes are sound, but incomplete as the verification problem is undecidable [9,11]. By resorting to action formalisms based on description logic, decidability can be achieved [1].

Verifying temporal properties of dynamic systems in the context of data management is studied by [5] for description logic knowledge bases. However, target establishment and planning components, and real-life environment settings are not considered.

The BDI model [24] is based on beliefs, desires and intentions, in which agents are viewed as being rational and acting in accordance with their beliefs and goals. There are many different agent programming languages and platforms based on it. Some works considered verifying properties of agents represented in these languages [4,12]. These approaches consider very complex architectures that even contain a plan library where plans are matched with the intentions or the agent's state and manipulate the intentions. Verification for such complex BDI architecture gets very challenging.

Verification of multi-agent systems with specifications defined in the epistemic logic is studied by [23], while our focus is on single agents with target determination and planning components which help in reasoning about the behavior of the agent in the environment.

Synthesizing and Verifying Plans. Synthesizing plans via symbolic model checking techniques was considered, e.g., in [3,6,7]. The approaches could solve difficult planning problems like strong planning and strong cyclic planning. Son and Baral [25] extend the action language $\mathcal{A}$ by allowing sensing actions and allow to query conditional plans. The latter are general plans that consist of sensing actions and conditional statements. They also consider a "combined-state" which consists of the real state of the world and the states that the agent thinks it may be in, while we combine the real states into one state if they provide the same profile for the agent. The equalization of states allows for omitting the details that are irrelevant to the behavior of the agent.

These works address a different problem than ours. Under nondeterminism and partial observability, finding a plan that satisfies the desired results in the environment is highly demanding. Our framework is capable of emulating the plans found by these works, and verifying policies relates to an intertwined plan generation and checking task.

Verifying whether a given plan is a solution to a planning problem considering knowledge-based programs as plans [21] or HTN plans [2] has been studied, while the policies that we focus on are more enriched, making use of target determination and outsourced planning.

Execution Monitoring. There are logic-based monitoring frameworks for plan execution and recovery in case of failure. Some of the approaches are replanning [10], backtracking to the point of failure and continuing from there [26], or diagnosing the failure and recovering from the failure situation [13,16]. These works consider the execution of a given plan, while we consider a given reactive policy that determines targets and uses (online) planning to reach them.

7   Conclusion and Future Work

In this paper, we described a high-level representation that models reactive behaviors, and integrates target development and online planning capabilities. Flexibility in these components does not bound one to only use action languages, but allows for the use of other formalizations as well. For future work, one could imagine targets to depend on further parameters or to incorporate learning from experience in the framework. Furthermore, to instantiate the framework for a range of action languages besides $\mathcal{C}$.

The long-term goal of this work is to check and verify properties of the reactive policies for action languages. In order to solve these problems practically, it is necessary to use techniques from model checking, such as abstraction, compositional reasoning and parameterization. Also, the use of temporal logic formulas is needed to express complex goals such as properties of the policies. Our main target is to work with action languages, and to incorporate their syntax and semantics with such model checking techniques. The general structure of our framework allows one to focus on action languages, and to investigate how to merge these techniques.

References

1. Baader, F., Zarrieß, B.: Verification of Golog programs over description logic actions. In: Fontaine, P., Ringeissen, C., Schmidt, R.A. (eds.) FroCoS 2013. LNCS, vol. 8152, pp. 181–196. Springer, Heidelberg (2013). doi:10.1007/978-3-642-40885-4_12

2. Behnke, G., Höller, D., Biundo, S.: On the complexity of htn plan verification and its implications for plan recognition. In: Proceedings of ICAPS, pp. 25–33 (2015)

3. Bertoli, P., Cimatti, A., Riveri, M., Traverso, P.: Strong planning under partial observability. Artif. Intell. **170**(4), 337–384 (2006)

4. Bordini, R.H., Fisher, M., Visser, W., Wooldridge, M.: Verifying multi-agent programs by model checking. Auton. Agents Multi-agent Syst. **12**(2), 239–256 (2006)

5. Calvanese, D., De Giacomo, G., Montali, M., Patrizi, F.: Verification and synthesis in description logic based dynamic systems. In: Faber, W., Lembo, D. (eds.) RR 2013. LNCS, vol. 7994, pp. 50–64. Springer, Heidelberg (2013). doi:10.1007/978-3-642-39666-3_5

6. Cimatti, A., Riveri, M., Traverso, P.: Automatic OBDD-based generation of universal plans in non-deterministic domains. In: Proceedings of AAAI/IAAI, pp. 875–881 (1998)

7. Cimatti, A., Riveri, M., Traverso, P.: Strong planning in non-deterministic domains via model checking. AIPS **98**, 36–43 (1998)

8. Clarke, E.M., Grumberg, O., Long, D.E.: Model checking and abstraction. ACM Trans. Program. Lang. Syst. (TOPLAS) **16**(5), 1512–1542 (1994)

9. Claßen, J., Lakemeyer, G.: A logic for non-terminating Golog programs. In: Proceedings of KR, pp. 589–599 (2008)

10. De Giacomo, G., Reiter, R., Soutchanski, M.: Execution monitoring of high-level robot programs. In: Proceedings of KR, pp. 453–465 (1998)

11. De Giacomo, G., Ternovskaia, E., Reiter, R.: Non-terminating processes in the situation calculus. In: Working Notes of Robots, Softbots, Immobots: Theories of Action, Planning and Control, AAAI 1997 Workshop (1997)

12. Dennis, L.A., Fisher, M., Webster, M.P., Bordini, R.H.: Model checking agent programming languages. Autom. Softw. Eng. **19**(1), 5–63 (2012)

13. Eiter, T., Erdem, E., Faber, W., Senko, J.: A logic-based approach to finding explanations for discrepancies in optimistic plan execution. Fundamenta Informaticae **79**(1–2), 25–69 (2007)

14. Eiter, T., Faber, W., Leone, N., Pfeifer, G., Polleres, A.: A logic programming approach to knowledge-state planning: semantics and complexity. ACM Trans. Comput. Log. **5**(2), 206–263 (2004). http://doi.acm.org/10.1145/976706.976708

15. Eiter, T., Ianni, G., Schindlauer, R., Tompits, H.: A uniform integration of higher-order reasoning and external evaluations in answer-set programming. In: Proceedings of IJCAI, pp. 90–96 (2005)

16. Fichtner, M., Großmann, A., Thielscher, M.: Intelligent execution monitoring in dynamic environments. Fundamenta Informaticae **57**(2–4), 371–392 (2003)

17. Fink, M., Germano, S., Ianni, G., Redl, C., Schüller, P.: ActHEX: implementing HEX programs with action atoms. In: Cabalar, P., Son, T.C. (eds.) LPNMR 2013. LNCS, vol. 8148, pp. 317–322. Springer, Heidelberg (2013). doi:10.1007/978-3-642-40564-8_31

18. Gelfond, M., Lifschitz, V.: Action languages. Electron. Trans. AI **3**(16), 193–210 (1998)

19. Giunchiglia, E., Lifschitz, V.: An action language based on causal explanation: Preliminary report. In: Proceedings of AAAI/IAAI, pp. 623–630 (1998)
20. Kowalski, R.A., Sadri, F.: From logic programming towards multi-agent systems. Ann. Math. Artif. Intell. **25**(3–4), 391–419 (1999). http://dx.doi.org/10.1023/A:1018934223383
21. Lang, J., Zanuttini, B.: Knowledge-based programs as plans - the complexity of plan verification. In: Proceedings of ECAI, pp. 504–509 (2012)
22. Levesque, H.J., Reiter, R., Lesperance, Y., Lin, F., Scherl, R.B.: GOLOG: a logic programming language for dynamic domains. J. Log. Program. **31**(1), 59–83 (1997)
23. Lomuscio, A., Michliszyn, J.: Verification of multi-agent systems via predicate abstraction against ATLK specifications. In: Proceedings of AAMAS, pp. 662–670 (2016)
24. Rao, A.S., Georgeff, M.P.: Modeling rational agents within a BDI-architecture. In: Proceedings of KR, pp. 473–484 (1991)
25. Son, T.C., Baral, C.: Formalizing sensing actions - a transition function based approach. Artif. Intell. **125**(1), 19–91 (2001)
26. Soutchanski, M.: High-level robot programming and program execution. In: Proceedings of ICAPS Workshop on Plan Execution (2003)
27. Turner, H.: Polynomial-length planning spans the polynomial hierarchy. In: Flesca, S., Greco, S., Leone, N., Ianni, G. (eds.) JELIA 2002. LNCS (LNAI), vol. 2424, pp. 111–124. Springer, Heidelberg (2002). doi:10.1007/3-540-45757-7_10

Correct Grounded Reasoning
with Presumptive Arguments

Bart Verheij[✉]

Artificial Intelligence, University of Groningen, Groningen, The Netherlands
Bart.Verheij@rug.nl

Abstract. We address the semantics and normative questions for reasoning with presumptive arguments: How are presumptive arguments grounded in interpretations; and when are they evaluated as correct? For deductive and uncertain reasoning, classical logic and probability theory provide canonical answers to these questions. Staying formally close to these, we propose case models and their preferences as formal semantics for the interpretation of presumptive arguments. Arguments are evaluated as presumptively valid when they make a case that is maximally preferred. By qualitative and quantitative representation results, we show formal relations between deductive, uncertain and presumptive reasoning. In this way, the work is a step to the connection of logical and probabilistic approaches in AI.

1 Introduction

There is a growing and productive research community in artificial intelligence focusing on argumentation. Some use artificial intelligence tools to study natural argumentation, others focus on computational properties, and there is work on formal foundations [12]. The present paper considers the formal foundations of argumentation, interpreted as reasoning with presumptive, possibly defeasible arguments. Studying the formal foundations of argumentation can help answering two questions:

1. **The semantics question.** How are presumptive arguments grounded in interpretations? This question is about *grounded argumentation*.
2. **The normative question.** When are presumptive arguments evaluated as correct? This question is about *correct argumentation*.

For deductive and uncertain reasoning, canonical answers to these questions exist. For deductive reasoning, arguments are interpreted in logical models (question 1), and logical validity characterizes correct deductive reasoning, such as formal proof (question 2). Uncertain reasoning is interpreted in probability distributions, and the probability calculus characterizes correct uncertain reasoning, such as Bayesian updating.

For reasoning with presumptive arguments, the answers to the two questions are less well-developed. In today's state of the art, a key role is played by Dung's

© Springer International Publishing AG 2016
L. Michael and A. Kakas (Eds.): JELIA 2016, LNAI 10021, pp. 481–496, 2016.
DOI: 10.1007/978-3-319-48758-8_31

ground-breaking work on abstract argumentation [11]. One can say that Dung's work provides an answer to the semantics question 1 by interpreting argument attack in directed graphs, and to the normative question 2 by formalizing an argumentative winning criterion in terms of argument admissibility. We distinguish two complications.

One complication is that these answers depend on the choice of one of the available abstract argumentation semantics. Dung himself suggested several extension types as interpretations of directed graphs (the grounded, complete, preferred, stable extensions; each based on the important notion of admissible set), and the number of proposals expanded quickly thereafter (see the review [3]).

A second complication is that these answers focus on argument attack, abstracting from argument support. Extending to include argument support has led to a variety of approaches, some referred to as structured argumentation. A recent special issue of the journal 'Argument and Computation' [5] usefully explains how four leading models connect in different ways to Dung's semantics: ABA [8], ASPIC+ [22], DeLP [13], deductive argumentation [6].

We propose case models and their preferences as a formal semantics used for the interpretation of presumptive arguments (answering question 1), and evaluate arguments as acceptable when they make a case that is maximally preferred (answering question 2). The proposed formalism is designed in close connection with classical logic and probability theory, in order to show formal relations between deductive, uncertain and presumptive reasoning. The formalism presented builds on an existing line of research [29–32]. [29,30] study formal connections between arguments, logic and probabilities, but do not provide a model-theoretic semantics as we do here. The case model semantics presented here formalizes ideas semi-formally presented in [31], which in turn is inspired by issues arising when modeling argument-based and scenario-based evidential reasoning about crimes using Bayesian networks [32] (cf. the discussion in Sect. 4).

2   General Idea

The argumentation theory developed in this paper considers arguments that can be presumptive (also called ampliative), in the sense of logically going beyond their premises. Against the background of classical logic, an argument from premises P to conclusions Q goes beyond its premises when Q is not logically implied by P. Many arguments used in practice are presumptive. For instance, the prosecution may argue that a suspect was at the crime scene on the basis of a witness testimony. The fact that the witness has testified as such does not logically imply the fact that the suspect was at the crime scene. In particular, when the witness testimony is intentionally false, based on inaccurate observations or inaccurately remembered, the suspect may not have been at the crime scene at all. Denoting the witness testimony by P and the suspect being at the crime scene as Q, the argument from P to Q is presumptive since P does not logically imply Q. For presumptive arguments, it is helpful to consider the *case made by*

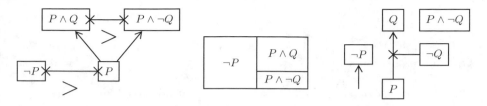

Fig. 1. Arguments and cases

the argument, defined as the conjunction of the premises and conclusions of the argument [28,29]. The case made by the argument from P to Q is $P \wedge Q$, using the conjunction of classical logic. An example of a non-presumptive argument goes from $P \wedge Q$ to Q. Here Q is logically implied by $P \wedge Q$. Presumptive arguments are often defeasible [20,27], in the sense that extending the premises may lead to the retraction of conclusions.

Figure 1 shows (on the left) two presumptive arguments from the same premises P. They make cases that are conflicting: one supports the case $P \wedge Q$, the other the case $P \wedge \neg Q$. The $>$-sign indicates that one argument makes a stronger case than the other, resolving the conflict: the argument for the case $P \wedge Q$ is stronger than that for $P \wedge \neg Q$. The figure also shows two assumptions P and $\neg P$, that can be considered as arguments from logically tautologous premises. Here the assumption $\neg P$ makes the strongest case when compared to the assumption P. Logically such assumptions can be treated as arguments from logical truth $\top$. In the figure on the right one sees which conclusions follow presumptively from which premises: $\neg P$ follows as an assumption, and Q follows from P. $\neg Q$ blocks the inference from P to Q. From premises $P \wedge \neg Q$ no further conclusions follow. The arguments make three cases: $\neg P$, $P \wedge Q$ and $P \wedge \neg Q$ (Fig. 1; middle). Their sizes suggest a preference relation.

The comparison of arguments and of cases are closely related in our approach, which can be illustrated as follows. The idea is that a case is preferred to another case if there is an argument with premises that supports the former case more strongly than the latter case. Hence, in the example in the figures, $\neg P$ is preferred to both $P \wedge Q$ and $P \wedge \neg Q$, and $P \wedge Q$ is preferred to $P \wedge \neg Q$. Conversely, given the cases and their preferences, we can compare arguments. The argument from P to Q is stronger than from P to Q' when the best case that can be made from $P \wedge Q$ is preferred to the best case that can be made from $P \wedge Q'$.

3   Formalism and Properties

We now formalize case models and how they can be used to interpret arguments (Sect. 3.1). Then follow qualitative and quantitative representation results (Sects. 3.2 and 3.3).

3.1   Case Models and Arguments

The formalism uses a classical logical language L generated from a set of propositional constants in a standard way. We write $\neg$ for negation, $\wedge$ for conjunction, $\vee$ for disjunction, $\leftrightarrow$ for equivalence, $\top$ for a tautology, and $\bot$ for a contradiction. The associated classical, deductive, monotonic consequence relation is denoted $\models$. We assume a finitely generated language.

First we define case models, formalizing the idea of cases and their preferences. The cases in a case model must be logically consistent, mutually incompatible and different; and the comparison relation must be total and transitive (hence is what is called a total preorder, commonly modeling preference relations [23]).

Definition 1. *A case model is a pair* $(C, \geq)$ *with finite* $C \subseteq L$, *such that the following hold, for all* φ, ψ *and* $\chi \in C$:

1. $\not\models \neg\varphi$;
2. *If* $\not\models \varphi \leftrightarrow \psi$, *then* $\models \neg(\varphi \wedge \psi)$;
3. *If* $\models \varphi \leftrightarrow \psi$, *then* $\varphi = \psi$;
4. $\varphi \geq \psi$ *or* $\psi \geq \varphi$;
5. *If* $\varphi \geq \psi$ *and* $\psi \geq \chi$, *then* $\varphi \geq \chi$.

The strict weak order $>$ standardly associated with a total preorder $\geq$ is defined as $\varphi > \psi$ if and only if it is not the case that $\psi \geq \varphi$ (for φ and $\psi \in C$). When $\varphi > \psi$, we say that φ is (strictly) preferred to ψ. The associated equivalence relation $\sim$ is defined as $\varphi \sim \psi$ if and only if $\varphi \geq \psi$ and $\psi \geq \varphi$.

Example. Figure 1 shows a case model with cases $\neg P$, $P \wedge Q$ and $P \wedge \neg Q$. $\neg P$ is (strictly) preferred to $P \wedge Q$, which in turn is preferred to $P \wedge \neg Q$.

Next we define arguments from premises $\varphi \in L$ to conclusions $\psi \in L$.

Definition 2. *An argument is a pair* (φ, ψ) *with* φ *and* $\psi \in L$. *The sentence* φ *expresses the argument's premises, the sentence* ψ *its conclusions, and the sentence* $\varphi \wedge \psi$ *the case made by the argument. Generalizing, a sentence* $\chi \in L$ *is a* premise *of the argument when* $\varphi \models \chi$, *a* conclusion *when* $\psi \models \chi$, *and a* position *in the case made by the argument when* $\varphi \wedge \psi \models \chi$. *An argument* (φ, ψ) *is* (properly) presumptive *when* $\varphi \not\models \psi$; *otherwise* non-presumptive. *An argument* (φ, ψ) *is an* assumption *when* $\models \varphi$, *i.e., when its premises are logically tautologous.*

Note our use of the plural for an argument's premises, conclusions and positions. This terminological convention allows us to speak of the premises p and $\neg$q and conclusions r and $\neg$s of the argument (p $\wedge$ $\neg$q, r $\wedge$ $\neg$s). Also the convention fits our non-syntactic definitions, where for instance an argument with premise χ also has logically equivalent sentences such as $\neg\neg\chi$ as a premise.

Coherent arguments are defined as arguments that make a case that is logically implied by a case in the case model.

Definition 3. *Let* $(C, \geq)$ *be a case model. Then we define, for all* φ *and* $\psi \in L$:

$$(C, \geq) \models (\varphi, \psi) \text{ if and only if } \exists \omega \in C: \omega \models \varphi \wedge \psi.$$

We then say that the argument from φ *to* ψ *is* coherent *with respect to the case model. We define, for all* φ *and* $\psi \in L$:

$$(C, \geq) \models \varphi \Rightarrow \psi \text{ if and only if } \exists \omega \in C: \omega \models \varphi \wedge \psi \text{ and } \forall \omega \in C: \text{ if } \omega \models \varphi, \text{ then } \omega \models \varphi \wedge \psi.$$

We then say that the argument from φ *to* ψ *is* conclusive *with respect to the case model.*

Example (continued). In the case model of Fig. 1, the arguments from $\top$ to $\neg P$ and to P, and from P to Q and to $\neg Q$ are coherent and not conclusive in the sense of this definition. Denoting the case model as $(C, \geq)$, we have $(C, \geq) \models (\top, \neg P)$, $(C, \geq) \models (\top, P)$, $(C, \geq) \models (P, Q)$ and $(C, \geq) \models (P, \neg Q)$. The arguments from a case (in the case model) to itself, such as from $\neg P$ to $\neg P$, or from $P \wedge Q$ to $P \wedge Q$ are conclusive. The argument $(P \vee R, P)$ is also conclusive in this case model, since all $P \vee R$-cases are P-cases. Similarly, $(P \vee R, P \vee S)$ is conclusive.

The notion of presumptive validity considered here is based on the idea that some arguments make a better case than other arguments from the same premises. More precisely, an argument is presumptively valid if there is a case implying the case made by the argument that is at least as preferred as all cases implying the premises.

Definition 4. *Let* $(C, \geq)$ *be a case model. Then we define, for all* φ *and* $\psi \in L$:

$(C, \geq) \models \varphi \rightsquigarrow \psi$ *if and only if* $\exists \omega \in C$:
1. $\omega \models \varphi \wedge \psi$; *and*
2. $\forall \omega' \in C: \text{ if } \omega' \models \varphi, \text{ then } \omega \geq \omega'.$

We then say that the argument from φ *to* ψ *is* (presumptively) valid *with respect to the case model. A presumptively valid argument is* defeasible, *when it is not conclusive.*

Circumstances χ *are* defeating *when* $(\varphi \wedge \chi, \psi)$ *is not presumptively valid. Defeating circumstances are* rebutting *when* $(\varphi \wedge \chi, \neg\psi)$ *is presumptively valid; otherwise they are* undercutting. *Defeating circumstances are* excluding *when* $(\varphi \wedge \chi, \psi)$ *is not coherent.*

Example (continued). In the case model of Fig. 1, the arguments from $\top$ to $\neg P$, and from P to Q are presumptively valid in the sense of this definition. Denoting the case model as $(C, \geq)$, we have formally that $(C, \geq) \models \top \rightsquigarrow \neg P$ and $(C, \geq) \models P \rightsquigarrow Q$. The coherent arguments from $\top$ to P and from P to $\neg Q$ are not presumptively valid in this sense.

Example. Arguments typically consist of multiple steps. Figure 2 shows a two step argument on the left. The first step is from P to Q, the second from Q to R. Both steps have defeating circumstances: the first $\neg Q$, the second $\neg R$.

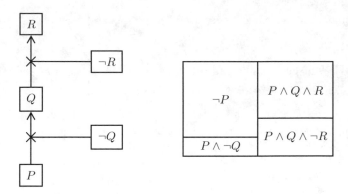

Fig. 2. An argument with two steps, each with exceptions

In the case model shown, Q follows presumptively from P since $P \wedge Q \wedge R$ is a (here: the) preferred case given P. From Q follows R. $\neg Q$ is defeating for the former presumptive inference, since there is no preferred case of $P \wedge \neg Q$ in which R holds. (That preferred case is $P \wedge \neg Q$.) $\neg R$ is a defeater for the second presumptive inference. Formally, we have:

$$(C, \geq) \models P \rightsquigarrow Q \qquad\qquad (C, \geq) \not\models P \wedge \neg Q \rightsquigarrow Q$$
$$(C, \geq) \models Q \rightsquigarrow R \qquad\qquad (C, \geq) \not\models Q \wedge \neg R \rightsquigarrow R$$

Note that in the case model also the following hold:

$$(C, \geq) \models P \rightsquigarrow Q \wedge R \qquad\qquad (C, \geq) \models Q \Rightarrow P$$
$$(C, \geq) \models R \Rightarrow P \wedge Q \qquad\qquad (C, \geq) \models R \Rightarrow Q$$
$$(C, \geq) \models \top \rightsquigarrow \neg P$$

The following properties follow directly from the definitions. Conclusive arguments are coherent, but there are case models with a coherent, yet inconclusive argument. Conclusive arguments are presumptively valid, but there are case models with a presumptively valid, yet inconclusive argument. Presumptively valid arguments are coherent, but there are case models with a coherent, yet presumptively invalid argument. The next proposition provides key logical properties of this notion of presumptive validity. Many have been studied for nonmonotonic inference relations [4,16,18]. Given a case model $(C, \geq)$, we write $\varphi \hspace{1pt}\vdash\hspace{-6pt}\sim \psi$ for $(C, \geq) \models \varphi \rightsquigarrow \psi$. We write $C(\varphi)$ for the set $\{\omega \in C \mid \omega \models \varphi\}$.

(LE), for Logical Equivalence, expresses that in a valid argument the premises and the conclusions can be replaced by a logical equivalent (in the sense of $\models$). (Cons), for Consistency, expresses that the conclusions of presumptively valid arguments must be logically consistent. (Ant), for Antededence, expresses that when certain premises validly imply a conclusion, the case made by the argument is also validly implied by these premises. (RW), for Right Weakening, expresses that when the premises validly imply a composite conclusion also the intermediate conclusions are validly implied. (CCM), for Conjunctive Cautious Monotony, expresses that the case made by a valid argument is still validly implied when an intermediate conclusion is added to the argument's premises. (CCT), for Conjunctive Cumulative Transitivity, is a variation of the related property Cumulative Transitivity property (CT, also known as Cut). (CT)—extensively studied in the literature—has $\varphi \mathrel{|\!\sim} \chi$ instead of $\varphi \mathrel{|\!\sim} \psi \wedge \chi$ as a consequent. The variation is essential in our setting where the (And) property does not hold generally (If $\varphi \mathrel{|\!\sim} \psi$ and $\varphi \mathrel{|\!\sim} \chi$, then $\varphi \mathrel{|\!\sim} \psi \wedge \chi$). Assuming (Ant), (CCT) expresses the validity of chaining valid implication from φ via the case made in the first step $\varphi \wedge \psi$ to the case made in the second step $\varphi \wedge \psi \wedge \chi$. (See [28,29], introducing (CCT).)

Proposition 5. *Let $(C, \geq)$ be a case model. For all φ, ψ and $\chi \in L$:*

(LE)   If $\varphi \mathrel{|\!\sim} \psi$, $\models \varphi \leftrightarrow \varphi'$ and $\models \psi \leftrightarrow \psi'$, then $\varphi' \mathrel{|\!\sim} \psi'$.
(Cons) $\varphi \mathrel{|\!\not\sim} \bot$.
(Ant)   If $\varphi \mathrel{|\!\sim} \psi$, then $\varphi \mathrel{|\!\sim} \varphi \wedge \psi$.
(RW)   If $\varphi \mathrel{|\!\sim} \psi \wedge \chi$, then $\varphi \mathrel{|\!\sim} \psi$.
(CCM) If $\varphi \mathrel{|\!\sim} \psi \wedge \chi$, then $\varphi \wedge \psi \mathrel{|\!\sim} \chi$.
(CCT) If $\varphi \mathrel{|\!\sim} \psi$ and $\varphi \wedge \psi \mathrel{|\!\sim} \chi$, then $\varphi \mathrel{|\!\sim} \psi \wedge \chi$.

Proof. (LE): Direct from the definition. (Cons): Otherwise there would be an inconsistent element of C, contradicting the definition of a case model. (Ant): When $\varphi \mathrel{|\!\sim} \psi$, there is an ω with $\omega \models \varphi \wedge \psi$ that is $\geq$-maximal in $C(\varphi)$. Then also $\omega \models \varphi \wedge \varphi \wedge \psi$, hence $\varphi \mathrel{|\!\sim} \varphi \wedge \psi$. (RW): When $\varphi \mathrel{|\!\sim} \psi \wedge \chi$, there is an $\omega \in C$ with $\omega \models \varphi \wedge \psi \wedge \chi$ that is maximal in $C(\varphi)$. Since then also $\omega \models \varphi \wedge \psi$, we find $\varphi \mathrel{|\!\sim} \psi$. (CCM): By the assumption, we have an $\omega \in C$ with $\omega \models \varphi \wedge \psi \wedge \chi$ that is maximal in $C(\varphi)$. Since $C(\varphi \wedge \psi) \subseteq C(\varphi)$, ω is also maximal in $C(\varphi \wedge \psi)$, and we find $\varphi \wedge \psi \mathrel{|\!\sim} \chi$. (CCT): Assuming $\varphi \mathrel{|\!\sim} \psi$, there is an $\omega \in C$ with $\omega \models \varphi \wedge \psi$, maximal in $C(\varphi)$. Assuming also $\varphi \wedge \psi \mathrel{|\!\sim} \chi$, there is an $\omega' \in C$ with $\omega \models \varphi \wedge \psi \wedge \chi$, maximal in $C(\varphi \wedge \psi)$. Since $\omega \in C(\varphi \wedge \psi)$, we find $\omega' \geq \omega$. By transitivity of $\geq$, and the maximality of ω in $C(\varphi)$, we therefore have that ω' is maximal in $C(\varphi)$. As a result, $\varphi \mathrel{|\!\sim} \psi \wedge \chi$.   □

We speak of *coherent premises* when the argument from the premises to themselves is coherent. The following proposition provides some equivalent characterizations of coherent premises.

Proposition 6. *Let $(C, \geq)$ be a case model. The following are equivalent, for all $\varphi \in L$:*

1. *$\varphi \mathrel{|\!\sim} \varphi$;*
2. *$\exists \omega \in C : \omega \models \varphi$ and $\forall \omega' \in C$: If $\omega' \models \varphi$, then $\omega \geq \omega'$;*
3. *$\exists \omega \in C : \varphi \mathrel{|\!\sim} \omega$.*
4. *$\exists \omega \in C : \omega \models \varphi$.*

Proof. 1 and 2 are equivalent by the definition of $\mid\!\sim$. Assume 2. Then there is a $\geq$-maximal element ω of $C(\varphi)$. By the definition of $\mid\!\sim$, then $\varphi \mid\!\sim \omega$; proving 3. Assume 3. Then there is a $\geq$-maximal element ω' of $C(\varphi)$ with $\omega' \models \varphi \wedge \omega$. For this ω' also $\omega' \models \varphi$, showing 2. 4 logically follows from 2. Assume 4. Hence $C(\varphi)$ is a finite, non-empty set, and 2 follows. $\qquad \square$

Hence coherent and presumptively valid arguments have coherent premises. The next corollary shows that logical generalisations of coherent premises are coherent.

Corollary 7. *Let $(C, \geq)$ be a case model. Then:*

If $\varphi \mid\!\sim \varphi$ and $\varphi \models \psi$, then $\psi \mid\!\sim \psi$.

In the representation result of the next subsection, additional properties are needed. We use the set of case expressions $L^* \subseteq L$ consisting of the logical combinations of the cases of the case model using negation, conjunction and logical equivalence (cf. the algebra underlying probability functions [23]).

(Coh), for Coherence, expresses that coherent premises correspond to a consistent case expression implying the premises. (Ch), for Choice, expresses that, given two coherent case expressions, at least one of three options follows validly: the conjunction of the case expression, or the conjunction of one of them with the negation of the other. (OC), for Ordered Choice, expresses that preferred choices between case expressions are transitive. Here we say that a case expression is a *preferred choice* over another, when the former follows validly from the disjunction of both. A *preferred case* given certain premises is a case that presumptively follows from those premises.

Proposition 8. *Let $(C, \geq)$ be a case model, and $L^* \subseteq L$ the closure of C under negation, conjunction and logical equivalence. Writing $\mid\!\sim^*$ for the restriction of $\mid\!\sim$ to L^*, we have, for all φ, ψ and $\chi \in L^*$:*

(Coh)   *$\varphi \mid\!\sim \varphi$ if and only if $\exists \varphi^* \in L^*$ with $\varphi^* \not\models \bot$ and $\varphi^* \models \varphi$;*
(Ch)   *If $\varphi \mid\!\sim^* \varphi$ and $\psi \mid\!\sim^* \psi$, then $\varphi \vee \psi \mid\!\sim^* \neg \varphi \wedge \psi$ or*
           $\varphi \vee \psi \mid\!\sim^* \varphi \wedge \psi$ or $\varphi \vee \psi \mid\!\sim^* \varphi \wedge \neg\psi$;
(OC)   *If $\varphi \vee \psi \mid\!\sim^* \varphi$ and $\psi \vee \chi \mid\!\sim^* \psi$, then $\varphi \vee \chi \mid\!\sim^* \varphi$.*

Proof. (Coh): By Proposition 6, $\varphi \mid\!\sim \varphi$ if and only if there is an $\omega \in C$ with $\omega \models \varphi$. The property (Coh) follows since $C \subseteq L^*$ and, for all consistent $\varphi^* \in L^*$, there is an $\omega \in C$ with $\omega \models \varphi^*$.

(Ch): Consider sentences φ and $\psi \in L^*$ with $\varphi \mid\!\sim^* \varphi$ and $\psi \mid\!\sim^* \psi$. Then, by Corollary 7, $\varphi \vee \psi \mid\!\sim \varphi \vee \psi$. By Proposition 6, there is an $\omega \in C$, with $\omega \models \varphi \vee \psi$. The sentences φ and ψ are elements of L^*, hence also the sentences $\varphi \wedge \neg\psi$, $\varphi \wedge \psi$ and $\neg\varphi \wedge \psi \in L^*$. All are logically equivalent to disjunctions of elements of C (possibly the empty disjunction, logically equivalent to $\bot$). Since $\omega \models \varphi \vee \psi$, $\models \varphi \vee \psi \leftrightarrow (\varphi \wedge \neg\psi) \vee (\varphi \wedge \psi) \vee (\neg\varphi \wedge \psi)$, and the elements of C are mutually incompatible, we have $\omega \models \varphi \wedge \neg\psi$ or $\omega \models \varphi \wedge \psi$ or $\omega \models \neg\varphi \wedge \psi$. By Proposition 6, it follows that $\varphi \vee \psi \mid\!\sim^* \neg\varphi \wedge \psi$ or $\varphi \vee \psi \mid\!\sim^* \varphi \wedge \psi$ or $\varphi \vee \psi \mid\!\sim^* \varphi \wedge \neg\psi$.

(OC): By $\varphi \vee \psi \mathrel{\vmid\hspace{-0.3em}\sim}^* \varphi$, there is an $\omega \models \varphi$ maximal in $C(\varphi \vee \psi)$. By $\psi \vee \chi \mathrel{\vmid\hspace{-0.3em}\sim}^* \psi$, there is an $\omega' \models \psi$ maximal in $C(\psi \vee \chi)$. Since $\omega \models \varphi$, $\omega \in C(\varphi \vee \chi)$. Since $\omega' \models \psi$, $\omega' \in C(\varphi \vee \psi)$, hence $\omega \geq \omega'$. Hence ω is maximal in $C(\varphi \vee \chi)$, hence $\varphi \vee \chi \mathrel{\vmid\hspace{-0.3em}\sim} \varphi$. Since $\chi \in L^*$, $\varphi \vee \chi \mathrel{\vmid\hspace{-0.3em}\sim}^* \varphi$.   □

3.2   Representation Results (Qualitative)

In this section, we show that an inference relation with the properties listed in the Propositions 5 and 8 can be represented by the presumptively valid arguments of a case model. The cases of the representing case model are the extensions of the inference relation, i.e., those valid consequences that are logically maximally specific:

Definition 9. *Let* $\mathrel{\vmid\hspace{-0.3em}\sim} \subseteq L \times L$, *and* φ *and* $\omega \in L$. *Then* ω *expresses an* extension *of* φ *when:*

1. $\varphi \mathrel{\vmid\hspace{-0.3em}\sim} \omega$; and
2. $\omega \models \varphi$; and
3. For all $\psi \in L$, if $\varphi \mathrel{\vmid\hspace{-0.3em}\sim} \psi$ and $\psi \models \omega$, then $\omega \models \psi$.

Proposition 10. *Let* $\mathrel{\vmid\hspace{-0.3em}\sim} \subseteq L \times L$ *have the property (Ant) (as in Proposition 5). Then, for all $\varphi \in L$, if $\varphi \mathrel{\vmid\hspace{-0.3em}\sim} \varphi$, there is an $\omega \in L$ that expresses an extension of φ.*

Proof. Consider the set of sentences $S = \{\psi \mid \varphi \mathrel{\vmid\hspace{-0.3em}\sim} \psi\}$ and pick a sentence $\omega \in S$ that is logically maximally specific. Such a sentence exists since S is not empty (as $\varphi \in S$) and L is assumed to be generated by finitely many propositional constants, hence has a finite number of logical equivalence classes. We show that ω is an extension of φ (Definition 9): (i) $\varphi \mathrel{\vmid\hspace{-0.3em}\sim} \omega$ since $\omega \in S$. (ii) By (Ant), $\varphi \mathrel{\vmid\hspace{-0.3em}\sim} \varphi \wedge \omega$; hence $\varphi \wedge \omega \in S$. Since ω is maximally specific in S, it follows that $\omega \models \varphi$. (iii) Consider $\psi \in L$ for which $\varphi \mathrel{\vmid\hspace{-0.3em}\sim} \psi$ and $\psi \models \omega$. Then $\psi \in S$. Since ω is maximally specific in S, $\omega \models \psi$.   □

We define the counterpart of the logical algebra L^* used in Proposition 8.

Definition 11. *Let* $\mathrel{\vmid\hspace{-0.3em}\sim} \subseteq L \times L$ *with the property (Ant) (as in Proposition 5), and $C \subseteq L$ the set of sentences expressing extensions. Then L^* denotes the closure of C under negation, conjunction and logical equivalence, and $\mathrel{\vmid\hspace{-0.3em}\sim}^*$ the restriction of $\mathrel{\vmid\hspace{-0.3em}\sim}$ to L^*.*

We can now formulate the representation theorem.

Theorem 12. *Let* $\mathrel{\vmid\hspace{-0.3em}\sim} \subseteq L \times L$ *have the following properties:*

(LE)   If $\varphi \mathrel{\vmid\hspace{-0.3em}\sim} \psi$, $\models \varphi \leftrightarrow \varphi'$ and $\models \psi \leftrightarrow \psi'$, then $\varphi' \mathrel{\vmid\hspace{-0.3em}\sim} \psi'$;
(Cons) $\varphi \mathrel{\not\vmid\hspace{-0.3em}\sim} \bot$;
(Ant)   If $\varphi \mathrel{\vmid\hspace{-0.3em}\sim} \psi$, then $\varphi \mathrel{\vmid\hspace{-0.3em}\sim} \varphi \wedge \psi$;
(RW)   If $\varphi \mathrel{\vmid\hspace{-0.3em}\sim} \psi \wedge \chi$, then $\varphi \mathrel{\vmid\hspace{-0.3em}\sim} \psi$;
(CCM) If $\varphi \mathrel{\vmid\hspace{-0.3em}\sim} \psi \wedge \chi$, then $\varphi \wedge \psi \mathrel{\vmid\hspace{-0.3em}\sim} \chi$;
(CCT) If $\varphi \mathrel{\vmid\hspace{-0.3em}\sim} \psi$ and $\varphi \wedge \psi \mathrel{\vmid\hspace{-0.3em}\sim} \chi$, then $\varphi \mathrel{\vmid\hspace{-0.3em}\sim} \psi \wedge \chi$;

(Coh) $\varphi \mathrel{\vert\!\sim} \varphi$ if and only if $\exists \varphi^* \in L^*$ with $\varphi^* \not\models \bot$ and $\varphi^* \models \varphi$;

(Ch)   If $\varphi \mathrel{\vert\!\sim^*} \varphi$ and $\psi \mathrel{\vert\!\sim^*} \psi$, then $\varphi \vee \psi \mathrel{\vert\!\sim^*} \neg\varphi \wedge \psi$ or
$\varphi \vee \psi \mathrel{\vert\!\sim^*} \varphi \wedge \psi$ or $\varphi \vee \psi \mathrel{\vert\!\sim^*} \varphi \wedge \neg\psi$;

(OC)   If $\varphi \vee \psi \mathrel{\vert\!\sim^*} \varphi$ and $\psi \vee \chi \mathrel{\vert\!\sim^*} \psi$, then $\varphi \vee \chi \mathrel{\vert\!\sim^*} \varphi$.

Then there is a case model $(C, \geq)$ with the property:

$\varphi \mathrel{\vert\!\sim} \psi$ if and only if $(C, \geq) \models \varphi \rightsquigarrow \psi$.

Proof. Given $\mathrel{\vert\!\sim}$ with the properties mentioned, we consider the set of all extension expressions $E := \{\omega \in L \mid \exists \varphi \in L : \omega$ expresses an extension of $\varphi\}$. Let C be a set containing one element for each logical equivalence class in E. For ω and $\omega' \in C$, define $\omega \geq \omega' := \omega \vee \omega' \mathrel{\vert\!\sim} \omega$. We show that the pair $(C, \geq)$ is a case model with the property of the theorem.

(i) $(C, \geq)$ *is a case model.*
We check the properties of the definition of a case model. 1. Let $\varphi \in C$. Then $\varphi \mathrel{\vert\!\sim} \varphi$. If $\models \neg\varphi$, by (LE) and (RW), $\varphi \mathrel{\vert\!\sim} \bot$, contradicting (Cons).

2 & 3. Consider φ and $\psi \in C$. Then $\varphi \mathrel{\vert\!\sim^*} \varphi$ and $\psi \mathrel{\vert\!\sim^*} \psi$. By (Ch), $\varphi \vee \psi \mathrel{\vert\!\sim^*} \neg\varphi \wedge \psi$ or $\varphi \vee \psi \mathrel{\vert\!\sim^*} \varphi \wedge \psi$ or $\varphi \vee \psi \mathrel{\vert\!\sim^*} \varphi \wedge \neg\psi$. Since φ and ψ are extensions, when $\varphi \vee \psi \mathrel{\vert\!\sim^*} \neg\varphi \wedge \psi$, $\varphi \models \neg\varphi$. When $\varphi \vee \psi \mathrel{\vert\!\sim^*} \varphi \wedge \psi$, $\varphi \models \psi$ and $\psi \models \varphi$, so $\varphi = \psi$. When $\varphi \vee \psi \mathrel{\vert\!\sim^*} \varphi \wedge \neg\psi$, $\psi \models \neg\varphi$.

4. Consider φ and $\psi \in C$. By (Ch), we have three cases: When $\varphi \vee \psi \mathrel{\vert\!\sim^*} \neg\varphi \wedge \psi$, by (RW): $\varphi \vee \psi \mathrel{\vert\!\sim^*} \psi$, i.e., $\psi \geq \varphi$. When $\varphi \vee \psi \mathrel{\vert\!\sim^*} \varphi \wedge \psi$, by (RW): $\varphi \vee \psi \mathrel{\vert\!\sim^*} \varphi$, i.e., $\varphi \geq \psi$ (and in this case also $\psi \geq \varphi$). When $\varphi \vee \psi \mathrel{\vert\!\sim^*} \varphi \wedge \neg\psi$, by (RW): $\varphi \vee \psi \mathrel{\vert\!\sim^*} \psi$, i.e., $\varphi \geq \psi$.

5. Consider φ, ψ and $\chi \in C$. Assume $\varphi \geq \psi$ and $\psi \geq \chi$. In other words, by the definitions, $\varphi \vee \psi \mathrel{\vert\!\sim^*} \varphi$ and $\psi \vee \chi \mathrel{\vert\!\sim^*} \psi$. Then (OC) gives $\varphi \vee \chi \mathrel{\vert\!\sim^*} \varphi$, i.e., $\varphi \geq \chi$.

(ii)   If $\varphi \mathrel{\vert\!\sim} \psi$, then $(C, \geq) \models \varphi \rightsquigarrow \psi$.
Assume $\varphi \mathrel{\vert\!\sim} \psi$. Then, by (Ant), $\varphi \mathrel{\vert\!\sim} \varphi \wedge \psi$. By (CCM), $\varphi \wedge \psi \mathrel{\vert\!\sim} \varphi \wedge \psi$. By Proposition 10, there is an $\omega \in C$ that is an extension of $\varphi \wedge \psi$. In particular, $\omega \models \varphi \wedge \psi$ and $\omega \in C(\varphi)$. Let $\omega' \in C(\varphi)$. Then $\omega \models \omega \vee \omega'$ and $\omega \vee \omega' \models \varphi$. Hence, by $\varphi \mathrel{\vert\!\sim} \omega$ and (CCM), $\omega \vee \omega' \mathrel{\vert\!\sim} \omega$, i.e., $\omega \geq \omega'$. In other words, ω is maximal in $C(\varphi)$.

(iii)   If $(C, \geq) \models \varphi \rightsquigarrow \psi$, then $\varphi \mathrel{\vert\!\sim} \psi$.
By definition, if $(C, \geq) \models \varphi \rightsquigarrow \psi$, there is an $\omega \in C$ with $\omega \models \varphi \wedge \psi$, maximal in $C(\varphi)$. Hence $\omega \models \varphi$ and, by (Coh), $\varphi \mathrel{\vert\!\sim} \varphi$. By Proposition 10, there is an $\omega' \in C(\varphi)$ that expresses an extension of φ. So $\varphi \mathrel{\vert\!\sim} \omega'$. By (RW) (and (LE)), $\varphi \mathrel{\vert\!\sim} \omega \vee \omega'$. Since ω is maximal in $C(\varphi)$, $\omega \geq \omega'$, i.e., $\omega \vee \omega' \mathrel{\vert\!\sim} \omega$. By (CCT), it follows that $\varphi \mathrel{\vert\!\sim} \omega$. So ω also expresses an extension of φ. Since $\omega \models \psi$, (RW) gives $\varphi \mathrel{\vert\!\sim} \psi$.   □

3.3   Representation Results (Quantitative)

In this section, we show that our notion of presumptively valid inference can also be quantitatively represented. We use the following lemma that the preference relations of our case models are exactly those that can be numerically represented.

Lemma 13. *Let $C \subseteq L$ be finite with elements that are logically consistent, mutually incompatible and different (properties 1, 2 and 3 in the definition of case models). Then the following are equivalent:*

1. *$(C, \geq)$ is a case model;*
2. *$\geq$ is numerically representable, i.e., there is a real valued function v on C such that for all φ and $\psi \in C$, $\varphi \geq \psi$ if and only if $v(\varphi) \geq v(\psi)$.*

The function v can be chosen with only positive integer values.

Proof. It is a standard result in order theory that total preorders on countable sets are the ones that are representable by a real-valued function [23]. In our finite setting, the numbers can be chosen as positive integer values. □

Definition 14. *Let $(C, \geq)$ be a non-empty case model and v a positive numeric function that represents $\geq$. Then we define, for all φ and $\psi \in L$:*

1. *$v(\varphi) := \max\{v(\omega) \mid \omega \in C, \omega \models \varphi\}$;*
2. *$w(\varphi) := \sum \{v(\omega) \mid \omega \in C, \omega \models \varphi\}$;*
3. *$s(\varphi) := w(\varphi)/w(\top)$;*
4. *$s(\varphi, \psi) := w(\varphi \wedge \psi)/w(\varphi) = s(\varphi \wedge \psi)/s(\varphi)$ (with $s(\varphi) > 0$);*
5. *$v(\varphi, \psi) := v(\varphi \wedge \psi)$.*

We say that $v(\varphi)$ is the value *of φ and $w(\varphi)$ its* weight. *We say that $s(\varphi, \psi)$ is the* strength *of the argument from φ to ψ, and $v(\varphi, \psi)$ its* value.

Corollary 15. *Let L^* denote the closure of C under negation, conjunction and logical equivalence. Then the function s restricted to L^* obeys the axioms of probability functions, i.e., for all φ and $\psi \in L^*$:*

1. *$s(\varphi) \geq 0$;*
2. *$s(\top) = 1$;*
3. *If $\varphi \wedge \psi \models \bot$, then $s(\varphi \vee \psi) = s(\varphi) + s(\psi)$.*

The coherence and conclusiveness of arguments can be represented in terms of these numeric functions, as in the following theorems.

Theorem 16. *(Coherence) Let $(C, \geq)$ be a non-empty case model and v and s as above. Then the following are equivalent, for all φ and $\psi \in L$:*

1. *The argument from φ to ψ is coherent;*
2. *$v(\varphi \wedge \psi) > 0$;*
3. *$s(\varphi \wedge \psi) > 0$.*

Proof. An argument is coherent if and only there is a case implying the case made by the argument. This is exactly so when the case made has positive value. This is equivalent to the strength of the argument having positive value. □

Theorem 17. *(Conclusiveness) Let $(C, \geq)$ be a non-empty case model and w and s as above. Then the following are equivalent, for all φ and $\psi \in L$:*

1. *The argument from φ to ψ is conclusive;*
2. $w(\varphi \wedge \psi) = w(\varphi) > 0;$
3. $s(\varphi, \psi) = 1.$

Proof. An argument is conclusive if and only if it is coherent and all cases implying the premises also imply the conclusions. This is exactly so when the cases implying the premises coincide with the cases implying the case made by the argument, i.e., when the weights of premises and case made are equal. That is exactly the case when the argument's strength is equal to 1. □

The next theorem characterizes presumptive validity using a value function v. We restrict to L^*.

Theorem 18. *(Presumptive validity; in terms of value) Let $(C, \geq)$ be a non-empty case model and L^*, v as above. Then the following are equivalent, for all φ and $\psi \in L^*$:*

1. *The argument from φ to ψ is presumptively valid;*
2. $v(\varphi \wedge \psi) = v(\varphi).$

Proof. An argument is presumptively valid if and only if there is a case implying the case made by the argument that is at least as preferred as all cases implying the premises. This is exactly so when the value of $\varphi \wedge \psi$ is equal to that of φ. □

In order to characterize presumptive validity in terms of a strength function s, we choose the value function from which it is derived with special care, as in this lemma:

Lemma 19. *Let α be a positive number. Then the function v in Definition 14 can be chosen such that, for all $\omega \in C$:*

$$v(\omega) > (\alpha + 1)w(\kappa), \text{ where } \kappa := \vee\{\omega^* \in C \mid \omega > \omega^*\}.$$

We say that v is α-separating.

Theorem 20. *(Presumptive validity; in terms of strength) Let $(C, \geq)$ be a non-empty case model and α the maximal number of elements in an equivalence class of the preference relation. Let L^*, v, w and s be as above, with v α-separating (as in the lemma). Then the following are equivalent, for all φ and $\psi \in L^*$:*

1. *The argument from φ to ψ is presumptively valid;*
2. $s(\varphi, \psi) > 1/(\alpha + 1).$

Proof. From 1 to 2: Let the argument from φ to ψ be presumptively valid. Then (and only then) the values of φ and $\varphi \wedge \psi$ are equal to the value $v(\omega)$ of a case $\omega \in C$ that is an extension of φ. The case ω can be chosen such that it implies the case made by the argument, but that makes no difference for the value $v(\omega)$. Let κ denote the disjunction of all cases of value smaller than $v(\omega)$ (cf. the use of κ in the lemma). We have the following inequalities:

$$\frac{w(\varphi \wedge \psi)}{w(\varphi)} \geq \frac{v(\omega)}{\alpha v(\omega) + w(\kappa)}$$

$$> \frac{v(\omega)}{\alpha v(\omega) + v(\omega)/(\alpha + 1)} = \frac{(\alpha + 1)v(\omega)}{\alpha(\alpha + 1)v(\omega) + v(\omega)}$$

$$= \frac{(\alpha + 1)}{\alpha(\alpha + 1) + 1} > \frac{(\alpha + 1)}{\alpha(\alpha + 1) + (\alpha + 1)} = \frac{1}{\alpha + 1}.$$

From 2 to 1: Let the argument from φ to ψ be presumptively invalid. Then (and only then) the value of φ, say $v(\omega)$ for a case $\omega \in C$, is higher than the value of $\varphi \wedge \psi$. Let κ be as before. Then we have these inequalities, completing the proof:

$$\frac{w(\varphi \wedge \psi)}{w(\varphi)} \leq \frac{w(\kappa)}{v(\omega)} < \frac{v(\omega)/(\alpha + 1)}{v(\omega)} = \frac{1}{\alpha + 1}. \qquad \square$$

4   Discussion and Conclusion

We set out to answer the semantics and normative questions for reasoning with presumptive arguments: How are presumptive arguments grounded in interpretations; and when are they evaluated as correct? Our formalism answers these questions, as follows.

As to the semantics question, we have proposed to interpret arguments in models consisting of cases and their preferences. Cases are structured expressions of what can be the case, formalized as consistent sentences in a classical logical language. Our cases are akin to exemplars, observations, precedents, situations, prototypes, schemes, scenarios, scripts, and other structured representations of parts of the world we live in. Our cases are to be contrasted with formal models or worlds that represent completely specified representations, in the sense that all properties are evaluated (as used for instance in preferential model semantics [16]). Key properties of our definition of cases are their logical consistency and mutual incompatibility. Hence, our cases can be thought of as distinguishable coherent combinations of properties. In a case model, the cases come with a preference relation expressing their relative value. Such values can be interpreted objectively, for instance as derived from frequencies or probabilities. However there is no reason to restrict to objective interpretations, and one can also think of subjective values, e.g., derived from utilities, as used in theories of decision making and preference-based choice.

The normative question is answered in terms of this case semantics. We have distinguished coherent, presumptively valid and conclusive arguments. For coherent arguments, there must be a case that implies the case made by the argument. For presumptively valid arguments, there must be a case implying the case made by the argument that is of at least as high value as the other cases implying the argument's premises. For conclusive arguments, there must be a case implying the case made by the argument, and all cases implying the premises should imply the argument's conclusions. When a presumptively valid argument is not conclusive, the argument is defeasible.

We have shown qualitative properties that characterize presumptively valid arguments. We have proven that coherence, presumptive validity and conclusiveness also can be defined in terms of quantitative interpretations. In particular, we have shown a characterization of presumptively valid arguments in terms of two kinds of numeric functions. The first (used in Theorem 18) is a value function v that maximizes (instead of sums) the values of cases. The second (used in Theorem 20) is an argument strength function s that obeys the probability axioms. This provides a probabilistic representation of presumptive validity, which is interesting now that our proposal does not exclude an interpretation of arguments for subjective, preference-based choices, more typically associated with utility functions. The value function v maximizes instead of sums the values of cases, hence reminds of how possibilistic logic [10] contrasts with probabilistic approaches (see also [29]).

By these answers to the semantics and normative questions, we have provided a theory of presumptive arguments with close ties to classical logic and standard probability theory. In contrast, in his influential work on argumentation in artificial intelligence [20,21], Pollock argued against approaches based on classical logic and standard probability theory. Before him, the philosopher and argumentation theorist Toulmin argued similarly [27], without developing an alternative formal and computational perspective, as did Pollock.

[6] focus on the development of the theory of deductive arguments, while our proposal emphasises ampliative argument in their relation to deductive (here: conclusive) and defeasible (here: presumptively valid) arguments. Compared to [19], who provide a framework of argumentation with preferences that can be instantiated with different abstract argumentation semantics, the present proposal gives a model-based formal semantics leading to a formal definition of presumptive validity. Connections between argumentation and uncertain reasoning have been investigated [14,15,17,26], several focusing on abstract argumentation. Our proposal has a model-based definition of presumptive validity that comes with both a qualitative and a quantitative interpretation.

This work connects semantics and properties of inference relations (cf. the research program proposed by [25]; see also [1]). [2] discuss the postulates closure, direct consistency and indirect consistency for the evaluation of argumentation formalisms. Analogs of these properties obtain for presumptively valid arguments. A property akin to closure under strict rules is that a presumptively valid argument remains valid when conclusive consequences of the case made are added. A property related to direct and indirect consistency is that in the present proposal extensions are consistent. A question that arises is how the present proposal is formally connected to related formalisms. In particular, it is natural to study connections with preferential modal logics. Also the place of this work among other studies of nonmonotonic inference relations [18] is a relevant topic of further study, in particular also [7].

The case model semantics presented here formalizes ideas semi-formally presented in [31]. That work was inspired by research using Bayesian networks for modeling argument-based and scenario-based reasoning with evidence [32], where well-known issues with Bayesian network modeling were encountered, namely first that such modeling typically requires many more numbers than are reasonably available, and second that—notwithstanding their transparent formal definition—Bayesian networks are easily misinterpreted, e.g., in causal terms (cf. [9]). In contrast with Bayesian networks, the present formalism is probabilistic, but does not require many numbers, and provides a formal interpretation of arguments in case models.

In conclusion, the present paper has contributed a logic of presumptively valid arguments using case models as semantics. The resulting formalism models correct grounded reasoning with presumptive arguments. As such, we have provided a perspective on how to formally combine logic, probability theory and argumentation, suggesting applications that require the representational power of logic, the data-analytic strength of probability theory, and the interactive social construction of argumentation.

By the combination of logical and probabilistic modeling primitives using an argumentation perspective, the present proposal is a step in the much-needed unification of logic and probability in AI [24].

References

1. Amgoud, L.: Postulates for logic-based argumentation systems. Int. J. Intell. Syst. **55**(9), 2028–2048 (2014)
2. Amgoud, L., Caminada, M.: On the evaluation of argumentation formalisms. Artif. Intell. **172**, 286–310 (2007)
3. Baroni, P., Caminada, M., Giacomin, M.: Review: an introduction to argumentation semantics. Knowl. Eng. Rev. **26**(4), 365–410 (2011)
4. Benthem, J. van: Foundations of conditional logic. J. Philos. Logic **13**, 303–349 (1984)
5. Besnard, P., García, A.J., Hunter, A., Modgil, S., Prakken, H., Simari, G.R., Toni, F.: Introduction to structured argumentation. Argument Comput. **5**, 1–4 (2014)
6. Besnard, P., Hunter, A.: A logic-based theory of deductive arguments. Artif. Intell. **128**, 203–235 (2001)
7. Bochman, A.: A Logical Theory of Nonmonotonic Inference and Belief Change. Springer, Berlin (2001)
8. Bondarenko, A., Dung, P.M., Kowalski, R.A., Toni, F.: An abstract, argumentation-theoretic approach to default reasoning. Artif. Intell. **93**, 63–101 (1997)
9. Dawid, A.P.: Beware of the DAG! In: Guyon, I., Janzing, D., Schölkopf, B. (eds.) JMLR Workshop and Conference Proceedings. Causality: Objectives and Assessment (NIPS 2008 Workshop), vol. 6, pp. 59–86 (2010). jmlr.org
10. Dubois, D., Prade, H.: Possibility theory, probability theory and multiple-valued logics: a clarification. Ann. Math. Artif. Intell. **32**(1), 35–66 (2001)
11. Dung, P.M.: On the acceptability of arguments and its fundamental role in nonmonotonic reasoning, logic programming and n-person games. Artif. Intell. **77**, 321–357 (1995)
12. Eemeren, F. H. van, Garssen, B., Krabbe, E.C.W., Henkemans, A.F.S., Verheij, B., Wagemans, J.H.M.: Argumentation in artificial intelligence. In: Eemeren, F. H. van, et al. (eds.) Handbook of Argumentation Theory. Springer, Berlin (2014)

13. García, A.J., Simari, G.R.: Defeasible logic programming: an argumentative approach. Theory Pract. Logic Program. **4**(2), 95–138 (2004)
14. Hunter, A.: A probabilistic approach to modelling uncertain logical arguments. Int. J. Approx. Reason. **54**, 47–81 (2012)
15. Hunter, A.: Probabilistic qualification of attack in abstract argumentation. Int. J. Approx. Reason. **55**, 607–638 (2014)
16. Kraus, S., Lehmann, D., Magidor, M.: Nonmonotonic reasoning, preferential models and cumulative logics. Artif. Intell. **44**, 167–207 (1990)
17. Li, H., Oren, N., Norman, T.J.: Probabilistic argumentation frameworks. In: Modgil, S., Oren, N., Toni, F. (eds.) TAFA 2011. LNCS, vol. 7132, pp. 1–16. Springer, Heidelberg (2012)
18. Makinson, D.: General patterns in nonmonotonic reasoning. In: Gabbay, D.M., Hogger, C.J., Robinson, J.A. (eds.) Handbook of Logic in Artificial Intelligence and Logic Programming, Nonmonotonic Reasoning and Uncertain Reasoning, vol. 3, pp. 35–110. Clarendon Press, Oxford (1994)
19. Modgil, S., Prakken, H.: A general account of argumentation with preferences. Artif. Intell. **195**, 361–397 (2013)
20. Pollock, J.L.: Defeasible reasoning. Cogn. Sci. **11**(4), 481–518 (1987)
21. Pollock, J.L.: Cognitive Carpentry: A Blueprint for How to Build a Person. The MIT Press, Cambridge (1995)
22. Prakken, H.: An abstract framework for argumentation with structured arguments. Argument Comput. **1**(2), 93–124 (2010)
23. Roberts, F.S.: Measurement Theory with Applications to Decisionmaking, Utility, and the Social Sciences. Cambridge University Press, Cambridge (1985)
24. Russell, S.: Unifying logic and probability. Commun. ACM **58**(7), 88–97 (2015)
25. Simari, G.R.: On the properties of the relation between argumentation semantics and argumentation inference operators. In: Parsons, S., Oren, N., Reed, C., Cerutti, F. (eds.) Computational Models of Argument, Proceedings of COMMA 2014, pp. 3–8. IOS Press, Amsterdam (2014)
26. Thimm, M.: A probabilistic semantics for abstract argumentation. In: Proceedings of the European Conference on Artificial Intelligence (ECAI 2012), pp. 750–755. IOS Press, Amsterdam (2012)
27. Toulmin, S.E.: The Uses of Argument. Cambridge University Press, Cambridge (1958)
28. Verheij, B.: Argumentation and rules with exceptions. In: Computational Models of Argument: Proceedings of COMMA 2010, Desenzano del Garda, Italy, 8–10 September 2010, pp. 455–462. IOS Press, Amsterdam (2010)
29. Verheij, B.: Jumping to conclusions. In: del Cerro, L.F., Herzig, A., Mengin, J. (eds.) JELIA 2012. LNCS, vol. 7519, pp. 411–423. Springer, Heidelberg (2012)
30. Verheij, B.: Arguments and their strength: revisiting Pollock's anti-probabilistic starting points. In: Parsons, S., Oren, N., Reed, C., Cerutti, F. (eds.) Computational Models of Argument. Proceedings of COMMA 2014, pp. 433–444. IOS Press, Amsterdam (2014)
31. Verheij, B.: To catch a thief with and without numbers: arguments, scenarios and probabilities in evidential reasoning. Law Probab. Risk **13**, 307–325 (2014)
32. Verheij, B., Bex, F.J., Timmer, S.T., Vlek, C.S., Meyer, J.J., Renooij, S., Prakken, H.: Arguments, scenarios and probabilities: connections between three normative frameworks for evidential reasoning. Law Probab. Risk **15**, 35–70 (2016)

Characterizability in Horn Belief Revision

Jon Yaggie[1](✉) and György Turán[1,2]

[1] University of Illinois at Chicago, Chicago, USA
jyaggi2@uic.edu
[2] MTA-SZTE Research Group on Artificial Intelligence, Szeged, Hungary

Abstract. Delgrande and Peppas characterized Horn belief revision operators obtained from Horn compliant faithful rankings by minimization, showing that a Horn belief revision operator belongs to this class if and only if it satisfies the Horn AGM postulates and the acyclicity postulate scheme. The acyclicity scheme has a postulate for every $n \geq 3$ expressing the non-existence of a certain cyclic substructure. We show that this class of Horn belief revision operators cannot be characterized by finitely many postulates. Thus the use of infinitely many postulates in the result of Delgrande and Peppas is unavoidable. The proof uses our finite model theoretic approach to characterizability, considering universal monadic second-order logic with quantifiers over closed sets, and using predicates expressing minimality. We also give another non-characterizability result and add some remarks on strict Horn compliance.

1 Introduction

The problem of belief change is how to modify a knowledge base of imperfect knowledge if new information is received. Belief contraction refers to the case when knowledge in the knowledge base should be removed. Belief revision refers to the case when new knowledge is to be incorporated into the knowledge base, which may be inconsistent with the current knowledge. The standard approach to the problem is to formulate rationality postulates, which should be satisfied by every belief change operator, and characterize the class of belief change operators satisfying those postulates. The basic example of this approach is the work of Alchourrón et al. [3]. Belief change operators satisfying the AGM postulates for belief contraction and belief revision have been characterized in many different ways (see, e.g., Hansson [13]).

Theorem 1 *(Katsuno, Mendelzon [16]). A belief revision operator satisfies the AGM postulates iff it can be obtained from a faithful ranking using minimization.*

The standard setup for the AGM framework is full propositional logic. Recent work also considered similar questions for other logics, in particular, for fragments of propositional logic such as Horn logic [1,5–7,9,10,12,17,24,25]. Most of the results on Horn belief change are about Horn belief contraction. Horn belief revision was considered by Delgrande and Peppas [8] and Zhuang et al. [26] and

© Springer International Publishing AG 2016
L. Michael and A. Kakas (Eds.): JELIA 2016, LNAI 10021, pp. 497–511, 2016.
DOI: 10.1007/978-3-319-48758-8_32

Horn belief merging was considered by Haret et al. [14]. Delgrande and Peppas gave a characterization of a class of Horn belief revision operators.

Theorem 2 *(Delgrande, Peppas [8]). A Horn belief revision operator satisfies the Horn AGM postulates and the acyclicity postulate scheme iff it can be obtained from a Horn compliant faithful ranking using minimization.*

Theorem 1 differs from Theorem 2 in two aspects. In Theorem 1 the preference structure has to be a total preorder, but the mapping of truth assignments to the elements of the total preorder is arbitrary. In Theorem 2 this is not the case: the mapping has to be Horn-compliant. The other difference is that the characterization of Theorem 1 is in terms of finitely many postulates, while that of Theorem 2 is in terms of infinitely many postulates, as the acyclicity postulate scheme has a postulate about cycles of length n for every $n \geq 3$.

As infinite postulate characterizations are unusual in belief revision, it is natural to ask whether it is necessary to use infinitely many postulates in Theorem 2. In this paper we give an affirmative answer to this question.

Theorem 3. *The class of Horn belief revision operators obtained from Horn compliant faithful rankings using minimization cannot be characterized by a finite set of postulates.*

This result is one of few non-characterizability results in belief revision. The first such negative results are due to Schlechta and Ben-Naim [4, 18, 22]. In [23] we developed a method to prove non-characterizability results using tools from finite model theory. Postulates are translated into a fragment of universal monadic second-order logic and Ehrenfeucht-Fraïssé games are used to prove undefinability. Impossibility results are also proved by Reis et al. [21].

The framework developed in [23] has to be modified for the present application, especially due to the constraint on Horn compliance. The version of universal monadic second order logic needed here has an unusual kind of quantifier, quantifying over *closed* subsets of the ground set consisting of truth assignments. Here closure is meant in the sense of being closed under componentwise intersection of truth assignments, the property characterizing Horn formulas. Also, the natural class of preference structures to consider (implicit in [8] and formalized here) goes beyond total, or even partial, preorders, and contains structures with cyclic substructures as well. This observation is due to [8], and the structures used in our proof generalize an example of that paper. The reason for infinitely many postulates is that finitely many postulates are not able to distinguish between Horn belief revision operators obtained from Horn compliant faithful rankings and those obtained from faithful structures which falsify some of the acyclicity postulates, but only those corresponding to long cycles.

A motivation to develop methods for proving non-characterizability is that the study of belief change for logics other than full propositional logic is "uncharted territory", where it is not clear what kind of characterizations can be expected. Horn belief revision with Horn compliant faithful rankings, considered in this paper, is a case in point. Another candidate is the class of Horn belief

revision operators with *strictly Horn compliant* faithful rankings, introduced by
Zhuang et al. [26]. Characterizability of this class of revision operators is an open
problem, and approaching it from the point of view of non-characterizability
might be useful. An understanding of the properties of strictly Horn compliant
faithful rankings might be helpful for the study of their characterizability, and
therefore we include some remarks on their properties and their connections to
classes of efficiently computable Horn belief revision operators introduced in [8].

The paper is structured as follows. Sections 2–6 develop the framework for
proving non-characterizability. Section 7 describes the structures used in the non-
characterizability proof. Section 8 contains the proof of Theorem 3 and the statement of another non-characterizability result. The final section contains remarks
on strict Horn compliance.

2   Preliminaries

We consider knowledge bases over a fixed finite set of propositional variables.
The set $\{0,1\}^n$ of truth assignments over n variables is denoted by T_n. The
weight of a truth assignment is the number of its ones. The *intersection* of two
truth assignments is the truth assignment formed by taking componentwise $\wedge$'s,
e.g., $(1,0,1) \cap (0,1,1) = (0,0,1)$. A Boolean function is a function of the form
$f : \{0,1\}^n \to \{0,1\}$. The set of truth assignments a for which $f(a) = 1$ is denoted
by $|f|$, and the set of truth assignments satisfying a propositional formula φ is
denoted by $|\varphi|$.

A clause is a disjunction of literals. A clause is *Horn* if it contains at most
one unnegated literal. A *Horn formula* is a conjunction of Horn clauses.

A Boolean function is a *Horn function* if it is represented by a Horn formula.
It is a basic fact that a Boolean function f is Horn iff $|f|$ is closed under intersec-
tion [15,20]. In what follows we refer to sets of truth assignments closed under
intersection as *closed*. Given a closed set A of truth assignments, $\langle A \rangle$ denotes
some Horn formula φ such that $|\varphi| = A$.

A *Horn knowledge base* H is a Horn formula. We write H_n to indicate that
H is over n variables. Given a Horn knowledge base H, a belief revision operator
$*$ assigns a Horn formula $H * \varphi$ to every Horn formula φ. Here φ is called the
revising formula, and $H * \varphi$ is called the revised knowledge base.

3   Pseudo-orders and Horn Revision by Minimization

A *pseudo-order* $R = (V, \leq)$ is a total binary relation over a finite ground set V,
i.e., for every $u, v \in V$ at least one of $u \leq v$ and $v \leq u$ hold. Thus, in particular,
pseudo-orders are reflexive. The strict order relation $u < v$ holds if $u \leq v$ but
$v \not\leq u$. It is convenient to think of a pseudo-order as a directed graph, containing
edges (u,v) such that $v < u$. (Thus edges between two vertices can go one way
or both ways.)

For a subset $S \subseteq V$, an element $u \in S$ is *minimal* in S if there is no $v \in S$
such that $v < u$. The set of minimal elements of S is denoted by $\min_{\leq} S$. Note

that $\min_\leq S$ may be empty. This happens, for example, if S can be covered with a set of directed cycles of edges (u, v) such $v < u$. As $\leq$ is always clear from the context, we write $\min S$ for $\min_\leq S$.

The notion of a pseudo-order is used in [8] informally, and the definition above is one of the possible formalizations. Another possible formalization would be to require reflexivity only, i.e., to allow for vertices having no directed edges between them. For our purposes both versions would work. The use of the term "order" in this general context is explained by the possibility of formulating minimality as above.

A total preorder $R = (V, \leq)$ is a total, transitive binary relation. A total preorder determines a partition $(V_1, \ldots, V_m)$ of its elements into levels: V_1 is the set of minimal elements, V_2 is the set of minimal elements in $V \setminus V_1$, etc.

Definition 1 *(Faithful structure). A faithful structure F for a Horn knowledge base H_n is a pseudo-order over T_n, such that $\min T_n = |H_n|$, and if $u \in \min T_n$ and $v \notin \min T_n$ then $u < v$.*

Definition 2 *(Horn compliance). A faithful structure is Horn compliant if for every Horn formula φ it holds that $\min |\varphi|$ is closed.*

In a Horn compliant faithful structure there are two relations: the preference relation $\leq$ of the underlying pseudo-order, and the componentwise partial ordering on truth assignments. The latter is only used implicitly when we refer to closed sets. The notion of a Horn compliant faithful structure generalizes that of a *Horn compliant faithful ranking*, where total preorders are considered instead of pseudo-preorders.

Definition 3 *(Horn revision by minimization). The revision operator $*_F$ for H, determined by a Horn compliant faithful structure F for H, by minimization is*

$$H *_F \varphi = \langle \min |\varphi| \rangle.$$

The assumption of Horn compliance guarantees that $H *_F \varphi$ is well-defined. Horn revision operators defined by some Horn compliant faithful structure are called *pseudo-order based*.

4 Horn Postulates and Characterizability

In order to be able to prove non-characterizability, one needs a formal definition of postulates and characterizability. These definitions are provided in this section. We begin with an example of a Horn postulate.

The acyclicity postulate scheme of Theorem 2 is the following. Here indices are meant cyclically, i.e., $n + 1 = 1$.

Definition 4 *(Acyclicity). The acyclicity postulate $Acyc_n$ for $n \geq 3$ is the following: if $(H * \varphi_i) \wedge \varphi_{i+1}$ is satisfiable for $i = 1, \ldots, n$ then $(H * \varphi_1) \wedge \varphi_n$ is also satisfiable.*

Theorem 2 also uses the Horn AGM postulates, which are slight modifications of the AGM postulates, and are not presented here.

We now give a general definition of a postulate for Horn logic. The difference between this definition and the general definition in [23] is that here we allow conjunctions only as arguments of the belief revision operator, instead of arbitrary Boolean combinations, as the class of Horn formulas is not closed under negation. The definition seems to be a natural one in the present context, but other definitions could be considered as well. For example, one could include predicates or functions on truth assignments, such as the componentwise partial ordering, in the language. A framework allowing the acyclicity scheme to be considered a single postulate would allow the inclusion of natural numbers and a variable number of formulas; this seems to be hard to deal with and it is perhaps less natural in view of the types of postulates used in belief revision.

Definition 5 *(Horn postulate).* *A Horn postulate $\mathcal{P}$ is a first-order sentence with unary predicate symbols $H, \varphi_1, \ldots, \varphi_\ell$ and $H * \mu_1, \ldots, H * \mu_m$, where $\mu_1, \ldots, \mu_m$ are conjunctions of $\varphi_1, \ldots, \varphi_\ell$.*

A Horn revision operator satisfies a postulate for a Horn knowledge base H if the postulate holds for all Horn revision formulas $\varphi_1, \ldots, \varphi_\ell$, with the variables ranging over the set of closed sets of truth assignments.

The acyclicity postulates can be rewritten in this form as follows:

$$\left(\bigwedge_{i=1}^{n} \exists x ((H * \varphi_i(x)) \wedge \varphi_{i+1}(x)) \right) \to \exists x ((H * \varphi_1(x)) \wedge \varphi_n(x)).$$

Theorem 2 gives a postulate characterization of Horn belief revision operators obtained from Horn compliant faithful structures. The framework to be developed applies to a generalization of this setup.

Definition 6 *($\mathcal{F}$-revision operator).* *Let $\mathcal{F}$ be a family of faithful structures. Let H be a Horn knowledge base and $*$ be a Horn revision operator for H. Then $*$ is an $\mathcal{F}$-revision operator iff there is a faithful structure $F \in \mathcal{F}$ for H such that $* = *_F$, i.e., F represents $*$ using minimization.*

Definition 7 *(Characterization, characterizability).* *Let $\mathcal{F}$ be a family of faithful structures. A finite set of Horn postulates $\mathcal{P}$ characterizes $\mathcal{F}$-revision operators if for every Horn knowledge base H and every Horn revision operator $*$ for H the following holds: $*$ satisfies the postulates in $\mathcal{P}$ iff $*$ is an $\mathcal{F}$-revision operator. The family of $\mathcal{F}$-revision operators is characterizable if there is a finite set of postulates characterizing $\mathcal{F}$-revision operators.*

The class considered in [8] is the following.

Definition 8. *Let $\mathcal{T}$ be the class of Horn compliant faithful rankings, i.e., the class of faithful structures where the underlying pseudo-order is a total preorder.*

Note that even if $\mathcal{P}$ characterizes $\mathcal{F}$-revision operators, it may happen that an $\mathcal{F}$-revision operator $*$ can also be represented by a faithful structure $F' \notin \mathcal{F}$. For example, for $\mathcal{T}$, Fig. 2 in [8] gives an example of a revision operator generated by a Horn compliant faithful structure based on a pseudo-order which is not a total preorder, such that the same revision operator can also be generated by a Horn compliant faithful ranking. The following concept is useful to deal with this phenomenon.

Definition 9. *For a family $\mathcal{F}$ of faithful structures let*

$$\widetilde{\mathcal{F}} = \{F : \ F \ is \ a \ faithful \ structure \ such \ that \ *_F \ is \ an \ \mathcal{F} - revision \ operator\}.$$

Thus $F \in \widetilde{\mathcal{F}}$ if there is an $F' \in \mathcal{F}$ such that $*_F = *_{F'}$

5 $H_{\min}$-Formulas and Translation

We define a translation of Horn postulates into sentences over an extension of the first-order language of pseudo-orders. The language of pseudo-orders contains the binary relation symbol $\leq$ and equality.

The translated sentences also contain additional unary predicate symbols $A_1, \ldots, A_\ell$, corresponding to Horn formulas $\varphi_1, \ldots, \varphi_\ell$ occurring in the postulates. In other words, the predicates $A_1, \ldots, A_\ell$ range over closed subsets of the ground set T_n.

Definition 10 *(Hat). Given a conjunction μ of $\varphi_1, \ldots, \varphi_\ell$, we denote by $\hat{\mu}$ the first-order formula obtained by replacing the φ's with A's.*

For instance, for $\mu(x) = \varphi_1(x)$ one has $\hat{\mu}(x) = A_1(x)$, and for $\mu(x) = \varphi_1(x) \wedge \varphi_2(x)$ one has $\hat{\mu}(x) = A_1(x) \wedge A_2(x)$.

Given a formula ν over the language $\leq, A_1, \ldots, A_\ell$ with a single free variable x we write $\min^\nu_\leq$ for a formula expressing that x is a minimal element satisfying ν, i.e.,

$$\min^\nu_\leq(x) \ \equiv \ \nu(x) \wedge \forall y(\nu(y) \rightarrow \neg(y < x)).$$

When $\leq$ is clear from the context it is omitted as a subscript. Minimal elements in the pseudo-order are defined by

$$\min(x) \ \equiv \ \forall y(\neg(y < x)).$$

We need the special cases when the formula ν is a conjunction of the unary predicates $A_1, \ldots, A_\ell$.

Definition 11 *($H_{\min}$-formula). A $H_{\min}$-formula over the unary predicate symbols $A_1, \ldots, A_\ell$ is a first-order formula built from the A_is and formulas of the form $\min^\nu_\leq(x)$, where the ν's are arbitrary conjunctions of the A_is.*

Now we can define the translation of a postulate.

Definition 12 *(Translation). The translation $\tau(P)$ of a Horn postulate P is the $H_{\min}$-sentence obtained from P by replacing*

1. *every occurrence of $H(x)$ with $\min(x)$*
2. *every occurrence $\mu_i(x)$ with its "hat" version*
3. *every occurrence of $H * \mu_i$ with $\min^{\hat{\mu}_i}(x)$.*

Note that Part 2 in the definition is redundant as the definition for φ_i is a special case of the definition for μ_i.

Example 1 (Translation of the acyclicity postulates). Applying Definition 12 we get the $H_{\min}$-sentence

$$\left(\bigwedge_{i=1}^{n} \exists x (\min^{A_i}(x) \wedge A_{i+1}(x)) \right) \rightarrow \exists x (\min^{A_1}(x) \wedge A_n(x)),$$

where, again, indices are meant cyclically.

The following is a direct consequence of the definitions, as τ is a simple syntactic transformation.

Proposition 4. *The mapping τ is a bijection between Horn postulates containing revising formulas $\varphi_1, \ldots, \varphi_\ell$ and $H_{\min}$-sentences over unary predicates $A_1, \ldots, A_\ell$.*

In order to interpret $H_{\min}$-formulas let us introduce the following.

Definition 13. *(ℓ-extension). Let $F = (X, \leq)$ be a faithful structure. An ℓ-extension of F is a structure*

$$F' = (X, \leq, A_1, \ldots, A_\ell),$$

where $A_1, \ldots, A_\ell$ are unary relations and every A_i is a closed set of truth assignments[1].

Given Horn formulas $H, \varphi_1, \ldots, \varphi_\ell$ and a faithful structure F for H, the definition of the $(\varphi_1, \ldots, \varphi_\ell)$-extension of F is standard, obtained by interpreting the unary predicate symbols $A_1, \ldots, A_\ell$ by $A_i(a) = \varphi_i(a)$. Again, the following proposition is a direct consequence of the definitions.

Proposition 5. *Let H be a Horn knowledge base, $F = (X, \leq)$ be a faithful structure for H and let $*_F$ be the Horn revision operator determined by F using minimization. Let $\varphi_1, \ldots, \varphi_\ell$ be Horn formulas and P be a postulate. Then P is satisfied by $*_F$ for $\varphi_1, \ldots, \varphi_\ell$ iff the $(\varphi_1, \ldots, \varphi_\ell)$-extension of F satisfies $\tau(P)$.*

---

[1] With an abuse of notation, we use the same notation for a predicate symbol and its interpretation over a structure, assuming that the structure is clear from the context.

6 $\forall MSO_{H_{\min}}$-Definability and Games

In this section we introduce the concepts needed from finite model theory (see, e.g., Ebbinghaus and Flum [11] and Libkin [19]).

A *universal monadic second-order ($\forall MSO$) sentence* is of the form

$$\Phi = \forall A_1, \ldots, A_\ell \, \Psi,$$

where $A_1, \ldots, A_\ell$ range over unary predicates (or subsets) of the universe, and Ψ is a first-order sentence using the unary predicate symbols $A_1, \ldots, A_\ell$ in addition to the original language (in our case $\leq$ and equality). An existential second-order ($\exists MSO$) sentence is of the form $\Phi = \exists A_1, \ldots, A_\ell \Psi$.

We will actually use the following modified version of monadic second-order quantifiers.

Definition 14 *(Closed set quantifier). The closed-set quantifiers $\forall^c$ and $\exists^c$ are generalized monadic second-order quantifiers interpreted in faithful structures, ranging over closed subsets of truth assignments.*

Definition 15 *($\forall MSO_{H_{\min}}$ sentence). A $\forall MSO_{H_{\min}}$ sentence is a second order sentence with universal closed-set quantifiers, of the form*

$$\Phi = \forall^c A_1, \ldots, A_\ell \, \Psi,$$

where Ψ is a $H_{\min}$-sentence.

The definition of $\exists MSO_{H_{\min}}$ sentences is analogous.

Definition 16 *($\forall MSO_{H_{\min}}$-definability). A family $\mathcal{F}$ of faithful structures is $\forall MSO_{H_{\min}}$-definable if there is a $\forall MSO_{H_{\min}}$ sentence Φ such that for every faithful structure F it holds that $F \in \mathcal{F}$ iff F satisfies Φ.*

The following theorem establishes the link between characterizability and definability. It follows directly from the definitions and its proof is omitted.

Theorem 6. *Let $\mathcal{F}$ be a family of faithful structures. The family of $\mathcal{F}$-revision operators is characterizable iff the family $\widetilde{\mathcal{F}}$ is $\forall MSO_{H_{\min}}$-definable.*

This theorem reduces questions about characterizability to questions about $\forall MSO_{H_{\min}}$-definability. We now develop tools for proving undefinability.

The q-round first-order Ehrenfeucht-Fraïssé game over two relational structures is played by two players, Spoiler and Duplicator. In each round Spoiler picks one of the structures and an element of that structure. Duplicator responds by picking an element in the other structure. After q rounds Duplicator wins if the substructures of picked elements in the two structures are isomorphic. Otherwise Spoiler wins. A basic result about this game is that a class of structures is first-order definable iff there is a q such that if the q-round game is played on a structure belonging to the class and a structure not belonging to the class, then Spoiler has a winning strategy.

The first-order Ehrenfeucht-Fraïssé game has a variant corresponding to $\exists MSO$ definability. Ajtai and Fagin [2] defined a modified version, which is easier to use for proving undefinability results.

We introduce a version of the Ajtai-Fagin game defined for faithful structures only. We refer to this game as the Horn-KM game. First let us introduce the notion of a variant.

Let $A_1, \ldots, A_\ell$ be unary predicate symbols. There are $L = 2^\ell$ conjunctions μ of $A_1, \ldots, A_\ell$. Let us pick unary predicate symbols $M_1, \ldots, M_L$ representing them.

Definition 17 *(ℓ-min-variant). Let $F = (X, \leq)$ be a faithful structure. An ℓ-min-variant of F is a structure*

$$F'' = (X, A_1, \ldots, A_\ell, M_1, \ldots, M_L),$$

where $F' = (X, \leq, A_1, \ldots, A_\ell)$ is an ℓ-extension of F, and $M_1, \ldots, M_L$ are the interpretations of the formulas $\min_{\leq}^\nu(x)$ in F', for conjunctions ν of the A_is.

Note that F'' is a structure with *unary* predicates only, the relation $\leq$ is *not* included, it is "forgotten". The relation $\leq$ is used, however, in the intermediate structure F' which determines the M_is. So F'' is not an extension of F; therefore, it is referred to as a variant.

Definition 18 *(($\mathcal{G}, \ell, q$)-$\exists MSO_{H_{\min}}$ game, or Horn-KM game). Given a class $\mathcal{G}$ of faithful structures and parameters ℓ and q, the ($\mathcal{G}, \ell, q$)-$\exists MSO_{H_{\min}}$ game is played by Spoiler and Duplicator as follows:*

1. *Duplicator picks a faithful structure $F_1 = (X_1, \leq_1)$ in $\mathcal{G}$,*
2. *Spoiler picks closed subsets $A_1, \ldots, A_\ell$ of X_1,*
3. *Duplicator picks a faithful structure $F_2 = (X_2, \leq_2) \notin \mathcal{G}$, and closed subsets $B_1, \ldots, B_\ell$ of X_2,*
4. *Form the ℓ-min-variant F_1'' of F_1 determined by the ℓ-extension $F_1' = (X_1, \leq_1, A_1, \ldots, A_\ell)$, and the ℓ-min-variant F_2'' of F_2 determined by the ℓ-extension $F_2' = (X_2, \leq_2, B_1, \ldots, B_\ell)$,*
5. *Spoiler and Duplicator play a q-round first-order Ehrenfeucht-Fraïssé game on F_1'' and F_2''.*

The following theorem shows how to use these games to prove undefinability (which, by Theorem 6, implies non-characterizability). The proof is standard and is omitted.

Theorem 7. *Let $\mathcal{G}$ be a class of faithful structures. Then $\mathcal{G}$ is not $\exists MSO_{H_{\min}}$-definable iff for every ℓ and q, Duplicator has a winning strategy in the ($\mathcal{G}, \ell, q$)-$\exists MSO_{H_{\min}}$ game.*

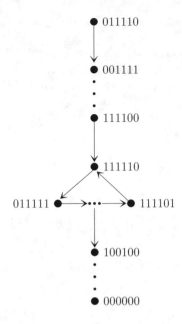

Fig. 1. An ab wheel for n = 6

7   Ab Wheels

After having developed the machinery to prove non-characterizability, we describe the structures used in the proof of Theorem 3. These structures generalize the example of Fig. 1 in [8].

Consider the knowledge base $H_n = \langle 0^n \rangle$. Let $C_n = \{a_1, \ldots, a_n\} \subset T_n$ be the set of truth assignments of weight $n - 1$, where a_i is the truth assignment with a zero in the i'th position. Let $U_n = \{b_1, \ldots, b_n\}$ be the set of truth assignments of weight $n - 2$ with two consecutive zeros. The truth assignment b_i has zeros in positions i and $i + 1$. Indices are meant cyclically, i.e., $b_5 = 01110$. Thus $a_i \cap a_{i+1} = b_i$, and so $\{a_i, a_{i+1}, b_i\}$ is closed. Finally, let G_n be the directed graph on the vertex set C_n, containing one-way edges (a_i, a_{i+1}) (where addition is again meant cyclically) and the other edges both ways.

Definition 19 *(Ab wheel[2]). An ab wheel W_n is a faithful structure for H_n with vertices T_n and $<$ corresponding to the following cases:*

1. *upper chain: truth assignments in U_n form a linear order and are greater than any other truth assignment,*
2. *cycle: truth assignments in C_n are below U_n and form the directed graph structure G_n as described above,*
3. *lower chain: all other truth assignments form a linear order and are smaller than any other truth assignment, with the all-zero truth assignment at the bottom.*

---

[2] The name refers to a gym tool resembling the structure.

Note that
$$\min\{a_i, a_{i+1}, b_i\} = \{a_{i+1}\}. \tag{1}$$

Lemma 1. *Every closed subset of T_n has a unique minimum in W_n.*

Proof. Let S be a closed subset of T_n. The statement is clear if S is contained in the upper chain, or if it has an element in the lower chain. Otherwise assume that S contains $k \geq 1$ elements in the cycle, and possibly some elements in the upper chain.

If $k = 1$ then the statement is clear again. If $k = 2$ and the two elements in the cycle are consecutive, i.e., of the form a_i, a_{i+1}, then the unique minimal element of S is a_{i+1}. Other cases are not possible: if $k = 2$ and the two elements are non-consecutive, or if $k \geq 3$, the closure of S implies that it contains at least one element from the lower chain.

Lemma 2. *The ab wheel W_n*

1. *is a Horn compliant faithful structure for H_n,*
2. *$*_{W_n}$ is Horn revision operator which is not in $\widetilde{T}$, i.e., it is not generated by any Horn compliant faithful ranking.*

Proof. For 1., only Horn compliance needs to be proved and it follows directly from Lemma 1. Part 2. follows from the facts that Horn compliant faithful rankings generate revision operators satisfying the acyclicity postulate scheme [8], and, on the other hand, $*_{W_n}$ falsifies $Acyc_n$. The latter claim follows from considering $\varphi_i = \langle\{a_i, a_{i+1}, b_i\}\rangle$. By (1) it holds that $(\min|\varphi_i|) \cap |\varphi_{i+1}| = \{a_{i+1}\}$, but

$$\min|\varphi_1| \cap |\varphi_n| = \{a_2\} \cap \{a_n, a_1, b_n\} = \emptyset.$$

The following statement is not used later on, but it may be of interest in itself.

Proposition 1. *The Horn revision operator $*_{W_n}$*

1. *satisfies the Horn AGM postulates,*
2. *satisfies the acyclicity postulates $Acyc_\ell$ for $3 \leq \ell \leq n - 1$.*

8   Proof of Theorem 3 and Statement of Another Non-characterizability Result

Theorems 6 and 7 yield the following "characterization of characterizability".

Lemma 3. *Let $\mathcal{F}$ be a class of faithful structures and let $\mathcal{G}$ be the class of faithful structures not in $\widetilde{\mathcal{F}}$. The class of $\mathcal{F}$-revision operators is not characterizable iff for every ℓ and q, Duplicator has a winning strategy in the $(\mathcal{G}, \ell, q)$-$\exists MSO_{H_{\min}}$ game.*

Thus to show that the class of $\mathcal{T}$-revision operators is not characterizable, we need to describe a winning strategy of Duplicator in the $(\mathcal{G}, \ell, q)$-$\exists MSO_{H_{\min}}$ game for $\mathcal{G}$, the class of faithful structures not in $\widetilde{\mathcal{T}}$.

In the first round Duplicator picks the ab wheel W_n for $n = 2^\ell + 1$. Assume that Spoiler picks closed subsets $A_1, \ldots, A_\ell$ of T_n in the second round.

Let $I \subseteq \{1, \ldots, \ell\}$. Then $S_I = \cap_{i \in I} A_i$ is closed and has a unique minimum m_I. Let $a_j \in C_n$ be a truth assignment which is never minimal, i.e., $a_j \neq m_I$ for every I.

The Horn compliant faithful structure picked by Duplicator in the third round is a linear order where the upper and lower chains are the same as in W_n, and the cyclic structure G_n between them is replaced by the linear order

$$a_j > a_{j+1} > \ldots > a_n > a_1 > \ldots > a_{j-1}.$$

In other words, the cycle G_n is cut and it is made into a chain (referred to as the *middle* chain) by placing a_j on top. The closed sets $B_1, \ldots, B_\ell$ are the same as the ones selected by Spoiler in W_n. (Note that closedness is defined in terms of the truth assignments only, independently of the underlying pseudo-preorder.)

We claim that the ℓ-min variants of the two structures are the same (as structures with unary relations over T_n), thus Duplicator wins the first-order game in the last part of the $Horn - KM$ game.

We need to show that for every $I \subseteq \{1, \ldots, \ell\}$ the set of minimal truth assignments in S_I and $S_I' = \cap_{i \in I} B_i$ are the same (in each case with respect to the corresponding pseudo-order). As we know that in both structures every closed subset has a unique minimum, it is sufficient to show that the minimal element m_I of S_I is also minimal in S_I'. This follows directly if m_I is in the upper or lower chain.

If m_I is in the cycle then we distinguish two cases. If m_I is the only element of S_I in the cycle, then all other elements of S_I are in the upper chain. In the second structure m_I is in the middle chain and all the other elements of S_I' are in the upper chain, so m_I is indeed minimal in S_I'.

Otherwise, it must be the case that S_I has two elements in the cycle, m_I and its predecessor m_I' on the cycle, and all other elements of S_I are in the upper chain. The choice of a_j guarantees that $m_I \neq a_j$, thus m_I' is greater than m_I in the second structure, and all other elements of S_I' are in the upper chain. Thus m_I is again minimal in S_I'. This completes the proof of Theorem 3.

We formulate a non-characterizability result for another class of Horn revision operators as well. Let

$$\mathcal{B} = \{F : F \notin \widetilde{\widetilde{\mathcal{T}}}\}$$

be the class of Horn compliant faithful structures not in $\widetilde{\widetilde{\mathcal{T}}}$.

Theorem 8. *The class of $\mathcal{B}$-revision operators is not characterizable.*

The proof is similar to the proof of Theorem 3, with the Duplicator starting with a sufficiently large linear order with truth assignments of weight $n - 3$ and

$n-1$ at the bottom, and producing a faithful structure similar to an ab wheel in the third round.

9   Remarks on Strict Horn Compliance

Strictly Horn compliant faithful rankings are introduced by Zhuang et al. [26]. In this section we make some observations on the properties of strictly Horn compliant faithful rankings and their connections to classes studied in [8].

Horn compliance for a faithful ranking is equivalent to the requirement that the intersection of two equivalent truth assignments is not above the two truth assignments [26]. A faithful ranking is *strictly Horn compliant* if the intersection of two *arbitrary* truth assignments is not above both assignments. The following is a direct consequence of the definitions.

Proposition 9. *Let R be a total preorder on T_n with level sets $V_1, \ldots, V_r$. Then R is strictly Horn compliant iff $V_1 \cup \ldots \cup V_i$ is closed under intersection for every i, $1 \le i \le r$.*

In other words, strictly Horn compliant total preorders can be thought of as a sequence of Horn formulas $\varphi_0, \ldots, \varphi_r$, where $\varphi_0 = H$ is the knowledge base, φ_r is identically true, φ_i implies φ_{i+1} for every i, and the level of a truth assignment is determined by the first formula it satisfies. This also implies that strictly Horn compliant total preorders have a syntactic definition as well, using the completeness of unit resolution for Horn formulas, as each formula can be obtained from the previous one using a sequence of unit resolutions and weakenings which preserve the Horn property of clauses.

Strictly Horn compliant belief revision operators turn out to be of interest from the point of view of relating contractions and revisions for Horn logic [26]. Strictly Horn compliant belief revision operators are related to basic and canonical Horn belief revision operators introduced in [8].

A faithful ranking is *basic* if truth assignments not in the knowledge base are ranked according to their weight, with lower weight truth assignments having lower rank. A *canonical* faithful ranking is specified by a Horn knowledge base H and a partition $(P_1, \ldots, P_r)$ of the variables. This determines a sequence $\varphi_0, \ldots, \varphi_{r+1}$ of Horn formulas, where $\varphi_0 = H$ and φ_i is obtained from H by adding the negations of every variable in $P_1 \cup \ldots P_i$ to every Horn clause of H. This, in turn, determines a total preorder on the truth assignments, where a truth assignment is on the i'th level if φ_i is the first formula it satisfies. There is an additional level added for truth assignments not satisfying φ_r.

It is clear, then, that both basic and canonical revisions are strongly Horn compliant. Proposition 9 implies that strictly Horn compliant revision operators, given their syntactic description, can be computed efficiently.

10   Conclusion

Delgrande and Peppas proved a characterization result for Horn belief revision related to the Katsuno-Mendelzon characterization of general belief revision operators. Their characterization, besides minor modifications of the AGM postulates, includes the acyclicity postulate scheme which contains infinitely many postulates. In this paper we showed that the postulates in their characterization cannot be replaced with a finite set of postulates. Thus any characterization of Horn belief revision operators obtained from a Horn compliant faithful ranking by minimization will inevitability include an infinite number of postulates.

Several open problems remain related to this topic. For instance, even though the formulation of Definition 5 was chosen to cover a broad spectrum of postulates, alternative definitions could be considered. One direction is to include the predicate for componentwise partial ordering of truth assignments, or other Boolean relations, in the language used by postulates. Considering alternative frameworks for characterizability could provide further insights into the logical structure of revision operators.

Strictly Horn compliant belief revision operators form a natural class based on total preorders with Horn "fallback sets" [8] having good computational properties. Characterizability of Horn revision operators obtained from such faithful rankings is an open problem. Should this class be non-characterizable, the approach of this paper offers a framework to prove such a result.

Finally, Horn logic is only one of many logics of interest in belief revision. The adaptation of the framework of [23] and this paper to other logics may yield further results.

References

1. Adaricheva, K., Sloan, R.H., Szörényi, B., Turán, G.: Horn belief contraction: remainders, envelopes and complexity. In: Proceedings of the 13th International Conference on Principles of Knowledge Representation and Reasoning (KR), May 2012
2. Ajtai, M., Fagin, R.: Reachability is harder for directed than for undirected finite graphs. J. Symbolic Logic **55**(1), 113–150 (1990)
3. Alchourrón, C.E., Gärdenfors, P., Makinson, D.: On the logic of theory change: partial meet contraction and revision functions. J. Symbolic Logic **50**(2), 510–530 (1985)
4. Ben-Naim, J.: Lack of finite characterizations for the distance-based revision. In: 10th International Conference on Principles of Knowledge Representation and Reasoning (KR 2006), pp. 239–248 (2006)
5. Booth, R., Meyer, T., Varzinczak, I., Wassermann, R.: A contraction core for Horn belief change: preliminary report. In: 13th International Workshop on Nonmonotonic Reasoning (NMR) (2010)
6. Booth, R., Meyer, T.A., Varzinczak, I.J.: Next steps in propositional Horn contraction. In: IJCAI, pp. 702–707 (2009)
7. Delgrande, J.: Horn clause belief change: contraction functions. In: 11th International Conference on Principles of Knowledge Representation and Reasoning (KR-2008), pp. 156–165. AAAI Press (2008)
8. Delgrande, J.P., Peppas, P.: Belief revision in Horn theories. Artif. Intell. **218**, 1–22 (2015)

9. Delgrande, J.P., Wassermann, R.: Horn clause contraction functions: belief set and belief base approaches. In: Proceedings of the Twelfth International Conference on the Principles of Knowledge Representation and Reasoning (KR 2010) (2010)
10. Delgrande, J.P., Wassermann, R.: Horn clause contraction functions. J. Artif. Intell. Res. (JAIR) **48**, 475–511 (2013)
11. Ebbinghaus, H.D., Flum, J.: Finite Model Theory. Springer Monographs in Mathematics. Springer, Berlin (2006)
12. Fotinopoulos, A.M., Papadopoulos, V.: Semantics for Horn contraction. In: Proceedings of the 7th Panhellenic Logic Symposium, pp. 42–47. Patras University Press (2009)
13. Hansson, S.O.: A Textbook of Belief Dynamics. Applied Logic Series. Springer, Netherlands (1999)
14. Haret, A., Rümmele, S., Woltran, S.: Merging in the Horn fragment. In: Proceedings of the Twenty-Fourth International Joint Conference on Artificial Intelligence, IJCAI 2015, Buenos Aires, Argentina, July 25–31, 2015, pp. 3041–3047 (2015)
15. Horn, A.: On sentences which are true on direct unions of algebras. J. Symbolic Logic **16**, 14–21 (1951)
16. Katsuno, H., Mendelzon, A.O.: Propositional knowledge base revision and minimal change. Artif. Intell. **52**(3), 263–294 (1991)
17. Langlois, M., Sloan, R.H., Szörényi, B., Turán, G.: Horn complements: towards horn-to-horn belief revision. In: AAAI National Conference on Artificial Intelligence (AAAI-2008) (2008)
18. Lehmann, D.J., Magidor, M., Schlechta, K.: Distance semantics for belief revision. J. Symbolic Logic **66**(1), 295–317 (2001)
19. Libkin, L.: Elements of Finite Model Theory. Texts in Theoretical Computer Science: An EATCS Series. Springer, Berlin (2004)
20. McKinsey, J.C.C.: The decision problem for some classes without quantifiers. J. Symbolic Logic **8**, 61–76 (1943)
21. Reis, M.D.L., Fermé, E., Peppas, P.: Construction of system of spheres-based transitively relational partial meet multiple contractions: an impossibility result. Artif. Intell. **233**, 122–141 (2016)
22. Schlechta, K.: Coherent Systems. Studies in Logic and Practical Reasoning. Elsevier Science, Amsterdam (2004)
23. Turán, G., Yaggie, J.: Characterizability in belief revision. In: Proceedings of the Twenty-Fourth International Joint Conference on Artificial Intelligence, IJCAI 2015, Buenos Aires, Argentina, July 25–31, 2015, pp. 3236–3242 (2015)
24. Zhuang, Z.Q., Pagnucco, M.: Horn contraction via epistemic entrenchment. In: Janhunen, T., Niemelä, I. (eds.) JELIA 2010. LNCS, vol. 6341, pp. 339–351. Springer, Heidelberg (2010)
25. Zhuang, Z.Q., Pagnucco, M.: Transitively relational partial meet Horn contraction. In: IJCAI, pp. 1132–1138 (2011)
26. Zhuang, Z., Pagnucco, M., Zhang, Y.: Inter-definability of Horn contraction and Horn revision. J. Philos. Logic (2016). doi:10.1007/s10992-016-9401-2

Short Papers

Formalizing Goal Serializability for Evaluation of Planning Features

Reza Basseda$^{(\boxtimes)}$ and Michael Kifer

Stony Brook University, Stony Brook, NY 11794, USA
{rbasseda,kifer}@cs.stonybrook.edu

Abstract. Evaluation of the properties of various planning techniques such as completeness and termination plays an important role in choosing an appropriate planning technique for a particular planning problem. In this paper, we use the already existing formal specification of two well-known and classic state space planning techniques, forward state space planning and goal stack state space planning techniques, in Transaction Logic($\mathcal{TR}$) to study their completeness. Our study shows that using $\mathcal{TR}$, we can formally specify the serializability of planning problems and prove the completeness of *STRIPS* planning problems for planning problems with serializable goals.

Keywords: Deductive planning · STRIPS planning · Transaction Logic

1 Introduction

Evaluation of different properties of planning techniques such as termination and completeness becomes more essential when, in many cases, different search strategies of a planning technique may affect the performance of planning process while different properties such as completeness and termination is required. For example, forward state space planning and goal stack space planning techniques may have different execution time when they are used by a robot in the famous block world example while Sussman Anomaly [1] shows that goal stack space planning is not guaranteed to succeed. Such considerations need appropriate formal frameworks to represent the planning techniques properly.

Using logical deduction to solve a planning problem has been a popular approach for more than three decades [2–6]. However, none of the existing logical frameworks of deductive planners are used to study the different properties of planning techniques because these planners are just relying on their corresponding inference systems to search for a plan and they are not expressive enough to formally represent more complicated planning techniques such as goal state space planning. Therefore, the requirement of a formal, neat, and expressive logical framework for such studies seems to be inevitable.

This work was supported, in part, by the NSF grant 0964196.

© Springer International Publishing AG 2016
L. Michael and A. Kakas (Eds.): JELIA 2016, LNAI 10021, pp. 515–521, 2016.
DOI: 10.1007/978-3-319-48758-8_33

In this paper, we are using the encoding of forward state space planning and goal stack state space planning techniques in Transaction Logic($\mathcal{TR}$) for the evaluation of their completeness. Our paper shows that $\mathcal{TR}$ is an appropriate logical framework for such evaluation. Unlike above mentioned logical frameworks, the well-defined model theory of $\mathcal{TR}$ together with its sound and complete proof theory let us easily prove different properties of planning techniques such as completeness. It also lets us formally redefine the concept of goal serializablity in planning that is used to examine the completeness of goal stack state space planning technique for planning problems. Our simple and straightforward proofs for two classic planning techniques, forward state space planning (called naïve[1]) and goal stack state space (called $STRIPS$[2]) are evidences for this claim.

The next section briefly characterizes a planning problem. The third section explains how we formally encode planning techniques in $\mathcal{TR}$ and the last section concludes our paper.

2 Characterization of a Planning Problem

In a $STRIPS$ planning problem, actions update the state of a system. We assume denumerable sets of variables $\mathcal{X}$, constants $\mathcal{C}$, and disjoint sets of predicate symbols, extensional ($\mathcal{P}_{ext}$) and intensional ($\mathcal{P}_{int}$) ones. A *term* is a variable or constant. Extensional (resp. intensional) ***Atoms*** have the form $p(t_1, ..., t_n)$, where t_i is a term and $p \in \mathcal{P}_{ext}$ (resp. $p \in \mathcal{P}_{int}$). A ***ground*** atom is a variable free atom. A ***literal*** is either an atom or a negated extensional atom, $\neg p(t_1, ..., t_n)$. Note that negative intensional atoms cannot form literals. A substitution θ is a set of expressions of the form $X \longleftarrow c$, where $X \in \mathcal{X}$ and $c \in \mathcal{C}$. Given a substitution θ, an atom $a\theta$ is obtained from atom a by replacing its variables with constants according to θ.

Intensional predicate symbols are defined by *rules*. A rule r, shown as $head(r) \leftarrow b_1 \wedge \cdots \wedge b_n$, consists of an intensional atom $head(r)$ in the head and a conditional body, a (possibly empty) conjunction of literals $b_1, \ldots, b_n$, where $b_i \in body(r)$. A ***ground instance*** of a rule, $r\theta$, is any rule obtained from r by a substitution of $head(r)$ and $body(r)$ with ground atoms $head(r)\theta$ and $body(r)\theta$ respectively. Given a set of literals $\mathbf{S}$ and a ground rule $r\theta$, the rule is *true* in $\mathbf{S}$ if either $head(r)\theta \in \mathbf{S}$ or $body(r)\theta \nsubseteq \mathbf{S}$. A (possibly non-ground) rule is *true* in $\mathbf{S}$ if all of its ground instances are true in $\mathbf{S}$. A set $\mathbf{S}$ of literals is ***consistent*** if there is no atom, a, such that $\{a, \neg a\} \subseteq \mathbf{S}$.

Definition 1 (State). *Given a set of rules* $\mathbb{R}$, *a consistent set* $\mathbf{S}$ *of literals is called a* **state** *if and only if*

1. *For each ground extensional atom a, either, $a \in \mathbf{S}$, or $\neg a \in \mathbf{S}$.*
2. *Every rule of $\mathbb{R}$ is true in $\mathbf{S}$.*

---

[1] Due to its simple nature.

[2] As it was originally proposed by [7] in $STRIPS$.

Definition 2 (*STRIPS* action). *A STRIPS action* $\alpha = \langle p_\alpha(X_1, ..., X_n),$ $Pre(\alpha), E(\alpha)\rangle$ *consists of an intensional atom* $p_\alpha(X_1, ..., X_n)$ *in which* $p_\alpha \in \mathcal{P}_{int}$ *is a predicate that is reserved to represent the action* α *and can be used for no other purpose, a set of literals* $Pre(\alpha)$, *called the* **precondition** *of* α, *and a consistent set of extensional literals* $E(\alpha)$, *called the* **effect** *of* α. *The variables in* $Pre(\alpha)$ *and* $E(\alpha)$ *must occur in* $\{X_1, ..., X_n\}$.

Note that the literals in $Pre(\alpha)$ can be both extensional and intensional, while the literals in $E(\alpha)$ can be extensional only.

Definition 3 (Execution of a *STRIPS* action). *A STRIPS action* α *is* **executable** *in a state* **S** *if there is a substitution* θ *such that* $\theta(Pre(\alpha)) \subseteq$ **S**. *A* **result of the execution** *(with respect to* θ*) is the state* **S'** *such that* **S'** $= ($**S** $\setminus \neg\theta(E(\alpha))) \cup \theta(E(\alpha))$, *where* $\neg E = \{\neg\ell | \ell \in E\}$.

Note that **S** is well-defined since $E(\alpha)$ is consistent. Observe also that, if α has variables, the result of an execution, **S**, may depend on the chosen substitution θ.

Definition 4 (Planning problem). *Given a set of rules* $\mathbb{R}$, *a set of STRIPS actions* $\mathbb{A}$, *a set of literals* G, *called the* **goal**, *and an* **initial state** **S**, *a* **planning solution** *(or simply a* **plan***) for the planning* $\Pi = \langle\mathbb{R}, \mathbb{A}, G, \mathbf{S}\rangle$ *is a sequence of ground actions* $\sigma = \alpha_1, ..., \alpha_n$ *such that for each* $1 \leq i \leq n$;

- *there is a substitution* θ_i *and a STRIPS action* $\alpha_i' \in \mathbb{A}$ *such that* $\alpha_i'\theta = \alpha_i$; *and*
- *there is a sequence of states* $\mathbf{S}_0, \mathbf{S}_1, ..., \mathbf{S}_n$ *such that*
  - **S** $= \mathbf{S}_0$ *and* $G \subseteq \mathbf{S}_n$ *(i.e., G is satisfied in the final state);*
  - α_i *is executable in state* $\mathbf{S}_{i-1}$ *and the result of that execution is the state* $\mathbf{S}_i$.

The following definition of **goal serializable planning** problems constitutes a measure that recognizing planning problems, for which the *STRIPS* planning technique is proven to be complete.

Definition 5 (Goal serializable planning problem). *Given a planning problem* $\Pi = \langle\mathbb{R}, \mathbb{A}, \mathbf{S}, G\rangle$, *let* σ *be the shortest solution plan for* Π *and* $G' \subset G$ *be any arbitrary set of literals such that* $G \neq G'$. *We call* Π *a* **goal serializable planning problem** *if and only if, for every* σ', *that is a planning solution for* $\Pi' = \langle\mathbb{R}, \mathbb{A}, G', \mathbf{S}\rangle$ *and the result of its execution is* **S'** *where* $|\sigma'| \leq |\sigma|$, *there is a planning solution* σ'' *for* $\Pi'' = \langle\mathbb{R}, \mathbb{A}, G, \mathbf{S'}\rangle$ *such that* $|\sigma''| < |\sigma|$.

A brief introduction to the *subset* of $\mathcal{TR}$ [8–11] has been appeared in [12–14]. Although such introduction is required to make our paper self-contained, we omit that introduction to save space and refer the reader to [14].

3   The $\mathcal{TR}$ Planners

The informal idea of using $\mathcal{TR}$ as a planning formalism and an encoding of *STRIPS* and naive planning as a set of $\mathcal{TR}$ rules first appeared in an unpublished report [8]. We extend and slightly modify the original methods to prove different properties of each planning technique.

Given a set of extensional literals G, we define $Enf(G)$ to be the set of elementary updates that makes G true. Next we introduce a natural correspondence between $STRIPS$ actions and $\mathcal{TR}$ rules.

Definition 6 (Actions as $\mathcal{TR}$ rules). *Let* $\alpha = \langle p_\alpha(\overline{X}), Pre(\alpha), E(\alpha) \rangle$ *be a STRIPS action. We define its* **corresponding** *TR* **rule***, $tr(\alpha)$, to be a rule of the form*

$$p_\alpha(\overline{X}) \leftarrow (\wedge_{\ell \in Pre(\alpha)} \ell) \otimes (\otimes_{u \in Enf(E(\alpha))} u). \tag{1}$$

Note that in (1) the actual order of action execution in the last component, $\otimes_{u \in Enf(E(\alpha))} u$, is immaterial, since all such executions happen to lead to the same state.

We now define a set of $\mathcal{TR}$ clauses that simulate naive and $STRIPS$ [7] planning techniques. Moreover, for convenience, we use $a \widehat{\otimes} b$ as a shorthand for $a \otimes b \vee b \otimes a$. This connective is called the *shuffle* operator in [8]. We define it to be commutative and associative and thus extend it to arbitrary number of operands.

Definition 7 (Naïve planning rules). *Given a STRIPS planning problem* $\Pi = \langle \mathbb{R}, \mathbb{A}, G, \mathbf{S} \rangle$ *(see Definition 4), we define a set of $\mathcal{TR}$ rules, $\mathbb{P}(\Pi)$, which simulate naive planning technique to provide a planning solution to the planning problem. $\mathbb{P}(\Pi)$ has two parts, $\mathbb{P}_{general}$, $\mathbb{P}_\mathbb{A}$, described below.*

- *The $\mathbb{P}_{general}$ part: contains a couple of rules as follows;*

$$\begin{aligned} plan &\leftarrow . \\ plan &\leftarrow execute\_action \otimes plan. \end{aligned} \tag{2}$$

  These rules construct a sequence of actions and bind them to the plan.
- *The $\mathbb{P}_{actions}$ part: for each $\alpha \in \mathbb{A}$, $\mathbb{P}_{actions}$ has a couple of rules as follows;*

$$\begin{aligned} p_\alpha(\overline{X}) &\leftarrow (\wedge_{\ell \in Pre(\alpha)} \ell) \otimes (\otimes_{u \in Enf(E(\alpha))} u). \\ execute\_action &\leftarrow p_\alpha(\overline{X}). \end{aligned} \tag{3}$$

  This is the $\mathcal{TR}$ rule that corresponds to the action α, introduced in Definition 6 and generally links an action to a plan.

Definition 8 ($STRIPS$ planning rules). *Let $\Pi = \langle \mathbb{R}, \mathbb{A}, G, \mathbf{S} \rangle$ be a STRIPS planning problem (see Definition 4). We define a set of $\mathcal{TR}$ rules, $\mathbb{P}(\Pi)$, which simulate STRIPS planning technique to provide a planning solution to the planning problem. $\mathbb{P}(\Pi)$ has three disjoint parts, $\mathbb{P}_\mathbb{R}$, $\mathbb{P}_\mathbb{A}$, and $\mathbb{P}_G$, described below.*

- *The $\mathbb{P}_\mathbb{R}$ part: for each rule $p(\overline{X}) \leftarrow p_1(\overline{X}_1) \wedge \cdots \wedge p_k(\overline{X}_n)$ in $\mathbb{R}$, $\mathbb{P}_\mathbb{R}$ has a rule of the form*

$$achieve\_p(\overline{X}) \leftarrow \widehat{\otimes}_{i=1}^n achieve\_p_i(\overline{X}_i). \tag{4}$$

Rule (4) is an extension to the classical STRIPS planning algorithm. It captures intentional predicates and ramification of actions, and it is the only major aspect of our $\mathcal{TR}$-based rendering of STRIPS that was not present in the original in one way or another.

- *The part* $\mathbb{P}_\mathbb{A} = \mathbb{P}_{actions} \cup \mathbb{P}_{atoms} \cup \mathbb{P}_{achieves}$ *is constructed out of the actions in* $\mathbb{A}$ *as follows:*
  - $\mathbb{P}_{actions}$: *similar to Definition 7.*
  - $\mathbb{P}_{atoms} = \mathbb{P}_{achieved} \cup \mathbb{P}_{enforced}$ *has two disjoint parts as follows:*
    - $\mathbb{P}_{achieved}$: *for each extensional predicate* $p \in \mathcal{P}_{ext}$, $\mathbb{P}_{achieved}$ *has the rules*

$$achieve\_p(\overline{X}) \leftarrow p(\overline{X}).$$
$$achieve\_not\_p(\overline{X}) \leftarrow \neg p(\overline{X}). \tag{5}$$

These rules say that if an extensional literal is true in a state then that literal has already been achieved as a goal.
  - $\mathbb{P}_{enforced}$: *for each action* $\alpha = \langle p_\alpha(\overline{X}), Pre(\alpha), E(\alpha) \rangle$ *in* $\mathbb{A}$ *and each* $e(\overline{Y}) \in E(\alpha)$, $\mathbb{P}_{enforced}$ *has the following rule:*

$$achieve\_e(\overline{Y}) \leftarrow \neg e(\overline{Y}) \otimes execute\_p_\alpha(\overline{X}). \tag{6}$$

This rule says that one way to achieve a goal that occurs in the effects of an action is to execute that action.
  - $\mathbb{P}_{achieves}$: *for each action* $\alpha = \langle p_\alpha(\overline{X}), Pre(\alpha), E(\alpha) \rangle$ *in* $\mathbb{A}$, $\mathbb{P}_{achieves}$ *has the following rule:*

$$execute\_p_\alpha(\overline{X}) \leftarrow (\widehat{\otimes}_{\ell \in Pre(\alpha)} achieve\_\ell) \otimes p_\alpha(\overline{X}). \tag{7}$$

This means that to execute an action, one must first achieve the precondition of the action and then perform the state changes prescribed by the action.
- $\mathbb{P}_G$: *Let* $G = \{g_1, ..., g_k\}$. *Then* $\mathbb{P}_G$ *has a rule of the form:*

$$achieve_G \leftarrow (\widehat{\otimes}_{g_i=1}^{k} achieve\_g_i) \otimes (\wedge_{i=1}^{k} g_i). \tag{8}$$

Given a *STRIPS* planning problem $\Pi = \langle \mathbb{R}, \mathbb{A}, G, \mathbf{S} \rangle$, each of Definitions 7 and 8 gives a set of $\mathcal{TR}$ rules that specifies the corresponding planning strategy for that problem. To find a solution for that planning problem, one simply needs to place the request (9) (resp. (10)) in the initial state and use the set of rules from Definition 7 (resp. Definition 8) and the $\mathcal{TR}$'s inference system to find a proof.

$$? - plan \otimes (\wedge_{g_i \in G} g_i). \tag{9}$$

$$? - achieve_G. \tag{10}$$

Completeness of a planning strategy means that, for any *STRIPS* planning problem, if there is a solution, the planner will find at least one plan.

Theorem 1 (Completeness of naive planning). *If there is a plan that achieves the goal* G *from the initial state* $\mathbf{D}_0$ *then the* $\mathcal{TR}$*-based naive planner will find a plan.*

520   R. Basseda and M. Kifer

Proof (Sketch). The proof is a direct consequence of $\mathcal{TR}$ inference system completeness.

Theorem 2 (Completeness of *STRIPS* planning). *Given a goal serializable planning problem $\Pi = \langle \mathbb{R}, \mathbb{A}, G, \mathbf{D}_0 \rangle$, if there is a plan that achieves the goal G from the initial state $\mathbf{D}_0$ then the $\mathcal{TR}$-based STRIPS planner will find a plan.*

Proof (Sketch). By induction on the length of the plan. The full proof can be found in the full report.[3]

4   Conclusion

This paper has demonstrated that the use of Transaction Logic opens up new possibilities for generalizations and considerations of the properties of existing planning techniques. For instance, we have shown that once the *STRIPS* algorithm is cast as a set of rules in $\mathcal{TR}$, the different properties of the framework can be studied, almost for free, to recognize and define such advanced concepts as goal serializability of planning. The concept of serializability, not only classifies planning problem regarding to the completeness of *STRIPS* planning technique, but also establishes further explorations in different areas such as algorithms and graph theory.

References

1. Sacerdoti, E.D.: The nonlinear nature of plans. In: Proceedings of the 4th International Joint Conference on Artificial Intelligence, IJCAI 1975, vol. 1, pp. 206–214. Morgan Kaufmann Publishers Inc., San Francisco (1975)
2. Bibel, W.: A deductive solution for plan generation. In: Schmidt, J.W., Thanos, C. (eds.) Foundations of Knowledge Base Management. Topics in Information Systems, pp. 453–473. Springer, Heidelberg (1989)
3. Kahramanoğulları, O.: On linear logic planning and concurrency. In: Martín-Vide, C., Otto, F., Fernau, H. (eds.) LATA 2008. LNCS, vol. 5196, pp. 250–262. Springer, Heidelberg (2008). doi:10.1007/978-3-540-88282-4_24
4. Cresswell, S., Smaill, A., Richardson, J.: Deductive synthesis of recursive plans in linear logic. In: Biundo, S., Fox, M. (eds.) ECP 1999. LNCS (LNAI), vol. 1809, pp. 252–264. Springer, Heidelberg (2000). doi:10.1007/10720246_20
5. Guglielmi, A.: Concurrency and plan generation in a logic programming language with a sequential operator. In: Hentenryck, P.V. (ed.) ICLP, pp. 240–254. MIT Press (1994)
6. Kahramanogullari, O.: Towards planning as concurrency. In: Hamza, M.H. (ed.) Artificial Intelligence and Applications, pp. 387–393. IASTED/ACTA Press (2005)
7. Fikes, R.E., Nilsson, N.J.: STRIPS: a new approach to the application of theorem proving to problem solving. Artif. Intell. **2**, 189–208 (1971)
8. Bonner, A., Kifer, M.: Transaction logic programming (or a logic of declarative and procedural knowledge). Technical report CSRI-323, University of Toronto, November 1995. http://www.cs.toronto.edu/~bonner/transaction-logic.html

---

[3] http://ewl.cewit.stonybrook.edu/planning/Goal-Serializability.pdf.

9. Bonner, A., Kifer, M.: A logic for programming database transactions. In: Chomicki, J., Saake, G. (eds.) Logics for Databases and Information Systems, pp. 117–166. Kluwer Academic Publishers, March 1998
10. Bonner, A.J., Kifer, M.: An overview of transaction logic. Theoret. Comput. Sci. **133**(32), 205–265 (1994)
11. Bonner, A., Kifer, M.: Transaction logic programming. In: International Conference on Logic Programming, Budapest, Hungary, pp. 257–282. MIT Press, June 1993
12. Basseda, R., Kifer, M., Bonner, A.J.: Planning with transaction logic. In: Kontchakov, R., Mugnier, M.-L. (eds.) RR 2014. LNCS, vol. 8741, pp. 29–44. Springer, Heidelberg (2014). doi:10.1007/978-3-319-11113-1_3
13. Basseda, R., Kifer, M.: Planning with regression analysis in transaction logic. In: Cate, B., Mileo, A. (eds.) RR 2015. LNCS, vol. 9209, pp. 45–60. Springer, Heidelberg (2015). doi:10.1007/978-3-319-22002-4_5
14. Basseda, R., Kifer, M.: State space planning using transaction logic. In: Pontelli, E., Son, T.C. (eds.) PADL 2015. LNCS, vol. 9131, pp. 17–33. Springer, Heidelberg (2015). doi:10.1007/978-3-319-19686-2_2

Rule-based Stream Reasoning for Intelligent Administration of Content-Centric Networks

Harald Beck[1]($\boxtimes$), Bruno Bierbaumer[2], Minh Dao-Tran[1], Thomas Eiter[1],
Hermann Hellwagner[2], and Konstantin Schekotihin[2]

[1] TU Wien, Vienna, Austria
{beck,dao,eiter}@kr.tuwien.ac.at
[2] Alpen-Adria-Universität Klagenfurt, Klagenfurt, Austria
bruno@itec.aau.at, {bruno.bierbaumer,hermann.hellwagner,
konstantin.schekotihin}@aau.at

Abstract. Content-Centric Networking (CCN) research addresses the mismatch between the modern usage of the Internet and its outdated architecture. Importantly, CCN routers use various *caching strategies* to locally cache content frequently requested by end users. However, it is unclear which content shall be stored and when it should be replaced. In this work, we employ novel techniques towards intelligent administration of CCN routers. Our approach allows for autonomous switching between existing strategies in response to changing content request patterns using rule-based stream reasoning framework LARS which extends Answer Set Programming for streams. The obtained possibility for flexible router configuration at runtime allows for faster experimentation and may result in significant performance gains, as shown in our evaluation.

1 Introduction

Various future Internet research efforts are being pursued for efficient multimedia distribution, among them *Content-Centric Networking* (CCN) [14]. The operation of a CCN network relies on two packet types, *Interest* and *Data*. Clients issue *Interest* packets containing the *content name* they want to retrieve. CCN routers forward the *Interest* packets until they reach a content provider, which answers with a *Data* packet. The latter travels back to the content consumer following the way of *Interest* packets. In addition, the CCN routers have the possibility to cache *Data* packets in their *Content Stores*. Thus, the *Interest* packets of another consumer can be directly satisfied out of a *Content Store*. These caches make it possible to satisfy popular content requests directly out of caches and reduce the network load [14].

A *caching strategy* defines which content is stored and for how long before being replaced. There is a rich literature of strategies for CCN [21,24]. Examples

---

This work was partly funded by the Austrian Science Fund (FWF) under the CHIST-ERA project CONCERT (A Context-Adaptive Content Ecosystem Under Uncertainty), project number I1402, as well as projects P26471 and W1255-N23.

L. Michael and A. Kakas (Eds.): JELIA 2016, LNAI 10021, pp. 522–528, 2016.
DOI: 10.1007/978-3-319-48758-8_34

of most popular strategies include: (a) *Least Recently Used* (LRU), which orders items in cache by access time stamps and replaces the oldest item; (b) *First-In-First-Out* (FIFO) implementing a queue; (c) *Least Frequently Used* (LFU) which orders items by access frequency and replaces the least accessed item; or (d) *Random* that replaces a random item in the cache. However, selection of an appropriate strategy is complicated.

Example 1. Consider a situation in which some music clips go viral, i.e., get very popular over a short period of time. In this case, network administrators may manually configure the routers to cache highly popular content for some time period, and to switch back to the usual caching strategy when the consumer interests get more evenly distributed. However, as this period of time is hard to predict, it would be desirable that routers autonomously switch their caching strategy to ensure high quality of service.   ∎

Evaluations, like [4,24], show that no "silver bullet" strategy is superior in all tested scenarios, since for every strategy there are conditions in which it works best. There conditions can often be characterized by parameters of a consumer interests distribution. Usually, the content popularity is described in the literature with a *Zipf* distribution [18]: $P(X = i) = \left(i^\alpha \sum_{j=1}^{C} 1/j^\alpha \right)^{-1}$, where C is a number of items in the content catalog, α is a value of the exponent characterizing the distribution and i is a rank of an item in the catalog. The variation of the exponent α allows to characterize different popularity models for consumers interests: (i) if α is high, the popular content is limited to a small number of items; (ii) if α is low, every content is almost equally popular.

As real CCNs are not deployed yet, there is currently no real-world experience to rely on, and developing selection methods for caching strategies is not well supported. Motivated by all this, we consider a router architecture that allows for dynamic switching of caching strategies in reaction to the current network traffic, based on *stream reasoning*, i.e., reasoning over recent snapshots of data streams.

Contributions. (i) We present an *Intelligent Caching Agent* (ICA) for the administration of CCN routers using stream reasoning, which allows for the first implementation of a local and dynamic caching strategy selection. (ii) To simulate various CCN application scenarios, router architectures and rule-based administration policies, we propose an extension of the well-known CCN simulator ndnSIM [15]. (iii) The evaluation results of our methods on two sample scenarios (as in Example 1) indicate a clear performance gain when basic caching strategies are dynamically switched by routers in reaction to the observed stream of requested data packets.

In summary, we provide a feasibility study for using logic-based stream reasoning techniques to guide selection of caching strategies in CCNs. Moreover, we also provide a detailed showcase of analytical, declarative stream reasoning tools for intelligent administration problems; to the best of our knowledge, no similar work exists to date.

2   Stream Reasoning

Router administration requires evaluation of streaming data. To the best of our knowledge, declarative *stream reasoning* [6] methods [2,11,12,16,23] have not been used.

Example 2 (con't). Consider the following rules to select a caching strategy. If in the last 30 s there was always a high $\hat{\alpha}$ value (some content is very popular), use LFU, and for a medium value, take LRU. Furthermore, use FIFO if the value is low but once in the last 20 s 50 % was real-time content. Otherwise, use Random.   ∎

Example 2 illustrates that a fully declarative, rule-based language would assist the readability of a router's module that controls (potentially far more complex) decisions. We employ the rule-based LARS [2] which can be seen as extension of Answer Set Programming (ASP) [3,10] for streams. In particular, it provides *window* operators to limit limit reasoning to so-called *snapshots* as in CQL [1]. We give a high-level intuition.

LARS. A LARS program is a set of rules of form $\alpha \leftarrow \beta_1, ..., \beta_j$, $\text{not } \beta_{j+1}, ..., \text{not } \beta_n$, $(n \geq 0)$ where $\alpha, \beta_1, \ldots, \beta_n$ are formulas and not denotes *negation-as-failure*. Let a be an atom and $t \in \mathbb{N}$. Then, the set $\mathcal{F}$ of LARS *formulas* is defined by the grammar $\varphi ::= a \mid \neg\varphi \mid \varphi \wedge \varphi \mid \varphi \vee \varphi \mid \varphi \rightarrow \varphi \mid \Diamond\varphi \mid \Box\varphi \mid @_t\varphi \mid \boxplus^w\varphi$. It uses the following:

- The *window operator* $\boxplus^w$ limits evaluation of a formula φ to the substream returned by a function w, which takes a stream and a time point. We only use a special window operator $\boxplus^k$ which returns the snapshot of the last k s.
- The *temporal quantifiers* $\Diamond$ and $\Box$ are used to query whether a formula φ holds at *some* time point in a selected window, or at *all* time points.
- The *@-operator* allows a jump in time, i.e., $@_t\varphi$ evaluates φ at time t.

Example 3. Figure 1 formalizes the rules of Example 2 in LARS, where atom $\hat{\alpha}(V)$ is used to retrieve from the router an estimation of the α value V. Similarly, $rtm50$ is true if at least 50 % of the content forwarded by the router was real-time. Rule (r_1) says the following. If in the last 30 s ($\boxplus^{30}$), at a specific (variable) time T ($@_T$) we had atom $\hat{\alpha}(V)$ for some value $V \geq 1.8$, then *high* is true at T. Then, rule (r_4) states that, if *high* is true at *all* ($\Box$) of the last 30 s,

$r_1 :\ @_T high \leftarrow \boxplus^{30} @_T \hat{\alpha}(V),\ V \geq 1.8.$ $r_5 :\ use(lru) \leftarrow \boxplus^{30}\Box mid.$

$r_2 :\ @_T mid \leftarrow \boxplus^{30} @_T \hat{\alpha}(V),\ 1.2 \leq V < 1.8.$ $r_6 :\ use(fifo) \leftarrow \boxplus^{30}\Box low,\ \boxplus^{20}\Diamond rtm50.$

$r_3 :\ @_T low \leftarrow \boxplus^{30} @_T \hat{\alpha}(V),\ V < 1.2.$ $r_7 :\ done \leftarrow use(lfu) \vee use(lru) \vee use(fifo).$

$r_4 :\ use(lfu) \leftarrow \boxplus^{30}\Box high.$ $r_8 :\ use(random) \leftarrow \text{not } done.$

Fig. 1. Program P deciding which caching strategy to use

then ($\leftarrow$) we shall use *lfu*. If $use(X)$ cannot by derived for any $X \in \{lfu, lru, fifo\}$ by rules $(r_4) - (r_6)$, the disjunction in (r_7) fails, thus *done* will not be derived, and due to (r_8) we will then use *random*.   ∎

3   System Description

As shown in Fig. 2, ICA extends the architecture of a common CCN router with a decision unit, which consists of three main components: (1) a database (DB) storing snapshots of parameters observed by the controller, (2) a knowledge base (KB) containing the ICA logic and (3) a reasoner that decides about configuration of the controller given the KB and a series of events in the DB. This architecture was implemented in ndnSim [15] and used in the evaluation as presented in Sect. 4.

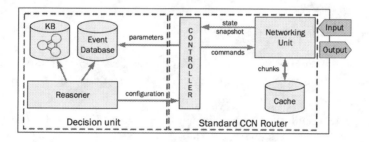

Fig. 2. Architecture of an Intelligent Caching Agent (ICA)

The components (2) and (3) are based on the LARS framework, which we implemented using DLVHEX 2.5 [9] as language of this system, i.e., higher-order logic programs with external atoms. We define an external atom $\&w[S, E, F](T, V)$ representing the described time-based LARS window operator. The terms $S, E \in \mathbb{N}$ define the time interval of the window and F is a string comprising a function name. Our DLVHEX plug-in evaluates the function over events registered in the database within the given time interval and returns its results as a set of tuples $\{(t_1, v_1), \ldots, (t_k, v_k)\}$, where t_i and v_i indicate the time point and the value of a function, respectively. E.g. for $F = $ alpha the estimated values $\hat{\alpha}$ of the parameter α of the Zipf distribution will be returned. To define rules that respect only recent events, we use an external atom $\&getSolverTime[](E)$ which has no inputs. It outputs the current system time E. The DLVHEX encoding for ICA is presented in Listing 1.1, which corresponds to the LARS encoding presented in Fig. 1 and could be in principle automatically generated from it.

```
1  intv1(S,E)  :- &getSolverTime[](E),  S=E-30.
2  intv2(S,E)  :- &getSolverTime[](E),  S=E-20.

3  val(high,S,E,T):- &w[S,E,alpha](T,V),  V>=18,  intv1(S,E).
4  val(mid,S,E,T)  :- &w[S,E,alpha](T,V),  12<=V,  V<18,  intv1(S,E).
5  val(low,S,E,T)  :- &w[S,E,alpha](T,V),  V<12,  intv1(S,E).
6  val(rtm50,S,E,T):- &w[S,E,rtc](T,V),  V>50,  intv2(S,E).

7  some(ID,S,E)    :- val(ID,S,E,_).
8  always(ID,S,E) :- val(ID,S,E,_),  val(ID,S,E,T):T=S..E.

9  use(lfu)  :- always(high,S,E),  intv1(S,E).
10 use(lru)  :- always(mid,S,E),  intv1(S,E).
11 use(fifo):- always(low,S1,E1),  intv1(S1,E1),  some(rtm50,S2,E2),
        intv2(S2,E2).

12 done  :- use(X),  X!=random.
13 use(random)  :- not done.
```

Listing 1.1. DLVHEX encoding for ICA

4   Evaluation

We selected the *Abilene* topology [20]. For every simulation run (see below), we connected 1000 consumers and all content providers randomly to one of the 11 routers.

Scenarios. As popularity change scenarios, we used (i) *LHL* that starts with $\alpha = 0.4$ (low), then changes to 2.5 (high), and then back to low; (ii) *HLH* is dual. The values are from [17,21]. Each simulation is 1800 s, α changes at 600 and 1200. Each consumer starts downloading a video at a random time point in each interval.

Caching Strategies. To measure the potential effect of switching strategies, we compare against the static ones *Random* and and LFU [21]. Dynamic strategy *Admin* is hypothetical, where all routers change their caching strategy exactly at phase changes L to H and H to L; in L they use Random, in H they use LFU. Finally, *Intelligent Caching Agent (ICA)* dynamically selects for each router a strategy due to locally observed data.

Simulation System Parameters. Following [14,17,19], we use 1000 users $\times$ 50 videos, in 1000 chunks of 10KB. Routers store 0.1, 0.5, 1, 4 or 10 % of all chunks.

Performance Metrics. The *cache hit ratio* should be high; it is the number of hits an *Interest* packet is satisfied by a router's content store per total number of requests. The *cache hit distance* should be low; it is the average number of *hops* for a *Data* packet from request to a router that returns it, i.e., the number of routers travelled between the router answering a request and the consumer that had issued it. See [24] for details.

Results. We determined 1 % of chunks to be a reasonable storage size. We observed that the reaction to changing content access for ICA was close to the

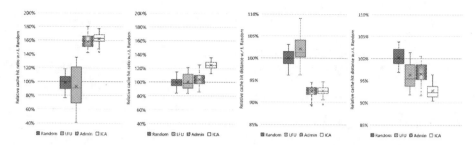

(a) LHL cache hit ratio (b) HLH cache hit ratio (c) LHL cache hit dist. (d) HLH cache hit dist.

Fig. 3. Aggregated evaluation results over 30 runs for each caching strategy

ideal preconfiguration of Admin. Interestingly, up to 5 routers used the Random strategy in the H phase under the ICA strategy. Here, the advantage of dynamic and *local* switching kicked in.

Figure 3 shows performance comparisons of caching strategies LFU, Admin and ICA in relation to Random (100 %), where plots show aggregated results over 30 individual runs. Figure 3a/b depict cache hit ratios for LHL/HLH; Fig. 3c/d show cache hit distances. In summary, dynamic switching is advantageous in all settings. ICA is at least as good as Admin for LHL scenarios, and proves to be the best strategy for HLH due to the advantage of choosing strategies locally for each router. Notably, both dynamic strategies lead to a decreased cache hit distance relative to the Random strategy.

5   Conclusion

In our paper we focused on a principled approach of automated decision making by means of high-level reasoning on stream data. This allowed us to design a purely declarative control unit for automated administration of CCN routers. A comprehensive feasibility study shows how reasoning techniques can be used for dynamic switching of caching strategies in reaction to changing user behavior may give significant savings due to performance gains. These observations clearly motivate the advancement of stream reasoning research, especially on the practical side. In particular, stream processing engines are in need that have an expressive power similar to LARS.

References

1. Arasu, A., Babu, S., Widom, J.: The CQL continuous query language: semantic foundations and query execution. VLDB J. **15**(2), 121–142 (2006)
2. Beck, H., Dao-Tran, M., Eiter, T., Fink, M.: LARS: a logic-based framework for analyzing reasoning over streams. In: AAAI (2015)
3. Brewka, G., Eiter, T., Truszczyński, M.: Answer set programming at a glance. Commun. ACM **54**(12), 92–103 (2011)

4. Cha, M., Kwak, H., Rodriguez, P., Ahn, Y., Moon, S.B.: Analyzing the video popularity characteristics of large-scale user generated content systems. IEEE/ACM Trans. Netw. **17**(5), 1357–1370 (2009)
5. Cisco Visual Networking Index: Forecast and Methodology, 2014–2019. White Paper (2016)
6. Della Valle, E., Ceri, S., van Harmelen, F., Fensel, D.: It's a streaming world! Reasoning upon rapidly changing information. IEEE Intell. Syst. **24**, 83–89 (2009)
7. Do, T.M., Loke, S.W., Liu, F.: Answer set programming for stream reasoning. In: Butz, C., Lingras, P. (eds.) AI 2011. LNCS (LNAI), vol. 6657, pp. 104–109. Springer, Heidelberg (2011). doi:10.1007/978-3-642-21043-3_13
8. Eiter, T., Fink, M., Krennwallner, T., Redl, C.: Domain expansion for ASP-programs with external sources. Artif. Intell. **233**, 84–121 (2014)
9. Eiter, T., Mehuljic, M., Redl, C., Schüller, P.: User guide: dlvhex 2.x. Technical report INFSYS RR-1843-15-05, TU Vienna (2015)
10. Faber, W., Leone, N., Pfeifer, G.: Recursive aggregates in disjunctive logic programs: semantics and complexity. In: Alferes, J.J., Leite, J. (eds.) JELIA 2004. LNCS (LNAI), vol. 3229, pp. 200–212. Springer, Heidelberg (2004). doi:10.1007/978-3-540-30227-8_19
11. Gebser, M., Grote, T., Kaminski, R., Obermeier, P., Sabuncu, O., Schaub, T.: Stream reasoning with answer set programming: preliminary report. In: KR, pp. 613–617 (2012)
12. Gebser, M., Kaminski, R., Kaufmann, B., Ostrowski, M., Schaub, T., Thiele, S.: Engineering an incremental ASP solver. In: Garcia de la Banda, M., Pontelli, E. (eds.) ICLP 2008. LNCS, vol. 5366, pp. 190–205. Springer, Heidelberg (2008). doi:10.1007/978-3-540-89982-2_23
13. Gelfond, M., Lifschitz, V.: Classical negation in logic programs and disjunctive databases. New Gener. Comput. **9**(3–4), 365–386 (1991)
14. Jacobson, V., Smetters, D.K., Thornton, J.D., Plass, M.F., Briggs, N.H., Braynard, R.: Networking named content. In: CoNEXT, pp. 1–12 (2009)
15. Mastorakis, S., Afanasyev, A., Moiseenko, I., Zhang, L.: ndnSIM 2.0: a new version of the NDN simulator for NS-3. Technical report NDN-0028, NDN (2015)
16. Mileo, A., Abdelrahman, A., Policarpio, S., Hauswirth, M.: Streamrule: a non-monotonic stream reasoning system for the semantic web. In: RR, pp. 247–252 (2013)
17. Rossi, D., Rossini, G.: Caching performance of content centric networks under multi-path routing (and more). Relatório técnico, Telecom ParisTech (2011)
18. Rossi, D., Rossini, G.: On sizing CCN content stores by exploiting topological information. In: IEEE INFOCOM, pp. 280–285 (2012)
19. Rossini, G., Rossi, D., Garetto, M., Leonardi, E.: Multi-terabyte and multi-gbps information centric routers. In: IEEE INFOCOM, pp. 181–189 (2014)
20. Spring, N.T., Mahajan, R., Wetherall, D., Anderson, T.E.: Measuring ISP topologies with rocketfuel. IEEE/ACM Trans. Netw. **12**(1), 2–16 (2004)
21. Tarnoi, S., Suksomboon, K., Kumwilaisak, W., Ji, Y.: Performance of probabilistic caching and cache replacement policies for content-centric networks. In: IEEE LCN, pp. 99–106 (2014)
22. Yu, H., Zheng, D., Zhao, B.Y., Zheng, W.: Understanding user behavior in large-scale video-on-demand systems. In: EuroSys, pp. 333–344 (2006)
23. Zaniolo, C.: Logical foundations of continuous query languages for data streams. In: Barceló, P., Pichler, R. (eds.) Datalog 2.0 2012. LNCS, vol. 7494, pp. 177–189. Springer, Heidelberg (2012). doi:10.1007/978-3-642-32925-8_18
24. Zhang, M., Luo, H., Zhang, H.: A survey of caching mechanisms in information-centric networking. IEEE Commun. Surv. Tutor. **17**(3), 1473–1499 (2015)

Inconsistency Management in Reactive Multi-context Systems

Gerhard Brewka[1], Stefan Ellmauthaler[1], Ricardo Gonçalves[2],
Matthias Knorr[2(✉)], João Leite[2], and Jörg Pührer[1]

[1] Institute of Computer Science, Leipzig University, Leipzig, Germany
{brewka,ellmauthaler,puehrer}@informatik.uni-leipzig.de
[2] NOVA LINCS & Departamento de Informática,
Universidade NOVA de Lisboa, Caparica, Portugal
{rjrg,mkn,jleite}@fct.unl.pt

Abstract. We address the problem of global inconsistency in reactive multi-context systems (rMCSs), a framework for reactive reasoning in the presence of heterogeneous knowledge sources that can deal with continuous input streams. Their semantics is given in terms of equilibria streams. The occurrence of inconsistencies, where rMCSs fail to have an equilibria stream, can render the entire system useless. We discuss various methods for handling this problem, following different strategies such as repairing the rMCS, or even relaxing the notion of equilibria stream so that it can *go through* inconsistent states.

1 Introduction

The occurrence of inconsistencies within frameworks that aim at integrating knowledge from different sources cannot be neglected, even more so in dynamic settings where knowledge changes over time. In this paper, we deal with *reactive Multi-Context Systems (rMCSs)* [5,6,13] that allow for integrating heterogeneous knowledge bases with streams of incoming information and to use them for continuous online reasoning, reacting, and evolving the knowledge bases by internalizing relevant knowledge. There are many reasons why rMCSs may fail to have an equilibria stream. These include the absence of an acceptable belief set for one of its contexts given its current knowledge base, some occurring conflict between the operations in the heads of bridge rules, or simply because the input stream is such that the bridge rules prevent the existence of such an equilibria stream. We address the problem of inexistent equilibria streams, also known as *global inconsistency*. We begin by defining a notion of coherence associated with individual contexts which allows us to first establish sufficient conditions for the existence of equilibria streams, and then abstract away from problems due to specific incoherent contexts and focus on those problems essentially caused by the way the flow of information in rMCSs is organized through its bridge rules. We introduce the notion of a *repair*, which modifies an rMCS by changing its bridge rules at some particular point in time in order to obtain some equilibria

© Springer International Publishing AG 2016
L. Michael and A. Kakas (Eds.): JELIA 2016, LNAI 10021, pp. 529–535, 2016.
DOI: 10.1007/978-3-319-48758-8_35

stream, which we dub *repaired equilibria stream*. We establish sufficient conditions for the existence of repaired equilibria streams and briefly discuss different possible strategies to define such repairs. However, repaired equilibria streams may not always exist, because, for example, some particular context is incoherent. To deal with such situations, we relax the concept of equilibria stream and introduce the notion of *partial equilibria stream*, which essentially allows the non-existence of equilibria at some time points. It turns out that *partial equilibria streams* always exist thus solving the problem of global inconsistency for rMCSs.

2   Inconsistency Management

We assume that the reader is familiar with rMCSs and refer to [5] for a thorough discussion of their background and the notation used in the following.

In [8], the authors addressed the problem of global inconsistency in the context of *managed multi-context systems (mMCSs)* [4]. Just as we do here, they begin by establishing sufficient conditions for the existence of equilibria. Then, they define the notions of *diagnosis* and *explanation*, the former corresponding to bridge rules that need to be altered to restore consistency, and the latter corresponding to combinations of rules that cause inconsistency. These two notions turn out to be dual of each other, and somehow correspond to our notion of repair, the main difference being that, unlike in [8], we opt not to allow the (non-standard) strengthening of bridge-rule to restore consistency, and the fact that our repairs need to take into account the dynamic nature of rMCSs. We start by introducing two notions of global consistency differing only on whether we consider a particular input stream or all possible input streams.

Definition 1. *Let M be an rMCS, KB a configuration of knowledge bases for M, and $\mathcal{I}$ an input stream for M. Then, M is* consistent *with respect to KB and $\mathcal{I}$ if there exists an equilibria stream of M given KB and $\mathcal{I}$. M is* strongly consistent *with respect to KB if, for every input stream $\mathcal{I}$ for M, M is consistent with respect to KB and $\mathcal{I}$.*

Obviously, for a fixed configuration of knowledge bases, strong consistency implies consistency w.r.t. any input stream, but not vice-versa. Unfortunately, verifying strong consistency is in general highly complex since it requires checking all possible equilibria streams. Nevertheless, we can establish conditions that ensure that an rMCS M is strongly consistent with respect to a given configuration of knowledge bases KB, hence guaranteeing the existence of an equilibria stream independently of the input. It is based on two notions – *totally coherent contexts* and *acyclic rMCSs* – that together are sufficient to ensure (strong) consistency. Total coherence imposes that each knowledge base of a context always has at least one acceptable belief set.

Definition 2. *A context C_i is* totally coherent *if $\mathbf{acc}_i(kb) \neq \emptyset$, for every $kb \in KB_i$.*

The second notion describes cycles between contexts which may be a cause of inconsistency. Acyclic rMCSs are those whose bridge rules have no cycles.

Definition 3. *Given an rMCS $M = \langle\langle C_1, \ldots, C_n\rangle, \mathsf{IL}, \mathsf{BR}\rangle$, $\lhd_M$ is the binary relation over contexts of M such that $(C_i, C_j) \in \lhd_M$ if there is a bridge rule $r \in BR_i$ and $j{:}b \in \mathrm{bd}(r)$ for some b. If $(C_i, C_j) \in \lhd_M$, also denoted by $C_i \lhd_M C_j$, we say that C_i depends on C_j in M. An rMCS M is acyclic if the transitive closure of $\lhd_M$ is irreflexive.*

These two conditions together are indeed sufficient to ensure strong consistency.

Proposition 1. *Let $M = \langle\langle C_1, \ldots, C_n\rangle, \mathsf{IL}, \mathsf{BR}\rangle$ be an acyclic rMCS such that every C_i, $1 \le i \le n$, is totally coherent, and KB a configuration of knowledge bases for M. Then, M is strongly consistent with respect to KB.*

These conditions can be rather restrictive since there are many useful cyclic rMCSs which only under some particular configurations of knowledge bases and input streams may have no equilibria streams. To deal with these, and recover an equilibria stream, one possibility is to repair the rMCSs by locally, and selectively, eliminating some of its bridge rules. Towards introducing the notion of *repair*, given an rMCS $M = \langle\langle C_1, \ldots, C_n\rangle, \mathsf{IL}, \mathsf{BR}\rangle$, we denote by br_M the set of all bridge rules of M, i.e., $br_M = \bigcup_{1 \le i \le n} BR_i$. Moreover, given a set $R \subseteq br_M$, denote by $M[R]$ the rMCS obtained from M by restricting the bridge rules to those not in R.

Definition 4 (Repair). *Let $M = \langle \mathsf{C}, \mathsf{IL}, \mathsf{BR}\rangle$ be an rMCS, KB a configuration of knowledge bases for M, and $\mathcal{I}$ an input stream for M until τ where $\tau \in \mathbb{N} \cup \{\infty\}$. Then, a repair for M given KB and $\mathcal{I}$ is a function $\mathcal{R} : [1..\tau] \to 2^{br_M}$ such that there exists a function $\mathcal{B} : [1..\tau] \to \mathsf{Bel}_M$ such that*

- *$\mathcal{B}^t$ is an equilibrium of $M[\mathcal{R}^t]$ given $\mathcal{KB}^t$ and $\mathcal{I}^t$, with $\mathcal{KB}^t$ inductively defined as*
  - $\mathcal{KB}^1 = \mathsf{KB}$
  - $\mathcal{KB}^{t+1} = \mathbf{upd}_{M[\mathcal{R}^t]}(\mathcal{KB}^t, \mathcal{I}^t, \mathcal{B}^t)$.

We refer to $\mathcal{B}$ as a repaired equilibria stream of M given KB, $\mathcal{I}$ and $\mathcal{R}$.

The notion of *repair* is quite general, and includes repairs that unnecessarily eliminate bridge rules, and even the *empty repair*, i.e., the repair $\mathcal{R}_\emptyset$ such that $\mathcal{R}_\emptyset^t = \emptyset$ for every t, whenever M already has an equilibria stream given KB and $\mathcal{I}$, ensuring that repaired equilibria streams properly extend equilibria streams.

Proposition 2. *Every equilibria stream of M given KB and $\mathcal{I}$ is a repaired equilibria stream of M given KB, $\mathcal{I}$ and the empty repair $\mathcal{R}_\emptyset$.*

It turns out that for rMCSs composed of totally coherent contexts, repaired equilibria streams always exist.

Proposition 3. *Let $M = \langle\langle C_1, \ldots, C_n\rangle, \mathsf{IL}, \mathsf{BR}\rangle$ be an rMCS such that each C_i, $i \in \{1, \ldots, n\}$, is totally coherent, KB a configuration of knowledge bases for M, and $\mathcal{I}$ an input stream for M until τ. Then, there exists $\mathcal{R} : [1..\tau] \to 2^{br_M}$ and $\mathcal{B} : [1..\tau] \to \mathsf{Bel}_M$ such that $\mathcal{B}$ is a repaired equilibria stream given KB, $\mathcal{I}$ and $\mathcal{R}$.*

Whenever repair operations are considered in the literature, e.g., in the context of databases [2], there is a special emphasis on seeking repairs that are somehow minimal, the rational being that we want to change things as little as possible to regain consistency. In the case of repairs of rMCS, we can establish an order relation between them, based on a comparison of the bridge rules to be deleted at each time point.

Definition 5. *Let $\mathcal{R}_a$ and $\mathcal{R}_b$ be two repairs for some rMCS M given a configuration of knowledge bases for M, KB and $\mathcal{I}$, an input stream for M until τ. We say that $\mathcal{R}_a \leq \mathcal{R}_b$ if $\mathcal{R}_a^i \subseteq \mathcal{R}_b^i$ for every $i \leq \tau$, and that $\mathcal{R}_a < \mathcal{R}_b$ if $\mathcal{R}_a \leq \mathcal{R}_b$ and $\mathcal{R}_a^i \subset \mathcal{R}_b^i$ for some $i \leq \tau$.*

This relation can be directly used to check whether a repair is minimal, and we can restrict ourselves to adopting minimal repairs. However, there may be good reasons to adopt non-minimal repairs, e.g., so that they can be determined *as we go*, or so that *deleted* bridge rules are not reinstated, etc. Even though investigating specific types of repairs falls outside the scope of this paper, we nevertheless discuss some possibilities.

Definition 6 (Types of Repairs). *Let $\mathcal{R}$ be a repair for some rMCS M given KB and $\mathcal{I}$. We say that $\mathcal{R}$ is a:*

Minimal Repair *if there is no repair $\mathcal{R}_a$ for M given KB and $\mathcal{I}$ such that $\mathcal{R}_a < \mathcal{R}$.*
Global Repair *if $\mathcal{R}^i = \mathcal{R}^j$ for every $i, j \leq \tau$.*
Minimal Global Repair *if $\mathcal{R}$ is global and there is no global repair $\mathcal{R}_a$ for M given KB and $\mathcal{I}$ such that $\mathcal{R}_a < \mathcal{R}$.*
Incremental Repair *if $\mathcal{R}^i \subseteq \mathcal{R}^j$ for every $i \leq j \leq \tau$.*
Minimally Incremental Repair *if $\mathcal{R}$ is incremental and there is no incremental repair $\mathcal{R}_a$ and $j \leq \tau$ such that $\mathcal{R}_a^i \subset \mathcal{R}^i$ for every $i \leq j$.*

Minimal repairs perhaps correspond to the ideal situation in that they never unnecessarily remove bridge rules. Sometimes, it may be the case that if a bridge rule is somehow involved in some inconsistency, it should not be used at any time point, leading to the notion of *global repair*. Given the set of all repairs, checking which are global is also obviously less complex than checking which are minimal. A further refinement – *minimal global repairs* – would be to only consider repairs that are minimal among the global ones, which would be much simpler to check than checking whether it is simply minimal. Note that a minimal global repair is not necessarily a minimal repair. One of the problems with these types of repairs is that we can only check whether they are of that type once we know the entire input stream $\mathcal{I}$. This was not the case with *plain* repairs, as defined in Definition 4, which could be checked *as we go*, i.e., we can determine what bridge rules to include in the repair at a particular time point by having access to the input stream $\mathcal{I}$ up to that time point only, important so that rMCSs can be used to effectively react to their environment. The last two types of repairs defined above allow for just that. *Incremental repairs* essentially impose that removed bridge rules cannot be reused in the future, while *minimally incremental repairs* further impose that only minimal sets of bridge rules can be added at each time point. Other types of repairs could be defined, e.g., based on a priority relation between bridge rules, or a distance measure between subsets of bridge rules. Repairs could also be extended to allow for the strengthening of bridge rules, besides their elimination, such as in [4,8].

Despite the existence of repaired equilibria streams for large classes of systems, two problems remain: first, computing a repair may be excessively complex, and second, there remain situations where no repaired equilibria stream exists, namely when the rMCS contains contexts that are not totally coherent. The second issue could be dealt with by ensuring that for each non-totally coherent context there would be some bridge rule with a management operation in its head that would always restore consistency of the context, and that such rule could always be *activated* through a repair. But this would require special care in the way the system is specified, and its analysis would require a very complex analysis of the entire system including the specific behavior of management functions. In practice, it would be quite hard – close to impossible in general – to ensure the existence of repaired equilibria streams, and we would still be faced with the first problem, that of the complexity of determining the repairs.

This can be addressed by relaxing the notion of equilibria stream so that it does not require an equilibrium at every time point. This way, if no equilibrium exists at some time point, the equilibria stream would be undefined at that point, but possibly defined again in subsequent time points, leading to the notion of *partial equilibria stream*.

Definition 7 (Partial Equilibria Stream). *Let* $M = \langle \mathsf{C}, \mathsf{IL}, \mathsf{BR} \rangle$ *be an rMCS,* KB *a configuration of knowledge bases for* M, *and* $\mathcal{I}$ *an input stream for* M *until* τ *where* $\tau \in \mathbb{N} \cup \{\infty\}$. *Then, a* partial equilibria stream *of* M *given* KB *and* $\mathcal{I}$ *is a partial function* $\mathcal{B} : [1..\tau] \nrightarrow \mathsf{Bel}_M$ *such that*

– $\mathcal{B}^t$ *is an equilibrium of* M *given* $\mathcal{KB}^t$ *and* $\mathcal{I}^t$, *with* $\mathcal{KB}^t$ *inductively defined as*

- $\mathcal{KB}^1 = \mathsf{KB}$
- $\mathcal{KB}^{t+1} = \begin{cases} \mathbf{upd}_M(\mathcal{KB}^t, \mathcal{I}^t, \mathcal{B}^t), & \textit{if } \mathcal{B}^t \textit{ is not undefined.} \\ \mathcal{KB}^t, & \textit{otherwise.} \end{cases}$

– *or* $\mathcal{B}^t$ *is undefined.*

Partial equilibria streams generalize equilibria streams and do always exist.

Proposition 4. *Every equilibria stream of* M *given* KB *and* $\mathcal{I}$ *is a partial equilibria stream of* M *given* KB *and* $\mathcal{I}$.

Proposition 5. *Let M be an rMCS,* KB *a configuration of knowledge bases for M, and $\mathcal{I}$ an input stream for M until τ. Then, there exists $\mathcal{B} : [1..\tau] \nrightarrow$ Bel$_M$ such that $\mathcal{B}$ is a partial equilibria stream given* KB *and $\mathcal{I}$.*

Partial equilibria streams not only do allow us to deal with situations where equilibria do not exist at some time instants, they also open the ground to consider other kinds of situations where we do not wish to consider equilibria, for example because we were not able to compute them on time, or simply because we do not wish to process the input at every time point, e.g., whenever we just wish to sample the input with a lower frequency than it is generated. To restrict that partial equilibria streams only relax equilibria streams when necessary, we can further impose the following condition on Definition 7: $\mathcal{B}^t$ is undefined $\Rightarrow$ there is no equilibrium of M given $\mathcal{KB}^t$ and $\mathcal{I}^t$.

3   Conclusions

Following the efforts done in the combination of knowledge bases integration and knowledge dynamics [1,3,7,9,10,12,14,16], this paper addresses the problem of how inconsistencies can be managed within the framework of reactive Multi-Context Systems (rMCSs). The occurrence of inconsistencies within rMCSs cannot be neglected, especially as we deal with dynamic settings where knowledge changes over time. Even with the power of management operations that allow the specification of, e.g., belief revision operations, many reasons remain why rMCSs may fail to have an equilibria stream. Since the absence of equilibria at certain time points ultimately render the entire system useless, we addressed this problem first by showing sufficient conditions on the contexts and the bridge rules that ensure the existence of an equilibria stream. In the cases where these conditions are not met, we presented two possible solutions, one following an approach based on repairs and a second by relaxing the notion of equilibria stream to ensure that intermediate inconsistent states can be recovered. In future work, we would like to explore an alternative to deal with inconsistent states, following a paraconsistent approach, as proposed for hybrid knowledge bases in [11,15].

Acknowledgments. R. Gonçalves, M. Knorr and J. Leite were partially supported by FCT strategic project NOVA LINCS (UID/CEC/04516/2013). R. Gonçalves was partially supported by FCT grant SFRH/BPD/100906/2014 and M. Knorr by FCT grant SFRH/BPD/86970/2012. G. Brewka, S. Ellmauthaler, and J. Pührer were partially supported by the German Research Foundation (DFG) grants BR-1817/7-1 and FOR 1513.

References

1. Alferes, J.J., Brogi, A., Leite, J., Moniz Pereira, L.: Evolving logic programs. In: Flesca, S., Greco, S., Leone, N., Ianni, G. (eds.) JELIA 2002. LNCS (LNAI), vol. 2424, pp. 50–61. Springer, Heidelberg (2002)

2. Arenas, M., Bertossi, L.E., Chomicki, J.: Consistent query answers in inconsistent databases. In: Vianu, V., Papadimitriou, C.H. (eds.) Proceedings of ACM SIGACT-SIGMOD-SIGART, pp. 68–79. ACM Press (1999)
3. Brewka, G., Eiter, T.: Equilibria in heterogeneous nonmonotonic multi-context systems. In: Proceedings of AAAI, pp. 385–390. AAAI Press (2007)
4. Brewka, G., Eiter, T., Fink, M., Weinzierl, A.: Managed multi-context systems. In: Walsh, T. (ed.) Proceedings of IJCAI, pp. 786–791. IJCAI/AAAI (2011)
5. Brewka, G., Ellmauthaler, S., Gonçalves, R., Knorr, M., Leite, J., Pührer, J.: Reactive multi-context systems: heterogeneous reasoning in dynamic environments (2016). http://arxiv.org/abs/1609.03438
6. Brewka, G., Ellmauthaler, S., Pührer, J.: Multi-context systems for reactive reasoning in dynamic environments. In: Proceedings of ECAI, pp. 159–164 (2014)
7. Brewka, G., Roelofsen, F., Serafini, L.: Contextual default reasoning. In: Veloso, M.M. (ed.) Proceedings of IJCAI, pp. 268–273 (2007)
8. Eiter, T., Fink, M., Schüller, P., Weinzierl, A.: Finding explanations of inconsistency in multi-context systems. Artif. Intell. **216**, 233–274 (2014)
9. Ellmauthaler, S.: Generalizing multi-context systems for reactive stream reasoning applications. In: Jones, A.V., Ng, N. (eds.) Proceedings of ICCSW, OASICS, vol. 35, pp. 19–26. Schloss Dagstuhl - Leibniz-Zentrum fuer Informatik, Germany (2013)
10. Ellmauthaler, S., Pührer, J.: Asynchronous multi-context systems. In: Eiter, T., Strass, H., Truszczyński, M., Woltran, S. (eds.) Advances in Knowledge Representation. LNCS, vol. 9060, pp. 141–156. Springer, Heidelberg (2015)
11. Fink, M.: Paraconsistent hybrid theories. In: Brewka, G., Eiter, T., McIlraith, S.A. (eds.) Proceedings of KR. AAAI Press (2012)
12. Gonçalves, R., Knorr, M., Leite, J.: Evolving bridge rules in evolving multi-context systems. In: Bulling, N., van der Torre, L., Villata, S., Jamroga, W., Vasconcelos, W. (eds.) CLIMA 2014. LNCS, vol. 8624, pp. 52–69. Springer, Heidelberg (2014)
13. Gonçalves, R., Knorr, M., Leite, J.: Evolving multi-context systems. In: Proceedings of ECAI, pp. 375–380 (2014)
14. Gonçalves, R., Knorr, M., Leite, J.: Minimal change in evolving multi-context systems. In: Pereira, F., Machado, P., Costa, E., Cardoso, A. (eds.) EPIA 2015. LNCS, vol. 9273, pp. 611–623. Springer, Heidelberg (2015)
15. Kaminski, T., Knorr, M., Leite, J.: Efficient paraconsistent reasoning with ontologies and rules. In: Yang, Q., Wooldridge, M. (eds.) Proceedings of IJCAI, pp. 3098–3105. AAAI Press (2015)
16. Knorr, M., Gonçalves, R., Leite, J.: On efficient evolving multi-context systems. In: Pham, D.-N., Park, S.-B. (eds.) PRICAI 2014. LNCS, vol. 8862, pp. 284–296. Springer, Heidelberg (2014)

Iteratively-Supported Formulas and Strongly Supported Models for Kleene Answer Set Programs

(Extended Abstract)

Patrick Doherty[1], Jonas Kvarnström[1], and Andrzej Szałas[1,2](✉)

[1] Department of Computer and Information Science, Linköping University,
581 83 Linköping, Sweden
{patrick.doherty,jonas.kvarnstrom,andrzej.szalas}@liu.se
[2] Institute of Informatics, University of Warsaw, Banacha 2, 02-097 Warsaw, Poland
andrzej.szalas@mimuw.edu.pl

Abstract. In this extended abstract, we discuss the use of iteratively-supported formulas (ISFs) as a basis for computing strongly-supported models for Kleene Answer Set Programs (ASP^K). ASP^K programs have a syntax identical to classical ASP programs. The semantics of ASP^K programs is based on the use of Kleene three-valued logic and strongly-supported models. For normal ASP^K programs, their strongly supported models are identical to classical answer sets using stable model semantics. For disjunctive ASP^K programs, the semantics weakens the minimality assumption resulting in a classical interpretation for disjunction. We use ISFs to characterize strongly-supported models and show that they are polynomially bounded.

1 Introduction

Classical answer set programming, ASP, has been intensively studied during the past three decades [3,5,9]. In addition, a great deal of attention has been devoted to ASP implementations [4,7,8,12,16]. One of the prominent techniques proposed earlier for computing answer sets is based on translating ASP programs into classical propositional formulas and then applying SAT solvers to generate answer sets. In [6,12] it is shown that Clark's completion together with loop formulas characterize answer sets for ASP programs. One of the obstacles in characterizing answer sets using propositional formulas is their Σ_2^P complexity. Loop formulas contribute to this because one may require exponentially many of them [10]. The current extended abstract provides an alternative to loop formulas, iteratively-supported formulas, that ameliorates this problem. Polynomial translations of normal ASP programs have also been considered in [11,13,14]. However, our translation is extended to disjunctive programs in a natural way.

In [15] a possible model semantics for disjunctive programs is proposed. It is formulated with the use of split programs and there can be exponentially many

© Springer International Publishing AG 2016
L. Michael and A. Kakas (Eds.): JELIA 2016, LNAI 10021, pp. 536–542, 2016.
DOI: 10.1007/978-3-319-48758-8_36

of them comparing to the original program. Similar semantics was independently proposed in [1] under the name of the possible world semantics. In [2] we have analyzed minimality and supportedness in the context of ASPs and proposed Kleene Answer Set Programs (ASP^K) using the concept of strongly supported models. The semantics used for Kleene Answer Set programs is based on Kleene logic, K_3, with an extra weak negation. In [2] it is shown that the problem of showing whether an ASP^K program has a strongly supported model is in NP (i.e., in Σ_1^P). This result applies to both normal and disjunctive ASP^K programs. For disjunctive ASP^K programs, the minimality assumption is relaxed, resulting in a classical interpretation of disjunction.[1] The ability to fine-tune the separation of supportedness and minimality in the disjunctive case results in a lower complexity for generating strongly supported models. In comparison to [15], ASP^K programs allow for strong negation and a three-valued model-theoretic semantics is provided. The presence of both default and strong negation in ASP^K provides a tool to close the world locally in a contextual manner, more flexible than possible model negation proposed in [15]. Though defined independently and using different foundations, both semantics appear compatible on positive programs, so the results of the current paper apply to possible model semantics of [15], too.

The main contribution of the current paper is the definition and use of ISFs to characterize strongly supported models for both normal and disjunctive ASP^K programs. Such formulas are shown to be polynomially bounded in both cases. As a derivative result, in the case of normal ASP programs and due to a correspondence between answer sets and strongly supported models, ISFs provide a more efficient alternative to loop formulas when using SAT solvers. For disjunctive ASP^K programs, the use of supported models and ISFs provide an efficient means for using SAT solvers, but with an alternative semantics that interprets disjunction classically due to a relaxation of minimality assumptions.

The paper is structured as follows. In Sect. 2 we introduce basic definitions related to both classical ASP programs and ASP^K programs in addition to strong supportedness. Section 3 introduces ISFs used to characterize normal and disjunctive ASP^K programs. Section 4 concludes the paper.

2   Kleene Answer Set Programs

In this paper, the syntax for Kleene ASP^K programs is identical for that of classical ASP programs. The semantics for Kleene ASP^K programs is based on the use of a three-valued Kleene logic K_3 and strongly-supported models presented in [2]. The semantics for classical ASP programs is based on stable model semantics [9]. For the sake of clarity we consider propositional programs only. Truth values are denoted by T (true), F (false) and U (unknown). The empty conjunction is T and the empty disjunction is F.

---

[1] Note that minimality is sometimes not required or may even be undesirable [2,3,15, 17], e.g., in the context of programs that use disjunctive rules.

Definition 1. By a *positive literal* (or an *atom*) we mean any propositional variable of $\mathcal{P}$. A *negative literal* is an expression of the form $\neg r$, where $r \in \mathcal{P}$. A *classical literal* is a positive or a negative literal. A set of literals is *consistent* if it does not contain a literal ℓ together with its negation $\neg\ell$.[2] By an *extended literal* we understand a classical literal or an expression of the form $not\ \ell$, where ℓ is a classical literal. If γ is an expression (formula, program, etc.) then $Lit(\gamma) \stackrel{\mathrm{def}}{=} \{p, \neg p \mid p \in \mathcal{P}$ occurs in $\gamma\}$ and $\mathcal{P}(\Pi) \stackrel{\mathrm{def}}{=} \mathcal{P} \cap Lit(\Pi)$.

An *interpretation* is a finite consistent set of literals. Interpretation I *satisfies* a classical literal ℓ iff $\ell \in I$ and I *satisfies* an extended literal $not\ \ell$ iff $\ell \notin I$. The satisfiability relation is denoted by $I \models \ell$.   ◁

Definition 2. By an ASP^K rule we understand an expression ϱ of the form:

$$\ell_1 \vee \ldots \vee \ell_k \leftarrow \ell_{k+1}, \ldots, \ell_m, not\ \ell_{m+1}, \ldots, not\ \ell_n, \tag{1}$$

where $n \geq m \geq k \geq 0$, $\ell_1, \ldots, \ell_k, \ell_{k+1}, \ldots, \ell_m, \ell_{m+1}, \ldots \ell_n$ are (positive or negative) literals. The expression at the lefthand side of '$\leftarrow$' in (1), denoted by $h(\varrho)$, is called the *head* and the righthand side of '$\leftarrow$', denoted by $B(\varrho)$, is called the *body* of the rule. The rule is called *disjunctive* if $k > 1$.

An ASP^K *program* Π is a finite set of rules. A program is *normal* if each of its rules has at most one literal in its head. If a program contains a disjunctive rule, we call it *disjunctive*. By $Disj(\Pi)$ we denote the set of disjunctive rules appearing in Π.

The set of rules with the empty body is denoted by $Fct(\Pi)$ and the set of rules with the empty head is denoted by $Ctr(\Pi)$. Members of $Fct(\Pi)$ and $Ctr(\Pi)$ are called *facts* and *constraints*, respectively. The set of rules whose bodies and heads are nonempty is denoted by $Rul(\Pi)$.

An interpretation I *satisfies* a rule ϱ of the form (1), denoted by $I \models \varrho$, if whenever $\ell_{k+1}, \ldots, \ell_m \in I$ and $\ell_{m+1}, \ldots, \ell_n \notin I$, we have $\ell_i \in I$ for some $1 \leq i \leq k$. An interpretation I *satisfies* an ASP^K program Π, denoted by $I \models \Pi$, if for all rules $\varrho \in \Pi$, $I \models \varrho$.   ◁

The following definition is needed to define strong supportedness (a construction similar in spirit is considered in [18]).

Definition 3. Given interpretations I and J, the *value of a formula A w.r.t.* (I, J), denoted by $(I, J)(A)$, is defined as follows:

$$(I, J)(A) \stackrel{\mathrm{def}}{=} \begin{cases} \mathrm{T} \text{ when } I \models reduct^J(A); \\ \mathrm{F} \text{ when } I \models reduct^J(\neg A); \\ \mathrm{U} \text{ otherwise.} \end{cases} \tag{2}$$

where $reduct^J(A)$ (respectively, $reduct^J(\neg A)$) is a formula obtained from A $(\neg A)$ by substituting subformulas of the form $not\ \ell$ by their truth values evaluated in J.   ◁

---

[2] We always remove double strong negations using $\neg(\neg\ell) \stackrel{\mathrm{def}}{=} \ell$.

Definition 4. An interpretation N is a *strongly supported model* of an ASP^K program Π provided that N satisfies Π and there exists a sequence of interpretations $I_0 \subseteq I_1 \subseteq \ldots \subseteq I_n$ where $n \geq 0$ such that $I_0 = Fct(\Pi)$, $N = I_n$, and:

1. for every $1 \leq i \leq n$ and every rule $\ell_1 \vee \ldots \vee \ell_k \leftarrow B$ of Π,
   if $\big(I_{i-1}, N\big)(B) = \mathrm{T}$ then a nonempty subset of $\{\ell_1, \ldots, \ell_k\}$
   is included in I_i;
2. for $i = 1, \ldots, n$, I_i can only contain literals obtained by applying point 1. ◁

3   Iteratively-Supported Formulas

Let p be a propositional variable. Then p_i (respectively $\bar{p}_i$) denotes the fact that in the i-th iteration, p (respectively, $\neg p$) is in the computed candidate for a strongly supported model. Thus, $\neg p_i$ (respectively $\neg \bar{p}_i$) denotes the fact that in the i-th iteration p_i (respectively, $\neg p_i$) is *not* in the computed candidate for a strongly supported model.

The number of different literals in heads of $Rul(\Pi)$ is denoted by $\#\Pi$. Since support can only be generated for up to $\#\Pi$ distinct literals, $\#\Pi$ iterations will be sufficient to provide support for all literals in any strongly supported model.

Definition 5. The translation function is defined as follows, where $1 \leq i \leq \#\Pi$ and ℓ is an extended literal:

$$Tr_\Pi(i, \ell) \overset{\text{def}}{=} \begin{cases} p_i & \text{when } \ell = p; \\ \bar{p}_i & \text{when } \ell = \neg p; \\ \neg p_{\#\Pi} & \text{when } \ell = not\, p; \\ \neg \bar{p}_{\#\Pi} & \text{when } \ell = not\, \neg p. \end{cases} \tag{3}$$

We extend the translation for bodies and heads of rules by setting:
$$Tr_\Pi(i, B) \overset{\text{def}}{=} \bigwedge_{\ell \in B} Tr_\Pi(i, \ell) \quad \text{and} \quad Tr_\Pi(i, H) \overset{\text{def}}{=} \bigvee_{\ell \in H} Tr_\Pi(i, \ell).$$

Definition 6. By a *support* of a classical literal ℓ in a normal ASP^K program Π at i ($i > 0$) we understand the formula:

$$Supp_\Pi^i(\ell) \overset{\text{def}}{=} \big[Tr_\Pi(i, \ell) \equiv \big(Tr_\Pi(i - 1, \ell) \vee \bigvee_{\varrho \in \Pi : \ell = h(\varrho)} Tr_\Pi(i - 1, B(\varrho)) \big) \big]. \tag{4}$$

Definition 7. By the *iteratively-supported formula* for a normal ASP^K program Π we understand the following formula of classical propositional calculus:

$$ISF(\Pi) \overset{\text{def}}{=} \bigwedge_{0 \leq i \leq \#\Pi} \bigwedge_{p \in \mathcal{P}(\Pi)} \neg\big(p_i \wedge \bar{p}_i\big) \wedge \tag{5}$$

$$\bigwedge_{F \in Fct(\Pi)} Tr_\Pi(0, h(F)) \;\wedge\; \bigwedge_{\ell \in Lit(\Pi) - \{h(F) | F \in Fct(\Pi)\}} \neg Tr_\Pi(0, \ell) \;\wedge \qquad (6)$$

$$\bigwedge_{1 \le i \le \#\Pi} \bigwedge_{\ell \in Lit(\Pi)} Supp_\Pi^i(\ell) \;\wedge \qquad\qquad\qquad (7)$$

$$\bigwedge_{\varrho \in \Pi} \big(Tr_\Pi(\#\Pi, B(\varrho)) \to Tr_\Pi(\#\Pi, h(\varrho)) \big). \qquad\qquad (8)$$

We have the following theorem for normal ASP^K programs.

Theorem 1. For any normal ASP^K program Π, I is a strongly supported model of Π iff there is a valuation v satisfying $ISF(\Pi)$ such that:
$$I = \{p \mid v(p_{\#\Pi}) = \mathrm{T}\} \cup \{\neg p \mid v(\bar{p}_{\#\Pi}) = \mathrm{T}\}. \qquad\qquad \lhd$$

Since for normal ASP^K programs strongly supported models are also classical answer sets, Theorem 1 applies to classical ASP, too.

Given a disjunctive ASP^K program Π, the support of literals appearing only in non-disjunctive heads remains unchanged. For literals appearing in disjunctive heads we have the following definition.

Definition 8. By a *support* of a classical literal ℓ occurring in a disjunctive head in an ASP^K program Π at i $(i > 0)$ we understand the formula:

$$Supp_\Pi^i(\ell) \stackrel{\mathrm{def}}{=} \big[Tr_\Pi(i, \ell) \to \big(Tr_\Pi(i-1, \ell) \vee \bigvee_{\varrho \in \Pi : \ell \in h(\varrho)} Tr_\Pi(i-1, B(\varrho)) \big) \big] \wedge$$
$$\big[Tr_\Pi(i-1, \ell) \to Tr_\Pi(i, \ell) \big]. \qquad (9)$$

For other literals, the support of ℓ is still specified by formula (4) in Definition 6. $\qquad \lhd$

Definition 9. By an *iteratively-supported formula* for a disjunctive ASP^K program Π we understand the formula (7) with $Supp_\Pi^i()$ understood as in Definition 8. $\qquad \lhd$

We now have the following generalization of Theorem 1.

Theorem 2. For any (normal or disjunctive) ASP^K program Π, I is a strongly supported model of Π iff there is a valuation v satisfying $ISF(\Pi)$ such that:
$$I = \{p \mid v(p_{\#\Pi}) = \mathrm{T}\} \cup \{\neg p \mid v(\bar{p}_{\#\Pi}) = \mathrm{T}\}. \qquad\qquad \lhd$$

Note that for any ASP^K program Π, the number of different literals in heads of $Rul(\Pi)$ (i.e., $\#\Pi$) is linear in the size of Π. Therefore we have the following lemma.

Lemma 1. For any (normal or disjunctive) ASP^K program Π, the size of $ISF(\Pi)$ is polynomial in the size of Π. $\qquad \lhd$

4   Conclusions

In this extended abstract, we have defined iteratively-supported formulas expressed in classical propositional logic and used them to characterize strongly supported models for ASP^K programs. For normal ASP^K programs, I is a classical answer set of the program iff I is a strongly supported model of the program. Since iteratively-supported formulas provide polynomially bounded characterizations of supported models for normal ASP^K programs, they also provide polynomially bounded characterizations of classical answer sets for normal ASP programs. In contrast, use of loop formulas could result in formulas of exponential size for normal ASP programs.

ISFs also characterize strongly supported models for disjunctive ASP^K programs and guarantee that all conclusions are grounded in facts or default reasoning based on extended literals (using default negation *not*). Additionally, due to a weakened minimization assumption, disjunction is interpreted classically which results in a semantics enjoying among other properties, a Σ_1^P complexity for computing strongly-supported models. This, together with a polynomial bound on ISFs, is a striking theoretical improvement compared to the Σ_2^P complexity of computing classical answer sets for ASP programs.

Acknowledgments. This work is partially supported by the Swedish Research Council (VR) Linnaeus Center CADICS, the ELLIIT network organization for Information and Communication Technology, the Swedish Foundation for Strategic Research (CUAS Project, SymbiKCloud Project), the EU FP7 project SHERPA (grant agreement 600958), and Vinnova NFFP6 Project 2013-01206.

References

1. Chan, P.: A possible world semantics for disjunctive databases. IEEE Trans. Knowl. Data Eng. **5**(2), 282–292 (1993)
2. Doherty, P., Szałas, A.: Stability, supportedness, minimality and kleene answer set programs. In: Eiter, T., Strass, H., Truszczyński, M., Woltran, S. (eds.) Advances in Knowledge Representation. LNCS, vol. 9060, pp. 125–140. Springer, Heidelberg (2015)
3. Ferraris, P., Lifschitz, V.: On the minimality of stable models. In: Balduccini, M., Son, T.C. (eds.) Logic Programming, Knowledge Representation, and Nonmonotonic Reasoning. LNCS, vol. 6565, pp. 64–73. Springer, Heidelberg (2011)
4. Gebser, M., Kaufmann, B., Neumann, A., Schaub, T.: *clasp*: a conflict-driven answer set solver. In: Baral, C., Brewka, G., Schlipf, J. (eds.) LPNMR 2007. LNCS (LNAI), vol. 4483, pp. 260–265. Springer, Heidelberg (2007)
5. Gelfond, M., Kahl, Y.: Knowledge Representation, Reasoning, and the Design of Intelligent Agents -The Answer-Set Programming Approach. Cambridge University Press, Cambridge (2014)
6. Lee, J., Lifschitz, V.: Loop formulas for disjunctive logic programs. In: Palamidessi, C. (ed.) ICLP 2003. LNCS, vol. 2916, pp. 451–465. Springer, Heidelberg (2003)
7. Leone, N., Pfeifer, G., Faber, W., Eiter, T., Gottlob, G., Perri, S., Scarcello, F.: The DLV system for knowledge representation and reasoning. ACM Trans. Comput. Log. **7**(3), 499–562 (2006)

8. Lierler, Y.: CMODELS – SAT-based disjunctive answer set solver. In: Baral, C., Greco, G., Leone, N., Terracina, G. (eds.) LPNMR 2005. LNCS (LNAI), vol. 3662, pp. 447–451. Springer, Heidelberg (2005)
9. Lifschitz, V.: Thirteen definitions of a stable model. In: Blass, A., Dershowitz, N., Reisig, W. (eds.) Fields of Logic and Computation. LNCS, vol. 6300, pp. 488–503. Springer, Heidelberg (2010)
10. Lifschitz, V., Razborov, A.: Why are there so many loop formulas? ACM Trans. Comput. Log. **7**(2), 261–268 (2006)
11. Lin, F., Zhao, J.: On tight logic programs and yet another translation from normal logic programs to propositional logic. In: Gottlob, G., Walsh, T. (eds.) Proceedings of the IJCAI-03, pp. 853–858. Morgan Kaufmann (2003)
12. Lin, F., Zhao, Y.: ASSAT: computing answer sets of a logic program by SAT solvers. Artif. Intell. **157**(1–2), 115–137 (2004)
13. Liu, G., Janhunen, T., Niemelä, I.: Answer set programming via mixed integer programming. In: Brewka, G., T., E., McIlraith, S. (eds.) Proceedings of the KR 2012. AAAI Press (2012)
14. Pelov, N., Ternovska, E.: Reducing inductive definitions to propositional satisfiability. In: Gabbrielli, M., Gupta, G. (eds.) ICLP 2005. LNCS, vol. 3668, pp. 221–234. Springer, Heidelberg (2005)
15. Sakama, C., Inoue, K.: An alternative approach to the semantics of disjunctive logic programs and deductive databases. J. Autom. Reasoning **13**(1), 145–172 (1994)
16. Simons, P., Niemelä, I., Soininen, T.: Extending and implementing the stable model semantics. Artif. Intell. **138**(1–2), 181–234 (2002)
17. Soininen, T., Niemelä, I.: Developing a declarative rule language for applications in product configuration. In: Gupta, G. (ed.) PADL 1999. LNCS, vol. 1551, pp. 305–319. Springer, Heidelberg (1999)
18. Son, T., Pontelli, E.: A constructive semantic characterization of aggregates in answer set programming. TPLP **7**(3), 355–375 (2007)

Forgetting in ASP: The Forgotten Properties

Ricardo Gonçalves, Matthias Knorr$^{(\boxtimes)}$, and João Leite

NOVA LINCS & Departamento de Informática,
Universidade Nova de Lisboa, Caparica, Portugal
{rjrg,mkn,jleite}@fct.unl.pt

Abstract. Many approaches for forgetting in Answer Set Programming
(ASP) have been proposed in recent years, in the form of specific operators, or classes of operators, following different principles and obeying different properties. A recently published comprehensive overview of existing operators and properties provided a uniform picture of the landscape,
including many novel (even surprising) results on relations between properties and operators. Yet, this overview largely missed an additional set
properties for forgetting, proposed by Wong, and this paper aims to close
this gap. It turns out that, while some of these properties are closely
related to the properties previously studied, four of them are distinct
providing novel results and insights, further strengthening established
relations between existing operators.

1 Introduction

Forgetting – or variable elimination – is an operation that allows for the removal,
from a knowledge base, of *middle* variables no longer deemed relevant, whose
importance is witnessed by its application to cognitive robotics [1,2], resolving
conflicts [3–5], and ontology abstraction and comparison [6,7]. With its early
roots in Boolean Algebra, it has been extensively studied within classical logic
[3,8].

Only more recently, the operation of forgetting began to receive attention in
the context of non-monotonic logic programming, notably of Answer Set Programming (ASP). It turns out that the rule-based nature and non-monotonic
semantics of ASP create very unique challenges to the development of forgetting
operators – just as with other belief change operators such as those for revision
and update, c.f. [9–12] – making it a special endeavour with unique characteristics distinct from those for classical logic.

Over the years, many have proposed different approaches to forgetting in
ASP, through the characterization of the result of forgetting a set of atoms from
a given program up to some equivalence class, and/or through the definition of
concrete operators that produce a program given an input program and atoms
to be forgotten [4,5,13–17]. These approaches were typically proposed to obey
some specific set of properties deemed adequate by their authors, some adapted
from the literature on *classical* forgetting [16,18], others introduced for the case
of ASP [5,13–15,17].

© Springer International Publishing AG 2016
L. Michael and A. Kakas (Eds.): JELIA 2016, LNAI 10021, pp. 543–550, 2016.
DOI: 10.1007/978-3-319-48758-8_37

The result is a *complex* landscape filled with operators and properties, that is difficult to navigate. This problem was tackled in [19] by presenting a systematic study of *forgetting* in ASP, thoroughly investigating the different approaches found in the literature, their properties and relationships, giving rise to a comprehensive guide aimed at helping users navigate this topic's complex landscape and ultimately assist them in choosing suitable operators for each application.

However, [19] ignores to a large extent the postulates on forgetting in ASP introduced by Wong in [13].[1] In this paper, we close this gap by thoroughly investigating them, their relationships with other properties and existing operators, concluding that, while some of them are straightforwardly implied by one of the previously studied properties, hence ultimately weaker than these and thus of less importance, others turn out to be distinct and provide additional novel results further strengthening the relations between properties and classes of operators as established previously.

2   Preliminaries

We assume a propositional language $\mathcal{L}_\mathcal{A}$ over a *signature* $\mathcal{A}$, a finite set of propositional atoms. The *formulas* of $\mathcal{L}_\mathcal{A}$ are inductively defined using connectives $\bot$, $\wedge$, $\vee$, and $\supset$:

$$\varphi ::= \bot \mid p \mid \varphi \vee \varphi \mid \varphi \wedge \varphi \mid \varphi \supset \varphi \tag{1}$$

where $p \in \mathcal{A}$. In addition, $\neg\varphi$ and $\top$ are shortcuts for $\varphi \supset \bot$ and $\bot \supset \bot$, resp. Given a finite set S of formulas, $\bigvee S$ and $\bigwedge S$ denote resp. the disjunction and conjunction of all formulas in S. In particular, $\bigvee \emptyset$ and $\bigwedge \emptyset$ stand for resp. $\bot$ and $\top$, and $\neg S$ and $\neg\neg S$ represent resp. $\{\neg\varphi \mid \varphi \in S\}$ and $\{\neg\neg\varphi \mid \varphi \in S\}$. We assume that the underlying signature for a particular formula φ is $\mathcal{A}(\varphi)$, the set of atoms appearing in φ.

Regarding the semantics of propositional formulas, we consider the monotonic logic here-and-there (HT) and equilibrium models [20]. An *HT-interpretation* is a pair $\langle H, T \rangle$ s.t. $H \subseteq T \subseteq \mathcal{A}$. The satisfiability relation in HT, denoted $\models_{HT}$, is recursively defined as follows for $p \in \mathcal{A}$ and formulas φ and ψ:

- $\langle H, T \rangle \models_{HT} p$ if $p \in H$; $\langle H, T \rangle \not\models_{HT} \bot$;
- $\langle H, T \rangle \models_{HT} \varphi \wedge \psi$ if $\langle H, T \rangle \models_{HT} \varphi$ and $\langle H, T \rangle \models_{HT} \psi$;
- $\langle H, T \rangle \models_{HT} \varphi \vee \psi$ if $\langle H, T \rangle \models_{HT} \varphi$ or $\langle H, T \rangle \models_{HT} \psi$;
- $\langle H, T \rangle \models_{HT} \varphi \supset \psi$ if (i) $T \models \varphi \supset \psi$,[2] and (ii) $\langle H, T \rangle \models_{HT} \varphi \Rightarrow \langle H, T \rangle \models_{HT} \psi$.

An *HT*-interpretation is an *HT-model* of a formula φ if $\langle H, T \rangle \models_{HT} \varphi$. We denote by $\mathcal{HT}(\varphi)$ the set of *all HT-models* of φ. In particular, $\langle T, T \rangle \in \mathcal{HT}(\varphi)$ is an *equilibrium model* of φ if there is no $T' \subset T$ s.t. $\langle T', T \rangle \in \mathcal{HT}(\varphi)$. Given two

---

[1] We use the term *postulate* to follow [13] and easily distinguish them from the *properties* discussed in [19]. However, their role is the same as the role of other properties.

[2] $\models$ is the standard consequence relation from classical logic.

formulas φ and ψ, if $\mathcal{HT}(\varphi) \subseteq \mathcal{HT}(\psi)$, then φ *entails* ψ in HT, written $\varphi \models_{HT} \psi$. Also, φ and ψ are *HT-equivalent*, written $\varphi \equiv_{HT} \psi$, if $\mathcal{HT}(\varphi) = \mathcal{HT}(\psi)$.

An *(extended) logic program* P is a finite set of *rules* r, i.e., formulas of the form

$$\bigwedge \neg\neg D \wedge \bigwedge \neg C \wedge \bigwedge B \supset \bigvee A \, , \qquad (2)$$

where all elements in $A = \{a_1, \ldots, a_k\}$, $B = \{b_1, \ldots, b_l\}$, $C = \{c_1, \ldots, c_m\}$, $D = \{d_1, \ldots, d_n\}$ are atoms.[3]

Given r, we distinguish its *head*, $head(r) = A$, and its *body*, $body(r) = B \cup \neg C \cup \neg\neg D$, representing a disjunction and a conjunction.

As shown by Cabalar and Ferraris [22], any set of (propositional) formulas is HT-equivalent to an (extended) logic program which is why we can focus solely on these.

The class of logic programs, $\mathcal{C}_e$, i.e., the set of all (extended) logic programs, includes a number of special kinds of rules r: notably if $n = 0$, then we call r *disjunctive*. Then, the class of *disjunctive programs*, $\mathcal{C}_d$ is defined as a finite set of disjunctive rules.

We recall the following from [19]. Given a class of logic programs $\mathcal{C}$ over $\mathcal{A}$, a *forgetting operator* is a partial function $f : \mathcal{C} \times 2^{\mathcal{A}} \to \mathcal{C}$ s.t. $f(P, V)$ is a program over $\mathcal{A}(P) \backslash V$, for each $P \in \mathcal{C}$ and $V \in 2^{\mathcal{A}}$. We call $f(P, V)$ the *result of forgetting about V from P*. Furthermore, f is called *closed* for $\mathcal{C}' \subseteq \mathcal{C}$ if, for every $P \in \mathcal{C}'$ and $V \in 2^{\mathcal{A}}$, we have $f(P, V) \in \mathcal{C}'$. A *class* F *of forgetting operators* is a set of forgetting operators.

Previous work on forgetting in ASP has introduced a variety of desirable properties and operators satisfy differing subsets of these. For lack of space, we refer to [19].

3   Wong's Properties of Forgetting

With all concepts and notation in place, we can now turn our attention to the postulates introduced by Wong [13]. These postulates were defined in a somewhat different way when compared to the properties presented in [19]. Namely, they only considered forgetting a single atom, were defined for disjunctive programs (the maximal class of programs considered in [13]), and used a generic formulation which allowed different notions of equivalence. Here, we only consider HT-equivalence, i.e., strong equivalence, as, in the literature, this is clearly the more relevant of the two notions considered in [13] (the other one being the non-standard T-equivalence) and in line with previously presented material here and in [19].

---

[3] Extended logic programs [21] are actually more expressive, but this form is sufficient here.

We start by recalling these postulates[4] adjusting them to our notation and extending them to the most general class of extended logic programs considered here.

(F0) F satisfies **(F0)** if, for each f ∈ F, $P, P' \in \mathcal{C}$ and $a \in \mathcal{A}$: if $P \equiv_{\mathsf{HT}} P'$, then $f(P, \{a\}) \equiv_{\mathsf{HT}} f(P', \{a\})$.

(F1) F satisfies **(F1)** if, for each f ∈ F, $P, P' \in \mathcal{C}$ and $a \in \mathcal{A}$: if $P \models_{\mathsf{HT}} P'$, then $f(P, \{a\}) \models_{\mathsf{HT}} f(P', \{a\})$.

(F2) F satisfies **(F2)** if, for each f ∈ F, $P, P' \in \mathcal{C}$ and $a \in \mathcal{A}$: if a does not appear in R, then $f(P \cup R, \{a\}) \equiv_{\mathsf{HT}} f(P', \{a\}) \cup R$ for all $R \in \mathcal{C}$.

(F2-) F satisfies **(F2-)** if, for each f ∈ F, $P \in \mathcal{C}$, and $a \in \mathcal{A}$: if $P \models_{\mathsf{HT}} r$ and a does not occur in r, then $f(P, \{a\}) \models_{\mathsf{HT}} r$ for all rules r expressible in $\mathcal{C}$.

(F3) F satisfies **(F3)** if, for each f ∈ F, $P \in \mathcal{C}$ and $a \in \mathcal{A}$: $f(P, \{a\})$ does not contain any atoms that are not in P.

(F4) F satisfies **(F4)** if, for each f ∈ F, $P \in \mathcal{C}$ and $a \in \mathcal{A}$: if $f(P, \{a\}) \models_{\mathsf{HT}} r$, then $f(\{r'\}, \{a\}) \models_{\mathsf{HT}} r$ for some $r' \in Cn_{\mathcal{A}}(P)$.

(F5) F satisfies **(F5)** if, for each f ∈ F, $P \in \mathcal{C}$ and $a \in \mathcal{A}$: if $f(P, \{a\}) \models_{\mathsf{HT}} A \leftarrow B \cup \neg C \cup \neg\neg D$, then $P \models_{\mathsf{HT}} A \leftarrow B \cup \neg C \cup \{\neg a\} \cup \neg\neg D$.

(F6) F satisfies **(F6)** if, for each f ∈ F, $P \in \mathcal{C}$ and $a, b \in \mathcal{A}$: $f(f(P, \{b\}), \{a\}) \equiv_{\mathsf{HT}} f(f(P, \{a\}), \{b\})$.

These postulates represent the following: Forgetting about atom a from HT-equivalent programs preserves HT-equivalence **(F0)**; if a program is an HT-consequence of another program, then forgetting about atom a from both programs preserves this HT-consequence **(F1)**; when forgetting about an atom a, it does not matter whether we add a set of rules over the remaining language before or after forgetting **(F2)**; any consequence of the original program not mentioning atom a is also a consequence of the result of forgetting about a **(F2-)**; the result of forgetting about an atom from a program only contains atoms occurring in the original program **(F3)**; any rule which is a consequence of the result of forgetting about an atom from program P is a consequence of the result of forgetting about that atom from a single rule among the HT-consequences of P **(F4)**; a rule obtained by extending with *not a* the body of a rule which is an HT-consequence of the result of forgetting about an atom a from program P is an HT-consequence of P **(F5)**; and the order is not relevant when sequentially forgetting two atoms **(F6)**.

Note that $Cn_{\mathcal{A}}(P)$ for **(F4)** is defined over the class of programs considered in each operator, and, likewise, that the kind of rules considered in **(F5)** is restricted according to the class of programs considered in a given operator.

The following proposition relates these postulates and the properties in [19].

Proposition 1. *The following relations hold for all* F*:*

---

[4] As mentioned before, we use the term *postulate* to follow [13] and ease readability. Technically, they are treated as every other *property*.

1. **(F1)** *implies* **(F0)**; *[13]*
2. **(F2)** *and* **(F1)** *imply* **(F2-)**; *[13]*
3. **(SE)** *implies* **(F0)**;
4. **(W)** *and* **(PP)** *together imply* **(F1)**;
5. **(SI)** *implies* **(F2)**;
6. **(PP)** *implies* **(F2-)**;
7. **(W)** *implies* **(F5)**.

Postulates **(F0)**, **(F2)**, **(F2-)**, and **(F5)** are implied by existing properties presented in [19], while **(F1)** is implied by a pair of these. This may impact on the question we investigate next, namely which classes of operators from the literature satisfy which of the new postulates. For that purpose, we verified for all classes of operators presented in [19] which of these postulates they satisfy. The results are summarized in the main theorem of our paper, illustrated in one easy-to-read table.

Theorem 1. *All results in Fig. 1 hold.*

It turns out that for three of the four postulates directly implied by existing properties, **(F0)**, **(F2)**, and **(F2-)**, the classes of operators that satisfy them coincide with their existing generalization (see Proposition 1). Also, postulate **(F3)** is always satisfied, which is not surprising given the definition of forgetting operators. Three of the remaining four properties, **(F1)**, **(F4)**, and **(F5)**, are in fact distinct (even though **(F5)** is implied by an existing property), and no other already existing property is satisfied by precisely the same set of classes of forgetting operators in each of these cases (see [19]). Notably, unlike the weaker property **(F0)** and the related **(SE)**, F_{SM} and F_{Sas} do not satisfy **(F1)**, most likely because the premise in the condition for satisfying **(F1)** is weaker than that of **(F0)**. Finally, postulate **(F6)** is not always satisfied, but it seems that this is solely tied to the incompatibility with the crucial property **(SP)**, further discussed in [23].

	(F0)	**(F1)**	**(F2)**	**(F2-)**	**(F3)**	**(F4)**	**(F5)**	**(F6)**
F_{strong}	×	×	✓	×	✓	✓	✓	✓
F_{weak}	×	×	✓	✓	✓	✓	✓	✓
F_{sem}	×	×	×	×	✓	×	×	✓
F_S	✓	✓	×	✓	✓	✓	✓	✓
F_W	✓	✓	✓	✓	✓	✓	✓	✓
F_{HT}	✓	✓	✓	✓	✓	✓	✓	✓
F_{SM}	✓	×	×	✓	✓	×	×	✓
F_{Sas}	✓	×	✓	✓	✓	×	×	×
F_{SE}	✓	✓	×	✓	✓	✓	✓	✓

Fig. 1. Satisfaction of properties for known classes of forgetting operators. For class F and property **(P)**, '✓' represents that F satisfies **(P)**, '×' that F does not satisfy **(P)**.

4   Conclusions

We have studied eight postulates of forgetting in ASP introduced in [13], to fill a gap in a recent comprehensive guide on properties and classes of operators for forgetting in ASP, and relations between these [19]. It turns out that four of them can safely be ignored because they either basically coincide with already existing properties or are trivially satisfied by any forgetting operator. The others are in fact distinct, and no other already existing property is satisfied by precisely the same set of classes of forgetting operators in each of these cases.

Left open is the investigation of these postulates for semantics other than ASP, such as [16] based on the FLP-semantics [24], or [15, 25] based on the well-founded semantics, as well as forgetting in the context of hybrid theories [26–28] and reactive/evolving multi-context systems [29, 30], as well as the development of concrete syntactical forgetting operators that can be integrated in reasoning tools such as [31–33].

Acknowledgments. All authors were partially supported by FCT under strategic project NOVA LINCS (UID/CEC/04516/2013). R. Gonçalves was partially supported by FCT grant SFRH/BPD/100906/2014 and M. Knorr by FCT grant SFRH/BPD/86970/2012.

References

1. Lin, F., Reiter, R.: How to progress a database. Artif. Intell. **92**(1–2), 131–167 (1997)
2. Rajaratnam, D., Levesque, H.J., Pagnucco, M., Thielscher, M.: Forgetting in action. In: Baral, C., Giacomo, G.D., Eiter, T. (eds.) Proceedings of KR. AAAI Press (2014)
3. Lang, J., Liberatore, P., Marquis, P.: Propositional independence: formula-variable independence and forgetting. J. Artif. Intell. Res. (JAIR) **18**, 391–443 (2003)
4. Zhang, Y., Foo, N.Y.: Solving logic program conflict through strong and weak forgettings. Artif. Intell. **170**(8–9), 739–778 (2006)
5. Eiter, T., Wang, K.: Semantic forgetting in answer set programming. Artif. Intell. **172**(14), 1644–1672 (2008)
6. Kontchakov, R., Wolter, F., Zakharyaschev, M.: Logic-based ontology comparison and module extraction, with an application to DL-Lite. Artif. Intell. **174**(15), 1093–1141 (2010)
7. Konev, B., Lutz, C., Walther, D., Wolter, F.: Model-theoretic inseparability and modularity of description logic ontologies. Artif. Intell. **203**, 66–103 (2013)
8. Larrosa, J., Morancho, E., Niso, D.: On the practical use of variable elimination in constraint optimization problems: 'still-life' as a case study. J. Artif. Intell. Res. (JAIR) **23**, 421–440 (2005)
9. Alferes, J., Leite, J., Pereira, L.M., Przymusinska, H., Przymusinski, T.: Dynamic updates of non-monotonic knowledge bases. J. Log. Program. **45**(1–3), 43–70 (2000)
10. Eiter, T., Fink, M., Sabbatini, G., Tompits, H.: On properties of update sequences based on causal rejection. Theor. Pract. Log. Program. (TPLP) **2**(6), 721–777 (2002)

11. Leite, J.A.: Evolving Knowledge Bases. Frontiers of Artificial Intelligence and Applications, xviii + 307 p. Hardcover, vol. 81. IOS Press (2003)
12. Slota, M., Leite, J.: A unifying perspective on knowledge updates. In: del Cerro, L.F., Herzig, A., Mengin, J. (eds.) JELIA 2012. LNCS, vol. 7519, pp. 372–384. Springer, Heidelberg (2012)
13. Wong, K.S.: Forgetting in Logic Programs, Ph.D. thesis. The University of New South Wales (2009)
14. Wang, Y., Wang, K., Zhang, M.: Forgetting for answer set programs revisited. In: Rossi, F. (ed.) Proceedings of IJCAI. IJCAI/AAAI (2013)
15. Knorr, M., Alferes, J.J.: Preserving strong equivalence while forgetting. In: Fermé, E., Leite, J. (eds.) JELIA 2014. LNCS, vol. 8761, pp. 412–425. Springer, Heidelberg (2014)
16. Wang, Y., Zhang, Y., Zhou, Y., Zhang, M.: Knowledge forgetting in answer set programming. J. Artif. Intell. Res. (JAIR) **50**, 31–70 (2014)
17. Delgrande, J.P., Wang, K.: A syntax-independent approach to forgetting in disjunctive logic programs. In: Bonet, B., Koenig, S. (eds.) Proceedings of AAAI, pp. 1482–1488. AAAI Press (2015)
18. Zhang, Y., Zhou, Y.: Knowledge forgetting: properties and applications. Artif. Intell. **173**(16–17), 1525–1537 (2009)
19. Gonçalves, R., Knorr, M., Leite, J.: The ultimate guide to forgetting in ASP. In: Baral, C., Delgrande, J.P., Wolter, F. (eds.) Proceedings of KR, pp. 135–144. AAAI Press (2016)
20. Lifschitz, V., Pearce, D., Valverde, A.: Strongly equivalent logic programs. ACM Trans. Comput. Log. **2**(4), 526–541 (2001)
21. Lifschitz, V., Tang, L.R., Turner, H.: Nested expressions in logic programs. Ann. Math. Artif. Intell. **25**(3–4), 369–389 (1999)
22. Cabalar, P., Ferraris, P.: Propositional theories are strongly equivalent to logic programs. TPLP **7**(6), 745–759 (2007)
23. Gonçalves, R., Knorr, M., Leite, J.: You can't always forget what you want: on the limits of forgetting in answer set programming. In: Fox, M.S., Kaminka, G.A. (eds.) Proceedings of ECAI. IOS Press (2016)
24. Truszczynski, M.: Reducts of propositional theories, satisfiability relations, and generalizations of semantics of logic programs. Artif. Intell. **174**(16–17), 1285–1306 (2010)
25. Alferes, J.J., Knorr, M., Wang, K.: Forgetting under the well-founded semantics. In: Cabalar, P., Son, T.C. (eds.) LPNMR 2013. LNCS, vol. 8148, pp. 36–41. Springer, Heidelberg (2013)
26. Knorr, M., Alferes, J.J., Hitzler, P.: Local closed world reasoning with description logics under the well-founded semantics. Artif. Intell. **175**(9–10), 1528–1554 (2011)
27. Gonçalves, R., Alferes, J.J.: Parametrized logic programming. In: Janhunen, T., Niemelä, I. (eds.) JELIA 2010. LNCS, vol. 6341, pp. 182–194. Springer, Heidelberg (2010)
28. Slota, M., Leite, J., Swift, T.: On updates of hybrid knowledge bases composed of ontologies and rules. Artif. Intell. **229**, 33–104 (2015)
29. Gonçalves, R., Knorr, M., Leite, J.: Evolving multi-context systems. In: Schaub, T., Friedrich, G., O'Sullivan, B. (eds.) Proceedings of ECAI, pp. 375–380. IOS Press (2014)
30. Brewka, G., Ellmauthaler, S., Pührer, J.: Multi-context systems for reactive reasoning in dynamic environments. In: Schaub, T., Friedrich, G., O'Sullivan, B. (eds.) Proceedings of ECAI, pp. 159–164. IOS Press (2014)

31. Gebser, M., Kaufmann, B., Kaminski, R., Ostrowski, M., Schaub, T., Schneider, M.T.: Potassco: the potsdam answer set solving collection. AI Commun. **24**(2), 107–124 (2011)
32. Ivanov, V., Knorr, M., Leite, J.: A query tool for $\mathcal{EL}$ with non-monotonic rules. In: Alani, H., et al. (eds.) ISWC 2013. LNCS, vol. 8218, pp. 216–231. Springer, Heidelberg (2013). doi:10.1007/978-3-642-41335-3_14
33. Costa, N., Knorr, M., Leite, J.: Next step for NoHR: OWL 2 QL. In: Arenas, M., et al. (eds.) ISWC 2015. LNCS, vol. 9366, pp. 569–586. Springer, Heidelberg (2015). doi:10.1007/978-3-319-25007-6_33

On Hierarchical Task Networks

Andreas Herzig[1], Laurent Perrussel[1], and Zhanhao Xiao[1,2]($\boxtimes$)

[1] University of Toulouse, IRIT, Toulouse, France
zhanhaoxiao@gmail.com
[2] AIRG, Western Sydney University, Penrith, Australia

Abstract. In planning based on hierarchical task networks (HTN), plans are generated by refining high-level actions ('compound tasks') into lower-level actions, until primitive actions are obtained that can be sent to execution. While a primitive action is defined by its precondition and effects, a high-level action is defined by zero, one or several methods: sets of (high-level or primitive) actions decomposing it together with a constraint. We give a semantics of HTNs in terms of dynamic logic with program inclusion. We propose postulates guaranteeing soundness and completeness of action refinement. We also show that hybrid planning can be analysed in the same dynamic logic framework.

1 Introduction

The two main approaches to deterministic AI planning are classical state-based planning [13] and Hierarchical Task Network (HTN) planning [5]. The former is based on action preconditions and effects. The latter is based on domain-specific heuristics about the decomposition of high-level actions ('compound tasks') into lower-level actions, until primitive actions ('primitive tasks') are obtained. It has no generally agreed semantics [7]. We here propose a semantics in terms of an extension of Propositional Dynamic Logic PDL [8] by a program inclusion operator. This framework sheds light on a problem that had not been investigated before: the soundness of HTN domain descriptions.

Let us illustrate HTNs and the soundness issue by an abstract example. Suppose the only method for high-level action α is $\langle \alpha, \langle \{(\beta, t)\}(t, p)\rangle\rangle$. The couple $\langle \{(\beta, t)\}(t, p)\rangle$ is a *task network*: (β, t) instantiates the action β by the temporal label t, and the constraint (t, p) stipulates that p should be true immediately after t. So the only way to perform α is by performing β, with postcondition p. Suppose moreover that β is also a high-level action and that its only method is $\langle \beta, \langle \{(b, t')\}(t', \neg p)\rangle\rangle$. So the only way to perform β is to apply b, with postcondition $\neg p$. No task involving α can ever be solved, and we call such an HTN domain description *unsound*. It is reasonable to expect HTN domain descriptions not to contain unsound methods. This is a simple example, and more complex unsound methods can be designed. In this paper we show that PDL provides a framework where we can characterise sound domain descriptions. The PDL semantics also allows us to study whether the set of methods for a high-level

© Springer International Publishing AG 2016
L. Michael and A. Kakas (Eds.): JELIA 2016, LNAI 10021, pp. 551–557, 2016.
DOI: 10.1007/978-3-319-48758-8_38

action α is *complete*, in the sense that when the precondition of α is true then there is a method for α that is executable.

Beyond traditional HTN planning, we can show that PDL with program inclusion also provides a semantics for so-called hybrid planning. There, domain descriptions have preconditions and effects not only for primitive actions, but also for high-level actions. Following [11,12], we consider that the effect of a high-level action is its main, *primary* effect. Indeed, it is not obvious to describe the effects of a high-level action α exhaustively. One of the reasons is that these effects depend on the way α is refined. For example, consider the high-level action of building a house. While its primary effect is that I have a house, its side effects depend on whether I build the house myself or hire a builder: I either have a bad back, or an empty bank account. We therefore consider that non-primitive actions are not described by their effects but only by their postconditions.

Our paper is organised as follows. In Sect. 2 we define PDL. In Sect. 3 we define HTN planning domains in PDL. In Sect. 4 we propose postulates of soundness, completeness and modularity. Section 5 concludes.[1]

2   PDL with Inclusion of Programs

We define syntax and semantics of a version of Propositional Dynamic Logic PDL having intersection and inclusion of programs and, for simplicity, with only boolean tests. Let Prp be a finite set of propositional variables, with typical elements p, q,... The set of boolean formulas built from Prp is noted $\mathtt{Fml_{bool}}$. Let Act be a finite set of actions, with typical elements α, β,... In examples we use capital letters for propositional variables (such as HasHouse) and small letters for actions (such as buildHouse).

The set of programs $\mathtt{Pgm_{PDL}}$ is defined by the following grammar:

$$\pi ::= \alpha \mid \pi;\pi \mid \pi \sqcup \pi \mid \pi \sqcap \pi \mid \pi^* \mid \varphi_0?$$

where $\alpha \in \mathtt{Act}$ and $\varphi_0 \in \mathtt{Fml_{bool}}$. The program operators ";", "$\sqcup$", and "$\sqcap$" are sequential, nondeterministic and parallel composition, "*" is bounded iteration, and "?" is test. The set of formulas $\mathtt{Fml_{PDL}}$ is defined by:

$$\varphi ::= p \mid \bot \mid \varphi \to \varphi \mid \langle \pi \rangle \varphi \mid \pi \sqsubseteq \pi$$

$\langle \pi \rangle \varphi$ reads "there is a possible execution of π after which φ is true" and $\pi' \sqsubseteq \pi$ reads "every execution of π' is also an execution of π". Subsets of $\mathtt{Fml_{PDL}}$ are called *theories*. As usual, $[\pi]\varphi$ abbreviates $\neg\langle \pi \rangle \neg\varphi$.

A model is a triple $M = \langle W, R, V \rangle$ where W is a non-empty set of possible worlds, $R : \mathtt{Pgm_{PDL}} \longrightarrow 2^{W \times W}$ associates accessibility relations R_π to programs, and $V : \mathtt{Prp} \longrightarrow 2^W$ is a valuation. The function R must satisfy some constraints:

[1] Our work is supported by CSC and CIMI. Thanks are due to the JELIA 2016 reviewers for their thorough comments. A long version of the paper with formal results and proofs is at www.irit.fr/~Andreas.Herzig/P/Jelia16htn.html.

$$R_{\pi_1;\pi_2} = R_{\pi_1} \circ R_{\pi_2} \qquad\qquad R_{\pi^*} = (R_\pi)^*$$
$$R_{\pi_1 \sqcup \pi_2} = R_{\pi_1} \cup R_{\pi_2} \qquad\qquad R_{\varphi_0?} = \{\langle w, w \rangle \ : \ M, w \Vdash \varphi_0\}$$
$$R_{\pi_1 \sqcap \pi_2} = R_{\pi_1} \cap R_{\pi_2}$$

Letting $R_\pi(w) = \{v \ : \ \langle w, v \rangle \in R_\pi\}$, the truth conditions for formulas are:

$$M, w \Vdash p \quad \text{iff} \ \ w \in V(p) \qquad\qquad M, w \Vdash \varphi \to \varphi' \ \ \text{iff} \ \ M, w \not\Vdash \varphi \text{ or } M, w \Vdash \varphi'$$
$$M, w \not\Vdash \bot \qquad\qquad\qquad\qquad M, w \Vdash \langle \pi \rangle \varphi \quad \text{iff} \ \ M, v \Vdash \varphi \text{ for some } v \in R_\pi(w)$$
$$\qquad\qquad\qquad\qquad\qquad\qquad\quad M, w \Vdash \pi \sqsubseteq \pi' \quad \text{iff} \ \ R_\pi(w) \subseteq R_{\pi'}(w)$$

For $\Gamma \subseteq \mathtt{Fml_{PDL}}$, we define $\Gamma \models \varphi$ as: for every model M, if $M \Vdash \psi$ for every $\psi \in \Gamma$ then $M \Vdash \varphi$, where $M \Vdash \varphi$ stands for: $M, w \Vdash \varphi$ for all $w \in W$.

3   HTN Planning in the PDL Framework

HTN planning presupposes that the set of actions Act is partitioned into two sets: the set of primitive actions $\mathsf{Act_0}$ and the set of high-level actions $\mathsf{Act} \setminus \mathsf{Act_0}$. We use $a, b, \ldots$ for typical elements of $\mathsf{Act_0}$ (and, as before, $\alpha, \beta, \ldots$ for arbitrary elements of Act). A *primitive plan* is a sequence of primitive actions. A *primitive program* is a program where only elements of $\mathsf{Act_0}$ occur.

We suppose that all actions have pre- and postconditions. The postconditions of primitive actions describe STRIPS-like effects in terms of add- and delete-lists. Non-primitive actions can have arbitrary boolean formulas as an postconditions. For example, the high-level action of leaving France may have postcondition $\neg\mathsf{InFrance} \land (\mathsf{InGermany} \lor \mathsf{InChina} \lor \ldots)$. In traditional HTNs, high-level actions have no postcondition, which can be captured by setting them to $\top$.

3.1   HTN Planning Domains

An *HTN planning domain* is a couple $\mathcal{D}_{\mathsf{htn}} = \langle \mathsf{Pre}, \mathsf{Post}, \mathsf{Ref} \rangle$ where $\mathsf{Pre}, \mathsf{Post} :$ $\mathsf{Act} \longrightarrow \mathtt{Fml_{bool}}$ and $\mathsf{Ref} : \mathsf{Act} \longrightarrow 2^{\mathtt{Pgm_{PDL}}}$ such that for every $a \in \mathsf{Act_0}$, $\mathsf{Ref}(a) = \emptyset$ and $\mathsf{Post}(a)$ is of the form $\left(\bigwedge_{p \in \mathsf{eff}^+(a)} p \right) \land \left(\bigwedge_{p \in \mathsf{eff}^-(a)} \neg p \right)$, for some $\mathsf{eff}^+(a)$ and $\mathsf{eff}^-(\alpha)$ such that $\mathsf{eff}^+(a) \cap \mathsf{eff}^-(a) = \emptyset$. The refinement function Ref associates to each α its methods: the set of programs refining α. For the introductory example we have $\mathsf{Ref}(\alpha) = \{(\beta; p?)\}$, $\mathsf{Ref}(\beta) = \{(b; \neg p?)\}$, $\mathsf{Ref}(b) = \emptyset$, and, say, that all pre- and postconditions equal $\top$, except that $\mathsf{Post}(b) = \neg p$.

Example 1. An domain that can be found in almost all papers on HTN is that of an agent travelling from A to B:

$\mathsf{Pre}(\mathsf{goAB}) = \mathsf{AtA}$	$\mathsf{Post}(\mathsf{goAB}) = \mathsf{AtB}$	$\mathsf{Ref}(\mathsf{goAB}) = \{\mathsf{taxiAB}, \mathsf{walkAB}\}$
$\mathsf{Pre}(\mathsf{taxiAB}) = \mathsf{AtA}$	$\mathsf{Post}(\mathsf{taxiAB}) = \mathsf{AtB}$	$\mathsf{Ref}(\mathsf{taxiAB}) = \{(\mathsf{rideAB}; \mathsf{pay})\}$
$\mathsf{Pre}(\mathsf{walkAB}) = \mathsf{AtA}$	$\mathsf{Post}(\mathsf{walkAB}) = \mathsf{AtB} \land \neg\mathsf{AtA}$	$\mathsf{Ref}(\mathsf{walkAB}) = \emptyset$
$\mathsf{Pre}(\mathsf{rideAB}) = \mathsf{AtA}$	$\mathsf{Post}(\mathsf{rideAB}) = \mathsf{AtB} \land \neg\mathsf{AtA}$	$\mathsf{Ref}(\mathsf{rideAB}) = \emptyset$
$\mathsf{Pre}(\mathsf{pay}) = \mathsf{Money}$	$\mathsf{Post}(\mathsf{pay}) = \neg\mathsf{Money}$	$\mathsf{Ref}(\mathsf{pay}) = \emptyset$

The last three actions are primitive. Note that Post(goAB) does not mention the possible effect ¬Money, which is only produced when goAB is refined to taxiAB.

An HTN planning domain is captured in PDL by the following theory:

$$\mathtt{Fml}(\mathsf{Pre}) = \{\langle \alpha \rangle \top \leftrightarrow \mathsf{Pre}(\alpha) \: : \: \alpha \in \mathsf{Act}\}$$

$$\mathtt{Fml}(\mathsf{Post}) = \{[\alpha]\mathsf{Post}(\alpha) \: : \: \alpha \in \mathsf{Act}\} \cup \{p \rightarrow [a]p \: : \: a \in \mathsf{Act}_0 \text{ and } p \notin \mathsf{eff}^-(a)\}$$

$$\cup \{\neg p \rightarrow [a]\neg p \: : \: a \in \mathsf{Act}_0 \text{ and } p \notin \mathsf{eff}^+(a)\}$$

$$\mathtt{Fml}(\mathsf{Ref}) = \{\langle \alpha \rangle \top \rightarrow \pi \sqsubseteq \alpha \: : \: \alpha \in \mathsf{Act}, \pi \in \mathsf{Ref}(\alpha)\}$$

So primitive actions behave like STRIPS actions, while high-level actions are less constrained, leaving room for conditional effects and other side effects. The theory of an HTN planning domain is $\mathtt{Fml}(\mathcal{D}_{\mathsf{htn}}) = \mathtt{Fml}(\mathsf{Pre}) \cup \mathtt{Fml}(\mathsf{Post}) \cup \mathtt{Fml}(\mathsf{Ref})$.

3.2   HTN Planning Problems and Their Solutions

A *HTN planning problem* is a triple $\mathcal{P}_{\mathsf{htn}} = \langle \mathcal{D}_{\mathsf{htn}}, \mathtt{I}, \pi \rangle$ where $\mathcal{D}_{\mathsf{htn}}$ is an HTN planning domain, $\mathtt{I} \in \mathsf{Fml}_{\mathsf{bool}}$ is a boolean formula, and $\pi \in \mathsf{Pgm}_{\mathsf{PDL}}$ is a program ('initial task network'). For our travelling domain we may e.g. have $\langle \mathcal{D}_{\mathsf{htn}}^{\mathsf{AB}}, \mathtt{I}, \mathsf{goAB} \rangle$ with $\mathtt{I} = \mathsf{AtA} \wedge \neg \mathsf{AtB} \wedge \mathsf{Money}$. (Usually $\mathtt{I}$ is a complete description of a state, but this is not necessary here.)

Traditionally, solutions of $\mathcal{P}_{\mathsf{htn}}$ are obtained by a fixed-point definition, in three steps. First, the *reduction* of a program π is:

$$\mathsf{red}(\mathcal{D}_{\mathsf{htn}}, \pi) = \{\pi^{\alpha}_{\mathsf{Pre}(\alpha)?;\pi'} \: : \: \alpha \text{ occurs in } \pi \text{ and } \pi' \in \mathsf{Ref}(\alpha)\}$$

where $\pi^{\alpha}_{\mathsf{Pre}(\alpha)?;\pi'}$ is obtained from π by replacing some occurrence of α in π by $\mathsf{Pre}(\alpha)?;\pi'$. For the introductory example: $\mathsf{red}(\mathcal{D}_{\mathsf{htn}}, (\beta; p?)) = \{(b; \neg p?; p?)\}$. Second, for a primitive π_0 we define its *completion* as follows:

$$\mathsf{compl}(\mathcal{D}_{\mathsf{htn}}, \mathtt{I}, \pi_0) = \{a_1; \cdots; a_n \: : \: \mathtt{Fml}(\mathsf{Post}) \models \mathtt{I} \rightarrow \langle (a_1; \cdots; a_n) \sqcap \pi_0 \rangle \top\}$$

For example, $\mathsf{compl}(\mathcal{D}_{\mathsf{htn}}, \mathtt{I}, (b; \neg p?; p?)) = \emptyset$. Third, the *solutions* of an HTN planning problem are primitive plans that are defined recursively as follows:

$$\mathsf{sol}^1(\mathcal{D}_{\mathsf{htn}}, \mathtt{I}, \pi) = \begin{cases} \mathsf{compl}(\mathcal{D}_{\mathsf{htn}}, \mathtt{I}, \pi) & \text{if } \pi \text{ is primitive} \\ \emptyset & \text{otherwise} \end{cases}$$

$$\mathsf{sol}^{k+1}(\mathcal{D}_{\mathsf{htn}}, \mathtt{I}, \pi) = \mathsf{sol}^k(\mathcal{D}_{\mathsf{htn}}, \mathtt{I}, \pi) \cup \bigcup_{\pi' \in \mathsf{red}(\mathcal{D}_{\mathsf{htn}}, \pi)} \mathsf{sol}^k(\mathcal{D}_{\mathsf{htn}}, \mathtt{I}, \pi')$$

Letting $\mathsf{sol}(\mathcal{D}_{\mathsf{htn}}, \mathtt{I}, \pi) = \bigcup_k \mathsf{sol}^k(\mathcal{D}_{\mathsf{htn}}, \mathtt{I}, \pi)$ we are able to connect the traditional solutions of HTN planning problems and logical consequence in PDL:

Theorem 1. *If* $a_1; \cdots; a_n \in \mathsf{sol}(\mathcal{D}_{\mathsf{htn}}, \mathtt{I}, \pi)$ *then* $\mathtt{Fml}(\mathcal{D}_{\mathsf{htn}}) \models \mathtt{I} \rightarrow \langle (a_1; \cdots; a_n) \sqcap \pi \rangle \top$.

4   Rationality Postulates for HTN Planning

We now introduce postulates of refinement soundness and completeness. Further postulates of modularity are discussed in the long report.

When α is executable then all refinements of α should guarantee the postconditions of α. This has to be conditioned: if $\mathsf{Pre}(\alpha)$ is false then there is no point in refining.

Definition 1. *Action α is* soundly refinable *at (M, w) if and only if either $M, w \not\Vdash \mathsf{Pre}(\alpha)$ or for every $\pi \in \mathsf{Ref}(\alpha)$ and $v \in R_\pi(w)$, $M, v \Vdash \mathsf{Post}(\alpha)$.*

Clearly, a reasonable HTN domain should be such that every action is soundly refinable at every pointed model (M, w). This can be characterised in PDL.

Theorem 2. *Let $\mathcal{D}_{\mathsf{htn}}$ be an HTN domain. An action $\alpha \in \mathsf{Act}$ is soundly refinable at every pointed model (M, w) iff $\mathsf{Fml}(\mathcal{D}_{\mathsf{htn}}) \models \mathsf{Pre}(\alpha) \to [\bigsqcup \mathsf{Ref}(\alpha)] \mathsf{Post}(\alpha)$.*

One may also define complete refinability: when the precondition of a high-level action is true then there should be a way of refining it.

Definition 2. *High-level action $\alpha \in \mathsf{Act} \setminus \mathsf{Act}_0$ is* completely refinable *at (M, w) if and only if either $M, w \not\Vdash \mathsf{Pre}(\alpha)$ or there is a $\pi \in \mathsf{Ref}(\alpha)$ such that $R_\pi(w) \neq \emptyset$.*

In other words, as long as the precondition of α is true, one of the programs refining α should be executable.

Theorem 3. *An action $\alpha \in \mathsf{Act} \setminus \mathsf{Act}_0$ is completely refinable at every pointed model (M, w) iff $\mathsf{Fml}(\mathcal{D}_{\mathsf{htn}}) \models \mathsf{Pre}(\alpha) \to \langle \bigsqcup \mathsf{Ref}(\alpha) \rangle \top$.*

As discussed in [12], even when some refinement is physically possible, there may be reasons for not including it in the Ref function. There are two possible such reasons: either the refinement is legally impossible, or it is not preferred. This former case of incompleteness can be illustrated with the help of Example 1: the primitive plan rideAB of taking the taxi without paying also achieves the postconditions of goAB. However, the domain designer did not want to allow such a refinement and deliberately omitted it from $\mathsf{Ref}(\mathsf{goAB})$.

Complete refinability can be weakened by requiring refinability *unless there is no primitive plan achieving the postconditions of* α. This is similar to what is called *planner completeness* in [12], which, as we understand it, requires that every solution that can be obtained by a classical planner is also obtainable by the HTN planner. It can be characterized by the PDL formula
$$\mathsf{Fml}(\mathcal{D}_{\mathsf{htn}}) \models \left(\mathsf{Pre}(\alpha) \wedge \langle (\bigsqcup \mathsf{Act}_0)^* \rangle \mathsf{Post}(\alpha) \right) \to \langle \bigsqcup \mathsf{Ref}(\alpha) \rangle \top.$$

5   Conclusion

We have proposed a representation of HTN in PDL with program inclusion, identifying HTN methods with PDL programs. We have formulated soundness and completeness postulates and have characterised them in PDL. It is clear that methods with linear constraints can be expressed in this way by sequential composition and tests. We leave the exact correspondence with more general constraints to future work and just note that the PDL program operators are expressive enough to capture the standard examples in the literature. Given results on grammar logics [2,4], our extension of PDL is undecidable, and it can be conjectured that fragments corresponding to regular grammars are decidable.

Previous work embedding HTN in the Situation Calculus [1,6,7] is discussed in more detail in the long report. Relations between HTN planning with the semantics of BDI logics are investigated in [3,9,10,14].

References

1. Baral, C., Son, T.C.: Extending ConGolog to allow partial ordering. In: Jennings, N.R., Lespérance, Y. (eds.) ATAL 1999. LNCS (LNAI), vol. 1757, pp. 188–204. Springer, Heidelberg (2000). doi:10.1007/10719619_14
2. del Cerro, L.F., Penttonen, M.: Grammar logics. Logique Et Analyse **31**(121–122), 123–134 (1988)
3. De Silva, L., Sardina, S., Padgham, L.: First principles planning in BDI systems. In: Proceedings of the 8th International Conference on Autonomous Agents and Multiagent Systems (AAMAS), vol. 2, pp. 1105–1112. International Foundation for Autonomous Agents and Multiagent Systems (2009)
4. Demri, S.: The complexity of regularity in grammar logics and related modal logics. J. Log. Comput. **11**(6), 933–960 (2001). http://dx.doi.org/10.1093/logcom/11.6.933
5. Erol, K., Hendler, J., Nau, D.S.: HTN planning: complexity and expressivity. In: Proceedings of the 12th National Conference on Artificial Intelligence (AAAI), vol. 94, pp. 1123–1128 (1994)
6. Gabaldon, A.: Programming hierarchical task networks in the situation calculus. In: Proceedings of the 5th International Conference on Artificial Intelligence Planning and Scheduling Systems Workshop on On-line Planning and Scheduling (2002)
7. Goldman, R.P.: A semantics for HTN methods. In: Gerevini, A., Howe, A.E., Cesta, A., Refanidis, I. (eds.) Proceedings of the 19th International Conference on Automated Planning and Scheduling, (ICAPS). AAAI (2009)
8. Harel, D., Kozen, D., Tiuryn, J.: Dynamic Logic. MIT Press, Cambridge (2000)
9. Herzig, A., Lorini, E., Perrussel, L., Xiao, Z.: BDI logics for BDI architectures: old problems, new perspectives. Künstliche Intelligenz (to appear)
10. Herzig, A., Perrussel, L., Xiao, Z., Zhang, D.: Refinement of intentions. In: Michael, L., Kakas, A.C. (eds.) JELIA 2016. LNCS (LNAI), vol. 10021, pp. xx–yy. Springer, Heidelberg (2016)
11. Kambhampati, S., Cutkosky, M.R., Tenenbaum, J.M., Lee, S.H.: Integrating general purpose planners and specialized reasoners: case study of a hybrid planning architecture. IEEE Trans. Syst. Man Cybern. **23**(6), 1503–1518 (1993)
12. Kambhampati, S., Mali, A., Srivastava, B.: Hybrid planning for partially hierarchical domains. In: Proceedings of the 17th National Conference on Artificial Intelligence and 12th Conference on Innovative Applications of Artificial Intelligence (AAAI/IAAI), pp. 882–888 (1998)

13. Nau, D., Ghallab, M., Traverso, P.: Automated Planning: Theory & Practice. Morgan Kaufmann Publishers Inc., San Francisco (2004)
14. Sardina, S., de Silva, L., Padgham, L.: Hierarchical planning in BDI agent programming languages: a formal approach. In: Proceedings of the 5th International Conference on Autonomous Agents and Multiagent Systems, pp. 1001–1008. ACM (2006)

Refinement of Intentions

Andreas Herzig[1], Laurent Perrussel[1], Zhanhao Xiao[1,2($\boxtimes$)], and Dongmo Zhang[2]

[1] IRIT, University of Toulouse, Toulouse, France
zhanhaoxiao@gmail.com
[2] AIRG, Western Sydney University, Penrith, Australia

Abstract. According to Bratman, future-directed intentions are high-level plans. We view such plans as high-level actions that can typically not be executed directly: they have to be progressively refined until executable basic actions are obtained. Higher- and lower-level actions are linked by the means-end relation, alias instrumentality relation. In this paper we extend Shoham's database perspective of Bratman's theory by the notions of refinement and instrumentality.

1 Introduction

Bratman highlighted the fundamental role of an agent's future-directed intentions: they are *high-level plans* to which the agent is committed [3,5]. Such high-level plans cannot be executed directly: they have to be *refined* as time goes by, resulting in more and more elaborate plans. The lower-level intentions that are inserted are *instrumental* for the high-level intention they refine [4]. At the end of the refinement process plans only have in *basic actions*: actions the agent can perform intentionally. Bratman's theory is at the basis of the by now huge literature on Belief-Desire-Intention (BDI) agents. However and as more extensively discussed in [12], the literature only contains few BDI logics where refinement is a central ingredient: essentially [2,14,17]. It is notably absent from Cohen and Levesque's logic [6] and Shoham's *database perspective* [15,18,19]. The latter is a simple account that is based on databases of time-indexed basic actions and beliefs. We believe it to be a promising basis for a logical analysis of intentions.

In order to extend Shoham's approach by an account of intention refinement, the first thing to do is to add high-level, temporally extended actions. We are also going to tackle another of its shortcomings, viz. that it does not solve the frame problem: the beliefs at time point t together with the intention at t fail to determine the beliefs at $t+1$. The reason is that Shoham's databases do not account for environment actions, alias events. We here add them to the picture. Just as in PDDL+ planning [10], we suppose that while the planning agent is proactive, the environment is reactive (or, more precisely, the planning agent

This work was partially supported by ANR-11-LABX-0040-CIMI within the program ANR-11-IDEX-0002-02 and CSC (Chinese Scholarship Council). A long version is available at www.irit.fr/~Andreas.Herzig/P/Jelia16db.html.

© Springer International Publishing AG 2016
L. Michael and A. Kakas (Eds.): JELIA 2016, LNAI 10021, pp. 558–563, 2016.
DOI: 10.1007/978-3-319-48758-8_39

believes so). Indeed, without such reactive events we would not be able to refine intentions. For example, consider the refinement of my intention to submit a paper to JELIA, which involves clicking Easychair's 'upload' button: I have to believe that my click action triggers the upload event in order to believe that clicking is a means for submitting. It is within this framework of high-level actions and reactive events we then study relations of refinement and instrumentality between intentions.

2 Belief-Intention Databases

Let $\mathsf{Act} = \{\alpha, \beta, \ldots\}$ be a finite set of actions. It contains a set of basic actions $\mathsf{Act}_0 = \{a, b, \ldots\}$: actions that can be directly executed by the planning agent. Let $\mathsf{Evt}_0 = \{e, f, \ldots\}$ be a finite set of basic events. Basic events and basic actions take one time unit to be executed. Let $\mathbb{P} = \{p, q, \ldots\}$ be a finite set of propositional variables. The language of boolean formulas built from $\mathbb{P}$ is noted $\mathscr{L}_\mathbb{P}$.

Definition 1. *A dynamic theory is a tuple* $\mathcal{T} = \langle pre, post \rangle$ *with* $pre, post : \mathsf{Act} \cup \mathsf{Evt}_0 \longrightarrow \mathscr{L}_\mathbb{P}$, *such that that the postconditions of basic actions and events are conjunctions of literals: there are functions* $eff^+, eff^- : \mathsf{Act}_0 \cup \mathsf{Evt}_0 \longrightarrow 2^\mathbb{P}$ *such that for every* $x \in \mathsf{Act}_0 \cup \mathsf{Evt}_0$, $post(x) = \left(\bigwedge_{p \in eff^+(x)} p \right) \wedge \left(\bigwedge_{p \in eff^-(x)} \neg p \right)$.

We extend the functions $pre, post, eff^+$ and eff^- to sets: $pre(X) = \bigwedge_{x \in X} pre(x)$. We say that a dynamic theory $\mathcal{T}$ is *coherent* if and only if for every $a \in \mathsf{Act}_0$ and $E \subseteq \mathsf{Evt}_0$, if $pre(\{a\} \cup E)$ is consistent then $post(\{a\} \cup E)$ is consistent.

Example 1. Alice has a high-level action **buy** of buying a movie ticket and a basic action of buying a ticket online buyWeb. There is an event deliver of the website delivering the electronic ticket. Here is its coherent dynamic theory:

$pre(\mathbf{buy})$	$= \top$	$post(\mathbf{buy})$	$= \mathsf{Ticket}$
$pre(\mathsf{wait})$	$= \top$	$post(\mathsf{wait})$	$= \top$
$pre(\mathsf{buyWeb})$	$= \top$	$post(\mathsf{buyWeb})$	$= \mathsf{PaidWeb}$
$pre(\mathsf{deliver})$	$= \mathsf{PaidWeb} \wedge \neg\mathsf{Delivered}$	$post(\mathsf{deliver})$	$= \mathsf{Ticket} \wedge \mathsf{Delivered}$

In the rest of the paper we suppose a fixed background dynamic theory $\mathcal{T}$.

An agent's database contains her (incomplete) beliefs about the facts and about event occurrences together with her intentions. Occurrence of event $e \in \mathsf{Evt}_0$ at time point $t \in \mathbb{N}$ is noted (t, e). We also consider the agent's beliefs about non-occurrence of events. For that we define the set of event complements $\overline{\mathsf{Evt}_0} = \{\bar{e} : e \in \mathsf{Evt}_0\}$ and write $(t, \bar{e})$ for non-occurrence of e at t. An *intention* is a triple $i = (t, \alpha, d) \in \mathbb{N} \times \mathsf{Act} \times \mathbb{N}$ with $t < d$. It represents that the agent wants to perform α in the time interval $[t, d]$: it should start at or after t and end before or at deadline d. We define $\mathsf{end}(t, \alpha, d) = d$. When $\alpha \in \mathsf{Act}_0$ then i is a *basic intention*.

Definition 2. *A belief-intention database is a finite set*

$$\Delta \subseteq (\mathbb{N} \times \mathscr{L}_\mathbb{P}) \cup (\mathbb{N} \times \mathsf{Evt}_0) \cup (\mathbb{N} \times \overline{\mathsf{Evt}_0}) \cup (\mathbb{N} \times \mathsf{Act} \times \mathbb{N}).$$

For example, $\Delta_A = \{(0, \mathbf{buy}, 3)\}$ is a database describing Alice's intention to buy a movie ticket within the temporal interval $[0, 3]$.

3   Semantics

The semantics of dynamic theories and belief-intention databases is in terms of *paths* defining for each time point which propositional variables are true, which basic events will occur, and which (single) basic action the agent will perform.

Definition 3. *A path is a triple* $\pi = \langle V, H, D \rangle$ *with* $V : \mathbb{N} \longrightarrow 2^\mathbb{P}$, $H : \mathbb{N} \to 2^{\mathsf{Evt}_0}$, *and* $D : \mathbb{N} \to \mathsf{Act}_0$. *It is a* $\mathcal{T}$*-model iff* $\mathcal{T}$ *is coherent and for every* $t \in \mathbb{N}$:

$$V(t{+}1) = \big(V(t) \setminus \textit{eff}^-(H(t){\cup}\{D(t)\})\big) \cup \textit{eff}^+(H(t){\cup}\{D(t)\})$$
$$H(t) = \{e \in \mathsf{Evt}_0 \mid V(t) \models \textit{pre}(e)\}$$
$$D(t) \in \{a \in \mathsf{Act}_0 \mid V(t) \models \textit{pre}(a)\}$$

So in a $\mathcal{T}$-model: (1) the state at $t{+}1$ is determined by the state at t and the basic action and events occurring at t; (2) event e occurs *iff* $\textit{pre}(e)$ is true (the environment is reactive); (3) basic action a occurs *implies* that $\textit{pre}(a)$ is true (the agent is autonomous and may or may not perform executable actions).

Definition 4. *A* $\mathcal{T}$*-model* $\pi = \langle V, H, D \rangle$ *satisfies intention* $i = (t, \alpha, d)$, *noted* $\pi \Vdash_\mathcal{T} i$, *if there are* t', d' *such that* $t {\leq} t' {<} d' {\leq} d$, $V(t') \models \textit{pre}(\alpha)$, $V(d') \models \textit{post}(\alpha)$, *and* $\alpha \in \mathsf{Act}_0$ *implies* $D(t') = \alpha$.

So π satisfies (t, α, d) if α is executable at some point after t and can end before the deadline at a point where the postcondition of α is true. Moreover, when α is basic then it conforms to the 'do'-function D of π.

Definition 5. *A* $\mathcal{T}$*-model* $\pi = \langle V, H, D \rangle$ *is a* $\mathcal{T}$*-model of* Δ, *noted* $\pi \Vdash_\mathcal{T} \Delta$, *if*

– $(t, \varphi) \in \Delta$ *implies* $V(t) \models \varphi$;
– $(t, e) \in \Delta$ *implies* $e \in H(t)$;
– $(t, \overline{e}) \in \Delta$ *implies* $e \notin H(t)$;
– $i \in \Delta$ *implies* $\pi \Vdash_\mathcal{T} i$.

We say that Δ is $\mathcal{T}$*-satisfiable* if there exists a $\mathcal{T}$-model of Δ. Δ is a $\mathcal{T}$-*consequence* of Δ', noted $\Delta' \models_\mathcal{T} \Delta$, if every $\mathcal{T}$-model of Δ' is also a $\mathcal{T}$-model of Δ. We write $\Delta' \models_\mathcal{T} i$ when Δ is a singleton $\{i\}$.

Proposition 1. $\mathcal{T}$*-satisfiability and* $\mathcal{T}$*-consequence are decidable, for every* $\mathcal{T}$.

4   Refining an Intention

A high-level intention cannot be executed directly by the agent: it can only be refined into lower-level intentions, until basic intentions are produced. For example, my high-level intention i to submit a paper to JELIA before its deadline June 30 is refined into the intention i_1 to register it on Easychair before June 30, the intention i_2 to upload it as a PDF file, etc.

Refinement consists in adding new intentions to the database while staying consistent. Intuitively, to refine an intention i means to add a minimal set of new intentions J to the database which, together with other intentions but i, suffice to entail i. Moreover, the deadlines of the refining intentions should be before that of the refined intention.

Definition 6. *Intention i is refinable to intention set J in Δ, noted $\Delta \models_\mathcal{T} i \triangleleft J$, iff*

1. *there is no $j \in J$ such that $\Delta \models_\mathcal{T} j$;*
2. *$\Delta \cup J$ has a $\mathcal{T}$-model;*
3. *$(\Delta \cup J) \setminus \{i\} \models_\mathcal{T} i$;*
4. *$(\Delta \cup J') \setminus \{i\} \not\models_\mathcal{T} i$ for every $J' \subset J$;*
5. *$\mathsf{end}(j) \leq \mathsf{end}(i)$ for every $j \in J$.*

For our running example we have $\Delta_A \models_\mathcal{T} (0, \mathbf{buy}, 3) \triangleleft \{(0, \mathsf{buyWeb}, 1)\}$.

Proposition 2. *It is decidable whether $\Delta \models_\mathcal{T} i \triangleleft J$.*

5   Refinement and Instrumentality

A higher-level intention and the lower-level intentions refining it should stand in a means-end relation: the lower-level means contribute to the higher-level end. This is also called the *instrumentality relation* [1,4,8,16].

Instrumentality cannot be defined from an action theory alone. First, the time point of action execution matters. For example, let us take up our intention of attending JELIA in November. Suppose I also have to go to the conference host city, Larnaca, in May, for some other reason. The postcondition of that action—to be in Larnaca—entails one of the preconditions of the attending JELIA action. However, my May intention does not contribute to my November intention. So the former is not necessarily instrumental for the latter. Second, the preconditions of the means are typically more demanding than the preconditions of the end; similarly, the postconditions of the means are more detailed than those of the end. For example, buying a movie ticket should *a priori* not require an adequate amount of money because there are other ways to buy a ticket, such as online with a credit card.

Formally, the instrumentality relation relates a refined high-level intention to a set of lower-level intentions, given a background database.

Definition 7. *Let Δ be a $\mathcal{T}$-satisfiable database. Let intention $i \in \Delta$ and let intention set $J \subseteq \Delta$. Then J is instrumental for i in Δ, noted $\Delta \models_\mathcal{T} J \triangleright i$, iff*

1. $\Delta \setminus J \not\models_T i$;
2. $(\Delta \setminus J) \cup \{j\} \models_T i$ for every $j \in J$;
3. $\mathsf{end}(j) \leq \mathsf{end}(i)$ for every $j \in J$.

When $\Delta \models_T J > i$ then J is a minimal set of intentions satisfying the counterfactual "if J was not in Δ then i would no longer be guaranteed by Δ" and all intentions of J terminate before or together with i. Note that when $\Delta \models_T J > i$ then J cannot be empty (because we require $i \in J$).

We now relate intention refinement and instrumentality: when $\Delta \models_T i \lhd J$ then every element of J is instrumental for i in the refined database $\Delta \cup J$.

Theorem 1. *If $\Delta \models_T i \lhd J$ then $\Delta \cup J \models_T \{i,j\} > i$ for every $j \in J$.*

The converse does not hold: instrumentality cannot guarantee that the added intentions are new, so item 1 of Definition 6 does not necessarily hold.

6   Conclusion

We have extended Shoham's database view by temporally extended high-level intentions and STRIPS-like reactive environment events. The successive refinement of high-level intentions into lower-level intentions relies on the consequence relation of our semantics. The refined databases contain high- and low-level intentions that are related by the instrumentality relation. We have shown that satisfiability and consequence checking are still decidable in our extended database perspective.

The closest domain concerning intention refinement would be Hierarchical Task Networks (HTN) [9] which considering refinement of actions in a predefined and primitive way. With an HTN planner, a BDI agent system has been developed [7,17]. In this paper we focus on refinement which is, in some way, a well-founded belief-intention database expansion. More general expansion may lead to unsatisfiable database and raises issues about withdrawal or revision of intentions. This is further explored in [13].

The next step is to investigate the revision of belief-intention databases. This is typically required when the agent learns a new piece of information about the environment. For example, suppose $(t, e) \in \Delta$ and the agent learns that e will not happen at t. This requires not only to contract other beliefs about facts and events, but also some of the agent's intentions. The instrumentality relation is of fundamental importance here: when $\Delta \models_T J > i$ then the end intention i is deeper entrenched in the belief-intention database Δ than the means J to achieve i. So the agent should only abandon i once all possible ways of refining i have turned out to be unavailable. One possible relational postulate for revision is that the end intentions in the revised database should be a subset of the end intentions of the original database. There is currently little work on linking intention revision with instrumentality, with the exception of [11,19]. However, these contributions are still preliminary as many issues are not yet solved, such as the frame problem or the relation between basic and non-basic actions. We intend to explore in future work the revision of a belief-intention database where rational change relies on instrumentality.

References

1. Audi, R.: A theory of practical reasoning. J. Am. Philos. Q. **19**, 25–39 (1982)
2. Baral, C., Gelfond, M.: Reasoning about intended actions. In: Proceedings of the 20th National Conference on Artificial Intelligence (AAAI), vol. 20, pp. 689–694. AAAI Press, MIT Press, Menlo Park, Cambridge, London (1999) (2005)
3. Bratman, M.: Intention, Plans, and Practical Reason. Harvard University Press, Cambridge (1987). Reedited 1999 with CSLI Publications
4. Bratman, M.: Intention, belief, and instrumental rationality. Reasons for action, pp. 13–36 (2009)
5. Bratman, M.E., Israel, D.J., Pollack, M.E.: Plans and resource-bounded practical reasoning. J. Comput. Intell. **4**, 349–355 (1988)
6. Cohen, P.R., Levesque, H.J.: Intention is choice with commitment. J. Artif. Intell. **42**(2), 213–261 (1990)
7. De Silva, L., Sardina, S., Padgham, L.: First principles planning in BDI systems. In: Proceedings of the 8th International Conference on Autonomous Agents and Multiagent Systems (AAMAS), vol. 2, pp. 1105–1112 (2009)
8. Dignum, F., Conte, R.: Intentional agents and goal formation. In: Singh, M.P., Rao, A., Wooldridge, M.J. (eds.) ATAL 1997. LNCS, vol. 1365, pp. 231–243. Springer, Heidelberg (1998). doi:10.1007/BFb0026762
9. Erol, K., Hendler, J., Nau, D.S.: HTN planning: complexity and expressivity. In: Proceedings of the 12th National Conference on Artificial Intelligence (AAAI), vol. 94, pp. 1123–1128 (1994)
10. Fox, M., Long, D.: Modelling mixed discrete-continuous domains for planning. J. Artif. Intell. Res. (JAIR) **27**, 235–297 (2006)
11. Grant, J., Kraus, S., Perlis, D., Wooldridge, M.: Postulates for revising BDI structures. Synthese **175**(1), 39–62 (2010)
12. Herzig, A., Lorini, E., Perrussel, L., Xiao, Z.: BDI logics for BDI architectures: old problems, new perspectives. Knstliche Intelligenz (to appear)
13. Herzig, A., Perrussel, L., Xiao, Z.: On hierarchical task networks. In: Michael, L., Kakas, A.C. (eds.) JELIA 2016. LNCS(LNAI), vol. 10021, pp. xx–yy. Springer, Heidelberg (2016)
14. Hunsberger, L., Ortiz, Jr., C.: Dynamic intention structures I: a theory of intention representation. In: Proceedings of Autonomous Agents and Multi-Agent Systems (AAMAS), vol. 16, no. 3, pp. 298–326 (2008)
15. Icard, T., Pacuit, E., Shoham, Y.: Joint revision of belief and intention. In: Proceedings of the 12th International Conference on Principles of Knowledge Representation and Reasoning (KR), pp. 572–574 (2010)
16. Lorini, E., Herzig, A.: A logic of intention and attempt. Synthese **163**(1), 45–77 (2008)
17. Sardina, S., de Silva, L., Padgham, L.: Hierarchical planning in BDI agent programming languages: a formal approach. In: Proceedings of the 5th International Conference on Autonomous Agents and Multiagent Systems (AAMAS), pp. 1001–1008. ACM (2006)
18. Shoham, Y.: Logical theories of intention and the database perspective. J. Philos. Logic **38**(6), 633–647 (2009)
19. Van Zee, M., Doder, D., Dastani, M., Van Der Torre, L.: AGM revision of beliefs about action and time. In: Proceedings of the 24th International Joint Conference on Artificial Intelligence (IJCAI), pp. 3250–3256 (2015)

GenB: A General Solver for AGM Revision

Aaron Hunter$^{(\boxtimes)}$ and Eric Tsang

British Columbia Institute of Technology, Burnaby, Canada
aaron_hunter@bcit.ca

Abstract. We describe a general tool for solving belief revision problems with a range of different operators. Our tool allows a user to flexibly specify a total pre-order over states, using simple selection boxes in a graphic user interface. In this manner, we are able to calculate the result of any AGM revision operator. The user is also able to specify so-called trust partitions to calculate the result of trust-sensitive revision. The overall goal is to provide users with a simple tool that can be used in applications involving AGM-style revision. While the tool can be demonstrated and tested as a standalone application with a fixed user interface, what we have actually developed is a set of libraries and functions that can flexibly be incorporrated in other systems. It is anticipated that this tool will be useful for experimentation, education, and prototyping to solve problems in formal reasoning.

1 Introduction

We describe GenB, a general tool for solving belief revision problems. While the theory of belief revision has been well-studied, there has been comparatively little work on the development of tools to calculate the result of revision. Moreover, the belief revision solvers that have appeared in the literature have commonly focused on implementing a specific revision operator as effeciently as possible. Our approach differs in that we develop a general tool that can capture *any* AGM revision operator.

Due to well-known results on the complexity of revision [4], it is certainly not possible to develop a solver that runs quickly for all instances of any given AGM revision operator. Nevertheless, we suggest that a general tool that can calculate the result of AGM revision would be useful in the development of prototype reasoning systems. For instance, many reasoning problems involve *selective revision*, where the input is pre-processed in some way [5]. Our tool can be extended to solve such problems. GenB can also be useful for solving inverse belief revision problems. For example, there are problems in which we have data about the revision that has occurred, and we want to determine what sort of plausibility ordering was used [9]. There are also problems where we know the revision operator, but we want to find a formula to announce in order to bring about a certain result [7]. Our tool can be useful for addressing this kind of problem.

© Springer International Publishing AG 2016
L. Michael and A. Kakas (Eds.): JELIA 2016, LNAI 10021, pp. 564–569, 2016.
DOI: 10.1007/978-3-319-48758-8_40

This paper makes several contributions to existing work. First, we present a fully general solver that can capture all AGM revision operators. The development of such a tool should, in principle, facilitate prototyping for systems that involve belief revision. Second, implementing a general solver allows us to explore a new approach to revision that can be used in cases where no faithful assignment is forthcoming. Finally, to the best of our knowledge, this is the first implemented system for solving problems involving *selective revision* and *trust*.

2 Preliminaries

Belief revision is the process in which an agent's beliefs change to incorporate new information. One of the most influential models of belief revision has been the AGM approach [1]. In AGM belief revision, the beliefs of an agent are represented by a *belief set*, which is just a set of formulas K that is closed under consequence. An AGM belief revision operator $*$ is a function that takes a belief set K and a new formula ϕ as input, and it returns a new belief set $K * \phi$. Moreover, an AGM revision operator must satisfy the so-called AGM postulates for revision.

We use the term *state* to refer to a propositional interpretation over the underlying signature, and we use the term *belief state* to refer to a set of states. A *faithful assignment* is a function that maps every belief set K to a total preorder $\preceq_K$ over states, where the models of K are minimal. A representation result has been proved to show that every AGM revision operator is characterized by a faithful assignment [8]. To be slightly more precise, for every AGM revision operator $*$, there is a faithful assignment such that $K * \phi$ is the set of formulas true in the $\preceq_K$-minimal models of ϕ. The converse also holds.

3 Implementation

We provide the user with a mechanism for entering a belief set and a new formula for revision. Each of these is entered as a propositional formula; the underlying vocabulary is just the set of proprositional variables that occur in the input. In addition to these inputs, the user must also specify a total pre-order over possible states. The basic revision algorithm operates as follows:

1. **Input:** sentence ϕ, comparator $\preceq$
2. **Set** $sentenceModels = \{M \mid M \models \phi\}$
3. **Set** $nearestModel = M'$ where M' is $\preceq$-minimal in $sentenceModels$
4. **Set** $nearestModels = \{M \mid M' \preceq M \preceq M'\}$
5. **Return** $nearestModels$

GenB is implemented in Kotlin, which is essentially a variant of Java[1]. Internally, we use a *Comparator* object to capture the ordering over possible states. However, in order to facilitate the use of our program, we give users a few basic revision operators to choose from. The GenB interface is actually inspired by the interface of COBA 2.0, a belief revision system described in [3]. The interface is displayed in Fig. 1.

---

[1] Technical documentation and download available at http://kotlinlang.org.

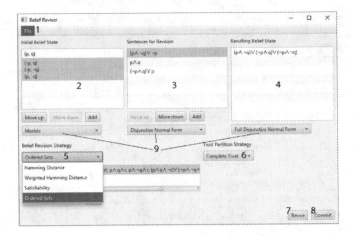

Fig. 1. GenB interface

The components identified in the interface above are as follows:

1. **File Menu:** Allows inputs to be loaded or saved to a file.
2. **Initial Belief State:** The initial beliefs of the agent can be entered and displayed as a set of models or a set of formulas.
3. **Sentences for Revision:** Entry and display can be through sets of models or formulas.
4. **Resulting Belief State:** Display can be through sets of models or formulas.
5. **Belief Revision Strategy:** This is a combo box that allows the user to specify different belief revision strategies, to be discussed below.
6. **Trust Partition:** Allows a trust partition to be specified, for trust-sensitive belief revision.
7. **Revise Button:** Pressing the revise button causes the revision to be performed, and displays the output.
8. **Commit button:** Pressing the commit button moves the new belief state to the initial belief box.
9. **Display Method:** Combo boxes for toggling between different ways to show information.

Users can toggle between the different display modes freely, switching from the model display to several different formula options.

4   Revision Strategies

4.1   Hamming Distance

GenB supports several different revision strategies. For the purposes of this paper, we focus primarily on the so-called Comparator-based revision strategies. These strategies correspond to AGM revision.

The first revision option is the Dalal revision operator based on the Hamming distance [2]. In order to use this operator, the user simply selects *Hamming Distance* from the combo box. No additional information is required for revision, because GenB is able to automatically define the comparator $\preceq$ by calculating the minimal Hamming distance from each state to a model of the input sentence.

Example 1. Suppose that we initially believe both p and q are true, but we want to revise by $\neg p \vee \neg q$. We proceed as follows:

1. Click *Add* on the *Initial Belief State* panel, enter p *and* q in the pop-up.
2. Click *Add* on the *Sentences for Revision* panel, enter $-p$ *or* $-q$ in the pop-up.
3. Select the *Hamming Distance* option.
4. Click the *Revise* button.

The resulting beliefs will be $\neg p \vee \neg q$, as expected.

4.2 Weighted Hamming Distance

In some cases, we want to use a variation of the Dalal operator where certain variables are understood to carry greater "importance." In GenB, this can be done by selecting the Weighted Hamming Distance, where each propositional formula has an associated priority. In this manner, the distance between two states will vary depending on the 'wieght' of the variables where they differ.

Example 2. Modifying the previous example, if we select the *Weighted Hamming Distance* at step 3, we will be prompted to list the propositional variables in order of importance. If we enter p, q as the ordering, then states are considered more plausible when the they differ on q as opposed to when they differ on p. As such, in this case, GenB will return q as the resulting set of beliefs.

4.3 Ordered Sets

The third revision option is based on Ordered Sets. When this option is selected, the user is prompted to provide an ordered list of formulas. Intuitively, the user is actually specifying the most plausible states for the comparator. Hence, if a user enters p, q in the corresponding dialog, they are saying that models of p are more plausible than models of q. It is possible (though tedious) to specify any total pre-order over states in this manner. The system also allows a randomized ordering, for users that do not want to produce a list.

We suggest that Ordered Sets revision can be used for experimentation. For example, we can iterated over all orderings and then look at credulous or skeptical reasoning. By using GenB as a library, we can address this kind of novel approach to revision.

4.4 Trust-Sensitive Revision

One issue with AGM revision for practical applications is the fact that the source of new information is always trusted. This can be addressed by *trust-sensitive* belief revision operators [6]. In trust-sensitive revision, we associate a partition Π over states with each information source. When we are given a sentence ϕ for revision, we first find $\{s \mid \Pi(s, s')$ and $s' \models \phi\}$. Rather than revising by ϕ, we then revise by this set. In other words, we consider ϕ to be evidence for every state that is Π-related to a model of ϕ. In this manner, the partition Π identifies the states that we trust a particular source to be capable of distinguishing.

GenB allows the user to define a trust-partition, and then perform trust-sensitive revision.

Example 3. Suppose that a particular agent is trusted on the value of the variable S, but not on the variable D. Using GenB, we can model and solve this problem as follows:

1. Click *Add* on the *Initial Belief State* panel, enter $-S$ *and* D in the pop-up.
2. Click *Add* on the *Sentences for Revision* panel, enter S *and* $-D$ in the pop-up.
3. Select the formula option on the *Trust Partition* combo box, enter S in the pop-up.
4. Click the *Revise* button.

Note that, if step 3 is omitted, then normal revision is performed and the result will include $-D$. However, using the trust-partition option, the result is not forced to include this information.

5 Discussion

In this preliminary report, we have described the development of an automated tool that can calculate the result of any AGM revision operator. To demonstrate potential applications, we included an implementation of trust-sensitive revision in our tool. We have addressed several interface design issues, such as providing the user a means for specifying a total pre-order in a flexible manner. In practice, however, we expect GenB to be deployed as a set of libraries that can easily be integrated into more complex reasoning systems.

There are several directions for future research. First, although the practical performance is strong, the effeciency of the system could be improved. Second, we are interested in using GenB to find propositional announcements for belief revision. Following the general approach in [7], we would like to use GenB to implement a practical robot controller involving public announcements. Finally, we would like to use GenB to address problems in security. To the best of our knowledge, no existing protocol verification tools actually implement any approach to belief revision. By implementing a general solver, we hope to explore the utlility of belief revision for security through exploration and experimentation.

References

1. Alchourrón, C.E., Gärdenfors, P., Makinson, D.: On the logic of theory change: partial meet functions for contraction and revision. J. Symbolic Logic **50**(2), 510–530 (1985)
2. Dalal, M.: Investigations into a theory of knowledge base revision. In: Proceedings of the National Conference on Artificial Intelligence (AAAI), pp. 475–479 (1988)
3. Delgrande, J.P., Liu, D.H., Schaub, T., Thiele, S.: COBA 2.0: a consistency-based belief change system. In: Mellouli, K. (ed.) ECSQARU 2007. LNCS (LNAI), vol. 4724, pp. 78–90. Springer, Heidelberg (2007). doi:10.1007/978-3-540-75256-1_10
4. Eiter, T., Gottlob, G.: On the complexity of propositional knowledge base revision, updates and counterfactuals. Artif. Intell. **57**(2–3), 227–270 (1992)
5. Fermé, E., Hansson, S.O.: Selective revision. Stud. Logica. **63**(3), 331–342 (1999)
6. Hunter, A., Booth, R.: Trust-sensitive belief revision. In: International Joint Conference on Artificial Intelligence (IJCAI), pp. 3062–3068 (2015)
7. Hunter, A., Schwarzentruber, F.: Arbitrary announcements in propositional belief revision. In: Proceedings of the Workshop on Declarative and Ampliative Reasoning (DARE) (2015)
8. Katsuno, H., Mendelzon, A.O.: Propositional knowledge base revision and minimal change. Artif. Intell. **52**(2), 263–294 (1992)
9. Liberatore, P.: Revision by history. J. Artif. Intell. Res. **52**, 287–329 (2015)

A Two-Phase Dialogue Game for Skeptical Preferred Semantics

Zohreh Shams[1] and Nir Oren[2(✉)]

[1] Department of Computer Science, University of Bath, Bath, UK
z.shams@bath.ac.uk
[2] Department of Computing Science, University of Aberdeen, Aberdeen, UK
n.oren@abdn.ac.uk

Abstract. In this paper we propose a labelling based dialogue game for determining whether a single argument within a Dung argumentation framework is skeptically preferred. Our game consists of two phases, and determines the membership of a single argument within the extension, assuming optimal play by dialogue participants. In the first phase, one player attempts to advance arguments to construct an extension not containing the argument under consideration, while the second phase verifies that the extension is indeed a preferred one. Correctness within this basic game requires perfect play by both players, and we therefore also introduce an overarching game to overcome this limitation.

1 Introduction

It has been argued that proof dialogues, while providing equivalent results to standard argumentation semantics, can decrease the gap between intuitive and formal accounts of argumentation [1,11–13], and have been used in human-computer interactions to aid understanding [4,6,16]. While the credulous acceptance problem under preferred semantics has been modelled using dialogue games in the past [3,7,12,16], the skeptical preferred semantics has received less attention.

In this paper, we propose a dialogue game for skeptical preferred acceptance that is similar to [10,16], but (i) differs from [16] in that it is not restricted to cases when the preferred and stable semantics coincide; (ii) differs to approaches such as [8,12] in that it does not use a meta-dialogue based approach; and (iii) also differs from existing approaches in that it uses argument labellings within the dialogue. Moreover, we believe that this dialogue is more intuitive than [8,10,12,16]. The principal aim of our dialogue is to facilitate explanation as to why an argument is — or is not — skeptically preferred to a human user (similar to the work of Caminada and Podlaszewski [5]).

Our dialogue utilises two phases. In the first, one participant (the opponent) identifies an extension in which the argument under discussion is not present. In the second phase, the other participant (the proponent) attempts to prove that the opponent has (in some loose sense) cheated — that the extension advanced is not a preferred extension. Under perfect play, this dialogue will identify whether

© Springer International Publishing AG 2016
L. Michael and A. Kakas (Eds.): JELIA 2016, LNAI 10021, pp. 570–576, 2016.
DOI: 10.1007/978-3-319-48758-8_41

an argument is skeptically preferred or not. In the presence of imperfect play, we extend this basic game to an overarching one, which allows the two phases to repeat until both parties are satisfied as to the presence or absence of the argument within all extensions.

Next, we introduce the argumentation system and labelling based semantics. Section 3 describes our dialogue. Note that a longer version of this paper containing proofs of our results, extensions of the basic dialogue, and additional details has appeared as a technical report [14].

2   Preliminaries

We begin with basic concepts from argumentation theory. Note that throughout this paper, we consider only finite argumentation frameworks.

Definition 1 (Argumentation Framework [9]). *An argumentation framework is a pair $AF = (Arg, Def)$, where Arg is a finite set of arguments and Def is a defeat relation between arguments: $Def \subseteq Arg \times Arg$.*

Argumentation semantics focus on arguments that are justified in an argumentation framework, whereas argument labellings (c.f., [15]) consider the status of all arguments. In Caminada's approach [2], an (partial) argument labelling is described as a function $\mathcal{L} : Arg \rightarrow \{in, out, undec\}$ such that $in(\mathcal{L}) = \{a \in Arg \text{ s.t. } \mathcal{L}(a) = in\}$, $out(\mathcal{L}) = \{a \in Arg \text{ s.t. } \mathcal{L}(a) = out\}$, and $undec(\mathcal{L}) = \{A \in Arg \text{ s.t. } \mathcal{L}(a) = undec\}$. Thus, a labelling may be presented as a triple of the form $(in(\mathcal{L}), out(\mathcal{L}), undec(\mathcal{L}))$. An equivalence exists between those arguments labelled *in* according to specific labelling procedures, and the various standard argumentation semantics. To define labelling procedures corresponding to the preferred extensions, we need to first recall the definition of legal and complete labellings.

Definition 2 (Labellings [2,12]). *Let $\mathcal{L}$ be a labelling for $AF = (Arg, Def)$. An argument belong to Arg is legally:*

- *in iff all its defeaters are labelled out;*
- *out iff there is at least one of its defeaters that is labelled in;*
- *undec iff not all of its defeaters are labelled out and there is none of its defeaters that is in.*

An argument is labelled illegally iff its label is not legal. We say that a labelling is legal if all its arguments are labelled legally.

A complete labelling is a non-partial labelling without arguments that are illegally in, out, or undec.

A complete labelling is called a preferred labelling iff its set of in-labelled arguments is maximal (with respect to set inclusion); or equivalently, iff its set of out-labelled arguments is maximal (with respect to set inclusion).

Note that an argument can only be labelled undecided if one or more of its defeater are also undecided, and none of its defeaters are labelled in.

For a given argumentation framework, multiple preferred labellings may be found. An argument is skeptically accepted under preferred labellings (and equivalently, semantics) if it is labelled *in* within every preferred labelling. If an argument is labelled *in* within a subset of labellings, then it is credulously accepted under the labelling.

3   A Dialogue Game for Skeptical Preferred Semantics

We now describe a dialogical proof procedure for the skeptically preferred semantics. Two players — P and O take part, with P seeking to prove that a single *focal argument* f is skeptically preferred. Our dialogue has two phases, and we describe the legal moves and protocosl for each phase.

Intuitively, within the first phase, O aims to find a preferred labelling where f is not *in*. In the second phase, P verifies that this labelling is maximally *in* or *out*. The first phase thus allows O to identify a labelling where the focal argument is not justified, and the second phase verifies that O did not cheat in Phase one.

Note that we need to consider only a subset of arguments in the framework, namely those arguments which directly or indirectly defeat or defend the focal argument[1]. We refer to the labelling of such arguments as a *sub-labelling*. Where the context is clear, we may refer to a sub-labelling as a labelling.

Definition 3 (Dialogue Moves). *The following moves are available to the dialogue participants.*

What is *— $WI(a)$. This move is used to request that a label be assigned to a, where $a \in Arg$.*
Claim *— $CL(\mathcal{L}(a))$. This move is used to assign a label $\mathcal{L} \in \{in, out, undec\}$ to a, where $a \in Args$.*

3.1   Phase One

In this phase, O seeks to create a complete sub-labelling of arguments in which the focal argument f is *undec* or *out*. If O fails to construct such a labelling, it loses the game. If on the other hand O succeeds, then the result of this phase is a complete sub-labelling, which is evaluated by P in the second phase to determine whether it is a preferred sub-labelling.

In this phase, P utters only *WI* moves, while O plays only *CL* moves. The proponent P initiates the dialogue with the move $WI(f)$, where f is the focal argument whose status is to be determined. Following this, O and P take turns

---

[1] i.e., only those arguments for which there is a directed path according to the defeat relation to the focal argument in the graph generated by the argumentation framework.

to make an utterance (with O making the second move). A $CL(\mathcal{L}(a))$ move by O provides a labelling for the directly preceding $WI(a)$ move of P, where $\mathcal{L}(a)$ is the label assigned to a. Note that WI moves (and therefore CL moves) cannot be repeated. The Phase one protocol is formally specified as follows.

Definition 4 (Phase One Dialogue). *Let $AF = (Arg, Def)$ be an argumentation framework. A phase one dialogue is a sequence $\Delta_o = [\delta_1, \delta_2, \cdots, \delta_n]$ $(n \geq 1)$ satisfying the following conditions:*

- *odd moves $(\delta_i, 1 \leq i \leq n, i \in 2\mathbb{Z}^+ + 1)$ belong to P and even moves $(\delta_i, 2 \leq i \leq n, i \in 2\mathbb{Z}^+)$ belong to O.*
- *$\delta_1 = WI(f)$, where f is the focal argument.*
- *each δ_i $(2 \leq i \leq n, i \in 2\mathbb{Z}^+)$ is of the form $CL(\mathcal{L}(a))$, where $\delta_{i-1} = WI(a)$.*
- *each δ_i $(3 \leq i \leq n, i \in 2\mathbb{Z}^+ + 1)$ is of form $WI(a)$ s.t. $\exists \delta_j = CL(\mathcal{L}(b))(j < i)$ and $(a, b) \in Def$.*
- *there exist no two WI moves δ_i and δ_j $(i \neq j)$ for which $\delta_i = \delta_j$.*

Phase one terminates when no more moves are possible. O loses the game if it

1. *utters $CL(in(x))$, where x is the focal argument in the dialogue; or*
2. *labels an argument in, having previously labelled one of its defeater in or undec; or*
3. *labels an argument undec, having previously labelled one of its defeaters in; or*
4. *when no more moves are possible, there is an argument labelled undec for which no defeaters are labelled undec; or*
5. *when no more moves are possible, there is an argument labelled out for which no defeaters are labelled in.*

If O does not lose the game when Phase one terminates, Phase two begins. Alternatively, if O loses the game, then P wins. If O does not lose the game during Phase one, then we must wait until Phase two terminates to determine whether O or P win the game.

3.2   Phase Two

Here, P tries to prove that the labelling of Phase one is not preferred. If successful, P wins the game and otherwise O wins. The latter occurs when O explores the consequences of claims made by P.

This phase utilises the same moves as previously. However, now P utters CL moves while O advances WI moves. As in Phase one, the proponent (P) and opponent (O) take turns to advance arguments. P makes the first move by putting forward $CL(in(x))$, where x was labelled *undec* in the Phase one. O responds to a CL move with a WI move, and P responds to such a move with a CL move.

As in Phase one, the argument of a WI move must be one that defeats the argument labelled by a CL move, with the additional constraint that a CL move may only be made over arguments which were labelled *undec* in Phase one. The *CL* move then changes the label of such an argument. Again, *WI* moves cannot be repeated. Formally, the second phase of the dialogue is described as follows.

Definition 5 (Phase Two Dialogue). *Let $AF = (Arg, Def)$ be an argumentation framework and $\Delta_o = [\delta_1, \delta_2, \cdots, \delta_n]$ ($n \geq 1$) be a Phase one dialogue in which O did not lose. A Phase two dialogue is a sequence of moves $\Delta_t = [\delta_1', \delta_2', \cdots, \delta_m']$ ($m \geq 0$) satisfying the following conditions:*

- *odd moves ($\delta_i', 1 \leq i \leq m, i \in 2\mathbb{Z}^+ + 1$) belong to P and even moves ($\delta_i', 2 \leq i \leq m, i \in 2\mathbb{Z}^+$) belong to O.*
- *$\delta_1' = CL(in(a))$ for $a \in Arg$ such that $\exists CL(undec(a)) \in \Delta_o$*
- *For any $2 \leq i \leq m$, $i \in 2\mathbb{Z}^+$, δ_i' is a move by O of the form $WI(a)$ where $a, b \in Arg$ and*
  - *$(a, b) \in Def$*
  - *$CL(\mathcal{L}(b)) \in \Delta_t$; and*
  - *$CL(undec(a)) \in \Delta_o$ but $CL(\mathcal{L}(a)) \notin \Delta_t$; and*

- *each δ_i' where $3 \leq i \leq m, i \in 2\mathbb{Z}^+ + 1$, is a move by P of form $CL(\mathcal{L}(a))$, where $\delta_{i-1}' = WI(a)$.*
- *there exists no two WI moves δ_i' and δ_j' ($i \neq j$) while $\delta_i' = \delta_j'$.*

The dialogue terminates when no further moves are possible. P wins the game iff it has made at least one move during Phase 2 and the labelling at the end of Phase two is legal. Otherwise, O is the winner.

The second phase requires P to demonstrate that the labelling advanced by O in Phase one is not a preferred labelling. Since such labellings are maximally *in*, P does so by changing the label of an argument labelled *undec* in Phase one to *in*. Once such a change is made, Phase two continues by relabelling the undecided defeaters of the changed argument until no further changes are required or possible. If P is able to perform the relabelling in such a way so that the resultant labelling is legal, then it wins the game as it has shown that the labelling advanced by O in Phase one is not maximally *in*. If P fails in doing this, then O wins the game.

Note that the relabelling in Phase two does not require all undecided arguments to be relabelled. Also, if no undecided arguments exist at the start of Phase two, the game ends immediately, with O winning the game. Finally, note that while P was required to relabel an *undec* argument to *in*, it would be equivalent to require *undec* arguments to be labelled *out*.

Theorem 1. *There is a winning strategy for P (under which they will win all games) iff the focal argument is skeptically preferred. Similarly, there is a strategy for O (under which O will win all games) iff the focal argument is not skeptically preferred.*

This theorem requires perfect play by O and P is required for the dialogue to correctly identify skeptically preferred arguments. However, as we describe in [14], it is possible to introduce a strategy, together with an extended form of the game, which guarantees that the dialogue will be sound and complete even under imperfect play, though at the cost of additional computational complexity (note that a single iteration of the dialogue has complexity linear in the number of arguments). Unsurprisingly, O's strategy in Phase one involves advancing a preferred labelling, while in Phase two, P should label the focal argument *in* and then proceed to label other *undec* arguments appropriately. Since pursuing such a strategy may be computationally infeasible, the extended form of the game (effectively) allows multiple games to take place, exploring alternative labellings until both parties are satisfied as to the outcome of the game.

4   Conclusions

In this short paper we introduced a dialogue game for the skeptical preferred semantics which exploits argument labellings. The basic game requires perfect play by both opponents, but is useful in human-computer interaction settings where argument status is explained by the computer to a human (c.f., [4]). As future work, we intend to investigate whether our approach can be more generally applied to any complete-based skeptical semantics (e.g., skeptical stable).

References

1. Caminada, M.: Dialogues and HY-arguments. In: Delgrande, J., Schaub, T. (eds.) 10th International Workshop on Non-Monotonic Reasoning, pp. 94–99 (2004)
2. Caminada, M.: On the issue of reinstatement in argumentation. In: Fisher, M., Hoek, W., Konev, B., Lisitsa, A. (eds.) JELIA 2006. LNCS (LNAI), vol. 4160, pp. 111–123. Springer, Heidelberg (2006). doi:10.1007/11853886_11
3. Caminada, M.W.A., Dvořák, W., Vesic, S.: Preferred semantics as socratic discussion. J. Log. Comput. **26**(4), 1257–1292 (2016). doi:10.1093/logcom/exu005
4. Caminada, M., Kutlak, R., Oren, N., Vasconcelos, W.W.: Scrutable plan enactment via argumentation and natural language generation. In: Bazzan, A.L.C., Huhns, M.N., Lomuscio, A., Scerri, P. (eds.) International conference on Autonomous Agents and Multi-Agent Systems, pp. 1625–1626 (2014)
5. Caminada, M., Podlaszewski, M.: Grounded semantics as persuasion dialogue. In: Verheij, B., Szeider, S., Woltran, S. (eds.) Computational Models of Argument, vol. 245, pp. 478–485 (2012)
6. Caminada, M., Podlaszewski, M.: User-computer persuasion dialogue for grounded semantics. In: Benelux Conference on Artificial Intelligence, pp. 343–344 (2012)
7. Cayrol, C., Doutre, S., Mengin, J.: Dialectical proof theories for the credulous preferred semantics of argumentation frameworks. In: Benferhat, S., Besnard, P. (eds.) Symbolic, Quantitative Approaches to Reasoning with Uncertainty, vol. 2143, pp. 668–679 (2001)
8. Doutre, S., Mengin, J.: On sceptical vs credulous acceptance for abstract argument systems. In: Delgrande, J., Schaub, T. (eds.) 10th International Workshop on Non-Monotonic Reasoning, pp. 134–139 (2004)

9. Dung, P.M.: On the acceptability of arguments and its fundamental role in non-monotonic reasoning, logic programming and n-person games. Artif. Intell. **77**(2), 321–358 (1995)
10. Dung, P.M., Thang, P.M.: A sound and complete dialectical proof procedure for sceptical preferred argumentation. In: LPNMR-Workshop on Argumentation and Nonmonotonic Reasoning, pp. 49–63 (2007)
11. Jakobovits, H., Vermeir, D.: Dialectic semantics for argumentation frameworks. In: Seventh International Conference on Artificial Intelligence and Law, pp. 53–62 (1999)
12. Modgil, S., Caminada, M.: Proof theories and algorithms for abstract argumentation frameworks. In: Simari, G., Rahwan, I. (eds.) Argumentation in Artificial Intelligence, pp. 105–129. Springer, US (2009)
13. Prakken, H.: Combining sceptical epistemic reasoning with credulous practical reasoning. In: Dunne, P.E., Bench-Capon, T.J.M. (eds.) Computational Models of Argument, vol. 144, pp. 311–322 (2006)
14. Shams, Z., Oren, N.: A labelling based dialogue game for skeptical preferred semantics, Technical report ABDN-CS-2016-02. http://homepages.abdn.ac.uk/n.oren/pages/abdn-CS2016-02.pdf
15. Verheij, B.: Two approaches to dialectical argumentation: admissible sets and argumentation stages. In: International Conference on Formal and Applied Practical Reasoning, pp. 357–368 (1996)
16. Vreeswik, G.A.W., Prakken, H.: Credulous and sceptical argument games for preferred semantics. In: Ojeda-Aciego, M., Guzmán, I.P., Brewka, G., Pereira, L. (eds.) JELIA 2000. LNCS (LNAI), vol. 1919, pp. 239–253. Springer, Heidelberg (2000). doi:10.1007/3-540-40006-0_17

Measuring Inconsistency in Answer Set Programs

Markus Ulbricht[1]([✉]), Matthias Thimm[1,2], and Gerhard Brewka[1]

[1] Department of Computer Science, Leipzig University, Leipzig, Germany
mulbricht@informatik.uni-leipzig.de
[2] Institute for Web Science and Technologies (WeST),
University of Koblenz-Landau, Koblenz, Germany

Abstract. We address the issue of quantitatively assessing the severity of inconsistencies in logic programs under the answer set semantics. While measuring inconsistency in classical logics has been investigated for some time now, taking the non-monotonicity of answer set semantics into account brings new challenges that have to be addressed by reasonable accounts of inconsistency measures. We investigate the behavior of inconsistency in logic programs by revisiting existing rationality postulates for inconsistency measurement and developing novel ones taking non-monotonicity into account. Further, we develop new measures for this setting and investigate their properties.

1 Introduction

Answer set programming (ASP, see [2] for an overview) is a popular non-monotonic formalism for knowledge representation and reasoning. We consider a finite set $\mathcal{L}$ of literals. An extended logic program P (over $\mathcal{L}$) is a set of rules of the form

$$r : \quad l_0 \leftarrow l_1, \ldots, l_k, \text{not } l_{k+1}, \ldots, \text{not } l_m. \tag{1}$$

with $l_0, \ldots, l_m \in \mathcal{L}$, $0 \leq k \leq m$. Let $\mathcal{P}$ be the set of all extended logic programs. We abbreviate $head(r) = l_0$, $pos(r) = \{l_1, \ldots, l_k\}$ and $neg(r) = \{l_{k+1}, \ldots, l_m\}$. For two sets M and L of literals, we say M satisfies L ($M \vDash L$) iff $l \in M$ for each $l \in L$. Now let P be a classical program (without default negation not). For a rule $r \in P$, $M \vDash r$ iff $M \vDash \{head(r)\}$ whenever $M \vDash pos(r)$ and $M \vDash P$ iff $M \vDash r$ for each rule $r \in P$. We let $\mathsf{Cl}(P)$ be the unique $M \subseteq \mathcal{L}$ with $M \vDash P$ and $M' \nvDash P$ for each set $M' \subsetneq M$.

Definition 1. *A set M of literals is called an* answer set *of a classical program P if $M = \mathsf{Cl}(P)$. M is an answer set of an extended logic program P if M is the answer set of P^M, where $P^M = \{head(r) \leftarrow pos(r) \mid r \in P, neg(r) \cap M = \emptyset\}$ is the* reduct *of P with respect to M.*

A set M of literals is called *consistent* if it does not contain both a and $\neg a$ for an atom a. A program P is called *consistent* if it has at least one consistent

© Springer International Publishing AG 2016
L. Michael and A. Kakas (Eds.): JELIA 2016, LNAI 10021, pp. 577–583, 2016.
DOI: 10.1007/978-3-319-48758-8_42

answer set, otherwise it is called *inconsistent*. Let $\mathrm{Ans}(P)$ denote the set of all answer sets of P and $\mathrm{Ans}_{Inc}(P)$ and $\mathrm{Ans}_{Con}(P)$ the inconsistent and consistent ones, respectively. Note that, motivated by the goals of this paper, our definition slightly differs from the original definition in [3] which allows for a single inconsistent answer set only, namely $\mathcal{L}$.

In the classical literature on inconsistency measurement—see e. g. [4,5,10]—inconsistency measures are functions that aim at assessing the severity of the inconsistency in knowledge bases formalized in propositional logic. Here, we are interested in measuring inconsistency for (extended) logic programs and only consider measures defined on those. Let $\mathbb{R}_{\geq 0}^{\infty}$ be the set of non-negative real values including ∞.

Definition 2. *An* inconsistency measure $\mathcal{I}$ *is a function* $\mathcal{I} : \mathcal{P} \to \mathbb{R}_{\geq 0}^{\infty}$.

The basic intuition behind an inconsistency measure $\mathcal{I}$ is that the larger the inconsistency in P the larger the value $\mathcal{I}(P)$. However, even in the setting of propositional logic, inconsistency is a concept that is not easily quantified and there have been a couple of proposals for inconsistency measures in this setting, see [10] for a recent survey.

The issue of measuring inconsistency in logic programs is more challenging compared to the classical setting due to the non-monotonicity of answer set semantics. This becomes apparent when considering the *monotonicity* postulate which is usually satisfied by classical inconsistency measures and demands $\mathcal{I}(P') \geq \mathcal{I}(P)$ whenever $P \subseteq P'$, i. e., the severity of inconsistency cannot be decreased by adding new information. Consider now the two logic programs P_1 and P_2 given as follows:

$$P_1 : \; b \leftarrow \mathrm{not}\; a. \qquad\qquad P_2 : \; b \leftarrow \mathrm{not}\; a.$$
$$\neg b \leftarrow \mathrm{not}\; a. \qquad\qquad \neg b \leftarrow \mathrm{not}\; a.$$
$$a.$$

We have $P_1 \subseteq P_2$ but P_1 is inconsistent while P_2 is not, so we would expect $\mathcal{I}(P_2) < \mathcal{I}(P_1)$ for any reasonable measure $\mathcal{I}$. Therefore, simply taking classical inconsistency measures and applying them to the setting of logic programs does not yield the desired behavior.

Many rationality postulates such as *monotonicity* from above are already disputed in the classical setting, cf. [1]. Taking non-monotonicity of the knowledge representation formalism into account, a rational account of the severity of inconsistency calls for a specific investigation, which we will undertake in the remainder of this paper. In particular, we will discuss rationality postulates for inconsistency measures in logic programs in Sect. 2 and propose some novel measures in Sect. 3. An extended version of this paper can be found online[1].

---

[1] http://www.mthimm.de/misc/utb_incasp.pdf.

2 Rationality Postulates

Research in inconsistency measurement is driven by *rationality postulates*, i.e., desirable properties that should hold for concrete approaches. There is a growing number of rationality postulates for inconsistency measurement but not every postulate is generally accepted, see [1] for a recent discussion on this topic. In the following, we revisit a selection of the most popular postulates—see e.g. [6,9]—and phrase them within our context of logic programs. To do so, we need some further notation.

Definition 3. *The* dependency graph D_P *of a program* P *is a labeled directed graph having all literals of the program as vertices and there is an edge* (l_i, l_j, s) *iff* P *contains a rule* r *such that* $head(r) = l_j$ *and* $l_i \in pos(r) \cup neg(r)$. *The label* $s \in \{+, -\}$ *indicates whether* $l_i \in pos(r)$ *or* $l_i \in neg(r)$. *For any literal* l, *let* $Path(P, l)$ *be the set of all literals* l' *(including* l *itself) such that there is a path from* l *to* l' *in* D_P.

Definition 4. *A set* U *of literals is called a* splitting set *[7] for* P, *if* $head(r) \in U$ *implies that all literals of atoms appearing in* r *are contained in* U, *for every rule* $r \in P$. *For a splitting set* U, *let* $bot_U(P)$ *be the set of all rules* $r \in P$ *with* $head(r) \in U$. *This set of rules is called the* bottom part *of* P *with respect to* U.

Definition 5. *A rule* $r^* \in P$ *is called* safe *with respect to* P *if the atom occurring in the head of* r^* *does not appear elsewhere in the program and* $pos(r^*) \cup neg(r^*)$ *is a subset of the literals occurring in* $P \setminus \{r^*\}$.

Now let $\mathcal{I}$ be an inconsistency measure. The postulate *Consistency* establishes that 0 is the minimal inconsistency value and that it is reserved for consistent programs.

Consistency. P is consistent iff $\mathcal{I}(P) = 0$.

Satisfaction of *Monotonicity.* is generally *not* desirable for ASP. However, as we still wish to require some form of monotonicity in special cases, we consider the weaker postulate *CLP-Monotonicity* (CLP stands for "classical logic program"). If a program does not contain any default negation and we only add new information without default negation, we are in the classical setting and monotonicity should hold. A stronger version of *CLP-Monotonicity* is *I-Monotonicity* which is applicable when the head of a new rule is independent of the defaults in the program. Similarly, *Split-Monotonicity* considers monotonicity with respect to the bottom part of splitting sets.

Monotonicity. $\mathcal{I}(P) \leq \mathcal{I}(P')$ whenever $P \subseteq P'$.
CLP-Monotonicity. If P is a classical logic program and r^* a classical rule, then $\mathcal{I}(P) \leq \mathcal{I}(P \cup \{r^*\})$.
I-Monotonicity. If r^* is a rule with $\mathsf{Path}(P \cup r^*, head(r^*)) \cap neg(P \cup r^*) = \emptyset$, then $\mathcal{I}(P) \leq \mathcal{I}(P \cup \{r^*\})$.
Split-Monotonicity. If U is a splitting set of P, then $\mathcal{I}(bot_U(P)) \leq \mathcal{I}(P)$.

Finally, *Safe-rule independence* demands that the addition of safe rules does not change the inconsistency value.

Safe-rule independence. If P is a logic program and r^* safe with respect to P, then $\mathcal{I}(P) = \mathcal{I}(P \cup \{r^*\})$.

3   Inconsistency Measures

We now propose concrete inconsistency measures for logic programs. Inconsistency of programs can occur due to two different reasons, namely because the program has no answer set at all or because all answer sets are inconsistent, cf. [8]. Different measures should assess those reasons differently. Furthermore, to measure inconsistency of a program, one could either take the program itself or the answer sets into account. We will cover both approaches.

Our first measure $\mathcal{I}_\pm$ aims at measuring the distance of the program to a consistent one. More specifically, it quantifies the number of modifications in terms of deleting and adding rules, necessary in order to restore consistency. Deleting certain rules can surely be sufficient to prevent P from entailing contradictions, but as already pointed out before, adding rules can also resolve inconsistency.

Definition 6. *Define* $\mathcal{I}_\pm : \mathcal{P} \to \mathbb{R}_{\geq 0}^\infty$ *via*

$$\mathcal{I}_\pm(P) = \min\{|A| + |D| \mid A, D \in \mathcal{P} \text{ such that } (P \cup A) \setminus D \text{ is consistent}\}$$

for all $P \in \mathcal{P}$.

Example 1. Consider the program P_3 defined via

$$P_3: \quad a_1 \leftarrow \text{not } b. \qquad\qquad a_1 \leftarrow \text{not } c. \quad a_1 \leftarrow \text{not } d.$$
$$\neg a_1 \leftarrow \text{not } b. \qquad\qquad \neg a_1 \leftarrow \text{not } c. \quad \neg a_1 \leftarrow \text{not } d.$$

and P_4 given as follows.

$$P_4: \quad a_1 \leftarrow \text{not } b. \qquad\qquad a_2 \leftarrow \text{not } b. \quad a_3 \leftarrow \text{not } b.$$
$$\neg a_1 \leftarrow \text{not } b. \qquad\qquad \neg a_2 \leftarrow \text{not } b. \quad \neg a_3 \leftarrow \text{not } b.$$

Note that P_3 contains three contradicting pairs of rules. Since one can delete one rule in each of them (or make the rule inapplicable by adding the corresponding fact), $\mathcal{I}_\pm(P_3) = 3$. Even though P_4 is similar, $\mathcal{I}_\pm(P_4) = 1$ since $P_4 \cup \{b.\}$ is consistent.

The measure $\mathcal{I}_\pm$ performs a *hypothetical* modification of the original program P itself to obtain consistency. Another approach is to relax the definition of answer sets and consider modifications of the reduct P^M instead.

Definition 7. *A consistent set M of literals is called a k-l-model of a classical logic program P if M is a model of $(P \cup A) \setminus D$ with $A, D \in \mathcal{P}$ and $|A| \leq k$, $|D| \leq l$. M is called a k-l-answer set of an extended logic program P if M is a k-l-model of P^M.*

Definition 8. *Define* $\mathcal{I}^{\pm} : \mathcal{P} \to \mathbb{R}^{\infty}_{\geq 0}$ *via*

$$\mathcal{I}^{\pm}(P) = \min_{M \subseteq \mathcal{L}} \{k + l \mid M \text{ is a } k\text{-}l\text{-answer set of } P\}$$

for all $P \in \mathcal{P}$.

Interestingly, however, these two different points of view—considering the reduct or the program itself—are equivalent.

Proposition 1. *For any extended logic program* P, $\mathcal{I}_{\pm}(P) = \mathcal{I}^{\pm}(P)$.

While for any program P, one can find a set M of literals such that M is a model of P^M, one cannot always guarantee M being the minimal model of the reduct. Our next measure minimizes the distance between M and $\mathsf{Cl}(P^M)$. We only consider the number of literals in the *symmetric difference* of two sets. Investigating other distances is left for future work. Recall that the symmetric difference d_{sd} of two sets M and M' is defined via $d_{sd}(M, M') = |(M \cup M') \setminus (M \cap M')|$.

Definition 9. *Define* $\mathcal{I}_{sd} : \mathcal{P} \to \mathbb{R}^{\infty}_{\geq 0}$ *via*

$$\mathcal{I}_{sd}(P) = \min_{M \in \mathit{ConCl}_P} d_{sd}(M, \mathsf{Cl}(P^M))$$

with $\mathit{ConCl}_P = \{M \subseteq \mathcal{L} \mid M, \mathsf{Cl}(P^M) \text{ is consistent}\}$ *and* $\min \emptyset = \infty$.

Example 2. If a program P contains two contradicting facts, $\mathcal{I}_{sd}(P) = \infty$ since in this case, $\mathsf{Cl}(P^M)$ is inconsistent for any set M of literals. For the programs P_3 and P_4 from Example 1, we have $\mathcal{I}_{sd}(P_3) = 3$ and $\mathcal{I}_{sd}(P_4) = 1$.

Our last measure $\mathcal{I}_{\#}$ takes the answer sets of a program into account rather than the rules. For this purpose, we need the following notion.

Definition 10. *A set* M *of literals is called* k*-inconsistent,* $k \in \mathbb{N} \cup \{0\}$, *if there are exactly* k *atoms* a *such that* $a \in M$ *and* $\neg a \in M$.

Furthermore, programs might have no answer set at all, which is a special case for $\mathcal{I}_{\#}$.

Definition 11. *Define* $\mathcal{I}_{\#} : \mathcal{P} \to \mathbb{R}^{\infty}_{\geq 0}$ *via*

$$\mathcal{I}_{\#}(P) = \min_{M \in \mathit{Ans}(P)} \{k \mid M \text{ is } k\text{-inconsistent}\}$$

with $\min \emptyset = \infty$.

Example 3. For $\mathcal{I}_{\#}$, we obtain $\mathcal{I}_{\#}(P_3) = 1$ and $\mathcal{I}_{\#}(P_4) = 3$.

Table 1 gives an overview on the compliance of our measures with respect to the rationality postulates from Sect. 2. Note that, naturally, none of our measures satisfies the classical *monotonicity* postulate which is also not desired for ASP.

Table 1. Compliance of inconsistency measures with respect to our rationality postulates

	$\mathcal{I}_{\pm} = \mathcal{I}^{\pm}$	$\mathcal{I}_{sd}$	$\mathcal{I}_{\#}$
Consistency	✓	✓	✓
Monotonicity	✗	✗	✗
CLP-Monotonicity	✓	✓	✓
I-Monotonicity	✓	✓	✓
Split-Monotonicity	✓	✓	✓
Safe-rule independence	✓	✓	✓

4   Summary

In this paper, we addressed the challenge of measuring inconsistency in ASP by critically reviewing the classical framework of inconsistency measurement and taking non-monotonicity into account. We developed novel rationality postulates and measures that are more apt for analyzing inconsistency in ASP than classical approaches. Intuitively, some of our measures take the effort needed to restore the consistency of programs into account ($\mathcal{I}_{\pm}$, $\mathcal{I}^{\pm}$), and our results show that it does not matter whether this is done on the level of the original program or on the level of the reduct. Others measure inconsistency in terms of the quality of the produced output, e. g., $\mathcal{I}_{\#}$ which considers the minimal number of inconsistencies in an answer set.

Acknowledgements. This work has been partially funded by the DFG Research Training Group 1763.

References

1. Besnard, P.: Revisiting postulates for inconsistency measures. In: Fermé, E., Leite, J. (eds.) JELIA 2014. LNCS, vol. 8761, pp. 383–396. Springer, Heidelberg (2014). doi:10.1007/978-3-319-11558-0_27
2. Brewka, G., Eiter, T., Truszczynski, M.: Answer set programming at a glance. Commun. ACM **54**(12), 92–103 (2011). http://doi.acm.org/10.1145/2043174.2043195
3. Gelfond, M., Lifschitz, V.: Classical negation in logic programs and disjunctive databases. New Gener. Comput. **9**(3/4), 365–386 (1991). http://dx.doi.org/10.1007/BF03037169
4. Grant, J., Hunter, A.: Measuring inconsistency in knowledgebases. J. Intell. Inf. Syst. **27**, 159–184 (2006)
5. Hunter, A., Konieczny, S.: Approaches to measuring inconsistent information. In: Bertossi, L., Hunter, A., Schaub, T. (eds.) Inconsistency Tolerance. LNCS, vol. 3300, pp. 191–236. Springer, Heidelberg (2005). doi:10.1007/978-3-540-30597-2_7
6. Hunter, A., Konieczny, S.: On the measure of conflicts: shapley inconsistency values. Artif. Intell. **174**(14), 1007–1026 (2010)

7. Lifschitz, V., Turner, H.: Splitting a logic program. In: Logic Programming, Proceedings of the Eleventh International Conference on Logic Programming, Santa Marherita Ligure, Italy, 13–18 June 1994, pp. 23–37 (1994)
8. Schulz, C., Satoh, K., Toni, F.: Characterising and explaining inconsistency in logic programs. In: Calimeri, F., Ianni, G., Truszczynski, M. (eds.) LPNMR 2015. LNCS, vol. 9345, pp. 467–479. Springer, Heidelberg (2015). doi:10.1007/978-3-319-23264-5_39
9. Thimm, M.: Inconsistency measures for probabilistic logics. Artif. Intell. **197**, 1–24 (2013)
10. Thimm, M.: On the expressivity of inconsistency measures. Artif. Intell. **234**, 120–151 (2016)

Author Index

Printed in the United States
By Bookmasters